D1453462

# ANCIENT WISDOM IN THE AGE
# OF THE NEW SCIENCE

Seventeenth-century England has long been heralded as the birth-place of a so-called 'new' philosophy. Yet what contemporaries might have understood by 'old' philosophy has been little appreciated. In this book Dmitri Levitin examines English attitudes to ancient philosophy in unprecedented depth, demonstrating the centrality of engagement with the history of philosophy to almost all educated persons, whether scholars, clerics, or philosophers themselves, and aligning English intellectual culture closely to that of continental Europe. Drawing on a vast array of sources, Levitin challenges the assumption that interest in ancient ideas was limited to out-of-date 'ancients' or was in some sense 'pre-enlightened'; indeed, much of the intellectual justification for the new philosophy came from re-writing its history. At the same time, the deep investment of English scholars in pioneering forms of late humanist erudition led them to develop some of the most innovative narratives of ancient philosophy in early modern Europe.

DMITRI LEVITIN is a Fellow of All Souls College, Oxford. Previously, he was a Fellow of Trinity College, Cambridge, and of the Centre for Research in Arts, Social Sciences and Humanities, also in Cambridge. He has also held positions at the Folger Library and at the University of Edinburgh.

IDEAS IN CONTEXT

*Edited by* David Armitage, Richard Bourke, Jennifer
Pitts, and John Robertson

The books in this series will discuss the emergence of intellectual traditions and
of related new disciplines. The procedures, aims, and vocabularies that were
generated will be set in the context of the alternatives available within the
contemporary frameworks of ideas and institutions. Through detailed studies of
the evolution of such traditions, and their modification by different audiences, it
is hoped that a new picture will form of the development of ideas in their
concrete contexts. By this means, artificial distinctions between the history of
philosophy, of the various sciences, of society and politics, and of literature
may be seen to dissolve. The series is published with the support of the Exxon Foundation.

*A list of books in the series will be found at the end of the volume.*

# ANCIENT WISDOM IN THE AGE OF THE NEW SCIENCE

*Histories of Philosophy in England, c. 1640–1700*

DMITRI LEVITIN

CAMBRIDGE
UNIVERSITY PRESS

# CAMBRIDGE
## UNIVERSITY PRESS

University Printing House, Cambridge CB2 8BS, United Kingdom

Cambridge University Press is part of the University of Cambridge.

It furthers the University's mission by disseminating knowledge in the pursuit of education, learning and research at the highest international levels of excellence.

www.cambridge.org
Information on this title: www.cambridge.org/9781107105881

First published 2015

Printed in the United States of America by Sheridan Books, Inc.

*A catalogue record for this publication is available from the British Library*

*Library of Congress Cataloguing in Publication data*
Levitin, Dmitri.
Ancient wisdom in the age of the new science : histories of philosophy in England, c. 1640–1700 / Dmitri Levitin.
pages    cm – (Ideas in context)
Includes bibliographical references and index.
ISBN 978-1-107-10588-1
1. Philosophy – England – History – 17th century.   I. Title.
B1131.L48   2015
192–dc23
2015008921

ISBN 978-1-107-10588-1 Hardback

# Contents

# Acknowledgements

This book began life as a doctoral thesis, researched and written while I was a member of Selwyn College, Cambridge, between October 2008 and September 2010. But as with any first monograph, its gestation lies further back, with the teachers who first inspired me to pursue the study of early modern intellectual history. In that respect, I am deeply grateful to David Smith, Richard Serjeantson, Quentin Skinner, Sylvana Tomaselli, and the late István Hont. Selwyn College quite rightly has a fine reputation as a centre for early modern history, and I was fortunate to be based there as both an undergraduate and graduate student. As I completed my PhD research, I was appointed to a Research Fellowship at Trinity College, Cambridge – in an age when specialised research in the humanities is increasingly threatened, that institution has offered a near-ideal venue for scholarship, which it is my pleasure and privilege to acknowledge.

While at Trinity, I have been particularly fortunate to have unrestricted access to the shelves in the Wren Library, and I must offer my deepest thanks to David McKitterick and his brilliant staff at the Library for all their assistance. As the list of manuscripts and *libri annotati* in the Bibliography indicates, I am also extremely grateful to the staff of many other libraries for affording me access to their collections and for assistance in using them. Special thanks are due to the staff in the Rare Books Room in Cambridge University Library, the Rare Books and Manuscripts Reading Rooms in the British Library, and the Special Collections section of the Bodleian Library. Final tweaks have been made while a Fellow at the Centre for Research in the Arts, Social Sciences and Humanities in Cambridge; many thanks are due to Simon Goldhill and everyone else at the Centre for allowing me to continue to pursue my research.

This book has been immeasurably improved by conversations with various friends and colleagues who have been kind enough to share their ideas with me, to send me early versions of their work, to indulge my questions with gracious answers, or to discuss historical issues with me when we have met. At the risk of accidentally neglecting to mention some, I must thank especially: Peter Anstey, Constance Blackwell, Bill Bulman, James Bryson, Louis Caron, Justin Champion, Karen Collis, Lyndsay Coo, Stephen Clucas, Conal

Condren, Sarah Day, Michael Edwards, Mordechai Feingold, Stephen Gaukroger, Elena Giusti, Anthony Grafton, Felicity Green, Wouter Hanegraaff, Nick Hardy, Peter Harrison, Ian Hunter, Sarah Hutton, Clare Jackson, Jill Kraye, Sachiko Kusukawa, Will Kynan-Wilson, Ceri Law, Marilyn Lewis, Rhodri Lewis, Scott Mandelbrote, John Marenbon, Joe Moshenska, Jon Parkin, Nicholas Phillipson, John Pocock, Jean-Louis Quantin, John Robertson, Jacqueline Rose, Hugh de Quehen, Paul Schuurman, Sophie Smith, Alex Walsham, Catherine Wilson, and Brian Young. Michael Hunter and Will Poole have been especially generous in supplying me with microfilms, unpublished works, and bibliographies, without which this book would certainly be much poorer.

The two anonymous readers for Cambridge University Press produced wonderfully useful reports. I am equally grateful to my academic editors and the staff of the Press for the care that they have expended on this book and the interest they have shown in it; special thanks here are due to John Robertson, Liz Friend-Smith, and Fleur Jones.

Three scholars in particular have contributed immeasurably to the present form of this book and to showing me what good historical scholarship should and can be. Sir Noel Malcolm acted as the external examiner of the doctoral thesis on which it is (now rather distantly) based: it is largely due to his meticulous attention, advice, and erudition that it has grown to be so much superior to the original version. Richard Serjeantson has now read various parts of this work more times than I care to remember: virtually every page reflects his immense learning and broad understanding of early modern intellectual history, which he has been kind enough to share with me since I first studied with him in 2006. Finally, I must acknowledge my great debt to my doctoral supervisor, Mark Goldie. With every passing year, I appreciate more and more his constant guidance and never-ending readiness to encourage me in my imperfect labours. His is a model of scholarly diligence and kindness that I am not the first to comment on, and which I can only hope, one day, to emulate.

My final debt is to my family and friends, who have tolerated my disappearances into scholarly solitude with only the promise of what must have seemed a largely metaphysical entity – 'the book' – to explain them away, and who have offered solace and fun when I have emerged back into the world. In this, I am above all grateful to my parents, to my sister, and to Maria Sbiti.

This small attempt at serious historical science is dedicated to D. V. Kviatkovsky†, O. N. Lavrovich, R. Z. Levitin†, and M. S. Levitina, who lived most of their lives in a criminal state that tried to deprive them of historical truth, but who nonetheless never lost their love for science.

# Abbreviations

| | |
|---|---|
| *Alum. Cantab.* | *Alumni Cantabrigienses*, part I: *from the earliest times to 1751*, eds., J. Venn and J. A. Venn (4 vols, Cambridge, 1922–27) |
| *Ath. Ox.* | Anthony à Wood, *Athenae Oxonienses*, ed. J. Foster (4 vols, London, 1891–92) |
| *BJHP* | *British Journal for the History of Philosophy* |
| *BJHS* | *British Journal for the History of Science* |
| BL | British Library, London |
| Bod. | Bodleian Library, Oxford |
| *Boyle Correspondence* | *The correspondence of Robert Boyle*, eds., M. Hunter, A. Clericuzio, and L. M. Principe (6 vols, London, 2001) |
| *Boyle Works* | *The works of Robert Boyle*, eds., M. Hunter and E. B. Davis (14 vols, London, 1999–2000) |
| *BUH* | *Bibliothèque universelle et historique*, ed. J. Le Clerc (26 vols, Amsterdam, 1686–1702) |
| CKS | Centre for Kentish Studies, Maidstone, Kent |
| *CMG* | *Corpus Medicorum Graecorum* (Leipzig and Berlin, 1907–) |
| *CTC* | *Catalogus translationum et commentariorum: Medieaval and Renaissance Latin translations and commentaries*, eds., P. O. Kristeller et al., (Washington, DC, 1960–) |
| CUL | Cambridge University Library |
| DK | *Die Fragmente der Vorsokratiker*, eds., H. Deils and W. Kranz, 11th edn (3 vols, Zurich and Berlin, 1952) |
| DL | Diogenes Laërtius, *Lives of eminent philosophers*. Unless otherwise stated, all English translations are from *Lives of eminent* |

|  | *philosophers*, ed. and trans. R. D. Hickes (Cambridge [MA], 1931). Greek is taken from *Lives of eminent philosophers*, ed. T. Dorandi (Cambridge, 2013) |
|---|---|
| *ESM* | *Early Science and Medicine* |
| ESTC | English Short Title Catalogue |
| Folger | Folger Shakespeare Library, Washington, DC |
| Hankins and Palmer | *The recovery of ancient philosophy in the Renaissance*, eds., J. Hankins and A. Palmer (Florence, 2008) |
| *HJ* | *Historical Journal* |
| *Hobbes Correspondence* | *The correspondence of Thomas Hobbes*, ed. N. Malcolm (2 vols, Oxford, 1994) |
| *IHR* | *Intellectual History Review* |
| *JHI* | *Journal of the History of Ideas* |
| *JHP* | *Journal of the History of Philosophy* |
| *JWCI* | *Journal of the Warburg and Courtauld Institutes* |
| K | Κλαύδιου Γαληνού Ἅπαντα = *Claudii Galeni opera Omnia*, ed. C. G. Kühn (20 vols, Leipzig, 1821–33) [=*CMG*, 1–20] |
| *LL* | *The library of John Locke*, eds., J. Harrison and P. Laslett (Oxford, 1971) |
| *Locke Correspondence* | *The correspondence of John Locke*, ed. E. S. de Beer (8 vols, Oxford, 1976–89) |
| Malcolm | Thomas Hobbes, *Leviathan*, ed. N. Malcolm (3 vols, Oxford, 2012) |
| *Newton Correspondence* | *The correspondence of Isaac Newton*, ed. H. W. Turnbull (7 vols, Cambridge, 1959–77) |
| *Newton Library* | *The library of Isaac Newton*, ed. J. Harrison (Cambridge, 1978) |
| *NRRS* | *Notes and Records of the Royal Society* |
| *ODNB* | *Oxford Dictionary of National Biography* |
| *OFB* | *The Oxford Francis Bacon* (2000–) |
| *Oldenburg Correspondence* | *The correspondence of Henry Oldenburg*, eds. and trans., A. R. Hall and M. B. Hall (Madison, 1965–86) |
| Pines | Maimonides, *The guide of the perplexed*, ed. and trans. S. Pines (2 vols, Chicago, 1963) |
| *PG* | *Patrologiae cursus completus. Series graeca*, ed. J.-P. Migne (Paris, 1857–1912) |

| | |
|---|---|
| Santinello I | *Models of the history of philosophy, vol. I: from its origins in the Renaissance to the "historia philosophica"*, eds., G. Santinello, C. W. T. Blackwell, and P. Weller (Dordrecht, 1993) |
| Santinello II | *Models of the history of philosophy, vol. II: from the Cartesian age to Brucker*, eds., G. Santinello and G. Piaia (Dordrecht, 2010) |
| *SHPS* | *Studies in the History and Philosophy of Science* |
| *System* 1845 | Ralph Cudworth, *The true intellectual system of the universe*, ed. J. L. Mosheim, trans. J. Harrison (3 vols, London, 1845) |

For the books of the Bible, standard abbreviations are used, and references and citations are from the Authorized Version, unless stated otherwise. Classical texts cited in the notes are only referred to by their short titles, usually as given in the *Oxford Classical Dictionary*, eds., S. Hornblower and A. Spawforth (4th edn, Oxford, 2005), and the appropriate book/section number (the editions used were those of the Loeb, Teubner, or Oxford Classical Texts series). Only in those cases when the text is relatively obscure, or when I have relied on a specific translation, have I offered a full reference to the relevant modern edition, which is then also listed in the 'Printed primary sources' section of the Bibliography.

# Notes on the text

*Dates* are in the Julian calendar (with the year dated from 1 January).

*Quotations* are given in the original spelling (with expanded contractions signalled), with the exception that medial 'u' (for 'v') and initial 'v' (for 'u') have been normalised. Manuscript transcriptions are diplomatic, with the following symbols used: insertions are signalled by <chevrons>, deletions with a ~~strikethrough~~, underlining as in the original.

*Bibliographical references* are all repeated in the Bibliography. First references to primary sources are given in full, with the short title used thereafter. In the interests of economy, first references to secondary sources are given in a contracted version, with a short title used thereafter. So what appears in the Bibliography as: Allen, D. C. 'The predecessors of Champollion', *Proceedings of the American Philosophical Society*, 104 (1960), 527–47, appears first in the text as: Allen, 'Predecessors of Champollion' (1960), and thereafter as: Allen, 'Predecessors'.

*Style* is academic, but I have attempted, to the best of my ability, to avoid the jargon that is so prevalent in the modern humanities. I make no apologies for the extensive scholarly apparatus, but I have attempted to confine discussion of secondary literature to the footnotes, unless it is particularly significant for my interpretation. An exception to this is the introductory first chapter: since many of my subsequent arguments depend on a revisionist account of seventeenth-century European and English intellectual culture more generally, it seemed preferable to set out that account at the start, rather than to allude to it constantly in the chapters themselves.

# 1    Introduction: histories of philosophy between 'Renaissance' and 'Enlightenment'

That the way humans see the past shapes their actions is not a new idea. It thus might be thought surprising that there has been no systematic investigation of how learned men and women conceived of the history of philosophy in a period that is supposed to have witnessed the development of a self-consciously '*new* philosophy'. The main objective of this monograph is to convey how much interest in, and engagement with, the history of ancient thought permeated English (as a subset of European) intellectual culture throughout the seventeenth century. Achieving this objective, it is hoped, will also lead to some major revisions to existing understandings of intellectual and religious change in this period, both in terms of developments that are often assumed to have led to something that one might or might not term 'enlightenment', and those that may or may not have constituted a part of a broadly conceived 'scientific revolution', in which England has always been assigned a very large role.

Such a simple formulation notwithstanding, this is a subject that touches on many other historiographical traditions and assumptions, and on the wider question of the nature of early modern English and European intellectual culture; some preliminary remarks are thus required. These will fall into three categories. The first will position this book within the disciplinary boundaries of intellectual history, especially as they have been applied to the study of early modern intellectual change. The second will chart some of the historiographical assumptions about the historiography of philosophy in the long period *c.* 1400–1800. The third will focus more narrowly on seventeenth-century English intellectual culture.[1]

## 1.1    Method: the history of scholarship, the history of philosophy, or the history of intellectual culture?

This book examines the history of historical scholarship and its wider dissemination. Given recent historiographical developments, this requires some

---

[1] This introductory chapter is not intended as a full survey of literature on early modern historiography of philosophy; many other references are provided in the chapters themselves. Those interested in a tangentially connected and wider discussion of similar themes to those discussed here might consult Levitin, 'From sacred history to the history of religion' (2012).

elucidation. As the best recent summary points out, the history of scholarship 'as a constituted branch of knowledge, an *episteme* . . . has, until quite recently, hardly existed at all'.[2] Classical scholars themselves have long examined, critiqued, praised, and reappraised the efforts of their predecessors, sometimes even in monographic format.[3] While classical scholars are of course well positioned to know what classical scholarship involves – not least because they possess the requisite technical skills – the limitations of these approaches, especially their tendency to ahistorical value judgements and insensitivity to context, have now begun to be recognised.[4]

A concomitant problem has been that the object of study of the history of scholarship when practised by classical scholars themselves, when not limited to individual scholars, has been the development of scholarly disciplines. To give an example relevant to us, two prominent recent studies of seventeenth-century English approaches to ancient Egypt and to ancient Zoroastrianism have sought to chart the 'birth' of a historical discipline (Egyptology or Zoroastrian studies).[5] This is to miss the basic point that those approaches cannot possibly have been contributions to those disciplines, which simply did not exist.[6] This is not just a point about anachronism; it is about the need to place scholarship within institutional and disciplinary contexts. It is only now that the history of scholarship is reaching a stage at which such an attempt can be made. The pioneering works that have defined the field as it has recently flourished – most notably Anthony Grafton's monumental intellectual biography of Joseph Scaliger (1983–93) – have understandably tended to focus on one figure, recreating their scholarly practices, intellectual networks, and charting their sources.[7] This has perhaps served to maintain an unwarranted distance between historians of scholarship and intellectual historians interested in broader patterns of change. But by building on such foundational studies, scholars can now use the history of scholarship to construct convincing, elaborate, and important long-term narratives that address such diachronic questions.

---

[2] Ligota and Quantin, 'Introduction' (2006), 1. For a more theoretical approach, see Güthenke, 'Reception studies and recent work in the history of scholarship' (2009).

[3] Sandys, *A history of classical scholarship* (1903–8); Pfeiffer, *History of classical scholarship* (1968, 1976); von Wilamowitz-Moellendorff, *History of classical scholarship* (1982 [1921]); Reynolds and Wilson, *Scribes and scholars* (1991). See also Jehasse, *Renaissance de la critique* (1976); Kenney, *The classical text* (1974); Timpanaro, *The genesis of Lachmann's method* (2005 [1963]).

[4] Ligota and Quantin, 'Introduction', 10–11.

[5] Stroumsa, 'John Spencer and the roots of idolatry' (2001) esp. 22–3; Stroumsa, 'Thomas Hyde and the birth of Zoroastrian Studies' (2002). Both reappear, in truncated versions, in Stroumsa, *A new science* (2010), 77–112. See similarly Parente, 'Spencer, Maimonides, and the history of religion' (2006).

[6] But see Ligota and Quantin, 'Introduction', 9. See also the comments in Quantin, 'John Selden et l'étude de l'Antiquité chrétienne' (2011), at 339–40.

[7] Grafton, *Joseph Scaliger* (1983–93); Toomer, *John Selden* (2009).

One recent example, Jean-Louis Quantin's study of seventeenth-century Anglican patristics, has set a new benchmark for how this can be achieved;[8] Professor Quantin's remarkable work is the closest methodological model for this book, and I can only hope to achieve a fraction of what is achieved there.

This book is thus first and foremost a contribution to the history of early modern English intellectual culture, and only by association to the fortune of various classical philosophical texts. A few studies of the historiography of classical philosophy in the early modern world have charted the afterlife of a specific text (or corpus of texts) within a specific timeframe.[9] This approach has the tendency, once again, to focus on texts that can easily be classified as 'scholarship': especially new editions and translations. It has generated very important results, essential to any student of the field. But 'to establish itself, however, [early modern] philology constantly had to engage with other disciplines, especially theology'.[10] In some sense, to point this out is to follow in reverse findings in other disciplines: for example, we are now aware of the great extent to which seventeenth-century 'political thought' was conducted in historical mode.[11] Indeed, the dominance of historical discourse in much of early modern intellectual culture is now being openly asserted in some quarters.[12] This book thus engages in the history of scholarship only to the extent that that discipline is essential to comprehending wider patterns of intellectual change, whether in the history of science, philosophy, theology, or historiography.

There is another quasi-methodological issue that concerns us, more familiar to intellectual historians than the issues raised by the history of scholarship. Anyone with a passing interest in early modern intellectual history will be aware that this is an age often defined by recourse to ancient ideologies, to the extent that one could believe that ancient Greece was being relived in seventeenth-century Europe. The period saw, we are told, the demise of 'Aristotelianism' in favour of any other number of 'isms': 'Epicureanism' in

---

[8] Quantin, *The Church of England and Christian antiquity* (2009). See also Toomer, *Eastern wisedome and learning* (1996).

[9] See e.g. Casini, 'The Pythagorean myth' (1996); Bercovitch, 'Empedocles in the English Renaissance' (1968); Kraye, 'Aristotle's God and the authenticity of "De mundo"' (1990). For further details on the transmission of *De Mundo*, see Kraye, 'Daniel Heinsius and the author of *De mundo*' (1988); Lorimer, *The text tradition of pseudo-Aristotle 'De mundo'* (1924).

[10] Hardy, 'The *Ars Critica* in early modern England' (2012), 21.

[11] The classic statement remains Pocock, *The ancient constitution and the feudal law* (1987 [1957]). See also Soll, *Publishing the prince* (2005); Bulman, 'Constantine's enlightenment' (2009), 160, *passim*; Levitin, 'Matthew Tindal's *Rights of the Christian Church* (1706)'. The pioneering work in this regard in the Restoration English context remains Champion, *The pillars of priestcraft shaken* (1992): although I disagree with its central thesis and many of its specific interpretations, its importance in this regard must be acknowledged.

[12] Mulsow and Zedelmaier, eds., *Die Praktiken der Gelehrsamkeit* (2001); Pomata and Siraisi, eds., *Historia* (2005).

moral and natural philosophy, 'Stoicism' in the same, 'Hermeticism' in sixteenth-century natural philosophy and natural magic, a revitalised or surviving 'Aristotelianism' in the universities and throughout all branches of philosophy.[13] What is remarkable is the extent to which such readings tend to take for granted the existence of essentialist 'isms' whose play through the course of a historical period can be charted. This kind of reification can be harmless, such as when an 'ism' is used simply as shorthand for an intellectual position: certainly someone who writes a commentary on the *Corpus Aristotelicum* can be usefully described as engaging with one or more of a variety of 'Aristotelianisms'.[14] But much more often these reified concepts become explanatory concepts, where as supposed historical phenomena they are attributed some kind of logical content. One need hardly delve deep into linguistic philosophy to make the obvious point that there was no such thing as 'Epicureanism' in seventeenth-century England, only attitudes to Epicurus. On the most abstract level, this is a point about the methodology of reception studies. To turn texts into 'ideologies' and then to chart the play of ideologies through various periods is tempting: it brings a familiarity to the material, and allows far easier descriptions of philosophical 'traditions' and their development through centuries of textual renegotiation. But this is to ignore the specificity of reception, and the fact that readers, in our case, seventeenth-century Englishmen and women, have unique and contingent attitudes towards philosophical texts.[15] Most importantly, by the seventeenth-century European intellectual culture had reached a stage at which ancient philosophy was *never* approached ahistorically. No one was an 'Epicurean' in some essentialist sense: even if they subscribed to the label, their ideas about what it meant were mediated through many layers of humanist historiographical tradition. One aim of this book is to challenge the facile use of ancient labels to describe early modern intellectual positions by examining what the early moderns themselves thought of the ancient positions: the results are often very surprising.

## 1.2    The historiography of the history of philosophy

As the historiographical proclivity to write early modern intellectual history through ancient labels suggests, men and women of letters throughout this

---

[13] The literature on these subjects is huge. On the diversity and survival of Aristotelianism, see the overview by Edwards, 'Aristotelianism, Descartes, and Hobbes' (2005); for the pedagogical context, see Feingold, 'Aristotle and the English universities in the seventeenth century' (1998); for Epicureanism and Stoicism, a good starting point are the essays in Osler, ed., *Atoms, pneuma, and tranquillity* (1991). For Hermeticism, see Merkel and Debus, eds., *Hermeticism and the Renaissance* (1988). On all these, see further below.

[14] The plural famously suggested in Schmitt, *Aristotle and the Renaissance* (1983).

[15] A useful discussion, with a specific focus on intellectual history, is Thompson, 'Reception theory and the interpretation of historical meaning' (1993).

period continued to live in a world in which the intellectual landscape was dominated by the past. Given this basic fact, it is again worth remarking upon how recent and sparse is investigation into the history of early modern history of philosophy. Pioneering works first appeared in France and Italy in the 1960s and 1970s.[16] They were followed by the encyclopaedic *Storia delle storie generali della filosofia* series.[17] These rich and erudite works remain essential to the field, often offering valuable expositions of texts unfamiliar to mainstream intellectual history. Yet in some sense they remain tied to the 'old' model of the history of scholarship, their ultimate aim being to chart the development of the 'discipline' of the history of philosophy.[18] As a result, they have almost nothing to say about the history of philosophy as it was practised by those who did not write works entitled *Historia philosophiae*, or the like.[19] Second, and connected, they subscribe to rather old-fashioned notions of wider intellectual change. Given that they are works about historical scholarship, the key markers of change remain, surprisingly, philosophical, especially Bacon and Descartes.[20] Finally, and again connected, they remain wedded to a model in which all pre-eighteenth-century history of philosophy is 'pre-enlightened', whereas the eighteenth century, especially in Germany, and especially in Johann Jakob Brucker's *Historia critica philosophiae* (1742–44), is said to witness the rise of a truly 'critical' or 'enlightened' history of philosophy.[21]

The last two decades have seen the crystallisation of this orthodoxy, with special focus devoted to histories of philosophy written in Germany between *c.* 1680 and 1750.[22] The stimulus has been twofold. First, a small academic

---

[16] Garin, *La filosofia come sapere storico* (1959); Braun, *Histoire de l'histoire de la philosophie* (1973); Del Torre, *Le origini moderne della storiografia filosofica* (1976); Gueroult, *Dianoématique: histoire de l'histoire de la philosophie* (1979–88).

[17] Santinello, ed., *Storia delle storie generali della filosofia* (1979–2004). The first two volumes have been translated as Santinello I and II.

[18] As made clear in Santinello, 'Preface', in Santinello, II, ix.

[19] An exception is Bayle: Piaia, 'Philosophical historiography in France from Bayle to Deslandes'. This point has already been made in the review by L. Catana, 'The history of the history of philosophy' (2012), at 621–2.

[20] As revealed by the very title of the second volume, and by comments at, e.g., Malusa, 'Renaissance antecedents to the historiography of philosophy', 3; Tolomio, 'The "Historica philosophica" in the sixteenth and seventeenth centuries', 66; Malusa, 'The first general histories of philosophy in England and the Low Countries', 163–71; Piaia, 'Foreword to the English edition', v; Piaia, 'The histories of philosophy in France in the age of Descartes', 3–4, and most explicitly in Piaia, 'Cartesianism and history: from the rejection of the past to a "critical" history of philosophy' (2012).

[21] Santinello, 'Preface', xi, betraying the influence of Paul Hazard, on whom, see below. Longo, 'A "critical" history of philosophy and the early enlightenment', does not reduce Brucker to post-Cartesian rationalism, as does Piaia, but still insists on the 'enlightened' nature of his criticism.

[22] Hochstrasser, *Natural law theories in the early Enlightenment* (2000), 150–9, 170–5; Lehmann-Brauns, *Weisheit in der Weltgeschichte* (2004).

industry has been devoted to the study of 'eclecticism': a self-defining school of thought that sought to synthesise the best elements of various philosophies.[23] This approach was inherently historical, and much of the original stimulus for it came from the scholarship of the polymathic Gerardus Johannes Vossius, whose *De philosophorum sectis* (1657) devoted a whole final chapter to the 'eclectic sect' whose putative founder was Potamon (it had only been mentioned in passing by Diogenes Laërtius).[24] An emphasis on the positive aspects of eclecticism was taken up by figures such as Jakob Thomasius, his son Christian, and then Brucker. But despite the strict chronological and geographic focus in the best scholarship,[25] there has been a somewhat careless tendency to reify eclecticism, and to assign it a massive role in the development of the history of philosophy as an intellectual exercise.[26] Eclecticism was a local phenomenon, whose broader importance should not be overplayed.

The other impetus for the recent upsurge in the study of German histories of philosophy is both more complex and has links to a much wider body of secondary scholarship, namely that concerned with what has solidified into a relatively widely accepted historical phenomenon: the 'early enlightenment'. German histories of philosophy are claimed as manifestations of a wider intellectual process:

In the latter part of the seventeenth century ... a revolution in the historiography of philosophy pioneered by Samuel Pufendorf (1632–94) and Christian Thomasius (1655–1728) and associated with a new understanding of 'eclecticism' in philosophy paved the way both for a coherent notion of philosophical progress and for the large, multivolume histories of philosophy written in the eighteenth century.[27]

This interest in Germany is unsurprising. The great 'enlightened' history of philosophy, famous across the continent, was Brucker's *Historia critica philosophiae*. Brucker is seen as the culmination of several 'enlightened' trends in the historiography of philosophy: the anti-syncretism of Thomasius (and others), and the propagation of Boyle's and Locke's natural philosophy by

---

[23] The key text is Albrecht, *Eklektik* (1994), which very much exaggerates the canon of supposed 'eclectics' (as admitted at 661). The best English summary is Schneider, 'Eclecticism and the history of philosophy' (1997), where many of the German-language secondary works are listed. See also Schneider's review piece, 'Eclecticism rediscovered' (1998), esp. the comments on Albrecht at 175. See further Blackwell, 'Sturm, Morhof and Brucker vs. Aristotle' (1998); and the brief remarks in Donini, 'The history of the concept of eclecticism' (1988).

[24] On Vossius, see Malusa, 'First general histories', 222–35; DL, I.21. Another key programmatic statement is that in Clemens Alexandrinus, *Strom.*, I.7.37; for a summary and discussion of the very few ancient references, see Hatzimichali, *Potamo of Alexandria and the emergence of eclecticism* (2011), 14–24.

[25] Schneider, 'Eclecticism'; Blackwell, 'Sturm, Morhof and Brucker'.

[26] See above all Kelley, *The descent of ideas* (2002). There is little evidence to support this attribution, and the book fails to justify its central thesis. It is particularly weak on England; for example, Theophilus Gale mutates into Thomas Gale within the duration of a sentence (50).

[27] Brooke, 'How the Stoics became atheists' (2006), 395.

Jean Le Clerc, as channelled through earlier German scholars like Johann Franz Buddeus.[28]

But were the new German developments really so revolutionary, and so intrinsically tied to 'enlightenment'? Recent scholarship has demonstrated that Brucker's celebrated delineation of independent 'systematic' philosophies – as opposed to 'syncretist' ones that confused philosophy and theology – derived from a specific background in Lutheran pedagogy.[29] More generally, we encounter here a larger set of assumptions, in which the history of humanist scholarship is seen as somewhat irrelevant to the history of 'enlightened' historiography and criticism, because the former was mere accumulation and pedantry, whereas the latter was truly critical and philosophical.[30] This is the case not just for the historiography of philosophy. It has been – and continues to be – a commonplace that attitudes to ancient religion, to the Bible as a historical text, and to paganism more generally did not become 'critical' until the early enlightenment, or a post-1680 'crise de la conscience européenne'.[31] This view, however, is the product of eighteenth-century propaganda, especially the French *querelle des anciens et des modernes*;[32] accordingly, we should be wary of adopting it.[33] Far from rejecting the work of their humanist predecessors, eighteenth-century freethinkers were more likely to plagiarise it. 'The bright weapons of eighteenth-century enlightened warfare were forged in the murky smithies of seventeenth-century erudition' – a conclusion that will be confirmed again and again in this study.[34] This book thus does not operate within the framework of the fetishisation of the post-1680 period that has dominated much of twentieth- and twenty-first-century European intellectual history.[35]

---

[28] Longo, 'Critical history'; Blackwell, '"Ideas" and their redefinition in Jacob Brucker' (1997), esp. 78–9; Blackwell, 'Thales philosophus: the beginning of philosophy as a discipline' (1997); Häfner, 'Das Erkenntnisproblem in der Philologie um 1700' (2001); Thouard, 'Hamann and the history of philosophy' (2006); Pocock, *Barbarism and religion*, v (2012), 199–200. Israel, *Enlightenment contested* (2006), 470–95, pushes these themes to extremes. The fullest studies are now those collected in Schmidt-Biggemann and Stammen, eds., *Jacob Brucker* (1998).

[29] Catana, *The historiographical concept 'system of philosophy'* (2008), 147–92.

[30] For prominent statements of this view, see e.g., Israel, *Enlightenment contested*, 473; Trevor-Roper, *History and the enlightenment* (2010), 1–16 ('The historical philosophy of the enlightenment' [1963]), at 1–2.

[31] Hazard, *La crise de la conscience européenne* (1935).

[32] Edelstein, *The Enlightenment: a genealogy* (2010); Fumaroli, 'Les Abeilles et les araignées' (2001); Norman, *The shock of the ancient* (2011), esp. 99–110.

[33] See now Quantin, 'Reason and reasonableness in French ecclesiastical scholarship' (2011), esp. 434–5; Bravo, '*Critice* in the sixteenth and seventeenth centuries' (2006); Hardy, '*Ars critica*'; Edelstein, *Enlightenment*; Levitin, 'Sacred history'.

[34] Serjeantson, 'Hume's *Natural history of religion* and the end of modern Eusebianism' (2011), 279.

[35] A fetishisation that no doubt also stems from the decline in Latin education, and thus a lack of familiarity with much pre-1680 material. It is worth noting the absence of this fetishisation in two old studies relevant to our topic: Diestel, *Geschichte des Alten Testamentes* (1869) and Glawe, *Die Hellenisierung des Christentums* (1912) (the latter is discussed in Ch. 6 below).

What does all this mean for the history of the history of philosophy? First, it means that the category of 'early enlightenment' needs – at least in this context – to be abandoned. It is a central claim of this book that the category obscures more than it reveals about seventeenth-century scholarship. This is not to say that Brucker and the German works were not central to the formation of the historiographical discipline of history of philosophy, which of course they were; rather, it is to escape altogether such disciplinary history, and instead examine seventeenth-century histories on their own terms. It emerges that many of the conclusions supposedly unique to the 'critical' and 'enlightened' historians – especially the rejection of Jewish and patristic narratives of pagan-Christian syncretism, and new attitudes to the relationship between ancient and modern natural philosophy – were not only present, but sometimes even commonplace, in the seventeenth-century discussions, and that there was no intrinsic connection between 'criticism' and heterodoxy. It is not only the fetishisation of 'enlightenment' that has led to neglect of this; it has been a problem from the side of Renaissance scholarship also. It remains customary to claim that Renaissance attitudes to ancient philosophy were 'syncretist', obsessed with developing narratives of a *prisca sapientia* or a *philosophia perennis*.[36] The seventeenth century then falls into the gaps, as scholars are unsure whether to classify seventeenth-century attitudes to the history of philosophy as 'syncretist' or 'enlightened'. However useful the terms *prisca sapientia* or *prisca theologia* are for the fifteenth century – and that itself is dubious – they will not be used here. Take for example the following different views: all philosophy derives from Moses or the ancient Israelites; certain natural religious truths descended from Noah to his children and then to the whole world; the Hebrews had vague foreshadowings of Christian doctrines like the trinity which then spread to some pagan philosophers; all pagans believed in God; all pagan *theists* were monotheists. All of these views have been labelled *prisca sapientia* or *prisca theologia* by modern historians, but they are all fundamentally different positions, and were recognised as such by seventeenth-century men of letters.

The true revolution in attitudes to paganism and its relationship to Judaism and Christianity occurred not at the end of the seventeenth century, but at the end of the sixteenth, in the chronological works of Joseph Scaliger, emulated and developed by scholars such as John Selden, G. J. Vossius, and Samuel Bochart in the next half-century.[37] Almost all of them rejected 'syncretism' in the manner it had been espoused by fifteenth- and sixteenth-century

---

[36] On this, see Vasoli, *Studi su Marsilio Ficino* (1999), 11–50 ('*Il mito dei* prisci theologi *come* ideologia *della* renovatio') (German trans. in Mulsow, ed., *Das Ende des Hermetismus* (2002), 17–60).

[37] Many of the landmarks and findings of this scholarship are discussed in Levitin, 'Sacred history', so I do not list them here. Restoration Englishmen were aware of the importance of

neoplatonists like Marsilio Ficino and Agostino Steuco,[38] a move that occurred not only in Casaubon's famous denunciation of the *Corpus Hermeticum* as a forgery.[39] In his chronological work, Scaliger inveighed against patristic distortions of the history of philosophy for the sake of Christian apologetics:

> Eusebius . . . to assert the truth of the Jewish (and thence the Christian) dispensation, has laid open the libraries of the ancient Egyptian, Phoenician and Greek philosophers, historians and theologians, so as either to disclose their foolishness, distant from the Word of God, or to show that the most ancient Egyptians, Chaldeans and Greeks drank from the fountain of the Hebrew prophets and thence quenched the thirst of their genius *[ingenium]*.[40]

These ideas became popularised in a new form of 'critical' Christian apologetics. A lovely summary of such intentions is available in a 1627 letter by G. J. Vossius, whose *De theologia gentili* (1641) would become probably the most important work on pagan religion to be published in the seventeenth century, and was extremely popular in England, as we shall see:

> I come now to the opinion that you asked about. I for my part, think that [Agostino] Steuco does a poor service to the Christian religion when he claims that its mysteries were known by the ancient pagan philosophers, especially Plato. And in order to claim this convincingly, he [Steuco] clearly twists Plato's words away from what that famous philosopher meant. Nor do I any more approve of the fact that he tries to establish these beliefs from [Hermes] Trismegistus and the Sibylline Oracles, where the secrets of the religion would be revealed much more clearly than in the revelations of the prophets . . . Heavenly truth, which is from Christ and from his Spirit, does not require falsehood . . . Hermes and the so-called Sibyls are spurious, as proven by both their contents and language . . . and I would here show this with many examples, if Casaubon (among others) had not already done it splendidly.[41]

---

Scaliger in this regard: see e.g. Robert Cary, *Palæologia chronica. A chronological account of ancient time* (London, 1677), sig. b$^r$.

[38] For literature on Ficino, Steuco, and others, see 3.1 below. The classic study of the 'ancient theology' remains Walker, *The ancient theology* (1972). It retains much value, avoiding the simplistic reductionism characteristic of many subsequent works, including many which cite it. But it still rests on the fundamental misconception that interest in ancient wisdom was characteristic of philosophical 'Platonism' rather than of professional scholarship much more widely (see e.g. the summary at 194–6).

[39] See 6.1 below.

[40] Joseph Scaliger, 'Animadversiones', in *Thesaurus temporum Eusebii Pamphili* (Leiden, 1606), 4–5, 'Quemadmodum igitur Eusebius in divinis commentariis Προπαρασκευή, ut legis Iudaicae, & inde Christianae veritatem assereret, omnes veterum Philosophorum, Historicorum, Theologorum Aegyptiorum, Phoenicum, & Graecorum Bibliothecas reclusit, ut aut eorum vanitatem ex lege Dei arguerer, aut vetustissimos Aegyptios, Chaldaeos, Phoenicas, & Grecos de prophetarum Hebraeorum fonte potasse, & sitim ingenii sui inde rigasse ostenderet'.

[41] G. J. Vossius to Abraham van der Meer, 13 Dec 1627, Bod. MS Rawl. letters 84c, fol. 7$^r$ (=*Gerardi Johan. Vossii et Clarorum Virorum ad eum Epistolae*, ed. P. Colomiès (London, 1690), 112b–113a): ' . . . venio ad judicium quod poscis. De Steuchio Eugubino equidem ita judico, male eum mereri de Religione Christiana, quando mysteria ejus cognita fuisse docet,

Vossius's published work was thus a form of Christian apologetic history of paganism – including pagan philosophy – without the syncretism he found in the previous neoplatonic apologists,[42] an aim Vossius shared with other major scholars.[43] This is a key point: whatever the apologetic aims such scholarship was put to, it relied on a contextualist recognition of *difference* between the ancient and modern worlds, a recognition that characterised late humanism more generally. This kind of scholarship has been largely neglected by the historiography of the history of philosophy because it was not immediately conducted in works explicitly devoted to the subject. But as we shall see throughout, the post-Scaliger 'critical turn' in biblical criticism, sacred history, and patristics was of central importance in the development of new histories of philosophy, directly leading to the reconsideration of the relationship between pagan wisdom and Jewish and Christian knowledge that has often been considered symptomatic only of 'enlightenment' works.

It is useful at this point to remind ourselves of the basic beliefs about ancient history held by virtually all educated Europeans in this period. Apart from a tiny and un-influential group of pre-Adamists, everyone believed in the gradual diffusion and subsequent corruption of Noachic belief: given the narrative offered in the Old Testament, how could anything else be the case? 'Prisca theologia' was not part of Christian 'orthodoxy', and challenges to it were not intrinsically 'heterodox'; nor, conversely, was it a preliminary stage to veneration of 'natural religion' only.[44] Anyone who used the Old Testament story was a diffusionist of one sort or another, totally irrespective of other political or ecclesiological preferences.

Antiquis Gentium Philosophis, imprimis Platoni: atque hoc ut persuasum eat, planè alioversum torquet verba ejus quàm Philosophus ille senserat. Nec magis probo, quod ea stabilire conatur, ex Trismegisto, ac Sibyllinis Oraculis: ubi multò apertiùs arcana Religionis proponuntur, quàm in Prophetarum Vaticiniis … Nec enim veritas coelestis, quae est à Christo, & Spiritu ejus, indiget mendacio, quod Patrem habet Diabolum. At Platonicos non id voluisse, quod Eugubinus putavit, nemo negabit, qui in Platone cum judicio fuerit versatus. Trismegistum autem, & Sibyllina, ut vocant Oracula, esse supposititia, & res clamat, & dictio ipsa arguit. Quod ego pluribus commonstrarem hoc loco, nisi inter alios luculentè id fecisset Casaubonus, exercitatione prima ad apparatum Annalium Baronii'.

[42] G. J. Vossius, *De theologia gentili, et physiologia Christiana; sive de origine ac progressu idololatriae* (Amsterdam, 1641), e.g. 10. The popularity and importance of Vossius's work is a recurring theme in this book: for a formal statement of his large reputation in England, see Thomas Pope Blount, *Censura celebriorum authorum, sive, Tractatus in quo varia virorum doctorum de clarissimis cujusque seculi scriptoribus judicia traduntur* (London, 1690), 680–1.

[43] See the important conclusion about Bochart and his counterparts in Shalev, *Sacred worlds*, 178–80: '[their] syncretism was very restricted … That Saturn hid the truth of Noah did not mean that they were equally valid narrations of the same story. It is therefore problematic to see in [Bochart] a promoter of syncretism, or even cabalism and "ancient theology", as some scholars do'.

[44] For the first view, see Harrison, *'Religion' and the religions in the English enlightenment* (1990), 131–2, *passim*; for the latter, Champion, *Pillars*, 133–69.

Many of the primary texts considered in this book – especially in Chapters 4 and 5 – were even further detached than theological ones from the world of 'scholarship' narrowly conceived, for they were works of philosophy itself, especially natural philosophy.[45] The vision of seventeenth-century European natural philosophy adopted in this book is not the traditional and still most frequently encountered one, in which one focuses on a small coterie of well-known figures (Descartes, Hobbes, Locke, and Leibniz, with Spinoza, Malebranche, Bacon, and Gassendi (if one is very lucky) as outliers).[46] Descartes did not usher in a sudden 'modernity' – in philosophy or in any other discipline.[47] The vast majority of philosophy in seventeenth-century Europe was conducted not by leading intellectuals working independently, but in institutions, usually at a relatively low level. Few university graduates *wanted* to be philosophers, for the discipline was considered a propaedeutic to one of the higher disciplines: divinity, law, or medicine (although the status of physicians as natural philosophers was much debated, as we shall see).[48]

This book rests on this institutionalised conception of early modern philosophy.[49] Throughout Europe, a vibrant late Aristotelianism continued to flourish;[50] its textbooks – often containing important introductory chapters on

---

[45] Throughout, I use 'natural philosophy' in favour of the anachronistic 'science'; indeed, I hope that this book makes a further contribution to showing that precision when dealing with such issues of generic and institutional identity is important if we are to achieve proper understanding of developments in the period.

[46] For a beautiful discussion of this problem, see Lüthy, 'What to do with seventeenth-century natural philosophy' (2000), discussing even the best overview, Garber and Ayers, eds., *Cambridge history of seventeenth-century philosophy* (1998) (see esp. Lüthy's judgement at 178). Recent synoptic studies continue to eschew an institutional perspective in favour of a focus on individuals: see e.g. (with some notable exceptions) the essays in Clarke and Wilson, eds., *The Oxford handbook of philosophy in early modern Europe* (2011); Anstey, ed., *The Oxford handbook of British philosophy in the seventeenth century* (2013); Nadler, ed., *A companion to early modern philosophy* (2002).

[47] For the early origins of this myth, see Schütt, *Die Adoption des 'Vaters der modernen Philosophie'* (1998).

[48] Serjeantson, 'Becoming a philosopher in seventeenth-century Britain' (2013); Holzhey, 'Der Philosoph im 17. Jahrhundert' (1998), Tuck, 'The institutional setting' (1998). For the fullest studies of law and medicine *qua* higher faculties, see Maclean, *Interpretation and meaning in the Renaissance* (1992); Maclean, *Logic, signs and nature in the Renaissance* (2002).

[49] A conception that has been elucidated by some heroic scholars, usually working on the boundaries between what used to be considered the history of science and the history of philosophy. See Lüthy, 'What to do', esp. 171–3; n. 52 below.

[50] Key works include: Randall, *The school of Padua and the emergence of modern science* (1961); Schmitt, *Aristotle*; Schmitt, *The Aristotelian tradition and the Renaissance universities* (1984); Lohr, *Latin Aristotle commentaries, II: Renaissance authors* (1988); Di Liscia et al., eds., *Method and order* (1997); Kessler, Lohr, and Sparn eds., *Aristotelismus und Renaissance* (1988); Blackwell and Kusukawa, eds., *Philosophy in the sixteenth and seventeenth centuries* (1999); des Chene, *Physiologia* (1996); Ariew, *Descartes and the last scholastics* (1999); Leijenhorst, *The mechanization of Aristotelianism* (2002); Sgarbi, *The Aristotelian tradition and the rise of British empiricism* (2013). Many other key works are discussed in Edwards, 'Aristotelianism'.

the history of philosophy[51] – were continually used in English pedagogy. I will have as much to say about the legacy of long-forgotten early seventeenth-century philosophical innovators[52] as about that of Descartes. It is no coincidence that the same historians who have made the most spectacular findings among the neglected sources of early seventeenth-century natural philosophy have also been those most sensitive to the historical assumptions of the philosophers they have studied.[53] It is my aim to show that such historical assumptions continued to inform the central ideas of natural philosophers through to the end of the century.[54]

Working with this conception of early modern natural philosophy may have some consequences that feel strangely unfamiliar to traditionally minded historians of philosophy or science. Although Hobbes, Boyle, Locke, and Newton are discussed, no special attention is devoted to them unless they made genuinely important contributions to the debates under consideration (as sometimes they did). Chapter 4, on histories of natural philosophical method, has as much to say about not particularly famous physicians as it does about heavyweight philosophers; indeed, one of its key arguments is that the most important re-historicisations of natural philosophical method occurred in institutionally anchored learned medicine. Concomitantly, while one of the main findings of these chapters is the continued engagement of the new experimental natural philosophers with texts of humanist scholarship, another subsidiary aim is to demonstrate that seventeenth-century men of letters would have encountered interpretations of the history of philosophy in the philosophical works they read at university, works such as Marcus Friedrich Wendelin's

---

[51] This subject is unstudied, but for pioneering studies of the broader relationship between natural philosophy and humanism, see Long, 'Humanism and science' (1988); Copenhaver, 'Did science have a Renaissance?' (1993); Grafton, 'The new science and the tradition of humanism' (1996); Grafton, 'Some late Renaissance histories of classical astronomy' (1997); Siraisi, *History, medicine, and the traditions of Renaissance learning* (2007); Hirai, *Medical humanism and natural philosophy* (2011), esp. 1–4 and the works cited there; see also the comments in Smith, 'Recent trends in the history of early modern science', 360–1.

[52] For important introductions to some of these, see Lüthy, 'Atomism, Lynceus, and the fate of 17th-century microscopy' (1996); Lüthy, 'Thoughts and circumstances of Sébastien Basson' (1997); Lüthy, *David Gorlaeus* (2013); Hirai, 'Jacob Schegk's theory of plastic faculty' (2007), 377–404; Shackelford, *A philosophical path for Paracelsian medicine* (2004); Michael, 'Sennert's sea change: atoms and causes' (2001); Newman, *Gehennical fire* (1994).

[53] See e.g. the stunning article by C. Lüthy, 'The fourfold Democritus on the stage of early modern science' (2000), which has served as the closest model for Chapters 4 and 5 of this book. See also Newman, 'Experimental corpuscular theory in Aristotelian alchemy' (2001), esp. 308–10 on Andreas Libavius's reading of Aristotle and Democritus; Hirai, 'Lecture néoplatonicienne d'Hippocrate chez Fernel, Cardan et Gemma' (2009).

[54] For broader emphasis on continuity between medieval, Renaissance, and early modern natural philosophy, see e.g. Newman, *Atoms and alchemy* (2006); Newman and Principe, *Alchemy tried in the fire* (2002); Hirai, *Le concept de semence dans les théories de la matière à la Renaissance* (2005), to pick only three studies which are relevant to Chapters 4 and 5 below.

*Contemplationes physicae* (1625–28), published in a Cambridge edition in 1648 specifically for the use of university students.[55]

## 1.3    English intellectual culture, *c.* 1640–1700

The previous sections have focused on European-wide aspects of intellectual culture. This has been deliberate: it is a major contention of this study that English intellectual culture simply cannot be understood without constant reference to developments on the continent. Nonetheless, this is a book about England; moreover, it is a book that depends on a revisionist vision of the nature of intellectual change in England in the seventeenth century. Some preliminary comments on this subject are thus in order, if only to avoid tiresome repetition of historiographical commentary in what follows.

In terms of synoptic narratives, the intellectual history of seventeenth-century England – especially of the second half of the century – has long been wedded to a totalising, progressivist narrative that stems from the nineteenth century, and which, despite some modifications, remains prevalent. This narrative seeks to forge a strong (and sometimes reductionist) connection between intellectual change and politics. It insists that a 'liberal' tradition stretched from divines like Hooker through to the 'Cambridge Platonists' and to the 'latitudinarians', and then to freethinkers and deists.[56] A combination of these groups is then said to constitute a distinctive English 'early enlightenment', which, while sometimes 'conservative', was still anchored to 'liberal', whig divinity.[57]

---

[55] See p. 62, n. 144.

[56] The roots of this story are in nineteenth-century whig history: see Tulloch, *Rational theology and Christian philosophy in England in the seventeenth century* (1874), I, 411–62, II, *passim*; Pattison, 'Tendencies of religious thought in England from 1688 to 1750' (1860); Stephen, *History of English thought in the eighteenth century* (1881). For a very important analysis of these whig histories and the survival of their assumptions, see Mandelbrote, 'Biblical hermeneutics and the sciences, 1700–1900' (2008). For varied modern manifestations, see e.g. Griffin, *Latitudinarianism in the seventeenth-century Church of England* (1992); Cragg, *From Puritanism to the age of reason* (1950), 61–113; Sykes, *From Sheldon to Secker* (1959), 146–52; McAdoo, *The spirit of Anglicanism* (1965), 81–315; Rivers, *Reason, grace, and sentiment* (1991), I, 25–88; Spellman, *The latitudinarians and the Church of England* (1993). Parkin, *Richard Cumberland* (1999) is far more subtle, but still, to my eyes, over-connects 'science' with 'latitudinarianism' (e.g. 173).

[57] Pocock, 'Clergy and commerce: the conservative enlightenment in England, (1985), at 530–1 (for a very idiosyncratic definition of 'high church' principles); see also 535, 550–1 (for the standard linking of 'Cambridge Platonism' and 'latitudinarianism' and, more puzzlingly, Socinianism); see also Pocock, 'Within the margins: the definitions of orthodoxy' (1995) (where, despite the instructive warnings about the cult of heterodoxy in Anglophone historiography at 33–5, the heroes are standard ones: Hobbes, Locke, Newton, the Cambridge Platonists, unnamed post-Chillingworth irenicists, Tillotson, Samuel Parker as a supposed 'Baconian'. That Parker was politically a persecutor and 'unenlightened' while still making

Whether these categories can help explain English ecclesiological history now seems very doubtful.[58] That they are of little use in explaining *intellectual* developments is a central assumption of this monograph. This is of particular importance for the history of English historiography. Previous studies have insisted that there was a specifically 'latitudinarian' attitude to ancient wisdom;[59] that the history of the concept of 'religion' in late seventeenth-century England can be told as a story not of historiography but of a set of theological–philosophical propositions witnessing the gradual rise of 'natural religion' from the Cambridge Platonists to the deists;[60] and that developments in the historiography of ancient ideas stemmed solely from 'liberal' theologians, anticlericals, and the heterodox.[61] The central misunderstanding generated by these studies is that intellectual change must stem from 'outsiders', and that all intellectual endeavour coming from politically non-'liberal' groups must have been counter-innovative. The most important discussion of Restoration Cambridge, for example, concludes that 'the influence of the high churchmen ... helped to strengthen a commitment to scholarship and academic rigour but their strong emphasis on tradition did little to promote intellectual innovation';[62] it then proceeds to tell a story of the opposition of 'reactive' forces to such 'progressive' developments as Cartesianism and the birth of the Royal Society, the exceptions again being rare islands of rationality such as the 'Cambridge Platonists' and the 'latitudinarians'.[63]

central contributions to European historiography is a central claim of Chs. 3, 5, and 6 below); and Pocock, 'Post-puritan England and the problem of the enlightenment' (1980), esp. 95–6, 100–2. For a sophisticated account of a later period that adopts views on Restoration intellectual culture structurally similar to Prof. Pocock's, see Young, *Religion and enlightenment in eighteenth-century England* (1998), 24.

[58] Spurr, '"Latitudinarianism" and the Restoration Church' (1988). Spurr's findings, based on exhaustive examination of the evidence, have never been seriously challenged, but are often ignored. Important accounts that do attempt a challenge are Rivers, *Grace*, 26, n. 5 and Marshall, *John Locke* (1994), 39 n. 12, but they do not, to my eyes, do much to disturb the evidence accumulated by Prof. Spurr. On the subjects of ecclesiology and toleration, it should be noted that Gilbert Burnet, who *did* consistently campaign for comprehension, was not representative but unique: see Greig, 'Gilbert Burnet and the problem of non-conformity' (1997); Claydon, 'Latitudinarianism and apocalypticism' (2008); 6.7 below.

[59] See the seminal article by Sarah Hutton, 'Edward Stillingfleet, Henry More, and the decline of *Moses Atticus*' (1992); also Levine, 'Latitudinarians, neoplatonists, and the ancient wisdom' (1992) and Levine, 'Deists and Anglicans: the ancient wisdom and the idea of progress' (1995) for the natural continuation of the same story.

[60] Harrison, *Religion*, 130–72.

[61] Champion, *Pillars*, esp. 133–69 for themes central to us. It should be noted that this work was nonetheless pioneering in its shift to charting the historical (rather than philosophical–rationalist) component of anticlericalism.

[62] Gascoigne, *Cambridge in the age of the enlightenment* (1988), 32–3.

[63] Ibid., 25–69. At 6, one finds cited the claim of Richard Westfall that 'The catastrophic decline of the university after the Restoration left it an intellectual wasteland as the Cambridge Platonists died off', from 'The role of alchemy in Newton's career' (1975), 194.

These attempts to connect intellectual change rigidly to politics are incompatible with the evidence. Seventeenth-century English universities demonstrated remarkable vitality in both humanism and the study of nature, without –
for the most part – any political implications.[64] The appeal to 'reason' was a
common shibboleth, not a preserve of 'liberal' theologians.[65] There was no
causal connection between the early Royal Society and an imagined
'latitudinarianism'.[66] On a European level, the republic of letters was not a
utopian force for political and religious liberalism, but a grouping of elitist
*érudits* concerned primarily with their own scholarship.[67]

Such a revisionist vision has major implications for the specific findings of
this book. Opposition to the Royal Society came not from an ingrained anti-
progressive attitude, but from institutional jealousies and insecurities on the
part of certain members of the universities and the College of Physicians;[68]
building on this, it is important to recognise that there was never a battle
between scientific 'moderns' and humanist 'ancients' who were 'already out
of date'.[69] As some of the best recent scholarship in Restoration intellectual
history has demonstrated, many of the most major developments came from the
interaction between natural philosophy and humanist modes of scriptural
exegesis;[70] a conclusion that is confirmed and expanded in this study. A
concomitant conclusion is that one did not have to be a 'Cambridge

---

[64] See the seminal studies by Feingold, 'The humanities' (1997); 'Mathematical sciences' (1997);
    also Toomer, *Eastern wisedome*; Frank, *Harvey*; Serjeantson, 'Introduction' (1999).

[65] Spurr, '"Rational religion" in Restoration England' (1988). See also Mulligan, '"Reason",
    "right reason", and "revelation" in mid-seventeenth-century England' (1984). Beiser, *The
    defense of rationality in the early English Enlightenment* (1996) repeats, with virtually no
    additions, the nineteenth-century whig story.

[66] As convincingly demonstrated in Hunter, 'Latitudinarianism and the "ideology" of the early
    Royal Society' (1990).

[67] The most important revisionist study, albeit one little concerned with ideas themselves, is
    Goldgar, *Impolite learning* (1995). See now the key comments in Malcolm, *Aspects of
    Hobbes* (2002), 457–546 ('Hobbes and the European republic of letters'), at 537–45;
    Malcolm, 'Kircher, esotericism, and the republic of letters' (2004). For the republic of letters
    and confessional disputes, see Jaumann, ed., *Die europäische Gelehrtenrepublik im Zeitalter
    des Konfessionalismus* (2001); van Miert, 'The limits of transconfessional contact in the
    republic of letters around 1600' (2011). For the most forceful version of the utopian view, see
    Marshall, *Early enlightenment culture* (2006); see further the discussion of Le Clerc at 6.8
    below.

[68] Feingold, 'Mathematical sciences', 390–2, 426–7; Hunter, *Science and society in Restoration
    England* (1981), 136–61 ('Science, learning and the universities'); Cook, *Decline*, 133–82;
    Cook, 'Physicians and the new philosophy' (1989); Cook, 'The new philosophy and medicine in
    seventeenth-century England' (1990).

[69] This claim is made in Spiller, *Meric Casaubon and the Royal Society* (1980), 1. The short-
    comings of this account are exposed in Hunter, 'Ancients, moderns, philologists, and scientists'
    (1982). For Casaubon's real attitudes, see Serjeantson, 'Introduction'.

[70] Scott Mandelbrote and William Poole are here at the forefront of research: see among their
    many publications, Mandelbrote, 'Isaac Newton and the writing of biblical criticism' (1993);
    Poole, *The world makers* (2010). See further esp. 3.7 below, including several key works on
    Newton.

Platonist', or in any way connected to the supposed group, to be interested in ancient thought.[71] In the *Storia delle storie generali della filosofia* series, England suffers especially because of this wrongheaded belief.[72] As is shown throughout this book, there was no such thing as a 'Cambridge Platonist' attitude to the history of philosophy. Indeed, the group's whole place in English intellectual history has been misunderstood and overemphasised. For a start, apart from Henry More, they were not 'professional philosophers',[73] but – like most senior university fellows – theologians and philologists who used philosophy when it suited them. Second, both their coherence and importance are predicated on the same nineteenth-century whig story that sought to trace a 'rationalist' lineage for 'liberal' Anglicanism.[74] The idea that they represent an anachronistic remnant of 'Renaissance humanism' in an otherwise 'modern' world is based on the old assumptions about 'ancients and moderns' and about traditions of Platonic 'syncretism' we met earlier. Their influence on divines such as Stillingfleet and Tillotson has been heavily inflated.[75] As will be seen, when we abandon this broad framework and terms like *prisca theologia*, the Cambridge group – which certainly existed as a loose set of acquaintances linked by tutorial relationships[76] and a strong anti-Calvinism (hardly unique in seventeenth-century England) – begins to lose both the intellectual coherence and importance attributed to it. Ralph Cudworth emerges not as an anachronistic 'Platonist' but as a cutting-edge European philologist (2.5, 3.6, 5.2, 6.6). Most importantly, a huge number of scholars, natural philosophers, and divines were acutely interested in ancient wisdom without having anything to do with the Cambridge group.

This book rests on a different vision of intellectual change in seventeenth-century England; one that finds far fewer connections between developments in intellectual life and in politics, and which accords a much more prominent role to the history of scholarship.[77] The old sweeping histories of scholarship

---

[71] Newton's interest in the history of ancient philosophy is consistently attributed to his supposed contacts with 'Cambridge Platonism', a conclusion challenged in 4.5 below.

[72] Malusa, 'First general histories', 279–370. Except for Thomas Stanley, all other historiographical endeavours are grouped under the banner of 'Cambridge Platonism'. To make matters worse, neither Theophilus Gale nor Thomas Burnet, who receive the bulk of the attention, can usefully be described as a 'Cambridge Platonist': see 3.5, 3.7 below.

[73] As claimed in Hedley, *Coleridge, philosophy and religion* (2000), 35. The foremost scholar of the group, Sarah Hutton, consistently presents them all as philosophers: see e.g. 'The Cambridge Platonists' (2002).

[74] Tulloch, *Rational Theology*, II, 1–488.  [75] For Stillingfleet, see 3.5 below.

[76] Now charted in great detail in Lewis, 'The educational influence of Cambridge Platonism' (2010). I am extremely grateful to Dr Lewis for sending me a copy of her thesis.

[77] Only very recently have attempts begun to be made to write English intellectual history from this perspective, the key contributions being Quantin, *Antiquity*; Hardy, '*Ars Critica*'; Haugen, *Richard Bentley* (2011), 12–55 ('Before Bentley: Restoration Cambridge'). The classic older studies are those of J. Levine: *Dr Woodward's shield* (1977); *The battle of the books* (1991); *Between the ancients and the moderns* (1999). While I would like to emphasise that Prof.

overlooked England because they could not find there editions of Greek and Latin authors in the classicists' canon.[78] But the realisation that that canon is a much later construction, and that in the seventeenth century the objects of 'scholarship' were as much post-Hellenic Greek, patristic, biblical, Hebraic, and oriental, has put England back on the scholarly map.[79] Indeed, this is particularly important in the case of England, where the institutional investment in scholarship on this model – 'a model far removed from the fixation on Greek and Roman eloquence and poetry that we associate with fifteenth- and sixteenth-century humanism'[80] – occurred simultaneously and very often in the tumultuous period of religio-political reform instituted by the 'avant garde' conformists who later amalgamated under Laud.[81] This is of course not to say that there was no such thing as Calvinist scholarship,[82] or, worse, that one had to be a Laudian sacerdotalist to practise it. But for the avant-garde conformists, investment in certain types of historico–theological scholarship had a strong polemical dimension. One was patristic. The clearest statements came in the 1620s from the pen of Richard Montagu, later bishop of Chichester and of Norwich, who did not simply affirm the Church of England's supposed patristic identity against the Catholics, as many had always done, but 'aimed also at countering that excessive reliance on modern, Calvinistic, systems of divinity … which Laudians made to be a part of Puritanism, as they now redefined it'.[83] This deliberate emphasis on antiquity against modern Calvinist divinity seems to have had a genuine impact on the theological studies of next-generation figures like Henry Hammond.[84] Montagu had worked as an assistant on Henry Savile's edition of the Greek works of Chrysostom (1613), but that work was more in the traditional humanist framework, addressing itself to the entire 'orbus Christianus' and avoiding overt theological controversy.[85]

Levine's extremely detailed work remains essential to the study of English historiography, I cannot agree with its overall interpretative framework, which to me still seems anchored in questions of 'ancients versus moderns' to an extent that is not justifiable by the evidence, and would have been alien to the subjects under study. Douglas, *English scholars* (1939) is in the old model of sweeping and judgemental history of scholarship, as is Brink, *English classical scholarship* (1986).

[78] See Grafton, 'Barrow as scholar' (1990), 291; also Hardy, '*Ars critica*', 15.

[79] For Grafton's early insistence on the importance of late antique sources to early modern scholars, see *Scaliger*, I, 134–60. Since then, see Grafton and Weinberg, *Isaac Casaubon* (2011); Quantin, *Antiquity*; Hardy, '*Ars Critica*'; Haugen, *Bentley*.

[80] Haugen, *Bentley*, 15.

[81] The foremost account is the magisterial Milton, *Catholic and Reformed* (1995). See also Milton, 'The creation of Laudianism: a new approach' (2002).

[82] For more general attitudes in the Elizabethan and Jacobean church, see Morgan, *Godly learning* (1986). For a useful study of how one of the technical scholarly disciplines that flourished in the seventeenth century already had roots in Reformed pedagogical culture, see Lloyd Jones, *The discovery of Hebrew in Tudor England* (1983).

[83] Quantin, *Antiquity*, 160.  [84] Ibid., 166–70; 6.3 below.

[85] Quantin, 'Du Chrysostome latin au Chrysostome grec' (2008); Hardy, '*Ars Critica*', 86–90.

Montagu and his colleagues were more influenced by the openly controversial and theologically charged patristics of the great émigré scholar Isaac Casaubon; this also led to a more historical conception of early Christianity than offered by Savile.[86]

In part this investment in patristic scholarship was simply part of the defence of ceremonialism,[87] but, more importantly for us, it also acquired a theological and sociological significance, as scholarship became identified both with a rejection of 'modern' (i.e. Calvinist) systems of divinity and with a rejection of putative 'puritan' anti-intellectualism. It was for this complex mix of reasons that Laud invested in a range of scholarship much wider ranging than just patristic, especially oriental.[88] The catastrophe of defeat only cemented the episcopalians' belief in the centrality of scholarship to their identity, partly because exile brought closer contact with continental – especially Dutch – scholars whom they had cultivated before the civil wars,[89] and partly because scholarship now became expressly associated with anti-puritanism and the assault on 'enthusiasm'.[90] Both trends are visible in the Grotius-inspired work of Henry Hammond, which was hugely important in redefining the theological identity of the exiled Church.[91] Just as important was the London Polyglot Bible, prepared mostly by a group of deprived divines led by Brian Walton. As Scott Mandelbrote has pointed out, this investment in philological and historical scholarship was also a statement about the sociology of knowledge:

Walton was no stranger to the debate over clerical authority in seventeenth-century England ... For Walton, the Hebrew text of the Old Testament was not the sole embodiment of the authority of Scripture. This rested instead in the combined testimony of all the versions of the Bible that had survived since antiquity. Taken together, these allowed the learned commentator to consider the true meaning of the text and to prepare suitable interpretations and translations for the people. One effect of Walton's position was to bolster the status of the clergy as interpreters of Scripture.[92]

---

[86] Quantin, *Antiquity*, 142–54. For the scholarship behind Casaubon's anti-Baronio *Exercitationes* (1614), see Grafton and Weinberg, *Casaubon*, 164–230; Hardy, '*Ars Critica*', 91–105. For his own theological status, see Campagnolo, 'Entre Théodore de Bèze et Erasme de Rotterdam' (2007); Reverdin, 'Isaac Casaubon et Genève' (1961).

[87] Quantin, *Antiquity*, 199–202; Milton, *Catholic and Reformed*, 275–6. See also somewhat more generally Lake, 'The Laudians and the argument from authority' (1992).

[88] Toomer, *Eastern wisedome*, 105–15; Feingold, 'Patrons and professors' (1994) for his promotion of oriental and Arabic scholarship. See also Hunt, 'Introduction' (1973), ix–xxxiv; Carter, *Oxford University Press* (1975), 26–36 for his (failed) attempt to establish a university press.

[89] Keblusek, 'Royalist and Anglican book culture in the Low Countries (1640–1660)' (2001); Keblusek, 'Royalist and Anglican experience of exile' (2010).

[90] The fullest treatment is Heyd, *The critique of enthusiasm* (1995), although it does not treat this scholarly dimension.

[91] See 6.3 below.

[92] Mandelbrote, 'The authority of the Word' (2004), 148–9; see also Laplanche, *L'écriture, le sacré et l'histoire* (1986), 322–8.

The vitriolic response of the Independent leader John Owen, while explicitly based on the authority of the Hebrew text alone, implicitly also repudiated this sociology of knowledge.

This is not to say that the Church's investment in continental scholarship was unproblematic. One of the central themes of this book, especially in Chapters 2, 3 and 6, is that it was precisely the tensions between this investment and the demands of religious and theological apologetics that stimulated many of the most important developments in English attitudes to ancient pagan philosophy and its relationship to the Judaeo-Christian ideas. But, crucially, this investment created a normalised intellectual culture where the discussion of issues like the Hellenisms in the New Testament was not limited just to scholars or to divines using scholarship for their own ends, but can be found even in the papers of someone like Robert Boyle.[93] By the Restoration, scholarship on the Scaliger-Casaubon-Grotius model had become institutionalised, and a central plank of conformist clerical identity.[94] Obvious senior examples are John Pearson in Cambridge[95] and John Fell and the circle around him in Oxford.[96] But just as important is the institutionalisation of criticism within a typical (successful) clerical career. Take the famous example of Edward Stillingfleet, who appears several times in what follows.[97] Stillingfleet's intellectual career has been seen as exemplifying the influence on a 'latitudinarian' branch of English divinity of Cartesianism, 'Cambridge Platonism' or 'rationalism' more generally.[98] This relies either on imagining intellectual contacts where there is no evidence for them,[99] or, more broadly, on attempting to spot those things we find 'modern' in someone who was key in the political development of that

---

[93] Robert Boyle, *Some considerations touching the style of the Scriptures* (1661), in *Boyle Works*, II, 450. On this debate, see 6.1 below.

[94] As also recognised in Haugen, *Bentley*, 13–14; aspects of the pre-history are told in Hardy '*Ars critica*'. For an explicit pre-1660 statement, see Brian Walton, *The considerator considered: or, a brief view of certain considerations upon the Biblia polyglotta* (London, 1659), 153–8.

[95] For Pearson, see 2.2, 6.3 below.

[96] See Carter, *OUP*, 53–132; Morison, *John Fell, the University Press and the 'Fell' types* (1967); Beddard, 'Restoration Oxford' (1997), 823–6, 861–3; Beddard, 'Tory Oxford' (1997), 870–6; Keene, 'John Fell: education, erudition and the English Church' (2003). Some very important observations will appear in Poole, 'John Fell's New Year Books again' (forthcoming). I am extremely grateful to him for sending me an early version of the paper.

[97] See 2.5, 3.5, 5.2, 6.5.

[98] Hutton, 'Science, philosophy, and atheism: Edward Stillingfleet's defence of religion' (1993), esp. 102–3, which explicitly downplays the importance of his 'scholarly humanism' and notes the *Origines sacrae* only as an 'intelligent, if bookish critique of Cartesianism'. See also the similar approaches in Popkin, 'The philosophy of Bishop Stillingfleet' (1971); Carroll, *The common sense philosophy of religion of Bishop Edward Stillingfleet* (1975). Stewart, 'Stillingfleet and the way of ideas' (2000) is the best account of Stillingfleet's philosophy in his conflict with Locke. Haugen, *Bentley*, 56, points out that 'Stillingfleet specialised in historical argumentation ... but he was very far from being an important classical scholar', but does not discuss his actual scholarship; cf. Champion, *Pillars*, 59–63.

[99] See p. 143, n. 157 for the lack of evidence of any contact between him and Henry More.

'modernity'. But Stillingfleet's early career is best characterised not by his allegiance to any philosophical position, but by the importance of developing a *scholarly* reputation for an aspiring careerist divine. The work that made his name, the hugely popular *Origines sacrae* (1662), consists almost entirely of historical argumentation, whether concerning the age of the world, the authenticity of the Old Testament texts, or the history of pagan idolatry.[100] When Stillingfleet said that Christianity was 'rational', he meant primarily that it was rational to believe the historical accounts in the New Testament: metaphysics, epistemology,[101] and 'natural religion' have very little to do with this. Rather, Stillingfleet drew on the latest scholarly discussions, some of them quite controversial, not least Isaac Vossius's preference for the Septuagint over the Masoretic chronology.[102] He continued to climb the clerical ladder partly by publishing more impressively erudite tomes, not least his *Origines Britannicae* (1685) on the history of British churches.[103] This work again required serious scholarly effort.[104]

The huge popularity of works like *Origines sacrae* in turn meant that the apologetic history of paganism – including pagan philosophy – became a genre that resonated throughout literate culture, with no obvious political or ecclesiological affiliation tying together those who practised it. John Evelyn, for example, wrote a huge *History of religion* for which he conducted much research in the original sources over almost forty years.[105] At the same time, scholar-divines who had not moved on to glittering ecclesiastical careers like

[100]   Edward Stillingfleet, *Origines sacrae, or, a rational account of the grounds of Christian faith, as to the truth and divine authority of the Scriptures and the matters therein contained* (London, 1662).

[101]   An earlier generation of historians obsessed about the role of 'moral certainty' in Restoration divinity, again connecting it to the 'rational' programme of the latitudinarians, esp. Shapiro, *Probability and certainty in seventeenth-century England* (1983); its importance is convincingly questioned in Spurr, 'Latitudinarianism', 72, 75.

[102]   Stillingfleet, *Origines*, 556–8. The only account to consider Stillingfleet from this perspective is Poole, *World makers*, 5, 13, 19–20, 34–5, 42, *passim*. For Vossius, see Grafton, 'Isaac Vossius, chronologer' (2012), and esp. Mandelbrote, 'Isaac Vossius and the Septuagint' (2012).

[103]   Edward Stillingfleet, *Origines Britannicae, or, the antiquities of the British churches* (London, 1685).

[104]   He searched extensively for new manuscript evidence (see e.g. Henry Dodwell to Thomas Smith, 6 Dec 1676, Bod. MS Smith 49, fols, 123$^r$–124$^r$, at 123$^v$, reporting on a MS of the *Vita Sancti Wilfrithi* lent to Stillingfleet by Thomas Gale).

[105]   Partially printed as John Evelyn, *The history of religion: a rational account of the true religion*, ed. R. M. Evanson (2 vols, London, 1850). Evelyn began the work in 1657 (BL MS Add. 78367, fol. 2$^v$), and worked on it through to the 1690s. See the notes in BL MSS Add. 78368 (esp. fols. 5$^r$–9$^v$ on the history of philosophy), Add. 78328 (e.g. fol. 41$^r$ for notes from Cudworth), 78332 (e.g. fols. 3$^v$, 8$^r$, 9$^v$). See also his lightly annotated copy of Theophilus Gale's *Court of the gentiles*, BL classmark: Eve.A.123, and his recommendation to go back to the original sources for the history of philosophy in a letter to Edward Thurland, 20 Jan 1657, in *The diary and correspondence of John Evelyn, F.R.S.*, ed. W. Bray (4 vols, London, 1854–57), III, 88.

Stillingfleet, but had either remained at or returned to the universities, continued to draw on the resources developed over the course of the century[106] to deliver scholarship of the highest calibre on issues directly relevant to us, whether John Spencer on the relationship between the biblical Hebrews and the Egyptians (3.6) or Thomas Hyde on ancient Persian religion and philosophy (2.7). These works have sometimes been classified as 'enlightened' but, to return to an earlier point, the institutional story I have just told makes it difficult to see why post-1680 works must be disconnected from the intellectual culture that gave birth to them.

## 1.4    The argument

As one of the scholars whose work has most inspired this book has written, 'A besetting sin of historians, especially anglophone, is their unwillingness or inability to count higher than two. In consequence they subtract arguments from one another, instead of multiplying and dividing them in their increasingly complex relationships.'[107] I agree with this judgement, and I have not attempted to subordinate the task of gathering and presenting evidence to that of producing an all-consuming argument.[108] I hope this is reflected in my own prose, where I have tried to convey the appropriate level of empirical evidence for each claim,[109] although no doubt I have allowed my language to mislead and to overplay the coherence of my story. Concomitantly, the extensive scholarly apparatus stems from my desire to convey what the subjects under study here were actually *doing* as historians: this has involved charting their sources, their precise engagement with contemporaries and European scholars more generally, and, whenever possible, documenting any evidence of them at work. Finally – at the risk of total hubris – I have attempted a degree of comprehensiveness. This is reflected in a slightly digressive style: where Chapter 2, for example, nominally deals with attitudes to ancient near-eastern philosophy, much of its first third is devoted to a more general analysis of Thomas Stanley, the first Englishman to publish an independent history of philosophy. I hope that the final interpretative results outweigh what might be considered a stylistic defect.

---

[106] For one important study of the build-up of such resources, see Reif, *Hebrew manuscripts at Cambridge University Library* (1997), 7–15.

[107] Pocock, 'Review of S. Pincus, *1688: The first modern revolution*' (2011), 188.

[108] For an overt statement of the contrary position, see e.g. Pedersen, 'Festschriftiness' (2011), 32: 'we need strong arguments, even wrong arguments: the job of the historian is to make persuasive claims and leave it to others to issue the caveats'. The logic of the claim does not reveal who these mysterious and inferior 'others' actually *are*: one assumes they cannot be other historians, who will be too busy making 'strong arguments'.

[109] If anyone requires methodological justification for this, please see Blau, 'Uncertainty and the history of ideas' (2011).

Given these caveats, there are some central themes that will be repeated, some of which have already been introduced: the continuing vitality of humanist traditions of scholarship; the centrality of historical arguments to debates about natural philosophical methods and doctrines; the importance of the post-Scaliger type of grand history of paganism for new ideas about the history of philosophy; the uselessness of categories like *prisca theologia* and 'ancients versus moderns' to describe seventeenth-century worldviews; the extreme precariousness of the category of 'enlightenment', at least on this subject; the weak connection between political–ideological aims and historiographical change. The last of these is again worth emphasising – while individuals may have developed historiographical positions for ideological reasons, those positions were then accepted or rejected primarily for scholarly reasons: that is to say, because people thought them historically *true*. This is not internalism: it is the recognition that not all early modern intellectual history has to be reduced either to politics or to a set of philosophical presuppositions.[110]

These themes can be subsumed into arguments that are synchronic and diachronic. The synchronic argument is that new histories of philosophy were developed within the framework of the English appropriation of late (i.e. post-Scaligerian) humanism both in its pure form (e.g. in Stanley and Marsham) and as it was applied to various professional disciplines: biblical criticism, apologetics, the study of early Christianity. This central theme runs through Chapters 2, 3 and 6. The first two of these chapters demonstrate the large-scale engagement of natural philosophers with these modes of scholarship. Chapters 4 and 5 focus more exclusively on natural philosophers, demonstrating that their methodological and doctrinal ideas were anchored in history. Here the humanist framework was broader than just the Scaligerian one, encompassing inheritances from Aristotelianism and anti-Aristotelianism, medical humanism, and historical defences of iatrochymistry (and historical attacks on it). If one particularly common starting point were to be identified it would be the works of Gassendi, but not as they are usually understood – that is, as a modified recapitulation of a coherent 'Epicureanism' – but as a wide-ranging set of very contextual historical reflections on ancient Greek natural philosophy.

The diachronic arguments are those of the chapters themselves; we may briefly summarise them here. Chapter 2 examines histories of near-eastern ancient philosophy, which, while they have received less attention, were just as prominent as claims about ancient Egypt. I commence with the treatment of the subject by Thomas Stanley, the fourth volume of whose *History of*

---

[110] See also the important parallel point made about the history of science in Malcolm, *Aspects*, 317–35 ('Hobbes and the Royal Society'), at 335.

*philosophy* (1655–62) treated 'Chaldaick Philosophy'. Stanley is an important, fascinating, but also very difficult and ambiguous figure: his *History* was the first vernacular work of the type. I place Stanley in the context of both European and royalist-episcopalian approaches to ancient history, and show how he combined the new critical approach and the use of Jewish sources (especially Maimonides) with what initially looks like the uncritical use of a classic forgery, the *Chaldean Oracles*. The history of ancient astronomy continued to be of great interest to practising natural philosophers, as we shall see from the edition of Manilius by Stanley's friend Edward Sherburne, from manuscript evidence from the archive of Henry Power, and from the natural philosophical networks around these works; indeed, these findings will allow us to form a very different picture of the 'scientific' culture of the 1650s than that in most of the existing literature. At the same time, we shall also cover the apologetic uses of near-eastern history of philosophy, before turning to the Latin edition of Stanley's work prepared by the Amsterdam-based Swiss scholar Jean Le Clerc, which inserted Chaldean philosophy into the debate about Judaic and early Christian syncretism. Finally, I offer a detailed treatment of the remarkable re-assessment of Zoroaster and Persian philosophy in Thomas Hyde's *Historia religionis veterum Persarum* (1700), the first Western discussion based extensively on Persian sources. It will be shown that for all of Hyde's pioneering methods, he must still be understood within the context of Church of England orientalism and seventeenth-century late humanism more generally.

Chapter 3 turns to histories of Egyptian and Jewish philosophy. This was a concern not just for scholarly or even apologetic reasons but also because it had been a traditional component of European natural philosophy and divinity to discuss the book of Genesis as a work of natural philosophy. I chart the 'historical turn' in English approaches to Genesis in the middle of the century. I then demonstrate that there was no 'Cambridge Platonist' approach to the history of ancient wisdom, whether Mosaic, Egyptian, or otherwise. Henry More was an outlier, whose vision of the history of Mosaic wisdom was highly idiosyncratic; it was implicitly opposed by many of his Cambridge colleagues. Indeed, the period witnessed a growing disenchantment with narratives of Judaic intellectual primacy, primarily because of the recognition – imported from continental critical scholarship – that the Jewish and early Christian sources of such a narrative were deeply untrustworthy. This trend found its peak in the revolutionary works of the young Anglican apologist Samuel Parker, the chronologer John Marsham (Stanley's uncle), and the Cambridge Hebraist John Spencer. These scholarly and religious themes were picked up by a host of natural philosophers in the 1680s and 1690s, as the debate about 'Mosaic philosophy' became *the* pre-eminent natural philosophical debate of the final years of the century.

While continuing this focus on natural philosophers as historians, Chapter 4 shifts to a more exclusively natural philosophical focus, examining how historical arguments were developed and deployed to articulate and defend specific methodological positions, especially in relation to what was coming to be called 'experimental philosophy'. It demonstrates the continuing importance of both Aristotelian and anti-Aristotelian historiographical traditions, whether in the methodological statements of William Harvey and his followers or of some members of the early Royal Society and its apologists. The key finding, however, is that the histories of natural philosophical method offered by the Royal Society apologists Thomas Sprat and Joseph Glanvill were – contrary to their continued historiographical prominence – remarkably unsuccessful. Instead, it is argued, the most important historical defence of the experimental method was offered at an institutional level, in the field of learned medicine. Physicians, drawing on long-established traditions in medical humanism, were able to present a history of their discipline that offered it an experimental identity while – crucially – not eroding its 'philosophical' status. This historical–methodological move filtered into wider natural philosophical discourse. Partially this occurred at the hands of those with strong medical interests: Thomas Willis, John Locke, and Thomas Sydenham. A similar move, albeit based on a different set of interests, was made by Isaac Barrow and his successor as Lucasian Professor of Mathematics at Cambridge, Isaac Newton, who offered histories of mathematics that demonstrated its relevance to natural philosophical explanation while at the same time equating it with observation rather than speculative hypothesising. All this will permit us to make some important contributions to the on-going debate about the methodological novelty – or lack thereof – of English natural philosophers.

Chapter 5 continues to focus primarily on natural philosophers, turning to histories of doctrine, specifically histories of matter theory and of animating principles. In contrast to a long historiographical tradition, we shall find that virtually no English natural philosopher – even of the many who accepted corpuscularianism[111] – believed themselves to be a successor of Epicurus, whose philosophy they tended to characterise as speculative and reductionist. Instead, they either drew on alternative genealogies involving a 'chymical' and 'experimental' Democritus, or concocted even more elaborate pre-histories for a non-reductionist corpuscularianism. Simultaneously, Gassendi's re-historicisation of Epicurus – the starting point for all historical treatments of matter theory – was rejected or heavily modified by heavyweight scholars such as Meric Casaubon and Ralph Cudworth. Gassendi had much more success in another field: the history of animating principles. He had suggested that virtually all the Greek philosophers had been animists. This radical conclusion

---

[111] The specifics of the terminology of microparticulate matter theories is treated at 5.1.

was taken up both by English scholars and theologians *and* natural philosophers, and blended more generally with the general interest in histories of
ancient idolatry of the Vossius type. It led – in adjusted form – to some of the
most famous programmatic statements about natural philosophy, by Willis, by
Boyle (especially in the *Free enquiry concerning the vulgar notion of nature*
(1686)), and by Newton (in the General Scholium, added to the second edition
of the *Principia* (1713)).

Chapter 6 returns primarily to scholars and divines. It demonstrates that the
realisation that early Christian theology was infected by Greek – specifically
Platonic – philosophy came not in the 'early enlightenment' but had been
gestating in English scholarship since the middle of the seventeenth century. It
was promoted precisely by the institutionalised investment in criticism described
in section 1.3 of this chapter, as English theologians attempted to amalgamate the
critical approach of Isaac Casaubon with their increasing postulation of a patristic
identity for the Church of England. This tension – exploited by both Reformed
and Catholic scholars on the continent – led to some remarkable syntheses, first
by a generation including Henry Hammond, Herbert Thorndike, and John
Pearson, then by an even more creative group including Samuel Gardiner,
Samuel Parker, Ralph Cudworth, Henry Dodwell, and George Bull; the heated
trinitarian debates of the 1690s were largely derivative of their scholarship. A
continued obsession was the relationship not only between Greek philosophy and
Christianity, but also between the former and Hellenistic Judaism. The chapter
again finishes with Le Clerc: it is argued his work had little to do with 'enlightenment', but simply adopted a standard Reformed position against the scholarly
tangles in which English scholarship had managed to embroil itself as it attempted
to walk the fine line between criticism and dogmatic theology, which remained a
central concern for Le Clerc too.

Readers may be surprised that I have not outlined the availability of the key
ancient texts. This important work has been ongoing for many years; it has
recently been very usefully summarised.[112] Each of the subsequent chapters
will provide an introductory summary of the debate as it had developed before
the mid-seventeenth century. I have also done this because it is often the case
that historians of the seventeenth and eighteenth centuries – especially of the
Anglophone world – still sometimes have a tendency to offer rather caricatured
and inaccurate descriptions of previous periods, a trap that I thought it particularly important not to fall into on this subject.

As for the sources, at this point it is sufficient to say that by the
seventeenth century an educated reader could quite easily obtain the

---

[112] Hankins and Palmer. A useful shorter summary is Grafton, 'The availability of ancient works'
(1988); see also Kraye, 'The legacy of ancient philosophy' (2003).

sources for almost any famous Greek philosopher, whether in Latin translation or in the original Greek. Extensive surveys are available for Plato,[113] Aristotle,[114] and now even their commentators.[115] The story of the recovery of Epicurus and Lucretius is too well known to require recapitulation;[116] Stoic[117] and sceptical[118] sources are equally well covered, as are famous pseudepigrapha like the *Hermetic Corpus* and the *Chaldean Oracles*.[119] Of course, these sources, and those for philosophers for whom little or no primary evidence survived (most notably those we – but not early moderns – call the presocratics), could be approached not through the primary evidence but through ancient anthologies of philosophical opinions,[120] whether those in the well-known and widely available texts of Aristotle, Cicero, or in Stobaeus's *Anthology*, in dedicated accounts like Philostratus's *Lives of the Sophists*, Pseudo-Plutarch's *De placitis philosophorum*,[121] or Iamblichus's *Vita Pythagorica*,[122] in the church fathers,[123] or in later compilations like the massive tenth-century Byzantine lexicon, the *Suda*, or Photius's *Bibliotheca*. From these and

---

[113] Hankins, *Plato in the Italian Renaissance* (1990). See also Hankins, 'Socrates in the Italian Renaissance' (2007).

[114] Cranz and Schmitt, *A bibliography of Aristotle editions, 1501–1600* (1984); Dod, 'Aristoteles Latinus' (1982), 45–79.

[115] See e.g. Cranz, 'Alexander Aphrodisiensis', *CTC*, I, 77–135, II, 411–22, VII, 296–8 (addenda by Carlo Vecce); Bossier, 'Traductions latines et influences du Commentaire *In de Caelo*' (1987); Schmitt, 'Olympiodorus', *CTC*, II, 199–204; Schmitt, 'Theophrastus', ibid., 239–322; O'Meara, 'Plotinus', *CTC*, VII, 55–74; Todd, 'Themistius', *CTC*, VIII, 57–102; Kraye, Ryan, and Schmitt, eds., *Pseudo-Aristotle in the Middle Ages* (1986); Lohr, 'Renaissance Latin translations of the Greek commentaries on Aristotle' (2000); Mahoney, 'Neoplatonism, the Greek commentators, and Renaissance Aristotelianism' (1982).

[116] Much of the earlier (principally Italian) literature is discussed in Prosperi, *La fortuna di Lucrezio* (2004); Solaro, *Lucrezio: Biografie umanistiche* (2000); and Fleischmann, 'Lucretius', *CTC*, II, 349–66. Greenblatt, *The swerve: how the Renaissance began* (2011) offers a spectacular narrative – perhaps too spectacular to be of much use.

[117] Boter, 'Epictetus', *CTC*, IX, 1–54; Hadot, 'La survie du Commentaire de Simplicius sur le *Manuel d'Epictète*: Perotti, Politien, Steuchus, John Smith, Cudworth' (1987).

[118] Floridi, *The transmission and recovery of Pyrrhonism* (2002); Schmitt, 'The rediscovery of ancient skepticism' (1983); Schmitt, *Cicero scepticus* (1972), 81–91.

[119] Dannenfeldt, 'Hermetica philosophica', *CTC*, I, 137–50, II, 423, III, 425 (addenda by M.-T. D'Alverny); Dannenfeldt, 'Oracula Chaldaica', ibid., 157–64, VII, 326–9 (very important addenda by I. Klutstein). See also Sider, 'Horapollo', *CTC*, VI, 15–30; Chevalier, ed., *Dionysiaca* (1937–50).

[120] For an introduction, see Runia, 'What is doxography?' (1999).

[121] Hankins and Palmer, 66–7; Mansfield and Runia, *Aëtiana. Vol. I: the sources* (1997), 1–41 offers a very informative discussion of the early modern reconstruction (primarily on the basis of ps.-Plutarch) of Aëtius (i.e. what for Diels became the key source). For Stobaeus, see also Stanwood, 'Stobaeus and classical borrowing in the Renaissance' (1985); Miller, 'Grotius and Stobaeus' (2005–7), esp. 107–8.

[122] Hankins and Palmer, 54–5.

[123] An important overview is Kraye, 'Pagan philosophy and patristics in Erasmus and his contemporaries' (2011).

other sources could be made new anthologies, most usefully Henry Estienne's (assisted by Scaliger) *Poesis philosophica* (1573).[124]

But of course most important was Diogenes Laërtius's *Lives of the eminent philosophers*, first translated from Greek by Ambrogio Traversari and published to immediate popularity in 1472, a text that publishers 'longed to reprint ... or even bring out their own edition'.[125] The Greek *editio princeps* was published by Froben in 1533; Latin-Greek editions with notes by scholarly heavyweights like Estienne and Casaubon followed before the end of the century.[126] The best new edition appeared in London in 1664 under the editorship of Gilles Ménage (with an improved edition in 1692): some aspects of the English contribution are discussed below.[127] The work was ubiquitous in learned culture. It was used to teach Greek at university[128] and was recommended as essential reading for aspiring divines, who could use Laërtius's encyclopaedic accounts of the various philosophical sects – or subsequent scholarship on the history of philosophy – to preach on the improvements over pagan wisdom brought by Christianity.[129] A portable

---

[124] Henri Estienne, *Poesis philosophica, vel saltem reliquiae poesis philosophicae* (Geneva, 1573). See Hankins and Palmer, 1; Kraye, 'Legacy', 340–1; Reverdin, 'Brève évocation de la Ποίησις φιλόσοφος' (1999); and most fully, Primavesi, 'Henri II Estienne über philosophische Dichtung' (2011). Scaliger had located many further fragments: Grafton, *Scaliger*, I, 298, n. 159; Primavesi, 'Estienne', 170–2.

[125] Tolomio, 'Historia philosophica', 154–60 is the best account of its popularity and many editions (quotation from 155). On Traversari, see Stinger, *Ambrogio Traversari* (1977), esp. 71–7 on the Laërtius translation, based on two manuscript copies collected in Constantinople by Guarino da Verona and Antonio da Massa; see also Gigante, 'Ambrogio Traversari interprete di Diogene Laerzio' (1988), 459. The Greek *editio princeps* was published by Froben in 1533. For the full manuscript tradition, see now Dorandi, *Laertiana* (2009). For the various editions judged by a modern scholar, see Knoepfler, *La Vie de Ménédème d'Érétrie de Diogène Laërce* (1991), 21–94.

[126] *Diogenis Laertii de vitis, dogmatis & apophthegmatis eorum qui in philosophia claruerunt, libri X ... cum annotationibus Henr. Stephani* (Geneva, 1570); *ibid ... Is. Casauboni notae ad lib. Diogenis, multo auctiores & emendatiores* (Geneva, 1593). Casaubon had first published his notes independently in 1583: see the brief discussion in Parenty, *Isaac Casaubon, Helléniste* (2009), 50–3. A superior Latin translation was published by Tomasso Aldobrandini in Rome in 1594.

[127] See 2.2, 5.2. More generally, see Maber, *The Ménage-Graevius-Wetstein correspondence* (2005); Piaia, 'Histories of philosophy in France', 72–7. For Ménage's *Historia mulierum philosopharum* (Lyon, 1690, then included in the 1692 DL), see the 'Introduction' in the translation by B. Zedler, *The History of women philosophers* (1984), iii–xxviii. From an English perspective, *Diogenis Laertii de vitis, dogmatibus et apophthegmatibus clarorum philosophorum libri X*, ed. M. Meibom (2 vols, Amsterdam, 1692), II, 557–66 contains collations by Thomas Gale of Trinity College, Cambridge MS R.9 18–19, fols. 132ʳ–240ᵛ and BL MS Arundel gr. 531 (on Gale and his interest in the history of philosophy, see 3.6 below).

[128] Porter, 'University and society' (1997), 68–9.

[129] As advised in Thomas Bray, *Bibliotheca parochialis: or, a scheme of such theological heads ... as are more peculiarly requisite to be well studied by every pastor* (London, 1697), 28. See also Henry Dodwell, *Two letters of advice I. For the susception of Holy Orders, II. For studies theological* (Dublin, 1672), 292 (for Dodwell, see 6.6 below). More generally,

octavo English translation appeared in 1688.[130] This was despite the serious concerns that scholars themselves had long held about the work: its seeming preference for arbitrary fact gathering rather than critical judgement; the presence of significant lacunae despite this approach; the doubtful chronologies.[131] Repairing these errors was one of the primary tasks the numerous editors of the text set themselves. At the same time, Laërtius's successions continued to inform and even drive interpretations of philosophical history, as we shall see; Table 1 summarises them for the convenience of the reader who might not be able to recall some of the more obscure names.

As for other connected subjects, the great surge of medical humanism in the sixteenth century had made available most of the key works in the Galenic and Hippocratic *corpora*.[132] As we shall see in Chapter 4, it was medical humanism above all that stimulated the idea that ancient thought had prioritised experience over theory and speculation. The case was somewhat different for mathematics, where although many texts were translated and published in the fifteenth and sixteenth centuries,[133] several, including parts of such crucial

---

Francis Brokesby, *Of education with respect to grammar schools, and the universities* (London, 1701), 86–8 expresses the desire for an introductory history of the diffusion of paganism after Noah, listing as his modern models Vossius and Bochart. For the use of Thomas Gataker's work on Stoicism and Meric Casaubon's on DL (5.2 below for both) in apologetics, see e.g. Daniel Whitby, *An endeavour to evince the certainty of Christian faith in general* (London, 1671), 348(=349)–50, 359, 363, 365, 366, 379.

[130] *The lives, opinions, and remarkable sayings of the most famous ancient philosophers*, trans. T. Fetherstone et al. (2 vols, London, 1688). A second edition of 1696 included lives of several other philosophers extracted from Eunapius's *Lives of the Sophists*. The work was obviously a commercial rather than scholarly venture, comparable to *The Apophthegmes of the ancients taken out of Plutarch, Diogenes Laertius, Elian, Atheneus, Stobeus, Macrobius, and others ... for the benefit and pleasure of the ingenious*, ed. J. Bulteel (London, 1683). Much earlier, Juan Luis Vives had hinted at the work's 'popular' nature by claiming that it was composed for a woman: *Vives: on education. A translation of the De trandendis disciplinis of Juan Luis Vives*, ed. and trans. F. Watson (Cambridge, 1913), 241, a claim repeated in England in Charles Blount, *Janua scientiarum, or, a compendious introduction to ... all genteel sorts of literature* (London, 1684), 64.

[131] Examples of early criticisms are offered in Tolomio, 'Historica philosophica', 155–6. See also *The lives of the ancient philosophers ... extracted from Diogenes Laertius, Casaubon, Menagius, Stanley, Gassendus, Charleton ...* (London, 1702), sigs. [A3]ʳ, [A4]ᵛ. Israel, *Enlightenment contested*, 422 claims that Le Clerc believed that 'So deficient was [the earlier humanists'] grasp of ancient systems of belief and thought ... that all their various editions of ... Diogenes Laertius ... were practically useless', citing Jean Le Clerc, *Ars critica ...* (2 vols, Amsterdam, 1697), II, 449–50. Le Clerc here says nothing of the sort, instead preaching caution about Laërtius's lists of various philosophers' writings, and actually praising Ménage on this score.

[132] Durling, 'Renaissance editions and translations of Galen' (1961) remains essential. See further 4.1 below for seminal works on medical humanism.

[133] Goulding, *Ramus, Savile, and the Renaissance rediscovery of mathematical history* (2010) is an excellent study, also discussing the available sources.

works as Apollonius' *Conics*, survived only in Arabic versions that only slowly became the subject of proper scholarship, a process that had a significant English component.[134] This is a process to whose history I do not have the technical skills to make a serious contribution; my discussion of histories of mathematics is mostly limited to the debate on the methodological relationship between mathematics and natural philosophy (4.5 below).

That the work of collecting the main primary sources was mostly complete, and that something further was needed to develop the history of philosophy, was recognised by learned Englishmen. John North, Regius Professor of Greek at Cambridge in 1672–74, and Master of Trinity College in 1677–83, planned to compose precisely such a work. He acknowledged that 'such an History was much wanted; but of Collectors and Transcribers of Sentences … there were more than enough' (although this did not prevent North from publishing some Pythagorean fragments).[135] Rather, what was required was to chart the

Originations, Connections, Transitions and Alterations of the Opinions, as also of the several Sects, how they sprung up, one under another, comparing their Tenets, and shewing wherein they agreed and disagreed, with their Squablings and Altercations; and so coming down so low as his own Time, to shew how the Moderns had borrowed from the Ancients, and what they had set up new of their own.[136]

At the same time, North planned 'an History of the Heathen Theology',[137] not only out of independent interest, but because pagan philosophy could not be understood outside the context of pagan religious culture. In holding these assumptions – that the history of philosophy had to be contextual, to make

---

[134] See esp. Mercier, 'English orientalists and mathematical astronomy' (1994) as well as the other essays in Russell, ed., *Arabick interest*, and Fried, *Edmond Halley's reconstruction of the lost book of Apollonius's* Conics (2011).

[135] See his translation of and notes on the very interesting fifth-century BC quasi-Doric tract Δισσοὶ λόγοι (which North knew by its alternate title, Διαλέξεις), in Thomas Gale, *Opuscula mythologica, ethica et physica* (Cambridge, 1671), 'Fragmenta quaedam Pythagoreorum' (separate pagination), 47–76. The *editio princeps* was published by Estienne in DL 1570; North's was the first ever translation and commentary. North's reasons for making the author a Pythagorean are a misreading (following Estienne) generating 'Μίμας' as the supposed name of the author (66) and the Doric language of the text (47, n. 1). It is possible that North edited the text as part of a campaign to succeed Gale as Regius, in which case it was a triumph.

[136] Roger North, *The life of the honourable Sir Dudley North … and … Dr. John North* (London, 1744), 258–60, 262. See also North's notes on 'Critica' in BL MS Add. 32514, fol. 183ʳ. North had all his notes and writings burned after his death, but one notebook survived: this is the neat transcript made by Roger North (fols. 167ʳ–227ᵛ); the rough notes can be found in BL MS Add. 32517. See further Kassler, *The honourable Roger North* (2009), 54–5.

[137] See the notes in BL MS Add. 32514, fols. 179ᵛ–182ᵛ.

connections rather than treat philosophers or sects individually, and that it could serve a didactic purpose without retreating into veneration for either 'ancients' or 'moderns' – North was typical of contemporary Englishmen well beyond the world of Greek scholars that he inhabited; we shall meet him on several occasions in what follows (4.4, 5.4, 6.6).

Following on from this point, it should be said that a list of sources as given above in a key sense negates one of the key purposes of this monograph: to demonstrate that educated seventeenth-century Englishmen (and some women) encountered the history of ancient philosophy not only in the classical works themselves, or in works of 'scholarship' narrowly defined, but virtually everywhere: in religious apologetics, in scriptural exegesis, and in philosophy textbooks (see 4.1). To be able to speak of the philosophical past was a cultural expectation. John Marsham, one of the heroes of this monograph (3.6 below), wrote in the 1660s a letter to his son before the latter left for university: in a rather moving example of male displacement of emotion into technical expertise, Marsham advises, 'When you have learned to frame a Syllogisme, and know the force of a Demonstration it will be worth y$^{or}$ consideration to reflect upon y$^e$ Author of this Art of reasoning; w$^{ch}$ actuates then y$^e$ Understanding noe lesse then dancing doth the feete, or fencing y$^e$ armes'. He proceeded to outline – in wonderful detail – how Plato's Socratic dialogue was replaced by Aristotelian syllogism and then the 'reputation y$^t$ Aristotle had in the Greeke Scholes' (listing famous commentators), the loss and rediscovery of learning under the Muslim conquests (again listing Arabic philosophers and astronomers), its subsequent reappearance in Europe, and the revival of Greek learning after 1453 (although he also praised the twelfth century 'shin[ing] forth' of y$^e$ liberall sciences, after a long eclipse' – a remarkable pre-empting of C. H. Haskins), and finished with an emotional plea – still grounded in history – for his son to continue his Greek studies.[138] Marsham was not an out-dated relic of a 'humanist' past: his work on Egyptian chronology was one of the most revolutionary European historical works of the period. That his son and his

---

[138] CKS MS U1121 E5/2: 'You see, by what is said, how Jo: Buriensis, not without cause, complayneth of the corrupt coppies of Aristotle, w$^{ch}$ he used: why in the Councill at Vienna (in France) a° 1311 . . . there was noe notice taken of the Greeks: you see how the great Doctors of the Schools, Aquinas, Scotus, and their Sectaries could not perfectly understand the author, upon whom they have made soe larg tracts: howe easy it was for them to run blindfold into absurdities, w$^{ch}$ being granted multiply infinitely. You see the reason why I formerly advised you to apply your self to the text, as the most compendious way of study; and not to neglect the Greek tongue w$^{ch}$ is of most excellent use in all kind of learning'. 'Jo: Buriensis' is John Boston of Bury, author of the *Catalogus Scriptorum Ecclesiae*; he had received prominence in Thomas Fuller's *Worthies of England* (1662), well known to Marsham from his work on the history of monasteries.

son's university colleagues were expected to have an automatic familiarity with the history of ancient and medieval philosophy, despite no doubt also being taught, and having an interest in, its modern counterpart, is a cultural fact that we must recover in the face of two (or more) centuries of historiographical erosion.

Table 1. *The successions of the philosophers in Diogenes Laërtius's* Lives of the Philosophers.

The list is selective: only the more prominent philosophers are included. These successions are very loose organisational structures employed by Laërtius, not designed – even by him – to have much causal or explanatory force. The long list of later Ionics, for example, is explicable solely by their stemming in the loosest sense from Socrates. Moreover, the level of interplay between the two successions becomes, at points, very large: as Laërtius makes clear, for example, Plato is heavily indebted to the Pythagoreans (III.6). This becomes even more of a problem with the so-called 'seven sages' (of whom there are more than seven because putative membership of the group varies): Thales, in particular, could be presented as being both the founder of the Ionic succession (due to his Milesian heritage) and as having a connection with the Italics (due to his contact with Pherecydes, another rather mysterious figure, sometimes reputed the teacher of Pythagoras). As we shall see, early modern scholars – especially Ralph Cudworth – used these ambiguities to their own interpretative advantage. Some figures who became prominent in early modern historiography, such as Ocellus Lucanus, are not included because they did not receive stand-alone treatment in Laërtius. SMALL CAPS indicate the founder of a school within the succession, followed by members of that school; e.g. Plato and after him seven Platonics. The group of Italics from Heraclitus to Timon were not formally members of any school. Dates (given for particularly prominent figures) are modern estimates: early modern scholars sometimes had very different chronological ideas.

**Seven Sages** Thales (c. 624–546 BC), Solon, Chilon, Pitacus, Bias, Cleobulus, Periander, Anacharsis, Myson, Epimenides, Pherecydes (6th c. BC)

| Italic Succession | Ionic/Milesian Succession |
| --- | --- |
| PYTHAGORAS (*c.* 570–495 BC) | ANAXIMANDER (*c.* 610–546 BC) |
| Empedocles (*c.* 490–430 BC) | Anaximenes (*c.* 585–528 BC) |
| Epicharmus | Anaxagoras (*c.* 510–428 BC) |
| Archytas | Archelaus |
| Alcmaeon | Socrates (*c.* 469–399 BC) |
| Hippasus | Xenophon |
| Philolaus | Aeschines |
| Eudoxus | ARISTIPPUS (*c.* 435–356 BC, founder of Cyrenaic sect) |
| Heraclitus (*c.* 535–475 BC) | PLATO (428–348 BC) |
| Xenophanes | Speusippus |
| Parmenides (early 5th *c.* BC) | Xenocrates |
| Melissus | Polemo |
| Zeno of Elea | Arcesilaus |
| Leucippus (first half 5th *c.* BC) | Bion |
| Democritus (*c.* 460–370 BC) | Carneades |
| Protagoras (*c.* 490–420 BC) | Clitomachus |
| Diogenes of Apollonia | ARISTOTLE (348–322 BC) |
| Anaxarchus | Theophrastus (*c.* 371–287 BC) |
| Pyrrho (*c.* 360–270 BC) | Strato (*c.* 335–269 BC) |
| Timon | Heraclides |
| EPICURUS (341–270 BC) | ANTISTHENES (*c.* 445–365 BC, founder of Cynic sect) |
| | Diogenes of Sinope |
| | Menippus |
| | Menedemus |
| | ZENO of Citium (334–262 BC, founder of Stoic sect) |
| | Aristo |
| | Dionysius |
| | Cleanthes |
| | Chrysippus |

## 2      Ancient wisdom I. The wisdom of the east: Zoroaster, astronomy, and the Chaldeans, from Thomas Stanley to Thomas Hyde

Historiographical interest in early modern approaches to ancient philosophy has focused primarily on discussions of ancient Egypt. We shall turn to this topic in Chapter 3. Here we may note that this historiographical focus is less the product of the early modern sources themselves and more of modern historians' own interests; perhaps most notably, of Frances Yates's belief that 'Hermeticism' was an identifiable movement or even 'ideology'.[1] In reality, early modern men of letters were just as interested in the supposed presence of philosophy throughout the orient – a perennial concern, for example, was the theological–philosophical wisdom of the Indian Brahmins.[2] But by far the most important group to receive such attention were the nations of the near east: Persia, Chaldea, Babylon, and, very often, the philosopher-sage who putatively stood behind them all – Zoroaster. Seventeenth-century England was not immune to this interest; indeed, English scholarship provoked some of the most important reconsiderations of Zoroaster and near-eastern intellectual history. The key figures in this story are (i) Thomas Stanley, author of the first vernacular history of philosophy, whose difficult and ambiguous text requires a prolonged contextualisation; (ii) Jean Le Clerc, a prominent Amsterdam-based Swiss scholar who republished Stanley's work on near-eastern philosophy in Latin translation, but also developed a complex re-interpretation of the evidence; and (iii) Thomas Hyde, an Oxford-based orientalist whose *Historia religionis veterum Persarum* (1700) was the first European work to attempt a history of ancient Zoroastrian theology on the basis of a systematic exploration of Persian texts. Interest in near-eastern philosophy was not, however, limited

---

[1] Yates, *Giordano Bruno and the Hermetic tradition* (1964). See Hanegraaff, 'Beyond the Yates paradigm' (2001); Gatti, 'Frances Yates's Hermetic Renaissance' (2002).

[2] The key classical source being ps.-Palladius, in England edited by Sir Edward Bysshe as Παλλαδίου, περι τῶν τῆς Ἰνδίας ἐθνῶν καὶ τῶν Βραγμανων. *Palladius de gentibus Indiae et Bragmantibus* ... (London, 1665, repr. 1668): as well as the stated texts, almost all known classical testimonies (Strabo, Cicero, Pliny, Plutarch, Arrianus, Apuleius, Clemens Alexandrinus, Porphyry, Philostratus) are supplied at sigs. b$^r$–[e4]$^r$. On Bysshe, see Sherlock, 'Bysshe, Sir Edward', *ODNB*. Bysshe appears to have been the first editor to ascribe the work (first published 1569) to Palladius Helenopolitanus (*c.* 363–425): Coleman-Norton, 'The authorship of the *Epistola de Indicis Gentibus et de Bragmanibus*' (1926), 154.

to such scholars, for it is also manifest among the natural philosophical *novatores* – specifically those interested in the history of astronomy – as well as among Christian apologists. Both groups, as we shall see, remained wedded to humanist forms of scholarship. Indeed, there was significant overlap of interests and intentions between some scholars and natural philosophers, an investigation of which sheds some important new light on the nature of mid-century intellectual culture.[3]

## 2.1     Zoroaster and near-eastern philosophy before 1600

'Real' Zoroastrianism is an Indo-Iranian religious system whose origins are early and obscure, but which served as the main religion of a major part of the Persian empires between the sixth century BC and the collapse of the Sassanid Empire in AD 651. It is a monotheistic faith that holds one, entirely good, supreme being, Ahura Mazda. However, this supreme being is in constant combat with a separately created evil principle, Angra Mainyu or Ahriman – the theological nature of this 'dualism' has been the subject of constant debate. Zoroaster himself is believed to be the divinely inspired prophet of the religion. He is said to have composed one portion (the 'Gathas') of the *Avesta*, the sacred texts of Zoroastrianism, written in the Avestan language. Only its liturgical elements now survive. In the third to tenth centuries AD, paraphrases and commentaries on the *Avesta* were developed in Middle Persian languages, especially in the Pahlavi script – the most important of these is the *Zand*. The oft-used expression 'Zend-Avesta' to refer to the *Avesta* is a mistaken extrapolation from *Zand-i-Avesta*, one of the manuscript forms in which the *Avesta* survived, in which the books are written together with their *Zand*. Zoroastrians consider fire and clean water as agents of ritual purity, and fire temples are the standard places of worship – this is not mentioned in the *Avesta*, and was a development of the Parthian era (250 BC–AD 226). In the tenth century, under renewed Islamic persecution, there was a mass migration of Zoroastrians to Persian cities on the margins of the salt deserts (especially Yazd and Kerman) and also to Gujarat in western India: the latter group became known as Parsees.[4]

---

[3] It should be noted at this point that the whole subject of Zoroaster's European reputation has been treated in compendious detail by the German scholar of religion Michael Stausberg (*Faszination Zarathushtra: Zoroaster und die Europäische Religionsgeschichte der Frühen Neuzeit* (1998)). We must be deeply grateful to Prof. Stausberg for his exhaustive treatment; I hope to add to his account something of the perspective of the early modern historian rather than the specialist on Zoroastrianism. In places, my argument, and the evidence that I use, thus differs significantly from his.

[4] This summary is based primarily on Boyce, *A history of Zoroastrianism* (1975–91); Boyce, *Zoroastrians: their religious beliefs and practices* (1979); Stausberg, *Die Religion Zarathustras* (2002–4).

Virtually none of this history or its textual products was known to the Graeco-Roman or Christian West; the *Avesta* was not made available until its publication by Abraham Hyacinthe Anquetil-Duperron in 1771. This did not prevent an elaborate and detailed historical picture emerging.[5] Two Zoroastrian *personae* developed: that of the religious leader or magus,[6] and that of the pioneering astrologer.[7] The first fit into a well-established Greek historiographical tradition concerning Persian religion and especially the magi;[8] the second, into the Greeks' and Romans' obsession with establishing exotic 'oriental' genealogies for their sciences, as Zoroaster was claimed as the fount from which Plato and Pythagoras drew their philosophies.[9] A particularly important discussion was that of Plutarch, who most explicitly discussed Zoroaster in the context of dualism and named the two principles as Oromazes and Areimanius;[10] as we shall see, dealing with Plutarch as a source was a central concern for early modern scholars. Zoroaster was also deemed the founder of one of the Roman mystery cults, Mithraism.[11] Christians, meanwhile, dealt with the Zoroaster that they inherited from Graeco-Roman historiography in a mostly negative way, associating him with the foundation of demonic or astrological magic and even with Noah's son Ham.[12] Just as importantly, variants of the heresy that became known as gnosticism (and its derivative Manichaeism) were attacked by their self-appointed 'orthodox' opponents for supposedly drawing on Zoroastrian dualism,[13] an accusation that would be of some importance for early modern scholars.

From all this speculation there emerged, in the second century AD, a text of great importance: the so-called *Chaldean Oracles*. This product of the unique philosophical–religious configuration of the first few centuries AD is a collection of Greek hexameter verses, supposedly originating in ancient Chaldea.

---

[5] The classic discussion is Bidez and Cumont, *Les mages hellénisés* (1938), whose claim that the Zoroastrian pseudipagraphia were partly the product of an Iranian diaspora in Anatolia is challenged in Beck, 'Thus spake not Zarathustra', (1991). For the fullest summary, see de Jong, *Traditions of the Magi* (1997). For the historiographical–cultural world that facilitated these speculations, see Momigliano, *Alien wisdom* (1971), esp. 141–8. For the early Christian reception, see Stausberg, *Faszination*, I, 439–50. I draw freely on all these for the following paragraphs.

[6] E.g. Plutarch, *Is. Os.*, 46–7; DL 1.6–9; Agathias, *Hist.*, II.23–5.

[7] See all the fragments collected in Bidez and Cumont, *Mages*, II, 137–263.

[8] E.g. Herodotus, 1.131–2; Strabo, *Geog.*, xv.3.13–15.

[9] E.g. Cicero, *Fin.*, v.29; Valerius Maximus, *Factorum ac dictorum memorabilium*, VIII.7; Pliny, *Hist. nat.*, xxx.2.3; Iamblichus, *Vita Pyth.*, 41; Plutarch, *Adv. Col.*, 14; Lactantius, *Div. inst.*, IV.2; Clemens Alexandrinus, *Strom.*, I.15.

[10] Plutarch, *Is. Os.*, 46–7. [11] E.g. Porphyry, *De antr. nymph.*, 6.

[12] Ps.-Clement, *Recogn.*, IV.27–9 (identification with Ham). See also ps.-Clement, *Hom.*, IX.4–5, identifying him with Nimrod as founder of astrology, who was killed by lightning and posthumously deified by the Persians. Cf. the variation in Augustine, *Civ. Dei*, XXI.14.

[13] Bidez and Cumont, *Mages*, II, 155–6. The truth is complex and remains disputed, based on evidence unavailable to early modern scholars; see Sundermann, 'How Zoroastrian is Mani's dualism?' (1997).

Their exact origin remains a mystery, the best evidence suggesting that they were first recorded by one Julian the Theurgist (*fl.* late second century), the evidence for which (*Suda*, 434) was available to early modern scholars. This, however, was not the opinion of their first readers, for it is 'of singular importance ... that the *Oracles* were regarded by the later neoplatonists— from Porphyry (*c.* 232–303) to Damascius (*c.* 462–537)—as authoritative revelatory literature equal in importance only to Plato's *Timaeus*':[14] it is through the quotations of these various neoplatonists that the *Oracles* survive. To give a sense of the mystical, anti-materialist, and mythological nature of the text, I will quote one fragment (fr. 56):

> Truly Rhea is the source and stream of blessed intellectual realities. For she, first in power, receives the birth of all these in her inexpressible womb and pours forth this birth on the All as it runs its course.[15]

Of particular importance to us is the *Oracles*' integration into western Christian discourse. Quoted by Platonising Christians such as Arnobius (*c.* 253–327) and Synesius (*c.* 370–413), they received extensive commentary by the Byzantine philosopher Michael Psellus (*c.* 1019–78), who gathered the scattered fragments and attempted to reconcile them with Christianity. The key role in their transmission to Western Europe was played by George Gemistos Plethon, an eighty-year-old court philosopher who arrived with the Byzantine Emperor John VIII Paleologus and the Orthodox Patriarch Joseph II to participate in the council on the reunion of Eastern and Western churches held in Ferrara in 1438.[16] Plethon was very important in developing the then rudimentary knowledge of Greek philosophy, especially Plato, among the Florentine humanists. But most important for us is his version of the *Oracles*, which he entitled the *Magical Sayings of the Magi, following Zoroaster*.[17] This was a key moment, for it was the first time that the *Oracles* had been attributed explicitly to Zoroaster.[18]

---

[14] Majercik, 'Introduction' (1989), in *The Chaldean Oracles* (1989), 2 (when not Stanley's, all English translations are taken from here). The standard critical edition is des Places ed., *Oracles chaldaïques, avec un choix de commentaires anciens* (3rd edn, rev. A. Segonds, Paris, 1996). See also Stausberg, *Faszination*, I, 44–57.

[15] *Chaldean Oracles*, 71. An obvious comparison presents itself between the *Oracles* and their more famous counterparts, the *Hermetica* – this comparison is often offered by modern historians of early modern historiography, but as we shall see, early modern scholars also had good reasons to suppose a qualitative difference.

[16] On Plethon, see the classic Woodhouse, *George Gemistos Plethon* (1986), and Tambrun, *Pléthon* (2006).

[17] For a modern edition, see Tambrun-Krasker, ed. and trans., Μαγικὰ λόγια τῶν ἀπὸ Ζωροάστρου μάγων ... *Recension de Georges Gémiste Pléthon* (1995); Woodhouse, *Plethon*, 48–61 has an English translation of Plethon's version and commentary.

[18] See Stausberg, *Faszination*, I, 35–44, 57–84, 278–83, 312–15, for Plethon and the *Oracles*. For a useful, if not always comprehensive, introduction to the *Oracles* in the Renaissance, see

Plethon's own religion probably consisted of an attempt to revive what he saw as Platonic paganism, but his work opened the door for the Platonic–Christian syncretism of Marsilio Ficino, who, after some earlier attempts, settled from 1469 on Zoroaster (*qua* author of the *Oracles*) as the earliest in a line of six proto-Christian sages (Zoroaster, Hermes Trismegistus, Orpheus, Aglaophamus, Pythagoras, and Plato).[19] Ficino saw Zoroaster as the founder of a good 'natural' (as opposed to 'demonic') magic; using some obscure phrases in the *Oracles* first noted by Plethon, he aligned Zoroaster with a proto-trinitarian, rather than dualist, scheme; he also claimed that the three μάγοι who followed the Star of Bethlehem to Christ (Matt. 2:1–12) were Zoroastrian magi.[20] Yet Ficino's vision was not particularly historical: 'he simply assumed a transmission of vision, a gentile equivalent, so to speak, of the apostolic succession; a line of theologians of the One and of the soul's journey to the One from the many, having escaped the trammels of the body by way of purgation and meditation'; the context for this semi-illuminationist view of pagan wisdom was in part a very optimistic view of the capacity of the human soul, in part the providential–astrological enthusiasm that was then sweeping Florence.[21] In many ways this context is also applicable to Giovanni Pico della Mirandola, the young Italian nobleman who in 1486 invited men of letters from around Europe to debate his 900 theses 'including his own and those of the wise Chaldeans, Arabs, Hebrews, Greeks, Egyptians, and Latins',[22] only to see the plan scuppered by the condemnation of Pope Innocent VIII in 1487. The great innovation in Pico's project was that it incorporated Christian Cabbala – Pico had been taught Hebrew and 'Cabbalistic' secrets by Flavius Mithridates, a Jewish convert to Christianity who told Pico as much of what the latter wanted to hear as what he found in Hebrew texts[23] – and Pico also claimed, in a letter to Ficino which would later become famous, that he possessed a copy of the *Oracles* in Aramaic, 'in which those things which are faulty and defective in the

Dannenfeldt, 'The Pseudo-Zoroastrian oracles in the Renaissance' (1957); also useful in this regard is Hanegraaff, *Esotericism and the academy* (2012), 29–76.

[19] The literature is extensive. For Ficino and the *Oracles*, essential is Klutstein, *Marsilio Ficino et la théologie ancienne* (1987), 3–18; see also Klutstein, 'Marsile Ficin et les "Oracles Chaldaïques"' (1976); Tambrun, 'Marsile Ficin et le "Commentaire" de Pléthon sur les "Oracles Chaldaïques"' (1999). For the general development of his view on the history of ancient wisdom, see Allen, *Synoptic art* (1998), 1–51 ('Golden wits, Zoroaster and the revival of Plato'); Hankins, *Plato*, II, 459–64 (app. 17, 'The development of Ficino's "ancient theology"').

[20] Allen, *Synoptic art*, 31–40; Stausberg, *Faszination*, I, 93–228, 235–41, 255–62, 273–7, 512–14.

[21] The quotation is from Allen, *Synoptic Art*, 41–2; for the soul, see Kristeller, *The philosophy of Marsilio Ficino* (1943), 377–80; for providential astrology in Florence, Weinstein, *Savonarola and Florence* (1970).

[22] Giovanni Pico della Mirandola, 'Preface', quoted and trans. in Farmer, *Syncretism in the West* (1998), 210–11.

[23] See now the essays in Perani, ed., *Gugliemo Raimondo Moncada alias Flavio Mitridate* (2008).

Greek, are read perfect and entire'.[24] The story emerged that Ficino found this manuscript upon Pico's death, but that it was illegible.[25] This story was used most prominently a century later by Francisco Patrizi, whose *Nova de universis philosophia* (1591) was a philosophical system designed to replace Aristotelianism with a philosophy based on pagan sources supposedly far closer to the Christian tradition.[26] As well as being a philosophical reformer (albeit an initially unsuccessful one – the work was prohibited in 1594), Patrizi was a far more serious historian than Ficino.[27] Not only did he give new scholarly life to the *Oracles*, supplementing existing collections with fragments from Proclus, Synesius, Olympiodorus, Damascius, and others (increasing the total to 324), he also developed a concerted historical explanation for their 'truths': Zoroaster was a son or grandson of Ham, and thus contemporary with Abraham, from whom he took philosophical wisdom; the *Oracles*, meanwhile, were not written, but only *translated* into Greek, by Julian the Theurgist.[28] Nonetheless, Patrizi's attitude to the *Oracles* was also in many ways even more optimistic than Ficino's, finding clear references to the trinity where Ficino had found only foreshadowings.[29]

These were far from the only discussions available, and the *Oracles* became a standard part of the ancient historiographical repertoire, especially given their wide availability in stand-alone publications.[30] They continued to shape discussion of near-eastern intellectual history in the seventeenth century, including in England.

## 2.2 Thomas Stanley as a historian of philosophy

### 2.2.1 The problem

Thomas Stanley (1625–78) has the honour of having written the first vernacular work exclusively devoted to the history of

---

[24] Dannnfeldt, 'Oracles', 15; Pico's correspondence was printed in his *Opera*, published in Basel in 1572. See also Stausberg, *Faszination*, 229–61.

[25] On this whole episode, see Wirszubski, *Pico della Mirandola's encounter with Jewish mysticism* (1989), 241–4.

[26] Muccillo, *Platonismo, Ermetismo e 'Prisca Theologia'* (1996), 73–194; Puliafito, 'Metaphysics of light and ancient knowledge in Francesco Patrizi da Cherso' (2002); Leijenhorst, 'Franceso Patrizi's Hermetic philosophy' (1998). For his influence as an anti-Aristotelian historian of natural philosophy, see Ch. 4 below.

[27] Mucillo, 'La biblioteca greca di Francesco Patrizi' (1993); Grafton, *What was history?* (2007), 126–42.

[28] Francesco Patrizi, *Nova de universis philosophia* (Venice, 1593 [1st edn=Ferrara, 1591]), 'Francisci Patricii Zoroaster et eius CCCXX Oracula Chaldaica' (new pagination), fols. 3$^r$–5$^v$ (Patrizi's interpretation), fols. 6$^r$–11$^v$ (his edition of the *Oracles*); see also *Discussionum Peripateticarum tomi IV* (4 vols, Basle, 1581), III, 292.

[29] This is well brought out in Leijenhorst, 'Patrizi's Hermetic philosophy', 139. See also Stausberg, *Faszination*, I, 291–395.

[30] Dannenfeldt, 'Oracula Chaldaica'; Stausberg, *Faszination*, I, 321–4.

philosophy.[31] Despite this fact, and despite the alluring nature of the subject, his work has received remarkably little scholarly attention. For the most part, the *History of philosophy* (1655–62) is presented as a rather bland foil for more enticing subjects, whether as the supposed conduit for Locke's knowledge of the works of Gassendi,[32] or as an unremarkable and uncritical contribution to the debate over the compatibility of Stoicism and Christianity,[33] or for any other number of seemingly more interesting issues.[34] The consequence of this approach is that the nature of Stanley's fascinating and subtle engagement with the history of philosophy remains entirely ambiguous: for some, he was an even more credulous version of Laërtius[35] or yet another 'syncretist' in the Renaissance Platonic mould;[36] for others, the *History* contributes to his status as nothing less than the 'most important proximate model for Richard Bentley's Greek projects of the 1690s'.[37]

There are good reasons for the confusion. Stanley's *History* is one of the most puzzling works of early modern scholarship. It was structured precisely on the model of Laërtius. Often, Stanley's contribution was simply to fill the holes left by the doxographer, such as the incomplete account of the Stoic

---

[31] Thomas Stanley, *The history of philosophy ... containing those on whom the attribute of wise was conferred* (4 vols, London, 1655–62); 2nd edn: *The history of philosophy: containing the lives, opinions, actions and discourses of the philosophers of every sect* (London, 1687); 3rd edn: ibid. (London, 1701); 4th edn: *The history of philosophy ... in which the innumerable mistakes ... of all former editions are corrected* (London, 1743). This last edition is based largely on the Latin translation by the German pietist Gottfried Olearius (1672–1715): *Historia philosophiae ... ex anglico sermone in latinum translata, emendata, variis dissertationibus atque observationibus passim aucta* (2 vols, Lepizig, 1711), the changes in and additions to which are well summarised in Malusa, 'First general histories', 178–9. The fourth edition is thus an unreliable witness to Stanley's own scholarship: unfortunately it is that which has been reproduced as Thomas Stanley, *The history of philosophy ... with a new introduction by Knud Haakonssen* (Bristol, 2000). The first edition was printed by Thomas Dring and Humphrey Moseley: Stanley authorised his banker to issue Dring £50 on 17 May 1663, and £95 to Dring's servant on 5 June 1663 (Stanley to John Morris, Bod MS Eng. lett.c.16, fols. 7$^r$, 8$^r$): it is unclear what these huge amounts relate to – perhaps Stanley's Aeschylus, also published by Dring? (Morris was a leading banker: Melton, *Sir Robert Clayton* (Cambridge), 45, 67–9, *passim*). The second edition was published by Thomas Bassett and the third by Awnsham Churchill. Both were re-set, but neither contains major changes beyond incorporation of errata. All citations from the third edition, unless stated otherwise.

[32] Kroll, 'The question of Locke's relation to Gassendi' (1984), convincingly disproved in Milton, 'Locke and Gassendi' (2000), 102–4.

[33] Brooke, 'How the Stoics became atheists', 394–5.

[34] E.g. Gaukroger, *Francis Bacon and the transformation of early modern philosophy* (2001), 17.

[35] Braun, *Histoire de l'histoire de la philosophie*, 69 ('Ce Diogène anglais est d'ailleurs aussi crédule que l'ancien'); Pocock, *Barbarism*, v, 141.

[36] Israel, *Enlightenment contested*, 475 and Gueroult, *Dianoématique*, ɪ, 275 (curiously enough drawing on the judgement of Hegel, *Geschichte der Philosophie*, xv).

[37] Haugen, *Bentley*, 24. John Edwyn Sandys (*Classical Scholarship*, 251) delicately avoided the issue by stating only that 'At the time of its publication, the field which it covered was almost untrodden ground'.

succession in Book VII.[38] At points, it demonstrates a remarkable degree of critical acumen (judged by contemporary standards), whether in its approach to some of the chronological problems raised by the conflicting evidence of the sources, or in the philologically sophisticated proposed emendations of the Greek. Yet at other points this critical acumen merges rather uncomfortably with what appears, at first sight, as a peculiarly accumulative attitude. Take, for example, Stanley's treatment of Socrates. In 1637, Leo Allatius (1586–1669), the Greek-born librarian of Cardinal Barberini who had managed the transportation to Rome of the Palatine library of Heidelberg in 1622 and would become Vatican librarian in 1661,[39] published from manuscript, to much fanfare, putative letters by Socrates and the Socratics. Since Plato explicitly stated that Socrates had left no writings, this was a major scholarly event. But to defend the Socratic provenance of the letters, Allatius had to engage in some rather tricky chronological manoeuvring. For example, one letter, purportedly written to Xenophon by a follower of Socrates who had been present at Socrates's trial and death, reported that the lost oration given against him at his trial was written by one Polycrates the Sophist.[40] But Laërtius (II.39) had reported that the authenticity of Polycrates's oration had been challenged by the Roman hermaphrodite sophist and philosopher Favorinus (c. AD 80–160) on the basis that it mentioned the rebuilding of the Athenian city walls by Conon, which 'did not take place till six years after the death of Socrates' in the last year of the archonship of Laches, or the first year of the ninety-fifth Olympiad (i.e. 399 BC), as reported in all the standard sources.[41] Allatius 'solved' the problem by extending Socrates's life by ten years, drawing especially on a passage in the Suda,[42] as well as on other peripheral sources, such as the *Vita Marciana*, a dubious life of Aristotle that claimed that he had been taught by Socrates.[43]

At the end of the century, Richard Bentley assaulted Allatius's scholarship in his famous *Dissertation upon the Epistles of Phalaris* (1697), not only demonstrating the absurdity of relying on the non-standard sources, but also providing a clever thesis to explain the issue of Polycrates's 'oration', which Favorinus had claimed as spurious but whose existence was confirmed by other sources,

[38]  Stanley, *History*, 344.
[39]  On Allatius's transfer of the Palatine library (supposedly on 200 mules), see Mazzi, *Leone Allacci e la Palatina di Heidelberg* (1893); for his scholarly activities in Rome more generally, which centred on promoting Roman-Greek union, see Rietbergen, *Power and religion in Baroque Rome* (2006), 395, 400, 424; Hartnup, *Leo Allatios and popular orthodoxy* (2004), esp. 27–67; *Dizionario biografico degli Italiani* (1960), II, 467–71, and above all Cerbu, 'Leone Allacci', esp. ch. 3.
[40]  Leo Allatius, ed., *Socratis, Antisthenis, et aliorum Socraticorum epistolae* (Paris, 1637), 32.
[41]  E.g. DL II.44 (also giving the testimony of Demetrius of Phalerum); Diodorus Siculus, *Bib. hist.*, XIV.37.7; Aristides, fr. 1K.
[42]  Allatius, *Epistolae*, 117.
[43]  Ibid., 122–3; P. Gigon, ed., *Vita Aristotelis Marciana* (Berlin, 1962), 2, 36.

most notably Isocrates.[44] This could be explained, Bentley affirmed, by the fact that although the oration was indeed genuine, it was written several years later by Polycrates as a typical sophist exercise in commending an unexpected subject, such as an illness, or, in this case, the killing of the revered Socrates; Plato, Xenophon, and others had, after all, also written dialogues in which Socrates was a character, which were hardly to be taken as literal history.[45] Bentley claimed that until him, 'this passage of *Favorinus* has not been yet rightly understood'; indeed, he added that since Allatius had published the epistles, 'no body, since, that ever I heard of, has brought the matter into controversie'.[46]

This was disingenuous. Bentley's argument had been made more than forty years previously by Stanley, with whose work he was undoubtedly familiar. Stanley's attack on Allatius in the *History* had been pioneering in defending the traditional authorities with support from the Parian Chronicle, recently made available through John Selden's catalogue of the Arundel Marbles.[47] However, there is a bigger point here than Bentley's plagiarism (previously unspotted by his many commentators). For Bentley drew a wider conclusion from the evidence: 'If *Socrates* died in *Laches's* Magistracy . . . not one Epistle only, but the whole bundle of them are spurious'.[48] Stanley, meanwhile, in a later section on Socrates's writings, listed '*Epistles*, some whereof are published by *Leo Allatius*', and then proceeded to offer English translations of the first seven of Allatius's letters, even including suggestions for emendations to the Greek![49] It is this mixture of critical acumen (Stanley's attack on Allatius even included corrections to the chronology of Scaliger himself) and a desire to squeeze the most out of *all* the sources – however spurious – that characterises Stanley's work, and requires contextual explanation.

---

[44] Isocrates, *Busiris*, XI.4.

[45] Richard Bentley, *A dissertation upon the Epistles of Phalaris, Themistocles, Socrates, Euripides, and others* (London, 1697), 94–9.

[46] Ibid., 95, 89.

[47] Stanley, *History*, 92a–b. There are even direct rhetorical parallels: 'there be not any thing in the *Greek* Story settled by better Authority, than the Years of *Socrates*' (Stanley, 92a); '*Socrates* was put to death Olymp. XCV, 1. when *Laches* was Magistrate. This is universally acknowledged; and to go about to prove it, were to add light to the sun' (Bentley, 99). For Bentley's knowledge of Stanley's other work, especially his notes on Callimachus (BL MS Harley 5676), from which he was accused of plagiarising, see Haugen, *Bentley*, 65; Lehnus, 'Callimaco redivivo tra Th. Stanley e R. Bentley' (1991). For Selden and the Arundel Marbles, see Toomer, *Selden*, I, 360–87.

[48] Bentley, *Phalaris*, 10 (Bentley's point is that since the other letters discuss events that *did* happen during Laches's archonship, they counteract Allatius's attempt at re-dating).

[49] Stanley, *History*, 99b–102b. He was criticised for this by Olearius, who drew on Bentley to offer an extended dissertation on the letters (*Historia*, 208–19).

## 2.2.2   Stanley's method

While some manuscript evidence has long been known – and more is here presented – the evidence for Stanley's scholarly practices is sparse, and our interpretation of the *History* must be based on a broader intellectual–biographical and contextual foundation.

Stanley, born into a rich gentry family in Hertfordshire, was something of a prodigy: his first publication, *Poems and translations*, appeared in 1647, when he was twenty-two, but biographical and manuscript evidence suggests that he had composed it *c.* 1642 (i.e. at seventeen), before leaving England for the continent at the outbreak of civil war, revising it extensively upon his return in 1646–47.[50] He attended Pembroke College, Cambridge between 1639 and 1643, but his education seems to have owed more – before, during, and after his time in Cambridge – to one William Fairfax, son of Edward Fairfax, the first translator of Tasso. There is little to support the contemporary accusation that the *History* was ghostwritten by Fairfax,[51] although it does seem to have been partly a product of Stanley's studies with his tutor:

> With scrutiny the Greeks we often vext,
> And disentangled oft the Romane Text,
> The old Philosophers we did excite
> To quarrel, whilst we smil'd to see the fight.[52]

These lines are from a poem entitled 'A Register of Friends', probably written towards the end of Stanley's life, in which he remembered many of those with whom he associated during the civil war and commonwealth periods.[53] From this poem we also learn that Stanley was part of a community of poets and scholars which met at his lodgings in the Middle Temple (where had taken up residence in 1646), which included his uncle William Hammond (himself a precocious Greek scholar), his cousin Richard Lovelace, the aforementioned Fairfax, the even more prodigious young northern poet John Hall, and

---

[50] See CUL MS Add. 7514, discussed in Crump, 'Thomas Stanley's manuscript of his poems and translations' (1958). The standard biographical discussions of Stanley are Crump, 'Introduction' (1962), esp. xxi–xxxiii; Flower, 'Thomas Stanley (1525–1678): a bibliography of his writings' (1950). On Stanley's poetry, see further Praz, 'Stanley, Sherburne and Ayres as translators and imitators of Italian, Spanish and French poets' (1925); Revard, 'Translation and imitation of Joannes Secundus' *Basia*' (2000); Wilson and Vinson, 'Thomas Stanley's translations and borrowings' (1958).

[51] See Osborn, 'Thomas Stanley's lost "Register of Friends"' (1958). I have been frustrated in my attempts to find more information on Fairfax. The entry on Edward Fairfax in *The Universal Magazine*, 94 (1794), 357 claims that William 'translated Diogenes Laertius out of Greek into English', but I have found no evidence for this. The same source claims that 'the greatest part' of Stanley's *History* was written by Fairfax, but given that it also ascribes to Stanley 'notes on Euripedes', when Stanley in fact published on Aeschylus, we may justly hold serious doubts regarding the value of the information.

[52] Thomas Stanley, 'A Register of Friends', in Crump, *Poems and translations*, 354–66 at 355.

[53] On its discovery, see Osborn, 'Register'.

additional poets Alexander Brome and Robert Herrick.[54] It is extremely likely that Stanley, with his doubly inherited income from his own family and from his marriage, acted as a patron to many of these figures, and also, recent evidence suggests, to Andrew Marvell.[55] The group was tied not only by poetry but by politics: all members (except Hall) were royalists, and it appears that Stanley established an 'Order of the Black Ribband', in which members wore a black armband to signify sympathy with the plight of the king.[56]

Beyond poetry and politics, there was a third dimension to this intellectual circle: scholarship. Stanley probably first turned to serious scholarship under the influence of Fairfax and Hammond,[57] but the classical interests of his closest friends, Sherburne and Hall, are also clear, not least in topics that directly concern us: Sherburne was interested both in ancient astronomy and Lucretius whilst Hall translated the commentary on the pseudo-Pythagorean *Golden Verses* by the neoplatonist Hierocles of Alexandria (see below for both). But Stanley's scholarly reputation extended well beyond the circle of the 'Black Ribband'. The *History* itself was dedicated to Stanley's uncle, John Marsham, who was, alongside Ussher, the leading English chronologer of the seventeenth century, and who Stanley said 'first directed me to this Design'.[58] As we shall see, there can be little doubt that Marsham's chronological interests rubbed off on Stanley. It may have been Marsham – well connected in royalist scholarly circles – who first introduced Stanley to the wider scholarly world: John Evelyn, for example, recorded meeting Stanley accompanied by Marsham and the famous antiquary and monastic historian Sir William Dugdale.[59] In

---

[54] Stanley, 'Register of Friends'; for the literary community reconstructed from the 'Register', see Revard, 'Thomas Stanley and "A Register of Friends"' (2000). Stanley had first met Hall on a trip north in 1641; Gause, 'Hammond, William', *ODNB*, incorrectly states that Hammond's younger sister, Mary, married 'the author Thomas Stanley'; in fact she married Stanley's eponymous father.

[55] McDowell, *Poetry and allegiance in the English civil wars* (2008), esp. 13–68.

[56] Flower, 'Stanley', 140–1; Crump, 'Introduction', xxvi–xxvii; McDowell, *Allegiance, passim*, including the interesting claim that 'The Black Riband was defined by its nostalgia for a courtly system of cultural patronage that had been wrecked by civil war' (62). For Sherburne's very *jure divino* monarchical readings of biblical passages, see BL Sloane 837, fols. 1$^r$–2$^r$.

[57] Crump, 'Introduction', xxiv.

[58] Stanley, 'To my Honoured UNCLE John Marsham, Esq', *History*.

[59] *The diary of John Evelyn*, ed. E.S. de Beer (6 vols, Oxford, 1951), III, 237; on Dugdale's scholarly life, see Parry, *The trophies of time* (1995), 217–48. It is also likely that Stanley may have had access to Marsham's library, which contained at his death 1,085 books even after having been 'considerably diminished by y$^e$ fire of London': See CKS MS U1121.E7, 'Catalogus librorum Bibliothecae Marshamianae' – which contains 459 books in folio, 211 in quarto, 369 in octavo, and 46 unclassified. Although the catalogue was composed several years after Marsham's death in 1685, it can be considered representative, for it contains few books after that date, the latest published in 1697 (see p. 21 of the Catalogue). The description of the library's contents is from CKS MS U1300 Z10, 'Robert Marsham's Biography of Sir John [Marsham]', fol. 1$^r$: which adds that the library is 'highly to bee valued for y$^e$ exquisite remarques on y$^e$ margins of most of y$^e$ Books' – unfortunately I have not been able to trace

1658, the royalist virtuoso Sir Thomas Browne was writing to yet another celebrated royalist antiquary (and astrologer), Elias Ashmole, to mention 'the honour' of a visit by Stanley and to remark on Stanley's friendship with Ashmole.[60] Stanley was very likely also in contact with John Greaves, the astronomer and orientalist who had travelled to Egypt and whose subsequent *Pyramidographia* (1646) showed a preference for 'down to earth explanations to fancier, metaphysical ones'.[61] As we shall see, the mix of critical interest in the learning of the ancient near east, in post-Scaligerean technical chronology, and in aspects of contemporary astronomy and natural philosophy that we find in Greaves is in many ways very similar to that of Stanley and his acquintances.

Stanley's reputation transcended even these wide royalist circles: through Hall, Samuel Hartlib invited him to become 'Orator' – the 'second place' after the President – of an 'Academy of Ingenuitys for Humane Learning'. When Stanley refused, because (as Hall reported it), '[he] himself hath a design Armilla Nigra [i.e. Black Riband], and forsooth will not be a ριψασπις ['Ripsaspis', a renegade]', Hall lamented the situation by comparing Stanley to the greatest gentleman-virtuoso of them all, Robert Boyle.[62] His work for his pioneering edition of Aeschylus, published in 1663, brought him into contact with three of seventeenth-century Europe's leading scholars: John Pearson, Isaac Vossius, and John Selden.[63] A passing reference confirms that he was acquainted with Sir John Cotton, possessor of effectively the greatest private library in the country.[64]

these annotated books, which would form perhaps the most important source for scholarly reading in seventeenth-century England if available. On Marsham, see 3.6 below.

[60] *The works of Sir Thomas Browne*, ed. G. Keynes (4 vols, London, 1928–31), VI, 293; on Browne's own scholarly world, see Parry, 'Thomas Browne and the uses of antiquity' (2008); Killeen, *Thomas Browne and the thorny place of knowledge* (2009).

[61] See the very informative article by Z. Shalev, 'John Greaves, the Great Pyramid, and early modern metrology' (2002) (quotation at 562). More broadly, see Toomer, *Eastern wisedome*, 127–41, 167–79. For the evidence of Greaves's contacts with Marsham and the chronologer John Bainbridge, see n. 146 below. The initial reasons behind Greaves' trip to Egypt, suggested by Bainbridge, were also historical – to check the results of the ancient Greeks: see Tyacke, *Aspects of English Protestantism* (2001), 244–61 ('Science and religion at Oxford before the Civil War'), at 251.

[62] Hall to Hartlib, 20 April 1647, HP, 60/14/32A–B; Hall to Hartlib, n.d. [1647], Hall to Hartlib, n.d. [1647], 60/14/35A; HP 60/14/39A. Hall had been attempting to ingratiate Hartlib with Stanley for several months: Hall to Hartlib, 11 Jan 1647, HP, 60/14/13B; Hall to Hartlib, 11 March 1647, HP 60/15/7B–8A. See further McDowell, *Allegiance*, 61–2; Turnbull, 'John Hall's letters to Samuel Hartlib' (1953).

[63] 'Life of Stanley', *History*, sig. d$^v$; Bod. MS Rawl. G.193; Bod. Auct. S.6.16; CUL Adv.e.44.2; CUL Adv.b.44.1–8; CUL MS Gg.3.7–15; Pembroke College, Cambridge, L.C.ii.159. Gruys, *The early printed editions of Aeschylus* (1981), 153–99 outlines Stanley's work on Aeschylus, correcting soundly the claim that all the work was done by Pearson, as made by E. Fraenkel in his 'Prolegomena', in Aeschylus, *Agamemnon* (1959), I, 36–44, 78–85. Tedeschi, 'Thomas Stanley, editore di Eschilo' (2010) now offers an exhaustive discussion.

[64] Stanley to Marsham, Feb 14 1663, CKS U1300 C1/13. For the Cotton library, see Tite, *The manuscript library of Sir Robert Cotton* (1994).

Stanley, then, was an important member of several scholarly networks, and hc was respected and admired within them. However, this only takes us so far in our attempts at understanding what Stanley may have seen himself as *doing* in the *History*: to achieve this, we must engage in a deeper contextualisation.

One possibility is that he was drawing on the Baconian idea of *historia literaria*, as suggested by Bacon in the *De augmentis scientiarum* (1623);[65] this model would influence the work of German polyhistors writing contemporaneously to Stanley.[66] Stanley did quote a passage from Bacon's *Advancement of learning* as a preface to the third volume of the *History* (1660), in which Bacon stated the need for a book *De antiquis philosophiis*, but the sole message of that quotation was that that book should consider each philosopher *in toto*, rather than 'collected by titles and handfuls as hath been done by *Plutarch*'.[67] There must have been other, deeper incentives for Stanley to write about the history of philosophy.

Some such deeper incentives have been suggested in the groundbreaking recent work of Kristine Haugen, as part of an examination of Bentley's seventeenth-century predecessors, of whom she finds Stanley to be the closest to the Master of Trinity. Professor Haugen compares Stanley to John Pearson and Thomas Gale in England, and Claude Saumaise, J. F. Gronovius, Henri Valois, Pierre Gassendi, Isaac Vossius, and Johann Scheffer on the continent, seeing them as representative of the type of scholarship which we introduced in 1.2:

> The English classicists directed their energies away from well-known poets, orators and historians . . . toward the periphery of the known world. The ancient texts that fascinated them most were late, not classical; pedestrian, rather than beautiful; and Greek, almost never Latin. Their motives for this study, while easily recognisable to specialist contemporaries, were similarly recondite . . . if the texts they studied were usually unfamiliar and strange, the English scholars were actually on the track of things more recondite still . . . the lost works of ancient poetry, philosophy, historiography, and scholarship that they knew had spanned nearly a millennium of Greek antiquity but that no one had seen for perhaps as long again.[68]

In all this, they followed a model that ultimately went back to Scaliger, and Professor Haugen demonstrates the importance of Scaligerian chronology to Stanley by charting how he used sources like the Arundel Marbles to show that Pythagoras could have studied with Thales, a classic problem in the doxographical tradition.[69] This was 'a particular triumph for his preferred scholarly

---

[65] This is the argument of Malusa, 'First general histories', 163–8.

[66] Grunert and Vollhard, eds., *Historia literaria. Neuordnungen des Wissens im 17. und 18. Jahrhundert* (2007).

[67] Stanley, *History*, 345, quoting Francis Bacon, *Of the proficience and advancement of learning, divine and humane* (London, 1605), fols. 35$^{r-v}$ (=*OFB*, IV (2000), 92). Stanley also quoted Montaigne, *Essais*, II.12.

[68] Haugen, *Bentley*, 15–16.   [69] Ibid., 18–23.

method, insofar as it turned not on rejecting ancient sources but rather on showing, through unexpected means, that in fact they were correct'. Moreover, this method explains his translation of sources that he must have seen as unreliable, such as the biographies of Pythagoras by Porphyry and Iamblichus, with their implausible tales of Pythagoras's golden thigh and wonder working, and, presumably, of the seven Socratic letters we met above. 'Where his sources passed out of the realm that could be plausibly addressed by his scholarly tools of comparison and fact-checking, Stanley followed a consistent policy of saying nothing.'[70]

We can amplify and amend some of these important conclusions. First, Stanley's engagement with chronology must be emphasised even more. It is not simply the case that Stanley 'checked the coherence of ancient statements of fact by referring to historical chronology' – although he did so for almost every philosopher covered.[71] More strongly, Stanley's whole project was anchored in chronology. His manuscripts reveal that he not only investigated independently the evidence for each philosopher, he also placed them in the framework of a new and more detailed chronology of Athens, based on a systematic attempt to establish synchronisms between the key sources tied to the dates of the archons (or, more specifically, to the *Archōn Epōnymos*) who had acted as chief magistrates for a year at a time. One surviving manuscript is a set of notes entitled 'Archontes Attici', where the sources for each archon are systematically gathered, drawing both on the most important discussions (Pausanias, Dionysius Halicarnassus, Eusebius, and the Arundel Marbles) as well as other ancient and modern sources (scholia to Pindar's *Pythian odes*, Thucydides, Clemens Alexandrinus, Antiochus, Plutarch, Philostratus, Diogenes Laërtius, Scaliger, and Meursius).[72] But even more important is the subsequent systematic presentation of that information, which survives in a series of tables copied 'from the notes of the most learned Stanley' ('è Schedis V. Cl. Th. Stanliis') by the voracious manuscript hunter Abednego Seller (1646–1705).[73] Here Stanley tabulated the results of his findings, allowing him to see where his sources disagreed, disagreements which could be resolved by reference to further sources noted on the facing folio.

It is very likely that this chronological project was inspired by Stanley's uncle Marsham. Indeed, we may go further, for since Stanley admitted that it was Marsham who had 'first directed' him to a history of philosophy, it is not unreasonable to suppose that the whole project was founded in this chronological scholarship. This would explain the relative lack of what one might anachronistically label 'historical criticism' in the books on Greek philosophy

---

[70] Ibid., 24.  [71] Ibid., 17.  [72] CUL MS Gg.3.16, no. 3, 'Archontes Attici', fols. 324^r–327^v.

[73] CUL MS Oo.6.91, no. 3 (new pagination) 'ARCHONTES'. On Seller, who also copied, for example, Selden's and others' scholarly correspondence (CUL MS Kk.5.38), see Handley, 'Seller, Abednego', *ODNB*; Seller's extensive Greek notes are CUL MS Ll.v.1.

(as we shall see, the situation was somewhat different for the work on the Chaldeans). Stanley's project was to collect all the evidence, suggest emendations to the Greek, and then reduce that evidence into chronological order. Discussion of causal relationships or contextual explanations was not, for the most part, the order of the day – unless, that is, it helped establish a chronological fact, such as the contextual explanation for Polycrates's anti-Socratic oration.

### 2.2.3 Critical histories of paganism and natural law: Stanley, Pearson, and Meric Casaubon after Vossius, Holstenius, and Grotius

And yet, we have still not arrived at a satisfactory answer for *why* Stanley felt that a history of philosophy was the specific project on which to deploy his chronological and philological skills. Dissatisfaction with Laërtius was one such motivation, but Stanley knew that the notes appended by Isaac Casaubon to the 1593 version of Henri Estienne's edition, or by Tommasso Aldobrandini to the 1594 Rome edition, had supplemented and corrected much of the work.[74] And while the history of philosophy certainly fits into the sort of broad subject matter that Professor Haugen has described mid-century scholars being interested in, there are also more specific – if difficult to trace – parallels between Stanley and some of his associates and contemporaries that somewhat qualify her image of Stanley as a direct predecessor to Bentley's 'secular' philology.

We have already encountered Stanley's friendship with John Pearson, like Bentley a future master of Trinity College, Cambridge, and recognised by contemporaries as one of the greatest scholars in seventeenth-century England. Pearson's scholarship was almost entirely ecclesiastical (most famously his *Vindiciae epistolarum S. Ignatii* (1672)), unsurprising for the man who became Lady Margaret Professor of Divinity (in 1661).[75] His only two publications on non-ecclesiological or theological topics directly concerned the history of philosophy: 'Prolegomena' to the edition of Hierocles's commentary on the pseudo-Pythagorean *Golden verses* and his *On providence and fate* published in London in 1654–55, and a dedication and preface to Gilles Ménage's edition of Diogenes Laërtius, published in 1664.[76] On both

---

[74] Stanley's lightly annotated edition of Aldobrandini's 1594 edition is CUL Adv.a.44.15.

[75] The fullest biographical account remains Churton, 'Memoir of the life and writings of John Pearson' (1844), which needs to be read with the usual caution required for works in the *Library of Anglo-Catholic Theology*. On Pearson as scholar, see Haugen, *Bentley*, 29–38; Hardy, '*Ars critica*', 240–1, 250–8; Quantin, *Antiquity*, 340–1, 363–4; de Quehen, 'Politics and scholarship in the Ignatian controversy' (1998).

[76] His extensive notes on Hesychius and the notes on Aeschylus from which Stanley benefitted remained in manuscript: Trinity College, Cambridge, MSS R.9.5–7 (Hesychius); Bod. MS Rawl. 193 (Aeschylus).

occasions Pearson solicited learned notes from Meric Casaubon, another disenfranchised Anglican-royalist cleric, forever living in the shadow of his father but now recognised as one of the key defenders of humanist learning in Interregnum and Restoration England.[77] Casaubon – who also knew Stanley[78] – not only contributed to Pearson's editions, but also made his own contributions to philosophical historiography, preparing English (1634) and Latin (1643) editions of Marcus Aurelius's *Meditations* and an edition of Epictetus's *Enchiridion* (1659), as well as offering important discussions throughout his other works.[79] What drove the Church of England divines Pearson and Casaubon to the history of philosophy, and might their motivations shed light on those of Stanley?

Hierocles's commentary on the *Golden verses* – a short hexameter poem consisting primarily of rather banal ethical commonplaces – had been published several times by the mid seventeenth century. His other major work, *On providence and fate*, was lost, but parts had been reconstructed through fragments preserved mostly by Photius.[80] Pearson supplied 'Prolegomena' to an edition of both, published in 1654–55 by Roger Daniel, former University Printer in Cambridge.[81] What Pearson was doing in this text sheds precious light on the aims of his friend Stanley.

The identity and dating of Hierocles had long been a mystery. Most of Pearson's 'Prolegomena' consisted of a complicated prosopography of no fewer than sixteen persons named Hierocles, a discussion that Professor Haugen interprets as 'stopping short of any clear statement about the nature and value of [Hierocles's and Pythagoras's] philosophy'.[82] This may be so, but Pearson's final identification of Hierocles was far less neutral than such a description implies. The real Hierocles, we now know, was a fifth-century Alexandrian neoplatonist.[83] Pearson, however, identified him with an early fourth-century proconsul of Bithynia and Alexandria who, early Christian

---

[77] Serjeantson, 'Introduction'.
[78] Casaubon must have known Stanley, because he had seen a pre-publication version of Stanley's Aeschylus, which he praises exuberantly in his *De nupera Homeri* (London, 1659), 40.
[79] See 5.2, 6.5 below.
[80] The *editio princeps*, with a translation by Fédéric Morel, appeared in 1597 (Hankins and Palmer, 56).
[81] Ἱεροκλέους φιλοσόφου ... *commentarius in aurea Pythagoreorum carmina* (London, 1654); *Hierocles de providentia & fato* (London, 1655), very often bound together. One contemporary English reader, Thomas Barlow, recorded on the front cover of his copy of the former (Bod. classmark: 8° A.72. Linc) that the work had been shown to be non-Pythagorean as early as 1510, by one of the first promoters of Greek learning in Italy, the Byzantine émigré Constantine Lascaris (1434–1501), in his *Institutiones* (Ferrara, 1510). On Daniel, see McKitterick, *A history of Cambridge University Press* (1992–2004), I, 168–90, *passim*.
[82] Haugen, *Bentley*, 33; more generally, the following account differs from the more secular reading offered there at 32–3.
[83] Schibli, *Hierocles of Alexandria* (2002).

sources reported, had inspired Diocletian's persecution of the Christians, and whose lost work *Φιλαλήθης* (*Lover of truth*) was well known as the first to compare Christ negatively to the pagan holy man Apollonius of Tyana: this Hierocles was the target of Eusebius's *Contra Hierocles*.[84] Like Johannes Curterius, whose 1583 commentary was included in the English edition, Pearson identified Hierocles the philosopher with *this* anti-Christian.[85] But even by seventeenth-century standards, this was not a convincing conclusion, and its weaknesses were quickly identified by both English and continental critics.[86] Not only did it involve completely mis-dating the references to Olympiodorus (*fl.* 412) and Plutarch of Athens (*c.* 350–430) in *On fate and providence*, but it also led Pearson into some rather curious readings. For example, in the important sixth-century geographical dictionary by Stephen of Byzantium entitled the *Ethnica*, there was a mention of yet another Hierocles, who was 'carried off from wrestling to philosophy' ('ἀπὸ ἀθλήσεων ἐπὶ φιλοσοφίαν ἀχθείς').[87] Pearson played on the ambiguity of 'ἀθλήσεις', which could mean something close to 'combat of the gymnasium', to suggest that it in fact meant 'combat against Christians', suggesting that this was further evidence for the identification of Hierocles the anti-Christian with

---

[84] The few relevant ancient sources are Eusebius, *Contra Hier.*; Lactantius, *Div. inst.*, v.3.18–21 and v.2.12 (which does not name Hierocles explicitly, but is accepted as referring to him in both early modern and modern accounts).

[85] John Pearson, 'Prolegomena de Editione, Autore, & Opere', in *Hierocles de Providentia & Fato*.

[86] See Johannes Jonsius, *De scriptoribus historiae philosophiae libri IV* (Frankfurt, 1659), 300–5; Jonsius replaces Pearson's conjecture with a stranger one of his own: that Photius's Hierocles is the same one attacked by Eusebius, and thus that that Eusebius was not Eusebius of Caesarea (for Jonsius, see p. 353, n. 136 below). Subsequent scholars refuted both Pearson and Jonsius: Ralph Cudworth, *The true intellectual system of the universe: the first part; wherein all the reason and philosophy of atheism is confuted* (London, 1678), 271–4 (tactfully attacking only Jonsius, despite knowing Pearson's conjecture); William Cave, *Ecclesiastici, or, the history of . . . the most eminent fathers of the church, that flourisht in the fourth century* (London, 1683), 8–9, again tactfully disagreeing only Jonsius while disagreeing with both him and Pearson (on Cave, see 6.6–8 below); Peter Needham, 'Praefatio', *Hieroclis Philosophi Alexandrini commentarius in Aurea Carmina, De Providentia & Fato*, ed. P. Needham (Cambridge, 1709), sigs. b4ᵛ–[b6]ᵛ. Needham's work was based on extensive collation of various continental manuscripts: see the account in the preface, the summary in the *Nouvelles de la république des lettres*, 48 (November 1709), 532–43 at 533–8, and *Remarks and collections of Thomas Hearne* (11 vols, Oxford, 1885–1921), ɪ, 296 (Needham to Hearne, 19 Aug 1706). The only major scholar that I have found accepting Pearson's conclusions is William Lloyd, in *A chronological account of the life of Pythagoras* (London, 1699), xxiv–xxvi. This work was written in the shadow of Bentley's work on the *Epistles of Phalaris*: see 3.8 below and the letter (14 May 1698) from Henry Dodwell to Lloyd in Bod. MS Cherry 22, fol. 56ʳ, as well as the letters (8 May, 30 June 1699) from John Wallis to Lloyd in Bod. MS Ballard 24, fols. 6ʳ, 110ʳ.

[87] Stephanus, *Ethnica*, β.v. Editions of the *Ethnica* had been produced at the Aldine press in 1502 and by Guilelmus Xylander in 1568; Lucas Holstenius, whom we shall meet forthwith, prepared posthumously published *Notae et castigationes postumae in Stephani Byzantii Ethnika* (Leiden, 1684).

Hierocles the philosopher – a suggestion for which he was soon mocked by many weaker scholars.[88]

Why did the otherwise usually cautious Pearson make these leaps? The answer, it seems to me, is because his work on Hierocles was not a mere exercise in mild humanist accumulation and emendation; rather, it was intimately tied to his ecclesiastical and theological vocation and to a set of wider presuppositions. As a practising theologian, Pearson was obsessed with the relationship between paganism (and especially pagan philosophers) and Christianity. In six Latin sermons later preached at Cambridge University in his capacity as Lady Margaret Professor of Divinity, Pearson used biblical starting points to address repeatedly issues such as: 'No novelty in Christianity'; 'The testimonies of the pagans and the Jews of Christ and primitive Christianity'; 'By what means the Gospel was spread among the gentiles'; 'The hostility of the philosophers to the teaching of Christ'.[89] Even more interesting is the set of extensive theological lectures on the divine attributes in which we find a similar concern to turn even hostile pagan testimony to apologetic advantage. Of the many examples given by Pearson, we should note in particular his use of Hierocles, whom he had so lovingly edited: the putative persecutor is now cited as evidence that 'the Gentiles knew of God's providence'.[90] (The Hierocles edition itself was prefaced by a quotation from Augustine on the compatibility of divine providence with human free will.)[91] Pearson, then, was using pagan philosophy as an apologetic crux despite his rejection of the Platonising syncretism of Ficino, Steuco, etc. His work is entirely 'critical' in this respect – the very fact that he was over-anxious to make Hierocles a critic of Christianity, where previous interpreters had aimed to read Christianity into him, is testimony to this.

---

[88] Pearson, 'Prolegomena', sigs. [*8]$^{v}$–**$^{r}$, [**5]$^{r–v}$. For challenges to this clear misreading, see e.g. Pearson, 'Prolegomena', in Needham, ed., *Commentarius*, xvii–xviii, nn. 24–5 (i.e. Needham's notes); André Dacier, *La vie de Pythagore, ses Symbols, ses Vers Dorez, & la vie d'Hierocles* (Paris, 1706), ccxl–ccxli, trans. into English as *The life of Pythagoras, with his Symbols and Golden Verses. Together with the Life of Hierocles* (London, 1707), 138–9.

[89] John Pearson, 'In Religione Christiana nulla novitas. In determinandis controversiis ad Ecclesiam primitivam respiciendum' (on Jer. 6:16), in *Theological works*, II, 3–4; 'Testimonia Ethnicorum atque Judaeorum de Christo et Christianitate primaeva' (on Joh. 5.31), 15–28; 'Quibus praecipue adjumentis Evangelium apud Gentes creverit' (on Acts 12.24), 29–40; 'Philosophorum in Christi disciplinam hostilis animus' (on Acts 17.18).

[90] Pearson, 'Lectiones de Deo et Attributis', in *Theological works*, I, 234. See also 74, where Hierocles' *De fato* is used to support the claim that the wisest pagans 'could think of no other cause for the creation of things, than God's goodness' ('Ad primum quod attinet, cum certu sit Deum non necessitate aliqua, vel extrinseca vel intrinseca, coactum, res creasse, et post infinita temporum spatia liberrime produxisse, nullam aliam causam hactenus excogitare potuerunt sapientissimi viri procreationis rerum, quam bonitatem').

[91] *Hierocles de Providentia*, 1, quoting Augustine, *Civ. Dei*, v.10.

The same may be said of Meric Casaubon, who supplied largely philological 'Notae & Emendationes' to Pearson's Hierocles edition. As one would expect from Isaac Casaubon's son, Meric had little time for facile ahistorical syncretisms between paganism and Christianity (see 6.5 below); nonetheless he commented in the short preface to his notes on Hierocles on those ideas in Hierocles, 'which come closest to the purity and sanctity of Christian doctrine, in so much as it is right to hope for from a non-Christian'.[92]

Pearson and Casaubon, then, as well as possessing the desire to produce editions of obscure and fragmentary Greek authors, were also driven by another aim: to establish the usefulness of pagan philosophy to the Christian reader while at the same time rejecting the uncritical syncretism of their sixteenth-century predecessors. Here we may place them in a wider current of European thought of the 1640s and 1650s. First mention must again go to G. J. Vossius, whom we met in Chapter 1 as the developer of an apologetic yet critical history of religion that sought traces of truth in a history of idolatrous error (1.2). Casaubon had corresponded extensively with Vossius in the 1630s and early 1640s (while Vossius was simultaneously updating Laud on the progress of his *Theologia gentilis*),[93] and had himself written a work entitled *De origine idololatriae*, unfortunately now lost.[94] Yet Vossius was not the only inspiration. Another was Lucas Holstenius, who had studied at Leiden but had converted to Catholicism in the early 1620s, moving to Rome and rising through the ranks of the circle of Cardinal Barberini until he was finally appointed to the premier scholarly position in Europe—first custodian of the Vatican library—in 1653.[95] Holstenius's conversion was stimulated, as he himself reported, by the Platonism he found in the church fathers, as espoused by Steuco and

---

[92] Meric Casaubon, 'In Hierocles Commentarium Notae, & Emendationes', in *Hierocles de Providentia*, 175: 'Ut dogmata omittamus, quae ad Christianae doctrinae puritatem & sanctitatem, quantum ab homine non Christiano sperare fas est, proxime accedunt'.

[93] As well as the many letters in *Gerardi Joannis Vossii ... epistolae*, 155, 158–9, 194–5, 196, 214–16, 225–6, 235–6, 247–8, 282–3, 303, 314, 336–7, 339–40, 386, 389–90, 398–9, 418–19, 451 (all first pagination), there are many unpublished (see van der Lem and Rademaker, *Inventory* (1993), sub nomine). For discussion of the *Theologia gentilis*, see Vossius to Casaubon, October 1638, Bod. MS Rawl. Letters 84f, fol. 114$^r$; Vossius to Laud, 5 July 1636, Bod. MS Rawl. Letters 83, fol. 81$^r$; Vossius to Laud, 12 Aug 1638, Bod. MS Rawl. letters 83, fol. 95$^r$; Vossius to Laud, 12 Apr 1639, Bod. MS. Rawl. letters 83, fol. 94$^r$. Vossius's letter to the Dean and canons of Canterbury (Nov 1641), including a copy and summary of the *Theologia gentili*, is Bod. MS Rawl. letters 84f, fol. 156$^r$. It is interesting that in his letter to Laud of October 1637 (Bod MS. Rawl. letters 83, fol. 79$^r$), Vossius names Lilius Geraldus as the pioneer of the history of paganism (no doubt thinking of *De Deis gentium varia et multiplex historia* (Basle, 1548)), for it was Geraldus's commentary on the Pythagorean *Sentences* that Pearson chose to print in his Hierocles edition (on Geraldus's history, see Enenkel, 'The making of 16th-century mythography' (2002).

[94] All the evidence is collected in Serjeantson, 'Introduction', 48–9 ('*De orig. Idololat.*' is the title assigned to the work in Meric Casaubon, *Of credulity and incredulity* (London, 1668), 170). See also Casaubon's *The originall cause of temporall evils* (London, 1645).

[95] Rietbergen, *Power*, 256–95; Herklotz, *Die Academia Basiliana* (2008), 38–40, 184–8, *passim*.

Bessarion.[96] And yet, as recently charted by Ralph Häfner, Holstenius's work on neoplatonism and its relationship to Christianity, which led to editions of Eusebius' attack on Hierocles (1628), Porphyry (1630), the Pythagorean *Sentences* (1638), and the *De diis et mundo* of Sallustius (1638), was very different from that of Steuco, Bessarion, or the other syncretists, finding traces of divine truth in the neoplatonists *despite* their anti-Christian attitude.[97] Casaubon had met Holstenius during the latter's stay in England (1622–24), during which the German learnt English and established contact with many English scholars,[98] and it is notable that Holstenius's edition of some of Porphyry's 'Pythagorean' writings was published in Cambridge in 1655.[99] Holstenius's work, then, was another spur to the study of neo-Pythagorean philosophy (not least Hierocles) in a way that was both 'critical' and prepared to deploy it for the services of Christianity.

There was a third recent source for such an approach: Hugo Grotius. Grotius's posthumously published *Sententiae philosophorum de fato* (1648)[100] collected passages from various philosophers (especially Stoic and neoplatonist), as well as church fathers and Jewish thinkers (e.g. Josephus and Maimonides), to demonstrate the compatibility of free will and divine providence. Particular emphasis was placed on Hierocles, whose strictures against those who deny the role of providence (i.e. the Epicureans) were to be particularly valued.[101] Once again, a 'critical' attitude – i.e. one entirely unimpressed by pre-Casaubonian syncretism – was being amalgamated with 'humanism' in its most traditional sense: the use of pagan sources as exemplars of virtue and truth, and an emphasis on similarity between the Christian and pagan traditions, in Grotius's case stimulated by his own neo-Stoic belief in 'common notions' (κοιναὶ ἔννοιαι).[102] Meric Casaubon offered exuberant

---

[96] See Holstenius to Nicolas-Claude Fabri de Peiresc, 9 July 1631, in *Lucae Holstenii epistolae ad diversos*, ed. J. F. Boissonade (Paris, 1817), 223–37, esp. 234, partially trans. in Rietbergen, *Power*, 265–6.

[97] Häfner, *Götter im Exil*, 81–174, esp. 113–15 (on Porphyry).

[98] Blom, 'Lucas Holstenius and England' (1984), 28.

[99] Although this edition was also motivated by financial considerations, as it was initially stimulated by a trip to Rome by the bookseller James Allestree, who asked Holstenius for assistance when he got in trouble with the Inquisition for importing four vernacular Bibles into Italy in 1650. See the letters from Allestree to Holstenius in Péllisier, 'Les amis d'Holstenius', (1891), 367–8, 372–4; the latter (2 Jan 1652) reports that the 1630 Rome edition of Holstenius's edition of Porphyry's *Vita Pythagorae* 'has sold here [England] for two crownes, and well is he that can get it at any rate'.

[100] For the possible circumstances of composition, see Nellen, 'An epistolary survey by Johan van Beverwijck' (1994), 736.

[101] See the first section, 'Hierocles de Deorum usu', in Hugo Grotius, *Philosophorum sententiae de fato* (Amsterdam, 1648), 1–17. This work has received almost no attention: see the sparse comments in Blom and Winkel, 'Introduction', in (2004), 4, 9–10.

[102] See the essays in Blom and Winkel, eds., *Grotius and the Stoa* (2004), esp. Miller, 'Innate ideas in Stoicism and Grotius', which surprisingly does not discuss the *Philosophorum sententiae*; the best discussion in a religious–scholarly framework is Häfner, *Götter im Exil*, 177–99.

praise of Grotius in his 'Notae' to Hierocles, and elsewhere explicitly adopted the concept of κοιναὶ ἔννοιαι, not to mention his extensive comments on the usefulness for Christian readers of the Stoic texts that he edited.[103]

And so if we are to judge Stanley by his known English counterparts in philosophical historiography, we might conclude that he was part of a group of royalist–episcopalian scholars who, under the inspiration of the latest continental scholarship, had adopted a critical approach that none-theless sought to emphasise similarities between paganism and Christianity from a non-dogmatic adherence to a broad theory of natural law of common notions.

This judgement can be confirmed from some of Stanley's other works, published and unpublished. In the commentary to his pioneering edition of Aeschylus, Stanley contextualised the tragedian as a Pythagorean. The dedica-tion proclaimed the poet as 'rich in a certain latent wisdom, close to that of the Pythagoreans', but Stanley's 'commentary tended to keep that wisdom latent, concentrating instead on matters of grammar and criticism'.[104] Stanley often rejected what he saw as overly facile patristic attempts at syncretism.[105] And yet, he still drew attention to those elements common to the Pythagorean and Judaeo-Christian traditions, when they stemmed from ideas common to all humanity. Similarly, he repeatedly 'interprets Aeschylus according to national and international law', with many references to Grotius.[106] The same mix of critical philology and a mild emphasis on natural law and *consensus gentium* appears in a hundred-page manuscript work, until recently unexplored, entitled 'Ἀκροθίνια. A philological exercise on the fourth verse of the seventh chapter of Hebrews, concerning the first yield and tithes of the spoils'.[107] The subject matter had been rendered particularly contentious by Selden's *Historie of tithes* (1618): Selden had deployed a painstaking examination to show that the payment of tithes was historically contingent, and did not exist by the law of

---

[103] Casaubon, 'Notae & emendationes', 175–6; *Temporall evils*, 1. Pearson similarly used Grotius, at 'Prolegomena', sigs. [***7]^{r–v}.

[104] Hardy, '*Ars critica*', 231, quoting Thomas Stanley, ed. and trans., *Aeschyli tragoediae septem: cum Scholiis Graecis omnibus* (London, 1663), sig. a2^r. For a very perceptive discussion, see Arnold, 'Thomas Stanley's *Aeschylus*' (1984), 231–8. Previous editors had been much keener to read Pythagorean allegoresis into Aeschylus, on the basis of Cicero, *Tusc.*, II.10.

[105] See e.g. the condemnation of Justin Martyr in Thomas Stanley, *Aeschyli tragoediae quae supersunt*, ed. S. Butler (4 vols, Cambridge, 1809–1816), III, 247 (not present in the original publication, as added by Butler from Stanley's manuscripts).

[106] Arnold, 'Stanley's *Aeschylus*', 246.

[107] CUL MS Gg.3.16 ('Ἀκροθίνια. Exercitatio philologica de primitiis ac decimis praedae ad versum IV capitis VII Epistolae ad Hebraeos'). It is now discussed, very acutely, in Hardy, '*Ars critica*', 270–2 (at 270, n. 753, it is noted that the reference on fol. 10^r to Stanley's Aeschylus commentary suggests a *terminus post quem* of 1663 – I have found no further evidence that could offer a more precise dating).

nature or by divine law.[108] Where 'Selden's philological particularism could not stomach the use of pagan sources to support natural law arguments for tithing', his numerous critics, 'by contrast, treated individual and occasional acts of consecration in a variety of different contexts as witnesses to a deeper, binding, and generally observed law which governed tithing as a whole, from the Old Testament Patriarchs to the late Roman Republic'.[109] Stanley's treatment of the subject was no less philologically advanced than Selden's, using a large array of Greek sources to gloss the term ἀκροθίνια ('tenth of the spoils'). Yet, ultimately, he sided with Selden's critics on natural law grounds: moving beyond the grammatical, the use of tithes could 'be shown from the authority of the whole of antiquity: the Greeks, Latins and Orientals observed [tithe payments]' in which 'we will show a remarkable *consensus gentium*'.[110]

To summarise: this combination of critical philology and mitigated respect for natural law arguments forms one of the three key elements of Stanley's scholarly method, the other two being his fixation with chronology and a 'maximalist' approach to classical sources that led him partially to rescue a dubious source (such as the Socratic letters) rather than dismiss it entirely, as long as that source did not blatantly contradict chronological or philological evidence. These principles were all put into operation in his treatment of Zoroaster and Chaldean philosophy.

### 2.3    Stanley and Zoroaster: the *Chaldean Oracles* in a rabbinic setting

Stanley had advertised the third volume (1660) of the *History* as the 'third and last' on the title-page, and our first question must be why he felt he had to add a fourth on Chaldean philosophy two years later, for not only did it go against his previous statements, but it also broke away from the Laërtian model which he had up to then followed so closely. Laërtius had begun with some brisk comments on those who claimed that philosophy 'had its beginnings among the barbarians' – whether Babylonian, Chaldean, Indian, Druidical, or Egyptian – before summarily dismissing these claims: 'These authors forget that the achievements which they attribute to the barbarians belong to the Greeks, with whom not merely philosophy but the human race itself began'

---

[108]  The literature is extensive: Toomer, *Selden*, I, 257–310; Toomer, 'Selden's *Historie of Tithes*' (2002); and Hardy, '*Ars critica*', 123–50, are the best analyses of Selden's scholarship. Cf. Woolf, *The idea of history in early Stuart England* (1990), 239; Parry, *Trophies*, 118–24. Other accounts focus on extrapolating political–ideological readings: see esp. Christianson, *The public career of John Selden* (1996), 63–82. For Selden on Hebrew tithing, see *The historie of tithes* (London, 1618), 11–24.

[109]  Hardy, '*Ars Critica*', 139–40. My debt to this discussion is large.

[110]  CUL MS Gg.3.16, fol. 16ʳ: 'Verum hactenus ad Grammaticorum metas hausisse videamur, progrediemur igitur, & ex optimis totius retro antiquitatis authoribus ostendemus quid in hac re a Graecis, quid a Latinis, quid ab Orientalioribus populis observatum, factum, in usu positum est, Demonstrabimus miro omnium gentium consensus … '.

(1.2–3). But this assumption had been eroded by generations of speculation on the eastern origins of philosophy.[111] Most interesting for us is the fact that this point was made by readers of Stanley's first volumes. The royalist and moderate Laudian bishop of Winchester, Brian Duppa (1588–1662), wrote to yet another prominent royalist scholar, Sir Justinian Isham (1611–75), on his initial reaction to reading the first volume of Stanley's opus, that,

He is very diligent and exact in his undertakings ... but he hath left so much unsaid ... for first he doth abruptly begin with those that vulgarly have the denomination of sages ... for all the learning that either those poets or philosophers had, came from the more eastern parts, and moved as the sun doth by degrees from the east unto the west, for before there was ... a Thales ... there was ... a Zoroaster ... and he might have done well to have begun with [him].

Duppa finished with the consummate modesty of a dilettante (which also further reveals the extent of Stanley's connections in royalist circles): 'If he and I may be acquainted, as I am promis'd by a third person that we shall be ... I shall (if he be counsailable) point out to him such particulars as may make his work more perfect'.[112] Whether Duppa managed to offer his counsel is unknown, but this is nonetheless evidence that there was something of an expectation in the scholarly circles Stanley moved in that a history of philosophy would consider oriental predecessors to the Greeks.

There was good reason for this expectation. The previous three decades had seen a new wave of interest in ancient near-eastern philosophy, partly stimulated by the new approach to the ancient Levant inspired by Scaliger, partly by the recovery of new sources. After Patrizi had published his expanded version of the *Chaldean Oracles*, it remained a commonplace to connect Zoroaster to Noah, his sons, or other elements of the sacred tradition. Only in England we may point to the presence of this conclusion in such disparate texts as Walter Raleigh's mammoth *History of the world* (1617), written during his imprisonment in the Tower, or the Pentateuch commentary of the separatist minister Henry Ainsworth (1627).[113] On the other hand, other theological and scholarly pressures could lead

---

[111] Both Isaac Casaubon and (no doubt following him) Ménage had argued that Laërtius was aggrandising the Greeks in response to contemporary Christian historiography, which emphasised the 'barbarian' origins of Greek philosophy: see 'Isaac Casauboni notae ad Diogenes Laertii libros ... ', 19 and 'Aegidii Menagii in Diogenes Laertius observationes et emendationes', 2, both in *Laertii Diogenes de vitis dogmatis et apophthegmatis eorum qui in philosophia claruerunt, libri X*, ed. G. Ménage (London, 1664), separate pagination for each.

[112] Duppa to Isham, 31 Dec 1657, in *The correspondence of Bishop Brian Duppa and Sir Justinian Isham, 1650–1660*, ed. G. Isham (Northampton, 1951), 147–8.

[113] Walter Raleigh, *The history of the world* (London, 1617 [1st edn=1614]), 80 (there were a further ten editions in the seventeenth century, one of which (1698) was an abridgement). For Raleigh and early modern historiography, see now Popper, *Walter Ralegh's* History of the world (2012). Henry Ainsworth, *Annotations upon the five books of Moses* (London, 1627), 19. Ainsworth is in need of further scholarship: for a start, see Moody, 'The reputation and

to other conclusions. The dean of Regensburg, Johannes Heinrich Ursinus (1608–1667) – a major Lutheran oriental scholar and pedagogue – argued in his *De Zoroastre Bactriano, Hermete Trismegisto, Sanchoniathone Phoenicio* (1661) that the three figures of his title were all younger than Moses (partly in response to La Peyrère's *Prae-Adamitae*), and that the *Chaldean Oracles* were late forgeries from the second century AD, thus explaining their similarities to Christian doctrine.[114] Ursinus was certainly not an uncritical scholar, but his aims were primarily theological: to defend the patristic argument for Mosaic intellectual primacy, and to dismiss claims of advanced pagan religious knowledge (he claimed the *Oracles* were tools of the devil) – here he was following in the footsteps of no less a Reformed titan than Theodore Beza, who had dismissed the *Chaldean Oracles* as 'semi-Christian' forgeries as early as 1565, in his commentary on Matt. 2 (the magi coming to Christ).[115] Even though Ursinus's work was published only a year before Stanley's *Chaldaick philosophy*, Stanley was familiar with its destructive argument, as well as with that of Beza.[116]

The study of ancient near-eastern philosophy and theology had also been transformed by another genre: the histories of religion written in the wake of Scaliger's *Thesaurus temporum*. Here, a particular inspiration was the incorporation of evidence from medieval Jewish and Arabic sources, especially the *Moreh Nevukhim* (*Guide for the perplexed*) of the famous twelfth-century rabbi Moses Maimonides. In Book III (chs. 29–33) of the *Guide*, Maimonides argued, against those who would ascribe the origin of the Mosaic Ritual Law to God's arbitrary and incomprehensible will, that it could be explained as the result of a God who was working rationally, through second causes. Maimonides drew on the theory of divine accommodation, well known to Christians from patristic writings (especially Augustine), but which Maimonides developed in a more historical manner.[117] The Ritual Law was the desire of a God working in and through history. The divine 'purpose' of the law was to abolish idolatry.

---

character of Henry Ainsworth', (1982); Muller, *After Calvin* (2003), 156–74 ('Henry Ainsworth and the development of Protestant exegesis in the early seventeenth century').

[114] Johannes Henricus Ursinus, *De Zoroastre Bactriano, Hermete Trismegisto, Sanchoniathone Phoenicio eorumque scriptis et aliis contra Mosaicae scripturae antiquitatem exercitationes familiares* (Nürnberg, 1661), 59–72. See Stausberg, *Faszination*, II, 625–34. On Ursinus as philosophical and religious historian, see also Häfner, 'Shaping early modern comparative studies' (2010), 9–10. His motivations were also anti-alchemical: Ganzenmüller, 'Wandlungen in der geschichtlichen Betrachtung der Alchemie' (1950), 145.

[115] *Iesu Christi D.N. Novum testamentum, sive Novum foedus*, ed. and trans. T. Beza (2nd edn, Geneva, 1582 [1st edn=1565]), sig. A.iiij^v (commentary on Matt. 2:12).

[116] Stanley, *Chaldaick philosophy*, 2b, 39a. That Stanley read Beza attentively is confirmed by CUL MS Gg.3.16.1, fol. 44^r. He may, however, have also known of his position from the description in Georg Horn, *Historiae philosophicae libri VII* (Leiden, 1655), 74 ('... *Beza* in cap. 2. *Matth.* Suspicatur, falso Zoroastris nomine editos illos versiculos'). On Horn, see 3.5. below.

[117] For an overview of the history of accommodationism, see Benin, 'The "cunning of God" and divine accommodation' (1984); Benin, *The footprints of God* (1993). For Augustinian accommodation, see 3.1 below.

Specifically, Maimonides claimed that it was designed to oppose the idolatry of the 'Sabians', whom Maimonides described as a widespread pagan people, drawing on the *Filahât al-Nabâtiyyah* ('Nabataean agriculture'), putatively translated from Syriac into Arabic by Ibn Waḥshiyya (d. 931), and which Maimonides believed to be a truly ancient Sabian work.[118] Too immersed in paganism to be left with no ritual at all, the Jews were 'condescended to' by God, who reversed the Sabian religion, a technique which Jan Assmann has usefully labelled 'normative inversion': 'If the Law prohibits an activity $x$ there must have existed an idolatrous community practicing $x$'.[119]

Maimonides' narrative concerning the Sabians was, from the perspective of his many early modern readers, rather ambiguous, jumping from the time of Abraham to that of Moses.[120] Nonetheless, he offered extremely tempting nuggets of putatively historical information, such as the claim that the source of Sabian idolatry was starworship.[121] Late sixteenth- and seventeenth-century Christian scholars became obsessed with discovering the true identity of the Sabians, and Maimonides was universally cited in discussions of ancient paganism.[122] Particularly important to us is the publication of the *Guide* in a new Latin translation by Johann Buxtorf (the younger) in 1629,[123] and the cementing of Maimonides's reputation as a key source for the history of idolatry with the 1641 publication of a Latin translation of his commentary on the Mishnah *Avodah Zarah* (the Mishnaic treatise on idolatry) by G. J. Vossius's son Dionysius (1612–33) – Vossius's own huge *Theologia gentilis* was published alongside it but ostensibly only as an accompanying commentary to the work of his son, who, befitting a child prodigy, died young, to be lamented by his father to Laud (the intended dedicatee) among others.[124]

---

[118] See now Hämeen-Anttila, *The last pagans of Iraq* (2006).

[119] Assmann, *Moses the Egyptian* (1997), 58.

[120] Maimonides, *Guide*, III.29 (Pines, 514–22). Thomas Hyde exploited this to suggest two Sabian corruptions: see 2.7 below.

[121] Maimonides, *Guide*, III.29 (Pines, 514).

[122] The best summary is still Chwolsohn, *Die Ssabier und der Ssabismus* (1856), I, 23–90; cf. Elukin, 'Maimonides and the rise and fall of the Sabians' (2001).

[123] Moses Maimonides, *Doctor perplexorum: Ad dubia & obscuriora Scripturae loca rectiùs intelligenda*, ed. Johann Buxtorf (Basel, 1629), discussed in Katchen, *Christian Hebraists and Dutch rabbis* (1984), 95–6; van Rooden, *Theology, biblical scholarship, and rabbinical studies* (1989), 117–18.

[124] Moses Maimonides, *De idololatria liber*, ed. Dionysius Vossius (Amsterdam, 1641); and the excellent discussion in Katchen, *Christian Hebraists*, 161–260 (although I am not sure that the conclusion that 'the ultimate impact of the *Mishneh Torah* on Christian scholars was far greater than that of the *Guide*' (viii) should apply to the seventeenth century). See also Rademaker, *Life and work of Gerardus Joannes Vossius* (1981), 338–9; Rooden, *Rabbinical studies*, 190–2. One can read the moving letter from Vossius to Laud, Feb 1634, at MS Rawl. letters 84f fols. 61$^r$–62$^r$, and MS Rawl. letters 84f, fol. 157$^r$, 9 Dec 1641 (=*Vossii Epistolae*, 383), sending the Maimonides edition and the *Theologia gentilis*.

One obvious solution to the problem of the Sabians' identity presented itself: that they were the Chaldeans. Not only was Chaldea the home of Abraham (Gen. 11:28), but the Old Testament even associated them with astrology and magic, and spoke of the 'learning of the Chaldeans' more generally (Dan. 1:4; 2:2; 4:7, 5:7). This could be combined with evidence from the best known ancient sources, not least Strabo's *Geography*, where 'Chaldeans' seemed to designate two things: the inhabitants of Chaldea (i.e. lower Mesopotamia), or more specifically, the members of the Babylonian priesthood.[125] So when Isaac Casaubon wrote to Scaliger to ask for the latter's opinion of the identity of the Sabians, Scaliger could confidently reply that they were Chaldeans, his authority enhanced by possession of a manuscript copy of the *Guide* in the original Judaeo-Arabic. 'The *Moreh Nevukhim*', he wrote, 'cannot be commended enough. I rate not only that book but also the works of that master so highly that I would say that he alone among the Jews has given up talking nonsense'.[126] This idea that Maimonides's 'historical' treatment was qualitatively different to the *nugae* of other Jewish interpretations would prove extremely popular. Meanwhile, when Scaliger's letter was printed, many scholarly giants followed the master's judgements, including Selden and Saumaise. A new element was introduced to the debate with the recovery of medieval Arabic sources, perceived as similar to the lost *Nabatean agriculture*. The Swiss Calvinist oriental scholar and theologian Johann Heinrich Hottinger (1620–1667), working with Scaliger's Judaeo-Arabic *Guide* and with a partial manuscript of the *Kitāb al-Fihrist* (938) by Ibn al-Nadīm that he had discovered among the papers of the pioneering Arabist Jacob Golius (1596–1667), aligned the Sabians not only with the Chaldeans but also with the pre-Islamic Arabs, a conclusion supported in other Christian Arabic scholarship by the likes of Edward Pococke and Golius himself.[127]

But what of Zoroaster? The crucial intervention here was by Stanley's acquaintance Selden, who in his *De jure naturali et gentium* (1640), inserted

---

[125] Cumont, *Astrology and religion among the Greeks and Romans* (1912), 26; Strabo, *Geog.*, XVI.1.6. For other particularly prominent discussions of this type, see Herodotus, I.181; Cicero, *Div.*, I.1.2. For this ambiguity in the Old Testament, perhaps under Hellenistic historiographical influence, see Roitman, '"This people are descendants of Chaldeans" (Judith 5:6): its literary form and historical setting' (1994). The Chaldeans were thus often classified as the first idolaters in seventeenth-century scholarship: for a nice example of the dissemination of such ideas in England, see its appearance in Peter Heylyn's popular *Cosmographie in four bookes: containing the chorographie and historie of the whole world* (London, 1652), III, 128, which serves as the source for the same conclusion in the commonplace book of Thomas Hatton, *c.* 1680, Folger MS V.b.154, 18.

[126] Quoted in Katchen, *Christian Hebraists*, 35 (see also the quotation from Selden's *De Diis Syris* in Toomer, *Selden*, 240, n. 226). For Scaliger and the Sabians, see Chwolson, *Ssabier*, 26–7. For Casaubon's reading of the *Guide* and interest in the Sabians, see Grafton and Weinberg, *Casaubon*, 112–13.

[127] Loop, 'Johann Heinrich Hottinger and the "Historia Orientalis"' (2008), 194; Chwolson, *Ssabier*, 28–31; see also Levitin, 'Spencer', 56–8.

Zoroaster into the Maimonidean narrative by asserting that he was the founder of Sabian/Chaldean religion. Selden was again drawing on a previously unknown Arabic source: the *Naẓm al-Jawhar* (The string of gems) by Sa'id ibn Batriq (877–940), or Eutychius, Melchite Patrarich of Alexandria, which Selden would make the first Arabic text (as distinct from isolated quotations) published in England in 1642 (partly because it could be used for an attack on episcopacy).[128] In his *De Diis Syris* (1617, 2nd edn=1629) Selden had already treated extensively both Maimonides's Sabians – whom he also aligned with the Chaldeans and placed at the origin of both astrology and starworshipping idolatry – and Zoroaster, whom he denied to have been the teacher of Pythagoras for chronological reasons.[129] Like Stanley he also accepted the usefulness of the *Chaldean Oracles* as a genuine source (even offering an emendation); he also used the commentary of Psellus. In the projected revised third edition of *De Diis Syris*, some of Selden's additions were directly relevant to Stanley, such as one on the relationship between Egyptian and Chaldean astronomy.[130] I have been unable to establish whether Stanley had any knowledge of this third edition; it was certainly known to royalist scholars with whom he was acquainted, such as Gerald Langbaine and Elias Ashmole.[131] In short, both Stanley's direct acquaintances and the scholarly world which was familiar to him were interested in the issue of ancient Chaldean/Sabian religion and

---

[128] John Selden, *De jure naturali & gentium, iuxta disciplinam Ebraeorum libri septem* (London, 1640), 211. A full version of the *Naẓm al-Jawhar*, jointly produced by Selden and Pococke, was published in 1658 (for the full context, see Toomer, *Eastern Wisedome*, 65–6, 164–5; Toomer, *Selden*, II, 600–14; Gabriel, 'Sa'id ibn Batriq, Selden, et la hiérarchie ecclésiale' (2011)) – the passage cited in *De jure naturali* is there reproduced in full: *Contextio Gemmaru, sive Eutychii Patriarchae Alexandrini Annales*, eds., J. Selden and E. Pococke (2 vols, Oxford, 1658), I, 62–3. Hottinger had made a transcription and translation of two long sections of the *Naẓm al-Jawhar* in 1645, and included discussion of it in both the *Historia Orientalis* and *Bibliotheca Orientalis* (1658) (Loop, 'Hottinger', 187). As well as Buxtorf's edition of the *Guide*, Selden also cited Agathias, *Hist.*, II.24.5–6 (Zoroaster as father of Persian religion), Scaliger's letter to Casaubon (Sabians=Chaldeans), DL, I.2 (Zoroaster as founder of the Persian magi), and the very interesting *De ecclesia ante legem* (Paris, 1630 [1st edn=Lyon, 1626]), by the Parisian Capuchin Jacques Boulduc, who, while a pioneer in the study of pagan-Judaic relations (see Malcolm, 'The name and nature of *Leviathan*' (2007), esp. 34–9), nonetheless saw Zoroaster as the great grandson of Cham (*Ecclesia*, 283). Selden also cites 'Justinus Lib. 30', but this seems to be a confusion, the best explanation for which I can think of is the discussion in Justinus, *Epit.*, I.1.

[129] John Selden, *De Diis Syris* (London, 1617), 120–1: 'Audire Zoroastrem non potuit, quippe Zoroastre aliquot saeculis recentior; uti ex Xantho apud Diogenem Laertium supputanti constat' (the reference is to DL, I.2); see also Toomer, *Selden*, I, 211–50, esp. 212 n. 14, 215–16, 222–5, 232–3. Stausberg, *Faszination*, discusses Selden only in a footnote (643, n. 414) and says nothing either of Scaliger or Hottinger.

[130] The manuscript of the third edition is Bod. MS Selden supra 106. The additions were incorporated in the version printed in *Joannis Seldeni jurisconsulti opera omnia*, ed. D. Wilkins (London, 1726) (cols. 261–2 for the addition discussed here). All the changes are tabulated in Toomer, *Selden*, II, 842–4.

[131] Toomer, *Selden*, II, 841.

philosophy, Zoroaster, and the *Chaldean Oracles*, treating it through newly available Jewish and Arabic sources.[132] As such, Stanley had very good reason to believe that a systematic new treatment was both necessary and desirable.

How, though, was such a treatment to progress? After a brief preface, *Chaldaick philosophy* goes on to discuss the chronology of Chaldean learning, the identity of Zoroaster, and the magi and their sects. It proceeds to the content of their philosophy, theology, astrology, and natural magic, drawn mostly from the *Chaldean Oracles*. The same process is then repeated for the Persians, and then the Sabians. Stanley finishes by printing the *Chaldean Oracles* in Greek and Latin as collected by Patrizi, before offering his own English translation, as well as English translations of Plethon's and Psellus's commentaries, and some philological conjectures.

The use of the *Chaldean Oracles* may lead one to suppose that Stanley had syncretist aims. This supposition might be further enhanced by Stanley's insistence on the Chaldeans' monotheism, grounded on a quotation from the most apologetic of early Christians, Eusebius:

> *Chaldees and Jews wise only, Worshipping*
> *Purely a Self-begotten God and King.*[133]

And yet, there is little else in the text that suggests such a reading. Straight after this quotation, Stanley pointed out that 'notwithstanding the Oracle', their 'Worship, though of the True God, was Idolatrous, [as] is beyond doubt'.[134] Stanley's aim was certainly not to defend the old uncritical, patristic ideas of Jewish primacy in the vein of Ursinus; elsewhere, for example, he was openly critical of Clemens Alexandrinus for distorting chronology to make Thales younger than the later prophets.[135] Nor is there any attempt at elaborate genealogies of wisdom: there is some discussion of Plato and Pythagoras obtaining Chaldean philosophical knowledge, but chronology again taught Stanley that they cannot have been 'fully acquainted with the depth of [Chaldean] Sciences', as his predecessors had commonly assumed.[136]

---

[132] This is also evident from a fascinating mid-1650s English commonplace book (Folger MS V.b.15), where rabbinic sources are used to shed light on the ancient '*Religio Chaldaeorum*' (162), Zoroaster's biography is examined (157), and, like Stanley (see below), the author draws on Jacques Gaffarel (167ff).

[133] Stanley, *Chaldaick philosophy*, 8b, 24b. As usual Stanley does not give the precise source, which is Eusebius, *Praep. Ev.*, IX.10.

[134] Stanley, *Chaldaick philosophy*, 25a. In any case, he knew that he was not quoting Eusebius directly, but a quotation taken by him from the anti-Christian Porphyry's lost *Philosophy from oracles*.

[135] Stanley, *History*, 2b, discussing Clemens Alexandrinus, *Strom.*, I.21.

[136] Stanley, *Chaldaick philosophy*, 30a. The discussion is rather puzzling. From Pliny, *Hist. nat.*, XXX.2 (Stanley mistakenly cited XXX.1), he knew that (the mythical) Osthanes first brought Persian learning into Greece, accompanying Xerxes's expedition. An elaborate chronological discussion confirms Diodorus Siculus's judgement (*Bib. hist.*, XI.1) that Xerxes set out in the fourth year of the seventy-fourth Olympiad (481 BC), after which Stanley comments: 'Hence it

Rather, a closer inspection shows that Stanley saw himself as a *critic* of what he perceived to be the over-simplistic connections between the pagan and the sacred tradition, and that he deliberately self-presented as a 'Scaligerian' reader of ancient history, much in the same way as had Selden.[137] In the short 'Preface' to *Chaldaick philosophy*, after commenting on the difficulty of the subject, Stanley went on to lament the lack of sources beyond the ambiguous *Chaldean Oracles*, themselves corrupted in the process of translation from Chaldean to Greek. The process of reconstruction was a difficult one, and key to it was 'taking care to reject such [sources] as are suppositious, or of no credit, as in the Historical Part, *Annius Viterbiensis, Clemens Romanus*, and the like: in the Philosophical, the *Rabbinnical Inventions*, which tho' incuriously admitted by *Kircher, Gaulmin*, and others, manifestly appear to have been of later Invention'.[138] Understanding precisely what Stanley meant by these accusations is important, and leads us to the heart of his project.

Stanley was sure that the Chaldeans were the oldest civilisation to develop a tradition of learning, even before the Egyptians.[139] Nonetheless, the true antiquity both of Chaldean philosophy and of Zoroaster was hugely problematic, for though that antiquity was 'such as other Nations cannot equal', it was 'far short of that to which they did pretend'.[140] In announcing this, Stanley was introducing a body of sources well known to early modern scholars for its complexity and uncertainty.[141] When Alexander the Great conquered the known world, he was accompanied by Aristotle's nephew Callisthenes, who dutifully reported back to his uncle on the learning of the eastern nations. The Chaldeans told Callisthenes that their astronomical observations stretched back an incredible 470,000 years. But the observations which Callisthenes actually brought back went back only 1,903 years (to 2234 BC), according to a later report by Porphyry.[142] This date had proved attractive to Christian chronologers because it fell just after the flood, demonstrating that pagan observations fit

---

appears that *Pythagoras* and *Plato* who were precedent in time to *Osthanes*, and in their Travels conversed with the *Persian* Magi, were not fully acquainted with the depth of their Sciences'. This fits Stanley's dating of Pythagoras (568–497 BC [*History*, 346a–7b, 641–3]), but, obviously, not that of Plato (*c*. 428–348 BC [156a–b, 651]). My only explanation is that Stanley meant that the Pythagorean *tradition*, including Plato, cannot have been directly influenced by Osthanes, but this is a very forced reading.

[137]  For Selden, see Toomer, *Selden*, I, 211–56, esp. 212–13 for Scaliger's acknowledged influence.

[138]  Stanley, *Chaldaick philosophy*, 'Preface'.

[139]  Ibid., 1a. The only sources given are DL I.1 (referring to the ps.-Aristotelian Μαγικός, which Stanley had ascribed to Antisthenes in the Preface, presumably on the authority of *Suda* A 2723), and Josephus, *Ant. Jud.*, I.8, but one supposes that this is part of a more general anti-Kircher reaction, discussed below.

[140]  Stanley, *Chaldaick philosophy*, 1b.

[141]  See e.g. the account in Grafton, *Defenders of the text* (1991), 134–7. See also Grafton, *Scaliger*, II, 265–8; Grafton, 'From apotheosis to analysis'; Popper, 'Abraham, Planter of Mathematics' (2006), esp. 91–2.

[142]  Reported in Simplicius, *In Cael.*, II.12 (to 293ᵃ4).

within the biblical framework. But there was another problem: all actually extant observations – i.e. those reported by Ptolemy – went back only to the era of Nabonassar, that is to 747 BC.[143] Even the great Scaliger had been too tempted by the biblical concurrence not to favour the former date; other late sixteenth- and early seventeenth-century readers continued to toy with speculations about the transmission of astronomy from the antediluvian patriarchs on the pillars supposedly erected by Seth, who had inherited astronomy from Adam himself.[144]

Stanley, on the other hand, doggedly followed the extant evidence, and favoured Ptolemy's dating, supporting it with a striking chronological conjecture:

> This [dating] indeed is beyond all exception; for we have them confirmed by the Authority of *Ptolomy*, who shews the Reasons and Rules for the Observations. What is more than this, seems to have been only hypothetical. And if we shall imagine a canicular Cycle, which consists of 1461 years (and are 1460 natural years) to have been supposed by *Porphyrius* to make up his Hypothesis, then there will want but 18 years of this number.[145]

This initially puzzling and seemingly innocuous statement is in fact testimony to both the brilliance and idiosyncrasy of Stanley's approach. What Stanley calls the 'Canicular cycle' is more commonly called the 'Sothic cycle', a period of 1,461 Egyptian years (of 365 days each, thus equalling 1,460 Julian years of 365.25 days) that the Egyptians used because the start of each year coincided with the heliacal rising of the star Sirius. It had been much discussed by Scaliger and by the English chronologer John Bainbridge, very likely also another acquaintaince of Marsham and Stanley.[146] When Stanley said that

---

[143] Ptolemy, *Alm.*, IV.6–7.

[144] For Scaliger: Grafton, *Defenders*, 134–5; Grafton, *Scaliger*, II, 264–6. For the pillars of Seth: Josephus, *Ant. Jud.*, I.2; Popper, 'Histories of mathematics'. This transmission could be posited in entirely mainstream philosophy textbooks, e.g. Marcus Friedrich Wendelin, *Contemplationum physicarum sectio I. Quae physiologiae generalis, de principiis & affectionibus corporis naturalis* (Cambridge, 1648), 9b.

[145] Stanley, *Chaldaick philosophy*, 2a.

[146] Grafton, *Scaliger*, II, 199–207. Marsham was very likely acquainted with the astronomer and chronologer Bainbridge (1582–1643), whose posthumous *Canicularia* (Oxford, 1648) offered important alterations to Scaliger's views on the Sothic cycle (Grafton, *Scaliger*, II, 207–8; Grafton, 'Barrow as scholar', 293–5), because Bainbridge was very close to John Greaves, who edited the *Canicularia* (Thomas Birch, 'An historical and critical account of the life and writings of Mr. John Greaves', in *The miscellaneous works of Mr. John Greaves* (2 vols, London, 1737), I, ii), whose work Stanley in turn praised (e.g. *History*, 9b), and who certainly knew Marsham well, using his library, and perhaps staying at his house (Greaves to Pococke, 25 March 1647 in Birch, 'Greaves', xxvi–xxvii). See also the dedication 'nobilissimo doctissimoque amico suo Johanni Marsham', in Greaves's *Astronomica quaedam ex traditione Shal Cholgii Persae una cum Hypothesibus Planetarum* (London, 1650), sigs. ¶3ʳ⁻ᵛ, which reveals that it was Greaves who persuaded Marsham to publish his *Diatriba chronologica* (London, 1649).

Porphyry used the canicular cycle, he was in effect saying that Porphyry had a set of observations with a precise point in the cycle, but no way of knowing *which* cycle they belonged to: he must have thus added 1,460 to the true year of those observations.

This still generates a gap of twenty-seven years between Porphyry's observation and the start of the era of Nabonassar:

$$2480 + 1460 = 3940 \text{ Julian} = 774 \text{ BC}$$

Stanley must, at some point, have made a mistake in his arithmetic. Yet far more important are the hints about his scholarly methodology that we can glean from this example. It shows us once again the emphasis Stanley placed on independent chronological verification. It shows us how hard he worked to get away from what he thought were unacceptable speculations on the connection between the history of the patriarchs and the history of pagan philosophy. And it shows us, yet again, how desperate he was to save all the sources available to him, rather than discount any testimony. There was no evidence whatsoever for Porphyry having used the canicular cycle; yet Stanley's explanation allowed him to reconcile the philosopher with Ptolemy, whose testimony was ultimately much more authoritative.

But, technical chronology aside, why was Stanley so keen to disconnect the history of near-eastern philosophy and sacred history? Here, we may fruitfully look at the ideas of those in his list of stated enemies: Kircher, Gaulmin, Annius, Clemens Romanus, and the 'rabbinical inventions'. The German Jesuit scholar Athanasius Kircher (1601–80) is well known; his works on the religion and philosophy of ancient Egypt, while often loudly ridiculed for their nonchalant attitude to source attribution, penchant for esotericism, sometimes wild philological conjectures, and borderline theological awkwardness, were often the source of conclusions accepted by ostensibly more sober historians.[147] Certainly, his works were widely read in England, and the fact that Stanley was engaging with them only a few years after their publication in Rome shows their widespread dissemination, and the complexity of Kircher's reception (despite his own rather ambiguous relationship with the international scholarly community).[148]

As he set out in the *Obeliscus Pamphilius* (1650) and *Oedipus Aegyptiacus* (1652–55), Kircher believed in a tradition of esoteric truth that began not with Moses but with Adam – it was transmitted through Noah and his sons to all the nations of the world, and although it descended into idolatry when the populace misunderstood the mysteries recorded in esoteric hieroglyphic writing, it

---

[147] The revisionist treatment of Kircher as an Egyptologist, begun by Iversen, *The myth of Egypt* (1993 [1961]), 92–102, is now completed in Stolzenberg, *Kircher*.

[148] For this relationship, see Malcolm, 'Private and public knowledge'.

contained the essential kernel of truth shared by Egyptian priests and Jewish Cabbalists. Kircher's focus was on Egypt, and on Hermes Trismegistus, whom he presented as a restorer of the original truth. He thus had to explain the origins of error, and this is where Zoroaster came in. Adam had transmitted two traditions, one true and transmitted via Seth, and one idolatrous, corrupted by his son Cain. These two traditions were combined by Noah's cursed son Ham, becoming the foundational belief systems of the various post-diluvian civilisations. Ham was none other than Zoroaster (and the authorship of the 'good' *Chaldean Oracles* had to be assigned to Hermes).[149]

The association of Zoroaster with Ham was not unprecedented: for example, Kircher cited the *History of the Franks* by the sixth-century Gallo-Roman historian Gregory of Tours. But the Jesuit was also aware that this kind of source was in this context not particularly impressive, so he cited a barrage of much more alluring ones – Christian, Jewish, and Arabic. Flying in the face of all contemporary scholarship, he used the most famous forgery of early modern historiography: Annius of Viterbo's pseudo-Berosus.[150] In his *Antiquitates* (1498), Annius's 'Berosus' expanded the account of Noah's drunkenness at Gen. 9:20–7, claiming that Ham – the same as Zoroaster – had castrated and sterilised the sleeping Noah and was thus cursed by his father to become the 'servant of servants', that is, the first idolater: here, thus, was the start of an idolatrous tradition that nonetheless preserved some of the original Noachic truths.[151] It is clear why this story appealed to Kircher, but his use of it as late as 1650 remains remarkable.[152] To the fake Berosus, Kircher added a list of sources which, it quickly becomes apparent, were precisely those attacked by Stanley: the Pseudo-Clementine *Recognitions* and a list of rabbinic and Arabic sources, including one Arabic manuscript ('Abenephius') which he may have invented himself.[153] As far as Stanley was concerned, Kircher's account was precisely the sort a sober, Scaligerian reading should seek to avoid.

---

[149]   Stolzenberg, *Kircher*, 135–6 offers the full evidence, which must be gathered from various *loci* in Kircher's works. For the most direct association of Zoroaster with Ham, see Athanasius Kircher, *Obeliscus Pamphilius, hoc est interpretatio nova et hucusque intentata Obelisci Hieroglyphici* (Rome, 1650), 13: 'Dicimus primo Zoroastrem illum famosum Magiae inventorem alium non fuisse, nisi Cham filium Noë'.

[150]   On Annius and his forgeries, see Ligota, 'Annius of Viterbo and historical method' (1987); Grafton, *Defenders*, 80–103.

[151]   Joannes Annius, *Antiquitatum libri quinque* (Wittenberg, 1612 [1st edn=Rome, 1498]), fol. 25ʳ.

[152]   See the discussion in Grafton, 'Kircher's chronology' (2004), at 175–6.

[153]   Kircher, *Obeliscus*, 14. The rabbinic sources are 'Rassi' (i.e. Sholmo Yitzhaki), Ibn Ezra, and 'Hannasse' (i.e. Yehudah HaNasi, chief redactor of the Mishnah). 'Abenephius' was an untraceable manuscript source that Kircher had claimed to possess since the early 1630s, and which gained him the patronage of Nicolas-Claude Fabri de Peiresc (see Stolzenberg, *Kircher*, 83–8). All these match on the list of sources attacked at Stanley, *Chaldaick philosophy*, 2a–b; cf. 4a, 34b–5a. A digression on the 'real' Berosus (5a–6a) is obviously also intended as a contribution to the anti-Kircher case.

And yet, it would be too simple to present Kircher as Stanley's sole target. Elsewhere, the Englishman offered broader condemnations of attempts to find direct links between near-eastern philosophy and the patriarchs. For example, although agreeing with Maimonides's claim that Abraham was educated in the system of the Sabians, Stanley went out of his way to deny 'Rabbinical Traditions, [which] are more particular herein', including the famous story from Midrash Rabba that Abraham survived the fire he was instructed to step into by Nimrod upon his refusal to worship it.[154] The same went for 'the *Arabians* who imitate the Jews in Relations of this kind, and fancy Superstructures of their own upon Fables of the Rabbins', such as the story of one 'Edris', a son of Enoch (himself a son of Cain), who supposedly left books to the Sabians but nevertheless refused Abraham's call to worship only the true God – this story Stanley attributed to 'Kissaeus', i.e. Muḥammad Abdullah al-Kisā'ī, whose *Qasas Al-Anbiya* ('Stories of the Prophets') (*c.* thirteenth century) Stanley knew from Hottinger (who had taken a manuscript of the work from Golius's library).[155] Stanley's other named opponent, Gilbert Gaulmin (1585–1665), was like Kircher an orientalist of some fame across Europe (Stanley's friend Isaac Vossius persuaded him to sell his library to Queen Christina); just like Kircher, he derived extravagant connections between pagan wisdom and sacred truth from the Arabic and Hebrew sources in his Cabbalistic notes to an edition of a rabbinic *De vita et morte Mosis* (1629) that he edited from manuscript.[156] Stanley, in short, thought that a key part of his historiographical task was to clear away the clutter of Judaeo-Arabic sources that had muddled the history of near-eastern philosophy with their dubious philology[157] and their Cabbalistic fables of direct patriarchal influence on the pagans.

Stanley was operating within the mainstream of European scholarship of his age, scholarship that was distinctly sceptical of Jewish historiographical

---

[154] Stanley, *Chaldaick philosophy*, 35a–b (Stanley also mentions variants of the story in Rashi and Nachmanides).

[155] Loop, 'Hottinger', 183. For Stanley's familiarity with Hottinger, see e.g. *Chaldaick philosophy*, 34b (mispaginated 26). Hottinger was then being lauded in English learned circles: see Oldenburg to Hartlib, 16 July and 13 Aug 1659 in *Oldenburg correspondence*, I, 282–3, 303.

[156] *De vita et morte Mosis, libri tres, cum observationibus*, ed. Gilbert Gaulmin (Paris, 1629), 173–409, esp. 390–1 for the alignment of Zoroaster with a Cabbala revealing Christ's incarnation. See further Secret, 'Gilbert Gaulmin et l'histoire comparée des religions' (1970), esp. 45–8. Gaulmin's work seems to have been relatively widely known in England: the richness of his manuscripts was later celebrated in a letter from Justel to Oldenburg, 8 Feb 1668, *Oldenburg correspondence*, IV, 154.

[157] Kircher had developed a convoluted Chaldean (i.e. Aramaic) etymology to arrive at צוראסתר ('Tsuraster'), 'the image of secret things' ('simulacrum rerum secretarum'), supposedly 'a name common to all, who practised esoteric science and magic' (*Obeliscus*, 12: 'Fuit igitur hoc nomen commune omnibus iis, qui abstrusarum rerum scientiam, ac magiam exercebant'). Stanley responded that the real meaning was probably the much more prosaic 'the son of the stars', from the Persian word for 'star' and the common prefix 'Zor' (2a).

traditions apart from the Maimonidean. There is a great irony to this, for the source which Stanley – along with virtually every other seventeenth-century scholar – thought of as the key to a sober contextual reading, the *Nabatean agriculture* as quoted by Maimonides, was of course part of the same Judaeo-Arabic tradition that he was condemning. Contextually, however, there is little surprising about this choice. Brought up on the chronology of Scaliger and the anti-syncretist conclusions of Casaubon,[158] Stanley would have found in Maimonides a way of interpreting near-eastern history that did not present the obvious chronological and evidential problems that plagued the linking of Ham and Zoroaster. This link had been made not only by Kircher and the Jewish and Arabic authorities cited by him, but also by Patrizi, the last editor of the *Chaldean Oracles*, who had argued that Zoroaster was the grandson of Ham and had learnt divine philosophy from Abraham.[159] In fact, claimed Stanley, there were no fewer than six Zoroasters.[160] This plurality was not a new conclusion,[161] but rather than worry about precise lines of transmission of a supposedly divine wisdom, Stanley placed it in the context of pagan religious culture as it had been investigated by Scaliger, Selden, and Vossius: that culture had always repeatedly given the same name to 'extraordinary Persons' who had been 'Authors of some Publick Benefit'.[162]

This contextualism was carried over into Stanley's actual treatment of Chaldean philosophy, in which 'safe' texts like the Bible could be built upon using the general cultural–historical framework available through Maimonides. Stanley summarised this hermeneutical principle and the limits to scholarship that it generated:

Since the *Chaldaick* Polytheism was not (like that of the *Greeks*) founded upon an imaginary Mythology, (tho' later Writers treat of it after the same manner) but had reference to the Celestial Bodies, which they worshipped under several Names and Idols; it is no less probable than Consonant to the Chaldaick Doctrine, that those other Assyrian Idols ... mentioned in the Scripture, were of the same kind with the rest, and belonged to several other of the Stars; but this conjecture is not easily evinced, in regard that there is little extant of those Idols more than the bare mention of their names.[163]

Stanley had developed a general theory about the progress of idolatry that was no less sophisticated than that of the conjectural historians of the eighteenth century, but one which at the same time meshed with his scholarly caution about what could be known from the 'little extant of those Idols'. And despite this caution, sometimes the evidence was available. When Stanley discussed the various sects of the Chaldeans, he drew on the account at Dan. 2:2 of

---

[158] Stanley, *History*, 159a–b, 232b.
[159] Francesco Patrizi, *Nova de universis philosophia*, 'Panaugia' (new pagination), fols. 22$^r$–23$^v$.
[160] Stanley, *Chaldaick philosophy*, 2a–3b.   [161] Stausberg, *Faszination*, I, 328–35.
[162] Stanley, *Chaldaick philosophy*, 3b.   [163] Ibid., 28a–b.

Nebuchadnezzar calling for the learned to interpret his dreams and pointed out that the four sects which were assembled (*hartumim, ashaphim, mechashphim, casdim*) must have been the four Chaldean philosophical schools. Only when such a 'safe' evidential base was available was it permitted to dive further into the evidence: '*casdim*' must have referred to the 'Chaldeans' as a distinct class of Chaldean society, that is to say the priestly families, as known from Diodorus Siculus and Hesychius.[164]

An even better example of Stanley building on the foundations Maimonides offered him is his discussion of the Chaldeans' theurgic magic and their use of talismans. Stanley once again began with a lengthy quotation from the rabbi, describing the Sabians' use of images that they erected in honour of the stars, matching earthly materials to the celestial bodies (a gold image for the sun, silver for the moon, etc.). This practice, Stanley conjectured, might shed light on the *teraphim*, the mysterious objects mentioned in the Old Testament that had been termed 'tsilmenaia' in the Targum Onkelos (this is Stanley's transliteration of the Aramaic 'צלמניא', translated 'imagines' in Walton's polyglot, undoubtedly Stanley's source), and 'idols' (εἰδωλα [Gen. 31:19]) or 'manifestations' (δήλους [Deut. 33:8]) in the Septuagint. All this, alongside some rabbinic testimonies, was evidence that in 'all these Interpretations ... they [the *teraphim*] were indued with the Gift of Prediction', confirmed by the mention of the King of Babylon using images for divination at Ezekiel 21:21, which Stanley took to be a reference to the *teraphim*.[165] This was not controversial, but what evidence was there for their use among the ancient Chaldeans, beyond Maimonides? Here Stanley turned to a rather more recent source: the *Curiositez inouyes sur la sculpture talismanique des Persans* (1629) by the French priest, orientalist, and astrologer Jacques Gaffarel. Gaffarel's very popular work aimed to defend astrology by claiming to delineate a Jewish-Cabbalistic astrological tradition, most strikingly by reading the Hebrew alphabet into the stars.[166] This in turn led him to discuss in detail the

---

[164] Ibid., 7a–b, 6a–b; Diodorus Siculus, *Bib. hist.*, II.24; Hesychius, ϰ 40 (which is in fact a unique reference to the Chaldeans as 'μάγοι' as opposed to a geographical area – see Schironi, *From Alexandria to Babylon* (2009), 46).

[165] Stanley, *Chaldaick philosophy*, 22a–b; cf. *Biblia sacra polyglotta*, ed. B. Walton (6 vols, London, 1655–57), I, 134–5.

[166] Jacques Gaffarel, *Curiositez inouyes sur la sculpture talismanique des Persans* (Paris, 1629). The book was immediately reprinted in both official and pirate editions: see the note on this in Leo Allatius, *Apes urbanae, sive de viris illustribus* (Rome, 1633), 140. Gaffarel was condemned by the Sorbonne on 1 August 1629, but Richelieu nonetheless made him his librarian. For his Cabbalistic interests, see further Campanini, 'Eine späte Apologie der Kabbala (2007); Dweck, *The scandal of Kabbalah* (2011), 157–60. An English translation was made by the scholar, hack, and ex-canon of Christ Church, Oxford, Edmund Chilmead (for whom, see Feingold and Gouk, 'An early critic of Bacon's *Sylva sylvarum*' (1983)): *Unheard-of curiosities: concerning the talismanical sculpture of the Persians* (London, 1650). One certain English reader who was a near contemporary to Stanley was Sir Thomas Browne: see the allusion in *Pseudodoxia epidemica* (London, 1646), 11.

history of pagan, especially Persian, talismans. This he did with reference not only to a barrage of real rabbinical sources, but also to ones he seems to have invented himself: one important chapter, 'Qu'à tort on a blasmé les Persans & les curiositez de leur Magie, Sculpture, & Astrologie', was based almost entirely on the supposed testimony of a seemingly spurious Hamahalzel, 'a Persian Astrologer translated into Hebrew by Rabbi Chomer'.[167] These were the exact sort of 'rabbinic fables' that Stanley was so keen to avoid (a sentiment no doubt enhanced by Gaffarel's sometimes vitriolic attacks on Scaliger). Yet at one point Gaffarel claimed that his illustrious friends – especially the French antiquarian Nicolas-Claude Fabri de Peiresc – could supply him with images of Persian talismans that would substantiate Maimonides's theory of the Sabian origins of talismans.[168] It is undoubtedly to this claim that Stanley referred. This use of a source that he would otherwise have condemned to confirm the testimony of Maimonides is further confirmation of Stanley's belief that the rabbi was the right foundation for a quasi-conjectural investigation into near-eastern philosophy.

Stanley's implicit argument, then, was that by combining the Maimonidean framework and the Greek (and other) sources, one could get away from the pointless guesswork of the 'rabbinical traditions' – guesswork that was unnecessary when one could show that 'there were anciently learned Persons in *Arabia*, skilful in natural Philosophy, Astronomy, and other Sciences, [which] is manifest from Testimonies far more authentick' than the Judaeo-Arabic ones.[169] This reliance on Maimonides also had a deeper consequence. Not only did it lead to a challenge to the fabulous tradition of Zoroaster's contact with the patriarchs, but it also generated a far more sober and qualified vision of early near-eastern philosophy. Yes, the Chaldeans had been astronomers, and yes, they had held an emanationist cosmology (as witnessed in the *Chaldean Oracles*), but that astronomy and cosmology were now revealed as the product of a specific religious–theological context, not a manifestation of an unfathomable wisdom.

This more sober view emerged from the chronological aspect of Scaliger's legacy; it merged with another. The Huguenot scholar had also addressed near-eastern philosophy in a very different work to the *Emendatio Temporum*: his edition of the *Astronomica*, the long astronomical poem by Marcus Manilius, a first-century Roman about whom almost nothing is known. Scaliger's edition (1579) was immediately recognised as revolutionary; not only did his critical apparatus make much of the text comprehensible for the first time, but he also developed a novel and provocative image of the history of astrology and

---

[167] Gaffarel, *Curiositez inouyes*, 97–8 : ' ... il faut que je monstre leur innocence, comme j'ay desia fait celle de leurs voisins. Je la tire de la Preface d'une Astrologie Persane, traduite en Hebreu par Rabbi Chomer ... Hamahalzel'.
[168] Gaffarel, *Curiositez inouyes*, 248–50.  [169] Stanley, *Chaldaick philosophy*, 36a.

astronomy. Far from representing a glorious past, near-eastern astronomy was pitifully primitive. Greek astronomy developed independently and was a great advancement; Manilius was interesting precisely because his text was some of the latest evidence of the primitive state of near-eastern astronomy before its Greek reformation.[170] While the first edition already implied this thesis, the second (1599–1600) made it explicit in 'Prolegomena de astrologia veterum Graecorum'.[171]

There can be no doubt that Stanley drew extensively on Scaliger's Manilius. Take, for example, Stanley's treatment of Chaldean astrology, and his claim that they divided the astrological signs into sections of 10 degrees, called *decani* in Latin and πρόσωπα in Greek. The proof that they had also been used by the Chaldeans was that '*Temer* the *Babylonian, an Author of great Antiquity, wrote concerning them*'.[172] 'Temer' is clearly a printer's error for the Babylonian whom Stanley elsewhere calls 'Teucer', and who had been identified as a believer in the decans only by Scaliger, drawing on the scholiast to the *Tetrabiblos*.[173] Scaliger's insistence on a progressivist history of astronomy is evident elsewhere in Stanley's *History*.[174] Most importantly, Stanley accepted Scaliger's general thesis: that while in astrology the Chaldeans had indeed taught the Greeks much, in astronomy they were 'far short of that height ... to which the *Greeks*, who brought it out of the East, improved it'.[175] Far from being a syncretist, Stanley was endorsing Scaliger's progressive view of the history of science. But Scaliger had never systematically treated the Chaldeans, using them only as a foil for his Manilius: Stanley surely saw himself as building on the work of the master who had taught him so much, placing the vision of ancient astronomy that Scaliger had developed in the theological–religious context offered by Maimonides, and filling the gaps that Scaliger had left with new evidence.

We have seen, then, that Stanley's aim was to follow in the footsteps of Scaliger, first by developing a chronologically viable history of near-eastern philosophy, second by promoting a progressivist attitude to the history of astronomy, third by rejecting as unfounded the Judaeo-Arabic speculations which had culminated in the work of the Jesuit Kircher. At the same time he sought to outdo the Huguenot by adding the contextual framework offered by Maimonides. Yet this leaves us with one great puzzle. It is very difficult to imagine Scaliger relying, as Stanley did, on that most dubious of sources: the *Chaldean Oracles*. Almost all of Stanley's long account of the Chaldean 'Theology and Physick', with their three orders of being and emanationist

[170] Grafton, *Scaliger*, I, 180–226.

[171] Much of which is usefully translated at Grafton, *Scaliger*, I, 214–15; see also II, 437–58.

[172] Stanley, *Chaldaick philosophy*, 18a.   [173] Grafton, *Scaliger*, I, 208.

[174] See e.g. the attack on Ramus's ascription of knowledge of the second to the fifth propositions of the fourth book of Euclid's *Elements* to Thales, at *History*, 9a.

[175] Stanley, *Chaldaick philosophy*, 16a (mispaginated 24).

metaphysics, was derived from exposition of the *Oracles*, and from Plethon's and Psellus's commentaries.[176] Why did Stanley accept this dubious source, whose veracity had already been challenged by Beza, Ursinus, and others? After all, he appreciated fully the possibility that it was '*forged by some Pseudo-Christian Greek*', not least because the obscure second-century gnostic Prodicus had claimed to possess 'secret Books of Zoroaster'.[177]

There are two reasons for Stanley's use of the source. First, he envisaged a qualitative difference between the *Oracles* and well-known forgeries like the *Hermetica* and the pseudo-Sibylline *Oracles*. The last two had been shown, most famously by Casaubon and in 1649 by the Amsterdam history professor David Blondel, to be certain Christian frauds.[178] Yet Stanley rightly countered that the case of the *Chaldean Oracles* was different. They lay 'dispersed among several authors'. More importantly, 'they have been held in great veneration by the Platonick Philosophers', who considered them divinely revealed.[179] These late antique neoplatonists were some of the best-known opponents of Christianity. Not only this, but they were intimately familiar with such literature. Were they likely to revere a Christian forgery? When the third-century Platonist Porphyry launched his vicious attack on the Christians, he accused them of forging Zoroastrian 'revelations' (ἀποκαλύψεις), 'concocted by the sectaries [i.e. gnostics] in order to pretend that the doctrines they had embraced were those of the ancient sage'; these forgeries, Porphyry trumped, had been exposed as spurious by himself, Plotinus, and Amelius.[180] What was crucial, Stanley cleverly pointed out, was that he had *not* accused the Christians of forging the *Chaldean Oracles*, which he of course cited many times himself.[181] To this Stanley added some subsidiary evidence: he wheeled out the old story of Pico possessing an Aramaic version of the *Oracles*, he correctly pointed out that their Greek was so full of 'harsh and exotick Expressions' that there must have been something 'Originally foreign' in them, and he reminded the reader that their translation into Greek by Julian was chronologically compatible with their introduction into Greece by the real Berosus. As for any similarities in terminology with later Greek thought, this only served to 'confirm that these Oracles were (as we said) Translated into Greek by Persons skilful in the Greek Phylosophy'.[182]

[176] Ibid., 8a–16a.

[177] Ibid., 38a (mispaginated 31), drawing on Clemens Alexandrinus, *Strom.*, I.15.

[178] David Blondel, *Des Sibylles célébrées tant par l'antiquité payenne que par les saincts perés* (Paris, 1649).

[179] Stanley, *Chaldaick philosophy*, 38a; at 38b, Stanley used the examples of the citations of the *Oracles* in Proclus, *In Tim.*, II.50 (=fr. 67), where Proclus speaks of them as 'the theology of the Assyrians . . . revealed to them by the gods'; and (with no acknowledgement of even the work being quoted), Proclus, *Theolog. Platon.*, 324 (= fr. 72), where it is claimed that Plato 'said the very things . . . revealed by the gods'.

[180] Porphyry, *Plot.*, 16.    [181] Stanley, *Chaldaick philosophy*, 38a.    [182] Ibid., 38a–b.

And yet, if we look closer, these justifications fall apart. Stanley never considered the possibility – which would surely have come to the mind of Casaubon and had already been voiced by Ursinus – that the spurious *Oracles*, whoever composed them, had fooled *both* the Christians and the pagan Platonists.[183] But this is where we can offer a second explanation that takes us away from the medium-term context of post-Scaligerian historical criticism and into the short-term context of mid-century Dutch and Anglican-royalist historiography. Stanley argued for the authenticity of the *Oracles* because he started from the presupposition that he shared with Pearson, Meric Casaubon, Grotius, and Vossius: that of a broadly universal *consensus gentium* on such basic principles as monotheism. The *Oracles* (read through the interpretations of Plethon and Psellus) allowed Stanley to argue that all of Chaldean natural philosophy, theurgy, astrology, and natural magic were ultimately related to their theology, which itself was an idolatrous corruption of a monotheism that was nonetheless traceable.[184] Precisely for this reason he could draw on Paul's message in the Epistle to the Romans: the gentiles knew the true God but 'changed the Glory of the uncorruptible God into an Image made like to corruptible Man' (Rom. 1:23), a testimony that Vossius had made central to his influential work.[185] At this point we should be clear: Stanley's was *not* a work of apologetics, and he certainly cannot be classed as a syncretist: as I have been at pains to show, he had certainly taken what may be called the 'Scaliger-Casaubon turn' and had rejected the fantasies of any so-called *prisca theologia*.[186] But even as a scholar – whether on the history of philosophy, of tithes, or of Greek poetry – he was working within a framework of loose philosophical–theological presuppositions, a set of presuppositions he shared with his closest Anglican-royalist collaborators and the European scholars who inspired them.

## 2.4 Histories of astronomy and the culture of English science: Stanley, Sherburne, and the natural philosophers

It is difficult to assess the level of familiarity with Stanley's work between the 1660s and the 1680s. It is not often cited, and there is some evidence of it being

---

[183] Porphyry, *Plot.*, 16, already has ' … πολλοὺς ἐξηπάτων καὶ αὐτοὶ ἠπατημένοι' ('[the Christians] deceived many, themselves first').

[184] See e.g. Stanley, *Chaldaick philosophy*, 8a–b, especially drawing on fr. 39; 24b–29a.

[185] Cited at Stanley, *Chaldaick philosophy*, 25a. Cf. Vossius, *Theologia gentilis*, 24–5, 252, and esp. 13: 'Mens igitur Apostoli est, nos ejus esse numinis progeniem, quod per Iovem intelligerent è gentibus saniores. Quod non diceret, nisi in nationibus etiam aliqui notitiam veri numinis habuissent. Et quomodo hoc sustinent negare, cum idem Apostolus dicat ad Rom.'

[186] See also Hardy, *'Ars critica'*, 275.

prohibitively expensive.[187] But Stanley's main themes – a new 'critical' verification of the identity of Zoroaster and a focus on Maimonides' 'Sabians' – were
adopted by many, albeit with variations based on their own interests and presuppositions. One group showing a serious interest were natural philosophers,
especially those with an interest in the history of astronomy. We have already had
cause to mention the pioneering intervention in this field of Scaliger's Manilius.
Its influence was vast, not only because of its radical philological and rhetorical
conclusions, but also because these conclusions became representative of
Scaliger's method, and thus archetypes for his admirers to emulate and prospective usurpers of his crown to challenge: major scholars who attempted a degree of
both included Gronovius, Huet, and Bentley.[188] Yet its relevance to astronomical
topics rendered it of interest to many beyond a narrowly 'scholarly' community.
Indeed, as we shall see, mid-century English 'scientific' culture was astonishingly captivated by the potential usefulness of the history of natural philosophy; a
finding that will in turn allow us to reach some further important conclusions
about Stanley and his scholarly acquintances.

An obvious manifestation of the impact of Scaliger's Manilius can be seen in
the work of one such acquaintance: Edward Sherburne's English translation of
the first book of the *Astronomica*, published in 1675 but begun in the mid
1650s. Sherburne had been tutored as a schoolboy by the well-known and well-
connected scholar Thomas Farnaby (*c.* 1575–1647); professionally, he succeeded his father as clerk of the Office of Ordnance in 1641 and was based in
the Tower for the rest of his long life, except the period 1642–60 when he first
served in Charles's army before moving (in 1645) to London and to the Middle
Temple, where he became very close to Stanley. It was with Stanley that he
moved to a country retirement in Hertfordshire, and like his younger friend
he also published translations of French and Italian poetry. In the early 1650s he
became tutor to the young Sir George Savile, and it was on his tour of Europe
that he began work on Manilius, in September 1656.[189]

---

[187]   By 1670, it was selling for the huge price of £3 (see the advertisements in Roger Manley, *The
        history of the late warres in Denmark* (London, 1670), sig. V2$^r$; *A catalogue of books printed
        for Thomas Basset* (London, 1672) (it was twice as expensive as all other works being sold by
        Basset (except legal anthologies)). The ESTC records significantly more extant copies of the
        1687 than the 1655–62 edition (and more again of the 1701 edition). Osler, 'Introduction'
        (1991), 7, calls Stanley's *History* 'immensely popular' without supplying any evidence.

[188]   For an overview from a later editor's mostly scornful perspective, see Housman, 'Introduction'
        (1937), I, xi–xix.

[189]   These biographical details are collected in van Beeck, 'Introduction' (1961), xvii–xlv; and de
        Quehen, 'Sherburne, Edward', *ODNB*; many ultimately deriving from Wood, *Fasti
        Oxonienses*, I. cols 30–2. For the first draft of Manilius, 'Begun 12$^{th}$ Sept 1656 at Paris', see
        BL MS Sloane 832, fols. 10$^r$–37$^v$ (quotation from fol. 11$^r$). The mock title-page for this draft
        shows that Sherburne initially intended to translate all five books (fol. 10$^r$), but he evidently
        quickly changed his mind (see the mock title-page at fol. 38$^r$). For Sherburne as translator of
        continental poetry, see Praz, 'Stanley, Sherburne and Ayres'. Farnaby is understudied, but see
        Serjeantson, 'Thomas Farnaby' (2001). Housman's dismissive judgement of Sherburne's

By contemporary standards, Sherburne would not have been seen as a leading scholar: unlike Stanley, for example, he never published an original-language edition of a classical text, preferring English translations, especially of the Senecan tragedies.[190] Nonetheless, we should not underestimate the extent to which he saw himself, and was seen by others, as at least engaging in scholarly practice. His library catalogues reveal a strong appetite both for the work of late humanist philologists and for the original classical texts.[191] Late in life he wanted to publish his Senecan translations at the Sheldonian press, home of Restoration scholarly editions.[192] He kept up with the work of the leading Oxford scholars, enquiring after Edward Bernard's doomed edition of Josephus; Bernard himself had earlier sent Sherburne not only copies of his works but also a collation of a valuable manuscript of the Gospels (the so-called Codex Pithaei or Codex Medicaeus). The young Bentley scoured Sherburne's library for such manuscripts at the start of his own scholarly career, and borrowed materials for his own Manilius.[193] And Sherburne clearly had a more ambitious contribution in mind even after the publication of the work, gathering variant readings from across Europe and inserting them in an interleaved copy of Scaliger's second edition.[194] How, then, should we understand his translation?

Manilius ('Introduction', xv) is negated by his mistakes (e.g. on the dating of the work) and the important evidence gathered in Reeve, 'Acidalius on Manilius' (1991), esp. 233–7.

[190] Seneca, *Medea*, ed. and trans. Edward Sherburne (London, 1648); Seneca, *Troades*, ed. and trans. Edward Sherburne (London, 1679); Edward Sherburne, *The tragedies of L. Annaeus Seneca the philosopher ... to which is prefixed the life and death of Seneca the philosopher* (London, 1702). Sherburne was certainly also interested in Stoic moral philosophy in itself: see his *Seneca's answer, to Lucilius his quaere; why good men suffer misfortunes seeing there is a divine providence?* (London, 1648) and his possession of excerpts from Simplicius' commentary on Epictetus's *Enchiridion* (BL MS Sloane 836, fols. 44$^v$–45$^v$) by the young high-church cleric George Stanhope (1660–1728), which would eventually become Stanhope's *Epictetus his morals, with Simplicius his comment* (London, 1694).

[191] BL MS Sloane 857 (commenced 1670), fols. 182$^r$–194$^v$, containing almost 900 vols (see also van Beeck, 'Introduction', xxxvii–xxxviii). See also the later catalogue, Bod. MS Rawl. Q.b.3 (for 1677–87). See Birrell, 'The library of Sir Edward Sherburne' (1997); importantly supplemented by Poole, 'Loans from the library of Sir Edward Sherburne' (2013).

[192] Sherburne to Wood, 12 Dec 1693, Bod. MS Wood. F.44, fol. 296$^r$.

[193] Sherburne to Wood, 1693 (no further date), Bod. MS. Wood F.44, fol. 298$^r$ (enquiring after Bernard's Josephus); Sherburne to Wood, 16 June 1688, Bod. MS Wood F.44, fol. 287 (Bernard had sent Sherburne his *De mensuris et ponderibus antiquis* (Oxford, 1688)); Bentley to Bernard, 26 Jan 1692, Bod. MS Smith 45, fol. 161$^r$ (scouring Sherburne's library; Bernard's collation); see also Bentley to Sherburne, undated (1693/4), BL Sloane MS 836, fol. 83$^v$; for their acquaintance and dealings over Manilius, see van Beeck, 'Introduction', xxxv–xxxvi; Reeve, 'Acidalius', 230–1. See also Sherburne's index of manuscripts in Italian, Spanish, and French libraries in one of his commonplace books: BL MS Sloane 836, fols 8$^r$–17$^v$, 18$^r$–24$^r$, 26$^r$–31$^r$, 33$^r$–35$^r$.

[194] CUL MS. Adv.d.44.5. One collation was by Bernard (now Bod. MS Linc. D.5.13, of the 'Pithoenaus', now Boston Public Library MS q.Med.20; see also Bod. MS Wood, F.44, fol. 251$^v$), another by Sherburne from Leiden Voss. Lat. O.3, and one of 'G.' (see Housman, vii), borrowed from Daniel Papebrochius. Bentley later used this copy (Reeve, 'Acidalius', 233–4).

To an extent, the work was certainly a product of Sherburne's scholarly interests and connections. The best example of this is the essay on the identity of the Roman poet included in the Preface, which challenges Scaliger's identification of him with the 'Manilius mathematicus' mentioned at Pliny, *Natural history*, XXXVI.10 in favour of the 'Manilius Antiochus' mentioned at XXXV.15 of the same work.[195] As Sherburne acknowledged, this whole discussion was in fact based on the thoughts of Isaac Vossius, to whom he had been advised to write for enlightenment on the subject by Stanley, and who obliged with a long response (a response whose length and promptness clearly upset Stanley, who had long been waiting for Vossius's notes on Aeschylus).[196] In the text itself, Sherburne's huge and copious notes, arranged carefully around the folio pages, also often offered new philological–historical readings, such as his correction of Scaliger's explanation for Manilius's reference to Venus as 'phosphorus'.[197] Many more of the notes were historical–contextual, identifying Manilius's implied targets[198] or drawing on the most recently translated Arabic sources, such as Ulugh Beg's famous star catalogue, *Zīj-i Sultānī* (1437) (which had been published in full for the first time, in Latin translation, by Thomas Hyde in 1665) to demonstrate that the pre-Greek ancients – including the Chinese – divided the day into hours.[199] In his manuscript notes we find him wrestling with the same problem of the age of Chaldean astronomical observations as had tormented Stanley and a host of others.[200]

And yet, this was not a work attempting to replace Scaliger's Manilius; that is to say, it was not a work of high scholarship or criticism as contemporaries understood it. Rather, the objective of the book was to use humanism – specifically the history of astronomy and philosophy more generally – as a

---

[195] Edward Sherburne, 'The preface', in *The sphere of Marcus Manilius* (London, 1675), sigs. b^r–[b2]^v.

[196] See Sherburne to Isaac Vossius, 11 Oct 1669, Bod. MS D'Orville 470, 107–8 (another copy is BL MS Sloane 836, fol. 46^r). Vossius's response is BL MS Royal Appendix 72, fols. 5^r–6^v; see also the account of it in Franciscus Junius to Thomas Marshall, 31 Dec 1669, Bod. MS Marshall 134, fol. 12^r. This letter claimed that Vossius had ready his Aeschylus notes for Stanley, but Stanley's subsequent exasperated pleading for the notes (Stanley to Vossius, 12 Feb 1670, Bod. MS D'Orville 470, 109) went unheeded.

[197] Manilius, *Sphere*, 14, note t. Scaliger had suggested that it was because it was the brightest celestial object in the night sky (i.e. not including the moon), but Sherburne countered that it was because it 'precedes the rising Sun, as being the Harbinger of Light', drawing on the account in Pliny, *Hist. nat.*, II.6 (II.8 in the older arrangement used by Sherburne).

[198] See e.g. the identification of Theophrastus as Manilius's target when discussing those who make the galaxy 'The Cement of the close-wedg'd Hemispheres' (49), for which the source is Macrobius, *In Somn.*, xv.

[199] See the huge note at 40, drawing extensively on the partial publication of the *Zīj-i Sultānī* by John Greaves: *Epochae celebriores, astronomis, historicis, chronologis Chataiorum ... ex traditione Ulugh Beigi* (London, 1650) (esp. p. 6), which was based primarily on a manuscript of an Arabic translation of the *Zīj* – the manuscript, with Greaves's annotations, is now at St. John's College, Cambridge, MS 91. See further Toomer, *Eastern wisedome*, 167–76.

[200] BL MS Sloane 829, fol. 26^v (see fol. 28^v for notes from Scaliger).

propaedeutic to incite gentlemanly readers to study astronomy. Anthony Wood's account of the gestation of the work, based on Sherburne's own comments, described it as 'chiefly intended by its author for the use of the young gentry and nobility of the land, to serve as their initiation in the first rudiment of spherical learning'.[201] This sentiment is echoed in Sherburne's preface, which answered the objection as to 'why, in an age wherein the learned World is so fruitful in Accurate Productions of this Kind, obtrude We upon the Reader a Piece of less curious and less knowing Antiquity?' by pointing out that many modern inventions were in fact 'but the Disguises and Alterations of elder Ingenuity', by arguing that it was easiest for a newcomer to a subject to start with its primitive origins before learning of its later development, and by citing a barrage of testimonies – including Scaliger's – about the usefulness of Manilius for 'youth ... to prepare their Way to the Elements of Spherical Learning'.[202]

To this, Sherburne added a list of topics on which Manilius summarised opinions which pre-empted modern astronomical discovery (later highlighting them in the notes): the fluidity of the heavens (as opposed to the Aristotelian solid orbs); the huge size of the sphere of the fixed stars and the variant distance of those stars from the earth, pre-empting Kepler; the self-luminosity of the fixed stars, pre-empting Galileo's 'so many suns'; the recognition that the Milky Way was simply a collection of stars, pre-empting through naked observation and reason a discovery that had been made more recently only through use of the telescope.[203] But this does not mean that Sherburne believed in the pre-eminence of the ancients. His whole work, with its myriad of notes, is testimony to a progressive view of the history of astronomy and of natural philosophy more generally. The point was that humanist scholarship was the best way of *conveying* that progress. Each natural phenomenon mentioned by Manilius received its own extensive note detailing the history of opinions on that subject. When Manilius mentioned thunder, Sherburne reported the ancient explanations of Anaximander and Metrodorus (that it was a wind breaking from inside a thick cloud), Anaxagoras (that it was a fiery matter making a noise as it was suddenly cooled by a cloud), the Stoics (that it was the noise made by two hollow clouds colliding), Descartes (a similar collision-based theory), and Hobbes (that it was the breaking of a frozen cloud – an explanation taken from Lucretius), before pointing out that 'much more consonant to Truth' was the recent chymical opinion that it was 'an Exhalation hot and dry, of a Sulphurous and Nitrous matter contracted within a cold and moist Cloud'.[204]

---

[201] Wood, *Fasti oxonienses*, II, col. 32. Sherburne supplied Wood with the information for the entry on him: see e.g. Sherburne to Wood, 8 Jan 1690, Bod. MS Wood F. 44 (Sherburne requests to see a draft of the entry).

[202] Sherburne, 'Preface', sigs. a$^v$, [a2]$^r$, c$^v$. [203] Ibid., sig. a$^v$; *Sphere*, 16, note a; 50, note b.

[204] Manilius, *Sphere*, 9, note q.

Similar histories were developed for Manilius's mentions of snow, hail, earthquakes, subterranean fire, rain, wind, and lightning, and a huge number of other topics.[205] At other points the notes were not didactic but simply historical, such as the history of those who held the world eternal and uncreated.[206] Sometimes they contextualised Manilius's own opinions, like Scaliger treating him not only as a Stoic but also as an inheritor of a more primitive ancient astronomy, but now also drawing on sources unavailable to Scaliger. These included Ulugh Beg, whom Hyde had also begun translating for natural philosophical reasons, on the request of Seth Ward, when Ward was Savilian Professor of Astronomy.[207]

In an appendix on 'The Original and Progress of Astronomy', Sherburne's debt to both Scaliger's and Stanley's progressivist views is evident (although unlike Stanley he indulged in speculation on the patriarchs' knowledge of astronomy and on the putative books of Enoch).[208] This was followed by a huge catalogue of 'The most eminent Astronomers, Ancient and Modern', which, while certainly lacking Stanley's chronological flair (Sherburne accepted the extended Septuagint chronology, no doubt under the influence of Vossius, but then proceeded to place figures within it arbitrarily, e.g. dating Zoroaster to 1990 BC), was nonetheless extremely thorough, running through to the 1660s.[209] Sherburne's purpose was, as I have emphasised, didactic, and so he finished with a discussion 'Of the Cosmical System', necessary because Manilius had not 'giv[en] any particular Description thereof'. But this description – accompanied by beautiful fold-out diagrams – also had to be couched in history, 'by representing the several Opinions, as well of the *Ancients* as *Moderns*, touching the same'.[210] And so Sherburne not only summarised the various ancient systems but also represented the most important ones (the Pythagorean, Platonic, Egyptian, and that of Philolaus, equivalent to the Copernican) with elaborate diagrams.

That Sherburne held a progressive view of the history of astronomy is not surprising. From the early 1650s he had been a keen mathematician and

---

[205]  Ibid., 9–10, nn. r–z.

[206]  Ibid., 11, note e, discussing Xenophanes, Parmenides, Melissus, and Aristotle.

[207]  Ibid., 13, note o (Manilius as Stoic); 18 (deities residing in each sign of the Zodiac an ancient Egyptian opinion inherited by the Arabs, drawing on Thomas Hyde, 'In Ulugh Beighi Tabulas Stellarum fixarum Commentarii', in Ulugh Beg, *Tabulae longitudinis et latitudinis stellarum fixarum*, ed. and trans. Thomas Hyde (Oxford, 1665), 30 (new pagination)); 35 (on the derivation of constellation names from Greek theology, drawing on a Greek inscription printed in Onoforio Panvinio's posthumous *De ludis circensibus* (Venice, 1600)). On Hyde, see 2.7 below; on his edition of the *Zīj*, see Toomer, *Eastern wisedome*, 249–50.

[208]  Edward Sherburne, 'The original and progress of astronomy', in *Sphere*, 1–6 (new pagination), esp. 1 (a clear direct textual similarity to Stanley, *Chaldaick philosophy*, 16a), 2 (the patriarchs), 4 (progressive history of Greek astronomy).

[209]  Edward Sherburne, 'A catalogue of the most eminent astronomers, ancient & modern', in *Sphere*, 6–126 (new pagination).

[210]  Edward Sherburne, 'Of the cosmical system', in *Sphere*, 127–212 (new pagination), at 127.

astronomer, and a friend and collaborator of Jonas Moore, the great patron and driving force behind the establishment of the Royal Observatory.[211] Both humanist history and astronomical practice confirmed the improvements in astronomy since the time of Manilius. But this was not the key point of Sherburne's edition – beyond those already mentioned, there are very few comparisons between ancient and modern astronomy. The real point was that humanist history, when presented attractively and in English, continued to be a spur for natural philosophical or mathematical endeavour, not because it revealed an ancient golden age to be emulated, nor because it contributed to a debate between ancients and moderns, but because it taught the reader about the principles on which previous attempts had been formulated. Precisely this was recognised and applauded in the review of the work in the *Philosophical Transactions of the Royal Society*.[212]

This concern was also shared by Sherburne's 'Dear Friend' Stanley.[213] It helps to explain the rather puzzling passages in Stanley's preface to both the *History of philosophy* proper, and to *Chaldaick philosophy*:

Nor is it unseasonable at this time to examine the Tenents [sic] of old Philosophers, when so great variety of Opinions daily spring up; some of which are but raked out of the Ruines of Antiquity, which ought to be restored to their first Owners; others being of late invention will receive addition, when advanced to such heights we look down to the bottom from which Philosophy took her first rise, and see how great a progress she hath made, whose beginnings are almost inscrutable.[214]

We are entering upon a Subject which I confess, is in it self harsh, and exotick, very unproper for our Tongue; yet I doubt not but they will pardon this, who shall consider, that other Philosophies and Sciences have been lately well received by several Nations Translated into their own Languages, and that this, as being the first, contributes not a little to the understanding of the rest.[215]

Once we examine Stanley's *History* through the lens of Sherburne's Manilius, these rather ambiguous statements make more sense. Critical humanist history can be a propaedeutic and handmaiden to the new natural philosophy, not because it reveals philosophical truth, but because it reveals the store of previous opinions and their development, and because it gives the modern natural philosopher both a better perspective on modern achievements and an attractive base from which to begin investigation.

---

[211] See the portion of his commonplace book devoted to mathematics and astronomy: BL Sloane MS 824, fols. 1$^r$–73$^r$, esp. the notes from Kepler at fols. 2$^r$–4$^r$. For Moore, see Willmoth, *Sir Jonas Moore* (1993) (146 on his friendship with Sherburne, for which see also van Beeck, 'Introduction', xxxiii).

[212] *Philosophical Transactions*, 110 (1675), 233–5 ('The learn'd and intelligent Author of this Work, rightly considering the great Importance of the mutual Helps, which the Knowledge of Antiquity and the Pursuit of New Discoveries of the present Times may afford to one another … ').

[213] Stanley is thus labelled in *Sphere*, 12, note k.   [214] Stanley, *History of philosophy*, 'Preface'.

[215] *Chaldaick philosophy*, 'Preface'.

This is certainly not *prisca sapientia*; nor has it anything to do with 'ancients versus moderns'. Yet it leaves the question of where such a specific image of the practical usefulness of the history of philosophy came from. In part, this is a false question: historical introductions to philosophy textbooks were commonplace (4.1 below) and the idea that vernacular humanism was a potent vehicle for instructing the nobility – and for gaining patronage[216] – was hardly a novel one. Nonetheless, there is a clear emphasis on *recent* philosophical novelty in both Stanley and Sherburne that suggests that they felt themselves to be doing something new. In his preface Sherburne cited Abraham Cowley's wish, in his *Proposition for the advancement of experimental philosophy* (1661), that in a school set up as an 'Apprenticeship in Natural Philosophy', children might be 'bre[d] up in Authors, or pieces of Authors, who treat of some parts of Nature, and who may be understood with as much ease and pleasure, as those which are commonly taught'.[217] As is well known, Cowley was highly sympathetic to the aims of the Royal Society (despite never becoming a member or attending meetings), and there is certainly some evidence linking Stanley and Sherburne to the Society. Stanley was elected FRS in August 1661, and Sherburne's *Manilius* was favourably reviewed in the *Philosophical Transactions*, as we have seen.[218] And yet this native English development also cannot have been the key influence, for both began their works in the mid 1650s, before the foundation of the Society, and when both were members of learned circles that were only tangential to the core groups behind the Society's formation. Similarly, while Sherburne certainly read Bacon,[219] there is as little evidence of Bacon being the key influence on his views on the usefulness of history as there is for Stanley.

It is, however, possible to make a case for the influence of one non-English figure in particular: Pierre Gassendi. As is well known, Gassendi developed a full and systematic natural philosophy on the basis of the surviving evidence for Epicurus: we shall meet English natural philosophers' deep engagement with Gassendi's rich humanist reinterpretations of ancient matter and causation theory in Chapter 5. But both Stanley and Sherburne began their histories before Gassendi's systematic statement of a neo-Epicurean philosophy – the *Syntagma philosophicum* (1658) – appeared. Rather, they had available to them

---

[216] Sherburne's catalogue finished with a notice of the recent building of an observatory in St Andrews (i.e. that commissioned by James Gregory in 1673), commenting 'which Heroick Example we hope may animate those of like Condition and Abilities [i.e. 'bishops, noblemen, and gentry'] in this Nation to incourage the promoting of the same Laudable Design amongst us'. See further the evidence discovered by Poole, 'Loans', 86 n. 26. For the fullest treatment of the St Andrews observatory, see Malet, 'Studies on James Gregorie' (1989), 80–5.

[217] Abraham Cowley, *A proposition for the advancement of experimental philosophy* (London, 1661), 45–6; Sherburne, 'Preface', sig. [c2]$^r$.

[218] Stanley was an inactive Fellow: Hunter, *Royal Society*, 148–9; n. 212 above for the review of Sherburne in the *PT.*

[219] BL Sloane 836, fols. 51$^r$–59$^v$ contains notes from Bacon's *Essays.*

Gassendi's *De vita, moribus, et doctrina Epicuri* (1647) and the *Animadversiones in decimum librum Diogenis Laertii* (1649), works of biography and textual commentary respectively. Far from presenting a systematic philosophy, these were historical readings of Epicurus's philosophy that placed it in the context of Greek philosophy more generally.[220] But at the same time, Gassendi – whose own investigations in astronomy and physics had by the 1640s led him to emphasise the importance of direct experience – repeatedly insisted that such history was of use to practicing natural philosophers, not necessarily because it revealed truth, but because it explained the conceptual apparatus that had been inherited by present generations.[221]

There is much evidence of Stanley's and Sherburne's deep engagement with Gassendi: Stanley's whole section on Epicurus was a translation from the Frenchman,[222] whereas Sherburne took extensive notes on the *Animadversiones* when in Paris in the 1650s.[223] But neither the history of Stanley, with his strict refusal to break Laërtian boundaries, nor that of Sherburne, with his vast independent mini-histories for each topic mentioned by Manilius, in fact much resembled Gassendi's contextualist and problem-based approach to Epicurus and to the history of philosophy.[224] Gassendi's influence on them lay elsewhere: in the belief that a critical history of philosophy, including emendations, variant readings, and the whole apparatus of humanist erudition, was directly relevant to the new philosophy. But where Gassendi had focused narrowly on Epicurus, Stanley and Sherburne believed that *all* philosophy had to go through the same process. This, it seems to me, is what Stanley meant in his statement – which has previously puzzled historians – in his dedication to Marsham, that,

The Learned *Gassendus* was my Precedent; whom nevertheless I have not follow'd in his Partiality: For he, tho' limited to a Single Person, yet giveth himself Liberty of Enlargement, and taketh occasion from this Subject to make the World acquainted with many excellent Disquisitions of his own. Our Scope being of a greater Latitude, affords less Opportunity to favour any Particular; whilst there is due to every one the Commendation of their own Deserts.[225]

---

[220] The best account remains that in Joy, *Gassendi the atomist* (1987), esp. 66–82. For further Gassendi historiography, see 5.1 below.

[221] Ibid., *passim*.

[222] It was a translation of parts of *De vita et moribus Epicuri* (1647) and the whole of the *Philosophiae Epicuri syntagma* (1649), an appendix to the *Animadversiones in decimum librum Diogenes Laertii* (Kroll, 'Question' incorrectly claims it to be a translation of the *Syntagma philosophicum* (1658)).

[223] BL MS Sloane 832, fols. $2^r$–$9^v$. Sherburne also began a translation of Lucretius (BL MS Sloane 837, fols. $7^r$–$19^r$) for which he again solicited notes from Vossius (Poole, 'Loans', 83).

[224] Joy, *Gassendi*, 77–8; ch. 5 below.

[225] Stanley, *History*, 'To my honoured uncle John Marsham, Esq.'

Pearson echoed this combination of praise for Gassendi's brilliant exposition of the tenth book of Diogenes Laërtius and a call for a similar project for the rest of the history of philosophy.[226] As I have been at pains to show, there is no single key to Stanley's *History*. Nonetheless, Gassendi's specific role in inspiring a belief that the history of philosophy was an important component of the recent developments in philosophy itself seems to have been one of the formative influences behind it.

Stanley and Sherburne were not mistaken in their assumption that a history of astronomy laden with marginal notes would appeal to practising mid-century natural philosophers and the gentry who were most likely to become virtuosi. Robert Hooke borrowed Sherburne's Manilius as soon as it was published;[227] John Flamsteed was receiving and reading it well before the final sheets had even been printed,[228] as was John Collins.[229] Pearson's Hierocles was likewise being read in natural philosophical circles.[230] On a wider level, there was an astonishing level of integration between humanist interest in the history of scientific disciplines and the activities of natural philosophical reformers themselves. Already in the early 1640s, John Wilkins, who would become the most important organisational force behind mid-century English natural philosophy, specifically called for a project of 'examination of ... old opinions' (citing Bacon's authority), and his works of that decade consist to a great extent of precisely such examinations,[231] a fact that was recognised by his contemporary continental editor.[232] The group that Wilkins led in 1650s Oxford, and which is commonly seen as the direct predecessor of the Royal Society, concerned itself at first with a project, led by Selden's friend Gerard Langbaine, to catalogue the books in the Bodleian, and in particular 'to make Medulla's [sic] of all Authors in reference to Experimental Learning'.[233] Stanley's friend John Greaves, who was Savilian Professor of Astronomy until forced to vacate in 1648, and who helped secure Seth Ward's election as

---

[226] John Pearson, 'Reverendissimo doctissimoque viro, Aegidio Menagio', in DL 1664, sig. [A3]ʳ.

[227] *The diary of Robert Hooke*, eds., H. Robinson and W. Adams (London, 1935), 86 (Hooke dined with Sherburne before picking up the book).

[228] Flamsteed to John Collins, 19 March 1673, in *The correspondence of scientific men of the seventeenth century*, ed. S. J. Rigaud (2 vols, Oxford, 1846), I, 161.

[229] Collins to John Beale, 20 Aug 1672, in ibid., 199–200.

[230] *Correspondence of scientific men*, II, 82.

[231] [John Wilkins], *A discourse concerning a new world & another planet* (London, 1640), sigs. [A4]ʳ⁻ᵛ. See further 3.3 below.

[232] 'Au lecteur', in John Wilkins, *Le monde dans la lune ... De la Traduction du Sr de la Montagne* (Rouen, 1656), sigs. [aiii]ʳ⁻[aiii]ᵛ, comparing Wilkins's work to Jean d'Espagnet's *La philosophie naturelle restablie en sa purete* (Paris, 1651), a project to revive the best of ancient natural philosophy.

[233] The key evidence is Langbaine's list of participants at Bod. MS Ashmole 1810; HP 28/2/5B (quotation there) and a letter from Seth Ward to Justinian Isham (who, we will recall, was one of Stanley's royalist-scholarly acquintances) printed in Robinson, 'An unpublished letter of Seth Ward' (1950), 69–70.

his successor, in his 1650 edition and translation of Maḥmūd Shāh Khaljī's Persian astronomical work, explicitly announced that one key purpose of such work was didactic: that is, to reveal the origins of obscure and confused astronomical terminology still in use.[234] This belief in the didactic value of the history of astronomy and natural philosophy more generally continued to manifest itself in institutional investment after the formation of the Royal Society. The Society entered into negotiations with Thomas Hyde, whose edition of Ulugh Beg's star catalogue we have met already, to produce an edition and translation of al-Ṣūfī's *Kitāb Ṣuwar al-kawākib al-thābita* ('Book of Fixed Stars', *c.* 964), negotiations which may have failed only because Hyde asked for the exorbitant sum of £20 or £30.[235] And they almost acquired the manuscript of the *Cronica de Matematici* (*c.* 1596) by the Italian Bernardino Baldi, which was seen as 'a design like Stanley's' and in the ultimately failed acquisition of which Sherburne was again involved: he was also prepared to invest £20 in the venture.[236]

Manuscript evidence allows us to reconstruct how practising natural philosophers actually engaged with historical scholarship. The best individual example is that of Henry Power, whose interest in natural philosophy was developed first through his medical studies in the 1640s and then through participation in the northern natural philosophical circle centred on the Catholic Towneley family based near Burnley. He was elected FRS in 1663, and is best known for his *Experimental philosophy* (1664), a collection of Power's experimental findings over the preceding decade in microscopy, air pressure, and magnetism fused with his own Cartesian and Helmontian views; he was also a keen practising astronomer.[237] A reader of that work would

---

[234] John Greaves, 'Ad lectorem', in *Astronomica*, sigs. [A5][r–v]; the discussion in Ben-Zaken, *Cross-cultural scientific exchanges in the eastern Mediterranean* (2010), 104–38 ('Converting measurements and invoking the "Linguistic Leviathan"') is useful on this; see also Gingerich, *An annotated census of Copernicus' 'De revolutionibus'* (2002), 262.

[235] Toomer, *Eastern wisedome*, 250; *Oldenburg correspondence*, II, 162–3, 177, 179, 180–1, Birch, *History*, I, 419.

[236] Collins to Beale, 20 Aug 1672, in *Correspondence of scientific men*, I, 199–200; Adrien Auzout to Henry Oldenburg, 14/24 Aug 1673, *Oldenburg correspondence*, X, 143–9 (the negotiations also involved Henri Justel (see ibid., 215–17); Sherburne, 'The Original and Progress of Astronomy', in *Sphere*, 70 ('And if the Manuscript now in possession of some of his Family, or a Copy thereof may be obtained; we may have then hopes that er'e long the Work will be communicated to the Curious of this Nation'). The manuscript is now Oklahoma University, MS 631: it was first printed as *Cronica de Matematici, overo Epitome dell'istoria delle vite loro* (Urbino, 1707).

[237] The only attempt at a serious account remains Webster, 'Henry Power's experimental philosophy' (1967), although of some use on Power's earlier medical work is Cole, 'Henry Power on the circulation of blood' (1957), 291–324. For Power's results from his own astronomical observations, see Henry Power to 'Dr Robinson', 30 Apr 1661, BL MS Sloane 1326, fols. 19[r]–20[r]; also fols. 134[v]–140[r] ('Observations made by H.P. 16th No[br] 1664. Of the Comet y[t] appeared in the south hemisphere'); fols. 23[v]–24[v] (correspondence with a glass grinder, 11 and 16 March 1660, re. building a telescope).

surmise that Power had few, if any, humanist interests.[238] But Power's archive (much of which remains preserved in the British Library) reveals a very different picture, not least in a library catalogue that lists almost 600 works and which contains, as well as the expected copies of Descartes and Hobbes, most of the works a diligent humanist interested in the history of philosophy would possess, not least Diogenes Laërtius.[239] It might be tempting to assume that Power's humanist interests were idiosyncratic in the natural philosophical community, a legacy of the early influence on him of Sir Thomas Browne.[240] But while Power certainly believed in the progress of knowledge, this did not stem from a dogmatic stance on ancients versus moderns. Nor did it preclude him from having deep humanist interests, in which he did not simply ape Browne (who had first advised him to take up medicine)[241] but through which he developed an independent fascination with ancient history. He wrote, for example, a lengthy 'Epitome Chronica rerum ab orbe Condito gestarum', which, while it sometimes depended more on semi-populist secondary works like Raleigh's *History of the world*, also drew extensively on the relevant primary sources (especially Josephus and Eusebius) and the more advanced modern discussions, such as the chronological work of Henry Bullinger (*Epitome temporum et rerum ab orbe condito* (1565)) and Scaliger's *Emendatione temporum*.[242] In many ways it is paradigmatic of the manner in which non-specialists practiced ancient history in the mid to late seventeenth century, drawing on a mixture of popular discussions, canonical works of critical humanist historiography, and some of the more widely available primary sources.[243]

It is in this light that we should approach a long letter written by Power to John Milner on New Year's Day 1656, 'on the subject of our last discourse ... the Antiquity of the Arts + Sciences, especially Astronomy'. Milner, then a preacher who had received clandestine episcopal ordination in 1649, was a highly competent Hebraist and chronologer in his own right, and that he took seriously Power's views on the history of ancient astronomy is testimony to the overlap between

---

[238] Henry Power, *Experimental philosophy, in three books containing new experiments microscopical, mercurial, magnetical* (London, 1664).

[239] BL MS Sloane 1346 (Henry Power, 'A Catalogue of all my Bookes Taken this 1st of September 1664 just before my removal to Wakefield'), fols. 1ʳ–16ʳ, at fols. 2ʳ (Hobbes), 3ʳ⁻ᵛ (Descartes), 6ʳ (Diogenes Laërtius).

[240] As is assumed in the best account: Webster, 'Power', 152–3, 155, 164, 166 (although it is also claimed that Power 'differed from Browne most noticeably in his spirited advocation of the "modern" ideology').

[241] Thomas Browne to Henry Power, n.d. [1646], in *Browne works*, IV, 255.

[242] BL MS Sloane 1326, fols. 50ʳ–75ᵛ (Henry Power, 'Epitome Chronica rerum ab orbe Condito gestarum'); for Power's ownership of Scaliger, see BL MS Sloane 1346, fol. 1ʳ.

[243] See e.g. Evelyn's notes for his *History of religion*, as discussed at 1.3 above.

learned–clerical and secular–natural philosophical branches of erudition.[244] In Power's letter we see the appearance of the exact same subjects that would later be treated by Stanley and Sherburne and which had been brought to the fore by Scaliger. Like them, he placed the origin of astronomy in Chaldea, and used the history of language and elaborate connections between pagan and sacred traditions to justify the view.[245] Like them, he examined the chronological problems raised by Callisthenes's and Ptolemy's varying reports on the age of Chaldean astronomical observation.[246] Like them, he could not resist antiquarian digressions, pointing out that while early Greece was indeed more primitive than the eastern nations, Raleigh cannot have been right that the early Greeks did not know of money, because Homer valued Glaucus's golden armour in Egyptian coins.[247] And like them, he took a mildly progressive view of the history of astronomy, admitting that while the Greeks originally had to learn from the Chaldeans, they later 'enlarged' the subject, especially in the period between Hipparchus and Ptolemy.[248] The work is also notable as an early English manifestation of the incorporation into such discussions of evidence from China.[249]

This kind of humanist speculation on the history of astronomy by a practising natural philosopher and astronomer was not just an idiosyncratic manifestation of Browne's influence on Power. Several decades later, the well-known plant anatomist and secretary of the Royal Society, Nehemiah Grew (1641–1712), also jotted down a similarly progressive narrative of the history of astronomy, once again engaging in the same chronological assessment of the antiquity of Chaldean observations and once again offering a narrative of near-eastern origins and Greek development after

[244] For Milner's biography, see Poole, 'Milner, John', *ODNB*. The best example of Milner's early scholarship is his Latin translation of the Targum on Chronicles I and II, at St. John's College, Cambridge, K.17, dated to November 1662 on p. 506 (it is assigned to Milner in Ralph Thoresby, *Vicaria Leodiensis* (London, 1724), 119). His later crowning scholarly achievement was his short *Conjectanea in Isaiam ix, I, II. Item in parallela quaedam veteris ac novi testamenti, in quibus versionis 70. Interpretum ... cum textu Hebraeo conciliationem* (London, 1673).

[245] Henry Power to John Milner, 1 Jan 1656, BL MS Sloane 1326, fols. 2$^r$–3$^r$, 6$^v$–8$^v$.

[246] Ibid., fols. 3$^v$–4$^r$.

[247] Ibid., fol. 5$^r$. The source is *Illiad*, VI.232. The Greek is ambiguous, referring to 'a hundred oxen' (χρύσεα χαλκείων, ἑκατόμβοι' ἐννεαβοίων), but that this referred to coins stamped with an ox is explained in Eustathius, 252.18, and *EM* 320.47 (Power was most likely relying on some more recent discussion). For Raleigh, who adopted a literal translation, see *History of the world*, 435.

[248] BL MS Sloane 1326, fols. 5$^v$–6$^r$.

[249] Ibid., fol. 4$^r$. Power suggested that the great knowledge of the Chinese stemmed from them not having been affected by the confusion of tongues at Babel, pre-empting the conclusions of John Webb, *The antiquity of China, or an historical essay, endeavouring a probability that the language of the empire of China is the primitive language spoken through the whole world before the confusion of Babel* (London, 1678), on which see Ramsey, 'China and the ideal of order in John Webb's *An historical essay*' (2001); Poole, 'Heterodoxy and Sinology' (2012), at 135–41.

Hipparchus[250] (Grew also certainly used Stanley's *History* while composing his own manuscript 'Short account of Thales, Solon, Socrates, and other antient philosophers, and their different systems of philosophy').[251] For all this emphasis on progress, neither Grew nor Power had rejected humanist history. English natural philosophers happily combined their interests with forms of semi-amateur humanist scholarship, especially on the history of the natural philosophy they were practising. Moreover, they did so not out of any quasi-Platonic belief in a *prisca sapientia*, nor out of an obsession with comparing ancients and moderns. Stanley and Sherburne, in other words, knew what they were doing when they wrote complex and critical histories of philosophy and astronomy with one eye on the new philosophers as their potential readers.

## 2.5     Near-eastern philosophy and apologetics

In the same year as Stanley published *Chaldaick philosophy*, there also appeared the first work by a clerical rising star, Edward Stillingfleet's *Origines sacrae* (1662), which according to his early eighteenth-century biographer was the work that 'made him known to the world'.[252] As we saw (1.3), this work, usually understood with reference to philosophical positions or 'latitudinarianism', was in reality the most successful work of historical apologetics published in seventeenth-century England; we shall encounter several of its themes again.[253] It was respected not just for its vigorous defence of religion (natural and revealed) and scripture, but also for its learning, to the extent that perhaps the most prominent European apologetic writer of the late seventeenth century, Pierre-Daniel Huet, was requesting a copy just before publishing his own *Demonstratio Evangelica* (1679).[254] Unfortunately, it is difficult to trace Stillingfleet's development as a scholar: his huge library survives – its *c.* 10,000 tomes formed the basis of Archbishop Marsh's library in Dublin – but there is a lack of marginalia or other signs of use; it is however worth pointing out the speed with which Stillingfleet snapped up Meric Casaubon's library when it became available.[255]

---

[250] BL MS Sloane 1950, fols. 46ᵛ–47ʳ. Grew's history stretched through to the Arabs (he mentioned Albategnius and Alfraganus), Alphonso of Castile, Peuerbach, Regiomontanus, Copernicus, Brahe, and Kepler.

[251] See BL MS Sloane 1950, fols. 13ʳ–34ᵛ. The epigram about Thales at fol. 13ʳ is exactly the translation offered in Stanley, *History*, 14b.

[252] [Timothy Goodwin [?]], 'The life and character of … Edward Stillingfleet', in Edward Stillingfleet, *Works* (6 vols, London, 1709–10), I, 1–53 at 5.

[253] See 3.5, 5.2, 6.5 below. Stausberg, *Faszination*, 641–5 discusses him on Zoroaster.

[254] Huet to Edward Bernard, 4 Jan 1677, Bod. MS Smith 5, fols. 131ʳ–132ʳ, at fol. 131ʳ.

[255] Stillingfleet was already sniffing out Casaubon's library two years before the latter's death: Dr. William's Library, MS 201/38, fol. 2ʳ. [Goodwin], 'Life', 3, notes that after he was appointed Fellow of St. John's College, Cambridge (31 March 1653, straight after obtaining his BA – he had entered the college in 1649), he 'made great use of a good Library belonging to that

The purpose of *Origines* is to defend the veracity of the Bible – the whole first book is devoted to demonstrating the historical reliability of the Old Testament in comparison with pagan sources – and to defend biblical chronology; Stillingfleet had read La Peyrère's *Prae-Adamitae* (1655) and probably also some of the continental attacks on it that had appeared in the preceding seven years.[256] Much of *Origines* is devoted to placing events from sacred and pagan history into the Septuagint chronology, and this inevitably brought Stillingfleet into contact with the history of pagan religion, historiography, and philosophy; the Chaldeans receive a whole chapter. There is the expected denunciation of their claims to the great antiquity of their astronomical observations, which would stretch to before the creation if accepted.[257] This leads to a discussion of their astronomy and astrology itself, which is dismissed as far more primitive than their claims to antiquity would lead one to expect; here Maimonides' Sabians are brought in – identified, citing Scaliger, with the Chaldeans – to explain that near-eastern astrology was only a subset of their idolatrous starworship.[258] Eutychius (via Selden) confirms that Zoroaster founded their theology. Up to here we have something very similar to Stanley, albeit in condensed form. Stillingfleet, however, takes an interesting detour, very briefly describing the *Avesta* itself by drawing on an account found in a work published in 1630 by Henry Lord, a chaplain with the East India Company who arrived in India in 1624 and was told about the *Avesta* and Zoroastrianism more generally by Parsees whom he interviewed.[259] Lord had mentioned the fire-worship of the Parsees: this led Stillingfleet to speculate that they were descended from the idolatrous Sabians.[260]

This was not enough for Stillingfleet's apologetic purposes, for he also offered a directly theological argument: the near-eastern proclivity for astronomy was a sign of God working by second causes, for it was this knowledge that later allowed the three magi (Matt. 2:1–12) to use a star to locate the newborn Christ.[261] As we shall see, he was not the last to use this old argument. Like Stanley, Stillingfleet abused Kircher for credulously believing rabbinic and Arabic sources, but unlike Stanley, Stillingfleet's aim is overtly

---

College', but I have not been able to obtain any specific details of his studies at this point (he proceeded MA in 1656, DD in 1668). His Tripos verses, 1657, were entitled *Homo naturâ est zōon politikon* ([Cambridge], 1657) [ESTC S5595].

[256] For a direct reference to the *Prae-Adamitae*, see Stillingfleet, *Origines sacrae*, 80.

[257] Ibid., 40–1. [258] Ibid., 42–3.

[259] Henry Lord, *A display of two forraigne sects in the East Indies vizt: the sect of the Banians the ancient natives of India and the sect of the Persees the ancient inhabitants of Persia* (London, 1630); see Firby, *European travellers and their perceptions of Zoroastrians* (1988), 98–105.

[260] Stillingfleet, *Origines*, 44–5. Sabianism also allows Stillingfleet to defend the historical rationality behind the Mosaic Law, at 219–20.

[261] Ibid., 47–8.

apologetic: to debunk Kircher's dangerously long ancient chronology.[262] Also unlike Stanley, Stillingfleet made no attempt to deny Zoroaster's dualism, which he thought inspired Manichaeism: it proved that the Judaeo-Christian tradition had a solution to the problem of evil which the pagans did not.[263] This is not a sign of a particular theological position or a systematic attitude to paganism, simply a function of Stillingfleet's specific apologetic aim: to show-case the uniqueness of the true faith. Stillingfleet's image of the philosophy of Zoroaster and the Chaldeans is one of a primitive astronomy stimulated by idolatry and the geographical accident of living in a flat land.[264] It was formulated to suit the needs of apologetics: to downplay the advancement, and thus the antiquity, of pagan civilisation against what he perceived to be the challenge recently posed by deviant chronologies. Yet Stillingfleet's work remains an excellent example of how apologetic works were still taken ser-iously not only as apologetics but also as scholarship. He was well read not only in the primary sources but also in all the relevant secondary discussions – Scaliger, Selden, Vossius, the travel literature – and showcasing that knowledge was a key step on the early part of a clerical career.

Stillingfleet remained silent on the *Chaldean Oracles*, but they were to be redeployed in another apologetic work: Ralph Cudworth's famous *True intel-lectual system of the universe* (1678). Cudworth – Master of Christ's College, Cambridge, from 1654 – appears more often in modern scholarship as a philosopher than as a philologist, but his professional and personal identity was much more closely tied to the latter discipline: he was, after all, Regius Professor of Hebrew.[265] One reason for the confusion is that Cudworth's huge and brilliant text was doing different things at different points: chapters I–III focus on the history of atheistic philosophy, while the huge chapter IV argues

---

[262] Ibid., 51–3. Stillingfleet then develops the clever thesis that the key sources for ancient Egyptian and Chaldean history, Manetho and (the real) Berosus, were written in response to the translation of the Old Testament into Greek. This interpretation posed serious chronological problems, which Stillingfleet solved ingeniously, if unconvincingly, through some variant readings. The *Letter of Aristeas* – the authenticity of which Stillingfleet accepted (48–50), no doubt on the authority of Isaac Vossius – dates the translation of the Septuagint to the reign of Ptolemy II Philadelphus (281–246 BC), whereas Berosus (as Stanley among many others had shown) had flourished at the end of the fourth or the very start of the third century BC. Using variant readings from the Paris edition of Eusebius (1627), Stillingfleet suggested that there was enough overlap between Ptolemy's reign and Berosus to accommodate his thesis.

[263] Stillingfleet, *Origines*, 492–3.

[264] Ibid., 42. This is surely a geographical variation on Herodotus, II.109, and its relative, Aristotle, *Met.*, I, 981$^b$21–5.

[265] For Cudworth as Hebraist, see ch. 3, n. 300 below. One attempt to understand Cudworth's historical–apologetic project is Popkin, 'The crisis of polytheism and the answers of Vossius, Cudworth and Newton' (1990), at 12–20, although it is in some respects unreliable. For the fullest philosophical reading, see Bergemann, *Ralph Cudworth—System aus Transformation* (2012). The fullest biographical treatment remains Passmore, *Cudworth* (1951). See further below.

that various pagan theologies were, for all their polytheistic elements, grounded in monotheism.

It is this chapter that concerns us here, for a significant component of Cudworth's historical case was that Zoroaster and the magi had, like all other theistic pagans, espoused a monotheistic philosophical theology that posited only one eternal and uncreated being, however many subordinate deities it amassed beneath him. For Cudworth, the Persians were of particular importance to this argument, for two reasons. First, they were the most famous of the putative dualists, primarily on the authority of Plutarch, and supposedly the pagan sources of Manichaeism. Second, Cudworth knew that the near-eastern story was now more important than ever, given that the traditional sources for Egyptian and Greek monotheism (as used by Steuco et al.), the *Hermetica* and the *Sibylline Oracles*, were now rejected as Christian forgeries.[266]

Cudworth's strategy was to denigrate the sources that offered a dualist interpretation and to emphasise the value of those that did not. This he did in unprecedented scholarly detail. The key account that required confutation was that of Plutarch. Having acknowledged that the Manicheans and the Marcionites were true dualists, Cudworth proposed that while 'learned men of later times, have for the most part look'd upon *Plutarch* . . . as a bare Relater of the [dualist] Opinion of other Philosophers', he was in fact 'heartily Engaged in this Opinion' – that is to say, that he was an unreliable source.[267] Thus, Cudworth proceeded, Plutarch systematically misrepresented the opinions of his predecessors – Plato, the Stoics, and the Persians – to align them with his own dualism, in turn tied to his eternalism, 'so that *God* was only the *Orderer*, or the *Methodizer* and *Harmonizer*' of pre-existent substance.[268] This was an original and pioneering reading of Plutarch that stimulated much debate throughout Europe for over a century.[269] We can see this from a comparison with the fullest available account up to that point, the 'Vita Plutarchi' by Joannes Rualdus, prefixed to the 1624 Paris edition of Plutarch's works (a text owned by Cudworth).[270] Rualdus acknowledged that Plutarch had

---

[266] Cudworth, *System*, 281: 'the Doctrine of the Greatest *Pagan Polytheists*, as well before Christianity as after it, was always the same, That besides their *Many Gods*, there was *One Supreme, Omnipotent* and *Only Unmade Deity*. And this we shall perform not as some have done, by laying the chief stress upon the *Sibylline Oracles*, and those reputed Writings of *Hermes Trismegist*, the Authority whereof hath been of late so much decried by Learned Men; nor yet upon such Oracles of the Pagan Deities, as may be suspected to have been counterfeited by Christians: but upon such Monuments of Pagan Antiquity, as are altogether unsuspected and indubitate'. For Cudworth's complex approach to the early Christian forgeries, see 3.6, 6.6 below.

[267] Ibid., 214. [268] Ibid., 214–18 (quotation from 215).

[269] See e.g. Johann Christoph Wolff, *Manichaeismus ante Manichaeos, et in Christianismo redivivus* (Hamburg, 1707), 138–9.

[270] *Bibliotheca Cudworthiana sive catalogus variorum librorum plurimus facultatibus* (London, 1692), 15. Rualdus's translation was used for the edition of the *Lives* prepared by a team led by

remained a pagan throughout his life, but also claimed that he had read the New Testament and 'condemned polytheism'.[271] Cudworth's judgement that as a historian of philosophy, Plutarch 'either out of design ... [or] to gain the better countenance and authority to a conceit, which himself was fond of' was an innovative move away from such readings.[272] It led Cudworth to propose – directly contrary to Stillingfleet among many others – that the Manicheans could not have drawn on true Zoroastrian traditions for their dualism. He pointed out that they themselves denied it (hardly surprising!);[273] more importantly, he noted, like Stanley, that Porphyry had attacked the Zoroastrian texts forged by the gnostics, speculating that the forgeries had been composed to misrepresent Zoroaster as a dualist.[274]

Where did that leave the 'real' Zoroaster? Unlike Stanley, Cudworth made no attempt to identify or date him precisely: a good example of the varieties of humanist approaches even within the same broad cultural milieu.[275] There could be no doubt that Zoroaster was an idolater – even his name might mean 'starworshipper', and near-eastern magic, astrology, and theurgy were all based on an idolatrous vision of a deified world.[276] There is no mention of the Sabians at this point, which is surprising because Cudworth, a leading Hebraist, had been a pioneer in promoting Sabian-centred contextualisation of the Mosaic Law in England.[277] Nonetheless, Cudworth proceeded to develop at great length a monotheistic reading of Zoroastrian theology and philosophy, and of near-eastern theological culture more generally. Some of Cudworth's arguments were very underdeveloped, such as his brief case that Persian dualism was invented by a monotheistic culture as an answer to the problem of evil.[278] Others, though, he developed in much greater detail. He noted a source missed by Stanley, Eubolus as quoted by Porphyry, which suggested that

---

Dryden: Plutarch, *Lives* (5 vols, London, 1684); see Levine, *Between the ancients and the moderns* (1999), 74–5.

[271] Joannes Rualdus, 'Vita Plutarchi Chaeronensis', in *Plutarchi Chaeronensis omnium quae extant operum* (2 vols, Paris, 1624), I, 15b–16a ('Addo ego, πολυθεϊσμό (quod certè maximum & primum nostrae religionis caput & fundamentum est) videri Plutarchum damnavisse, ac unum anovisse Deum mente ac ratione praeditum ... '). For Plutarch's reading of scripture, Rualdus draws on the standard patristic source, Theodoret of Cyr's *Peri Archēs*.

[272] Cudworth, *System*, 223.   [273] Ibid., 223, drawing on Augustine, *Cont. Faust.*, xx.3

[274] Cudworth, *System*, 291. Contrast with Stillingfleet, *Origines*, 492–3.

[275] Cudworth, *System*, 285: '[he] was of so great Antiquity, that Writers cannot well agree about his Age'.

[276] Ibid., 286.

[277] R[alph] C[udworth], *A discourse concerning the true notion of the Lords Supper* (London, 1641), 71. Indeed, he would later be attacked for such Maimonidean readings: John Turner, *Boaz and Ruth ... with a discovery of several things, as well in the Eastern, as the Roman antiquities, never yet explained or understood by any* (London, 1685), 240–1; see further Levitin, 'Spencer', 89–90.

[278] Cudworth, *System*, 213.

Zoroaster consecrated worship to Mithra as the creator of the world; extrapolating, Cudworth conjectured that the Persians' sun worship was thus only a manifestation of their reverence for God's creation. Eubolus seemed a good source because elsewhere Porphyry claimed that he had written a history of the Mithraic mysteries (it was much later that scholars realised that this was the Roman mystery religion that flourished from the first to the fourth centuries AD).[279] Even if the Persians *had* worshipped fire as a corporeal object, it was because they were animists like the Stoics, and thus worshipped one God anyway – this fitted Cudworth's elucidation of a widespread animism among the pagans (see 5.4.3 below). The last interpretation was developed on the basis of a Latin altar inscription (also from the Roman Mithra cult).[280]

But for all these interesting sources – Cudworth also drew on the Arabic testimonies that had been collected by Pococke, and on the obscure neoplatonist Damascius (*c.* 458–538), whom he consulted in manuscript[281] – his key testimony was that of the *Chaldean Oracles*, which give a 'clear acknowledgement of a *Divine Monarchy,* or *One Supreme Deity*'.[282] Like Stanley, Cudworth believed that their being cited so much by pagans proved them not to have been written by Christians, and agreed that their late translation (by Julian) also led to this conclusion. But he also developed a powerful new argument: there was enough paganism in the *Oracles* to render it highly unlikely that they were Christian forgeries.[283] The example he gave was their references to the goddess Hecate, who in several fragments of the *Oracles* is referred to as a female principle responsible for material creation.[284] Here, then, was a perfect example of a Persian source which, while undoubtedly pagan, 'nevertheless ... carr[ied] along with [it] ... a clear acknowledgment of a *divine Monarchy,* or *One Supreme Deity*'.[285]

---

[279] Ibid., 286, drawing on Porphyry, *De antr. nymph.*, II, and *De abst.*, II.56 respectively.

[280] Cudworth, *System*, 286–7. The inscription ('Deo Soli Invicto Mithrae'), for which Cudworth does not give a source, was available to him in Jan Gruter's *Inscriptionum Romanarum corpus absolutissimum* (Paris, 1616), xxxv, the 'seventeenth century's standard epigraphic corpus' (Grafton, *The footnote* (1997), 180).

[281] Cudworth, *System*, 291–2. Damascius's *De principiis* was well known in various manuscripts in the seventeenth century, all copied from a manuscript in the possession of Cardinal Bessarion. Cudworth very likely used the copy made by Thomas Gale: Trinity College, Cambridge, MS O.4.23, which is copied from Corpus Christi College, Oxford, MS 158. The Oxford manuscript was also used by Thomas Hyde (see below), *Historia religionis veterum Persarum, eorumque Magorum* (Oxford, 1700), 291. For a full account of all the manuscripts, see Ruelle, 'Praefatio' (1889), at iii–xvii.

[282] Cudworth, *System*, 293.  [283] Ibid.

[284] Ibid. Hecate is associated with 'nature' in fr. 54. Fr. 206 refers to the 'magic wheel of Hecate', and Cudworth's reference to the 'Hecatine circle' is surely to this fragment, allowing him to state that it is 'manifest' that 'there is something of the Theurgical Magick mixed together with Mystical Theology in these Oracles'. Those who wish to familiarise themselves with all the relevant fragments may consult Johnston, *Hekate soteira* (1990).

[285] Cudworth, *System*, 293.

Cudworth, writing in apologetic mode, makes explicit some of the presup-positions we had to dig deep to find in Stanley. It is again worth emphasising that there is nothing 'Platonic' about this: both Cudworth and Stanley accepted the *Oracles* not because the text was a neoplatonic forgery, but *despite* their knowledge that this might have been the case and that the Greek certainly represented a later philosophical language. Nor were they attempting to develop a Ficino or even Patrizi-esque philosophical system on the basis of such sources: they recognised them as the products of a long-gone idolatrous pagan culture, but sought nonetheless to extract a limited apologetic message from them considered as historical artifacts (Cudworth much more explicitly than Stanley). In short, they were both operating within the Casaubonian paradigm.

## 2.6    Jean Le Clerc, after Stanley

The second edition of Stanley's *History* was published by Thomas Bassett, future publisher of Locke's *Essay*, in 1687. As befitting a major scholarly work by that period – albeit not always one written in English – it was immediately greeted with reviews in the learned journals, all of them positive.[286] Of these, by far the longest was that by Jean Le Clerc in his *Bibliothèque universelle et historique* (1687). Within three years, Le Clerc had fulfilled his own wish, expressed in the review, that 'someone translate this work in Latin, and cite all the sources in the original languages',[287] publishing in Amsterdam a Latin translation of the section on Chaldean philosophy only, with notes and a philological index.[288]

Le Clerc was born and educated in the learning necessary for a clerical career in Geneva, but his theological idiosyncrasies led him to early 1680s sojourns to Saumur and London before Philipp van Limborch helped him obtain a post at the Remonstrant seminary in Amsterdam as professor in the arts.[289] We know

---

[286] [Jean Le Clerc], *Bibliothèque universelle et historique* [=BUH], 7 (1687), 1–48; [Henri Basnage de Beauval], *Histoire des ouvrages des sçavans*, 1 (December 1687), 423–39; *Acta eruditorum quae Lipsiae publicantur supplementa*, 2 (1696), 356–61. It was Basnage's review which formed the majority of the 'Life of Thomas Stanley esq.' that was appended to the 1701 English edition (Malusa, 'First general histories', 179 is thus correct to point out that it was this 'Life', and not a new biography, which was included in the Latin edition published in Leipzig in 1711, but fails to identify the original source).

[287] *BUH*, 7, 4, 'Il seroit à souhaiter que quelcun traduisit cet Ouvrage en Latin, & citât tous ces endroits dans les Langues originales'.

[288] Thomas Stanley, *Historia philosophiae orientalis. Recensuit, ex Anglica lingua in Latinam transtulit, notis in oracula Chaldaica & indice philologico auxit Joannes Clericus* (Amsterdam, 1690). The work was then incorporated into Le Clerc's *Opera philosophica* (Amsterdam, 1698) (further edns, 1704, 1710, 1722).

[289] The best biographical treatment remains Barnes, *Jean Le Clerc* (1938). Cf. Golden, *Jean Le Clerc* (1972).

less about Le Clerc's practices and conclusions as a scholar than we do about his role as a journalist and editor in the republic of letters,[290] and his methodological claims.[291] His engagement with English scholarship (see also 6.8 below) allows us to form a new, fuller picture of this important figure.

Le Clerc's ability to read English made him a particularly important conduit for the dissemination of English works,[292] and his correspondence reveals a continuing fascination with and respect for English intellectual culture. This is the case not just with Locke, whose friendship with him is well known, but perhaps more importantly with a group of English scholars and clergymen connected less by any politico-ecclesiastical stance than by reverence for the scholarly achievements of the preceding century, particularly in the fields of biblical criticism and ecclesiastical history, and from whom Le Clerc never quite stopped hoping for preferment for a clerical position.[293] It is clear that *Chaldaick philosophy* was the part of Stanley's *History* that Le Clerc was most interested in, for forty-three of the forty-seven pages of his review concern it directly.[294] As was usual for Le Clerc, the review is mostly descriptive and infrequently interspersed with his own comments. Stanley is much praised: he is compared with his uncle, 'the famous *Marsham*', and with John Spencer.[295] Attention is drawn to Stanley's attack on the 'ridiculous fables' of Annius's pseudo-Berosus: it is remarkable that this was still being celebrated in the late 1680s.[296] Yet what is most curious about Le Clerc's review is a digression in which he comments that the Chaldeans' theology, and their thoughts about good and evil angels, 'are not so far removed from that of the Hebrews', instancing the discussion of 'diverse orders' of angels in the New Testament and the government of parts of the earth by angels in the book of Daniel.[297] This similarity, Le Clerc suggested, might be attributed to the 'Jews

---

[290] Bots et al., eds., *De 'Bibliothèque Universelle et Historique'* (1981); Wijngaards, *De 'Bibliothèque Choisie' van Jean Le Clerc* (1986). Pocock, *Barbarism*, v, esp. 89–114 and Marshall, *Early enlightenment*, 504–5, *passim*, tie some of his activities and ideas into a narrative of early enlightenment; this view is not adopted here.

[291] Pitassi, *Entre croire et savoir* (1987); Asso, 'Alcune osservazioni sulla filologia Neotestamentaria de Jean Le Clerc' (2004).

[292] Preliminary investigation is begun in Bots, 'Jean Leclerc as journalist of the Bibliothèques: his contribution to the spread of English learning on the European continent' (1984).

[293] The story of his tragic attempts is well told in Brogi, 'Jean Le Clerc et l'église anglicane' (2007), so I do not repeat the details here. See further 6.8 below.

[294] Malusa, 'First general histories', 199 and Stausberg, *Faszination*, I, 388–9 offer only cursory summaries that do not capture the complexity of Le Clerc's argument.

[295] *BUH*, 7, 2, 42. For Marsham and Spencer, see 3.6; for Le Clerc's deep admiration for both, see 3.7, 6.8.

[296] Ibid., 4.

[297] Ibid., 22: 'On peut voir par ce detail de la Theologie Caldéenne, que leurs pensées touchant les bons & les mauvais Anges, n'étoient pas fort éloignées de celles des Hebreux'. For Daniel, see Dan. 10:12–21. The extraction from the Bible of an angelic hierarchy derives from ps.–Dionysius, *De Coelesti Hierarchia*, but became very prominent in scholastic theology; see e.g. Aquinas, *Summa theologica*, I.108.

having borrowed this knowledge, and other things, during the Babylonian captivity'.[298] This focus on specific intercultural borrowing transcended Stanley's more vague Maimonidean narrative, and requires explanation.

From the 1680s, Le Clerc was engaged in a concerted historical project: to identify historically the mental and cultural world of the early Christian writers, specifically as they had or had not sought to express the Christian message in terms of pagan – especially Platonic – philosophy. This brought him into contact with a wealth of other English scholarship that we shall chart in detail in Chapter 6. Yet in all these discussions, spread between book reviews in French and larger Latin works, but uniformly controversial, Le Clerc was always reticent to posit a pre-history for the specific beliefs about the nature of the divinity which he found the church fathers adopting from the Platonists. 'We shall not dwell', he at one point wrote, 'on seeking from where *Plato* might have learned this Doctrine [the subordination to God of a series of spiritual creatures], whether from the *Chaldeans*, whose Theology can be seen in the seventh volume of this journal [i.e. the review of Stanley], or from the Old Testament, as some of the church fathers believed'.[299] This casually phrased set of options was far from neutral. The second – that any congruence between Platonism and Christianity was explicable by Plato having borrowed those truths from the Jews, to whom they had originally been revealed – was indeed a standard patristic position. The first, however, was highly provocative: it implied that those Christian doctrines that bore similarity to paganism had pagan origins. In another review, Le Clerc made it clear which opinion he favoured: after again noting that the church fathers opted for Judaic primacy, he commented that he could support the opposite view with evidence 'at least as strong as that which the fathers bring to prove the contrary ... perhaps, another day, I shall publish a dissertation about it, in one of the volumes of this *Bibliothèque*'.[300]

Yet it appears that Le Clerc chose a different format to defend this position,[301] for there are clear signs that this is precisely what he was doing in his

---

[298] *BUH*, 7, 23, 'Aussi quelques Savans ont conjecturé que les Juifs avoient emprunté d'eux ces connoissances & quelques autres semblables, dans la Captivité de Babylone'.

[299] *BUH*, 10 (1688), 389: 'On ne s'arrêtera pas à rechercher de qui Platon pouvoit avoir pris cette doctrine, si c'est des Caldéens, dont on a pu voir la Théologie, au commencement du VII. Volume de cette Bibliotheque, ou du Vieux Testament comme quelques-uns des Peres l'ont cru'. These words come in a review of an edition of Eusebius published in Cologne in 1688: for the full context, see 6.7 below.

[300] *BUH*, 10 (1688), 201: 'On pourroit apporter des preuves de cette conjecture, pour le moins aussi fortes que toutes celles que les Peres ont apportées, pour prouver le contraire, mais comme ce seroit trop s'écarter de principal sujet, dont il s'agit ici, on n'entreprendra point d'entrer en cettre matiére. Peutêtre qu'on en pourra donner quelque jour une Dissertation, dans l'un des volumes suivans de cette *Bibliothèque*'. The review is of an edition of Clement of Alexandria published in Cologne in 1688.

[301] Le Clerc's disdain for claims about Jewish intellectual primacy are evident throughout his writings: for another interesting example in connection with English scholarship, see his review of James Windet's *De vita functorum statu, ex Hebraeorum atque Graecorum*

1690 Latin edition of Stanley. With Le Clerc's usual predilection for striking methodological statements, the short preface to that edition explains that a contextual approach is required to understand early Christian controversies:

We were not the first mortals to be born, and we did not come up with the opinions that we hold; rather, we received from others the opinions that they had been taught by people of an earlier period. Therefore, in order for us to know whence various dogmas that are now accepted by some Christians draw their origins, we need to follow the traces of them, so to speak, from our age to the immediately preceding age, and then again into the remoter past, until we arrive at the source. Those who rescue the opinions of the ancient peoples of the east from the mustiness of antiquity, and place them in a clear light, either point to the source, or point to streams that are extremely near to the source.[302]

But in reality, the story was even more complex, for there was a double infiltration of Chaldean ideas. First, they had appeared in Second Temple Judaism:

If someone, for example, is ignorant of what kind of philosophy flourished above all among the Hebrews after the release from the Babylonian Captivity, and among the early Christians, then however much he holds in his memory all the more famous events of their history, he will nevertheless not see how it happened that previously unknown or very obscurely known dogmas became popular and exercised the minds of the wise so much. Being ignorant of this, it is unavoidable that one is ignorant of the origin and kindling of the most serious controversies, which gave birth to the greatest disturbances . . . The Jews seem to have taken the doctrine of Demons and of 'the possessed' (ἐνεργούμενοι) from the Chaldeans, which is why they mentioned them so often after their return from the Captivity, something that happened hardly, or not at all, before.[303]

---

*comparatis sententiis concinnatus* (London, 1663) in *Bibliothèque choisie*, 1 (1703), 354–79, with many sarcastic comments about Windet's argument (that Greek opinions about the post-mortem state of the soul were taken from the Jews). Windet is a fascinating figure about whom it would be good to know more: he graduated MD in Leiden in 1655 and proceeded to practise medicine as a member of the College of Physicians in London, but his passion appears to have been oriental languages and Greek (*Fast. Ox.*, cols. 193–4), particularly as they related to the history of ideas, for he also translated, and provided a commentary on, Olympiodorus's *Vita Platonis*, which appeared in the 1692 edition of Ménage's DL (582–8), from a manuscript taken from Isaac Casaubon's papers.

[302] Le Clerc, 'Praefatio', in *Philosophia orientalis*, sigs. *5ᵛ–[*6]ʳ. 'Quoniam autem primi mortalium non sumus nati, neque opiniones, quas tuemur, invenimus, sed ab aliis accepimus quas ab antiquioribus ipsi edocti fuerant; ut sciamus unde originem ducant varia quae nunc recepta sunt, apud nonnullos ex Christianis, dogmata, nos oportet vestigia eorum, ut ita dicam, à saeculo nostro in proximè praeteritum, & rursus in remotius sequi, donec ad fontem pervenerimus. Fontem porrò aut indicant, aut rivos fonti admodum vicinos, qui Veterum Orientis Gentium opiniones è Vetustatis situ eruunt, atque in clara luce collocant'.

[303] Le Clerc, 'Praefatio', sig. *5ᵛ: 'Si quis, exempli causa, ignoret quae potissimùm inter Hebraeos à Captivitatis Babylonicae solutione, & Christianos primaevos, floruerit Philosophia; is, quamvis eventus omnes eorum Historiae celebriores memoriâ teneat, attamen qui factum ut dogmata antea ignorata, aut obscurissimè nota communia postmodum evaserint, & doctorum ingenia tantopere exercuerint, non videbit. Hoc ignorato, gravissimarum originem & fomites controversiarum, quae maximas turbas pepererunt, ignoret necesse est. Atque hujus rei exempla suppeditabit is, quem Latinè edimus, *Thomae Stanleii* viri eruditissimi libellus. Doctrinam

Yet there was also a second infiltration, from the neoplatonists of the first four centuries AD, for whom the *Chaldean Oracles* were so important:

Likewise, the ancients, when occupied with other points, always refer to certain opinions in their histories and in other writings. Unless these opinions are already known from another source, it will remain hidden to us what those writers that we read wanted to say in their own texts. It is known that most of the early fathers, especially the Greeks, were addicted to Platonic philosophy, and everywhere looked back to it and then borrowed its expressions. And so those who want to understand them, must first read Plato and the Platonic writers. Certainly, no one would otherwise understand what the essential point at issue was in the disagreement between the Orthodox and the Arians, unless he knew what they [sc. Plato and the Platonists] thought about 'the three primal hypostases' [περὶ τῶν τριῶν ἀρχικῶν ὑποστάσεων[304]] ... The *Chaldean Oracles* can give us considerable help in understanding certain terms, as will be clear enough from the remarks which I have made about those matters.[305]

Stanley had noted that the Chaldeans' emanationist theology, with its steps of degradation to lesser degrees of reality, resembled 'a triple triad'.[306] No doubt impressed by Stanley's refusal to connect this to Christian trinitarianism, Le Clerc insinuated that it was this idolatrous emanationism that lay at the root both of the demonology of the later books of the Old Testament and the speculations on the nature of the Godhead found in the neoplatonists and the Greek fathers. This fit with his broader views on the origins of idolatry, expressed elsewhere, which he attributed to the reification of God's messengers (angels, etc.) into full divinities.[307] It also involved him in a complicated attitude to the *Chaldean Oracles*. On the one hand, they were clearly semi-corrupt, representing the Platonism of the sources from which they were taken: Patrizi was chastised for failing to recognise this.[308] Many of Le Clerc's notes point to similarities between the theology of the *Oracles* and that of the late

---

de Daemonibus & ἐνεργουμένοις inter alia à Chaldaeis videntur accepisse Judaei; unde post reditum è Captivitate tam frequens eorum mentio, quae antea aut tenuis, aut nulla prorsus occurrit'.

[304] A reference to the terminology introduced into Plotinus by Porphyry (*Enn.*, v.1; *Plot.*, 25).

[305] Le Clerc, 'Praefatio', sig. *5ᵛ: 'Veteres quoque aliud agentes, in Historiis & quibusvis aliis Scriptis, passim ad opiniones quasdam respiciunt; quae nisi aliunde notae sint, quid sibi velint, iis in locis, quos legimus Scriptores nos prorsus latet. Notum est plerosque primorum saeculorum Patres, praesertim Graecos, Platonicae Philosophiae addictos fuisse, & passim eò respicere atque inde voces mutuari; quo fit ut iis, qui eos intelligere cupiunt, prius Plato & Platonici Scriptores sint evolvendi. Nemo sane, quanam in re situs esset controversiae inter Orthodoxox & Arianos nodus intelligat, nisi quid περὶ τῶν τριῶν ἀρχικῶν ὑποστάσεων senserint ... Atque ex Oraculis Chaldaïcis non levia, ad quasdam voces intelligendas subsidia, duci posse ex iis quae ad ea notavimus satis apparebit'.

[306] Stanley, *Chaldaick philosophy*, 9a–b (mispaginated 17); *BUH*, 7, 13–14.

[307] Jean Le Clerc, *Compendium historiae universalis* (Amsterdam, 1698), 9. As with so many of Le Clerc's works, this one was very quickly translated into English: *A compendium of universal history* (London, 1699), 8–9.

[308] Jean Le Clerc, 'Notae interpretis in Oracula Chaldaica', *Philosophia orientalis*, 157.

antique Platonists (and early Christians).[309] On the other, they had to be at least semi-representative of the lost Chaldean originals, so as to explain the presence of their theology in Second Temple Judaism. Both in his edition, and in a later letter to Locke, Le Clerc thus identified some of the *Oracles* as truly Chaldean and entirely free from Platonic corruption (Locke, in turn, took great interest in the matter).[310]

This message is not explicit in the *Philosophia orientalis* itself, and it is only by gathering statements Le Clerc scattered elsewhere that we have been able to recover it. One reader, however, seems to have grasped the point. Gilbert Burnet, who was by then bishop of Salisbury and to whom the work was dedicated (Le Clerc had met him during Burnet's exile in Holland, 1685–88), acknowledging Le Clerc's exuberant dedication, wrote: 'Your Notes and Index are worthy of you and that is all I can say: the designe in them is so deep that perhaps every one will not reach it'.[311] This was true, but as we shall see (6.7–8), both Le Clerc and Burnet would later offer far less ambiguous statements about the place of pagan philosophy in early Christianity that would land them in hot water, despite their own belief that they were beating antitrinitarians at their own game. The key point at this stage is that Le Clerc was not simply 'using' Stanley's forty-year-old *History*: he valued it and thought that he was continuing the Englishman's work. There is no sign that he saw what he was doing as a radical 'enlightened' break.[312]

## 2.7    Thomas Hyde[313]

When Pierre Bayle added an entry on Zoroaster to the second edition of his *Dictionnaire*, he mentioned all the well-known ancient sources and most of the key seventeenth-century scholars and travellers we have encountered: Stanley (in Le Clerc's edition), Huet, Lord. But his fullest comments were reserved for 'un des plus beaux ouvrages qui se pût faire sur un tel sujet', the *Historia*

---

[309] See Le Clerc, 'Notae interpretis', *passim*, and 160 (comparison with the Arians), 164 (with the Valentinians [one of the early gnostic movements]).

[310] Le Clerc, 'Notae interpretis', 179; Le Clerc to Locke, 16/26 Aug 1692, *Locke correspondence*, IV, 502–3; see also *BUH*, 7, 23–4, 41. Locke copied Le Clerc's judgement into a commonplace book, under the title 'Chaldaica philosophia' (Bod. MS Locke. c. 42B, 218). For other notes from the *Chaldaick philosophy* (Locke used the 1687 English and 1690 Latin edns [LL 2755, 758, pp. 238, 111]), see Bod. MS Locke, f. 32 (Book of notes on the Old Testament), fol. 141ʳ (notes on Dan. 2.2, under the specific heading 'soothsayers'); Bod. MS c. 42B, p. 210 (against Annius' ps.-Berosus). See also Bod. MS Locke, f. 33 for an independent note on the Magi, drawing on a reading of Josephus, *Ant. Jud.*, x.11.

[311] Burnet to Le Clerc, 18 July 1690, in Jean Le Clerc, *Epistolario*, eds., M. Grazia and M. Sina (4 vols, Florence, 1987–97), II, 21.

[312] For the same conclusions regarding his use of the works of Henry Hammond, see 6.8.

[313] As I was conducting research on Hyde, William Poole, of New College, Oxford, supplied me with his notes on Hyde's manuscripts and bibliography. If there is anything of value in what follows, it is due almost entirely to his remarkable generosity.

*religionis veterum Persarum* published in Oxford in 1700 by Thomas Hyde (1626–1703).[314] Hyde was one of the foremost orientalists of the seventeenth century, with a huge range of interests to which the historiography has barely begun to do justice – what follows is only a preliminary attempt to scratch the surface of the remarkable work that is the *Historia*.[315]

After a brief dalliance with medicine,[316] Hyde was convinced by his father to proceed with oriental studies – of all seventeenth-century orientalists, he is unique in obtaining such a huge array of languages without spending time in the Levant (in a letter written late in life, Hyde, expressing the typical innocent surprise of a prodigy, complained that so few were now learning eastern languages when he himself had happily devoured them in his youth).[317] Originally studying at Cambridge (with Abraham Wheelock, himself a noted orientalist), he quickly moved to Oxford, working (at age twenty) on Walton's polyglot, being appointed Hebrew Reader at Queen's College, and becoming Librarian of the Bodleian in 1665, a post he would hold until 1701. In 1691 he succeeded the great Pococke as Laudian Professor of Arabic, obtaining the Hebrew chair as well in 1697. His achievements and abilities in those languages were nowhere near those of his predecessor – a fact commented on by some Oxford contemporaries[318] – but he had secured himself some degree of wider renown with his edition of Ulugh Beg (2.4 above). It was his knowledge of other eastern tongues, including Turkish, Malay, Armenian, and especially Persian, that stimulated much contemporary interest and correspondence, not least with Robert Boyle.[319] Most remarkably, he even acquired some competence in Chinese, in summer 1687 entertaining, in Oxford, Shen Fuzong (1658–91), a converted Chinese brought to Europe by the Jesuits,

---

[314] Pierre Bayle, *Dictionaire historique et critique* (2nd edn, 3 vols, Amsterdam, 1702), III, 3077–83, at 3081, n. F.

[315] For Hyde's biography, see George Sharp, 'Προλεγομενα de vita et scriptis doctissimi viri Thomae Hyde, S.T.P', in Thomas Hyde, *Syntagma dissertationum*, ed. George Sharp (Oxford, 1767), i–xxiv, supplemented by Marshall, 'Thomas Hyde: stupor mundi' (1982). For an overview of his work as an orientalist, see Toomer, *Eastern wisedome*, 248–50, 295–8; Feingold, 'Oriental studies' (1997), at 495–7. By far the fullest account of the *Historia* is Stausberg, *Faszination*, II, 680–717, although it considers none of the extensive manuscript material and is not particularly sensitive to contextual issues; see also Stroumsa, 'Hyde'.

[316] See Hyde's own autobiographical testimony inserted into the copy of Anthony Wood, *Athenae Oxoniensis. An exact history of all the writers and bishops who have had their education in the ... University of Oxford ... The second edition*, ed. T. Tanner (London, 1721), Bod. MSS Top. Oxon.b.8–9, between cols. 972–3 and 974–5. The discovery of this testimony is entirely that of William Poole.

[317] Hyde to John Ellis, 1698, BL MS Add. 28927, fols. 94$^{r-v}$.

[318] Some examples are gathered in Toomer, *Eastern wisedome*, 296, 298.

[319] Boyle seems to have been first notified about Hyde by John Wallis: Wallis to Boyle, 27 March 1663, *Boyle correspondence*, II, 72. The first letter in their extensive correspondence is Hyde to Boyle, 14 Feb 1667, ibid., III, 298–9, which in passing already shows Hyde's interest in Zoroaster. Boyle sponsored Hyde in producing a translation of the Gospels in Malay (1677): see Hunter, *Boyle*, 195–6.

with whom Hyde discoursed in Latin and who provided Hyde with descriptions of the Bodleian's Chinese books.[320] All this learning was paraded in Hyde's publications on Chinese weights and measures, oriental games, and Hebrew cosmography.[321]

Hyde repeatedly told Boyle and others that his oriental learning was ultimately intended to serve biblical exegesis;[322] this is precisely what one would expect from a seventeenth-century orientalist in the Laudian tradition, but it nonetheless poses questions about the genre of the *Historia*. Although it contained an apologetic dimension (as we shall see), it was certainly not a work in the same genre as, say, Cudworth's *System*. Its first purpose was purely scholarly – a contribution, based on a mass of previously unavailable evidence brought from the near east[323] – to a topic which by then had stimulated much interest in the European republic of letters. However, there is also strong evidence that Hyde believed the work to be of interest to a wider readership: not only the ultimately disastrous publication by subscription,[324] but also his subsequent claim that an English translation would appeal to 'our English Gentry'.[325] This was undoubtedly a major reason for the inclusion of so many elaborate plates depicting various religious practices of the ancient Persians, their clerical garb and inscriptions, as well as Persian plants and the scripts of many other unconnected nations.[326]

It is difficult to trace precisely when Hyde conceived of, and began working on, the *Historia*. When the Oxford antiquary Thomas Smith went to

[320] See the brief discussion in Toomer, *Eastern wisedome*, 249.

[321] Thomas Hyde, 'De mensuris & ponderibus Sinensium epistola', in Edward Bernard, *De mensuris et ponderibus antiquis libri tres* (Oxford, 1688); Abraham ben Mordechai Farissol, *Igeret orḥot shalem, id est, Itinera mundi, sic dicta nempe cosmographia*, ed. and trans. Thomas Hyde (Oxford, 1691), Thomas Hyde, *De ludis orientalibus* (Oxford, 1694).

[322] Hyde to Boyle, 23 Oct 1671, *Boyle correspondence*, IV, 220–1; Hyde to Boyle, 24 Feb 1684, ibid., VI, 7; Hyde to Tenison, 9 March 1701, LPL MS 953, no. 67; Hyde to Sloane, 24 Jan 1702, BL MS Sloane 4038, fol. 292ʳ.

[323] Hyde sold many manuscripts to the Bodleian in 1692: these are listed in [Edward Bernard], ed., *Catalogi librorum manuscriptorum Angliae et Hiberniae* (Oxford, 1697), 286–7, sometimes with Hyde's own short descriptions. For a catalogue of Hyde's most important oriental books and papers *c.* 1703, see BL MS Sloane 3323, fols. 270ʳ–272ᵛ. The best evidence for Hyde's ceaseless quest after eastern manuscripts are the letters to Captain Thomas Bowrey, free merchant in India 1669–88, in BL MSS APAC Eur. E.192a J.763 (letters from 1700–2).

[324] See Thomas Hyde, *Historia religionis veterum Persarum, eorumque magorum prospectus* ([Oxford], 1699) [Wing H3872A]. Hyde's desperate attempt to shift books can be followed through letters between him and Thomas Smith (Bod. MS Smith 50, fols. 227–32, MS Smith 63, 121–7) and then several letters to Sloane between 5 August 1700 and the despairing letter of 24 January 1702 (BL Sloane MS 4038, fols. 89ʳ–90ʳ, 148ʳ, 199ʳ, 292ʳ ('I am heartily sorry and ashamed to have given you so much trouble about my Books … ').

[325] Hyde to Humfrey Wanley, Easter Monday [1702?], BL MS Sloane 4066, fol. 386ʳ. Hyde wanted Wanley, his former assistant at the Bodleian, to write the translation, which would contain further additions.

[326] On these plates, see also the letters to Smith in Bod. MS Smith 50, fols. 229–31 (also available in *Syntagma dissertationum*, II, 491–4).

Constantinople in 1668, Hyde, as well as warning him to 'be very careful of what you eat or drink when you are abroad, both for the quantity and the quality', asked him to 'enquire into the Religions of any ... sorts of strange people, as you have occasion, and especially if you can get the authentic books of their Religions written in their own language'.[327] Yet in a 1675 letter outlining his publication plans to Sir Joseph Williamson, Hyde made no mention of a work like the *Historia*, instead proposing an edition of Sharaf ad-Dīn's Persian biography of Tamerlane, a history of the Persian monarchy reconciled with the Greek chronology, a translation of Abū 'l-Fidā's *History*, and a biblical commentary, adding that 'the end of all our studies ought to tend to the glory of God'.[328] By 1684, however, he was telling Boyle of plans to write books on both the 'History of the Kings of Persia' and 'the Religion of the old Persians'.[329] On the other hand, as late as May 1692 John Woodward had heard rumours that Hyde was writing only 'a treatise de Lingua et Literis Persarum'.[330] But his information was probably out of date, for by February 1693 Hyde was telling Edmond Halley that he was 'writing a Book about the Religion of the Old Persians'[331] and by 1694 he had informed Anthony Wood that the work was finished.[332]

As befitting a work long in gestation and founded primarily on a desire to communicate new source information, it is somewhat miscellaneous in character, including chapters on the names and epithets of the ancient Persian angels, on their calendar, and a digressive chapter on the Vesta cult among the Greeks and Romans.[333] Most generally, it can be described (anachronistically) as a cultural history of Persian religion, its chapters dealing not only with theology and belief (Mithra, the names and attributes of God, sects and heresies, etc.), but also with religious biography (Abraham, Darius Hystaspes, Zoroaster) and ritual practice (fire worship, the priesthood of the magi, marriage, baptism, and funeral rites).

[327] Hyde to Smith, 8 June 1668 (diet); Hyde to Smith, 18 July 1668 (religious books), in *Syntagma dissertationum*, II, 483–4. On Smith, see 3.8 below.

[328] Philip, 'Letter from Thomas Hyde' (1950–51). The Tamerlane would have been based on Hyde's own MS, now Bod. MS Hyde 36. Hyde printed two pages as a specimen: *Historia Timûri Arabicè ac Latiné* (Oxford, 1675) [Wing H3879A].

[329] Hyde to Boyle, 24 Feb 1684, *Boyle correspondence*, VI, 7.

[330] Woodward to Edward Lhuyd, 7 May 1692, Bod. MS Ashmole 1817B, fol. 350ᵛ.

[331] Hyde to Edmond Halley, 9 Feb 1693, RS MS EL/H3/79.

[332] *Ath. Ox.*, IV, col. 526, 'Books of Dr. Hyde now in 1694 ready for the press ... '. This information must have come from a list sent by Hyde, now lost, slightly different to a later list in Hyde's hand inserted into Thomas Tanner's edition of the 1721 edition of the *Athenae* (Bod. MSS Top. Oxon. b. 8–9, insert between II, cols 972–3 and 974–5). The discovery of Hyde's manuscript list, and its collation and dating against the published list, is entirely the work of William Poole.

[333] Hyde, *Historia*, chs. xii (names of the angels) xiv–xx (the calendar and its connection to religion), vii (Greek and Roman Vesta cult).

Yet it also put forward a concerted thesis. According to Hyde, the history of Persian religion underwent a tripartite evolution. At first, the Persians followed Shem and Elam in worshipping only the one true eternal God. This original religion was quickly corrupted by 'Sabianism', instituting the second stage. Sabianism, however, was not the true idolatry that the later Arabs (i.e. as cited by Maimonides)[334] thought it was – although it reverenced the celestial bodies, it did not worship them as divine. Abraham, called directly by God, reformed this religion back to its primitive state, but there was soon an 'interpolatio Sabaitica secunda'. Nonetheless, even this Sabianism involved worship of the true God. Third, the religion was again reformed by Zoroaster, who lived in the time of Darius, son of Hystaspes (late sixth century BC). As well as re-introducing a strict monotheism, Zoroaster reformed the Persian practice of fire worship. But this fire worship had always been *pyrodulia* rather than *pyrolatria* – that is to say, it was a 'civil worship', respecting fire as a symbol of divinity, but little more.[335] The same was the case with Mithra, who represented not only the sun, but also, ultimately, God himself. As for the Persians' putative 'dualism', it was in fact a mistaken description of their belief in the battle between one uncreated good principle (who ultimately became Oromasdes in Greek) and a created evil principle, Ahâriman (Arimanius in Greek).[336] Later, genuinely dualist sects did emerge – most importantly, Mazdaism and Manichaeism. It was these 'heresies' that misled the Greeks, especially Plutarch, into thinking that 'orthodox' (Hyde uses these terms) Zoroastrianism was dualistic.[337] The true Persian tradition was always monotheistic.

At all points Hyde was at pains to support this remarkable narrative from a variety of non-Western sources, of which we can only give a few examples. That Abraham had been a monotheistic pioneer was confirmed not only by the Qur'an's famous references to *millatu Ibrāhīm* (faith of Abraham), but also by unpublished Arabic works such as Abū 'l-Fidā's *History*, by the *Farhang-i-Sūrūri*, a Persian dictionary composed in 1599, and by an Islam catechism written in Turkish which was owned by the Cambridge scholar Thomas Gale.[338] The monotheism of Zoroaster was defended with reference to the

---

[334] Hyde had planned to publish a version of the *Guide* in the Arabic it was originally written in, transcribed from the Hebrew characters of a manuscript. This was a project he inherited from Pococke, but it collapsed when the Delegates of the Oxford press refused to pay him for his labour. See Toomer, *Eastern wisedome*, 277–9, and, as well as the evidence gathered there, Thomas Bennet to Thomas Tanner, 22 Dec 1696, Bod. MS Tanner 24, fol. 170ʳ (still hoping for Hyde's edn). For Hyde on the Sabians, see also Chwolson, *Ssabier*, 43–5.

[335] The most concise summary is that at *Historia*, 3–4.

[336] This is the theme of *Historia*, ch. ix, 161–9.

[337] Ibid., 280–90. The most important source is al-Shahrastānī, on whom see below.

[338] Ibid., 33–6. Gale's MS is Trinity College, Cambridge, R.13.32, fols. 96ᵛ–98ᵛ.

*Zarātusht-Nāmah*, an important thirteenth-century Pahlavi compendium of later Zoroastrianism which Hyde also owned in manuscript.[339]

And yet, as is so often the case with the vast tomes of the late humanists, we can identify some central sources lying at the core of Hyde's argument. One was the testimony of contemporary Persian Zoroastrians and Parsees as delivered by his contacts in the east. Particularly valuable – and thus oft repeated – was the testimony of one such unnamed contact in India:

> Lest I seem to say this about their worship and religion [i.e. that they were monotheists] gratuitously: a friend of mine staying in India, on my urging and advice, seriously questioned the priests of the ancient Persians on the worship accorded to Mithra, asking 'At what time and with what ceremonies they worship the sun?' They answered that they never worshipped the Sun, and completely repudiated such worship, soon adding that they did not present divine worship to the sun, moon or planets, but they only turned toward the sun during prayer ... because the sun comes closer to the essence of fire.[340]

Hyde placed much emphasis on such first-hand testimony – not only from well-known published travellers' reports by Pietro della Valle, Thomas Herbert, Johann Albrecht von Mandelslo, Jean de Thévenot, André Daulier-Deslandes, Jean-Baptiste Tavernier, and Henry Lord,[341] but also by personal acquaintances such as the Armenian merchant Shafraz di Avedik, who settled in London in the 1680s and who supplied him with information on the state of the modern Zoroastrian clergy.[342] Hyde may have met Avedik through the auspices of the most important traveller to Persia of them all, the Huguenot merchant Sir John Chardin, who had settled in England in 1681 and whose tales of his visits to Persia and India – including his having to disguise himself as a missionary to avoid customs searches before a subsequent exposure by an over-amorous Mingrelian princess – attracted much interest in the Royal Society and elsewhere.[343]

---

[339] See esp. Hyde's description of the *Zarātusht-Nāmah* at *Historia*, 329–30. His MS is now BL Roy. 16B.viii.

[340] Hyde, *Historia*, 5: 'Ne autem de eorum Cultu & Religione haec gratis dixisse videar, Veterum Persarum Sacerdotes in Indiâ meo suasu & consilio de illo cultu quem *Mithrae* tribuunt seriò interrogati à singulari Amico nostro in Indiâ tunc degente, *Quibus temporibus quibúsque Ceremoniis Solem adorarent?* Responderunt, *Quòd nunquam adorabant Solem,* & talem Adorationem planè negarunt: & mox addiderunt, *Se non exhibere Divinam aliquam Adorationem Soli aut Lunae aut Planetis; sed tantùm erga Solem se convertere inter orandum:* hocque ... *quòd Sol propiùs accedat ad naturam Ignis'.* I have been unable to identify this friend with certainty: it may have been Thomas Bowrey or Jean Chardin (see n. 323 above and n. 343 below).

[341] See the discussion, with all the relevant citations of the *Historia*, in Stausberg, *Faszination*, 683–4.

[342] Hyde, *Historia*, 351 (not mentioned by Stausberg); on Avedik, see Aslanian, *The global trade networks of Armenian merchants from New Julfa* (2011), 76, 81.

[343] Hyde's acquaintance with Chardin, to whom he spoke Persian, is reported in Hyde to Boyle, 5 March 1690, *Boyle correspondence*, VI, 331. Chardin is also referred to as 'singularus amicus' at *Historia*, 519. Williams, 'Hyde, Thomas', *Encyclopaedia Iranica* (1982–), XII, fasc. 6, 590–2,

A second key source was the *Sad-Dar* ('Hundred Doors/Chapters'), a miscellaneous late collection of Zoroastrian religious customs and beliefs, written in Persian but derived from the Pahlavi texts. Once again Hyde possessed it in manuscript, in several variants, the flyleaf of one of which reveals it to have been copied by a Parsee priest in secret from his co-religionists, 'at night, when all eyes were shut and asleep'.[344] So central was this text to Hyde that he translated it into Latin for publication in the *Historia*.[345] He considered it a 'collection of canons and precepts taken from the works of Zoroaster about two hundred years ago, for the use in the church of the magi'.[346] Aware of its limitations (he called it 'a hodgepodge of the good and the bad, [containing] much that is good and pious, but also much superstition and mere nonsense'),[347] Hyde nevertheless valued it extremely highly because he believed it to offer a Persian summary of the Zoroastrian beliefs which were otherwise hidden away in a language preserved only for the priestly caste.[348] Its greatest importance was that it allowed Hyde to extract a monotheistic, non-idolatrous reading of Zoroastrianism, in direct contrast to the Greek and Islamic authors, who, Hyde claimed, could not have known the true nature of the religion due to the secrecy of the Zoroastrian priests and the non-availability of translations such as the *Sad-Dar*.[349] For example, the compilation instructed only the

is thus wrong to say that there is 'no mention' of Chardin in Hyde's work (591). On Chardin, see Firby, *European travellers*, 57–68; Ferrier, *A Journey to Persia* (1996); Labib-Rahman, 'Sir Jean Chardin, the great traveller' (1977–82). The intellectual connections between Chardin and Hyde merit further study. The fullest version of Chardin's travels, *Voyages de monsieur le chevalier Chardin en Perse et autres lieux de l'orient* (3 vols, Amsterdam, 1711), contains a long section 'De la religion des Persans' (II, 165–496), and like Hyde, he believed that scholarship on Persia was essential for better biblical exegesis: his manuscript notes were used extensively in Thomas Harmer, *Observations on divers passages of Scripture ... the second edition ... enlarged with many new observations* (2 vols, London, 1776 [1st edn=1764]). For their differences on Zoroastrian dualism, see below.

[344] de Menasce, 'Zoroastrian Pahlavi writings' (2000), at 1186–7. A modern edition is B. N. Dhabhar, ed., *Saddar Nasár and Saddar Bundehesh* (Bombay, 1909); an English translation by E. W. West is in *Pahlavi Texts* III (Oxford, 1885), 253–361. Hyde's manuscripts are BL MS Roy. 16 B.xv, vi, vii, i (the last has the story about the nocturnal priest, in the hand of whichever merchant obtained it).

[345] Hyde, *Historia*, 429–88.

[346] Ibid., 431: 'Liber SAD-DER est Canonum & Praeceptorum ex Zerdushti seu Zoroastris operibus collectio circa ducentis abhinc annis facta in usum Ecclesiae Magorum'.

[347] Ibid., sig. [b4]ʳ: 'In eo est bonorum ac malorum farrago: sc. multa valdè bona & pia, & alia valdè superstitiosa & merae nugae'.

[348] Ibid., 431–2; see further Stausberg, *Faszination*, 685–92.

[349] See e.g. Hyde, *Historia*, 5: 'Graeci quidem & Mohammedani affatim Persis impingunt Divinam Adorationem Solis & Planetarum & Ignis. Atqui haud mirum est si fallantur, cùm exteri non satis intelligant Ritus Persarum veterum; quippe qui studiosè suam Religionem celant, quia Religioso Zoroastris Pracepto in Libro *Sad-der*, vetitum est vel eam vel veterem ejusdem Linguam & Scripturam cuivis extero revelare & docere'. See also 27, 121, 169, 292, 326–7, 396–402 (the last is a long set of quotations in both Persian and Latin, and subsequent discussion, forming the centerpiece of ch. xxxiii, 'A summary of the ancient Persian faith').

upkeep of the sacred fire and *not* its worship – supposedly proof that the rituals around it were 'civil' rather than divine.[350]

If these two key sources were Zoroastrian (albeit modern), the last was somewhat different. We have already seen Hyde using a very large variety of Arabic sources, but one in particular was a constant favourite of his: the *Kitāb al-Milal wa al-Niḥal* ('The Book of Sects and Creeds') by the eleventh-century Persian historian al-Shahrastānī. This hugely valuable history of religion had first been utilised by Pococke,[351] but Hyde expanded that use significantly. Not only did it support his revisionist reading of the Sabians, but much of his key Chapter 22 – 'The opinions of the primitive Persians on the first principles of their Religion' – was also based upon it. Most importantly, it presented Hyde with a non-dualist interpretation of Zoroaster.[352] That interpretation could be contrasted with that of the Greeks, especially Plutarch, who did not have the necessary sources available to him.[353] Hyde's reliance on al-Shahrastānī in this respect was not missed by later critics.[354]

Yet Hyde's full narrative was even more spectacular, and reveals the theological assumptions behind this pioneering work. After an entertaining passage in which he conjectured that the name of Zoroaster's mother (*Dughda*) was an allusion to the dodo bird, which he then described in loving natural historical detail on the basis of an exemplar preserved in the Oxford anatomy school,[355] Hyde concluded, again from Arabic sources, that Zoroaster could reform the Persian religion because he had learnt true religion from the Jews. Specifically, his childhood poverty had led to him becoming a servant to the prophet Ezra. From thence Zoroaster proceeded back to Persia, to the court of King Gushtasp (i.e. Vištāspa), where he used his knowledge to reform the by now corrupt Persian religion, reasserting that the supreme God was the creator of both good and evil and condemning any dualist tendencies.[356] He also reformed the Persian fire cult, 'augmenting and enlarging it'.[357] It was this that explained the deep similarities between Persian and Hebrew theology and sacred history (creation, the flood,

---

[350] Hyde, *Historia*, 140: 'Ut autem Persae in aeternum liberentur à falsâ illâ imputatione colendi Ignem, velim ut Lector adeat supra citata Capita 43 & 93 [=West, 39 and 92] inter Praecepta Zoroastris . . . in Libro *Sad-der*, ubi tantùm praecipitur *cura & custodia* Ignis, & Deum orare juxta eum: nulla autem Ignis adoratio ibi praecipitur'.

[351] Toomer, *Eastern wisedome*, 161. Stroumsa, 'Hyde', asserts that it was 'edited by Pococke' (219), but it was not published until 1842; I have used: Muḥammad al-Shahrastānī, *Livre des religions et des sectes*, eds. and trans., D. Gimaret, G. Monnot, and J. Jolivet (2 vols, Paris, 1986).

[352] See esp. the extremely long quotation in Hyde, *Historia*, 298–300 (=*Livre des religions*, 642–5). See also 294–6. Al-Shahrastānī's dismissal of Zoroaster as an impostor is put down to his Muslim faith at 326. See also Stroumsa, 'Hyde', 227: 'Hyde invented the concept 'dualismus', in order to translate Shahrastānī's *thanawiyyia* [sic (=Ṯhanawīya)]'.

[353] Hyde, *Historia*, 290–301, esp. 292.   [354] Bayle, *Dictionaire*, 3081.

[355] Hyde, *Historia*, 312. This specimen had been donated to Oxford by one 'Mr Camden, engineer', in 1634: Frank, 'Medicine' (1997), 542.

[356] Hyde, *Historia*, 316–30, 164, 298–9.   [357] Ibid., 4.

terrestrial paradise, etc.).[358] This pioneering late seventeenth-century discussion thus returned to that most ancient of Judaeo-Christian themes: the derivation of pagan theological truth from the Jews.

The only prominent Anglophone investigation of Hyde has concluded that he was 'effecting a dramatic detheologization of the study of religious phenomena', key to the 'paradigm shift which allowed the birth of the modern study of religion' as it occurred during the Hazardian *crise de la conscience européenne*, of which Hyde's work was 'a typical product'.[359] This judgement, it seems to me, requires significant modification. There can be no doubt that Hyde's use of Persian material, and of the *Sad-Dar* especially, was without precedent. But even on this question of sources, Hyde can be read somewhat differently. On the most primitive level, his use of the Zoroastrian material was qualitatively different from that achieved by Anquetil-Duperron seventy years later. He could not read Avestan and had to resort to the most basic form of early modern philological conjecture to explain the title of the *Zand-i-Avesta*, of which he knew from travellers' reports, claiming that it was a mélange between the Arabic زند (*Zend* – 'flint') and the Aramaic אשתא (*Eshta* – 'fire'), 'and so those who these days try to coax the meaning of this exotic expression out of Persian, where in reality it is not, work in vain'.[360] He had access to two manuscripts of the *Yasna*, the primary liturgical collection of texts of the *Avesta*, but hardly made reference to them; the same goes for a manuscript of the *Khordeh Avesta*, a selection of verses used by the laity.[361] He considered the Old Persian cuneiform inscriptions recorded by Chardin and the East India Company agent Samuel Flower (the latter published in the *Philosophical Transactions*) to be only ornamental, a somewhat ironic reversal of the common early modern practice of taking spurious Roman 'hieroglyphs' for true Egyptian ones (see 3.8 below); Hyde may have reached his conclusion from excessive fear of being mocked like Kircher.[362]

These *ex post facto* judgements are of course of little value for understanding the historical Hyde. But there is another sense in which Hyde's use of the

---

[358] Ibid., 170–7, 290–301.

[359] Stroumsa, 'Hyde', 230, 218, see also Stroumsa, *A new science*, 101–12. The dismissive comments in Harrison, *Religion*, 155 are certainly unwarranted.

[360] Hyde, *Historia*, 331–2 ('Ideóque in hujus exoticae Voculae significatione hodiè frustrà laborant, conando eam elicere ex linguâ Persicâ, ubi reverà non est' [332]).

[361] Ibid., 340, supplemented in the Appendix, 530. The two manuscripts are BL MS Roy. 16B.5 (Hyde's own, listed in BL MS Sloane 3323, fol. 270ʳ, item iii.5) and Emmanuel College, Cambridge, MS 3.2.6, brought to England in 1633 by a merchant named Nannaby Moodie, and inscribed 'This Booke is called Ejessny, written in the language Jenwista, and contains yᵉ Religion of yᵉ Antient Parseys'. I have not been able to trace any more information on Moodie. Hyde's *Khordeh Avesta* is BL MS Roy.16B.6. For short (outdated) descriptions of both the BL manuscripts, see Sachau, 'Contributions to the knowledge of Parsee literature' (1869), at 266–9.

[362] Hyde, *Historia*, 526; Flower's inscriptions, copied in 1667, are in *Philosophical Transactions*, 17 (1693), 775–7; see also RS MS EL/H3/79.

sources was more the product of a specific context than modern scholars have realised. Hyde was dogmatically adamant that the Persian and Arabic sources he was using were a vast improvement on the long-available Greek sources. It was this dogmatism that led him to reject unequivocally the *Chaldean Oracles*, an important difference from the directly theological rejections of Beza, Ursinus, and Huet.[363] In part, this anti-Greek attitude was one means of challenging the dualist reading of Zoroastrian theology, as we have seen.[364] But it also stemmed from a strong belief that not only the Persian but also the Arabic sources had preserved a historiographical tradition that offered invaluable and otherwise lost access to ancient history (not just Zoroastrian). Hyde is perhaps the epitome of this form of pan-European historiographical enthusiasm about the value of Arabic sources for ancient history, which we can date roughly to *c.* 1640–1730 (we have already met one manifestation of it in the fascination with Eutychius's *Naẓm al-Jawhar* of Selden, Pococke, and Hottinger). Hyde's use of sources like al-Shahrastānī and Abd-al-Barr, previously used (less fully) by Pococke, was a clear inheritance of this tradition. Indeed, several of his key arguments had been preceded, albeit in far more fragmentary form, by earlier seventeenth-century Christian Arabists. Thomas Erpenius had been the first European to set forth the characterisation of Zoroaster as a reformer of Persian religion as early as 1625, when he published the *al-Majmu` al-Mubarak* ('The blessed collection') of the thirteenth-century Arabic Christian historian al-Makīn Ǧirǧis al-'Amīd, discussed by Hyde and even noted by Stanley;[365] moreover, the non-dualist interpretation of Zoroaster's doctrine had already been extracted out of various Arabic sources by Pococke.[366] Indeed, this whole period of optimism about the potential of Arabic ancient historiography may be said to culminate in Hyde, as well as in the Dutch philologist Albert Schultens, whose works (published between 1706 and 1740) promoted the idea that Arabic would reveal the primitive Semitic tongue and thus explain much of early biblical history.[367]

This optimism, although part of mainstream seventeenth-century philology, manifested itself in some scholarship that was, by wider contemporary standards, peculiar. Take, for example, Hyde's claim that Zoroaster had studied with Ezra. It

---

[363] Hyde, *Historia*, sig. [b4]ʳ, referring to the Persians' 'genuina ... Praecepta (nisi cum aliis loquendo, *Oracula* vocare mavis)'; undoubtedly a reference to the *Chaldean Oracles*.

[364] As well as the examples above, see e.g. the discussion at *Historia*, 90, challenging Strabo's claim that the Persians worshipped the elements (*Geog.*, xv.3.13).

[365] al-Makīn Ǧirǧis al-'Amīd, *Historia Saracenica*, ed. and trans. Thomas Erpenius (Leiden, 1625). Erpenius had translated only the second part of the work, beginning with Muḥammad, but Hyde was also familiar with the first part (from the Creation), although he did not have a high opinion of it (*Historia*, 325, 528–30). For Stanley, see *Chaldaick philosophy*, 3a.

[366] Edward Pococke, *Specimen historiae Arabum, sive Gregorii Abul Farajii Malatiensis, de origine & moribus Arabum* (Oxford, 1650), 147–9.

[367] For the controversy engendered by Schultens, see Fück, *Die arabischen Studien in Europa* (1955), 108–24.

is clear that for Hyde this finding explained the similarities between Persian and Hebrew theology that would otherwise have seemed dangerously inexplicable. Yet it also posed problems. Hyde in fact had the choice of three different Arabic narratives: that Zoroaster had been the servant of Ezra (from Abū Moḥammed Mustapha), of a disciple of Jeremiah (al-Tabari), or of Elijah (Abu'l-Faraj).[368] For chronological reasons, Hyde favoured the first.[369] Yet this left his whole work in a chronological mess. He had asserted, again on the basis of his precious Arabic sources, that Zoroaster had been contemporary with Darius Hystaspes (late sixth-early fifth century BC).[370] But generations of European scholars, obsessed with the identity and role of 'Ezra the scribe' (because of his role in histories of transmission of the text of the Old Testament), had identified Ezra as flourishing *c.* 480–440 BC.[371] Hyde's Zoroaster thus supposedly lived before the Jew to whom he was meant to have been a servant. Hyde's devout belief in the privileged status of the Arabic sources prevented him from seeing these basic faults, obvious to his near-contemporary readers.[372]

This brings us to a more fundamental point about Hyde's approach to these sources. As we have seen, and will see many times again, one of the great developments of seventeenth-century scholarship on such topics was the rejection of overly simple narratives of transmission from the sacred to pagan. Stanley had rejected Jewish and Arabic accounts of direct sacred influence on the Chaldeans as fables; Le Clerc had gone further, contextualising the intentions behind the patristic sources that argued for a Jewish origin for near-

[368] Hyde, *Historia*, 313–16. See also Stausberg, *Faszination*, 700; like Prof. Stausberg, I have been unable to identify 'Abu Mohammed Mustapha', from whose 'Vita *Gushtaspis*' Hyde quotes in Arabic. For Abu'l-Faraj, see Pococke, *Specimen*, 147; Pococke, *Historia compendiosa dynastiarum, authore Gregorio Abul-Pharajio* (Oxford, 1663), 54.

[369] Hyde, *Historia*, 314: 'Rectiùs forte supradictus Abu Mohammed Mustapha referens *Zerdushtum fuisse servum عزير Ozair* seu *Ezrae*, quod verisimilimum videtur'. Elijah (*fl.* 9th cent. BC) was obviously out of the question, explicitly rejected by Hyde ('tempus non patitur, cùm iste propheta 400 annis ante illum vixerit'). He offered no such explicit rejection of the 'disciple of Jeremiah' thesis, which would have made more sense given Jeremiah's flourishing *c.* 626–587 BC on the standard accounts.

[370] Hyde, *Historia*, 308. The key source is Agathias, *Hist.*, II.23–5. That Darius was the son of Hystaspes was itself contentious, but had been pretty firmly established by this point: the definitive discussion of Zoroaster's chronology is that in John Marsham, *Chronicus canon Aegyptiacus, Ebraicus, Graecus et disquisitiones* (London, 1672), 139–40. On Marsham, see 3.6 below.

[371] Although it is possible that Hyde differentiated between Ezra the scribe and Ezra the prophet, as had been attempted by Jacques d'Auzolles de Lapeyre in 1632: see Hamilton, *The apocryphal apocalypse* (1999), 101–2, 225.

[372] Humphrey Prideaux spotted the problem, preferring the 'disciple of Jeremiah' reading and claiming that that disciple was Daniel, whose extremely long life (Dan. 10:1 claims that he was still alive in the third year of Cyrus, i.e. 533 BC) allowed a degree of overlap with Zoroaster (*The Old and New Testament connected in the history of the Jews and neighbouring nations* (4th edn, 2 vols, London, 1718 [1st edn=1716–18]), I, 213). On Prideaux, see below. See also John Leland, *The divine authority of the Old and New Testament asserted* (2 vols, London, 1739–40), II, 305.

eastern philosophy and theology. Hyde was familiar with Le Clerc's approach,[373] but he entirely failed to share in it. From the moment the *Historia* came off the press he was criticised for this: as early as November 1699 the Dutch scholar and diplomat Gisbert Cuper, who must have had a very early version of the work, wrote to the highly regarded Utrecht-based *erudit* Johann Georg Graevius to state that Hyde's sources for the monotheism of the Persians were all late, and that he found it doubtful that the worship of Mithra was purely 'civil'.[374] Once this criticism was made publicly and much more sharply by Bayle in the second edition of the *Dictionaire*[375] it became a commonplace.

In part, this was a product of scholarly jealousy: those who could not read Arabic were immediately more suspicious about grandiose claims to the superiority of Arabic over Greek sources when the latter were often a millennium or more older. But it was also a product of a methodological shift: the recognition that late claims to chronological primacy were to be treated with great caution. Stanley and Le Clerc, among many others (see Chs. 3 and 6 below), had made this clear for the patristic/Jewish narrative of Judaic primacy, but the resources for such a scepticism about Hyde's 'new' sources for Zoroaster were also available. Hyde's friend Chardin, when his reports from Persia were finally published, would emphasise the ignorance of contemporary Zoroastrians as to the true history of their religion, claiming that they distorted its real dualism into a more monotheistic version so as to placate the Muslims under whose rule they lived.[376] Surely he had told Hyde of his views? Such a contextual explanation for the contemporary Zoroastrians' claim to monotheism was even conjectured by Bayle before Chardin's full memoirs were published.[377]

---

[373] See Hyde to Thomas Smith, 13 May 1700, in *Syntagma dissertationum*, ii, 491, responding to Smith's criticisms of Hyde's Latin in the samples for the *Historia*: 'I am not writing eloquence or orations, but only plain matter ... if any word or phrase doth slip, I do not value it ... I observe that le Clerk and other critics, who write a great deal, are subject to the same exceptions of sometimes small failures by writing hastily'.

[374] Gisbert Cuper to Johann Georg Graevius, 23 Nov 1699, Bod. MS d'Orville 478, pp. 169–70. On Cuper, see now Chen, 'Gisbert Cuper as servant of two republics' (2011), esp. 90–2 on his interest in near-eastern antiquities and consequent connections with Oxford scholars.

[375] Bayle, *Dictionaire*, 3077–83. For Bayle on Zoroaster, see Stausberg, *Faszination*, ii, 724–35. The claim in Stroumsa, 'Hyde', 226 that 'Bayle basically presented Hyde's main idea about Iranian original monotheism' cannot be accepted; the case is in fact the opposite.

[376] See the very full and useful account in Firby, *Travellers*, 63–6.

[377] Bayle, *Dictionaire*, iii, 3081, n. F: 'Je conjecture que ses sectateurs lui ont prété charitablement, & pour leurs propres interêts la creation du mauvais principe, & qu'ils en ont usé de la sorte depuis qu'ils ont été soumis à la dure domination des Mahometans qui les abhorrent, & qui les traitent d'idolâtres & d'adorateurs du feu. Ne voulant point s'exposer encore plus à leur haine, & à leurs insultes, sous pretexte qu'ils reconoitroient une nature incrée, & souverainement mechante, & independante de Dieu, ils ont trouvé à-propos de donner une autre interpretation à cette partie de leur système; car pour nier absolument qu'il ait admis deux principes, ils ne pourroient pas'.

As for the Arab sources – and especially their constant reference to the Sabians – their reliability had been challenged several times, even just in England, in the years between Stanley and Hyde.[378] Far from being particularly 'modern', then, Hyde's attitude to the sources on ancient Zoroastrianism was part of a specific scholarly context: the professional Arabists' (rather self-serving) claim that Arabic sources held the key to ancient history.

There is another reason for questioning an overly modernising reading of Hyde, and for contextualising him in a rather narrower fashion. It is sometimes claimed that his interpretation depended on an ecumenical or even positive attitude towards paganism. Usually this is combined with the story of how he urged one of his correspondents in the east to tell the Parsees that he was 'a great lover of their religion'.[379] Yet the full quotation reveals a rather different picture, for in it Hyde asks his correspondent to procure manuscripts from the Parsees, who are 'very close and not apt to impart any thing', by 'a little Bribing of one of their Preists with a little mony, and telling him its for me who is a great lover of their religion'.[380] I have found no evidence to suggest that Hyde was anything other than the typical Oxford Anglican that one would expect from his acquaintances, or that his theological attitude to paganism was anything other than one of condescension.

More puzzling are the specifics of his religious reading of Zoroaster. Although Hyde paid lip service to Zoroaster's achievements in astronomy, he showed remarkably little interest in him as a philosopher, focusing almost entirely on his status as a religious reformer. There were several sources for this shift. In part, it must have been a response to Hyde's long-standing interest in China: famously, some of the Jesuits in China had defended their accommodation to Chinese religious customs by arguing that the Confucian rites of the elite mandarins were 'civil' rather than religious ceremonies (a position adopted by Matteo Ricci, developed by Martino Martini, and culminating in the *Confucius Sinarum philosophus* (1687) by a team led by Philippe Couplet), and Hyde's description of Zoroastrian fire and Mithra worship as 'cultus civilis & caeremonialis' is too similar to the Jesuit approach to be coincidental.[381] But it seems to me that the deepest influence was not the work of the Sinologists but the new approaches to the

---

[378] Levitin, 'Spencer', 89–90.

[379] See e.g. Marshall, 'Hyde, Thomas', *ODNB*, 'Hyde collected religions as well as languages and was broadly tolerant in his attitude to non-Christian beliefs'; Marshall, 'Hyde', 8–9; cf. Stausberg, 'Von den Chaldäischen Orakeln zu den Hundert Pforten und darüber hinaus' (2001), 271.

[380] Hyde to Thomas Bowrey, BL MS APAC Eur.E.192, no. 12, fol. 1ʳ.

[381] Hyde, *Historia*, 120, *passim*. The best account of Jesuit accommodationism remains Mungello, *Jesuit accommodation and the origins of Sinology* (1985). Hyde had certainly read *Confucius Sinarum philosophus* (see n. 388 below); in addition, as early as 1673 he had received from Melchisédec Thévenot a 'Confucii librum de Scientiis Sinensium', which must be Thévenot's French translation of Prospero Intorcetta's *Sinarum scientia politico-moralis* (1667–69) [=Melchisédech Thévenot, *Relations de divers voyages curieux* (4 vols, Paris, 1663–72), IV, 1–24] (Hyde to Thévenot, 24 June 1673, *Syntagma dissertationum*, II, 464). The similarity

figure of Moses that were being developed in the second half of the seventeenth century. We shall see in the next chapter that under the influence of Maimonidean accommodationism in particular, Moses was more and more defined as a legislator, this identity subsuming that of philosopher, a trend that reached a peak in England in the 1680s and 1690s. The most prominent scholarly proponent of this step was John Spencer, and there are obvious connections between his and Hyde's work, not least the similarly wide definition of 'Sabianism'.[382]

But this raises an obvious problem. The whole idea of Moses the lawgiver was founded on the premise that the Jews were God's chosen people and that Moses was an instrument of a God working by second causes to reform Judaism. Why could the same model apply to Zoroaster? One possibility was that he was simply a plagiarist, applying to the Persians what he learnt with the Hebrews. But Hyde went further than this, taking the logical, if unexpected step. The Persians, he asserted, were *also* a chosen people. Not only had Zoroaster learnt from the Jews, but he had been blessed with his own revelation, so as to better be able to reform corrupt Persian religion.[383] The three μάγοι who visited Christ upon his birth (Matt. 2) were Persian magi, acting upon prophetic knowledge of the coming of the Messiah.[384] These claims had been made (on the basis of very different sources) by Ficino;[385] by the late seventeenth century, they opened one up to the charge of naïve enthusiasm. Hyde defended this reading through biblical reference, and through a vision of an omnipotent God ('who from eternity has foreseen what would happen from his ordination')[386] working through second causes. Had Cyrus the Great not been prophesised by Isaiah two hundred years before his birth (Isa. 44:28), and had he not then ordered the rebuilding of the temple (Ezra 6:3–5, leading to the designation of Cyrus as a 'Messiah' in Isa. 45:1–6)?[387] And was it so strange to find Zoroaster prophesising the coming of Christ when the gentile Balaam had done so too?[388] God was preparing the world

---

between Hyde and the Jesuits was first pointed out by Bayle (*Dictionaire*, III, 3083, n. H), and again in Stroumsa, *New science*, 107.

[382] Compare Hyde, *Historia*, 4–5 ('Verum quidem est quòd totus fere Mundus tunc fuit pessimo Sabismo involutus … ') with John Spencer, *De legibus Hebraeorum ritualibus et earum rationibus, libri tres* (The Hague, 1686 [1st edn=Cambridge, 1683–5]), II, 213. For Spencer, see 3.6 below. It is also worth noting that Hyde must have known Thomas Burnet, another key player in the 'Moses as lawgiver' debate (see 3.7), because he dedicated a plate to him (see the plate of Nabataean script keyed to p. 521) (I am very grateful to Scott Mandelbrote for drawing this to my attention).

[383] Hyde, *Historia*, sig. [b3]$^r$, 382.    [384] Ibid., 377–9.

[385] Allen, *Synoptic art*, 37–40. The key source for Zoroaster's foreknowledge of the Messiah was Abū'l-Faraj (already discussed in Pococke, *Specimen*, 147, 149–50).

[386] Hyde, *Historia*, 380: ' … qui ab omni aevo praeviderat quid ex suâ ordinatione futurum esset'.

[387] Ibid., 380–1.

[388] Ibid., 384. Balaam's seven prophecies are at Num. 23:7–10, 18–24; 24:3–9, 14–19, 20, 21–2, 23–4. Hyde also believed that Confucius had prophesied Christ, drawing on Philippe Couplet's 'Philosophorum Sinensium principis Confucii vita', in *Confucius Sinarum philosophus sive scientia Sinensis* (Paris, 1687), xcvii–cxxiv (*Historia*, 385–6).

for the coming of Christ, and the Persians were a tool in this endeavour – even their skill in astronomy was planned by God to facilitate their finding the Messiah by following the star of Bethlehem (as Stillingfleet had claimed almost forty years previously).[389] Contrary to Ficino, then, this was not a story about the illumina-tionist capacity of human reason, but about God's operation in the world; ultimately, Hyde felt that the reason 'why God condescended to favour the Persians before all over pagans with such a revelation, He Himself knows best'.[390] This did not prevent him from being very optimistic that the discovery and translation of further Zoroastrian texts would reveal more prophecies con-cerning Christ – if only the money were to be found.[391] These words do not make Hyde an 'apologist' or render his work 'unhistorical'. While Hyde did briefly advertise the apologetic usefulness of his work,[392] there is no evidence that this was his main purpose. Like Stanley, he was a scholar who nonetheless worked with a set of theological presuppositions, albeit unlike his predecessor, ones which he made much more overt.

## 2.8    Conclusion

The work of Le Clerc (and thus Stanley) was much read and cited in the eighteenth century; Hyde's, meanwhile, eventually became very popular throughout Europe, a sad irony given his initial troubles shifting the book. We have already met Bayle's forceful emphasis on a dualist reading of Zoroastrianism – that debate continued unabated with ever more polemic and ever less scholarship, culminating in Voltaire's ironic treatment in the *Dictionnaire philosophique* (1764), plagiarising (and misrepresenting) Hyde extensively to defend his thesis of a universal deism.[393] A much more interesting side-avenue was Isaac de Beausobre's revisionist treat-ment of Manichaeism (*Histoire critique de Manichée et du Manichéisme* (1734–39)), which drew extensively on seventeenth-century Zoroaster scholarship, especially Hyde.[394] In England, Hyde's work also became embroiled in the deist debates, as freethinker and orthodox bashed each other over the head with their misunderstandings of the *Historia*, each party now celebrated by modern historians, depending on political

---

[389] Hyde, *Historia*, 379.

[390] Ibid., 379: 'Cur Deus Persas prae aliis Gentibus dignatus est favere tantae Revelationis, ipse meliùs novit'.

[391] Ibid., sig. b2ᵛ. See also Hyde to Sloane, 24 Jan 1702, BL MS Sloane 4038, fol. 292ʳ, 'I being (if God grants me 2 or 3 years) engaged in some Notes upon the Scripture ... and also about the workes of Zoroastres, if mony is contributed'.

[392] Hyde, *Historia*, sig. [b3]ʳ.

[393] For the eighteenth-century story, see Stausberg, *Faszination*, ii, 718–946 (901–46 on Voltaire).

[394] Stroumsa, 'Isaac de Beausobre revisited' (2000); Laursen, 'Isaac de Beausobre and the Manicheans' (2003); Pocock, *Barbarism*, v, 137–62.

preference.[395] Most interesting is the treatment given in *The Old and New Testament connected in the history of the Jews and neighbouring nations* (1716–18) by Humphrey Prideaux, an ex-fellow of Christ Church, Oxford (where he had spied on Locke) and member of the same Oxford scholarly community around Thomas Smith and Edward Bernard as Hyde, who was a competent Hebraist and an aspiring if largely incompetent Arabist. Prideaux rejected the Hebrew chair in 1691 in favour of an ecclesiastical living and thence turned from scholarship to scholarly apologetics (the *Life of Mahomet* (1697) and the work under discussion here).[396] The *Connection* is tied together by an ingenious thesis: that the foreknowledge of Christ possessed by the patriarchs was in fact the source of pagan idolatry. 'The necessity of a Mediator between God and Man was a general Notion, which obtained among all mankind from the beginning' because it was recognised that they could not 'have any access to the all holy, all glorious, and supreme Governour of all things'; but because 'no clear Revelation being then made of the Mediator, whom God had appointed', the pagans 'took upon them to address unto him by Mediators of their own chusing', picking the celestial bodies.[397] Prideaux thus struck at both historical–chronological challenges to religion and antitrinitarianism at the same time. As this shows, Prideaux was not dismayed by Hyde-esque speculations on (vague) pagan foreknowledge of Christ and he willingly followed Hyde's account of Zoroaster, praising the evidence 'supplied by the *Persians* and *Arabs*' which filled the large gaps left by the Greek sources.[398] But he deviated in one great

---

[395] E.g. [Thomas Morgan], *The moral philosopher* (London, 1737), 236, 348–9; Leland, *Divine authority*, I, 336–8, II, 234–6, 297–306, both wilfully mispresenting Hyde's arguments. For Hume's use of Hyde, see Stausberg, *Faszination*, II, 715, 718–23.

[396] For his biography: [Anon.], *The life of the Reverend Humphrey Prideaux* (London, 1748); de Quehen, 'Prideaux, Humphrey', *ODNB*. For his oriental scholarship: Toomer, *Eastern wisedome*, 289–92; Holt, 'The treatment of Arab history by Prideaux, Ockley and Sale', (1962), esp. 290–4. For a more contextual analysis of Prideaux's place in Oxford intellectual life, see Feingold, 'Oriental studies', 474–5, 493–6. There is further manuscript evidence for his Oxford network: see e.g. Bod. MS Smith 53, fols. 111ʳ, 113ʳ for letters from Prideaux to Smith. Prideaux's dissatisfaction with Oxford and with Christ Church, which led him to reject the Hebrew chair (see E. M. Thompson, *Letters of Humphrey Prideaux, sometime dean of Norwich, to John Ellis* (London, 1875), 150), may have been stimulated by the actions of John Fell (see the slightly ambiguous statement in John Aubrey to Anthony Wood, 30 Dec 1679 [Bod. MS Wood F. 39, fol. 334ʳ]) (there is much more Oxford evidence to be mined). For his spying on Locke, see Woolhouse, *Locke* (2007), 177.

[397] Prideaux, *Connection*, I, 177–8; see also Kidd, *Before nationalism* (1999), 47–8.

[398] Prideaux, *Connection*, I, xxii–xxiii. For Prideaux's deviation from Hyde on the identity of Zoroaster's Jewish master, see n. 372 above; his general superiority to Hyde in matters chronological is revealed by the discussion of the subject in the preface (i–xvi).

way from Hyde: far from being a true prophet and reformer like Moses, Zoroaster, for all his learning from the Jews, was a power-hungry impostor in the vein of Muḥammad. All the similarities between his doctrine and that of the Jews were pure theft. As for the supposed prophecies about Christ, 'all this seems to be taken out of the *Legendary* [i.e. incorrect] writings of the Eastern Christians'; Hyde's key Arabic source, Abū'l-Faraj, was after all a Christian.[399] This was certainly an adequate resolution to Hyde's theological idiosyncrasies, but it only exacerbated the problem of the reliability of the Arabic sources which had plagued Hyde. The whole field was of course transformed by Anquetil-Duperron's publication of the *Avesta*; the Frenchman's long preface discussed Hyde at length, for the most part with condescension.[400]

It is worth pausing at this point to summarise some of the themes we have encountered, for they will reappear in the following chapters. One is the uselessness of labels like *prisca theologia*. Another is the continuing interest and investment of natural philosophers in humanist scholarship on the history of philosophy, free from any speculations about ancients and moderns.[401] Finally, the extended treatments of Stanley, Le Clerc, and Hyde show that the category of 'enlightened' history seems a particularly empty one at this point. Le Clerc has most often been placed within it, but his continued reliance on the *Chaldean Oracles* seems the height of childish naïvety when compared to Hyde's use of the sources. And yet Hyde's approach to the intentionality behind the sources he used is fundamentally lacking in the critical insight deployed by Le Clerc. Far more fruitful is an approach that appreciates these scholars' local contexts – the mix of scholarship and subtle theological arguments among interregnum royalists, the anti-patristic historiography of Dutch Arminianism, or the optimism about near-eastern ancient historiography in Restoration Oxford – while recognising that they were operating in a larger context that had nothing to do with 'modernity' or overt political, ecclesiological, or other ideological battles: the scholarly fascination with the history of ancient paganism that so infected the republic of letters

---

[399] Prideaux, *Connection*, I, xxiii, 210–31 (quotation from 230).

[400] Abraham Hyacinthe Anquetil-Duperron, *Zend-Avesta, ouvrage de Zoroastre, contenant les idées théologiques, physiques & morales de ce législateur, les cérémonies du culte religieux qu'il a établi, & plusieurs traits importans relatifs à l'ancienne histoire des Parses* (3 vols, Paris, 1771), I, iv–v, cccclix–cccclxii, cccclxxxviii–di.

[401] Although this was the use Le Clerc's edition of Stanley was put to by Pierre Coste, who argued that it showed that while 'everyone was in agreement that Philosophy came from the Orient' and was originated by the Chaldeans, their philosophy 'barely merits the name', for 'it may be more justly titled a *superstitious Theology*': 'Discours sur la philosophie ancienne et moderne où l'on fait en abregé l'histoire de cette science', in Pierre-Sylvain Régis, *Cours entire de philosophie ou système général selon les principes de M. Descartes* (Amsterdam, 1691), sig. A2$^r$ ('cette premiére Philosophie étoit si informe, qu'à peine merite-t-elle ce nom. On pourroit l'appeller à plus juste titre *une Théologie superstitieuse*').

from the late sixteenth century. The 'ideology' that was most important to the transformation of attitudes to near-eastern philosophy was not a religious heterodoxy or 'liberalism' that led to a 'comparativist' mentality; rather, it was a curiosity about the subject matter on the part of scholars, their readers, and those who used their scholarship for other tasks, all grounded in the culture of late humanism that had made the subject matter interesting in the first place.

# 3    Ancient wisdom II: Moses the Egyptian?

From histories of near-eastern philosophy we move southwards, to histories of Egyptian and Judaic wisdom. On this subject, a historiographical common-place was established very soon after the events we shall chart, in the German histories of philosophy of the eighteenth century. In 1743, Brucker cemented his own reputation for a 'critical' approach to the history of philosophy by outlining, at the end of the *Historia critica philosophiae*, how his predecessors had all stumbled into the death-trap of 'syncretism'. In fewer than thirty pages, Brucker aligned three hundred years of scholarship into three groups: those who combined the 'Platonic philosophy with the Pythagorean and the Cabbalistic'; those who sought to build a 'Scriptural Philosophy'; and the 'theosophists'. From Ficino and Giovanni Pico della Mirandola to Thomas Burnet, varying degrees of scholarly endeavour had been employed to unravel the putative mysteries of the ancient sages. But all three groups were misled by the myths of ancient wisdom of the Cabbalists; all indulged in 'philosophical romances'; and all damaged both religion and philosophy by not confining them to their respective spheres.[1]

Brucker's reading has proved remarkably influential: both historians of 'enlightenment' and of the late Renaissance present the whole ancient wisdom narrative as something of a fish: it survived in the sea of *quattrocento* Florence, was dragged out by Isaac Casaubon (in his attack on the dating of the Hermetic corpus), flapped around a little on the deck of the seventeenth century (indulged by some out-of-date doters), and was finally put of its misery by the 'enligh-tened' mallet of Brucker and his German counterparts.[2]

---

[1]  Johann Jakob Brucker, *The history of philosophy, from the earliest times to the beginning of the present century*, trans. W. Enfield (2 vols, London, 1791 [1st edn=Leipzig, 1742–44]), II, 483–509. For the explicit linkage of Burnet with a putative programme of restoring 'Alexandrian Platonism' of Ficino, Patrizi, and Cudworth, see I, xxv.

[2]  See Blair, 'Mosaic physics and the search for a pious natural philosophy in the late Renaissance', 57–8 (explicitly following Brucker), and Copenhaver's learned 'Introduction' (1992), 1, jump-ing from Casaubon to Brucker within the space of a sentence. From the perspective of a German enlightenment, see e.g.: Israel, *Enlightenment contested*, 472; Israel, 'Philosophy, history of philosophy, and *l'histoire de l'esprit humain*' (2004); Blackwell, 'Thales'; Lehmann-Brauns, *Wisheit in der Weltgeschichte*. See further 1.2 above.

There may, however, be good reason to rethink this narrative, and to reconsider when the real revolution in attitudes to Mosaic wisdom took place. Brucker was of course aiming to advertise the novelty of his own work, and this led him to downplay the key methodological development of seventeenth-century approaches to ancient Egyptian and Jewish wisdom: the realisation that Moses had to be understood contextually, and that traditional Jewish and patristic claims about the relationship between Mosaic and pagan wisdom were far from always trustworthy. This development, first promulgated by scholars, was soon picked up by theologians and biblical critics, and then spread throughout the educated world. It proved particularly important for natural philosophers, as in the wake of the collapse of Aristotelianism the compatibility of various competitors for its replacement with the creation narrative offered in the Book of Genesis was considered in historical terms. By the end of the century, the narrative of Judaic primacy and of Moses as pioneering philosopher-sage was almost dead. This happened not under the aegis of heterodoxy or 'early enlightenment', but from the slow dissemination of new sources, from new approaches to the existing sources, and from the theological pressures that shaped these scholarly developments. English scholarship played a particularly crucial role in this process because historical criticism of the Old Testament was especially welcomed by a church wishing to distance itself from Reformed modes of exegesis, whose scholarly stars in turn disseminated this historicism to various lay thinkers, whether to scholars such as John Marsham, or to the natural philosophers who made Moses's status as a philosopher such a burning issue at the end of the century.

## 3.1    Egyptian and Mosaic philosophy before 1640

The textual resources on the subject available to an early modern scholar were even more complex that those for the near east. Greek historians were from an early stage interested not only in the ancient Egyptians but also in constructing direct lineages between their own philosophy and a supposed stock of 'barbarian' wisdom preceding them; from Hecateus in the fourth century BC onwards it became a commonplace that Plato, Pythagoras, and numerous other Greek philosophers had travelled to Egypt (and elsewhere in the east) in search of enlightenment.[3] As late antique neoplatonism moved from school traditions of philosophy to a more open religiosity, historical narratives in turn became more about the Greek philosophers' receipt not just of philosophical truth, but also of

---

[3]  Momigliano, *Pagans, Jews and Christians* (1987), 31–57 ('The origins of universal history'), at 42–3; Iversen, 'Egypt in classical antiquity' (1994); Kákosy, 'Egypt in ancient Greek and Roman thought' (1995); Burstein, 'Images of Egypt in Greek historiography' (1996). Hopfner, *Orient und griechische Philosophie* (1925), 1–9, lists almost all the key sources for the idea that Greek philosophers took from the east; see also Kákosy, 'Plato and Egypt. The Egyptian tradition' (1993).

divine revelation from their oriental predecessors. Although far less cited by the neoplatonists than the *Chaldean Oracles*, the collection of Egyptian-Greek wisdom texts attributed to Hermes Trismegistus and known as the *Hermetica* belong to the same context.[4]

As Christianity spread and incorporated literate elites, its apologists developed narratives to counter pagan accusations of anti-intellectualism. These took two forms, both of which were to be of great importance for early modern scholars. The first was the assertion of Judaic, and especially Mosaic, intellectual primacy. Here they inherited a Jewish historiographical tradition – that Moses had been a pioneering sage and patron of both Egyptian and Greek philosophy and civilisation had already been asserted by Jewish apologists like Eupolemus, Artapanus (who implied that Moses *was* Hermes), Josephus, and Philo Judaeus.[5] Starting with Justin Martyr, the Christian appropriation of this tradition found its apogee in the fourth century in the works of Eusebius.[6] An important development was the incorporation of an esoteric component, as Clement of Alexandria and Origen in particular argued that Christianity, like ancient Egyptian wisdom, contained a strand of hidden philosophical wisdom known only to the elite; Origen thus promoted an allegorical scriptural exegesis in which the literal meanings were only a 'veil' for the spiritual and philosophical.[7]

The second apologetic approach was more directly tied to biblical exegesis. It was most prominently developed by Augustine in his *De Genesi ad litteram*. Like Clement and Origen, Augustine was concerned that the biblical creation account might seem absurd to potential converts. Unlike Origen, he rejected allegory in favour of a literal reading. Yet that literal reading could be rendered compatible with natural philosophy by adopting the accommodationist hermeneutic. The scriptural text had been accommodated to the limited understandings of the original audience: the Bible had a spiritual purpose – inculcating belief – not a philosophical one. Nonetheless, the literal reading was still true in a phenomenalist sense: when Genesis talked of 'two great lights' (Gen. 1:16), Augustine argued that this did not imply an incorrect assumption about the moon's size, only a description of the relative appearance to the human eye.[8] There was always a degree of ambiguity: was the accommodation performed by God operating through Moses or by Moses himself? Augustine seemed to stress the former; as we saw in Chapter 2 a potentially more historical narrative

---

[4] Copenhaver, ed., *Hermetica*; Festugière, *La révélation d'Hermès Trismégiste* (1950); Fowden, *The Egyptian Hermes* (1986).

[5] Droge, *Homer or Moses?* (1989), 12–47; Eusebius, *Praep. Ev.*, IX.27.6 (for Moses as Hermes).

[6] Droge, *Homer or Moses*, 49–71 (Justin), 168–93 (Eusebius).

[7] E.g. Origen, *Cels.*, I.12, *Princ.*, I.2; Clemens Alexandrinus, *Strom.*, V.7. For the esoteric theology and philosophy of the Egyptians, the most popular source was Plutarch, *Is. Os.*, 8.

[8] Augustine, *De Gen. ad litt.*, II.16. See Howell, 'Natural knowledge and textual meaning in Augustine's interpretation of Genesis' (2008); Benin, *Footprints*, 94–112.

was offered in the twelfth century by Maimonides, who defended the rationality of the Mosaic ritual law by claiming that it was accommodated to the primitive and still pagan mindsets of the contemporary Hebrews. It is worth noting at this point the possible incompatibility of the two forms of Christian apologetics: the first assumes great wisdom on the part of the biblical Jews, the second assumes their backwardness (the reason they required divine condescension in the first place).

Ficino translated the *Corpus Hermeticum* (publ. 1471), and assigned both Hermes and Moses places in his pantheon of six earliest sages.[9] Giovanni Pico della Mirandola adopted this perspective, but combined it with the Jewish mysticism taught to him by Flavius Mithridates, giving birth to what is now known as 'Christian Cabbala',[10] which had a long and contentious afterlife in the sixteenth century, most prominently in the hands of Johannes Reuchlin, Guillaume Postel, and Cornelius Agrippa.[11] The origins of Cabbala lie in medieval Spain; its foundational work, the *Zohar*, includes mystical interpretation of the Torah and metaphysical speculations. It was probably composed by the thirteenth-century Spanish Jew Moses de León – although he assigned its writing to the second-century rabbi Shimon bar Yochai, its key historical claim was to be derived from the oral traditions delivered to Moses on Mount Sinai. A much fuller cosmological–metaphysical framework was added in the wake of the work of Isaac Luria (1534–72), now known as 'Lurianic Cabbala'. Its quasi-emanationist metaphysics of the divine naturally appealed to Platonically inclined Christians; most importantly for us, it contributed significantly to the historiographical narrative of Moses's philosophical endowments and of a tradition of esoteric metaphysical wisdom later inherited from the Jews by the pagans, not least Plato and Pythagoras.[12] This also informed iatrochymical authors in the Paracelsian tradition who posited great antiquity – often Egyptian – for their discipline.[13] But their claims were challenged in the majestic *De Hermetica Aegyptiorum vetere et Paracelsicorum nova medicina liber unus* (1648) by the Lutheran Hermann Conring. Conring, drawing on

---

[9] Allen, 'Marsilio Ficino, Hermes Trismegistus and the *Corpus Hermeticum*' (1990); Gentile, *Marsilio Ficino e il ritorno di Ermete Trismegisto* (1999); Salaman, 'Echoes of Egypt in Hermes and Ficino' (2001).

[10] On Pico and Cabbala, see most fully Wirszubski, *Jewish Mysticism*.

[11] See now most fully, Schmidt-Biggemann, *Geschichte der christlichen Kabbala* (2012); landmark older studies are Blau, *The Christian interpretation of the Cabala in the Renaissance* (1944); Secret, *Les Kabbalistes Chrétiens de la Renaissance* (1964); and Scholem, 'The beginnings of the Christian Kabbalah' (1997).

[12] As well as the works above, see on this in particular, Idel, 'The magical and neoplatonic interpretations of the Kabbalah in the Renaissance' (1983); Idel, 'Jewish Kabbalah and Platonism in the Middle Ages and Renaissance' (1992); Idel, 'Prisca theologia in Marsilio Ficino and some Jewish treatments' (2001); Idel, 'Jewish thinkers versus Christian Kabbalah' (2003). Idel's unilinear/multilinear interpretation is challenged in Hanegraaff, *Esotericism*, 58–9.

[13] See Ch. 4, p. 239 below.

Scaliger and Casaubon's scepticism about pseudepigrapha like the *Corpus Hermeticum* and about self-aggrandising Jewish and Christian pre-histories, denied the whole Egyptian pre-history of chymistry, and found the origins of the science in Hellenistic Alexandria; he also ridiculed the idea of finding a glorious proto-Paracelsianism and aligned ancient Egyptian natural philosophy with their idolatrous theology.[14] We shall encounter the great impact of Conring's book – perhaps no smaller than Casaubon's – among both English scholars and natural philosophers in both this and the next chapter.

We should not fall into the common trap of assuming that 'Hermeticism' was the standard Renaissance approach to the figure of Moses.[15] First, as in all other philosophical issues, the intellectual mainstream was dominated by a vibrant and varied Aristotelianism. In the sixteenth century, the Aristotelians produced a series of commentaries on Genesis that often addressed its relationship to natural philosophy – these included Hieronymus Zanchius's *De operibus Dei* (1591), David Pareus's *In Genesin Mosis commentarius* (1609), and the most popular and important, Benedict Pereira's *Commentariorum et disputationum in Genesin tomi quatuor* (1589–98).[16] Although they often had recourse to the Augustinian accommodationist hermeneutic, this was rarely extended in a full historical–contextual direction, even in the case of such a pioneering exegete as Pereira, an influential early critic of the Cabbala who was still being celebrated by Richard Simon at the end of the seventeenth century.[17] While they often trumpeted Moses' supposed intellectual capacities, they were more likely to read Aristotelian philosophy into Genesis while explaining away contentious passages as accommodated, rather than actually ask *why* the process of accommodation was required or place Moses in the context of contemporary theological and philosophical culture. This approach filtered into more general natural philosophy textbooks, including those still being used in mid-seventeenth-century England.[18] There was also a more narrowly defined genre of 'Mosaic physics', in which figures such as Otto Casmann,

---

[14] Hermann Conring, *De Hermetica Aegyptiorum vetere et Paracelsicorum nova medicina liber unus* (Helmstadt, 1648), and an expanded version: *De hermetica medicina libri duo* (Helmstadt, 1669), discussed briefly but usefully at Siraisi, 'In search of the origins of medicine: Egyptian medicine and Paduan physicians' (2001), 257–9.

[15] As pointed out in Vasoli, *Quasi sit Deus*, 11–50 ('Il mito dei *prisci theologi* come *ideologia* della *renovatio*'); more generally, see Maclean, 'Foucault's Renaissance episteme: an Aristotelian counterblast' (1998).

[16] See Williams, *The common expositor: an account of the commentaries on Genesis, 1527–1633* (1948), which, despite its old-fashioned approach, remains in places wonderfully useful.

[17] See Williams, *Common expositor*, 174–98, esp. 175–6. For the Cabbala, see Blum, 'Benedictus Pererius critico della magia e della cabala' (2007); Richard Simon, *Histoire critique du vieux testament* (Paris, 1680 [1st edn=1678]), 475 (=*A critical history of the Old Testament*, trans. [H. Dickinson] (London, 1682), III, 84. For this translation, see p. 191, n. 400).

[18] See e.g. Wendelin, *Contemplationes physicae*, 30a, discussing the relationship between the Mosaic chaos and Aristotelian prime matter. See also Thomas White, *Institutionum peripateticarum ad mentem summi viri clarissimique philosophi Kenelmi Equitis Digbaei, pars*

Johann Heinrich Alsted, Conrad Aslacus, and most famously Johannes Amos Comenius based their natural philosophy on scriptural passages that described natural objects; as one might expect, the practical results of this approach were limited.[19]

Moreover, the humanist approach to ancient Egypt was not limited to neoplatonic mysticism. Some of the key rediscovered ancient sources did indeed encourage esoteric readings of the indecipherable hieroglyphs – most importantly, Horapollo's *Hieroglyphica* – or of ancient Egyptian religion – Plutarch's *Isis and Osiris* and Macrobius's *Saturnalia*. Yet other texts offered much more rounded pictures: Pliny's *Natural history*, Apuleius's *Metamorphoses*, the works of Josephus (with the extremely important surviving fragments of the 'History of Egypt' of Manetho), Herodotus's *Histories*, and perhaps the most frequently used source on Egypt, the *Bibliotheca* of Diodorus Siculus.[20] Just as importantly, the antiquarian approach that had been developed in other fields was also applied to Egypt: travellers brought back not only reports of pyramids and crocodiles but also actual fragments of mummies, whose medicinal values were reported as late as Boyle.[21] John Greaves's sceptical attitude to narratives of grand esoteric Egyptian wisdom was partly an inheritance of these more sober approaches.[22] The obelisks which had been brought to imperial Rome still survived – particularly prominent after the vast project of urban renewal initiated by Sixtus V (Pope 1585–90) – and were a source for speculation on Egypt's past from the time of Niccolo Niccoli (1364–1437) and Leon Battista Alberti (1404–72).[23] A large antiquarian literature on hieroglyphic symbolism developed; in the hands of Michele Mercati (*Degli obelischi di Roma* [1589]) and Lorenzo Pignoria (*Vetussimae tabulae explicatio* [1605]), fantastic speculation gave way to a cautious attitude which, while acknowledging that the hieroglyphs probably hid great wisdom, refused to speculate on its contents, preferring more prosaic analysis.[24] The new critical northern humanism challenged the textual sources for the

---

*theorica: item appendix theologica de origine mundi* (London, 1647), 1–60 (2nd pagination) (=*Peripaticall Institutions* (London, 1656), 345–430). On White, see 4.4, 5.3 below.

[19] Blair, 'Mosaic Physics', esp. 52 on its limitations; Crowther, 'The Mosaic physics of Levinus Lemnius (1505–1568) and Francisco Valles (1524–1592)' (2008). This was recognised as a separate genre in mid-century England: see John Prideaux, *Hypomnemata logica, rhetorica, physica, metaphysica, pneumatica, ethica, politica, oeconomica* (Oxford, 1650), 215–19.

[20] Curran, *The Egyptian Renaissance* (2007), 15–26; Stolzenberg, *Kircher*, 41–8; Iversen, *Myth*, 57–123; Dannenfeldt, 'Egypt and the Egyptian antiquities in the Renaissance' (1959), at 8–9; see also Allen, 'The predecessors of Champollion' (1960).

[21] El Daly, 'Mummies as medicine' (2000); Dannenfeldt, 'Egypt', 16–21; Shalev, 'Greaves'.

[22] See 2.2 above.

[23] Curran, 'The Renaissance afterlife of ancient Egypt' (2003), 105; Curran and Grafton, 'A fifteenth-century site report on the Vatican obelisk' (1995); Allen, *Mysteriously meant* (1970), 111–12.

[24] Stolzenberg, *Kircher*, 45–6; Mulsow, 'Antiquarianism', esp. 187–97.

neoplatonic-philosophical reading of Egypt. Scaliger, for example, was sceptical about stories of great ancient Egyptian wisdom – and the Cabbala that was
used to support them – as early as the 1570s.[25] This trend found its apogee in
Isaac Casaubon's famous denunciation of the *Hermetica* as a late forgery in
1614,[26] which we now know was the culmination of a process that had been
ongoing since the mid-sixteenth century.[27] This was a scepticism born out of a
general mistrust of the products of Hellenistic historiography, ranging roughly
from the *Letter of Aristeas* to Eusebius; the importance of this source-critical
scepticism will be a constant theme in this and other chapters. Nonetheless, the
vision of esoteric Egyptian wisdom lived on, most prominently in the 1650s
works of Athanasius Kircher. Until recently, these were dismissed as a particularly spectacular example of outdated Renaissance neoplatonic folly; recent
work, especially by Daniel Stolzenberg, has taught us that Kircher should be
seen as combining the philosophical and antiquarian approaches to Egyptian
history that had characterised the previous centuries.[28] We shall find that the
English reception of Kircher was similarly dual-faced.

## 3.2 The turn to history

As this brief account shows, it is important to note the variety of genres in
which Egyptian or Mosaic philosophy could be discussed: technical biblical
commentary, apologetics, natural philosophy and metaphysics, and late humanist antiquarianism. Approaches differed significantly and delineating a single
narrative is somewhat risky. Some of the most interesting developments
occurred when conclusions from one genre were imported into another.

In England, a key stage was the early to mid-seventeenth-century shift to a
more historical approach to the Old Testament. From the late sixteenth century
to the 1640s, the dominant approach to the scriptural text was still one that can
loosely be described as inspired by Reformed theology, especially by the
doctrines of total inspiration of the scriptures and scripture as its own interpreter. The consequence was an emphasis on God – rather than on any historical
human agent like Moses – and on theological exposition that searched for
interrelations between the passage under discussion and other passages,

---

[25] Grafton, 'Rhetoric, philology and Egyptomania in the 1570s' (1979), esp. 189; Dijkstra,
'Mysteries of the Nile? Joseph Scaliger and ancient Egypt' (2009). This scepticism was well
familiar to Englishmen with a casual interest in ancient history: see e.g. the mid-1650s commonplace book at Folger, MS V.b.15, p. 162.

[26] Grafton, 'Protestant versus prophet: Isaac Casaubon on Hermes Trismegistus' (1983), now
supplemented by Grafton and Weinberg, *Casaubon*, 30–42.

[27] See the essays in Mulsow, ed., *Das Ende*.

[28] Stolzenberg, *Kircher*. The revisionist approach to Kircher began in earnest with Iversen, *Myth*,
92–102. For the limits of Kircher's Coptic – in which he believed he had found the key to
deciphering the hieroglyphys – see Hamilton, *The Copts and the West* (2006).

especially in the New Testament.[29] As the Separatist minister Henry Ainsworth (1569–1622) put it in his popular *Annotations* (1616), upon Genesis, 'The things which Moses wrote, were not his owne, but the Law of the Lord by his hand'.[30] This did not imply a lack of philological skill: Ainsworth was one of the leading Hebraists of the early seventeenth century and eagerly praised Maimonides as an exegetical guide; but the philology only served as a starting point to establish the precise meaning of words before they were placed in a theological framework.[31] A host of Genesis commentaries published in the 1640s and 1650s – some by even more eminent Hebraists like John Lightfoot and Christopher Cartwright – broadly followed this method.[32] When these works did ask the question of how Moses came to have knowledge of the creation, they tended to answer cautiously that even if he had it by historical tradition, it was supplemented by revelation.[33] While some accounts relied sporadically on accommodationism, it was always God, rather than Moses, who was doing the accommodating.[34] The few attempts to explain Moses' words through natural philosophy did so simply by using Aristotelian categories, without explaining historically what Moses himself might have been doing.[35] And yet, we should not assume that historical questions were entirely foreign to the Reformed tradition. Perhaps the most important Calvinist

---

[29] Muller, *Post-Reformation Reformed dogmatics.* II: *Holy Scripture* (2003), esp. 230–54, 490–502.

[30] Henry Ainsworth, *Annotations upon the first books of Moses* (Amsterdam, 1621 [1st edn=1616]), 'A Preface concerning Moses writings', sig. [A4]ʳ. For the popularity of the *Annotations*, see John Wilkins, *Ecclesiastes, or, a discourse concerning the gift of preaching* (3rd edn, London, 1651 [1st edn=1646]), 43, where it is one of the two 'starred' items on the Pentateuch.

[31] Ainsworth, *Annotations*, sig. [A6]ᵛ. For the purely theological reading of Gen. 1:1, see 1–7.

[32] George Walker, *The history of the creation, as it is written by Moses in the first and second chapters of Genesis, plainly opened and expounded* (London, 1641), 2; John Lightfoot, *A few, and new observations, upon the booke of Genesis* (London, 1642), 1–2; Arthur Jackson, *A help for the understanding of the Holy Scripture . . . the first part. Containing certain short notes of exposition upon the five books of Moses* (Cambridge, 1643); Christopher Cartwright, *Electa thargumico-rabbinica; sive, annotationes in Genesim* (London, 1648), sigs. aʳ–a3ʳ, 1–5; Henry Walker, בראשית *The creation of the world being an exposition on the Hebrew in the first chapter of Genesis* (London, 1649); Benjamin Needler, *Expository notes, with practical observations: towards the opening of the five first chapters of the first book of Moses called Genesis* (London, 1655 [i.e. 1654]); John Richardson, *Choice observations and explanations upon the Old Testament . . . to which are added some further and larger observations of his upon the whole book of Genesis* (London, 1655); John White, *A commentary upon the three first chapters of the first book of Moses called Genesis* (London, 1656). For a later example, see Francis Bampfield, *A grammatical opening of some Hebrew words and phrases in the beginning of the Bible* (London, 1684).

[33] E.g. White, *Commentary*, 2–3.

[34] E.g. Jackson, *A help for the understanding*, 1–2, 10; Needler, 'Directions for the right understanding of the Scriptures', in *Expository notes*, 264; Richardson, *Choice observations*, commentary on Gen. 3:24.

[35] E.g. Walker, *The history of creation*, 11–12; Lightfoot, *Observations*, 1–2; Richardson, *Choice observations*, commentary on Gen. 1:1.

Genesis commentary in Europe – widely used in England – André Rivet's *Theologicae et scholasticae exercitationes ... in Genesin* (1633), while devoting almost all its discussion of Gen. 1:1 to the question of whether it adumbrated the trinity (by comparison with John 1:1), at least acknowledged that it was 'another question' – that is, a historical one – whether the Jews for whom Moses wrote could have understood the text in the same way.[36] Calvinist exegetes were not unaware of the historical setting of scripture but for the most part they sought to deal with statements applied to specific 'subject, time, place or persons' by 'sort[ing]' them through the 'art of analysing' (i.e. logic), as explained in the equally popular *Annotationes in Biblia* (1607) by the Genevan Calvinist Giovanni Diodati.[37]

Just as important, historical interpretations of the Pentateuch and of Moses as an author had long been available, spurred on by the famous controversy over the Hebrew vowel points.[38] Some of the Jesuit Genesis commentaries that engaged with such issues were certainly circulating in English pedagogical circles by mid-century – particularly popular was the *Pentateuchus Moysis commentario illustratus* (1625) by Jacobus Bonfrerius (Jacques Bonfrère).[39] Reformed theologians like Cartwright were also familiar with the more widely available rabbinic literature such as Menasseh ben Israel's popular *De creatione problemata XXX* (1635), which discussed extensively the nature of Moses's knowledge of the creation; they simply chose not to deploy these more historical discussions in their own works.[40]

---

[36] André Rivet, *Theologicae et scholasticae exercitationes CXC in Genesin* (Leiden, 1633), 3–12 (Gen 1:1) at 6a ('Concludiamus ergo apud Mosem & Joannem, principii vocem eodem sensu accipi, & ex utroque conjunctim necessarium duci argumentum pro Christi Deitate ... Sed quamvis illud argumentum solidum sit, ex collatione & conjunctione dictorum Mosis & Joannis, quod apud eos qui novum Testamentum recipiunt magni ponderis esse debet: alia quaestio est, an ex hisce Mosis verbis seorsim sumptis, ubi adversus Judaeos, qui Mosem recipiunt, & novum Testamentum abjiciunt agendum est, possit firmum argumentum deduci, quo Trinitas personarum in divinis possit sufficienter probari?'). Rivet answered that they could, on the basis of the Cabbala (6a–b). For Rivet's favour among English Presbyterians in the 1640s, see Mortimer, *Reason and religion in the English revolution* (2010), 108–10. For the popularity of his Genesis commentary, see Wilkins, *Ecclesiastes*, 44, where it is a starred item on the reading list for Genesis. For an equally Reformed list of recommended expositors of Genesis (Rivet, Pareus, Calvin, Peter Martyr, Willet, Ainsworth), see Edward Leigh, *A treatise of divinity* (London, 1646), 48.

[37] Giovanni Diodati, *Pious annotations, upon the Holy Bible* (London, 1643), sig. [A6]ʳ. See further sig. [A6]ᵛ for the importance of establishing definitions, and sig. [A7]ʳ, 1–2 for a theological exposition of Genesis on the basis of Moses's direct inspiration. The original is *Annotationes in Biblia* (Geneva, 1607).

[38] Muller, 'The debate over the vowel points and the crisis in orthodox hermeneutics' (1980); Malcolm, *Aspects*, 383–431 ('Hobbes, Ezra, and the Bible: the history of a subversive idea'), at 415–18.

[39] See e.g. Jacobo Bonfrerio, *Pentateuchus Moysis commentario illustratus* (Antwerp, 1625), 95 (on Gen. 1:1), also recommended in Wilkins, *Ecclesiastes*, 43.

[40] Menasseh ben Israel, *De creatione problemata XXX* (Amsterdam, 1635), esp. 24–8; Cartwright cites Menasseh at *Electa thargumico-rabbinica*, 8. Menasseh's huge importance in European

However, something of a revolution was occurring. As part of the drive away from continental Reformed theology (see 1.3 above), the biblical criticism of the deprived episcopalian divines became far more overtly anti-Calvinist, and far more openly historical. They drew on the work of the Oratorian Jean Morin, the Huguenot Louis Cappel (who had spent two years at Oxford), and the Leiden professor Daniel Heinsius and his friend Hugo Grotius, who promoted historical readings of the Bible that (speaking rather generally) forsook the doctrine of the immediate divine revelation of the whole of scripture in favour of textual history and a focus on the historical intentionality behind specific passages, while attempting to maintain the theological value of their commentaries by reconfiguring the use of typological exegesis.[41] This is not to say that their interest manifested itself in the directly 'historical' questions of Mosaic intentionality that will concern us below: the two greatest products of this movement – the London Polyglot (1657) edited by Brian Walton and the *Critici Sacri* (1660), a nine-volume compilation of biblical commentaries published by John Pearson – were most concerned with questions of textual transmission and historical comparison of various versions (Masoretic, Septuagint, Samaritan, etc.).[42] But Grotius's *Annotationes in Vetus Testamentum* (1644–50) (reprinted in the *Critici Sacri*) in particular, with their constant comparison of Judaism with contemporary paganism,[43] shaped the approach of the next generation of clerical exegetes.[44]

scholarly circles deserves more attention; for a start, see the essays in Kaplan et al., eds., *Menasseh ben Israel and his world* (1989). See also 3.4 below.

[41] See Nellen, 'Growing tension between church doctrines and critical exegesis' (2008), esp. 808–16; van Rooden, *Rabbinical studies, passim*, esp. 49–93; Drouin, *L'exégèse allégorique à l'âge des Lumières* (2010), esp. 99–109, whose readings of Grotius as highly iconoclastic are tempered by Hardy, '*Ars critica*', 186–93. For the reception of Grotius's commentaries in England, see Mortimer, *Reason and religion*, 122–3, 145, 153–4, 209, 215–16; and more generally Barducci, 'Political and ecclesiological contexts for the early English translations of Grotius's *De Veritate*' (2012); Barducci, 'Clement Barksdale, translator of Grotius', *The Seventeenth Century*, 25 (2010); for the reception of Heinsius, see Sellin, *Daniel Heinsius and Stuart England* (1968) (with the additions at Hardy, '*Ars critica*', 195); see also Hardy, '*Ars critica*', 201, 203–8 on the Anglo-Irish response to Morin, especially that of Ussher.

[42] Brian Walton, 'Prolegomena', in *S. S. Biblia sacra polyglotta*, I; *Critici sacri: sive doctissimorum virorum in SS. Biblia annotationes, & tractatus*, ed. J. Pearson (9 vols, London 1660). On the English polyglot, see Miller, 'Antiquarianisation'; Keene, 'Critici Sacri: biblical criticism in England c. 1650–1710' (2004), 57–115 (although I cannot agree that the Polyglot had much to do with an 'orthodox counter-attack' on Hobbes [57]). Pearson's own views – including his high estimation of Cappel and Morin – are best represented in his 'Praefatio Paraenetica', in *Η Παλαιά Διαθήκη κατά τους Εβδομήκοντα Vetus Testamentum Graecum ex versione Septuaginta interpretum* (Cambridge, 1665), 1–19. See further Mandelbrote, 'Authority'.

[43] Laplanche, 'Grotius et les religions du paganisme dans les *Annotationes in Vetus Testamentum*' (1994).

[44] As revealed, for example, by the divinity lectures of Joseph Beaumont, Regius Professor of Divinity in Cambridge from 1674: see Tyacke, *Aspects*, 330. See also the notes on Judaism in CUL MS Add. 8861[3], *c.* 1660? many of them taken from Cappel, Scaliger, and

As an addendum, it is worth noting that this kind of scholarship was extremely sceptical about the historical claims of the Cabbala. In part this was a coincidental consequence of another debate, for the *Zohar*'s discussions of the vowel points made it tempting for opponents of Masoretic purity to classify it as late pseudepigrapha;[45] more generally it was part of a trend of anti-Cabbalism that had been evident in the works both of leading Christian scholars like Scaliger and Casaubon[46] and of some high-profile anti-Cabbalistic Jews, like Leon Modena (1571–1648).[47] This anti-Cabbalism is visible in a strong denunciation in Walton's 'Prolegomena' to the London Polyglot; as we shall see, it would come to shape much of English attitudes towards narratives of ancient Jewish or Egyptian wisdom.[48]

## 3.3    Scientists confront scripture I

Before the impact of this move could be felt, the debate over 'Mosaic philosophy' had already manifested itself in natural philosophical discussion. Galileo had used the Augustinian accommodationist hermeneutic to defend heliocentricism against the strictures of the Roman church, especially in his *Letter to the Grand Duchess Christina* (1615, first printed 1636).[49] Certainly, no such dramatic interventions were required in England, where heliocentricism was gradually accepted, including at an institutional level.[50] Nonetheless, one prominent defence was penned by John Wilkins, the doyen of mid-century science whose deep interest in the history of philosophy we have encountered already (2.4 above). Wilkins's heliocentricism was attacked by Alexander Ross, a dogmatic Aristotelian whose wide-ranging publications still displayed a good level of familiarity with contemporary erudition, not least in the sphere

Johannes Leusden's *Philologus Hebraeus* (1656), which are a perfect demonstration that neither Spinoza nor Simon were requisite for advanced historical speculation on the biblical Israelites, including on the authorship of the Pentateuch (8). See also CUL MS Dd.4.52 ('Loci communes theologiae', mid-century), fols. 15ᵛ–16ʳ, entry headed 'An Hebraica Biblia corrupta sunt. Bellarm[ine]'. See also Richard Kidder, *A commentary on the five books of Moses: with a dissertation concerning the author or writer of the said books* (London, 1694), which, while generally defensive (xxiv identifies Hobbes, La Peyrère, and Spinoza as his main opponents) is constantly historical in approach (see esp. lv–lvii), and insists that Moses, rather than God, was doing the accommodating (iv; and see the exuberant praise of Maimonides at sig. bᵛ).

[45] Blau, *Cabala*, 108–9, on Cappel.

[46] For Casaubon, see Grafton and Weinberg, *Casaubon*, 89–92; for Scaliger, see n. 25 above.

[47] Dweck, *Scandal*.

[48] Walton, 'Prolegomena VIII' (separate pagination), in *Biblia sacra polyglotta*, 52b–54b; see also Walton, *Considerator considered*, 38–9, 239, 246. On a more popular level, see e.g. John Gaule, *Pus-mantia the mag-astro-mancer, or, the magicall-astrologicall-diviner posed, and puzzled* (London, 1652), 3, attributing the invention of allegorical–astrological readings of Genesis to the Cabbalists (Gaule was a royalist minister: Clark, 'Gaule, John', *ODNB*).

[49] For a starting point, see Finocchiaro, 'The biblical argument against Copernicanism and the limitation of biblical authority' (2008).

[50] For this, see Feingold, *The mathematicians' apprenticeship* (1984), 16.

of Genesis exegesis.[51] Ross's *Commentum de terrae motu circulari* (1634) was directed against defenders of heliocentricism, both continental (especially Johan Philip Lansberge) and English (especially Nathaniel Carpenter), on the basis of Aristotelian natural philosophy and biblical authority.[52]

As the debate had been raging in Europe for some time, Ross could deploy a host of heavyweight Jesuit Aristotelians to his cause.[53] Yet he was particularly keen to defend the proposition that scripture reveals natural philosophical truth, leading him to make two claims relevant to us. The first was that Pythagoras was a dangerous charlatan and necromancer. Copernicus had famously presented his own view as 'Pythagorean', and Ross was at pains to show the dangers of the Pythagorean tradition; rather inconsistently he also claimed that there were no ancient sources which confirmed that Pythagoras himself had held heliocentrism.[54] More important was his claim that accommodationism, and the belief that Scripture speaks only 'ad vulgi captum', was a dangerous conceit.[55] Scripture was full of natural truths, as revealed by the history of philosophy, for if it had not been Moses who had given astronomy to the Egyptians, it must have been one of the earlier figures from sacred history, whether Abraham, Jacob, or Joseph, in the same way that Daniel taught it to the Chaldeans.[56] In short, Ross believed in the great philosophical proficiency of the early Jews and that this in turn proved the usefulness of scripture to natural philosophy.[57]

---

[51] Alexander Ross, *The first booke of questions and answers upon Genesis* (London, 1620) (2–3 for a defence of geocentricism); interestingly, the work was dedicated to Bacon. See also his *Rerum Judaicarum memorabiliorum* (4 vols, London, 1617–32). Ross (1591–1654) was educated in Aberdeen; he became master of Southampton grammar school in 1616, and chaplain to Prince Charles in 1622. Allan, 'Ross, Alexander', *ODNB* is somewhat unreliable, misdating the *Questions* and claiming that Ross attacked Spinoza [!], and that he received patronage from Laud, a claim then disputed in Allan, 'Alexander Ross and the defence of philosophy' (2001), 72. The latter receives further correction in Malcolm, 'The 1649 English translation of the Koran' (2012), 268, n. 28; this article also demonstrates that Ross was probably not the translator of the 1649 Qur'an, to which he added a short dissertation, and that far from being 'high Laudian', he happily espoused Calvinist theology and accommodated himself to Presbyterian ecclesiology (266–72). Johns, 'Prudence and pedantry in early modern cosmology: the trade of Al Ross' (1997), adopts a sociological reading which is somewhat blighted by mistaken assumptions about Ross's allegiances (esp. at 23–4).

[52] McColley, 'The Ross-Wilkins controversy' (1938), remains the most useful (if highly whiggish) introduction to the debate.

[53] See e.g. Alexander Ross, *Commentum de terrae motu circulari* (London, 1634), 9, citing Zabarella and Pereira.

[54] Ross, *Commentum*, 62 (the key source for Pythagoras as necromancer is Augustine, *Civ. Dei*, VII.35, cited by Ross, but followed by 'Sed mihi videmini vigilantes somniare, nam nec Laertius, nec ullus altius vetustus scriptor quem ego legerim, quique de vita & dogmate Pythagorae scripserunt, hoc phantasma illi adscribunt: quin contrarium censisse [sic] videtur senex Samius, dum ex conversione orbium quandam harmoniam fingit'). See also Ross, *The new planet no planet* (London, 1646), 6–7.

[55] Ross, *Commentum*, 16–21.    [56] Ibid., 17.

[57] See further his later reply to Wilkins, *New planet*, 44: 'If the Gentile Philosophers had not found much Philosophy in Scripture, they had never conveighed so much out of it, (as they did) into their Philosophicall books'. This perspective may partly explain Ross's fondness for Walter

Wilkins responded, implicitly and explicitly, in *The discovery of a world in the moone* (1638) and *A Discourse concerninge a new planet* (1640) respectively. These works are often described as 'populist', because they were written in English, and because of the seemingly fantastic subject matter of the first, leading to comparisons with Francis Godwin's utopian fiction, *The man in the moone* (1638).[58] But these texts are perhaps better read as the first public ventures into natural philosophy of a recent graduate (Wilkins had graduated MA in 1634 and stayed on as a tutor at Magdalen Hall, Oxford until 1637): they are packed with references to reading among the ancients and their commentators and are a fine example of how a standard university education, rich in humanism, could produce one of the most important patrons of 'new' natural philosophy in seventeenth-century England. As we have seen, Wilkins explicitly insisted on the importance of the study of the history of philosophy for improving the modern-day discipline.

Indeed, these early works contain less natural philosophy and more humanism and biblical exegesis. For example, Wilkins suggested that the weakness of Aristotle's arguments for geocentricism and only one inhabitable world stemmed from his desire to impress his patron Alexander the Great, who despaired at the possibility of other worlds when he had not yet managed to conquer one.[59] His key argument, however, was that scripture had nothing to do with philosophy. Again and again, he insisted that its words were accommodated to the capacities of its original audience, citing a huge range of authorities, from Aquinas to Calvin, to more recent Jesuit commentators, to defenders of heliocentricism, and especially Augustine's *De Genesi at litteram*.[60] All this, he argued, was confirmed by the history of philosophy. In a neat argument, Wilkins suggested that scripture did not mention heliocentricism *because* it had not yet been discovered by Pythagoras.[61] More importantly, he argued that there was no evidence for the philosophical accomplishments of Moses or the ancient Jews more generally; the only time they were 'supernaturally indowed with humane Learning' was when divine providence required 'particular ends': the apostles were given the knowledge of languages so they could evangelise; Moses might have been knowledgeable in the learning of the Egyptians (Acts 7.22), but that learning was only

Raleigh's *History* (see 2.1 above): see *The marrow of historie* (London, 1650) (Raleigh's *History* abridged by Ross); Alexander Ross, *The history of the world the second part* ... *being a continuation of the famous history of Sir Walter Raleigh* (London, 1652).

[58] For Wilkins's later reading of Godwin's work and connections between them, see Poole, 'Introduction' (2009), 45–9.

[59] [Wilkins], *Discovery*, 24–8; the source for Alexander's despair is Plutarch, *De tranquilitate animi*, IV.1. For the tradition of ascribing errors in Aristotle's philosophy to the influence of Alexander, see 4.1 below.

[60] [Wilkins], *Discovery*, 36–9; [Wilkins], *A Discourse concerning a new planet* (London, 1640), 1–12, 10–14, 30–5, 46–61.

[61] [Wilkins], *Discourse*, 61.

'imperfect'; Job was 'strangely gifted with all kinde of knowledge' only to teach the moral lesson of its vanity (Eccl. 1:18), but even he could not answer the basic natural philosophical questions God set him.[62] The whole idea of ancient Jewish wisdom and biblical philosophy was a rabbinic fable; it had misled many of the church fathers, but was now the preserve of a 'Rabbi or Chymicke'.[63]

These last words remind us of Bacon, but Wilkins, as befitting a recent university graduate with an eye on a clerical career, seems to have been much more widely informed about the relevant textual traditions; when mocking the Cabbala, for example, he cited the *Bechinath Happeruschim* (1624) of the influential German Hebraist Wilhelm Schickard.[64] Wilkins's positing of accommodationism and Judaic primitiveness against narratives of a great Hebraic philosophical past in many ways foreshadows the conclusions that were to be developed in England over the next half-century; it is fair to say that his complete denial of Hebrew philosophical accomplishment was one of the most radical published in the seventeenth century. And yet it lies somewhat to the side of the subsequent debate, for two reasons. First, it was published before the impact of Hebrew biblical commentary had fully been felt in England; as we shall see, Maimonidean accommodationism led to a significantly more 'historical' picture than the Augustinian variety – Wilkins was still anchored in the textual resources of late-scholastic Genesis commentary. More importantly, Wilkins, for all his personal moderation and willingness to accommodate to ecclesiological circumstance, was (at least at this point) theologically within the Reformed tradition; consequently, he was more or less uninterested in historical arguments about Mosaic intentionality, because for him it was not Moses but the Holy Spirit that was doing the accommodating.[65] However, from the 1650s a new focus developed on Moses himself as a historical figure.

### 3.4     Henry More and the non-existence of 'Cambridge Platonism'

This occurred, as I have suggested, under the influence of Anglican investment in continental humanist modes of exegesis. It was shared by some figures who have traditionally been classed as 'Cambridge Platonists'. This label has been

---

[62] Ibid., 10–14.

[63] [Wilkins], *Discovery*, 120–1; see also 39–40; [Wilkins], *Discourse*, 28–9, 55, 77–88.

[64] [Wilkins], *Discourse*, 77–80. For Schickard's learned discussion of the Cabbala, see הפירושים בחינת *Bechinath Happeruschim, hoc est examinis commentationum Rabbinicarum in Mosen prodromus* (Tübingen, 1624), 60–79, which is critical without being entirely dismissive, but does conclude (61) that 'hodie à Judaeastris in superstitiosum Abusum tracta, & partim in inania mysteria puerilesque nugas conversa, partim ad Medicinam, Incantationes adeòque Magiam (ignoratae veriori Cabalae, ab ipsis perfidè substitutam) turpiter abrepta'. For his fame as a Hebraist in England, see Nelson, *The Hebrew republic* (2010), 40–3.

[65] Wilkins, *Discovery*, 39; [Wilkins], *Discourse*, 10, 30–1, 46–7, 61. See also *Ecclesiastes* [1646 edn], 9, 25, for insistence on the key Reformed exegetical principle of *analogia fidei*.

somewhat misguiding in its implication that members of the group shared a vision of the history of philosophy.[66] Examining them individually reveals a rather more nuanced state of affairs.

One of the oldest members of the putative group, Nathaniel Culverwell, in his *Discourse of the light of nature* (written in the late 1640s as a set of lectures on Proverbs 20:27 but published posthumously in 1652 by his brother and by William Dillingham, a contemporary at Emmanuel College), does indeed include a theme that was typical of his Cambridge colleagues: the use of reason in religion, where that reason was defended, from the Proverbs passage, as 'the candle of the lord'. This was understood as the ability of the rational soul to partake in the divine understanding, presented as a *via media* between the illuminationism of the sectarians and the mechanistic ratiocination of the Socinians.[67] But there was little 'Platonic' about this claim, which was grounded in traditional scholastic ideas (albeit stripped of the epistemological superstructure of intelligible species, etc.).[68] And so we should not be surprised by the fact that Culverwell actually rejected 'Platonic' views of the history of philosophy. The idea that philosophy had to have Judaic origins was, for him, a Jewish fabrication that resembled the irrational claims of the Calvinists to the exclusivity of divine light: the Jews 'imagine and suppose that the light of *Nature* shines only upon themselves originally and principally, and upon the Gentiles only by way of Participation and dependence upon them: They all must light their candles at the Jewish lamp'.[69] The traditional stories of Pythagoras and Plato taking from the Jews, and even of Aristotle having lectures read to him by the high priest Simeon, were all rabbinic 'pretty stor[ies]'.[70] Culverwell's key source here was evidently John Selden, who although sometimes partial to finding Judaic origins for Pythagorean ideas,

---

[66] See e.g. Hutton, 'Decline', esp. 69 ('As with other liberal theologians of the Renaissance, the particular synthesis of pagan philosophy and Christianity which the Cambridge Platonists adopted was that known now as the *prisca theologia*, the ancient theology'); Goldie, 'The Cambridge Platonists' (they believed in 'pure original truth, which Moses had possessed, and which had passed from him to the Egyptians and thence to Plato and the Greeks'); Harrison, *Religion, passim*; Webster, *Great instauration*, 145; see further 1.3 above.

[67] William Dillingham, 'To the reader', in Nathanial Culverwell, *An elegant and learned discourse of the light of nature* (London, 1652), sig. A4ᵛ (publication details); 7, 11 (against Socinians and illuminationists). On Culverwell's biography, see Greene and MacCallum, 'Introduction' (1971), now valuably supplemented by Day, 'Nathaniel Culverwell's *Elegant and learned discourse on the light of nature* (1652) in institutional and philosophical context' (2009) (I am extremely grateful to Ms Day for sending me a copy of her work).

[68] See Greene and MacCallum, 'Introduction', xlvii; Greene, 'Whichcote, the candle of the Lord and synderesis' (1991), esp. 632, 640–1, 644; for Culverwell's rejection of innate ideas, direct refutations of Plato and Origen, and explicit belief that Aristotle 'better clarified' the soul's relationship to the divine than Plato, see *Discourse*, 88–94.

[69] Culverwell, *Discourse*, 63. The source for Pythagorean circumcision is Clemens Alexandrinus, *Strom.*, 1.66.2. See also Lagrée, 'Lumière naturelle et notions communes: Herbert de Cherbury et Culverwell' (1996).

[70] Culverwell, *Discourse*, 64–8 (quotation at 66)

had also strongly attacked narratives of Judaic primacy as part of his emphasis on a universal natural law equivalent to the Noachic precepts, and as part of his wider appreciation of the critical methods of Scaliger and Casaubon.[71]

Here, then, we have evidence not only of the variety of views among the Cambridge group, but also of the influence of Christian Hebraist scholarship. This is corroborated by the case of John Smith (1618–52), who like Culverwell had the double misfortune of dying young and of being rather crudely lumped together with his Cambridge counterparts by modern historians. While Smith was employed at Queens' College, Cambridge as a mathematics lecturer, and while he did have some interest in Cartesianism,[72] his one extant (posthumous) publication, the *Select discourses* (1660),[73] based on lectures delivered in the college chapel, is less philosophical and more historical–theological in character, dealing with knowledge of God, superstition, atheism, prophecy, righteousness, and the nature of Satan. Its greatest achievement – at least in the eyes of contemporaries – was the discourse 'On prophecy', which 'cost [Smith] more pains … than any of the other',[74] for it drew extensively on rabbinic commentaries, especially Maimonides, to provide perhaps the most detailed mid-century discussion on the epistemological differences between natural reason, divine inspiration, and enthusiasm, again posited against the dual threats of illuminationism and Socinianism.[75]

As for his view on the history of philosophy, Smith's few surviving manuscript notes show him to have had an interest in Egypt,[76] but in the *Discourses* he expressed no high opinion of ancient Egyptian or Jewish philosophy. Instead, he attacked the Cabbalistic–allegorical reading of Genesis, abusing Philo Judaeus for 'sailing between Cabbalisme and Platonisme [and] grop[ing] after an Allegorical and Mystical meaning' in the words of Moses.[77] In this, he was not saying

---

[71] See p. 148 below.

[72] Saveson, 'Descartes' influence on John Smith' (1959); Saveson, 'Differing reactions to Descartes among the Cambridge Platonists' (1960), at 564–7; challenged by Patrides, 'Introduction' (1979), viii. Also Hutton, 'Smith, John', *ODNB*.

[73] Brought to the press by John Worthington, another fellow of Emmanuel, who divided the work into the 'Discourses' it appears in (Worthington, 'To the reader', in John Smith, *Select discourses* (London, 1660), v). Worthington, interestingly, *did* believe in the philosophical accomplishments of Moses: see p. x (citing Josephus).

[74] Worthington, 'To the reader', xxii. Jean Le Clerc – hardly a fan of Platonism – liked Smith's discourse so much that he translated and included it in his *Veteris testamenti prophetae … cum ejusdem commentario philologico et paraphrasi* (Amsterdam, 1731). It is worth noting that despite Smith's reputation as a forefather of 'liberal' theology, Oxford sacerdotalists also happily cited the *Select Discourses* (e.g. Henry Dodwell, 'An answer to six queries proposed to a *gentlewoman* of the Church of England, by an emissary of the Church of ROME, fitted to a gentlewomans capacity' (separate pagination), in *Two short discourses against the Romanists* (London, 1676), 268).

[75] Smith, *Select discourses*, 169–284; see also discourses vi and viii for further displays of Smith's Hebraic erudition (esp. 288–307). That erudition is also evinced by the books Smith bequeathed to Queens', a catalogue of which is available in the College Library.

[76] See the surviving commonplace book, CUL MS Dd.9.44, e.g. fol. $2^r$ for an Egyptian dynasty list, and fol. $130^v$ for notes from Diodorus Siculus.

[77] Smith, *Discourses*, 186.

anything different than his older Cambridge colleague Benjamin Whichcote, who recorded in his commonplace book that Philo derived his absurd allegorical method from reading too much Plato, and virulently condemned the Platonists' view on the soul and their tendency, adopted by 'Some of the Ancient Jewes ... & some later writers among Chr[i]s[tia]ns' to believe that 'Man was Created a Kind of Hermaphrodite': in the latter group he placed such notorious Renaissance neoplatonists as Steuco and Francisco Giorgi.[78]

Unlike Whichcote, Smith was familiar with Cabbalistic authors, and even knew the *Zohar*; although he believed it to be 'one of the ancientest monuments we have of the Jewish learning', he nonetheless saw it as a mystical justification for the barren legalism ('legal righteousness') of Judaism which was opposed by Paul (as reported in Acts).[79] Instead, Maimonides taught him that scripture was accommodated to the vulgar, revealing '*Moral* and *Theological*', rather than '*Philosophical* or *Physical*' truths.[80] Some pagans had 'partake[n] of the Divine Nature' by purifying their souls in the same way as Christ but this was not a skill derived from the Hebrews or in any way connected to the sacred tradition. Rather, it was developed independently, as was evident from the *paideiai* they had their students undertake: Pythagoras did not initiate his students into 'the sublimer Mysteries of Philosophy' until they had proved the '*sedateness* and *Moral* temper of their Minds'; the Platonists thought 'the Mindes of men could never be purg'd enough from those earthly dregs of Sense and Passion' before they proceeded to the study of 'their divine *Metaphysics*'; Aristotle forbade the study of moral philosophy until 'the heat and violent precipitancy of his youthful affections was cool'd and moderated'; all insisted on the importance of mathematics as a spiritual exercise by which 'the Souls of men might farther shake off their dependency upon Sense'.[81]

This group of Cambridge scholars, then, had rejected the syncretist reading of the history of philosophy: none of them believed in any great Mosaic wisdom, and all were sceptical of the Cabbala and similar stories of transmission from Jews to Greeks. Concomitantly, Henry More – who *did* believe in what he called a 'philosophical Cabbala' – is an idiosyncratic case, as he is on so many other issues.[82] More's argument, as it was developed in the *Conjectura Cabbalistica* (1653) and its defences, an 'Appendix to the Philosophick Cabbala' (in the *Collection of several philosophical writings* (1662) and the 'Apology' printed in

---

[78] Folger MS V.a.326, fol. 45$^r$ rev. (my foliation) (Philo), 45$^v$–46$^r$ rev. (Steuco and Giorgi). Giorgi (1466–1540) was a Venetian Franciscan and prominent Christian Cabbalist: see Campanini, 'Le fonti ebraiche del *De harmonia mundi* di Francesco Zorzi' (1999).

[79] Smith, *Select Discourses*, 246, 304–7.

[80] Ibid., 172 (then quoting *Guide*, I.26 (Pines, I, 56)), 171–86.

[81] Smith, *Discourses*, 10. For Aristotle on moral philosophy, see *Nic. Eth.*, I, 1095$^a$2, an early modern commonplace (e.g. Shakespeare, *Troilus and Cressida*, II.2).

[82] Although the only modern scholar adequately recognising More's idiosyncrasy is A. R. Hall, in his *Henry More: magic, religion and experiment* (1990), 127.

the *Modest enquiry into the mystery of iniquity* (1664)), is simply summarised. Genesis could be subjected to a tripartite reading: literal (the 'Literal Cabbala'), natural philosophical and metaphysical (the 'Philosophick Cabbala'), and mystical (the 'Moral Cabbala'). The second of these Cabbalas was illuminated by the history of philosophy: Descartes had revived Democriteanism; Democritus had inherited the physical parts of Pythagoreanism; Pythagoras had taken from Egyptians who had been influenced by Judaism, or from the Jews directly, and the Jewish account was originally Mosaic. This, then, was an argument for Mosaic primacy.[83] Despite calling his scheme a 'Cabbala', More was completely unfamiliar with the *Zohar* or any other real Cabbalistic material.[84] In Part III of the *Principia philosophiae* (1644), Descartes had offered a hypothetical cosmology based on his own physical principles; although he had stressed that this was only a thought experiment, a host of his followers attempted actually to read Cartesianism into Genesis.[85] In the late 1640s and early 1650s, More was still in his enthusiastically pro-Cartesian phase and became the first Englishman to attempt such a marriage,[86] although his own 'philosophical' re-telling of Genesis was far more elaborate than Descartes's: *creatio ex nihilo* of immaterial substance only (the first day), the ordering of the material potentiality of this substance (day two), and the creation of the 'reall material Earth' (day three), the celestial bodies (day four), animals (five), and man (six).[87] This obviously differed hugely from the actual text, and so the 'literal' (or 'historical') Cabbala was an accommodation to the capacities of the vulgar in which Moses spoke not of the *mundus philosophorum* but the *mundus plebeiorum*.[88]

How did More arrive at and justify his historical thesis? It is not the case that More was just another Renaissance theorist of *prisca theologia*; nor is it the case that his historical scheme was, like Descartes's, a fiction that was not

---

[83] It is thus not quite right that More argued 'for the priority and purity of pagan revelation' (Grafton, *Defenders*, 18). More believed that God had first revealed the Cabbala to Adam, and then again to Moses on Sinai: *Conjectura Cabbalistica or, a conjectural essay of interpreting the minde of Moses* (London, 1653), 85; elsewhere he remained ambiguous on whether Moses had the creation narrative by tradition as well as revelation (136–7).

[84] For the development of More's knowledge of Cabbalistic texts, see Coudert, 'Henry More, the Kabbalah, and the Quakers' (1990); also Hutton, 'Henry More, Anne Conway and the Kabbalah' (1999).

[85] For England, see (taking into account the qualifications below) Harrison, 'The influence of Cartesian cosmology in England' (2000).

[86] Ibid., 169–71. For More and Cartesianism, see Gabbey, 'Philosophia Cartesiana triumphata' (1982), 171–250; Pacchi, *Cartesio in Inghilterra* (1973), 3–48; Webster, 'Henry More and Descartes: some new sources' (1969).

[87] More, *Conjectura*, 22–33. As far as I can tell, the huge idiosyncracy of this Creation narrative has not been recognised in the historiography: while More certainly aligned his account with that of Descartes, it was in many respects very different (I differ on this score from Harrison, 'Cartesian cosmology', 169–70).

[88] These are the terms used in Henry More, 'The apology of Dᵣ. Henry More', in *A modest enquiry into the mystery of iniquity* (London, 1664), 481–567, e.g. 484.

intended to be taken literally.[89] While More did read Ficino in his earliest Platonic phase, during his studies for his MA degree (*c.* 1635),[90] even his earliest philosophical poems already betray little use of the Florentine tradition.[91] On the second score, More was insistent that he *had* discovered a true historical Cabbala, and that the only reason to discuss the Greek philosophers at all was because they offered elucidation on Moses.[92]

More's whole method of scriptural exegesis was entirely different from that of the Renaissance Platonists, drawing on resources unavailable to them; his opinions on the history of philosophy, meanwhile, were at points directly critical of the Renaissance readings, especially concerning the central figure of Pythagoras. There was nothing peculiar about explaining Genesis by means of contemporary natural philosophy, and More was familiar with a large array of scholastic and late humanist Genesis commentators who had done just that.[93] Like them, More resorted extensively to the technique of accommodation to explain why the literal word of scripture did not present directly the philosophical truths hidden within. But unlike them, he went significantly further in distancing the accommodated sense from the philosophical one, by combining the accommodationist hermeneutic with an esoteric-'Cabbalistic' one. Certainly, More often spoke in traditional terms of the literal sense still being phenomenalistically 'true': 'the very Letter of the History is true, though delivered with due advantages to ... the Vulgar Apprehension ... so that there is not the least clash ... betwixt the *Historical* Cabbala and *Philosophical*'.[94] But More wanted to have his cake and eat it. For as well as claiming that scripture contained an esoteric philosophy, he also claimed, like Wilkins, that the literal sense was entirely *un*philosophical:

And by the [literal Cabbala] there is a very charitable provision made for them that are so prone to expect rigid precepts of Philosophy in Moses his outward Text. For this Literal Cabbala will steer them off from that toil of endevouring to make the bare letter speak consonantly to the true frame of nature: Which while they attempt with more zeal then knowledge, they both disgrace themselves and wrong Moses ... Wherefore to men

---

[89]  The first option is proposed by More's best biographer: Crocker, *More*, 70; see also Hutton, 'Moses atticus', 69–70 among others. The second option is proposed by Peter Harrison in 'Cartesian cosmology', 179.

[90]  Henry More, 'Praefatio generalissima', in *Opera omnia* (London, 1679), vii.

[91]  See the very precise discussion in Jacob, 'Henry More's *Psychodia Platonica* and its Relationship to Marsilio Ficino's *Theologia Platonica*' (1985).

[92]  See e.g. *Conjectura*, sigs. A8$^{r-v}$; 106; 190–1; More, 'Appendix', 126.

[93]  See e.g. the list offered in More, 'Apology', 484, encompassing Rupert Tuitiensis (*c.* 1090–1135), almost certainly known by More through Pereira's *In Genesin* (1606)), Gregory of Valencia, Pereira himself, Augustine, Calvin, François Vatable, Johannes Drusius, Grotius, and Sebastian Castellio (for Castellio's influence on the young More, via More's tutor Robert Gell, see Crocker, *More*, 9–10).

[94]  More, 'Apology', 485. See also More, *Conjectura*, 100–1. Calvin's standard view is then cited at 103.

recovered into a due command of their reason, and well-skill'd in the contemplation and experience of the nature of things, to propound to them such kinde of Mosaical Philosophy, as the boldnesse and superstition of some has adventured to do for want of a right Literal Cabbala to guide them, is as much as in them lies, to hazard the making not only of Moses, but of Religion it self contemptible and ridiculous.[95]

Just before writing the *Conjectura*, More had been involved in a fierce debate with the Welsh royalist mystic, alchemist, and philosopher Thomas Vaughan. Vaughan was much influenced by the alchemical–illuminationist tradition of Cornelius Agrippa (via the work of the Polish alchemist Michael Sendivogius);[96] against this whole tradition, More retorted that reading philosophy into scripture was the preserve of the enthusiast.[97] The philosopher had to free himself from the literal sense: 'the first impressions of the Literal Text, which is so plainly accommodated to the capacity of meer children and Idiots, by reason of custome have so strongly rooted themselves in the minds of some, that they take that sense to be more true, then the true meaning of the text indeed'.[98]

With this juxtaposition of the 'literal' and the 'true' meaning, More seemed to be diverging from the one cornerstone of Protestant hermeneutics: literalism. This idea that the literal text was not quite true at all was exacerbated by More's frequent references to Moses as a 'politician' or 'lawgiver' who had to offer a rival cosmology to that of the Egyptians, with their Isis and Osiris as the sun and the moon: 'this was true and sound Prudence, aiming at nothing but the glory of God, and the good of the poor ignorant people'.[99] Prudence it may have been, but prudence was a long way from truth, and these passages were some of the most attacked by More's many critics (see below).

More's combination of accommodationism and esotericism was novel and a product of specific circumstances, but More himself thought of it as the culmination of a long Jewish exegetical tradition. For accommodationism he cited Maimonides;[100] more important was his source for esoteric exegesis: the first-century Alexandrian Jew Philo Judaeus. We have already seen that More's

---

[95] More, *Conjectura*, sig. B2$^r$.

[96] See Newman, 'Thomas Vaughan as an interpreter of Agrippa von Nettesheim' (1982), repr. in Debus, ed., *Alchemy and early modern chemistry* (2004).

[97] [Henry More], *Observations upon Anthroposophia Theomagica* (London, 1650), 64 ('What profane boldnesse is this to distort that high Majesty of the holy Scripture to such poor and pitifull services, as to decide the controversies of the World and of Nature?'). Vaughan had published under the pseudonym 'Eugenius Philalethes'. More's first attack on him, under the pseudonym 'Alazonomastix Philalethes', was the *Observations*; Vaughan replied with *The man mouse taken in a trap* (London, 1650); More countered with *The second lash* . . . (London, 1651); the final blast was to be Vaughan's in *The moor scour'd again* (London, 1651). On the debate see Burnham, 'The More-Vaughan controversy' (1974); Guinsburg, 'Henry More, Thomas Vaughan and the late Renaissance magical tradition' (1980). For More's ambiguous relationship with 'enthusiasm', see Crocker, 'Mysticism and enthusiasm in Henry More' (1990).

[98] More, *Conjectura*, 91–2. See also the insistence that the Cabbala is not understood through direct inspiration: sig. A7$^v$.

[99] Ibid., 99–100; and also sig. A8$^v$, 93–4.     [100] Ibid., 107.

Cambridge colleague John Smith was extremely sceptical about Philo's exegetical method; more generally, Christian scholars had by this point recognised that Philo stood at the apex of the tradition of Hellenistic Jewish syncretism, and were correspondingly very wary (see 6.1 below). More, on the other hand, was extremely positive, constantly referring to the Alexandrian's authority.[101] Indeed, he even hinted that Philo was his archetype for the ideal of a metaphysician–priest: that is to say, not one who simply used philosophy as a propaedeutic for theology but actively continued philosophical speculation as part of a holy life.[102] The philosophical–allegorical strand of Judaism represented by Philo had almost always stood in opposition to the rationalist strand represented by Maimonides. But a recent attempt to synchronise them *had* been made by the Amsterdam-based rabbi – and friend of many European Hebraists – Menasseh ben Israel, who, like More, placed much emphasis on supposed later pagan appropriation of the Cabbala, especially by Pythagoras.[103] In his *De creatione problemata* (1635), Menasseh had defended the pre-existence of the soul by drawing on a supposed Cabbalistic tradition that was to be found in Plato and Pythagoras; More was citing him as early as 1647, before meeting him in London in the late 1650s, later admitting the rabbi's influence upon him.[104] It is no coincidence that the two quotations on the title-page of More's 'Defence of the Threefold Cabbala' are from Philo and Maimonides.[105]

But even if Menasseh was More's key contemporary model, More's own exegetical method was novel and idiosyncratic. The same can be said for the

---

[101]  Ibid., 97, 138, 144, 153, 157, 160, 195, 226–7; More, *Collection*, v–vi; More, 'Appendix', 107, 117, 120–1; More, 'Apology', 485. I thus slightly disagree with the claim that Origen was More's central exegetical model in the *Conjectura* (Hutton, 'Iconisms, enthusiasm, and Origen: Henry More reads the Bible' (2006), esp. 194, 204–5). More was certainly partial to Origen, especially because he offered strong support for the pre-existence of the soul: see already *Conjectura*, 180–1 (but see the prior use of Philo for the same purpose, 168). But he also thought that Origen, unlike Philo, was a poor model for the natural philosophical exegesis of scripture: *Collection*, xxii–xxiii. Philo never explicitly expounded a threefold scheme of exegesis, but it was easily deduced from his works: see the discussion of the relevant sources in Wolfson, *Philo* (1947), i, 117–33 (notwithstanding the challenge by de Lubac, *Exégèse médiévale* (1959–61), i, 204ff). The standard editions of Philo were those of Sigismund Gelen (*Philonis Iudaei ... lucubrationes omnes* (Basle, 1561), which were not held in high esteem (see e.g. Smith, *Discourses*, 186). For Gelen, see Bietenholz, 'Sigismundus Gelenius of Prague' (1985), 84–5.

[102]  More, *Collection*, v–vi.

[103]  Menasseh ben Israel, *De creatione*, 61–6. See Dan, 'Menasseh ben Israel: attitude towards the Zohar and Lurianic Kabbalah' (1989) (although this deals only with Menasseh's Hebrew work, *Nishmath Ḥayyim*); Idel, 'Kabbalah, Platonism and *prisca theologia*: the case of R. Menasseh Ben Israel' (1989) (focusing especially on Menasseh's Jewish sources).

[104]  See [Henry More], 'Annotations', in George Rust, *Two choice and useful Treatises* (London, 1682), 27. More was already citing Menasseh as a key source as early as his 'The praexistency of the soul', in *Philosophical Poems* (Cambridge, 1647), 225, undoubtedly there drawing on Menasseh ben Israel, *De creatione*, 61–9; see also the use of Menasseh in *Conjectura*, 113. See the very useful account of their relationship in van den Berg, 'Menasseh ben Israel, Henry More and Johannes Hoornbeeck on the pre-existence of the soul' (1989), esp. 98–112.

[105]  More, *Conjectura*, 80.

vision of the history of philosophy that he used to justify it. Of course, he cited all the usual Jewish and patristic sources for the Mosaic origins of Pythagorean and Platonic philosophy.[106] But he was aware that more was required of him, for he was not simply asserting Judaic primacy but also insisting that the pagans had preserved – better than the Jews themselves – a natural philosophical reading of Genesis that conformed with a neo-Cartesian cosmology. The key figure in his narrative was Pythagoras, and this has led to the assumption that More was part of a standard Renaissance tradition of esoteric–mystical historiography. But More's reading of Pythagoras was entirely novel and in fact critical of the Renaissance tradition. In More's 'philosophical Cabbala', the account of the fourth day of Creation (i.e. Gen. 1:14–19) was central because it revealed the key cosmological truth of heliocentricism as well as the movement of celestial bodies through the operation of vortices in an aether.[107] That Pythagoras had been a heliocentricist was a commonplace, but how to connect this to the Genesis narrative? What More called the 'one great Key'[108] for understanding Genesis was an interpretation of the famous Pythagorean tetractys (τετρακτύς), a mystical symbol comprising the numbers one to four which played a central role in the Pythagorean oath:

> I swear by him [i.e. Pythagoras] who gave to us the tetractys,
> which has the source and root of everlasting nature.[109]

Renaissance exegetes had obsessed over the tetractys; the standard 'readings' were arithmological mysticism and the alignment of it with the Hebrew Tetragrammaton, יהוה (*YHWH*), the name of God.[110] More entirely rejected this whole tradition: 'There is no likelihood that so wise a man as Pythagoras was, should lay any stress upon such [numerical] trifles, or that his Scholars should be such fools as to be taken with them'; 'that it is a *Number*, not a *Name*, all the rest of the Numbers of the *Pythagorick* Denary will bear witness'.[111] More showed in great detail how the Greek names of the various Pythagorean numbers did not refer to names: this was by far the most philologically

---

[106] See the vast list of authorities at ibid., 185–6. More did believe that the pagans had introduced their own corruptions, e.g. transmigration of souls (see e.g. ibid., 82–3).

[107] Ibid., 28–9, 149–156, *passim*.    [108] Ibid., 137.

[109] Variants can be found in Stobaeus, *Ecl*. 58 B 15 [=*DK* 282ᵇ2], Sextus Empiricus, *Adv. math.*, vii.94, Iamblichus, *Vit. Pyth.*, 150, 162, Porphyry, *Plot.*, 20. More first quotes it at *Conjectura*, 154.

[110] For Pythagoras in the Renaissance, see Joost-Gaugier, *Pythagoras and Renaissance Europe* (2009); Celenza, 'Pythagoras in the Renaissance: the case of Marsilio Ficino' (1999); Heninger, *Touches of sweet harmony* (1974); and esp. Heninger, 'Some Renaissance versions of the Pythagorean tetrad' (1961); also Schmidt-Biggemann, 'History and prehistory of the Cabala of JHSUS' (2006). For number symbolism more generally, see Brach, 'Mathematical esotericism: some perspectives on Renaissance Arithmology' (2009), 75–90. For More, see also Brown, 'The mere numbers of Henry More's Cabbala' (1970).

[111] More, *Conjectura*, 154–5; More, 'Appendix', 106–7.

impressive part of his discussion. But this was because he took all that evidence from the *Denarius Pythagoricus* (1631) by Johann Meursius. Meursius (1570–1639) had held one of Europe's leading scholarly chairs, the history professorship at Leiden, and the *Denarius* is a suitably learned and sober analysis of the labyrinth of sources on the Pythagorean numbers and their various names. Its criticism was destructive by accumulation; refusing to engage in mystical speculation, Meursius instead patiently charted the various uses of the numbers, usually showing that their philosophical meaning was aligned with metaphysical or natural philosophical ideas.[112] More relied on this scholarship, picking out the natural philosophical interpretations of the numbers that fitted his own theory and condemning the rest as the inventions of late, corrupt, Pythagoreanism.[113] Meursius's chapter on the tetractys had remained pointedly silent on connections with the Tetragrammaton; More used it to attack such interpretations, replacing them with an entirely different explanation for what was transferred from the Jews to Pythagoras: that is to say, More's own idiosyncratic reading of Genesis.

Both in his approach to Moses and to the history of Greek philosophy, then, More was deviating significantly and self-consciously from any Renaissance interpretations. This was surely an attempt to distance himself from a type of scholarship that had for some time been coming under severe scrutiny. But it did not prevent his own scholarship from having some major peculiarities, to say the least. The most serious we have already hinted at: More's very dangerous flirtation with a total abandonment of literalism, the central plank of all Protestant exegesis. Protestants had always been happy to accept accommodationism because it was *historical*, that is to say, part of the literal sense. When Genesis suggested that the earth was made on the third day and the sun on the fourth and yet light had existed before the sun, generations of exegetes had happily answered that the account was at least phenomenologically true – either the original light had been a miraculous light (the view of Calvin), or the later appearance of the sun at Gen. 1:16 was only the revealing of the extant sun, re-described to suit the capacities of the vulgar. Yet More went much further, and claimed that the order in the text was simply wrong when compared with the philosophy hidden beneath:

And it had been a needless Miracle, and it may be impossible, to contrive one and the same Text to answer in accurate Order to the popular Appearances of things, to the severity of Philosophick Truth, and the Moral Allegory at once. With all which this Text of *Moses* is charged, & does to admiration make good the design as to all considerable

---

[112] Johannes Meursius, *Denarius Pythagoricus. Sive, de numerorum, usque ad denarium, qualitate, ac nominibus, secundum Pythagoricos* (Leiden, 1631). The only remotely useful analysis that I am familiar with is Neumann, 'Atome, Sonnenstäubchen, Monaden. Zum Pythagoreismus im 17. und 18. Jahrhundert' (2008), at 213–15.

[113] E.g. More, 'Appendix', 106–25.

intents & purposes: but an exact concatenation of the Series of things throughout is more then ought to be expected, no such Accuracy being industriously intended, but only that the *Order* of Numbers according to their *significancy* should be a *Repository* of *Notes* and *Remembrances*; but the management of the *Cabbala* it self, (that is, of the ancient Philosophy of the *Jewes*,) left to the skill of the *Mystagogus*, when he was consulted, who would not fail to declare all things in a due and natural Method.[114]

The history of philosophy seemed to be trumping the authority of scripture. These difficulties in reconciling the literal and the philosophical senses,[115] combined with More's talk of Moses as a 'politician', would soon get him into trouble. But neither was his approach to the history of post-Mosaic philosophy free from such scholarly leaps of faith. Take for example his argument that the history of pagan philosophy better revealed the content of the 'philosophical Cabbala' than did Judaic tradition. More was aware that this claim would be perceived as a weakness, and attempted to respond. Without offering any evidence, he argued that the Jews' literalism blinded them to the philosophical sense hidden beneath.[116] He must have known that this was weak, for he did attempt one proof that heliocentricism 'was once the hidden Doctrine of the learned of that Nation'. Numa Pompilius (753–673 BC), the semi-legendary second king of Rome, had, according to Plutarch, instituted the Vestal temple, 'where the perpetual fire was kept, of a circular form, not in imitation of the shape of the earth, believing Vesta to be the earth, but of the entire universe, at the centre of which the Pythagoreans place the element of fire, and call it Vesta and Unit'.[117] Plutarch had also intimated that Numa was originally a Lacedemonian. More jumped on this, pointing out that both the Old Testament and Josephus had stated that the Jews and Lacedemonians were 'of one stock' (1 Macc. 12:21), and that Numa's 'heliocentric' worship was taken from the Jews.[118] The threads of this story were thin indeed: virtually nothing was known of the supposed Jewish-Lacedemonian connection,[119] whereas the connection between Numa and Pythagoras was somewhat ruined by the fact that the philosopher lived not only in a different part of Italy but also a century later than the lawgiver, as Cicero and Livy had both pointed out in antiquity.[120]

---

[114] More, 'Appendix', 145.

[115] See also More's very defensive attempt to justify the reconciliation of the literal and philosophical accounts of the first day of creation, supposedly entirely immaterial ('Appendix', 130–1).

[116] More, 'Appendix', 127.    [117] Plutarch, *Vit. Num.*, 11.1.

[118] More, 'Appendix', 128–9; Plutarch, *Vit. Num.*, 1.3; Josephus, *Ant. Jud.*, XII.4, XIII.5 (More mistakenly cited XIII.11). For the long afterlife of Numa's reputation as a civil religious lawgiver, see Silk, 'Numa Pompilius and the idea of civil religion in the West' (2004).

[119] For the fullest scholarly discussion of the Jewish-Lacedemonian relationship that might have been available to More (that I am aware of), see Hugo Grotius, *Annotationes ad Vetus Testamentum* (Paris, 1644), 389 (in the note to 1 Macc. 12:7).

[120] Cicero, *De oratore*, II.154, *De re publica*, II.29. Livy, *Ab urbe condita*, I.18. See also Plutarch, *Vit. Num.*, 1.2–3; More was aware at least of Plutarch's discussion ('Appendix', 128).

But this was nothing when compared to More's justification for discovering all of Cartesianism in Pythagoras. The great problem here was proving that Pythagoras had held the same micro-particulate matter theory as Descartes.[121] More 'solved' it by claiming that Democritus – certainly an atomist – had been a student of Pythagoras, from whom he must have taken his doctrine. This was a classic problem: Laërtius had pointed out that a lost source, Thrasylus, stated that Democritus 'seemed an admirer of the Pythagoreans ... if chronology did not stand in the way, he might have been thought his pupil' (ix.38). Laërtius never resolved this issue; neither did he ever claim Pythagoras was an atomist. Yet More ignored all this, instead pointing out that when Plato sought to burn all the extant works of Democritus he was dissuaded by two Pythagoreans.[122] Unfortunately, More neglected to mention the key reason given by his source (DL ix.40): not that the Pythagoreans had an affection for Democritus, but that they thought 'there was no advantage in doing so, for already the books were widely circulated'. On the basis of this childish reasoning, More proceeded to read whatever Democritean doctrines he wanted to into Pythagoras, including the infinity of worlds and atoms and vortical motion.[123] Pythagoras must, in turn, have taken this all from the Jews, proving that 'the *Mosaical* Philosophy in the Physiological part thereof is the same with the *Cartesian*'.[124] This backwards-working methodology broke all the rules of early modern historiography.

Finally, More appeared even more credulous when he recited the old pagan testimonies for Pythagoras having performed miracles, an ability More claimed was part of his inheritance of the Jewish Cabbala.[125] More's own attitude to natural magic and the world of spirits is well studied[126] but this is not one of its manifestations, for he expressly denied that Pythagoras acted as a magician; rather, it was a direct providential intervention, for God desired that Pythagoras, 'having got the knowledge of the holy *Cabbala*, which [He had] imparted to *Adam* and *Moses* ... should countenance it before the Nations by enabling him to do Miracles'.[127] This whole reading was bizarre: why would God keep the

---

[121] More, 'Appendix', 103–4. For histories of matter theory, see 5.1–3 below. More's interest in matter theory and its history was of course not limited to Descartes; on 5 Nov 1649 he wrote to Hartlib to ask if he could 'procure me out of France with any tolerable speed a Copy of Gassendus his ~~naturall~~ <Epicurean> Philosophy', for which he would 'willingly pay what it shall cost' (HP, 18/1/36A). But by the end of the year his scholarly laxity had got the better of him, after seeing a sample: 'Gassendus is too tedious a Philologer for me. Ὁ βίος βραχύς ['life is short']. I am glad you did not send for it for me'.

[122] More, 'Appendix', 103.

[123] More, 'Appendix', 103–4. The key to More's interpretation was the translation of 'φέρεσθαι δ' ἐν τῷ ὅλῳ δινουμένας' (DL ix.44) as '*they* [i.e. atoms] *are moved in the Universe after the manner of* Vortices'.

[124] More, 'Appendix', 104.    [125] More, *Conjectura*, 85–6, 186–90.

[126] Crocker, *More*, 127–42; Hall, *More*, 128–45, *passim*; Fouke, *The enthusiastical concerns of Dr. Henry More* (1997), *passim*.

[127] More, *Conjectura*, 86.

Cabbala secret if he then wanted Pythagoras to reveal it by his miracles? It was clearly designed by More as further proof that Pythagoras had received Jewish traditions, but it was so ill thought out that More's later critics responded with genuine incredulity that he had ever conceived of it.

### 3.5     Questioning Mosaic primacy

Historians have tended to claim that the reception of More's early works was politically motivated.[128] Certainly, some of the opposition was led by a coterie of episcopalian churchmen in the circle of the prominent Laudian ex-bishop Matthew Wren: Joseph Beaumont (whom Wren had installed as Master of Peterhouse in 1663), Anthony Sparrow (at that point vice-chancellor of Cambridge), and Herbert Thorndike, a leading scholar (he had special responsibility for the Syriac portion of the London polyglot) who had been reinstated as a fellow of Trinity College, Cambridge following the Restoration.[129] Their attacks were indeed partly predicated on the belief that More's whole philosophical and theological scheme was liable to bring down episcopacy and incite heresy.[130] But they, and a host of other opponents who did not hold their ideological views, did not base their attacks primarily on a political agenda, for they also held a much more fundamental belief: that More was wrong.

For example, Beaumont, who circulated his critique of More around the university in manuscript and only stepped into print when More made it public, questioned the logic of More's use of accommodationism, commenting on the distance between More's 'literal' and 'philosophical' senses and pointing to his confused attitude to the historical Jews: were they primitive (and thus in need of divine condescension), or were they advanced esoteric philosophers?[131] These questions stemmed not from political or ecclesiological differences but from Beaumont's background in a different exegetical tradition to More. His surviving lectures as Regius Professor of Divinity (appointed 1674) show him to have been firmly imbued with the

---

[128] See e.g., Crocker, *More*, 85–9; Dockrill and Lee, 'Reflections on an episode in Cambridge Latitudinarianism: Henry More's Epistle Dedicatory to Gilbert Sheldon of his *Enchiridion Metaphysicum*' (1994), and the classic Nicolson, 'Christ's College and the latitude men' (1929).

[129] The relevant evidence is collected in Crocker, *More*, 86–9. For this circle at Cambridge, see Gascoigne, *Cambridge*, 29–33. For Thorndike as a scholar, see 6.3 below.

[130] See e.g Joseph Beaumont, *Some observations upon the apology of Dr. Henry More* (Cambridge, 1665), 52–85, 168–83 (on church government), 143–67 (on liberty in religion); Herbert Thorndike, *The principle of comprehension: or a petition against the Presbyterian request for a comprehensive act in 1667*, in *The theological works of Herbert Thorndike*, ed. J. H. Parker (6 vols, Oxford, 1844–56), v, 313–14 (placing More's belief in pre-existence, pagan salvation, and questioning of the resurrection of the same body in the context of an argument against comprehension and toleration).

[131] Beaumont, *Observations*, 6–7.

historical–theological approach of Grotius.[132] Beaumont was taking as his base the new approach to the biblical text developed in continental philology, against which More must have looked not only primitive, but positively deranged.

That politics was not a key driving force behind the attacks on More is confirmed by the fact that exegetes from the opposite ecclesiological background were similarly critical. In the preface to the *Analytical exposition of the whole first book of Moses* (1672) by the deprived interregnum minister George Hughes, his brother offered a not very thinly veiled (but previously unnoticed) attack on More.[133] Both Hughes's and his brother's theological orientation was far more Reformed than Beaumont's; consequently, they placed less emphasis on the person of Moses than on God speaking through him.[134] In the preface, Hughes's brother asserted that Hughes would have been happy to see defended the idea 'that the Philosophy which had so much puffed up the gentiles had lighted its Torch at the holy Lamp': Judaic primacy remained a preference among Reformed scholars, as we shall see in the case of Theophilus Gale. But even here More's whole attempt to address philosophical debates through scripture was dismissed, for the Bible was not 'designed by the Spirit to furnish the world with a body of Physicks . . . to seek philosophy here was to seek the dead among the living. Our author therefore medleth not with the threefold Cabbala to make the word more prolificall of mysteries then either the Spirit or Moses intended it.' It is worth noting that More was obliquely referred to as a 'supercilious Philosopher'; this is a good sign of professional demarcation, for More, who had rejected ecclesiastical preferment and must have always seemed rather jejune in refusing to move on from philosophy, repeatedly faced accusations of meddling in a discipline he was unqualified to partake in.[135]

Henry Stubbe, whose deep interest in the history of philosophy we shall meet in Chapter 4, went much further, attacking More's historical and exegetical method after the latter had written in support of the Royal Society against Stubbe's earlier attacks. Stubbe, who was a careful scholar, pointed to many of the absurdities we have already identified in More's account, reacting with

---

[132] CUL MS Kk.3.1 (Beaumont's lectures on Romans); see e.g. fols. 30$^{r-v}$, discussing Paul's intended audience (on the basis of Rom. 1:5). When applied to theological *quaestiones*, however, humanist methods were subsumed to the demands of controversial theology: CUL MSS Add. 697–9 (divinity exercises set by Beaumont). I am working on a study of Beaumont's theological tuition.

[133] Hughes had been suspended by Laud in 1636, active during the Interregnum and again ejected in 1662, and imprisoned in 1665. See Wolffe, 'Hughes, George', *ODNB*.

[134] George Hughes, *An analytical exposition of the whole first book of Moses, called Genesis . . . delivered in a mornings exercise on the Lords Day* (London, 1672), sig. [\*\*\*6]$^r$ (God spoke through Moses). But Hughes was also indebted to the latest continental scholarship, especially Hottinger: sig. \*\*\*4$^r$; 1–12 on the creation.

[135] Hughes, *Genesis*, sig. [\*\*\*5]$^r$. See also Beaumont, *Observations*, 51–2. More repeatedly defended his status as a philosopher: 'Apology', 482; *Collection*, v; 'Appendix', 150–1.

particular incredulity at the idea of Pythagorean miracles.[136] That More's exposition of Pythagorean number theory was being cited to defend transmutational alchemy cannot have enhanced its reputation.[137] More was even attacked by a Lutheran professor of theology at Marburg, Samuel Andreae: More considered this the most important attack on the *Conjectura*, refuting it at length in Scholia added to the 1679 *Opera*. Andreae quickly identified the central issue: More claimed that the philosophical Cabbala was to be accommodated to the context of the scriptural words, but in reality he had 'violently infer[red]' it from them.[138] It was impossible to extract a unified 'Cabbala' from the philosophers in whom More claimed to find it; not only did their opinions disagree with each other but there was also no evidence for such a Mosaic tradition in the first place.[139] More, according to Andreae, was only the latest in a tradition that stemmed from Philo and Origen to fall for the Platonic myth of allegorical–philosophical interpretation of scripture.[140]

In England, most important were the earlier attacks by two prominent young careerist clerics, Edward Stillingfleet and Samuel Parker.[141] We shall recall that Stillingfleet's aim in the *Origines sacrae* (1662) was to defend the veracity of the biblical account; his interest in Moses was thus as a human author whose reliability had to be verified. Part of that verification involved showing that Moses could not 'be ignorant of the things which he writ of', because he was a

---

[136] Henry Stubbe, *A reply unto the letter written to Mr Henry Stubbe in defense of the history of the Royal Society* (Oxford, 1671), 50, 73–4, 76–7.

[137] William Simpson, *Hydrologia chymica* (London, 1669), 228. On Simpson, see 5.3 below.

[138] Samuel Andreae, *Examen generale Cabbale philosophicae D. Henrici Mori* (Herborn, 1670), sig.):():(ʳ ('*Philosophiam*, quae à nauseantibus Philosophis & viris literatis, per applicationem eorum quae de materiâ subjectâ apud alios legerunt aut ceu vera admiserunt, literae ac verborum contextui est accommodanda, vel potius (ut specimen Morianum ostendit) violenter inferenda'). For More's responses, see the 'Scholia' to the 1679 *Opera omnia*, as they appear untranslated in the *Collection of several philosophical writings* (London, 1712), esp. 114–20, 124–31, *passim* (More was by this point drawing on knowledge of the real Cabbala he had acquired from the translations of Christian Knorr von Rosenroth). I do not know of a single discussion of Andreae or More's response in the historiography, no doubt because both remain untranslated (even the 1712 editor felt the Scholia were 'fitted rather for the use of the Learned' – perhaps a statement of embarrassment at their contents). On Andrae more generally, see Gundlach, *Catalogus professorum Academiae Marburgensis* (1927), 24–5, and the brief comments in Kaehler, 'Der Kampf zwischen Theologie und Philosophie, 1680–1702' (1927).

[139] Andreae, *Examen*, sig.):():(2ʳ.

[140] Ibid., 3: 'Ad hanc verò sunt revocandi quotquot Philonem Judaeum & Judaeorum traditiones de בראשיתמעשה ut vocant, seu *Opere Creationis*, atque *Originis, Augustini* aliorumque veterum allegorias incauta sequuntur, aut caetero quin in mundi opficio describendo ratiociniis suis & principiis Philosophicis plus quàm par erat tribuunt'.

[141] Stillingfleet's attack on More was first noted and discussed in Hutton, 'Moses Atticus', esp. 73–4. This seminal article is much cited in the prominent secondary literature (see e.g. Grafton, *Defenders*, 19), but my own reading differs from its conclusions quite significantly. For Stillingfleet, see 1.3, 2.4, 5.2, 6.5. The key passages which reveal that Stillingfleet's target was More are at *Origines sacrae*, 425–6, 440, 510.

'person of more then ordinary judgement, wisdom, and knowledge'.[142] Here
Stillingfleet relied on Acts 7:22 ('Moses was learned in all the wisdom of the
Egyptians'), but he did so in a novel and critical manner. Deeply sceptical about
claims to great Egyptian wisdom, Stillingfleet repeatedly mocked Kircher for
credulously swallowing the belief of an esoteric philosophy hidden beneath the
hieroglyphs[143] and instead naturalised Egyptian intellectual history. First, the
annual flooding of the Nile required them to learn the geometry and natural
philosophy required for irrigation;[144] second, the presence of a priestly caste
with the necessary leisure facilitated the rise of contemplative science.[145] Their
learning reflected these contextual conditions: they were good geographers and
physicians but poor natural philosophers, since their knowledge of the natural
world was corrupted by their idolatrous anthropomorphism. Their mathematics
cannot have been so advanced if Pythagoras, who spent twenty-two years in
Egypt, still sacrificed a hundred oxen upon discovering his famous theorem.[146]
Yet this was enough evidence to defend Moses: 'Can we now imagine such a
person as *Moses* was bred up in all the *ingenous literature* of *Aegypt* . . . should
not be able to pass a judgement between a mere *pretence* and *imposture*, and
*real* and *important Truths*?'[147] Of course, a narrative of Mosaic primacy and
great Egyptian wisdom would have suited Stillingfleet's apologetic purposes
even more, but he had read Conring's *De Hermetica Aegyptiorum*, which had
rendered him very sceptical to such narratives and no doubt influenced his

[142]  Stillingfleet, *Origines*, 120.
[143]  For direct attacks on Kircher, see e.g. *Origines*, 129 (hieroglyphs), 31 (mocking Kircher's
claim to have seen an original version of Sanchoniathon's *History* (preserved only in Greek in
Philo of Byblos, himself preserved in Eusebius [*Praep. Ev.*, I.9–10])). For similar mockery of
Kircher's use of Sanchoniathon, from whom he took 'quotations' unavailable to anyone else,
see e.g. Cudworth, *System*, 413. As an example of the false wisdom in the hieroglyphs,
Stillingfleet gives one from 'Diospolis' (i.e. Thebes) consisting of a child, an old man, a
hawk, a hippopotamus, and a crocodile, supposedly meaning the prosaic 'O ye that come into
the world, and that go out of it, God hates impudence'. Although he does not give the source,
the whole story is clearly derived from Clemens Alexandrinus, *Strom.*, V.7.
[144]  Stillingfleet, *Origines*, 124. This interpretation had already been implied by Herodotus, II.108–
9. Also Diodorus Siculus, *Bib. hist.*, I.37–8; Strabo, *Geog.*, XVII.3, both of which were cited by
Stillingfleet (who does not include Aristotle, *Met.*1.981$^b$20–6). The same origin for philosophy
is posited in Nehemiah Grew's 'Short account of Thales, Solon, Socrates, and other antient
philosophers, and their different systems of philosophy', BL MS Sloane 1950, fols. 13$^r$–34$^r$,
at 13$^r$.
[145]  Stillingfleet, *Origines*, 125–6; the key source is again Strabo, *Geog.*, XVII.3. Diodorus Siculus,
*Bib. hist.* I.74 had delineated another class of learned men in Egypt, but Stillingfleet expressly
favours the reading of Strabo, on the advice of Isaac Casaubon: Strabo, *Res Geographia*, ed.
I. Casaubon (Geneva, 1587), 220b.
[146]  Stillingfleet, *Origines*, 127–9. For Pythagoras's twenty-two years in Egypt, see Iamblichus,
*Vita Pyth.*, 11; for his sacrificing a hecatomb, see DL, VIII.12 (but disputed by Cicero, *Nat.
Deor.*, III.36 on the basis of Pythagoras's vegetarianism).
[147]  Stillingfleet, *Origines*, 129–30.

negative opinion of Kircher.[148] This is a nice example of how the scholarly conclusions of one genre – Scaligerian criticism – could shape those of another – medical history – which in turn shaped those of a third – apologetics.

Moses, accordingly, was for Stillingfleet only a moderately learned man, whose learning allowed him to appreciate the veracity of the traditions about the creation that he had received from his predecessors. Like the continental scholars and Hebraists, Stillingfleet had shifted emphasis from Moses as a direct receiver of revelation to a faithful historian who, 'setting aside Divine revelation', had received a tradition that was not only transmitted by the Jewish patriarchs but also by their descendants among other peoples (albeit the Jewish tradition was not mired by the '*confusion* in the *tradition* of other Nations').[149] This precluded the need for More's Cabbalistic explanations. First, it was absurd to read Pythagorean esotericism into Moses's intentions: unlike the former, the latter nowhere 'gives us . . . the least intimation that he left behind him such *plaited picture* in his *History* of the *beginning* of the *world*, that if you look *straight forward*, you may see a *literal Cabbala*, on the *one side* a *Philosophical*, and on the other a *Moral*'.[150] The whole esoteric Cabbalistic narrative was unnecessary when it could be acknowledged that both Moses and Pythagoras drew on a near universal tradition. The Egyptians themselves had always believed in the world's creation.[151] More importantly, it was common opinion among not just the Pythagoreans but also all the early Greek philosophers, as Aristotle complained when promoting eternalism.[152] Was it likely that they too were all in possession of an esoteric Mosaic Cabbala? Stillingfleet focused on the case of Thales, the founder of the Ionic succession, and his idea of water as a first principle; drawing on an interpretation by Grotius that would prove very popular he argued that Thales's ideas were probably derived from those of his Phoenician ancestors.[153] 'I do not see any reason to aver', Stillingfleet concluded, 'as some do, that those *Philosophers* who spake any thing consonantly to *Moses*, must presently *converse* with the *Jews* . . . or have it conveyed to them in some secret *Cabbala* of the *Creation*'; far more likely, they drew on the '*universal tradition* of the first *ages* of the *world*, which was

---

[148]  See e.g. ibid., 121–2, where Stillingfleet admits his great debt to Conring; many of the later examples are clearly taken without acknowledgement from the *De Hermetica Aegyptiorum*. See also the use of Casaubon's attack on Hermes at 33–6, esp. 35.

[149]  Stillingfleet, *Origines*, 132–3. The lineal descent ran thus: Adam conversed with Noah, Noah's son Shem 'probably' overlapped with Jacob or Isaac, and from there the line to Moses was easily proved. This claim was in fact rather peculiar, for the biblical ages of the patriarchs did not allow Adam to speak to Noah, but required postdiluvian man to have contact with Adam only through Methuselah or Lamech. Indeed, the narrative would have been even more complicated by Stillingfleet's preference for the Septuagint chronology. Of course, this reading did not stop Stillingfleet from accepting Mosaic miracles as proof of his divine mission (140).

[150]  Ibid., 510.    [151]  Ibid., 425, drawing on DL, Proem. 10.

[152]  Stillingfleet, *Origines*, 423, citing Aristotle, *De caelo*, 1.10 (279[b]12–15).

[153]  Stillingfleet, *Origines*, 424–9. For other uses of this idea, see 5.3 below.

preserved far better among the *Phaenicians, Aegyptians, Chaldeans*, and others then among the *Greeks*.[154] As for Pythagoras, he may have spoken with the Jews (especially during his eastern travels, simultaneous to the Babylonian captivity); but that *all* of Pythagoreanism should be read back into a spurious Mosaic Cabbala was historiographically absurd: both Pythagoras' supposed circumcision and fancy for pre-existence were better attributed to the influence of the wrong-headed Egyptians.[155]

Stillingfleet's vision was fundamentally different from that of More.[156] This is not surprising when we remember that Stillingfleet was working in a very different world to that of his predecessor. More had been educated in the 1630s, when Calvinist–scholastic exegesis was dominant; his rebellion against such traditions led him to what he felt was an opposing Jewish tradition characterised by the mystical rationalism of Philo. By the time Stillingfleet went to study at Cambridge in the late 1640s to the mid 1650s the scholarly world had changed: as he himself said about previous visions of Egyptian wisdom, 'the world is now grown wiser'.[157] Brought up on a diet of recent Dutch biblical commentators and sacred historians (Grotius, G. J. Vossius, Isaac Vossius), Stillingfleet had no need to resort to More's speculations. Like these scholars and the other pioneers of the first half of the seventeenth century, he had decided that narratives of Judaic primacy and Cabbala were the invention of Philo, misled by his own syncretism.[158] Far from representing a slow outgrowth from 'Cambridge Platonism', Stillingfleet represented the appropriation of continental scholarship into apologetics against the idiosyncrasies of More – a phenomenon which has little to do with any purported 'latitudinarianism'.

Indeed, such a conclusion brings Stillingfleet close to More's other great opponent, Samuel Parker (both are also not very dissimilar from Beaumont,

---

[154] Ibid., 424.    [155] Ibid., 424–5.

[156] My interpretation here differs from that offered in Hutton, 'Moses atticus', 69–71.

[157] Stillingfleet, *Origines*, 122. Stillingfleet's education is somewhat obscure, but we know that his sponsor was Samuel Pickering (see Mayor and Scott, *Admissions to the college of St John the Evangelist* (1882–93), 90; [Goodwin?], 'Life', 2 is thus wrong to claim Pickering was Stillingfleet's tutor, an error followed by Fishman, 'Edward Stillingfleet, Bishop of Worcester' (1977), 1), fellow from 1647 (*Alum. Cantab.*, III, 360). Pickering stayed on to receive a D.D. in 1669, while Peter Gunning was still Regius Professor of Divinity, and he was still Rector of Brant Broughton upon his death in 1671 (Lincolnshire Archives, MS Tur.14.1.7), suggesting conformist sympathies. Stillingfleet's tutor was Henry Eyre (*Admissions*, 90), for whom there is a lack of evidence, although his academic progression (M.A. 1645, fellow 1647, taxor 1649, bread and beer bursar 1655, senior bursar 1657, M.D. 1658) may possibly suggest more sympathies for the interregnum regime, even if the evidence is too sparse for any strong conclusions (see *Report presented to the Cambridge antiquarian society* (1865), 99). The idea that Stillingfleet knew More at Cambridge is unsubstantiated; importantly, the long-standing claim that More's letters in Ward, *Life*, 149–59 are to Stillingfleet is wrong: they are clearly to William Sherlock, since there are direct references to Sherlock's *Discourse concerning the knowledge of Jesus Christ and our union and communion with him* (London, 1674)).

[158] Stillingfleet, *Origines*, 426. Andreae already recognised the fundamental difference between Stillingfleet and More: *Examen*, 10.

and would have appreciated the pedagogical programme he would institute in Cambridge). Parker – one of the most intolerant clerics of the Restoration – is best understood not as a 'latitudinarian',[159] but rather, like Stillingfleet, as a product of a 1650s education (albeit at Oxford). Having rejected both Calvinism and Aristotelian natural philosophy, he instead found the intellectual foundations of the clerical vocation in a mixture of the new critical humanism, elements of the new philosophy including its experimental method (in doctrine, he was particularly keen on Gassendi and heavily opposed to Descartes), and traditional neo-scholastic natural theology.[160] For all these he was respected: he became the Royal Society's youngest non-armigerous fellow in 1665, his scholarship was valued by far more advanced scholars, and his early publications secured the patronage of Archbishop Sheldon.[161]

Parker's opposition to More (and Joseph Glanvill) was partly motivated by a general theological preference for emphasising God's omnipotence over that of his goodness or rationality as well as the more widespread distaste for such unorthodox opinions as pre-existence and philosophies that emphasised abstract reasoning over sense experience.[162] But it was also motivated by historical scholarship; indeed, we will see throughout (5.2, 5.4.3, 6.5) that Parker was one of the most original and influential historical thinkers in seventeenth-century England, and even Europe. The end of his *Free and impartial censure of the Platonick philosophie* (1665) contained a historical section entitled 'The supposed Agreement between Moses and Plato disproved'. Parker was evidently familiar with the case he was opposing: citing Ficino, Patrizi, Bessarion, and Pico, he offered the first Anglophone history of

---

[159] *Pace* Parkin, *Cumberland*, 37–45; Parkin, 'Hobbism in the later 1660s: Daniel Scargill and Samuel Parker' (1999), 85–108 esp. 96–108; Crocker, *More*, 201–2.

[160] See Levitin, 'Rethinking English physico-theology: Samuel Parker's *Tentamina de Deo*' (2014). For his political opinions, Rose, 'The ecclesiastical polity of Samuel Parker' (2010) surpasses all previous discussions.

[161] Levitin, 'Physico-theology'. For respect from serious scholars, see e.g. the correspondence with Henry Dodwell at Bod. MS Eng. letters c. 28, fols. 3$^r$–6$^r$; Bod. MS Cherry 23, fols. 322$^r$–324$^r$. These were not empty platitudies: Dodwell openly cited Parker's works in his own scholarly endeavours (see e.g. *Dissertationes in Irenaeum* (Oxford, 1689), 12). The only modern historian even to touch on this aspect of Parker's intellectual identity is J. P. Rosenblatt, who summarises fairly that Parker's work comprised 'equal parts of sound scholarship and bad temper' and notes his repudiation of Selden (*Renaissance England's chief rabbi* (2006), 118–19). See further 5.2, 5.4, 6.5 below.

[162] See especially Parker's *Account and nature of the divine dominion and goodnesse,* appended to the second edition of the *Free and impartial censure* (Oxford, 1667), but also published separately; also Crocker, *More*, 116–19. The thesis in Jacob, *Robert Boyle and the English revolution* (1977), 159–64 that Parker was attacking the circle around Sir John Heydon is unsupported by the evidence. For a response to Parker on divine goodness, see Henry Hallywell, *Deus justificatus; or, the Divine goodness vindicated and cleared* (London, 1668), 254–9. Glanvill planned to respond to Parker, but was talked out of it by John Beale (Lewis, 'Glanvill', 287). The *Censure* was building on the earlier *Tentamina*, as Parker acknowledges at 2.

the Florentine neoplatonic revival.[163] Like Stillingfleet, Parker believed that the Egyptians were not necessarily primitive but that those who believed in their great wisdom were only deceived by forgeries like the *Hermetica*. Like Stillingfleet, he placed Kircher and his readings of the hieroglyphs at the apex of such credulity.[164] Like Stillingfleet, he suggested that Acts 7:22 was to be read with caution and not as a license to speculate on Judaeo-Egyptian Cabbalas.[165] And like Stillingfleet, he attributed the whole idea of a grand Jewish philosophical past to the Hellenistic Jews, although rather than focus on Philo he was more concerned with those who had most influenced the church fathers into this erroneous opinion; in particular, Josephus and Aristobulus.[166]

Yet in two respects he went further than his predecessor. First, he explicitly challenged the dating of the real Cabbala, arguing that it was a late rabbinical invention. He took this argument so far that he ended up conflating Cabbalism with the foundational idea of Rabbinic Judaism: that Moses had received at Sinai,

A twofold Law, תורה שבכתב, The *Written Law* and תורה שבעל פה, The *Vocal Law*, which is the Mystical and Enigmatical meaning of the Former, but by reason of its extraordinary sacredness was not exposed to the rude People, but only whispered and conveyed in the slender Pipe of Auricular Tradition from age to age among the great Sanhedrim and the Prophets down to the time of *Esdras*, by whom (and the great Synagogue, of which many of the latter Prophets were members) it was committed to writing, least by reason of their frequent dispersions and captivities it should by some ill fortune perish: which carried its stream out of the private Channel, in which it run before, and soon spread it abroad among Forreign Nations, especially in Egypt and Chaldea.[167]

An accurate description of the Cabbala this was not, but it was a good representation of the disdain for *all* oral tradition that had by then become prominent in the most advanced scholarly circles; indeed, Parker's argument bears a striking resemblance to that developed by Walton in his 'Prolegomena' to the London Polyglot, which was in turn almost certainly building on the conclusions of Louis Cappel.[168]

---

[163] Samuel Parker, *A free and impartial censure of the Platonick philosophie* (Oxford, 1666), 32–3; also 35–6.

[164] Ibid., 97, 104–6 (Reuchlin is also attacked here).   [165] Ibid., 96–9.

[166] Ibid., 100–1 (almost all the surviving fragments of Aristobulus are in Eusebius, *Praep. Ev.*, VIII.10, XIII.12). There is a further implicit attack on Eusebius at 101–2. See further 6.5 below.

[167] Parker, *Censure*, 93–4.

[168] Walton, 'Prolegomena VIII', in *Biblia sacra polyglotta*, 52b, explicitly admitting that 'Cabalam Masorae subjungimus', and continuing, 'Legem etiam distinguunt in Scriptam, et Traditam sive Oralem. Illam in quinque libris Mosis contineri dicunt, hanc a Mose voce traditam volunt: undè Legem Oralem, sive תורה שבעל פה τον εν στοματι νομον appellant; quam a Mose continuâ successione ad Ezram, et ab illo ad ipsos quasi manu traditam a majoribus dicunt'. Walton was very likely drawing on the discussion in Louis Cappel, *Arcanum punctationis revelatum* (Leiden, 1624), 25–37. See also CUL MS Add. 8861[3], 36: 'The Jews say yᵉ Law was twofold, written & Kabbala, both delivered by God to Moses in mount Sinai, but yᵉ later was deliverd from Moses to Joshua, from him to yᵉ Elders, from yᵐ to yᵉ Prophets, from yᵉ Prophets to those of yᵉ great Synagogue & successively to after Ages till at last it was digested

But perhaps even more important was Parker's attack on the whole idea of the Greeks borrowing from the Jews. Like Stillingfleet, he suggested that 'we find as great a consonancy of the opinions of the *Wise men* of other Nations with the *Hebrew Writings*, where there appear no foot-steps of commerce between them'.[169] But he also went further than his clerical colleague in denying *any* contact between the Greeks and the Jews. For all the huge eagerness of the Greeks to admit their intellectual debt to the orient, their records 'are scarce more silent in any thing, then the *Jewish Nation*'. Parker cited a passage from Lactantius that chided them for this neglect of Israelite knowledge; this was the only patristic testimony that denied Greek contact with the Jews, and as we shall see, it would soon become a favourite among scholars.[170] As for the theory recently made prominent by the work of Samuel Bochart, that the '*Grecians* might confound *Judea* with *Phaenicia*' – it only proved how little knowledge the Greeks had of the Jews themselves.[171] Parker pushed this idea to its extreme, taking to task not only obvious scholarly charlatans like More but also heavyweights like Selden. He rose to the challenge, pointing out that the best foundation for Selden's conjecture that the seven books of Numa found when his tomb was dug up in 186 BC showed Jewish influence because they contained Pythagorean philosophy was 'the (deserved) greatness of his [Selden's] own *name* and *authority*': 'if such a licentious latitude may be allowed in historical *guesses, Quidlibet ex Quolibet* will soon be as warantable a *maxime* in History, as 'tis in the *Epicurean Philosophie*'.[172] Parker's parenthetical praise of Selden shows that he knew that caution was required in expressing these conclusions and it is true that no one in England had ever before stated them so bluntly. Nonetheless, they were the product of discernible drift in the scholarship. A year earlier, he had already attacked not only the neoplatonists but even Scaliger and Vossius for being too eager to find syncretisms between pagan literature and the Bible.[173]

Exceptions to this drift came only from those who were excluded – or excluded themselves – from the scholarly mainstream, such as Theophilus

---

into one book ... Kabbala as it is distinguished from y$^e$ Talmud, signifies only some subtilties & Mysterys w$^{ch}$ are obscure from y$^e$ different writing, transposing, & arithmatick of some letter in y$^e$ Script' (this manuscript elsewhere contains many notes from Cappel).

[169] Parker, *Censure*, 103.    [170] Ibid., 102–3, citing Lactantius, *Inst. Div.*, IV.2.

[171] Parker, *Censure*, 103. For Bochart, see Shalev, *Sacred words*, 141–204.

[172] Parker, *Censure*, 103–4. For Selden, see *De jure naturali*, 13. For the sources of the story, see Pliny, *Hist. nat.*, XIII.13; Plutarch, *Vit. Num.*, 22; Livy, XL.29.

[173] Parker, *Tentamina*, 268–82. The chapter is tellingly entitled 'Gentilium theologiam historicam plerumque sacrae historiae perperam accommodari', and goes on: 'Sed quicunque primus auctor extitit [i.e. of the practice of adapting sacred history and pagan theology to each other], eam postea insigniter nobilitarunt Veneranda *Scaligeri, Seldeni, Bocharti, Grotii, Vosii*, aliorumque doctissimorum nomina, qui impensissimo studio hujusmodi *Philologiae* rationem adornarunt; inde fit ut si quis inter *Philologiae Antistites* nomen suum recenseri affectaret, sese protenus accingeret res *Graecanicas Hebraicis* quoquo modo accommodare'.

Gale. Gale's *Court of the gentiles* (1669–77) and *Philosophia generalis* (1676) in fact comprise the largest English contribution to the history of philosophy in the seventeenth century, the four volumes of the former totalling 2,003 pages and the rather turgid Latin of the latter a further 976.[174] Gale (1628–79) had entered Magdalen Hall, Oxford in 1648, where he associated with Thomas Goodwin (then president of the college) and Goodwin's close colleague John Owen (then vice-chancellor), adopting both their Independency and Calvinism; there he became a logic lecturer and dean of arts. In 1657 he was appointed preacher in Winchester Cathedral, relinquishing the position at the Restoration.[175] In 1662 he took a position as tutor to the two sons of Philip, fourth Baron Wharton, a noted interregnum supporter of Parliament and patron of nonconformists. Gale took the boys to Caen, where they attended the Protestant College – his surviving correspondence with Wharton is a treasure trove of information on mid-century tutor–client relations, as Gale requested deliveries of seasonal clothes, informed on the elder son's attendance at a masque despite Gale's express prohibition, reluctantly acquiesced to Wharton's requests for the boys to receive fencing and dancing tuition in addition to the literary studies Gale was feeding them, and incessantly pestered his patron for money, both before and after his dismissal in summer 1664, ostensibly for failing to segregate the boys upon a case of smallpox but clearly because his strictness had entirely frustrated both his charges and their father.[176] Gale began the *Court* sometime during his time at Oxford, later planning to adapt it for his tutees; the *Philosophia generalis*, meanwhile was also clearly written with education in mind, designed for students at the Dissenting academy he established in Newington Green.

---

[174] The publication history of the *Court of the gentiles: or a discourse touching the original of human literature ... from the Scriptures, and Jewish church* is complex. There are four volumes: *I: Of philologie* (1st edn=Oxford, 1669; 2nd edn=Oxford, 1672); *II: Of philosophie* (1st edn=Oxford, 1671; 2nd edn (renamed *Of barbaric and Grecanic philosophie*)=London, 1676); *III: The vanitie of pagan philosophie* (1st edn=Oxford, 1671; 2nd printing=London, 1677); *IV: Of Reformed philosophie* (London, 1677), with a supplement, *Of Divine predetermination* (London, 1678). Reference will be made to the second editions. Each volume consists of parts, with separate pagination; references will be given to volume, part, and page number. And *Philosophia generalis, in duas partes disterminata* (London, 1676), in which 1–209, 695–74 recapitulate the history of philosophy from *Court*, II.

[175] For Gale's biography, see Pigney, 'Theophilus Gale' (2007). The best overall account is Pigney, 'Theophilus Gale and historiography of philosophy' (2010), supplemented by Wallace, jnr, *Shapers of English Calvinism, 1660–1714* (2011), 87–120 ('Theophilus Gale: Calvinism and the ancient theology'), although the latter is unreliable on Gale's historical work, repeating several mistaken generalisations about 'ancient theology' (e.g. 91: 'it was also an attempt to form a more universal and tolerant approach to religion'), and ignoring Gale's Latin works.

[176] Bod. MS Rawl. letters 59, fols. 1$^r$–286$^v$; MS Rawl. letters 52, fols. 281, 343, 359, 362; MS Rawl. letters 53, fol. 198; MS Rawl. letters 54, fol. 5, 39; MS Rawl. letters 104, fol. 2.

On first impression everything about these works suggests a high degree of scholarly acumen: from their great length, to the Latin prefatory poems, to the copious quotations in Greek and Hebrew, to the large library of Hebraica he left to Harvard.[177] However, all of this is misleading. Gale's work is often compared, not least by himself, to Stillingfleet's *Origines sacrae*.[178] But the theological differences between them meant that their accounts were in fact fundamentally different. Stillingfleet, as we have seen, believed that knowledge of the creation was a universal tradition that had passed through a natural historical process to various pagan philosophers – he said nothing about *all* philosophy being derived from the Hebrews and dismissed such narratives as the fancy of the Hellenistic Jews. Gale, on the contrary, was the seventeenth century's most concerted defender of Judaic primacy. All knowledge, sacred and secular, had been revealed to the Jewish patriarchs Adam, through Seth, Enoch, Abraham, Joseph, Solomon, Job, and above all Moses; these 'first human Instituters, or Authors of Philosophie', were 'indeed Divine, and divinely illuminated'.[179] From Moses in particular it descended to the pagans, who corrupted it either with their own idolatrous speculations (the orientals) or with their sophistic wrangling (the Greeks), a process that Gale charted over thousands of pages of scholarship that was, by the standards of its time, supinely credulous and out of date.

For example, not content with the usual sources for Pythagoras and Plato plagiarising from the Jews, Gale also claimed such a status for Aristotle, citing the authority of Aristobulus – one of the Hellenistic Jews who was known as the first exponents of Judaic primacy – who had reported of one Clearchus (*c*. 300 BC), an Aristotelian who claimed that Aristotle had conversed with a Jew.[180] At this point Gale had the temerity to mis-cite Selden in support of his case, whose actual words are worth quoting in full:

Furthermore, from the authority of Aristobulus it is said that the Peripatetic philosophy (whose founder was Aristotle and follower Aristobulus himself) 'was derived from the law of Moses and other prophets'.[181] Certainly there is an ancient Hebrew fiction, that the dying Aristotle taught his disciples not only about the immortality of the soul, but also about [post-mortem] rewards and punishments, as if he had been taught by the descendants of Shem, that is to say the Jews. Then there is the story that having been

---

[177] Gale gave the theological part of his library, consisting of over 1000 volumes. Unfortunately, they were lost in the fire that decimated Harvard Hall in 1764: Potter, *The library of Harvard University* (1915 [1903]), 14–15, 120. The Harvard donations and library records do not hold an inventory of the books donated (I am very grateful to Barbara Meloni and Robin Carlaw for assistance in this matter).

[178] Gale, *Court*, I, sig. *2$^r$ (although Gale admits the difference between them at sigs. **$^{r-v}$).

[179] Gale, *Court*, II.1, 7–22, quotation at 7.

[180] Aristobulus's claim is preserved in Josephus, *Ap.*, I.22, from there adopted in Eusebius, *Praep. Ev.*, IX.5.

[181] Clemens Alexandrinus, *Strom.*, V.14.

admonished by the High Priest Simeon the Just, he changed his early opinion, 'in all points in which he previously thought contrary to the law and doctrine of the Hebrews, and thenceforth changed into a completely different man' . . . This latter story they quote from a book found long ago in Egypt, which they are not afraid to attribute to Aristotle himself. But there is no reason why we should believe these fictions.[182]

Selden *did* believe that pagans like Pythagoras had taken some theology from the Hebrews, but his acceptance of the findings of the latest critical scholarship led him to dispute the tendency of the Hellenistic Jews and their rabbinic followers to stretch this idea to absurdity. Gale heeded no such warning, merrily approving of the claims not only of Aristobulus, but also of Philo – in direct contrast to Stillingfleet – even adopting the long-abandoned claim that he had spoken with the apostles.[183]

This entirely uncritical attitude was also adopted in the case of the pre-Greek pagans. In the case of the Egyptians, Gale was alone among all the figures we have considered in citing Kircher when it suited his thesis that Moses had given the Egyptians esoteric wisdom preserved in the form of hieroglyphs.[184] As for near-eastern traditions, not only did Gale repeat all the old claims about Abraham's vast proficiency in mathematics and subsequent teaching of the Chaldeans that had been ignored by Stanley (2.3), he also accepted the stories of the philosophical books of Enoch that the royalist scholar had dismissed as late Judaeo–Arabic fables.[185] Gale, then, was operating in a fundamentally different world to Stillingfleet and the conformists who were amalgamating the latest continental scholarship into their conclusions – his claim to be following

---

[182] Selden, *De jure naturali*, 14–15: 'Quinetiam ex Aristobuli illius authoritate dicitur, Philosophiam Peripateticam (cujus princeps Aristoteles & sectator ipse Aristobulus) . . . *ex Lege Mosaica atque aliis pendere Prophetis.* Certe & vetustum liquet esse Ebraeorum aliquot commentum, Aristotelem jam moribundum discipulos suos tum animae immortalitatem tum poenae ac praemii rationem velut a peculiaribus Semi posteris, id est Judaeis, edoctum docuisse, tum a Simeone Justo pontifice monitum, pristinas mutasse sententias . . . *in universis de quibus ante senserat contra legem ac doctrinam Ebraeorum, & in hominem inde planè alium migrasse* . . . Alterum illud de Simeone Justo, ex libro citant veteri in Aegypto antiquitùs reperto quem nec Aristoteli ipsi tribuere verentur. Utcunque autem fictis hisce non sit cur credamus . . . '. The sources Selden refers to are the pre-tenth century ps.-Aristotelian Arabic *Risālat al-Tuffāha* (*The Book of the Apple*) which he consulted in manuscript in Hebrew translation (see Toomer, *Selden*, ii, 494, n. 29) and the *Kitab al Khazari* by the Spanish Jewish philosopher Rabbi Judah ha-Levi made available in a Hebrew translation (which was used by Selden) by Judah b. Tibbon as הכוזרי (Venice, 1594) and ed. and trans. Johannes Buxtorf, jnr as *Liber Cosri* (Basel, 1660) (see there, 30–1). Contrary to Selden's intentions, the impressive obscurity of this testimony later rendered it attractive to other defenders of Judaic philosophical primacy apart from Gale: see e.g. Hermann Witsius, *Aegyptiacam et ΔEKAΦYΛON. Sive de Aegyptiacorum sacrorum cum Hebraicis collatione libri tres* (Amsterdam, 1696), 272–3.

[183] Gale, *Court*, ii.3, 262 (the original source is Eusebius, *Hist. Eccl.*, ii.17.1–2; see 6.5 below).

[184] Gale, *Court*, ii.1, 34. This argument is expanded in *Philosophia generalis*, 67–79, where, on the authority of Steuco, Gale suggests that the world/snake/wing hieroglyph represented the trinity.

[185] Gale, *Court*, ii.1, 67–8, 9.

in a long and proud scholarly tradition (into which he threw not only Stillingfleet but such luminaries as Scaliger) has been far too easily accepted by his modern readers, for it was nothing more than disingenuous self-promotion.[186] He even appended to the second edition a short defence against the argument that there was no evidence of Graeco–Jewish contact: although he is not named, there can be no doubt that the target here is Parker.[187] Gale's rather pathetic explanation – which did not even directly answer the original objection – was that the Hebrew truths had been so corrupted by pagan mythology that their trace was only faint.[188]

The reason for Gale's scholarly backwardness is that his whole historical picture was subservient to theological ends that were becoming outdated in the Restoration; specifically, to a version of Reformed covenant theology.[189] After Adam's fall the pagans unconsciously attempted to use philosophy to make up for their lack of grace: 'the grand Designe of Ethnic Philosophie . . . was to put men under a Covenant of Workes'. This was a rationalistic hubris that was directly mappable onto Christian heresy:

> How apt is every man by nature to run himself on a Covenant of Workes, and deifie some righteousnesse of his own, though never so unrighteous! What latent venes of *Pelagianisme* are there in the hearts of al by nature! whence, according to *Augustin, Pelagianisme is the Heresie of Nature.* Now what was the πρῶτον ψεῦδος or *prime Error* of al *Ethnic* Philosophie but this, so to *cultivate, refine* and *elevate* corrupt nature, as to render it a fit Temple of the Deitie, without the superaddition of Medicinal Grace?[190]

Pagan philosophy was an attempt to counteract the defects of pagan theology, an attempt doomed to failure because of the incapacity of human reason. This sounds close to pure fideism, but the story is not so simple, because Gale *did* believe in a role for philosophy and developed his own vision of what he called a 'Reformed philosophy' in Part IV of the *Court* and in the *Philosophia*

---

[186]  Gale, *Court*, I, sig. *2ʳ; *Court*, II.1, 94–6.

[187]  My reading is thus the opposite of that in Wallace, *Shapers*, 110 ('Perhaps the unnamed "discourse" that Gale had come across which disagreed with his argument . . . had come from the Cambridge group or one of their sympathizers').

[188]  Gale, *Court*, I.3, 111–15. For the explanation for this addition ('having . . . met with a Discourse of a learned man, which directly tendes to the subversion of my main *Hypothesis*, I could not but conceive my self under an essential Obligation, to adde what I could for the confirmation of the same'), see *Court*, I, 'Advertissements', sigs. **ᵛ–**2ʳ.

[189]  This is very well demonstrated in Pigney, 'Gale', 88–92, on which I draw. For Gale's direct thoughts on covenant theology, see his 'A summary of the two Covenants', in William Strong, *A discourse of the two covenants*, ed. Theophilus Gale (London, 1678), sigs. [A3]ʳ–[(a4)]ʳ. For Gale's Reformed-influenced scholarly conservativeness, see his defence of the purity of the Masoretic text of the Bible in his *Idea theologiae, tam contemplativae quam activae, ad formam s. Scripturae delineata* (London, 1673), 65–70.

[190]  Gale, *Court*, III, sigs. [A3]ʳ⁻ᵛ. I know of no place where Augustine speaks directly of 'haeresis naturae', but Gale was probably simply thinking of Augustine's *De natura et gratia* in general. For Gale on the philosophical origins of Christian heresy, see 6.5 below.

*Generalis*.[191] This philosophy, he claimed, put him in a lineage of 'reformed' philosophers stretching from Wycliffe and Jan Hus, through Pico, Savonarola, Melanchthon, Ramus, and finally Cornelius Jansen, of whom Gale was one of the most important early English followers.[192] What was in need of reform was Aristotelian scholasticism, which Gale associated especially with the Jesuits; its replacement should, he claimed, be a cautious form of Platonism.[193] This has led to some confusion, Gale being aligned with 'Cambridge Platonism'.[194] A closer reading reveals that what Gale called 'Platonism' was simply a version of Reformed scholasticism that had little to do with what anyone else in the seventeenth century called Platonism. Take for example his treatment of 'Platonic' ethics. Discussing human liberty and the will, he extensively quoted Suárez, Bradwardine, Aquinas, and Jansen (among others) and incorporated an attack on Pelagianism: unsurprisingly the 'Plato' that emerges is closer to a Reformed neo-scholastic, with all the emphasis on divine omnipotence that that entails; the supporting evidence from Plato is the discussion in the *Republic* (IX.952$^b$) of a 'pattern [of an ideal city] laid up in heaven', which to Gale confirms that 'God is the measure of all things and the most perfect model'.[195] When he came to discuss 'Platonic' natural philosophy, Gale moved straight to extracting it from Genesis, not on the basis of any historical assumptions about Mosaic intentionality but on the old-fashioned Reformed model of extracting whatever natural historical facts he could from the text – all this supposedly 'ex mente Mosis & Platonis'.[196] An even better example is the case of metaphysics. For several generations, metaphysicians had debated whether Aristotle's definition of metaphysics as study of 'being' (τὸ ὄν) meant a study of all being or something more akin to 'natural theology' as the study of God's essence and attributes.[197] For theological reasons Gale favoured the latter: 'May we not take it for granted, that nothing properly belongs to Metaphysics, but what is supernatural, as the name importes?'[198] And so, ignoring all the technical debate that came before him, he simply assigned that definition to Plato, claiming that the confusion in Aristotle must have stemmed from his corruptions of his master, who himself of course possessed the original tradition from the Jews.[199] Yet the

---

[191] See most explicitly his defence of this move at *Court*, III, sig. (b)$^v$. See also Gale, 'Dissertatiuncula Prooemialis', *Philosophia generalis*, 8 (separate pagination).

[192] Gale, *Court*, IV, sigs. A2$^{r-v}$. For Gale's Jansenism, see his *The true idea of Jansenisme, both historick and dogmatick* (London, 1669).

[193] Gale, *Court*, IV, sigs. A4$^{r-v}$, *passim*.

[194] Malusa, 'First general histories', 292–5; Pigney, 'Gale', 79–80, 86; Hutton, 'Moses Atticus', 71. But cf. Wallace, *Shapers*, 113.

[195] Gale, *Philosophia generalis*, 447–52, 528. I also draw on the discussion at Malusa, 'First general histories', 316–17, 325.

[196] Gale, *Philosophia generalis*, 304–6.     [197] See 4.2 below.     [198] Gale, *Court*, IV, 210

[199] Ibid., IV, 237–8; see also 210–12, *Philosophia generalis*, 658–60.

metaphysics Gale actually presented was based entirely on the standard neo-scholastic discussions of Suárez and others.[200]

Far from being in the scholarly tradition of Vossius or Stillingfleet, then, Gale's whole history of philosophy was very different, and a propaedeutic to a neo-scholastic Reformed divinity. The real pre-history of Gale's work lies not with these figures but in the approach of his mentor John Owen, the leading Independent minister whom we have met already as an opponent of the historical assumptions behind the London Polyglot. Owen's *Theologoumena pantodapa* (1661) was, like Gale's *Court*, an attempt to reconcile the new continental approach to the history of religion and theology with a scheme of Reformed covenant theology; it proved popular among nonconformists (Lucy Hutchinson, for example, made a translation of the first two books).[201] Like Gale, Owen betrayed the scholarship he was appropriating by resorting to a naïve assertion of Judaic primacy. This he did either by relying uncritically on the church fathers,[202] or by directly challenging the findings of the latest scholarship, such as when he insisted that biblical Hebrew was the primitive language, contrary to the assertion of Vossius and a host of others, all of whom had followed Scaliger's finding that Samaritan characters preceded Hebrew.[203] Like Gale, Owen launched a fideist historical attack on the intrusion of philosophy into theology at the same time as developing a sophisticated Reformed scholastic philosophical theology of his own.[204]

This is not to say that Gale did not draw on other Reformed sources: his key source for the existence and putative brilliance of ancient Jewish philosophy was the *Historia philosophica* (1655) by the respected German scholar Georg Horn (1620–1670), who in 1654 inherited the chair of history at Leiden once held by Scaliger and Vossius and is notable as probably the seventeenth century's most important world historian (*Arca Noae* [1666]).[205] As this all

---

[200] Gale, *Court*, ɪv, 250; Gale, *Philosophia generalis*, 658–94.

[201] John Owen, *Theologoumena pantodapa, sive, de natura, ortu progressu, et studio verae theologiae, libri sex* (Oxford, 1661). There are no studies of this work as a piece of religious historiography, but from a theological perspective, see Rehnman, *The theological methodology of John Owen* (2002). For Lucy Hutchinson, see her *On the principles of Christian religion, addressed to her daughter; and on theology*, ed. J. Hutchinson (London, 1817), 141–347 (the MS is unlocated).

[202] See e.g. Owen, *Theologoumena*, 73–4.

[203] Ibid., 288–301 (Owen was also particularly concerned by Kircher's suggestion of the antediluvian antiquity of Egyptian hieroglyphs). For the Hebrew/Samaritan story, see Cornelius, *Languages in seventeenth- and early eighteenth-century imaginary voyages* (1965), 5–24; Droixhe, 'La crise de l'hébreu langue-mère au XVIIe siècle' (1992).

[204] Owen, *Theologoumena*, 509–21. For Owen's Reformed scholasticism, see Rehnman, 'John Owen: a Reformed scholastic at Oxford' (2001); van Asselt, 'Covenant theology as relational theology' (2012). This does not mean that Owen was not an able humanist in a more general sense: see Gribbe, 'John Owen, Renaissance man?' (2012).

[205] Klempt, *Die Säkularisierung der universalhistorischen Auffassung im 16. und 17. Jahrhundert* (1960), 114–23; van der Zande, 'August Ludwig Schlözer and the English *Universal History*'

suggests, Horn was a far more critical scholar than Gale; he rejected, for example, the idea that Plato had directly available to him any form of Mosaic tradition, attacking the Jewish and patristic authors that had suggested this.[206] But the broadly Calvinist Horn had still insisted that the history of philosophy was the history of the dual Adamic legacy: a combination of diminished rational capacity and hubristic over-rationalising sophistry.[207] (Whether one episode from Horn's later insanity, which involved him running naked through Leiden shouting 'And have you ever seen a man from paradise? I am that Adam' is connected to this is unclear.)[208] Accordingly, Horn believed that the patriarchs from Abraham to Moses were directly illuminated with theological–philosophical wisdom: Gale's section on 'Jewish philosophy' is nothing more than a series of extended quotations from Horn's discussion.[209]

Gale's work testifies less to the vitality of nonconformist scholarly culture, and more to its increasing obsolescence by the 1670s. His history of philosophy shows that Owen's descendants struggled to amalgamate new continental scholarship with their theology as much as the other great nonconformist leader, the Presbyterian Richard Baxter, struggled with similar developments in Anglican patristics (mocked for his obsolete efforts by Parker among others).[210] The history of philosophy was of course a far less charged field than patristics but even here the exclusion from the formalised centres of learning, combined with a refusal to surrender Reformed scholasticism,[211] led to scholarly stagnation.

---

(2003), at 137–8. For the *Historia philosophica*, see Malusa, 'First general histories', 236–59. Horn's contacts with England remain largely unexplored, but he worked there in 1645–46 as an aristocratic tutor, subsequently publishing *De statu ecclesiae Britannicae hodierno, liber commentarius; una cum appendice eorum, quae in Synodo Glasguensi contra episcopus decreta sunt* (Danzig, 1647), with the obvious pro-Presbyterian line implied in the title, as well as the *Rerum Britannicarum libri septem* (Leiden, 1648). He was in frequent contact with Hartlib, sending him the *Historia philosophica* on 17 January 1655 (HP, 16/2/9A).

[206] Horn, *Historia philosophica*, 190–2.

[207] See e.g. ibid., 52: 'Cum primi parentes nostri, fraude Diaboli, omni solida sapientia penitus excidissent, dubium non est, quin, detumescente indies dolore, cum quod factum, infectum fieri non posset, animum ad scientias excolendas adjecerint, quarum adhuc scintillae quaedam & rudera non contemnenda in ipsorum animis errant'.

[208] For the source of this story, see Mandelbrote, 'Vossius and the Septuagint', 98.

[209] Gale, *Court*, II.1, 7–22, which finishes with a translated quotation from Horn, *Historia philosophica*, 112: 'Sapientia, ut notum, in ipso primitus Paradiso exorta, postmodum à sanctis Patribus exculta, & ad posteros propagata est. Deus enim semper aliquos suscitavit, qui, relictis profanorum erroribus, instaurationem imaginis Dei, etiam Sapientiae studio, molirentur. Quales post Noachum Ebraei dicti sunt, quorum postea appellatio usque ad natum Christum obtinuit. Igitur ex Semi posteris Abrahamus erat, vir divino ingenio & admiranda rerum perita insignis. In cujus familia clarissimum Philosophiae domicilius ac sedes fuit. Abrahamus enim non inter suos modo, sed & in toto Oriente, clarissimi propter Sapientiam nominis habitus est'.

[210] Quantin, *Antiquity*, 314–18.

[211] For Baxter's belief that he could trump history with logic-chopping, see Quantin, *Antiquity*, 314–15; for his self-avowed scholasticism more generally, see Burton, *The hallowing of logic: the trinitarian method of Richard Baxter's Methodus Theologiae* (2012), esp. 65–72.

## 3.6    The assault on Jewish primacy and a new Egypt

The previous section has shown that in England the idea of a Judaic philosophical primacy was dying by the mid-seventeenth century, confined only to those with their own peculiar agenda, whether More with his pseudo-Cabbala or Gale with his covenant theology. This may be confirmed by the reaction among scholars to Pierre-Daniel Huet's *Demonstratio Evangelica* (1679). Huet – a bishop in the French church from 1685 – was a respected figure in the republic of letters: he had published a new edition of Origen in 1668, based partly on new manuscripts, and edited the famous edition of the Latin classics known as the 'Delphin Classics'.[212] The *Demonstratio* was a large apologetic work, whose main argument (mainly against chronological challenges to scriptural authority as well as Spinoza's more thoroughgoing politicisation of Moses) was that all pagan history and mythology were based on the Old Testament, near-eastern and Asian deities representing either Moses or, if female, his wife Zipporah. Like Gale he had been much inspired by the work on the Phoenicians by Bochart, who had taught him and whom he had accompanied as a young man to the court of Queen Christina.[213] Despite this similarity Huet was far more judicious in his thesis than the nonconformist Englishman – he did not push the Mosaic origins of philosophy, merely of 'leges, ritus, ac historiae'.[214] Nonetheless, he was not averse to piling up the old Jewish and patristic testimonies for Pythagoras and Plato having taken from the Hebrews – even citing Aristobulus's story of Aristotle speaking with an Israelite.[215]

Huet sent his great work to the leading Oxford scholar Edward Bernard, whom he had met while the latter was unhappily tutoring Charles II's two sons by the duchess of Cleveland in Paris in 1676–78; by this point he was back in England (having 'been soe affronted and abused by that insolent woman that he hath been forced to quit that imployment and return') and Huet had to send the *Demonstratio* with John Locke, himself returning to England just as Huet's book was coming off the press in April 1679.[216] From a later letter from Huet

---

[212] The fullest account is now Shelford, *Pierre-Daniel Huet and European intellectual life* (2007).

[213] The fullest study of the *Demonstratio* remains Dupront, *Pierre-Daniel Huet et l'exégèse comparatiste au xviie siècle* (1930); see also Walker, *Ancient theology*, 214–20; Shelford, 'Thinking geometrically in Pierre-Daniel Huet's *Demonstratio evangelica* (1679)' (2002); C. Ligota, 'Der apologetische Rahmen der Mythendeutung im Frankreich des 17. Jahrhunderts' (1984).

[214] Pierre-Daniel Huet, *Demonstratio evangelica ad serenissimum delphinium* (Paris, 1679), 124.

[215] Ibid., 46. Clearly sensitive to the anti-syncretist backlash that had become prominent in the preceding decades, he also frequently qualifies such views (as here: 'Verum etiamsi alia nos indicia destituerent, vel sola Platonicae doctrinae cum Mosaica consensio, alterius ab altera propagationem ostenderet').

[216] Huet to Isaac Vossius, 4 March 1679, Bod. MS D'Orville 470, p. 138; Huet to Bernard, 5 March 1679, Bod. MS Smith 5, fols. 137$^r$–138$^r$ (in both promising to send the *Demonstratio*, also explaining that a copy will go to Pearson); Huet to Vossius, Bod MS D'Orville 470, p. 141 (it has been sent with Locke). That Huet met Bernard in Paris is confirmed by an earlier undated

we know that Bernard was not particularly impressed by Huet's case, complaining that there was no evidence that the pagans had counted Moses among their deities and that Huet had overvalued the primacy and ubiquity of Hebrew.[217] Bernard is perhaps the leading representative of the combination of Greek and oriental scholarship that became so prominent in Oxford in the second half of the century and is thus an important barometer of scholarly opinion. In the 1660s he studied Hebrew privately with Isaac Abendana, but like his Oxford colleagues Edward Pococke, Thomas Smith, and Thomas Hyde, his interests ranged further across many things Greek and oriental.[218] His greatest scholarly undertaking was an edition of the Greek text of Josephus's *Jewish Antiquities* first commissioned by John Fell in 1669; unfortunately the truncated version that finally appeared in 1700 has no reflections on Josephus's penchant for asserting Judaic primacy.[219] But Bernard was at the centre of a group of Oxford scholars – most prominent of whom was the much younger Humphrey Hody – who played the key role in the dismantling of another myth of Hellenistic Judaism: the *Letter of Aristeas* purporting to explain the origin of the Septuagint; these critics 'in particular ... criticised the reliance on the testimony of Josephus which had marked earlier attempts to defend the authenticity of the *Letter of Aristeas*'.[220] The Hellenistic–Jewish sources of Judaeo-centred apologetics were coming under sustained attack from entirely 'orthodox' figures. On a broader level it is probably more significant that Bernard informed Huet that English *theologians* were also unimpressed with the *Demonstratio*.[221] Finding Judaism in all pagan history was falling out of fashion with those to whom the tactic was most meant to appeal. For if England in the 1650s and 1660s had seen a gradual marginalisation of any hyperbolic claims to Mosaic philosophy and Jewish influence on the history of philosophy, the 1670s and 1680s saw the solidification of this

---

letter: Bod. MS Smith 6, fols. 129ʳ–130ʳ. Bernard evidently knew Locke quite well, because he wrote to him twice about his project to edit Josephus, the second time with a specimen: Bernard to Locke, 3 Jan 1679, *Locke Correspondence*, ii, 661; Bernard to Locke, 8 Mar 1679, ibid., 691–3. For the story about Bernard and the Duchess, see *Letters of Humphrey Prideaux to John Ellis 1674–1722*, ed. E. M. Thompson (London, 1875), 58.

[217] Huet to Bernard, July 1682, MS Smith 72, fols. 5ʳ–6ʳ. Bernard's thoughts on the development of scripts, which show that he favoured the post-Scaliger tendency to prioritise Samaritan, are available in the single engraved sheet *Orbis eruditi literaturam à charactere Samaritico hunc in modum favente Deo deduxit Eduardus Bernardus* (Oxford, 1689).

[218] The fullest source for Bernard's biography is Smith's *Vita clarissimi et doctissimi viri, Edwardi Bernardi* (London, 1704); see Toomer, *Eastern wisedome*, 299–305; Feingold, 'Oriental studies', 491–2; Mandelbrote, 'Vossius', 102–5, 112–15. For his library at death, see the auction catalogue, *Bibliotheca Bernardina* (London, 1697).

[219] Flavius Josephus, *Antiquitatum Judaicarum libri quatuor priores, et pars magna quinti*, ed. E. Bernard (Oxford, 1700). See Carter, *OUP*, 88–90; Toomer, *Eastern wisedome*, 299–300.

[220] Mandelbrote, 'Vossius', esp. 114–5 for Bernard's influence on both Hody and Antonie van Dale (quotation from 114).

[221] Huet to Bernard, Jul 1684, Bod. MS Smith 72, fol. 8ʳ.

consensus in some canonical works of scholarship, the most prominent of which were John Marsham's *Chronicus canon* (1672), John Spencer's *De legibus Hebraeorum* (1683–85), Ralph Cudworth's *True intellectual system* (1678), and Thomas Tenison's attack on Cudworth in his *Of idolatry* (1678), all of whom, in one way or another, engaged with, drew on, or shared the conclusions reached by the young Samuel Parker in the 1660s.

Together Marsham's and Spencer's works consist of over two thousand pages of dense scholarly Latin. Marsham's was a work of technical chronology, Spencer's a detailed investigation into one episode of sacred history (the giving of the Ritual Law to the post-Exodus Hebrews). This difference between the two is worth bearing in mind,[222] because from their earliest reception they have been treated together due to their sharing one notorious thesis: that much of Jewish religion and intellectual culture derived *from* that of the Egyptians. Although the history of ancient thought was only part of their huge works, this thesis is obviously of great importance to our story, as it certainly was to their first readers. Both set the development of Egyptian and Israelite culture within a wider scheme of historical development and cultural progress.

Marsham (1602–85) made his name outside the academy, pursuing a diplomatic and political career.[223] We have already seen the influence his chronological interests had on his nephew Stanley; he was similarly prominent in royalist–Anglican scholarly circles (albeit without Stanley's verve for dispensing patronage), writing the preface to Sir William Dugdale's *Monasticon Anglicanum* (1655), an important work in reasserting the place of monasteries in medieval English life.[224] He was also close to the clerical scholarly world, around 1660 showing Herbert Thorndike unpublished works by Isaac Vossius.[225] Through Henry Oldenburg he was in contact with the important

---

[222] Although it is also interesting to note that the German editors of the 1676 edition of Marsham advertised it as a 'Liber non Chronologicae tantùm, sed & Historicae Antiquitatis reconditissima complexus' on the title page (*Canon chronicus … nunc longè emendatior in Germaniâ recusus* (Leipzig, 1676)).

[223] He attended St John's College, Oxford in the early 1620s before being admitted a student at the Middle Temple. He was present in attendance on Sir Thomas Edmondes during the signing of the Treaty of Fontainebleau. In 1638, he was appointed one of the six clerks in chancery but after following the king to Oxford during the civil war – supposedly losing *c.* £6,000 in sequestrations – he retired to his estate in Cuxton, like so many royalists devoting himself to scholarship (although he did sit as an MP for Rochester in the Convention Parliament which restored the monarchy). The fullest biography is that of his son: 'Robert Marsham's biography of Sir John [Marsham]' (CKS MS U1300 Z10), mildly supplemented by Hull, 'John Marsham, a forgotten antiquary' (1968). Black, 'Marsham, John', *ODNB* has '£60,000'.

[224] On this work, see Parry, *Trophies*, 217–48. Marsham's long preface was clearly thought of as an important *apologia* for the medieval monks: as late as 1695, William Wake considered Thomas Tanner's *Notitia monastica* (Oxford, 1695) its first replacement (Wake to Tanner, 11 Apr 1695, Bod. MS Tanner 24, fol. 6ʳ).

[225] See Thorndike to Vossius, *c.* 1660, MS D'Orville 470, p. 33. Thorndike referred to Marsham showing him the beginning of Vossius's 'Aegyptiaca', which would help confirm the authenticity of scripture. It is unclear what this refers to: Vossius did publish in 1666 a work *De Nili et*

Maurist antiquarian and scholar Luc d'Achery.[226] He had a large library, containing at his death 1,085 books even though it had been 'considerably diminished by y$^e$ fire of London'; it was valuable enough to have manuscripts stolen from it by the Master of University College, Oxford, Obadiah Walker.[227] He was also a keen numismatist, leaving a large collection of coins to his son and frequently using antiquarian evidence in his work.[228]

Marsham's chronological studies had already produced by 1649 a short *Diatriba chronologica* for resolving some chronological issues in the Old Testament,[229] but it is the *Chronicus canon* that propelled him to European fame. Although branded a work on Egyptian, Jewish, and Greek chronology, it is clear from the outset that Marsham's central concern was with one particular issue that had flared up in the republic of letters since the early years of the century. As the centrepiece of his revolutionary *Thesaurus temporum* (1606), Scaliger produced a reconstruction of the Greek version of Eusebius's *Chronicle* based on the excerpts that had survived in the Byzantine world chronicle of George Syncellus. Here he found the list of thirty-one Egyptian dynasties preserved by the Egyptian priest Manetho. These were difficult sources: Syncellus provided different lists of the dynasties to those of Eusebius and Julius Africanus, and to another very different list by the Alexandrian polymath Eratosthenes. But there was an even greater problem: the dynasties stretched back to before the creation, to 5285 BC. Yet Manetho seemed a genuine source, and Scaliger's partial 'solution' was to publish the dynasty lists while announcing a prior period of 'proleptic time'.[230] This was hardly satisfactory and a long debate ensued. Some, like Denis Petau, simply dismissed the veracity of the lists (*Opus de doctrina temporum* (1627)). But a new stage in the debate was

---

*aliorum fluminum origine*, but this seems an unlikely match. Stanley wrote to Marsham on 14 February 1663 to mention Vossius's presence in England, working in the Cotton library (CKS MS U1300 C1/13). For letters from Vossius to Marsham, see CKS MS U1300 C1/14, 15.

[226] CKS MS U1300, C1/6, 11, 12 (d'Achery is throughout named 'De Carcary', which has prevented his previous identification). The letters are not in the *Oldenburg correspondence* (one of Marsham's replies is in XI, 361).

[227] See CKS MS U1121.E7, 'Catalogus librorum Bibliothecae Marshamianae', containing 459 books in folio, 211 in quarto, 369 in octavo, and 46 unclassified. Although the catalogue was composed several years after Marsham's death in 1685, it can be considered representative, for it contains few books after that date, the latest being published in 1697 (see p. 21 of the Catalogue). The description is from CKS MS U1300 Z10, fol. 1$^r$. The story of the supposed theft (Walker claimed Marsham gave it to him) is told in Edmund Gibson to Arthur Charlett, 9 Jul 1694, Bod. MS Ballard 5, fol. 52$^r$ (the work in question is a manuscript of ps.-Ingulf, which formed the basis of the edition in *Rerum Anglicarum scriptorum veterum*, eds., William Fulman and Thomas Gale (Oxford, 1684) (see there, sig. a3$^r$)) – Gibson claimed that 'the old gentleman [i.e. Walker] has too much of the spirit of an antiquarie and a great scholar to think stealing a manuscript any sin'.

[228] E.g. Henry Futter to Marsham, Feb 1665, CKS MS C1/7.

[229] Marsham, *Diatriba chronologica*.

[230] For a brief introduction, see Grafton, 'Joseph Scaliger and historical chronology' (1975), at 170–3; for a full discussion, see Grafton, *Scaliger*, II, 491–743, esp. 711–20.

reached when G. J. Vossius suggested that some of the dynasties were not successive but parallel and could thus be squeezed in not only after the creation but even after the flood; Manetho had misunderstood the ancient hieroglyphic records he was transcribing.[231] All this was rendered less of a scholarly and more a theological problem by La Peyrère's pre-Adamite hypothesis and by the rise in popularity of the Septuagint chronology (longer by 1,200 years than the Masoretic), especially in the hands of Marsham's friend Isaac Vossius.[232]

Marsham had no time for Petau's scepticism. 'It seems to me', he wrote, 'that these dynasties must neither be extended immeasurably, nor rejected altogether'.[233] Although he clearly had a desire to see them fit the biblical chronology – the Masoretic one at that – and although his argument was based on following Vossius's parallel-dynasties thesis, Marsham's work in many ways returned the debate to the field of technical chronology and away from apologetics. There can be no doubt that it was his work that kicked off the debate over Egyptian chronology that engulfed the republic of letters over the next hundred years.[234]

G. J. Vossius defended his thesis of simultaneous dynasties only on the basis of conjecture about Manetho's method of source acquisition. Marsham defended it by what we might call a 'reverse chronology': starting towards the end of the dynasty lists he showed that because events known from other sources matched perfectly on to a simultaneous-dynasty scheme, it must also apply to the earlier periods. There were four dynasties: Thebes, Theis, Memphis, and Tanis (or Lower Egypt).[235] Every chronologer knew that at one point during the reign of Tutimaeus, Egypt had been conquered – with the exception of Thebes – by some 'shepherds' (also known as 'Hyksos'),[236] but

---

[231] Grafton, *Scaliger*, ii, 719–20; Grafton, 'Discipline'. See Vossius, *Theologia gentilis*, 206–12, esp. 210–12 (the majority of Vossius's reasoning (206–10) actually depends on a theory about the Egyptians' shifting understanding of the canicular year).

[232] For the response to La Peyrère, see the entertaining n. 103 in Allen, *Noah*, 136; Klempt, *Säkularisierung*, 95–6; Rossi, *Abyss*, 138–52; Jorink, *Reading the book of nature in the Dutch golden age* (2010 [2006]), 97–105, 301–8. For Vossius, see now Grafton, 'Isaac Vossius, chronologer'.

[233] Marsham, *Canon*, 1: 'Mihi visum est Dynastias istas neque in immensum extendi debere, neque omnino rejici'. This comes directly after a citation of Petau's rejection of the dynasty lists, from *De doctrina temporum* (2 vols, Paris, 1627), ii, 181 ('Aegyptiorum origines, ac Dynastias, quas Africanus & Eusebius scriptis prodiderunt, fabulosas, &, quod ad vetustatem attinet, ementitas esse, cùm res ipsa loquitur, tùm nos breviter suo loco significavimus'), and a discussion of Scaliger.

[234] This makes it all the more surprising that it has received no detailed treatment. A few useful remarks can be found in Rossi, *The dark abyss of time* (1984 [1979]), 124–5; also briefly but usefully, see Buchwald and Feingold, *Newton and the origins of civilization* (2013), 204, 226–8. The copious manuscripts in the CKS have, to my knowledge, until now gone entirely untapped.

[235] Marsham, *Canon*, 24–9.

[236] Manetho, *Aegyptiaca*, fr. 42, i.75–79.2; Josephus, *Ap.*, i.73, also i. 93; i.227 (the account in Josephus, supposedly taken from Manetho, is slightly longer).

when that conquest had occurred was unclear. Yet one piece of philological trickery seemed, at least to Marsham, to solve the problem. If the last ruler of Lower Egypt before the conquest was called not Tutimaeus (or 'Timaeus', as he was by Josephus), but Concharis (a name that appeared before the first shepherd pharaoh in Syncellus), then a synchronism emerged between him and Nitocris, who must have been the last ruler of Memphis before its conquest by the shepherds (because Africanus listed no rulers after her). Since Eratosthenes also listed Nitocris in his Theban catalogue, she must have combined the rule of both Thebes and Memphis. Here a brilliant synchronism occurred: the two rulers listed before Nitocris by both Eratosthenes and Africanus had ruled for one year and one hundred years respectively. Even though they had completely different names, this was surely unlikely to be a coincidence: 'This equal inequality of reigning is far too unusual to believe that it happened fortuitously, twice and simultaneously!'[237] From this remarkable congruence could be built the dynasty lists for all four locales, stretching back to the founder of them all, Menes, all conveniently presented in clear and elegant tables.

Yet this involved problems. It meant identifying the last pharaoh of a united Egypt (after the expulsion of the shepherds), Sesostris, with the biblical conqueror Susac (1 Kings 14:25, 2 Chron. 12:1–2), a move that was critiqued by numerous scholars in the following decades.[238] It involved rather arbitrarily claiming that Africanus had deliberately elongated his list of dynasties.[239] And most importantly for us, it took the Egyptian dynasties right back to the first days after the flood, meaning that Menes had to be identified with Noah's son Ham rather than with Ham's son Mizraim (Gen. 10:6), as was usual.[240] Egypt, then, while not quite antediluvian, was very ancient indeed – much more so than the other civilisations.

What did this great antiquity imply for the history of the arts and sciences? In his newly reconstructed dynasty lists, the second ruler of Thebes and of Theis was Athothes/Thoth. Thoth had long been identified with Mercury/Hermes,[241] and Marsham felt obliged to explore precisely the nature of the learning he had bestowed upon the Egyptians. This was certainly not the Trismegistus of the Renaissance: Marsham explicitly accepted Casaubon's judgement that the *Poemander* 'was assembled from Plato and Holy Scripture': 'long ago perished

---

[237] Marsham, *Canon*, 85: 'Ista regnandi aequalis inaequalitas nimis insolita est, ut illam bis & simul fortuitò contigisse credamus'.

[238] Ibid., 352–69. See e.g., in England, Richard Cumberland, *Origines gentium antiquissimae; or, attempts for discovering the times of the first planting of nations in several tracts* [c. 1680] (London, 1724), xi–xii. But the conjecture was later accepted by Newton in his chronological work: Buchwald and Feingold, *Civilization*, 226.

[239] Marsham, *Canon*, 4–5. Marsham sometimes justified this by comparing Africanus to Manetho (see e.g. 391–2, where Africanus's eleventh, twelfth, and nineteenth dynasties are discarded for this reason), but this went against his usual practice.

[240] Marsham, *Canon*, 22–3.

[241] Fowden, *Egyptian Hermes*, 22–31 charts the relevant ancient sources.

the genuine Hermetic books, and long ago crept in the spurious ones'.[242] His Hermes was the inventor of the alphabet, of Egyptian worship and sacrifices, and the first observer of the stars, facts preserved among the Greek tradition but mixed with what Marsham saw as the spurious Greek myths of their own deity Hermes.[243] To complicate matters, Hermes's alphabet was hieroglyphic and mystical: 'from this occult Symbology was born the mad Egyptian theology and their monstrous images of the Gods';[244] indeed Thoth himself was placed among the mysterious chthonic deities known as the Cabeiri.[245] The confusion between Hermes and Moses that stemmed from Eusebius was the result of the fact that there was a *second* Thoth/Hermes, roughly contemporary with the prophet (Marsham's chronology showed that he in fact came slightly after), who divulged some of the secret arts of the first.[246]

This broad scheme established, Marsham turned to the cultural relationship between the Egyptians and the Jews. His starting point was Luke's statement that 'Moses was learned in all the wisdom of the Egyptians'. 'What then', asked Marsham, 'was this "wisdom of the Egyptians"? The second Hermes had not yet divulged the secret arts of Thoth, for he came later than Moses'.[247] Philo, the other Hellenistic Jews, and their Christian followers had all supposed that Moses was learned in all sorts of philosophical and astronomical truths, but as over half a century of the best scholarship had agreed, 'credit is not to be given recklessly to these claims'.[248] The reality was very different: 'The Israelites were up to this time an obscure people, without name, a country, a law, magistrates. Moses, the author of their liberty, was their leader on their journey, and their legislator'.[249]

---

[242] Marsham, *Canon*, 234–5: 'Jamdudum perierunt genuini Hermetis libri: jamdudum irrepserunt supposititii ... Librum illum è Platone & S. Scripturis concinnatum esse docuit V. Cl. Is. Casaubonus'. See also 40.

[243] Marsham, *Canon*, 34–44. Marsham's key source is Diodorus Siculus, *Bib. hist.*, 1.16, despite the acknowledgement that 'Diodorus autem hic Mercurium Aegyptium cum Graeco miscet' (36–7). For the invention of writing, this is supported by such 'safe' sources as Pliny, *Hist. nat.*, VII.56 and Sanchoniathon as in Eusebius, *Praep. Ev.*, I.9.

[244] Marsham, *Canon*, 38: 'Ex occultâ hâc Symbolologiâ orta est insana Aegyptiorum Theologia, & monstrosa Deorum simulacra'.

[245] Ibid., 35–6. The Cabeiri deities were usually classified as Greek, but Marsham noted the obscure scholium on Apollonius's *Argonautica*, 1.916 for the connection of the four Cabeiran deities with Demeter, Persephone, Hades, and Hermes.

[246] Marsham, *Canon*, 38–9; 231–5. The key source for two separate Hermes is the spurious *Book of Sothis*, also supposedly by Manetho, in Syncellus, 72–3 (=*The chronography of George Synkellos: a Byzantine chronicle of universal history from the creation*, eds. and trans., W. Adler and P. Tuffin (Oxford, 2002), 54–5). Marsham (34–5) maps these on to the five Hermes in Cicero, *De natura deorum*, III.56 (three are dismissed as later Greek additions).

[247] Marsham, *Canon*, 136–7: 'Quaenam verò fuit ista *Aegyptiorum Sapientia*? Nondum enim Mercurius Secundus absconditas Thoti artes evulgaverat. Mercurius enim iste ... est Mose recentior'.

[248] Ibid., 142: 'Istis verò fides temere non est adhibenda'.

[249] Ibid., 140: 'Israelitarum gens hucusque obscura fuit; sine Nomine, sine Patriâ, sine Lege, sine Magistratu: Moses, Libertatis auctor, Dux erat itineris; & Legislator'.

But what of the great claims to philosophical profundity of Moses and the Jews and their influence on the Greek philosophers? Marsham offered a long catalogue of these claims, recognising that they all stemmed from the Hellenistic Jews like Aristobulus, Josephus, and Philo.[250] But, he countered, chronology and cultural history simply rendered these claims absurd.[251] Like Parker, he pointed out that there was no evidence for Greek contact with the Jews, citing exactly the same key passage from Lactantius to that effect. The Greeks had no interest in philosophy before the time of the Babylonian captivity, whereas after the captivity the Jewish state was obscured under the Persian, 'so that even their name was unknown to the Greeks in the time of Herodotus'.[252] From the Jewish perspective this was hardly surprising, for 'if we examine the customs of the Jews, we find that their familiarity with foreigners was non-existent: no one visited them, nor was visited by them'.[253] The Hellenistic Jews, seeking to combat the idolatry of their gentile neighbours, rewrote the history of philosophy to universalise the impact of the Mosaic law – the product of this was not only their incorrect histories of philosophy but also the Septuagint and the forged *Letter of Aristeas* used to promote it.[254]

But this left a fundamental question: 'since it is not likely that the Greeks ... were taught by the Jews' but since 'nevertheless there was so much similarity between Greek and Jewish philosophy', might it not be the case that each of them 'agrees so closely with some third body of teaching that the way in which it developed from that one may start to become clear?'[255] That *tertium quid* was of course the philosophy of the Egyptians. Moses had been learned in some of the wisdom of the first Thoth. But even more fundamentally,

---

[250] Ibid., 144–6.

[251] Marsham, *Canon*, 146: 'If we examine either the Jewish state or their customs, it will not appear credible that the Platonic or Pythagorean philosophy was taken from a Jewish source' ('Neque verisimile videbitur Philosophiam Platonicam aut Pythagoricam ex fonte Judaico derivatam fuisse; si vel Judaeorum Rempublicam, vel illorum Mores examinemus'). See also CKS MS U1121 Z25/1, which shows that one of Marsham's sources for this idea was Scaliger's discussion of Hellenistic Judaism in *Elenchus Trihaeresii Nicolai Serarii ... eiusdem delirium fanaticum & impudentissimum mendacium, quo Essenos Monachos Christianos fuisse contendit, validisssimis argumentis elusum* (Franeker, 1605), specifically 199 on Philo: 'Scripta enim ejus pigmentis Platonicis condita, & multis luminibus Hellenismi lita esse nemo negaverit ... '.

[252] Marsham, *Canon*, 146–7: 'Ante Captivitatem Babylonicam, sive VII Sapientum aetatem, Graeci non solùm Philosophiae, sed & rerum suarum, magìs Exterarum, incuriosi fuerunt. Post reditum è Babylone, Judaeorum Respublica sub Persis adeò obscura fuit, ut vel Nomen eorum (aetate Herodoti) Graecis inauditum fuerit', citing Lactantius, *Inst. Div.*, IV.2.

[253] Marsham, *Canon*, 147: 'Si mores Judaeorum inspiciamus; nulla fuit iis consuetudo cum Exteris; neque visebant eos, neque ab iis visebantur'.

[254] Ibid., 147–8.

[255] Ibid., 148: 'Cùm igitur non sit verisimile Graecos, vetustioribus Persarum temporibus, à Judaeis edoctos fuisse; nihilominùs tanta sit Philosophiae Graecae Judaicaeque congruentia, ut Josephus, Clemens, alii illam ex hâc prognatam esse arbitrati fuerint: Videamus an non utraque ità conveniat in Tertiâ aliquâ disciplinâ, ut ex illâ propagationis ratio elucescere possit'.

We learn from the sacred writings that the Hebrews were for a long time inhabitants of Egypt: we can suspect, not without reason, that they did not entirely cast aside Egyptian customs, and that some relics of Egyptian teachings endured. Many of the laws of Moses derive from ancient customs. Whatever impeded the worship of the true God was strictly prohibited. Moses abolished the majority of the Egyptian rites, but he also altered some, some held to be indifferent, and some he permitted, and even commanded. This indifference [ἀδιαφορία] towards Egyptian customs is to be seen most in those that most resemble the customs of the Hebrews, of which there are not a few, although there is a great shortage of evidence.[256]

In the face of this 'shortage of evidence', how *could* Marsham justify this striking conclusion? One important source was Maimonides. Marsham adopted his Sabian thesis, modifying it in two ways. First, he simply equated the Sabians with the Egyptians: '[Maimonides] says that the Sabian people filled the entire world: that is to say, it was Egyptian superstition that extended far and wide'.[257] Second, he implied that Moses not only *opposed* Sabian idolatry but also some-times took some of their acceptable rites, such as those concerning sacrifices.[258]

Marsham also used some of the old sources in new and creative ways. In a short section in his *De abstinentia* (IV.10), Porphyry discussed the (real) Egyptian ritual of the Judgement of the Dead, a post-mortem process of sacrifice, embalming, and absolution. The rite involved an 'apology' to the Gods in which one of the priests spoke on behalf of the deceased, promising that they had honoured their parents, not committed homicide, not stolen, nor 'committed any other atrocious deed', and that if 'I have eaten or drunk things which it is unlawful to eat or drink, I have not erred through myself, but through these', at which point he pointed to a chest containing the deceased's entrails, which was then thrown into the Nile. These elements, which sounded suspiciously like a mix of some of the Ten Commandments and the ritual prohibitions on food, proved perfect fodder for Marsham, who spent many

---

[256] Ibid., 149: 'Ex Sacris etiam Literis cognoscimus Ebraeos diutinos fuisse Aegypti incolas: Illos autem mores Aegyptios non penitus exuisse, sed mansisse aliquas disciplinae Aegypticae reliquias non immeritò suspicari possumus. Multae Mosis Leges ex antiquis moribus. Quicquid verum Numinis Cultum impediret, strictè interdicitur. Moses plerosque Aegyptiorum ritus abrogavit, quosdam immutavit, quosdam pro indifferentibus habuit, quos-dam permisit, imò & jussit. Ista rerum Aegyptiacarum ἀδιαφορία in iis maximè cernitur quae ad Ebraicas propriùs accedunt; cujusmodi occurrunt non paucae, tametsi de rebus istis magna sit auctorum penuria'.

[257] Ibid., 195: 'Dicit *gentem Zabiorum implevisse totum Orbem:* id est, Superstitiones Aegyptias longè latéque fuisse propagatas'. Marsham argued this on the basis that there was an old medieval tradition of labelling Maimonides' key source, the *Nabatean agriculture* (see 2.3 above), as the *Egyptian Agriculture*, of which he knew from Buxtorf's edition of the *Guide*: Maimonides, *Doctor perplexorum*, 425 ('Celeberrimus inter hos est Liber, qui vocatur הנבטית העבודה (h.e. ut alii transferunt, *de Agricultura Aegyptiorum*), quem transtulit *Aben vachschi-jah*'). See also *Canon*, 156: 'Zabiorum autem nomine, Aegyptios, maximè Mendesios, intelli-gere videtur'.

[258] Marsham, *Canon*, 194–7.

pages proving that not only the Mosaic Laws but even the earlier 'praecepta Noachidarum' were connected to this 'funebris Aegyptiorum Apologia'.[259]

But there was one other way in which the history of philosophy specifically served Marsham's case. We have seen that Henry More worked by a kind of historical enthymeme: (A) Pythagoras took from the Jews; (B) therefore anything held by Pythagoras must have been held by Moses. Marsham reversed this, adopting the logic that (A) Pythagoras and the Jews both took from the Egyptians; (B) therefore anything held by both the Jews and Pythagoras must have been first held by the Egyptians. For example, the injunction to honour one's parents must have come to the Jews from the Egyptians because it was also mentioned in the *Golden verses* of Pythagoras.[260] The Sabbath was connected to Egyptian veneration for numbers, which was provable by the Pythagoreans' obsession with number mysticism.[261] When Pythagoras was circumcised, it was following an Egyptian rather than a Jewish custom.[262] Even the immortality of the soul was another 'notable Egyptian invention': the Jews were so backward that 'post-mortem conditions little troubled them'.[263] Needless to say, none of this undermined the Jews' status as a chosen people: indeed, it demonstrated the lengths to which God would go to protect them.

A prominent recent account has claimed that Marsham, 'Reviving the esoteric Renaissance conflation of Moses with the mystic wisdom of Hermes Trismegistus . . . argued that before the Exodus Moses had been well versed in Egyptian magical arts. Despite the outward orthodoxy of Marsham's staid, steady chronological study, his discreet drawing on distinctly unorthodox notions of *prisca theologia* implicitly undermined rather than reinforced the authority of the Bible'.[264] This judgement could hardly be further from the truth: it inverts directly the two fundamental aspects of Marsham's scholarship. As we have seen, Marsham's most famous idea – that the Jews had taken from the Egyptians – was based on an almost pathological mistrust of claims to anything resembling 'prisca theologia', which he presented as Hellenistic Jewish propaganda that broke all historiographical rules. As for his 'implicit undermining' of the Bible, it was because of his dogmatic adherence to the Masoretic chronology that he had to develop his most elaborate chronological manouverings, and it was for that adherence that he was most attacked.

---

[259] Ibid., 151–82.    [260] Ibid., 181.    [261] Ibid., 188.

[262] Ibid., 208. The source for Pythagorean circumcision is Clemens Alexandrinus, *Strom.*, I.66.2. Marsham had previously challenged the claim in Gen. 17:10–27 that Abraham first instituted the practice (72–4).

[263] Marsham, *Canon*, 217: 'Nobilissimum autem eorum inventum fuit *immortalitas animae*; ita ut de Vita spem aliquam haberent, etiam post hujus vitae interitum . . . Ebraeorum autem veterum sapientia in sui Juris prudentia posita erat . . . De statu post Mortem illi minus erant solliciti'. Marsham's source for the Egyptians is Herodotus, II.123, where Herodotus is in fact rather sceptical about the Egyptians' claims to priority.

[264] Sutcliffe, *Judaism*, 63.

The attempt to place Marsham in a story of 'enlightenment' simply does not do justice to the world in which he was operating. He is much better understood by placing his work's subject matter in institutional and cultural context. Technical chronology was for the most part considered subservient to 'real' history and theology, its achievements summarised in Scaliger and Petau and to be used instrumentally by theologians. Marsham and Stanley, as independent gentleman scholars, could ignore this disciplinary hierarchy and continue with the sort of scholarship epitomised by Scaliger and by Marsham's friend John Bainbridge.[265] Marsham's originality stemmed from entering fully into a technical discipline that was used only as a propaedeutic by the cleric–scholars who mostly debated these issues.

Spencer's book was even more renowned than Marsham's, being known to virtually every European intellectual to discuss these issues for the next 150 years. His aims, however, were just as distant as Marsham's from those of the enlightenment. His central thesis derived partly from long-established Catholic scholarly traditions about the amalgamation of pagan rites into early Christianity and partly from a desire to attack nonconformist scripturalism and anti-ceremonialism: if the ancient Jews had taken some indifferent rites from the Egyptians, then it was fine for the English church to preserve some previously Catholic rites; at the same time, it was also fine for her to deviate from certain biblical practices – especially strict Sabbatarianism – which various 'puritan' groups had been clamouring for.[266] Here we must focus only on Spencer's treatment of Moses in the difficult and ambiguous eleventh chapter of the first book of *De legibus Hebraeorum*.

Unlike Marsham, Spencer made his career within the academy.[267] As we have seen, mid-century Cambridge was a relatively good place to become a Hebraist and he cultivated the company of such heavyweights as Lightfoot and Cudworth. This background in clerical scholarship is evident in Spencer's work, which is devoted to a central issue of biblical interpretation, namely the reasons behind the 613 Mosaic ritual laws, many of which seem to have no 'rational' purpose at all. But denying such a purpose and surrendering to the unfathomable will of God – as Spencer knew had been done by both Jewish and

---

[265] For this culture of chronology, see the extensive account in Buchwald and Feingold, *Civilization*, 107–25; for Marsham's friendship with Bainbridge, see 2.2 above.

[266] This is proved at length in Levitin, 'Spencer'.

[267] Entering Corpus Christi College, Cambridge, in March 1645, rising to mastership of the college by 1667, vice-chancellorship of the university in 1673, and becoming Dean of Ely in 1677. For his student commonplace book, consisting mostly of standard declamations on the value of rhetoric and philosophy, see LPL MS 870 ('Jo. Spenceri Literae et Declamationes in Acad. Cantabrig.'). His tutor was Richard Kennet, on whom see R. Masters, *The history of the college of Corpus Christi* (Cambridge, 1753), 167. Kennet's proficiency as a Hebraist is unknown, but he did donate Buxtorf's pioneering *Lexicon Hebraicum et Chaldaicum* (1615) and *Concordantiae Bibliorum Hebraicae* (1632) to Corpus (see Masters, *Corpus*, 325).

Calvinist exegetes[268] – was unacceptable. Like so many others, Spencer turned to the accommodationism of Maimonides: the Law was 'rational' in a historical sense, designed to combat the idolatry of the Sabians. Maimonides was present in his work to a far greater extent than in Marsham's: even when he did not cite him for a conclusion, we find the appropriate passage in his copy of the *Guide* marked with a dog-eared page folding.[269] This also fit Spencer's general preference for emphasising God's general providence (working by second causes) over special providential intervention.[270]

As we saw in Chapter 2, the standard identification of the Sabians was as the Chaldeans. But Spencer used the work of Hottinger and other recent Christian Arabists to show that medieval Arabic writers used 'Sabians' to refer to an array of pagans known to them, especially the Harranians.[271] Using this fact, alongside the statement (unsupported by any evidence) that 'the Chaldeans once filled the world with their colonies and victories, or at least their rites and mysteries', Spencer claimed that Scaliger had been wrong: the Arabs referred to the Sabians not as a people but as a loose set of doctrines. To Ibn Waḥshiyya (Maimonides's self-proclaimed main source) and the other Arabic scholars the Sabians must have meant not only the Chaldeans but also the 'Egyptians, Nabateans, Charaneans, Syrians and others addicted to the dogmas and rites

---

[268] See Spencer, *De legibus*, I, sig. (a)ʳ, in the first category placing Joseph Albo's popular exposition of the principles of Judaism, *Sefer ha-'Iḳḳarim* (1425), and in the latter the *Hierozoicon* (1663) of Samuel Bochart. These are already contrasted with the call for rationalism in Maimonides, *Guide*, III.26 (Pines, 506). For the full publication history of the work, see Levitin, 'Spencer'. Spencer had already adumbrated some of his key conclusions in his *Dissertatio de Urim & Thummim* (Cambridge, 1669) (reissued 1670).

[269] See Spencer, *De legibus*, I, 39–40, 118, claiming that the Sabbath was primarily instituted by God to remind the Hebrews of the creation, and thus to direct them away from the idolatrous worship of created things as practised by the Sabians. The idea that the Sabbath commemorates 'that the world has been produced in time' is already present in *Guide*, III.43 (Pines, 570) – although this is unacknowledged by Spencer in the text, his copy of Buxtorf's 1629 edition (Parker Library, Corpus Christi College Cambridge [=PL CCCC], classmark: M.8.33) is folded at the corner to mark the passage.

[270] John Spencer, *A discourse concerning prodigies* (Cambridge, 1663); Spencer, *A discourse concerning vulgar prophecies* in *A discourse concerning prodigies* (2nd edn, Cambridge, 1665) (seperate pagination). See Gascoigne, 'Wisdom', 177–8; Burns, *An age of wonders* (2002), 58–70; Burns, 'John Spencer and the controversy over prodigies' (1995).

[271] Spencer, *De legibus*, II, 213, citing: Johann Heinrich Hottinger, *Historia orientalis: ex variis orientalium monumentis collecta* (Zürich, 1651), 165 (on Sabians as Harranians) (Hottinger's own source can be found at Muḥammad ibn Isḥāq Ibn al-Nadīm, *The Fihrist of al-Nadīm: a tenth-century survey of Muslim culture*, ed. and trans. Bayard Dodge (2 vols, New York, 1970), II, 745); Golius's commentary on the *Compendium of astronomy* (*c.* 833) by al-Farghānī, which he translated from Arabic to Latin: *Muhammedis Fil. Ketiri Ferganensis, qui vulgo Alfraganus dicitur, elementa astronomica, Arabicè & Latinè* (Amsterdam, 1669), 251 (on Sabians as Harranians); Pococke's translation of Gregory Abū'l Faraj, *Historia compendiosa dynastiarum* (3 vols, Oxford, 1663) (contemporary Sabians are similar to ancient Chaldeans [Spencer cites the original Arabic at II, 281, but in fact simply uses Pococke's Latin commentary from I, 184]).

of the Chaldeans'.[272] This reasoning for Spencer's jump from the Sabians to the Egyptians may strike us as shaky – even if 'Sabian' is broadened to mean 'pagan', what evidence is there for extending it to include Egyptian?[273] The answer is that this discussion of the Sabians was designed to fit into an already prepared conjecture about Egypto–Hebraic contact.

Daniel Stolzenberg has shown that it was Kircher, rather than Spencer, who, broaching the subject of the extensive concord between Egyptian and Hebrew ritual, first systematically suggested the possibility that the borrowing may not have indicated simple Judaic primacy: 'the Hebrews have such an affinity to the rites, sacrifices, ceremonies and sacred disciplines of the Egyptians, that I am fully persuaded that either the Egyptians were Hebraicizing or the Hebrews were Egypticizing', a passage cited by Spencer in both his earlier *Dissertatio de Urim et Thummim* (1669) and in *De legibus*; Kircher also used Maimonides' Sabian thesis to claim that 'it is evident that the law of the Hebrews was almost parallel to the false laws of the gentiles'.[274] Spencer clearly grew somewhat ashamed of his use of Kircher, because he advertised it far more in *Urim et Thummim* than in *De legibus*, but in private he remained committed to the Jesuit as an invaluable source: his copious marginal additions to his own copy of *De legibus* (intended for a new edition) show that despite a surface distancing he continued to work with his copies of all of Kircher's major tomes at hand, reminding himself of Kircher's conclusions in almost every chapter.[275]

At the same time, there were also vast differences between the two men's works: where Kircher posited shared ritual and philosophy between Egypt and Israel to explain later Israelite idolatry or the mutual inheritance of an antediluvian Cabbala and talked of two philosophically advanced societies, Spencer explained the sharing simply through God's accommodation to the tastes of the Hebrews, a backward and slavish people. To explain these differences we must turn to Spencer's treatment of Moses, philosophy, and mystery in the dense and complex chapter 11 of Book I: 'Of the secondary end

---

[272] Spencer, *De legibus*, II, 213: 'Chaldæi coloniis, victoriis, aut saltem ritibus & mysteriis suis, olim impleverunt omnia ... His argumentis inductus, Scaligeri sententiae veritati maximè consentaneam esse judicarem, nisi quòd Zabiorum nomine *solos* Chaldæos intelligendos asserit. Sententia (si quid ipse judico) veritate proprior, haec est: Zabiorum nomine, Chaldaeos in primis, Ægyptios etiam, Nabatæos, Charanæos, Syros, alios Chaldæorum dogmatis & ritibus addictos, censendos esse'.

[273] Like Marsham, Spencer drew on the medieval tradition of calling the *Nabatean Agriculture* the *Egyptian Agriculture* (*De legibus*, II, 217), at the same time playing on the ambiguity of the book's name in Hebrew, חעבודה הנבטית – the meaning of עבודה can be either 'agriculture' or 'cult', which Spencer extended to 'religio'. He might also have been thinking of the conquests of Egypt by Ninus and Semiramis as described in Diodorus Siculus, *Bib. hist.*, II.2.3; II.16.1.

[274] Kircher, *Oedipus*, I, fol. b1ᵛ, 248; Stolzenberg, 'Athanasius Kircher and the hieroglyphic doctrine' (2001), esp. 162–3.

[275] CUL Adv.a.44.11 (Spencer's annotated copy of *De legibus* [1683–85 edn]), 519, 548, 552, 614, 615, 639, 677, 694, 745, 888, 994, 1014; CUL MS Add. 2610 (MS notes for a new edition of *De legibus*), fol. 117ʳ contains notes from Kircher's *Mundus Subterraneus* (1664).

of the Mosaic law and rites'.[276] Spencer stated that the Law had 'primary' and 'secondary' ends: the primary was the abolition of idolatry, the secondary was the adumbration of 'certain mysteries'.[277] The idea that the Law had a secondary typological sense (i.e. that it prefigured New Testament figures or events, especially Christ) was a mainstay of both Protestant and Catholic exegesis.[278] Spencer discussed why God might have wanted a secondary meaning in the Law, how he might have enacted it, and what sort of mysteries might be contained within it. He then offered some reflections on excessive allegorical interpretation, which at points strike a very critical tone, attributing its origin to the incorporation of Greek (especially Platonic) philosophy into Hellenistic Judaism, finishing:

Origen, Clement [of Alexandria], Cyril of Alexandria and others, most learned in the literature and the writings of the more ancient Historians: what kind of torch might they have carried in front of us, who are investigating the meaning of the Mosaic Laws, if, having thrown out their empty allegories, they had turned their minds to the investigation of the primary sense and scope of the Laws? We have perhaps lost the reason for several of the Laws for eternity, because the Ancient Historians, who had recorded the customs of the Egyptians and Assyrians (the reason for those Laws), are lost today; and in the writings of those Fathers, those Mosaic matters, lacking the light of antiquity, are distorted to another purpose by allegorical sophistries.[279]

Yet the same set of authorities is sometimes used by Spencer to *defend* the existence of an esoteric meaning in the Law, especially when Spencer argues that the Hebrews inherited an esoteric wisdom from the Egyptians. This complexity has confused modern readers into claiming that Spencer believed that Moses had appropriated the true religion from the Egyptians[280] or that he was a closet Socinian who denied typology,[281] claims that I have elsewhere disproved.[282] As we shall see in Chapter 6, dismissing overly allegorical readings as the inheritance of Hellenistic Platonism was a favourite tactic of Anglican anti-nonconformist polemic, and Spencer fits precisely in that

---

[276] Spencer, *De legibus*, I, 153–73.

[277] Ibid., 153: 'PRIMARIA erat, ut Lex ea medium esset Ordinarium, quo Deus, ad idololatriam abolendam, & Israëlitas in Ipsius fide cultúque retinendos, uteretur: SECUNDARIA erat, ut Legis illius ritus & instituta mysteriis quibusdam adumbrandis inservirent'.

[278] More work is needed on the survival of typology in Protestant 'literal' exegesis: a good introduction is Muller, *Dogmatics*, II, 477–82, and now Drouin, *L'exégèse allégorique*.

[279] Spencer, *De legibus*, I, 167: 'Qualem nobis, Legum Mosaïcarum sensus indagantibus, facem praetulissent, Origenes, Clemens, Cyrillus Alexandrinus, alii, literis & Historicorum antiquiorum scriptis instructissimi; si, missis allegoriis suis inanibus, animos suos ad Legum earum sensum & scopum primarium investigandum appulissent? Legum nonnullarum ratio nos forsan in aeternum latebit, quòd Historici Veteres, qui ritus Ægyptios & Assyrios (Legum earum occasiones) memoriae mandârant, hodiè desiderentur; & in Patrum illorum scriptis, Mosaïca illa, quae luce antiquitatis egent, argutiis allegoricis aliò detorqueantur'.

[280] Assmann, *Moses*, 79, followed by Sutcliffe, *Judaism*, 70.

[281] Parente, 'Spencer', 296–9, 303; Mulsow, 'Orientalistik'.    [282] Levitin, 'Spencer'.

pattern, placing the search for allegory at the root of enthusiast pathology: 'many books and sermons call the common herd of Christians to that mystical and allegorical theology, and rather vehemently encourage them to the study of *glorious types* (as they put it)' but this only causes 'their minds to remain wretchedly anxious and suspenseful' as they do not know how to dig out the mystical meanings.[283] In the meantime, atheists pounce on this hermeneutic and 'are responsible for the mockery of the Laws of God', claiming that they contain nothing more than allegorical Egyptian hieroglyphs.[284] Spencer limited the scope of allegorical interpretation not from a closet Socinianism but from a desire to attack what he presented as nonconformist exegetical techniques. More widely, this move aligned him with a broader scholarly tradition associated most with Grotius and Cappel, for it was they who had most actively connected typological interpretation with Hellenistic allegorising (without entirely rejecting the former). Traditional typology, after all, rested not on allegory but on the supposed historicity of both type and antitype, but Grotius in particular had confused the issue by suggesting that the practice of reading New Testament events into the Old in fact derived (at least partly) from an ancient Jewish custom: the allusion in the form of citation; when this was misunderstood, over-enthusiastic typology was born.[285]

But what of Moses, and those philosophical secrets revealed to him? Spencer offered seven reasons for God hiding mysteries in the Law, of which only some are relevant to us.[286] First, the Israelites, 'having been recently liberated from the house of slavery', were not prepared to understand heavenly things, and so a veil was placed over those things in the same way that Moses placed a veil over

---

[283] Spencer, *De legibus*, I, 168: 'Nam plurimi libri & conciones, Christianorum vulgus ad theologiam illam mysticam vocant & allegoricam, eósque ad *typorum* (utì loquuntur) *gloriosorum* studium impensiùs adhortantur ... Eorum interim animi miserè anxii & suspensi manent, quòd ipsi sensus mysticos eruere nesciant ... ' Spencer's argument was not all polemical exaggeration – for the survival of allegorical methods in Reformed exegesis, see Luxon, *Literal figures* (1995).

[284] Spencer, *De legibus*, I, 168. See also the discussion (at 169), again based on study of Philo and Hellenistic Judaism, of why 'Haec opinio [quòd scilicet Leges Mosaïcae mera sint ænigmata & mysteria verbis simplicibus ubique dissimulata] nullo non aevo Leges illas literaliter spectatas in contemptum duxit, & authoritate omni apid plebem spoliavit'.

[285] For the broad context see Drouin, *Théologie*, esp. 99–109 (but see the moderating comments in Hardy, '*Ars critica*', 186–93). Spencer seems to have realised the value of Cappel's work to his own conclusions after the publication of the first edition of *De legibus*: see the marginal note to Cappel's *Commentarii et notae criticae in Vetus Testamentum* in CUL Adv.a.44.11 (Spencer's annotated copy of *De legibus* [1683–85 edn]), 179 (i.e. when discussing the secondary end of the Law). Spencer only owned the 1689 edition of this work – his copy is PL CCCC Classmark: B.1.21. He had almost certainly read Cappel's famous *Critica Sacra* (Paris, 1650), a copy of which was donated to Corpus by Henry Montague (d.1681), son of the Chancellor of the University, classmark: E.4.9. For an English 'freethinker' who did (mis)use Grotius to attack *all* typological reading, see the discussion of Anthony Collins in Reventlow, 'English deism and anti-deist apologetic' (2008), 862–4.

[286] Levitin, 'Spencer', for the others.

his face upon coming down from Sinai (Exodus 34.33).[287] Second, Spencer deviated from his usual emphasis on the primitiveness of the post-Exodus Jews and argued that '[t]he Mosaic Law was given to the whole nation of the Jews, in whom the primitive and ignorant were mixed up with the educated and intelligent'.[288] He then drew on the standard discussion from Eusebius's *Praeparatio Evangelica* to assert that Moses gave the literal law for the satisfaction of the masses, but preserved a mystical sense for the learned, although Spencer's language shifts Eusebius's emphasis on the lawgiver to God himself.[289] This standard historical point led Spencer down two rather more original avenues. He pointed out that 'God handed down many things in the Law which were wrapped up in coverings of types and figures, perhaps so that the Mosaic Law might harmonise with the actual cast of mind and education of Moses'. He drew on the classic passage of Philo favoured by all allegorists, that Moses was imbued with the hieroglyphic literature in Egypt – 'among many other kinds of knowledge'.[290] But rather than ask the standard question about what was being transferred, Spencer inquired into what God was *doing*: 'why shouldn't we believe that God handed down many things through symbols and sacred types (*figuras*) in the Law, so that they might be more accommodated and congruous to Moses's cast of mind, which was accustomed to symbols and more secret writings?'[291] God enacted a double accommodation: not only did he accommodate the rites his messenger Moses delivered to the Israelites to *their* mindsets, he also accommodated his own communications to the mindset of the messenger. This allowed Spencer to explain the famous incident of God first calling Moses through the burning bush (Exod. 3:2): God 'managed him [Moses] just as a man who was brought up on the hieroglyphic letters of Egypt, showing him the mystery of divine providence as something to be contemplated in the symbol of a bush that burned but was not consumed'.[292]

---

[287] Spencer, *De legibus*, I, 155–6: 'Israëlitæ, nuper è servitutis domo liberati, res cœlestes, nude & quasi retectâ facie propositas, intueri non poterant aut æstimare'.

[288] Ibid., I, 156: 'Lex Mosaïca toti Judaeorum Genti data erat, in qua rudes & indocti politis & ingenio valentibus immiscebantur'.

[289] Ibid., I, 156, citing Eusebius, *Praep. Ev.*, VIII.10 (Spencer mis-cited this as VII.10). This is also the point of the seventh reason for God's inclusion of a mystical sense (159).

[290] Spencer, *De legibus*, I, 156–7: 'Deus multa in Lege typorum & figurarum tegumentis involuta tradidit, forsan ut Lex Mosaïca cum ipso Mosis ingenio & educatione consensum coleret ... è Philone discimus, Mosem literatura hieroglyphicâ in Ægypto imbutum, & inter plures alias scientiae species, τὴν διὰ συμβόλων φιλοσοφίαν ibi didicisse', citing Philo, *Vit. Mos.*, I.23.

[291] Spencer, *De legibus*, I, 157: 'Quidni itaque credamus, Deum multa per symbola & figuras sacras in Lege tradidisse, ut Mosis ingenio, symbolis & literis secretioribus assueto, eò magis congrua essent & accommodata?'

[292] Ibid.: 'Præterea, Cùm primùm Deus ad munus propheticum Mosen evocavit, eum tanquam virum hieroglyphicis Ægypti literis innutritum tractavit, ei providentiæ divinæ mysterium, in rubi ardentis sed non consumpti symbolo, contemplandum præbens.'

This was a brilliant and truly original explanation, but it stemmed from a familiar concern: to explain God's operation in the world – even on men's minds – entirely through second causes. And it led Spencer to his longest and most controversial explanation for the secondary meaning of the Law: 'It seems that God handed down certain rather holy things in the Law covered with veils of symbols and types, on account of the related practice that was common among the sages of the Gentiles, especially the Egyptians'.[293] The Jews, acculturated in the customs of the surrounding gentiles, would have expected a mysterious element to the Law, and so God provided one, 'so as to accommodate his ordinances to the taste and use of the age'.[294] The beauty of this explanation was that it allowed Spencer to deploy the old (and standard) sources for his new purpose. That the ancient pagans practised a system of esoteric truth was a commonplace, and Spencer deployed a barrage of sources: Strabo, Clemens Alexandrinus, Plutarch, Iamblichus, Francesco Patrizi, Kircher, and most intriguingly, Ole Worm's *Danicorum monumentorum libri sex* (1643), which claimed that the ancient eastern practices were maintained in the rune-inscribed stones in Norway, Sweden, and Denmark.[295] Clemens had of course written with the purpose of refuting pagan claims of anti-intellectualism against Christianity and thus maintained that it possessed a mystical sense like all models of ancient wisdom.[296] Spencer turned his claims to a different apologetic purpose: demonstrating how God operated in the world with perfect efficiency by supplying a secondary meaning to the Law that was both historically necessary *and* typological.

All this explains Spencer's deviation from Kircher. Like Stillingfleet, Marsham, and his friend Samuel Parker,[297] Spencer had taken the critical turn that had eluded the Jesuit: recognising that narratives emphasising the philosophical sophistication of the biblical Jews were an invention of the allegorising Hellenistic Jews and their patristic followers. His genius was to re-historicise Mosaic allegoresis: no longer was it the sign of hidden Cabbalistic truth, but only the symptom of Moses's cultural–historical context. This had nothing to do with

---

[293] Ibid.: 'Verisimile est Deum sacratiora quaedam, symbolorum & typorum velis obducta, in Lege tradidisse, ob morem affinem inter Gentium, Ægyptiorum praecipuè, sapientes usitatum'.

[294] Ibid.: 'Cùm itaque Philosophia quaedam sacra figuris mysticis obsepta, & Religio aliud in summo monstrans, aliud in imo premens, apud Ægyptios & alios, Hebraeorum temporibus obtinuerit; æquum est opinari, Deum religionem, carnalem quidem in frontispicio, sed divinam & mirandam in penetrali, Judæis tradidisse, ut instituta sua ad seculi gustum & usum accommodaret, nec quicquam sapientiæ nomine commendatum, Legi vel cultui suo deesse videretur'

[295] Ibid. On the popularity of Worm's work in England, partly because it could offer hints on the origin of Stonehenge, see Parry, *Trophies*, 284.

[296] Clemens Alexandrinus, *Strom.*, v.4, which contains the passage cited by Spencer.

[297] For Parker's letters to Spencer, including discussion of Spencer's work, see LPL MS 942, 33; 674, 27. Spencer was also close to Nathaniel Bisbie, to whom Parker had dedicated two works (LPL MS 674, 35).

heterodoxy or diminishing the status of the Bible: as Spencer's first Anglican readers noted, it was an ingenious way of saving typology in a historicist inter-pretation.[298] It was only later, when others misunderstood or misused Spencer's work, that it became associated with heterodoxy.

Ralph Cudworth's treatment of Egyptian and Jewish philosophy in the *True intellectual system of the universe* might look, on a cursory reading, as the direct antithesis of the work of Marsham and Spencer; one might even take it as a manifestation of Henry More-like 'syncretist' tendencies.[299] But there are also very good reasons for doubting this. Some of these are biographical: Cudworth, like Spencer, was a leading Cambridge Hebraist who also participated in Abendana's *Mishnah* project, was respected in his youth by no less a Hebraist than Selden, was pioneering in introducing explanations for Mosaic rites based on Maimonidean contextualism into English scholarship, and was named Regius Professor of Hebrew at the university in 1645, at the age of twenty-eight.[300]

Moreover, Cudworth's historical method and sense of criticism were fundamentally different to those of his friend More. He did not believe that

---

[298] William Outram, *De sacrificiis libri duo* (London, 1677), 207–8 (citing Spencer's *Urim & Thummim*). Outram, a prebend at Westminster (1626–79), had previously been a fellow of Christ's College, Cambridge: see B. D. Spinks, 'Outram, William', *ODNB*. His extensive scholarly library, totalling some 2,760 volumes (closer to 3,000 if bound pamphlets are considered separately) is detailed in William Cooper, *Catalogus librorum ... Guliemi Outrami* (London, 1681); see esp. 15–16 for his collection of thirty-eight Hebrew works and 9 for Spencer's *Urim & Thummim*.

[299] A direct contrast between Cudworth and Spencer is drawn in Sutcliffe, *Judaism*, 68–70. See further 2.5 above.

[300] Katz, 'The Abendana brothers and the Christian Hebraists of seventeenth-century England' (1989), 41. See letters from Cudworth to Selden in Bod. MS Selden supra 109, fols. 272ʳ (12 Apr [1642]); 264ʳ (19 Sep 1642); 262ʳ (25 Oct 1642); 260ʳ (13 Feb 1643); 266ʳ (14 Nov 1643); 268ʳ (21 Nov 1643); 270ʳ (28 Nov 1643); 258ʳ (5 Dec 1643); Selden supra 108 fol. 1ʳ (13 Jul 1647); for details (their mutual interest was in Karaite manuscripts), see Toomer, *Selden*, II, 575–6, 627–9, 822. For his extensive early reliance on Maimonides' Sabian thesis, see his *Lords Supper*, 71 (the work was popular enough to be reprinted in 1670). His eighteenth-century biographer, Thomas Birch, claimed that upon his appointment as Regius, he 'aban-doned all the functions of a minister, and applied himself only to his academical employments and studies, especially that of the Jewish antiquities' ('Account of the life and writings of Ralph Cudworth', in R. Cudworth, *The true intellectual system of the universe*, ed. T. Birch (4 vols, London, 1820), I, 9). He appears to have been active as Regius, for John Worthington covered for his scheduled lectures in February 1652 (*The diary and correspondence of Dr John Worthington*, eds., J. Crossley and R. C. Christie (2 vols, London, 1847–86), I, 48). He also contributed several Hebrew poems in various congratulatory collections presented by the university (Reif, *Hebrew manuscripts*, 5–7, 13). See also his commentaries on the Book of Daniel, BL MSS Add. 4986–7. Unfortunately, the auction catalogue of Cudworth's library is not a reliable source for his Hebraism, because as the auctioneer informed the reader, Cudworth gave away the 'Rabbinical Part' separately in his will: Edward Millington, 'To the Reader', *Bibliotheca Cudworthiana*, sig. [A]ᵛ. Indeed, Cudworth's will shows that he also gave his English books to his wife, to be passed on to his daughter (Damaris Masham): PRO Prob/11/392, fol. 230ᵛ. All this, I hope, dispels the idea that Cudworth 'evinced almost no interest in rabbinics' (Sutcliffe, *Judaism*, 69).

philosophy had been revealed by God to Moses (or anyone).[301] He refuted any attempt to extract an esoteric philosophy from Genesis, like his scholarly contemporaries attributing the idea to those Hellenistic Jews – especially Philo – who had 'Platonized to[o] far'.[302] He did believe that some *theological* truths had come down from the Jews to the pagans, but even here he directly disagreed with More, claiming that all mystical–numerical readings of the Pythagorean Tetrad were futile, for it 'was really nothing else but the Tetragrammaton, or that proper name of the supreme God amongst the Hebrews'.[303] More, who had by this point finally got his hands on some genuine Cabbalistic texts through the mediation of Franciscus Mercurius van Helmont, would subsequently add some new scholia to the Latin translation of the *Conjectura* in his posthumous *Opera*, one of which attempted to disagree with Cudworth.[304] But by this point virtually no one (at least in England) was listening to him.

Cudworth, then, was no Renaissance syncretist or Cabbalist – hardly surprising, given that this was a man who was correcting Scaliger's chronology in letters to Selden at the age of twenty-six.[305] And yet, Cudworth disagreed with perhaps the most famous finding of the new critical historiography: Casaubon's proof of the spuriousness of the *Hermetica*. His ideological reasons for doing so are clear: the whole fifty-page discussion of Egypt came in the giant fourth chapter, in which he sought to demonstrate the ubiquity of monotheism among even those pagans who held multiple subordinate deities (see also 2.5 above, 5.4 below). But how could a leading Hebraist and historical philologist justify such a conclusion on a scholarly basis?

To answer this, we must recognise, first of all, that Cudworth was sure that Egyptian belief in 'one uncreated Deity' was manifest from other sources, sources with which he demonstrated his great familiarity before turning to the *Hermetica*. For all their extended chronologies, the Egyptians must have believed in a creation in time, for why else would the anti-Christian Simplicius have labelled the Old Testament an 'Egyptian fable'?[306] As Herodotus had clearly stated, they believed in the soul's immortality: thus they must have also held immaterial substances.[307] Plutarch regularly spoke of the Egyptians' 'one supreme Deity' (τὸν πρῶτον Θεὸν), and the foremost

---

[301] Cudworth, *System*, 12. This is despite Cudworth's alignment of Moses with Moschus the atomist; see 5.2 below.

[302] Ibid., 554.    [303] Ibid., 375–6.

[304] Henry More, 'Scholia in Cap.II. Sect. I.' in 'An appendix to the Defence of the Philosophic Cabbala', in *A collection of several philosophical writings of Dr. Henry More* (London, 1712), 127 (new pagination). More claims that Cudworth's interpretation in fact agreed with his – how he reached this conclusion I am at a loss to explain.

[305] Cudworth to Selden, 5 Dec 1643, Bod. MS Selden supra 109, fol. 258ʳ.

[306] Cudworth, *System*, 313, quoting Simplicius, *In Phys.*, VIII.1.

[307] Cudworth, *System*, 313–14, drawing on Herodotus, II.123.

'Egyptological' source, Horapollo, spoke of a παντοκράτωρ and a κοσμοκράτωρ ('ruler of all').[308] Plutarch had also preserved a temple inscription at Sais (Sa el-Hagar) which read 'I am all that hath been, is, and shall be, and my *peplum* or veil no mortal hath ever yet uncovered';[309] even more impressive was the inscription to Isis 'still extant at Capua':

TIBI

UNA. QUAE.

ES. OMNIA.

DEA. ISIS

It was unclear why evidence for ancient Egyptian theology was to be found inscribed in Latin in southern Italy, but it was impressive nonetheless.[310] While Cudworth evidently marshalled much of his evidence himself, it is also clear that he was working within the tradition of histories of paganism established over the last half-century. For example, his thesis that Ammon was another name for the Egyptian supreme deity and that this might offer a better explanation for Jer. 46:25 ('The Lord of hosts, the God of Israel, saith; Behold, I will punish the multitude of No, and Pharaoh, and Egypt, with their gods, and their kings'), where 'multitude' (in Hebrew אמון ['âmôn']) was to be replaced with 'Ammon' as the titular deity of the city of No (i.e. No-Amon, Thebes) was clearly taken, without acknowledgement, from Bochart's *Geographia sacra* (1646).[311] All this only served to buttress the impression of an impressive array of evidence for the monotheism of the Egyptians.

Just as importantly, Cudworth was at all points careful to show that he was not engaging in the more disreputable type of uncritical Egyptology. Nowhere is this clearer than in his treatment of Egyptian esotericism. He cited three robustly 'safe' sources – Origen, Clemens Alexandrinus, and Plutarch; all either natives of Alexandria or acknowledged experts on Egypt – to the effect that the Egyptians, 'besides their Vulgar and Fabulous Theology' also held 'another ... *Arcane and Recondite Theology*', available only to the pharaohs and the priestly elite (hence their placing of sphinxes in

---

[308] Cudworth, *System*, 334–5, quoting Plutarch, *Is. Os.*, II, 351ᵉ–352ᵃ and Horapollo, *Hieroglyphica*, I.61. The *Hieroglyphica* (*c.* fifth century AD) was rediscovered in 1419, with the *editio princeps* published by Aldus Manutius in 1505: see Sider, 'Horapollo', in *CTC*, VI, 15–29, and VII, 325.

[309] Cudworth, *System*, 341, quoting and translating Plutarch, *Is. Os.*, II, 354ᵇ ('Ἐγώ εἰμι πᾶν τὸ γεγονὸς καὶ ὂν καὶ ἐσόμενον καὶ τὸν ἐμὸν πέπλον οὐδείς πω θνητὸς ἀπεκάλυψεν').

[310] Cudworth, *System*, 410. Assmann, *Moses*, 86, 88–9 claims great originality on Cudworth's part for using such evidence, but it had already been marshalled by Vossius in the expanded edition of the *De theologia gentili ... editio nova* (Amsterdam 1668), VII.2 (new pagination for each book), 156. The full inscription is in fact dedicated by a Roman senator (=*Corpus inscriptorum Latinarum*, X 3800).

[311] Compare Cudworth, *System*, 339–40 with Samuel Bochart, *Geographia sacra* (Caen, 1646), 6. The source for Ammon as the 'Zeus' of the Egyptians is Herodotus, II.42.

front of temples).[312] And if, as Herodotus had taught, the Egyptian priests had been the first to assert the immortality of the soul, what could this 'higher kind of Philosophy' have been concerned with if not incorporeal substances?[313] As everyone knew, the Egyptians concealed their knowledge 'from the Vulgar Two manner of ways, by Fables or Allegories, and by Symbols or Hieroglyphics' – since hieroglyphs did not answer 'to sounds or words, but immediately represent[ed] the Objects and Conceptions of the Mind', they were likely to be 'one and the same thing with their *Arcane Theology* or *Metaphysicks*'.[314] This may seem a peculiar jump, but the idea that hieroglyphics 'had a direct, isomorphic, relationship with the things and notions they represented' was a late Renaissance commonplace not just among the wilder fringes but also for more mainstream figures such as Bacon and Thomas Browne.[315] Cudworth immediately applied his theory of esoteric philosophical meaning to perhaps the most famous ancient Egyptian artifact of the Renaissance, the Mensa Isiaca or 'Bembine Tablet', a bronze tablet depicting Egyptian cult scenes that had been discovered in Rome in the 1520s and acquired by Cardinal Pietro Bembo – it had received its fullest treatment of many in Lorenzo Pignoria's *Vetustissimae tabulae explicatio* (1605) (it is now known to be a product of Imperial Rome, and the 'hieroglyphs' are nonsensical).[316]

In an eighty-page interpretation, Kircher had claimed that it was a sacred altar in an Isiac temple that contained the twenty-one sacred signs of the alphabet of Thoth and 'adumbrated the entire "Egyptian theosophy" which he understood in terms of a neoplatonic metaphysics of archetypal, celestial, and elementary worlds, animated by the radiating power of the transcendent divinity'.[317] Cudworth was deeply sceptical, censuring Kircher for 'arrogating too much to himself, in pretending to such a certain and exact Interpretation of it'.[318] Instead of a fully developed interpretation he presented what he claimed was a safely mitigated reading:

---

[312] Cudworth, *System*, 314. The sources cited are Origen, *Cels.*, I.12; Clemens Alexandrinus, *Strom.*, v.4–5; Plutarch, *Is. Os.*, II, 354[b–c]. For previous uses of these commonplaces, see Curran, *Egyptian Renaissance*, 93–4.

[313] Cudworth, *System*, 313.    [314] Ibid., 316.

[315] Lewis, *Language, mind and nature* (2007), 13 (quotation from there), 70, 74, 76, 120–1. See also Allen, *Mysteriously meant*, 107–34; Rolet, 'Invention et exégèse symbolique à la Renaissance' (2002); Stolzenberg, *Kircher*, 57–63; Curran, *Egyptian Renaissance*, 228, 234–5. Pignoria had already condemned the 'far-fetched interpretations of the Platonists' (Curran, 'Renaissance afterlife', 123).

[316] See Leospo, *La Mensa Isiaca di Torino* (1978); Curran, *Egyptian Renaissance*, 231–3; Iversen, *Myth*, 55–6. Cudworth owned the 1608 edition: *Bibliotheca Cudworthiana*, 44.

[317] Stolzenberg, *Kircher*, 143–6 (quotation at 145).

[318] Cudworth, *System*, 317. For more scepticism on Kircher's use of Arabic and Aramaic sources for trinitarian readings of the Pamphilian obelisk in Rome, see 413.

Now as it is reasonable to think, that in all those Pagan Nations where there was another Theology besides the Vulgar, the principal part thereof, was the Doctrine of *One Supreme and Universal Deity the Maker of the whole World* ... can it not well be conceived, what this ... should be other than a kind of *Metaphysicks* concerning God, as *One Perfect Incorporeal Being, the Original of all things.*[319]

It is important to recognise that Cudworth allowed himself this sort of rhetorical confidence because he was sure that he wrote not as a speculative reviver of an esoteric philosophy, as had the Jesuit Kircher, the enthusiast Robert Fludd, or even his friend More, but as a qualified historical philologist asserting the simple historical truth that ancient philosophy was grounded in immaterialist monotheism. He had reconstructed not an esoteric philosophy but a broad cultural history of a superstitious yet nonetheless philosophically curious and monotheistic people.

It is in light of all this that we must approach Cudworth's defence of the *Hermetica*. In his discussion of Casaubon's challenge Cudworth mercilessly mocked Kircher for ignoring the great scholar's work, for accepting the whole of the *Hermetica* and for 'greedily swallow[ing]' other forgeries, such as the pseudo-Aristotelian *Theology*, which Cudworth knew had long been proven as 'unquestionably pseudepigraphous'.[320] His own defence was based on the same mitigated cultural historical approach he had adopted throughout. The main argument was that 'every Cheat and Imposture must needs have some *Basis or Foundation of Truth* to stand upon'. Casaubon had thus been wrong to dismiss the whole of the corpus—only three of the sixteen treatises were forgeries.[321] That was not to say that the treatises were genuinely written by a Hermes; only that they contained enough scraps of truly Egyptian philosophy and theology to be useful sources. This conclusion was based on two arguments. The first was that there really was a Thoth/Hermes who had played an important enough role in the cultural history of Egypt to be deified and to have numerous books assigned to him. Not one of Cudworth's numerous modern interpreters has recognised that almost the whole of Cudworth's argument – down to the idea that there was a second Hermes just after the time of Moses – was taken, without acknowledgement, from Marsham.[322] Yet this is important evidence that Cudworth saw himself not as a reviver of antiquated Renaissance scholarly traditions but as a partaker in the conclusions of the latest research.

---

[319] Ibid., 317.

[320] Ibid., 320. For ps.-Aristotle in the Renaissance, see Kraye, 'The pseudo-Aristotelian *Theology* in sixteenth- and seventeenth-century Europe' (1986); for Kircher's use of it, see Stolzenberg, *Kircher*, 146, 205, 211–12, 215–16.

[321] Cudworth, *System*, 320.

[322] Compare Cudworth, *System*, 322–4 with Marsham, *Canon*, 231–5. That Cudworth had read Marsham carefully is confirmed by BL MS Add. 4986, fol. 4ʳ.

Second, Cudworth adopted the same tactic as he had with the *Chaldean Oracles* (2.5 above): by pointing out the genuinely pagan elements in the text, it could be proved that it was not (entirely) a gnostic or Christian forgery. The twelfth treatise, for example, spoke in pantheistic terms of a return and regeneration upon death – a characteristically Egyptian opinion, and certainly not a Christian one.[323] Cudworth offered many more such examples. It is crucial to recognise that through doing so, Cudworth felt that he was beating Casaubon at his own game. Casaubon's argument was primarily philological, dependent on finding anachronistic Greek phrases in the text.[324] But an answer to that objection was already available in the ancient neoplatonist Iamblichus, who had asserted that the Hermetic books often 'speak the language of philosophers [i.e. Greek]' because they had been translated out of Egyptian by those familiar with Greek philosophy.[325] Iamblichus had been published in Latin by Ficino and this argument had been known to Casaubon, and even deployed against him by Kircher.[326] But Cudworth had a trump card: he was, he proudly announced, working with a new manuscript of Iamblichus's *De mysteriis*, very soon to be published as the *editio princeps* by his Cambridge colleague Thomas Gale, who had acquired it from Isaac Vossius.[327] This manuscript

---

[323]  Cudworth, *System*, 333 (=*Hermetica*, xii.16, 46–7).

[324]  Grafton, 'Protestant versus prophet'.    [325]  Iamblichus, *Myst.*, viii.4.

[326]  Hankins and Palmer, 54–5; Isaac Casaubon, *De rebus sacris & ecclesiasticis exercitationes XVI* (Frankfurt, 1615 [1st edn=London, 1614]), 55b; Kircher, *Obeliscus Pamphilius*, sig. c2ʳ.

[327]  The original manuscript for Gale's edition is now Leiden University Library, MS Voss. Q 22. Gale had an exemplar of the manuscript from Isaac Vossius, as well as variant readings from a Parisian manuscript supplied to him by Edward Bernard and Jean Mabillon, as well as from a Basel manuscript belonging to Sebastian Feschius, as explained in Iamblichus, *De mysteriis liber*, ed. T. Gale (Oxford, 1678), sigs. **ᵛ–**2ʳ (see also Sicherl, *Die Handschriften, Ausgaben und Übersetzungen von Iamblichos 'De Mysteriis'* (1957), 107–11 (on Vossius), 195–8 (on Gale)). Vossius's interest in Iamblichus seems to have been stimulated by his acquiring from Holstenius and Claude Sarrau in Paris manuscripts of the *De mysteriis aegyptiorum* and the very rare *Chronicon Babyloniaca* for Queen Christina of Sweden, in whose court he was 1648–54 (see Åkerman, *Queen Christina of Sweden and her circle* (1991), 96–7, 104–5; Blok, *Isaac Vossius and his circle* (2000 [1999]), 313–15). The earliest subsequent notice of it that I know of is a letter from Samuel Tennulius, who himself produced an edition of Iamblichus's *In Nichomachi arithmeticam introductionem* (Arnhem, 1668), who was asking Vossius for readings in June 1657 (Bod. MS D'Orville 470, p. 89) – there are sporadic further references to Iamblichus in this correspondence (pp. 304, 306). The first note of Gale's work on Iamblichus is a letter to Bernard of 22 March 1670 (Bod. MS Smith 8, fol. 131ʳ) from which it is clear he had been working on it for some time; later correspondence with Bernard reveals his hope for finding relevant manuscripts among the Barocci collection in the Bod. (Bod. MS Smith 8, fols. 143ʳ–144ʳ). On 3 June 1672 he wrote to Vossius to say that he had not yet received the copy of the latter's manuscript (Bod. MS D'Orville 470, p. 115). Not atypically, John Fell appears to have annoyed the contributors to his press, for he managed to solicit both Tennulius and Gale to produce editions of Iamblichus, to the great frustration of the former (writing to Bernard on 3 Jan 1677, Bod. MS Smith 8, fols. 23ʳ–24ʳ), which Gale attempted to quell (Gale to Bernard, undated, but before the publication of his edn, MS Smith 8, fols. 147ʳ–148ʳ). The full involvement of Fell and Bernard is not fully clear to me, and I fear will remain a mystery until a full study of Bernard's copious papers is undertaken. Gale's

allowed Cudworth to answer a difficult textual problem, and at the same time to question the quality of Casaubon's conclusions. Iamblichus's work was a response to a letter by Porphyry, of which only fragments survived, to an Egyptian priest named Anebo, in which Porphyry challenged the value of theurgy. In one passage, preserved in Eusebius, Porphyry reported that another Egyptian priest, Chaeremon, had stated that the Egyptians were materialists who believed the Gods to be the celestial bodies.[328] This was obviously a major blow to Cudworth's case for Egyptian monotheism. But Gale had not only painstakingly reconstructed the letter to Anebo,[329] but had also solved the whole problem. Cudworth could follow him in scoffing that Ficino, whose edition Casaubon was using, had completely misunderstood the proper name 'Χαιρήμων', translating it as the first person imperfect subjunctive of the verb 'to choose' ('optarem').[330] More importantly, he could now make fuller sense of the passage in Iamblichus (VIII.4) where the authenticity of the Hermetic books was defended: Porphyry's doubts about their authenticity depended on a dubious authority (Chaeremon) who could not even correctly represent Egyptian theology, never mind verify the authenticity of their books. Iamblichus meanwhile, 'who had made it his business to inform himself thoroughly concerning the Theology of the Egyptians', had offered the most reliable early account. Cudworth's conclusion could not be clearer:

> To conclude, *Jamblichus* his judgment in this case, ought without controversie, to be far preferred before *Casaubon*'s, both by reason of his great Antiquity, and his being much better skilled, not only in the Greek, but also the Egyptian Learning; That the Books imputed to *Hermes Trismegist* did Ἑρμαικὰς περιέχειν δόξας, *really contain the Hermaick Opinions*, though they spake sometimes the Language of the Greek Philosophers.[331]

Cudworth's overall argument – that the *Hermetica* contain traces of genuinely Egyptian doctrine – has the virtue of being correct.[332] But much more

---

variants are usefully included in Iamblichus, *De mysteriis*, ed. and trans. E. C. Clarke, J. M. Dillon and J. P. Hershbell (Leiden, 2004). For Gale as a scholar, the only discussion of importance is that in Haugen, *Bentley*, 39–48 (39–41 on Iamblichus).

[328] Eusebius, *Praep. Ev.*, III.4 (=Porphyry, *ad Aneb.*, II.12–13 [=Porphyry, *Lettera ad Anebo*, ed. and trans. A. R. Sodano (Naples, 1958), 23–5];=Chaeremon, fr. 5 [=*Chaeremon: Egyptian priest and Stoic philosopher: the fragments*, ed. and trans. P. W. van der Horst (Leiden, 1984), 14–15]).

[329] 'Porphyrii epistola ad Anebonem Aegyptium', in Iamblichus, *De mysteriis*, ed. Gale, sigs. b2ʳ–d2ʳ (with the testimony of Augustine, *Civ. Dei*, x.11 appended at sigs. [d2]ᵛ–eʳ).

[330] Cudworth, *System*, 318, following Iamblichus, *De mysteriis*, ed. Gale, 303b. Casaubon (*Exercitationes*, 55b) had also argued, on the basis of a reference to books called the 'Salmeschiniaka' (τοῖς σαλμενισχιακοῖς) that Iamblichus's 'Hermetica' must have been produced in Athens, which was close to Salamis. Cudworth (325–6) followed Gale's conjecture of 'ἐν τοῖς Ἀλμενιχιακοῖς' ('almanacs') (160 and 304b–305a, where Gale admits that all his manuscripts had the former reading). The debate is ongoing: see e.g. *On the mysteries*, ed. Clarke et al., 317, versus Fowden, *Egyptian Hermes*, 139, n. 103.

[331] Cudworth, *System*, 327.      [332] Fowden, *Egyptian Hermes*.

importantly, by sidestepping philosophical labels like 'Platonism' or 'Hermeticism', we have been able to recover, to an extent, what Cudworth was actually *doing*. This was an attempt to appropriate the history of Egyptian philosophy for apologetic purposes without falling into the 'zeal' of Kircher and by following the methods of 'the Learned of the Latter Age': i.e. those like Casaubon.[333]

Nonetheless, the move to discredit Cudworth, and to bring him closer to the uncritical More, began before the ink on the sheets of the *System* was dry. For there exists a major (but previously unnoticed) critique in a book published in the very same year by another Cambridge man, Thomas Tenison, future Archbishop of Canterbury and by then a Chaplain in Ordinary to the King.[334] It has been claimed that when Tenison entered Corpus Christi College, Cambridge as an undergraduate in 1653 he was 'probably influenced by the Cambridge Platonists, who sought to lift religion from a dispute over theological niceties to a set of universal principles. A particular influence ... was Ralph Cudworth.'[335] This judgement, typical of the vague associations that still plague Restoration intellectual history, is not founded on any evidence. There is a much more solid proof for a different connection: Tenison was the closest friend of none other than John Spencer.[336] Tenison's work is of a different genre to Spencer's, being more in the vein of Stillingfleet's scholarly apologetics. His claim, by then a commonplace, was that histories of pagan idolatry and of philosophy went hand in hand: the intrusion of erroneous natural philosophy led to natural theological error. The Egyptians produced black statues to signify the invisibility of the divine essence; their mathematics eventually led to the institution of mystical hieroglyphics which then inspired further idolatrous worship; the pyramids were first constructed on the basis of 'philosophical considerations' and were directed towards sun-worship (confirmed by recent travellers' reports of pyramids with the same purpose in Mexico); their astrology led to the deification of the stars. Indeed, as soon as a natural cause removed an annoyance of any sort the Egyptians ascribed such effects 'with

---

[333] Cudworth, *System*, 285, 320.

[334] Carpenter, *Thomas Tenison* (1948), while dated, remains the best overall introduction. For Tenison as a scholar, I know of no work except the scattered comments in Sheehan, 'Idolatry' (2006). Nonetheless, he was certainly at this point in contact with the scholarly community: see e.g. his letter to Henry Dodwell of 29 April 1678 (Bod. MS Cherry 23, fols. 337$^r$–339$^r$), concerning the latter's work on Stephanus of Alexandria, on whom Tenison offers some remarks, saying he has many more (Dodwell's work was published in the Appendix to his *Dissertationes Cyprianicae* (Oxford, 1684), 128–41 (new pagination)).

[335] Marshall, 'Tenison, Thomas', *ODNB*. Further similarity is claimed because both attacked Hobbes.

[336] Masters, *Corpus*, 167, 170. Tenison was the sole executor of Spencer's will, in charge of the publication of the fourth edition of *De legibus*. For correspondence between the two, see LPL MSS 674, 870 (Spencer's papers at Lambeth also came through Tenison). Tenison's own copy of *De legibus* is BL, shelfmark: 3105 f.1.

Divine Praises, to the vain and insufficient Talisman'.[337] None of this would have been denied by Cudworth, and like his Cambridge colleague, Tenison also suggested that ancient pagan religious culture – especially Egyptian – was esoteric, and that the hidden doctrine probably tended to monotheism.[338]

And yet, a 'Review and Conclusion' appended to the end of the book after the printing of the rest consists of what is clearly a scathing critique of the historical aspects of Cudworth's *System*. Consisting of a dialogue between 'A' and 'B' (Tenison himself), it begins with the former asking about a work providing the 'acknowledgment of one Supreme God amongst the Gentiles' which has 'appear'd since your Papers were under the Press'. This must be a reference to Cudworth. Much of the critique has a theological dimension (see 6.5 below) but more generally Tenison also sought to portray Cudworth's work as the fancy typical of the 'Ficinus's of this age', a hermeneutic that he traced, like so many others, to the Hellenistic Jews.[339] What is most ironic is that Tenison trained his guns on the notion that Moses or Jewish philosophy more generally had influenced the Greeks – a thesis which, as we saw, was not central to Cudworth's argument. Nonetheless, Tenison could attack the association of the Pythagorean tetrad with the Tetragrammaton: the Pythagorean sign symbolised nothing but the four elements of the physical world and the Greek philosophers hardly had to conceal the name of God, given that various pagan forms of God's name were 'no mystery among the Greeks'.[340] Moschus the Phoenician was clearly a far later figure than Moses.[341] All in all, there was no evidence to show that either Pythagoras or Plato had 'Mosaize[d]'.[342]

Tenison was patently unfair to Cudworth. Cudworth never argued that all Greek philosophy was a direct product of Mosaic wisdom. As for such theological inheritances as the tetractys, even the great Selden had not denied the genuine similarity. But for us this is precisely the point: Tenison sought to align Cudworth with the unacceptable, 'allegorical' expositors such as More and Kircher, a reading that has become standard since. For the friend of Spencer, any account that even suggested the philosophical proficiency of the biblical Jews was a piece of Platonic–syncretist chicanery. History and the Bible showed that God had to accommodate to an entirely primitive people: 'the Israelites doted on such a gross manner of expressing their devotion. And seeing they must needs offer Sacrifice, it pleased God to give them a Law which might at once indulge them in their inclination, and restrain them from

---

[337] Thomas Tenison, *Of idolatry: a discourse, in which is endeavoured a declaration of, its distinction from superstition; its notion, cause, commencement, and progress* (London, 1678), 25, 30, 42–3, 70, 328. The source for Mexican pyramids is Thomas Gage, *A new survey of the West-Indies* (London, 1677), 113–14, suggesting that Tenison composed the work relatively quickly, which supports the interpretation below.
[338] Tenison, *Idolatry*, 142, 55–8.     [339] Ibid., 397, 105.     [340] Ibid., 404–7.     [341] Ibid., 407–8.
[342] Ibid., 407–9. This is a misrepresentation of Cudworth's argument: see 5.2 below.

sacrificing unto Idols.'[343] Historical apologetics did not need to find theism in all the pagans when one could instead demonstrate the wisdom behind God's providential operation in human history.

## 3.7    Scientists confront scripture II

In the 1680s the debate suddenly switched from a clerical–scholarly one to one driven by the concerns of natural philosophers. More's resounding failure at a historical–philosophical explanation of Genesis in the 1650s seemed to be forgotten as a new generation of natural philosophers – much more experiment-oriented than him – turned to the problem. The history of this debate, the most prominent 'scientific' debate in late century England, has been written several times,[344] but its historical component has not been systematically considered, and as a preliminary we can identify some common features of particular relevance to us. First, there was a near ubiquitous reliance on the hermeneutic of accommodation, almost always citing Maimonides rather than Augustine or any of the older Christian authorities. This confirms the speed with which the textual authority of mid-century rabbinica was disseminated not only among scholars but also among the learned community more generally. Second, almost everyone agreed that the creation narrative was part of a universal tradition that had survived from before the flood. Again, this is an outgrowth of early to mid-century continental biblical scholarship and apologetics.[345] Finally, there was a concomitant degree of liberty about drawing comparisons between Moses and Genesis and pagan figures and cosmographies. As we have already seen there was nothing intrinsically heterodox about such moves, but it is not difficult to see how they could eventually lead to trouble.

As always, there are exceptions. One is the remarkable merchant of Dutch origin Francis Lodwick (1619–94), a member of both the Hartlib circle and the Royal Society. Thanks to recent meticulous work on Lodwick's manuscripts (which unfortunately are difficult to date, but must stem from *c.* 1660–90), we now know that he subscribed to more heresies than probably any other figure in seventeenth-century England (at least among the learned), among them a very

---

[343] Ibid., 100; see also 101–2, 328–9.

[344] The best account, based on much new evidence, is now Poole, *World makers*; see also Poole, 'The Genesis narrative in the circle of Robert Hooke and Francis Lodwick' (2006). For older monograph treatments, see: Porter, *The making of geology* (1977), 1–89; Rappaport, *When geologists were historians* (1997); Rossi, *Abyss*, 3–122. See also Roger, 'The Cartesian model and its role in eighteenth-century "Theories of the earth"' (1982); Tuveson, 'Swift and the world makers' (1950); Taylor, 'The English worldmakers of the seventeenth century and their influence on the earth sciences' (1948). Works on specific figures are cited in the appropriate places below.

[345] For shifting attitudes to the flood more generally, see the essays in Mulsow and Assmann, eds., *Sintflut und Gedächtnis* (2006).

idiosyncratic antitrinitarianism, pre-Adamism, and the belief in the great antiquity of the world.[346] To defend his reading of Genesis, Lodwick *did* use accommodationism: it was 'not likely' that God only created the sun and moon on the fourth day; rather, 'things are described according to humane understanding and not allwayes according to their truth'.[347] Yet he offered no real historical justification for this beyond one short passage elsewhere in his notes where he noted that 'The Bookes of Moses intend chiefly a history of the Jewish nation and therefore the Author thereof is the shorter in the history of the Original of all creatures and of man' – clearly his Moses was not a philosopher.[348] For all Lodwick's heterodoxies, there is something decidedly old-fashioned about his approach to the Bible. He was not really concerned with putting biblical events in historical context; rather, he would reach a theological conclusion based on internal comparison of biblical passages, only then offering any kind of 'historical' explanation.[349] In this respect, he was still a product of standard Reformed hermeneutics, however much he moved away from Reformed orthodoxy.

### 3.7.1 Thomas Burnet

This was very different to the approach taken by the most important of the 'world-makers', Thomas Burnet. It was Burnet's *Telluris theoria sacra* (1681, 1689) that really kicked off the controversy, not only because of its content but also because of its presentation. Much of Restoration natural philosophy had been offered in natural historical format, but Burnet proposed his work as a 'theory', undoubtedly giving it a sense of fashionable mystique comparable to that generated by the English publication of Bernard Fontenelle's *Conversations on the plurality of worlds* (1686), assisted by a literary style that would draw praise from both Addison and Steele.[350] The *Theoria* was an

---

[346] See now Francis Lodwick, *On language, theology, and utopia*, eds., F. Henderson and W. Poole (Oxford, 2011) [=*LTU*]. See also Poole, 'Genesis Narrative'; Poole, 'Francis Lodwick's creation' (2005).

[347] Lodwick, 'A suppoisal of the manner of creation', in *LTU*, 254.

[348] Lodwick, 'Concerning the originall of mankind', in *LTU*, 200.

[349] Although an exception is his forging of connections between the pagans making their Gods aspects of one God, Jewish beliefs on angels, and Christian trinitarianism ('Concerning Religion', in *LTU*, 226–7). His favourite example here was Hierocles, whom he was reading in Hall's 1655 English translation ('Observations on Hierocles', 233–6).

[350] For the methodological distinction between natural history and 'theory', see Anstey, 'Experimental versus speculative natural philosophy' (2005); ch. 4 below. On this aspect of Fontenelle's reception, see Terrall, 'Natural philosophy for fashionable readers' (2000). Burnet had studied at Cambridge and moved from Clare to Christ's College to follow Cudworth in 1655, where he taught Cartesian philosophy in his lectures; after travelling on the continent, he became a private tutor and then Master of Charterhouse School in 1685: Mandelbrote, 'Burnet, Thomas', *ODNB*; Lewis, 'Educational influence', 55–7; Thomas Sharp, *The life of John Sharp ... Archbishop of York*, ed. T. Newcome (London, 2 vols, 1825), I, 10–11 (Sharp attended Burnet's lectures in the early 1660s).

attempted integration of the earth sciences, Cartesian vortex theory, and scripture. Most basically, Burnet argued that the primitive earth had existed in the form of a smooth egg, had cracked and changed its axial alignment at the time of the flood, and had released huge torrents, which shaped the earth into its current mountainous state.[351] The theory was 'sacred' because it sought to reconcile natural history with the history of man's sin: the flood occurred at the moment of man's greatest sinfulness. Crucially, this involved prioritising the account of the earth given at 2 Peter over that of Genesis, as well as an idiosyncratic approach to the millennium.[352]

Of most importance for us is that Burnet believed that selected fragments from the history of philosophy could function as evidence of a scattered memory of this theory; the theory would in turn explain puzzling passages in the works of the ancient philosophers. As he put it in the English version, 'as when one lights a Candle to look for one or two things which they want, the light will not confine it self to those two objects, but shows all the others in the room'.[353] Famously, the theogonies and cosmogonies of the ancient Greek poets and philosophers all posited a primordial chaos (Aristotle had summarised this in *Metaphysics*, XIV, $1091^b–1092^a$): Burnet argued that this could be explained as the inheritance of a vague tradition of the creation of the earth, which he believed had been made from pre-existent matter.[354] The ancient philosophers also spoke of the earth's egg-shape; here there was even testimony for the Egyptians, for Eusebius had recorded their account of the Demiurge Cneph producing an egg from his mouth, which was the world.[355] Perhaps most impressively one could now explain why Anaxagoras, Empedocles, Leucippus, and Democritus all seemed to believe that the earth's poles were in a different place to that usually acknowledged: this was because previously they had been, and the philosophers' testimonies were evidence that this occurred 'after the world was formed and inhabited'.[356] Crucially, this was not a narrative of good philosophising but of the accidental preservation of

---

[351] For a very full description and analysis, see Poole, *World makers*, 55–63.

[352] See now the very useful analysis in Magruder, 'Thomas Burnet, biblical idiom, and 17th-century theories of the earth' (2008), at 463–5. The classic study of Burnet's whole approach remains Mandelbrote, 'Isaac Newton and Thomas Burnet: biblical criticism and the crisis of late seventeenth-century England' (1994). See also Jacob and Lockwood, 'Political millenarianism and Burnet's *Sacred theory*' (1972), which is flawed in its political determinism but useful for some of the evidence it brings forward.

[353] Thomas Burnet, *The theory of the earth: containing an account of the original of the earth* (2 vols, London, 1684, 1690), I, 263. It was originally published in Latin as *Telluris theoria sacra: orbis nostri origenem & mutationes generales* (2 vols, London, 1681, 1689). There are significant variations between the Latin originals and English translations, some of them noted below.

[354] Burnet, *Theoria*, I, 232–47.    [355] Ibid., I, 283–6; Eusebius, *Praep. Ev.*, III.11.

[356] Burnet, *Telluris*, I, 292–3, from 292 ('Primò quoad mutatum Telluris situm supersunt apud Philosophos aut eorum historiae & dogmatum Scriptores, testimonia satìs illustria; notántque speciatim versùs partes meridionales aut polum Antarcticum inclinatum & depressum fuisse

scraps of truth. As Burnet put it to one critic: 'The Theorist does not cite these Authors to learn of them the causes ... of that *Inclination*, or change of posture in the Earth, but only matter of Fact. To let you see, that, according to their testimony, there was a Tradition in that time, which they took for true, concerning a change made in the posture of the Earth.'[357]

It did not take long for Burnet's *Theory* to become subject to criticism. Some of it concerned his employment of Cartesian vortex theory, which was then in the process of being discredited.[358] But more important were the queries concerning scriptural compatibility, for Burnet's emphasis on 2 Peter and on his own natural philosophical theory seemed to undermine the most important account of all: that of Moses.[359] It is an important sign of the continued importance of humanism to late seventeenth-century natural philosophical culture that Burnet replied not with further 'scientific' reasoning but with a work on the history of philosophy, the *Archaeologiae philosophicae*, published in 1692. Already in the 1684 English version of the *Theoria* Burnet had suggested that he had 'not mention'd *Moses's Cosmopoeia*, because I thought it deliver'd by him as a Lawgiver, not as a Philosopher; which I intend to show at large in another Treatise, not thinking that discussion proper for the Vulgar Tongue'.[360] In the late 1680s and early 1690s he embarked on a programme of systematic reading in the history of philosophy and theology, as witnessed by his copiously self-annotated copy of the 1689 Latin *Theoria*, which contains references not only to classical philosophers, but also the church fathers, medieval rabbis like Maimonides and Nachmanides, Christian exegetes like

mundum, elevato altero polo in eum, quo jam est situm: Neque id ab ipso principio rerum contigisse sed post mundum formatum, cultum, & animalibus repletum').

[357] [Thomas Burnet], *An answer to the late exceptions made by Mr. Erasmus Warren* (London, 1690), 32.

[358] Schuster, 'Descartes' vortical celestial mechanics' (2005); Dear, 'Circular argument: Descartes' vortices and their crafting as explanations of gravity' (2005); Magruder, 'Burnet', 473–5.

[359] This is well brought out in Poole, 'Sir Robert Southwell's dialogue on Thomas Burnet's theory of the earth', at 81: 'it is significant that although Burnet concluded his first two books with a discussion of his critical attitude to Moses, Southwell's interlocutors commence upon this topic, signalling how central and how problematic Burnet's critical assumptions were to his earliest readers'. See also Herbert Croft, *Some animadversions upon a book intituled, The theory of the earth* (London, 1685), esp. 2–3, 81–2, 110–11. For another example, see Erasmus Warren, *Geologia: or a discourse concerning the earth before the deluge* (London, 1690), 41–2. Warren was the obscure incumbent of two country parishes in Suffolk, but Burnet considered his attack important enough to issue a full bad-tempered reply: *Answer*, esp. 12, 20–1, 28–9, 31–7, 40–1, 44, 84 on the history of philosophy and the tradition concerning the creation. Warren responded with *A defence of the Discourse concerning the earth before the flood* (London, 1691); Burnet again countered with *A short consideration of Mr. Erasmus Warren's defence* (London, 1691), which now contains few historical claims, except at 40. Warren had the last word in his *Some reflections upon the Short consideration* (London, 1691). The fullest biography of Warren is that in Lewis, 'Educational influence', 177–81.

[360] Burnet, *Theory*, I, 288–9. This passage is not in the 1681 Latin.

Bellarmine, and the latest 'secondary' literature on the history of philosophy, especially Cudworth and Huet.[361]

The *Archaeologiae* is divided into two books and the key to understanding it lies in the final chapter of Book I, 'De origine Philosophiae Barbaricae'.[362] Everyone agreed that the Greeks took philosophy from the barbarians, Burnet began, but there were two very different standard theses about the nature of barbarian philosophy: either they had developed it 'by their own talent', or it had been 'derived from the Hebrews to other peoples'.[363] The latter opinion had been developed by the Jews themselves – especially Hellenistic ones like Josephus – but whether they referred the origins of philosophy back to Moses or to Abraham did not matter, for the whole story was an imposture. 'The Hebrews were famous neither for natural science, nor for mathematics, yet they still want the Egyptians to have been taught by themselves ... this sort of thing is said by Josephus not only without cause but also contrary to any appearance or likeness of truth.'[364] Elsewhere, Burnet cited the same passage from Lactantius concerning the Greeks' ignorance of the Israelites as had been cited by Parker, Marsham, and Spencer; he is thus just one figure in the general trend of rejecting Theophilus Gale-like claims to Judaic primacy, and attributing such claims to Hellenistic Jewish pious fraudulence.[365]

But the possibility that the pagans had developed their own philosophy from scratch also had to be rejected, albeit for very different reasons. The history of philosophy had to be placed within a developmental cultural history:

Whoever is even moderately versed in the literature and texts of the ancients is sufficiently informed that the custom of those ancient sages was not to found theories,

---

[361] Thomas Burnet, *Telluris theoria sacra ... Libri duo posteriores* (London, 1689), CUL, Classmark: Adv.c.27.4.

[362] Thomas Burnet, *Archaeologiae philosophicae: sive doctrina antiqua de rerum originibus* (London, 1692). An English translation was published in 1736, in two separate parts: *Archaelogiae philosophicae: or the ancient doctrine concerning the originals of things* (London, 1736) and *Doctrina antiqua de rerum originibus: or, an inquiry into the doctrine of the philosophers of all nations* (London, 1736). The former is a translation of Book I, the latter a rearranged translation of Book II (Chs I.1–4 map onto chs II.7–10 in the 1692 edn; chs II.1–6 onto their equivalents). While generally faithful, the translation sometimes exaggerates Burnet's ironic tone to suit a mid-eighteenth-century audience; I have therefore referred only to the 1692 Latin edition. The fullest previous account of Burnet as a historian of philosophy is Malusa, 'First general histories', 330–70, which suffers rather badly from attempting to squeeze him into a 'Cambridge Platonist' straitjacket.

[363] Burnet, *Archaeologiae*, 190–1: 'Duae sunt opiniones, maximè communes, de Philosophiae Barbaricae origine. Nonnulli statuunt ab ipsis illis gentibus, suopte ingenio, inventam fuisse: alii ab Hebraeis deductam & derivatam ad ceteras gentes: à Mose scilicet, aut Abrahamo: omnium scientiarum, ut volunt, principibus'.

[364] Ibid., 195–6: 'Neque scientiâ naturali, neque Mathematicâ, celebres fuere Hebraei: & à se tamen edoctos esse volunt Aegyptios, qui, in his disciplinis, facile caeteras omnes gentes olim superâsse perhibentur: Haec non tantùm gratis dicuntur à *Josepho*, sed etiam contra omnem veri speciem aut similitudinem'.

[365] Ibid., 43.

nor to demonstrate their dogmas through cause and effect, as modern philosophers do. The philosophy of the ancients was less painstaking ... As human customs and life in general were simple in the first centuries, so was knowledge, of which [they were] satisfied with little ... the ancient barbarian philosophy was easier and shorter, proceeding by question and answer rather than argument and contention, as the Greeks did later.[366]

Ancient philosophy, like ancient culture more generally, proceeded 'by tradition', an idea repeated again and again by Burnet. The origin of that tradition could only be the knowledge disseminated throughout the world by the progeny of Noah, who had delivered it from the antediluvian patriarchs. This was not an excuse to engage in wild speculations about the lost books of Enoch, pillars of Seth, or any of the ideas we have seen critiqued by Stanley and others. Rather, it was a simple anthropological and cultural historical fact – even if the Noachic tradition had been 'spattered with many blemishes' over the ages.[367]

Of course, Burnet had very good personal reasons for believing this: he wanted to defend his own 'theory' of the creation as one inherited from an antediluvian tradition. Accordingly, one would expect the chapters on the history of philosophy (chs 1–13) to be openly self-justifying. However, Burnet did something rather more interesting. Rather than search for scraps of 'his' truth, he offered a more general cultural history of philosophy, the purpose of which was more to present a series of conditions of possibility in which his theory could have been preserved. This was a clever step, for it allowed him to avoid the sort of esoteric searches and absurd leaps of scholarship practised by the likes of More in favour of a more critical history. Burnet was an acute and cautious historian who verged on the side of scepticism when in doubt: just as he refused to engage in speculation on the true age of the world given the different accounts offered in the Masoretic Bible, the Septuagint, and the Samaritan version, so he rejected the *Chaldean Oracles* (and the wilder stories about Zoroaster more generally) and any attempts to 'read' anything into Pythagorean number theory.[368] His dismissal of the Cabbala – about which he clearly made some effort to find out – includes some of the most

---

[366] Ibid., 192–3: 'Qui enim in literaturâ & lectione veterum, vel mediocriter versati sunt, satis nôrunt, moris non fuisse priscis illis sapientibus, *Theorias* condere, neque dogmata sua per Causas aut Effecta demonstrare, ut solent hodierni Philosophi. Minus operosa fuit primorum hominum Philosophia ... Utì mores hominum, & vita humana, ita cognitio pariter, in primis saeculis, simplicior erat, & paucis contenta. Rectè notat Clemens Alexandrinus, Philosophiam antiquo-barbaram fuisse facilem brevemque, per quaesita & responsa: non argumentativam & contentiosam, ut erat postea Graeca' (see also 4). The reference is to Clemens Alexandrinus, *Strom.*, viii.1. This 'argumentative' view of Greek philosophy played an important role in attacks on it by Royal Society apologists: see Chapter 4 below.

[367] Burnet, *Archaeologiae*, 196–7: 'Haec & hujusmodi capita complexa est priscorum philosophia; Quae, licet multis maculis conspersa, aut fordibus involuta, ad nos seros homines, ultimam ferè Noachidarum progeniem, post aliquot millennia, pervenerit'.

[368] Ibid., 21–3 (*Chaldean Oracles* and Zoroaster), 154–60 (Pythagorean numbers).

genuinely humorous passages of early modern scholarship. Lurianic Cabbala included a discussion of the beards (*dikna*) of God (Arich Anpin) that contained thirteen levels of divine mercy, with every hair representing a power of contraction (*Tzimtzum* [צמצום]) of the light emanated by God. 'So much for the beard, and the little beard', commented Burnet after quoting Luria; 'if you ask them about the nose, the head and other parts, they answer in the same splendid way, equally unconnected to any vestige of human understanding'.[369] His focus on cultural development sometimes led to truly novel and critical conclusions, such as when he asserted (contrary to much seventeenth-century speculation) that the Phoenicians cannot have developed atomism because 'that way of philosophising by hypotheses and systems of principles does not seem to reflect the character of the ancient times'; it took the speculative mindset of the Greeks to develop such doctrines.[370]

The great pay-off for Burnet was that any similarities between the pagan and the Mosaic creation accounts now appeared not as the product of an esoteric and unscholarly search but as the vague remnants of an ancient tradition revealed by a sceptical and critical history. He refused to speculate on the contents of the philosophies of peoples whose texts had not survived (the Celts, Scythians, Indians, Chinese, Assyrians, etc.) but it was clear from later reports and from what the Greeks took from the east that a vague tradition of constructing cosmogonies or theogonies had dominated primitive natural philosophy. Moreover, these cosmogonies inevitably referred to a chaos, creation from pre-existent matter, and the formation of the first humans from a primordial slime. Once again, the point was not to 'decipher' these primitive stories but to illustrate the existence of an early tradition.[371] The only textually daring step that Burnet had to take was to insist on the important role of Orpheus. The Orphic texts had been classified as *spuria* by several scholars throughout the century, most importantly by G. J. Vossius, drawing on the scepticism already expressed in antiquity by Cicero and Aristotle.[372] But Orpheus was crucial for Burnet's narrative of a cultural transfer between the 'barbaric' nations of the Mediterranean to the Greeks, and so he defended the authenticity of some of his

---

[369] Ibid., 61: 'Haec de Barbâ & Barbulâ. Si praetereà de *naso*, de *cranio*, caeterisque partibus interrogentur, praeclara itidem respondent, & ab omni intelligentiâ humanâ non minùs aliena'.

[370] Ibid., 40: 'Praetereà non videtur mihi sapere indolem antiquissimorum temporum iste modus philosophandi per *hypotheses* & principiorum *systemata*; quem modum, ab introductis Atomis, statim sequebantur philosophi. Haec Graecanica sunt, ut par est credere, & sequioris aevi'.

[371] See e.g. the discussion of Greek theogonies, and their relationship to 'barbarian' cosmogonies, at ibid., 117–18.

[372] For scepticism about Orpheus, see Walker, 'Orpheus the theologian and Renaissance Platonists' (1953); for Isaac Casaubon's doubts, see Grafton, *Defenders*, 161; for Vossius, see G. J. Vossius, *De artis poeticae natura, ac constitutione liber* (Amsterdam, 1647), 78–9 (drawing on Cicero, *Nat. Deor.*, 1.38 which cited the lost second book of Aristotle's *Poetics*), challenged by Burnet at *Archaeologiae*, 132–5. Cudworth had previously developed a long and typically elaborate defence at *System*, 294–8.

statements at length.[373] All this contributed to the defence of specific doctrines of Burnet's theory in Book II of the *Archaeologiae*. When all the philosophers before Aristotle spoke of a primordial chaos, of the battle of the elements, or of an ancient deluge, they were not necessarily representing the pure truth, but they were taking part in a philosophical tradition that went back to the earliest times.[374] Even more rewarding were the specific examples. When Plato spoke of a twofold age of the world, for example, and even of something resembling a flood, he was not developing his own ideas but adding his own contribution to a universal tradition.[375]

This was a major contribution to the history of philosophy, for Burnet's thesis of cultural development, while not unprecedented, was original in its general application: Brucker was certainly mistaken to claim that this was an old-fashioned excursion into Renaissance syncretism. However, it was entirely overshadowed by Burnet's second main argument: that Moses had not philo-sophised, but acted as a 'lawgiver'. His case rested on four foundations: (A) the primitiveness of the post-Exodus Israelites; (B) what had been written by previous authorities; (C) what befits the nature of God; and (D) a contextual comparison with other nations. The first three were not controversial. Resting on the authority of Maimonides in particular, Burnet suggested that God, who acted by second causes rather than by constant miracles, weaned the Israelites off pagan idolatry by having his lawgiver, Moses, deliver a creation narrative whose first purpose was the celebration of his own glory.[376] It was only the fourth argument that cost Burnet his reputation and his career. He drew on a large array of sources to make the generally accepted point that the sages of ancient cultures usually concealed their truths under symbols, hieroglyphs, allegories, etc. This was particularly the case with such difficult physico-theological truths as the creation, which would always be rejected in favour of simpler fables.[377] Again, there would be nothing new in claiming that Moses possessed an esoteric doctrine, as long as it was confirmed that the literal text – and Burnet consistently defended his interpretation as literal, not requiring recourse to the allegorical hermeneutics of the Alexandrian Jews and church fathers[378] – was still true in a phenomenalist sense. But Burnet seemed repeat-edly to suggest that Moses had acted as just another lawgiver (he consistently used such political terminology) preserving the true creation account that he inherited for himself, while accommodating a fable to the backward Israelites. For example, when Moses had proposed geocentricism there was no way a reading could save the heliocentric truth; rather, the text had to be read politically: '[Moses] rightly looked out for the safety of the state, and,

---

[373] Burnet, *Archaeologiae*, 119–35.     [374] Ibid., 202–7, 209–10, 245–8.     [375] Ibid., 250–9.

[376] See e.g. the extensive reliance on Maimonides at ibid., 334–6.     [377] Ibid., 330–2.

[378] See e.g. ibid., 296.

neglecting philosophy, concerned himself with graver deliberations and deci-
sions of greater importance' – that is to say, the preservation of the Israelites
from idolatry.[379] This was a history of ethics, not physics.[380]

Even more controversially, Burnet seemed to favour the tradition he had
delineated in his history of philosophy over the Mosaic account. For example,
where the pagan philosophers discussed the matter pre-existing before the
creation of the world, Moses only focused on the earth so as to avoid confusing
the masses, who would never have distinguished between the creation of the
universe and of their world.[381] This argument seems remarkable, but it is less
surprising when we remember that Burnet's original problem, as he himself
presented it, was that his account differed substantially from the Mosaic.[382]
Nonetheless it left Burnet in the obvious quandary that he seemed to be saying
that Moses was tactically lying: as one of his many future critics was to put it,
Burnet seemed to give every ancient civilisation a Cabbala *except* the Jews.[383]
Burnet knew this, and sought to defend the Mosaic account as more 'true' than
that of the other pagan lawgivers. But on every single occasion that he did this it
emerged that 'truth' consisted in the politico-theological truth of worshipping
the true God, not in any physical truths concerning the creation.[384] Indeed,
context dictated that Moses had to act in this way, for since the 'neighbouring
pagans had their own cosmogonies, for the most part depraved and inimical to
true religion', Moses had to supply an alternative to prevent their easy seduc-
tion by idolatrous others: 'If you do not give your daughter a marriage, she will
search for a husband herself, perhaps among the servants or the lowest
masses'.[385]

---

[379] Ibid., 298: 'Qua in rectè consuluit saluti publicae, & neglectâ philosophiâ, gravioribus con-
siliis, & majoris momenti rationibus, adhaesit'.

[380] Ibid., 314: 'Haec mihi videtur ratio utriusque Cosmopoeïae, Physicae & Ethicae: ita enim
appello Mosaicam: cùm non tam φυσικῶς quàm ἠθικῶς, institui & ordinari videatur'.

[381] Ibid., 306: 'Neque mirum videri debet haec non distinxisse Mosem, aut Universi originem non
tractâsse seorsim ab illâ mundi nostri sublunaris: Haec enim non distinguit populus, aut
separatim aestimat'. See also 315–16.

[382] Ibid., 298: 'Conveniunt quidem Hexaëmeron & Theoria in primis rerum staminibus, ut ita
dicum: quòd utrumque supponat Chaos pro substratâ mundi materia ... In caeteris autem, ut it
formâ & limitibus mundi producti, in modo, tempore, aliisque, non parùm discrepant. Quae
jam pluribus sunt examinanda'.

[383] John Woodward, *Of the wisdom of the antient Egyptians ... a discourse concerning their arts,
their sciences, and their learning* (London, 1777), 65. On this work, including the dating of
composition, see below.

[384] Burnet, *Archaeologiae*, 312–13, 323.

[385] Ibid., 321: 'Habuerunt Gentes circumvicinae suas Cosmogonias, suam Historiam, aut
Physiologiam, de Mundi origine: in plerisque vitiosam, & verae religioni inimicam. Atque
has, similesve, Traditiones, aut Mythologias, secuti fuissent, nisi aliter edocti, Israelitae. Si
nuptum non dederis filiam, ipsa sibi maritum quaeret, è famulis forsan, aut humili plebe: & nisi
populo dederis suam fidem, dogmata, & opiniones, ipsi sibi fingent, quisque pro suo ingenio,
pro suo affectu, aut pro suis vitiis'.

It seems impossible to explain Burnet solely on the basis of any potential predecessors or influences upon him.[386] He may well have been influenced by his tutor Cudworth both in his Cartesianism and in his critical scholarship (fundamentally different to that of More); more intriguing is the fact that Cudworth also wrote a manuscript work entitled 'A Discourse of the Creation of the World', unfortunately now lost.[387] This has little to do with 'Platonism', and Burnet was in fact far more critical of Platonic physics than either More or Cudworth.[388] His Moses was certainly not the esoteric Cabbalist of More, and he explicitly rejected allegorical readings of Genesis. The possibility that he was heavily influenced by Spencer's De legibus is more difficult to assess. We know that Burnet read the book because there are two references to it in his self-annotated copy of the 1689 Theoria;[389] moreover, his language concerning the backwardness of the Israelites strongly resembles Spencer's. But there is also a significant chronological problem, because Burnet was espousing a 'hard' (i.e. non-phenomenalist) accommodationism as early as 1680–81, in his correspondence with Newton, several years before the publication of De legibus.[390]

Given the lack of conclusive evidence, we must descend into speculation. My own theory is that Burnet took his idea that Moses was a lawgiver like all other near-eastern lawgivers from Spencer's claim that God adapted Moses's knowledge to contemporary intellectual culture (the germ of this claim was already available in Spencer's Urim & Thummim of 1669). If this is the case, he completely misunderstood Spencer's argument, for Spencer never claimed that Moses was promoting a pragmatic civil religion like that of the pagans.

### 3.7.2    The debate after Burnet

The impact of Burnet's work on late century natural philosophical discourse was staggering: it is difficult to find a major natural philosopher who did not

---

[386] For the claim that he should be treated as a late 'Cambridge Platonist', see Malusa, 'First general histories', 330–70 and Harrison, The Bible, Protestantism, and the rise of natural science (1998), 142; for the claim that he was a direct follower of Spencer, see Gascoigne, 'Wisdom', 180–3, 185–6. I discount the third possibility that Burnet's idea of Moses qua lawgiver stemmed in any way from the Machiavellian civil religion tradition.

[387] Birch, 'Cudworth', xx. For an (imperfect) account of Cudworth's manuscripts, see Passmore, Cudworth, 107–13; see also 5.4 below.

[388] Burnet, Archaeologiae, 177–8.

[389] The notes do not concern the central issues covered in Archaeologiae: one concerns the millenarian meaning of the Sabbath, another the role of the high priest in the Jewish theocracy. See CUL Adv.c.27.4, p. 182, MS note to De legibus, 1685 edn, 141 (presumably Burnet disagreed with Spencer's claim that the Sabbath was a purely anti-idolatrous measure) and p. 202, MS note to De legibus, 1685 edn, 224).

[390] For this correspondence, which commenced when Burnet sent Newton a copy of the Latin Telluris, see Mandelbrote, 'Biblical criticism'.

have at least a cursory interest. At the same time, the theological implications of his work meant that the subsequent debate could never be restricted to natural philosophers, as more and more theologians also waded in, especially after a translation of the most contentious chapters of the *Archaeologiae* were published in Charles Gildon's edition of Charles Blount's *Oracles of reason* (1693) (Burnet, meanwhile, had to resign his place at court).[391] It is worth noting that alongside Burnet, Blount also invoked Spencer to attack theories of Jewish primacy and to compare the Israelites to other pagans.[392] Continental critics – almost always Reformed in theological orientation – at this point started to claim that Spencer's thesis was heterodox, creating the myth of him as a Socinian.[393] This approach was followed by the notoriously rigorous Calvinist Cambridge divine John Edwards, who claimed that Marsham, Spencer, and Burnet made 'the True God most diligently and precisely tread in the steps of the false Gods and Idols'.[394] This was a complete misrepresentation of their arguments, but it demonstrates the complexities that the historical form of the accommodationist hermeneutic, by then accepted by almost everyone, was throwing up. From a clerical–theological perspective, one could of course simply dismiss Burnet's whole framework: if the Bible was not written to expound natural philosophy, what use was Burnet's deconstruction?[395] Or, *contra* Spencer, why would God use pagan rites to eradicate pagan idolatry?[396] But scholarship had moved on and if a theologian was to make a convincing argument he had to engage with the history of theology and of philosophy. In his commentary on Genesis, designed to demonstrate the truth of the scripture 'without forsaking the literal sense, and betaking to I know not what allegorical interpretations', the Bishop of Ely, Spencer's associate Simon Patrick, claimed that far from being a universal tradition, the creation narrative

---

[391] The full circumstances remain unclear – the fullest discussion is Mandelbrote, 'Biblical criticism', 164–5.

[392] Charles Blount, *The oracles of reason*, ed. C. Gildon (London, 1693), 1–77; and 'The original of the *Jews*' (126–34), where Spencer is implicitly invoked to attack the theories of Jewish primacy promoted by 'Bochartus . . . Stillingfleet . . . not to mention Theophilus Gale': 'Most of the *Iewish* Laws and Rites were practised among the *Gentiles* indifferently, or at least did not much vary from them, as the diligent Searchers into Antiquity well know' (133). A separate anonymous English manuscript translation of the inflammatory seventh book of the *Archaeologiae* is BL MS Sloane 1775, fols. 144ʳ–155ᵛ.

[393] For a full summary, see Levitin, 'Spencer'. The most important early critique is in Witsius, *Ægyptiaca*, esp. 282–4 (Witsius rather confusedly combined the voluntarist claim that God could have arbitrarily turned the hearts of men as he pleased with a 'traditional' Maimonidean 'inversion' of pagan rites in the accommodation process). For a long list of others who defended Hebrew primacy against Spencer, see C. M. Pfaff, 'Dissertatio praeliminaris', in John Spencer, *De legibus Hebraeorum ritualibus* (Tübingen, 1732), sigs. d2ᵛ–d3ʳ.

[394] John Edwards, *A compleat history: or, survey of all the dispensations and methods of religion* (London, 1699), 246–50 at 249.

[395] 'E.g. Robert St. Clair, 'To the Reader', in *The Abyssinian philosophy confuted: or, Telluris theoria neither sacred, nor agreeable to reason* (London, 1697), sigs. a7ʳ⁻ᵛ.

[396] Edwards, *Compleat history*, 246–50.

*was* in fact a uniquely Jewish possession but one that was passed on to the pre-Mosaic Egyptians through Abraham and Joseph during their time there (Gen. 19.9–20, Gen. 41.44–46). But they, presumably, had received it by tradition from the earlier patriarchs, so it is not clear how this argument differed significantly from Burnet's, at least on this topic.[397]

A more convincing response was to resort to traditional 'phenomenalist' accommodationism and to reassert that Moses was acting as both lawgiver *and* philosopher. This was the argument of the relatively obscure but prolific rector of Selsey William Nicholls, who argued against Burnet's 'political' interpretation of Genesis by reassuring readers that the text was in fact 'the most noble piece of Philosophy, which ever the World was acquainted with'.[398] But Nicholls also had to resort to scholarly traditions that had been tainted with the accusation of heterodoxy. Admitting, like Burnet, that Gen. 1:1 referred not to the whole universe but only to the sun and the planets, he thus suggested that Gen. 1:16 had been modified by a later rabbinical commentator to add a reference to the late creation of the stars, drawing for this thesis of textual emendation on the famous *Histoire critique du Vieux Testament* (1678) by the Oratorian Richard Simon.[399] This move had allowed Simon both to explain inconsistencies in the text and to defend Roman Catholic traditionalism, but he was quickly associated with heterodoxy, especially Spinoza, not least in England (even if only two copies of the suppressed French edition initially reached English shores).[400] For Nicholls, the sacrifice was worth making. The integrity of the text was forsaken but Moses was rescued: he 'took the middle and the wisest Course' between lying and confusing the masses, and was nothing like the Egyptian priests who wrapped everything in mystery and double meaning.[401] Nicholls, who had studied at St Paul's with Thomas Gale

---

[397] Simon Patrick, *A commentary upon the first book of Moses, called Genesis* (London, 1695), 'Preface', sigs. A1ʳ, A2ʳ.

[398] William Nicholls, *A conference with a theist* (London, 1696), 98. Nicholls's biography is worth further research; Cornwall, 'Nicholls, William', *ODNB* offers a skeletal beginning.

[399] Nicholls, *Conference*, 99–101 (use of Simon), 109, 126–8, 252. Simon had argued that the Pentateuch had been composed over time by public scribes who edited the text and other biblical books, and were prevented from making serious errors by providential guidance. On Simon, the best study remains Auvray, *Richard Simon* (1974); more recently also Bernier, *La critique du Pentateuque de Hobbes à Calmet* (2010), 250–63.

[400] Charles-Marie de Veil, *A letter to the Honourable Robert Boyle ... defending the divine authority of the Holy Scripture* (London, 1683); Evelyn to John Fell, 18 March 1682, *Evelyn correspondence*, III, 264–6 (curiously, Evelyn associated Marsham with Simon and Spinoza). On the details behind the publication of Simon in English in 1682 (n. 17 above), see Ward, '*Religio Laici* and father Simon's *History*' (1946); Harth, *Contexts of Dryden's thought* (1968), 48, 57–9, 67–8, 174–88, 190–214, 273–6; Reedy, *The Bible and reason* (1985), 90–118, 145–55; Champion, 'Richard Simon and biblical criticism in Restoration England' (1999); and for corrections to these and for the fullest collection of evidence on the clerical-scholarly reception, Mandelbrote, 'Vossius', 99, 101–2, 104–6, 110–11, 112 n. 112.

[401] Nicholls, *Conference*, 128.

and attended Oxford in the early 1680s, was of the generation that happily accepted the need to historicise both Moses and the biblical text; the key debates were going on within a wide and scholarly advanced Anglican orthodoxy. Nonetheless, there is an important development here, for Nicholls's popular work (it was reprinted several times), written in English, with attractive illustrations of his own explanation of Genesis and published in cheap octavo, was presented to the general reading public as an easily digestible dialogue effectively rewriting the Bible to defend Moses from the charge of being a bad philosopher.[402] The scholarly mentality that had provided the English church with so much of its identity since Laud was bubbling over into wider literate society. Its older statesmen, like Pococke, were shocked to find its results being discussed in coffee-houses.[403]

It was perhaps this sense of intellectual free-for-all that encouraged natural philosophers to believe that they were as qualified as theologians to contribute to the debates. The key challengers to Burnet were John Woodward (*An essay toward a natural history of the earth* (1695)) and William Whiston (*A new theory of the earth* (1696)), but each was embedded in a circle of friends, acquintances, and rivals, almost all of whom were sceptical about the compatibility of any of the others' accounts with that of Moses. The amount of time dedicated to reading and discussing relevant texts was evidently immense; Robert Hooke's reading of Burnet, for example, led to lengthy coffee-house discussion with colleagues including Lodwick and to the publication of an epitome of the *Archaeologiae* in the *Philosophical Transactions* after it had been read at a meeting of the Royal Society on Burnet's own permission.[404] Nonetheless, that reading was always targeted: as his notes demonstrate, Isaac Newton read Cudworth's *System* diligently but also ransacked it precisely for what he desired, namely data on the history of natural philosophy, Egyptian idolatry, and the nature of Moses' intellectual development.[405]

Although he never developed a concerted answer to Burnet, Newton is important to our story both as Whiston's mentor and as a natural philosopher obsessed with the history of Egyptian and Mosaic philosophy and theology. The outlines of Newton's history – now scattered across the world in

---

[402] See also ibid., 122: 'So that I should rather think ... instead of finding fault with *Moses* for a *Plebian* Philosopher, [we] should admire him for an excellent *Vertuoso*'. The work was reprinted (with additions) in 1698, 1703 and 1723.

[403] See Mandelbrote, 'Vossius', quoting Pococke's letter to Narcissus Marsh of Feb 1680, from L. Twells, 'The life of ... Pococke', in *The theological works of ... Pocock*, ed. L. Twells (2 vols, London, 1740), I, 74.

[404] Poole, 'Genesis Narrative', 51. On Hooke, see below.

[405] See Newton's 'Out of Cudworth', William Andrews Clarke Memorial Library, MS fn563Z, fol. 1ʳ–2ᵛ, printed, with some imperfections, in Force and Popkin, *Essays* (1990), 207–13. See Sailor, 'Newton's Debt to Cudworth' (1988). A further part of the MS is Trinity College, Cambridge, MS R.16.38, fol. 438ʳ.

manuscript fragments – have been sketched many times: God had revealed to Adam a primitive and minimalist ur-religion that went hand in hand with certain natural philosophical truths; the practical manifestation of this religion was worship in circular temples surrounding a central fire, preserving the truth of heliocentricism. Restored in the time of Noah, this belief was corrupted by Euhemeristic worship of the patriarch and his progeny and spread to all the pagans, meanwhile preserving scraps of truth. Since philosophical and religious truth was thus united, it was 'y$^e$ Priests [who] anciently were above other men well skilled in y$^e$ knowledge of y$^e$ true frame of Nature & accounted it a great part of their Theology'.[406] Yet it was this philosophical–religious truth that spread the seeds of a second type of idolatry: the worship of the elements themselves: 'y$^e$ frame of y$^e$ heavens consisting of Sun Moon & Stars being represented ~~by~~ <in> the Prytanæa as y$^e$ real temple of the Deity men were led by degrees to pay a veneration to these sensible objects & began at length to worship them as the <visible> seats of divinity'.[407]

The idea that the rise of idolatry went hand in hand with natural philosophical error was not new, having been propounded most fully by Vossius; it is no surprise to find that Newton's copy of the *Theologia gentilis* appears to be one of his most used books, marked with almost constant dog-earing.[408] Yet he was also familiar with the more recent work that we have covered above. His copies of both Marsham's *Canon* and Spencer's *De legibus* survive and we have already encountered his correspondence with Burnet.[409] Accordingly, Newton did develop views on both the question of the Israelites' intellectual

---

[406] Newton, 'The original of religions' [*c.* early 1690s], NLI MS Yahuda 41, fol. 7$^r$. Unless otherwise stated, the datings and transcriptions of the Newton manuscripts are those given at the Newton project (www.newtonproject.sussex.ac.uk).

[407] NLI MS Yahuda 41, fol. 8$^r$. The fullest treatment remains Goldish, *Judaism in the theology of Sir Isaac Newton* (1998). See also Buchwald and Feingold, *Civilization*, 126–63; Mandelbrote, *Footprints of the lion* (2001), 91–2, 109–10; Knoespel, 'Interpretative strategies in Newton's *Theologiae gentilis origines philosophicae*' (1999); Force, 'Newton, the Lord God of Israel and knowledge of nature' (1993); Gascoigne, 'Wisdom'; Popkin, 'Crisis of polytheism'; Popkin, 'Newton and Maimonides' (1988); Popkin, 'Some further comments on Newton and Maimonides' (1990); Popkin, 'Polytheism, deism and Newton' (1990). Manuel, *Isaac Newton, historian* (1963), is at points still useful, but was written before the re-emergence of the Yahuda manuscripts. I do not here consider Newton's post-1700 historical works, much more concerned with questions of chronology and population growth, and now analysed in great detail by Buchwald and Feingold.

[408] Trinity College, Cambridge, classmark: NQ 8.46. Newton's foldings suggest that he took far more interest in G. J. Vossius's historical commentary than in the actual translation of Maimonides's *Mishnah* commentary by Dionysius, indicative of his reliance on modern interpretations.

[409] John Marsham, *Canon chronicus … nunc longè emendatior in Germaniâ recusus* (Leipzig, 1676), Linda Hall Library for Science, Engineering and Technology, Kansas City, Missouri, classmark: D59.M36 1676; John Spencer, *De legibus Hebraeorum ritualibus* (Cambridge, 1683–5), Trinity College, Cambridge, classmark: NQ 17.18 (Westfall, *Never at rest: a biography of Isaac Newton* (1980), 351–2, n. 56, claims that 'Newton could [not] have read the work before autumn 1689' – the reasons given are convincing, if not conclusive). Newton's

relationship with Egypt and on the nature of 'Mosaic physics'. There is little evidence, however, to suggest that he was heavily influenced by Spencer's ground-breaking thesis.[410] Newton's actual use of Spencer, whom he cited only twice in all his copious manuscripts, shows a significant misappropriation, for far from being inspired to modify or even rethink his position he simply slotted Spencer's conclusions into his own narrative, ignoring the marked differences between them. The first reference to Spencer is in a Latin manuscript bundle from the late 1680s or early 1690s, preserved at the National Library of Israel: 'If the Mosaic rites were derived from the Egyptian, as Spencer broadly shows, it should be said that the Egyptians certainly took the same by tradition from the patriarch Noah, and that this religion is the oldest and truest of them all'.[411] This usage is repeated and accentuated in an English manuscript from the early 1690s on 'The Original of Religions'.[412] But Spencer never stated that Moses retained the 'true' elements of Egyptian theology, only indifferent ceremonies which helped the process of accommodation. And he certainly did not claim any congruence between Noachic and Mosaic religion – indeed, quite contrary to Newton, he offered a remarkably naturalised explanation for the initial origin of religious rites.[413] Newton's copy of Marsham contains far more dog-earring than that of Spencer, but he also seems to have used it only as a repository of useful data, ignoring Marsham's overall conclusions.

copies of Burnet are Trinity College, Cambridge, NQ 16.150A–B (*Theoria*); NQ 8.56 (*Archaeologiae*).

[410] I thus differ here from Gascoigne, 'Wisdom', and Mulsow, 'Orientalistik', 51, which claims close friendship between them and Burnet ('Die drei Männer [i.e. Spencer, Newton and Burnet] hatten nämlich enge Beziehungen untereinander, und man diskutierte ungetrennt voneinander naturwissenschaftliche, historische und religiöse Fragen'); I am not aware of any evidence for this friendship. A continuing myth is that Newton was in charge of the posthumous publication of a new edition of *De legibus*, but the evidence adduced for this shows the exact opposite: Newton to Otto Mencke, 22 Nov 1693, in *Newton correspondence*, III, 291: 'Et cum Spencerus noster non multo post ex hac luce migraret expectabam aliquamdiu donec ejus Executores convenire liceret ut quaenam ejus opera posthuma in lucem edentur ex iis cognoscerem et tibi significarem. Edetur autem ejus liber de legibus Hebraicis duplo fere auctior quam prius in duobus voluminibus, quorum secundum continebit librum quartum omnino novum'. Turnbull translates 'Spencerus noster' as 'our friend Spencer' (292) but I see no warrant for this. Mencke had reviewed *De legibus* in the famous journal which he edited: *Acta eruditorum* (Leipzig, 1686), 113–19 (that the anonymous review was by Mencke himself is shown in Laven, *The 'Acta Eruditorum' under the editorship of Otto Mencke* (1990 [1986]), 311). See also Newton to Locke, 13 December 1691, in *Newton correspondence*, III, 185: 'Dr Spencer ye Dean of Ely has perused ye specimen of Le Clerk's latin version of ye Old Testament and likes ye designe very well but gives me no remarks about it'. Newton's copy of *De legibus* shows no sign of having been given by the author.

[411] Isaac Newton, 'Further notes on ancient religion', NLI MS Yahuda 17.3, fol. 11$^r$: 'Si Sacra Mosaica ab Ægyptiacis desumpta sint ut <fuse> probavit Spencerus dicendum erit Ægyptij vero eadem a patre Noacho didicerant per traditionem acceperant <sitque hac [sic?] religio verissima omnium antiquissima aeque ac verissima>'.

[412] NLI MS Yahuda 41, fol. 5$^r$.    [413] Spencer, *De legibus*, 118–33.

There is no evidence, then, that Newton believed the Jews to have taken a great deal from the Egyptians. Nonetheless, he was also not a Theophilus Gale-esque espouser of Mosaic primacy.[414] Saying that aspects of true *theology* derived from Noah (as Newton did) was one thing; saying that all *philosophy* was derived from Moses and the Jews (à la Gale) was quite another. There are clear signs that Newton had inherited the critical attitude towards such assumptions. He spoke, for example, of Artapanus 'ascrib[ing] some things to Moses w^ch does not well agree to him', an obvious attack on the self-serving philosophical history deployed by the Hellenistic Jews.[415]

Far more than Gale, Newton was prepared to enter into the sort of comparisons between Moses and other pagans made by Burnet, albeit with the proviso that the Genesis account was true on a phenomenalist level.[416] As with most post-Calvinist exegetes this involved a comparative–contextual focus on the historical figure of Moses:

When the ancient Sages ~~prepared~~ <would have> one thing to be represented by another, they framed a Metamorphosis of the one into the other, & thence came all the ancient Metamorphoses recited by Ovid & others. This was their way of making Parables, & Moses in this Parable of the Serpent speaks in the language of the ancient ~~sages~~ wise men, being skilled in all the learning of the Egyptians.[417]

Such statements surely reveal the influence of either Spencer or Burnet, and for all of Newton's differences from both, his ideas on the subject of Mosaic philosophy would undoubtedly have faced a challenging reception if made public.

Something of that reception was reserved for Newton's disciple William Whiston, of whose scheme – much more directly posited at answering the problem set by Burnet – Newton was said to have 'well approved' (albeit by Whiston himself).[418] Whiston had in his youth been impressed by Burnet's Cartesian theory, but after his conversion to Newtonianism he argued that the flood was caused by the near passing of a divinely guided comet which had also transformed the earth's orbit from circular to elliptical.[419] Like Newton, he was

---

[414] As is claimed in Mandelbrote, 'Newton and the writing of biblical criticism', 290, n. 47.

[415] NLI MS Yahuda 41, fol. 25^v. Newton's full statement is rather curious, for it assigns Artapanus' error to his 'being a Christian' – perhaps a mistake stemming from his only appearing in Christian authors like Eusebius and Clemens Alexandrinus?

[416] Snobelen, 'Isaac Newton, the scriptures, and the hermeneutics of accommodation' (2008), 508; Mandelbrote, 'Crisis', 162.

[417] Isaac Newton, 'Treatise on revelation' [*c.* mid to late 1680s], NLI Yahuda MS 9.1, fol. 21^v.

[418] William Whiston, *Memoirs of the life and writing of Mr William Whiston . . . the second edition, corrected* (London, 1753 [1st edn=1749–50]), 38.

[419] For Whiston's early sympathy for Burnet's hypothesis, see William Whiston, 'A discourse concerning the nature, stile, and extent of the Mosaick history of Creation', in *A new theory of the earth* (London, 1696), 78 (separate pagination); Force, *William Whiston* (1985), 37, and more generally, 32–62.

cautious to portray his accommodationism as phenomenalist and thus 'literal': he claimed to be providing a reading that lay between those who only believed the 'common and vulgar' exposition and those that 'have ventur'd to exclude it from any just sense at all, asserting it to be a meer Popular, Parabolick, or Mythological relation' – an obvious barb at Burnet.[420] But Whiston was clearly less interested in the contextual–historical approach to Moses adopted by Burnet and Newton, and content to rely on the Maimonidean assumption that was by then commonplace: the Mosaic account was explicable as a 'Historical Journal or Diary' – true from the viewers' perspective – designed to wean the primitive Israelites off their idolatrous starworship.[421] This rather loose framework was flexible enough to support simple natural philosophical explanations: the appearance of the celestial bodies on the fourth day in fact referred only to their appearance to the beholder, when 'the Air was rendered ... transparent'. At other points, more intricate philological manoeuvering was required: the passages at Gen. 1:14–17 that suggested that God had made light before the heavenly bodies needed to be reinterpreted with the knowledge that Hebrew had no pluperfect tense and that the perfect tense had been used instead, generating: 'And God having (*before*) made two great lights, the greater light to rule the day, and the lesser light to rule the night; and having (*before*) made the stars also, God set them in the firmament of Heaven to give light upon the Earth, &c'.[422] Nonetheless, Whiston could not escape the deeper historical question of what precisely the historical Moses was doing – he decided that Moses knew the truth, but being 'so far from deeming his People capable of understanding the intire System ... esteem'd it improper to say a word about the internal Constitution and Parts of our own Earth'.[423] Moses, then, was still an advanced philosopher who knew the truth; how he knew it remained unsaid.

This issue clearly continued to plague the whole debate. It was raised by one of Burnet's earliest and most perceptive critics, the Anglo–Irish diplomat, civil servant, and future president of the Royal Society Robert Southwell, who was in correspondence with Burnet and many other figures interested in the issues, including Hooke and Woodward.[424] 'Can wee think that Moses if he knew [the truth]', asked Southwell, 'did designedly take care by a misrepresentation to obstruct that Glory, and to leave the Generations now of above 3000 yeares in the dark?'[425] Moses's identity as a lawgiver could not subsume that of philosopher. Others sought to develop this implication more fully. The rector of Wolington in Suffolk, Erasmus Warren, sought to defend both the truth of a literal reading of Genesis and of Moses's status as a philosopher by recourse to

---

[420] Whiston, 'Mosaick History', *New theory*, 1–2; see also the further attacks on Burnet at 76–7.
[421] Ibid., 30.     [422] Ibid., 15.     [423] Ibid., 83–4.
[424] See the extremely full biographical evidence collected in Poole, 'Southwell', 76–7. Also Levine, *Shield*, 25, 44–5, 63, 107.
[425] Southwell, 'Dialogue', 87.

the Cabbala.[426] Aware that it had been denounced as a form of late Jewish allegoresis, he distanced himself from Pico and Reuchlin by citing a barrage of standard Jewish testimonies – Ibn Ezra, Rashi, Nachmanides, Menasseh ben Israel, and the Talmud – to the effect that the Cabbala was compatible with a literal reading. This had been attempted by Buxtorf (jnr) forty years before – both Buxtorfs, while sceptical of the Cabbala's tendency to anti-literalism, had defended it because they thought it offered independent witness to the antiquity of the vowel points.[427] But the world had changed significantly since such arguments had been taken seriously and Warren's recourse to them is a nice example of the tensions stimulated by Burnet's work.

An even more idiosyncratic historical explanation was developed by John Beaumont (c. 1640–1731), a Somerset-based physician, natural philosopher, and geological collector who had been in regular contact with leading naturalists since the 1670s, had numerous publications in the *Philosophical Transactions*, and had been FRS since 1685.[428] His *Considerations on ... The theory of the earth* (1693) – dedicated to Hooke – challenged Burnet's *Theory* book by book, forcing him to engage with Burnet's history as well as his philosophy. Beaumont's first historical case was ingenious. Where Burnet had argued that the philosophical culture of the ancients was 'traditional' and that their ideas must thus represent scraps of a long inheritance, Beaumont responded that on the contrary, the ancients had consistently conducted independent search for explanatory *causes*; after all, no less an authority than Plutarch had complained about the fact.[429] Even better, the report of Pythagoras's teaching on geological change in Ovid's *Metamorphoses* mentioned him finding seashells far from the ocean: clearly there was evidence enough for the ancient philosophers to deduce events like the flood without tradition.[430] The upturn of this was that the Mosaic account must be much more singular than supposed by Burnet; indeed, this singularity, and the impossibility of giving a full philosophical account of Genesis, proved the events miraculous.[431] Burnet's search for a universal 'tradition' was based on faulty scholarship that spotted false similarities: while many ancients had

---

[426] For Warren, see n. 359 above.

[427] Warren, *Geologia*, 58–61. See e.g. Johann Buxtorf, *Tractatus de punctorum vocalium ... in libris Veteris Testamenti* (Basle, 1648), 68–75, 104; S. G. Burnett, 'Later Christian Hebraists', in *Hebrew Bible*, ed., Sæbø, II, 785–801, at 788.

[428] The scant evidence for Beaumont's biography is collected in Mandelbrote, 'Beaumont, John', *ODNB*.

[429] John Beaumont, *Considerations on a book, entituled The theory of the earth* (London, 1693), 9–10, quoting Plutarch, *Def. Or.*, 48.

[430] Beaumont, *Considerations*, 3–4, drawing on Ovid, *Met.*, xv.259–63 (not xiii, as cited by Beaumont). The idea was first proposed by Hooke: see below.

[431] Beaumont, *Considerations*, 7–8, 19–20, 147–8.

talked about the creation of an egg, some had meant by it the universe, others the earth, others the primordial chaos.[432]

All this would have been a powerful historical argument against Burnet had Beaumont not supplemented it with a peculiar addition: as well as having a literal sense, Genesis also contained an allegorical meaning. Not only this, he claimed that 'it is too manifest to be brought in dispute, that many of the [Gentiles] were initiated in Prophetick Mysteries (the Spirit of Prophecy being *inter dona gratis data*)', listing among the putative recepients Orpheus, Homer, Hesiod, Theocritus, Virgil, Ovid, Lucan, Claudian, the Sibyls, magi, and the druids (themselves supposedly Pythagoreans), 'and many of the *Platonists*.'[433] Allowing such prophetic insight to pagan philosophers and poets was well outside the realm of acceptability. This belief surely stemmed from Beaumont's own rather mystical and spiritualist brand of Roman Catholicism.[434] That he cited Henry More to defend his view is testimony to how *outré* More's vision was by the standards of English Protestant scholarship.[435]

The natural philosophical elements of Beaumont's attack on Burnet – especially his calculations concerning the volume of water required for a universal flood – were appreciated by John Ray (unsurprisingly, he found Beaumont's historical arguments to 'sme[ll] rank of the Enthusiast').[436] Ray was one of the most important natural philosophers of the Restoration, especially in his work on botany and geology with his former colleague at Trinity College, Cambridge, Francis Willughby (Ray left Trinity in 1662).[437] Ray was entirely unimpressed by Burnet, whose work he claimed not to have read as late as May 1691 because 'by w[ha]t I have heard of it I think it needs no great confutation'.[438] Given his repeated complaints about Burnet in his correspondence, his deep familiarity with the issues, and his friendship with other naturalists engaging with them, this seems an exaggeration (by 1696 he was openly saying that Burnet charged Moses with a

---

[432] Ibid., 154–9.    [433] Ibid., 170.

[434] Unfortunately, the evidence is sparse: Hans Sloane revealed Beaumont's Catholicism in a short biography (BL MS Sloane 4039, fols. 94$^r$–103$^r$ at 96$^v$). This, as well as other relevant circumstantial evidence, is charted in Mandelbrote, 'Beaumont'.

[435] Beaumont, *Observations*, 181–2.

[436] John Ray to Edward Lhuyd, 1 June 1694, in *The further correspondence of John Ray*, ed. R. W. T. Gunther (London, 1928), 245; Ray to Lhuyd, 26 Dec 1693, ibid., 242 ('a great deal of stuffe he hath about the mysticall & Allegorical Physiology of the Ancients, wch I understand not, nor I believe himself neither'). There is no sign that Ray knew of Beaumont's religious affiliations, although he probably knew him personally since he was looking forward to the *Considerations* before they were published (236–7); see likewise the praise for Beaumont in Ray to Hans Sloane, 25 May 1692, in *The correspondence of John Ray*, ed. E. Lankester (London, 1848), 250.

[437] Raven, *John Ray* (1950), much supplemented in Mandelbrote, 'Ray, John', *ODNB*.

[438] Ray to Lhuyd, 27 May 1691, in *Further correspondence*, 218.

'fable').[439] Although Ray's *Miscellaenous discourses concerning the dissolution and changes of the world* (1692) and its expansion, the *Three physico-theological discourses* (1693) were based on much older work and did not directly address the whole of Burnet's theory, some of their historical themes clearly engage with Burnet's ideas, for Ray discussed ancient pagan testimony for the primordial chaos, the flood, and the general conflagration.[440] In the early 1690s Ray had begun a programme of reading on 'ancient & modern learning'.[441] Like Burnet he rejected the idea that these traditions stemmed from Moses only, tracing them back to the spread of Noah's progeny.[442] And like Burnet, he offered many pagan poetic and philosophical testimonies for creation from a primordial chaos.[443] The difference between the two was that while Burnet had preferred the pagan testimonies to the Mosaic, Ray claimed them for one 'true' tradition, with varying degrees of corruption: the Mosaic *Tohu wa bohu*, for example, had become pagan 'chaos' after 'the Primitive Patriarchs of the World delivered [it] to their Posterity, who, by degrees annexing something of fabulous [*sic*] to it, imposed upon it the name of *Chaos*'.[444] This was obviously much preferable to Burnet's apparent favouring of pagan over scriptural testimony, but it left the problem that unlike Burnet, Ray was quite limited in the extent to which he could use textual sources to support his natural historical ideas: it is striking that Moses makes virtually no appearance in these works. This reflected Ray's cautious piety[445] but it also demonstrated the dawning of the gradual realisation that in this field, the history of philosophy might cause more problems than it solved.

But the issues could not be avoided, because theology and the spectre of heterodoxy kept rearing their heads. Blount's use of Burnet was accentuated in the anonymous *Two essays sent in a letter from Oxford* (1695), for a long time – but still inconclusively – associated with John Toland.[446] The thesis of the work was encapsulated on the first page: 'the Sacred *Writers* spoke to a Generation of

---

[439] In a lost letter to Tancred Robinson, 8 July 1696, summarised from a manuscript list by William Derham (the first editor of Ray's papers) in *Further correspondence*, 301. Already in a lost letter of 3 August 1691 to Robinson, Ray had advertised his dislike for Burnet's theory (295).

[440] They were based on lectures delivered at Great St Mary's thirty years earlier (Ray to Lhuyd, 25 Sep 1691, in *Further correspondence*, 222). For the development of Ray's thoughts on the natural philosophical issues, see Poole, *World makers*, 116–18, 130–3, 163–6, *passim*. The *Miscellaneous discourses* (London, 1692), discusses only the testimonies for the Flood and the Conflagration; those on the chaos were only added to the *Three physico-theological discourses* (London, 1693), as explained at sigs. [A4]$^{v-r}$, and 1–2.

[441] Lost letter to Robinson, Dec 1690, in *Further correspondence*, 294.

[442] Ray, *Miscellaneous discourses*, sigs. [A6]$^v$–[A7]$^r$; 37–8; Ray, *Three discourses*, sigs. [A4]$^v$–a$^v$.

[443] Ray, *Three discourses*, 2–5.     [444] Ibid., 7.

[445] Well brought out in Poole, *World makers*, 132–3.

[446] The attribution was first made in Carabelli, *Tolandiana* (1975), 20–1. The subsequent historiography is summarised and questioned in the judicious piece by Rappaport, 'Questions of evidence: an anonymous tract attributed to John Toland' (1997).

Men, who were never famous in Arts and Sciences; therefore they adapted all their sayings to the vulgar Idea's of that Time and Nation; their design being not to compose a Natural system of the World, but to establish the true *Theocracy*, and good *Morals*'.[447] This was defended by Burnet-esque contextualism: the swerving of truth 'to sweeten and allure the minds of men' was a 'kind of *Philosophy* ... first made use of amongst the *Eastern Nations*' whose intellectual culture dominated Moses' world. The author then complained of the 'unjust Calumnies [that] have been thrown upon the *Worthy Master of the Charter-House*', praised Spencer, and snidely compared the just deceptions of the ancient philosophers with the self-serving manipulations of the modern clergy.[448]

This amalgamation of Spencer and Burnet into a dangerous hybrid appeared even more threatening when it came not in a noisy pamphlet but in a serious scholarly work, as it did in a new translation and commentary on Genesis by Jean Le Clerc, first published in Amsterdam in 1693, to which he appended twelve prefatory dissertations, retracting his earlier denial of Mosaic authorship of the Pentateuch.[449] When Le Clerc identified the key influence on his own method he pointed to the work of Spencer, who in turn approved of Le Clerc's work just before his death.[450] Although his commentary touches on many subjects, we may reconstruct his view on the history of Jewish philosophy, and of Moses's relationship to it, with some accuracy. Moses did not write his words 'like the writings of Mathematicians'. Rather, he accommodated his text to a specific people: the primitive Hebrews. At the same time, 'he considered the opinions and customs of neighbouring peoples, which he approved or opposed according to whether they were consistent with truth or probity'.[451]

---

[447] L. P., *Two essays sent in a letter from Oxford* (London, 1695), i–ii.

[448] Ibid., 15–16, 31, 34.

[449] *Genesis sive Mosis prophetae liber primus*, ed. and trans. Jean Le Clerc (Amsterdam, 1693). For Le Clerc, see 2.6, 5.3. 6.8. It was expanded into *Pentateuchus, sive Mosis prophetae libri quinque* (Amsterdam, 1696). For his earlier denial of Mosaic authorship, see [Jean Le Clerc], *Sentimens de quelques theologiens de Holland sur l'Histoire Critique du Vieux Testament* (Amsterdam, 1685), 125–9, some elements of which were disseminated in English as [Jean Le Clerc], *Five letters concerning the inspiration of the Holy Scriptures* (London, 1690). For a clerical critique, see William Lowth, *A vindication of the divine authority and inspiration of the writings of the Old and New Testament* (Oxford, 1692). That Le Clerc was the author was quickly known in England: see e.g. Henri Justel to Thomas Smith, 8 Jan 1686, Bod. MS Smith 46, fol. 412ʳ.

[450] [Le Clerc], *Sentimens*, 'Sentimens ... sur l'Histoire Critique en général', 14–15 (for the wider methodological significance of this, see 6.8). For emphasis on the influence of Spinoza, see Pitassi, *Le Clerc*, 12–13; Bravo, 'Historical criticism', 192–4; Israel, *Contested*, 425. The key primary evidence in fact demonstrates the strong negativity of Le Clerc's initial reaction to Spinoza: le Clerc to Limborch, 6 Dec 1681, *Epistolario*, I, 31 (I am very grateful to Anthony Grafton for reminding me of this); Simon he thought entirely unoriginal: Le Clerc to Limborch, 10 March 1682, *Epistolario*, I, 41. For Spencer's approval, see Newton to Locke, 13 Dec 1691, *Newton correspondence*, III, 185.

[451] Le Clerc, *Genesis*, sig. e3ᵛ ('De Scriptore Pentateuchi Mose'): 'Si possemus rescire omnia Mosis in scribendo consilia, multò majoris hoc esset momenti, ad ejus librorum

This obviously conforms to much of what we have encountered already, but Le Clerc also developed some further reasoning of his own. The Old Testament showed the paucity of biblical Hebrew, which was 'meager, ambiguous, and lacking elegance'.[452] The later rabbis had to invent a huge vocabulary to explain their Bible: 'no one is ignorant' that Buxtorf's rabbinical thesaurus was ten times larger than the biblical one.[453] The historical explanation for this was key: 'where arts and sciences are spurned and little written, there it is unavoidable that there will be a very great lack of vocabulary where many subject-matters are concerned'; in the same way that the Greeks had a sparse vocabulary before they cultivated philosophy and Cicero had to admit to coining Latinisations of Greek philosophical terms, the Hebrews' linguistic deficiency showcased their intellectual limitations.[454]

From evidence scattered throughout his 1690s works it is evident that Le Clerc had a clear vision of the intellectual development of the Jews: from the intellectual backwardness of the Egyptian captivity through to the Babylonian captivity; the subsequent infusion of Babylonian philosophy and theology; to the non-Hebraic and deeply allegorical culture of the Hellenists.[455] Moses and the other prophets thus had to accommodate their language to the original cultural backwardness.[456] The question remained whether the Genesis account had been revealed directly to Moses or whether he had received it by tradition. In line with recent scholarship, Le Clerc adopted the latter position, also insisting that the tradition was a written rather than an oral one.[457] Many of these writings, Le Clerc conjectured, were poetical, on the basis not only of

---

interpretationem; neque enim hîc sunt libri Mathematicorum Scriptis similes, in quibus dogmata tantum generalia, quae neque ad certa loca, ac tempora, neque ad certos homines pertineant, neque ad alia alludant, contineantur. Moses scripsit in gratiam certi cujusdam populi, Israëlitarum, nimirum; quamquam non nego divinâ Providentiâ factum, ut innumeris aliis Gentibus libri ejus postea inservierint. Itaque multa dixit, in ejus populi usum, quae omissa fuissent, si res aliter sese habuisset. Respexit ad opiniones & mores vicinorum populorum, quibus assensus est, aut adversatus, prout cum veritate, aut probitate consentanea erant'.

[452] Ibid., sig. [b4]$^r$: 'inopem eam, ambiguam, & parum cultam fuisse existimamus'.

[453] Ibid., sig. [b4]$^r$: 'Nemo nescit minimum decies plures esse in *Rabbinico Thesauro Joan. Buxtorfii*, quàm in ejusdem *Biblico Lexico*, dictiones'.

[454] Ibid., sig. [b4]$^v$: 'Si quaeramus causam inopiae Linguae Hebraïcae, eandem inveniemus, quae est in aliis Linguis observata. Ubi spernuntur disciplinae & artes, & pauca scribuntur, ibi necesse est esse plurimis in rebus summam vocabulorum penuriam ... Exempli causâ, antequàm Graeci Philosophiam diligenter colerent, innumera erant de quibus homines non cogitarant, & quibus experimendis defissent vocabula, nisi ficta fuissent. Idem contigit Latinis, cùm primùm de rebus Philosophicis Latinè scribere coeperunt' (Le Clerc goes on to quote Cicero, *Acad.*, I.7). See also Le Clerc, 'Remarques sur le livre de Jean Selden, intitule "Des Dieux des Syriens"', *Bibliotheque Choisie*, 7 (1705), 80–146, esp. 112–13.

[455] For the Babylonian context, see 2.6 above. For the Hellenistic period, see the clear statement at *Genesis*, sig. c2$^r$, as well as the attack on Philo at sig. c3$^v$; see further 6.8 below.

[456] See Le Clerc, *Genesis*, sig. c$^v$.

[457] Ibid., sigs. e$^{r-v}$, where it is affirmed that the only people who assume direct revelation are 'rabbis, who were never ashamed to lie, and to whom we thus pay no attention' ('quos nunquam mentiri puduit, & quos proinde non moramur') – a dig at Calvinist exegesis?

internal evidence but also because 'among almost *all* peoples the fragments of the most ancient history were certainly preserved in verse, as learned men have shown'.[458] Here also Le Clerc was contributing to an old debate.[459] As for the claim that Moses both opposed and accepted some elements of the worldview of his neighbours, especially the Egyptians, it is clear that Spencer was an inspiration (Le Clerc elsewhere accepted the Englishman's identification of the Sabians with the Egyptians).[460] Nonetheless he again developed his own reading. Partly, Moses sought to oppose the wildly long chronologies of the Egyptians.[461] But Genesis was also designed to oppose Egyptian esoteric philosophy and theology: Moses instructed the open reading of the law every seventh year (i.e. שמיטה (*Shmita*—the year of remission of Deut. 31:10)) to counteract the esotericism of the Egyptian priests, a conclusion Le Clerc reached by drawing on his own edition of Stanley and on Marsham.[462] Moses, in short, was not a philosopher but an inheritor of a poetic tradition responding to the philosophy of his idolatrous neighbours.

In further dissertations Le Clerc applied these principles to certain exegetical debates, like the universality of the flood, which he denied. Although he was clearly familiar with English natural philosophy[463] the post-Burnet debate was not his main focus. But Le Clerc was not in control of his English reception. The poet and hack Thomas Brown translated Le Clerc's twelve dissertations into English and published them in a cheap octavo edition in 1696, tearing them away from their initial presentation in a large biblical commentary published in folio. Even worse, Brown appended a polemical preface in which he placed the work in the middle of the English debates. Where Whiston, Woodward, and

---

[458] Ibid., sig. e⁵: 'Certè apud omnes paenè Gentes, antiquissimarum historiarum fragmenta versibus continebantur, ut ostenderunt viri docti'. As for the intenal evidence, see e.g. the note on Gen. 4:24 (p. 41b) where Le Clerc finds a case of poetic ὁμοιοτέλευτον (similarity of termination of clauses) in the so-called 'Song of the Sword' of Lamech (Gen. 4:23–4).

[459] See Haugen, 'Hebrew poetry transformed, or, scholarship invincible between Renaissance and enlightenment' (2012), esp. 21–2.

[460] Stanley, *Historia philosophiae orientalis*, sigs. O4ᵛ–[O5]ʳ (index entry for 'Sabaei'); for similar admiration for Marsham, see e.g. *Genesis*, sig. [e4]ᵛ.

[461] Le Clerc, *Genesis*, sig. [e4]ʳ⁻ᵛ; see also the note on Num. 13:23 (338a).

[462] Ibid., sig. [e4]ᵛ ('Videtur etiam non modò scriptâ Lege, sed etiam editâ, atque additis mandatis, quibus eam singulis septenniis legi jubebat, Deut. Cap. XXXI.10. tacitè Aegyptiorum sacerdotum mores reprehendisse, apud quos erant arcani ritus, & arcana dogmata, quae in vulgus efferre nefas habebatur'). See also the long note on Gen. 41:8 (260a–261b) where Le Clerc explains the חרטמים (*hartumim*; 'magicians' in the KJV) of the pharoah's dream as equivalent to the 'magicians' (i.e. Chaldean magi) referred to in Dan. 1:20, and thus to the corresponding Egyptian esoteric priests, as referred to in Herodotus, II.171 and Diodorus Siculus, *Bib. hist.*, III.3, 5 (drawing directly on Marsham, *Canon*, 231).

[463] He cited Halley's recent *Philosophical Transactions* piece on air pressure to refute the possibility of a universal flood generated by air turning into water: Le Clerc, *Genesis*, 60a (note on Gen. 7:19); see Edmund Halley, 'A discourse of the rule of the decrease of the height of the mercury in the barometer', *Philosophical Transactions*, 16 (1686), 104–16. See also 5.3 below.

Nicholls had used Moses as a peg for their own philosophies, 'pollut[ing] him with their own mixtures, and mak[ing] him act what part they please, in any habit, or under any mask, as best serves their Scenes and Opera's', Le Clerc and Burnet had both 'left *Moses* pure, free, and undefiled as ... [they] found him'. Where they had followed a contextual–historical explanation, the other English naturalists and divines had ignored the injunction of Paul against 'vain Philosophy ... by introducing their own Chimerical *Hypotheses* into them'.[464] This was surely deliberately provocative, as were Brown's footnotes informing the reader that when Le Clerc stated that Moses usually remained quiet on philosophical details but 'sometimes sprinkles a few things, which he judged would more easily persuade the Israelites to the observation of the law', the Swiss scholar was writing 'much to the same purpose' as 'the Learned Master of the *Charter-house* in his *Archaeologiae*'.[465] Unlike Whiston and almost all others, Le Clerc was not looking to save the phenomena but to offer a historical explanation for the scriptural text; this was enough for Brown to align him with Burnet (and to include a mildly anticlerical preface).[466]

It is worth pausing on this development, for while many undoubtedly still read Le Clerc in the large Latin folio he intended them to, some Englishmen, even among the more scholarly, first heard of him through Brown's English translation.[467] The more 'popular' natural philosophical debate was merging with the scholarly and theological ones, and all felt free to comment on the issues *in toto*. A nice example is that of John Harris, an Oxford graduate and FRS who was now rector of Winchelsea and soon to be appointed a Boyle lecturer.[468] A keen searcher for heterodoxy – his aim was to answer L.P., whom he incorrectly outed as Tancred Robinson – Harris was nonetheless a perceptive reader of the debate. He realised that the central issue was the line beween phenomenalist and 'hard' accommodationism: 'It's quite a different thing to *omit* giving *account* of a Matter; or to do it only *summarily* and *in general*, and to do It *falsely and precariously*'.[469] Crucially, the fact that Moses was not a philosopher did not mean that he was not telling the truth: 'For whoever looks into it with a careful and unprejudiced mind will very clearly see, that though it

---

[464] [Thomas Brown], 'Preface', in *Twelve dissertations out of Monsieur Le Clerk's Genesis* (London, 1696), sig. A4$^{r-v}$.

[465] Le Clerc, *Genesis*, sig. [e3]$^r$; *Twelve dissertations*, 134.

[466] For Brown's status as a particularly scholarly member of the Grub Street wits (he had graduated from Oxford), see Jones, 'Brown, Thomas', *ODNB*.

[467] See Gilbert Budgell to Arthur Charlett, 8 Feb 1696, Bod. MS Ballard 39, fol. 67$^r$, asking for information on 'w$^t$ Station M$^r$ Clerke the late Corrector of Moses, holds in Holland'. Budgell, a graduate of Trinity College, Oxford, held a D.D, and was by this point rector of Simondsbury in Dorset: *Fasti*, II, 318, 335; Gilbert Budgell, *A discourse of prayer* (London, 1690).

[468] Stewart, 'Harris, John', *ODNB*; Stewart, *The rise of public science* (1992), 72–5, 108–14.

[469] John Harris, *Remarks on some late papers relating to the universal deluge* (London, 1697), 6. Harris's natural philosophical aim was to defend the account of Woodward, whom he knew (see the reference to a supposedly forthcoming work by Woodward at 65–6).

were not the *Great Author's* design *primarily* to teach the Jews *Philosophy*, yet he hath no where delivered any thing that *contradicts* the *Phaenomena* of *Nature'*.[470] Just because ancient oriental philosophy was fabulous should not suggest that Moses emulated it or that he was a lawgiver like Numa.[471] Intriguingly, this led Harris to defend Le Clerc from association with L.P.: there was a fine but important difference between acknowledging that a historically sensitive literal reading sometimes found in the text 'the way of Instruction by Fables and Parables' as not only Le Clerc but also Grotius and Simon had done, and L.P.'s claim that 'the *Holy Scriptures are altogether Mysterious, Allegorical and Aenigmatical'*.[472]

In this highly complex whirlwind of subtle distinctions it is not surprising that someone attempted to cut through the complexity by resuscitating More's long-discredited scheme: this task fell to Thomas Robinson, a former student at Christ's College, Cambridge, where he surely fell under More's influence.[473] According to Robinson, all of the confusion had been caused by ignorance of the history of philosophy:

> If the learned Authors of the new Theories and Essays had but taken the Pains to have consider'd better of those great Advantages of Learning and Education which *Moses* (the greatest Philosopher that ever was in the World, and the first Describer of its Creation) had beyond any of those learned Philosophers of later date, who have writ upon the same Subject; they would have entertain'd a greater Veneration and Esteem for his short, but most comprehensive System.[474]

After Moses had been educated among the 'Hierophanthae' at Pharaoh's court, 'most skilled in the Knowledge of mystical as well as natural Philosophy', and had studied with his father-in-law Jethro, who taught him the philosophical secrets of creation passed down from the antediluvian patriarchs (which he himself derived from his ancestor Abraham), he had a 'most excellent System' in which 'Philosophy, Divinity and Mystery seem to be so closely interwoven that it wou'd be a Matter of great Difficulty (if not Impossibility) for any, unless such as are well skill'd in the Cabalistical Traditions and Mythology, to unravel the Contexture and distinguish its parts'. This esoteric practice was passed on to the pagans who 'imitate[d] Moses'. Its content was a threefold Cabbala. The story of Adam and Eve had a literal sense (i.e. the story as it appeared), a real 'Philosophical sense' in which they signified 'a Generation of Men and Women', and a 'Mystical sense' in which they signified 'Reason and Sense,

---

[470] Harris, *Remarks*, 6.    [471] Ibid., 63–4, 67–8.    [472] Ibid., 70–1.

[473] *Alum. Cantab.*, III, 474. His interest in geological and natural philosophical questions was partly stimulated by William Nicolson: Nicolson to Woodward, 6 Dec 1697, in William Nicolson, *Letters on various subjects*, ed. J. Nichols (2 vols, London, 1809), I, 95.

[474] Thomas Robinson, *New observations on the natural history of this world of matter* (London, 1696), sigs. [A6]^{r–v}.

or the Superior, and Inferior Faculties of the Soul'.[475] Given that he elsewhere even more openly professed polygenesis,[476] Robinson was lucky that he was only mocked for his More-like mysticism.[477]

Others were rather more in tune with the way the scholarly wind was blowing. Archibald Lovell – a pensioner at Charterhouse, where Burnet was still Master – managed to identify the issues very precisely. Burnet had preferred the accounts of the pagans to that of Moses, yet he could not 'Excuse this by saying, that *Moses* spake Figuratively' since he had always insisted on literalism – 'unless to tell a Lye be to make a Figure'.[478] Lovell had pinpointed the central tension in Burnet's account. This dilemma – matching a phenomenalistically true, non-allegorical Mosaic account onto a body of natural philosophy – was starting to seem unsolvable. Perhaps the best example of the exegetical complexities of the problem, and the humanist energy devoted to solving them even by naturalists, appears in the work of John Woodward, Gresham Professor of Physic from 1692.[479] Woodward's *Essay toward a natural history of the earth* (1695) argued that God suspended gravity at the time of the Flood, causing the temporary disintegration of non-biological matter and the stratification of different types of biological matter on the basis of their differerent specific gravities. The reactivation of gravity led to the settling of fossils in the positions in which they were being discovered, and a great strength of Woodward's thesis was its accounting for fossil evidence – a prominent topic since the publication of Nicolas Steno's *Dissertationis pro-dromus* (1669) (some of which it emerged Woodward had plagiarised) but one

---

[475] Ibid., sigs. [A6]$^V$, [A7]$^r$–a$^r$, a3$^r$. I spent many fruitless hours searching for a source for Robinson's peculiar belief that Abraham was a direct ancestor of Jethro, finally arriving at the claim in Raleigh, *History of the world*, 266 that Jethro was descended from Abraham because he was of the Kenite clan (Judg. 4:11, 17) and a priest of Midian (Ex. 3:1) (the Kenites were thus Midianites, descended from Midan, one of Abraham's sons by his second wife Keturah, and the Kenites were probably named after her). That Robinson relied on works like this shows his scholarly backwardness.

[476] Thomas Robinson, *The anatomy of the earth* (London, 1694), 3–4, again combined with the claim that 'Moses was certainly the greatest Philosopher that ever was in the World'.

[477] Harris, *Remarks*, 152–3 ('And first, Sir [Robinson], I would have you, before you write another Book, endeavour to understand *Something* of the *Subject* you treat about: Which the World will never believe you do, till you can write intelligibly, and will condescend to strip your self of that clumsie Veil of Mystery, Allegory, Metaphor and Darkness, which you now are wholly wrap'd up in'). The issue is confused by Harris also attacking Tancred Robinson (who he thought was 'L.P.') and who had in fact supplied 'some hasty Annotations off hand' to Thomas Robinson when shown a manuscript of the *New observations* (Tancred Robinson, *A Letter sent to Mr. William Wotton ... concerning some Late Remarks* (n.p., n.d. [1697]), [2] (unpaginated)).

[478] Archibald Lovell, *A summary of material heads which may be enlarged and improved into a compleat answer to Dr. Burnet's Theory of the earth* (London, 1696), 23–4.

[479] FRS 1693, MD 1695. Levine, *Shield* remains the essential study. See also Poole, *World makers*, esp. 64–7; Rossi, *Abyss*, 217–22, 251–4; Jahn, 'A bibliographical history of John Woodward's *Essay*' (1974).

entirely ignored by Burnet.[480] Woodward was sure that contrary to Burnet and Whiston, his natural history (he detested anyone labelling it a 'theory') 'evinced the Fidelity and Exactness of the Mosaick Narrative of Creation'.[481] Yet the *Essay* contained far less speculation on Moses himself than the work of any of the other 'world makers' – only a short 'digression' against any that would suspect his ideas on the flood of 'not well squar[ing] with the Mosaick Description of it', based on Gen. 3:17–19, 23, 4:2, which he thought could be 'reduced to two plain and short Propositions': (A) 'That *Adam's* Revolt drew down a Curse upon the Earth'; (B) 'That there was some sort of Agriculture used before the Deluge'.[482] This, claimed Woodward, fit with his gradualist history of the relationship between sacred and natural history: the earth was created in a perfectly fertile state before Adam's sin brought two punishments that only came into effect over time: natural death, and the gradual defertilisation of the earth culminating in the all-destructive flood. Like Burnet, 'Woodward too appeared to date the completion of punishment of sin to the Flood and not the Fall'.[483]

There is a simple explanation for Woodward's reluctance to offer a fuller reading: he planned a vast, ultimately unfinished, work that would encompass a full historical, theological, and natural historical account of the ante- and post-diluvial earth and would incorporate evidence from the history of the arts and sciences. Some of the evidence for this work survives, but more is lost, and we must reconstruct Woodward's historiographical assumptions from fragmentary evidence and from his works on other subjects.[484] Most importantly for us, Woodward had strong opinions both on the nature of Moses's knowledge and on its relationship to the philosophies of the surrounding pagans. Although he agreed with Burnet that 'there was a *Tradition* amongst the *Ancients*, both *Jews*

---

[480] For the fossil debate, see Poole, *World makers*, 115–33, and the works cited there. For Woodward's collecting of fossils, beginning with shellfish *c.* 1688–89, see Levine, *Shield*, 23–4, 93–102. Much of his collection survives in the original cabinets in the Sedgwick Museum of Earth Sciences, Cambridge.

[481] John Woodward, *An essay toward a natural history of the earth* (London, 1695), sigs. [A7]$^{r-v}$.

[482] Woodward, *Essay*, 98–107 (the whole 'digression') at 98–9.     [483] Poole, *World makers*, 66.

[484] Woodward published a defence of the *Essay* against the German Elias Camerarius: *Naturalis historia telluris* (London, 1714). This was translated into English by Benjamin Holloway as *The natural history of the Earth, illustrated, inlarged, and defended* (London, 1726). As well as otherwise unavailable quotations from Woodward's papers, this edition includes a list of other relevant works by Woodward, intended for his 'greater Work' (which is first mentioned in Holloway's 'Introduction', 1–2): 1. 'Notes on the first Chapter of Genesis, wherein he has justified the Mosaic Account of the Creation'; 2. 'A Representation of the State of Mankind in the first Ages after the Deluge', especially concerned with America; 3. 'Of the Wisdom of the antient Aegyptians' (104–8). The second of these is likely to be closely related to the 'Discourse concerning the Migration of Nations, and the re-peopling of the World after the Deluge by the Posterity of Noah, particularly that mighty tract of America' mentioned in Harris, *Remarks*, 65–6, suggesting that Woodward was composing these works directly after publishing the *Essay* (a connected project is already mentioned at *Essay*, 105)

and *Gentiles*' about the flood, he disagreed with his rival – and with virtually everyone else by this point – in suggesting that Moses's knowledge of the events described in Genesis did not come by tradition but directly by revelation.[485] Just as importantly, he entirely rejected the post-Spencer assumption that Moses had adopted Egyptian customs and ideas in a work entitled *Of the wisdom of the antient Egyptians*, which survives because it was printed after being read at the Society of Antiquaries in the mid-1770s.[486] Woodward argued that Spencer had inspired the vision of Moses as tactical lawgiver espoused by Burnet.[487] This was clearly still part of the 'world makers' debate: Woodward claimed that his *Essay* had shown that the Mosaic account 'every where stood ... the test of nature ... as constantly as that theory [Burnet's] where it differs from them [has] failed'.[488] Nonetheless, his protracted treatment of the subject, and the fact that his main target was Spencer rather than Burnet, demonstrates how central the purely humanist component remained.

Woodward admitted that the fruitfulness of the Nile allowed the Egyptians the most leisure to develop an intellectual culture of all the ancient peoples.[489] But what 'most favoured the opinion of their learning' was their hieroglyphs. Woodward was familiar with a large body of Renaissance work on Egyptian antiquities, such as the images of canopic jars depicted in Antonio Lafreri's *Speculum Romanae magnificentiae* (1547), the mummy shrouds depicted in an

---

[485] See the very long quotation from Woodward's 'larger work' in Holloway's 'Introduction', 39–49.

[486] Woodward, *Wisdom*; see Levine, *Shield*, 75–9. The work was read to the Society by the antiquary Michael Lort (1724/5–90), who says (5) that he obtained it from 'Mr Herbert', undoubtedly the bibliographer and printseller William Herbert (1718–95). There is no trace of the manuscript in any of the catalogues of the sale of Herbert's library (*Catalogue of books in various languages ... among others ... [the] library of the late Mr. William Herbert* (London, 1795); *Catalogue of the library of William Herbert* (London, 1796); *Catalogue of the entire and curious library of a late well-known collector* (London, 1798); *Catalogue of a choice and valuable library, the property of a gentleman* (London, 1798)), nor in the book-lists scattered throughout CUL MS Add. 3313–18, nor in Lort's correspondence in the Society of Antiquaries of London, MS 447.2. There is a clear reference to it in a letter to Woodward from one 'Jos. Eyles' (CUL MS Add. 7647, no. 145), but it is dated only '12 July', with no year. A late reference is in a Latin letter from a Parisian physician-antiquary, Claude Genebrier, 5 June 1716 (CUL MS Add. 7647, no. 148), suggesting quite a wide manuscript circulation (on Genebrier, see Haskell, *History and its images* (1993), 66–7). Woodward showed William Nicolson a manuscript of 'his History of America; wherein he endeavours to point at the certain time when those people went out of Europe, from that Share of our most early Inventions and Knowledge which they have in Common with us' (i.e. no. 2 in the list in n. 484 above) on 4 January 1705, in which, Nicolson reported, 'he takes occasion to run down the Egyptians, as mistaken Masters of antient Learning', and on 31 December 1705 Nicolson saw the manuscript of *Wisdom* (*The London diaries of William Nicolson, Bishop of Carlisle, 1702–1718*, ed. C. Jones (Oxford, 1985), 271, 344). From internal evidence, the *terminus post quem* for the work is 1697 (41). On the basis of all this, it must have been composed in the late 1690s/early 1700s.

[487] Woodward, *Wisdom*, 60–6 (Marsham is offered mitigated criticism). Whiston is subsumed into the attack at 69–72.

[488] Ibid., 69.      [489] Ibid., 9, 15–16.

appendix on Egyptian funeral shrouds in the Florentine edition of Lucretius prepared by Giovanni Nardi (1647), and of course the many objects outlined by Kircher.[490] Moreover, as a keen antiquarian collector, he had himself acquired Egyptian antiquities.[491] In one fell swoop, he rejected the 'symbolical construction' of the hieroglyphs, whether assumed by the ancients (Diodorus Siculus, Plutarch, Clemens Alexandrinus, Horapollo) or in the modern 'voluminous and fanciful works' of Valeriano, Caussin, or Kircher.[492] As Woodward summarised on a manuscript scrap:

All who have set forth the Hierogliphicks as any thing other than meer History-Paintings ... are very wrong. The later Egyptians did that to the Greeks and Romans that made inquiry into the affair. But either the[y] [sic] were Ignorant and knew not yᵉ primitive Intention of them, those of their Times being meer Copyes and Imitations of the Antients, Or else they deluded and imposed up<on> them. There needs no surer proof of this than-that-the <than that> when brought together they each contradict the other, and no two of them agree.[493]

The disdain for allegorical reading that we have met so often had now spread into a full rejection of *any* meaning to the hieroglyphs; accordingly, Herodotus was wrong to report that the Egyptians had even possessed writing.[494] The hieroglyphs were basic pictograms depicting their absurd religious superstition, which Woodward discussed at great length, drawing on all the classical and patristic sources.[495] Just as basic were the pyramids, which only survived so long because of favourable environmental conditions (Woodward here included a long note on the damage caused by coal smoke to London buildings).[496] The few things the Egyptians *were* good at, such as preserving corpses, were part of their idiotic religion: since they believed in the transmigration of souls and their subsequent return to their original bodies after 3,000 years, their poor souls must have returned to bodies 'destitute of brains, and the greater part of the bowels', which, Woodward quipped, 'surely would have afforded [them] but a very indifferent habitation'.[497] Even the mummies, like the pyramids, disintegrated in the wrong climate: Woodward claimed to have seen one that 'after it had been for some time in our more humid air, began to

---

[490]  Ibid., 11–12. See Giovanni Nardi, 'De funeribus Aegyptiorum', in Lucretius, *De rerum natura*, ed. Giovanni Nardi (Florence, 1647), 627–58.

[491]  Woodward, *Wisdom*, 23; CUL MS Add. 7570 ('Sylloge rerum antiquarum quas collegit Joh: Woodwardus', 1727), pp. 4–5, 8 and the pasted-in slip on p. 7. He continued to be interested in Egypt late into life: see Thomas Shaw to Woodward, 20 Dec 1725, BL MS Egmont 47131, fols. 92ʳ–95ᵛ, describing a journey from Cairo to the Sinai Peninsula. For Woodward as collector, see Levine, *Shield*, 93–113.

[492]  Woodward, *Wisdom*, 13.     [493]  CUL MS Add. 7646, no. 145, verso.

[494]  Woodward, *Wisdom*, 14; Herodotus, II.36.4.     [495]  Woodward, *Wisdom*, 29–59.

[496]  Ibid., 18.

[497]  Ibid., 26–7. For the 3,000-year soul cycle, see Herodotus, II.123.2. For the pre-preservation evisceration, Woodward draws on Diodorus Siculus, *Bib. hist.*, I.91.5; Herodotus, II.86.3–4; Porphyry, *De abst.*, IV.10; Sextus Empiricus, *Pyrr.*, III.24.

corrupt and grow mouldy, emitted a foetid and cadaverous scent, and in conclusion putrified and fell to pieces'.[498] This must have been the mummy donated to the Ashmolean in 1681 by Aaron Goodyear, a merchant trading in Turkey.[499] But what of the Egyptians' superiority to the Jews, on which Spencer had rested his argument? Here Woodward replied with an old move, positing the case of Joseph's appointment as vizier in Egypt (Gen. 41:40–4): this, he countered, was hardly evidence of the mean status allotted to the Hebrews in Egyptian eyes by Spencer. Moreover, the post-Exodus building of the temple of Solomon, 'built of stone made ready before it was brought thither' [1 Kings. 6:7–9], cannot have been done 'without common geometry, mathematicks, architecture, and the several arts subservient to it'.[500]

This dual emphasis – on Moses's direct inspiration and on Jewish philosophical accomplishment – might on first glance appear as a sign of a Reformed attitude comparable to Theophilus Gale's. But Woodward never adopted Gale's uncritical use of the sources, and the extent of Israelite philosophical accomplishment that he posited was in fact quite limited. Indeed, he clearly overestimated the degree of difference between himself and Spencer: nowhere had Spencer insisted on the absolute wisdom of the Egyptians, only on their *relative* wisdom when compared with the Hebrews. That Woodward was unsympathetic to Reformed exegesis, meanwhile, is evident from a rather comical correspondence with Thomas Baker, a nonjuror who had returned to his old Cambridge College, St John's. Baker's anonymously published *Reflections upon learning* (1699) was a self-acknowledgedly semi-serious romp through various disciplines to show the inadequacies of human reason and the necessity of revelation; in it he considered the recent theses of the world makers and although he praised Woodward's as the best, he still found it a 'theory' rather than a sound 'hypothesis'.[501] Woodward, perennially incapable of accepting criticism, reacted furiously when he was shown a passage of Baker's work by one 'Dr Gaulter'. There ensued a tragicomedy in which 'Gaulter' and then Woodward wrote to Baker, while the replies came from both Baker and the anonymous 'author' of the *Reflections*. Baker – convinced that 'Gaulter's' letters were in fact by Woodward forging a different handwriting – consistently denied authorship of the *Reflections* and claimed to pass on Woodward's letters to the real 'author', who in turn wrote brief letters because 'not being good at counterfeiting a hand, nor willing my own should be known, [he] must be

---

[498] Woodward, *Wisdom*, 27.

[499] Anthony à Wood, *The life and times of Anthony Wood, antiquary, of Oxford, 1632–1695* (5 vols, Oxford, 1891–1900), III, 56.

[500] Woodward, *Wisdom*, 76–8; 99–100.

[501] [Thomas Baker], *Reflections upon learning* (London, 1699), 82–4. On Baker, an important antiquary whose book shows him only at his most mischievous, see Korsten, 'Thomas Baker's *Reflections upon learning*' (1984); Korsten, *A catalogue of the library of Thomas Baker* (1990).

short'.[502] Woodward went to Baker's bookseller to verify Baker's handwriting.[503] Baker, in turn, had good reason to be suspicious, for towards the end of the correspondence he again received a letter purporting to be from 'Gaulter' which demanded a public recantation, even going so far as to supply a full draft of one: it was all written in Woodward's hand and included a superscription from Woodward's servant. Unsurprisingly, Baker at this point told Woodward exactly what he thought of him and his draft recantation: 'In short, S$^r$, it is thro' the whole thread of it, such an abject piece of meaness, as he [i.e. the 'author' of the *Reflections*] would dye a thousand Deaths, rather than submit to so mean a thing'.[504] Woodward, for his part, pretended to know nothing of the requested recantation, both to Baker and in private.[505] For all this posturing, the correspondence did contain a serious intellectual point. Woodward accused Baker of a historical scepticism that would lead either to atheism, enthusiasm, or Rome if applied to the Bible.[506] Baker replied that French and Dutch Protestants did not resort to history but defended the Bible using 'Internal Arguments, from the Intrinsic evidence of the Books themselves'.[507] Woodward's reply was telling: they were members not of the French or Dutch but of the English church, which allowed 'reason [to] be still reason'.[508] Historical scholarship was essential to proving the veracity of scripture. Baker responded by positing a qualitative difference between sacred and profane texts that was by this point simply out of date.[509]

Woodward's vision, then, did not stem from a fundamentally different perspective on the nature of theology or exegesis to that of Spencer. In part, it stemmed from the necessities of his philosophical vision: for example, because his hypothesis required a universal flood, it was more difficult to envisage even Noah knowing of its true nature, for how could he know what

---

[502] [Baker] to Woodward, 1 Aug 1699, CUL Add. 7647, no. 28.

[503] Woodward to Baker, 13 Nov 1699, ibid., no. 34.

[504] [Baker] to Woodward, 18 May 1700, ibid., no. 42.

[505] Woodward to Baker, 21 May 1700, ibid., no. 43; see also his description of the whole controversy at no. 26. I am more suspicious of Woodward than is Prof. Levine, who takes his claims at face value (*Shield*, 58–62).

[506] Woodward to Baker, 13 Nov 1699, ibid., no. 34: 'The best we could do would be to recourse either to Rome or Enthusiasm: as take our information from Oral Tradition, or y$^e$ Light within'.

[507] [Baker] to Woodward, 15 Apr 1700, ibid., no. 35.

[508] Woodward to Baker, 23 Apr 1700, ibid., no. 36.

[509] [Baker] to Woodward, 25 Apr 1700, ibid., no. 37 ('I cannot but put a great difference betwixt Civil & Ecclesiastical History, especially in the main points of Religion. The Authors that treat of the Canon are generally men of the greatest piety & uprightness, & consequently their Integrity cannot possibly be suspected: The Books they speak of, are of the utmost concern to the peace & welfare of mankind, w$^{ch}$ is very different from a story in Herodotus or Livy: The Books themselves were in the Hands of all, they were read publicly & dispers'd over the face of the whole world, they had the force of Laws, & were constantly appeald to in all controversies of Religion; & consequently they that treated of them could not want Information. And lastly the Providence of God was concern'd with their preservation, & that men should not be deceiv'd after an impartial search. What is there like this in prophane history?').

was occurring in the whole world?[510] Direct revelation was thus simply necessary. More fundamentally, it depended on a developmental vision of the history of civilisation that Woodward had been advancing since the early 1690s, primarily on the basis of his antiquarian research. The barrenness of the earth after the flood meant almost all time had to be spent in agriculture, which greatly 'curtail[ed] and retrench[ed] the ordinary means of Knowledge and Erudition'.[511] There was a general trend to the development of civilisation, to be demonstrated in the (lost) work on 'The State of Mankind in the first Ages after the Deluge' which would focus on in particular on the Americans, who 'preserv'd the Memory of Things, by Hieroglyphic Representations' not just like the Egyptians, but also 'the most antient *Asiatic, African,* and *European* Nations, [and] the *Chineses*'.[512] There was an apologetic purpose to this: it showed that for all the differences between peoples (difference of skin colour had been a key argument for polygenicists), all came 'originally from one and the same Stock'; moreover, it offered a naturalistic explanation for the similarities between the Jews and the Egyptians.[513] But it also functioned as a heuristic for all antiquarian scholarship. When Woodward came into possession of some Roman urns found in London, he used them to build a whole theory about the development of the city. Both those who thought ancient London a flourishing city and those who thought it entirely a Roman construction were wrong.[514] The urn was found inside the city walls, but the Romans always buried outside city perimeters: thus early British London was so primitive as not even to have a city wall.[515] Drawing on all the available sources Woodward concluded that the druids were therefore 'barbarous, and wholly unciviliz'd', and that any who 'entertain'd very lofty Thoughts of that Order of Men' were entirely incompetent judges of the history of the sciences.[516] This should not surprise anyone, 'when 'tis known that several other great Nations were likewise so till lately: nay, that all Mankind quite round the Globe were once so, I mean at their first Original, in the Ages that ensued next after the Deluge'.[517] This was the reason that it was so important for Woodward to prove that the plough was not invented until after the Deluge, a point first made in the *Essay* and then painstakingly defended, with reference

---

[510] Holloway, 'Introduction', 41.    [511] Woodward, *Essay*, 94–5.
[512] Holloway, 'Introduction', 106.    [513] Ibid., 105; Woodward, *Wisdom*, 78–81.
[514] The former view represented for Woodward by Geoffrey of Monmouth's *Historia Regum Britanniae*, the latter by Stillingfleet's posthumous *Discourse of the true antiquity of London* (London, 1704): see John Woodward, *An account of some Roman urns, and other antiquities … with brief reflections upon the antient and present state of London* (London, 1713), 2–3; 16–17. For a full discussion, see Levine, *Shield*, 133–50.
[515] Woodward, *Urns*, 26.
[516] Ibid., 17–19. That Woodward had developed this view early is confirmed by his letter to Edward Lhuyd, 12 Dec 1693, Bod. MS Ashmole 1817b, fols. 365$^r$–366$^v$.
[517] Woodward, *Urns*, 23–4.

to a barrage of classical sources, in a long letter to John Edwards (in a correspondence that led to yet another falling out): the tool was unnecessary before, and the primitive post-diluvian peoples took time to develop it.[518] Consequently, Moses *had* to have had the Genesis account by revelation, because he was writing in what was still a primitive time: 'The World was not then thorowly settled, Things sufficiently establish'd, or Arts so far advanc'd as to afford Leisure to Curiosity, or such Kinds of Speculation'.[519] In turn, where pagan notions matched Genesis – such as in their frequent recourse to a primordial chaos – they were derived from misunderstandings of Moses.[520]

Woodward's theory, although at first glance appearing as a 'conservative' response to Spencer and Burnet, was radically new. To break the impasse generated by Burnet's work he cut through the mass of inconclusive source material by developing a conjectural history of the development of the arts and sciences in *all* civilisations.[521] His novelty can be confirmed by a comparison with another natural philosopher who attempted to resolve the debate by defending – at great length – Mosaic intellectual primacy. This was Edmund Dickinson (1624–1707), an Oxford-educated physician (including to Charles II and James II) who had participated in the Oxford experimentalist group in the 1650s, became an inactive FRS, and was a long-term believer in transmutational alchemy;[522] the work in question is his *Physica vetus et vera* (1702), written in the 1690s but rewritten after the first draft was accidentally burnt.[523] Dickinson's actual cosmogony was a complex speculative atomic system in which the particles were stimulated by a double motion, one forming basic compound corpuscles, the other giving them a circular motion ultimately creating the revolution of the heavens; this was combined with a theory of seminal principles that explained the formation of life. Although scattered throughout the work, Dickinson's historical thesis was summarised in the final two chapters. Whether it had been revealed to him by God or by patriarchal tradition, Moses knew what occurred at the creation in its full natural philosophical complexity. Moses 'was very skilled in all parts of Physics, but

---

[518] Woodward, *Essay*, 84–5; Woodward to Edwards, 26 June 1699, CUL MS Add. 7647, no. 118, pp. 17–45; Levine, *Shield*, 66–72.

[519] Holloway, 'Introduction', 43.    [520] Woodward, *Naturalis historia*, 44–9, 68.

[521] For the wider place of schemes like Woodward's in the development of conjectural history, see Levitin, 'Egyptology, the limits of antiquarianism, and the origins of conjectural history' (2015).

[522] W. N. Blomberg, *An account of the life and writings of Edmund Dickinson* (London, 1739), supplemented by Principe, 'Dickinson, Edmund', *ODNB*; Principe, *The aspiring adept* (1998), 101–3, 119. The overlord of mid-century Oxford chymistry, Peter Stahl, was exuberant in his praise for Dickinson's abilities: Folger MS V.a.291 (John Ward diaries, vol. XIII, 1661–62), fol. 10ʳ.

[523] There is a useful account of this work in Collier, *Cosmogonies of our fathers* (1934), 149–65.

especially Chymistry and Astrology'.[524] These sciences flourished at the time in Egypt, and this was undoubtedly the meaning of Acts 7:22. Moses must have known chymistry, for how else could he have melted the golden calf in a solution that was then drinkable (Ex. 32:20), or prepared vast quantites of anointing oil and incense (Ex. 30:25, 34)? No doubt he had learnt the skill from the chymical sages then living in Arabia.[525] No matter that the first recorded use of the word 'alchemy' was in the fourth century (in Julius Firmicus),[526] for it was clearly far more ancient: here Dickinson trotted out the old arguments, long ago dismantled by Conring, about Tubal-cain being an alchemist, even quoting Abū'l-Faraj from Pococke's translation (Dickinson impressively managed to get hold of Arabic types).[527] This was supported by a long and original argument that Dickinson was clearly very proud of: that the source of light in Noah's ark could not have been the one window it was fitted with, nor an oil lamp or a torch or a particularly glittering jewel, but only a light made of a 'fiery or sulphurous liquid' suspended in individual pods hung in each of the rooms: Noah himself was thus a skilled adept.[528] Inheriting this alchemical knowledge, as well as astrology, Moses was the best equipped philosopher in all of human history to describe the creation, celebrated by such authorities as Clement of Alexandria and only opposed by hubristic or even atheistic pagans like Aristotle.[529]

As old-fashioned as this theory was, Dickinson did know that recent scholarship had provided a major stumbling block with its consensus that Moses had spoken not philosophically but accommodated his language to a primitive people.[530] Dickinson's answer was unique and remarkable. Abraham was

---

[524] Edmund Dickinson, *Physica vetus et vera* (London, 1702), 317: ' ... partes omnes Physicae perbenè calleret, praesertim Chemiae, ac Astrologiae'.

[525] Ibid., 317–22, esp. 318: 'Nec dubitandum est quin Moses, qui quadraginta annos inter Aegypti, totque porrò inter Arabiae sapientes degeret (quibus egregiè nota fuerunt Chemiae secreta) retrusas atque abditas omnium rerum solvendarum vias intellexerit, maximè cùm certum sit, Chemiam fuisse non exiguam partem istius sapientiae, in qua Moses educatus fuit'.

[526] Julius Firmicus, *Matheseos*, III.15; Dickinson's source is Bochart, *Geographia sacra*, I, 234.

[527] Dickinson, *Physica*, 322–4; the translated quotation, unacknowledged by Dickinson, is taken from Abū'l-Faraj, *Historia compendiosa dynastiarum*, I, 22. A similarly unsuccessful attempt to confute Conring had already been made in England in John Webster's *Metallographia: or, an history of metals* (London, 1671), 2–15, esp. 11.

[528] Dickinson, *Physica*, 325: 'Doctiores interpretes igitur hic vehementer exoratos velim, ut mihi condonarent modestè concipienti, lumen illud fuisse eximium quendam splendorem, cujusdam liquoris ignei sulphureique, per artificium ipsius Noae confecti; quam Noa vasculis è lapide speculari vel è crystallo vel fortè vitro paratis inclusit; & in singulis Arcae tabulates suspendi jussit; ità ut animantium cellas, aut mansiones omnes illuminare valeret'. The full argument is at 324–30, also depending on the ambiguity between the two references to the light source in the ark: Gen. 6:16 has the ambiguous צהר (*tsohar*) while Gen. 8:16 has the clearer חלון (*halon*—'window'): this is a classic exegetical problem, and Dickinson thought he had found the true meaning of the former.

[529] Dickinson, *Physica*, 331–2.

[530] See the description of the problem at ibid., 271–3; although not naming them, he was surely thinking of Spencer and Burnet.

such a wise philosopher that all his descendants could not fail to follow in his learned footsteps. Even in Egypt, all the Israelites were educated in natural philosophy in such a way that made them perfectly suited to understanding the creation account – Dickinson here brought out the old Jewish fables of Aristotle speaking to wandering Jewish philosophers, long ago dismissed by Selden and others.[531] But what about the disastrous period of slavery during the Egyptian captivity? Dickinson responded by undercutting the whole Judaeo–Christian historical tradition: the slavery began late and was not particularly arduous (although he consented to admitting that the slaughter of male infants had been a blow). Certainly the 'condition of the Egyptian populace was no better'; moreover, the Israelite priests were probably excluded from slavery anyway.[532] It was only the 'impious' who, seeking to 'impale Mosaic theology and physics through their sides', insisted on the 'stupidity and ignorance' of the Israelites.[533] To save the idea of Moses the philosopher, Dickinson had entirely reinvented the most formative event in Jewish history.

Although they were making essentially the same case, it is difficult to imagine two arguments more different in approach than Woodward's and Dickinson's. The latter was very elderly, and in many ways the relic of an older generation: as an MA student Dickinson had studied sixteen hours per day to learn oriental languages before publishing his *Delphi phoenicizantes* (1655), which, heavily influenced by Bochart, argued that Greek mythology, when traced through its Phoenician roots, in fact revealed its Hebraic origins.[534] Scholarship had simply moved on (Dickinson did not make any serious attempts to answer the challenge from the 'critical' history of alchemy offered by Conring). Woodward's work, meanwhile, in many ways anticipates the conjectural approach that would become so popular in eighteenth-century Scotland.

Yet this could not hide the basic fact that the distance between natural history and any history of Moses *qua* actor in human history was looking increasingly unbroachable. Even Woodward's close acquintances – who had seen or heard about his 'historical' manuscript works – were unconvinced. Even before it had appeared, Edward Lhuyd expected Woodward's hypothesis to be different not only to 'the Theory of D$^r$ Burnet', but also to 'the History of Moses'.[535]

---

[531] E.g. ibid., 284, reporting Aristobulus's claim, as in n. 180 above.

[532] Ibid., 286–303, esp. 291 ('Nec melior ex illa parte fuit plebis Aegyptiacae conditio'); 294–7 (the priests).

[533] Ibid., 303: 'Israëlitas etenim vilibus hisce stupiditatis & inscientiae notis inusserunt homines impii, ut per eorum latera transfoderent Theologiam simul & Physicam Mosaicam'.

[534] Edmund Dickinson, *Delphi phoenicizantes sive, tractatus, in quo Græcos, quicquid apud Delphos celebre erat . . . è josuæ historiâ, scriptisque sacris effinxisse rationibus haud inconcinnis ostenditur* (Oxford, 1655); Blomberg, *Life*, 7–8 (on his MA studies).

[535] Lhuyd to Martin Lister, 1 Jan 1695, Bod. MS Lister 36, fol. 109$^r$. For Lister's engagement with Woodward's work, see Roos, *Web*, 364–75, suggesting that Lister may have been 'L.P.', which seems unlikely.

William Nicolson became the latest to receive an epistolary shouting down from Woodward when he dared to suggest that both he and Whiston agreed that 'the old vulgar exposition is not to be stood to'.[536] Although he remained politely placatory, in private Nicolson was far more open about the difficulties created by the world makers:

Our late refiners upon the Creation and the Deluge are unanimously agreed, that the old interpreters of Moses were all blockheads: and which of them will furnish us with a more rational and lasting exposition, time must show. Whether Dr. Burnet's roasted egg, Dr. Woodward's hasty pudding, or Mr. Whiston's snuff of a Comet, will carry the day, I cannot foresee.[537]

In light of this, it is unsurprising that some began virtually to ignore Moses altogether. One such figure was Robert Hooke, who had developed his views on the earth's historical mutations over a longer period than any other theorist, in lectures read to the Royal Society that spanned from the late 1660s to 1700, entitled a 'A Discourse of Earthquakes' in his posthumous *Works* (1705).[538] Contrary to the flood-centred theories of Burnet and Woodward, Hooke argued that polar wanderings had caused great geomorphological changes, especially as a result of earthquakes. Although he claimed that he 'could give a very plausible account concerning the manner of [the] Deluge, as it is expressed by *Moses*', he never did so.[539]

But the history of philosophy remained central to his work. The natural philosophical circle in which Hooke operated keenly devoured the latest works of criticism; Hooke, for example, read Marsham's *Canon* with some relish (it was originally recommended to him by Thomas Sydenham during a ride in the country) and dicussed it at length with Marsham's brother; he even possessed a manuscript version of Diogenes Laërtius.[540] Although he was initially sceptical, Hooke came to believe – like Burnet – that scraps of geological truth could

---

[536] Nicolson to Woodward, 4 Dec 1697, *Nicolson letters*, I, 91–2. The angry nature of Woodward's (lost) response is indicated by Nicolson's placatory letter of 13 January 1698 (100).

[537] Nicolson to Lhuyd, 31 Jan 1698, *Nicolson letters*, I, 108. For very similar comments from a more openly hostile figure, see John Arbuthnot, *An examination of Dr. Woodward's account of the deluge* (London, 1697), 29.

[538] Robert Hooke, *The posthumous works of Robert Hooke*, ed. Richard Waller (London, 1705), 279–450. Waller's editorial practices were extremely loose: the lectures are sorted into chronological order and mapped onto other relevant evidence in Rappaport, 'Hooke on earthquakes: lectures, strategy and audience' (1986), at 143–6 (all references to the lectures will includes dates and cross-references to Rappaport's list). The fullest account remains the classic piece by Ito, 'Hooke's cyclic theory of the earth in the context of seventeenth century England' (1988); see also Poole, *World makers*, 104–13, 118–24, 127–30, *passim*.

[539] Hooke, *Works*, 409 (lecture 13, 22 Feb 1688). For a partial attempt to use Genesis, see 412–15 (lecture 14, 29 Feb 1688), but there is no attempt to position Moses historically.

[540] *Hooke diary*, 163 (Sydenham tells him of Marsham, 8 Jun 1675), 245 (discussion with Marsham's brother, 18 Oct 1676), 266 (lends Marsham to Abraham Hill – 7 Jan 1677). For Laërtius, see 89 (27 Feb 1674: 'Mr. Scot borrowd Diogenes Laertius MS' – I have been unable to identify this manuscript). Intriguingly, Hooke owned the 1676 Leipzig edition of Marsham's

be found in the ancient philosophers and theogonic poets. Indeed, it was probably reading Burnet's *Theoria* that stimulated him into the move.[541] His key sources were the Atlantis story in Plato's *Timaeus-Critias* and the theogony of Ovid's *Metamorphoses*: as Yoshi Ito has demonstrated, he was far from novel in using these as evidence for cyclic change in the earth.[542]

Nevertheless, he did see himself as doing something new. First, he felt that for the first time Plato's Atlantis narrative could now be verified by the famous navigation account of Hanno the Carthaginian known as the *Periplus*, recently re-published by Abraham Berkelius in Leiden.[543] Hanno had mentioned flaming islands west of the straits of Gibraltar that Hooke triumphantly took to be equivalent to the final stages of Plato's Atlantis, identifying the volcanic Mount Teide on Tenerife as the last visible remains of the island.[544] Crucially, this proved that Plato was offering 'a true History and not a Romance'.[545] This reading could then be applied at length to Ovid, whose purpose was not purely poetical but 'to relate what were the most celebrated Opinions concerning [the world's] Formation and first Ages, and as I conceive more particularly that of *Pythagoras*, who had spread and left his Doctrines in *Italy* long before *Ovid's* time'.[546] Hooke later sought to confirm these views with testimonies from

*Canon*, as well as the old 1566 Plantin edition of Laërtius (Feisenberger, ed., *Sale catalogues of libraries of eminent persons: vol.* XI: *scientists* (1975), 62, 44).

[541] For the development of Hooke's views on this matter, see the evidence collected in Rappaport, 'Earthquakes', 137–9. This account underestimates the extent of engagement with Burnet, as shown in Ito, 'Cyclic theory', 301, 304 n. 54. Furthermore, Rappaport claims that Hooke's turn to history was stimulated by criticisms made by John Wallis and the Oxford Philosophical Society in 1687 (see Wallis to Halley, 4 March 1687, in Turner, 'Hooke's theory of the Earth's axial displacement: some contemporary opinion' (1974), 168: 'Yet so vast a change as is now suggested, could not possibly have been (within the reach of Histories now extant) but that some foot steps thereof would certainly have been found in History. Since it is so many Hundred years (not to say thousands) since Astronomers have been curiously inquiring into such matters'). But these criticisms referred only to Hooke's theory of axial shift: he had been suggesting that evidence from Plato and Ovid would support his *overall* theory much earlier (*Works*, 320, 323, 328 [lecture 1, 1667–68]; also Trinity College, Cambridge, MS O.IIa.1). Hooke also read a long account of Burnet's *Archaeologiae* to the RS (BL MS Sloane 3828, fols. 217ʳ–229ᵛ [='An account of a book', *Philosophical Transactions*, 17 (1693), 796–812]) and was one of the very few to make positive comments about it, specifically its historical dimension: *Works*, 395 (lecture 10 – Rappaport claims that this was read 14 December 1687 (on the basis of Birch, *History*, IV, 557) but this is obviously incorrect: it belongs to one of the 1693 lectures [lectures 20–2]).

[542] Ito, 'Cyclic theory', 299–300.

[543] Abrahamus Berkelius, *Genuina Stephani Byzantini De urbibus et populis fragmenta ... accredit Hannonis Carthaginensium Regis Periplus* (Leiden, 1674), 66–98. The most important English scholarly engagement with this difficult text was that of Henry Dodwell, whose 'Dissertatio prima. De vero Peripli, qui Hannonis nomine circumfertur, tempore' was included in the edition prepared by John Hudson: *Geographiae veteris scriptores graeci minores* (Oxford, 1698), 1–41 (separate pagination). For a full account of the Renaissance textual history, see Mund-Dopchie, 'Hanno', *CTC*, XIII, 49–55.

[544] Hooke, *Works*, 375–6 (lecture 9, 7 Dec 1687); Rappaport, 'Earthquakes', 138.

[545] Hooke, *Works*, 374 (lecture 9, 7 Dec 1687).    [546] Ibid., 380 (lecture 11, 4 Jan 1688).

Herodotus and Aristotle, but he never really lived up to his claim that he could prove Ovid 'to be the Epitome of the Theories of the most antient and most approv'd Philosophers ... by Quotations out of other Authors among the Antient'.[547] Neither was he sure on the epistemology behind this history, wavering on whether this knowledge had been achieved observationally – like his supporter Beaumont after him, he mentioned Pythagoras finding shells on mountains and even suggested that earlier humans had possessed much greater mental capacity – or by 'tradition, whether Oral or Written'.[548]

Nonetheless, the idea that mythology represented a coded natural philosophy was not disreputable. The foremost Restoration mythographer, Thomas Gale, Regius Professor of Greek at Cambridge, was a close friend of Hooke's partly through his secretaryship of the Royal Society in 1679–81 and 1685–93.[549] Gale's *Opuscula mythologica, ethica et physica* (1671) collected many Greek mythological fragments, although he himself remained frustratingly ambiguous about their value, commenting (in a later edition) only that 'the custom of teaching the youth through fables is old and long-established'.[550] In private he was rather sceptical about the use of myth in the search for truth.[551] Nonetheless, he seemed to become something of an in-house specialist on myth in the Royal Society.[552] He responded with mitigated scepticism to Hooke's project. At the meeting where Hooke first made his claims about the *Periplus*, Gale expressed doubts as to the Carthaginian origins of the text because all the place-names were Greek (he was probably familiar with debates on the text, as his acquaintance Isaac Vossius had also been planning to work on it).[553] Hooke clearly solicited his advice more directly, for in a personal note Gale warned him about matching mythical terms onto Septuagint vocabulary, since the translators 'lived among Greeks at *Alexandria*: And they were desirous to shew that the Bible was not unacquainted with the Greek Stories' (Hooke promptly ignored this advice).[554] But just as importantly, Gale felt that

[547] Ibid., 381 (lecture 11, 4 Jan 1688).    [548] Ibid., 384, 379–80 (lecture 11, 4 Jan 1688).

[549] Gale was elected FRS on 6 Dec, 1677: Hunter, *Royal Society*, 196–7. For Hooke spending time 'at Dr. Gales,' see e.g. Henderson, 'Unpublished material from the memodrandum book of Robert Hooke' (2007), 150 (on 17 Aug 1681). It was Gale who first read an account of Burnet's *Theoria* to the RS, 27 Apr 1681 (Birch, *History*, IV, 69, 83).

[550] Thomas Gale, *Opuscula mythologica, ethica et physica* (Cambridge, 1671); Gale, *Opuscula mythologica, ethica et physica* (Amsterdam, 1688), sig. *5ʳ: 'Vetus est & receptissimus mos informandi puerorum animos per fabulas'.

[551] Gale to Bernard, 12 Apr 1671, Bod. MS Smith 8, fol. 133ʳ.

[552] RS MS Hooke Folio, p. 559, reporting on a meeting on 2 Aug 1682 where 'Dʳ. Gale' spoke on the 'various ways of fables' in response to a paper on 'fables from the Indians' (this goes unmentioned in Birch, *History*, IV, 157–8).

[553] Birch, *History*, IV, 555–6. For Vossius, see Mandelbrote, 'Vossius', 87, quoting Paul Colomiès, *Opuscula* (Utrecht, 1669), 141–2.

[554] Thomas Gale, 'Concerning Giants', in Hooke, *Works*, 384. The issue at stake was whether the Septuagint 'Γίγαντες' of Gen. 6:4 was equivalent to the נפילים (*Nephilim*) in the Masoretic text (Gale in fact speaks of רפאים (*Rephaim*) of Gen. 14:15, 15:20 – both can be translated as

Hooke's idea that the war of the giants ('gigantomachia') represented an earthquake was not unfounded, because he thought that 'γίγας' 'tho commonly taken for a Greek word, is indeed of Hebrew or Phaenician Original': thus the poets *may* have been referring to a much earlier geological tradition.[555]

Hooke, then, was working on the boundary of scholarly acceptability. Yet the problem, as ever, was Moses. It is difficult to know exactly why Hooke was so silent about him: the suggestion that he favoured the longer chronologies offered in the pagan narratives is based on a misreading of the evidence.[556] More likely is that like Burnet, he simply got carried away with what looked like remarkably convenient pagan testimonies of the sort that could not be found in Genesis. In some senses 'science' had trumped scripture, but this manifested itself in silence more than in open heterodoxy.[557] However, this was not a development that could go unnoticed: within weeks of Hooke's 1687 lectures, John Wallis was writing to report on the Oxford philosophers' views on the incompatibility of Hooke's theory with Moses: 'Which we think cannot be, without over throwing the credit of all History, sacred & profane'.[558]

This inability for anyone to succeed even remotely in convincing a signifi-cant proportion of their readership or auditors about the compatibility of their theories with Moses – despite the huge exegetical effort that went into doing so – may explain the drift towards silence of Wallis's correspondent: Edmond Halley. Like Hooke he presented his ideas in lectures to the Royal Society (1694–95), and like those of his friend these were only published much later, due to fear of 'incur[ring] the Censure of the Sacred Order'.[559] Halley thought

---

'giants', but the word is ambiguous). Gale pointed out that in using the word the Septuagint translators were probably thinking of the 'Τιτᾶνες' so prominent in Greek mythology. Hooke goes on with his hypothesis at 385.

[555] Gale, 'Concerning Giants', in Hooke, *Works*, 384.

[556] Ito, 'Cyclic theory', 303, claims that Hooke's mention of the long chronologies of the Chaldeans, Egyptians, and Chinese (*Works*, 395 – lecture 10, 1693) means that he 'suggested that the age of the world was much greater than that recorded in the Bible'. But Hooke never accepted these opinions, and his most open discussion of pagan chronologies in fact stated that Plato's long chronology rendered his whole work a possible 'fiction', but that the debate was unresolved 'till we are certain what space of Time is there signified by a Year' (*Works*, 404 – lecture 12, 12 Feb 1688). See also his scepticism about the self-aggrandising chronologies of the pagans at 328, 372–3, 408.

[557] See also Poole, *World makers*, 106–8, and the brilliant case study of Hooke's scriptural exegesis at 110–11.

[558] Wallis to Halley, 26 April 1687, in Turner, 'Axial Displacement', 170; also Wallis to Halley, 4 March 1687, in ibid., 168–9. On the whole debate, see also Oldroyd, 'Geological controversy in the seventeenth century' (1989).

[559] The key publications are: Edmond Halley, 'A short account of the cause of the saltness of the ocean ... to discover the age of the world', *Philosophical Transactions*, 29 (1714–16), 296–300; Halley, 'Some considerations about the cause of the universal deluge', *Philosophical Transactions*, 33 (1724–25), 118–23; Halley, 'Farther thoughts upon the same subject', ibid., 123–5 (quotation from 125). See now Levitin, 'Edmund Halley and the eternity of the world revisited' (2013), which functions as a corrective to Schaffer, 'Halley's atheism and the end of

Burnet's hypothesis absurd; his own various theories are usefully summarised by William Poole: 'that the earth, hollow, enclosed a smaller sphere, the motions of which caused variations in the magnetic poles; that extrapolation back from the current salinity of lakes could act as a dating mechanism for creation; that the flood might have been due to the impact of a comet'.[560] Only at one point did Halley make his attitude to the Mosaic text explicit:

The Account we have of the universal Deluge is no where so express as in the Holy Scriptures; and the exact Circumstances as to point of Time, do shew that some Records had been kept thereof more particularly than is wont in those things derived from remote Tradition, wherein the Historical *Minutiae* are lost by length of Time. But the same seem much too imperfect to be the Result of a full Revelation from the Author of this dreadful Execution upon Mankind, who would have spoke more amply as to the Manner thereof, had He thought fit to lay open the Secrets of Nature to the succeeding Race of Men; and I doubt not but to all that consider the 7th Chapter of *Genesis* impartially, it will pass for the Remains of a much fuller Account of the *Flood* left by the Patriarchs to their Posterity, and derived from the Revelation of *Noah* and his Sons. It must be granted, that there are some Difficulties as to the Construction of the *Ark*, the Reception and Agreement of the *Animals* among themselves, and Preservation of it in so immense and boundless an Ocean, during that *Wind* which God sent to dry the Water away, especially when it first came on Ground: But it must also be allowed, that length of Time may have been added, as well as taken away many notable Circumstances, as in most other Cases of the Story of remote Times and Actions.[561]

Halley here managed to run through the full gamut of options: that Moses was at least partially inspired, that he relied on earlier patriarchal traditions, and that the text had been corrupted.[562] What this might mean in practice is only revealed in another lecture, when Halley explained that he believed that ''tis no where revealed in Scripture' how long each of the days of creation had lasted.[563] This complete abandonment of any pretence of literalism is a sign of Halley's refusal to engage in the debates about Mosaic intention that had engrossed everyone else, as is his countenancing of the opinion offered 'by a Person whose Judgment I have great Reason to respect' that the shock which shaped the earth occurred 'before the creation [i.e. of man]'.[564]

---

the world' (1977); see also Kollerstrom, 'The hollow world of Edmond Halley' (1992); Poole, *World makers*, 108–10.

[560] Poole, 'Genesis narrative', 45. For Halley on the absurdity of Burnet, see 'Some considerations', 120–1.

[561] Halley, 'Some considerations', 118–19.

[562] Poole, *World makers*, 108–9 suggests the influence of Richard Simon; while not impossible, it is worth noting that Halley did not own Simon's work, although he did later own an English edition of Simon's New Testament (1730): Feisenberger, *Sale catalogues*, 189. As we have seen, he could have derived such a view from even more mainstream discussions.

[563] Halley, 'Cause of saltness', 296.

[564] Halley, 'Further thoughts', 123. Schaffer, 'Halley', 27, n. 51 suggests the unnamed person was Isaac Newton; given Newton's literalism, this seems distinctly improbable, and Poole's suggestion of Hooke is a much better fit (*World makers*, 108).

Yet this does not mean that he abandoned the critical humanist dimension to the search for the world's origins: indeed, we would be surprised if this were the case from a man who was educated by Gale at St Paul's, learnt Arabic to reconstruct the lost book of Apollonius's *Conics* (1710), and more generally displayed all the signs of humanist learning.[565] Like Burnet, Hooke, and others, Halley believed that pagan philosophers had preserved scraps of evidence about physical reality. Unlike them, the sources he referred to were astronomical. Ancient astronomical observations had of course been in continuous use as sources of data for practising astronomers, but Halley's use depended on a historical thesis. During the application process for the Savilian Professorship for Astronomy, rumours had spread that Halley believed in the eternity of the world.[566] In a series of lectures given 1691–93, Halley (who eventually lost out on the job to David Gregory) defended himself by arguing – partly on the basis of an idiosyncratic reading of Newton's findings in the *Principia* – that gravity and the resistance of the aether would lead the earth very gradually to slow down, travelling in a spiral until it collapsed into the sun, thus invalidating eternalism.[567] A corollary of this was that the years would gradually get longer (or as Halley later realised, shorter – the theological conclusion was the same). But this was not evident from the ancient astronomical observations of the Chaldeans as cited in Ptolemy (which Halley dated *c.* 700 BC – see 2.3 above), Hipparchus (c. 150 BC) and al-Battānī (*c.* AD 900). Ingeniously, Halley solved this by claiming that they had modified their observations to create an artificial concord: Ptolemy, for example, 'was obliged to suppose Babylon nearer to Alexandria by about half an hour than the same author in his Geography hath placed it'.[568] The history of philosophy had proved eternalism wrong, a case that Halley stuck to in a further lecture, despite changing his mind on natural philosophical particulars.[569] However, the history of philosophy could only take Halley so far. Moses remained lost, and it is with Halley's case that we can first say that science has trumped scripture.

---

[565] See now Fried, *Halley's reconstruction*. See also Chapman, 'Edmond Halley's use of historical evidence in the advancement of science' (1994); Cohen and Ross, 'The commonplace book of Edmond Halley' (1985).

[566] Halley to Abraham Hill, 22 June 1691, in *The correspondence and papers of Edmond Halley*, ed. E. F. MacPike (Oxford, 1932), 88. All the evidence is now collected in Levitin, 'Halley'.

[567] There is a full account in Schaffer, 'Halley', 22–4.

[568] 'Concerning the motion of light by Mr Halley, 19 October 1692', RS MS RBC 7.391, reproduced in Schaffer, 'Halley', 30–1; MacPike, *Halley*, 229 reproduces the appropriate Journal Book entry.

[569] 'Some observations on the motion of the sun, 18 October 1693', RS MS RBC 7.364, reproduced in Schaffer, 'Halley', 32–3. Levitin, 'Halley', corrects the misreading of this manuscript in Schaffer, 'Halley' and the subsequent historiography.

## 3.8     The scholarly response

We have already seen that Gale was sceptical at best about Hooke's efforts and that Le Clerc's reputation could only be dragged into the debate by some creative editing. This reflects the general pattern of scholarly response, as far as the limited evidence can tell us. If Bernard was unimpressed with the Mosaic speculations of a serious apologist like Huet, his opinion of the efforts of the natural philosophers was unsurprisingly altogether more scathing. Burnet wrote 'more for his own sake, $y^n$ either $y^t$ of truth or of Moses'; Whiston had written 'a mad booke ... Derogatory to holy Moses, & voyd of good mathematiques as well as theology'.[570] He was more optimistic about the possibility of a new history of Egypt, writing to Gale in Cambridge to encourage him to follow in the footsteps of Selden, Vossius, and Bochart in working on Egypt and Chaldea, about which Plutarch, Clemens Alexandrinus, and Eusebius transmitted information only 'confusedly and in no order', and which was characterised not by true religion but by idolatrous starworship.[571] We see here all the main themes that we have already encountered: the influence of the continental histories of religion, anti-syncretism, and scepticism about patristic histories of paganism.

Even more apt in this regard is a 1698 letter to Samuel Pepys – Royal Society president in 1684–86 and himself a keen student of the exegetical issues raised by Burnet[572] – from Bernard's close acquaintance at Oxford, Thomas Smith, by now a nonjuror and unofficial librarian of the Cotton Library.[573] The letter concerns a hieroglyph-inscribed wooden board from an ancient Egyptian coffin, donated in 1681 to Oxford University by Robert Huntington (in 1683 it passed to the newly formed Ashmolean Museum, where it still lies).[574] Huntington was one of Pococke's most brilliant oriental students: on the latter's recommendation he successfully applied in 1670 for the post of chaplain to the Levant Company in Aleppo, a post he used – after an initial near-catastrophic encounter with Greek corsairs on his journey there – to travel extensively, establish a major network of advisers and informants across the middle east, and obtain a vast amount of manuscripts (Arabic, Hebrew, Coptic, Syriac, Samaritan, Persian, and Turkish),

---

[570] Bernard to Thomas Smith, 16 January 1693 and 26 June 1696, Bod. MS Smith 47, fols. 124ʳ, 203ʳ.

[571] Bernard to Gale, pre-1672, BL MS Add. 4292, fol. 127ʳ⁻ᵛ. See also Haugen, *Bentley*, 40.

[572] Pepys, 'Notes of discourses touching religion', Bod. MS Rawl. A7171, fol. 217ʳ; Poole, *World makers*, 34, 43, 62, 138, 175. The manuscript is now discussed and reprinted in Loveman, 'Samuel Pepys and "Discourses touching religion" under James II' (2012). The following discussion is much expanded in Levitin, 'Egyptology and conjectural history'.

[573] They corresponded regularly in the 1690s, primarily on antiquarian matters: all the letters except the one under discussion here are contained in Bod. MS Smith 65, fols. 10ʳ–67ʳ. They shared Thomas Gale as an acquaintance and correspondent.

[574] Item 1836.482. The board is from the coffin of the priest Kha'hap, dating from the third century BC. See Whitehouse, *Ancient Egypt and Nubia in the Ashmolean museum* (2009), 109–10.

most of which were sold to Oxford for almost £1100 in 1692.[575] Huntington's modesty and diffidence led him to publish only one thing in his life, but we can still tentatively reconstruct his views on the hieroglyphs and Egyptian wisdom.[576] His one publication was a short letter to the Royal Society published in 1684 on 'the Porphyry Pillars in Egypt', that is to say the three obelisks (not actually made of porphyry) now in London, Paris, and New York known as 'Cleopatra's Needles'; the subject of how the ancients had carved and transported the stone had for some time been of considerable interest to the Royal Society.[577] In this article Huntington also posited a short explanation for the hieroglyphs on the pillars: they may have been the 'Aboriginal *Aegyptian* Letter, long since worn out of common use in the Country', in the same way that Samaritan had died out to be replaced by Hebrew among the Jews, or that the Chinese still formed their script 'where each note represents a word': both, after all, were written from top to bottom, as was exemplified by the board he had rescued from its use as a door in Saqqara.[578]

Learned readers would have immediately recognised the implications of this. That Hebrew was not an original ur-language but developed from others had become a commonplace by mid-century.[579] As for the comparison with Chinese, this was to follow in the tradition of José Acosta, who had posited the western invention of the alphabet as significant progress from what he called the 'painting and ciphering' of the Chinese. This was in direct contrast to those like John Webb, who had partially followed Kircher in seeing Chinese as a pure natural language (Kircher had explicitly connected Egyptian hieroglyphs and Chinese characters as forms of a putative advanced philosophical language) and whose works were well known in the Royal Society and beyond.[580]

---

[575] The fullest account is in Smith's 'Huntingtoni vita' appended to *D. Roberti Huntingtoni, Episcopi Rapotensis, epistolae*, ed. T. Smith (London, 1704), iii–iv for the attack by the Greek 'pessimi latrones'. See Hamilton, 'Huntington, Robert', *ODNB* and for the fullest account of his activities on his travels, Toomer, *Eastern wisedome*, 281–6. In 1683 he was appointed provost of Trinity College, Dublin; rector of Great Hallingbury in 1691; and Bishop of Raphoe in July 1701, twelve days before his death. Many letters survive in the Bodleian, often complaining of what he called his 'Celtic exile'.

[576] His diffidence is well brought out in Toomer, *Eastern wisedome*, 282, 286, although I would disagree with the claim that by 1692 Huntington 'had finally abandoned oriental studies, and indeed academic life', for he wrote to his close friend Pierre Allix on 21 March 1696 that '[n]o one is more willing than me to help in working for the republic of letters; if only strength could be equal to spirit' ('Nemo me libentius succurreret pro Republica literaria laborantibus, si modo vires suppeterent animo pares' [*Epistolae*, 61]).

[577] R[obert] H[untington], 'A Letter from Dublin … concerning the porphyry pillars of Egypt', *Philosophical Transactions*, 14 (1684), 624–9; see Martin Lister, 'The manner of making steel … with a guess at the way the ancients used to steel their picks, for the cutting or hewing of porphyry', *Philosophical Transactions*, 17 (1693), 865–70; the discussion within the RS in fact went back to at least 1666 (Birch, *History*, II, 73).

[578] Huntington, 'Pillars', 627–8.    [579] Droixhe, 'Crise'.

[580] José de Acosta, *The natural and morall histories of the East and West Indies* (London, 1604), 440. I was led to this source by the key account in Poole, 'Heterodoxy and Sinology'. For

Even without knowing any of these languages it would not be difficult to see that these comparisons are flimsy: alphabetic, logographic, and iconographic ideas are combined into one. But this was precisely the point: the idea of hieroglyphs containing advanced esoteric philosophy was being replaced by a developmental theory of language and of culture more generally. This is not to say that this immediately led to Woodward-esque anti-Egyptian polemic – Huntington still felt that the construction and movement of the vast monuments demonstrated that Egypt was 'the Mother of the Mathematics' – but it certainly undermined a central component of the idea of 'Egyptian wisdom' as it had been developed since antiquity.

Smith's letter to Pepys, to which was attached a drawing of the board (which Smith thought perhaps '<one of> the greatest reliques of that antient sort of amusing & intricate Learning at this time in Christendome') drew on and developed Huntington's ideas.[581] Some had supposed 'that the old Aegyptian alphabet might bee collected' from the hieroglyphs. This was fundamentally mistaken, for they were better compared with other primitive forms of written communication:

it seems to mee by the great variety of them both here and elsewhere, that they cannot fall under that denomination, and that they rather stand for entire words, like those of the Chineses, tho not so perplexd and intricate. This old Aegyptian way of preserving the secrets of religion and philosophy ... (which I will thus suppose also ... to bee the designe of this bord) is made up, as it appears here, both of the Chinese way of writing by meare phantastick characters, without any regard to rules of art in the framing of them, or to the values of the things, which they are designed to represent, and of the Mexican way of describing their thoughts and notions of things by picture and image: both which, it may bee, at first owed their original to their ignorance of reducing the severall articulate sounds, by which words are formed, to a certain number of letters, and of inventing severall marks and figures, to expresse first, and then distinguish their powers, so as they might bee comprised in an alphabet.[582]

The hieroglyphs were to be compared to the primitive ideograms not only of the Chinese but also the Mexicans and Peruvians – a clear nod to the kind of ethnographic interpretation pioneered by Acosta. However, the Egyptians were not as primitive as these peoples, for it was 'unquestionably certaine, that they from the first beginnings of their Monarchy ... had the knowledge and use of letters': this was evident from those letters of the Coptic alphabet which did not have Greek counterparts and which must have expressed characters 'which they could not part with' because they signified 'severall distinct and unusual sounds of words'.[583]

---

Webb, see his *Historical essay*, esp. 47, 53, 86–117 for the history of Chinese learning that acts as context for the theory.

[581] Smith to Pepys, 7 Sep 1698, Bod. MS Smith 88, fol. 51ʳ.      [582] Ibid., fol. 51ᵛ.

[583] Ibid., fol. 53ʳ. Smith added that Herodotus's ambiguous reference to the right-to-left writing of the Egyptians (II.36.4) must have been referring to 'these common characters, and not [to]

This raised the historical question of *why* the hieroglyphs had been developed. Moreover, it concerned one of the central issues of our discussion: 'whether the great and inspired Lawgiver, Moses ... [was] versed and practised in this mysticall sort of writing'. This idea was dismissed for the same reason as so many others had become reluctant to class Moses as a philosopher: it was the invention of the Hellenistic Jews like the 'florid Rhetorician and Sophist' Philo, from whom Christian writers like Clement of Alexandria and Justin Martyr had 'unwarily taken up the same opinion.' Indeed, it was entirely absent from Josephus, 'notwithstanding his profound researches ... [in] the antiquity and history of his own nation'.[584] This repudiation of the fathers was 'no denigration' to Moses for it was much more likely that 'this hieroglyphicall way of writing is owing wholly to the imbecility of the Egyptian Priests' who sought to aggrandise themselves 'as being the onely interpreters of those ιερά or ... sacred letters or writings, under the disguise of which long hid, as they pretended, the great mysteryes of their theology especially, and of other sciences'. The existing interpretations in Horapollo showed these putative great mysteries to be 'inconsiderable'. It was to be regretted that the existing evidence – Manetho, Herodotus, and Diodorus Siculus – was so sparse as to render any attempt to date the origins of the hieroglyphs 'vaine and idle'.[585] The only thing that was certain was that Kircher had 'phantastically explained' the hieroglyphs and that such interpretations were unacceptable.[586] In the hands of Huntington and then Smith, we see both the demystification of the hieroglyphs and deep scepticism about ever achieving a higher level of understanding about Egyptian wisdom and Moses's relationship to it, even if Huntington hoped that if the inscriptions on the pyramids 'were but exactly copyed, it might be then lawful to hope, that the Language so long since dead and buried in the House of Bondage, might have its resurrection in the Land of Liberty'.[587]

This mix of historical scepticism and disdain for any claims to great esoteric wisdom among the early pagans manifested itself in one other scholarly debate of the 1690s: the re-examinination of Pythagoras, who, as we have seen, was almost inevitably a key component of any such narratives. After the high point of the 1640s–50s and Pearson's work on Hierocles, the study of Pythagoreanism had seemed to come to something of a halt. When John Locke enquired in the 1670s about the best available work on the subject he was directed, by no less a figure than Lord Carbery, President of the Royal Society, to the *De natura et constitutione philosophiae Italicae, seu Pythagoricae* (1664) by the Swedish humanist Johannes Gerhard

mythicall Sculptures'. This was essentially a correct interpretation, for Coptic contains seven characters derived from Demotic (ⳟ, ⳋ, ⳉ, ⳃ, ⳍ, ⳏ, ⳁ). For Huntington as a collector of Coptic manuscripts, see Hamilton, *Copts and the West*, 256–8.

[584] Ibid., fols. 53$^{r-v}$.   [585] Ibid., fol. 53$^v$.   [586] Ibid., fol. 51$^r$.   [587] Huntington, 'Pillars', 628.

Scheffer.[588] Scheffer was an important scholar, but his work on Pythagoras, 'printed only because of the constant urging of the author's patroness, Queen Christina', was not particularly pioneering;[589] to take only one example, he was rather ambiguous about whether Pythagoras had derived his ideas from Hermes Trismegistus.[590] More generally, scholars faced a serious source problem: the key source for Pythagoras's life was Iamblichus's *Vita Pythagorica* – not least because it was the only source that offered a full chronology for his biography – and yet this was the same Iamblichus who ascribed to Pythagoras such patently improbable miracles as his display of a golden thigh to Abaris.

There was thus incentive for more work; an opportunity was provided by the 'ancients and moderns' controversy. I share entirely Kristine Haugen's judgement of the controversy – a literary debate that began in France and migrated to 1690s England – as 'unserious, trivial, and disingenuous'.[591] It nonetheless remains true that its polemical and semi-popularising dimension had some consequences for historical scholarship and how it was perceived (as everyone now knows, the key representatives of the 'moderns' were not anti-historical scientists but critical humanists who believed that the ancients could be understood better than they had understood themselves). William Temple's initial blast in the debate was, as contemporaries realised, entirely trivial; in the history of philosophy he wrote of Brahmins impressing Alexander the Great with 'Magical Operations' and from thence deduced that Pythagoras had learnt all he knew from them rather than the Egyptians.[592] The real debate was between a set of Christ Church, Oxford men who published a new edition (1695) of the *Epistles* of Phalaris – praised by Temple as containing 'more Force of Wit and Genius' than any modern writings – and Richard Bentley, who – spurred by a backhanded compliment in that edition – promptly composed an attack on the authenticity of the *Epistles* for the second edition of William Wotton's *Reflections upon ancient and modern learning* (1697); riposte and counter-riposte swiftly followed.[593]

---

[588] Bod. MS Locke d. 11 ('Lemmata physica') fol. 68ʳ: 'Pithagorian philosophy Scheffer de na[tur]a & constitutione philosophia Italica. It is the best account we have of the Pithagorian philosophi: L^d Carbery'.

[589] See Tolomio, 'Historica philosophica', 150–3, quotation at 150.

[590] Johann Scheffer, *De natura et constitutione philosophiae Italicae, seu Pythagoricae* (Uppsala, 1664), 57–8 ('Caterum Pythagoras hausisse istaec ab Aegyptiis videtur, si modo Mercurius ille, vulgo Trismegistus, cuius opera nonnulla extant, & fragmenta servant Stobaeus aliique, fuit Aegyptius, & non unus ex philosophiae Platonice, vel quod paene idem, est, Pythagoricae studiosis').

[591] Haugen, *Bentley*, 277, n. 45. On England, Levine, *Battle*, remains the classic account, surveying a great deal of the print and manuscript material.

[592] William Temple, 'Upon ancient and modern learning', in *Miscellanea … the second part* (London, 1690), 18, 20–1.

[593] Levine, *Battle*, 47–120 for the full story.

Importantly for us, since Phalaris was a putative contemporary of Pythagoras, some attention was diverted to the Samian philosopher. Bentley devoted forty pages to him in his much extended *Dissertation upon the Epistles of Phalaris* (1699); although his arguments were primarily technical–chronological they also contained hints of a broader historical attitude. When he did discuss Pythagoras's life in detail, he seemed to present him as a charlatan more than a philosopher, dwelling on the famous episode in which Pythagoras hid underground for seven years being fed food and news by his mother so that he could pretend to have travelled to Hades upon his re-emergence. Even more importantly, Bentley was deeply critical of the biography of Iamblichus: ''Tis a wonder, that in so short a work he sould be so often inconsistent with himself'.[594] And as his previous publication – the *Epistola* to John Mill (1691) – had shown, Bentley was entirely intolerant of Christian–pagan syncretisms, seeing them as Jewish frauds foolishly accepted by the early Christians.[595]

This attitude – specifically applied to Pythagoras – manifested itself even more strongly in the work of William Lloyd, then bishop of Coventry and Lichfield; Lloyd's work almost certainly informed that of Bentley. Lloyd was considered 'one of the most deepe learned Divines of the Nation, in all sorts of literature';[596] respected especially for his chronological scholarship, which he had conducted in tandem with his friend Henry Dodwell.[597] His scholarship thus had nothing to do with the ancients–moderns controversy, but his *Chronological account of the life of Pythagoras* (1699) was obviously a publication stimulated by it, consisting mostly of an 'epistle' to Bentley concerning the two key sources for Pythagoras's life apart from Diogenes Laërtius:

---

[594] Richard Bentley, *A dissertation upon the epistles of Phalaris, with an answer to the objections of the honourable Charles Boyle* (London, 1699), 63–5; 85–7 (quotation at 87).

[595] Richard Bentley, 'Cl. Viro Joanni Millio', in Ἰωάννου Ἀντιοχεως του επικλην Μαλάλα χρονικη ιστορια *Joannis Antiocheni cognomento Malalae historia chronica* (Oxford, 1691), 2–14. The fullest discussion remains Grafton, *Defenders*, 13–21; see also Haugen, *Bentley*, 92–3. One of Bentley's arguments on Orpheus (2–3), based on a reading from a manuscript of Damascius (Corpus Christi College, Oxford MS 158), may well take off from Cudworth, *System*, 306. Dodwell wanted Gale to produce a Latin translation of this manuscript: Dodwell to Gottfried Christian Goetz, Sep 1700, Bod. MS Cherry, 23, fol. 108ʳ. Gerard Langbaine had already noted its value and begun a transcription: see the letters to Ussher of 1 January and 15 March 1651, in *The whole works of the most Rev. James Ussher, D.D.*, ed. C. R. Elrington (17 vols, Dublin, 1847–64), xvi, 568, 570.

[596] *Evelyn diary*, iv, 172–3. Evelyn himself had an interest in hieroglyphics: as early as 1646 he had sent to Kircher, via Thomas Henshaw, a drawing of hieroglyphics on a stone from Egypt given to him in Venice by one 'Captain Powell': he was distraught to find Kircher describing the drawing without acknowledging him and with only a slight acknowledgement for Henshaw (BL MS Add. 78351, fol. 101ʳ; for his earlier meeting with Kircher, see Darley, *John Evelyn* (2006), 48–50).

[597] Much useful information is gathered in Levine, *Battle*, 90–3, although it does not consider the manuscripts in the Gloucestershire Record Office (see esp. D3549/2/4/24 for detailed chronological notes). See also his correspondence with the Franciscan chronologer and ecclesiastical historian Antoine Pagi, CUL MS Kk.5.38, *passim*.

Porphyry and Iamblichus. Both, Lloyd argued, had offered hagiography, describing 'him as a very extraordinary Person ... above all, they magnifie his knowledge of the Gods, and of the things of Religion'.[598] In reality they were virtually useless as sources. First, there were purely formal faults, especially internal inconsistencies. Lloyd admitted that Iamblichus's precise chronology seemed wonderfully useful: '[it] did, I confess, not a little rejoice me, when I first met with it'.[599] And yet, closer inspection revealed the most basic faults. Iamblichus claimed that Pythagoras had been taken to Egypt by Cambyses's soldiers and from there went straight to Babylon – this seemed very convenient, for 'there is nothing better known in ancient History' than that Cambyses conquered Egypt either at the end of the third or the start of the fourth year of the sixty-third Olympiad. At the same time, Iamblichus reported that Pythagoras had gone to Italy during the sixty-second Olympiad. Yet by adding up the other years mentioned by Iamblichus, one could derive the meaning that Pythagoras had gone to Italy not seven years before going to Babylon, but sixteen years after.[600]

Even more serious was Lloyd's second criticism: Iamblichus and Porphyry were not really historians at all but religious propagandists whose biographies of Pythagoras were designed as part of their all-consuming hatred of Christianity. Seeing the traditions of Greek learning trumped by a Jewish carpenter, they realised that the only way to counterattack was to 'like[n]' Pythagoras to 'the great things that are said of Christ'.[601] The genre of their works was thus not history, but the pagan apologetics of the type perfected by Philostratus (c. 170–245), the great opponent of Christianity who had posited Apollonius of Tyana as a miracle-worker comparable to Christ. Lloyd included a long digression on Philostratus, arguing (correctly) that he wrote his fabrications on the orders of the Empress Julia, adding (incorrectly) that she probably wanted to 'draw off her Son ... from the esteem he had of the Christians' due to having a Christian slave wet-nurse – either that or to 'countenance her wicked design of drawing her Son to her Bed', a known practice of the Magi.[602] Iamblichus's account of Pythagoras could be re-contexualised politically in the same way; the one difference was that he lived initially under Christian emperors, and thus adopted the more careful tactic of picking the biography of an existing sage, Pythagoras, and 'add[ing] out of his own Invention, whatever he thought would either adorn his Subject, or promote the design of his

---

[598] Lloyd, *Pythagoras*, iv.      [599] Ibid., xlvii–xlix.

[600] Ibid., xlix–l (Lloyd here mistakenly places Cambyses's conquest at Ol. LXIV.3, but silently corrects this to LXIII.3 in the chronological account, at 14). See also Iamblichus, *Vit. Pyth.*, 35–6.

[601] Lloyd, *Pythagoras*, xix–xx.

[602] Ibid., xl–xli. The source for Caracalla's Christian nurse is Tertullian, *Ad Scapulam*, iv (not Eusebius, *Hist. Eccl.*, VI, as claimed by Lloyd). For Magi incest, the source is Sextus Empiricus, *Pyrr.*, III.205 (Lloyd has III.24).

Writing . . . [i.e.] to subvert the Christian Religion'. Although he never admitted it, this polemical aim was fully revealed upon the accession of Julian the Apostate, who wrote more letters to Iamblichus 'than to any other while he was living'.[603] That the genre of Iamblichus's *Vita* was not history but propaganda could then be confirmed by internal evidence: could it be a coincidence that in his account Pythagoras had a virgin mother, had his birth prophesised, performed miracles, and was likened to a son of God (Apollo) or to the God himself? Was this anything but an 'Abusive imitation of the Gospel'?[604] Who could be surprised that his 'sources' were entirely untraceable? 'To conclude', finished Lloyd, 'I do not lay any weight at all upon the Testimony of *Jamblichus*, nor much on that of his Master *Porphyry*'.[605]

Lloyd's history – with its mix of technical chronology and critical source analysis – became the most sophisticated available. The concern with the contextually understood intentions of the neoplatonists was as methodologically advanced as anything being offered by Le Clerc and others at the same time. Yet there was also something deeply paradoxical about it. On the one hand, Lloyd appreciated that his criticism was fundamentally destructive: 'There is not in all my Collection, any one certain year in which any thing happen'd to him, or was done by him'.[606] Yet on the other, he *did* posit a very strong vision of Pythagoras, whom he classified as an impostor in the vein of Muḥammad, making up stories of the transmigration of his soul, hiding in cellars to pretend that he had travelled to Hades, and tricking Abaris out of his money.[607] This contradictory attitude was not missed by contemporaries; as John Wallis wrote to Lloyd: 'As to Pythagoras, according to the account of Porphyry & Jamblicus [sic], I am of your Lordships opinion that he must have been a very great Cheat. But if those stories be only the Forgeries of those authors (without any Foundation of Truth) Pythagoras might perhaps have deserv'd a better Character'.[608]

But from our perspective, this is precisely the point. Anti-syncretism had become a dogma of a historical criticism that was otherwise tending towards scepticism. There were few things in early Greek history that the leading scholars of the 1690s would admit to being sure of,[609] but one of them was

---

[603] Lloyd, *Pythagoras*, xliii–xliv.     [604] Ibid., xliv–xlvi.     [605] Ibid., lvii.     [606] Ibid., iv.

[607] Ibid., v–viii, x–xiii (the comparison with Muḥammad is at x). See also the similar move in William Wotton, *Reflections upon ancient and modern learning* (London, 1694), 92–8.

[608] Wallis to Lloyd, 30 June 1699, Bod. MS Tanner 21, fol. 110ʳ.

[609] The more prominent manifestation of this scepticism perhaps being Dodwell's first Camden lecture of 1688, printed as 'Quam nupera sit, quamque imperfecta, antiquissima Graecorum historia', in Henry Dodwell, *Praelectiones academicae in schola historices Camdeniana* (Oxford, 1692), 1–31. Dodwell *did* believe he could prove the existence of a Phalaris against Bentley and was dismayed by his old friend Lloyd's implicit defence of Bentley's view (Levine, *Battle*, 89–90); nonetheless, he supported Lloyd's attack on the reliability of Iamblichus for Pythagoras's life (*De veteribus Graecorum Romanorumque cyclis* (2 vols, Oxford, 1701–2), i, 138–9).

that the stories about the Greek philosophers offered by the Hellenistic Jews, the church fathers, and the late antique neoplatonists were a pack of lies.

## 3.9    Conclusion

Brucker was wrong. The idea of 'Mosaic philosophy' and its afterhistory was not the same at the end of the seventeenth century as it was at the start; indeed, it had been fundamentally revolutionised. But neither was the development the result of a 'crisis' or of anything that merits the name 'enlightenment'. More than anything it was the outgrowth of a critical attitude to a set of sources – Jewish, early Christian, and neoplatonic – that had emerged in the late sixteenth century (and that we will return to in Chapter 6), the use of new sources (especially Maimonides), and the dissemination of 'anti-Egyptian' works like Conring's.[610] By the end of the century the anti-syncretist attitude had become normalised not just among scholars but also among theologians and even natural philosophers. Figures like Henry More and Theophilus Gale, previously considered representatives of movements such as 'Cambridge Platonism', or, in Gale's case, as respected scholars, were in fact outliers, their works disrespected or ignored by virtually everybody.

As was so often the case, however, a new historiographical orthodoxy could destabilise orthodoxies elsewhere. We have already seen how Burnet's mismanaged appropriation of Spencer led directly to accusations of heterodoxy and use of his work by those who really were heterodox; this trend only continued in the first decades of the eighteenth century. The discourse moved away from natural philosophy and back to apologetics and the history of religion, as John Toland in particular started to imply that Moses himself was an Egyptian political lawgiver while positing himself as a defender of the pioneering Anglicans Marsham and Spencer against the out-of-date claims of Pierre-Daniel Huet.[611] Spencer's accommodationist hermeneutic became appropriated as license for ecclesiological relativism.[612] Under these circumstances it is no surprise that scholarship became subordinated to ideology; Warburton's *Divine legation of Moses* (1738–42) – now often incorporated into a story of 'religious enlightenment' – was a populist attempt at turning Spencer's conclusions to their original purpose. Hume was still battling about Mosaic primacy in the 1750s.[613] But that battle was only a faint after-skirmish of the great campaigns of the seventeenth century.

---

[610] See e.g. Wotton, *Reflections*, 116–35, much of which is a paraphrase of Conring.
[611] John Toland, *Dissertationes duae, Aedeisidaemon et origines Judaicae* (The Hague, 1709), esp. 198–9. See Champion, 'English theories of "imposture" from Stubbe to Toland' (1996).
[612] Levitin, 'Tindal'.    [613] Serjeantson, 'Eusebianism'.

# 4    Histories of natural philosophy I. Histories of method

Having already encountered much natural philosophical engagement with the history of philosophy, we turn to histories of natural philosophy proper. In Chapter 5 we will consider historical approaches to key natural philosophical doctrines, specifically to matter theory and theories of causation (mechanical or otherwise), undoubtedly the two most important fields of contention in seventeenth-century physics. Yet for early modern natural philosophers such questions of doctrine – important as they were – took second place to questions of philosophical *method*.[1] In particular, the role of observation, experience, and experiment was continuously discussed. This was the case for many reasons, not least because what came to be known as 'experimental philosophy' did not fit the traditional neo-Aristotelian definition of natural philosophy as a speculative (or contemplative) science of causes, a definition that could be and was defended historically in England even in the late seventeenth century.[2]

It is well established that the terms 'rationalist' and 'empiricist' are not only anachronistic but also actively misleading when discussing early modern methodology debates. Alternatives, specifically for seventeenth-century England, have recently been posited.[3] It will be suggested here that setting such precise terminological boundaries may be at least partially futile. We shall see that not only were these methodological debates almost always conducted in historical mode, but also that in many cases the key development was less the

---

[1] For introductions, see Di Liscia et al., eds., *Method and order*; Dear, 'Method and the study of nature' (1998). For various approaches, see Chalmers, 'Intermediate causes and explanations' (2012); Gaukroger, *The emergence of a scientific culture* (2006), 352–99; Dear, *Discipline and experience* (1995), among many others. Key 'methodological' statements by post-1660 Englishmen are still most usefully approached via Hunter, *Science and the shape of orthodoxy* (1995), 169–80 ('The early Royal Society and the shape of knowledge').

[2] See e.g. BL Sloane MS 3433, 'Disciplinae physicae', dated 1685, fol. 1$^r$, defending the proposition that 'physica apud philosophos' is a 'philosophica Theoretica', as evidenced by both Plato and Aristotle. More generally, see Dear, 'What is the history of science the history *of*?' (2005), esp. 393–7.

[3] Anstey, 'Experimental versus speculative'. Developed in Anstey, 'Francis Bacon and the classification of natural history' (2012); Anstey and Vanzo, 'The origins of early modern experimental philosophy' (2012); Anstey, *John Locke and natural philosophy* (2011); Anstey, Campbell, and Jacovides, 'Locke's experimental philosophy' (2013). Discussed at 4.6 below.

rejection of ancient methods and terminology, but more their transformation and appropriation for new ends. The rejection of metaphysical intrusion into natural philosophy was presented as an outgrowth of the 'true' Aristotelian inheritance, even by dogmatic anti-Aristotelians (4.2). Natural philosophical reformers advanced their ideas as a return to pre-sophistic practice. And most importantly, the successful integration of experimental methods into the mainstream of seventeenth-century English natural philosophy depended, at least in part, on the ability of learned physicians to rewrite the history of medicine as a history of observational – yet still philosophical – endeavour. This was a crucial step because it occurred within the institutions in which natural philosophy was still most practised: university medicine faculties and the Royal College of Physicians. And it was in contrast with the failure of the Royal Society apologists to offer a convincing historical genealogy for a wider process of methodological reform, a failure that stemmed from their misuse of the humanist tools that they tried to put to the task. A large amount of literature in the last two decades or so has demonstrated the prevalence of emphasis on experience in late Renaissance natural philosophy and medicine.[4] And yet, attempts to draw direct connections between that emphasis and the 'experimental philosophy' proper have been inconclusive. It is hoped that the discussion here will supply at least some such connections. As usual, before we turn to the debates themselves, an introduction to the key sources and their prior interpretation is required.

## 4.1    Sources

(A) *The Aristotelian tradition.* For most of our period, arts course philosophy can still be labelled, in a wide sense, Aristotelian.[5] This is the case both for domestic textbooks, and those continental textbooks – produced by both Protestants and Catholics – which remained standard within English (and indeed Scottish) universities.[6] Aristotelianism had its humanist turn in the early to mid-sixteenth century,[7] and this tendency carried through into the textbook format that became popular in the late sixteenth century.[8] The history of philosophy was therefore very often discussed either in prefaces that directly addressed the subject, or for particular topics. The extent of this engagement

---

[4] A very useful historiographical summary can be found in Siraisi, 'Medicine, 1450–1620, and the history of science' (2012), esp. 499–505.

[5] On the vitality and variety of Renaissance Aristotelianism, the literature is now huge; the best introduction remains Schmitt, *Aristotle*.

[6] For Aristotle in seventeenth-century English universities, see Costello, *The scholastic curriculum* (1958); Feingold, 'Aristotle and the English universities'.

[7] Again, the literature is large; for a start, see Kessler, 'The transformation of Aristotelianism during the Renaissance' (1990).

[8] Schmitt, 'The rise of the philosophical textbook' (1988).

varied greatly. Very basic textbooks might address historical issues extremely sporadically,[9] but even one level up from this works like Franco Burgersdijk's much-used *Collegium physicum* could do so at length, adding glosses from Laërtius and a host of commentators.[10] Even basic logic textbooks would show students that doing philosophy depended on appreciating the contradictions and internal structure of ancient texts.[11] More advanced textbooks, of the sort more likely used on M.A. courses, would often contain extensive historical digressions, often with untranslated Greek quotations. Marcus Freidrich Wendelin's *Contemplationes physicae*, first published in Hanau in 1625 and read by advanced natural philosophy students (probably at M.A. level) in Cambridge from an edition published there in 1648, is an excellent example.[12]

[9] Robert Sanderson, *Physicae scientiae compendium* (Oxford, 1671) has no history at all; Francis Willis, *Synopsis physicae tam Aristotelicae, quam novae ad usum scholae accommodata* (London, 1690), is equally basic, but still historicises Aristotle at 44–5 (Aristotle followed Ocellus Lucanus on the world's eternity). Aristotle's eternalism could be more fully historicised in actual divinity tuition: see Henry Fairfax's divinity commonplace book (Folger MS V.b.108), p. 142 (in a section 'De erroribus circa Creationem'). At the start of the century, a Cambridge philosophy commencement thesis could still involve arguing that 'The world, according to Aristotle, is not eternal' ('Mundus secundùm Aristotelem non est æternus', 1600): Bod. shelf-mark G. Pamph. 1688(6) [ESTC S124768]; I have found little evidence of such syncretic aims later in the century.

[10] Franco Burgersdijk, *Collegium phyiscum, disputationibus XXXII* (Cambridge, 1650 [1st edn=Leiden, 1632]), 12, 14–18, 23–4, 319, 344–6; John Prideaux, *Hypomnemata logica, rhetorica, physica, metaphysica, pneumatica, ethica, politica, oeconomica* (Oxford, 1650), 44, 215–19; Adrian Heereboord, *Meletemata philosophica* (Amsterdam & London, 1680 [1st edn=Amsterdam, 1665]), 1a–6a, 22a–6b, 104a–5a, 183a–5b, 385b, 408a, 415a–19b (this last section is entitled 'De origine et progressu philosophiae') (The 1665 Amsterdam edition was already being used in English universities: the copy in CUL [shelf-mark: N.3.41] is marked on the inside flyleaf as the property of a student of Corpus Christi College [the name of the student has been torn out]). The manuscript philosophy course belonging to Hugh Smith, 'Philosophia universalis, vulgo metaphysica' (1664) (CUL MS Kk.6.7) includes extensive treatment of the history of philosophy at pp. 5–13 (Smith is not listed in *Alum. Cantab.*). See also the very popular Johann Magirus, *Physiologiae Peripateticae libri sex cum commentariis* (Cambridge, 1642 [1st edn=Frankfurt, 1597]), e.g. 271–6 for a long list of various ancient philosophical opinions on the soul, and commentary upon them. Magirus's textbook was used by the undergraduate Newton, whose notes are in CUL MS Add. 3996, fols. 16ʳ–26ᵛ. While they were not deemed worth including in *Certain philosophical questions: Newton's Trinity notebook*, eds., J. E. McGuire and M. Tamny (Cambridge, 1983), aspects of them are discussed in Wallace, 'Newton's early writings' (1988) and Levitin, 'Newton and scholastic philosophy' (2015).

[11] See e.g. John Flavel, *Tractatus de demonstratione methodicus & polemicus ... in usum Juventutis in Collegio Wadhami apud Oxonienses privati praelectionibus traditus*, ed. A. Huish (Oxford, 1619, repr. 1624, 1651 (references to this last edn)), 1–11, explaining that the *Corpus Aristotelicum* provides two types of demonstration (i.e. those of *Anal. Post*, i.8 and ix.1), with reference to many commentators both ancient (e.g. Themistius) and modern (e.g. Zabarella). See also the discussion at 97–100 under the heading 'An sit scientia de novo?', where Aristotle is said to follow Plato's idea that the soul arrived with all knowledge and was only then corrupted by the body, an idea which then inspired the Manichean heresy and the errors of Origen.

[12] See e.g. the copy at CUL, shelf-mark: Peterborough 2.2, inscribed on the title-page: 'Ex libris Iohannis Patricke Reginalensis. Iuly: 1. 1650' – Patrick took his BA from Queens' in 1650, MA

We shall find that some of the historiographical features which have been considered unique to the *novatores* were in fact textbook commonplaces.

(B) *Learned medicine*. In the late Renaissance, medicine was – like theology, its colleague among the higher faculties – presented as an outgrowth of preparatory philosophical studies, specifically in natural philosophy.[13] Hippocrates, Galen, and Aristotle (predominantly through the few lines of the *De sanitate et morbo* preserved in the *Parva naturalia*) were all viewed as *philosophical* physicians, and Hippocrates was credited with founding medicine as a rational art.[14] Medical conclusions had to conform to the standards of (Aristotelian) philosophical explanation: that is to say, they had to provide a discussion of cause.[15] This was of great importance, for the identity of medicine was tied into its history, specifically the methodologies adopted by the three ancient sects known primarily from the works of Galen (but also from the long preface to Celsus's *De medicina*).[16] They were (1) the Rationalists (or Dogmatics), who believed that the physician must use reason to investigate the causes of disease and physiological phenomena; (2) the Empirics, who derided theory and the search for causes and claimed that long clinical experience is the only root of medical practice; and (3) the Methodics, who proposed that a full medical training could be acquired on the basis of a few simple rules in six

in 1654. Wendelin was also read at university in 1650 by Francis Willughby, later a leading member of the RS: see his commonplace book, Nottingham University Library, MS Mi LM 15/1, 572. I am very grateful to Richard Serjeantson for supplying me with this reference; the significance of this commonplace book will be explored in his 'The education of Francis Willughby' (forthcoming).

[13] See Schmitt, 'Aristotle among the physicians' (1985), esp. 12–15 on the dictum, associated with Aristotle, 'Ubi desinit physicus, ibi medicus incipit'. For uses of this phrase in our period to defend learned medicine from attacks by other medical practitioners, see e.g [Eleazar Duncon], *The copy of a letter written by E.D. Doctour of physicke to a gentleman ... The latter is a discourse of emperiks or unlearned physitians* (London, 1606), 22–6 (drawing on Galen, *Meth. Med.* 1.2, K.x.11–12) (apothecaries are aligned with Empirics at 18); Walter Harris, *Pharmacologia anti-empirica* (London, 1683), 36; Everard Maynwaring, *Medicus absolutus adespotos* (London, 1668), 46. For Maynwaringe, see below.

[14] Schmitt, 'Aristotle among the physicians', 2–3; for the Renaissance debate on whether medicine is an art or a science: Maclean, *Learned medicine*, 70–6; Mikkeli, *Jacopo Zabarella on the nature of the arts and sciences* (1992), 135–47. For the earlier availability of Hippocratic texts, see Kibre, *Hippocrates Latinus* (1985).

[15] Maclean, *Learned medicine*, 70–1.

[16] There is a full discussion, with many of the relevant Galenic *loci* identified, in von Staden, '*Haeresis* and heresy: the case of the *haireseis iatrikai*' (1982); see also the essays in van der Eijk, ed., *Ancient histories of medicine* (1999), esp. von Staden, 'Hellenistic reflections on the history of medicine'. The fragments for the Empirics are collected in K. Deichgräber, *Die griechische Empirikerschule: Sammlung der Fragmente und Darstellung der Lehre* (Berlin, 1965). For Celsus, see Temkin, 'Celsus' "On medicine" and the ancient medical sects' (1935); von Staden, 'Celsus as historian' (1999). Maclean (*Learned medicine*, 76) states that in c. 1530–1630, Celsus's 'account does not seem often to be quoted'. This situation certainly changed in the seventeenth century: a systematic study of Celsus's reception in the Renaissance is a *desideratum*. The *editio princeps* was published in Florence in 1478.

months.[17] The Empirics were the chief *bête noire* of methodological discussions, their lack of philosophical acumen presented as both intellectually shallow and dangerously irresponsible.[18] The stakes were further raised in this debate by the identification of Paracelsian physicians with the Empirics, both by opponents and sometimes even by themselves.[19]

But even more important was the development – directly caused by humanist reforms – of a sense that Rational physic had been more practical or experiential than medieval and Arabic physicians had recognised.[20] The appearance of the Greek Aldine edition of Galen in 1525, which revealed the importance of anatomy to Galenic physic,[21] and Andreas Vesalius's famous conclusion in the preface to his *De humani corporis fabrica* (1543) that Galen had dissected apes rather than humans, were perhaps the most spectacular manifestations of this shift. Vesalius developed two historical conclusions from his finding: first, that there was required a revival of the lost anatomy of the 'prisci anatomiae professores' of Alexandria; second, that for all their differences, all three medical sects had agreed on the importance of the use of the hands, and the real degeneration of physic had occurred 'after the devastation of the Goths', when 'the most fashionable physicians . . . despising the use of the hands, began to relegate to their slaves those things which had to be done manually', until 'they promptly degenerated from the earlier physicians, leaving the method of cooking and all the preparation of the patients' diet to nurses, the composition of drugs to apothecaries, and the use of the hands to barbers'.[22]

Throughout Europe, these assumptions became commonplace among both learned physicians and their critics, such as the apothecaries and barber-surgeons, who were gaining prestige and market share in the increasingly populated cities and beginning to bridle at the medical monopolies of the physicians. Medical humanism thus led to an almost universal (if contested) focus on the value of practical experience, and even to scepticism about the usefulness of causal theorising, over a century before the Royal Society apologists started making these claims systematically for natural philosophy *tout court*. The Pisan physician Giovanni Argenterio, for example, was by the mid-sixteenth century complaining that the only people who believed that medicine's position as a healing *ars* rendered its status less than that of the speculative *scientiae* were 'lazy philosophers' who 'affect[ed] to consider such

---

[17] The Methodic sect was also linked to Pyrrhonism by Sextus Empicus: *Pyrr.*, I.237.

[18] Siraisi, *Traditions*, 85.    [19] See the examples in Maclean, *Learned medicine*, 78.

[20] See e.g. the examples collected in Siraisi, *Avicenna in Renaissance Italy* (1987), 66, 70, 73–5; Siraisi, *Girolamo Cardano and Renaissance Medicine* (1997), 27–8; Maclean, *Learned medicine*, 20–1, 339–40.

[21] Durling, 'Galen' remains essential.

[22] I use the translation of Vesalius's preface offered in O'Malley, *Adreas Vesalius* (1964), 317–24, at 317–8.

activity inferior to contemplation';[23] other humanist physicians constantly insisted that ancient physicians had practised not only botany and pharmacy but many other 'practical' medical disciplines and that far from being split into specialist roles like the physician and apothecary, the ancient model had been that of the total *medicus*.[24] Moreover, the initial reception of Vesaslius, combined with the humanist tendency to return *ad fontes*, also saw a new focus on Hippocrates as a the source of a true, pre-corrupted medicine; the physician of Cos's tendency for aphoristic expression and case histories in turn intensified the reflexive awareness of a historical component to debates over medical methodology.[25] It is a central theme of this chapter that the long familiarity of the learned physicians (and their opponents) with these kinds of historical justifications for 'practical' knowledge of nature, while at the same time maintaining that that knowledge remained 'philosophical', made their defences of such knowledge much more effective than that of the Royal Society apologists.

(c) *Anti-Aristotelianism*.[26] From the thirteenth century, the use of Aristotle in the schools was challenged, first on a primarily rhetorical basis (Petrarch, Valla), but by the sixteenth century also from a systematic philosophical and deeply historically informed perspective. The subsequent debates permeated almost all philosophical discourse, but a canon of key texts can be identified: Valla's *Dialecticae disputationes* (1439);[27] books IV–VI of Gianfrancesco Pico della Mirandola's fideistic *Examen vanitatis* (1520);[28] Juan Luís Vives's *Censura de Aristotelis operibus* (1538);[29] Mario Nizolio's *De veris principiis et vera ratione philosophandi contra pseudophilosophos* (1553);[30] and, in greatest detail of all, Francesco Patrizi's *Discussiones Peripateticae* (1571).[31]

---

[23] Siraisi, 'Giovanni Argenterio and sixteenth-century medical innovation' (1990), quoting Argenterio, *In artem medicam Galeni*, in *Opera* (1592), I, 42: the work was first published in 1566, Argenterio having worked on it for twenty years by that point (Siraisi, n. 11).

[24] See the examples offered in Findlen, *Possessing nature* (1994), 246, and the discussion of this issue in Levitin, 'The Society of Apothecaries' (2015).

[25] Maclean, *Learned medicine*, 77; Nutton, 'Greek texts and Renaissance anatomists' (1988), 123–4; Nutton, 'Hippocrates in the Renaissance' (1989); Lonie, 'The "Paris Hippocratics"' (1985). For the importance of reading to mid-seventeenth-century medical training, see Frank, 'The John Ward diaries' (1974).

[26] Martin, *Subverting Aristotle* (2014) is the now the fullest treatment of this subject: it appeared very late in the process of composition of this book, and I have attempted to incorporate its conclusions as much as possible.

[27] See now most fully, Nauta, *Lorenzo Valla's humanist critique of scholastic philosophy* (2009).

[28] Schmitt, *Gianfrancesco Pico della Mirandola and his critique of Aristotle* (1967).

[29] Noreña, *Juan Luis Vives* (1970), esp. 166–73.

[30] Schmitt, *Mirandola*, 161–3; Breen, 'Introduction' (1955).

[31] The best treatments on Patrizi's anti-Aristotelianism, and his attitude to the history of philosophy more generally, are Wilmott, 'Francesco Patrizi da Cherso's humanist critique of Aristotle' (1984); Deitz, 'Francesco Patrizi da Cherso's criticism of Aristotle's logic' (2007); Deitz, 'A sixteenth-century critic of Aristotle—Francesco Patrizi da Cherso on privation, form, and matter' (1997), esp. 228–9; Vasoli, *Francesco Patrizi* (1989), 149–80; Muccillo, 'La storia

Needless to say, each had its own focus and characteristics, but a set of six central and repeated themes can be identified: (1) *ad hominem* attacks on Aristotle's life and character; (2) the repeated accusation that he plagiarised what was best in his works from his predecessors and scurrilously misrepresented them in his critiques; (3) stylistic attacks, in particular the claim that in his more speculative works (*Metaphysics, Physics, De anima,* etc.) Aristotle was deliberately obscure and ambiguous;[32] (4) protracted treatments of the reception and textual uncertainty of the *Corpus Aristotelicum,* often including the claim that Aristotle's fame derived from his acquaintance with Alexander the Great, and also elaborating on the standard transmission histories in Plutarch and Strabo;[33] (5) detailed commentaries on the incompatibility of various Aristotelian doctrines with Christian theology; and (6) detailed treatments of the supposed internal inconsistencies and contradictions within Aristotle's works.

It is worth re-emphasising the historical character of these criticisms, based on extensive engagement with the Greek sources and on detailed contextual treatments of Greek philosophical culture. The anti-Aristotelian tradition generated English successors such as William Pemble's *De formarum origine* (1629), as well as the work of the Irish-based physicians Gerard and Arnold Boate, *Philosophia naturalis reformata* (1641), both of which were read and used both in English academic philosophy and by the *novatores* to the end of the century.[34] It is important to recognise that one did not have to be a concerted

---

della filosofia presocratica nelle "Discussiones peripateticae" di Francesco Patrizi da Cherso' (1975).

[32] See also Schmitt, 'Aristotle as a cuttlefish: the origin and development of an image' (1965).

[33] Plutarch, *Vit. Sul.*, 26; Strabo, *Geog.*, XIII.68. See also Cicero, *De fin.*, v.5.13; *Disp. Tusc.*, IV.5.9. The fullest discussion with which I am familiar of the mutation of the tradition is Moraux, *Der Aristotelismus bei den Griechen von Andronikos bis Alexander von Aphrodisias* (1975–84), I, 1–94.

[34] William Pemble, *De formarum origine* (London, 1629, repub. Cambridge, 1650 and Oxford, 1669) which, although it shows little historical interest, concludes (30–2), as did Patrizi, that Aristotle's confusions on 'form' meant that he could only have meant 'accident'. On Pemble, a divinity reader at Magdalene Hall, Oxford (1591/2–1623), see Greaves, 'Pemble, William', *ODNB*. For extensive later pedagogical engagement with *De formarum origine*, see Heereboord, *Meletemata philosophica*, 162–86; its conclusions are directly accepted in George Meldrum (*praeses*), *Theses philosophicae quas posuerunt adolescentes, laureæ Magisterialis candidati, in inclyta universitatis Aberdonensis* (Aberdeen, 1659), 14. It was still being read *c.* 1700: see the anonymous commonplace book containing much philosophical and theological reading, Folger MS V.b.254, where Pemble's book is listed under the heading 'Form' (189). For the Boates, see G. Boate and A. Boate, *Philosophia naturalis reformata. Id est, philosophiae Aristotelicae accurata examinatio, ac solida confutatio. Et novae ac verioris introductio* (Dublin, 1641), esp. 36–7, 93–101 for similar conclusions to Pemble on form (also drawing on Basson, e.g. at 23). There is no satisfactory work on the Boates: a few useful comments can be found in Coughlan, 'The project for a natural history of Ireland' (1994), 299–300. My colleague Michael Edwards is preparing a study of the Boates. Boyle knew Gerard Boate, who supplied him with recipes for herbal remedies in the late 1640s (see e.g. RS BP28,

anti-Aristotelian to engage with these issues. For one, they grew out of the problems encountered by Aristotelian humanists when editing the Greek texts. Second, they generated much reflection within the Aristotelian philosophical tradition: my examination of textbooks available in England leads me to disagree with the judgement of the leading Anglophone Patrizi scholar that seventeenth-century Aristotelians 'paid little heed to Patrizi's criticisms'.[35]

Particularly important for us are the two great appropriations of the humanist anti-Aristotelian literature. The first was Pierre Gassendi's *Exercitationes paradoxicae adversus Aristoteleos* (1624): Gassendi's reputation ensured a very wide readership, even if (or perhaps because) the work itself was mainly a reorganised compendium of Patrizi.[36] The second was that of Francis Bacon, in his *Advancement of learning* (1605) and especially in the *Novum Organum* (1620).[37] Bacon's vision was both closely related to the anti-Aristotelian tradition, and at the same time idiosyncratic. He approached the history of philosophy through what he called 'signs',[38] allowing him to examine Greek philosophical culture – and he deliberately identified the Greek as formative[39] – as a totality, rather than a set of disparate sects. If there was one word to capture the identity of Greek philosophers it was 'sophists' – in reality, they only differed from the orators that they so labelled in that whilst the latter travelled and collected fees, the philosophers opened schools and did not charge.[40]

p. 311 (from 'Memorialls philosophicall beginning this newyears day 1649/50')); for references to the *Philosophia naturalis reformata*, see *Usefulness of experimental natural philosophy* (1662), in *Boyle works*, III, 338. Locke considered the Boates's work 'tres bon' (Locke, 'Excerpts from Journals', in *An early draft of Locke's essay, together with excerpts from his journals*, eds., R. I. Aaron and J. Gibb (Oxford, 1936), 111, note from March 1678).

[35] Deitz, 'Patrizi's Criticism', 249. As early as 1607, a Cambridge philosophy commonplace book (CUL MS Add. 102, belonging to 'Edmundus Læus' [fol. 2$^r$]), under the heading 'An Mundus sit aeternus?' ascribes Aristotle's eternalism to his debt to the obscure Pythagorean Ocellus Lucanus, as had been done by Patrizi (see n. 379 below) (for the compiler of the commonplace book, see now Serjeantson, 'The philosophy of Francis Bacon in early Jacobean Oxford' (2013)); see also Willis, *Synopsis*, 44–5; for extensive textbook engagement with Patrizi and other anti-Aristotelians, see Wendelin, *Contemplationes physicae*, 11b–13a, 107a–9b.

[36] Pierre Gassendi, *Exercitationes paradoxicae adversus Aristoteleos* (Amsterdam, 1649 [1st edn=Grenoble, 1624]) is the edition cited throughout. See Joy, *Gassendi*, 30–7. Gassendi's debt to Patrizi was recognised by near contemporaries; see e.g. [Richard Simon], *Bibliothèque critique* (4 vols, Paris, 1708–10), IV, 100.

[37] The literature on Bacon is vast. The best treatment of his attitude to the history of philosophy remains Rossi, *Francis Bacon* (1968 [1957]). See also Gaukroger, *Bacon*, 104–18; Whitaker, 'Francesco Patrizi and Francis Bacon' (1990). In what follows I cite only those works of Bacon that were available to later seventeenth-century readers; needless to say, a full discussion of Bacon on the history of philosophy would incorporate many more texts.

[38] Rees and Wakely, 'Introduction' (2004), lvii–lxi; Fattori, '*Signum* in Francis Bacon: dal mondo del sacro al mondo degli uomini' (1999).

[39] Francis Bacon, *Novum organum* (London, 1620), aph. LXXI, 83 (=*OFB*, XI, 112): 'Scientiae, quas habemus, ferè à Graecis fluxêrunt. Quae enim Scriptores Romani, aut Arabes, aut Recentiores addiderunt; non multa, aut magni momenti sunt: & qualiacunque sint, fundata sunt super basin eorum quae inuenta sunt à Graecis'.

[40] Ibid., aph. LXXI, 83 (=*OFB*, XI, 112–14).

Drawing on the anti-Aristotelian tradition, Bacon could then portray Aristotle as the archetypal sophist.[41] The only exception were the philosophers who would, in the nineteenth century, gain the name 'presocratics': Empedocles, Anaxagoras, Leucippus, Parmenides, Heraclitus, Xenophanes, Philolaus, and above all Democritus, who 'did not open schools (as far as we know); but directed themselves to the search for truth more quietly, seriously and simply- that is, with less affectation and ostentation';[42] unfortunately, these were quickly 'corrupted and rendered useless by arguments and the ambition to novelty'.[43] Bacon's argument was quickly summarised by an early admirer in the 1620s: 'the *Grecians*, and among them *Aristotle*' had been 'very defective in the *historicall* part' of natural philosophy; in the speculative, meanwhile, 'both himselfe & his followers seeme to referre it rather to *profession* & disputation . . . then use & practice'. At this point the Baconian solution seemed clear: 'to mixe and temper practice & speculation together'.[44] But what, in reality, did that mean? By the 1660s, the answer had become rather confused, and the attempts to build on Bacon's vision of the history of philosophy, and especially to delineate a specifically Greek 'speculative' phase, came under severe strain, as we shall see.

(D) *The chymical tradition.* While it may have derived in part from Patrizi,[45] Bacon's praise for the presocratics probably also owed a debt to another 'anti- establishment' tradition: that of the post-Paracelsus chymists. In Chapter 3, we have already met the illuminationist Hermeticism of Paracelsus and some of his followers, drawing less on the *Hermetica*, and more on alchemical treatises of Arabic origin attributed to Hermes, such as the *Tabula Smaragdina*, still being analysed by Newton at the end of our period.[46] Paracelsus combined this focus with elements of humanist anti-Aristotelianism and illuminationism to arrive at

---

[41] Ibid., aph. LXIII, 72–3 (=*OFB*, XI, 98–9); aph. LXXVII, 89–90 (=*OFB*, XI, 120); Bacon, *Advancement*, 29–30 (=*OFB*, IV, 86).

[42] Bacon, *Novum organum*, aph. LXXI, 83–4 (=*OFB*, XI, 114): 'Antiquiores illi ex Graecis, Empedocles, Anaxagoras, Leucippus, Democritus, Parmenides, Heraclitus, Xenophanes, Philolaus, reliqui -scholas, quod novimus, non aperuerunt: sed maiore silentio & severiùs, & simpliciùs, id est, minore cum affectatione & ostentatione, ad inquisitionem veritatis se contulerunt'.

[43] Ibid., aph. LXXIX, 93 (=*OFB*, XI, 124–6): 'At ipsissima illa periodus temporis, in quâ inquisi- tiones de Naturâ viguerunt, contradictionibus & novorum placitorum ambitione corrupta est, & inutilis reddita'. The best discussion of this complex subject remains Rees, 'Atomism and "subtlety" in Francis Bacon's philosophy' (1980).

[44] George Hakewill, *An apologie of the power and providence of God in the government of the world* (Oxford, 1627), 246. See esp. Poole, 'The evolution of George Hakewill's *Apologie*' (2010).

[45] As suggested in Ligota and Quantin, 'Introduction', 19, n. 97.

[46] Dobbs, 'Newton's *Commentary* on *The Emerald Tablet*' (1988). The *editio princeps* was contained in *De alchemia* (Nuremberg, 1541), and was frequently reprinted thereafter. For its use in seventeenth-century England, see also Hessayon, *Gold tried in the fire* (2007), 273–4, 277, 344; Schuler, 'Some spiritual alchemies of seventeenth-century England' (1980), 313–16.

a regressive history of philosophy: 'The sciences had made a promising start among the sages of the east, ending with Hippocrates, who were truly pious men, being rewarded with great mysteries and *magnalia*; but Plato and Aristotle fell under a dark cloud, their imitators in subsequent times achieving rhetorical effect without the backing of substance'.[47] Paracelsus was as much a medical as a philosophical reformer and he combined his methodological critique with a doctrinal one: Galen's self-serving sophistry led him to develop the entirely imaginary theory of humours.[48]

This tradition was elaborated, often either by the positing of a further 'pious' heritage for chymistry (e.g. in England in Richard Bostocke's *Of the ancient and later phisicke* (1585))[49] or through the use of the Bible as a source, such as the reference to Tubal-cain as 'instructer of every artificer in brass and iron' (Gen. 4.22), accepted even by serious academic philosophers who were not particularly sympathetic to Paracelsianism, such as Daniel Sennert.[50] Meanwhile, the idea that Empiric medicine had its origins in ancient Egypt, while controversial, had serious scholarly support, such as Prospero Alpino's *De medicina Aegyptiorum* (1591), unsurprising given the ancient authority for such a claim.[51]

Even more important was the philosophical and medical 'sanitisation' of Paracelsus after his translation into Latin and publication in the 1560s and 1570s: the main figures here are Petrus Severinus, Gerhard Dorn, Joseph du Chesne (Quercetanus), and Johannes Albertus Wimpenaeus.[52] In contrast to Paracelsus himself, they attempted to render Paracelsian chymistry more philosophical by placing it within a full physical system; this involved writing a pre-history of such a system, the best and most influential example of which is the chapter on 'De ortu & progressu artis medicae, medicorumque diversis

---

[47] Webster, *From Paracelsus to Newton* (1982), 52. See also Pagel, *Paracelsus* (1982), 58–9. The fullest account of chymical historiography is still the very valuable study by R. Halleux, 'La controverse sur les origines de la chimie, de Paracelse à Borrichius' (1980).

[48] Pagel, *Paracelsus*, 129–32.

[49] R[ichard] B[ostocke], *The difference between the auncient phisicke, first taught by the godly forefathers ... and the latter phisicke proceeding from idolaters, ethnickes, and heathen* (London, 1585), obviously stimulated by a Reformed theological agenda; see Debus, 'An Elizabethan history of medical chemistry' (1964).

[50] See e.g. Daniel Sennert, *De Chymicorum cum Aristotelicis et Galenicis consensu ac dissensu* (Paris, 1633), 39–40

[51] Siraisi, 'Origins', at 237–41, 245–7 (on Alpino, who was stimulated by his own visit to Egypt in 1581–84), and 241–2 on the classical sources (she lists those collected in Polydore Vergil, *De inventoribus rerum*, I.20, most importantly Clemens Alexandrinus, *Strom.*, VI.4 and Diodorus Siculus (which must be *Bib. hist.*, I.82.1–3), as well as Galen, *Int.* (K XIV.674–6); but neglects the most important: Herodotus, II.84).

[52] On the development of Paracelsianism, see Debus, *The French Paracelsians* (1991); Debus, *The English Paracelsians* (1965) and Grell, ed., *Paracelsus: the man and his reputation* (1998), esp. the ch. by S. Pumfrey.

sectis' which begins Severinus's *Idea medicinae philosophicae* (1571).[53] Severinus offered a conjectural history of medicine. It began as a collaborative learning from observation in response to the needs of daily life. Hippocrates inherited this observational medicine; after him it degenerated into sectarianism; Galen was able to rescue it from this sectarianism but only by modelling it on geometry and reducing it to 'principles and axioms' – from this move emerged the doctrines of the balance of the four elements, the four qualities, and humoral pathology.[54] It is probably from Severinus that Bacon adopted the image of a natural historical Hippocrates, the 'discontinuance' of whose 'auncient and serious diligence' was a chief cause of the 'deficiences' of medicine.[55]

Other chymical theorists attempted to align their discipline with presocratic philosophy.[56] Perhaps most important here was the figure of Democritus the dissecting naturalist, derived not from the traditional sources (themselves sparse and fragmentary) but from two unconnected pseudographia: (1) the *Epistola ad Damagetum*, a pseudo-Hippocratean forgery that reports on Hippocrates coming across the supposedly insane Democritus in a forest only for it to emerge that Democritus is practising comparative anatomy, which Hippocrates then proceeds to learn from the Abderite; and (2) the *Physica et mystica*, which presents Democritus as a patron of Egyptian alchemists. Together, they allowed many early modern chymists and chymical physicians to present an image of a Democritus who followed 'an experimental approach to resolution that involved microscopical anatomy, chemical analysis, and mechanistic model-building'.[57] This, for example, is the exact image offered by the influential chymical physician Andreas Libavius.[58] The extent to which these *spuria* were accepted not just by natural philosophers but also by early modern scholars is remarkable; I know of only one explicit repudiation of the authenticity of the *Epistola ad Damagetum* before the middle of the seventeenth century, by the Bolognese anatomist Joan Baptista Cortesius in 1625;

---

[53] Severinus's philosophical transformation of Paracelsus is the theme of Shackelford, *Severinus*, esp. 143–210, and 250–85 for the British reception.

[54] My account combines Petrus Severinus, *Idea medicinae philosophicae* (Basle, 1571), Dedicatory Epistle to Frederick II (conjectural history of medicine) and 1–8 (the history of medicine proper). For a fuller treatment, see Shackelford, *Severinus*, 143–59.

[55] Bacon, *Advancement*, 88 (=*OFB*, IV, 99). See Smith, *The Hippocratic tradition* (1979), 18.

[56] Joly, 'Les references à la philosophie antique dans les débats sur l'alchimie au début du XVIIe siècle' (1995). The most popular example might be Joseph Quercetanus, *Liber de priscorum philosophorum verae medicinae materia* (Geneva, 1603), an English translation (not entirely reliable) of which was produced very quickly: *The practise of chymicall, and hermeticall physicke*, trans. T. Timme (London, 1605); see also his *Ad veritatem Hermeticae medicinae ex Hippocratis veterumque decretis ac therapeusi* (Paris, 1604); for the context, see Debus, *French Paracelsians*, 53–7.

[57] See the brilliant account in Lüthy, 'Democritus' (the quotation is from 470). That Democritus was the teacher of Hippocrates is also asserted in Celsus, *De medicina*, Prooem., 7–8.

[58] See the quotation from his *Rerum chymicarum epistolica forma* (1595), 157, in Newman, *Atoms and alchemy*, 73, and the discussion in Lüthy, 'Democritus', 475–7.

Stanley translated the whole text in his *History*.[59] It was this Democritean *persona* that was inherited by Bacon; we shall find it deployed repeatedly in English methodological debates.[60]

The Vesalian narrative of Galen's corruption of Hippocratic method and subsequent introduction of humoral doctrine was very influentially repeated and expanded by J. B. van Helmont in his *Ortus medicinae*, posthumously published in 1648. As well as the quasi-Baconian attacks on logic and Greek speculativeness,[61] van Helmont offered a fuller narrative: the exiled Adam encouraged his sons to investigate nature for the improvement of life, giving birth to agriculture – 'the first philosophy'; as their descendants grew more proficient at preventing natural ills they invented astrology, but when Hippocrates began recording his observations, ambition crept into the discipline, finding its apogee in the figure of Galen, whose hubristic desire to establish 'first qualities' led to the invention of the doctrine of the elements and their constant battle.[62] But the same year that Helmont's work was published also saw the appearance of the very learned attack on the antiquity of chymistry by Conring that we already met in Chapter 3. However, even Conring's scholarship was challenged, in learned works published in 1668 and 1674 by the prominent Danish professor of philology and natural

---

[59] Stanley, *History*, 456–60; for an eighteenth-century edition, see *The laughing philosopher. Being a letter from Hippocrates the physician to his friend Damagetus, concerning the madness of Democritus* (London, 1736). For Cortesius: Joan Baptista Cortesius, *Miscellaneorum medicinalium decades denae* (Messina, 1625), 9–10. Cortesius based his argument on the fact that even though Laërtius does mention a meeting between Hippocrates and Democritus (IX.42), chronology dictated that by the time of the meeting, Democritus would have been 'decrepit, and no longer fit for dissection' ('quo tempore iam Democritus erat decrepitus, nec amplius aptus sectioni cadaverum') (Cortesius assumed birthdates of 492 BC [Democritus] and 436 BC [Hippocrates]). Cortesius is not mentioned by Lüthy, but he does report on the doubts of Scaliger ('Democritus', 463, n. 49), and also on the widespread scepticism about the *Physica et mystica*. The only useful discussion of Cortesius's biography that I know of is in Gurlt, *Geschichte der Chirurgie und ihrer Ausübung* (1898), II, 553–8.

[60] The translation of continental works also propagated these stories in England: see e.g. Simeon Partliz, *A new method of physick: or, a short view of Paracelsus and Galen's practice*, trans. N. Culpeper (London, 1654), 14–15, 17, 18–19, 31–7 (a trans. of *Medici systematis harmonici* (Frankfurt, 1625)).

[61] Jan Baptist van Helmont, *Ortus medicinae* (Amsterdam, 1648), 7–8; 45–50. See also the Baconian attack on 'logica inutilis' at 41–5. See Pagel, *Joan Baptista van Helmont* (1982), 20, 36–43; Debus, *The chemical philosophy* (1977), II, 312–14; Browne, 'J. B. van Helmont's attack on Aristotle' (1979). The *Ortus medicinae* was translated into English, relatively reliably, as *Oriatrike or, physick refined* (London, 1662). On Helmont in England, see Clericuzio, 'A study of the transmission of Helmontian chemical and medical theories in seventeenth-century England' (1993). He was certainly being discussed in mainstream medical tuition by the mid-1650s: see BL MS Sloane 3309, fol. 64ʳ (a medical thesis discussed under the tuition of Francis Glisson on 7 June 1656). See also 5.4 below. While most condemned Galen for applying Aristotelianism to medicine, the Boates emphasised the differences between him and the Stagirite: *Philosophia naturalis reformata*, 192–4.

[62] Van Helmont, *Ortus medicinae*, 164–8. This history of medical theory had the obvious defect of not accommodating a critique of the influence on medicine of Aristotelian natural philosophy.

philosopher Olaus Borrichius.[63] These works generated great interest in England, receiving wide readership and long reviews in the *Philosophical Transactions*;[64] as we shall see they were repeatedly invoked in English debates about natural philosophical method.

## 4.2    Historicising natural philosophy's break from metaphysics

The sixteenth and early seventeenth centuries witnessed much debate among academic philosophers about the proper relationship of the various philosophical disciplines, and – since so much of philosophy was being practised in an Aristotelian framework – about the relationship of Aristotle's various philosophical books. A key issue was the place of metaphysics. This was a debate that had its origins, at least to some extent, in Aristotle himself, for in the *Metaphysics* he offered two definitions of πρώτη φιλοσοφία (first philosophy): (A) that it is a science which studies 'being *qua* being' (ὂν ᾗ ὂν [*Met.* IV, 1003ᵃ21]), or a science of universal principles; (B) that it is 'theology' (θεολογική [*Met.* VI, 1026ᵃ19–20]), or the science of eternal causes and immutable and immaterial entities. With the development of Reformed scholasticism from the middle of the sixteenth century, the simultaneous rise of Jesuit metaphysics, and the growing theological pressure of both inter- and intra-confessional disputes, the debate became ever more complex, but with a general tendency for the neo-Scotists (especially important representatives included Francisco Suárez and his Lutheran adapter, Christoph Scheibler) to adopt the former definition, while those following one of Suárez's Jesuit counterparts, Benedict Pereira, postulated that 'metaphysics proper' had as its subject only God and immaterial being, and thus equated it with *theologica naturalis*.[65] As always there were important exceptions, including in English

---

[63] Olaus Borrichius, *De ortu, et progressu chemiae dissertatio* (Copenhagen, 1668), much expanded in Borrichius, *Hermetis Aegyptiorum et chemicorum sapientia ab Hermanni Conringi animadversionibus vindicata* (Copenhagen, 1674). For Borrichius's biography, see Schepelern, 'Introduction' (1983).

[64] [Henry Oldenburg], 'An account of some books', *Philosophical Transactions*, 3 (1668), 779–88 and 19 (1675), 296–301 (both reviewing Borrichius). Borrichius was also reviewed in the *Journal des Sçavans*, 3 (1675), 209–11, which is where Locke learnt about his work (Bod. MS Locke, f. 15 [Memorandum book, 1677–78], p. 48). Locke also recorded Henry Stubbe's judgement that Borrichius was 'Learned & inquisitive' and noted works on the consent of chymistry with Arisotle and Galen by Gregorius Martinius and on Egyptian chymistry by Johann Becher (i.e. *Oedipus chymicus* (Amsterdam, 1664)) (Bod. MS Locke, d. 11 'Lemma Physica', fols. 9ᵛ, 13ᵛ, 14ᵛ; another note on Borrichius is Bod. MS Locke. c. 42A [Medical and scientific commonplace book, 1679–94], p. 140). John Beale wrote to Oldenburg on 12 October 1668 suggesting Borrichius be translated (*Oldenburg correspondence*, IV, 81).

[65] Lohr, 'Metaphysics' (1988), at 605–38; Leijenhorst, *Mechanisation*, 17–27, esp. 22–7. For a widely circulated contemporary British discussion of the whole issue, see Robert Baron, *Metaphysica generalis* (London, 1658), 5–8. Baron (1593–1648) was a philosophy professor

pedagogy.[66] Bacon drew on the second tradition when he criticised Aristotle and Plato for mixing the metaphysical (i.e. understood as 'natural theological') study of final causes with natural philosophy.[67] The echoes of this debate resonated among three of the most prominent English *novatores*: Thomas Hobbes, Kenelm Digby, and Thomas More.

Hobbes, who needs little introduction,[68] engaged with this issue in depth; we can summarise his position briefly because it has already been excellently treated by Cees Leijenhorst.[69] Hobbes is of course famous for his attacks on Aristotle and his followers[70] but on this issue he presented himself as reviving the true, uncorrupted Aristotle. His position was broadly consistent between the early draft of *De Corpore* (MS Chatsworth A 10 [early-mid 1640s?], the *Anti-White* (*c.* 1643), *Leviathan* (1651), *De Corpore* itself (1655), and the *Six lessons* (1656).[71] His main case was twofold: (A) the contents of Aristotle's *Metaphysics* were *philosophia prima*, contrary to scholastic corruption of it into something theological or transphysical; and (B) Aristotle's *philosophia prima* was contained both in the *Physics* and the *Metaphysics*, because it was equivalent to *physica generalis*, the first part of natural philosophy.[72] The

---

at St. Andrews and Aberdeen, with clear Calvinist preferences (see e.g., ibid., 305). The work was popular, with printings in 1657, 1658, and 1660 and a Cambridge printing as late as 1685; it was being read by Calvinist divines into the eighteenth century (see e.g. the notebook of the Dissenting minister John Rastrick, Folger MS V.a.472, fol. 62$^v$). Wendelin, *Contemplationes physicae*, 2a, is as always interesting, claming that the Stoics divided 'physics' into three: metaphysics, physics '*in specie*', and mathematics; his source is a very unorthodox reading of Cicero, *De fin.*, IV.2.4. For a late example of the Scotist reading in English pedagogy, see Andreas Frommenius, *Synopsis metaphysica*, ed. Peter Claussen (Oxford, 1669, repr. 1691), 1, citing Suárez, Scheibler, and others.

[66] See the very popular textbook by Thomas Barlow, *Exercitationes aliquot metaphysicae, de Deo: quod sit objectum metaphysicae* (Oxford, 1658 [1st edn=1637]), who, despite his use of Scheibler, concludes (101): 'Sed hoc manifestius patet ex Aristotele, qui *lib. 6. Metaphys. cap.* I. & II. *Metaphys. cap.*6. appellat Metaphysicam θεολογία φυσική Theologiam naturalem ... '. For metaphysics in the curriculum more generally, see Costello, *Scholastic curriculum*, 71–80. See also Hatfield, 'Metaphysics and the new science' (1990).

[67] Bacon, *Advancement*, 29–30 (=*OFB*, IV, 86). See Kusukawa, 'Bacon's classification of knowledge' (1996), at 56–8.

[68] Malcolm, *Aspects*, 1–26 ('A summary biography of Hobbes').

[69] Leijenhorst, *Hobbes*, 17–55, on which I draw freely for the below. See also Sorell, 'Hobbes and Aristotle' (1999).

[70] See 6.4 below.

[71] I use Thomas Hobbes, *Critique du De mundo de Thomas White*, eds., J. Jacquot and H. W. Jones (Paris, 1973); Hobbes, *Elementorum philosophiae sectio prima de corpore* (London, 1655); Hobbes, *Six lessons to the professors of the mathematiques* (London, 1656). For *Leviathan*, I give references to the 1651 London edition and the 1668 Amsterdam edition of the Latin, followed by the equivalent passage in Malcolm. Unlike Prof. Leijenhorst, I do not consider the *Short tract* Hobbesian (on the authority of Malcolm, *Aspects*, 80–145 ('Robert Payne, the Hobbes manuscripts, and the "Short tract"') and Raylor, 'Hobbes, Payne, and a Short tract on first principles' (2001)) – it does not affect the issues at stake here.

[72] MS Chatsworth A 10, in *Critique du De Mundo*, 486; *Critique*, 169–71; *Leviathan*, 371 (=Malcolm, III, 1076); *Six lessons*, 14–15. This discussion is removed from the Latin *Leviathan*. Leijenhorst adds a third dimension: 'with respect to its method *philosophia prima*

difference between the principles of natural philosophy and metaphysics is therefore entirely eroded: both are the study of the principles of physical bodies.

Hobbes buttressed this with a philological point: the title τῶν μετὰ τὰ φυσικὰ was either used by Aristotle because he wrote these books after the *Physics*, or, 'as the majority of most learned think', it was assigned by his later followers.[73] This kind of philological–historical speculation on the naming of the *Metaphysics* had its Renaissance *locus classicus* in Patrizi's *Discussiones Peripateticae*. Pointing out that the first mentions of μετὰ τὰ φυσικὰ were found only in Nicolaus of Damascus (second half of the first century BC) and after him Plutarch, Patrizi suggested that the name came from Aristotle's first century BC editor, Andronicus of Rhodes.[74] It has been persuasively suggested that Patrizi was one of Hobbes's 'most learned' sources, along with Samuel Petit (uncle of Hobbes's close friend Samuel Sorbière) whose *Miscellanea* (1630) included similar historical speculations.[75] Gassendi's *Exercitationes* also contains traces of this polemic but since the relevant philological discussion only appears in his *Syntagma* (1658) we can probably discount it as a direct source at this point.[76]

Hobbes himself was probably less concerned with these issues than with the assault it allowed him to make upon what he claimed was the absurd essentialism of scholastic philosophy. It was the error specifically of metaphysicians (i.e. those with a corrupt understanding of what Aristotle's metaphysics was) to abstract essences from the copula 'is', and subsequently to reify accidents.[77] In short, the history of metaphysics revealed it either as a source of essentialist error (i.e. in its corrupt scholastic version) or as a *philosophia prima* that was

proceeds by means of definitions of basic philosophical terms' (*Hobbes*, 17, 37–55), but we shall not consider this here.

[73] Hobbes, *Critique*, 170: 'Contigit autem libros illos de philosophia prima, hoc est de philosophiae elementis, inscribi τῶν μετὰ τὰ φυσικὰ, vel ab ipso, quòd ab eo scripti fuerint tempore posteriùs quàm libri eius physici, vel quod doctissimorum plerique censent, à successoribus eius, qui eos libros inventos sine inscriptione, eo ordine in operibus eius disposuerunt, ut libros physicos sequerentur'; *Leviathan*, 371 (=Malcolm, III, 1076).

[74] Francesco Patrizi, *Discussiones Peripateticae*, 62. Patrizi and the philological–historical discussion of the *Metaphysics* is very usefully introduced in Reiner, 'Die Entstehung der Lehre vom bibliothekarischen Ursprung des Namens Metaphysik' (1955), 79–80. Patrizi did not give a source, but must have been adopting a liberal interpretation of Porphyry, *Vit. Plot.*, 24.

[75] Leijenhorst, *Hobbes*, 21–2.

[76] Gassendi, *Excercitationes*, 126, 154–5; *Syntagma philosophicum*, in *Opera omnia* (6 vols, Lyon, 1658), I, 133–4 (the similarities between the latter and Hobbes are discussed at Leijenhorst, *Hobbes*, 37).

[77] Hobbes, *De corpore*, 20–2; *Leviathan*, 372–3 (=Malcolm, III, 1078–82) (Hobbes here seems to attribute the error more to Aristotle than to his mistaken followers, suggesting that Aristotle's essentialism may have been an accommodation to pagan religion); *Latin Leviathan*, 319–21 (=Malcolm, III, 1075–91). In the very early notes for *De corpore*, 'De principiis', Hobbes absolved Aristotle of the error of reifying accidents: printed in *Critique*, 449–60 ('Aristotle's definition (Accidens inest in subjecto non tanquam pars sic tamen ut sine subjecti interitu abesse potest) is right' (453)).

only an investigation of the basic concepts of natural philosophy (i.e. in its 'true' Aristotelian version). Under no circumstance must metaphysics understood as natural theology be allowed to intrude into natural philosophy. This was a point that had already been made by more naturalistically inclined Renaissance Aristotelians such as Jacopo Zabarella.[78]

Before any of Hobbes's sentiments on this issue had appeared in print, it had already been addressed by another leading English *novator*, Hobbes's friend Kenelm Digby.[79] Digby's *Two treatises ... [on] the nature of bodies [and] the nature of mans soule* (1644) was immediately acknowledged as a key text of the new philosophy.[80] Although it is well known that Digby was a leading late Aristotelian (if an idiosyncratic one, especially in his matter theory), existing studies have treated his attitude to Aristotle and the history of Aristotelianism in a rather unsatisfactory way; it is thus worth examining in some detail.

Digby presented himself as returning to Aristotle's true and uncorrupted doctrine.[81] The confusion over this doctrine had stemmed, according to Digby, primarily from the erroneous conflation of Aristotle's physics with his metaphysics and logic. The doctrines of prime matter, forms, and privations were all accretions from Aristotle's metaphysics, which were 'to be sett apart, as higher principles, and of an other straine, then neede be made use of for the actuall composition of compounded thinges, and for the resolution of them into their material ingredients, or to cause their particular motions'.[82] It was the great

---

[78] E.g. Jacopo Zabarella, *De naturalis scientiae constitutione* (Venice, 1586), 42–3 (compare with Hobbes, *De corpore*, 6–7). For Zabarella, see Jardine, 'Keeping order in the school of Padua' (1997), 195.

[79] For the extent of our knowledge about Digby's early relations with Hobbes, see Malcolm, 'Biographical register', in *Hobbes correspondence*, II, 829–30. Digby may have been aware of Hobbes's thoughts on Aristotle when he was writing the *Two treatises*, for he had read Hobbes's 'Logike' (Digby to Hobbes, 17 Jan 1637, *Hobbes correspondence*, I, 42–3; Malcolm suggests that this was 'probably an early version of the first part of *De corpore*; possibly to be identified with the notes 'De principiis' (see n. 77 above)). Digby himself remains understudied: while far from complete, by far the best intellectual biographical treatment is Foster, 'Sir Kenelm Digby as man of religion and thinker' (1988), in all things preferable to Petersson, *Sir Kenelm Digby* (1956). On his self-avowedly 'Aristotelian' atomism, see 5.3 below.

[80] See e.g. Isaac Barrow's M.A. oration (1652), 'Cartesiana hypothesis de materia et motu haud satisfacit praecipuis naturae phaenomenis', in *The theologial works of Isaac Barrow, D.D.*, ed. A. Napier (9 vols, Cambridge, 1859), IX, 79–104, at 80–1; also Walter Needham to Richard Busby, 1655, BL MS Add. 4293, fol. 85$^r$ (' ... the three new systemes, y$^t$ have most prevailed in this last age, I meane, Chartes, Gassendus & Digby'); Payne, 'Sir Charles Scarburgh's Harveian Oration, 1662' (1957), 163.

[81] As well as the frequent claims in the *Two treatises*, see his advice about the seriousness required when reading philosophy: Digby to ?, n.d., BL MS Harl. 4153, fols. 39$^{r-v}$: 'Lucian and Rabelais may be slightly and cursorily runne over after dinner, to laugh out the digestion of a fulle meale; whilst Plato & Aristotle require to be read fasting, and perused devoutly, and every expression reverently turned on every side; so to conceive the weight and true force of it'.

[82] Kenelm Digby, *Two treatises, in the one of which, the nature of bodies; in the other, the nature of mans soule; is looked into: in way of discovery, of the immortality of reasonable soules* (Paris, 1644), 344. The work was reprinted in London in 1658, 1665, and 1669.

fault of the 'latter sectatours, or rather pretenders of Aristotle' to confuse logical categories such as 'qualities' for some 'reall positive entity or thing, separated (in its owne nature) from the maine thing or substance in which it was'.[83] Aristotle himself, after all, had separated the predicate of quality from that of substance or quantity (*Categories*, $1^b25$); what the understanding reifies as heat is in fact nothing other than the substance of the fire itself, or a 'continuall streame of partes issuing out of the maine stocke of the same fire'.[84] Our questions are straightforward: (i) why did Digby resort to Aristotle's authority at all? (ii) why did he historicise Aristotle in this manner?

The answer to the first of these questions has traditionally been taken as equally straightforward: Digby was an Aristotelian because he was a Roman Catholic. Digby's aim was to 'provide philosophical underpinning for the Catholic doctrine of the *natural* immortality of the soul', and his use of Aristotle derived from the fact that for him, 'Aristotelianism was one of the traditions of the Catholic Church'.[85] I would like to offer a different reading. Digby's previously wavering Catholicism had led him to a serious course of patristic study[86] – study which was very unlikely to convince him that Aristotelianism was an unchanging part of Catholic tradition (indeed, the closest person to asserting something like this was the arch anti-Catholic Hobbes – see 6.4 below). Moreover, both Catholics *and* Protestants usually insisted that the natural immortality of the soul was to be treated as the last part of natural philosophy.[87]

Digby's reading of Aristotle is better understood in the context of the long-term, cross-confessional debate within late Aristotelianism about the correct method for proving the soul's natural immortality in the wake of Pietro Pomponazzi's well-known attack on philosophy's ability to offer such proofs. According to Pomponazzi, Aristotle maintained that the doctrine is to be studied as part of physics, and as physics deals only with bodies, it is impossible

---

[83] Ibid., 344. See further 345–6, the summary at the start of Book II (350–1), and 70: 'For Aristotle and S$^t$ Thomas, and their intelligent commentators, declaring the notion of *Quality*; tell us that *to be a Quality* is nothing else but to be the determination or modification of the thing whose quality it is'. For an anti-Digby defence of the claim that for Aristotle, '*accidents* are *reall entities*', see Alexander Ross, *The philosophical touch-stone: or observations upon Sir Kenelm Digbie's discourses* (London, 1645), 5–6.

[84] Digby, *Two Treatises*, 72–3.

[85] These are the conclusions in the important and valuable studies by John Henry: 'Sir Kenelm Digby, recusant philosopher' (2010), 43–4, 51, and 'Atomism and eschatology' (1982), 233. It should be added that I do not deny that some of Digby's secondary conclusions about the nature of the post-mortem soul may have fed into his Catholicism; but this did not impact on the overall philosophical project of the *Two treatises*.

[86] *Letters between the Lord George Digby, and Sir Kenelm Digby knight concerning religion* (London, 1651); Foster, 'Digby', 48–9; Quantin, *Antiquity*, 240.

[87] The fullest introduction can be found in Serjeantson, 'The soul' (2011).

to prove the soul's immortality on Aristotelian terms.[88] The challenge of responding to Pomponazzi generated two methodological solutions. One was pioneered by Crisostomo Javelli, who in his *Tractatus de animae humanae indeficientia* (1536) argued that the immortality of the soul is a position rationally demonstrable not in physics but in metaphysics.[89] Variants of this approach were widely adopted, for example in the much-read Aristotle commentaries produced by the Jesuits at Coimbra (1592–98), which, rather than discuss the rational soul's immortality as part of the commentary on Aristotle's *De anima*, treated it separately in an appended *Tractatus de anima separata*, where it was explained that Aristotle did not treat the separate soul in his text, and that 'discussion of the soul considered as separate from the body belongs more properly to *metaphysica* than to *physiologia*'.[90] An alternative position, adopted by Franciscus Toletus and most influentially by Francisco Suárez, explicitly rejected this view and again sought proofs of the rational soul's immortality in Aristotelian physics.[91]

Digby's attack on 'metaphysical' intrusions into a physical treatment of the soul can be understood as a late contribution to this debate. This is made clear at the beginning of the preface to the whole work, when, responding to the hypothetical 'objection' of 'why I should spend so much time in the consideration of bodies' (i.e. when writing on the soul, an immaterial substance), he responded that he was following in the footsteps of Aristotle but rejecting 'a current of doctrine that at this day, much raigneth in the Christian Schooles, where bodies and their operations, are explicated after the manner of spirituall thinges'. Such explications depended on analysing the qualities of substances as if they were separate entities: the error imported from logic that we have already found Digby castigating.[92] In reality, Aristotle's metaphysics was simply 'the science above physics ... [and so must] declare the principles of Physickes'.[93] In other words, Digby had reached the same conclusion as Hobbes, albeit for different reasons.

Digby had interjected into the late Aristotelian debate over whether the immortality of the human soul was to be discussed in physics or in metaphysics

---

[88] See e.g. Pietro Pomponazzi, *Tractatus de immortalitate animae* (Bologna, 1516), VIII, 'Cum Aristoteles tam diligens naturae per scrutator in poesi in Rhetoricis & in multis aliis fuerit tam diligens & in re tam excellenti negligens'. The secondary literature is large: for a start, see Kristeller, *Aristotelismo e sincretismo nel pensiero di Pietro Pomponazzi* (1983); Kessler, 'The intellective soul' (1988).

[89] Lohr, 'The sixteenth-century transformation of the Aristotelian natural philosophy' (1988), 90–1; Lohr, 'Metaphysics', 604–5.

[90] See the very informative discussion in Fowler, *Descartes on the human soul* (1999), 195.

[91] Ibid., 195–7.

[92] Digby, *Two treatises*, 'Preface', sig. [iiiij]$^{r-v}$. That Digby was reading the late scholastics in the late 1630s is confirmed by the letter to Père Hilaire, Lector of Theology at the Carmelites, Tours, 8 Jan 1638, BL MS Harl. 4153, fols. 91$^{r-v}$.

[93] Digby, *Two treatises*, 24. See also Digby to ?, n.d., BL MS Harl. 4153, fols. 65$^{v}$–66$^{r}$.

by claiming that he was reviving the 'true' Aristotelian approach that worked from physics outwards to prove the soul's immortality. We might further speculate on the relationship of this approach to Digby's attitude to Descartes, although this is complicated by the primitive state of our knowledge about the composition of the *Two treatises* and the development of Digby's thought.[94] Following those scholastics who confined the study of the rational soul to metaphysics, Descartes confined it to his *prima philosophia*.[95] Marin Mersenne, upon receiving the manuscript of the *Meditationes* in late 1640, had been particularly perturbed by Descartes's failure to treat the immortality of the soul as part of natural philosophy, writing to Descartes on the subject and then repeating his criticisms in the *Objections* which appeared with the published version of the *Meditationes* (1641).[96] Digby, an early and careful reader and critic of Descartes, and a member of the Mersenne circle, may well have held similar sentiments.[97]

We can be more sure that Digby's view of the history of philosophy was constructed as a late response to the Pomponazzi question, which Digby again saw as an outgrowth of older tendencies in the history of philosophy. He wanted

---

[94] The standard position is that Digby wrote the *Two treatises* (or at least the part 'on body') while in prison between November 1642 and July 1643 (see e.g. Malcolm, 'Biographical Register', 830). Foster suggests a very early date for the writing of 'On souls', claiming that it 'was largely written' during Digby's period at Gresham College (1633–5) ('Digby', 45, 104). His evidence is (a) the rather inconclusive claim that it 'shows preoccupation with Venetia's death' (Digby's wife, Venetia, had died on 1 May 1633, causing his spiritual reawakening); and (b) a letter to George Hakewill of 13 May 1635 (BL MS Harl. 4153 fols. 6$^r$–13$^v$ [printed in Gabrieli, *Sir Kenelm Digby, un inglese italianato nell'età della controriforma* (1957), 278–83]), in which, as part of a challenge to Hakewill's argument that 'naturally [i.e. not by God's will] the worlde decayeth not, nor groweth old and towards an end', Digby argued that 'Out of a PHYLOSOPHICALL consideration of the naturall operations of a humane soule, one may peradventure by undeniable reason conclude the immortality of it' (fols. 7$^v$–8$^r$). But, as this suggests, the debate was not, as Foster thinks, about the immortality of the soul *per se*, but about the naturalness of the Conflagration (for Hakewill, see now Poole, 'Hakewill', esp. 9 on Hakewill and Digby). Of more direct relevance to the argument of the *Two treatises* is BL MS Harl. 4153, fols. 14$^r$–18$^r$, a discussion of the nature of the soul – unfortunately it is undated. Given the evidence of the correspondence with Mersenne (see below), it seems safer to say that 'On soul' was begun *c.* 1640.

[95] Fowler, *Descartes on the soul*, 200.  [96] Ibid., 187–92 collects all the evidence.

[97] For Digby's relationship with Descartes and Mersenne, see Foster, 'Digby', 50–2 (suggesting that Hobbes introduced Digby to Mersenne); Malcolm, 'Biographical register', 828–32 is more sceptical. That Digby's work was written with Cartesian ideas (e.g. animal reasoning) in mind seems clear from the letter to Mersenne written during its composition, 14 Feb 1640, *Mersenne correspondence*, IX, 120: 'pour exactement traitter cette affaire, il faut monstrer à l'oeil comment toutes les operations se font entre les corps, et jusques où elles peuvent arrive, pour ainsi s'acquiescer à accorder que quelques operations que font quelques bestes, qui semblent provenir de raisonnement, ont origine de principes corporels et materiels; et aussi, par là, determiner les derniers limites ausquels les agents materiels peuvent atteindre'. Digby had earlier written objections to Descartes's proof of God (*Mersenne Correspondence*, VII, 312, 419; VIII, 63, 113). My colleague Joe Moshenska is preparing an edition of Digby's correspondence that will showcase much new evidence concerning Digby's relationship with Mersenne and his circle.

to attack the Pomponazzian denial of philosophy's ability to discover the soul's natural immortality, without descending into the metaphysical corruptions of Aristotle that we have seen him ascribing to the scholastics. He made this clear in the treatise on the soul, pointing out that he wanted 'to encounter [those that held Pomponazzi's view] with their owne weapons' – that is to say, by considering the soul as the subject of physics rather than metaphysics.[98] Here Digby further elucidated his view of the history of Aristotelianism and its corruption. He claimed that the error of denying the soul's immortality stemmed not from Pomponazzi himself but from the third-century Aristotelian commentator Alexander of Aphrodisias, and specifically from his claim that all the knowledge in the rational soul must come from the imagination; thus with the extinction of the body comes the extinction of the soul.[99] Alexander had indeed argued, in his *De anima*, that man's reason in inseparable from the body and that the soul is thus mortal. This theory was known and sporadically condemned throughout the middle ages but became a central topic of dispute after the publication of the first Latin translation in 1495.[100] Pomponazzi used Alexander's *De anima*, and the subsequent affair naturally thrust it into the spotlight.[101] For Digby, the Alexandrian move was one that failed to appreciate the full content of Aristotelian physics, for it was to 'embrace and stike to one *Axiome* of their Patrone [i.e. Aristotle]', that nothing is known except through the senses, but to neglect another, that 'a substance is for its operatione ... so likewise ... *Matter* is for its *forme*'.[102] The priority of form renders Alexandrian–Pomponazzian mortalism absurd. Digby acknowledged that the Aristotelian texts were ambiguous but attributed this to later interpolations. He added that if Aristotle's dialogue *Eudemus* (or *On the soul*) had survived, it would support natural immortality, for who would write a dialogue on the soul upon the death of a friend (the eponymous Eudemus) without first believing in immortality? This is a reference to a lost work, listed in Laërtius, the circumstances of whose composition are mentioned in Plutarch's *Life of Dion*.[103]

---

[98] Digby, *Two treatises*, 429.    [99] Ibid., 428–9.

[100] The fullest treatment is now Pluta, 'The transformations of Alexander of Aphrodisias' interpretation of Aristotle's theory of the soul' (2001); see also Cranz, 'Alexander Aphrodisiensis'. Alexander's surviving *De anima*, not to be confused with his lost commentary on Aristotle's *De anima*, was translated by Hieronymus Donatus, now appearing with an introduction by E. Kessler as *Alexander Aphrodisias: enarratio de anima ex Aristotelis institutione* (2008).

[101] Pluta, 'Alexander', 157–65.

[102] Digby, *Two treatises*, 431. There is no equivalent statement in Aristotle, the closest parallel being *Met.*, VII, 1035$^{a-b}$, but I suspect Digby was drawing on Aquinas, *Summa contra gentiles*, II.89 or a later derivative, where the corresponding claim is made directly. Digby praises Aquinas as an interpreter of Aristotle in BL MS Harl. 4153, fols. 91$^{r-v}$.

[103] Digby, *Two treatises*, 431 (not citing any sources). See DL v.22; Plutarch, *Dion*, XXII.5. Benjamin Whichcote also noted the existence of this book from Plutarch: Folger, MS V.a.326, fol. 43$^v$ (my foliation).

Digby thus presented his mechanical Aristotelianism as based on a 'true Aristotle' who was a mid-point between two corruptions: the metaphysical–logical corruptions of some scholastics and the mortalist–materialist corruptions of Alexander of Aphrodisias. This was a clear contribution to the post-Pomponazzi debate on the relationship of Aristotelian physics and metaphysics. Even if Digby's specific doctrines fell by the wayside, no doubt the popularity of his work helped spread the idea that the history of Aristotelian natural philosophy was in part a history of its corruption by metaphysics and logic.

In Hobbes and Digby we have met two neoterics who sided with those Renaissance Aristotelians who aligned Aristotle's metaphysics with a *physica generalis*. But one other major English philosopher took the other route, using his interpretation of the Stagirite to claim that metaphysics should be a *theologia naturalis*. This is the argument offered by Henry More in his *Enchiridion Metaphysicum* (1671), a text in which he self-consciously distanced himself from his earlier Cartesianism by emphasising the causal agency of a 'Principium hylarchicum' or 'Spirit of nature'.[104] As we have already noted, the focus on More's 'Platonism' has obscured his engagement with other traditions from the history of philosophy, in this case the Aristotelian. More knew of the double tradition of metaphysics as natural theology and as a science of first principles.[105] He also knew that at the origins of these traditions lay a philological confusion: the title τὰ μετὰ τὰ φυσικὰ, 'incorrectly and ignorantly prefixed to a certain Aristotelian work'.[106]

More wanted to return to the definition of metaphysics as natural theology.[107] He attempted to justify this by claiming that Aristotle's *philosophia prima* was the study of incorporeal substances as first causes (of which God is the first), referencing Aristotle's well-known statement at *Metaphysics* 938ᵃ8 ('a science is divine if it is peculiarly the possession of God, or if it is concerned with divine matter. And this science alone fulfils both these conditions'), as well as the description of the science as 'θεολογικὴν'.[108] Defending this definition of metaphysics naturally led him into the problem of Aristotle's definition of it as the science of being *qua* being. More's solution was to claim that this definition must have stemmed from Aristotle's confused insertion of logic into an inappropriate

---

[104] The best introduction to the *Enchiridion* remains Jacob, 'Introduction' (1995). See further 5.4 below.

[105] Henry More, *Enchiridion metaphysicum, sive, de rebus incorporeis succincta & luculenta dissertatio* (London, 1671), 'Ad Lectorem Praefatio', sig. Aᵛ.

[106] Ibid., 1: 'Quod ad Nomen *Metaphysicae* attinet, est sane significantissimum; desumptum verò à Titulo Tractatui cuidam *Aristotelico* perperàm & imperitè praefixo: Inscribitur enim, τὰ μετὰ τὰ φυσικὰ'.

[107] Ibid.: 'Metaphysica est Ars rectè contemplandi res Incorporeas quatenus è Lumine Naturae Facultatibus nostris innotescunt. Itáque Metaphysica *Theologia quasi* quaedam Naturalis est'.

[108] Ibid., 2, 4.

domain.[109] More here silently drew on the humanist anti-Aristotelian tradition. His most likely source was Gassendi's *Exercitationes*; in a chapter offering a taxonomy of the inappropriate subject matter of the *Metaphysics* the Frenchman had often pointed to its logical elements.[110] The consequence was that what More called 'metaphysics' seemed to merge with what had emerged as the genre of 'physico-theology'. Whichever way one turned, metaphysics was being squeezed out.

Digby's, Hobbes's, and More's re-historicisations of the relationship between Aristotelian metaphysics and natural philosophy were different, and driven by different agendas. But they all shared some elements: an engagement with the late Aristotelian tradition and with the humanist anti-Aristotelian tradition, and a sense that the identities of the various fields (metaphysics, natural philosophy, *philosophia prima*, natural theology) had to be more clearly demarcated because of the confusion created by Aristotle and his followers. This turned into a blasé commonplace amongst the experimental philosophers, but this should not obscure their debts to the debates within late Aristotelianism. We can see an early appropriation of these debates by an experimentalist in the case of Ralph Bathurst, a leading member of the Oxford natural philosophers of the 1650s. In a set of Oxford medical lectures of 1654, in a *quaestio* on 'whether all sense is touch?' Bathurst argued the affirmative. The opposing view, that perception occurred by 'faculties, qualities, species and the like', was the product of the 'abstractions of metaphysicians ... unworthy' of physicians and physiologists.[111] As had Hobbes, Bathurst was affirming that an incorrect demarcation of philosophical boundaries had led metaphysics to corrupt natural philosophy. Bathurst was close to Hobbes, explicitly praising the latter's anti-Aristotelianism and writing a commendatory poem for *Human nature* (1650); subsequently he came under the patronage of William Cavendish, first duke of Devonshire and eldest son of Hobbes's patron the third earl of Devonshire.[112] The experimentalists were not

---

[109] Ibid., 1 (speaking of the *Metaphysics*: ' ... sed aut *Logica* plerumque, aut alîus alicujus Artis aut Scientiae'); and the extended discussion at 5–18.

[110] Gassendi, *Exercitationes*, 154–5: 'Verum & superiùs jam innuimus ex libris XIV. Quibus opus illud continetur, sola V. posteriora 12. Libri capita Metaphysica propriè esse. Ex quo sequitur, ut caetera omnia aliena, ac superflua sint ... III. IV. V. VI. VII. Totius sparsìm organi: VII.IX. ac X. & ipsius organi, & physicorum plurimum'. For More's abortive reading of Gassendi's later works, see p. 137, n. 121 above.

[111] Ralph Bathurst, 'Tres quaestiones in Comit. Oxon. 1654', in Thomas Warton, *The life and literary remains of Ralph Bathurst, M.D.* (2 vols, London, 1761), I, 227: 'Nam ut dicat aliquis haec omnia fieri per facultates, qualitates, species et similia, verba sunt tantùm in summis labris natantia, quaeque dant *sine mente sonum* ... Quae licèt in umbraticis metaphysicorum abstractionibus locum suo jure vendicent, medicis tamen et physiologis ad penitiora contendentibus, indignum prorsus est huiusmodi commentis acquiescere'.

[112] Thomas Warton, 'The life of Ralph Bathurst', in *Bathurst*, I, 48–50; *Hobbes correspondence*, I, 180.

immune to adopting the historical–methodological reflections of systematisers like Hobbes.[113]

## 4.3     Histories of natural philosophical method before 1660

Bathurst, it is worth emphasising, was writing not in an overtly natural philosophical but rather a medical context. For all the importance of Baconianism, it was in fact in learned (i.e. institutionalised) medicine that the most important justifications for experimental method and practice developed in the 1640s and 1650s. As we have seen, humanist physicians had been insisting on the unique combination of experience and philosophical learning among the ancient *medici* for over a century. New developments accentuated the need for such insistence. William Harvey's discovery of the circulation of the blood stimulated much debate about the nature of medical research throughout Europe: this inevitably led to reflection about the history of medical method and practice and the history of the relationship between physicians and natural philosophers. As we shall see, few followed Harvey's own historical justifications. But the issues raised resonated in methodological debate through to the end of the century. It was medical language that facilitated the most convincing arguments for the historical importance of experience – and then 'experiment'.

### 4.3.1     *Harvey and experimental medicine before 1660*

Our concern here is with Harvey's well-known methodological justification for his own novelty, as it was presented in the preface to the *Exercitationes de generatione animalium* (1651),[114] specifically the section where that methodology is putatively elucidated 'according to Aristotle' (*ad mentem* Aristotelem). In the wake of both domestic and continental criticism of his discovery of the forceful systole and of the blood's circulation as unphilosophical and even

---

[113] Although he makes no historical claims, it seems to me that this is the debate Locke is implicitly referring to in *Some thoughts concerning education* (London, 1693), 225: '*Natural Philosophy* being the Knowledge of the Principles, Properties, and Operations of Things, as they are in Themselves, I imagine that there are Two Parts of it, one comprehending Spirits with their Nature and Qualities; and the other *Bodies*. The first of these is usually referr'd to *Metaphysicks:* But under what Title soever the consideration of *Spirits* comes, I think it ought to go before the study of Matter, and Body, not as a Science that can be methodized into a System.' For Newton's virulent antipathy to, and historiciastion of, metaphysics, see 5.4.5 below.

[114] The landmark studies of *De generatione* and its preface are: Webster, 'Harvey's *De generatione*' (1967); Wear, 'William Harvey and the "way of the anatomists"' (1983); Schmitt, 'William Harvey and Renaissance Aristotelianism' (1984); and for the dating, Whitteridge, 'Introduction' (1981), xix–xxv, concluding (xxiv), 'the period of time during which it seems most probable that Harvey collected his notes and assembled them into a coherent whole is between 1628 and 1642'.

Empiric (since no cause in the Aristotelian sense was evident), Harvey sought to defend the claim that 'observation itself was a type of knowledge'.[115] Although it was not always correct to follow the ancients slavishly in matters of specific doctrine, in matters of method they 'undoubtedly offered a light for our studies' by 'searching by indefatigable labours into various experiments [*experimenta*] of things ... to the extent that almost everything exceptional that we have learned in philosophy so far has flown down to us from the assiduity of the ancient Greeks'.[116] The best light was offered by Aristotle. The problem as Harvey presented it was that Aristotle had seemed to suggest two modes of knowledge-formation. In Book I of the *Physics* ($184^{a}16$–$25$) knowledge was said to stem from moving from things which are best known (universals) to those which are least (particulars), but in the *Posterior Analytics* (Harvey does not give a specific reference, but the general locus is II.19), Aristotle states that singulars are better known to us, because first in the senses.[117] Harvey reconciled the two by claiming that for Aristotle, sensation produces universals.[118] Although, he noted, *Posterior Analytics* $71^{a}1$ again seemed to claim that knowledge 'comes from antecedent knowledge',[119] the problem could be resolved: Aristotle believed that while certain knowledge is produced by syllogism from first principles, those first principles could only stem from observation, which produces in turn memory, compound memory, experience, and from experience, first principles.[120]

Harvey developed this reading with some interesting examples: *Metaphysics* (I, $980^{a}$–$981a5$) (animals' intelligence depends on the capacity of their respective memories),[121] and *Generation of animals* (III, $760^{b}28$–$33$) (where Aristotle seems to suggest that the causal question of the generation of bees would not be fully resolved until the accumulation of further data was complete).[122] Harvey seems to have found these himself (I have been unable to find a secondary source), but more generally he was here adopting a modified version of the *regressus* method as it had been developed in the Paduan Aristotelianism in which he was educated, the key works being those of

---

[115] French, *William Harvey's natural philosophy* (1994), 316, and *passim* for the English and continental reception.

[116] William Harvey, *Exercitationes de generatione animalium* (London, 1651), sig. B$^v$: ' ... veteres Philosophi (quorum nos etiam laudamus industriam) contrarium prorsus iter institerint; atque indefessis laboribus varia rerum experimenta inquirentes, haud dubiam lucem studiis nostris praetulerint. Adeò ut, quicquid ferè hactenus in Philosophia eximii compertíque habemus, id ipsum ad nos ab antiquae Graeciae sedulitate profluxerit'.

[117] Ibid., sigs. B2$^{r-v}$.

[118] Ibid., sig. [B4]$^r$: 'Hic enim doctrinam omnem, & disciplinam dianoéticam, ex antecedente cognitione fieri, asserit'.

[119] Ibid., sig. B2$^v$: 'Licèt enim in moni cognitione à sensu ordiamur, quia (ut ibidem Philosophus) sensibilia singularia sensui notiora sunt; ipsa tamen sensatio est universalis'.

[120] Ibid., sig. [B4]$^{r-v}$, citing *Anal. Post.*, $99^{b}26$–$100^{a}9$.  [121] Harvey, *De generatione*, sig. C$^r$.

[122] Ibid., sig. C$^v$.

Jacopo Zabarella.[123] In short, to discover causes from effects, sense data is reduced to first principles; the process is then reversed, and one can go from the newly established first principles to explain the effects.[124] Zabarella explicitly attributed these dual 'methods' to Aristotle.[125] Harvey adopted the outlines of this Zabarellan reading but significantly enhanced the emphasis on observation as an end in itself, remaining silent on the role of syllogism. This was probably an outgrowth of his debt to the Paduan Aristotelian anatomical tradition of his teacher Hieronymus Fabricius ab Aquapendente.[126] Despite these differences there is one important element of continuity between Harvey and Zabarellan *regressus* theory: neither drew on the image of Aristotle as natural historian, author of the *History of animals*. In the *regressus* tradition these natural historical works were categorically separated from the philosophical treatment of cause in the *Parts of animals*.[127] Although Harvey was not so explicit it is clear that he also wanted to defend his observational results as philosophical and not merely natural historical. Later English defenders of Aristotle would sometimes cite Harvey (by then canonical) alongside their references to Aristotle's natural historical works; in doing this they went beyond Harvey's own intentions.

It was probably Harvey's exposure to Paduan Aristotelianism that rendered him unique: his historical Aristotle found no supporters, even amongst his own followers, all of whom defended the key role of observation and experience for the learned physician.[128] But by this point medical humanism had generated plenty of other ways of doing this. In 1650s England, and especially in Oxford, this humanist language began to be expanded beyond medical circles and to the defence of observational methods in natural philosophy *tout court*.[129]

---

[123] Harvey's debt to the *regressus* method is treated in Schmitt, '*Praefatio*', esp. 129–32; French, *Harvey*, 313–15; Sgarbi, *British empiricism*, 180–4.

[124] The classic studies of *regressus* are Randall, *School of Padua*; Jardine, 'Galileo's road to truth and the demonstrative regress' (1976); see now also, among many studies, Mikkeli, *Aristotelian response*, esp. 92–106.

[125] Jacopo Zabarella, *Opera logica* (4th edn, Venice, 1600 [1st edn=1578]), col. 169: '... duae igitur scientificae methodi oriuntur, non plures, nec pauciores, altera per excellentiam demonstrativa methodus dicitur, quam Graeci κύριον ἀποδείξιν, vel ἀποδείξιν τοῦ διότι vocant, nostri, potissimam demonstratione, vel demonstrationem propter quid appelare consue verunt, altera, quae ab effectu ad causam progreditur, resolutiva nominatur, huiusmodi enim progressus resolutio est, sicuti a causa ad effectum dicitur compositio, methodum, hanc vocant Graeci συλλογισμὸν τοῦ ὅτι, vel διὰ σημεῖον, nostri demonstrationem quia, vel syllogismum a signo, vel secundi gradus demonstrationem'. For the philological manoeuvring employed by Zabarella so as to claim that Aristotle was discussing 'method' at all, see Gilbert, *Method*, 167–70.

[126] Wear, 'Way'; Cunningham, *The anatomical Renaissance* (1997), 167–90 (183–4 on Harvey).

[127] See Jardine, 'Order', 205–7; Mikkeli, 'The foundation of an autonomous natural philosophy: Zabarella on the classification of arts and sciences' (1998), 223.

[128] For the general context, see Frank, *Harvey*, 41–3.

[129] On the general importance of Oxford, I agree broadly with the conclusions in Feingold, 'The origins of the Royal Society revisited' (2005), 181–3.

Harvey's first English followers reflected little on the history of natural–philosophical method, perhaps because although they were dissatisfied with Harvey's model they could not find another; nonetheless, the little evidence we have is still of considerable interest. In his *Apologia pro circulatione sanguinis* (1641), George Ent, Harvey's first major defender in England, compared Harvey not to Aristotle but to Democritus and also claimed that he had 'strengthened the foundations of the Methodic sect, and offered a new torch to the Dogmatic'.[130] This alignment with the Methodics would have greatly perturbed Harvey. It was part of Ent's far more thoroughgoing rejection of school philosophy and medicine, which he believed was based on Aristotle's erroneous confusion of final and efficient cause, and subsequent introduction of 'faculties' to explain phenomena.[131] The reference to Democritus is to the anatomist of the *Epistola ad Damagetum*. It is important that Democritus is a medical experimentalist who is still a philosopher, and thus not tainted with the lowly reputation of the Empirics: we shall find him being used in this way again.

Harvey's most important early follower, because the most institutionally established, was Francis Glisson, Regius Professor of Physic at Cambridge from 1636. Not only did he accept circulation, he also had further reason to develop a justification for new research, for his own pioneering work was on rickets, universally acknowledged to be a 'new' disease and thus by definition requiring precisely such research.[132] Paracelsian iatrochymists had for several generations claimed that diseases had changed so much from the ancient world that ancient methods were rendered useless; it was thus a particular challenge for a learned physician within the establishment to develop a counter-history. In his printed medical works Glisson rarely reflected on the methodology or history of his own discipline. But he did at one point claim that Galen had united the 'practical' and 'speculative' roles of the physician, a clear nod towards the learned tradition. Glisson was clearly thinking about the way in which the learned physician could incorporate new sensory data without descending to Empiricism, for he focused on Galen's use of 'indications'

---

[130] George Ent, *Apologia pro circulatione sanguinis* (London, 1641), Dedication to Harvey, sig. A3$^r$: 'Edidisti jamdudum de circuitu sanguinis libellum (sine cerussa dicam) verè aureum; quo Methodicae sectae fundamenta confirmâsti, & Dogmaticae novam facem praetulisti. Mirabantur Medici, tam insignem veritatem tam diu in *Democriti* puteo delituisse'. For Ent's intellectual biography and the circumstances around the composition of the *Apologia*, see French, *Harvey*, 168–78; Frank, *Harvey*, 22–3, 109–11.

[131] Ent, *Apologia*, 28 ('Dico autem, à vera philosophia alienum esse, finalem causam pro efficiente assignare'); 40 ('Tandem ad Facultatem, magnum illud Philosophorum subterfugium pervenimus ... Quod quid aliud est, quàm Deos advocare in theatrum, ut solvant nodum fabulae?' [the marginal note refers to Aristotle, *Met.*, 1.2]) This is part of a 'Digressio' on attraction, discussed more broadly in French, *Harvey*, 172–4.

[132] Stevenson, '"New diseases" in the seventeenth century' (1965), esp. 7.

(ἔνδειξις) – the identification of those signs that allowed the physician to make rational inferences from what can be observed to discover what cannot[133] – which he presented as 'that noble instrument of the method of medicine ... by whose use the Dogmatic sect especially want to separate themselves from the Empirics'.[134] In *De motu cordis* (1628), Harvey had briefly referred to Galen working from both 'experiments and reasoning', and 'proving' things 'by experiment';[135] Ent had happily referred to Galen's famous binding of foetal arteries as an 'experimentum'.[136] Glisson here expanded on this theme, a staple of Renaissance medical epistemology.[137]

Of even greater interest is a piece of evidence preserved among the *c.* 5000 manuscript pages of Glisson's lectures at the College of Physicians and Cambridge. One of these lectures was devoted to showing that 'The dogmatic *praxis* excels in medicine' (*Praxis dogmatica praepollet medendo*). Introducing the three ancients sects, Glisson pointed out that some now characterised the chymists as a fourth, but that the Dogmatics excelled all of them. The Empirics rejected the search for causes, but this search was a prerequisite for a *methodo medendi*. Hippocrates was claimed back for the Dogmatics; Galen only developed his method.[138] Glisson was probably the most influential prominent medical teacher in late seventeenth-century England and his amalgamation of experimentalism and the learned tradition was very influential, as we shall see below.[139]

Another example of the ambiguities engendered by Harvey's legacy is that of Nathaniel Highmore, part of the group of experimentalists at Trinity College, Oxford in the 1640s, atomist, friend of Boyle, and self-professed follower of Harvey.[140] His *Corporis humani disquisitio anatomica* (1651), advertised as a

---

[133] Maclean, *Learned medicine*, 306–15. See also an academic respose by Glisson (discussed further below), BL MS Sloane 3309, fol. 343ᵛ ('Methodus enim medendi indicans et indicatum termini abstracti sunt: et quidem indicans <abstrahitur> a causa aut essential morbi, cum viribus aestimata').

[134] Francis Glisson, *De rachitide, sive, morbo puerili* (London, 1650), 295–6: 'Indicatio, ἔνδειξις, nobile illud methodi medendi instrumentum, (cujus usu Dogmatici sectam suam ab Empiricis maximè disciminari volunt) ad partes Rationis etiam venit accensenda'. Glisson cites Galen, *Meth. med.*, II.4 (K x 100–3) for the definition of ἔνδειξις and *Ad Thrasybulus*.

[135] William Harvey, *Exercitatio anatomica de motu cordis et sanguinis in animalibus* (Frankfurt, 1628), 11 ('Quid itaquere respondeant Galeno, qui librum scripsit, Natura sanguinem contineri in arteriis ... sicut ab experimentis, & rationibus *in eodem libro* facile colligere licet').

[136] Ent, *Apologia*, p. 13; the implied reference is to *De usu part.*, VI.21 (K III.509–10).

[137] Maclean, *Learned medicine*, 306–15.

[138] BL Sloane MS 3309, fols. 344ʳ–349ᵛ (fols. 346ʳ–48ᵛ are preparatory notes for the lecture, inserted in the middle of the lecture itself), 'Praxis dogmatica praepollet medendo'. Glisson's lectures comprise BL Sloane MSS 3309–15.

[139] As pointed out by Giglioni, 'Glisson, Francis', *ODNB*, Glisson's lectures incorporated much of his work 'on a project of anatomising the organs of nutrition and digestion'; see also the case of Sprackling below.

[140] Highmore deserves more attention: only Oster, 'Highmore, Nathaniel', *ODNB*, and Frank, *Harvey*, 97–101 (and *passim*) are of value. Of Highmore's two early works, the *Corporis*

post-circulation anatomy text, contained almost no methodological self-justification, except the claim, made against James Primrose's request that Harvey demonstrate the arteries-to-veins transit, that medicine deals with probabilities rather than demonstrations.[141] This was again a clever way of deploying a standard assumption of Galenic learned medicine to the service of an experimental research programme.[142] But it was combined with a very much more novel and even crude vision of the history of natural philosophy more broadly conceived. For Highmore believed that all the ancients were hylomorphists and modern philosophy was effectively defined by the break from hylomorphism.[143] This vision, and Highmore's philosophy more generally, has been attributed, without much evidence, to the influence of Gassendi.[144] However, the manuscript drafts of the *Disquisitio anatomica* (which was initially entitled 'Anatomia restaurata') show that his anti-Aristotelianism derived from a different French atomist: Sébastien Basson.[145] This is excellent evidence of how the 1650s witnessed the coming together of the by then well-established experiential language of medical humanism with the more iconoclastic historicisations offered by recent natural philosophical innovators. Highmore's neighbour Boyle also cited Basson as an early inspiration[146] and this may be further evidence that his work was more influential than previously recognised; manuscript evidence shows that it was even being discussed and used in a pedagogical context.[147] At the very least, we have here an explanation

---

*humani disquisitio anatomica* (The Hague, 1651) was dedicated to Harvey, and *The history of generation* (London, 1651) to Boyle.

[141] French, *Harvey*, 317, discussing Highmore, *Disquisitio anatomica*, 149.

[142] The key discussion is Maclean, *Learned medicine*, 290–330. Central Galenic *loci* for the conjectural/probabilistic character of medicine include *Meth. med.* IX.16 (K x.653); *Loc. Aff.* (K VIII.14); see further the *loci* gathered in Boudon-Millot, 'Art, science et conjecture chez Galien' (2003).

[143] Highmore, *The history of generation*, 1–4.  [144] Frank, *Harvey*, 93, 100; Oster, 'Highmore'.

[145] BL MS Sloane 546, 'Anatomia restaurata, sive corpus humani disquisitionis anatomicae liber primus', fols. 7ᵛ–8ʳ; BL MS Sloane 547, 'Anatomia restaurata', corrected draft, fols. 6ᵛ–7ʳ. These references to Basson's *Philosophiae naturalis adversus Aristotelem libri XII* (Geneva, 1621) (on which see Lüthy, 'Basson') are not in the printed version. On Basson see p. 12, n. 52 above; for his claim that non-hylomorphist ancient philosophy was disastrously corrupted by Aristotelian hylomorphism, see Basson, *Philosophia naturalis*, esp. 4–17. Unfortunately, Highmore's later manuscripts on the nature of medicine (BL MS Sloane 528, fols. 1ʳ–32ᵛ ('Observationes de signis morborum'); fols. 33ʳ–7ʳ ('Observationes de methodo medendi')) contain no historical discussions, even if they clearly stem from much reading (see the early commonplace book, MS Sloane 543, e.g. the entry from Averroës at fol. 22ʳ).

[146] Boyle, 'Essay of the Holy Scriptures', in *Boyle works*, XIII, 190; see also *The origin of forms and qualities* (1666–67), in *Boyle works*, V, 295; for Highmore's possible influence on Boyle, see Hunter, *Boyle*, 90–1.

[147] See BL Sloane 1324 (anonymous treatise on natural philosophy, mid-seventeenth century), fol. 24ʳ; and the extensive notes, taken in the early 1650s, from the 1649 Amsterdam edition of Basson's *Philosophia naturalis adversus Aristotelem* by John Patrick at CUL MS Add. 84, fols. 2ʳ–12ʳ (I am very grateful to Richard Serjeantson for drawing the second of these to my attention). See also n. 34 above.

for Highmore's dissent from the Aristotelianism of his friend Harvey, and from the more general nods to the learned tradition by Glisson.

More influential than Highmore's idiosyncratic thoughts were the medical lectures delivered in Oxford in 1650–51 by William Petty, who had been made D.M. there in March 1650 and appointed Tomlins Reader in anatomy late that year. Petty had a central role in the Wilkins group and in the development of experimental natural philosophy at Oxford (most famous is his role in the 'resuscitation' of Anne Greene in December 1650).[148] Upon appointment as D.M., he read six lectures which, alongside the anatomy lectures of the following year, reveal his unabashed adherence to 'new' doctrines and methods: iatrochymistry, circulation, and mechanistic physical explanations.[149] The first of the six lectures introduces the discipline through its history, and given Petty's clear experimental proclivities one might expect a pro-Empiric attitude. In fact, the exact opposite is the case: although the Methodics were considered the worst in antiquity, the reality, Petty suggests, is that the most dangerous sect was the Empiric.[150] Both proceeded haphazardly rather than systematically from indications.[151] Only the Dogmatic/Rational sect combined the correct level of systematical observation and 'deduction' from said observations.[152] The Paracelsian chymists claimed to render the old methods entirely obsolete, but in reality they offered no better explanations of the causes of illnesses than the Galenists.[153] This was because the theoretical superstructure behind Rationalism – the four elements, substantial forms, etc. – was irrelevant to its clinical efficaciousness. Rational *method* was entirely compatible with the incorporation of new natural philosophical *doctrines*.[154]

The importance of this kind of 'pragmatic' defence of learned medicine – suggesting that its methods did not depend on its doctrines – cannot be overstated. As we shall see, the key historical–methodological defence of experimentalism came from the further development of this alignment of the learned medical tradition with observational and even experimental practice. Petty and Glisson were engaged in the same enterprise of rendering the learned tradition compatible with natural-philosophical research and the incorporation of new findings, while defending it from the challenge of unlearned (that is to say, not trained in university natural philosophy) Empirics. This was a battle

---

[148] Frank, *Harvey*, 50, 52–6, 66–7, 75, 91–2, 95, 101–3, 106, 107, 116, 128, 171–3; Mandelbrote, 'Medical and political reform in Commonwealth Oxford' (2005); Purver, *The Royal Society* (1967), 119–20; Lewis, *William Petty on the order of nature* (2012), 1–10, 22–70; Webster, 'More and Descartes', 367–73. I do not list the many works on Petty as an economist.

[149] The lectures are BL MS Add. 72891, fols. 1$^r$–7$^v$ (lecture 2), 10$^r$–21$^v$ (lecture 1), 113$^r$–191$^v$ (fair copy of lecture 2 and lectures 3–6). The anatomical lectures are fols. 22$^r$–78$^r$, and further anatomical and osteological lectures are fols. 268$^r$–326$^r$. See the essential discusson at Frank, *Harvey*, 101–3.

[150] BL MS Add. 72891, fol. 10$^v$.  [151] Ibid., fol. 12$^r$.  [152] Ibid., fols. 4$^v$–5$^v$; 17$^r$–18$^r$.

[153] Ibid., fols. 1$^v$–2$^r$.  [154] Ibid., fols. 4$^v$–5.

that had been going on in England, on and off, for some time: in the 1630s the apothecaries had already been using the tools of medical humanism to insist, in lectures delivered at Apothecaries Hall, that it was they, rather than the physicians, who were closer to the model of the total *medicus* of antiquity; this involved a lowering of the status of the 'speculative' or 'theoretical' parts of medicine (physiology, pathology, and semiology) in favour of the 'practical' (prophylactic and therapeutic), in part by drawing on some of the same Galenic *loci* that seemed to insist on the compatibility of Rationalism and Empiricism.[155] The learned physicians were responding not only by reasserting the value of natural philosophy and semiotics, but also by demonstrating the compatibility of these disciplines with new findings. That this argument was successful is evident from its use by other members of the Oxford group of experimentalists: delivering Medical Act Verses in 1657, William Quatremaine responded negatively to the question 'Whether recent anatomical discoveries have changed the *methodus medendi?*', while denying that the four humours make up the blood.[156] Ironically, the idea that the philosophy underpinning Galen's medical practice was in some senses utilitarian had recent precedent in Harvey's *negative* reception. As Roger French has shown, both in England (James Primrose) and abroad (Jean Riolan), part of the critical response to circulation involved a newly pragmatic reading of the ancients:

As for Riolan, so for Primrose, the argument is that the doctrines of the forceful systole and of circulation add nothing to benefit practice and indeed destroy the foundation of practice . . . Harvey's doctrines were, for his opponents, novelites that did not agree with an extant scheme of things and were therefore, they concluded, wrong. It followed for them that Havey's *method* of producing these novelties, what we are here calling his natural philosophy, must also have been at fault. It was Primrose's complaint that Harvey took no note of medicine as an autonomous activity: of how the thought of its founders had been bound into an intelligible and trustworthy system of understanding and, importantly, practice, which circulation could only disturb.[157]

But this pragmatic reading was quickly picked up by neoterics like Petty and Glisson to *defend* innovation.

It was this new focus on the incorporation of novelty that meant that medical humanism could be easily adapted for wider purposes. Petty may have been defending experimentalism in a formal medical–pedagogical setting but his

---

[155] Levitin, 'Apothecaries'.

[156] Bod. MS Nep/supra/Reg. Qa [Register of Congregations, 1647–59], fol. 154ʳ, 'Ob nuper inventa Antomica Methodus medendi immutanda sit? Neg. Dentur quatuor humores massae sanguinea constitutive? Neg'. But Quatremaine was more radical than Petty, answering positively to the question 'Placita Dogmaticorum Sectae Empiricae Superadditae plus damni-quam utilitatis attulerint Medicina?' For his place among the Oxford physiologists of the 1650s, see Frank, *Harvey*, 86–7, 104–6.

[157] French, *Harvey*, 116–17, 227–8.

methods were shared more widely among the *novatores*. His friend Christopher Wren, a key member of the Oxford virtuosi, talked in his inaugural oration as Gresham Professor of Astronomy (1657) of the Hippocratean aphorisms as being 'diligently collected from the *Brasen-Tables*, from Experiments deriv'd in Succession from his aged Preceptors before him, and from his own unerring Industry'. This aphoristic–experimental knowledge derived from the east, from whom the otherwise speculative Greeks 'receiv'd much of their Art of healing'. The existence of this experimental method was confirmed by Democritus's anatomising as described in the *Epistola ad Damagetum*.[158] In Oxford, such claims were still standard in the late 1660s.[159] The fervour and devotion that the Oxford physiologists of the 1650s and their friends devoted to natural science was unprecedented, and did indeed herald a new autonomy for the *persona* of the experimental natural philosopher,[160] but the language they used very often remained that of the medical humanists of the last century and a half.

### 4.3.2    Histories of philosophy in intellectual reform debates

We have so far focused on continuity and on those 'establishment' figures who, for all their novelty, remained for the most part within the ambit of university natural philosophy. But however much one stresses continuity it is impossible to ignore the fact that the political events of the two decades between 1640 and 1660 had major consequences for intellectual life – not because political and philosophical ideas were tied up in an all-encompassing web, but because political changes brought major disruption to the universities, allowing previously ignored reformers to crawl out of the woodwork, and modulating the conditions of operation for those who managed or were willing to stay on.[161]

The many educational reform programmes published or conceived in these two decades were almost always ultimately about institutional authority:

---

[158] Christopher Wren, 'Inaugural oration as Gresham Professor of astronomy' (1657), in Stephen Wren, *Parentalia* (London, 1750), 202–3. See also the very similar reference to Democritus the anatomist in William Petty, 'Anatomy lecture' (delivered in the late 1660s to the Dublin College of Physicians), in *The Petty papers.*, ed. Marquis of Landsdowne (2 vols, London, 1927), II, 174. Wren's *Parentalia* must be read in light of the guidelines in Bennett, 'A study of *Parentalia*' (1973), as well as more generally Davies, 'The youth and education of Christopher Wren' (2008).

[159] Bod. MS Nep/supra/Reg. Qb [Register of Congregations, 1659–69], fol. 176ᵛ, from the Act of 1669, where Thomas Jameson of Wadham argued negatively to the question 'Propter inventa nuper Anatomica mutanda sit medendi methodus?'.

[160] See also Feingold, 'Science as calling? The early modern dilemma' (2002).

[161] For this much-studied topic, see Webster, *Great instauration*; Frank, *Harvey*, 45–92; the chapters by Webster, Clericuzio and Pumfrey in Greengrass et al., eds., *Samuel Hartlib and universal Reformation* (1994); Worden, *God's instruments* (2012), 91–193 ('Politics, piety, and learning: Cromwellian Oxford').

reformers challenged traditional university education and chymical physicians campaigned for their own official recognition. Within these debates the relationship of natural philosophy to other disciplines – especially theology and medicine – appeared again and again. It was almost always in this context that the history of natural philosophy was considered. Even at the risk of over-accentuating a stereotype, it can be said that those reformers whom Charles Webster subsumed under the label of 'puritan' did not make many significant references to the history of philosophy, beyond anti-Aristotelian common-places almost always directly cribbed from Bacon.[162] Sometimes these were combined with a Baconian call for the study of the history of philosophy as a means of learning about natural history and ways in which it could be improved (of the type we met in 2.4), or with an attempt to resuscitate supposedly lost, non-Aristotelian wisdom. Hartlib himself, so virulently anti-Aristotelian that he revelled in the Oxford disputations against Aristotle,[163] was nonetheless particularly hopeful on this score.[164] The prominent ex-physician and projector Benjamin Worsley, who may have played a central role in the shadowy Invisible College that met in London in the late 1640s, similarly announced himself to be revealing the 'great Secret' of 'the Ancient Philosophers' on the subject of the influence of the celestial bodies, almost in the same breath that he chastised 'our University Professors' for 'stand[ing]' to 'Tradition . . . without further doubt or question'.[165] Often, the reformers offered ahistorical complaints about the 'paganism' of those ancient philosophers whom they did not want to see on university curricula – a direct inheritance from the Paracelsian tradition, via English Paracelsian reformers like Fludd.[166] But since these

---

[162] See e.g. Johannes Amos Comenius, *A reformation of schooles designed in two excellent treatises* (London, 1642), 34 (the standard claim that Aristotle had unfairly disparaged his predecessors).

[163] E.g. Hartlib, Ephemerides, 1640, HP 30/4/61A.

[164] Hartlib, Ephemerides, 1639, HP 30/4/35A, insisting that 'Critici should labour to explicate' Pliny better as he has best preserved ancient natural history, but 'his Text is most corrupt'; 30/4/10A, stating that a pansophia should begin with 'an accurate Censura of all the Ancient Learning'; and again in 1641, 30//4/71A. More generally, Hartlib was clearly interested in forming judgements on books about the history of philosophy, preferring Saumaise to Lipsius on the history of Stoicism (Ephemerides, 1639, HP 30/4/19A; the reference is to Saumaise's long and interesting 'Notae et animadversiones in Epictetum et Simplicium', in *Simplicii commentarius in enchiridion Epicteti ex libris veteribus emendatus* (Leiden, 1640)) and commenting rather negatively on Gassendi's project to revive Epicureanism, which Hartlib considered sectarianism (Ephemerides, 1640 and 1641, HP 30/4/49B, 70A: how Hartlib derived this early knowledge of Gassendi's plans is not clear).

[165] HP 33/2/5A–B, 'Dr. Worsley's physico-astrologicall letter, Dublin, October 20th, 1657'. For Worsley's natural philosophical interests more generally, the fullest account is now that in Leng, *Benjamin Worsley* (2008), 95–117.

[166] See e.g. Comenius, *Reformation*, 21 (but see also his explanation for sometimes using pagan works in his pansophia at 31, 33); or for a particularly virulent statement: William Dell, 'A plain and necessary confutation of divers gross and antichristian errors', in *The tryal of spirits both in teachers & hearers* (London, 1653), *passim*. For Fludd, see e.g. *Philosophia Moysaica*

claims were often allied to historically unconvincing lineages of 'divine' philosophy,[167] and because they rarely clearly explained precisely *why* being a pagan made one unqualified to produce good natural philosophy,[168] their opponents could dismiss them with little discussion.[169]

There are two exceptions to this general pattern. One was those intellectual reformers who came from a specifically iatrochymical background, and who re-deployed variants of van Helmont's history of physic and natural philosophy. These can be found in the *Mataeotechnia medicinae praxeos* (1651) by the obscure medical reformer Noah Biggs[170] and in two works promoting chymical medicine by Robert Boyle's American collaborator in chymistry, George Starkey (*Natures explication and Helmont's vindication* (1657) and *Pyrotechny asserted* (1658)).[171] Here we find the standard Helmontian claims, adjusted (especially in Starkey) to the language of 'experimentalism': Hippocrates was the first who 'left any thing to us upon record of usefull experimental practice', but Galen took Hippocratic 'art' and 'digested [it] into a Method', turning it into 'idle specula-tion'. This 'method' was then combined in the school into 'one aery lump of Natural Philosophy'.[172] Biggs, as well as chastising Galen's ambition and ignor-ance of chymistry and his supposed reduction of all natural principles to the contraries of hot and cold, claimed that it was Chrysippus (of all people) 'who was the first that pulled Physick out of experience, & put it into opinion'.[173] I have been unable to trace Biggs's source for this peculiar chronology.

---

(Gouda, 1638), fol. 5[r] (=*Mosiacall philosophy grounded upon the essential truth, or eternal sapience* (London, 1659), 10).

[167] For examples of alchemical illuminationism in the Hartlib papers, see e.g. the undated 'Short treatice [sic] proving Urim et Thummim to be perfected by Arte ... ', HP 27/23/1A–4B, esp. 4A, and the 'Treatise of the most hidden secret of the Ancients', HP 16/7/1A–18B.

[168] One partial exception is John Dury, who, although he only offered the usual commonplaces about the pagan 'monkishness' of the extant curriculum in his published calls for educational reform (see esp. *The reformed librarie-keeper, with a supplement to the reformed-school* (London, 1650), 1–9), did, in private, conduct research into the precise nature of how pagan theology affected natural philosophy: HP 68/6/1A–10B ('A demonstration that the Lutherans are not Idolaters'), esp. 1B–2A.

[169] E.g. Thomas Hall, *Vindiciae literarum, the schools guarded, or the excellency and usefulnesse of humane learning in subordination to divinity* (London, 1654), sigs. [A5]ᵛ–[A6]ʳ.

[170] Biggs was possibly 'Henry Biggs', a dockyard surgeon: the fullest treatment is Debus, 'Noah Biggs and the problem of medical reform' (1974); also Cook, *Decline*, 122–5.

[171] On Starkey, see Newman, *Gehennical fire*.

[172] The quotations are from George Starkey, *Natures explication and Helmont's vindication* (London, 1657), 9, 12. For Galen as sophistic corrupter of Hippocratic medicine see also J[ames] T[hompson], *Helmont disguised: or, the vulgar errours of impericall and unskilfull practisers of physick confuted* (London, 1657), 46 (see also the ubiquitous claim that Galen did not perform anatomy, citing Vesalius, at 77). Also [Anon.], *Anthropologie abstracted: or the idea of humane nature reflected in briefe philosophicall, and anatomicall collections* (London, 1655), 171–2 (the Greeks ignored chymistry); also n. 61 above.

[173] Noah Biggs, *Mataeotechnia medicinae praxeos, the vanity of the craft of physick ... with an humble motion for the reformation of the universities* (London, 1651), 11–12, 15.

The second exception was those rare reformers who tried to substantiate their arguments with extended historical examples, of whom by far the most important was John Webster.[174] Webster was clear that the purpose of his examination of Aristotle was practical, for it was 'the *Philosophy* which the *Schools* use and teach', and it was thus worth examining 'the ground and reasons why it should be imbraced'.[175] Chapter 6 of his *Academiarum examen* (1654, actually published late 1653) offered a long and detailed attack on the Stagirite. Webster accused him of various un-Christian errors: anthropomorphising God, binding the deity to fate, eternalism, denying creation *ex nihilo*, denying the possibility of resurrection, and denying the immortality of the soul. From there he moved to *ad hominem* attacks: Aristotle betrayed his country to the Macedonians, was ungrateful to his master Plato and unjustly chastised the other ancients, and he was intemperate, voluptuous and lived in an obscene manner. His high reputation was unjustified for he was both rejected in favour of other philosophers by pagans (Cicero and Quintilian) and attacked by the church fathers. There was huge uncertainty over the transmission and integrity of his works. The works themselves were obscure in both style and doctrine, being 'verbal, speculative, abstractive, formal and notional', and lacking experimental and chymical evidence.[176]

We need not search for the sources of this attack, for it is quite clear that for all his citations of the primary sources, Webster was shamelessly plagiarising (even in the loose early modern sense of the word), primarily from Gassendi's *Exercitationes Peripateticae*. As much was pointed out in Seth Ward's well-known reply, *Vindiciae Academiarum* (1654): Ward included a helpful table outlining Webster's plagiarisms.[177] Unlike the anti-Aristotelian histories of

---

[174] On Webster and his debate with Wilkins and Ward, the best introduction remains Debus, 'Introduction' (1970). For Webster's biography, the fullest account is Elmer, *The library of Dr. John Webster* (1986), 1–15.

[175] John Webster, *Academiarum examen, or the examination of academies* (London, 1654), 52.

[176] Ibid., 52–68, 78–83.

[177] [Seth Ward] and [John Wilkins], *Vindiciae academiarum containing some briefe animadversions upon Mr Websters book stiled, The examination of academies* (Oxford, 1654), 33. Ward (who wrote the body of this work) claimed that the gap in the attack on Aristotle (i.e. 68–77) was due to the non-Latinate Webster's translator having 'failed him, who should have brought it to him altogether'. Ward's claim that Webster could not read Latin was unfounded: Webster had been a master of a grammar school in Clitheroe in 1643–47, and his library contained numerous Latin works (Elmer, *Library*). Ward's claim was based on Webster's mistranslation of Gassendi's quotation from 'one who usually prefaces Aristotle's works' ('quae vulgo jam praefigitur operibus Aristoteleis'): 'Accedebat ad haec, ingenium viri tectum, & callidum, & metuens reprehensionis, quod inhibebat eum, ne proferret interdùm apertè quae sentiret' ('To these [i.e. Aristotle's many positive qualities] was added the protective and crafty nature of the man, afraid of criticism; which sometimes inhibited him from advancing openly what he was thinking') (Gassendi, *Exercitationes*, 86–7). The quotation, offered by both Gassendi and Webster without attribution, is from Juan Luis Vives's oft-reprinted preface to Aristotle's works (see e.g. Vives, 'De Aristotelis operibus censura', in Aristotle, *Opera* (12 vols, Venice, 1560), I, sig. B^v). Ward's accusation was based on the fact that Webster's translation

Glanvill and Sprat, to which we shall come forthwith, Webster did not even amend his uses of the anti-Aristotelian tradition to suit a methodological agenda: since the basis of his attack was that the universities slavishly adhered to Aristotle, he felt that all he had to do was regurgitate anti-Aristotelian commonplaces. The only hint of other sources is a negative historicisation of Galen in which the Roman physician was dismissed as a fame-seeking corrupter of Hippocrates; this was again clearly a simple paraphrase of van Helmont.[178]

Webster's accusations had little impact, not because they were based on unsound scholarship but because they were premised on the idea that Aristotle was still dominant in English universities, an idea that Wilkins and Ward could easily refute (conveniently absolving them of any need actually to engage with Gassendi's philology). The only anti-Webster reading of Aristotle of interest in this respect was an anonymous interpretation of Aristotle's logic incorporated into a response to Webster by the presbyterian minister Thomas Hall, *Vindiciae literarum* (1654).[179] Hall's defence of the usefulness of philosophy contained the usual claims for philosophy's biblical sanction and references to the putative philosophical learning of Moses, Solomon, and the church fathers.[180] But the anonymous section on Aristotle's logic went rather further in challenging Webster's assertion that Aristotle's logic was obscure and confused on account of its reduction of all modal propositions to four types (necessary, impossible, possible, and contingent), when all adjectives could in fact be moods.[181] The author argued that Webster has erred in thinking that Aristotelian moods were types of propositions when they were in fact 'generall Rule[s] for all the species [of proposition]'.[182] Hall was certainly exaggerating when he advertised on his title page that this was an 'elaborate defence of logick by a learned pen', for this was a standard reading of Aristotle, available in the most widely read textbooks.[183]

---

began, 'There happened to these things, the closs wit of the man ... ' Webster had missed that 'accedere' followed by 'ad' means 'added to', wrongly preferring 'to happen', and leading Ward to claim (*Vindiciae*, 33–4) that this was the only passage translated by Webster himself.

[178] Webster, *Academiarum examen*, 73. Ward did not spot this plagiarism, but recognised (*Vindiciae*, 33) that some of Webster's anti-Aristotle comments (*Academiarum examen*, 65–7) were also taken from Helmont (i.e. *Ortus medicinae*, 46).

[179] Hall, *Vindiciae Literarum* (Hall claimed that he would not have published the work, given the sufficient defence by Ward and Wilkins, had he not received the defence of logic: see the preface to *Histrio-mastix. A whip for Webster*, incorporated into Thomas Hall, *Vindiciae literarum* from 197, at sig. O3ʳ). For Hall's biography and the context, see Debus, *Debate*, 49–51; Hughes, 'Popular presbyterianism in the 1640s and 1650s' (1998).

[180] Hall, *Vindiciae Literarum*, 11–13, 38.

[181] Webster, *Academiarum examen*, 32–8, esp. 36. See Aristotle, *De interpretatione*, chs. 7–8.

[182] [Anon.], *Histrio-Mastix. A whip for Webster* in *Vindiciae Literarum*, 226–8.

[183] E.g. Robert Sanderson, *Logicae artis compendium* (Oxford, 1615), 104–9. This work was regularly reprinted throughout the seventeenth century.

Far more important and consequential than the arguments of those who wanted to reform the universities were those closer to the traditional mainstream who nonetheless wanted to reform natural philosophy. The most important of these was Robert Boyle, not only because of his vast influence on the culture of Restoration natural philosophy but also because the surviving evidence allows us to demonstrate the variety of historical viewpoints that could lead to a preference for what Boyle himself would start calling 'experimental philosophy'.[184] Readings of Boyle's early turn to natural philosophy have differed significantly between presenting him as a radical sectarian iconoclast and a relatively mainstream figure of the type prominent in 1650s Oxford.[185] His views on the history of philosophy reveal much on this score.

Late in life, Boyle recounted that his interest in natural philosophy was sparked by reading Diogenes Laërtius.[186] Indeed, he was not the only major Restoration natural philosopher to supply such an intellectual autobiography, for John Beale also described how 'in my youth I read in Laertius ... ye characters' of the philosophers.[187] This is only further confirmation that Stanley and Sherburne were not misguided in believing their works would be of interest to aspiring natural philosophers (2.4 above). Boyle's formative years have been well charted: his preoccupation, from the mid-1640s, with moralising romances, his interest in biblical exegesis and personal piety from the early 1650s onward, his turn to natural philosophy as he set up a laboratory at his house in Stalbridge in 1649–50, and his subsequent interest in chymical experimentation in particular, as he worked with Starkey and with Samuel Hartlib's son-in-law, Frederic Clodius.[188] His views in this period on the history of philosophy reflected those interests. It is certainly right to call him an 'anti-Aristotelian', but what precisely he considered to be the source of Aristotle's error is harder to pinpoint, as the early work in which he explained

---

[184] The historiography on Boyle and his influence is now vast; landmarks are Hunter, *Boyle*; Hunter, *The Boyle papers* (2007); Hunter, *Robert Boyle: scrupulosity and science* (2000); Hunter, ed., *Robert Boyle by himself and his friends* (1994); the essays in Hunter, ed., *Robert Boyle reconsidered* (1994) and Dennehy and Ramond, eds., *La philosophie naturelle de Robert Boyle* (2009); MacIntosh, ed., *Boyle on atheism* (2005); Harwood, ed., *The early essays and ethics of Robert Boyle* (1991); Sargent, *The diffident naturalist* (1995); Anstey, *The philosophy of Robert Boyle* (2000); Wojcik, *Robert Boyle and the limits of reason* (1997); Principe, 'Virtuous romance and romantic virtuoso' (1995); Newman, 'The alchemical sources of Robert Boyle's corpuscular philosophy' (1996). For further references to studies of Boyle's corpuscularianism by Newman and Clericuzio, see Ch. 5 below.

[185] There is a useful overview of the debates in Hunter, 'Boyle's early intellectual evolution: a reappraisal' (2015).

[186] 'Burnet memorandum' in *Boyle by himself*, ed. Hunter, 26.

[187] Beale to Oldenburg, 31 Jan 1662, *Oldenburg correspondence*, II, 16. On Beale, see 6.4 below.

[188] Hunter, 'How Boyle became a scientist', in Hunter, *Scrupulosity*, 15–57; Principe, 'Virtuous romance'; Harwood, 'Introduction', in *The early essays*. On his early chymical interests, see Principe, *Aspiring adept*, 159–62; Hunter, *Boyle*, 76–9.

'what I thinke of the Philosophy of Aristotle' has not survived.[189] Similarly, at several points in his 1650s manuscripts Boyle refers to his reading of Aristotelian commentaries, but it is never clear how extensive this reading was (although he later cited Julius Caesar Scaliger's work with some approval).[190] Unsurprisingly there are hints of a Baconian/Helmontian attitude: references appear to Aristotle's 'sophisticall Ravings', and, interestingly, criticisms of Aristotle are on several occasions followed by deleted references to Galen, suggesting a Helmontian influence on the issue which was then suppressed.[191]

Yet Boyle's anti-Aristotelianism also had an idiosyncratic streak in that he associated Aristotle's natural philosophy with theological hubris, whether in its original form,[192] in the hands of scholastic theologians,[193] or (in particular) in the hands of Pomponazzi and the Socinians.[194] These tendencies towards an anti-philosophical fideism never left Boyle, as we see from later manuscripts. They certainly have a familial relationship with the scepticism of the mid-century reformers about philosophy as a preparative to theology, a scepticism which had its ultimate origins in the Renaissance fideism of Savonarola and Gianfrancesco Pico della Mirandola: it is no coincidence that we find Boyle citing Mirandola's dictum about the dependence of wisdom on divine truth: 'The Hebrews drinke at the Fountaine, the Greekes of the streames, & the Latines of the Puddles; says the excellent Prince de la Mirandola'.[195]

Still, Boyle's attitude must be carefully differentiated from that of the mid-century reformers.[196] Like them, he found in the history of Christianity the

---

[189] This work is referred to in Boyle, 'Essay of the holy Scriptures' (*c.* 1652), in *Boyle works*, XIII, 190. I assume that this may have been the essay 'Of naturall philosophy & filosofers', listed in the catalogue 'Materials & addenda', 25 January 1649/50', in *Boyle works*, XIV, 329, although another possibility is the essay 'Of antiquity & new-light', also listed there.

[190] For references to Aristotelian commentators: Boyle, 'Of the study of the book of nature' (*c.* 1652), in *Boyle works*, XIII, 154–5; Boyle, 'Essay of the holy Scriptures', 190–1, 201. For Scaliger, see e.g., *The origin of forms and qualities* (1666–7), in *Boyle works*, v, 339–40.

[191] See e.g. Boyle, 'Essay of the holy Scriptures', as in the original manuscript (RS BP7, fol. 51$^r$): 'When the Adorers of Aristotle & ~~Galen~~ <his Scholiasts>, shall by their Masters Principles make out those Effects of Nature … ' and fol. 55$^r$: '[I] dare allow my self the Liberty of thinking Aristotle ~~& Galen~~ or any that *Confine* themselves to his Principles, none of the Competent'st Judges of what Nature, or God by his, can & cannot doe' (for these passages in normalised transcription, see *Boyle Works*, XIII, 201, 203).

[192] Boyle, 'Essay of the Holy Scriptures', 191.  [193] Ibid., 200–1, 203.

[194] Ibid., 187 (Pomponazzi), 191 (on Socinians borrowing from the 'Scholiasts of Aristotle'). See e.g. RS BP1, fols. 160$^r$, 162$^r$, where all ancient philosophers' attempts to describe God's perfection are dismissed as hubristic self-projection onto him, and their failure to say anything worthwhile about infinity is remarked on (in 'Papers on the idea of an infinitely perfect being and related topics', 1670s-80s, fols. 159$^r$–162$^r$). For general emphasis on this theme, see Wojcik, *Limits*.

[195] Boyle, 'Study of the book of nature', 153–4. For such sentiments later in Boyle's life, see Boyle, 'Letter to Mr. H[enry] O[ldenburg]' (*c.* 1675?), in *Boyle Works*, XIV, 270.

[196] On this theme in general, see the nuanced discussion in the Appendix to Hunter, 'Became', 51–7.

lesson of the danger of excessive theological rationalism.[197] But unlike them he never moved to a fully fledged anti-intellectual fideism. Partly this was a response to the realisation that scriptural exegesis depended on philologically precise historical contextualism, a realisation imprinted on him by his discussions with Selden and especially with Ussher.[198] Analogously, Boyle never adopted a fully fideist attitude to philosophy's potential to serve theology. He found a historical precedent for this potential in the ancient philosopher-priests: 'The Indian Brachmanes & Gymnosophists, the Persian Magi, the Old Gaules Druides, <not> to mention other Instances, were both their Philosophers & Priests; & in almost all Nations; Philosophy & Priesthood were so ally'd, that those whose Profession should give them most interest in the Deffinition of Man; made a more strict Profession of celebrating & serving God'.[199]

It should be noted that this idea of philosopher-priests has attracted attention, both in Boyle's case[200] and more widely; it has recently been accorded a very large degree of novelty and importance, with claims that it was only conceivable in a radically post-scholastic world: 'Such an understanding of natural philosophers is possible only on the basis of a wholly new conception of the enterprise, and a wholly new conception of those who commanded the requisite authority to undertake it'.[201] Adopting a wider contextual view, we may want to temper some of these claims. That the ancient eastern sages had combined natural philosophy and theology was a commonplace in entirely standard Aristotelian natural philosophy textbooks, many of which were available in England. Not particularly scholarly, they often traced the history of such practices back to Adam himself (Solomon was also a favourite, as he was for Boyle).[202] We can find such a narrative in Wendelin's *Contemplationes physicae*. In the preface, students would have learnt that 'the study of nature is clearly a divine and sacred thing', a sentiment demonstrated by a long list of those who came to the veneration of God through the study of nature, from the

---

[197] See e.g. 'Essay of the Holy Scriptures', 193: 'Philosophy did Christianity more mischiefe then Persecutions'.

[198] Hunter, *Boyle*, 80. It was Selden who convinced him, 'both in private conference & in his Excellent Tract of the Syrian Dietys', that 'divers Passages of the Mosaicall Law' could only be understood through reference to the 'Religion of the ancient Zabians' (Boyle, 'Essay of the Holy Scriptures', 181–2, 218). For Boyle's later use of the Sabians, see below. In the 'Essay of the Holy Scriptures' we find Boyle engaging in remarkably up-to-date discussion of biblical typology, which modern scholars have yet to analyse fully (211–15).

[199] Boyle, 'Of the study of the book of Nature', 153.

[200] Ben-Chaim, 'Robert Boyle and the moral economy of experiment' (2002); H. Fisch, 'The scientist as priest' (1953).

[201] Gaukroger, *Emergence*, 152–3 (see also 227), and Harrison, *Rise*, 197–9, also placing this supposedly transformative moment in the mid-seventeenth century, and giving special emphasis to Boyle. For a similar conclusion reached in a different way, see Corneanu, *Regimens of the mind* (2012), esp. 138–40.

[202] Boyle, 'Study of the book of nature', 147–8; 'Essay of the Holy Scriptures', 196–7.

long-living patriarchs through to the Chaldeans and Egyptians (who mingled true veneration with their own idolatry) and then the Greeks.[203] Very similar, if less detailed, narratives were available in John Prideaux's *Hypomnemata* (1650) and would later appear in Adrian Heereboord's *Meletemata philosophica* (1665, English edn, 1680).[204]

I give these examples not to suggest that Boyle drew on them but to show that his vision of pre-Greek natural philosophy as a spiritual exercise was far from a unique one: it did not depend on a new physico-theological view of the world intimately tied to the new philosophy. Boyle's main source came from the apologetic tradition whose late sixteenth-century *locus classicus* was Philippe de Mornay's *Traité de la vérité de la religion chrétienne* (1581), very often reprinted in England in either Latin or English translation.[205] It was Mornay who supplied Boyle with the idea that the ancient Philosophers 'still'd [sic] the World a Temple', with his references to Galen's *De usu partium* (whose semi-providential analysis of the body made it a favourite for these kinds of Christian natural-philosophical apologetics), and with his reference to the spuriously Aristotelian *De mundo*, particularly attractive to Christians because of its providentialism (making it unique in the 'Aristotelian' corpus), which Boyle presented as Aristotle's modification of his earlier 'sophisticall Ravings', a modification accomplished once the Stagirite had acquainted himself with a 'Philosophy which he learnt of the Creatures'.[206] Mornay even supplied Boyle

---

[203] Wendelin, *Contemplationes physicae*, sigs. A3$^r$–[A5]$^r$. The quotation forms the first line of the dedication (sig. A3$^r$: 'Res sacra & planè divina *Naturae* studium est').

[204] Prideaux, *Hypomnemata*, 215–19; Heereboord, *Meletemata philosophica*, 1b. For an off-hand English appropriation, see e.g. Cary, *Palaegologia chronica*, 4.

[205] Mornay was first translated into English, partially by Sir Philip Sidney, as *A worke concerning the trewness of the Christian religion* (London, 1587); further editions followed in 1592, 1604, and 1617.

[206] Boyle, 'Study of the book of nature', 150–1 (world a temple, drawing on Mornay, *Trewnesse*, 38–9); 156, 162 (Galen's *De usu partium*, drawing on Mornay, *Trewnesse*, 169); 162 (ps.-Aristotle's *De mundo*, drawing on Mornay, *Trewnesse*, 35). Peter Harrison has claimed that 'it is likely that Boyle found these ideas [i.e. the world as temple] in ancient writers', citing Macrobius and Philo (*Rise*, 198, n. 194). This judgement ignores the manuscript evidence, and thus fails to recognise Boyle's direct use of Mornay for these commonplaces. For the popularity of Galen in Protestant pedagogy, in part because he was so amenable to providentialist apologetics, see Nutton, 'Wittenberg anatomy' (1993). Around the same time, Benjamin Whichcote recorded in his notebook that 'Galen ascribes y$^e$ system of mans Body to a great minde, so writes a Booke de usu partium & entitles it Hymnes Deo Conditore' (Folger, MS V.a.326, fol. 39$^v$ rev. (my foliation). In 1651, William Rand found *De usu partium* to be so popular that he could not buy a copy (Rand to Benjamin Worsley, 11 Aug 1651, HP, 62/21/1A–2B). But I have found one exception, which I am at a loss to explain: the commonplace book of Henry Oxenden, *c.* 1640s–60s, Folger MS V.b.110, p. 56: 'Galen will not approve of y$^e$ Christian Religion quia demonstratione caret. He was an Atheist'. The ps.-Aristotelian *De mundo* had by this point come under significant philological doubt (Kraye, 'Aristotle's God'; Kraye, 'Heinsius'), but it was a favourite citation for the *novatores*: see e.g., Walter Charleton, *The darkness of atheism* (London, 1652), 50–1; Evelyn, *History of religion*, I, 5 (adding 'if it be his'); Boyle 'Essay of the holy Scriptures', 187. Locke found Boyle's attribution of *De mundo*

with his similar references to Hermes Trismegistus performing natural philosophy as a spiritual *paideia*. James R. Jacob claimed Boyle's discussion of Hermes is evidence of engagement with Interregnum sectarianism, because one of Boyle's references to Hermes came from a translation of the *Corpus Hermeticum* by John Everard.[207] Everard was indeed a sectarian (specifically a Familist), and a practising alchemist who saw the Hermetical–alchemical tradition as a means for allowing one direct contact with the divine: his other works contain references suggesting an illuminationist reading of Hermes.[208] However, the edition of the *Corpus Hermeticum* used by Boyle was published after Everard's death and contains far less of the mystical spiritualism that marked Everard's unpublished commentaries on the Hermetic material. Boyle simply amalgamated Hermes into the image of him presented by Mornay, and thus into the canon of those who 'were curious to contemplate God in his Workes'.[209] The language of physico-theology stemmed not from a radical shift of worldview, but from the appropriation of long-familiar humanist commonplaces.[210]

Before 1660, then, the key steps taken in the historical justification of experimental method were either those of the post-Harvey learned physicians or of Boyle in his private manuscripts. The aggressive historical elements of Baconian rhetoric had been usurped by the institutional reformers like Webster, who combined them with Gassendi's humanist anti-Aristotelianism: they were easily opposed not because the historical arguments were not convincing but because defenders of the universities could simply bypass the whole issue by denying that the curriculum was particularly Aristotelian. It was not until the 1660s, and the rise of the Royal Society and the problems faced by the Royal College of Physicians, that a full historical debate about natural philosophical method broke out.

## 4.4    Histories of natural philosophical method after 1660

It emerges – somewhat to this historian's surprise – that the situation did shift rather fundamentally in the 1660s. The key components of the debate did not change much. What did change was that these components were re-deployed towards a new focus on *method*. Where someone like Webster had used

---

to Aristotle interesting enough to note it in a commonplace book under the heading 'Aristoteles': Bod. MS Locke f.14 [notebook, *c.* 1659–67], p. 34.

[207] Jacob, *Boyle and the English revolution*, 311 (Jacob's claims are already convincingly challenged in Hunter, 'Became').

[208] On Everard's religiosity, see Schuler, 'Some spiritual alchemies', esp. 308–17.

[209] Boyle 'Study of the book of nature', 153–4 (see also 168); 'Essay of the Holy Scriptures', 182; *Usefulness*, 270–1 (all these clearly derived from Mornay).

[210] See further Levitin, 'Parker'.

the anti-Aristotelian tradition indiscriminately to chastise the universities for using Aristotle, defenders of the newly formed Royal Society like Thomas Sprat and Joseph Glanvill re-focused and re-deployed it as an *ex post facto* defence of experimental method. Similarly, various medical reformers shifted from a broad and unfocused anti-Galenism to a more concerted vision of the history of medical method and its relationship to natural philosophy. However, this raised problems, especially for the Royal Society apologists: the anti-Aristotelian tradition as it stood was not designed for the methodological task they put it to, and they found themselves on the ropes when faced by philologically equipped opponents who were not constrained by similar methodological straitjackets. The learned physicians were able to adapt far better, partly because they were already used to examining the history of their own discipline and its methodology, and to defending its 'practical' components.

The Royal Society was not a united body with a homogenous ideology, whether political, religious, or natural philosophical, and no text, and certainly not Sprat's semi-official *History of the Royal Society* (1667), can be read as a manifestation of such an ideology.[211] After a promising and optimistic beginning, by the late 1660s the Society entered into what has fairly been labelled a 'crisis', with dwindling enthusiasm and membership, attacks from without, and other institutional problems. Some of these were linked to the Society's struggle to defend its supposed intellectual identity, which we shall consider here.[212]

The Royal College of Physicians faced different, if related, problems. In April 1664 it failed to pass in Parliament a bill giving statutory authority to a new College charter.[213] The charter had been opposed not only by traditional institutional competitors, the Society of Apothecaries and the Barber-Surgeons' Company, but also, it seems, by some who favoured the new experimental philosophy and who were able to garner support at court.[214] In mid-1665, also at court, attempts were made (led by Thomas O'Dowde) to establish a Society of Chemical Physicians: signatories of the petition included some of the medical reformers of the 1650s.[215] Opponents of learned medicine invariably claimed that their methods were more

---

[211] Hunter, 'Ideology'.

[212] Hunter, *Royal Society*, 38–41; Hunter and Wood, 'Rival strategies for reforming the early Royal Society' (1989), 185–244.

[213] Cook, *Decline*, 133–41.

[214] Cook, 'The Society of Chemical Physicians, the new philosophy, and the Restoration court' (1987). For the relationship between the new philosophy and medicine in general, the essential study remains Cook, 'The new philosophy and medicine'.

[215] Cook, 'Society'; see also Rattansi, 'The Helmontian-Galenist controversy in Restoration England' (1964); Webster, 'A background to the "Society of Chymical Physitians"' (1967).

'experimental' than the bookish or speculative approaches of the physicians. But the divisions were not simple, for five groups can be identified: (1) the extreme critics of existing learned physic and supporters of chymical medicine (Marchamont Nedham, Edward Bolnest, Thomas O'Dowde, George Starkey, George Thomson); (2) virtuosi-physicians who practised both learned medicine and the new philosophy, and were thus often members of the both the Royal Society and the College of Physicians (e.g. Daniel Coxe, Timothy Clarke, Christopher Merrett, Jonathan Goddard); (3) virtuosi who concerned themselves, publicly or privately, with the state of physic (Boyle, Thomas Willis, John Locke); (4) the staunch defenders of learned medicine and the privileges of the College of Physicians (John Twysden, Robert Sprackling, Henry Stubbe); and (5) the Royal Society apologists who sometimes commented on medical matters (Sprat, Glanvill). All had recourse to historical arguments, and it is with their debates that we shall begin.

### 4.4.1    The historical challenge to learned medicine

The natural-philosophical and medical stories run parallel, have many interconnections, and converge on the figure of Henry Stubbe. At the risk of privileging narrative convenience over interpretative precision, we shall tell them serially, beginning with the medical. But we might begin with a concurrence here too: the section in Boyle's *Usefulness of experimenal natural philosophy* (1663) entitled 'Of its usefulness to physick' (written during the late 1650s).[216] Boyle read directly in the primary sources when writing this work;[217] most importantly, his argument – that experimental philosophy would bring benefits to physic – involved concerted engagement with the history of medical method, and particularly the relationship between Empiric and Rational medicine.

Boyle drew extensively on Celsus's preface to *De medicina*, twice quoting long passages that claimed that the origin of medicine lay in un-theorised experience, as well as citing positively the Empiric dictum quoted by Celsus, that 'it does not concern us what causes the disease, but what removes it'.[218] Combined with some rather disparaging comments about the 'imperfect Method' of the 'generality of Physitians' and a focus on chymical over Galenic medicine,

---

[216] For the dating: *Boyle works*, III, xxii-iv, liv-viii. The most important studies of Boyle and medicine are Hunter, 'Boyle versus the Galenists' in Hunter, *Scrupulosity*, 187–222, and Kaplan, *The medical agenda of Robert Boyle* (1993).

[217] See e.g. BP8, fols. 3ᵛ–4ʳ.

[218] Robert Boyle, *Some considerations of the usefulnesse of natural philosophy. II, I* (1663), in *Boyle works*, III, 428, 468–9 (the Empiric origins of medicine, drawing on Celsus, *De med.*, Prooem., 33, 35); also 459.

the text took on, at points, a reformist tone.[219] But as was often the case, Boyle wanted to have his cake and eat it: to resuscitate the reputation of those who had for so long been disparaged by philosophers (i.e. Empirics), while at the same time also claiming that what he was promoting was still 'philosophy'. So he also cited a separate passage from Celsus that suggested that '[a]t first the science of healing was held to be part of philosophy' and that Pythagoras, Empedocles and Democritus were all philosopher–physicians before Hippocrates 'severd Physick from Philosophy, and made it a distinct Discipline'.[220] Indeed, so desperate was Boyle that his readers were not put off by his use of the 'name of Emperick' that he misattributed a saying to Aristotle to support the sect.[221] This ambiguity would lead to a tug of war over his reputation between opponents and defenders of academic medicine in the debate that ran from the mid-1660s.[222]

Lying behind this moderate tone, however, was a far more critical attitude to Galen and his method, to be found in Boyle's suppressed attack on academic medicine, begun *c.* 1664–68.[223] The plans for this critique contain one important historical claim: that 'where specificks are knowne there deseases very formidable are successfuly cured without the help of a method built on Artificiall Indications which Gallen <& Sennertus> ~~him~~themselves confesses not to take place in such cases namely in the wounds of scorpions vipers, mad Dogs & in other deseases springing from poisons'.[224] Boyle did not offer a citation but it is clear that he was referring to Galen's *De methodo medendi*, IV.3 (K X.244–7). There, Galen discussed *prokatarktic* (προκαταρκτικός) causes, which he elsewhere defined as causes 'which befall from without', to be distinguished from *proegoumenic* (προηγούμενος) causes, 'which exist in the actual body of the animal'.[225] Method dictated that *prokatarktic* causes were

---

[219] Boyle, *Usefulnesse*, 458. At 439–40, Boyle cited Galen, *De simp. med. fac.*, VI.3.10 (K XI.859–60) (a peony amulet cures epilepsy) to claim that Galen himself sometimes favoured proto-chymical medicines.

[220] Boyle, *Usefulnesse*, 437, quoting Celsus, *De med.*, Prooem., 6.

[221] Boyle, *Usefulnesse*, 469: 'And lest the mistaken name of Emperick should make you under-value so useful a Consideration, which not the nature of their Sect, but that of the thing, suggested to them; I shall adde ... a sentence ascrib'd to *Aristotle* (and in my opinion, one of the best that is ascrib'd to him,) *Ubi res constat, si opinio adversetur rei, quarendam rationem non rem ignorandam*'. The quotation in fact comes from Julius Caesar Scaliger's commentary on Aristotle's *On plants*: *Julii Ceasaris Scaligeri in libros duos, qui inscribuntur de Plantis, Aristotele authore, libri duo* (Marburg, 1598), 218. Boyle read and admired Scaliger (n. 190 above), but he may have been misled on this score by Sennert, whom he read even more extensively: see Daniel Sennert, *Opera omnia* (4 vols, Lyon, 1656), I, 138a.

[222] Hunter, 'Boyle versus the Galenists', 162–5.  [223] Ibid., 166ff.

[224] Boyle, 'Considerations & doubts touching the vulgar method of physick' (BP8, fols. 133–4, at fol. 134ʳ), printed as Appendix 1 to Hunter, 'Boyle versus the Galenists', 187–9 at 188–9. The reference to Sennert is superscript, and I believe it was a later addition, for the reasons given below.

[225] Galen, *Meth. med.*, I.8 (K X.65–6) (see also *Caus. morb.*, II.5 (K VII.10)).

irrelevant to the therapeutic and prophylactic parts of medicine, which dealt with things that exist or will exist. That is because the indication (ἔνδειξις) of a disease 'takes its origin from the nature of the matter'. It is a logical 'reflection . . . of what is consequent', and thus 'whatever is distinct from experience is all called indication'.[226] In the passage under discussion, Galen states that Empirics take the *prokatarktic* cause as part of the whole syndrome when dealing with bites of rabid dogs or venomous creatures, and that some Dogmatics also treat such things from experience alone, rather than from the 'logical indication'. He admits that *prokatarktic* causes can contribute to the diagnosis of a condition (it helps to know that someone has been stung by a scorpion), but only if there is some knowledge lacking of the actual condition: they can thus be useful for diagnosing conditions, but not as indications for therapy.

Boyle's usage seriously distorted Galen on artificial indications: there was no mention that the reference came in a discussion of *prokatarktic* causes, and Galen's caveats were ignored. This was because it was clearly an attempt to show that even Galen was an inheritor of the 'Empiric' roots of medicine that Boyle hinted at in the published text of the *Usefulnesse*. But Boyle was here developing a long-running humanist theme, begun by the Parisian physician Jean Fernel (1497–1558). Fernel's *De abditis rerum causis* (1548) became famous throughout European medical circles for proposing a new medical theory based on a pneumatology that emphasised the operation of occult morbific causes; Fernel had insisted on the physician's 'experimental' duties in response to men's inability to discover the causal operation of many occult diseases, laying particular stress on rabies and scorpion stings.[227] Fernel's manipulation of Galen on causes was taken up by many (in England the apothecaries used it in the 1630s to insist on the priority of experience over natural philosophical theorising in medicine),[228] including the author named by Boyle, Daniel Sennert, in whom we can see a desire to render Galen more experiential by softening some of the potentially anti-experiential implications of his rhetoric about indications.[229] Sennert never offered this specific textual

---

[226] Galen, *Meth. med.*, III.1 (K x.157); II.7 (K x.126–7). For the Renaissance debate over indications, see Maclean, *Learned medicine*, 306–15. For a later extensive discussion, based on a close reading of Galen, see Daniel Sennert, *Institutionum medicinae libri quinque* (Wittenberg, 1644), 1067a–1068a (on the use of Sennert in English medical faculties, see Frank, 'Medicine', 535–7).

[227] See Jean Fernel, *On the hidden causes of things*, eds. and trans., J. M. Forrester and J. Henry (Leiden, 2005), esp. 611–13, 735; see also Forrester and Henry's 'Introduction', 50–3.

[228] Levitin, 'Apothecaries'.

[229] E.g., Sennert, *Institutiones medicinae*, 1068a–b (directly after the long examination of Galen on indications): 'Non autem hoc ita accipiendum, quasi Medicus dogmaticus planè non utatur experientia aut analogismo: sed ideo solùm haec Galenus addidit, ut hunc per indicationes inveniendi remedia modum, qui dogmaticorum proprius est, & ex affectus per caussas cognitione proficitur, ab aliis secerneret. Indicatio enim sola proprium Medici dogmatici ad invenienda auxilia instrumentum est. Experientia verò & analogismus cum aliis ipsi communis.

example from Galen, so it appears that Boyle worked directly from the source (it is possible that reading Sennert inspired him to examine Galen). Thus even the relatively iconoclastic Boyle was directly inheriting the experiential rhetoric of the medical humanists of the sixteenth century.

Boyle's name was repeatedly used in the 1660s debates over medical practice, but the medical reformers' histories of medicine and natural philosophy usually took on slightly different forms to his. The debate had its textual starting point in the *Medela medicinae*, a long tract calling for medical reform, and especially for the introduction of Helmontian chemical medicine, by Cromwell's former chief publicist Marchamont Nedham, dated 1665 but published in late 1664, shortly after the Royal College of Physician's failure to obtain their charter.[230] The work contained two key historical arguments. The first was that because so many new diseases had developed since antiquity on account of the 'spreading of the *Venerous* and *Scorbutick* Ferments', ancient methods were unsuitable to the tasks of modern medicine.[231] This was in direct contradiction to what Glisson was teaching about the applicability of Galenic method to new diseases like rickets (4.3.1 above).

Second, Nedham developed at some length a vision of the history of medical method. On the relatively simple structure of Hippocrates, Galen built a 'fictitious' theory of humours, qualities, and contraries, all for the sake of worldly renown: the schools inherited this cumbersome system.[232] This was pure Helmont. But Nedham also went further in his desire to present a historically convincing *ad hominem* attack, drawing on the rather hostile *Epitome* (1554) of Galen's work by Andreas Lacuna, which endowed Nedham's reformist text with an aura of learned authority badly lacking from the chymical tradition.[233] From Lacuna, he took the claim (resonant of the anti-Aristotelian

---

Nam cum nocens seu indicans incognitum est, indicatione uti non possumus: itaque tum ad experientiam & analogismum confugere licet'.

[230] M[archamont] N[edham], *Medela medicinae. A plea for the free profession, and a renovation of the art of physick* (London, 1665); Cook, 'Society'; King, *The road to medical Enlightenment* (1970), 145–54; Jones, *Ancients and moderns* (1961), 206–10. Nedham's use of Hippocrates, and the response of Sprackling, is briefly discussed in Cunningham, 'The transformation of Hippocrates in seventeenth-century Britain' (2002), at 97–102 (for qualifications of this discussion, see below).

[231] Nedham, *Medela medicinae*, 29–203 (62–5 on 'Venereous and Scorbutick Ferments'); Cook, *Decline*, 146–7; Stevenson, 'New diseases', 15–17.

[232] Nedham, *Medela medicinae*, 240–1, drawing (with acknowledgement) on Helmont, *Ortus medicinae*, 8ff. See also 246–7, where it is denied that Hippocrates held a four-elements theory, drawing on the commentary by Johan van Heurne, in Hippocrates, *Prolegomena, et prognosticorum libri tres* (Leiden, 1597), 81.

[233] Andreas Lacuna, *Epitome omnium rerum et sententiarum, quae annotatu dignae im commentariis Galeni in Hippocratem extant* (Lyon, 1554). Lacuna is almost totally unstudied: he is entirely missing from Temkin, *Galenism: rise and decline of a medical philosophy* (1973); for some very brief comments, see Maclean, *Learned medicine*, 218, 230 (I have been unable to

tradition) that Galen was said to have 'made it his business to rail at others that were before him': Herostratus, Asclepiades, Protagoras, Erasistratus, Herophilus, and even his own master Quintus, who was – no less – an Empiric. This was, so to speak, in Galen's blood: 'his Mother having been such another perpetual Clack to his Father, as *Xantippe* was to *Socrates*'; itself only known because Galen besmirched her in his *Affections of the mind*.[234] Needless to say, Vesalius's proof that Galen had never performed human anatomy also made an appearance.[235]

These nuggets are of less importance than the historical framework Nedham placed them in. Building on Boyle's few positive references to the Empirics, Nedham expanded by presenting Hippocrates as a champion of that sect, drawing on the *Precepts*, a late pseudo-Hippocratean work whose first section emphasised that medicine must be based on 'experience combined with reason' rather than 'theories' (λογισμοί).[236] The Empiric refusal to search for causes, as reported by Celsus, made them far more adaptable to studying new diseases, the central motif of Nedham's treatise.[237] This attack on the over-readiness to search for causes was supported by the example of the ancient physicians' most absurd causal search: their attribution of events in the course of a disease to decretorial and critical days. Here even Hippocrates was to be condemned, as he already had been by the Epicurean physicians Asclepiades and by Nedham's favourite Celsus. To defend Celsus, Nedham entered directly into humanist controversy, challenging (correctly) the richly documented assertion of the Jewish Galenist Abraham Zacuto (1575–1642) that Celsus had at this point only reported Asclepiades's judgement, not his own.[238] Boyle's use of Celsus had clearly spurred reformers like Nedham to conduct their own historical investigations and to incorporate them into the standard Helmontian narrative of Empiric origins and post-Hippocratean collapse.

Nedham's work was much read, acting as the textual catalyst for a debate that lasted until the end of the decade, much of which engaged with and expanded on his historical arguments. There was, however, a historical element of the reformist case not made by Nedham but which first appeared in a treatise

---

obtain a copy of Joaquín Olmedilla y Puig, *Estudio histórico de la vida y escritos del sabio segoviano Andrés Laguna* (Madrid, 1887)).

[234] Nedham, *Medela medicinae*, 241, drawing on Lacuna and Galen, *Aff. dig.*, VIII (K v.40–1).

[235] Nedham, *Medela medicinae*, 366–7.

[236] Ibid., 217, quoting Hippocrates, *Precepta*, II.9–10: 'Be not slack to inquire and learn even from Idiots, if they have any thing that seems to promote a Cure upon occasion' (Nedham's translation).

[237] Nedham, *Medela medicinae*, 228–9.

[238] Ibid., 318–20, drawing, without citation, on Celsus, *De med.*, III.4.11–15. See Zacutus Lusitanus, *De medicorum principum historia*, in *Opera omnia* (2 vols, Lyon, 1657 [1st edn=1649]), I, 979b. Zacuto's work was the fullest available history of medicine in the mid-seventeenth century: see Friedenwald, *The Jews and medicine* (1944), II, 307–17.

entitled *A letter concerning the present state of physick* (1665), by one
'T.M.'[239] The author classified himself as a 'virtuoso', and his proposal has
been described as one of 'remaking the College [of Physicians] in the image of
the Royal Society'.[240] His whole argument was based on the historical case first
developed by Vesalius and the other medical humanists who had from the
sixteenth century insisted on the need for physicians to re-engage with the
practical components of the healing arts. Modern physic suffered because of its
deviation 'from the *ancient Form* and *Method* of *Practice*'.[241] It was necessary,
'for the effective application of the principles of a better Philosophy to the
noble *Experiments* of *Physick* ... to bring again those *Experiments* into
the hands of such persons who know how to manage and employ them'.[242]
This meant a return to 'those Ages' when the physician was not separate from
the apothecary, and 'did not think it too mean a work to ... *compound
Medicines, with his own hands*'.[243] This was the practice of both Hippocrates
(in the *Epistola ad Damagetum* he asks for simples to help him concoct a cure
for Democritus), and Galen, who travelled to Cyprus to collect medicinal
ingredients and scolded those 'who contented themselves to know Simples
out of Books'.[244] Those who claimed that apothecaries were a separate profession in Galen's Rome had misunderstood the word '*pharmacopola*', 'which in
those times signifi'd not an *Apothecary*, but such a person we now call a
*Mountebank*' (cleverly, the evidence presented is the opening lines of
Horace's satire of adultery and sexual profligacy, where *pharmacopolae* are
listed alongside beggars, strippers, and 'the federated flute-girls' union' as
those who lament the passing of Tigellius the singer).[245] Learned physicians
had long argued the opposite – that is, that the apothecary had always been a
separate, subordinate profession – using elaborate readings of various Galenic
*loci* to insist that while ancient physicians did indeed make their own medicines, they also had subordinate medical practitioners.[246] T.M.'s argument thus
had obvious polemical valency.

[239] T.M.'s identity has been the subject of some inconclusive dispute. That he was *not* Christopher
Merrett or Timothy Clarke is suggested by, respectively, Roberts, 'Jonathan Goddard,
*Discourse concerning physick and the many abuses thereof by apothecaries*, 1668: A lost
work or a ghost?' (1964), 191 and Cook, *Decline*, 141.
[240] Cook, *Decline*, 142; T.M., *A Letter concerning the present state of physick* (London, 1665), 7–8.
[241] T.M., *Letter*, 9–10. [242] Ibid., 13. [243] Ibid., 10.
[244] Ibid., 20–1 (Hippocrates); 23–4 (Galen). Much is made of the *Epistola ad Damagetum*, to
which the author says he was introduced by an anonymous 'Dr'. I have been unable to identify
who this might be.
[245] T.M., *Letter*, 25, citing Horace, *Sat.*, 1.2.1–3 (I quote from the translation by Niall Rudd
(London, 1979), 44).
[246] See e.g. John Securis, *A detection and querimonie of the daily enormities and abuses comitted
[sic] in physic* ([London], 1566), sigs. D.ii$^v$–D.iii$^r$, D.iv$^v$–D.v$^v$, drawing on Galen, *In Hipp.
Epid.* (=*CMG* v 10.2.2, 257)), and John Cotta, *A short discoverie of the unobserved dangers of
severall sorts of ignorant and unconsiderate pracitsers of physicke* (London, 1612), 47–8
(citing exactly the same passage from Galen). For the European picture more broadly, see

After the treatises of Nedham and T.M. we find the same historical themes adumbrated again and again by proponents of medical reform and chemical medicine. Indeed, some tension can be seen between their attacks on the ancients as unprepared to deal with 'new' diseases and their frequent insistence that modern medical method was a deviation from an earlier Hippocratic or even (uncorrupted) Galenic version, which was experiential.[247] This is a manifestation of the fact that their polemics were trying to do two things at once: attack specific Galenic doctrines, and make a pronouncement about correct method. Helmont had conflated the two by suggesting that Galenic humours and contraries were an outgrowth of his corruption of Hippocratic method, but the 1660s reformers were not always so consistent.[248] Nevertheless, tens of pages were repeatedly devoted towards the history of medicine, especially to the claim that the ancients had combined the *personae* of the physician and apothecary and made their own medicines, a refrain repeated both by the chemical physicians and by members of the College of Physicians (and often simultaneously of the Royal Society) who were sympathetic to a more 'experimental' medicine. Among others, these claims were reasserted by Jonathan Goddard, a leading Glisson-trained physician, important member of the scientific community in 1650s Oxford, and founding member of the Royal Society.[249] Most, as I say, were derivative, but

Findlen, *Nature*, 247–8; Brockliss and Jones, *The medical world of early modern France* (1997), 94–5, 128–9, 217–18.

[247] E.g. Edward Bolnest, *Medicina instaurata, or, a brief account of the true grounds and principles of the art of physick* (London, 1665), at sig. [A6]ʳ, labelling Hippocrates and Galen as 'dreamers', yet at 86 claiming that '*Galen* and *Hippocrates* ... intended not their Labours ... as ... a *non plus ultra*', and going on to quote Hippocrates to the effect that medicine has not 'attained to so great Perfection, that nothing could be added to it' (Bolnest does not offer a citation, and I have been unable to locate the quotation in Hippocrates). Bolnest was a chymical physician who signed O'Dowde's petition: Cook, *Decline*, 152–3.

[248] For historicisations of Galen undoubtedly derived from Helmont, see George Thomson, *Galeno-pare: or, a chymical trial of the Galenist, that their dross in physick may be discovered* (London, 1665), 1–3 (Galen's 'indirect course' of discovery by reducing everything to contraries; his ambition and distortion of Hippocrates; his non-performance of human anatomy and lack of knowledge in botany); see also the very Helmontian attack on contraries at 65–9. On Thomson, who studied in Leiden in the late 1640s after being unable to afford his College of Physicians membership fee, and on his Helmontianism, see Webster, 'The Helmontian George Thomson' (1971). On his 1660s works and his activities during the plague, see Cook, *Decline*, 150, 155–6, 158–60. No doubt because of his clear borrowings from Helmont, he was accused of not even having read Galen in William Johnson, *Agyrto-Mastix, or, some brief animadversions upon two late treatises; ... Galeno-Pale; ... the Poor man's physitian* (London, 1665), 4.

[249] See e.g., Johnson, *Agyrto-Mastix*, 129–34, explicitly accepting the history in T.M.'s *Letter*, but then offering a compromise solution; Jonathan Goddard, *A discourse setting forth the unhappy condition of the practice of physick in London* (London, 1670), 8–9 (this work was in fact composed *c.* 1665 – see 57); [Daniel Coxe], *A discourse wherein the interest of the patient in reference to physick and physicians is soberly debated* (London, 1669), 320–1, clearly drawing, without acknowledgement, on T.M., *Letter*, 20–4. Goddard was a member of the Royal Society who was openly arguing against the apothecaries, but obviously intended the Royal College of Physicians to adopt a more experimental approach (Cook, *Decline*, 169–70). On his contacts with the Oxford experimentalists and his experimental work on respiration and contraction, see Frank,

some showed a high degree of original engagement with the sources, such as the lengthy account of ancient physicians' training and of the history of the apothecary–physician split in the attack on apothecaries by Gideon Harvey, who was not a member of either the College of Physicians or of the Royal Society, but a successful private practitioner with strong sympathies for natural philosophical novelty.[250]

### 4.4.2    The response of the learned physicians: Dogmatism becomes experimental

As the example of Gideon Harvey suggests, there was a high degree of overlap about the history of medicine between chymical reformers and more experimental 'establishment' physicians. Nonetheless, the latter, and their more defensive College of Physicians colleagues, also developed extensive counter-histories to defend the historical role of learned medicine and to expose the dangers of a return to Empiricism. In this, they followed their continental humanist predecessors, and the arguments we have already found being developed in an institutional context by Glisson and Petty, who were sometimes their teachers. But they also drew on the tension present in the reformers' accounts between a historical critique of doctrine on the one hand and of method on the other. This is evident in the first major reply to Nedham, the *Medela ignorantiae* (1665) of Robert Sprackling, a candidate for the College of Physicians.[251] Like every other participant in our debate, Sprackling did not deny that important discoveries had been made since antiquity.[252] Nonetheless, he presented the historical groundwork of Nedham's attack as entirely unstable, at the same time advertising his own learned status by mocking Nedham's translations and by claiming that his own readings of the ancients would be mediated

---

Harvey, 54, 56, 151, 159–61, 233. Coxe was a chymical physician, active member of the Royal Society, and associate of Boyle (Cook, *Decline*, 167–8; Hunter, *Royal Society*, 172–3; Clericuzio, 'From Van Helmont to Boyle', 327).

[250] [Gideon Harvey], *The accomplisht physician* (London, 1670), 40–3, 48–9, 50–3. Harvey was educated in the Low Countries, came to Oxford in 1655 but left without a degree in 1657 to study medicine in Leiden, and established himself in London in the early 1660s. Further study is certainly required: Wallis, 'Harvey, Gideon', *ODNB*, offers the basic biographical details Cunningham, 'Thomas Sydenham: epidemics, experiment and the "Good Old Cause"' (1989) at 182, 187 is concerned only with Harvey's later attacks on Sydenham, without mentioning that they were part of a larger dispute with the Royal College of Physicians over their joint treatment of Lord Mohun; Cantlie, 'Gideon Harvey' (1921), is anecdotal and whiggish, but remains the best source for the primary evidence, including the attribution of the anonymously published *Accomplisht physician* to Harvey (213).

[251] Cook, *Decline*, 147; Jones, *Ancients and moderns*, 210–11; for his biography: Munk, *The Roll of the Royal College of Physicians, vol.* I (1861), 306.

[252] Robert Sprackling, *Medela ignorantiae: or a just and plain vindication of Hippocrates and Galen from the groundless imputations of M. N.* (London, 1665), 51.

not through 'private conjectures' but through 'their received meaning, in the judgment of both ancient and modern Interpreters and Commentators'.[253]

Sprackling's whole case depended on the argument we found being developed both in Oxford (Petty) and in Cambridge (Glisson): Rationalist method was correct, even if specific ancient doctrines were now untendable. The 'common Doctrine of elements, humours, and temperaments' could 'explain the appearances of bodies, and their affections in a gross and general manner, without descending to more particular explications of abstruse and occult causes'.[254] Atomism was a great improvement on this 'common doctrine', but history had shown that full natural philosophical precision was not a prerequisite for medicine: 'it must be granted by all, that these gross notions of humors and temperaments, have served eminently to the Cure of great Diseases for many hundreds of years'.[255] In claiming that elements and humours could be reduced to corpuscularian explanation, Sprackling undoubtedly drew on the tradition of Galeno–chymical syncretism epitomised by Sennert. But he also drew on the same pragmatic view of the relationship between Galenic theory and practice we have found being espoused in the 1650s. To attack specific Galenical doctrines was to misunderstand what Galen was doing; that is to say, building a physiological system that was geared towards medical practice. It was to ruin medicine through philosophical dogmatism: in other words, Sprackling here turned the accusation the chymists were levelling at the learned physicians back onto themselves.

On the other hand, Sprackling continued, Rationalist method was just *philosophical enough*. Responding to Nedham's critique of the doctrine of critical days, Sprackling acknowledged 'that this Philosophy is now exploded', but added: 'But what doth this signifie to you, who are so far from assigning any cause, that you frontlessly deride the very name of *Crisis* it self, and argue out of late Authors by the help of their *Indices* against the cause imagined by *Galen*'.[256] Why criticise Galen's ignorance of human anatomy (à la Vesalius), if you consider anatomy and the search for internal causes useless?[257] In reality, the ancients *had* practised anatomy, for that is what Hippocrates found the allegedly insane Democritus doing in the forest by Abdera.[258] Their conclusions might have been wrong, but their method of learned medicine – the one taught at the universities and promoted by the Royal College of Physicians – was the right one.

---

[253] Ibid., 76–7, 2.   [254] Ibid., 45.

[255] Ibid. See also 147–9, where it is claimed that the chymical principles (spirit, sulphur, salt, water, and earth) are the same as the Aristotelian–Galenic elements.

[256] Sprackling, *Medela ignorantiae*, 15–16.   [257] Ibid., 117–18.

[258] Ibid., 124. Sprackling is being disingenuous here, for the *Epistola ad Damagetum* is clear that Democritus was performing *comparative* anatomy.

The continuity between the arguments of Sprackling and the institutionalised *novatores* of the 1650s was not coincidental. While he was studying with Glisson, he had offered as his 1662 D.M. thesis the case that 'The doctrine of the circulation of the blood in no way changes the ancient *methodus medendi*'.[259] This is an exact analogue of the claims being made by Petty and others in Oxford. What is particularly interesting in this case is that Glisson's sporadic notes on Sprackling's spoken thesis survive, as does the full version of Glisson's response. Glisson agreed with Sprackling that 'the doctrine of the circulation in no way changes the *methodus medendi* of the ancients'.[260] This could be proved in two ways. First, the discovery of the circulation could be portrayed as 'elucidating' (*enodat*) rather than rendering redundant Galenic physiology, specifically the doctrine of the 'vital faculty'. The latter 'is like some occult quality of which [circulation] speaks openly, explaining that on which the formerly occult nature was based'.[261] This reference to occult qualities requiring empirical verification was, as we have seen, a reference to the arguments for the necessity of experience popularised by Fernel.

But, Glisson acknowledged, this might still leave therapeutic discrepancies between the two positions,[262] and so a second argument was of greater importance:

In medical praxis not only are the *indicans* and *indicatum* to be considered, but also the *materia medica* which answers to the *indicatum*; and this certainly is to be discovered not by a *methodus*, but by *experientia*. Indeed, although reason contributes much to that discovery, knowledge of the thing itself is exceedingly unsure and slippery until confirmed by *experientia*. Whence it is little to be wondered at if that praxis which is pointed out by *experientia* is firmly enough based, even if the assigning of cause and essence is worth slight trust and commonly merits correction. For my part, therefore, I would reckon that the true reason why the praxis of the ancients remains, for the most part, established, although their theory is greatly modified, is that the former is more extensively and firmly founded on the *experientia* from which *materia medica* is taught than on their theoretical *methodus* which merely serves the occasion of seeking out such *materia*.[263]

Glisson was defending the ancients by arguing for what might seem as a radical break between their (philosophical) 'theoretical method' (*methodo eorum theoretica*) and their experiential (one is tempted to say 'experimental') practice. He concluded:

---

[259] BL MS Slonae 3309, fols. 341ʳ–343ᵛ. It is usefully transcribed and translated in Boss, 'An unpublished manuscript (1662) by Francis Glisson on implications of Harvey's physiology' (1978). The transcription is for the most part accurate, if extremely difficult to follow due to the symbols utilised. I will give references to both the manuscript and to Boss, using his translations unless stated otherwise.

[260] BL MS Sloane 3309, fol. 343ᵛ (=Boss, 324, 334).

[261] BL Sloane MS 3309, fols. 341ʳ, 343ʳ (=Boss, 318–319, 328–9).

[262] BL Sloane MS 3309, fol. 343ʳ (=Boss, 312–21, 329–32).

[263] BL Sloane MS 3309, fols. 343ʳ⁻ᵛ (=Boss, 322, 332).

From what has been said, we may take as established that the ancient *methodus medendi* can be taken in two ways, as an abstract *methodus* or as something concrete and applicable to individual illnesses. The former is valid continuingly and in all ages; the latter drifts and is changed day by day as more certain knowledge of the causes and essences of diseases is acquired, and as the more certain vindication of remedies by *experientia* and use is studied.[264]

We will recall that Glisson in his lectures emphasised that the Dogmatic/ Rationalist sect was the correct one, and that the Empiric refusal to search for causes could not lead to a true *methodus medendi*. Rationalism, in short, was the position most safely grounded in *experientia*. In reality, Glisson was simply placing emphasis on the Galenic *loci* that insisted on the importance of methodical investigation of each particular case, *loci* in which Galen admits this to be a similarity between Empiric and Rationalist approaches.[265] Humanist medical pedagogy had a long-standing tension: *practica* was treated in devoted manuals that listed diseases and treatments while not acknowledging that this was antithetical to true Galenic method, which emphasised the importance of methodical investigation of each particular case.[266] Glisson emphasised the latter, allowing him to make the polemical point that while the philosophy underpinning the ancient *methodus medendi* might be faulty, the practice should not be abandoned in favour of the radically new medicines being promised by the iatrochymists.

Sprackling, then, was not a reactionary 'conservative' allergic to novely, but was in fact adopting the key defence of experimental medical research as it had been developed by some of the most important neoterics of the 1650s. It is important to recognise how much of a consensus developed around this historical interpretation. This is hardly surprising when we consider that generations of physicians passed through Glisson's hands, and ingested the similar ideas being taught by Petty and others in Oxford. By emphasising the distinction between theory and practice, the learned physicians could present Galenic *methodus medendi* as a *via media* opposed to both philosophical reductionism and Empiric anti-intellectualism. We find variants of this historicisation throughout the 1660s responses to the chymical physicians. William Johnson, the College's own chymist, asserted like Sprackling that Galen's acceptance of Aristotelian tenets was not central to the validity of his method.[267] John Twysden, a recently elected fellow, went further in developing a full historical defence of a learned, 'rationalist' medicine that could nonetheless accommodate experimentalism. Twysden directly challenged Nedham's

---

[264] BL Sloane MS 3309, fol. 343$^\mathrm{v}$ (=Boss, 324, 333–4).
[265] See Galen, *Meth. Med.*, 3.7, K.x.206–9; *De. dign. puls.*, K.viii.8–9; *De diebus decret.*, K.ix.932.
[266] See the brilliant account in Bylebyl, 'Teaching *Methodus medendi* in the Renaissance' (1991).
[267] Johnson, *Agyrto-Mastix*, 44. On Johnson, who already had experience in attacking the reformers from the 1650s, see Webster, *Instauration*, 312–4; Cook, 'Society of Chymical Physicians', 67–8.

aligning of Hippocrates with the Empirics, attempting to return him to the Rationalist fold.[268] Like Sprackling he claimed that the 'ancient Hermetick Philosophers' actually combined four-elements theory with the chymical theory of sulphur and mercury as base elements. His Galeno–chymical syncretism clearly went further than a reading of Sprackling, for he also cited Sendivogius (i.e. the Polish alchemist Michał Sędziwój) and the *Physica Restituta* (i.e. the *Enchiridion physicae restitutae* (1623) by the French lawyer and alchemist Jean d'Espagnet).[269] We have a nice barometer of intellectual change here, because the last author to recommend directly these two authors together was the avowed Hermeticist Thomas Vaughan – hardly a mainstream member of the Royal College of Physicians, as Twysden was.[270] Again we have the crucial development: Rationalist *method* is defended by abandoning Galenic *doctrine*.

Even fuller was the positive re-historicisation of learned medicine offered by Nathaniel Hodges, a candidate for the College of Physicians who would later be chosen as one of four College nominees to stay in London to treat plague victims. Hodges was displeased with Boyle's positive comments about Empirics.[271] In response he drew a sharp distinction between the Empiric, 'who, *without consideration of any rational Method undertakes to cure Diseases*', and the Hippocratean tradition, which relied on '*true Experience … constituted of Reason and Sense*', and whose epistemological foundations had echoes of Harvey's 'Paduan' Aristotle, now freely amalgamated with the language of 'experiment': 'for as a *judicial observation of sensible Experiments* produceth apt *Theorems*, so thereby the *Intellect* forms *Universal conceptions* and essays their confirmation by repeated *experimental Operations*, whence issued what men call *Science*, together with all its *eternal* and *immutable Truths*'.[272] Hippocrates's and Galen's use of '*Humors, Qualities*,

---

[268] Twysden, *Medicina veterum vindicata*, 26: 'So that tis clear, that *Hippocrates* here joyns Empirical Medicines with Rational discourses, tells you that reason is to compound and assume one thing after another'. On Twysden, who had been elected a fellow in 1664, see King, *Medical enlightenment*, 154–60.

[269] Twysden, *Medela medicinae*, 162–3, 164–5. He acknowledges that he has drawn on Sprackling's 'vindication' of Galen and Hippocrates at 127.

[270] Eugenius Philalethes [Thomas Vaughan], *Anima magica abscondita: or a discourse of the universall spirit of nature* (London 1650), 55; see Newman, *Gehennical fire*, 222–3; Newman, 'Vaughan'. Twysden was elected a fellow of the RCP on 20 October 1664 (Moore and Wallis, 'Twysden, John', *ODNB*).

[271] Nathaniel Hodges, *Vindiciae medicinae et medicorum* (London, 1665), 24–5. Hodges paraded his knowledge of humanist medical commentaries: see e.g. the discussion of Hippocrates on phlebotomy in pregnant women: 163–6. For Hodges's biography and his sympathies towards chemical medicine, see Cook, *Decline*, 151–2, 156; King, 'Hodges, Nathaniel', *ODNB*. Hodges calls for a mild chymical–Galenist syncretism at *Vindiciae medicinae*, 104.

[272] Hodges, *Vindiciae medicinae*, 3–4.

and the like *Sentiments'* was irrelevant to the acceptance of the *'substantials* of [their] *Physick'*.[273] For sure, they made their own medicines, but this just confirmed that it was the learned physician rather than the Empiric chymist who was to be the office-bearer of medical progress.[274] This conclusion reflected a broader structural tension in apothecary–physician polemics. By this point, medical humanism had led most figures on both sides to argue that the ancient physician was a total *medicus* practising all the medical subdisciplines. But the conclusions they reached from this were the opposite: one side insisted that this justified the learned physicians' monopoly; the other that only the practical experience of the apothecary could match up to the ancient ideal.

This near-universal emphasis on the value of experience naturally fused with more specific issues emerging from the new philosophy, as can be seen from the work of George Castle, an M.D. and graduate of All Souls, Oxford, whose syncretic ideals were advertised in the very title of his work, *The chymical Galenist* (1667), and in his effusive praise for Sennert.[275] For all his chymical sympathies, Castle suggested that the biggest danger to modern medicine was not 'an over-fondness of Antiquity', but 'the other Extream, a fancy of rejecting the wisdom of the Ancients'.[276] Like all the other defenders of learned medicine he meant not that that 'wisdom' had not been improved on but that it represented an appropriate method for the physician.[277] This was proved by a conjectural history of medicine, which Castle derived from an assortment of classical sources. 'Remedies at first were either found out by Chance, or learnt from wild Beasts'. Virgil, Plutarch, and Pliny all reported, after all, that the use of dittany to extract splinters from wounds had been modelled on the practices of Cretan goats; the Egyptian Ibis bird had invented the enema, and the swallow taught men the use of celandine for eye conditions by dropping its juice into the eyes of its blind fledglings.[278] Far from depending on speculative system building, 'ancient Medicines' derived from this kind of long experience,

---

[273] Ibid., 7.

[274] Ibid., 49–50 (quoting in Greek, without a citation, Hippocrates, *Decorum*, x.292.9–17); see also 117.

[275] George Castle, *The chymical Galenist: a treatise wherein the practise of the ancients is reconcil'd to the new discoveries in the theory of physick* (London, 1667), 10–11, where Sennert's *De Chymicorum cum Aristotelicis et Galenicis consensu* is much praised (as also at 134, 178), and an attempt is made to bring Boyle into the same camp (citing *Sceptical chymist* (1661) (=*Boyle works*, II, 340)). Castle had been a member of the Oxford Experimental Philosophy Club, had significant chymical interests, and was elected FRS in 1669 (Frank, *Harvey*, 68–9, 195–6; Principe, 'Castle, George', *ODNB*). His attitude to the history of corpuscularianism is discussed at 5.3 below.

[276] Castle, *Chymical Galenist*, sig. [A6]ʳ.

[277] For Castle's admissions of significant medical progress since antiquity, see e.g. ibid., 1.

[278] Castle, *Chymical Galenist*, 20–1, quoting Virgil, *Aen.*, XII.415, and alluding to Plutarch, *Moralia*, 974D; Pliny, *Hist. nat.*, XX.156. For the Ibis bird and the swallow, the unacknowledged sources are Pliny, *Hist. nat.*, VIII.41.97 and Dioscorides, *De materia medica*, II.211.

rather than from attempts 'to give the true reason of their Composition'.[279] If the physiology and pathology of the ancients is 'insufficient' for knowing 'the true cause of Diseases and their Symptoms', it remains that 'much of the[ir] Method certainly is not grounded upon them, but was long in use before those notions of Causes were invented'.[280] Crucially, though, that method was not 'bare Empericism', but was based on 'induction from observations' – that is to say on 'Method and Reason'.[281] In Castle's hands, as in others', the traditional Galenic focus on experience had been turned to showing that learned physic was not incompatible with natural philosophical innovation. It was this observational method that had been followed in the 'Colledges and Universities', and their conclusions were thus 'not easily to be laid aside'.[282] Once again, the chymical reformers' dual attack on Galenic doctrine and Galenic method has been turned upon itself, and a tradition of learned medicine continuous from antiquity and based on observation is presented as the *via media*.

By this point, the defenders of learned medicine had turned the whole tradition they were defending into an experimental medicine that nonetheless had to be distinguished from the method-less experimentation of the Empirics. The language of Galenic *method* – of semiotic, indications, and reason – could be preserved without concession to Galenic *doctrine*.[283] Yet it is clear that this, combined with many of the College of Physicians defenders' acceptance of the idea that the apothecary and the physician had been joined in antiquity, in turn led to the easy resuscitation of ancient Empiricism as a potential counter-model to the institutionalisation of learned medicine. Nowhere is this clearer than in the very detailed historicisations offered in three works by Everard Maynwaring between 1668 and 1671. Maynwaring had earned his M.D. in Dublin but set up as a private practitioner in London in 1663 and supported O'Dowde's proposed Society of Chymical Physicians.[284] He is an excellent example of the complex institutional allegiances that underpinned methodological debates in the 1660s, for while he clearly felt

---

[279] Castle, *Chymical Galenist*, 131.  [280] Ibid., 127 (see also 171, 196).

[281] Ibid., 127–8 (Castle is here drawing on Thomas Willis's *De febribus*, on which see below).

[282] Ibid., 49.

[283] See e.g. Hodges, *Vindiciae medicinae*, 3, defining an 'Empirick' as someone 'who, *without consideration of any rational Method undertakes to cure Diseases* . . . and his *proof of Receipts* seem to him more satisfactory then the *Scholastick odd rules of practices:* but what can be expected from such *rude Experimentings*, not respecting any *Indications*, or other *circumstances* very considerable in the right effecting of a *Cure*?' (my emphasis). See also the remarkably pragmatic approach to the keeping of ancient terms in Castle, *Chymical Galenist*, 134 (ultimately drawing on Sennert).

[284] Very little work has been done. For the biography, see Clericuzio, 'Maynwaring, Everard', *ODNB*; for his participation in the Society of Chymical Physicians, see Rattansi, 'Helmontian-Galenist Controversy', 21–3; Cook, 'Society', 71.

that the 'learned' status on which the institutional authority of the College of Physicians was based was a false one, he also fully supported Merrett's attack on the apothecaries. His approach to the history of medicine reflected this complexity, although this should not lead us to conclude that that history was purely a polemical tool; Maynwaring clearly took some care over it, drawing on such staples of humanist medical writing as Rodericus a Castro's *Medicus-politicus* (1614).[285]

As a good Helmontian, Maynwaring ascribed divine origins to physic, but then moved to what we have labelled the conjectural history of medicine: 'the medicinal virtues of many things were found out by chance; and by observation of the brute Creatures'.[286] Maynwaring even suggested reviving the ancient practice of making medical 'Experiments upon condemned Malefactors'.[287] Hippocrates inherited and developed this experimental physic; from him it passed on to Diocles of Carystus, Praxagoras, Chrysippus, Herophilus, and Erasistratus, and came to be divided into three parts: 'diaeteticam, pharmaceuticam & chirurgicam'.[288] This was not a neutral list, for it deliberately made no mention of the two other 'theoretical' parts of the usual five parts of medicine, physiology and semiotics.[289] As this art spread, Maywaring continued, different sects arose, all of which could be reduced to the Empirics, the Methodics, and the Rationalists, the latter of which might be divided into Galenic and Chymical.[290] The Empirics relied on experience, which itself could be defined in three ways: accidental (when all things happen by chance); *ex proposito* ('when one does purposely and designedly make a tryal'); and *Experientia imitatrix* ('when a Physitian useth

---

[285] Everard Maynwaring, *Medicus absolutus adespotos* (London, 1668), 7–8. On a Castro and his work (on medical ethics), see Maclean, *Learned medicine*, 50–1, 65. Maynwaring's notes on Stubbe's attacks on the Royal Society (see below) are in BL Sloane MS 1786, fols. 116$^r$–129$^v$.

[286] Maynwaring, *Medicus absolutus*, 10. Maynwaring claims that among the ancient Indians, 'there was Law, that if any person had committed a Crime, and did not find out some medicinal Remedy, he was put to death; but if he did find out some such Experiment, he was rewarded and advanced by their Kings'. Maynwaring has here misunderstood or misremembered Strabo, *Geog.*, xv.1.22, where it is in fact stated that the punishment and reward apply only if someone discovers anything deadly.

[287] Maynwaring, *Medicus absolutus*, 11–12. No source is provided, but I assume Maynwaring was thinking of the famous story of Mithridates, as it was elaborated on in Galen, *Ant.*, ii.1 (K xiv.108).

[288] Maynwaring, *Medicus absolutus*, 15. Maynwaring's account here is not a neutral one: [Ps.-] Galen, *Int.* (K xvi 683) had explicitly listed Diocles as a 'Rationalist'. Maynwaring may be favouring the account in Pliny, *Nat. hist.*, xxvi.6.10–11. See further the discussion in Van Der Eijk, *Diocles of Carystus* (2001), ii, 19.

[289] The two key *loci* for the five-fold division are Galen, *Int.* K xiv.689 and *Def. med.*, K xix.351; for the early modern re-appearance of the division and its various consequences, see the very useful discussion in Mikkeli, *Hygiene in the early modern medical tradition* (1999), 32–40, as well as Maclean, *Learned medicine*, 69–70; Siraisi, *Avicenna*, 101–2; Levitin, 'Apothecaries'.

[290] Maynwaring, *Medicus absolutus*, 16.

or rejecteth those things, which in like cases he has found to do good or hurt'). It was in the third sense – which was in fact rather contested among the ancient Empirics, some of whom considered its inferential assumptions an unhealthy concession to Rationalism[291] – that it was used by the ancient Empirics, who thus did not search for causes but nonetheless did not rely on blind individualism. But in this they differed from *modern* Empirics, who 'pretend not only Experience, but great Knowledge, when they are very ignorant in Philosophy and the Tongues'.[292] The Rational method was thus the correct one and Galen was right to attack the Empirics and Methodics. Unfortunately he went too far, both because he did not build his superstructure 'upon a right [philosophical] foundation', but also because unlike the difficult chymical combination of reason and experience, Galen's 'speculative' method offered an 'easier life'.[293] Chymical rationalism, however, derived from Hermes in Egypt, where Empiricism also had its strongest roots.[294] Its learned heritage was confirmed by its uptake by a select elite of Greek philosophers: Zosimus, Olympiodorus, and Democritus.[295] As for medical practice, it was certainly well after Galen's time that the apothecary emerged as a separate producer of medicines.[296] Maynwaring could thus construct a syncretic canon of practising and experimental physicians: Asclepius, Hermes, Hippocrates, Diocles (whom Galen had snatched for the Dogmatists), and Galen himself.[297] Chymical medicine was subsumed into the Rationalist tradition.[298] By 1670, the step foreshadowed by Petty in his 1650s lectures had been taken.

---

[291] The Greek phrase is 'ἡ τοῦ ὁμοίου μετάβασις'. For this debate among the Empirics, see the classic discussion of the sources in Deichgräber, *Die griechische Empirikerschule*, 164–5 and more recently Hankinson, *Cause and explanation in ancient Greek thought* (2001), 311–14; Perilli, *Menodoto di Nicomedia* (2004), 154–76.

[292] Maynwaring, *Medicus absolutus*, 16–17.

[293] Ibid., 20–1, 33–4. See also 40–1, where Hippocrates is claimed for the anti-Empiric side.

[294] Ibid., 17–18 (Egyptian Empiricism), 24–5 (on the antiquity of chymistry). It is clear that for Egyptian 'Empiricism', Maynwaring is extrapolating from Herodotus, II.84. For the Empirical origins of learned medicine, see also Maynwaring's *Praxis medicorum antiqua et nova* (London, 1671), 7.

[295] Maynwaring, *Medicus absolutus*, 26. Only the first of these is now treated seriously as an alchemist, but I know of no early modern doubts about Olympiodorus's authorship of the fourth book of the commentary on Aristotle's *Meteorology* (where ps.-Olympiodorus's 'alchemical treatise' can be found). For doubts about Democritus the alchemist, see 4.1 above. Boyle used the name 'Zosimus' in some of his dialogues, on the implications of which see Principe, *Aspiring adept*, 51–2, 74.

[296] Maynwaring, *Medicus absolutus*, 56–7, 89–90 (explicitly drawing on Hodges, a nominal 'opponent'), 106; Edward Maynwaring, *The pharmacopoeian physician's repository* (London, 1670), 61–4, 118; Maynwaring, *Praxis medicorum*, 3–5, 16–17, 44.

[297] Maynwaring, *Praxis medicorum*, 4 (for Galen on Diocles, see *Alim. fac.*, I.1 (K VI.455)).

[298] Maynwaring, *Praxis medicorum*, 9–10; Maynwaring, *Repository*, 65. See also 4.7 below.

### 4.4.3    Histories of medical method by natural philosophers

Experimental philosophy had become equated with the classical Rationalist medical tradition.[299] This was a major step, for it allowed far wider natural philosophical research programmes to be conducted under the ambit of mainstream, institutionalised medicine. Moreover, the medical debates about method in the 1660s had wide resonances, not least because so many of the neoterics were either practising physicians, or had strong interests in the method of physic and its connections to natural philosophy (as we have already seen with Boyle). As might be expected, they adopted and adapted the historical ideas being developed in the more concretely medical debates. This is evident in the cases of three of the most famous *novatores*: Thomas Willis, John Locke, and Thomas Sydenham.

Willis is the least well known of the three but was the one with the greatest contemporary importance (at least until the burgeoning of both Locke's and Sydenaham's reputations in the early eighteenth century). He graduated BA from Oxford in 1639; like his fellow royalist Bathurst, he may have shifted from divinity to medicine due to the Civil War, graduating MD in 1646. He became a successful practising physician in Oxford, but most importantly for us, he developed an early interest in advanced and new natural philosophy, especially in Helmontain iatrochymistry and post-Harveian anatomy – carrying out experiments with Bathurst and John Lydall as early as the late 1640s – and was a core member of the Oxford Experimental Club of the 1650s. Gilbert Sheldon arranged for his appointment as Sedleian professor of natural philosophy in 1660.[300] Willis's first published works were the *Diatribae duae medico-philosophicae* (1659), containing *De fermentatione* (completed by 1656) and *De febribus*. These works not only developed causal explanations for both fermentation and, subsequently, for the circulation of the blood, but also couched them in a quasi-corpuscularian language.[301]

Willis had a strong sense that Harvey's discoveries required a new theoretical foundation grounded in further experimental work.[302] Unlike Harvey, he never sought to defend such a research programme in Aristotelian terms; rather,

---

[299] William Simpson, in his *Hydrologica chymica* (London, 1669), 192 still attempted to defend chymical physicians as 'empirical in their practice', but his is a solitary voice. For the fullest study of Simpson's ideas and relationship to the Royal Society, see Roos, *The salt of the earth* (2007), 114–31.

[300] Two biographies are available: Hughes, *Thomas Willis* (1991), and Isler, *Thomas Willis* (1968 [1965]), of which the second is the fuller. For Willis's connections in Oxford medical and natural philosophical circles, see Frank, *Harvey*, 28–9, 50, 66–7, 166–9, and 282–3 for Willis's high reputation at his death.

[301] For Willis on corpuscularianism, see 5.3 below.

[302] Thomas Willis, *Diatribae duae medico-philosophicae* (London, 1659), sig. H2*v (in the preface to *De febribus*).

he developed a history of natural philosophy and medicine that we can now see was a direct counterpart to the debates of the 1660s. From Harvey's reception, Willis knew that he had to answer a possible objection to a new theory of fevers: that they had been 'happily cured' by ancient remedies, and that 'new things' were thus 'reckless and unsafe'.[303] Willis's response was a conjectural history of medicine. The discipline was originally Empiric, finding remedies only through frequent trials rather than through 'general precepts'. This method of 'observations and experiments' was followed by Hippocrates, and would have led to great success had the ancients continued it, but unfortunately it was corrupted by those who made physic into a 'general method, as if it were some kind of speculative science'. Willis thus felt justified in following a method of 'induction of observations'.[304]

But, Willis continued, physic's Empiric origins should not conceal the need for 'method and reason' to supplement 'naked Experience'.[305] As his career progressed and he became more institutionally secure, and as he developed important new anatomical results from his collaboration with Richard Lower in the 1660s, Willis sought further to amalgamate his work with what he presented as the learned tradition. As the history of medicine offered in his *Pharmaceutice rationalis* (1674) explained, although physic had at first been purely Empiric (*merè empiricam*)[306] – as testified by Herodotus's reports from Egypt – it was then reduced to a 'method', 'so that therapeutic indications

---

[303] Willis, *Diatribae duae*, sig. H3*$^v$: 'Quod vero objicitur, iisdem remediis, & simili medendi methodo, ab Hippocratis & Galeni temporibus in hunc usque diem febres sat feliciter curates fuisse; ideoque opus temerarium & minus tutum videri, ut posthabita tot saeculorum experientia res novas moliremur, pracipue cum de corio luditur humano'.

[304] Willis, *Diatribae duae*, sigs. H3*$^v$–H4*$^r$: ' ... medicina fuit primitus empirica, & remedia crebro singularium tentamine, minimeque praeceptis generalibus, aut Analogia fuerunt inventa: atque si Hippocratis exemplo ducti, posteri ejus observationes tantum & experimenta recoluissent, proculdubio ars medica cum majori aegrotantium fructu, melius & ornatium accrevisset. Quod vero lumen ab antiquis clare accensum cito praeclusit, posterorumque oculos obfuscavit, fuit prae posterum illorum studium qui proper nimis Ιατρική in methodum generalem, ad modum scientiae alicuius speculativae, tantum non ex ingenio suo efformabant: namque hac ratione, priusquam fundamenta firma ponerentur, speciosa satis, at fallax & instabilis struebatur doctrinae moles ... Atque hinc defensionem satis locupletem paratam mihi spero; si enim veterum scita prorsus erronea non obstiterint, quin praxis medicinae, observationum inductione quadam primo instituta, commode satis processerit; multo minus theoria veritate subnixa damni aliquid languentibus apportabit; aut a tramite illo, quem longa aetas nobis laudatum dedit, medicinam facientes transverses rapiet'.

[305] Willis, *Diatribae duae*, sigs. H4*$^{r-v}$: 'Interim non dissimulandum est, nudam Empiricam sine methodi rationisque subsidiis parum valere ... '.

[306] Thomas Willis, *Pharmaceutice rationalis, sive, diatriba de medicamentorum operationibus in humano corpore* (Oxford, 1674), 1: 'Artem medicinalem à primâ inventione, usque ad Hippocratis secula merè empiricam fuisse, ejusdem annales consulentibus compertum est' (see also the preface, sigs. [a]$^{r-v}$). It is interesting to note that in the 1684 English translation, *merè empiricam* becomes 'merely Experimental' (Thomas Willis, *Pharmaceutice rationalis* in *Dr. Willis's practice of physick* (London, 1684), 1 [new pagination]).

concerning the use of medicines were properly delineated'.[307] Thus the true physician's role was to accept his Empiric heritage but then to go beyond it with a search for the *causes* of the operation of medicines.[308] Once again, as for Glisson, Galenic indications had become the key link between naked experience and scientific explanation.

We see here a clear modification of the Helmontian story of post-Hippocratean 'speculative' corruption. Indeed, we might talk of the 'sanitisation' of the Helmontian story, as Hippocrates emerges as a middle ground between the Empirics and the speculators (Willis was careful never to condemn Galen by name, and it is never made clear when the 'speculative' corruption occurred), while at the same time justifying a programme of experimental research; a programme that, moreover, explicitly permits and encourages the search for philosophical causes. Again, experimentalism and Rationalism were being folded into each other. Indeed, this is the implicit message of the very title of the book: pharmacy, after all, had traditionally been classed as one of the three 'practical' (as opposed to the 'theoretical') of the five parts of medicine.

But while this historical approach certainly led to a consensus about the experimental origins and nature of physic, that consensus could incorporate a range of philosophical–methodological positions, as we see in the case of Locke. Locke had trained as a physician from the late 1650s, reading extensively, attending Willis's lectures at Oxford, and learning chymistry from Boyle and Peter Stahl.[309] While it used to be thought that Sydenham was a major methodological influence on Locke, it has recently been argued that the reverse was the case, a conclusion accepted and expanded here.[310]

---

[307] Willis, *Pharmaceutice rationalis*, 1: 'Postquam verò, accrescente indies observationum cumulo, Ιατρική in praecepta & methodum redigi coepisset … ut Indicationes Therapeuticae, circa supellectilis medicamentalis usum rite designarentur'. The 1684 English translation (1–2) is again of interest: '[so] that the Reasons or Circumstances, why and when they [medicines] were to be used, might be as plainly known'. This does not reflect Willis's technical vocabulary of 'therapeutic indications', but this may be an interesting example of the vernacular transformation of classical concepts.

[308] Willis, *Pharmaceutice rationalis*, 2–3; see also Thomas Willis, *Pharmaceutice rationalis … pars secunda* (Oxford, 1675), sig. a3ʳ: 'Enimvero rationibus, quibus medicamenta operantur, non rite expensis, Jatrice omnis quasi adhuc merè empirica, casu ac fortuna potius quam consilio regitur'.

[309] Anstey, 'John Locke and Helmontian medicine' (2010); Anstey, *Locke*, 169–88, *passim*; Walmsley, 'John Locke's natural philosophy', (1998), 20–137, *passim*; Dewhurst, ed., *Thomas Willis's Oxford lectures* (1980); Meynell, 'Locke as pupil of Peter Stahl' (2001). The key older treatment is Dewhurst, *John Locke, physician and philosopher* (1963), although many of its conclusions have to be amended due to subsequent redating and re-attribution of several manuscript works. For the relevant notebooks, a good starting point is Meynell, 'A database for John Locke's medical notebooks and medical reading' (1997). Further studies are cited below.

[310] See esp. Anstey and Burrows, 'John Locke, Thomas Sydenham, and the authorship of two medical essays' (2009).

The key texts for us are two manuscript treatises, 'Anatomia' (1668) and 'De arte medica' (1669).[311] In the latter, Locke became the latest to turn to the history of medicine to justify his research method. Like Willis, he pointed out that medicine began in observation, and that 'had this method beene continued', physic 'had been in a far better condicion then now it is'.[312] Yet hubris derailed 'proud man, [who] not content with that knowledg he was capable of & was useful to him, would needs ~~prie~~ <penetrate> into the hidden causes of things lay downe principles & establish maximes to him self about the operacions of nature'.[313] Although Locke stated that 'this vanity spread its self into ~~all the~~ <many of> usefull parts of naturall philosophy',[314] it is clear that he was here thinking in Helmontian fashion, for he had two folios earlier equated the 'uselesse ~~notions~~ speculations' with the 'long & elaborate discourses of the ancients ~~about the humours~~': the final tactful deletion has resonances of Boyle's suppressions in his anti-Galenic tract.[315]

Despite their acceptance of a modified Helmontian history, Locke and Willis drew different conclusions from that history. Unlike Willis, Locke considered the search for causes as hubristic and futile.[316] Strangely enough, this may be because Willis, remembered more as a physician and anatomist, was far more positive than Locke, remembered as a philosopher, about the potential for philosophy to set up foundations for the physician by discovering the 'hidden causes of things'. Locke suggested that it was in 'the large field of <natural> phylosophy where perhaps the foundation of the mischeif was first laid' – very likely a reference to the idea that it was the incorporation of Aristotelian philosophical principles that misled Galen.[317] Unlike Willis, and even unlike those 1660s medical reformers who we have met (e.g. Maynwaring), Locke never attempted to amalgamate his promotion of experimental method with the traditional language of indications and of philosophy as a counter-balance to Empiricism. It has been claimed that in 'De arte medica' Locke 'is careful not

---

[311] The fullest treatment, with precise dating, is now Anstey and Burrows, 'Authorship'. Unfortunately, Locke's fullest earlier medical manuscript, 'Morbus' (1667), does not contain any thoughts on the history of medical methodology (the best and most accessible transcription is in Walmsley, '"Morbus"—Locke's early essay on disease' (2000), at 390–3).

[312] John Locke, 'De arte med[ica] 1669', in Walmsley, 'Locke's natural philosophy', 287–95, at 290. Having consulted the manuscript (PRO 30/24/47/2, fols. 47$^r$–56$^r$), I have verified that Walmsley's is the best of the available transcriptions.

[313] Locke, 'De arte medica', 290–1.　[314] Ibid., 291.　[315] Ibid., 289.

[316] See more generally Walmsley, 'Locke's natural philosophy', 123–8; Anstey, Locke, 28–45, esp. 33–4 on the difference between Locke's strong claims in 'Anatomia' and his later, more mitigated statements.

[317] Locke, 'De arte medica', 293. Locke's projected design for the full 'De arte medica' – unfortunately never completed – would have involved a much fuller history of medicine, considering the historical contributions of '1 Experience. 2 Method founded upon phylosophy & Hypothesis 3 Botaniques. 4 Chymistry. 5 Anatomy' (293).

to be dismissive of the medical wisdom of the past',[318] but, contextually speaking, Locke's rejection of the search for causes and his claim that the philosophical search for them was the historical root of error in physic were, as far as legitimations of experimental method went, well towards the radical side of the scale. Like Helmont and Bacon, he offered as a historical–contextual explanation for the speculative corruption of physic the disputational intellectual culture of the ancients (one assumes he was thinking of the Greeks): 'they accommodated them selves to the fashion <of> & their times and contrys … their being busy & subtile in imag disputeing upon certain alloud principles was but to be imploid in the way of fame & reputacion & the learning of that valued in that age'.[319] Moreover, in the 'Anatomia' manuscript, he went further than Willis or the medical reformers by ascribing the ancient philosophers' futile search for causes to their theologico–philosophical principles (see 5.4 below).

Unlike Locke, and despite Locke's influence on him, Sydenham did invest in the image of a historical *via media* between Empirics and speculative Rationalists that developed in the 1660s.[320] Sydenham's first publication, the first edition of the *Methodus curandi febres* (1666), already contains certain important passages where Sydenham eschewed the search for causes and, most importantly for us, rejected the *persona* of the philosopher.[321] But Sydenham's engagement with methodological issues, and concomitantly with their history, expanded rapidly after the beginning of his friendship with Locke around mid-1667. The key texts are the Preface to the third edition of the *Observationes medicae* (1676), almost certainly jointly written with Locke,[322] the *Epistolae* to Robert Brady and Henry Paman published in 1680, the *Dissertatio epistolaris* to William Cole (1682), and the methodological section of his treatise on gout and dropsy, the *Tractatus de podagra et hydrope* (1683).[323]

As we would expect from a work co-authored with Locke, the Preface to the third edition of the *Observationes medicae* is highly sceptical about the potential for knowledge of the primary causes of disease, with a preference for looking for 'immediate and conjunct' (*immediatas … & conjunctas*)

---

[318] Anstey and Burrows, 'Authorship', 13.  [319] Locke, 'De arte medica', 288–9.

[320] For Sydenham's biography, see Dewhurst, *Dr Thomas Sydenham* (1966), significantly modified and supplemented by Meynell, *Materials for a biography of Dr Thomas Sydenham* (1988).

[321] Thomas Sydenham, *Methodus curandi febres* (London, 1666), 90: 'Ego Philosophi nomen non ambio; & qui titulum illum se mereri existimant, atque me fortassis hoc nomine cupandum putabunt, quòd in haec penetralia non irrumpere conatus sim' (=*Methodus Curandi Febres … with English translation from R. G. Lathan (1848)*, ed. G. G. Meynell (Folkestone, 1987), 101–2). For further examples, see Walmsley, 'Locke's natural philosophy', 99–101.

[322] Meynell, 'John Locke and the Preface to Thomas Sydenham's *Observationes medicae*' (2006).

[323] For the circumstances of the three *Epistolae*, see Dewhurst, 'The physician', in Dewhurst, *Sydenham*, 45–6.

causes; that is, those available to the senses.[324] This was the true *methodus medendi*. It was to be built not on particular instances but on an extensive natural history of disease.[325] This, claimed Sydenham, was precisely the method followed by Hippocrates. Works such as *On diseases* and *Affections* were works of natural history, whereas the *Aphorisms* and the *Coan prenotions* (another pseudo-Hippocratean aphoristic collection) contained 'certain rules taken from the observation of this method'.[326] To some extent Sydenham was here playing fast and loose with traditional classifications of Hippocrates's work. The *Coan prenotions* and the *Aphorisms* had, since Galen, been classified as part of semiotic, of which Hippocrates was said to be the founder.[327] Therefore, Sydenham's presentation of them as second-order works based on initial observation was not unjustified. But the idea that *On diseases* and *Affections* were works of natural history deliberately designed as a first step in this process was surely forced: *Affections*, for example, as well as containing disease descriptions, also contains suggestions for treatment, as well as more theoretical considerations. Sydenham's claim that Hippocrates himself saw the foundation of medicine as a non-hypothetical natural history depends on a very forced reading of the latter's famous statement that '[t]he body's nature is the physician in disease'.[328] Yet for all its scholarly deficiencies this was a polemically powerful reading, for it suggested that the heart of traditional medicine – semiotic – was founded on natural history. It is impossible to know whether this was one of the passages supplied by Locke,[329] but there are good reasons for thinking that it was: first, we know that Locke had previously supplied Sydenham with the more 'learned' parts of his works;[330] second, Locke's wider interest in semiotic.[331] It would have

---

[324] Thomas Sydenham, *Observationes medicae circa morborum acutorum historiam et curationem* (London, 1676), Praefatio, sigs. (b)ᵛ–(b4)ʳ (=*The works of Thomas Sydenham*, ed. and trans. R. G. Latham (2 vols, London, 1848–50), I, 18–20 (this translation is rather loose in places; I have amended it when required)). Quotation is from sig. (b4)ʳ.

[325] Sydenham, *Observationes medicae*, sigs. [(a5)]ʳ–(b)ᵛ (=*Works*, I, 15–18).

[326] Sydenham, *Observationes medicae*, sigs. [(a6)]ᵛ–[(a7)]ʳ: 'Regulas etiam quasdam tradidit ex observatione methodi istius' (=*Works*, I, 16).

[327] Galen, *Hipp. Epid.*, III (K XVIIA, 579); Maclean, *Learned medicine*, 276–332.

[328] Sydenham, *Observationes medicae*, sig. [(a6)]ʳ: '*Hippocrates* ... hanc Arti Medicae insuper struendae solidam ac inconcussam substernens basim, viz, Νούσων φύσιες ἰητροί ... id egit ut morbi cujuslibet Phaenomena apertè traderet, nullâ Hypothesi adscitâ, & in partes per vim adactâ' (=*Works*, I, 16). The source is Hippocrates, *Epid.*, VI.5.1.

[329] All such known passages, derived from text concordances, are listed in Meynell, 'Locke and the Preface'.

[330] Meynell, 'Sydenham, Locke and Sydenham's *De peste sive febre pestilentiali*' (1993).

[331] Serjeantson, '"Human understanding" and the genre of Locke's *Essay*' (2008), esp. 170–1. As well as the evidence presented there, see also Locke's multiple manuscripts on the 'Division of the sciences', where the place of semiotics is delineated: e.g. Bod. MS Locke c. 28, fols. 155ʳ–156ʳ; 157ʳ–158ʳ.

suited Locke's purposes to have the doctrine of signs founded on Baconian natural history.[332]

Whether this section was by Locke or not, Sydenham certainly ascribed to these beliefs personally, later adding that this Hippocratean method was a happy middle ground between that of the Empirics (who rejected both the natural history of diseases from which indications could be taken and the *methodus medendi*) and that of the speculative 'smatterers' in knowledge.[333] Sydenham's fullest statement of this supposedly 'Hippocratean method' came in the *Tractatus de podagra et hydrope*, where he not only reaffirmed its place between Empiricism and speculative medicine but also rescued some of Hippocrates's rather more Empiric-sounding statements. For example, when Hippocrates (in *Ancient medicine*) castigated recent physicians and philosophers for asserting that 'nobody can know medicine who is ignorant what man is', he intended, according to Sydenham, not a return to Empiricism but simply an anti-hubristic withdrawal from the search for ultimate causes (i.e. exactly as suggested by Sydenham himself), and an injunction to spend as much time in the 'diligent observation' of natural phenomena.[334] This Hippocratean *persona* was then posited against the chymists, whom he accused of preferring the concoction of new chymical medicines to the hard search for indications of diseases themselves.[335]

A prominent commentator has written:

In the later part of the seventeenth century, the name of Hippocrates rather than Galen conjured up intellectual excitement and an aura of the frontiers of knowledge. The change is significant, for Galen's reputation had come to rest on his medical rationalism, while that of Hippocrates stemmed from his empiricism. At least that is how Paracelsus, Francis Bacon, Van Helmont, and others portrayed Hippocrates, and by the middle of the seventeenth century that is how most people thought of him: the collector of case studies, the compiler of medical details, the inductivist, the early founder of the true methods of natural history whose achievements had been devalued by the rationalist practitioners following him.[336]

This view depends on the idea, developed in the most thorough study of Hippocrates's afterlife, that Sydenham's Hippocrates was directly

---

[332] See also Anstey, 'Locke, Bacon and natural history' (2002). As shown in Serjeantson, 'Genre', 165, Locke's *Essay* was self-consciously a work of semiotics grounded on the natural history of the understanding.

[333] Thomas Sydenham, *Epistolae responsoriae duae* (London, 1680), 52–3: 'Luditur enim, quod ajunt, de corio Humano plus satis, cùm hinc Empirici, neque Morborum historiam, nec Methodum medendi callentes, & Receptis tantùm freti; isthinc Sciolorum vanissimi spem omnem in affectato Artis ambitu, & speculationibus utrinque pari ferè momento disceptatis ponentes … Ea demum Praxis, eaque sola aegris mortalibus opem feret, quae Indicationes curatives ex ipsis morborum Phaenomenis elicit, dein firmat experientia: Quibus gradibus magnus *Hippocrates* ad coelum ascendit' (=*Works*, II, 22). See also 77–8.

[334] Thomas Sydenham, *Tractatus de podagra et hydrope* (London, 1683), 154–8 (=*Works*, II, 171), discussing Hippocrates, *Vet. med.*, xx.

[335] Sydenham, *Podagra et hydrope*, 160–3 (=*Works*, II, 172). [336] Cook, *Decline*, 185.

Baconian.[337] There can be no doubt that Sydenham inherited Bacon's Hippocratean rhetoric, as we have seen. But like the near contemporaries we have met, he reconfigured it to present Hippocrates not as an Empiric but as the founder of the *true* Rationalism, a Rationalism that differed from Empiricism through systematic observation and which could thus be packaged with the traditional terms of Rationalist medicine: indications and semiotic. These terms were stripped of the extensive psychological and epistemological baggage they had acquired in the Renaissance. But their continued use was a mark of the success of the new virtuoso-physicians in reconfiguring the identity of traditional medicine. This is an important distinction that the above passage, with its anachronistic talk of 'empiricism' and its conflation of Bacon and the Restoration physicians, fails to represent.

By the 1670s, the learned physicians had amalgamated the rhetoric of experimentalism with that of a 'learned' tradition. When John Mapletoft – a close acquaintance of Locke and Sydenham and FRS from 1676 – became Gresham Professor of Physic in 1675, his Latin inaugural lecture included a long history of medicine that traced its roots back to the 'heroic age' of the Assyrians and Egyptians who 'began to search out experience'.[338] When Strabo and Herodotus asserted that these nations lived without physicians, they only meant that everyone who suffered an illness learnt by experience how to treat it and then passed on the knowledge: these were societies of physicians.[339] The Greeks had inherited this practice of physic by tradition from those they labelled 'barbarians'.[340] This practice was called Empiricism.

---

[337] Smith, *The Hippocratic tradition*, 13–23 (cited at Cook, *Decline*, 185); Cunningham 'Hippocrates', citing this passage from Cook at 91. Cunningham also claims (102) that 'the greatest transformation … that Hippocrates underwent occurred at the hands of … Sydenham', but as I hope the discussion above has shown, Sydenham added little to the general move made by the establishment learned physicians. In general, I see a far less 'radical' Sydenham than that presented in Cunningham, 'Good Old Cause'. But for the realisation that the key was to show a Hippocrates who was *not* an Empiric, see French, *Medicine*, 190–2, albeit again focusing only on Sydenham.

[338] 'Praelectiones Johannis Mapletoft M. D. in Collegio Greshamensi, ann. Dom. 1675', in John Ward, *The lives of the professors of Gresham College* (London, 1740), 123 (separate pagination): 'Praeter jam dictos etiam Cadmus Agenorides, qui et primus litterarum inventor dicitur (quarum ope inscitiae atque ignorantiae, gravissimis animorum morbis, medicina paratur) apud Phoenices suos, apud Samothraces alii, alii denique apud Assyrios atque Aegyptios, herbarum naturam ac vires, vel ipso heroico saeculo, observatione sedula atque iterata, saepe experientia indagare coeperunt; atque ita demum ubique terrarum per varios casus artem experientia fecit, exemplo monstrante viam'. For Mapletoft, see Meynell, *Materials*, 27, 41, 84; Wallis, 'Mapletoft, John', *ODNB*.

[339] Mapletoft, 'Praelectiones', 123. See Herodotus, I.197; Strabo, *Geog.*, XVI.20.

[340] Mapletoft, 'Praelectiones', 123–4: 'Quinimo non desunt, qui medicinam apud Aegyptios natam esse affirmant; et ab illis primum ad Graecos, ex exinde de manu in manum per scriptores Romanos, Arabas, caeterosque a Romanis pro barbaris habitos (prout illi ipsi a Graecis olim habebantur) ab his, inquam, Aegyptiis ad nostra usque tempora manasse illustria

It was continued by the Greeks, who upon recovering from an illness not only sacrificed a cock to Asclepius, but also placed votive tablets in his temple in which they recoded the disease and the remedy. Hippocrates, who was no more skilful than his predecessors, was the first to record together all these tablets and so to found the art of medicine.[341] These ideas had irreproachable ancient testimonies to back them up,[342] but finishing an academic discussion on the history of physic with this story would have been unthinkable less than half a century previously. In the hands of the academic physicians, the history of natural philosophy became a successful defence of experimental method as a respectable tradition. Having charted this success, we can now contrast it with a simultaneous failure: the attempt of various Royal Society apologists to produce similar historical justifications for experimental method not just in medicine, but also in natural philosophy *tout court*.

### 4.4.4    *Sprat, Glanvill, and the failed historical justification of experimental philosophy*

The tradition of early apologetics for the experimental philosophy is well known. Boyle's *Usefulness* served as an early semi-official manifesto. The Royal Society had no 'ideology', but its institutionalisation and some of its members' desires to respond to early criticisms led to the commissioning, in 1663, of Thomas Sprat's *History of the Royal Society* (1667).[343] Joseph Glanvill, meanwhile, in 1665 dedicated to the Society his *Scepsis scientifica*, a reworking of his *Vanity of dogmatizing* (1661), leading to his election. This

---

aliquot hujus artis axiomata, quale est illus apud Hippocratem: Πέπονα φαρμακεύειν καὶ κινέειν, μὴ ὠμά, μηδὲ ἐν ἀρχῆσιν, ἢν μὴ ὀργᾷ· τὰ δὲ πλεῖστα οὐκ ὀργᾷ. Quod quidem Aegyptiorum placitum fuisse nos docet Aristoteles, qui in *Politicis* haec habet: καὶ ἐν Αἰγύπτῳ μετὰ τὴν τετρήμερον κινεῖν ἔξεστι τοῖς ἰατροῖς, ἐὰν δὲ πρότερον, ἐπὶ τῷ αὐτοῦ κινδύνῳ'. The quotations are from Hippocrates, *Aph.*, I.22; Aristotle, *Pol.*, III, 1286ᵃ13–14.

[341] Mapletoft, 'Praelectiones', 124: 'Hisce initiis, ut ingentia flumina a pusillis ac vix dum conspicuis aquarum scaturiginibus in unum corrivata, ars medica ortum debuit suum; secta nempe omnium prima, quae emperica ideo est appellata, quod ab usu solo, posthabita quacunque ratiocinatione, artem peteret: quae quidem ab omni retro antiquitate ubique fere invaluit viguitque, quam olim Graeci, satis apposite, τηρητικὴν *observatricem*, et μνημονευτικὴν *memorem*, dixeris, pro rei ratione insigniverunt. Cumque apud priscos homines in more positum esset, ut qui a morbo evasissent, non tantum gallo facerent Aesculapio sanitatis, ut putabatur, instauratori; sed in ejus templo votivas suspenderent tabulas, in quibus tum morbi, quo fuerant detenti, naturam ac morem describerent; tum etiam remediorum formulas, quorum ope convaluerant, fideliter atque accurate subnotarent; ut qui in posterum simili afficerentur aegritudine, pari modo possent restitui: Hippocrates, vir nec igenio, nec arte, nec facundia cuiquam aut antenatorum, aut etiam posterorum secundus, tabulas hasce omnium primus ex scripsisse, atque ex iisdem invicem collatis medicam artem condidisse concinnasseque vulgo perhibetur'. I have been unable to identify what specific classical source – if any – the Greek terms are allusions to.

[342] Strabo, *Geog.*, XIV.19; Pliny, *Hist. nat.*, XXIX.2.

[343] On Sprat: Wood, 'Methodology and apologetics' (1980); Hunter, 'Ideology'.

was followed by his even more explicitly pro-Society *Plus ultra* (1668), which was initially greeted with some enthusiasm by important Society veterans such as John Beale.[344]

Part I of Sprat's book, completed by late 1664, was both presented and read as a history of philosophy. Glanvill, meanwhile, adopted the status of the historian of philosophy, appending a 'Letter to a friend concerning Aristotle' to *Scepsis*.[345] And yet, perhaps because of the tendency to see their works as expressions of a more widely held ideology, I know of no attempts to examine what they, as individuals, were actually doing in their histories.[346] In the absence of manuscript evidence we must attempt to recreate their working processes from internal textual evidence. Indeed, it must even be a question as to why Sprat felt that his 'official' history of the Royal Society should include a history of philosophy. My suspicion is that he was drawing inspiration from the oration format. As we have already seen, inaugural orations by new incumbents of learned chairs invariably began with histories of the relevant disciplines; even more relevant, inaugural orations pronounced by rectors or professors in university commencement ceremonies would often begin with a historical introduction.[347] Sprat may have felt that he was composing the equivalent of an extended celebratory oration, with a historical introduction both demanded by the genre and convenient for his methodological agenda.

Both Sprat and Glanvill undoubtedly approached their tasks with a Baconian historical framework. Athenian philosophy was rooted in a sophist culture. This led to a philosophy that was hasty, not based on observation and prone to

---

[344] Lewis, 'Glanvill' is now the best account. Cope, 'The cupri-cosmits: Glanvill on latitudinarian anti-enthusiasm' (1954) is now outdated, and Cope, *Joseph Glanvill: Anglical apologist* (1956) must be used with caution.

[345] Thomas Sprat, *The History of the Royal Society* (London, 1667), 120 (dating); 4, advertising Part I as giving 'a short view of the *Antient*, and *Modern* Philosophy'; see also Oldenburg to Boyle, 24 Nov 1664, in *Oldenburg correspondence*, II, 320–1: 'ye Author hath divided his discourse into 3. generall Heards: ye first giveth a short view of ye Ancient and modern Philosophy . . . [to show] what moved y$^m$, to enter upon a way of Inquiry, different from y$^t$, on w$^{ch}$ the former [i.e. the Royal Society] have proceded'. Glanvill later insisted that knowledge of the history of philosophy was a mark of the best divines of the Restored Church of England: 'Anti-fanatical religion, and free philosophy, in a continuation of the NEW ATLANTIS', in *Essays on several important subjects in philosophy and religion* (London, 1676), 8 (new pagination). John Ward used Glanvill precisely as a mine of historical data on the history of anatomy: Folger MS. v.a.295 (Diary of John Ward, vol. XII, fols. 102$^r$–110$^v$) (see also Frank, 'Mirror', 171–2).

[346] A partial exception is Gaukroger, *Emergence*, 222–4, discussed below. For a powerful critique of the tendency to read Sprat's *History* as an expression of a wider 'ideology', see Hunter, 'Ideology'.

[347] See the many examples offered in Serjeantson, 'Hobbes, the universities, and the history of philosophy' (2006), at 128–9. For an English example, to which I was led by n. 82 of that article, see Samuel Fell, *Primitiae, sive oratio habita Oxonia in schola theologica* (Oxford, 1627), 3–14.

over-eager systematisation.[348] But Sprat and Glanvill defended and augmented this historical conclusion in ways that significantly transcended Bacon's, and differed from each other.

Sprat offered a dual explanation. After offering the commonplace observation that 'all Learning and Civility were deriv'd down to us, from the *Eastern* parts of the World', he suggested that 'as to them we owe the *Invention*; so from them proceeded the first *Corruption* of knowledge'. The Assyrians, Chaldeans, and Egyptians wrapped their knowledge in mystery and hieroglyphics. This was an obscurantism that was self-serving, designed so 'that they might the better insinuate their opinions into their hearers minds'. When philosophy passed to Greece, these 'ornaments of *Fancy*' were preserved (hence the first Greek wisemen – Orpheus, Linus, Musaeus, Homer – were also poets). This inheritance 'gave the *Grecians* occasion ever after of exercising their wit, and their imagination, about the works of Nature, more then was consistent with a sincere Inquiry into them'.[349] While it is tempting to speculate about possible sources for this addition by Sprat to the Baconian narrative, the idea that philosophy came to Greece from the east was, as we have seen, such a commonplace that such speculation would be fruitless.[350] We see further evidence, however, that even among non-specialists the history of philosophy was moving towards a general history of culture.

Sprat's second addition to Bacon was to expand on the latter's focus on Athens. The Athenians possessed an 'active humour' and were 'Masters of the Arts of *Speaking*': this made them particularly fit 'for the reducing of Philosophy into *Method*'. Their city was famed for political education, something that produced scholars 'in a short time' and created a temper fitted for making '*sudden* Conclusions' and convincing hearers 'by argument'. This political culture could hardly breed interest in the 'diligent, private, and severe examination of those little and almost infinite Curiosities, on which the true Philosophy must be founded'. Sprat rather cleverly adapted the usual description of Socrates as the inventor of moral philosophy to proclaim him typical of the Athenian desire to make philosophy 'serviceable to the affairs of men, and the uses of life'. Socrates's dialectical method incited his followers to sectarianism, which only exacerbated the problem by engendering more 'subtilties of confuting' from the 'Talkative Sects'.[351]

Previous commentators have surprisingly not noted that this emphasis on the practical sources of Athenian error directly contradicted Bacon. The

---

[348] Sprat, *History*, 6–9, 30; Joseph Glanvill, *Plus ultra, or, the progress and advancement of knowledge since the days of Aristotle* (London, 1668), 20–30.

[349] Sprat, *History*, 5–6.

[350] Sprat himself noted that the history of ancient philosophical method had been considered by 'several *Great Men*' before him (ibid., 4).

[351] Ibid., 8–9.

Athenians' speculation has become the product not of their distancing from the world, but of their political engagement. It is difficult to identify a precise source for this rather surprising conclusion: such a contextual explanation for Athenian philosophical culture does not appear in any of the standard anti-Aristotelian works that I am familiar with. However, there is one interesting (and rather surprising) possibility. Sprat's claim that the errors of Athenian natural philosophy can be linked to their active political culture is in some ways reminiscent of Hobbes's claims in chapter 46 of *Leviathan*. Although Hobbes did say that philosophy only developed in Athens after the victories over the Persians had generated enough leisure (pointing out that the Greek cognates of *schola* and *diatriba* signified '*Leasure*' and '*Passing of the time*' respectively), he did also imply that it was particularly suited to the disputatiousness of Greek city states – it was, after all, partly the imbibing of Aristotelian political philosophy that had led to civil war in England.[352] There is some reason to suspect that Sprat valued Hobbes's opinions on the political culture of ancient Athens. He prefaced his 1659 poetic retelling of Thucydides' account of the Athenian plague with Hobbes's translation of the relevant section of the Greek historian.[353] The poem itself was modelled on the 'Pindarick way' of Abraham Cowley, under whose literary influence Sprat had fallen in 1657, and who had himself composed an anti-Aristotelian Pindaric ode to Hobbes.[354] If there were both intellectual and personal reasons for Sprat to draw on Hobbes, there was also good reason for his qualified dissent from him (and from Bacon), and for his even greater emphasis on the active political culture that had given birth to his version of vain philosophy, for in the more political sections of his *History*, Sprat emphasised the importance of 1650s Oxford in the pre-formation of the Royal Society so as to give it a sense of political quiescence and loyalist withdrawal.[355] I thus tentatively propose that Sprat drew on Hobbes's political–contextual explanation for the failures of Athenian philosophy and modified it to suit his own end: the defence of the (supposed) methodology of the Royal Society virtuosi.

---

[352] Hobbes, *Leviathan*, 368–9 (=Malcolm, III, 1056). For further details, see Malcolm, III, 1057, nn. k–l. Hobbes, *Leviathan*, 110–11 (=Malcolm, II, 334) connects Aristotelian philosophy with popular politics. In *De corpore*, 'Epistola Dedicatoria', sigs. A2ᵛ–A3ʳ, Hobbes connects Greek sophistry and the culture of their philosophical schools with their 'political philosophy' (*Philosophia Civilis*), without adding a further cultural explanation. I tentatively propose that Sprat was most influenced by the last of these.

[353] Thomas Sprat, *The plague of Athens* (London, 1659), 1–4.

[354] Morgan, 'Sprat, Thomas', *ODNB*; Anselment, 'Thomas Sprat's *The plague of Athens*' (1996); Abraham Cowley, 'To Mr. Hobs', *The works of Mʳ Abraham Cowley* (5th edn, London, 1679 [1st edn=1668]), 26–8. Sprat's emulation of Cowley led to him being monickered 'Pindaric Sprat': *Ath. Ox*, IV.727.

[355] Sprat, *History*, 53; Morgan, 'Science, England's "Interest" and universal monarchy: the making of Thomas Sprat's *History of the Royal Society*' (2009), 35–6.

Although their discussions of the history of philosophy reached similar conclusions (and thus are often treated together), a detailed examination reveals that Glanvill took a different approach to Sprat. Where Sprat's compositional strategy is difficult to retrace, it is relatively easy to see what Glanvill was doing: he adopted the Baconian framework, then buttressed it with a large quantity of material from the humanist anti-Aristotelian tradition. Evidence for Glanvill's early philosophical development is sadly lacking,[356] and we must rely primarily on his published works: *The vanity of dogmatizing* (1661), its slightly modified reissue, *Scepsis scientifica* (1665) – now dedicated to the Royal Society and including two new sections, 'Scire\i tuum nihil est, or, the author's defense of *The vanity of dogmatizing*', and 'A letter to a friend concerning Aristotle', both intended as rebuttals to Thomas White's 1663 attack on the *Vanity* – and *Plus ultra, or, the progress and advancement of knowledge since the days of Aristotle* (1668), conceived as an apology for the Royal Society supplementary to Sprat's *History*.

The first two of these works were designed to promote a moderate scepticism, and their engagement with the history of philosophy was limited to a series of anti-Aristotelian commonplaces, clearly cribbed from Gassendi's *Exercitationes*.[357] The reader is presented with a catalogue of largely unconnected contradictions, absurdities, and impieties supposedly to be found in Aristotle. The only hint of a methodological agenda comes when Glanvill claims that Aristotle's philosophy was incapable of making discoveries. The animal books – obviously problematic to this claim – were dismissed as 'not much transcending vulgar observation' used only 'to suffrage' previously formulated hypotheses.[358] This was a weak argument, and Glanvill later retracted it in favour of a more standard attitude of praise for these books as a rare escape from fruitless speculation on Aristotle's part.[359]

Glanvill's attacks on Aristotle were here only one part of a larger anthropological and methodological argument about the necessity of recognising the limits of man's knowledge. He stated that *Vanity* began as an overly long preface to an ultimately unpublished treatise on the immortality of the soul;[360] since Glanvill only graduated MA in 1658, it is not an unreasonable assumption that that treatise itself stemmed from notes taken in training towards that

---

[356] The claim that Glanvill could not understand Greek in Burns, 'Glanvill, Joseph', *ODNB* does not seem to be based on any evidence, and is distinctly unlikely. There is no evidence of contact with the Oxford natural philosophical circles during his time there in the 1650s, and he spent much of the 1660s in the West Country (see also Parkin, *Cumberland*, 120–2).

[357] Glanvill, *Vanity*, 148–88; Joseph Glanvill, *Scepsis scientifica* (London, 1665), 109–40 (Glanvill admits his debts to Gassendi at *Vanity*, 156, 184). Glanvill added a caveat at the beginning of the first anti-Aristotelian chapter of *Scepsis*, signalling that he was not writing a history of the fortunes of various classical philosophies (109).

[358] Glanvill, *Vanity*, 179; Glanvill, *Scepsis*, 131–2.  [359] Glanvill, *Plus ultra*, sigs. [B5]$^{r-v}$.

[360] Glanvill, *Vanity*, sigs. A3$^r$–A4$^r$.

degree, and that the anti-Aristotelian themes that Glanvill discovered in Gassendi were simply incorporated into a wider project (perhaps only upon reading Gassendi's *Opera* of 1658).

However, Glanvill was forced to prioritise these aspects of his work by the critical response of Thomas White, *Sciri, sive sceptices & scepticorum a jure disputationis exclusio* (1663).[361] Unlike Glanvill, White developed a full statement of natural philosophical methodology, itself based on a considered and idiosyncratic presentation of the historical Aristotle. He immediately recognised the debt of Glanvill's anti-Aristotelianism to Gassendi.[362] His own position was that Aristotle had been dangerously misrepresented by the later Aristotelians, and that he and his friend Digby had revived the true Stagirite.[363] This involved him in revisionist readings of specific Aristotelian doctrines, especially his matter theory (see 5.2 below). But it also involved him in an extensive interpretation and defence of Aristotle's philosophical method, which White placed, as had the anti-Aristotelians, in the context of classical Greek philosophy.

In direct contrast to the anti-Aristotelians, White claimed that Aristotle reacted *against* the sophistic intellectual culture of classical Athens. Socrates had been 'merely a Dialectician and a Doubter', and his school had been divided into two by Plato and Aristotle. The former, relying on his 'most pure eloquence', spoke speciously about the principles necessary for human life. The latter, however, hunted after truth through experiments, and married to the inspection of nature the power to deduce consequences. While Athens was a democracy the orators held power, and Aristotle was not valued, only achieving esteem later.[364] It is clear that White was deliberately reversing what had by then become an anti-Aristotelian commonplace: that his success was contingent on his tapping into the rhetorical and sophistic culture of contemporary Athens.

This contextualisation led White to develop some interesting readings of specific Aristotelian natural philosophical doctrines, so as to defend his claim that far from being a sophist, Aristotle defined his terms more clearly than any other philosopher.[365] For example, he simply equated Aristotelian

---

[361] Thomas White, *Sciri, sive, Sceptices & scepticorum jure disputationis exclusio* (London, 1663), trans. as *An exclusion of scepticks from all title to dispute: being an answer to The vanity of dogmatizing* (London, 1665). The translation is generally faithful although it often adopts a less academic prose style: I give references to both. The fullest treatment is Southgate, *The life and work of Thomas White* (1993), but it is not always reliable on White's relationship with the Renaissance Aristotelian tradition from which he emerged.

[362] White, *Sciri*, 13–14 (=*Scepticks*, 1–2). At 104–5, White claims that Glanvill has simply picked out the best of Gassendi's anti-Aristotelian arguments (the English version, 60–1, is rather more polemical).

[363] White, *Sciri*, 74–5, 88–9 (=*Scepticks*, 41, 50).    [364] White, *Sciri*, 95–7 (=*Scepticks*, 55–6).

[365] White, *Sciri*, 105–7 (=*Scepticks*, 61–2).

'form' – which Glanvill had presented as a paradigmatic example of Aristotelian obfuscation – with figure: form thus became accident.[366] This was certainly a way to save Aristotle from the charge of obfuscation, but it was also to accept precisely the reading offered by such arch anti-Aristotelians as Patrizi or, in England, William Pemble, who had claimed that this was the only salvageable interpretation of the nature of 'form' that Aristotle's confusions allowed.[367] Elsewhere, White had to resort to more philological defences, such as in his response to Glanvill's attack on the supposed absurdity of defining light as 'the act of a perspicuous body' – Glanvill's translation of 'ἐνέργεια τοῦ διαφανοῦσ' of *De anima* 418$^b$9.[368] White responded – fairly – that a far better English translation of ἐνέργεια was 'operation' (i.e. of a transparent body).[369]

More important was White's reinterpretation of Aristotle's method. White's Aristotle resembles Harvey's: he used experiments to establish general principles. Collecting experiments for their own sake is the work of craftsmen (*artifices*), not philosophers.[370] Glanvill had stated that 'we cannot know any thing of *Nature* but by an *Analysis* of it to its *true initial causes*';[371] jumping on this, White asserted that this was precisely what Aristotelian metaphysics was designed to offer. Unlike the dreamer Descartes, Aristotle 'by contemplation deduced into method what he discovered in nature': it was metaphysics that acted as a base for natural philosophy, for example by defining rarity and density, or a vacuum as impossible.[372] That it was a set of first principles for natural philosophy may be a controversial interpretation of the role of Aristotelian metaphysics, but as we saw above (4.2) it was a common one in late Renaissance Aristotelianism, accepted even by Hobbes (whom White of course knew personally).

White's Aristotelian philosophy has been presented as idiosyncratically defined by its opposition to scepticism, itself tied in with his anti-Anglican theological polemics.[373] Yet the idea that Aristotle had developed his natural philosophical method as a way of establishing solid first principles against an otherwise prevalent scepticism was in fact present in a variety of late Renaissance Aristotelian works across the theological spectrum, such as the Calvinist Wendelin's advanced textbook, which we have already met. Wendelin claimed that all the pre-Aristotelian philosophers were sceptics, for they did not consider physics a science. Heraclitus, Cratylus, Pythagoras,

---

[366] White, *Sciri*, 109–10 (=*Scepticks*, 64).   [367] See n. 34 above.   [368] Glanvill, *Vanity*, 156–7.
[369] White, *Sciri*, 112–13 (=*Scepticks*, 65–6).   [370] White, *Sciri*, 126–7 (=*Scepticks*, 73–4).
[371] Glanvill, *Vanity*, 210.
[372] White, *Sciri*, 131–2 ('Aristoteles enim quae in naturâ insita invênit, Contemplatione in Methodum conclusit') (=*Scepticks*, 76–7).
[373] Southgate, *White*, 66–137; Southgate, 'Blackloism vs scepticism' (1992); Henry, 'Atomism and eschatology', 233.

and Plato were all dualists who believed in an intelligible world in which resided truth and a sensible (and thus illusionary) world, the subject of physics. The Sceptics and Academics eroded not just natural, but all knowledge. Democritus, Anaxagoras, Empedocles, and even Ptolemy could be counted among the sceptics.[374] Only Aristotle recognised that the intellect could produce universals and that physics was a science because it investigated causes – even if Aristotle was only a man who naturally also made mistakes.[375] Needless to say, this 'Aristotle versus the sceptics' history of natural philosophy could be questioned on many historical particulars.[376] There can be little doubt, however, that White was following an established Europe-wide interpretation, an interpretation not limited to seventeenth-century English theological polemics.

White's reading forced Glanvill to address the issue of Aristotle head on. We can recreate Glanvill's actions with some degree of reliability, for where *Vanity* (and thus *Scepsis*) relied almost entirely on Gassendi, the two anti-White tracts appended to *Scepsis* displayed familiarity with a wide range of earlier humanist anti-Aristotelian works: Glanvill must have engaged in a systematic programme of reading such works between the appearance of White's *Sciri* in 1663 and mid-1664. The result, even if entirely derivative, was the fullest ever statement of English anti-Aristotelianism. Some elements were simply further extractions from Gassendi, such as the continued insistence on the internal

---

[374] Wendelin, *Contemplationes physicae*, 2b–3a: 'Ad tertium, *An Physica sit scientia?* Capitis causam, pro Physica, contra veteres & recentes nonnullos Physicos, orare libet. E veteribus, qui Physicam scientiam esse negârunt, permulti fuere: *Heraclitus Ephesius, Cratylus, Pythagoras, Socrates, Plato:* qui duos statuebat mundos: unum intelligibilem, in quo veritas habitaret: alterum sensibilem, quem visu tactúque perciperemus: in cujus contemplatione Physici versarentur: In hoc veri-similitudinem seu opinionem dominari contendebat. Accedit tota *Scepticorum & Academicorum* familia, quae non rerum tantùm naturalium, sed omnium scientiam sustulit, verámque veri notitiam augustiorem longè esse, quàm ut humani sensûs & judicii angustiis capi posset, affirmavit. *Democritus*, referente *Lactantio*, veritatem in puteo, cui fundus non sit, demersam latitare quiritatur. *Anaxagoras* impenetrabili circumfusam caligine exclamat. *Empedocles* veritatis notitiam in animum, per angustas sensuum vias, descendere posse inficiatur. *Arcesilae* quatuor sunt dogmata paradoxa: unum, *Nihil posse comprehendi*: alterum, *Sapientem nulli rei unquam assensurum*: tertium, *Omnia esse aequaliter incerta, obscura, incognita, improbabilia*: quartum, *Sapientem nihil probaturum, nihilque opinaturum*. Priora duo amplexus, quoque *Carneades*. In posterioribus dissensit, & inter omnino incertum & omnino comprehensum statuit medium, probabile & verisimillimum, quod probaturum, opinaturum & secuturum sapientem dixit: ità tamen ut se non scire, sed opinari, non verum comprehendere, sed veri-similitudinem sequi & intelligat ipse, & simpliciter apertéque profiteatur. Mathematicorum princeps *Ptolemaeus* in *Scepticorum* sententiam quoque inclinâsse videtur: Nam & Theologiam & Physicam contemtui duxisse fertur, quòd illam praesigni rerum excellentiâ imbecillitas humana consequi haud posset'.

[375] Ibid., 3a–b, 13b–14a.

[376] Wendelin used the fideist Gianfrancesco Pico della Mirandola for his history of scepticism (ibid., 2b–3a, 7a–b, 13a); Pico he aligned with the most radical sceptic of them all, Xeniades (7a–b). For Xeniades, see Sextus Empiricus, *Ad. Math.*, VII.388, 399; for Pico's scepticism, see Schmitt, *Pico*, esp. 84–127.

absurdities and contradictions in Aristotle's works.[377] However, Glanvill now added further *ad hominem* assaults on Aristotle's putative contrariness, sodomy, avarice, scurrility, and traitorousness, drawing on Patrizi in particular.[378] He focused especially – as had several generations of anti-Aristotelians – on Aristotle's relationship with his predecessors, arguing that he misrepresented them when he disagreed with them (as in the case of the atomists and of Plato's doctrine of ideas), while plagiarising much of his doctrine from them at the same time, especially from the two obscure Pythagoreans Archytas and Ocellus Lucanus. This much-used argument, of great interest to seventeenth-century English natural philosophers,[379] religious apologists,[380] and scholars,[381] was derived entirely from Patrizi.

---

[377] Glanvill, 'The authors defence of the Vanity of dogmatizing', in *Scepsis*, 64–6.

[378] Ibid., 58–9; Glanvill, 'A letter to a friend concerning Aristotle', in *Scepsis*, 90. Glanvill admitted that Patrizi, Pico and Gassendi were key sources for him in his *Praefatory Answer to Mr. Henry Stubbe* (London, 1671), 142.

[379] Glanvill, 'Aristotle', in *Scepsis*, 84–7, 91. By Archytas, Glanvill meant Plato's correspondent Archytas of Tarentum (i.e. as described in DL VIII.86 and whose fragments are preserved in Simplicius (see Ps.-Archytas, *Über die Kategorien. Texte zur griechischen Aristoteles-Exegese*, ed. T. A. Szlezák (Berlin, 1972)), but who, Patrizi speculated, himself drew on the ideas of an 'older Archytas', a follower of Pythagoras (i.e. that mentioned in Iamblichus, *Vit. Pyth.*, 104, and whose mock-Doric work on the ten categories had been brought out in 1561 by Domenico Pizzimenti), whom he aligned (for reasons inexplicable) with the more famous Pythagorean Ocellus Lucanus (*On the nature of the universe*, Latin trans. by Joannes Boscius (1554) (Hankins and Palmer, 50). But a more popular edition was the Greek–Latin *Ocelli Lucani de universi natura libellus*, ed. L. Nogarola (Venice, 1559)). See esp. Patrizi, *Discussiones Peripateticae*, II, 182–3, and the excellent discussion in Deitz, 'Patrizi's criticism', 117–20. That Aristotle had stolen from Archytas was (on the basis of Iamblichus, *Myst.*, 302.18–303.30; Simplicius, *In. cat*, II.9) already a commonplace: see Lorenzo Valla, *Dialectical disputations* [1439], eds. and trans., B. P. Copenhaver and L. Nauta (2 vols, Cambridge [MA], 2012), I, 14–15. But it was the accusation that he plagiarised from Ocellus – with whom he shared the unappealing doctrine of the world's eternity – that dominated seventeenth-century English discussions: see e.g. nn. 9 and 35 above, and the notebook of Benjamin Whichcote (Folger MS V.a.326, fol. 44$^v$ rev. (my foliation)).

[380] E.g. Herbert of Cherbury, *De religione gentilium, errorumque apud eos causis* (Amsterdam, 1663), 63; David Lloyd, *Dying and dead mens living words published* (London, 1668), 53; Stillingfleet, *Origines sacrae*, 430 (taking directly from Nogarola's edition, rather than Patrizi); Boyle, *The excellency of theology* (1674), in *Boyle works*, VIII, 86; Matthew Hale, *The primitive origination of mankind, considered and examined according to the light of nature* (London, 1677), 256; Cudworth, *System*, 119, 251; Charles Blount, *Anima mundi, or, an historical narration of the opinions of the ancients concerning man's soul after this life* (London, 1679), 10.

[381] E.g., Thomas Pope Blount, *Censura celebriorum authorum*, 4; John Harris, *The atheistical objections against the being of God and his attributes fairly considered and fully refuted* (London, 1698), 8 (4th pagination, accusing Hobbes of plagiarising from him!); Nicholls, *Conference*, 18–22; Robert Jenkin, *The reasonableness and certainty of the Christian religion* (London, 1700), xxiii–xiv. Bentley had brought renewed attention to him by postulating that the work was originally in Doric Greek: *Phalaris*, 47–50. He was promptly accused of plagiarism (Charles Boyle, *Dr. Bentley's Dissertations on the epistles of Phalaris . . . examin'd* (London, 1698), 54–6) from Charles Emmanuel Vizzanius's preface to *Ocellus Lucanus philosophus De universi natura*, ed. and trans. C. E. Vizzanius (Bologna, 1646): a comparison

Glanvill also paid much attention to Aristotle's reputation and reception. First, he simply turned White's point that Aristotle was not valued in classical Greece to a different purpose, aligning his rise with the 'barbarism' that 'overr[a]n *Rome* and *Athens*'.[382] And he showed his zeal by accepting the most radical conclusion available about the history of the Aristotelian corpus: that of the Brescian humanist Mario Nizolio (1488–1567), who argued in his *De veris principiis et vera ratione philosophandi contra pseudophilosophos* (1553) that the surviving Aristotelian texts were only 'compendia' or 'epitomes' made by his son Nicomachus.[383] Glanvill combined this with the far more standard criticism (again most fully developed by Patrizi), derived from the transmission histories of the *Corpus Aristotelicum* in Strabo and Plutarch, that the *Corpus* had been gradually corrupted by a series of editors including Theophrastus, the first century AD book-collector Apellicon of Teos, the grammarian Tyrannion of Amisus, and finally Andronicus of Rhodes, who had prepared a new edition of the *Corpus*.[384] But when it came to method, Glanvill made no concerted effort to tailor these anti-Aristotelian topoi to an 'experimentalist' agenda, the sole exception being when he deliberately ignored White's natural philosophical interpretation of Aristotelian metaphysics in favour of the theological one, allowing him to argue, à la Bacon, that Aristotle had confusingly intermingled theology (i.e. metaphysics so defined) and natural philosophy.[385] Glanvill's attacks on Aristotle do not, at this point, seem to be representative of a new and singularly post-Baconian mentality;[386] rather, they were late salvoes in the humanist debate over the historical Aristotle.

This state of affairs changes markedly in the *Plus Ultra*, where Glanvill followed Sprat in attempting to develop a history of classical philosophy that systematically demonstrated the qualitative difference between the (sophistic) aims of classical Greek philosophers and the truth seeking of the '*Modern Experimenters*', who 'think, That the *Philosophers* of elder Times, though their *Wits* were excellent, yet the way they took was not like to bring much

---

with that text, combined with what we have learnt about his other 'borrowings' from previous scholars on Greek philosophy (2.2 above), seems to confirm the justness of the accusation. Dodwell and William Lloyd were at that time also discussing the Doric context of Pythagoreanism, the former developing an elaborate thesis: Dodwell to Lloyd, 14 May 1698, MS Cherry 22, fols. 54$^{r-v}$ (see further 3.8 above).

[382] Glanvill, 'Aristotle', in *Scepsis*, 79–80.

[383] Ibid., 82–3, drawing on Mario Nizolio, *De veris principiis et vera ratione philosophandi contra pseudophilosophos libri IV* [1553], ed. Q. Breen (2 vols, Rome, 1956), II, 167. Nizolio's 'sources' are *Suda*, 398; DL, VIII.88 and, most important, Cicero, *Fin.*, v.5.12.

[384] Glanvill, 'Aristotle', in *Scepsis*, 81–3, drawing, with acknowledgement, on Gianfrancesco Pico della Mirandola, Patrizi, and Gassendi. The classical sources are Strabo, *Geog.*, XIII.1.54; Plutarch, *Sulla*, XXVI.

[385] Glanvill, 'Defence', in *Scepsis*, 71.

[386] I thus dissent from the reading of Glanvill in Gaukroger, *Emergence*, 198.

*advantage* to *Knowledge*, or any of the *Uses* of *humane Life;* being for the most part *that* of *Notion* and *Dispute*, which still runs round in a *Labyrinth* of *Talk*, but *advanceth nothing*'.[387] Examining systematically a series of natural philosophical disciplines, Glanvill claimed that following a bright 'observational' start they were all turned into sophistic wrangling in the century or two around the flourishing of Athens, until they were gradually revitalised, culminating in modern experimental philosophy. His first case study was chymistry. It had been developed by Hermes or by the ancient Egyptians at least, 'but it was not at all in *use* with *Aristotle* and his *Sectators*', and was generally unknown to 'the *Grecians*, or the *disputing Ages*'.[388] This was not Glanvill's worst claim, but as we shall see he was later roundly embarrassed on this score by Henry Stubbe, who was far more *au fait* with the latest literature on the antiquity of chymistry. But Glanvill's scheme also forced him into errors that can be detected through examining his own text alone. For example, he claimed that anatomy went entirely unpractised by the ancients. He offered the usual post-Vesalius commonplace about Galen's ignorance of human anatomy and the prohibition of anatomy in ancient Rome, but he also added the claim that '*Democritus* was fain to excuse his *Dissection* of *Beasts*, even to the great *Hippocrates*'.[389] Glanvill here clearly mangled the narrative offered in the *Epistola ad Damagetum* (4.1 above), whose message is surely that Democritus and Hippocrates *did* practise anatomy.

Such misuse of evidence is also evident in his discussion of the history of mathematics. As usual, Glanvill sought out the latest and best humanist treatments, in this case G. J. Vossius's recent (1650) history of the discipline. Once again, he claimed that although the discipline had a promising beginning (with Pythagoras), it was soon bogged down in '*idle Speculation*', from which it was brought out only by Euclid, Apollonius of Perga,[390] and Archimedes, whose nonspeculative methods were then taken up by Diophantus and Hero of Alexandria.[391] But once again, this narrative involved Glanvill in some absurd

---

[387] Glanvill, *Plus ultra*, 7. It was this passage above all that so infuriated Henry Stubbe: see below.

[388] Ibid., 10–11.   [389] Ibid., 12–13.

[390] Glanvill made a further mistake here, citing the recent (1661) Florentine translation of Books v–vii of the *Conics* (which were lost in the original Greek and only available in Arabic), and claiming that it was based on a manuscript '*Iacob Golius* procured out of the *East*', when in fact it was based on the manuscript brought to Rome by Ignatius Ni'matallah in 1577 (see Toomer, *Eastern wisedome*, 23, 25). Golius's manuscript was finally transported to England by Edward Bernard, and translated by Edward Halley in 1710, for which, see Toomer, *Wisedome*, 289 and Fried, *Reconstruction*.

[391] Glanvill, *Plus ultra*, 26–9. Archimedes' and especially Hero's expertise in mechanics had long rendered them attractive to those who emphasised the philosophical value of practical disciplines: see Hall, 'Hero's *Pneumatica:* a study of its transmission and influence' (1949). Glanvill's belief that the ancient Greeks knew algebra, and the special focus on Diophantus, was an early modern commonplace (see n. 483 below); for the anti-Arabic motivations behind the birth of this commonplace, and the importance of Diophantus, see Cifoletti, 'The creation

mistreatments of the sources, as he was forced to claim that before this revival classical Greek mathematics, as developed by Archytas and Eudoxus, was stuck in '*abstractive Contemplations*' and that these mathematicians 'were scared from the *Mechanical* and *Organical Methods*'.[392] There was nothing to support this in their respective biographies in the classical sources; rather, Laërtius reported that Archytas 'was the first to bring mechanics to a system by applying mathematical principles; he also first employed mechanical motion in a geometrical construction' (VII.83). This embarrassment can only have been amplified by the fact that John Wilkins, the doyen of mid-century English science, had lauded Archytas and his mechanical inventions, especially his famous flying wooden dove, as ideal models for modern endeavours.[393] It is clear that Glanvill made these embarrassing errors because he wanted to place the two most famous mathematicians aligned with classical Athenian philosophy into the 'speculative' category.

It has been worth spending this time on Sprat and Glanvill; their works are well known and still often cited as statements of a general Royal Society 'attitude' towards ancient philosophy, but we have now been able to reconstruct, at least to some extent, what they were actually doing in their historicisations. It should by now be clear that their texts were the products of deliberate and reflexive engagement with the classical sources and with various interpretative traditions. Unfortunately for them, their iconoclastic histories could not stand up either to historical–philological or to a broader cultural critique. Part of the problem was that such dismissive comments about the ancients were by then being associated with the dangerously speculative approach of Descartes. This manifested itself directly in methodological–historical commentary. For example, Isaac Barrow – hardly a reactionary – announced in 1661 that Aristotle had developed a philosophy based 'not on arbitrary figments of the mind, and which does not resort to impercetible causes, does not slip into inconsistent hypotheses, does not feed the mind with chimaeras ... [but rather] one open to nature, and accommodated to the appearances grafted onto the mind, to the infallible standard of experience, to common sense and to the comprehension of those learning it'; all this in contrast to a 'certain new fashioned philosophy, which blunts the apprehension

---

of the history of algebra in the sixteenth century' (1996). Vossius's discussion is in *De quatuor artibus popularibus de philologia et scientiis mathematicis cui operi subjungitur chronologia mathematicorum* (Amsterdam, 1650). Practising mathematicians in England read this work with interest: John Collins, for example, was curious whether it would be enlarged by Isaac Vossius: letter to Wallis, 17 Jun 1669, *Correspondence of scientific men*, II, 515.

[392] Glanvill, *Plus ultra*, 27–8.

[393] Wilkins, *Mathematical magick*, 191–9. The standard sources for Archytas's dove are late: Aulus Gellius, *Noct. Att.*, x.12.8–10, quoting Favorinus, fr. 66, although some doubt as to which Archytas wrote on mechanics is introduced by DL VIII.80.

with too much "Meditation", breaks the force and retards the alacrity of the growing intellect'.[394] Just as White would assert against Glanvill, Barrow argued that Aristotle had avoided both scepticism and speculative dogmatism by building principles on the basis of observation.[395] Those 'tricksters' who defiled Aristotle with the title of 'sophist' (Barrow cannot have been unaware he was condemning Bacon) were wrong; reading Aristotle was the best method for 'carefully clearing sophistical tricks', not least because he had so 'expanded the huge repository of natural history'.[396]

Barrow was at this point Regius Professor of Greek and his defence of Aristotle against Cartesian cavilling had an institutional–pedagogical agenda; this was also the case in the two most prominent responses to the Royal Society apologists: those by the cleric and scholar Meric Casaubon and the prolific Warwick physician Henry Stubbe.[397] These negative responses were the product not of an intellectual backwardness but of institutional tensions, as Casaubon and Stubbe concerned themselves with the putative threat posed by the Royal Society to the universities and to learned medicine.[398] In Stubbe's case in particular this involved them in an extensive treatment of the history of natural philosophical method.

Casaubon was eminently qualified to challenge the *novatores'* vision of the history of philosophy, given his work on Laërtius, Hierocles, and various Stoic texts, and his general philological learning.[399] But the section challenging Glanvill in the *Letter to Peter du Moulin* (1669) is rather sparse, no doubt

---

[394] Isaac Barrow, 'Oratio sarcasmica in schola Graeca' (1661), in *Theological works*, IX, 165–6: 'Non ut novitia quaedam philosophemata meditatione nimiâ obtundit aciem, frangit vim, retardat impetum, alacritatem extinguit ingenii pubescentis ... Philosophia quippe haec non ad figmenta mentis arbitraria exigitur; non ad insensiles causas recurrit; non ad absonas hypotheses delabitur; nullis chimaeris pascit animos ... Ad naturae indolem apertam, ad mentis insitas species, ad experientiae infallibilem normam, ad popularem sensum, ad captum se discentis accommodat'. I have slightly amended the partial translation in Osmond, *Isaac Barrow* (1944), 94–5.

[395] Barrow, 'Oratio', 166.

[396] Ibid., 167 ('quidni enim sycophantae mihi audient, Aristotelis qui toties venerandum nomen Sophistae titulo aspergunt?'), 165–6: ('... ad sophisticas praestigias caute eluendas ... Naturalis Historiae thesaurus ingens expanditur').

[397] Stubbe studied with Glisson and became an admirer of Willis after his expulsion from Christ Church, Oxford, in 1660 (Frank, *Harvey*, 237–8). Jacob, *Henry Stubbe* (1983) should be read with extreme caution: almost all the conclusions are rendered precarious by attempts to crowbar Stubbe's into the category of political radical, often verging on conspiracy theory. On the subjects of learned medicine and the RS, much preferable is Cook, 'Stubbe'.

[398] The best introduction remains Hunter, *Science and society*, 136–61, ('Science, leaning and the universities'), which lists many other less full responses with similar concerns at 137–8; for Stubbe's institutional allegiances and concerns, see Cook, 'Stubbe'. See also the case of James Duport's 'Apologiae pro Aristotele, contra novos philosophos. Seu pro veteribus contra nuperos Novatores', in *Musae subsecivae, se, poetica stromata* (Cambridge, 1676), 47–8, brilliantly contextualised in Feingold, 'Barrow', 9–15.

[399] See 2.2, 5.2, 6.5.

because Casaubon's aim was not to challenge the *novatores* per se but to show the value of the full range of university learning so as not to 'allow [the new philosophy] … to usurp upon all other learning, as not considerable in comparison'.[400] Casaubon's only serious foray into the debate of the history of philosophical method was a brief defence of Aristotle. Challenging Glanvill's claim that Aristotle was a slave to his speculative theories, Casaubon stated that Aristotle had 'prefer[red] *experience* without *art* or knowledge, before *art* and knowledge, without *experience*; though indeed otherwise he doth make art of it self, (that is, general rules and maxims grounded at first upon reiterated experience) … which doth look into the causes, and can give satisfactory reasons of events, more commendable, then illiterate or irrational, though successful experience'.[401] This is the standard image of the 'observational' Aristotle as mid-way between the Empirics and the system builders that we found in Harvey, and Casaubon underlined the medical sources of the topos by citing Hippocrates's 'ἡ δὲ πεῖρα σφαλερή' ('perilous experience') as part of the tradition that 'meer *Empiricks* have always been accounted dangerous'.[402] He did this only in passing, but we have here the hint of a key conclusion of this chapter: where the learned physicians carefully presented their experimentalism and focus on observation as the culmination of a long tradition, the Royal Society apologists appeared to be riding roughshod over these traditions, whilst entirely misrepresenting them. This was the case made loudly and powerfully by Henry Stubbe.

Stubbe remains a slightly troubling figure, partly because of his complex political views and partly because of the continuing prevelance of the idea that anyone who opposed the Royal Society so virulently must have had a 'conservative' agenda of some sort or another.[403] However, as Harold Cook has shown, Stubbe's work was the product less of idiosyncratic politics (whether 'radical' or 'conservative') than of institutional tensions and of the 1660s methodological debate about the relationship between physic and natural philosophy.[404] Stubbe was immediately incensed by Glanvill's *Plus ultra* (to

---

[400] Meric Casaubon, *A letter … to Peter du Moulin* (Cambridge, 1669), 30. As is well known, he also suggested that it might lead to atheism (also 30).

[401] Ibid., 10.   [402] Ibid.

[403] The best example of this confusion is Jones, *Ancients and moderns*, 245. But for more a more recent case, see e.g., Crocker, *More*, 164, n. 50. Stubbe himself accurately defined the issues at stake in his *Reply*, 48–9: 'All this deliberation could not qualifie him [i.e. Glanvill] so, as to understand the right state of the Question betwixt us: which is not, *Whether Aristotle did know all things?* Nor, *Whether the latter Ages knew more then the precedent?* But, *Whether Antiquity was shie and unacquainted with Anatomy? Whether the Grecians, disputing Ages, and Sectators of Aristotle, did know any thing of Chymistry? In fine, Whether the Ancient Aristotelian Philosophy hath Advanced Nothing of Practical and Beneficial Knowledge?*'

[404] Cook, 'Stubbe'.

which he was supposedly introduced at a dinner party). His outrage was twofold. First, Glanvill's self-advertised progressivism had led him to dismiss traditional practices like phlebotomy as dangerously outmoded. But more importantly, Glanvill had suggested that the whole of learned physic was based on ancient traditions which were 'speculative' rather than experimental or practical. All of Stubbe's extensive excursions into the history of natural philosophy and physic can be seen as challenges to this vision of the history of method, which he associated with the dangerous assaults of the medical reformers.

Stubbe's learning eclipsed that of Sprat and Glanvill (not particularly difficult), or even of the other learned physicians that we have considered.[405] That is not to deny that he sometimes made claims that were either outdated or could not be supported by the evidence, such as when he claimed that Hippocrates knew of the circulation of the blood.[406] At other points he seemed to revel in proving Glanvill's history wrong for its own sake, such as in his response to Glanvill's aforementioned treatment of Democritus the anatomist, where, as well as pointing out Glanvill's error, Stubbe also suggested that the whole story might be spurious (such a conclusion would of course play into Glanvill's hands).[407] But for the most part, Stubbe devoted himself to showing systematically that the history of philosophical method developed by the Royal Society apologists was simply absurd when the evidence was considered. He mocked their obsession with ancient Athens and their attempts to present all Greek philosophy as the product of Athenian sophistry – Stubbe reminded them of the Ionic tradition, into which he smartly incorporated Hippocrates because of the physician's use of Ionic dialect. Where Sprat and Glanvill tried to separate Athenian from the rest of Greek philosophy, Stubbe deflated their claims by moving the heart of the Greek tradition to Alexandria, therefore immediately appropriating for his side the Alexandrian mathematicians and physicians, who could hardly be dismissed as 'speculative'.[408] Moreover, Sprat

---

[405] The catalogue of Stubbe's very extensive library is BL MS Sloane 35.

[406] Henry Stubbe, *The Plus Ultra reduced to a Non Plus* (London, 1670), 100–2. Stubbe's argument depends for the most part on *Nat. oss.*, 11 and *Nutr.*, 22 (Stubbe mistakenly cites 12). From his text and citations, it is also clear that he is drawing on similar claims by Harvey's first continental readers, especially Walaeus and Riolan, on whom, see Pagel, *New light on William Harvey* (1976), 120–1; French, *Harvey*, 273. We can appreciate how niche this position was in England via a letter of Henry Power to Ralph Widdrington of 1 January 1656, in which, although suggesting that Cesalpino (rather than Harvey) discovered circulation, he characterised those who 'strive to prove all the Doctrine of the Circulation out of some fragments of Hippocrates & ill applyed texts of <Plato> Aristotle & Galen' as 'splenetick & malitious writers' (BL MS Sloane 1326, fols. 9ʳ–10ᵛ).

[407] Stubbe, *Reduced*, 89–90; Glanvill himself pointed out this tendency: *Praefatory answer*, 13: 'there are acknowledgements due to him, for the *Reading*, and *shew* of *Learning*, that I find in his Discourse; and I may say of it, *Bene disputat, sed nihil ad rem*'.

[408] Henry Stubbe, *Legends no histories* (London, 1670), sig. [A4]ʳ⁻ᵛ.

was a complete 'stranger . . . in the *History of Philosophy*' if he thought Athenian philosophy could be explained through their obsession with rhetoric.[409] The Greek philosophers all wrote in different dialects, and even the Athens-based Plato and Aristotle coined new terms (Stubbe offered the well-known examples of Λόγος and ἐντελέχεια respectively): 'Read over, Oh! *tres-haute* & *tres-agreeable virtuosi* Diogenes Laertius, & Foesius before you tell these stories'.[410]

Even more damaging than this challenge to Athens-centred history was Stubbe's response to Glanvill's histories of chymistry and physic. For the former, Stubbe challenged Glanvill's narrative of promising experimental beginnings in ancient Egypt, followed by Greek ignorance, and subsequently by gradual revival. The great antiquity 'pretended to' by the alchymists was entirely forged, for it is based on 'entitling several *spurious* books to *Hermes, Moses*, (and *Miriam his Sister*) *Democrtius, Plato, Aristotle*'. Chymistry did begin in Egypt, but much later than the Paracelsians claimed: the first mentions of it appear only in the fourth century AD, even if there were slight earlier traces. Even more damaging to Glanvill was the argument that from these late Egyptian beginnings, chymistry *did* pass on to Greeks – Stubbe listed Zosimus, Olympiodorus, Stephanus, and Synesius as early Greek practitioners – it was from them that it came to the Arabs, and even the term *chymia* had a Greek origin. Although he admitted that their knowledge was limited to metallurgy rather than chymical medicine, the Arabs who first 'accommodated *Chymistry* in an eminent manner to *Physick*' were working in an Aristotelian context.[411] The reason for Stubbe's detail and historical superiority over Glanvill and Sprat is simple: he relied on the anti-Paracelsian work of Conring, whom he cited copiously. But while Conring had sought to attack neo-Paracelsian claims towards the Egyptian antiquity of chymistry, Stubbe cleverly used his research to emphasise the role of the Greeks: 'Out of all which it is evident, that neither the *Grecians*, nor the *disputing Ages* were so ignorant of *Chymistry*, as Mr. *Glanvill* asserts'.[412] One ironic consequence

---

[409] Sprat, *History*, 7, had written that because the Athenians 'were the Masters of the Arts of *Speaking*, to all their Neighbours [they] . . . might well be inclin'd, rather to choose such Opinions of Nature, which they might most elegantly express; then such, which were more useful, but could not so well be illustrated by the ornaments of Speech'.

[410] Stubbe, *Legends*, sigs. [A4]ᵛ–aʳ. Anutius Foesius was the premier sixteenth-century translator of Hippocrates.

[411] Stubbe, *Reduced*, 51–4. Stubbe's source for the philological point about χημεία was G. J. Vossius, *De philosophia et philosophorum sectis libri II* (The Hague, 1658), 66–7, where Vossius cites as his sources Suidas and Photius's entry on Zosimus. There is indeed an entry on 'χημεία' in the Suda, but Photius only has an entry on Zosimus the Byzantine historian, not Zosimus of Panopolis.

[412] Stubbe, *Reduced*, 57. See also, after the long discussion at 58–62, the statement at 64: 'Out of all which it is *evident* that *Chymistry* was a practice *known* and in *use* among the *Sectators* of *Aristotle:* and that the *Grecian* and *disputing Ages* were not unacquainted with *those Processes*,

of all this is that Stubbe, opponent of the Royal Society, was offering a far more progressivist history of chymistry than Glanvill, the Society's most outspoken defender.

Glanvill's and Sprat's attempts to divide the history of natural philosophy into a speculative and rhetorical Greek period and observational and experimental periods coming before and after were similarly undermined by Stubbe's approach to the history of physic. Unsurprisingly, he had recourse to the image of Hippocrates the observational physician which, as we have seen, was then becoming so popular among almost all types of physicians. Indeed, for a supposedly 'conservative' figure, Stubbe offered a relatively radical reading, claiming that Hippocrates was uninterested in 'all *disputes* about *Natural Philosophy* that did not refer to *practice*' and that he was a philosophical syncretist, adopting at different times whichever philosophical method best suited clinical experience.[413] The Greek tradition could then be presented as following in the Hippocratean paradigm. For sure, Vesalius had been right that Galen had not anatomised, and attempts to exonerate him (e.g. that of Sylvius) were 'ridiculous'. But this did not disprove 'that the *Method* he took (however founded on false *principles*) was *secure* and *good*'. He resurrected the Hippocratean research programme – how else could he have discovered the recurrent nerve?[414] More importantly, Stubbe could again demonstrate, *contra* Glanvill, that far from being unknown to the Greeks, anatomy 'was very ancient amongst them', being practiced by Alcmaeon (mid-fifth century BC), although the evidence for this was a late and rather ambiguous statement in Chalcidius's *Timaeus* commentary (*c.* AD 321).[415] The same passage in Chalcidius far less ambiguously attributed human dissections to Herophilus and to the Aristotelian Calisthenes, which Stubbe revelled in.[416] The objections to anatomy in Celsus's *De medicina* 'were put into his mouth by the *Methodists*, as well as *Empirics*'.[417]

---

though these *latter times* have been more *various* and *inquisitive*, and have reduced that *Art* into better *Method*'.

[413] Ibid., 73–4.

[414] Ibid., 93. Although he did not offer a primary citation, Stubbe must be referring to *Loc. aff.* (K VIII.53) and the famous account of the silencing of the squealing pig by the compression of its recurrent nerve in *Praen.* (K XIV.627–30). Stubbe's own citations were to Vesalius's *De humani corporis fabrica*, IV.9 (see e.g. the edn of Basle, 1555, 524 for the relevant discussion of Galen) and Realdus Columbus's *De re anatomica*, XIV (see e.g. the edn of Paris, 1562, 472), making Stubbe a rather nice fit to be a late participant in the 'anatomical renaissance' of Cunningham, *Anatomical renaissance*.

[415] Stubbe, *Reduced*, 77–8. For Chalcidius, see *Chalcidii V.C. Timaeus de Platonis translatus*, ed. J. Meursius (Leiden, 1617), 340: 'quique primus exsectionem aggredi est ausus', and Meursius's extensive discussion of the passage in his 'Notae', 33–6 (new pagination). The ambiguities of the passage remain debated: see e.g. Longrigg, *Greek Rational medicine* (1993), 58–9.

[416] Stubbe, *Reduced*, 175. Chalcidius's is the only known reference to Calisthenes.

[417] Ibid., 84, discussing Celsus, *De med.*, Prooem. 40–4, 74–5. Remarkably, Stubbe was here somewhat pre-empting modern scholarship: e.g. Deuse, 'Celsus im Prooemium von "De

Stubbe, then, destroyed the Royal Society apologists' claim that the Greeks had rejected observational and experimental knowledge. All that was left was to justify the latter's theoretical output. Here, he followed the reading developed by Petty, Glisson, and the many others whom we have already met: 'of the *Methods* of Ancient *Science* there were *two*, the one consisting of more *general principles*, or *rules*; the other making up a *particular Systeme* or *hypothesis*, such as the *Aristotelian* and *Galenical philosophy* (with its *variations* and *discrepancies*) accommodated to *Physick*'.[418] Whatever the validity of the particular systems (and Stubbe had already shown that they had borne much fruit), the key point was that the ancients' general *method* held as its key principle that 'the *final determination* of *philosophical truthes* (relating to *material beings*) is SENSE'.[419] This was by now a standard conclusion: Stubbe supported it by twisting some of the classic anti-Aristotelian commonplaces on their head. Aristotle's association with Alexander, for example, was in fact a point in his favour, for Alexander provided him with thousands of collectors of natural historical data.[420] Although Stubbe did not point it out, this point had already been made in a defence of operative philosophy by Sprat's patron Wilkins, who had also praised Aristotle for combining pure mathematics with practical mechanics (albeit on the basis of the spurious *Mechanical questions*).[421] Sprat and Glanvill ignored the possibility of such narratives in favour of an attempt to wrench the anti-Aristotelian humanist tradition to the service of the methodological rhetoric of the Royal Society; ill fated and unsuited to the task as this attempt was, it shows how strong were the inroads that that tradition had made.

When he attempted to respond to Stubbe, Glanvill could only offer a mixture of backtracking and confusion. He admitted that the ancient physicians followed '*Observation*, and *Experiment*', and claimed that he had only attacked the ancient '*Natural* Philosophers, and *their* Methods, which were made up of *Notion*, and ministred to everlasting Disputes'.[422] Elsewhere, he was forced to admit that Aristotle had also followed observation.[423] Yet his counterattack

---

medicina": Römische Aneignung griechischer Wissenschaft', 835–7. I have been unable to discover an earlier precedent than Stubbe's for this interesting claim.

[418] Stubbe, *Reply*, 37–8. See also 42: 'if Hee [Glanvill, when he speaks of ancient disputatiousness] means *Logical*, or *Metaphysical disputes*, who was obliged to understand him about them, when the Question was about *Natural philosophy*, and *practical knowledge?*'

[419] Ibid., 38. Stubbe cited two of the classic *loci* for Galenic insistence on a balance between reason and experience: *Meth. med.*, IX.6 (K x.628–30) and VI.2 (Stubbe was surely thinking of the attack on the Methodics at K x.389–90, 400–1).

[420] Stubbe, *Reduced*, 21.

[421] John Wilkins, *Mathematicall magick, or the wonders that may be performed by mechanicall geometry* (London, 1648), 6–7, 12, 196–7.

[422] Joseph Glanvill, *A further discovery of M. Stubbe* (London, 1671), 11.

[423] Glanvill, *Answer*, 94–5.

continued to insist that the discoveries that he now admitted had been made by the ancients had not been the result of their 'notional' philosophy. As an increasingly exasperated Stubbe complained, what this actually meant seemed ever less clear – either the ancients had made discoveries based on observation, or they had not.[424] It is not surprising that even Glanvill's acquintances dismissed his anti-Aristotelian works as childish.[425]

## 4.5     Historical justifications for the mathematisation of experimental natural philosophy

As far as it was developed, the historical justification of what after 1660 came to be called 'experimental philosophy' had – like the method itself – reached something of an impasse. Its identity rested on a separation from Greek philosophy – supposedly speculative, system building, dogmatic, hypothetical, and sophistic – but not only was this view historically indefensible, how much 'philosophy' that separation left at all was questionable. There were two solutions. One, as we have seen, was developed by learned physicians who were also adherents of the new philosophy: they grafted experimentalism onto the Rationalism of traditional medical method. A second was to make one's historical statements so vague as to be unchallengeable. This was the move adopted by Hooke in the famous dedication 'To the Royal Society' that the Society instructed him to append to his *Micrographia* (1665):

The Rules YOU have prescrib'd YOUR selves in YOUR Philosophical Progress do seem the best that have ever yet been practis'd. And particularly that of avoiding *Dogmatizing*, and the *espousal* of any *Hypothesis* not sufficiently grounded and confirm'd by *Experiments*. This way seems the most excellent, and may preserve both *Philosophy* and *Natural History* from its former *Corruptions*.[426]

But what precisely those 'former *Corruptions*' were remained unsaid. In his other methodological writings, Hooke offered a much simpler narrative than other Royal Society apologists: the ancients were lacking not quantitatively but only qualitatively, for they simply did not produce enough natural history before they began hypothesising, partly out of self-aggrandisement and the desire to please,

---

[424] See e.g. Glanvill, *Further discovery*, 13: 'They proceeded, no doubt, by *General Rules*, drawn from *Observations* in their *Art*, and therefore acted not as *pure Empericks*; But that the *Scientifical Theory* they were *directed by*, was any *Hypothesis* in *Philosophy*, you must prove; Till *then*, I shall be unconcern'd in your *goodly Demonstrations*'. For Stubbe's exasperated question as to what Glanvill actually *meant* by 'notional' philosophy, see e.g. Stubbe, *Reply*, 42.

[425] As early as 1661, John Worthington was (politely) expressing such opinions: *Worthington diary*, I, 299–301.

[426] Robert Hooke, *Micrographia, or, some physiological descriptions of minute bodies made by magnifying glasses* (London, 1665), sig. [A2]ᵛ. For the RS's instructions to Hooke, see Birch, *History*, I, 490–1.

partly because so many of them believed in innate ideas.[427] Glanvill and Sprat's attempts to utilise the tools of humanist anti-Aristotelianism to defend the Royal Society's methods were abandoned. The key fault lay not with the classical Greeks but with their slavish followers.[428] Hooke was far more comfortable with hypotheses than the rhetoric of the Society's apologists would have allowed him to be,[429] so it is unsurprising that he also abandoned the details of their historicisation in favour of his own, rather vague, vision.

One more ambitious attempt to adapt the anti-Aristotelian tradition to the defence of the Royal Society programme was developed in the late 1660s and early 1670s, in private, by the Greek scholar and serious historian of philosophy John North (see 1.4 above). From his notes, it is clear that North – who had enough interest in natural philosophy to talk to Barrow about mathematics, to complain that the standard university curriculum only encouraged the study of natural philosophy at an early stage (rather than as a mature discipline), and to make extensive judgements on Cartesian vortex theory[430] – was a strong supporter of the Royal Society. The correct method was to 'procee[d] in $y^e$ way of Experiment, to collect a natural history, as Verulam directed'.[431] This he justified via a virulently anti-Aristotelian history of philosophy, self-avowedly informed by the critiques of Agrippa, Ramus, Bacon, and Hobbes.[432] With much more skill than Glanvill or Sprat, North attempted to combine the critique of Aristotelian doctrine with a methodological message. Like Bacon, he believed that the 'old phisici' – of whom Democritus was the best – explored nature in the simplest way, '[e]xplaining things by Matter & motion' only.[433] Aristotle, holding to the sophist desire 'to dispute firmly on both sides', brought in logic, which had not previously been invented, and infused it into every discipline. This logic led not only to disputatiousness but also to the reification of forms and qualities: and so it 'it was his logick [that] spoyled all'.[434] This, then, was a more concise way of combining the doctrinal and the methodological critiques of Aristotelianism. But it still left unanswered the question of why Aristotle had produced more natural history than any other Greek philosopher. Even more importantly, it left hanging the most significant issue:

---

[427] Robert Hooke, 'A general scheme, or idea of the present state of natural philosophy, and how its defects may be remedied', in *Works*, 3–4.

[428] Ibid., 4–5.

[429] See his comments, from RS MS CP 20 50a, printed in Oldroyd, 'Some writings of Robert Hooke' (1987), 145–67, esp. 151–2, 158, and Oldroyd's comments at 160–1; also Hesse, 'Hooke's philosophical algebra' (1966); Feingold, '"Experimental philosophy": the history and meaning of a concept' (forthcoming) (I am very grateful to the author for sending me a draft version of this piece).

[430] North, *Life of North*, 260–1; BL MS Add. 32514, fols. 190$^{r-v}$, 202$^v$ (university pedagogy); 203$^v$–204$^v$ (vortex theory).

[431] BL MS Add. 32514, fol. 190$^v$.   [432] Ibid., fols. 191$^r$, 192$^v$–193$^v$.   [433] Ibid., fols. 200$^r$, 192$^v$.

[434] Ibid., fols. 192$^{r-v}$, 193$^r$–194$^v$, 199$^v$–200$^r$.

how was the neo-Baconian methodology of the Royal Society going to produce any body of philosophy at all? As North summarised:

Really considering y$^e$ ... Method of my Lord Verulam, tho y$^e$ most true, in whose stepps this [Royal] society treads, one can hardly Imagin an exact acc$^t$ should ever be given of natural philosophy because the history of nature, can never be experimented by one man in y$^e$ whole, and Improvement in philosophy hath ever bin advanced by single persons, to w$^{ch}$ the successors of each sect, have added little or nothing considerable. My Judgm$^t$ of the Greshamites is, that tho they never reach a body of <reall> philosophy, yet by Conversing so much with & varying Experiments, they may discover notable, and more advantageous things for y$^e$ use of Mankind. ffor if so brave inventions, as especially printing Gunpowder &c. have owned their original to chance, certainly much more Noble attainmen$^t$ cannot escape an Industrious search.[435]

The Royal Society was unlikely every to build a 'reall' philosophy, only to make improvements in the operative knowledge of nature. According to North, history had shown that philosophical progress was made by individuals, but Baconian method had closed the door to such progress.

This kind of history would not have had much success had it been published. At an institutional level, very different narratives were being used to justify the new philosophy. In his 1675 inaugural lecture as Sedleian Professor of Natural Philosophy, Thomas Millington (knighted 1680), who had been a member of the Oxford physiologists of the 1650s, where he had taken part in several important research programmes before becoming a leading physician, turned the anti-Aristotelian commonplaces on their head. Aristotle would indeed have been nothing had he not borrowed liberally from his predecessors, especially Democritus. But science depended on this kind of accumulation, and Aristotle was to be celebrated rather than condemned for his actions. It was his accumulative methods that had been revived by Bacon and then Galileo.[436]

The next generation of natural philosophers inherited the methodological problem identified by North, but were rather more reflexive about trying to pinpoint precisely what experimental philosophy actually was. Apart from the ideas of the physicians, there was another solution: the mathematisation of natural philosophy effected by Newton and by his Trinity colleague and predecessor in the Lucasian Chair of Mathematics, Isaac Barrow.[437] This topic is

---

[435] Ibid., fols. 202$^v$–203$^r$.

[436] CUL MS Add. 8861.2 [Thomas Millington, Inaugural lecture as Sedleian Professor of Natural Philosophy, 12 Apr 1675], fols. 3$^{r-v}$ (my foliation). As far as I can tell, this source was previously unknown to scholarship. Wood, from whom the dating comes, said the lecture was 'much commended' (*Life and times*, II, 343).

[437] For Barrow, see the essays in *Before Newton*, especially the essential biographical essay by Feingold. For Barrow's methodological influence on Newton, see Kargon, 'Newton, Barrow and the hypothetical physics' (1966); Malet, 'Isaac Barrow on the mathematization of nature' (1997); Dunlop, 'What geometry postulates' (2012); it is also discussed in most of the works in the note directly below.

both complex and well studied;[438] we may usefully quote the summary of Peter Dear:

Newton's version of 'experimental philosophy' postulated the actual production of particular phenomena so as to allow the formation of a universal science from singulars; the trick lay in that final stage and was accomplished, to the extent that it could be accomplished, by framing the issues in terms of physico-mathematics. The difficulties in attributing to contrived events a philosophical meaning that enabled them to have relevance to the establishment of universal knowledge-claims had left the Royal Society's enterprise at something of an impasse; Newton's work retrospectively validated the experimental program that Boyle had advocated and that the Royal Society had largely exemplified. It placed event experiments into the frame of the expanding mathematical sciences by providing them with a new meaning constructed from the methodological language that those sciences had already developed for themselves.[439]

Barrow's mathematical lectures of 1663–69 defended the relevance of mathematics to natural philosophy, and its status as a *scientia*, in terms that Newton would later echo and develop. The lectures would have been delivered to undergraduates who would have had little more than familiarity with Euclid's *Elements*, and thus discussed generally 'mathematics as a body of learning and as a mode of reasoning, fixing its place and role in the catalogue of the sciences'.[440] This generality made them perfect for wider methodological reflection. At the same time, Barrow – Regius Professor of Greek from 1660 to 1663 – was a very able scholar;[441] his comments often demonstrate an investment in antiquity that has nothing to do with preference for 'ancients' over 'moderns', but is similar to that we encountered in many of the scholars and natural philosophers of the 1650s in particular (2.4 above):

To preserve ancient authors, the inventors of the sciences, from destruction seems an important task for their modern followers, who would otherwise earn a reputation for ingratitude. True, their contents can in large part be derived more rapidly or constructed more concisely by modern techniques [i.e. in this case the post-Viète algebraic analysis]; yet reading them retains its value. First, it seems pleasant to examine the foundations from which the sciences have been raised to their present height. Second, it will be of some interest to sample the sources from which virtually all the discoveries of the moderns are derived; for it was by studying or imitating the clever and subtle methods of the ancients that the industry of the latter reached its eminence.[442]

---

[438] Key studies are Dear, *Discipline*, 210–44; Garrison, 'Newton and the relation of mathematics to natural philosophy' (1987); Shapiro, *Fits, passions, and paroxysms* (1993), 31–6; Shapiro, 'Newton's "experimental philosophy"' (2004); Guicciardini, *Certainty* (2009); Ducheyne, *Business* (2011).

[439] Dear, *Discipline*, 242.

[440] Mahoney, 'Barrow's mathematics: between ancients and moderns' (1990), 183.

[441] Grafton, 'Barrow as a scholar'.

[442] Ibid., 299, quoting and translating Isaac Barrow, 'Epistola lectori', in *Archimedis opera; Apollonii Pergaei conicorum libri IIII; Theodosii Sphaerica* (London, 1675), sig. A2[r]. For the composition of these editions in 1653, see Feingold, 'Barrow', 44–5.

We could not ask for a more precise summary of the assumptions about the usefulness of a historical grounding for natural philosophy than we have already found being expressed by many others, both scholars and natural philosophers.

As for Barrow's point about mathematics, it 'was part of a more general conception of knowledge in which the mathematical sciences tended to assume priority in the understanding of all branches of natural philosophy', and because of which 'what he called either "physico-mathematics" or "mixed mathematics" [w]as applicable to all areas of natural philosophy, insofar as all parts of physics implicated considerations of quantity'.[443] In defending the status of mathematics as a *scientia* (in Aristotelian terms), Barrow was taking part in a long debate that had its roots in the mid-sixteenth century: he was still attacking some of the same Aristotelians (such as Benedict Pereira) who had argued that because mathematics does not consider the essential qualities of objects, it cannot be a causal *scientia*, as had the earlier Jesuit defenders of mathematics like Christopher Clavius.[444] Barrow extended this point further, arguing simply that 'since magnitudes appear everywhere ... geometry will be required everywhere and the mathematical sciences will embrace almost the whole of natural philosophy'.[445]

This involved historical claims that were internal to mathematics, but also touched directly on claims made by reformist natural philosophers. Boyle, for example, had been sceptical about mathematics' usefulness to experimental philosophy.[446] For this conclusion, he was very likely indebted to the chymical tradition: van Helmont, among others, had virulently attacked mathematics as incompatible with his reformed–experimental method, leading him to make the rather peculiar claim that Aristotle and Galen had over-mathematised nature.[447]

---

[443] Dear, *Discipline*, 223.

[444] E.g. Isaac Barrow, *Lectiones mathematicae XXIII, in quibus principia matheseôs generalia exponuntur* (London, 1685), 89–90, 108–9 (throughout, I will also give references to the translation: *The usefulness of mathematical learning explained and demonstrated*, trans. J. Kirkby (London, 1734) [here 80, 97–8]; this translation is usually faithful, and I usually quote from it [as '*ML*'], sometimes with minor changes. However, it has the large defect of not including Barrow's Greek quotations from the original sources). For this debate, see the very clear account in Mancosu, *Philosophy of mathematics and mathematical practice in the seventeenth century* (1996), 10–33 (20–4 on Barrow); also Feldhay, 'The use and abuse of mathematical entities' (1998).

[445] Malet, 'Geometrical Optics'.

[446] Robert Boyle, *Certain physiological essays* (1661), in *Boyle works*, II, 74–5; also Boyle, *Hydrostatical paradoxes* (1666), in *Boyle works*, V, 194–5, 197. See (with some caution) Shapin, 'Boyle and mathematics' (1988). Interestingly, Boyle had held the opposite position before his turn to experimentalism: see e.g. 'Of desseins & undertakings' (late 1640s), in *Boyle works*, I, 129.

[447] See e.g. van Helmont, *Ortus medicinae*, 38b ('Et licet ante nata Euclidis elementa, Mathesis rudior esset? tamen Aristoteles in hac, quam in natura, longe peritior, naturam subter illius scientiae Regulas, subigere annisus est'); 7b (on Galen). See Debus, *Chemical philosophy*, 311–17; Debus, 'Mathematics and nature in the chemical texts of the Renaissance' (1968).

This historical point was also made more widely: Gassendi had attacked the claim that *any* discipline – including natural philosophy – could be classed as a *scientia*, praising Epicurus precisely for avoiding the hubristic search for certainty.[448] Unconvinced by the anti-mathematical and seemingly inconclusive probabilism of the major Royal Society *virtuosi* and figures like Gassendi, Barrow and Newton sought to develop a model of experimental philosophy which could deliver certainty through mathematisation.[449]

Barrow developed a counter-history in which mathematics was presented as a near-universal intellectual propaedeutic. He began with the definition of 'mathematics', pointing out its derivation from μάθημα, translating it as 'Disciplines' (*disciplinae*, i.e. 'study'/'teaching'). Rejecting the explanation of Proclus that this ambiguous term stemmed from the nature of the reasoning involved, Barrow suggested that there was a good reason for its use: 'when the *Grecians* first begun to apply themselves to the Study of Arts, these only [i.e. mathematics] were delivered in the Schools; the other Arts being not yet invented for the Instruction of their Youth'.[450] Grammar and rhetoric only came to flourish at the time of Plato and Aristotle; logic began with Zeno of Elea and 'scarcely was reduced by *Aristotle* to the Method of an Art' and was certainly unknown to Pythagoras.[451] Philosophy, while it of course existed, was a higher discipline reserved for the learned: indeed, mathematics was preparative to it. Pythagoras and Plato, as was well known, had insisted on this role for mathematics (Barrow could cite a ream of impressive and sometimes obscure commentators to confirm this).[452]

Apart from the level of detail, this argument was not particularly novel: even in England the few proponents of physico-mathematics among the early Royal Society had deployed similar themes from the history of philosophy- a good example can be found in Christopher Wren's 1657 inaugural oration as Gresham Professor of Astronomy.[453] But Barrow also pushed it forward in a

---

[448] Joy, *Gassendi*, 165–94.

[449] Guiccardini, *Certainty*, 19–30; *passim*; Feingold, 'Mathematicians and naturalists' (2001).

[450] Barrow, *Lectiones*, 5 (=*ML*, 4).

[451] Barrow, *Lectiones*, 5–6 (=*ML*, 5). For the late invention of rhetoric, Barrow cited Cicero's statement that it was invented by Corax and Tisias (fifth century BC) (*de Inventione*, II.6; *Brutus*, 46). For grammar, he argued that Plato's famous reference to its invention by Thoth in *Philebo* 18^b was a reference to the invention of writing, grammar being developed only in Aristotle's time. For Zeno as the inventor of logic, he was probably thinking of DL VIII.57, IX.25. For Pythagoras' ignorance of logic, he cited Aristotle, *Met.*, I.6: there is certainly no such claim made there.

[452] Barrow, *Lectiones*, 6–8 (=*ML*, 6).

[453] Christopher Wren, 'Oratio inauguralis, habita Londini in collegio Greshamensi', in John Ward, *The lives of the Professors of Gresham College* (London, 1740), App. XIII (new pagination), 29–37 at 31: 'Hanc methodum secuti veteres scientiarum inventores, mathematicas reliquis prius ediscendas praeposuere. Quis nescit scholae Platonicae programma, sive statutum potius, μηδεὶς ἀγεωμέτρητος εἰσίτω? Quis gradus, quos Pythagorei suscipiebant; qui primo

new direction. The ancients, starting from Pythagoras and Plato, divided mathematics into pure and mixed upon recognising that quantities (the subject matter of the discipline) could be considered either abstracted from matter 'or as they inhere in some particular Subject'.[454] As knowledge developed, more subjects were added to mixed mathematics, first by Aristotle (who added optics, mechanics, and geodesy) and culminating in the scheme of Geminus (first century BC), 'which yet most Mathematicians of a later Date do embrace'.[455] Barrow considered the growth of this division a key source of error. 'In reality every one of its [mathematics'] Objects are at the same time both intelligible and sensible in a different respect; intelligible as the Mind apprehends and contemplates their universal Ideas, and sensible as they agree with several particular Subjects occurring to the Sense'.[456] This was the case on Aristotle's own terms, for he had admitted that 'the mental *Abstraction* we spake of is not the only Property of *Mathematics*, but is common to all Sciences'.[457] The conclusion was clear: '*Mathematics*, as it is vulgarly taken and called, is adequate and co-extended with *Physics*'.[458] Even medicine 'itself will [thus] be a Part of Mathematics', as had been noted by both Aristotle and Hippocrates, who advised his son to study geometry.[459]

Not only was mathematics a *scientia*; it was the premier causal *scientia*.[460] Contrary to the claims of Pereira et al., Aristotle strongly believed in the certainty of mathematics. Here we have our first example of the weakness of Barrow's reading, for the *loci* Barrow produced for this undermined his

---

ἀκουσικοὶ, et, quinquenii silentio peracto, mathematici nominabantur, deinde physici, postremo politici? Quanto matheseως amore flagravit Plato? quanto Aristoteles? Neque enim scripsisset Aristotles mechanicam, opticam, musicam; itemque plurima de Pythagorae et Archytae philosophia, περὶ σοιχέιων; neque hypotheses planetarias, quas Eudoxus invenerat, cum Callippo correxisset; neque Alexandrum monuisset, ut, capta Babylone, Chaldaeorum, observationes coelestes annorum fere bis mille, coctilibus laterculis inscriptas, in Graeciam mitteret (haec scilicet optima orientis spolia a philosopho expetita sunt) neque bini demum Aristotelis discipuli, Eudemus et Theophrastus, geometria et astronomica scripsissent: nisi sanctum prorsus et inviolabile Platonicis omnibus fuisset, αγεωμετρητον in scholam non admittere'. This passage is not in the English version (n. 158 above). For Wren's dissimilarity from most of his early RS colleagues in this regard, see Shapiro, *Fits*, 31.

[454] Barrow, *Lectiones*, 11 (=*ML*, 10–11): Barrow extrapolates the division from Plato, *Philebus*, 56ᵈ–57ᵃ.

[455] Barrow, *Lectiones*, 15–22 (=*ML*, 14–20). The key source for Geminus is Proclus, *In Eucl.*, 38–9.

[456] Barrow, *Lectiones*, 21–2 (=*ML*, 19).

[457] Barrow, *Lectiones*, 13–14 (=*ML*, 13), quoting the explicit comparison of physics with mathematics at *Met.*, XI.1 1061ᵃ29–1061ᵇ5; and *Lectiones*, 22 (=*ML*, 19), quoting *Anal. Post.*, I.24, 86ᵃ13–15.

[458] Barrow, *Lectiones*, 30 (=*ML*, 26). On the precise meaning of this, see Dear, *Discipline*, 223, n. 41.

[459] Barrow, *Lectiones*, 25 (=*ML*, 21) (the sources are a very forced reading of *Anal. Post.*, I.13, 79ᵃ15–16) and the certainly spurious (and by then known to be so) Hippocratic *Letter to Thessalus*.

[460] For the repudiation of Aristotle's theory of causation that this involved, see Malet, 'Geometrical Optics'.

argument for mathematics' usefulness to natural philosophy, since in them Aristotle only argued for the *accuracy* of the subject, and even commented on its difference from physics in this respect.[461] Indeed, Barrow continued, the only ancient philosophers apart from the sceptics to doubt the capacity of mathematics for causal demonstration were the Epicureans: no wonder that Proclus remarked on Posidonius's attack on the Epicurean Zeno of Sidon.[462] Barrow concluded that 'some of the Moderns tread in the same Footsteps': I highly suspect this to be a reference to Gassendi.[463] Barrow had thus defined the high historical status of mathematics against both its scholastic critics and the *novatores*. This also meshed with his broader defence of Aristotle's natural philosophical method (4.4 above). 'By pursuing to its logical conclusion the assumption ... that all natural phenomena ... are caused by matter and its motions in space, Barrow was able to justify the mathematization of all nature'.[464] Moreover, he defended this as the method of the ancient mathematicians, revising Euclid's scheme of postulates to make it inextricable from physical reality: 'Barrow argues that the activity by which material things are brought into accord with mathematical description is enjoined by geometry's first principles, specifically its postulates'.[465] Postulates, in fact, are indistinguishable from hypotheses, 'And every Action, Motion or Mode of Being that falls under Observation, or may be apprehended by Experience, is the Subject of *Hypotheses*. Especially ... *Mathematical Hypotheses*, which we principally respect, is extended to all the affections of Magnitude obvious to any Sense'.[466]

The radical nature of this re-historicisation of mathematical method is revealed by Barrow's treatment of number theory. His belief in the pre-eminence of geometry as the science of magnitude led him to subsume even arithmetic to geometry.[467] In part, this was a way of sidelining the new algebra, which he reduced to the status of a useful tool like logic; this may have been another move in the argument against abstraction (Cartesian or otherwise) from the physical world.[468] But defending this position historically was difficult: all the ancient mathematicians had clearly differentiated arithmetic from geometry; most

---

[461] Barrow, *Lectiones*, 74–5 (=*ML*, 67), incorrectly citing *De caelo*, II.7 (the correct reference is III.7, 306ᵃ18–21) and the last chapter of *Met.*, I (i.e. what is now II, 995ᵃ15–16, which is of extremely dubious usefulness to Barrow's argument ('τὴν δ' ἀκριβολογίαν τὴν μαθηματικὴν οὐκ ἐν ἅπασιν ἀπαιτητέον, ἀλλ' ἐν τοῖς μὴ ἔχουσιν ὕλην')). See also Barrow, *Lectiones*, 108–10 (=*MW*, 97–9).

[462] Barrow, *Lectiones*, 75 (=*ML*, 67), drawing on Proclus, *In Eucl.*, 199–200, 214–18.

[463] That Gassendi may have been one of Barrow's targets has already been suggested in Mancosu, *Philosophy of mathematics*, 23–4, without identifying this precise passage.

[464] Shapiro, *Fits*, 33.

[465] See the discussion in Dunlop, 'What geometry postulates', 77–82 (quotation from 79).

[466] Barrow, *Lectiones*, 150 (=*ML*, 134). See also the illuminating analysis in Stewart, 'Mathematics as philosophy: Barrow and Proclus' (2000), esp. 162–78.

[467] Barrow, *Lectiones*, 33–56 (=*ML*, 29–49); Mahoney, 'Barrow's mathematics', 186.

[468] As suggested by Mahoney, 'Barrow's mathematics', 201.

importantly, both Aristotle and Euclid supported a strict division between number and magnitude, a division reflected in the separation of the geometric and arithmetic material in Euclid's *Elements*.[469] Barrow was aware of this problem and sought to alleviate it by manipulating some of the evidence. Instead of citing the mathematical tradition as it was commonly understood, Barrow quoted a very ambiguous fragment from the obscure Pythagorean Archytas, which stated that arithmetic was only the 'sister' to geometry. Yet had Barrow been honest, he would have admitted that the same source which contained this fragment – Nicomachus's *Introduction to arithmetic* – also stated that Archytas believed that 'arithmetic seems to be far superior to the other arts', geometry in particular.[470] Barrow was effectively twisting the truth on its head, and this kind of scholarship is impressive neither by modern nor by early modern standards: certainly, it was an idiosyncratic reading in the seventeenth century.[471]

These weaknesses were only exacerbated by Barrow's further claims. A brief passage in Plato's *Philebus* supposedly confirmed that he believed abstract numbers – traditionally the object of mathematics – to be different from real numbers that could not be independent of things counted;[472] this, Barrow speculated, was probably a true tradition derived from the Pythagoreans, because Aristotle also 'seems to intimate' it, 'when he says in a *Mathematical Number* no one Unit differs from another'.[473] Barrow did not offer a citation at this point, and with good reason, for the passage of the *Metaphysics* at which Aristotle says this in fact condemns the opinion.[474] Soon after he had to acknowledge that Aristotle had announced arithmetic to be more accurate than geometry. Aristotle's argument was based on the idea that arithmetic is simpler (a point, unlike a unit, has to have a location), and Barrow could now come back to his old criticism: the properties of numbers were rooted in objects;

---

[469] See Neal, *From discrete to continuous* (2002), 12–27 (the ancient sources), 121–2 (on Barrow, although it is not correct that 'he could . . . cite no examples of a classical source that agreed with his point of view', as we see now).

[470] Barrow, *Lectiones*, 33–4. The source is Nicomachus, *Intr. Arith.*, I.3.4 (=*Introduction to Arithmetic*, trans. M. L. D'Ooge (London, 1926), 184–5). Barrow cites fr. 1 ('ταῦτα γὰρ τὰ μαθήματα δοκοῦντι ἔμμεναι ἀδελφεά') but Archytas' real belief is given in fr. 4 (καὶ δοκεῖ ἁ λογιστικὰ ['logistics', i.e. arithmetic] ποτὶ τὰν σοφίαν τῶν μὲν ἀλλᾶν τεχνῶν καὶ πολὺ διαφέρειν, ἀτὰρ καὶ τᾶς γεωμετρικᾶς ἐναργεστέρω πραγματεύεσθαι ἃ θέλει'). The Archytas fragments were published by Henri Estienne in an edition of Aristotle and Theophrastus (1557), and they appeared in the many popular collections of Pythagorean fragments published in the sixteenth and seventeenth centuries (Hankins and Palmer, 51).

[471] For the recognition that the ancients had made arithmetic prior to geometry, using some of the standard sources, see e.g. John Wallis, *Mathesis universalis* [1657], in *Opera mathematica* (3 vols, London, 1693–99), I, 53.

[472] Barrow, *Lectiones*, 45–6 (=*ML*, 40–1), quoting Plato, *Philebus*, $14^c 11$–$14^d 1$; Mahoney, 'Barrow's mathematics', 186–7.

[473] Barrow, *Lectiones*, 46 (=*ML*, 41).

[474] Aristotle, *Met.*, XIII ($1080^a 22$). See the discussion in Cleary, *Aristotle and mathematics* (1995), 346–57.

in Aristotelian terms a point could not be compared to a number but only to an 'Arithmetical Nothing'.[475]

Barrow's mathematisation of nature thus involved a quite radical, and ultimately unconvincing, rewriting of the history of mathematics. Newton built on this to develop a historical identity for mathematics that tied it even closer to natural philosophy, as recently charted by Niccolò Guicciardini;[476] it is my thesis that he also developed some of his key historical assumptions and terminology in an attempt to avoid the scholarly traps that had snared his mentor. As is well known, in the *Principia* Newton eschewed any mechanical explanation for gravity, instead offering a 'mathematical' investigation of force, based on general propositions (Books I and II) and the application of those propositions to celestial motion (Book III). The very status of such an approach as 'philosophical' required some justification. In the first words of the preface to the *Principia*, Newton placed his mathematical natural philosophy within the ambit of a putatively ancient 'rational mechanics':

Since the ancients (according to Pappus) considered *mechanics* to be of the greatest importance in the investigation of nature and since the moderns—rejecting substantial forms and occult qualities—have undertaken to reduce the phenomena of nature to mathematical laws, it has seemed best in this treatise to concentrate on *mathematics* as it relates to natural philosophy. The ancients divided *mechanics* into two parts: the *rational*, which proceeds rigorously through demonstrations, and the *practical*. Practical mechanics is the subject that comprises all the manual arts, from which the subject of *mechanics* as a whole has adopted its name. But since those who practise an art do not generally work with a high degree of exactness, the whole subject of *mechanics* is distinguished from *geometry* by the attribution of exactness to *geometry* and of anything less than exactness to *mechanics*. Yet the errors do not come from the art but from those who practise the art. Anyone who works with less exactness is a more imperfect mechanic, and if anyone could work with the greatest exactness, he would be the most perfect mechanic of all. For the description of straight lines and circles, which is the foundation of *geometry*, appertains to *mechanics* . . . The ancients studied this part of mechanics in terms of the five powers that relate to the manual arts, and paid hardly any attention to gravity (since it is not a manual power) except in the moving of weights by these powers. But since we are concerned with natural philosophy rather then manual arts and are writing about natural rather than manual powers, we concentrate on aspects of gravity . . . and forces of this sort, whether attractive or impulsive. And therefore our present work sets forth mathematical principles of natural philosophy.[477]

---

[475] Barrow, *Lectiones*, 53–4 (=*ML*, 47–8), citing *Met.*, I.2, 982ª26 and *Anal. Post.*, I.27 (87ª35–7).

[476] Guicciardini, *Certainty*, 291–328. Also Domski, 'Newton as historically-minded philosopher' (2010). Except the qualification I make below, I must acknowledge my deep indebtedness to these studies, as well as to Garrison, 'Relation' and Dear, *Discipline*, 210–44.

[477] Isaac Newton, *The Principia. Mathematical principles of natural philosophy* [1687], eds. and trans., I. B. Cohen and A. Whitman (Berkeley, 1999), 381–2. I have slightly modified the translation of the first line, removing the unwarranted 'and science' after 'nature' ('Cum Veteres *Mechanicam* (uti Author est *Pappus*) in rerum Naturalium investigatione maximi fecerint . . . ').

We have here the same theme we found in Barrow: geometry is reunited with the study of physical reality, and those who divided them are chastised. Moreover, Newton has added the important language of 'analysis and synthesis' that he would use throughout his mathematical manuscripts of the 1690s – where he repeatedly assigned such analytic and synthetic methods to the ancients – and in the methodological sections of the Queries to the *Opticks*: as in mathematics so in natural philosophy investigation should proceed first by analysis, which consists of making experiments and observations, generating general conclusions by induction; subsequently, in synthesis (or composition), those general conclusions are taken as principles and new phenomena are derived and proved by them.[478]

This was both a further contribution to the Renaissance defence of mathematics as a study applicable to natural philosophy, and an anti-Cartesian salvo in the vein of Barrow.[479] But we also have a major development: that study is now labelled 'rational mechanics', and the ancients' failure to produce a *philosophiae naturalis principia mathematica* is explained by their application of that rational mechanics to other subjects, principally to the manual arts. The division between 'practical' and 'rational' mechanics was well known to the seventeenth century, but Newton developed it in a new, hyper-mathematical direction.[480] In the manuscripts for the treatise on geometry that Newton attempted to write in the 1690s, this emphasis on the philosophical status of mechanics in antiquity was re-emphasised: 'Pappus said that mechanics was held by philosophers to be worthy of the highest praise, and all mathematicians studied it seriously'.[481] Newton further developed these ideas in a draft preface to a new edition of the *Principia* written in the later 1710s, where he 'justified

---

The reference to Pappus is to *Collectio*, VIII (=*Pappi Alexandrini collectionis quae supersunt e libris manuscriptis edidit*, ed. and trans. F. Hultsch (3 vols, Berlin, 1876–78), III, 1022–3).

[478] Other key *loci* include *Principia*, 382, 943 (the latter is from the General Scholium); *The mathematical papers of Isaac Newton*, ed. D. T. Whiteside (8 vols, Cambridge, 1967–81), VII, 212–16 (a draft for a tract on 'Analysis Geometrica', *c.* 1691), 249–51 (a draft preface to 'Geometriae Libri tres', early 1690s); VIII, 442–59 (=*Principia*, 49–54) (drafts for a new preface to the *Principia*, 1710s); the famous passage in I. Newton, *The opticks* (Dover, 1952) [based on the 1730 edition], 404–5; the drafts for this *Opticks* passage in CUL Add. 3970, fols. 242ᵛ–243ʳ, 480ᵛ; that adduced in Pelseneer, 'Une opinion inédite de Newton sur l'analyse des anciens' (1930). The most important studies are Shapiro, 'Newton's "experimental philosophy"' and Guicciardini, *Certainty*, 309–327.

[479] Guicciardini, *Certainty*, 293–305; Domski, 'The constructible and the intelligible in Newton's philosophy of geometry', (2003), 1114–24.

[480] See Gabbey, 'Between *ars* and *philosophia naturalis*: reflections on the historiography of early modern mechanics' (1993); Gabbey, 'The *Principia*: a treatise on "mechanics"?' (1992).

[481] Newton, 'Draft preface to *Geometriae libri duo*', in *Mathematical papers*, VII, 340: 'Ait Pappus Mechanicam a Philosophis maxima laude dignam existimatam esse et omnes Mathematicos non mediocri studio in eam incubuisse'. See also the further examples in Guicciardini, *Certainty*, 300–2, especially the key anti-Cartesian use of the ancients in *Mathematical papers*, VII, 342: 'Et si authoritas novorum Geometrarum contra nos facit, tamen major est authoritas Veterum'.

the geometrical style of the *Principia*, stating that he wanted to adhere to the ancients' way of presenting their theorems by synthesis', and that 'the ancients, too, conceived geometrical objects as generated by motion, subsuming geometry under mechanics'.[482] Newton believed that the ancients had a form of analysis equivalent to algebra, a view common in seventeenth-century England and beyond.[483] But, like Barrow, he was sceptical about algebra's explanatory capacities: 'He made it clear that a problem is solved only though composition [i.e. 'synthesis' in the above quotation from the *Principia*], and that in composing its solution no space needs to be given to algebraic criteria', an idea he also attributed to the ancients.[484] Natural philosophy mapped on to this practice: 'As Mathematicians have two Methods for doing things w^ch they call Composition & Resolution & in all difficulties have recourse to their method of resolution <before they compound> so in explaning the Phaenomena of nature the like methods are to be used'. Resolution 'consists in trying experiments & considering all the Phaenomena of nature relating to the subject in hand ... until you come to the general properties of things'; 'composition' would 'explain the causes of Phaenomena as follow from' these principles.[485] The mathematical model supposedly practised by the ancients offered a way of preserving both the experimental and the causal status of natural philosophy.

Where did Newton get these historical ideas? Even the best recent treatments have suggested that they were a function of his idiosyncratic 'attempt to re-establish the lost wisdom of the ancients', and 'was certainly characteristic of the Cambridge Platonism tradition in which Newton was schooled'.[486] But as this whole book has aimed to suggest, one did not need to be a 'Cambridge Platonist' to be interested in ancient precursors for one's own philosophy. Interestingly enough, there is no evidence of a connection in Newton's eyes between those ancients who knew the natural philosophical truths of the *Principia* because they were conveyed through an originally divine tradition from Noah (3.7 above), and the Greek mathematicians who had a

---

[482] Guicciardini, *Certainty*, 303–4; the key passages are in *Mathematical papers*, viii, 452–5.

[483] See e.g. René Descartes, *Regulae ad directionem ingenii*, in *Oeuvres de Descartes*, eds., C. Adam and P. Tannery (12 vols, Paris, 1897–1910), x, 376–7; John Wallis to Gerard Langbaine et al., 20 Dec 1656, *The correspondence of John Wallis*, eds., P. Beeley and C. J. Scriba (3 vols, Oxford, 2003–12), i, 265; Fermat to Digby, Feb 1657, ibid., 275–6; John Wallis, *A treatise of algebra, both historical and practical. Shewing, the original, progress, and advancement thereof* (London, 1685), 1, 3–4. This belief was reinforced by Fermat's new edition of Diophantus (1670): see e.g. Collins to John Gregory, 25 March 1671, in *Correspondence of scientific men*, ed. Rigaud, ii, 218.

[484] Guicciardini, *Certainty*, 310.

[485] CUL Add Ms. 3970, fol. 480^v (*c.* 1704), first discussed in McGuire, 'Newton's "Principles of philosophy"' (1970), and treated in combination with much related material in Guicciardini, *Certainty*, 315–18; Shapiro, 'Newton's experimental philosophy'.

[486] Guicciardini, *Certainty*, 312–13; see also Guicciardini, *Reading the Principia* (1999), 31–2; Domski, 'Newton as historically-minded philosopher', 77.

correct vision of the methodological relationship between geometry and mechanics. Finally, as I have shown in detail elsewhere, it seems unlikely that Newton was applying the *regressus* of the Aristotelians to mathematics.[487] Instead, I hope to have offered here a rather simpler, and biographically more convincing, exaplantion: that the passages in the *Principia* and in the manuscripts on the history of mathematics were an attempt to formulate a pre-history for a mathematical natural philosophy that was more convincing than that offered by Barrow, whose scholarly contortions we have charted, and the deficiencies of which Newton is very likely to have recognised.

## 4.6    Conclusion

Outside observers who found other elements of Stubbe's polemic undesirable praised his treatment of Aristotle and the ancients.[488] The publication of *Plus ultra* saw Beale distancing himself from Glanvill,[489] and while Wallis attempted to placate Oldenburg about the possible damage from Stubbe's attacks,[490] real damage was done.[491] Glanvill was even forced to point out that his 'Letter concerning Aristotle' had nothing to do with the Royal Society.[492] Although some of the *novatores* stuck to a fully fledged anti-Aristotelianism and anti-Hellenism (mostly in private),[493] many resorted to

---

[487]  Levitin, 'Newton and scholastic philosophy'.

[488]  [Anon], *A Letter to Mr. Henry Stubs, concerning his censure* (London, 1670), 2–3.

[489]  Oldenburg to Boyle, 7 April 1668, in *Oldenburg correspondence*, IV, 307.

[490]  Wallis to Oldenburg, *Oldenburg correspondence*, 15 Apr 1669, V, 493–4. Oldenburg clearly remained worried (see Wallis to Oldenburg, 24 Apr 1669, ibid., 499–500: note that Wallis, while being placatory, advises Oldenburg that the Royal Society should drop the rhetoric of no experimental philosophy being done at the universities, again demonstrating the key institutional nature of the debate).

[491]  Hunter, 'Universities', Cook, *Decline*, 179–80; Frank, 'Medicine', 550–1.

[492]  Glanvill, *Answer*, 'Postscript', sig. O2$^v$ (new pagination). For Glanvill's later, much-tempered anti-Aristotelianism, see 'Continuation of the NEW ATLANTIS', 49–50 (new pagination).

[493]  See e.g. for Locke: Bod. MS Locke c. 28, fol. 117$^r$ (a passage projected as an addition to ch. III.10 of Locke's *Essay, c.* 1694–5 [?]): 'By this learned art ~~the rules of Logic too of the Schooles~~ h of abuseing words and shifting their significations the rules left us by the ancients for the conducting our thoughts ~~and~~ in the search or at least the examination of truth have been defecti~~d~~ve' (I take Locke to mean that it was the ancients' logic, rather than a later corruption of it, that offered a defective research method). The amateur Cartesian philosopher Roger North (1651–1734) similarly considered Aristotle's logic the sophistic corruption of a prior, non-logical natural philosophy: BL MS Add. 32546 (Notes by Roger North on natural philosophy), fols. 207$^v$–208$^r$: 'The ancientest of the Greek philosophers . . . setting aside Democritus & after him Epicurus, are not now taken notice of, were certainly in a better way of philosophising then their successors, who all at last fell in with Aristotle. Logick as not knowne in their time but was invented afterwards and by Aristotle turned in to an useless, I might say pernicious art of Wrangling. W$^{ch}$ did not subserve y$^m$ much of knowing, but of disputing. And was at best, but a means of defence, against the . . . Sophists'. On North, see Korsten, *Roger North* (1981), Chan and Kassler, *Roger North: materials for a chronology of his writings* (1989); *The life of the lord keeper North by Roger North*, ed. M. Chan (Lewiston [NY], 1995) and 5.3 below.

the old technique of praising Aristotle's natural historical works while castigating the theoretical ones as typical of Athenian speculativeness.[494] Some
went further: Nehemiah Grew, in his manuscript account of the history of
philosophy, dismissed the anti-Aristotelian commonplace that the Stagirite
burned the books of his predecessors;[495] Matthew Hale offered a full defence
of Aristotle as a natural historian.[496]

The failure of the Royal Society apologists was one of the factors that
precipitated the crisis of the Royal Society of the late 1660s and early 1670s.
There were of course many reasons for the backfiring of Sprat and Glanvill's
*apologiae*, but their defeat in the historical arena must certainly be classified as
one of them. Once again, this had nothing to do with 'ancients versus moderns' – it was a debate about the history of natural philosophical method. Like
the scholarly and scientific figures we met in Chapter 2, the figures under
discussion here shared the cultural assumption that foundational natural philosophical debates were best conducted historically, not out of reverence for the
ancients, but because unpacking the inheritance of antiquity was the most
profitable and most natural method for exploring the presuppositions of the
present.

Having established this, we must contrast the learned physicians' success in
presenting new methods as continuations of a long tradition with the Royal
Society apologists' failure to construct a convincing historical narrative. The
physicians drew on several centuries of humanist medical reflection on ancient
method, which offered them a more 'experimental' Hippocrates, Galen, and
even Aristotle, while maintaining their traditional opposition to Empiricism.
Sprat and Glanvill meanwhile, sought to defend an adapted Baconian history,
which portrayed classical Greek philosophy as speculative and rhetorical, with
a tool that was unsuited for the job: the humanist anti-Aristotelian tradition that
berated Aristotle's philosophical and theological errors, rather than focusing on
his method *per se*. It would of course be unduly hyperbolic to credit the writing
of the history of philosophy with a formative role in the fortunes of the Royal

---

[494] See e.g. William Simpson, *Philosophical dialogues concerning the principles of natural bodies*
(London, 1677), 13 (for Simpson's thoughts on the history of corpuscularianism, see 5.3).
Ralph Bohun, in his *Discourse concerning the origine and properties of wind* (Oxford,
1671), 1–2, 4–5 condemned Aristotle as a '*Philosophicall Monarch*' who wanted to reign by
'destroy[ing] all his Bretheren first', typical of the '*Athenian* Sages'. He expanded the criticism
in a letter of 1 August 1667 to John Evelyn (BL MS Add. 78314, fols. 16$^r$–20$^v$, at fols. 16$^v$–17$^r$),
but then condemned the 'vogue' for anti-Aristotelianism in the Royal Society, and explained
why he would continue to teach Aristotle to Evelyn's son, whom he was tutoring.

[495] Grew, 'History of Philosophy' (BL MS Sloane 1950, fols 13$^r$–34$^v$), at fol. 26$^v$: 'A meer forgery
y$^t$ he burnt y$^e$ antient Philosophers books, for any y$^t$ reads Cicero will find, they were most of y$^m$
extant in his time'.

[496] [M. Hale], *Observations touching the principles of natural motions* (London, 1677), sig. A4$^v$;
Cromartie, *Sir Matthew Hale* (1995), 196 (see further 5.4 below).

Society and of learned medicine, but it is still significant that the late 1660s and early 1670s saw a sharp decline in the activity of physicians in the Society.[497] The neoterics among the physicians had managed to justify their activities more successfully, partly by more convincingly presenting themselves as continuators of an ancient and learned tradition. It is significant that no attempt was made to offer a historical justification of experimentalism by the next generation of natural philosophers. Instead, Barrow and Newton developed a rather different pre-history for the natural philosophical revolution they were claiming to be participants in.

The sort of discussion conducted above can only be truly important if it allows a wider contribution to debates in the history of science, so I will finish by relating my findings to what seem to me to be the two most prominent and important recent discussions of English natural philosophical methodology. The first is that of Stephen Gaukroger, who makes much of the *novatores'* attacks on the 'moral failings' of the ancient philosophers. As we have seen, this was indeed an important theme. Professor Gaukroger seems to suggest that this critique stemmed from the Renaissance moral philosophical debate over the advantages of active or contemplative lives, as it was channelled by Bacon, a reading he derives primarily from texts like Sprat and Glanvill's *apologiae* (he does not include medicine in his discussion of the rise of 'experimental philosophy').[498] I make no claims about Bacon himself, but I have found little evidence to suggest that the debates about natural philosophical method in England from *c.* 1640 had much to do with Renaissance moral philosophy. They *did* have another connection to the Renaissance, but to the rather more predictable field of Renaissance natural philosophy and, especially, humanist physic, which had been trumpeting the value of practical experience for over a century and a half.

More quantitatively substantial is the evidence assembled by Peter Anstey for his claim that English philosophy in the second half of the seventeenth century was centred on the distinction between 'experimental' and 'speculative' philosophy. This distinction had, according to Professor Anstey, an important historical component, for those who classified themselves as experimentalists 'distance[d] themselves from the *old* speculative way of proceeding in physics'.[499] He has undoubtedly demonstrated the widespread use of the

---

[497] Hunter, *Royal Society*, 38 ('medical men ... seem to have been particularly prone to withdraw').

[498] Gaukroger, *Emergence*, esp. 196–207. Glanvill, as 'one of the most prominent apologists for the Royal Society', is said to depend 'pivota[lly]' on Bacon at 198. Medicine is discussed only in the context of 'The scope of mechanism' (346–52) – even Harvey is conspicuous only by his absence.

[499] Anstey, 'Speculative versus experimental', 221 (my emphasis), followed (222) by citation of the exact Glanvill passage (n. 387 above) that so annoyed Stubbe.

distinction. But what we have seen here is how difficult it was to maintain the key historical element of it in light of evidence to the contrary. If we go back to one of our medical case studies, Everard Maynwaring, we find him explicitly deploying the speculative–experimental vocabulary.[500] But we also find him claiming to be an inheritor of the ancient tradition of learned medicine. This belief he derived from sources that pre-dated not only the experimental–speculative distinction, but also Bacon. The justificatory rhetoric for the new philosophy – including its historical element – came from many sources: claiming that the experimental–speculative distinction was '*the* fundamental dichotomy in discussions of natural philosophical methodology during the period'[501] may be to simplify the complex relationship that the new philosophers had with the ancient philosophical tradition as they conceived it. If the method of experimental philosophy consisted of the claim that 'natural philosophy, i.e. theory, is only to be developed once the history, generated through observation and experiment, has been, or is nearing, completion',[502] then it is understandable why the university natural philosophers and physicians balked at the claims to novelty made by figures like Sprat and Glanvill. As early as 1476, Theodorus Gaza had insisted, in his edition of the *Corpus Aristotelicum*, that Aristotle had first composed his *History of animals*, and only then the *Parts of animals* and the *Generation of animals*, precisely because the two later books deal with causes, building on the historical knowledge of the thing itself delivered in the first.[503] The experimental philosophers of seventeenth-century England were certainly doing something new. But until quite late in the period, they were not always very good at explaining why, methodologically speaking, that was the case.

---

[500] Maynwaring, *Praxis medicorum*, 9–10 ('Solid knowledge in Natural Philosophy, is the most necessary qualification, preparatory to make a good *Physician:* now this *Philosophy* must be experimental, solid, and certain: the *notional Theorems* in *Philosophy*, the World hath too long insisted on, and spent much time to little purpose, in vain *ratiocinations, speculative conjectures*, and *verbal probations'*).

[501] Anstey, 'Speculative versus experimental', 216, emphasis in original.

[502] Anstey, 'Philosophy of experiment in early modern England' (2014), 111.

[503] Theodorus Gaza, 'In libros de animalibus praefatio', *Aristotelis Stagiritae operum, tomus secundus* (Leiden, 1549), sig. aa3$^r$: 'Historia primum obtinet locum, atque ut nomen ipsum significat, expositionem continet rei, quod est, sive ut sit … mox libri de partibus, ac de generatione, causam cur ita sit, declarant: alteri finale praecipuè, alteri agentem'. I was led to this source by the very interesting discussion in Deer, 'Academic theories of generation in the Renaissance' (1980), 133–4.

# 5 Histories of natural philosophy II. Histories of doctrine: matter theory and animating principles

We move now from natural philosophers' attitudes to ancient method to their attitudes to specific ancient doctrines. Our focus will be on their approaches to two subjects that were undoubtedly at the heart of the monumental developments that took place in seventeenth-century natural philosophy: matter theory and theories of causation. These were the greatest areas of contestation, in part because the abandonment of hylomorphism had led to great uncertainty about any of the fundamentals of the structure of matter and the cause for its motion, especially the seemingly teleological quality of natural life. The field is also rendered more complicated by major recent historiographical revisions. Several generations of historians of science assumed that the new, corpuscularian matter theory was virtually interchangeable with mechanism – all change in nature being explained by the meetings of inert matter characterised by shape, size, and motion only – which had been imported from physics into all other natural philosophical disciplines.[1] Recent work, however, has demonstrated both the ubiquity of 'non-mechanical' microparticulate structures in various early modern natural philosophies[2] and the variety of philosophical approaches that could lead to them, especially chymical.[3] And yet despite this revisionism, there has been little debate as to whether the ancient tags which were so easily applied to seventeenth-century English natural philosophers might now need reconsideration. The most recent major study, for example, has concluded that Boyle can be classed as an 'Epicurean', and more broadly that 'Epicureanism' –

---

[1] Classic statements include Hall, 'The establishment of the mechanical philosophy' (1952); Hall, *Robert Boyle and seventeenth century chemistry* (1958); Westfall, *The construction of modern science* (1971); Hall, *The revolution in science* (1983).

[2] A seminal revisionist piece is Henry, 'Occult qualities and the experimental philosophy' (1986). For an earlier period, see Clucas, 'The atomism of the Cavendish circle: a reappraisal' (1994).

[3] See especially the works of William Newman and Antonio Clericuzio, cited below. For broader revisionism about the identity of alchemy, see Newman and Principe, 'Alchemy vs. chemistry' (1998).

as it grew in England in particular – lay at 'the origins of modernity'.[4] This, of course, follows a long and distinguished historiographical tradition.[5]

Conversely, it will be shown here that both English scholars and English natural philosophers for the most part rejected Epicurus as a model of natural philosophical endeavour and doctrine. The vision of Epicureanism as an observational, probabilistic and non-speculative philosophy presented by Pierre Gassendi was repudiated both by scholar-divines and, more importantly, by natural philosophers themselves, who mostly saw Epicurus and his atomism as reductionist, speculative, and dogmatic. In addition, the reification of 'English Epicureanism' has rested partly on vague associations between literary works (especially translations of Lucretius) and natural philosophical texts, associations often made by literary scholars who do not engage fully with the specific conclusions of practising natural philosophers, and which are thus often unwarranted by the extant evidence.

Early modern historicisations of causation theory and active principles have received less attention than the history of microparticulate matter theory, the assumption being that the narrative is clear: the 'scientific revolution' saw a shift from a teleological to a mechanistic model. Where Aristotelians ascribed rational agency to nature, the moderns removed all such agency, withholding it solely for God (if that); concomitantly, they pointed to the unnecessary teleologies in ancient philosophy. On the purely philosophical level, this picture has again been complicated by recent scholarship, especially that which emphasises the perseverance of quasi-teleological principles (such as *semina*) in the thought of many of the neoterics.[6] By examining the new philosophers' historical assumptions (and their sources), we shall find that the revisionist story needs to be taken further. The very idea that a teleological or animistic 'ancient' natural philosophy had been replaced by a 'new' philosophy that preserved the distance between God and nature was the creation of the *novatores* themselves, drawing heavily on the humanist genre of the history of idolatry.

## 5.1     Histories of matter theory

It would be impossible to chart in full here the varieties of matter theory available to an educated and well-supplied reader in mid-century

---

[4] Wilson, *Epicureanism at the origins of modernity* (2008), esp. 224–51.

[5] Mayo, *Epicurus in England* (1934), 142 ('the apologists for the New Science of the Royal Society . . . availed themselves of his [Epicurus's] useful atomic theory even as they rejected with such virtuous heat the theological and ethical conclusions which he had drawn from it'); Kargon, *Atomism in England from Hariot to Newton* (1966), 77–117.

[6] Henry, 'Occult qualities'; the key work on *semina* is now Hirai, *Le concept de semence*; further works on *semina* theories in England are cited below.

England.[7] Suffice to say, Aristotelian matter theory, as it was variously presented in pedagogical texts, depended on the analysis of substance into matter and form (thus the anachronistic term 'hylomorphism').[8] Aristotle had criticised Democritean atomism for positing mathematically impossible indivisibles; he was both the main ancient critic of atomism, and one of the key sources for its historical development.[9] Instead of microparticulate structure, Aristotelian substances possess substantial forms which have the capacity to turn different materials into a single homogeneous substance.

By the 1640s our hypothetical reader would have had a large array of alternatives to hylomorphism, most of which could be grouped under the vague label 'particulate'. But the variety of these positions – very often attached to ancient names – requires emphasis: not only the indivisible and variously shaped atoms of Epicurus and Democritus but also, to name but a few, Aristotelian *minima naturalia* (promoted in the much-read work of Julius Caesar Scaliger, among many others),[10] themselves presented as Democritean by the hugely influential Wittenberg professor of medicine and chymist Daniel Sennert (yet without a full commitment to indivisibility),[11] the 'two-element' atomism of David Gorlaeus,[12] and the theologically charged atomism of Sébastien Basson.[13] This is not to mention Bacon's ambiguous statements about atomism and its history.[14]

---

[7] The landmark overview studies in the history of early modern atomism are Lasswitz, *Geschichte der Atomistik* (1890); van Melsen, *From atomos to atom* (1960 [1949]); Gregory, 'Studi sull'atomismo del Seicento' (1964–67); Kargon, *Atomism*; Clericuzio, *Elements, principles and corpuscles* (2000); Lüthy et al., eds., *Late medieval and early modern corpuscular matter theories* (2001); Newman, *Atoms and alchemy*. The best historiographical introduction is Lüthy, Murdoch and Newman, 'Introduction' (2001); see also Lüthy, 'Atoms and corpuscles. Kurd Lasswitz and the historiography of atomism' (2003). Pyle, *Atomism and its critics* (1995) is an overview from a philosophical perspective. From herein, I use 'atomist' to signify specifically those matter theories positing indivisibility of minimal parts, 'corpuscularianism' for the deliberately ambiguous system devised primarily by Boyle, and 'microparticular matter theories' as a catch-all.

[8] For extensive treatments: Lüthy and Newman, '"Matter" and "form": by way of a preface' (1997), and the subsequent papers in that special volume of *ESM*; Pasnau, 'Form, substance, and mechanism' (2004); and the essays in Manning, ed., *Matter and form in early modern science and philosophy* (2012), esp. Manning, 'Three biased reminders about hylomorphism'.

[9] Hasper, 'Aristotle's diagnosis of atomism' (2006); Murdoch, 'Aristotle on Democritus's argument against infinite divisibility' (1999).

[10] Lüthy, 'An Aristotelian watchdog as avant-garde physicist' (2001).

[11] Michael, 'Daniel Sennert on matter and form' (1997); Michael, 'Sennert's sea change'; further studies are cited below.

[12] Lüthy, 'Gorlaeus' Atomism'; Lüthy, *Gorlaeus*.

[13] Nielsen, 'A seventeenth-century physician on God and atoms' (1988); Ariew, *Late scholastics*, 133–6; and above all Lüthy, 'Basson'.

[14] The best introduction is Manzo, 'Francis Bacon and atomism' (2001), especially the historiographical exposition at 209–10.

Yet it was not only the variety of 'atomisms', but also the lack of evidence for microparticulate structure, that complicates our attempts to explain the shift from hylomorphism:

It is not yet entirely clear by what exact mechanism the corpuscular theory, despite the obvious lack of experimental support, was able to win so many adherents among those who considered themselves empirical scientists after only a few decades of vigorous pros and cons.... The acceptance of corpuscularianism cannot be reduced to a single cause, and least of all to the experimental progress of science alone. The arguments and rhetorical stratagems in defense of atomism operated ... on many different levels simultaneously. They came from epistemological, mathematical, and empirical points of view, not to mention the theological and metaphysical ones.[15]

To the list offered at the end of this quotation we must add the historical arguments. We shall see that while a few English natural philosophers did follow Pierre Gassendi into a highly positive characterisation of ancient atomism, and specifically of the philosophy of Epicurus, many more responded to him by characterising it – alongside the other philosophies of antiquity – as overly speculative and reductionist. The situation is further complicated by the religious and scholarly response to the new histories of atomism (especially that of Gassendi); this response is charted in section 5.2.

### 5.1.1     Gassendi's Epicurus

This is not the place for the much-needed full examination of Gassendi's influence on English natural philosophy (which was vast). I confine myself to the far more limited task of examining to what extent Gassendi's reinterpretation of Epicurus and Epicureanism was accepted by English natural philosophers and scholars. Gassendi's 'baptising' of Epicurean philosophy has been well documented: he denied the Epicurean doctrines of the eternity of the world, the infinitude of atoms, the mortality of the soul, and the existence of the atomic *clinamen* (swerve), which had been necessary to account for the impact of atoms with an inherent downwards gravitational motion.[16] Less studied, but more important, was Gassendi's elaborate scholarly reconstruction of the historical Epicurus, the culmination of several centuries of revisionism of (mostly patristic and Ciceronian) anti-Epicurean commonplaces after the rediscovery of Lucretius and of Diogenes Laërtius,

---

[15] Meinel, 'Early seventeenth-century atomism' (1988), 103.

[16] Osler, 'Baptizing Epicurean atomism' (1985); Osler, 'Gassendi's Epicurean project' (1993); Joy, *Gassendi*, 66–82, 130–94, *passim*; Palmerino, 'Pierre Gassendi's *De Philosophia Epicuri Universi* rediscovered' (1998); Blundell, *Pierre Gassendi* (1987), 48–82; Johnson, 'Was Gassendi an Epicurean?' (2003); Lolordo, *Pierre Gassendi and the birth of early modern philosophy* (2007), esp. 20–4.

Book X of whose *Lives* is devoted exclusively to the philosopher of the garden.[17]

Gassendi's strategy, spread between his *De vita, moribus, et doctrina Epicuri* (1647), his vast commentary on Book X of Laërtius (1649), and his *Syntagma philosophicum* (in the *Opera* (1658)), can be characterised as two-fold: first, a rehabilitation of Epicurus's moral philosophy, which he claimed had been unfairly characterised as hedonistic; second, a complete reconstruction of Epicurus' natural philosophy to render it probabilistic, non-dogmatic, based on sense-perception, and compatible with recent experimental findings (i.e. diametrically opposite to the image of Aristotelianism offered in the *Exercitationes*). Rescuing Epicurus from the charge of hedonism was easy, for it simply involved repeating the assertion in several classical sources, most notably Laërtius, that Epicurus's emphasis on pleasure as the end of life was an emphasis on measured friendship and contemplation, in contrast to the true hedonism of the Cyrenaics, especially Aristippus.[18] Gassendi, again following Laërtius, claimed that the negative conflation of Epicureanism and Cyrenaicism was nothing more than Stoic propaganda: there was nothing particularly novel about this, for it was a common conclusion from the mid-fifteenth century – it became a commonplace in England, repeated both by those inspired by Gassendi and by others writing independently.[19]

---

[17] Although Joy, *Gassendi*, is an excellent exception. Influential anti-Epicurean patristic *loci* are collected in Jungkuntz, 'Fathers, heretics and Epicureans' (1966); Cicero's many anti-Epicurean statements are summarised in Roskam, *A commentary on Plutarch's* De latenter vivendo (2007), 49–69.

[18] Aristippus's hedonism was famous enough in seventeenth-century England for him to be the subject of a satire by Thomas Randolph, where the philosopher is dismissed in favour of the sweet wine colloquially known by his name: *Aristippus, or, the joviall philosopher presented in a private shew* (London, 1630).

[19] See the huge discussion in Pierre Gassendi, *Animadversiones in decimum librum Diogenis Laertii* (3 vols, Lyon, 1649), III, 1181–1768. For a contemporary English version, see Gassendi, *Three discourses of happiness, virtue, and liberty collected from the works of the learn'd Gassendi, by Monsieur Bernier* (London, 1699), esp. 46, 51, 63 (this work is a translation of François Bernier's abridgement of the 'Ethics', which comprised the last part of the *Syntagma*). For direct appropriations of this idea from Gassendi, see Stanley, *History*, 633; John Evelyn, *An essay on the first book of T. Lucretius Carus De rerum natura* (London, 1656), sig. [A8]ʳ. See also Samuel Gott, *An essay of the true happiness of man in two books* (London, 1650), 112; William Brent, *A Discourse upon the nature of eternitie* (London, 1655), 26. For those that *did* conflate the 'hedonism' of Epicurus and Aristippus, see e.g. Richard Younge, *The drunkard's character* (London, 1638), 18, 628; John Milton, *The reason of church-government urg'd against prelaty* (London, 1641), 62–3; Henry Hammond, *Of superstition* (Oxford, 1645), 6; Nathaniel Ingelo, *Bentivolio and Urania in four bookes* (London, 1660), sig. Cʳ, 110. D. C. Allen long ago dismissed the notion that the moral rehabilitation of Epicurus was a seventeenth-century phenomenon: 'The rehabilitation of Epicurus' (1941); see also Jones, *The Epicurean tradition* (1989), 148–9; Joy, 'Epicureanism in Renaisance moral and natural philosophy' (1992). Gassendi's unwarranted later reputation as a libertine is charted in Osler, 'When did Gassendi become a libertine?' (2005).

In the case of Epicurus's natural philosophy, Gassendi's strategy was far more novel, ingenious, and philologically daring. He brilliantly extrapolated already available pro-Epicurean *loci* to construct a rich contextual image of Hellenic philosophy which explained Epicurus's own doctrines as a reaction to the confused physics of the Stoics, Sceptics (both Academic and Pyrrhonist), and Peripatetics.[20] Most importantly, the historical atomism of Epicurus emerged as a philosophy grounded in sense perception and free from geometrical or logical intrusions, in contrast to all of its competitors. Gassendi achieved this by commenting in great detail on two supposed historical 'misinterpretations' of Epicurus. The first, stemming from Aristotle, was that he was a mathematical point atomist. There was a long tradition of defending Epicurus against this argument,[21] regularly adopted by early modern atomists before Gassendi.[22] But Gassendi expanded this defence by subsuming it into an historical image of Hellenic philosophy as divided into competing mathematical and physical models of nature, contextualising Epicurus in the debate over indivisibility between the Middle Academy and the Stoa related by Plutarch and aiding himself by suggesting some emendations (from manuscript) to the relevant discussion at DL x.57.5–57.10. Gassendi emphasised that 'mathematical and physical notions of infinite divisibility had been conflated with one another in ancient Greek debates', and that this 'conflation explained why Epicurus' concept of atoms had frequently been misconstrued'.[23]

A second step was a reconstruction of Epicurus's lost epistemological–logical work, the *Canon*, summarised at DL x.31–4. Comparing Epicurus's use of the term 'σημεῖον' ('sign') with other Greek systems of logic, Gassendi argued that Epicurus had held a probabilist view of knowledge formation.[24] This again allowed Gassendi to claim that he had defeated anti-atomic scepticism, which, he argued, misrepresented Epicurus's epistemology as offering the necessary truths of geometry, rather than the probable truths of physics.[25] This meshed perfectly with the anti-Aristotelian accusation, much propagated by Gassendi among others, that the Stagirite and his followers had misled themselves in their hubristic search for demonstrative *scientia*.[26]

---

[20] See the brilliant account in Joy, *Gassendi*, 83–194.

[21] See esp. *Gen. et corr.*, 315$^b$26. For details, see the extremely full discussion in Murdoch, 'Aristotle on Democritus's argument'.

[22] See 5.3 below on Sennert.    [23] Joy, *Gassendi*, 156; and more generally, 152–62.

[24] Ibid., 171. See further Blundell, *Gassendi*, 84–103, which, unlike most Gassendi scholarship, draws on the manuscript evidence.

[25] Joy, *Gassendi*, 167–73, esp. 172.

[26] Interesting in this regard is Gassendi's attitude to medicine, discussed in French, *Harvey*, 328–33.

## 5.1.2    Gassendi's Epicurus in England

While the influence in England of Gassendi's philosophical system *in toto* was very great indeed,[27] his attempt to provide an image of an experimental atomist Epicurus was unsuccessful. It found an early vernacular articulation in Stanley's section on Epicurus in volume III (1660) of his *History of philosophy*, which was in fact a direct translation of parts of Gassendi's *De vita et moribus Epicuri* (1647) and of the whole *Philosophiae Epicuri syntagma* (1649). Well-known translations of Lucretius appeared from John Evelyn (1656), Lucy Hutchinson (begun by 1658 at the latest), and Thomas Creech (1682).[28] There has been a consistent tendency to equate such 'literary' or 'cultural' Epicureanism with the natural philosophical revival of atomism and even with the scientific revolution more generally.[29] This connection is rather forced, depending on the reification of a vague 'Epicurean culture'. Of course, Evelyn and Hutchinson had natural philosophical interests. But accounts of Epicurus's philosophy had been available to natural philosophers for several centuries. Lucretius, meanwhile, had long been considered a premier Latin poet worth translating for literary reasons alone. It was not translating Lucretius but engaging in detail with Gassendi's vision of Epicureanism that was a sign of a serious natural philosophical interest in ancient matter theory.[30] Remarkably, only one positive engagement of this type appeared from an English pen: that of the royalist physician Walter Charleton.[31]

---

[27] As well as the works cited throughout, see Levitin, 'Parker'. For the circulation more generally, see Kirsop, 'Prolégomènes à une étude de la publication et de la diffusion des *Opera omnia* de Gassendi' (2000).

[28] Evelyn, *Essay*. See Hunter, *Shape of orthodoxy*, 66–98, 'John Evelyn in the 1650s: a virtuoso in quest of a role', esp. 87–92; Repetzki, 'Preface' (2000); Thomas Creech, ed. and trans., *T. Lucertius Carus the Epicurean philosopher, his six books De natura rerum done into English verse, with notes* (Oxford, 1682), on which, see Real, *Untersuchungen zur Lukrez-Übersetzung von Thomas Creech* (1970). For Hutchinson, see now Barbour and Norbrook, 'Introduction' (2012), xxiii for the dating. See also Barbour, 'Anonymous Lucretius' (2010). For the broader context, see also Gillespie, 'Lucretius in the English Renaissance' (2007).

[29] Mayo, *Epicurus*, 54, *passim*; Kargon, *Atomism*, 80–92, claiming vast influence for Charleton (89) without providing any evidence; Wilson, *Epicureanism*, 230–46 (offering a psychoanalysis-based 'Epicurean' Boyle); Kroll, *The material word* (1991); Barbour, *English Epicures and Stoics* (1998); Barbour and Norbrook, 'Introduction', xxviii–xxxiii; all at least partially following in the footsteps of Harrison, 'The ancient atomists and English literature of the seventeenth century' (1934).

[30] Wolff, 'L'utilisation du texte du Lucrèce par Gassendi dans le *Philosophiae Epicuri Syntagma*' (1999) brings out well the non-literary use of Lucretius by Gassendi. As we saw in Chapter 2, Gassendi's work did also stimulate a wider cultural interest in the history of philosophy that meshed with the interests of the new philosophers. But the difference between the works of Stanley and Sherburne and more literary enterprises is still significant.

[31] Charleton had been made DM 1643, came under the influence both of Harvey and of Helmontian iatrochmistry (the latter perhaps under the aegis of Sir Theodore Turquet de Mayerne, the senior royal physician to whom he occasionally worked as an assistant), began medical practice in London in the late 1640s, published two Helmontian translations and a

Charleton's three key 'Epicurean' texts were all in English: *The darkness of atheism* (1652), the *Physiologia Epicuro-Gassendo-Charltoniana* (1654), and *Epicurus's morals* (1656). His interest in Epicurus seems to have been stimulated by the Cartesian, Hobbesian, and Gassendist philosophies with which he had recently become familiar.[32] The first of these was not really a work of natural philosophy, but of natural-theological apologetics self-avowedly in the vein of Mornay or Grotius, stimulated, as Charleton himself admitted, by the religious upheavals of the civil wars (it is not impossible that Charleton was attempting to distance himself from the sectaries, in response to criticism that had apparently fallen upon his earlier Helmontian works).[33] In its treatment of the history of philosophy, its primary aim is a version of the argument for theism from near-universal consent.[34] It should be noted here that although he did often simply plagiarise Gassendi, Charleton was also, throughout his life, a serious humanistic reader of the ancient sources himself,[35] as well as such major scholarly works as Marsham's *Chronicus canon.*[36]

In *Darkness*, there was an ambiguity in Charleton's treatment of Epicurus. He was chastised for his belief in creation by the chance collision of internally motive atoms and his subsequent denial of providence.[37] The historical explanation for this is unambiguous: Epicurus 'and the rest of that miscreant crew' were seeking to promote atheism.[38] On the other hand, Charleton praised Epicurus for developing an explanatory system (atomism) which accounted for the evidence of the senses with 'more of probability' than the principles of

---

Helmontian treatise in 1650, and probably became acquainted with the philosophers around the Mersenne circle during an early 1650s trip to Paris. He became one of the earliest FRS, elected 15 May 1661. See most fully, Sharp, 'Walter Charleton's early life' (1973); Fleitmann, *Walter Charleton: Leben und Werk* (1986); Booth, *The medical world of Walter Charleton* (2005); Hunter, *Royal Society*, 148–9.

[32]    Charleton, *Darkness*, sigs. b3$^{v-r}$; Sharp, 'Charleton', 323–4.

[33]    Charleton, *Darkness*, sig. a$^{r-v}$. In 1674, Charleton sent a portrait of Grotius to the Bodleian as a present (letter to Thomas Hyde, 14 May 1674, Bod. MS Smith 13, p. 63).

[34]    Charleton, *Darkness*, 47–9; 103–4; 350–2.

[35]    See the notes from classical authors in the commonplace book, BL MS Sloane 3413, fols. 2$^{r}$–8$^{r}$. See also Walter Charleton, *Chorea gigantum, or … Stone-Heng, standing on Salisbury Plain, restored to the Danes* (London, 1663) (for the reputation of this work, which argued (primarily on the authority of Ole Worm) that Stonehenge was Danish, see Booth, *Charleton*, 19, n. 92; and Golden, 'Dryden's praise of Dr Charleton' (1966)), and the appendix in Walter Charleton, *The harmony of natural and positive divine laws* (London, 1682), 'A short history of the Jews Talmud', 209–19, for which the draft is Bod. MS Smith 13, no. 20. See also Fleitmann, *Charleton*, 325.

[36]    See his notes in Bod. MS Smith 13, no. 31.    [37]    Charleton, *Darkness*, 40–3.

[38]    Ibid., 96–7. Charleton then quotes Epicurus's own words – in Gassendi's paraphrase – as proof ('ut mens ex perspectis causis conquiescat, neque aliam eamque divinam subesse causam suspicando, felicitatem interturbet'). Gassendi had attempted to diffuse the atheistic implications of this statement: *Animadversiones*, 727–8. Charleton believed at this point that Epicurus was only the last in a canon of deliberate atheists stretching from Leucippus, Democritus, Dicaearchus, Strato, Ennius, Lucretius, Velleius, and Lucian, for all of whom he offers citations (95–6).

Aristotle, Plato, or the Stoics; all that was required was the additional recognition 'that God created that first *Matter* out of *Nothing*' and then providentially guided it.[39]

This final theme was elaborated in the *Physiologia*, a combination of direct translations out of Gassendi[40] and experimental evidence of Charleton's own.[41] By this point Charleton had abandoned his earlier fears that Epicurus's intentions were atheistic – indeed, his translations of Lucretius render Epicureanism far more compatible with Christian monotheism than those of the same passages in Evelyn's version of the poem.[42] Epicurus's *Canon* is presented as having laid down the basis of a philosophy of sense experience and probabilism, from which the tenets of atomism could be inferred.[43] This is supplemented by the commonplace praise of the eclectic sect as practitioners of non-dogmatic philosophy, an example we have met already in Boyle (4.3), although unlike him Charleton probably drew on the much fuller discussion in G. J. Vossius's *De philosophia et philosophorum sectis* (1657–58).[44]

Finally, *Epicurus's morals* consists, as one would expect, of a full presentation of the revisionist version of Epicurean ethics, whose aim is said to be moderate pleasure and tranquillity; Epicurus was certainly not the 'Patron of Impiety, Gluttony, Drunkennesse, Luxury and all kinds of Intemperance, as the common people (being mis-informed by such learned men as either did not rightly understand, or would not rightly represent his opinions) generally conceive him to be'.[45] The historical themes are almost entirely confined to the 'Apologie for Epicurus . . . Written in a Letter, to a Person of Honour'.[46] As well as denying outright Epicurus's atheism, Charleton sought to alleviate 'three Capitall Crimes whereof he is accused': his espousal of the mortality of the soul; his belief that 'Man is not obliged to . . . worship God . . . out of any hope of any Good or feare of any evill . . . but merely in respect of the transcendent Excellencies of his Nature'; and his defence of suicide.[47] Clearly under the influence of Gassendi, Charleton's defence was deeply

---

[39] Charleton, *Darkness*, 44. Charleton acknowledged his debt to Gassendi's *Animadversiones* at sig. B5[r], and also adopted Gassendi's important re-contextualisation of Epicurus on fate and causation (291–320), discussed at 5.4 below.

[40] For a tabulation of Charleton's borrowings from Gassendi, see Fleitmann, *Charleton*, 416–17.

[41] Clericuzio, *Elements*, 96–7.

[42] See the tabulation at Fleitmann, *Charleton*, 412–15, especially the comparisons of the translations of *Rer. nat.*, I.47–9 and v.168–73.

[43] Walter Charleton, *Physiologia Epicuro-Gassendo-Charltoniana* (London, 1654), esp. 19–20.

[44] Charleton, *Physiologia*, 1–8. Lewis, 'Walter Charleton and early modern eclecticism' (2001) attempts to explain Charleton's whole intellectual development through his adherence to a reified 'eclecticism', failing to realise that this was a scholarly commonplace.

[45] Walter Charleton, *Epicurus's morals* (London, 1656), sigs. A3[v]–[A4][r].

[46] This is likely to have been Thomas Belassis, Viscount Fauconberg; a presentation copy survives with a 'Letter Dedicatory' to him (Bod. Shelfmark: 4°Rawl. 49); Sharp, 'Early life', 332–3.

[47] Charleton, *Epicurus's morals*, sigs. a[r–v].

historical–contextual. Epicurus was certainly a mortalist, but those Greek philosophers who did defend the immortality of the soul were no better in that they believed, unlike Christians, in its later return to a universal *anima mundi*.[48] The refusal to worship a providential God was simply an overreaction to the 'sottish Idolatry' of his Greek contemporaries, and Epicurus needed to be understood as a brave opponent of pagan idolatry and 'polytheisme' before the light of revelation had made the need for that task clear.[49] Similarly, suicide was not 'repugnant to the Law of *Nature*', but only to divine law; that the Stoics had promoted it far more widely was surely incontrovertible evidence of this.[50]

Charleton is often portrayed as part of a general English Epicurean movement of the 1650s,[51] but his acceptance of Gassendi's observational Epicurus was unique and needs to be separated from his more general rehabilitation of Epicurus's ethics and religiosity. Even his friend John Evelyn, a fellow early experimentalist and admirer of the philosopher of the garden, did not include in his commentary on his Lucretius translation 'any of the sense of excitement about the simplicity and clarity of Lucretius's atomistic view of nature'.[52] Evelyn seems to have been more attracted by the image of Epicurus's natural philosophy as a process of *askesis* and virtue acquisition, where the *telos* of natural philosophy is a moderate, philosophical happiness and freedom from irrational fear.[53] This distinction between Epicureanism and hedonistic Cyrenaicism was repeatedly emphasised, even by those for whom there is no evidence that they came under the influence of Gassendi.[54] It has been suggested that this vision of Epicureanism appealed to the royalists Charleton, Evelyn, and Stanley because of its emphasis on a dignified contemplative life, attractive to those deprived of the opportunity to hold public office.[55] There is only a limited extent to which these questions of motivation can be answered, but we can certainly find a degree of reflexive self-awareness about the Epicurean identity among these figures: Stanley's close friend John Hall published an 'Epicurean Ode' in a volume dedicated to Stanley; the

---

[48] Ibid., sigs. [a3]$^v$–c$^v$. The very wide-reaching implications of this argument, first made by Gassendi, are discussed in 5.4 below.

[49] Ibid., sigs. c2$^r$–[c3]$^r$.

[50] Ibid., sigs. d$^v$–d3$^r$. For a near-contemporary contextual discussion of the Stoics on suicide, see Meric Casaubon, 'Notes', in *Marcus Aurelius Antoninus the Roman emperor, his meditations concerning himselfe* (London, 1634), 42–3 (this work is discussed further at 5.2 below).

[51] E.g. Wilson, *Epicureanism*, 9, follows Kargon, 'Walter Charleton, Robert Boyle and the acceptance of Epicurean atomism in England' (1964) in claiming Charleton as a key source for Boyle.

[52] Hunter, *Shape of orthodoxy*, 90. For Charleton's long friendship with Evelyn, who was probably sending him new French philosophy in the early 1650s, see Sharp, 'Early life', 314, 324–5, 336–7.

[53] See e.g. Stanley, *History*, 605: 'that which is of Nature would be useless, unless it conferr'd to the End of Life with an Ethical Consideration'. See also Whitelocke Bulstrode, *An essay of transmigration, in defence of Pythagoras* (London, 1692), sig. [A6]$^v$.

[54] Stanley, *History*, 633; Evelyn, *Essay*, sig. [A8]$^r$.

[55] Hunter, 'Evelyn', 70; Kroll, *Material Word*.

Epicurean garden built by Evelyn had at its entrance a statue of the goddess Venus, representing 'nature' in *De rerum natura*; in a rather misogynistic letter, Ralph Bohun complained to Evelyn of the 'Amor' of a common female acquaintance whose 'whole discourse is of Clysters & retirement', which he attributed 'more [to] a designless & stupid contempt of fortune, then $y^t$ her soul is raised enough to relish a contemplative life' or 'ye Epicurean Felicity, Tranquility of mind & Negation of Trouble'.[56] Again, I am reluctant to read into this fashion for Epicurean moral philosophy the wide cultural importance that some literary scholars have discovered there.[57] It appears to have been limited to this mostly royalist circle; for example, I have found no evidence of it penetrating university moral–philosophical pedagogy. Most importantly, whatever they thought of the revisionist view of Epicurean moral philosophy, Gassendi's account was not accepted in full by any natural philosopher apart from Charleton, as we shall see. It was also challenged on a scholarly level, a challenge to which we now turn.

## 5.2    Scholarly and religious responses to Gassendi's history of matter theory

Undoubtedly the most learned English (and perhaps even European) response to Gassendi came from the pen of the scholar–cleric Meric Casaubon, whose antagonism to the Royal Society apologists we have treated already (4.4). While it is tempting to subsume Casaubon's opposition to Epicurus to his opposition to the new philosophy *tout court*,[58] the reality that is revealed by examining all the evidence is both more complex and more interesting. Casaubon's critique appeared not only in his well-known *Of credulity and incredulity* (1668 and 1670) and the *Letter to Peter du Moulin* (1669), but was first developed at length in his 'Notae & Emendationes' to Ménage's edition of Diogenes Laërtius (1664). Since this was prepared before the key *apologiae* for the Royal Society were published, it seems to render unlikely the

---

[56] John Hall, *Poems* (Cambridge, 1646), 42–3, sigs. A2$^{r-v}$; Small and Small, 'John Evelyn and the garden of Epicurus' (1997), 201; Bohun to Evelyn, 1 Aug 1666, BL MS Add. 78314, fols. 4$^{r-v}$. For women and Epicureanism more generally, see Barbour and Norbrook, 'Introduction', xxxiii–xlii.

[57] Especially Kroll, *Material word*; Barbour and Norbrook, 'Introduction'.

[58] See e.g., Spiller, *Meric Casaubon and the Royal Society*, 80–104, esp. 81–2 ('it is probable that his fear and hatred [of Epicurus] were stimulated only by his observation of the close relations between some aspects of Epicurus's theories and the new philosophy after 1660'). See likewise Mayo, *Epicurus*, 140–2; Wilson, *Epicureanism*, 238; Westfall, *Science and religion in seventeenth-century England* (1973), 23. Spiller knew about the 'Notae', but appears to have misunderstood their content ('Casaubon's [later] harshness is remarkable, for he had himself contributed scholarly notes to ... Diogenes Laertius' *Lives*' [*Casaubon*, 81]); he is followed in this by Repetzki, 'Preface', xcv.

possibility that Casaubon's anti-Epicureanism was simply a part of his broader antagonism to the new philosophy, and compels us to undertake a broader examination of his earlier works.

Casaubon was most likely invited to participate in that edition by Pearson.[59] He later suggested that his views on Gassendi's Epicurus were formed on the basis of reading the *Vita Epicuri* (1647) and before the publication of Gassendi's *Animadversiones* (i.e. 1649).[60] As we shall see, Casaubon's negative attitude to Epicurus in fact first appeared in his Greek–Latin edition of Marcus Aurelius (1643). From all this we might conclude, in ascending order of speculativeness, that (A) his attack on Epicurus had, at least in its formative stage, little to do with his attitude towards experimental philosophy or the Royal Society; and (B) he was asked to contribute to Ménage's Diogenes Laërtius by Pearson because the latter knew about his thoughts on Epicurus and valued his qualifications as a historian of philosophy more generally.[61]

In the section on DL x in the 'Notae', Casaubon deviated from the narrowly philological approach of the rest of his text to offer a virulently reductionist interpretation of the historical evidence preserved there: 'In my view (so that I might say freely what I think) in all this discussion of nature, which is contained in the first two Epistles [i.e. the letters to Herodotus and to Pythocles], Epicurus appears not so much to speak or to write as to rave from an unrestrained hatred of piety and divine worship'.[62] This was contrasted not only with Judaeo–Christian belief but also with the Stoics' respect for God's omnipotence.[63] The

---

[59] See 2.2. above. Incidentally, it was Pearson who later informed Casaubon that Thomas Gataker's edition of Marcus Aurelius had been published: BL MS Burney 369, fol. 104[r] (Pearson to Casaubon, 27 Jan [1652]).

[60] Casaubon, *Credulity* [68], 226–7: 'Since this written, I bethought my self, that *Gassendus* happily, in those large Comments and *Animadversions* upon *Epicurus* his *Philosophy*, (if we may so call it, which deserveth better to be called, *dotage and madness*) set out some years after, in three *Tomes*; might retract some of those notorious *mistakes*, if any man can think them so. I have searched, but I find, that instead of *retracting*, he doth *repeat*, and endeavour to confirm'. Casaubon then goes on (227–9) to challenge two of Gassendi's arguments in the *Animadversiones*, based on the testimony of Jerome and Porphyry, but it is clear that these are genuinely later additions to Casaubon's main case, which is based on the *Vita Epicuri*. For Casaubon's library, see Birrell, 'The reconstruction of the library of Isaac Casaubon' (1980), esp. 62.

[61] He would not have been the only one. As early as September 1638, the puritan minister Nathaniel Ward (who would later compile the first constitution in North America) wrote to Casaubon with questions on Ocellus Lucanus, Plato, and Marcus Aurelius, initiating a detailed scholarly correspondence that lasted until September 1639 (BL MS Burney 369, fols. 178[r]–186[v]). Pearson himself saw Gassendi's work as a landmark episode in the historiography of philosophy which nonetheless required expanding beyond Epicurus: see his laudatory preface to Ménage in DL 1664, sig. [A3][r].

[62] Meric Casaubon, 'Notae, & emendationes', in DL 1664, 24b (new pagination): 'Mihi certè (ut quod censeo liberè dicam:) in tota hâc de naturâ disputatione, quae duabus prioribus *Epistolis* continetur; non tam loqui, aut scribere; quàm ex impotenti pietatis, & divini cultus odio, rabere videtur Epicurus'.

[63] Ibid., 24b, quoting (without acknowledgement) Cicero, *Nat. Deor.*, III.39.

third letter (i.e. to Menoeceus), on ethics, was simply dismissed as a cover for Epicurus's hedonism.[64]

These themes were heavily expanded in the part of *Credulity and incredulity* published in 1668, Casaubon from the outset advertising himself as a patron of the 'traditional' anti-Epicurean view, incredulous at the recent revisionism, by which he obviously meant Gassendi.[65] Further evidence that he was not directly concerned with the Royal Society is that the focus was very much on Epicurus's moral philosophy and theology: although he made some cursory attempts, Casaubon's criticisms of Epicurus's natural philosophy were no more than the most basic commonplaces (e.g. that Epicurus considered the sun the same size as it appeared (from DL x.91)), failing almost entirely to engage with Gassendi's sophisticated reinterpretation of Epicurean physics.[66] The counter-revisionist treatment of Epicurean moral philosophy and theology, on the other hand, is long, detailed, and philologically sophisticated. At all points Casaubon followed what is clearly recognisable as a concerted interpretative strategy: to downplay the importance of Laërtius's account and to revitalise the accounts of those whom Gassendi (and others) had accused of misrepresenting Epicurus. According to Casaubon, Laërtius's testimony was unreliable because he was a 'professed Epicurean' – a common judgement in early modern scholarship.[67] Expanding on Laërtius, Gassendi had attributed much of the (supposedly unfounded) opprobrium against Epicurus to the calumnies of Cicero.[68] Casaubon systematically rehabilitated Cicero as a source. Comparison revealed that some of Cicero's statements about Epicurus's hedonism were actually matched by those in Laërtius.[69] Moreover, context dictated that Cicero could hardly have lied, for his Epicurean friends – 'who were many, and of the best he had' – would have immediately seen through the fraud if, as '*Gassendus* would have us to believe ... those were spurious writings, or interpolated, and

---

[64] Casaubon, 'Notae', 24b–25a; the rest of the notes on 25a–b are philological.

[65] Casaubon, *Credulity* [68], 201; see also *Generall learning*, 149–50.

[66] Casaubon, *Credulity* [68], 202–3. Spiller is thus precisely wrong in his claim that 'whereas the traditional condemnation of Epicurus relied upon his reputation for voluptuousness and immorality, Casaubon, in allying himself with it, usually makes Epicurus' physical theories his target, the theories which were, of course, precisely the point of contact of Epicurean philosophy and the new science' (*Casaubon*, 82).

[67] Casaubon, *Credulity* [68], 206–7. For the same judgement, see e.g. Ménage, 'In Diogenem Laertium observationes et emendationes', in DL 1664, 2a (new pagination) ('... Epicuro tribuit laudes immodicas; quin & inde Epicureum fuisse conjicimus'); Blount, *Janua scientiarum*, 64. Casaubon also overplayed his hand, wrongly accusing Gassendi of having mistranslated the already biased views of Laërtius (207, claiming that contrary to Gassendi, *Vita Epicuri*, 140, the words about Epicurus's accusers at DL x.9 (Μεμήνασι δ' οὗτοι ['But these peole are stark mad']) only referred to the last accusation (of despising all men except himself) – there is no solid philological reason to suppose this).

[68] E.g., Gassendi, *Vita Epicuri*, 224–8; *passim*.

[69] Casaubon, *Credulity* [68], 207, citing the example of the quotation from Epicurus offered at DL x.6 and matched at Cicero, *Disp. Tusc.*, III.41; *De fin.*, II.3.7.

corrupted by the *Stoicks*'.[70] The same was true of Plutarch, a key source of anti-Epicurean testimony, especially valuable because his ideas could not be dismissed as Stoic prejudices. Gassendi had devoted a whole chapter to him, ingeniously claiming that his anti-Epicurus statements were not his own but only reports of common opinion,[71] an argument that was tendentious at best, as Casaubon gleefully pointed out.

Even more interesting was Casaubon's clever (if daringly speculative) solution to the problem of the two varying accounts of Epicurus' death. Laërtius (x.22) quoted a deathbed letter by Epicurus to Idomeneus in which Epicurus dismissed the pains of death in favour of 'gladness of mind at the remembrance of our past conversations'. Yet Plutarch reported that the dying Epicurus 'found compensation in being escorted on his journey by the recollection of the pleasures he had once enjoyed', elsewhere showing his familiarity with the *Letter to Idomeneus*.[72] Gassendi had sensibly argued that Plutarch's reading was a corrupt one, especially given that even Cicero repeated Laërtius's reading.[73] But Casaubon correctly pointed out that in another place, Cicero also appeared to support Plutarch's reading.[74] Casaubon suggested that either the *Letter* included two different readings, or that there were two different versions of the *Letter* itself; either way, '*Cicero* made use of either reading, as he saw occasion'. Speculating on the origins of this double reading, Casaubon suggested that the *Letter* had been doctored by 'some of *Epicurus* his friends, or disciples' when it first appeared, for they were 'ashamed' of the true reading: the alteration never became available to Plutarch (hence his not mentioning it), but reached Laërtius.[75]

Finally, Casaubon dealt with Seneca, whose testimony was notoriously problematic because it seemed to waver between condemnation and relatively firm praise for Epicurus. Casaubon explained that Seneca *had* condemned Epicurus's theology: only in his weaker moments did he praise Epicurus, understandable given that he was the least constant of the Stoics, one who 'gave too much occasion to the world'. This was typical of the move away from Seneca amongst those interested in Stoicism in the mid-seventeenth century; it also allowed Casaubon to suggest a correct emendation of Lipsius's reading of a passage in the *Epistulae morales*.[76] As for Epicurus himself, the advice

---

[70] Casaubon, *Credulity* [68], 208.     [71] Gassendi, *Vita Epicuri*, 98–101.

[72] Plutarch, *Non posse suaviter vivi secundum Epicurum*, 1099D; *Adv. Col.*, 1117E, 1127E (for a modern discussion of Plutarch's knowledge of the letter, see Westman, *Plutarch gegen Kolotes* (1955), 189–92, 225–7).

[73] Gassendi, *Vita Epicuri*, 52–4, 100–101; Cicero, *De fin.*, ii.96.

[74] Casaubon, *Credulity* [68], 213–14; Cicero, *Disp. Tusc.*, v.26.

[75] Casaubon, *Credulity* [68], 214–15.

[76] Ibid., 203–5, 218–19, 222–3. Discussing Seneca, *Ben.*, iv.19 Casaubon correctly suggested reading 'extra mundum' where Lipsius had 'extra metam' (*Opera omnia* (Antwerp, 1600), 473).

towards temperance that was so often quoted by his defenders was in fact not a denial of hedonism but the 'advice to others of his crew ... that the right and sober management of such pleasures, was the way to enjoy them long, and to make them more pleasing'.[77] Or it was possible that his oft-reported abstinence was simply a means of allowing him to 'return to ... *wallowing*, more fresh and vigorous'.[78] As always, Casaubon supported these speculations with philology, even defending the veracity of a blatantly spurious letter of the philosopher–concubine Leontium (from Alciphron's *Epistles*) which reported Epicurus's lechery; this letter had been dismissed not just by Gassendi.[79]

If his original aim was not a serendipitous assault on the new philosophy, when and why did Casaubon develop his counter-revisionist image of Epicurus, which he must have known was working against the latest scholarship? To this question we must add another, previously unrecognised intellectual biographical problem. In the notes to his pioneering English edition of Marcus Aurelius's *Meditations* (1634) – the first attempt fully to place the emperor in his Stoic context[80] – Casaubon briefly offered the standard Laërtian revisionist defence of Epicurus as a seeker of virtue whose views had suffered later misrepresentation at the hands of his Stoic enemies.[81] Why did he change his mind?

---

[77] Casaubon, *Credulity* [68], 202.     [78] Ibid., 219–20.

[79] Ibid., 220–1 (contrast Gassendi, *Vita Epicuri*, 170). Casaubon's argument was that Leontium's accusations against the aged Epicurus fit well with Plutarch's descriptions of ways he had devised 'to prolong and maintain lust and leachery' (Casaubon does not offer a source; I can only speculate that he is misusing *Quaest. conv.*, III.6.1 653B). Leontium is mentioned in the standard sources (e.g. DL x.4–7, 23); the issue of women philosophers and Epicureanism is an interesting and complex one: the key sources are usefully summarised in Taylor, *Jewish women philosophers* (2003), 202–5.

[80] The best discussion is Kraye, 'Marcus Aurelius and his *Meditations* from Xylander to Diderot' (2000), 110–14. The work is subjected to a narrowly political interpretation in Barbour, *Ancient legacies*, 156–61, based on a very loose reading of the short dedicatory epistle to Laud – Prof. Barbour fails to note that the 1643 Greek–Latin edition was dedicated to Selden, hardly signalling a consistency of political purpose. In a letter to G. J. Vossius of July 1634, Casaubon mentioned no political motivations, but said that he undertook the edition 'to understand him [i.e. Marcus Aurelius]' ('Nobis tamen Antoninus legentibus, ipsum intelligere') and 'to please the mind' ('animi oblectandi causa à me factum est') (Bod. MS. Rawl. Letters 84f, fol. 143[r] [=*Vossii epistolae*, 130 (2nd pagination)] (See also Casaubon to Vossius, early 1634 [Bod. MS Rawl. Letters 84f, fol. 40[r]]). Vossius's reply again treats it as a work of scholarship and mentions no political implications (Bod. MS Rawl. Letters 84f, fols. 74–5 [=*Vossii Epistolae*, 235 (1st pagination)]). Moreover, as already pointed out in Kraye, 'Marcus Aurelius', 110–11, Casaubon's work was probably also connected to his father's work on Marcus Aurelius for his edition of Persius (1605). Later, one reader *was* interested in Casaubon's Latin-Greek edition for political reasons: Queen Christina of Sweden wanted a copy because she wanted to learn to emulate the Emperor (Johann Freinsheim to Isaac Vossius, 3 Oct 1648, Bod. MS D'Orville 468, p. 361 (the letter in general concerns the attempt to lure Vossius to Sweden))

[81] Marcus Aurelius, *Meditations concerning himselfe*, ed. and trans. Meric Casaubon (London, 1634), 38–9. That Casaubon was carefully reading Laërtius for contextual information when preparing the English Marcus Aurelius is clear from the comments in the letter to Vossius, Bod. MS. Rawl. letters 83, fol. 143[r] [=*Vossii epistolae*, 130 (2nd pagination)]. Both Spiller (*Casaubon*, 84) and Mayo (*Epicurus*, 142) vaguely associate Casaubon's anti-Epicureanism with his Stoicism,

The answer, I propose, is that Casaubon was influenced by another piece of scholarship, intimately connected to his own interest in Stoic philosophy of the 1630s–50s: the edition of Marcus Aurelius that was published in Cambridge in 1652 (after forty years of work) by the moderate Reformed priest and brilliant scholar Thomas Gataker, who had wisely preferred to remain in his country rectory when offered the Mastership of Trinity College, Cambridge.[82] Casaubon visited Gataker before embarking on the Latin version of his Marcus Aurelius (1643) and received Gataker's fulsome encouragement, and, more generously, Gataker's extensive notes.[83]

The key text here is Gataker's 'Praeloquium' to his edition, 'in which the Stoic teaching, is compared with that of the other Sects: the Peripatetic and that of the Old Academy, and especially the Epicurean'.[84] Here we find that in defending his argument that 'to bring together closely . . . Epicurus' garden with Zeno's portico . . . is clearly inadmissible',[85] Gataker deployed arguments – extensively documented – that bear a striking resemblance to those that Casaubon would later deploy against Gassendi. Where the Stoics aimed for virtue, the Epicureans were, for all their rhetoric, hedonists.[86] Following Cicero,

but neither discusses the relevant evidence. Some of Casaubon's original positive feelings towards the Epicureans also manifest themselves in *A treatise concerning enthusiasme* (London, 1655), 49–51, where he seems to posit some 'refined *Epicures*', such as the friends of Cicero, who were less debauched. But further evidence of Casaubon having changed his mind by the early 1640s is his *Originall cause of temporall evils* (London, 1645), sigs. A3ᵛ–[A4]ʳ.

[82] Gataker is understudied, and it is unfortunate that we cannot consider him in full here. The fullest biographical account is Usher, 'Gataker, Thomas', *ODNB*; see also T. Gataker, 'Vita, propriâ manu scripta', in *Opera philologica et critica* (2 vols, Utrecht, 1697–8), ii, sigs. Ccʳ–Cc2ᵛ. As for Gataker's scholarship as a whole, the discussion in Brink, *English scholarship*, 10–20 (esp. 15–16) is, as the chapter title suggests ('The way to Bentley'), concerned almost entirely with prolepti- cally measuring to what extent Gataker was or wasn't similar to the scholar who *did* take up the Trinity Mastership. On his Marcus Aurelius, Kraye, 'Marcus Aurelius' (114–18) is again the most useful discussion, expanded in Kraye, 'Thomas Gataker's edition of Marcus Aurelius's *Meditations*' (2007); see also Brooke, *Philosophic pride* (2012), 97–9, 134–5. Barbour, *Ancient legacies*, 236–8 again offers political motivations for which there is scant evidence. In a letter to Edward Bernard of 12 May 1696, Theodoor Jansson van Almeloveen, who was informed of the progress of the Utrecht edition of Gataker's works, said that Gataker's surviving manuscripts and books were mutilated (Bod. MS Smith 8, fols. 106ʳ).

[83] Kraye, 'Marcus Aurelius', 114.

[84] Thomas Gataker, 'Praeloquium', in Marcus Aurelius, *De rebus suis, sive de eis quae ad se pertinere censebat*, ed. and trans. T. Gataker (Cambridge, 1652), sig. *3ʳ: 'In quo de Disciplina Stoica, cum Sectis aliis, Peripatetica & Academica Vetere, Epicurea verò praecipuè collata'. I have systematically amended Gataker's idiosyncratic non-use of 'u' after 'q' (on the curious reasons for which, see Kraye, 'Marcus Aurelius', 116).

[85] Gataker, 'Praeloquium', sig. [*4]ᵛ: 'Caeterùm Epicuri hortulos cum Zenonis porticu, *Voluptatis* Magistros cum *Virtutis* patronis, molles cum rigidis, discinctos & dissolutos cum altè cinctis, arctè strictis committi & in certamen descendere, indignissimum plane videtur, & à ratione omni alienum non immeritò habeatur'.

[86] Ibid., sig. **ʳ: 'Medicus siquidem valetudini prospicit, nè in morbum mutet; Epicureus volup- tati, nè in dolorem vertat; Stoicus virtuti, nè à tramite istius vel tantillum declinando, in vitium protinus proruatur'.

Gataker dimissed Epicurus's castigations of debauchers (*asotos*) as warnings against an over-indulgence that would lead to ruin.[87] Epicurus's profession and practice of abstinence stemmed not from moral concerns, but was only a way to avoid 'entirely exhausting the faculties';[88] or it was simply preparation for periods of debauchery.[89] On all accounts, Cicero's testimony was to be preferred to the contradictory statements of Seneca, which could be explained by his being the least of the three great Stoics: himself, Epictetus, and Marcus Aurelius.[90]

These similarities should not lead to the conclusion that Casaubon followed Gataker slavishly: it is quite clear that his reading of Gassendi inspired him to examine the sources in great detail by himself, and he added many points not found in Gataker. However, the praise for Epicurus that we found in the English edition of Marcus Aurelius is missing from the Greek–Latin, and although Epicurus is now barely mentioned in the commentary there is one overtly anti-Epicurean passage, like Gataker emphasising the value of Cicero's testimony on Epicurus's fraudulent claims to virtue.[91] It is an interesting question as to whether Gataker was acquainted with Gassendi's late-1640s works: he gives no references to them and although they were widely available in England, Gataker had permanently retired to his rectory in Surrey after illness in 1645 and may not have had access to the latest imported literature. However, his preference for a Ciceronian over a Senecan (or Laërtian) reading of Epicurus was inherited by Casaubon, who deployed it deliberately and repeatedly against the Frenchman. Once again we find that a debate that has previously been interpreted solely in the context of the new philosophy in fact had deeper roots in humanist scholarship. Moreover, these counter-revisionist arguments could change minds: Evelyn, for example, also abandoned the positive vision of Epicurean ethics in favour of the Ciceronian one.[92]

---

[87] Ibid., sigs. \*\*$^v$–\*\*2$^r$.    [88] Ibid., sigs. \*\*2$^{r-v}$ ('facultates funditus exhauriuntur').

[89] Ibid., sig. \*\*3$^r$.

[90] Ibid., sigs. \*\*$^{r-v}$; \*\*\*3$^{r-v}$ (esp. sig. \*\*\*3$^v$: 'Verúm non est unius ejusdémque ubique coloris; nec par omnia constat sibi').

[91] Meric Casaubon, 'In Marci Antonini De seipso & ad seipsum libros, notae', in *Marci Antonini Imperatoris De seipso et ad seipsum libri XII* (London, 1643), 104–5 (a note on ix.41 [ix.36 in Casaubon's edition], discussing Epicurus's death – Casaubon here completely misinterprets the verb which he analyses, καταφρυάττεσθαι): 'Porrò ejusdami argumenti apud Dio. Laertium extat Epistola, quam moriens Epicurus ad Idomeneum quondam scripsisse perhibetur: de quâ quod Ciceronis jam olim judicium fuerit, digna res est quae à prudenti lectore, ne sibi ab infami impostore verba dari patiatur, diligenter animadvertatur. Extat illud Tuscul. Quaest LV' (the references are to DL x.22 and Cicero, *Disp. Tusc.*, v.26.73). At 'Notae', 91, i.e. the equivalent note on the use of φιλόσοφος in viii.1 to the one in the English edition where Casaubon had praised Epicurus, he now seems to distance himself from that edition: 'De multipici vocum φιλόσοφος & φιλοσοφίας apud Graecos scriptores acceptione quaedam in Notis Anglicis pridem monuimus; sed multò plura parata habemus, ex quibus non parva lux haud paucis authorum locis vel obscuris vel à Latinis interpretibus male acceptis inferri posit'.

[92] Evelyn, *History of religion*, I, 325.

Casaubon's attack on Gassendi was the most scholarly attempt to deal with the issues of Epicurus's moral philosophy and theology. Many even among the learned clergy simply continued to chastise Epicurus's denial of providence, which they claimed was as good as an admission of atheism.[93] Of such treatments, perhaps the most scholarly example is John Smith's *Select Discourses*.[94] Although Smith deployed the standard counter-Epicurean arguments for the existence of God and the immortality of the soul, his historical assessment of Epicurus as a closet atheist and hedonist in the vein of the Cyrenaics is derived entirely from Cicero, simply ignoring Laërtius's counter-evidence.[95] His only addition was that Epicurus deliberately concealed his atheism so as to avoid the fate of Protagoras, whose scepticism about the Gods led to him being 'put to Death, and his books burnt in the streets of *Athens*'[96] – a bizarre conclusion, since all versions of DL ix.51–2 are clear that Protagoras was expelled (ἐξεβλήθη) rather than executed.

Smith is usually characterised as a 'Cambridge Platonist', but as we have seen, there is little similarity between either his and More's views on the history of philosophy or their motivations for writing them. Smith was regurgitating standard (mostly Ciceronian)[97] anti-Epicurean sentiments that he had probably kept in his commonplace book since his youth, whereas More had developed a whole history of atomism that allowed him to combine his own apologetic aims (by the late 1650s mostly anti-Hobbesian) with his penchant for Cartesian natural philosophy. More's attitude to the history of atomism we have already met (3.4) – a proto-Cartesian Mosaic 'Cabbala' containing both atomism and immaterialism was adopted by Pythagoras before being corrupted by Democritus and Epicurus into materialism.[98] More's evidence for this thesis was meagre, but it is of interest to us here because of its structural similarity to the much more scholarly history of atomism offered by his friend Ralph Cudworth (see below).

Far more sophisticated histories of the relationship between matter theory and religion than More's were offered in the popular genre of historical apologetics, specifically in Stillingfleet's *Origines sacrae* and Cudworth's *System*, which we have met already, and in Samuel Parker's *Tentamina de*

---

[93] See the discussion in Mayo, *Epicurus*, 115–46.    [94] See 3.4 above.

[95] Smith, *Select discourses*, 45–6 (mispagination of 44–5), 53. See also John Worthington's comments in 'To the reader', xxi.

[96] Smith, *Select discourses*, 46 (mispagination of 45). See also the comparison with the Cyrenaics at 53.

[97] E.g. ibid., 45–6 (i.e. 44–5), misquoting Cicero, *Nat. Deor.*, 1.30. This use of Cicero was later plagiarised by Creech in his notes: see 'Notes upon the first book', in *Lucretius his six books of epicurean philosophy and Manilius his five books containing a system of the ancient astronomy and astrology together with the philosophy of the Stoicks* (London, 1700), 2 (new pagination).

[98] As well as the evidence cited at 3.4 above, see *The immortality of the soul* (London, 1659), 347.

*Deo* (1665), which we have not. Stillingfleet and Parker both began – without admitting it – with the claims made at the very start of Vossius's *Theologia gentilis*. As part of his defence of a near-universal theism, Vossius had argued that the Greek materialists – those like Theodorus, Bion, Diagoras, Euhemerus, Protagoras, and especially Epicurus – had not in fact been atheists but had been labelled as such because they rejected the superstition and idolatry of pagan religion.[99] This assertion, stemming from a passage in Clemens Alexandrinus, would later lie at the heart of Pierre Bayle's argument about the existence of virtuous atheists.[100] English clerics wrestled with it no less vigorously than would the Huguenot. Stillingfleet agreed with much of Vossius's general argument. Like Vossius, he set himself the question, 'if this knowledge of [the] truth [of God's existence] be so great, so natural ... whence comes so much of the world to be over-run with Ignorance and Barbarism ... ?',[101] and like the Dutchman he suggested that one answer was that pagan idolatry was built on the edifice of truth: specifically the two truths of the existence of God and the immortality of the soul.[102] And yet when Stillingfleet reached the Greek materialists, he consciously deviated from Vossius's attempt to discover a truly universal theism. So monstrous was the idolatry constructed on top of the common principles that when 'many *considerative heathen*' examined it, they threw the baby out with the bathwater, 'not being able ... through the want of *divine revelation* to deduce any certain *instituted worship*'.[103] Those who offered the '*Apology* usually made for *Protagoras, Diagoras*, and such others of them who were accounted *Atheists*' – that is, 'that they only rejected those heathen Deities, and not the belief of the Divine nature' – were wrong. The same was the case with Anaxagoras and the other Ionics, who, even if they spoke of an eternal Mind (νους), probably '*imbrace[d]* [it] only as an *hypothesis* in *Philosophy* to *solve* the *phaenomena* of *nature* with, but yet not to make this *eternal mind* the *object of adoration*'.[104] Epicurus, it followed, could be

---

[99] Vossius, *Theologia gentilis*, 4–6.

[100] The key *locus* is Clemens Alexandrinus, *Protr.*, 2, 'ὧν δὴ χάριν 'οὐ γὰρ οὐδαμῶς ἀποκρυπτέον θαυμάζειν ἔπεισί μοι ὅτῳ τρόπῳ Εὐήμερον τὸν Ἀκραγαντῖνον καὶ Νικάνορα τὸν Κύπριον καὶ Διαγόραν καὶ Ἵππωνα τὼ Μηλίω τόν τε Κυρηναῖον ἐπὶ τούτοις ἐκεῖνον 'ὁ Θεόδωρος ὄνομα αὐτῷ καί τινας ἄλλους συχνούς, σωφρόνως βεβιωκότας καὶ καθεωρακότας ὀξύτερόν που τῶν λοιπῶν ἀνθρώπων τὴν ἀμφὶ τοὺς θεοὺς τούτους πλάνην, ἀθέους ἐπικεκλήκασιν, εἰ καὶ τὴν ἀλήθειαν αὐτὴν μὴ νενοηκότας, ἀλλὰ τὴν πλάνην γε ὑπωπτευκότας, ὅπερ οὐ σμικρὸν εἰς ἀλήθειαν φρονήσεως ζώπυρον ἀναφύεται σπέρμα', directly cited by Vossius, Stillingfleet, and Parker, and much adumbrated in [Pierre Bayle], *Lettre à M. L. A. D. C. Docteur de Sorbonne, où il est prouvé par plusieurs raisons ... que les cometes ne sont point le presage d'aucun malheur* ([Rotterdam], 1682), 395–7 [=*Pensées diverses sur la comète: edition critique*, ed. A. Prat (2 vols, Paris, 1939), II, 107–10], adducing exactly the same list of 'atheists': Diagoras, Theodorus, Euhemerus, Hippon, and Epicurus. Bayle, like Stillingfleet, disagreed with Clemens; Vossius and Parker agreed; see further below.

[101] Stillingfleet, *Origines sacrae*, 6.    [102] Ibid., 7–8.    [103] Ibid., 9–10.

[104] Ibid., 10–11; see also 364–5.

similarly classified, and Cicero's testimonies for Epicurus's self-contradictory statements regarding theology and ethics could once again be redeployed: 'the *reason* why many of them did to the *world* own a *Deity*, was, that they might not be *Martyrs* for *Atheism*'.[105]

Why this deviation from Vossius, on whom Stillingfleet drew so much, and with whom he shared so many basic assumptions? First, there is the importance of Cicero, who remained a common source for anti-Epicurean arguments in mid-century English pedagogy.[106] Stillingfleet, undoubtedly a diligent scholar, may have consciously picked Cicero over Vossius because he could not abandon the old anti-Epicurean sources on which he was brought up and which even 'all the pains that *P. Gassendus* hath taken in the vindication of the *life* and *opinions* of *Epicurus*, hath not been able to wipe off';[107] he may also have been influenced by Casaubon, whom he knew and whose books he inherited.

But there is also a second possible explanation, which stems from Stillingfleet's acceptance of Descartes's famous proof of God's existence from the Third Meditation: since whatever is contained objectively in an idea must be contained either formally or eminently in the cause of that idea, I can be the cause of any of my own ideas; but since the idea of God is the idea of an infinite substance, and I am only a finite substance, I cannot be the cause of the idea of an infinite substance – that cause must be God, and the idea of God must be innate (rather than adventitious or imaginary).[108] Stillingfleet rightly understood that this proof depended on the fact that 'this *Idea* [of God] is of such a *nature* as could not be *formed* from the *understandings consideration* of any *corporeal phantasms*', and that consequently, 'this *Idea* ... must be a pure *act* of *Intellection*, and therefore supposing there were no other *faculty* in man but *imagination*, it would bear the greatest *repugnancy* to our *conceptions*'.[109] And yet, as any reader of Laërtius knew, a key theme of Epicurus's *Letter to*

---

[105] Ibid., 11–12. But see also 365–6, where, drawing entirely on Cicero's, *Nat. Deor.*, I.44, Stillingfleet argues that 'after all the labours of *Epicurus*, he knew it was to no purpose to *endeavour* to *root* out wholly the *belief* of a *Deity* out of the world, because of the unanimous *consent* of the *world* in it; and therefore he admits of it as a necessary *Prolepsis* or *Anticipation* of *human nature*': nice evidence of the confusions that dependence on Cicero engendered.

[106] See e.g. BL Sloane MS 2514, 'Cursus physici pars posterior sive specialis de variis corporum speciebus', fol. 8$^r$, attacking Democritus and Epicurus, and telling the student to read the second book of *De natura deorum* for further details. See also the appearance of Ciceronian commonplaces about the usefulness of the study of nature for divinity in Wendelin, *Contemplationes physicae*, sigs. A3$^r$, A4$^v$. Of course, Cicero remained a key source for *consensus gentium* arguments too (*Nat. Deor.*, II.2.4), even in philosophy textbooks: e.g. Heereboord, *Meletemata philosophica*, 51. For such arguments making their way into actual theological pedagogy, see e.g. the theological commonplace book of Henry Fairfax, composed while studying for his B.D. (awarded 1666): Folger MS V.b.108, p. 31.

[107] Stillingfleet, *Origines Sacrae*, 454.     [108] Ibid., 367–74; Pacchi, *Cartesio*, 66–73.

[109] Stillingfleet, *Origines*, 372–3.

*Herodotus* was that no phenomena could be classified as pure acts of a 'rational' soul disembodied from elementary sensations (imagination was part of the sensitive soul). And so, according to Stillingfleet, 'it would be according to the *principles* of *Epicurus* and some modern *Philosophers*, a thing wholly *impossible* to form an *Idea* of *God*, unless with *Epicurus* we imagine him to be *corporeal*, which is to say he is no *God*'. All this brought Stillingfleet back to Cicero: 'which was the reason that *Tully* said *Epicurus* did only *nomine ponere, re tollere Deos*, because such a notion of *God* is repugnant to natural light'.[110] And so in an argument that emphasised near universal consent, Epicurus was an atheist because his philosophy denied the psychological principles on which such consent could be based. It is often assumed that 'orthodoxy' invariably depended on the argument from universal consent.[111] As we see here, the reality was somewhat more complex. Writers of apologetics had historiographical traditions to draw on that could find atheists in the classical philosophical past, and yet turn that finding to their own apologetic ends.

This is further demonstrated by a fascinating but almost entirely unknown text, which is of great interest to us, not least because at points it engages directly with Stillingfleet's treatment of the same issues. The work in question is Samuel Parker's *Tentamina physico-theologica de Deo: sive theologica scholastica ad normam novae & reformatae philosophiae concinnata* (1665 [*Physico-theological esssays on God, or scholastic theology adjusted to the standard of the new and reformed philosophy*]). We have already encountered Parker's erudite attack on narratives of Mosaic intellectual primacy (3.5); we shall later encounter his very astute comments on the relationship between Greek philosophy and early Christianity (6.5). Both of these, however, came in the well-known *Censure of the Platonick philosophie* (1666); the *Tentamina*, a passage in which inspired the *Censure*,[112] has gone almost entirely unexamined, as has its expanded follow-up, the *Disputationes de Deo* (1678).[113] This is a disservice to the book, which secured Parker election to the Royal Society – making him the youngest non-armigerous fellow – and received a glowing review in the first volume of the *Philosophical Transactions*, where Oldenburg commended it as essential reading for those 'who either please themselves with that fond opinion, *That Philosophy is the Apprentiship of Atheisme*; or hearken to the aspersions, that are generally laid upon the *Reformation of Philosophy*'. Indeed, so highly did Oldenburg value the work that he suggested that it should

---

[110] Ibid., 373.

[111] E.g. Israel, *Enlightenment contested*, 67, 70–1, 73–5; Harrison, *Religion*, 39–40; Kidd, *Before nationalism*, 41–2.

[112] As admitted at Parker, *Censure*, 2.

[113] An exception is Pacchi, *Cartesio*, 118–35, which is useful but only examines the anti-Cartesian elements of the work. For a full analysis of the *Tentamina*, see now Levitin, 'Parker'.

be 'joined and compared with the truly Noble Mr. *Boyle's* Considerations in his *First Part* of the *Usefulness of Experimental Natural Philosophy*' – high praise indeed.[114] For the nascent Royal Society, this up-and-coming careerist cleric – whose book was dedicated to Archbishop Sheldon – must have been quite a coup.

*Tentamina* is comprised of two books: 'Of the existence of God, against atheists', and 'Of his essence and attributes'. It is a rich mixture of the intellectual resources available to a university-educated man of letters: humanism, late scholasticism, and the new philosophy (especially the life sciences). Parker's later opponent Andrew Marvell would disparage the *Tentamina* as a 'transcript of his Common place book';[115] this might have been a shrewd assessment, for it seems very probable that it was written on the basis of Parker's studies towards the priesthood: Parker is a fine example of the contemporary ideal of the 'generall scholar', working from the M.A. towards his B.D.[116] We remain so ignorant of pedagogical culture at seventeenth-century theology faculties that it is difficult to know standard patterns of reading, but as we have found in the case of Cicero, and as can be seen from published guides to budding divines, it appears that anti-atheistic disputation was a standard part of the course.[117]

Parker saw Epicurean non-providential atomism as the major threat to be confuted through the argument from design, which he developed in chapter 2, the 'Disputation against atheists', drawing extensively on the latest findings of the new philosophy. But even here Parker could not resist involving himself in humanist debates. Most of his criticisms of Epicurus's creation theory had already been made by Gassendi, on whom Parker clearly drew.[118] But in

---

[114] *Philosophical Transactions*, 1 (1665–66), 324–5. For Oldenburg's ownership of Parker's *Tentamina*, see Malcolm, 'The library of Henry Oldenburg' (2005), 47. For further early praise of Parker amongst RS fellows, see Oldenburg to Boyle, 8 June 1666, *Boyle correspondence*, III, 168; Beale to Boyle, 31 October 1666, *Boyle correspondence*, III, 260. Beale was still praising Parker to Boyle in the 1680s: see the letters of 26 June and 1 July 1682, in *Boyle correspondence*, V, 299–300, 306.

[115] Andrew Marvell, *The rehearsal transpros'd. The second part* (London, 1673), 182.

[116] Serjeantson, 'Introduction', 19.

[117] See e.g. Dodwell, *Two letters*, 204–5; Edward Reyner, *A treatise of the necessity of humane learning for a Gospel-preacher* (London, 1663); Bray, *Bibliotheca parochialis*, 26–7 (recommending Parker's later expansion of the *Tentamina*, the *Disputationes de Deo* (London, 1678), alongside Cudworth's *System*, as 'proper to be first Read upon this Subject, as giving an Historical Account of Atheism and its Authors, as well as a Confutation of their Opinions'). For the recommendation of the *Tentamina* in one such guide, see John Wilkins, *Ecclesiastes: or, a discourse concerning the gift of preaching ... the seventh edition*, ed. J. Williams (London, 1690), 189.

[118] Samuel Parker, *Tentamina physico-theologica de Deo: sive, theologica scholastica ad normam novae & reformatae philosophiae concinnata & duobus libris comprehensa* (London, 1665), 34 (infinite atoms incompatible with void), 35 (causal fortune), 42–3 (variety of atoms); see also 44–5 for the standard conclusion that Epicurus's non-providential world would be chaos. All these issues had been raised by Gassendi.

one respect Parker deviated from the Frenchman and made an important contribution to the English reception both of Gassendi and of Epicurus. Gassendi had supported Epicurus's belief in inherent atomic weight (*pondus*), which allowed atomic motion.[119] Crucially, he had presented this as an observational conclusion, not because atoms are perceptible to the senses but because atomic motion can be inferred from our experience of the behaviour of material things; all this was part of a defence of the historical Epicurus as an observational philosopher. But Gassendi was well aware that this had long ago been questioned by Cicero, who in his dialogue *De fato* mocked the arbitrariness of Epicurean motion theory.[120] The Frenchman had failed to find a philosophical response and had turned to historical reasoning instead: accepting that Epicurus had taken arbitrary steps, he attributed this to all the pagan philosophers' ignorance of the first cause; had not the Aristotelians and the Stoics also been unable to explain the origins of material motion?[121] The better-informed Christian philosopher could keep the core of Epicurus's system but adjust those things about which the ancients could not know: specifically, he could attribute the origin of atomic weight to God. But, Parker objected, it was all very well to point out that Epicurus was no worse than his pagan counterparts, but why accept the rest of his hypothesis about atomic weight? Was this not to undermine the principle of relying on sense experience that Gassendi had so vigorously defended? 'What else is this, than assigning causes without cause?'[122] This is not our last encounter with the important conclusion that Gassendi's Epicurus was far more observational than the sources could justify.

And yet, Parker did not accept Cicero's characterisation of Epicurus as a hedonistic atheist. Chapter 1 of the *Tentamina* is entitled 'Of the ancient philosophers, who were considered atheists by the vulgar'. It is a learned excursion into the history of philosophy, whose apologetic purpose is to show that atheists are misguided if they believe that the ancient philosophers shared their opinions. Here again is proof that this type of argument did not rely in the slightest on any 'neoplatonic' assumptions: Ralph Cudworth would more famously attempt something similar in his *System* (and he almost certainly knew and used Parker's work during composition)[123] but we would hardly

---

[119] The fullest discussion of Gassendi on atomic motion remains Messeri, *La fisica di Pierre Gassendi* (1985), 74–93. But see now also Lolordo, *Gassendi*, 140–52; Osler, *Divine will and the mechanical philosophy* (1994), 180–200.

[120] Cicero, *Fat.*, esp. x.22–3; xix.45; xx.46–7.

[121] Gassendi, *Syntagma philosophicum*, in *Opera omnia*, I, 275b.

[122] Parker, *Tentamina*, 38: 'hoc enim quid aliud est, quàm causas sine causis assignare?'

[123] See e.g. *System*, 118, 'Now we shall take notice of an Objection, made by some late Writers, against this Aristotelick Accusation of the old Philosophers [i.e. that the Ionic sect was atheists; see below] . . . ': Parker had done precisely this, citing the passage from *Met.* I.3, 984$^b$12–15 on which Cudworth rested his argument (*System*, 112–13), and replying 'Quid autem Authoritatis homini dandum est, qui ut ipse solus principatum obtineret, nihil in omni Philosophiâ, tam assiduè conatus est, quam ut omnium qui antecesserunt existimationem imminueret', before

align Parker – the most virulent anti-Platonist in seventeenth-century Europe – with any Platonic sympathies.

Parker began by considering whether those Greek philosophers usually classified as atheists – he listed Anaxagoras, Theodorus, Bion, Diagoras, Euhemerus, Protagoras, and especially Epicurus, that is to say the list given by Clemens Alexandrinus and then taken up by Vossius – were indeed unbelievers. He then offered the thesis that even if they had been atheists, these philosophers were wiser than those Greeks who shared the 'insane superstitions of the Vulgar'.[124] Parker's defence of this rather striking proposition was that superstition is more hurtful to God than atheism[125] – note that we have an entirely orthodox Anglican cleric arguing a variant of what Bayle would famously propose almost two decades later, to much modern historical fanfare. He did not continue with this line of argument, but proceeded to argue that the philosophers accused of atheism attacked not all religion, but only pagan superstition.[126] Parker cited Clement,[127] but it is clear that his main source was Vossius. Indeed, he quoted one of the foundations of Vossius's argument: 'It is more fitting to reason, that they [philosophers accused of atheism] were named atheists, even by ourselves, from reading this in the pagans; but the pagans only called them atheists because they did not hold the gentile gods to be true gods'.[128] The accusers of the putative 'atheists' did not charge them with attacking all religion, but only certain ceremonies. And the Athenians produced more ceremonies and superstitions than any other ancient city; concomitantly, their laws for protecting the superstitions were the harshest.[129] Even 'the pious and honest were accused of atheism, only because they openly shuddered at their wild superstitions' – here the figure of Socrates unsurprisingly made an appearance.[130] Once he had reconstructed the world of pagan religious culture, Parker could proceed to defending each of the philosophers

---

going on to challenge Aristotle at length (*Disputationes de Deo*, 11–14). Moreover, this raises intriguing questions about the history of the composition of Cudworth's *System*: as is well known, the imprimatur was by Parker, and dated 29 May 1671. Could the delay in publication have been caused by Cudworth waiting for Parker's updated work to be ready, so that he could enagage with its arguments?

[124] Parker, *Tentamina*, 1.     [125] Ibid., 1–2.

[126] Ibid., 5–6: 'Verum enimvero plusquam verisimile videtur praedictos Philosophiae Antistites non omnem Religionem, sed solum Idola, Gentilitios Deos, & Graecanicam δεισιδαιμονιαν derisui habuisse, atque idcirco αθεϊστές damnari'.

[127] Clemens Alexandrinus, *Protr.*, 2, cited at Parker, *Tentamina*, 3–4. See n. 100 above.

[128] Vossius, *Theologia gentilis*, 4: 'Rationi magis consentaneum est, atheos vocatos, à nostris quidem, quia sic apud gentiles legissent; à gentibus verò, quia Deos Gentium pro Diis non haberent', quoted in Parker, *Tentamina*, 5–6.

[129] Parker, *Tentamina*, 6–9.

[130] Ibid., 9–10: 'Postremo quod qui illos Atheismi accusarunt, aliis, quos pientissimos fuisse abunde novimus, pari vehementia Atheismi scelus intentarunt, solum quod aperte a vesana eorum superstitione abhorruissent'.

on his list individually, devoting greatest attention to Epicurus. Contextualising Epicurus's famous denial of God's providential interference in the world within the historical framework of the split between pagan philosophy and religious culture which he had set up in the beginning of the chapter, he concluded that Epicurus's did not 'deliberately do away with God and religion, or stray out of contempt for them'.[131] Epicurean moral philosophy was not hedonistic but had as its *telos* pleasure in mental tranquillity, contrary to the true hedonism of Aristippus.[132] Epicurus's letter to Menoeceus proved that belief in God was one of his first principles.[133] His negative reputation was in fact the result of the jealousies of the Stoics, who forged letters in which Epicurus attacks all other philosophies and promotes atheism.[134]

Parker's intentions were tripartite. First, he had developed a convincing argument from universal consent of the Vossian variety. Second, he clearly felt that he was adopting the best historical–philological case. We have encountered the serious scholarly attempt to uphold Cicero's reading of Epicurus in Gataker and Casaubon, but major continental scholars had adopted the revisionist reading independently of or alongside Gassendi (whose work Parker also knew well).[135] Of these, Parker drew on Gilles Ménage's extensive notes on Laërtius (printed in the same edition as Casaubon's), and on Johannes Jonsius's *De scriptoribus historiae philosophicae* (1659).[136] But there was also a third, more immediate, context for Parker's rescuing of the Greek atheists. Aware that pagans had thrown the accusation of atheism as much at the early Christians as at the Greek materialists whom he had condemned, Stillingfleet had been forced to argue that 'when the Heathens accused the *Christians* of *Atheism*', the cause had been Christian rejection of pagan ceremonies only; in the case of the Greek materialists, he found this limited aim 'not in the least pretended to by any of the[m]', for they had rejected both the ceremonies and the beliefs that underpinned them.[137] Parker saw this as dangerously fallacious: 'If the accusations of the gentiles are credible, not even Christians are acquitted; if not, the philosophers are innocent. Each is

---

[131] Ibid., 16–17: 'Caeterum Ego utcunque fateor *Epicuri* opinionem ab aestimatione Dei Deo prorsus indigna ortam esse (censuit enim Dei faelicitatem mundi cura & gubernatione turbatam esse, at quam anile est credere immensam sapientiam ulla cura vexari posse!) utcunque insuper agnoscam quicquid Dei Providentiam mundo abrogaverit proclives ad atheismum efficere, & universum Deo cultum abolere, tamen inficias eo *Epicurum* aut consulto Deos & religionem sustulisse, aut ab contemptu de iis erravisse'.

[132] Ibid., 21.      [133] Ibid., 23, citing DL x.123.      [134] Parker, *Tentamina*, 19.

[135] For Parker's extensive engagement with Gassendi on other subjects, see Levitin, 'Parker'.

[136] See Ménage, 'Observationes et emendationes', 258–83 (new pagination), drawing extensively on Gassendi, as admitted at 258; Jonsius, *De scriptoribus*, 195–6 (explicit attacking Cicero). On Jonsius, see Micheli, 'The history of philosophy in Germany in the second half of the seventeenth century', in Santinello I, at 388–97; Dal Pra, 'Giovanni Jonsio' (1948).

[137] Stillingfleet, *Origines*, 10.

condemned with the other, or neither'.[138] It was the consistency of the religious culture he had identified that explained the accusations of atheism levelled at Christians by those like the Emperor Julian: like the philosophers they rejected pagan ceremonies and like them they were accused of atheism.[139] Parker's personal and intellectual dislike of Stillingfleet would continue throughout his career.[140] However, there is no evidence of a personal animosity before the publication of *Tentamina*, so we must assume that Parker's reasons were at this point intellectual.

Partly, the difference was simply philological–historical: Parker was right to point out that his interpretation stemmed from a much more consistent vision of pagan religious culture. But there was also a more fundamental philosophical–theological issue at stake. Chapter 5 of the *Tentamina* included undoubtedly the most important early systematic critique of Descartes published in England.[141] Parker saw Descartes's proof of God's existence as an absurd piece of Platonic optimism that failed to recognise that all knowledge derived from sense experience, suggesting that Descartes was hubristically led to it by his proficiency in mathematics.[142] Parker's stated reason for challenging the Cartesian proof of God was that it had recently been adopted in English apologetics, namely in More's *Antidote*, Charleton's *Darkness of atheism*, and most importantly in Stillingfleet's *Origines sacrae*.[143] As we saw, Stillingfleet had denied that an Epicurean model of the understanding could lead to knowledge of God. Yet the whole of the theology developed by Parker in Book II of the *Tentamina* (i.e. the 'scholastic theology' of the title) depended on a strictly sense-based and anti-innatist model of the understanding. For Parker, spirit was unknowable, and God was to be known only through his effects (discussed by Parker

---

[138] Parker, *Tentamina*, 10–11: 'si itaque fidem mereantur Gentilium delationes, ne quidem Christiani absolvantur, sin minus, insontes Philosophi, adeo utrosque damnare par est, aut neutros'

[139] Ibid., 10: 'Cuius rei perquàm luculentissimi sunt testes, quotquot libros aut *Apologeticos* pro Christianis, aut *adversus Gentes* scripsere, quibus licet impensè desudatum sit, ut Christianum nomen ab ἀθεότητος criminatione perpurgarent, nihilo minus in plerosque, qui quoniam nomina Christianismo, ideo quoque paenas dederunt, tanquam Atheos atque omnimodae religionis hostes, animadversum est: & *Julianus*, teste *Sozomene*, ipsum Christianismum ἀθεότητος nomine designare solitur est'.

[140] As well many comments in his printed works, see Parker to Dodwell, 13 Nov 1680, Bod. MS Eng. letters c. 28, fols. 3ʳ–4ʳ.

[141] Pacchi, *Cartesio*, 118–35; Levitin, 'Parker', 55–9, which shows that Parker's argument was certainly derived from Gassendi.

[142] Parker, *Tentamina*, 157. Henry More had already repeatedly attributed Descartes's errors to over-mathematising: Gabbey, 'More', 186, 217. This sort of critique was also connected to the idea that Descartes was a philosophical 'enthusiast', well developed by this point (see Heyd, *Enthusiasm*, 109–43). For Parker's alignment of Descartes's proof with the Platonic idea that the intellect somehow acquired knowledge without sensation, see *Tentamina*, 163.

[143] Henry More, *An antidote against atheisme* (London, 1653), 6–8; Charleton, *Darkness*, 6–38; Stillingfleet, *Origines*, 367–74.

through the traditional Thomist–scholastic *via causalitatis, via eminentiae* and *via remotionis*).[144] Of course, this raised the spectre of materialism, which Parker evaded by simply accusing Epicurus (alongside the Stoics and Tertullian) of the same hubris as those who claimed to know that the soul *was* immaterial.[145] His whole philosophico–theological outlook – inspired as it was by Gassendi and by a tradition of scholastic nominalism – was fundamentally incompatible with Stillingfleet's, partly explaining their conflicting attitude to the Greek materialists. We thus emerge with a curious situation, where Stillingfleet, a convinced innatist and Cartesian, denies the argument from universal consent, whereas Parker, a dogmatic anti-innatist, argues for the theism of the traditional Greek 'atheists'. If this teaches us anything, it is that attempts to reduce early modern theological ideas to philosophical and ideological categories are doomed to over-simplification.

Understanding this also allows us to adopt a fresh perspective towards the fullest clerical-scholarly history of ancient matter theory published in seventeenth-century England: Ralph Cudworth's *True intellectual system*. We have dealt already with aspects of the huge fourth chapter (2.5, 3.6, also 5.4, 6.6 below); we turn now to the first three. The historiographical obsession with labelling Cudworth a 'Platonist' has obscured the fact that the contemporary with whom he engaged most on the issue of matter theory was Gassendi.[146] This should not be particularly surprising, since Cudworth's aim – like Parker's – was to show that the history of atomism would not offer succour to atheists; specifically, he argued, a host of early philosophers had combined atomism and a belief in immaterial substances before Democritus (and then Epicurus) turned that atomism into a pure atheistic materialism. This materialism in turn underpinned the determinism that was the overall target of the projected three volumes of the *System*.[147] Historically, Cudworth claimed, atheism had been either

---

[144] Parker, *Tentamina*, 295–304; Levitin, 'Parker'.    [145] Parker, *Tentamina*, 299–300.

[146] It should be noted, however, that three recent studies have slightly broken away from the Platonist mould to ask what Cudworth was actually doing as a scholar: Sellars, 'Stoics against Stoics in Cudworth's *A treatise of freewill*' (2012); Sellars, 'Cudworth on Stoic theology' (2011); Osborne, 'Ralph Cudworth's *The true intellectual system of the universe* and the presocratic philosophers' (2011): none of these recognises the debts to Gassendi.

[147] The *System*, whose aim is an attack on atheism and a proof of the existence of God, was only one part of a projected three-part work against 'fatal necessity', the rest of which is either lost or remains in manuscript in the British Library (see the description at *System*, sigs. [A4]$^{r-v}$). Part II was to deal with the existence in nature of objective moral distinctions; Part III with the reality of human freedom (draft versions of these parts are the *Treatise concerning eternal and immutable morality*, published from a now-lost manuscript in 1731, and the extensive manuscript notes in BL MSS Add. 4978–82, of which 4978 was published as *A treatise of freewill* in 1838. See Cudworth, *A treatise concerning eternal and immutable morality* (London, 1731); Cudworth, *A treatise of freewill*, ed. J. Allen (London, 1838), both available in an edition ed. by S. Hutton (Cambridge, 1996), which is that cited hereafter. The other manuscripts remain unpublished). Cudworth was planning a work on the objective existence of moral distinctions

materialist–atomist (either Democritean or 'Hylopathian') or animist ('Hylozoic' or 'Cosmoplastic'). What connected the two groups was materialistic determinism, based on a denial of God's operation in the world and the existence of immaterial substance; what differentiated them was the physical basis of their materialisms.[148] In turn, each atheism was a corruption of a previously theistic version of that philosophy.[149]

| General type of atheism | Specific type of atheism | Theistic precursor |
| --- | --- | --- |
| Atomist | Democritic–Epicurean | 'Pious' atomism (Moschus and the Italics) |
| Atomist | Hylopathian (Anaximander) | Thales |
| Animist | Hylozoic (Strato) | Aristotle |
| Animist | Cosmoplastic (some Stoics) | Uncorrupted Stoics (e.g. Zeno) |

Our concern at this point is with Cudworth's history of immaterialist atomism and its corruption into Democritean materialism. This history was targeted at what 'hath been of late confidently asserted … that never any of the ancient Philosophers dream'd of any such thing as Incorporeal Substance … [for] it was nothing but an upstart and new fangled Invention of some Bigotical Religionists'.[150] This can mean no one except Hobbes, although at first it appears that Cudworth is confused, conflating Hobbes's claim in chapter 4 of *Leviathan* that there can be no such thing as incorporeal substance with the critique of essentialist philosophy in chapter 46.[151] But elsewhere, Hobbes attributed the invention of incorporeal substance to Plato and Aristotle, making it clear that their pagan predecessors had held spirit to be

in the mid-1660s, leading to a falling out with Henry More, who began a similar project after finding out about Cudworth's, which had initially been preached as a college sermon (see the letters in *Worthington diary*, II, 157–67).

[148] For Cudworth's taxonomies of determinism, see esp. *System*, sig. A3$^{r-v}$. Determinism was not limited to atheists, for the theistic Stoics (sig. A3$^v$) and Calvinists (see Cudworth, *Immutable morality*, 14–15) also fell into its trap. For Cudworth's virulent anti-Calvinism, see his letter to Limborch: Universiteitsbibliotheek Amsterdam MS M.21.a (recounting his and the university's turn away from Calvinism). Linking Calvinist predestinarianism with Stoic determinism was an old anti-Calvinist polemical tool: for its appearance in England as early as the 1610s, see the notebook of a pupil of John Overall's, CUL MS Gg.1.29, fol. 52$^v$ rev. For a Cambridge contemporary of Cudworth making the same claim, see John North's notes in BL MS Add. 32514, fols. 173$^r$, 177$^v$–178$^r$.

[149] This is a slightly modified version of a similar table offered at Sellars, 'Cudworth on Stoic theology', 129.

[150] Cudworth, *System*, 18.

[151] Hobbes, *Leviathan*, 17, 207, 371–4 (=Malcolm, II, 60; III, 610, 1076–86). This has led to the confusion at Osborne, 'Cudworth and the presocratics', 224 (including the improbable assertion that Bacon may have been the target).

a very thin substance;[152] Cudworth clearly extrapolated from this that Hobbes thought that the pre-Platonic philosophers were corporealists.

On some points Cudworth simply followed Gataker, Casaubon, and Stillingfleet in relying on Cicero. For example, while it seems an obvious problem that Cudworth categorised Epicurus as a Democritic fatalist when Epicurus had unambiguously maintained the freedom of the will (DL x.133), Cudworth 'solved' it by parroting Cicero and claiming that Epicurus had introduced liberty of will into his philosophy from 'a Mind to Innovate Something, that he might not seem to have borrowed from Democritus', thus introducing a fundamental 'Contradictio[n] to the Tenour of his own Principles'.[153] Like Casaubon, Cudworth rejected entirely the revisionist attempt to resuscitate Epicurus's moral philosophy, in favour of the traditional Ciceronian view.[154]

If here Cudworth was adding little new, the real significance of his history of atomism was its detailed and critical defence of the narrative first proposed in print in a very primitive version by his friend More: that the atheist–materialist atomism developed by Leucippus and Democritus was only a corruption of a prior philosophy that combined atomist physics with immaterialist pneumatology. Cudworth's case is both philologically and philosophically very complex, but in reality can be broken down into two arguments. The first is strictly historical–philological: atomism was originally combined with immaterialism, and so was not an atheistic philosophy. This was true of Moses, but especially of Pythagoras and his followers, and then Empedocles. In short, this was the case for all the Italic philosophers in Laërtius's classficiation. They were to be counterpoised to the Ionian succession, whose later members descended into atheism because they did not recognise that all qualities were the productions of atomic motion, leading them to reify forms and qualities into actual entities, removing the need for immaterial substance. Cudworth's second argument might be called a semi-conjectural historical argument. From the philological–historical fact that the ancient philosophers all held *ex nihilo nihil fit* as a basic principle, Cudworth hypothesised that they must all have been

---

[152]   Hobbes, *Leviathan*, 211 (=Malcolm, III, 622); see also a similar passage inserted into the Latin *Leviathan*, 56 (=Malcolm, II, 167–9).

[153]   Cudworth, *System*. sig. *ᵛ; the unstated source is Cicero, *Fat.*, xx.48.

[154]   A neat summary is at BL MS Add. 4979, fol. 13ʳ: 'ffor though Epicurus hath been defended of late as if he had avowed yᵗ yᵉ pleasure of virtue, & tranquility of the mind arising from thence were yᵉ chiefest good, yet Torquatus in Tully tells us that it was his Maxime That *omnis voluptatis Animi strictur a voluptatibus corporis* yᵗ he acknowledged no other pleasure of yᵉ mind than such as did arise & proceed from yᵉ pleasures of yᵉ body'. See also *System*, 60–1; 83–4. Cudworth thought that Epicurus developed his system as an overreaction to the extreme immaterialism of Plato, using a rather loose paraphrase of Cicero, *Nat. Deor.*, I.8. This reading was common: see the variant in Richard Baxter, *The reasons of the Christian religion the first part . . . also an appendix defending the soul's immortality against the Somatists or Epicureans and other pseudo-philosophers* (London, 1667), 576 (also following Lactantius, *De ira Dei*, 13). Baxter's critique was important for popularising the term 'somatic atheist'.

atomist-immaterialists. This allowed the canon of atomist-immaterialists to be much expanded. Atheistic corruptions of atomic-immaterialism (i.e. those of Democritus and Epicurus) could be shown to stem, in part, from misunderstanding this principle.

Although he never stated it explicitly, and although his history of philosophy – founded on patterns of atheism rather than on doxography – is very un-Laërtian, Cudworth was still operating with Laërtius's divisions. His whole argument depended on the idea that Democritean atheist-atomism was a corruption of the pious atomism of those whom Laërtius placed at the heart of the Italic succession: Pythagoras and Empedocles. This has been obscured by Cudworth's famous invocation of Mo[s]chus/Moses as the originator of this pious atomism. However, it is clear that this was only a semi-speculative and unimportant addition to Cudworth's schematic, based primarily on his reading of Selden; it is certainly not the case that for Cudworth, 'the Greeks ... reached this understanding not just by the pure light of reason, but with assistance from God, indirectly mediated by way of Moses',[155] for Cudworth is very careful to point out that even if the philosophy was held by Moses, it had nothing to do with revelation.[156] Neither is it the case that there was something essentially neoplatonic about this conclusion:[157] the available discussions of Moschus, who first appeared in European scholarship in the edition of Iamblichus's *Life of Pythagoras* (1598) by the Frisian friar Johannes Arcerius, were by no means neoplatonic.[158] The whole idea that Cudworth was obsessed with Judaic primacy must be abandoned (see also 3.6 above).

---

[155] Osborne, 'Cudworth and the presocratics', 222. The same misreading is even more pronounced in Sutcliffe, *Judaism*, 68.

[156] Cudworth, *System*, 12: 'Some Phantastick Atomists perhaps would here catch at this, to make their Philosophy to stand by Divine Right, as owing its Original to Revelation; whereas Philosophy being not a Matter of Faith but Reason, Men ought not to affect (as I conceive) its Pedigree from Revelation'.

[157] As claimed in the much cited article by Sailor, 'Moses and atomism' (1964).

[158] Mentioned at DL, I.1; Strabo, citing Posidonius, is the source for the association with atomism and the pre-Trojan War chronology (*Geog.*, XVI.757); also Josephus, *Ant. Jud.*, 1.107. Isaac Casaubon also suggested that Mochus could be read as Moschus/Moses, but for philological reasons; he certainly did *not* align the Phoenician with the person of the prophet. The first to take that claim seriously was John Selden, from whom it passed to More and Cudworth (and Pierre-Daniel Huet). In the meantime, most serious scholars disputed the Moschus/Moses link (e.g. G. J. Vossius, Samuel Bochart), content simply to point out that there was a Phoenician naturalist or atomist who may or may not have had contact with the Hebrews. It was this line of thought that was picked up by Daniel Sennert; Gassendi considered the thesis, before deciding that Leucippus and Archelaus were the true first atomists, but by this point it had proved popular enough to enter pedagogical traditions: Adrian Heereboord's Aristotelian–Cartesian textbook synthesis also providing a Moschical lineage for corpuscularianism. This narrative is intended as a corrective both to the facts and the interpretation offered in Sailor, 'Moses', and the oft-cited article by McGuire and Rattansi, 'Newton and the "Pipes of Pan"' (1966), at 130.

But how could Cudworth achieve his main aim: to prove that the whole Italic succession consisted of atomists? First, he took as a sign of atomism not explicit statements of matter theory *per se*, but simply the idea that secondary qualities have no existence within the object, only in the perceiver. For this he cited Aristotle's well-known statement that 'the former Physiologers were generally out in this, in that they thought there was no Black or White without the Sight, nor not Bitter or Sweet without the Taste'.[159] This step was ingenious, as it allowed Cudworth to find this supposed 'sign' of atomism in many in whom there is no mention of atomic matter theory. The first figure who Cudworth interpreted on these terms was Protagoras.[160] But Cudworth's most important examples were Pythagoras and Empedocles, as he himself summarised his argument in the preface: 'it is certain, that divers of the *Italicks*, and particularly *Empedocles*, before *Democritus, physiologised atomically*'.[161] On the basis of an obscure passage in Stobaeus and an even more obscure epigram by Automedon, as well as some passages in Aristotle, he showed that the 'famous Pythagorean' Ecphantus, and the Pythagoreans more generally, held their famous monads to be atoms.[162]

This brilliant argument, however, is derived almost entirely from Gassendi.[163] Cudworth's debt to Gassendi – whose case that the presocratic philosophers had all been atomists was itself only an expansion of similar arguments to be found in natural philosophical defences of atomism like that of Daniel Sennert[164] – has never been recognised, but it confirms that there is little 'neoplatonic' about his narrative. Gassendi was also Cudworth's starting source for the claim that Empedocles had been an atomist, although here

The relevant sources are Iamblichus, *De vita Pythagorae, & protrepticae orationes ad philosophiam*, ed. J. Arcerius (2 vols, [Heidelberg], 1598), II, 4 (new pagination); Isaac Casaubon, *Animadversiones in Athenaei Dipnosophistas* (London, 1600), 151 (the original edition of Athenaeus of 1597 does not include Casaubon's commentary); John Selden, *De jure naturali*, 22–3; Henry More, 'An Appendix to the Defence of the Philosophick Cabbala', in *A collection of several philosophical writings* (London, 1662), 102–3 (new pagination); Pierre-Daniel Huet, *Demonstratio evangelica* (3rd edn, Paris, 1690 [1st edn=1679]), 53–4, 189; G. J. Vossius, *De historicis Graecis libri quatuor* (London, 1624), 307–8; Samuel Bochart, *Geographia sacra* (3rd edn, London, 1692 [1st edn=1646]), col. 777 (Theophilus Gale claimed that Bochart told him that Moschus's philosophy 'was nothing else, but the Historie of the Creation' [*Court, II. Of philosophie*, 62]); Sennert, *Hypomnemata*, 89; Gassendi, *Animadversiones*, 180; Gassendi, *Syntagma philosophicum* in *Opera*, I, 257; Heereboord, *Meletemata philosophica*, 385b.

[159] Cudworth, *System*, 9–10, quoting and translating Aristotle, *De anima*, III.2, 426ᵃ20–2 ('ἀλλ' οἱ πρότερον φυσιολόγοι τοῦτο οὐ καλῶς ἔλεγον, οὐθὲν οἰόμενοι οὔτε λευκὸν οὔτε μέλαν εἶναι ἄνευ ὄψεως, οὐδὲ χυμὸν ἄνευ γεύσεως'); Mosheim misidentifies Cudworth's source at *System* 1845, 15, n. 9.

[160] Cudworth, *System*, 10–11, slightly mis-quoting Plato, *Theaetetus*, 153ᵈ–154ᵃ.

[161] Cudworth, *System*, sig. *2ʳ.

[162] Ibid., 13, 16; Stobaeus, *Ecl.* I.21.3 (=DK 51a2–5); Aristotle, *Met.*, 1080ᵇ9; Automedon in *Anth. Gr.*, 11.50.

[163] Gassendi, *Syntagma*, in *Opera*, I, 256a.    [164] See 5.3 below.

Cudworth added his own evidence, including an impressively obscure verse fragment of which Mosheim wrote despairingly, 'Where the learned Doctor got this verse of Empedocles, I leave to others to find out, having in vain searched for it with great care in a number of books both ancient and modern',[165] but which we can now identify as coming from Simplicius's *Physics* commentary (=fr. 16).[166] After a short listing of additional putative atomists (Xenocrates, Heraclides, Asclepiades, Diodorus, and Metrodorus Chius), Cudworth could now make his main historical conclusion: that the key source for Democritus and Leucippus being the first of the atomists, Aristotle, in fact only meant that the two were 'the first that ever made this Physiology to be a complete and entire Philosophy by it self', that is to say, without incorporeal substance.[167]

All that was left was to show that the Italic atomist lineage he had just identified also incorporated immaterial substances into their philosophy.[168] Particularly important was the example of Pherecydes of Syros (*fl. c.* 540 BC),

---

[165] *System* 1845, I, 27, n. 9.

[166] Cudworth, *System*, 14–16 (14–15 for the citation of Simplicius, *In phys.*, 33.18). For Gassendi on Empedocles: *Syntagma*, in *Opera*, I, 257b. The fragments of Empedocles had been collected in Estienne, ed., *Poesis philosophica*, 17–31 (with emendations by Scaliger at 216), but fr. 16 was not included. Cudworth then adduced a host of further evidence, in particular to demonstrate that Empedocles's four elements could have been made up of atoms, and that his theory of vision was also atomic – here Cudworth drew a clever parallel between Plato's description of Empedocles's theory of vision as containing 'ἀπορροὴ σχημάτων' (an 'effluence of figures') and Aristotle's description of Democritus's atoms as 'σχήματα' (Cudworth, *System*, 15, citing Plato, *Meno*, 76ᵈ). Cudworth does not offer a citation of Aristotle, but I suspect he was thinking of *Part. an.*, I.1, 640ᵇ29–31; 641ᵃ5. Cudworth also recognised that Aristotle was more generally favourable to his case, as he often compared Empedocles and Democritus (e.g. he cites *De caelo*, III.7, 305ᵇ1–5).

[167] Cudworth, *System*, 16–17 (see also the positing of the original problem at 8–10, quoting, without citation, *Met.*, I, 985ᵇ5; *De anima*, I, 404ᵃ2–9; *Gen. corr.*, I, 315ᵇ7–13 (also relevant is 325ᵃ1–3)). Cudworth also extracted a more positive argument from Aristotle: eliding *De sens.*, 442ᵃ30–442ᵇ1 and 442ᵇ11–13, he had Aristotle stating that 'Democritus *and most of the Physiologers … make all Sense to be Touch, {and resolve sensible Qualities into the Figures of insensible Parts or Atoms}*' (9 – I have placed the amalgamation from 442ᵇ11–13 in braces – this passage is then cited again when the 'Aristotle on atomism' problem is discussed at 17). To achieve this meaning, Cudworth had to change, in his Greek quotation, the singular verb 'ἀνάγει' (here 'resolve') in 'εἰς δὲ τὰ σχήματα ἀνάγει τοὺς χυμούς' into the plural 'ἀνάγουσι'. This led Mosheim (*System* 1845 14, n. 8) to breathless accusations of duplicity, but Cudworth's sense is surely mitigated by Aristotle's preceding 'οἱ δὲ τὰ ἴδια εἰς ταῦτα ἀνάγουσιν, ὥσπερ Δημόκριτος·'.

[168] Cudworth spent some time (18–20) showing that this was the case for Plato and Aristotle, although it is not clear why, since they were not included in his canon of atomists; the same can be said for his treatment of Thales, whom he links to Phoenicia by drawing, without acknowledgement, on the notes to the classic work of seventeenth-century apologetics, Grotius's *De veritate*. Cf. Cudworth, *System*, 21, with Hugo Grotius, *De veritate religionis Christianae. Editio nova, additis annotationibus, in quibus testimonia* (Leiden, 1640), 'Annotationes' (separate pagination), 33–46. Both include the same parallel between 'מרחפת' (in Gen. 1:2) and Sanchoniathon's 'ἠράσθη τὸ πνεῦμα τῶν ἰδίων ἀρχῶν' (Eusebius, *Praep. Ev.*, I.10).

of whom Cicero said that that he was the first to believe in the immateriality of the soul. For Cudworth, not only did this offer a chronologically early immaterialism, but Laërtius had also stated that Pherecydes may have taught Pythagoras: obvious grist for Cudworth's mill.[169] He then again evoked the obscure Pythagorean Ecphantus, the evidence for whom (to be found in Stobaeus) was particularly convenient, as it suggested that Ecphantus was an atomist who simultaneously proposed a world 'ordered and governed by a divine providence'.[170] The main scholarly achievement of this section, however, was a long attempt to rescue Empedocles from the charges laid upon him by Aristotle: making knowledge purely sensory, compounding the soul out of the four elements, and attributing the formation of animals to chance. Modern scholarship knows Empedocles as the author of two poems in hexameter verse, *On nature* and *Purifications*, the former focusing primarily on natural phenomena, the latter written as the autobiography of a divine being.[171] Recognising this division was not beyond early modern scholars;[172] although Cudworth never did so explicitly, it is notable that his attempt to discredit Aristotle and to present Empedocles as a member of the Italic tradition of atomist-theism is based almost entirely on the fragments now ascribed to *Purifications* (this even led him to speculate that the anti-Empedoclean sections of Aristotle were later corruptions).[173] Cudworth's scholarship is not always fair to Aristotle, but his assessment of Empedocles's having a relationship to Pythagoreanism and being a theist was both correct and pioneering.[174]

The evidence Cudworth gathered for the atomism and immaterialism of those we would now call the presocratics was impressive, even if it depended on linguistic fluidity, turning all talk of microparticulate structure into 'atomism'. The problem, however, was that the more scholarly miracles he performed to fill in the gaps in this attractive general picture, the more incomplete it looked: if one had to work so hard to turn Pythagoras and Empedocles into

---

[169] Cudworth, *System*, 21, quoting (without acknowledgement) Cicero, *Disp. Tusc.*, 1.16 and alluding to DL. 1.119. See also *System*, 195, 370, 529, 727.

[170] Cudworth, *System*, 26; Stobaeus, *Ecl.* 1.21.3 (=DK 51a2–5).

[171] Although some now consider them as one; the key new source, not available to early modern scholars, is the Strasbourg papyrus: Martin and Primavesi, eds., *L'Empédocle de Strasbourg* (1999).

[172] Stanley, *History*, 432, has 'he wrote Books concerning *Nature* and *Lustrations*, which extended to 5000 verses'. See also [Thomas Birch?], 'Empedocles', in Pierre Bayle, *The general dictionary, historical and critical* (10 vols, London, 1734–41), v (1737), 25–9, esp. 27. Cudworth speaks of '*Empedocles* his Poems' (25, my emphasis). All, I suspect, stem from Estienne's introduction in *Poesis philosophica*, 6–7.

[173] Cudworth, *System*, 22–6, esp. 25. See further the useful discussion in Osborne, 'Cudworth and the presocratics', 226–7.

[174] See e.g. *System*, 26 for Cudworth's use of the obscure but relevant fragment from Tzetzes, *Chiliades*, XIII.464.80 (=fr. 134), although in this case he may have got it from Estienne, *Poesis philosophica*, 30.

atomists, what of the other philosophers? It is no surprise that scholars from Mosheim to the present day have smirked at Cudworth's attempt to construct a lineage for pre-Democritean atomism. But, it seems to me, they have all misunderstood Cudworth's case. For as well as the examples of Pythagoras and Empedocles, Cudworth offered a second, semi-conjectural historical argument. It was semi-conjectural because, while it depended on philosophical reasoning, that reasoning rested on a philological–historical base. This base prefigured the key finding of nineteenth-century scholarship on the presocratics: that their natural philosophies were responding to the proposition that *ex nihilo nihil fit*.[175] Once again, Cudworth was here drawing on Gassendi, who had offered a large compendium of ancient philosophers who had held the doctrine.[176] Following Gassendi, Cudworth (correctly) identified Parmenides as the originator of the doctrine, tracing it through Melissus, Zeno of Elea, Xenophanes (in short, the Eleatics), then Anaxagoras and Empedocles, finishing with the crowning quotation from Aristotle, that it was a common opinion 'that it is impossible, that any thing should be made out of nothing'.[177] Like Gassendi, Cudworth proceeded from this incontestable fact to the claim that this general doctrine was a propaedeutic for 'establishing some atomical physiology or other ... as takes away all Forms and Qualities of Bodies (as Entities really distinct from the Matter and Substance)'.[178]

The logic is clear – if qualities cannot arise from nothing, they must arise from matter.[179] This hardly leads to an *atomic* physics (with indivisible particles, etc.). But Cudworth was not really concerned with atomism as a physical theory *per se*, but with the dualism that he claimed underpinned it. 'This very same Principle of Reason which induced the Ancients to reject Substantial Forms and Qualities of Bodies, and to Physiologize Atomically, led them also unavoidably to assert Incorporeal Substances.'[180] Seeing that life (including animal life) could not be explained either by matter or by new qualities, the atomists had to posit an incorporeal substance: 'And now it is already manifest, that from the same Principle of Reason before mentioned, That *Nothing of it self can come from Nothing nor go to Nothing, the Ancient Philosophers were induced likewise to assert the Soul's Immortality, together with its Incorporeity or Distinctness from the Body*'.[181] Indeed, it was this thought-process that led

---

[175] See e.g. Rapp, 'Friedrich Nietzsche and pre-Platonic philosophy' (2011), 352–4.
[176] Gassendi, *Syntagma*, in *Opera*, I, 232b–234a; it was also discussed by Gataker, in 'Annotationes', in *De rebus suis*, 130a–b (commenting on IV.4, 'οὐδὲν γὰρ ἐκ τοῦ μηδενὸς ἔρχεται, ὥσπερ μηδ' εἰς τὸ οὐκ ὂν ἀπέρχεται').
[177] Cudworth, *System*, 31–2, quoting Aristotle, *De caelo*, III.1, 298ᵇ14 (Parmenides and Melissus); Simplicius, *In phys.*, I.4, 34ᵛ26–8 (Parmenides), [ps.-]Aristotle, *De Meliss. Xenoph. Gorg.*, i; Stephanus, *Poesis philosophica*, 36 (Xenophanes); [ps.-]Aristotle, *De Meliss. Xenoph. Gorg.*, ii (Empedocles); Aristotle, *Phys.*, I.4, 187ᵃ26.
[178] Cudworth, *System*, 32.     [179] Cf. Gassendi, *Syntagma*, in *Opera*, I, 234a–41a.
[180] Cudworth, *System*, 35.     [181] Ibid., 35–8, quotation from 38.

the ancient incorporealists to posit the pre-existence of souls, for it would have been inconsistent for them to believe in the production of souls *ex nihilo*; a conclusion that it would still be rational to accept were it not for the revealed knowledge that souls are 'Created by God immediately, and infused in Generation'.[182]

Proceeding from *ex nihilo nihil fit* thus led the ancients logically to an incorporealist atomism; Empedocles was again the star witness.[183] Democritus and Epicurus misunderstood and corrupted this generally accepted doctrine, using it to limit God's creative powers.[184] This was an even more ingenious turning of Gassendi's findings to apologetic ends, and, ironically, against Gassendi's beloved Epicurus.

All in all, this was a brilliant piece of historical speculation, with a clear pay-off. However, there is an obvious issue on which Cudworth seems genuinely susceptible to contextually valid criticism. This is his easy assumption of a logical move from *ex nihilo nihil fit* to substance dualism. Why might the ancients not have considered seminal atoms – much publicised by Gassendi and others[185] – as the principles of life, negating the need for an immaterial substance? Cudworth dealt with vitalist atheism in great length elsewhere in the *System*, but he assigned it not to the atomists but either to the corrupters of Aristotelian hylomorphism (Strato of Lampsacus) or the later, 'cosmoplastic' Stoics (5.4 below). Why could those who held *ex nihilo nihil fit* as a principle not also have been vitalists, attributing independent powers of life to matter, as Mosheim would later keep asking with increasing degrees of exasperation?[186]

Mosheim failed to understand the complexity of Cudworth's story however, because he did not read chapter one in the light of chapter three, as was Cudworth's intention. Here Cudworth argued that Italic atomists wrote against those whom he variously labels as the 'old materialists', 'atheistic Materialists', and, ultimately, the 'hylopathian' atheists. The great error of these materialists was precisely that of reifying qualities separate from matter, and so,

taking it for granted, that *Matter* or Extended Bulk is the only *Substance*, and that the *Qualities* and *Forms* of Bodies, are Entities really distinct from those Modifications of Magnitude, Figure, Size, Motion or Rest . . . [thence] conclud[ing], that the *Souls* of all Animals, as well as those other *Qualities* and *Forms* of Bodies, were *Generated* out of the Matter, and *Corrupted* again into it, and consequently that every thing that is in the whole World, besides the *Substance* of *Matter*, was *Made* or *Generated*, and might be again *Corrupted*.[187]

---

[182] Ibid., 38–9, 43.    [183] Ibid., 40–1.

[184] Ibid., 30–2, quoting Lucretius, *Rer. nat.*, I.149, 159, 215; DL, IX.44 (Democritus); DL, X.38–9 (Epicurus).

[185] Hirai, *Concept*; Hirai, 'Le concept de semence de Pierre Gassendi' (2003).

[186] E.g., *System* 1845, 77, n. 8: 'Nor do I understand, why he who considers nothing to perish but to pass merely into a new form, cannot allow forms and qualities to matter'.

[187] Cudworth, *System*, 115–6.

Cudworth's reasons for delineating this hylopathian atheism have always been murky: Mosheim was puzzled as to their difference from the hylozoists;[188] others tend simply to ignore them. We see now that they were the atheistic 'Other' of Cudworth's Italic atomists, their error being the reification of qualities partly from a misunderstanding of the logical consequences of *ex nihilo nihil fit*.[189] In turn, the Italic atomists could now be understood as arguing 'in way of opposition to those atheistic Materialists', from a correct understanding of that same basic principle.[190]

What was the textual evidence for the existence of this hylopathian atheism, which no one had previously identified? Cudworth found it in a highly creative reading of Aristotle. He offered a set of well-known passages in which Aristotle condemned those who only assigned a material cause for all the activity in the universe, and thus could not account for the origin of motion.[191] As Cudworth knew, this could just as easily have applied to Democritus and Leucippus. But, he argued, Aristotle would hardly have described them (as he did at *Metaphysics* 938[b]7) as 'some of the first philosophers' ('τινὲς τῶν πρώτων φιλοσοφησάντων'); moreover, the Stagirite never mentioned atoms when discussing these early materialists, but only their resolution of all things into ὕλη (matter) and πάθη τῆς ὕλης (a phrase never used by Aristotle, and rather broadly translated by Cudworth as 'the passions or affections, qualities and forms of matter').[192] Aristotle must have meant someone else, and Cudworth found his answer in the same long passage from *Metaphysics* 983[b]. In *De caelo*, discussing materialist theories of generation and corruption, Aristotle briefly mentioned Hesiod as a proponent of the view that all matter, having been produced from one original substance, was in a constant state of flux (III, 298[b]27–34). In this *Metaphysics* passage (983[b]7–984[a]17), he linked the view that 'the principles which were of the nature of matter were the only principles of things' with (A) 'the ancients who ... first framed accounts of the gods' making 'Ocean and Tethys the parents of creation' (i.e. those like Hesiod); (B) with the philosophy of the Ionic sect, derived from Thales, through to Anaximenes and Anaxagoras. On (A), early modern scholars devoted much labour to attempts to decipher the theology contained in the ancient poets.[193]

---

[188] *System* 1845, I, 179, n. 7.     [189] Cudworth, *System*, 116; see also 113–14.

[190] Ibid., 114; see also 116: 'these Materialists [i.e. the Hylopathians] being sometimes assaulted by the ... Italick Philosophers'.

[191] Cudworth, *System*, 111–16, citing *Met.*, I, 983[a]7–12; 948[b]10–15.

[192] Cudworth, *System*, 123.

[193] Although this scholarship remains largely unexplored, for a start that could be much supplemented, see Stroumsa, *New science*, 49–61. An important English example not discussed there (or anywhere else) is James Windet's *De vita functorum statu* (p. 92, n. 301 above): see e.g. the argument about Homer at 7–8 and the long comparison of the Hebrew underworld, She'ol (שאול) and Greek *materia prima* – supposedly found in the works of both poets and philosophers – at 19–71.

Cudworth drew not only on his own reading of Homer, but also on the older work of Saumaise on Aristophanes's discussion of the world's beginning with Chaos and Night (*Birds*, 693–700), which the French scholar had interpreted as a report of a materialistic account of generation derived from the Egyptians.[194] Yet Cudworth's main interest was not theogonic poetry, but philosophy. So he simply followed in greater detail the rest of the discussion from the *Metaphysics* passage, and ascribed hylopathian atheism to the Ionic sect *in toto* (Anaximander, Anaximenes, Diogenes, and Hippon).[195] The Italic atomists thus opposed the 'hylopathian' Ionics.[196] Cudworth's one deviation from Aristotle was to exculpate Thales from Aristotle's accusation of being the 'founder' of the atheistic philosophy, given the statements to the contrary in Laërtius and Cicero; here he followed a standard early modern pattern.[197]

From a few fragments in Aristotle, Cudworth thus reconstructed an atheist philosophy – tied to the Ionic succession – that is a direct counterpoint to the immaterialist atomism of the Italics. This obviously served Cudworth's overall aims: modern materialist atheism could now be presented as the repeat of an Ionic error that had already been defeated by the Italics. Just as importantly, this account offered Cudworth a wonderful degree of historical consistency. We can see this from his treatment of Anaxagoras. As Cudworth had explained in chapter 1, Anaxagoras had been the one atomist who *had* adopted the philosophy of qualities, with his doctrine of *homeomeria*, where the atoms constituting a substance have the properties of that substance. Anaxogaran *homeomeria* had been mocked by Lucretius, and early modern commentators followed this mockery, not least Cudworth: 'These Atoms being supposed to be endued originally with so many several Forms and Qualities Essential to them, and Inseparable from them, there was indeed a wide difference betwixt his

---

[194] Cudworth, *System*, 120–3 (123 mispaginated as 117). Cudworth, without giving a citation, was thinking of Claude Saumaise, *Plinianae exercitationes in Caii Iulii Solini Polyhistora* (Paris, 1629), 435b (although this is not listed in *Bibliotheca Cudworthiana*): ' ... secundum Aegyptios terra posterius creata quam coelum & astra. Eadem antiquissimorum Graecorum fuit sententia, ab Aegyptiis sumpta. Nam avium genus prius editum quam terra esset condita crediderunt, ut ex his Aristophanis versibus patet'. The discussion is of Aristophanes, *Birds*, v.413.

[195] Cudworth, *System*, 124–9. Hippon, not mentioned in Aristotle, would have fitted Cudworth's scheme not only because Simplicius reports that he was an atheist, but also that he held the universe to be generated from fire; Cudworth does not give a source, but he was surely using Simplicius, *In phys.*, xxiii.21–9.

[196] Cudworth, *System*, 380, using a perfectly apt quotation from Iamblichus, *Protr.*, Symbol 36 (=Iamblichus, *Exhortation to philosophy ... including the letters of Iamblichus and Proclus' commentary on the Chaldean oracles*, eds. and trans., T. M. Johnson and S. Neuville (Grand Rapids, 1988 [1st edn=1907]), 110): 'reverence above all the Italic philosophy, which speculates upon incorporeal essences in themselves, in preference to the Ionic, which chiefly investigates bodies'.

[197] Cudworth, *System*, 123–9; see also e.g., Stanley, *History*, 6a–b; Parker, *Disputationes de Deo*, 14.

Philosophy and the Atomical'.[198] So Cudworth was pushing at an open door when he castigated Anaxagoras, but his interpretation was novel: Anaxagoras had fallen into error from 'not being able to understand the [Italic] Atomical *Hypothesis*'. Crucially, this was because as well as being a failed atomist, Anaxagoras was a successor of the Ionics. When Cudworth came to the discussion of the hylopathians in chapter 3, he could explain Anaxagoras's deviation from Italic atomism through the residual influence of the Ionic philosophy of reified qualities. And so he could reinterpret perhaps the most famous statement of all about Anaxagoras: Aristotle's claim that he was unique in making νοῦς (mind) an ordering force (*De anima*, I, 405$^b$20). By this, Cudworth explained, Aristotle simply meant that Anaxagoras was the first *of the Ionics* to add this theistic element to his philosophy; plenty of other philosophers had been theists before him.[199]

There is one other issue in his history of atomism on which Cudworth was, from his earliest reception, accused of inconsistency. In 1.42, he finally came to explain the disappearance of Pythagoric atomism, attributing its decline to its double corruption by Democritus and Leucippus on one hand and Plato and Aristotle on the other. The former adopted only the materialist atomism, the latter only the 'Theology and Doctrine of Incorporeals, but Unbodied, and Devested of its most Proper and convenient Vehicle, the Atomical Physiology'.[200] The explanation for Democritus's and Leucippus's departure from Pythagoric atomism was that 'being Atheistically inclined [they] quickly perceived that they could not in the ordinary way of Physiologizing, suffi-ciently secure themselves against a Deity, nor effectually urge Atheism upon others'.[201] Mosheim reserved one of his more scathing footnotes for this explanation.[202] More importantly for us, his critique was already being pre-empted by Cudworth's near-contemporaries in England. In the British Library, there is a copy of the *System*, beautifully bound in red morocco leather, with extensive annotations by John Sheffield (1647–1721), third earl of Mulgrave and future first duke of Buckingham.[203] Sheffield's interest in the ancient atomists was strong enough for him later to write a translation of Epicurus's *Letter to Menoeceus*.[204] One assumes that it is in preparation for this work that he made annotations on Cudworth, for the notes are almost entirely on the passages on ancient atomism (although he was also interested in Cudworth's discussion of the history of trinitarianism in chapter 4). The notes are generally

[198] Cudworth, *System*, 16; Lucretius, *Rer. nat.*, 1.891–2. One exception is Daniel Sennert, who claimed that Anaxagoras, like Empedocles and Democritus, believed in the emergence of new forms upon mixture; he offered no evidence (*Hypomnemata physica*, 121–2).
[199] Cudworth, *System*, 380; see also 117.     [200] Ibid., 51.     [201] Ibid.
[202] *System* 1845, 93, n. *.     [203] Sankey, 'Sheffield, John', *ODNB*.
[204] John Sheffield, Duke of Buckingham, *The works of John Sheffield, Earl of Mulgrave, Marquis of Normandy, and Duke of Buckingham* (London, 1723), 239–48.

fair-minded, supporting and attacking Cudworth in equal measure. However, beside Cudworth's claim that Democritus and Leucippus adopted atomism only to 'secure their Atheism', Sheffield anticipated Mosheim's remarks almost exactly:

This is a strange supposition of the Authour, as if Democritus &c made theyr Atomick scheme only for the sake of Atheism; whereas Atheism seems only a necessary consequence of theyr philosophy; tho it appears that the first Atomicks did not thinck it so, & therefore were no Atheists; but pretended at least to beleeve something besides matter for the cause of all Cogitation.[205]

Other early readers made the same criticism in print.[206] What all these critics failed to recognise was that Cudworth was not, as they claimed, assuming *a priori* the atheism of Democritus and Leucippus. Rather, he placed them in the context of an ancient Greek theological battle between atheists and theists, which, he believed, ran alongside the history of philosophy. His evidence for this was a passage from Plato's *Laws* (x.888$^c$), where the Athenian stranger proposes to admonish a depraved youth by telling him that 'you and your friends are not the first nor the only persons to embrace this tenet as your doctrine about gods'. Cudworth proposed that 'friends' here was an allusion to Democritus, Leucippus, and Protagoras; more importantly, he could use it, alongside other evidence, as proof of an ancient theist–atheist battle in Greek culture.[207] The 'hylopathian' poets of the 'fabulous age', such as Hesiod, were further testimony to this ancient battle. Both the hylopathians and the Democritean atheists thus designed their philosophical systems as a contribution to this age-old debate between theists and atheists. Indeed, the atheistic atomists knew about the hylopathians, but deviated from them because they 'were really convinced, that it [the atomic hypothesis] was not only more Ingenious, but also more agreeable to Truth; [than] the other by Real Qualities and Forms', as indeed it was.[208]

The full elegance of Cudworth's history of atomism now emerges. Its sophistication and originality – the debts to Gassendi notwithstanding – is worth noting: it was no less elaborate than would be the nineteenth-century attempts to forge connections between the various presocratics. Summarised, it was a narrative of a battle between Greek theists and atheists that simultaneously mapped on to

---

[205] Cudworth, *System* (BL, Shelfmark: 676.g.17), 131.
[206] M. S. [Matthew Smith?], *A philosophical discourse of the nature of rational and irrational souls* (London, 1695), 1.
[207] Cudworth, *System*, 111; see also 18, quoting from *Soph.*, 246$^a$7–$^b$2 (on materialists), although Cudworth offers no justification for his claim that Plato here 'tells us, that there had been always, as well as then there was, a perpetual War and Controversie in the World ... betwixt these two Parties or Sets of men [i.e. incorporealists and corporealists]'; it is far more natural to assume that Plato was simply referring to Democritus, etc.
[208] Cudworth, *System*, 131.

Laërtius's division between the Italics (immaterialist atomists) and the Ionics (hylopathian atheists). Confused Anaxagoras straddled the two, but was nonetheless a theist. Italic atomism was corrupted by Democritus and Leucippus into atomist materialism, and by Plato and Aristotle into pure pneumatology. Despite these corruptions, this Italic philosophy offered an answer to all atheist objections, demonstrating the existence of created material and immaterial matter from the basic principle of *ex nihilo nihil fit*, on which everyone agreed.

|  | **Theism** | **Atheism** |
| --- | --- | --- |
| **Pre-history** | Moschus | Homer and Hesiod |
| **Philosophical history** | Italics (atomists) | Ionics (hylopathians) |
|  | Pherecydes | *Thales* |
|  | Pythagoras | Anaximander |
|  | Empedocles | Anaximenes |
|  | Ecphantus | Hippon |
|  |  | Diogenes |
|  | *Anaxagoras* | *Anaxagoras* |
| **Corrupt philosophies** | Plato | Democritus |
|  | Aristotle | Leucippus |
|  |  | Epicurus |

It is a triumph of Cudworth's scholarship that the only exception that needs to be made to the above schematic is Thales's theism; this is no loss, since Laërtius himself was ambiguous about whether Thales or Anaximander should be held as the founder of the Ionic succession.[209]

On the other hand, it is clear why Cudworth's history of atomism has baffled so many of its readers, from contemporaries through to Mosheim and to the present day. As we have seen, a full context for Italic atomism, introduced extensively in chapter 1, only becomes available upon the encounter with hylopathian atheism in chapter 3. Hylopathian atheism meanwhile, with its errors stemming from reified forms and qualities, sounds a lot like the vitalist atheism that Strato Lampsacus supposedly derived from his perverted Aristotelianism (see 5.4 below), as even Cudworth acknowledged.[210] Just as important is the question of form and genre. As a work of scholarship, even heavyweights like Mosheim struggled to keep up. As a work of apologetics, there was little hope, and we shall find Cudworth being plundered for whatever a reader wanted, with the bigger picture inevitably becoming lost. Crucially, however, Cudworth believed that contemporaries *would* understand him because he was building on the successful model of Gassendi. Cambridge 'Platonism' this was not.

---

[209] DL, I.13.    [210] Cudworth, *System*, 130–1.

## 5.3    Natural philosophical histories of matter theory

Natural philosophers certainly concerned themselves with this kind of scholarship and religio–historical speculation on the ancient atomists; not only Newton's reading of Cudworth (see below), but also Boyle's extensive notes on Epicureanism – made in preparation for an ultimately unwritten treatise 'On atheism' – testify to this.[211] But for the most part, they were far more concerned with ancient atomism *qua* natural philosophy, only bringing up the theological consequences once they had decided that the philosophy was unstable.[212] Some of Gassendi's conclusions were widely accepted. That Democritus and Epicurus were physical rather than point atomists became a commonplace, to the extent that I have been able to find only one post-1650 natural philosopher claiming the contrary.[213] Speculation about *semina*, which Gassendi had done much to propagate, took on a life of its own, outside of his Epicurean–atomist framework.[214] However, this did not lead to an acceptance of Gassendi's observational Epicurus *tout court*. Several traditions of English natural philosophy came together so that by the 1670s, it was widely held that Epicurus's atomism was a speculative quasi-metaphysical system whose results were incompatible with experimental method.

### 5.3.1    Aristotle the atomist: Digby and White

Before we tell that story, we must investigate another 'failed' tradition: that of Aristotle the atomist. Discussing Anaxgoras's philosophy in *Physics*, I.4 ($187^{b}13$–$188^{a}5$), Aristotle suggested that there is a smallest size of matter on which a form can impose itself. These *minima naturalia* enjoyed a varied reception and interpretation in medieval and Renaissance philosophy, and certainly helped pave the way for later microparticulate theories.[215] Meanwhile, in book I of *De generatione et corruptione* ($328^{a}10$–12), Aristotle had asserted that a true mixture occurred when the ingredients combined to produce true homogeneity, rather than a mere juxtaposition of parts. Traditional scholastic

---

[211] *Boyle on atheism.*

[212] I thus disagree with the overall argument in Mayo, *Epicurus* (see e.g. 112: 'As the traditional vehicle of the atomic physics, Epicureanism had affiliations with both Descartes and the Baconians of the Royal Society. But in its essential spirit it was so radically antagonistic to the Christian attitude as to get itself quite consistently deplored and abused by the Church and its philosophic allies'). Following Mayo, most of the literature has concentrated on the natural philosophers' *religious* concerns about Epicurus: see e.g. Wilson, *Epicureanism*, 224–5; Osler, 'Baptizing'.

[213] This exception is John Twysden, in his *Medicina veterum vindicata* (London, 1666), 141, 144, directly repeating the accusation at Aristotle, *Physics*, v, $265^{b}29$. On Twysden, see below.

[214] See e.g. the account of Parker in Levitin, 'Parker', 52–5, and the discussion below.

[215] The best summary is now Murdoch, 'The medieval and Renaissance tradition of *minima naturalia*' (2001).

interpretation suggested that the mixture had its own new substantial form. But a deviant alchemical tradition, epitomised in the *Summa perfectionis* of Geber (supposedly eighth-century Arabic, but actually composed at the end of the thirteenth century), argued that 'an [Aristotelian] homoemerous substance is one where the juxtaposed particles retain their own identity but are united with sufficient cohesion that they resist the analytical agents at the alchemist's disposal'.[216] In the sixteenth and early seventeenth centuries, the alchemical and the *minima naturalia* readings of Aristotle came to be combined, leading to a variety of microparticulate readings of Aristotle.[217]

This tradition of a corpuscularian Aristotle was inherited by two major English philosophers of our period: Kenelm Digby and Thomas White.[218] This is not to say that it could not be found elsewhere, including in a pedagogical context. In Scotland, for example, by the 1650s an M.A. candidate at Aberdeen, although he explicitly rejected Sébastien Basson's rehabilitation of the pre-Aristotelian atomists, drew on the anti-Aristotelian William Pemble (4.1 above) to equate the elements with the constituent parts of bodies, rejecting both prime matter and substantial forms as later scholastic additions to Aristotle's own doctrine.[219] Whilst I have not found any textbooks widely available in England promoting an atomist Aristotle, I do not rule out that further investigation might discover a larger pedagogical reach of this image.[220]

With White and Digby, the problem is establishing the lines of influence.[221] White's *De mundo* (1642) contains references to *particulae minimae*, but a key passage reveals that these were cribbed from Digby's *Two treatises*, of which White almost certainly saw a manuscript version.[222] Whence, then, did Digby obtain his belief in Aristotle the atomist?

---

[216] Newman, 'Experimental corpuscular theory', 297.

[217] Ibid.; Newman, *Atoms and alchemy.*     [218] See 4.2 and 4.4 above.

[219] Meldrum, *Theses philosophicae*, 14: 'Corporis partes essentiales, dicuntur principia. De quibus, discrepantes adeo, et ridiculae proponuntur veterum sententiae, ut cachinno potius excipiantur, quam ratione. Nec mirum, cum ex *Aristoteles* (quem sublestae in hoc puncto fidei arguunt quidam nominatim *Sebat. Basso.*) colligantur scriptis. Corpus naturae ex atomis heterogeneis componi, communis fuerat veterum, ante exortum *Aristotelem*, sententia. Hanc in corpore misto *Aristotelicae* praeferendam censemus. Elementa autem sunt corpora simplicia. Sed de his infra redibit sermo. Nec enim materiam primam, nec formam substantialem materialem, agnoscimus. Verum, ne in *Aristotelicorum* scriptis peregrini videamur, has, juxta ipsorum hypotheses, subjungemus positiones ... His èt similibus, de materia et forma quaestionibus, inutilibus satis, utramque implen paginam Aristotelici, illud anxia (ut recte *Pembelius*) indagine investigantes, quod nisi in Philosophorum cerebri, librisque, est nusquam'.

[220] For the influence of *minima naturalia* theories on some important late scholastic texts, including some being used in England, see Ariew, *Late scholastics*, 131.

[221] The best discussion remains Jacquot and Jones, 'Introduction' (1973) at 25–31.

[222] Thomas White, *De mundo dialogi tres* (Paris, 1642), 56–8; this passage is usefully discussed in Jacquot and Jones, 'Introduction', 26. However, see also White's scepticism about microparticulate explanations at 176.

Digby certainly believed that Aristotle had held an atomic physics: 'Let any man read his [Aristotle's] bookes of Generation and Corruption, and say whether he doth not expressly teach, that mixtion (which he delivereth to be the generation or making of a mixt body) is done *per minima*; that is in our language and in one word, by atomes'.[223] The same view, Digby added, could be found in Aristotle's *Parva naturalia*, in the pseudo-Aristotelian *Problems*, 'and in all other places, wheresoever he hath occasion to render Physically, the cause of Physicall effects'. Anyone who disagreed, Digby continued, had adopted the logical and metaphysical readings of Aristotle that we have already found him castigating (4.2). The same atomism was held, he added, by 'Hippocrates and Galen ... their Master Democritus, and with them the best Physicians ... [the] Alchymistes, with their Master Geber ... all naturall Philosophers, eyther auncient commentatours of Aristotle, or else moderne inquirers into naturall effects'.[224]

Digby developed this idiosyncratic historical reading not from the mainstream university Aristotelian tradition, but from the chymical tradition with which he must have engaged deeply during his time at Gresham (1633–35), where he had his own well-stocked laboratory.[225] He drew on the unorthodox reading of Aristotle on mixture developed in twelfth-century Salernitan medical texts and in the alchemical *Summa perfectionis* of pseudo-Geber, and his references to Galen and Hippocrates stem from a medieval tradition of atomic readings of Galen's *De elementis secundum Hippocratem*.[226] The reference to Democritus as 'Master' of Hippocrates, meanwhile, is a clear allusion to the tradition deriving from Celsus and the *Epistola ad Damagetum* (4.1 above).

White, meanwhile, had fully accepted Digby's atomistic reading of Aristotle by the time of his *Institutiones Peripateticae* (1646).[227] In his attack on Glanvill of 1663, he again presented Digby's atomism as a revival of the genuine Aristotle.[228] We shall remember that he saw Glanvill as little more than a cipher for Gassendi; it is therefore unsurprising to find him mocking Democritus's variously shaped atoms as a futile attempt to save the phenomena – surely, he

---

[223] Digby, *Two treatises*, 343. For the fullest analysis of Digby's matter theory, see Dobbs, 'Studies in the natural philosophy of Sir Kenelm Digby, I' (1971), at 18–25.

[224] Digby, *Two treatises*, 343–4.

[225] Dobbs, 'Studies in the natural philosophy of Sir Kenelm Digby, II' (1973); Foster, 'Digby', 42–5.

[226] As shown convincingly in Newman, 'Experimental corpuscular theory', 305–6 (but the page numbers in references to the *Two treatises* are given incorrectly). For the medieval tradition, see Jacquart, 'Minima in twelfth-century medical texts from Salerno' (2001), 40–1. For the early modern printing history of the Greek text and Latin translations of *De elementis*, see *CMG* v 1, 2, 37–41.

[227] White, *Institutiones peripateticae*; Clericuzio, *Elements*, 85–6.

[228] White, *Sciri*, 74–5 (=*Scepticks*, 41).

asked, any such shape could be composed of parts?[229] Little here suggests that White was doing anything other than slavishly following Digby and adapting him to his own polemical ends: he certainly makes no appeal to the chymical Aristotelian tradition, as Digby had, and there is no evidence that he engaged with it. Nonetheless, we meet here a key theme of what is to come: that the speculation on microparticulate structure with which classical Democritean and Epicurean atomism was associated could easily be dismissed as a reductionist thought experiment.

Digby and White's reading of Aristotle as an atomist was opposed by Alexander Ross and Glanvill, both of whom made the obvious retort that Aristotle had condemned Democritus and atomism.[230] Their reasons are clear: the former was a hylomorphist Aristotelian who, while clearly familiar with the *minima naturalia* Aristotelian tradition, simply stated that Aristotle 'never affirmed, that all *actions, passions, motions, mutations* are performed by them [i.e. *minima*]'.[231] Glanvill, saturated in the Italian anti-Aristotelian tradition, refused to countenance the possibility that the Stagirite shared any of the positive accomplishments found in the history of natural philosophy. More interesting is the question of why the *minima naturalia* or atomist Aristotle traditions did not gain more of a foothold in England, given their popularity in late Renaissance Aristotelian thought. The answer, in part, is the low amount of academic natural philosophy produced in the country; as we have already seen, most was to be found not in the arts but in the medicine faculty or outside the universities altogether; textbooks were imported from the continent. A second reason is the quick assimilation of Gassendi's Epicurean project into English philosophical culture,[232] which shifted focus back to the classical atomists, as did the association of them with Descartes. A third – and perhaps the most important – reason is that the most *avant garde* Aristotelian thought was shifting in another direction, towards an anti-reductionist vitalism.

### 5.3.2    Harvey and his followers

Other neoterics in the Aristotelian tradition did not take Digby's route; instead, they strenghthened a historical reading that threw doubt on the ancient

---

[229] White, *Sciri*, 81–2 (=*Scepticks*, 46). See also the comparison of Aristotelianism with Cartesian vortex theory at *Sciri*, 126–7 (=*Scepticks*, 74–5).

[230] Ross, *Touch-stone*, 60; Glanvill, *Scepsis*, 'Scire/I tuum nihil est: or, the authors defence of the Vanity of dogmatizing; against the exceptions of the learned Tho. Albius' (new pagination), 36–7. See also S. W., *A vindication of the doctrine contained in Pope Benedict XII* (Paris, 1659), 104–5 (this work is attributed to John Sergeant in both the ESTC and in Tutino, *Thomas White and the Blackloists* (2008), 34, but, given the sharp criticism of Digby and White, this seems questionable).

[231] Ross, *Touch-stone*, 60. For Ross's biography, see 3.3 above.

[232] For Gassendi in the universities, see Levitin, 'Parker'.

atomists' ability to explain natural phenomena. One such group were the followers of Harvey. Harvey's own *De generatione animalium* (1651) was a radical critique of most contemporary theories of animal reproduction: Harvey presented himself as offering a modified version of Aristotelian epigenesis (the development of an animal from an initial principal part through the successive formation of parts). Contemporary medical orthodoxy, meanwhile, was pre-formationist (the parts of organisms are all initially present in miniature), following Galen's critique of epigenesis in his *De semine*.[233] Harvey rejected any materialist approach to embryology as inadequate for explaining the teleological development of the foetus, explicitly linking such materialism to ancient philosophies:

> Truly, I can scarcely limit myself, without criticising and carping at the followers of Empedocles and Hippocrates (who want all similar bodies generated from the congregation of the four contrary elements (as if they were mixtures) and corrupted by their segregation); and no less Democritus, and his followers the Epicureans, who likewise build all bodies from the congregation of atoms of various figures.[234]

No one, Harvey went on, not even his favourite Aristotle, had ever demonstrated by experience that either elements or atoms had independent existence, or that they were basic principles.[235] Harvey's epigenesis went further than Aristotle's: his extremely vitalistic conception of blood led him to diverge from Aristotle's classification of blood as a humour. And so he presented Aristotle's error as due to over-indebtedness to the materialist tradition: 'As [Harvey] saw it, the ancient view of semen and blood as elemental compositions and mixtures, the result of a process of adding according to certain quantities and ratios, implied a *preformationist* principle'.[236] He explicitly pointed out Aristotle's debt to Empedocles, a debt that everyone knew in the case of four-element theory, but which Harvey extended to the question of generation.[237] Even more importantly, he offered an image of ancient atomism especially as overly *reductionist*, unable to explain the operations of nature in the generation of life in particular, 'as if generation was nothing else but the separation,

---

[233] The fullest discussion of Harvey on this issue, with many instructive comparisons with near-contemporaries, remains Pagel, *Harvey's biological ideas* (1967), 233–78. See now also the essays in Smith, ed., *The problem of animal generation in early modern philosophy* (2006), esp. Smith's 'Introduction', and for Harvey, Lennox, 'The comparative study of animal development'.

[234] Harvey, *Exercitationes*, 254: 'continere me sanè vix possum, quin *Empedoclis*, & *Hippocratis* etiam sectatore (qui corpora omnia similaria, ex quatuor elementis contrariis (ceu mista) congregatione generari, & segregatione corrumpi volunt) vellicem, ac perstringam: nec minus *Democritum*, eúmque sequutos *Epicureos*, qui ex diversarum figurarum atomis simul congregatis omnia componunt'.

[235] Ibid., 255: 'Neque *Aristoteles* ipsemet, aut alius quispiam unquam demonstravit, elementa in rerum naturâ separatim existere, aut principia esse corporum similarium'.

[236] Pagel, *Biological ideas*, 265.   [237] Harvey, *Exercitationes*, 298.

congregation and layout of things'.[238] 'Those who philosophise in this way' were also reductionist in assigning everything to a material cause, thus abrogating from the glory due to God.[239]

The debate over reductionism of this sort was as old as the second book of Aristotle's *Metaphysics*, but it became particularly prominent from the late sixteenth century as most natural philosophers (however pro- or anti-Aristotelian) came to realise that classical hylomorphism was being replaced by other matter theories. This was one of the topics on which Gassendi had been compelled to expand significantly on Epicurus, preserving his preformationism only through a theory of providentially guided *semina*.[240] We have already met Harvey's institutional influence, even if his methodological allegiance to Aristotle was not adopted by his followers. There is evidence of a similar phenomenon in respect to matter theory. With the exception of Glisson,[241] none of Harvey's followers adopted his supra-Aristotelian vitalism. However, many do seem to have inherited his doubts about the reductionism supposedly latent in ancient atomism. An interesting example is that of Walter Needham, who would become one of the leading Restoration medical theorists with the publication of his *Disquisitio anatomica de formato foetu* (1667), which, while based on work he had done in Cambridge in the 1650s, was also self-avowedly indebted to Harvey and the Oxford physiologists.[242] In letters written while studying for his M.A. to his old tutor at Westminster, Richard Busby, in 1655, Needham reported that he was reading Aristotle in the original texts, for he had realised that his commentators had 'been generally those Monkes, Friars, or Jesuites' who 'have lived only in Colledges & y$^e$ like places'; hardly conducive to an understanding of nature itself. While Aristotle had established 'general maxims', his followers had neglected his observational method until 'succeeding ages, seeing so small a progresse in so great a time, began to despair of going any further, & set up their rests in occult qualities & hidden qualities'. We need not look far for the origins of these views, for Needham offered long supporting quotations from Bacon. More

---

[238]  Ibid., 29: 'Quasi generatio nil aliud foret, quàm separatio, aut congregtio, aut dispositio rerum'. Democritus and Empedocles are again singled out in the preceding section of this passage.

[239]  Ibid. In her translation, Gweneth Whitteridge renders Harvey's 'qui hoc modo philosophantes materialem duntaxat caussam assignant' as 'those who, *as they spin philosophies in this manner*, assign only a material cause' (my emphasis), but I see no warrant for the overly ironic interpretation of 'qui hoc modo philosophantes'.

[240]  Hirai, 'Le concept de semence de Pierre Gassendi'; Fisher, 'Gassendi's atomist account of generation' (2003). See also Hirai, 'Atomes vivants, origine de l'âme et génération spontanée chez Daniel Sennert' (2007).

[241]  Temkin, 'The classical roots of Glisson's doctrine of irritation' (1964), repr. in *The double face of Janus* (1977), 290–316; Pagel, 'Harvey and Glisson on irritability' (1967). See further 5.4.1 below.

[242]  Frank, *Harvey*, 180–1, 198–200.

interesting is his opinion of the *novatores*, whom he took to be simply reviving ancient philosophies – 'y$^e$ Democriticall & Epicurean systemes diversly altered & disguised by Gassendus, Magnenus, Des Chartes & others'. All these rested on the claim that they 'doe depend more upon experiment, than any ordinary philosophy'. But this was an illusion, and their anti-Aristotelian conclusions (Bacon is quoted and attacked) 'might be easily refuted by reducing those principles, w$^{ch}$ Aristotle hath laid downe, to practise'.[243] This led Needham to propose a remarkable project: 'y$^e$ bestowing of such a Commentary upon some peeces of Aristotle as Gassendus hath upon Epicurus. So y$^t$ those men may find they have no so great an advantage over us in y$^e$ experimentall part of philosophy as they thinke'.[244] It is a great shame that there is no evidence of such a project ever being carried out. However, it is worth noting that in a later letter Needham takes as archetypal of the non-experimentalism of the *novatores* the claim that animal life could be explained materially.[245] Although this is an obvious reference to Descartes, it is clear that Needham considered it typical of the reductionism of the ancient materialists and their revivers. In a much later manuscript treatise entitled 'Institutiones Medicae', evidently intended as a relatively basic introduction to the subject, Needham demonstrated his mild allegiance to Aristotle by still offering a closely Aristotelian description of the four elements, although he disagreed with the Stagirite on whether the forms of the elements remain in mixture.[246] This is the kind of deliberately mildly agnostic and anti-reductionist attitude to matter theory that would characterise much of Restoration natural philosophy.

It was not only natural philosophers who drew on this kind of scepticism about the capacity of atomism to explain natural phenomena. Meric Casaubon appended to his 'Notae' to Diogenes Laërtius 'addenda quaedam' in which he quoted at length one of Harvey's attacks on ancient materialist accounts of generation. Wrenching it out of its natural philosophical and medical context, Casaubon claimed it for the side of the pious who recognised God's providential operation.[247] We are reminded not only that the barrier between natural philosophical, scholarly, and theological concerns could, at points, be very porous, but also that it was the issues of generation and growth that often excited the most vigorous and wide-reaching debate among all these groups.

---

[243] Walter Needham to Richard Busby, 5 Feb 1654[/5], BL MS Add. 4292, fols. 84$^v$–85$^r$.

[244] Ibid., fol. 85$^v$.    [245] Needham to Busby, 2 May 1655, BL MS Add. 4292, fol. 87$^r$.

[246] BL MS Sloane 656 (Walter Needham, 'Institutiones medicae' (1670s)), fols. 4$^v$–5$^v$.

[247] Casaubon, 'Notae', 26a–b. See also the very similar use of the same passage in Stillingfleet, *Origines*, 453–4.

### 5.3.3   Boyle and followers on ancient matter theory

In his classic study of the 'Oxford physiologists', Robert Frank suggested that English natural philosophy post-Harvey was shaped by a Harveian research programme conducted through non-Harveian mechanistic principles, particularly as they were derived from Gassendi. There remains much truth to this, but as we shall see, English natural philosophers consistently presented Epicurus as an unsuitable model in questions of matter theory and *principia rerum*. In part this was an inheritance from Harvey or from Glisson, who clearly exerted a large pedagogical influence. It was also an inheritance from a different tradition, whose impact on English natural philosophy has only recently begun to be fully explored: chymistry. The latter, like medicine, brought to the fore the subject of organic change, a subject that any early modern natural philosopher would have known had particularly vexed atomists from antiquity onwards.

Mid-seventeenth century Englishmen were in possession of differing chymical theories of matter; while far from all pushed in a corpuscularian direction, all shared an emphasis on the possibility of retrieving initial constituents of bodies by means of analysis, contrary to classic scholastic theories of mixture.[248] The godfather of early modern chymistry, Paracelsus, was certainly no corpuscularian; his *tria prima* (mercury, sulphur, salt) were principles rather than substances. Van Helmont, whose great influence in England we have already had cause to mention, attacked both the four elements of Aristotle and Galen and the Paracelsian principles. He proposed that the two principles of all bodies are water and *semina*, which 'operate not as physical agents, but according to the ferment they contain'.[249] Some of Van Helmont's statements on mixture have encouraged a corpuscularian reading;[250] we need not enter this debate here, but need only point out that his theory explicitly precluded reductionist interpretations of particulate mixture: all composition required the 'work of a spiritual agent' which 'promotes' the matter into transmutation.[251]

At the same time, from the late sixteenth century, some chymists – especially those with academic affiliation and thus a desire to advertise their 'philosophical' pedigree – had suggested that chymistry and atomism were historically close allies. Key figures here were the Germans iatrochymists Andreas Libavius and Daniel Sennert. As early as 1595, the former was drawing on

---

[248] Kangro, 'Erklärungswert und Schwierigkeiten der Atomhypothese und ihrer Anwendung auf chemische Probleme' (1968).

[249] Clericuzio, *Elements*, 58–9.

[250] For a corpuscularian reading of Helmont, see Newman, *Gehennical fire*, 110–14, 141–51; for a more sceptical response, Clericuzio, *Elements*, 56–9.

[251] van Helmont, *Ortus medicinae*, 67b: 'Quidquid enim in compositum abire, & ex diversis, in hoc aliquid, converti oportet, necesse, hoc fiat spirituum agentium opera, & eatenus se complectentium, quatenus materiam, in novam generationem trasmutando, promovent'.

the pseudo-Democritean sources we have already met to present Democritus as a chymical philosopher both in his observational methods and in his particulate matter theory, which Libavius linked with *semina*.[252] Sennert, in his *De chymicorum cum Aristotelicis et Galenicis consensu ac dissensu* (1619), also claimed compatibility between chymistry and the philosophy of Democritus, while following Libavius in associating the Abderite's atoms with Aristotle's mixts.[253] Since these works were well known to English natural philosophers, there was a strong reason to explore the supposed relationship between ancient atomism and modern chymistry. At the same time they also had strong reasons to suspect classical atomism of a reductionism that precluded the full explanation of natural phenomena. This was the internal struggle that shaped the attitude to classical atomism of many English natural philosophers.

A key intervention was made by Thomas Willis. His breakthrough work, *De fermentatione* (1659) – which maintained that many central aspects of life, including the heat of the blood, were generated by fermentation – is often described as 'mechanist' or even 'atomic'.[254] But in the first chapter, 'De principiis rerum naturalium', Willis offered a rather different picture. The history of philosophy, he proclaimed, offered three opinions on matter theory: the four elements of Aristotle and his followers, the variously shaped atoms of Democritus and Epicurus, and the five principles of the chymists (spirit, sulphur, salt, water, earth). The first he classified as the product of a philosophy that was not interested in penetrating the secrets of nature, but only in saving the phenomena.[255] More interesting are his comments on classical atomism, which, he argued, 'presupposed, rather than demonstrated' its principles, speculating on atomic shape and generally moving far from the senses.[256] Instead, the less reductionist principles of the chymists were preferable.

---

[252] Newman, 'Experimental corpuscular theory', 306–17; Newman, *Atoms and alchemy*, 76–7.

[253] Newman, 'Experimental corpuscular theory', 317–25; Newman, *Atoms and alchemy*, 92–3; Hirai, 'Atomes vivants'.

[254] E.g. Frank, *Harvey*, 165–6 (which is nonetheless extremely useful for showing the contemporary importance of Willis's work); Frank, 'Thomas Willis and his circle' (1990), 118–19, despite recognising Willis's conscious distancing from Epicurus, still claims Gassendi as a key source; see also Dewhurst, 'Introduction' (1983), xix. But cf. Clericuzio, *Elements*, 100.

[255] Willis, *Diatribae duae*, 3: 'Quoad quatuor *Elementa* & primas qualitates inde deducendas, fatendum est pro explicandis naturae phaenomenis, hanc opinionem aliquatenus conducere, verum crasso adeo modo, & sine peculiari respectu ad secretiores naturae recessus rerum apparentias solvit'.

[256] Ibid., 3–4: '*Altera sententia*, quae tantum *Epicureae* philosophiae subtegmen est, quatenus mechanice res explicandas suscipit, & instrumenta velut artificis manu fabrefacta naturae accommodat, ac sine recursu ad occultas qualitates, Sympathiam, & caetera ignorantiae asyla, difficiles aliquot scientiarum nodos & aenigmata feliciter & perquam ingeniose extricat, laudem certe non levem meruit. At quoniam principia sua supponit potius, quam demonstrat, docetque qualis figurae elementa ista corporum sint, non quae ipsa fuerint, atque etiam notiones inducit valde subtiles & a sensu remotas, quaeque naturae phaenomenis, quando ad particularia descenditur, non satis quadrant.'

Crucially, these principles were 'not the most simple' or homogeneous entities, but 'only those substances into which physical things are resolved—the least perceptible parts, as it were'.[257] Later, in his *De anima brutorum* (1672), Willis characterised modern theories of animal souls that rendered them purely mechanical – i.e. those of Descartes, Digby, Gassendi, and Gometius Pereira before them – as revivals of Epicureanism, invalid not for religious reasons but because they were 'ingeniously produced' but not consonant with truth, since their reductionism was unable to explain the phenomena in the same way as his own fermentation-based solution.[258] Chymistry and considerations from life science were rendering Epicurus unattractive.

What is immediately striking is how the doctrinal anti-reductionist rhetoric of Harvey and the chymists has fused with the methodological anti-speculative rhetoric we met in Chapter 4; Epicurus emerges as an un-observational system-builder, in opposition to the self-limited and sense-grounded conclusions of the chymists. Willis was not the only one of the Oxford physiologists to make this comparison. In a discourse to the Royal Society presented *c.* 1664, Christopher Wren drew a very similar contrast between the speculations of the 'mechanical philosophy' and the natural philosophical research that is 'actually done' by chymists.[259] By 'mechanical philosophy' Wren probably meant Cartesianism as well as ancient atomism: given Descartes's frequent invectives against the central tenets of Epicureanism such as the vacuum, it is remarkable how often English naturalists conflated the two. Of course, this stemmed partly from the religious fear of all 'mechanist' philosophies (e.g. as it did for Henry More), but it is clear that there was also a methodological agenda here: both were presented as promoters of a speculative and reductive matter theory. If this view was only tentatively expressed before *c.* 1660,[260] it became mainstream in English natural philosophy after the publication of the works of Robert Boyle. In the second edition of the *Diatribae duae*, Willis acknowledged that some had

---

[257] Ibid., 4: '*Principiorum* nomine intelligo, haud Entia simplicissima & omnino incomposita, sed ejusmodi tantum substantias in quas veluti partes ultimo sensibiles res physicae resolvuntur'.

[258] Thomas Willis, *De anima brutorum quae hominis vitalis ac sensitiva est, exercitationes duae* (London, 1672), 3–7, esp. 7: 'Verum enim vero istae (i.e. Epicurus-like) φαινομένων difficulium solutiones, rationumque συλλογαί pro mechanico animalium animarumque apparatus, ab Authoribus illis affabrè licet effictae, menti veritatis avidae haud satisfacere videntur'. Smith, *Divine machines* (2011), 80, misunderstands the passage at 3–4, which does not, as he claims, signal an agreement with the Epicurean opinion, but simply describes it, Willis then making it clear that he does not share it.

[259] *Memoirs of the life and works of Sir Christopher Wren*, ed. J. Elmes (London, 1823), 152–3.

[260] See e.g. the well-known example of William Petty's correspondence with Henry More: Webster, 'More and Descartes'. A remarkably early example is [Hartlib?] to Comenius, 7 Dec 1640, HP 7/78/1A–4B: 'Ita Democriteam de Atomis doctrinam in theatrum nostra tempestate reducere coepit Cartesius sed non prospero admodum successu, ut ex brevi quodam Anonymi cujusdam scripto adversus ipsum apparet'.

attempted to reconcile chymistry and atomism, but announced that he would not engage in such speculation, rather churlishly linking it to 'dream philosophy'.[261] Willis's target, I propose, was Boyle, who suggested in both his *Sceptical chymist* (1661) and *Certain physiological essays* (1661) that there was a historical connection between microparticulate matter theory and chymistry. A passage in the preface to the former work chastising those academic natural philosophers who had too readily adopted the chymists' principles was very likely directed at Willis.[262] But if this was a dissent from Willis, the similarities were also strong: the Willis of *De fermentatione* and the Boyle of the early 1660s shared the belief that ancient atomism (as opposed to what Boyle called corpuscularianism) was reductionist and incompatible with experimentalism.

This was not a position that Boyle arrived at immediately. During his earliest phase of natural-philosophical interest, he adopted a favourable attitude to Epicurean atomism. In the much-discussed 'Of the Atomicall Philosophy' (*c.* 1653, later endorsed by one of Boyle's amanuenses: 'These Papers are without fayle to be burn't'), Boyle defended Epicurus from the charge of mathematising nature, deploying an elaborate historical elucidation:

The Atomists seeme not without reason to complaine that the same envy which mov'd Aristotle to represent the Placits of his preceders under a disadvantageous notion has very injuriously represented the opinions of Democritus & Epicurus as if by Atomes they understood those Mathematicall points which being suppos'd absolutely indivisible & without any quantity can not consequently become constituent parts of a body ... whereas by Atoms the Assertors of them understand not indivisible or Mathematicall points which are so void of quantity that the subtle rasor of Imagination it selfe cannot dissect them but minima Naturalia or the smallest particles of bodyes which they call Atomes not because they cannot be suppos'd to be divided into yet smaller parts (for they allow them both quantity & figure as wee shall see anon) but because tho they may be further divided by Imagination yet they cannot by Nature, which not being able in her resolutions of Naturall bodyes to proceed ad infinitum must necessarily stop somewhere & have some bodyes which shee can possibly no further subdivide & which therefore may be justly termed Atomes.[263]

[261] Thomas Willis, *Diatribae duae medico philosophicae ... editio secunda, ab authore recognita, atque ab eodem multiplici auctario lucupleta* (London, 1660), 4: 'Si vero objiciat aliquis principia atmoeidea, & nostra spagyrica omnino subordinari; Nimirum ut haec, licet ultimo sensibilia, in ista (conceptu tantum designanda) resolvantur: huic non multum repugno, modo ostendat conceptus istos reales esse. Lusciosus ego atque hebes, lynceis accuratiora relinquo; eatenus sapere contentus, quousque rationi sensus externi operam praestitere; procudere enim, aut somniare philosophiam me nolle lubens profiteor.' By early 1660 it was known that Boyle was planning to amalgamate 'Chymicall experiments with Atomicall notions': Robert Southwell to Henry Oldenburg, 20 Feb 1660, *Oldenburg correspondence*, I, 355.

[262] Robert Boyle, *The sceptical chymist* (1661), in *Boyle works*, II, 208; Clericuzio, 'Carneades and the chemists' (1994), 80–1; Principe, *Adept*, 35–51.

[263] Boyle, 'Of atomicall philosophy' (*c.* 1653), in *Boyle works*, XIII, 227–8.

We know that despite his impressive list of *novatores* at the start of the manuscript – Gassendi, Magnen, Descartes, and Digby – the actual experimental evidence for atomism that Boyle deployed in the manuscript was derived from the work of Daniel Sennert, specifically his 'reduction to the pristine state' experiments.[264] This was also the case with Boyle's history of atomism, for in his *Hypomnemata physica* (1636), Sennert pre-empted Gassendi in arguing that *all* pre-Aristotelian philosophers held a physical atomism which was mistakenly attacked with mathematical arguments by Aristotle.[265]

But Boyle would never again defend Epicurus so openly as he had in the early 1650s, and from Essay IV of *The usefulness of natural philosophy* (1663), 'Containing a Requisite Digression concerning those that would exclude the Deity from intermeddling with Matter', Boyle became increasingly hostile to the philosopher of the garden. What changed? One suggestion is that Boyle was reacting to the doctrine of inherent atomic motion as it had been espoused by Gassendi, Charleton, and Margaret Cavendish.[266] Yet this hardly explains Boyle's total refusal to commit to the central tenets of Epicurean atomism: indivisibility and the void. More convincing is the explanation of William Newman: Boyle, following through the implications of his reading of Sennert, realised that his chymically derived corpuscularianism – one that allowed for subordinate physical causes (beyond the size, shape, and other affections of atoms) – was far more methodologically sound than reductionist Epicurean atomism.[267]

This is confirmed by the evidence of Boyle's historical ideas. From the late 1650s, Boyle decided that the historical baggage of Epicurean atomism derived from the fact that Epicurus himself espoused a speculative, reductionist, and dogmatic atomism that did not represent the values of the experimental philosophy. When Boyle was concerned with specific Epicurean doctrines he found erroneous, he explained them as the consequence of such a reductionist approach. For example, he repeatedly sought to emphasise that his own corpuscularian philosophy was compatible with (and indeed encouraged) the argument from design, and should not be confused with Epicurus's strictly non-teleological atomism. In Boyle's mind, teleology was synonymous with complexity; atomism with reductionism. This can be seen from his contrast of Harvey's discovery of the function of the venous valves with the Roman Epicurean physician Asclepiades of Bithynia (*c.* 124–40 BC), who, had he

---

[264] Newman, 'Alchemical Sources', 577–80; Newman, *Atoms and alchemy*, 160–70.

[265] Sennert, *Hypomnemata physica*, 91.

[266] Clericuzio, *Elements*, 120; Clericuzio, 'Gassendi, Charleton and Boyle on matter and motion' (2001).

[267] Newman, *Atoms and alchemy*, 173ff. For how this belief actually shaped Boyle's experiments, see the interesting account in Cecon, 'Boyle's experimental programme' (2015).

come across them, 'might have thought himself well grounded, to look upon them as Superfluous Parts'.[268] The point is not just a religious one; any educated seventeenth-century reader interested in philosophy would have known that almost all the evidence for Asclepiades's life was to be derived from Pliny's *Natural history* (XXXVI.12–20), where he is criticised for adopting an overly theoretical approach to medicine, to which he supposedly turned only to enrich himself after becoming impoverished as that most archetypal of sophists – a professor of rhetoric.

Examining further passages, it quickly becomes evident that by the 1660s, Boyle came to classify Epicurus and his atomistic philosophy as speculative and reductionist. So in the *Certain physiological essays* (1661), when comparing the fruits of non-speculative chymistry and medicine with the non-productiveness of 'the speculative Devisers of new Hypothesis', Boyle named Leucippus, Epicurus, and Aristotle (along with the moderns Telesio and Campanella) as examples of the latter.[269] He summarised his thoughts on the 'Epicurean hypothesis' in 1669: 'it [i]s a Precarious and Chimærical Fancy of the Atomists, to imagine, that in Solid, and as to sense, Quiescent Bodies, there should be any intestine Motion of the component Particles, neither the Motions nor the Corpuscles themselves being to be seen, and both of them being therefore as well incredible as invisible'.[270]

This approach fundamentally distinguished Boyle from the Gassendist defence of Epicurus: indeed, Oldenburg wrote to Spinoza about Boyle's rejection of Gassendi's speculations about atomic shape.[271] Boyle was not alone in refusing to admit Epicurus into the canon of those who philosophised on the basis of sense experience. In Cambridge University Library there is a copy of Charleton's *Physiologia*, copiously annotated by William Brouncker, first president of the Royal Society, and presented to him by the author.[272] Brouncker's marginal comments repeatedly chastise Charleton's over-eager reduction of various phenomena to atomistic explanations, expressing a polite

---

[268] Boyle, *A disquisition about the final causes of natural things* (1688), in *Boyle works*, XI, 142–3.

[269] Boyle, *Certain physiological essays* (1661), in *Boyle works*, II, 87. See further Boyle, *Atheism*, 345: 'there being so many thousands of those requisite to make up the least Body of a visible bulke, that a single Atome must needs be Invisible: as is confessed by Epicurus himselfe' (Boyle was probably thinking of Epicurus, *Ep. Hdt.*, in DL x.56; see also Lucretius, *Rer. nat.*, IV.110–28). See also Boyle, *Atheism*, 371–2. These passages were written in the 1670s–80s. See also RS BP8 fol. 165ʳ, where Aristotelianism and Epicureanism are cited as the two extremes of reductionism (in 'Sections of an essay of various degrees or kinds of the knowledge of natural things', fols. 165ʳ–170ʳ).

[270] Boyle, *Of absolute rest in bodies* (1669), in *Boyle works*, VI, 194–5.

[271] Oldenburg to Spinoza, 3 April 1663, *Oldenburg correspondence*, I, 41–2.

[272] Walter Charleton, *Physiologia Epicuro-Gassendo-Charltoniana* (London, 1654), CUL, Classmark: Adv.a.27.7. Brouncker's note on the title page explains that it was given to him personally by Charleton, and points out that his disagreement from the author should not signify 'any breach of Freindship'.

but persistent scepticism and refusing to replace Charleton's hypothesis with one of his own.[273] Although there is no direct evidence of Boyle and Brouncker discussing these matters, it appears that in the early Royal Society, with its deliberate emphasis on natural historical methods, there existed a current of opposition to Epicurean atomism on the grounds of its speculative nature.[274] Boyle's refusal to class Epicurus amongst the experimentalists was a formative event in the history of Epicurus's reception and the development of corpuscularianism in seventeenth-century England.

But this is not the end of the issue. In later published works, Boyle delineated a tradition of supposed pre-Aristotelian corpuscularians. They were exalted less for their positive doctrine and more for their approach to nature, as is evident from this important passage in the *Excellency of theology* (1674):

> Nor is it onely in the Credit of mens Opinions about Philosophical Matters, that we may observe an Inconstancy and Vicissitude, but in the very Way and Method of Philosophizing; for Democritus, Plato, Pythagoras, and others, who were of the more sincere and ingenious Cultivators of Physicks among the Greeks, exercis'd themselves chiefly either in making particular Experiments and Observations, as Democritus did in his manifold Dissections of Animals; or else apply'd the Mathematicks to the Explicating of a particular Phænomenon of Nature, as may appear (not to mention what Hero teaches in his Pneumaticks,) by the Accounts, Democritus, Plato, and others, give of Fire and other Elements, from the Figure and Motion of the Corpuscles they consist of. And although this way of Philosophizing were so much in request before Aristotle, that (albeit he unluckily brought in another, yet) there are manifest and considerable footsteps of it to be met with in some of his Writings, (and particularly in his Books of Animals, and his Mechanical Questions).[275]

Boyle claimed that a host of pre-Aristotelian philosophers had, in contrast to the Stagirite's speculative systematising, promoted an experimental natural philosophy; moreover, this manifested itself in corpuscularian explanations of natural phenomena. Why did Boyle believe that all the pre-Aristotelians were corpuscularians? And why did he associate some of the presocratics,

---

[273] See e.g. Brouncker's note at CUL Adv.a.27.7, p. 19, where he questions Charleton's Epicurean claim that a vacuum is necessary for the motion of particles (he refers back to this point at pp. 24–5), and his note at p. 26 suggesting that the space taken up in an air-compression experiment could just as possibly be explained by 'Fire or Aether' as by a vacuum.

[274] On the shared influence between Boyle and the early Royal Society, and the centrality of natural history, see Hunter, 'Robert Boyle and the early Royal Society' (2007); Anstey and Hunter, 'Robert Boyle's "Designe about natural history"' (2008).

[275] Boyle, *The excellency of theology, compar'd with natural philosophy* (1674), in *Boyle works*, VIII, 87–8 (see also the very similar passage at 85–6). For the reception of Hero, see Hall, 'Hero's *Pneumatica*'. Aristotle's 'books of animals' are of course the *History of animals* and *On the parts of animals*; the 'mechanical questions' is a reference to the spurious *Mechanica*. The latter was mostly accepted as Aristotelian, although this attribution was questioned by Girolamo Cardano and Francesco Patrizi: see Rose and Drake, 'The pseudo-Aristotelian Questions of Mechanics in Renaissance culture' (1971).

especially Democritus, with an experimental approach? Did Democritus not hold the same view as the speculative Epicurus?

There was of course one prominent model for Boyle's association of the presocratics with a more experimental approach: Bacon. But even if he was partially inspired by Bacon, Boyle was doing far more than simply aping him. Although the standard sources emphasised the continuity between Democritus and Epicurus, we have seen that there also existed a Democritean *persona* derived not from the traditional sources but from the *Epistola ad Damagetum*, a collection of (spurious) letters by Hippocrates, and from the *Physica et mystica*, a similarly spurious work which presented Democritus as a follower of Egyptian alchemists (4.1 above). It was this Democritean *persona* that we find Boyle inheriting, and it is particularly instructive that he identified with it again in his drafts for an ultimately unpublished work on the use of reason and experience in natural philosophy: 'In the controversy between Aristotle and Democritus [about atoms and indivisibility] . . . I take not upon me to determine here any thing about the Truth of the Opinions, but only about the goodness of the Argumentations. And tho I fear that neither has opin'd well, yet Democritus seems to have Philosophis'd the better of the two'.[276]

This is clearly a reference to (pseudo-)Democritus's supposedly experimental credentials. Elsewhere, we find Boyle accepting that Democritus was the teacher of Hippocrates.[277] Importantly, this claim was made when discussing the value of natural philosophy to medicine. We have already met Boyle's semi-repressed thoughts on the relationship between medicine and the new philosophy, and it is important to remind ourselves that he was operating in a context in which many medical reformers were arguing that philosophy – as a search for causes – had nothing to do with physic. Boyle was similarly critical of those traditional authorities he disagreed with, here Galen, for being slaves to their theories, and often contrasted their lack of results with the positive results of those with no theories at all – in this case practitioners of primitive pagan medicine.[278] At the same time, he was also careful to differentiate himself from the bare mechanic, artisan, or primitive physician.[279] By presenting Democritus the philosopher as a pioneering physician and by reminding his readers that his own non-speculative corpuscularianism still had a philosophical heritage, Boyle reasserted his role as a philosopher, while differentiating

---

[276] RS BP9 fol. 106ʳ (in 'Further material relating to the use of reason and experience in natural philosophy', 1670s–80s, fols. 96ʳ–128ʳ).

[277] Boyle, *Usefulness of natural philosophy I, II* (1663), in *Boyle works*, III, 437. Boyle also added that Pythagoras and Empedocles were medically skilled philosophers.

[278] Boyle, *Usefulness of natural philosophy I, II*, 426.

[279] See Shapin, *A social history of truth* (1994), 396; see also the comments on Boyle's depiction of his relationship to practical chymistry in Newman and Principe, *Alchemy*, 17–18.

himself from the metaphysical speculations with which 'philosophy' had become associated by the middle of the seventeenth century.

This sort of fashioning was also performed by those who packaged Boyle's works, for in the 'Advertisement to the Reader' of the *Usefulness of natural philosophy*, Boyle's friend, the Anglican churchman and fellow natural historian Robert Sharrock, directly compared Boyle to the experimentalist Democritus, and went on to celebrate the fortune of Boyle's readers for living in an age of print, lamenting that printing would have 'sav'd that Excellent Book of *Democritus*, which he inscribed his ΧΕΙΡΌΚΜΗΤΑ or Experiments ... so utterly lost, that the Name of the piece is not mention'd among the Catalogue of his Writings in *Laertius*'.[280] This was one way of turning a scholarly inconvenience to one's advantage: Laërtius had not mentioned the work because it was only referenced in the spurious *Epistola ad Damagetum*. There is no reason to suspect Sharrock and Boyle of scholarly disingenuousness: as we have seen, the Democritus of the *Epistola* remained a commonly accepted figure even among scholars in the mid-seventeenth century (4.1). Among natural philosophers, Christopher Wren had similarly evoked the figure of Democritus the experimental anatomist in his inaugural lecture as Gresham Professor of Astronomy in 1657.[281] As far as mid-seventeenth century natural philosophers were concerned, presocratic experimentalism was a real historical phenomenon.

But Boyle had even deeper philosophical reasons for suggesting this lineage, reasons that transcended his desire to emulate Bacon or any of the other defenders of presocratic experimentalism. In his 1660s works, the earliest figure that Boyle deployed in his genealogy of positive corpuscularianism was Moschus the Phoenician, whom we have already met in Cudworth. In the 'Attempt to make *chymical experiments* useful to illustrate the notions of the corpuscular philosophy' in the *Certain physiological essays*, Boyle sought to reconcile the 'Atomical & Cartesian Hypotheses' – precisely the reconciliation that Willis was sceptical about. Acknowledging that they differed over the notion of body, the possibility of a vacuum, the origin of motion, and infinite indivisibility, Boyle nevertheless asserted that due to their common opposition to Aristotelianism, their deduction of 'all the Phaenomena of Nature from Matter and local Motion', and the fact that their disagreements stemmed from 'rather Metaphysical than Physiological Notions', their doctrines may be classified 'by a Person of a reconciling Disposition ... [as] ... one Philosophy ... call'd Corpuscular'. But he did not stop at these philosophical

---

[280]  Robert Sharrock, 'The publisher to the reader', in Boyle, *Usefulness of natural philosophy I, II*, 194, referring to DL, IX.46–9.
[281]  Wren, 'Oratio inauguralis', 33. For a later English attack on the veracity of 'Democritus the alchemist', see Wotton, *Reflections*, 126–7.

reasons, for he also offered a historical genealogy for this non-dogmatic 'corpuscular philosophy': 'I sometimes style it the Phoenician Philosophy, because some ancient Writers inform us, that not only before *Epicurus* and *Democritus*, but ev'n before *Leucippus* taught in *Greece*, a Phoenician Naturalist was wont to give an account of the Phaenomena of Nature by the Motion and other Affections of minute Particles of Matter'.[282]

This 'Phoenician naturalist', Boyle went on to explain, was Moschus. Still in the *Physiological Essays*, Boyle twice claimed that Moschical corpuscularianism was particularly consistent with chymistry, including its alchemical ambitions.[283] Then, in the *Sceptical chymist*, he discussed van Helmont's thesis that water is the ultimate principle of nature.[284] Boyle pointed out that 'though the Arguments be for the most part his, the Opinion it self is very Antient, For *Diogenes Laertius* and divers other Authors speak of *Thales* as the first among the *Grecians* that made disquisitions upon nature'.[285] The reference to Laërtius was familiar: any reader who had got as far as the first few pages of the doxographer's tome would have known of Thales's belief in water as a first principle.[286] But Boyle did not stop there. Relying on Plutarch and Justin Martyr, he suggested that the opinion was older than Thales, and some ingenious use of relatively obscure testimonies (a scholiast on Apollonius and Athenagoras) led him to attribute the opinion to the ancient poets, Homer, Hesiod, and the poet-philosopher-sage Orpheus. Once he had travelled so far back, he could hardly stop: its true antiquity, Boyle continued, went back to Phoenicia, where it was well known Thales had travelled. He could therefore return to the figure of Moschus; moreover he suggested that the Phoenicians, who had 'borrow'd most of their Learning from the *Hebrews*', were in fact influenced by the creation account into believing that water was the first principle.[287]

The scholarly points are all, in fact, from Grotius, who had used them to defend the truth of the creation.[288] But far more important is the historical–methodological point. Boyle was here offering what amounts to a historical reconciliation between Helmontian chymistry and corpuscularianism. Indeed, so strong was his belief in an early chymically compatible corpuscularianism that he was even prepared to break his rule of not reading philosophy into

---

[282] Boyle, *Certain physiological essays*, 87.     [283] Ibid., 91.
[284] For background, see Webster, 'Water as the ultimate principle of nature' (1965); for more on Boyle's debt to Van Helmont, see Clericuzio, 'Transmission'.
[285] Boyle, *Sceptical chymist*, 259.
[286] DL, I.27. Boyle supplemented this with Cicero, *Nat. Deor.*, I.10.
[287] Boyle, *Sceptical chymist*, 259–61.
[288] See Grotius, 'Annotationes', in *De veritate*, 33–46. This story proved extremely popular among both natural philosophers and apologists. See 5.2. above for its use by Cudworth and below for its use by Mayow, taking it from Theophilus Gale. See also e.g. Stillingfleet, *Origines*, 427–8.

scripture to justify the claim.[289] We need not assume that Boyle was at this point drawing on Cudworth, or partaking in a broader 'neoplatonic tradition'.[290] As well as the scholarship of Grotius, Boyle's would have found a precedent for citing Moschus as a 'chymical corpuscularian' in Sennert.[291] Elsewhere in the *Sceptical chymist*, Boyle announced that in their theory of mixture, the chymists 'agree with most of the Antient Philosophers that preceded *Aristotle*', directly referencing the 'Writings of *Sennertus*'.[292] It is through this route that we can explain the seemingly bizarre previous list of supposed corpuscularians – Democritus, Plato, Pythagoras, Anaxagoras – they are all listed as corpuscularians in Sennert.[293] Ultimately, Boyle's, Sennert's, and Bacon's readings originated from the same tradition, a particularly apt example of which can be found in the *Idea medicinae philosophicae* (1571) of Petrus Severinus.[294] Boyle simply added the philological story he found in Grotius onto this chymical base.

All this was not simple humanist ornamentation, but lay at the heart of Boyle's understanding of his own corpuscularianism. Boyle saw Epicurus's reduction of all phenomena to atoms as symptomatic of a speculative dogmatism. His rejection of this kind of reductionism has been the subject of heated debate, with some major historians of science (especially Alan Chalmers)

---

[289] Boyle, *Sceptical chymist*, 263–4. For the rule of not reading philosophy into scripture, see e.g., Boyle, 'An examen of the greatest part of Mr. Hobbs's Dialogus physicus de naturâ aëris' (1662), in *Boyle works*, III, 163.

[290] *Pace* Sailor, 'Moses and atomism', 13: [Boyle's] personal ties with the Cambridge Platonists were considerable and their influence on him inescapable. Thus, he reiterated Cudworth's history of ancient atomism fairly closely'. But Boyle was discussing Moschus in print no fewer than seventeen years before Cudworth's *Intellectual system* was published. Moreover, the claim that Boyle had strong personal ties with the Cambridge group is not well attested: Cudworth was first in contact with him on 27 May 1664 (*Correspondence*, II, 276) and only once from then on; Henry More similarly only wrote to him sporadically before their falling out over More's later disingenuous use of Boyle's experimental evidence, on which see Henry, 'Henry More versus Robert Boyle' (1990).

[291] Sennert, *Hypomnemata physica*, 89: 'Inter alias autem opiniones, quae Democrito, ut Empedocli, aliisque pluribus nobilissimis Philosophis antiquis tribuuntur, est, quòd atomos principia rerum naturalium constituerint, ex quarum varia unione reliqua corpora orta sint. Atque haec sententia antiquissima fuit, & jam Monacho cuidam Phoenicio, quem ante Trojae excidium floruisse memorant, tribuitur; imò commune ferè fuisse Philosophorum ante Aristotelem sententiam, ex initio *lib*.8.*de generat. & corrupt.* [sic – it is book II] patet. Primus Aristoteles ab hac sententia recessit, statuitque, corpora illa minima non solùm in mistione uniri, sed & per mutuam actionem & passionem inter se ita alterari & affici, ut desinant esse id, quod ante mistionem erant'.

[292] Boyle, *Sceptical chymist*, 266–7.

[293] Sennert, *Hypomnemata physica*, 89–91, Sennert, *Epitome scientiae naturalis*, in *Opera*, I, 4.

[294] Severinus, *Idea medicinae philosophicae*, 94–5: 'Ubi Annales temporum evolverimus, Philosophos ejus aetatis Democritum, Heraclitum, Empedoclem, Anaxagoram, Parmenidem, antiquae, primae & sacrae Philosophiae alumnus fuisse apparebis, naturaeque penetralia superatis umbris debitè didicisse: quemadmodum & hoc loco Hippocratem fecisse demonstravimus'.

claiming that Boyle's anti-reductionism was fundamentally incompatible with his corpuscularian and mechanical philosophy and that Boyle was aware of this; others (especially William Newman) have fiercely opposed this interpretation.[295] Our analysis of Boyle's view of the history of 'experimental corpuscularianism' makes it clear that the latter position approaches far closer to the truth, for Boyle clearly believed that such a non-reductionist mechanical corpuscularianism was not only possible and desirable, but had actually existed in history. He saw his chymical corpuscularianism as valuable precisely because it was non-reductionist, and it is worth noting that in his most general methodological discussion of hypothesis formation (which remains in manuscript), Boyle again contrasted the 'deduction' of Epicureanism (and Cartesianism) with 'y$^t$ knowledge of the works of nature y$^t$ Physicians, Chymists & others pretend to'.[296] Professor Chalmers has attempted to minimise the difference between Boyle and Epicurus (and Descartes), writing that 'the main difference lies in the stress Boyle put on the role of God in devising and sustaining the world-order ... nevertheless, the important differences notwithstanding, the mechanical philosophies of Epicurus, Descartes and Boyle were alike'.[297] But Boyle's anti-Epicurus sentiments, in contrast to those of contemporaries like Casaubon and Cudworth, were not primarily religious, but methodological (although he also repudiated Epicurean theology).[298] If Boyle had believed in a likeness between himself and Epicurus, he would have adopted one of the historiographical narratives available to him (e.g. in Gassendi) to support that claim. Instead, he went down a different historiographical path.

The conclusion that ancient atomism was reductionist and speculative became a commonplace after Boyle, transcending the boundary between those who fully ascribed to Boyle's corpuscularianism, those who remained Helmontians, and those who attempted an amalgamation between the two.[299]

---

[295] The current debate consists of the following articles: Chalmers, 'The lack of excellency of Boyle's mechanical philosophy' (1993); Chalmers, 'Experiment versus mechanical philosophy in the work of Robert Boyle' (2002); Chalmers, 'Boyle and the origins of modern chemistry' (2010); Chalmers, 'Understanding science through its history' (2011); opposed by Newman, 'Alchemical Sources'; Newman, *Atoms and alchemy*; Newman, 'How not to integrate the history and philosophy of science' (2010). See also Clericuzio, 'A redefinition of Boyle's chemistry and corpuscular philosophy' (1990); Anstey, 'Robert Boyle and the heuristic value of mechanism' (2002); Anstey, 'Boyle on seminal principles' (2002).

[296] RS BP8, fols. 184$^r$–185$^r$ (in sections of 'An essay of various degrees or kinds of the knowledge of natural things', 1660s–80s, fols. 184$^r$–187$^r$).

[297] Chalmers, 'Understanding science', 151–2.

[298] Newman, 'How not to integrate', 209–10 also discusses the important RS BP8, fols. 165$^r$–70$^r$, which, he concludes, 'was intended to separate [Boyle] from what he viewed as an excessively deductive and non-experimental type of mechanical philosophy as practised by certain unnamed Epicureans and Cartesians'.

[299] I adopt this tripartite division from Clercicuzio, 'Carneades and the chemists', 85–6.

Wren's aforementioned contrast between chymistry and mechanical modelling was very likely indebted to his acquaintance Boyle. That this conclusion could be accepted on competing sides in the medical debates of the 1660s is testimony to its popularity.[300] Marchamont Nedham resoundingly critiqued Galenic and Aristotelian matter theory, and regularly spoke of 'atoms', but he never once aligned them with either Epicurus or Democritus; unsurprising, since for him they were not physical principles but akin to morborific particles in the vein of *semina* (Sennert was again a key source).[301] George Castle, an acquaintance of Boyle's from Oxford, despite his opposition to Nedham, was also clearly inspired by Willis and Sennert. In his *Chymical Galenist* (1667), he mocked the Helmontian *archeus* and even *semina*, and argued that 'the advantages which came from *Chymistry* to Medicine, were very slender and incosiderable, till it fell into the hands of Rational Learned Men . . . adapting it to the *Atomical Philosophy*'.[302] But he still made sure to align this with the 'chymical' Democritus rather than with Epicurus.[303] Base mechanism was out of the question: nitro-sulphurous salts were, 'as it were, the Soul of the World'.[304]

Most interesting in this respect is the case of John Twysden, an Oxford-educated Fellow of the College of Physicians. Twysden knew not only Boyle, but also Gassendi, with whom he claimed to have 'frequently converse[d]' during a period in Paris.[305] Rather remarkably he claimed that Gassendi 'would never declare his opinion to agree with that of *Epicurus*, onely resolving to write his Life and Philosophie'.[306] This was obviously intended to support Twysden's own fulsome rejection of Epicurean matter theory. Among many criticisms, he even accepted the Aristotelian one that Epicurean atoms were mathematical points and thus could not be indivisible: this was a major dissent from his friend Gassendi, but may also have stemmed from Twysden's own mathematical interests.[307] The

---

[300]  For medical matter theories, see now Anstey, 'The matter of medicine' (2011).
[301]  Nedham, *Medela medicinae*, 113–14, 185–203; Anstey, 'Matter of medicine', 68–70.
[302]  Castle, *Chymical Galenist*, 9–10. See also 5, 6–7, 10–11, 134, 136, 176–8; Anstey, 'Matter of medicine', 70–2; Frank, *Harvey*, 195–6.
[303]  Castle, *Chymical Galenist*, sigs. A3$^v$–A4$^r$.     [304]  Ibid., 127.
[305]  John Twysden, *Medicina veterum vindicata, or, an anwer to a book, entitled Medela medicinae* (London, 1666), 138–9. For friendship with Boyle, see Anstey, 'Matter of medicine', 77, n. 16. For his biography, see Moore and Wallis, 'Twysden' – although the details are shady, he appears to have been in Paris between 1645 and *c.* 1650 (graduating MD at Angers in 1646).
[306]  Twysden, *Medicina veterum vindicata*, 139.
[307]  Ibid., 141, and more fully, 136–56. See John Twysden, 'To the reader', in Samuel Foster, *Elliptical, or azimuthal horologiography* (London, 1654) (which Twysden edited after Foster's death in 1652); Samuel Foster, *Miscellanies, or mathematical lucubrations of Mr. Samuel Foster published and many of them translated into English by . . . John Twysden* (London, 1659); John Twysden, *Problematum quorundam mathematicorum . . . analytica solutio, et constructio* (London, 1659); Twysden, *The use of the general planishpere, called the analemma* (London, 1685). As the title of Twysden's anti-Nedham work suggests, he was a keen student of antiquity: see also his *Disquisition touching the sibyls and the sibylline writings* (London, 1662).

true 'ancient' opinion, he claimed, was an amalgam of the chymical principles of sulphur and mercury and Galenic four-elements theory: 'the ancient Philosophers did conceive and hold, that their *Sulphur* and *Mercury* is something that lies hid in the heart of that matter which is a compound of the four Elements'.[308] Unlike Epicurean atomism, such non-reductionist explanations actually fitted with medical experience.[309]

The reductionism of ancient atomism now came to be a standard assumption in the most prominent works of experimental philosophy. A particularly curious way of viewing the history of philosophy through the refracting glass of reductionism was adopted by the important physiologist of respiration John Mayow, yet another product of the Oxford natural philosophical circle (although he began his study of chymistry slightly later than the Oxford heyday, *c.* 1667).[310] In his 'On nitrous salt, and the nitro-aerial spirit', printed in the *Tractatus quinque medico physici* (1674), which developed his earlier work on aerial nitre as the source of life through respiration, Mayow implicitly adopted a quasi-corpuscularian, but not atomic, matter theory: 'Mayow clearly assumed that ultimate particles had distinct properties, properties that were not derived from their magnitude or figure. In this sense, in his belief in the real distinctiveness of saline-sulphurous corpuscles, or nitro-aerial particles, he was closer to the corpuscular philosophy of Boyle, and even more so to that of Willis, than to the French mechanists'.[311] He justified this with a strikingly simple history of matter theory:

Let us look over ... what role the nitro-aerial spirit ... has in causing fire. Upon this our opinion is that *the form of the flame chiefly proceeds from the nitro-aerial spirit set in motion*. For I do not think the recent philosophers should be agreed with, in whose opinion fire can be started by intensely agitating the subtle particles of any matter whatsoever. For while once the Peripatetics assigned some distinct quality for almost any natural operation, and multiplied entities unnecessarily, the Neoterics on the other hand think that each natural effect comes from the same material, merely through changes in its form and its state of motion or rest, and that consequently anything can be made from anything. But in truth this new philosophy appears to recede exceedingly from the doctrine of the ancients; and it seems preferable to me, to pursue a *via media*. By all means it is right to suppose that some material particles, not different except in their form and most compact and solid contexture, are indeed so different from others, that no natural power can change one into the other, and that the elements are made up from specific and primary particles of this type.[312]

---

[308] Twysden, *Medicina veterum vindicata*, 164–5. His key source is Jean d'Espagnet's *Enchiridion physicae restitutae* (Paris, 1608).

[309] Anstey, 'Matter of medicine', 74–6.

[310] Partington, 'The life and work of John Mayow' (1956); Frank, *Harvey*, 224–32, 262–72.

[311] Frank, *Harvey*, 272–3; see also Clericuzio, *Elements*, 150–1, which drew my attention to the quotation below.

[312] John Mayow, *Tractatus quinque medico-physici* (Oxford, 1674), 22–3: 'Despiciamus nunc autem proxime, quas partes spiritus nitro-aereus, sive, quod idem est, pars nitri aerea in igne

All of Boyle's long agonising over the ancient atomists has gone, in favour of the simplest story: the ancients (i.e. Aristotelians) multiplied qualities without cause, the moderns (by which is surely meant Descartes rather than Boyle)[313] have gone too far in reducing all natural phenomena to homogeneous principles. It seems pointless to ask whether Mayow was a 'mechanist': he was not operating with the same categories as we do, which are the product of a different worldview. Mayow's ambiguity about matter theory – which has so frustrated his interpreters – is probably of more importance: according to him it was the fault of both the qualitative ancients and the reductionist moderns to posit overly speculative particulate explications for phenomena and there was no experimental evidence to justify further speculation on the microparticulate constituents of nitro-aerial particles.

Even clearer on the issue was William Simpson, a physician from York who settled in London and developed a chymistry of fermentation on a Helmontian–corpuscularian base, seeing Helmontian *semina* as 'corpuscles containing a spiritual formative principle'.[314] In his *Zymologia physica* (1675) Simpson made it clear that his matter theory was different from that of Epicurus, or for that matter of Descartes, both of whom made 'a pleasant *Mathematical Scheme*' – note that Epicurus is being accused of mathematising nature, precisely the methodological accusation Gassendi had battled so hard to save him from.[315] The question of infinite divisibility was irrelevant: the natural philosopher was to examine those 'parcels of matter as ... come nearest to be perceptible to the acutest Organs of our Sense' and which could be produced by experimental division. Reductionism to shape, size, and motion simply could not explain 'the whole business' of natural phenomena.[316] This message was expanded in the *Philosophical dialogues concerning the principles of*

---

excitando fortitur. Super hoc nostra fert opinio, *Flammae formam à Spiritu Nitro-aereo, in motum concito, praecipuè dependere.* Neque enim nuperis Philosophis assentiendum esse arbitror, ex quorum sententia ignis à particulis materiae cujusvis subtilibus, valde commotis conflari potest. Nimirum cum olim Peripatetici pro operatione fere quavis naturali qualitatem quandam distinctam assignarunt, & Entia sine necessitate multiplicarunt; Neoterici è contra effectus quosque naturales ab eadem materia, figurâ ejus, statuque motûs; aut quietis tantum variatis, provenire statuunt; & consequenter quidlibet ex quolibet fieri posse. Verum enimvero Philosophia haec nova à veterum doctrina nimis recedere videtur; mihique potius visum est, mediâ viâ insistere: Quippe opinari fas sit, particulas materiae aliquas non alio, quàm figurae, & partium suarum contexturae, maxime compactae, solidaeque, respectu, ab aliis adeo diversas esse; ut hae in illas nullâ vi naturali commutari possint: atque à particulis istiusmodi peculiaribus, primariisque *Elementa* constituta esse. Hinc ignem non, nisi à certi generis particulis, conflandum esse arbitror: id quod vel exinde liquet, quoniam idem sine particulis nitro-aereis excitari prorsus nequeat'.

[313] In this judgement, I follow Clericuzio, *Elements*, 151, rather than Partington, 'Mayow', 406.

[314] Clericuzio, *Elements*, 153–4. By far the fullest treatment is now Roos, *Salt of the earth*, 108–54.

[315] William Simpson, *Zymologia physica, or, a brief philosophical discourse of fermentation* (London, 1675), sigs. [A6]$^{r-v}$.

[316] Ibid., 2–3.

*natural bodies* (1677), where the religious and methodological critiques of ancient atomism were combined. Being atheists, Epicurus, Democritus, and Leucippus were happy to build a world in which atoms came together randomly; thus their reductionism and failure to recognise the need for chymical analysis of fermentation and the search for *semina*.[317] Their system was again classified as speculative–mathematical because Democritus assigned a pyramidic form to fire atoms; but how could a pyramid 'always made up of Lines, Superficies, and Profundities (the natural sequels of Solids)' be indivisible?[318] This is of course a rehash of Aristotle's claim that Democritus had proposed mathematical indivisibles: it is instructive to find it being recycled for anti-atomist use by the chymical corpuscularians. Simpson contrasted this atomic reductionism with his own theory that 'acidic spirits in water reacted with sulphureous and fiery components of matter to ferment and produce "the formations and transformations of Bodies"', for which he found a precedent in the safely 'experimental' Hippocrates. 'The great *Hypocrates* himself has given touches thereof, while in his Book *de Dicta* he tells us, *Constituuntur tum omnia animantia, tum homo ipse ex duobus, igne & aqua* ... So that it appears that *Fermentation* in our sense, is the same with his *Spiritus impetum faciens* ... Fire hid in bodies'.[319] This Hippocratic comparison had already been made by Helmont to offer a historical precedent for his *archeus*, but Simpson's source was the *Hippocrates chymicus* (1669) by Otto Tachenius, a Venice-based iatrochymist from Westphalia;[320] Simpson was not the only Englishman to make it.[321]

Perhaps the most interesting case is that of Thomas Sherley, who had possibly studied with Oldenburg in the 1650s and gone on to obtain an MD in France, returning to practise medicine in London in the late 1660s and seemingly becoming physician-in-ordinary to Charles II in the early

---

[317] Simpson, *Philosophical dialogues*, 32, 80–2.

[318] Ibid., 155. Simpson made a strange mistake here, for every source says Democritus held fire atoms to be spherical: Aristotle, *De anima*, 403$^b$31–404$^a$3; Aristotle, *De Caelo*, 303$^a$12–16; Philoponus, *In phys.*, 25.21–26.8, 228.28–229.2; Philoponus, *In Gen. Corr.*, 12.31–13.2. No doubt he was misled by some later variant on the discussion of fire in Plato, *Timaeus*, 61$^d$–62$^a$ (where there is no mention of Democritus).

[319] Simpson, *Zymologia*, sigs. A4$^{r-v}$. Roos, *Salt of the earth*, 116 also discusses this passage. See also the comparable use of Hippocrates made by Josephus Thomas Rosetti in the eighteenth century: French, *Medicine before science* (2003), 242–3.

[320] van Helmont, *Ortus medicinae*, 548b ('Adeoque Archeum esse impetum facientem, apud Hippocratem extraque ... '). That Tachenius was Simpson's source is admitted in *Zymologia*, sig. A4$^r$, and discussed at Roos, *Salt of the earth*, 116; see esp. Otto Tachenius, *Hippocrates chymicus* (Lyon, 1671 [1st edn=Venice, 1666]), sig. *6$^v$. Tachenius's work was reviewed in *Philosophical Transactions*, 4 (1669), 1019–21; for Boyle's reaction, see Hall, 'Acid and alkali in seventeenth-century chemistry' (1956). A popular English translation was later produced: *Otto Tachenius his Hippocrates chymicus*, trans. J[ohn] W[arr] (London, 1677 [2nd edn, 1696; 3rd, 1696]) (Warr's autograph manuscript of the translation is RS BP32).

[321] Cf. Nedham, *Medela medicinae*, 40.

1670s.[322] His *Philosophical essay declaring the probable causes whence stones are produced in the greater world* (1672) was partly inspired by Boyle, whom Sherley knew; it has been described as a 'fusion of Helmontian doctrines with the corpuscular philosophy'.[323] Sherley held water and *semina* as the basic principles and claimed Boyle towards this Helmontian view, citing the historical passage from the *Sceptical chymist* that we have met.[324] He explained that he sought 'to explicate ... the Origin of Bodies, by the *Mechanical* Principles', but that he differed from those mechanists who 'leave out the first principle of Natural Motions; viz. the Seminal principle'.[325] And so his pre-history for this finding, offered in the final section of the work, discussed not Epicurus or even Democritus, but was devoted to showing that this 'doctrine ... is no Novel conceit; but so Ancient, that we shall find that it was held, [and by them transmitted to Posterity] not only by *Plato, Timaeus Locrus, Parmenides, Pythagoras, &c.* Philosophers of the Academick and Italick Sect; but also by *Orpheus, Thales* the *Milesian*, and also by *Mochos*, and *Sanchoniathon*, the great, and Ancient *Phoenician* Philosophers; nay, by that Divinely illuminated Man, *Moses*'.[326] Beginning with Gen. 1:2 ('and the spirit of God moved upon the face of the waters'), he claimed that in the original Hebrew, the verb מרחפת ('moved'),

properly signifieth not a bare motion, but such a motion as we call Hovering, or Incubation, as Birds use to do over their Eggs to hatch them ... in all probability, the sence of the Expression is, that at that time ... God infused into the bosome of the waters, the seeds of all those things, which were afterwards to be made out of the waters, setting them their constant Laws, and Rules of acting.[327]

He then proceeded to match various expressions of the Phoenician and Greek philosophers onto the same 'seminal' reading. He repeated the same evidence for Sanchoniathon, Mochus, Orpheus, and Thales as had been offered in this regard by Boyle from Grotius. But he also went further, offering evidence for Pherecydes and claiming that Pythagoras's 'first matter' (ὕλη) was equivalent to Sanchoniathon's primordial slime (μὼτ). Plato's *anima mundi* was given a materialist–vitalist interpretation rendering it equivalent with Stoic *logoi spermatikoi*, and Platonic 'ideas' were categorised as the paradigms of the *semina* in God's mind.[328]

One is immediately suspicious about Sherley having completed this philological journey alone, and a comparison reveals that he had cribbed and mangled the account offered in Theophilus Gale's *Court of the*

---

[322] Clericuzio, 'Sherley, Thomas', *ODNB*, is the fullest biographical discussion.
[323] Clericuzio, *Elements*, 153; see also Debus, 'Thomas Sherley's *Philosophical essay*' (1980).
[324] Thomas Sherley, *A philosophical essay declaring the probable causes whence stones are produced in the greater world* (London 1672), 57.
[325] Ibid., sig. *ʳ.    [326] Ibid., 23.    [327] Ibid., 111–12.    [328] Ibid., 113–21.

*gentiles.*[329] Sherley's appropriation of Gale, however, is truly ingenious. As we have seen, the nonconformist divine had used Bochart and his own scholarship for theological ends: to assert Judaic intellectual primacy (3.5). Sherley stripped his account of this message entirely and simply used what was for him a fortuitous coincidence: that Gale's Mosaic archetype – the interpretation of מרחפת as 'hovering' or 'incubation' (which Gale derived from the Genesis commentary of Paul Fagius (1542))[330] – fitted so conveniently his Helmontian purposes. Gale had done the philological hard work of matching the ancient philosophers' doctrines to those of Moses (although Sherley also often made them more materialistic, and thus compatible with *semina* theory, than Gale had). It is important to emphasise that the main pay-off for Sherley was not religious–theological but philosophical–methodological: plundering Gale allowed him to propose a counter-history to that which encompassed the '*Atomical, Cartesian, or Corpuscularian* Philosophers', which while being 'very ingenious', was ultimately the resort only of those who 'desire[d] of being accounted witty Disputants'.[331]

Epicurus and his ancient atomist counterparts were thus presented as speculative and reductionist, not dissimilar to Aristotle amongst the ancients and Descartes among the moderns. So far we have charted this conclusion mostly among medical and chymical authors; as always, the real significance came when it became a commonplace. Already by 1671, Ralph Bohun, in his *Discourse concerning the origine and properties of wind*, dismissed Epicurus as the creator of a 'theory' no less speculative than Aristotle.[332] Matthew Hale made the case even more explicitly.[333] In the case of Roger North (1651–1734), a lawyer of very wide intellectual interests who became a nonjuror after 1689,[334] we can chart how the conclusion reached him. In the British Library there survive hundreds of pages of a treatise by North on natural philosophy, and notes towards it, composed in the last decade of the seventeenth century and the first decade of the next.[335] North was the last great English Cartesian, fuelled at least in part by his strong dislike of Newtonianism.[336] This Cartesian

---

[329] Theophilus Gale, *Court . . . Part I. Of Philologie*, III (new pagination), 40–3; *Court . . . Part II. Of Philosophie*, 56, 111–13, 118–26, 162–3, 240, 313–15, 319–26.

[330] Gale, *Court I*, III, 42; Paul Fagius, *Exegesis sive expositio dictionum Hebraicarum literalis & simplex, in quatuor capita Geneseos, pro studiosis linguae hebraicae* (Isny im Allgäu, 1542), 11–12.

[331] Sherley, *Philosophical essay*, 123–4. It is clear that by 'corpuscularian' Sherley did not mean the same as Boyle, but something similar to 'atomist'.

[332] Bohun, *Wind*, 49. See also the explicit condemnation of Epicurean atomism as non-observational in Evelyn, *History of religion*, I, 55–6.

[333] [Hale], *Natural motions*, sigs. [A5]ʳ⁻ᵛ.    [334] See p. 325, n. 493 above.

[335] Korsten, *North*, 29–56; Chan and Kassler, *North chronology*.

[336] Although North himself claimed that his interest in Cartesian natural philosophy was stimulated during his time at Jesus College, Cambridge (1667–8) (BL MS Add. 32506, fols. 18ᵛ–19ʳ), thus predating his anti-Newtonianism.

allegiance did not stop him taking an interest in the history of philosophy: he speculated – with more originality than many we have met – on the causes of Aristotle's success in the ancient world,[337] and even attempted to defend Descartes from the charge of philological philistinism: 'It is most apparent from Cartesius applying himself both in his Geometry, & philosophy to the Notions, defects and the ... discoverys of the ancients, that he was very conversant with them, and was as nice a Critic in their severall texts & the designe of them, as any what ever'.[338]

North, however, was no dogmatic Cartesian, for in his notes and drafts we find a remarkably resolute scepticism about Cartesian microparticulate explanations, repeated again and again: 'that [Cartesian] sect however coming nearest truth in general, yet in $y^e$ formed hypothesis have assumed for principles certain stated formes & figures, as well as motions of imperceptible matter, $w^{ch}$ are so open to a prompt denyall as makes all $y^e$ usefull inventions of Descartes of less authority'.[339] This is all the more remarkable given his (mitigated) acceptance of Cartesian vortex theory, by then *the* archetypal 'speculative' hypothesis.[340] Most importantly for us, North argued that it was a lesson from the history of philosophy that speculation on microparticulate structure was fruitless. The ancient atomists' proposal of variously shaped particles was pure fancy, an improvement on Aristotle only in that they saved the phenomena (although even for this they had to posit not only entirely unobserved microparticulate shapes but also such *dei ex machina* as innate principles of gravitation and the *clinamen*).[341] Just as with Boyle, this reading

---

[337] BL MS Add. 32546 ('More notes on naturall philosophy'), fol. 208$^{r-v}$: 'I doe beleeve the heathen priests thought Aristotles phisicks least hurtfull to their trade, and the other way, more dangerous, ffor Aristotle was sufferd $y^e$ best in $y^e$ world to teach $y^e$ heathen religion, deserving hardly the name of a philosopher, as Meddling onely with a few appearances here on Earth, leaving vastly $y^e$ Greater of $y^e$ univers to be Managed by God or petty Intelligences. And all his Qualitys, Naturall Endowments, Gravity ... were referr'd to $y^e$ deity' (North goes on to mention that the systematic nature of the Aristotelian corpus also made him an easier guide than the fragmentary and obscure works of Plato and Epicurus). This interpretation may have been influenced by Hobbes, whose anti-scholasticism is later mentioned (fols. 209$^v$–210$^r$) (but cf. the criticism of Hobbes's attack on immaterial substances at fol. 266$^v$).

[338] BL MS Add. 32546, fol. 214$^r$. North goes on to give the example of Descartes's engagement with Pappus's problem (i.e. the problem mentioned in Pappus, *Collectio*, vii.33.40, dealt with at length by Descartes in *La Géométrie*, the appendix to the *Discourse on Method* (1637)); to claim that Descartes, deliberately in opposition to the eternalism of the ancients, 'found a way to shew that the same laws as maintained [the world] might possibly be the means of bringing it together'; and to insist on Descartes's supposedly deliberate correction of ancient atomism.

[339] BL MS Add. 32544 (PHYSICA: an essay on natural philosophy), fols. 10$^{r-v}$. See also e.g., BL MS Add. 32545 ('Autobiographical notes, and draughts, more or less imperfect, of essays on natural philosophy'), fol. 11$^v$; BL MS Add. 32548 ('Loci phisiologici, ordine fortuito'), fols. 10$^{r-v}$; BL MS Add. 32546, fols. 29$^v$, 143$^r$.

[340] BL MS Add. 32546, fols. 94$^v$–100$^r$. For the fate of vortex theory, see p. 183, n. 358 above.

[341] BL MS Add. 32544, fols. 9$^v$–10$^r$, 87$^{r-v}$, 96$^v$; BL MS Add. 32546, fol. 143$^r$; BL MS Add. 32548, fol. 18$^{r-v}$.

of the ancient atomists sat alongside the claim that Aristotle had corrupted the natural philosophy of his predecessors – especially Democritus – with logic and sophistry.[342] The history of philosophy taught the need for self-limiting in matter theory: 'diverse have ... used this Hypothesis, $w^{ch}$ is called $y^e$ Corpuscular, but few or rather none with that justice, & Retention as ought to be; that is to carry it on so far as a just reasoning will warrant & no further; & as for $y^e$ rest to sit down contended $w^{ch}$ is better than to spoil all with doubtefull guessing';[343] even Boyle, 'after all his reiterated examination of Compound Body, with the consequent separations, and distinctions of salt, oyles, flegme, & I know not what, he could never discover what any one of those products consisted of'.[344]

North had clearly thought about this issue independently and in detail. However, one work is cited repeatedly when discussing it: Jean Le Clerc's *Physica sive de rebus corporeis* (1696). We have met Le Clerc as a scholar, but on this occasion we are dealing with a natural philosophy textbook designed as part of a series of textbooks – very popular in England – covering the whole of the philosophy component of the arts course.[345] Le Clerc was undoubtedly influenced by the methodological rhetoric of Boyle and Locke, both of whom he knew.[346] In his preface he chastised ancient philosophy for neglecting experiment and instead focusing on speculation, for evidence of which one only had to 'cast one's eyes to Diogenes Laërtius', and which he ascribed to the intellectual culture of the Greeks.[347] Of specific relevance for us is how this attitude manifested itself in the final, fifth book of the work, 'De corpore in

---

[342] BL MS Add. 32546, fols. 207$^v$–208$^r$: 'Aristotle must in his physicks have fallen into Democritus way ... but his logick spoyled all'; also fols. 209$^r$; 300$^r$.

[343] BL MS Add. 32544, fols. 9$^{r-v}$.    [344] BL MS Add. 32548, fol. 55$^r$.

[345] Other texts were the *Ontologia et pneumatologia* (Amsterdam, 1692) and the *Logica: sive ars ratiocinandi* (London, 1692). They were published in many editions in London and Amsterdam between 1690 and 1720. The first edition to contain them all was the *Opera philosophica* (Amsterdam, 1698). The popularity of Le Clerc's works in English pedagogy is testified by the *Physica* being one of the first works printed at the new Cambridge University Press for the London bookseller Timothy Child in an edition of 1700; further editions followed in 1705 and 1708, totalling a print run of 2500: McKenzie, *The Cambridge University Press, 1696–1712* (1966), I, 100, 161, 166, 255; McKitterick, *CUP*, II, 84.

[346] See *Boyle correspondence*, VI, 258, 292, 328–30 (which reveals that he taught philosophy for two hours a day at the Remonstrant seminary); a letter from as early as 1682 is unfortunately lost (*Boyle correspondence*, V, 284).

[347] Jean Le Clerc, *Physica, sive, de rebus corporeis* (London, 1696), sig. [*8]$^v$: 'Veteres etiam celerius aequo, non sat multis edoctos experimentis, circa rerum naturalium causas, conjecturis nimiùm indulsisse iidem demonstrarunt. Ac sanè plerorumque Veterum dogmata Physica adeò inficeta erant, ut aut vocabulis obscuris ab ineptissimis vulgi opinionibus duntaxat differrent; aut si clariùs proponerentur, & novi quidpiam complecterentur, palam absurda ut plurimùm essent, quod exemplis illustrare non necesse est, cùm oculos vel in *Diogenem Laërtium* conjicienti ingens se eorum statim ingerat seges ... Si quis rationem tantae, hoc in negotio, Veterum caecitatis quaerat, ea paritm in levitate Graecorum, qui quàm primùm ad unguem omnia tenere videri volebant, partim in rei ipsius obscuritate inveniri poterit'.

genere'. Le Clerc went through all the available matter theories, condemning each for excessive speculation: Aristotelian prime matter; the four elements of Empedocles, 'which position no one approached, except in a dream';[348] the five principles of the chymists; and most importantly, the atomism of the ancients and moderns. The hypothesis of one common element was preferable to the others, but in reality the systems of Democritus and Epicurus had been no less speculative than those of their Greek counterparts: their hypothesis of solid atoms was just an 'invention' (*figmentum*) that was 'equally easy to deny as to affirm'.[349]

The result was less a traditional textbook and more a series of discussions of possibilities, whose main message was summarised in the final paragraph:

> This brings to an end the fifth and final book of our *Physics*, from which it is clear that it has not yet been possible to find the hypotheses, which, had they been posited, would have offered an account of the properties of all corporeal bodies, and that the whole of this discipline swarms with uncertain conjectures, although there are many splendid discoveries, & more discovered daily. And so it should neither be scorned too much, nor held in too great esteem. It is more useful to be ingenious men who, like Democritus, wear away life in experiments and the search for truth, so as to light the way for others.[350]

Here we have all the themes we have met already: pessimism about the possibility of full corpuscularian explanations and condemnation of ancient atomism as yet another speculative theory, combined with an exhortation towards experimentalism defended on the authority of one of those atomists, Democritus. That this vision of the history of matter theory, developed most fully by the aristocratic virtuso Boyle and taken up by the Amsterdam scholar and textbook writer Le Clerc, inspired North – perhaps the most devoted English Cartesian – testifies to its power to convince late seventeenth-century natural philosophers.

Since the 1980s, a strand of the historiography has wanted to present the English corpuscularians as somewhat self-contradictory in their countenancing

---

[348] Ibid., 365: 'Verùm cùm ea loca nemo umquam adierit, nisi somniando, nihil nos cogit somniis *Empedoclis* aut aliorum fidem adhibere'.

[349] Ibid., 378: 'Suppositio atomorum solidarum, ita ut comminui nequeant, merum est *Democriti*, quem *Epicurus* sequutus est, figmentum, quod aequè facilè negari potest, ac affirmatur'. So ingrained was this attitude by then that Le Clerc did not feel the need to offer much of an argument, beyond God's omnipotence ('Deinde circa ejusmodi Atomos moveri possunt omnes quaestiones quae ad divisibilitatem materiae pertinent, nam quamvis atomi actu non dividerentur, tamen à Deo possent dividi, non aliter ac majores materiae moles').

[350] Ibid., 491: 'Hîc finem statuemus huic quinto eidemque ultimo Physicae nostrae Libro; ex quo satis liquet nondum potuisse inveniri Hypotheses, quibus positis proprietatum omnium rerum corporearum ratio redderetur; & totam hanc disciplinam scatere incertissimis conjecturis, quamvis multa praeclara inventa sint, & quotidie inveniantur. Itaque ut nequaquam spernenda est, sic neque nimio in pretio habenda. Utile est esse viros ingeniosos qui, *Democritii* instar, in experimentis, & investigatione veri vitam terant, ut aliis facem praeferant'.

of active principles like *semina*, and in their ambiguity about microparticulate structure.[351] Inevitably, this accusation has depended on comparisons with the 'pure' atomism of the ancients; Andrew Pyle, for example, has organised a whole monograph on the history of atomism as a history of deviations from or approximations to classical atomism, 'an *ideal* Atomist position capable of serving as a sort of landmark for future reference'.[352] Yet we have seen time and time again that English natural philosophers did *not* see ancient atomism as an ideal. This was not primarily for reasons of religion or even natural philosophical doctrine, but for reasons of method. For some, it led to a total rejection of microparticulate theory; more often, it led to a mitigated and cautious corpuscularianism – a position that Peter Anstey has demonstrated Locke to have held, usefully labelling it 'corpuscular pessimism'.[353] Even more importantly, Newton, as we shall see, saw Democritus and Epicurus as speculators who had to introduce arbitrarily the concept of innate atomic gravitation to explain the cause of movement, a cause which their atomic predecessors had refrained from speculating about (5.4.5). Those who continued to hypothesise about atomic structure after the 1660s, such as William Petty, were mostly met with derision.[354] When English natural philosophers did see ancient atomism as a yardstick it was usually only as a measure of the possible results of speculative system building.

In this, they were influenced primarily by lessons learnt from chymistry and the life sciences. This, I hope, helps sheds some light on the supposed tension between English corpuscularianism and residual 'animist' influences within it. This tension was not necessarily evident to seventeenth-century English natural philosophers because they did not seek to place themselves on a scale somewhere from 'pure' ancient atomism to (by implication) 'corrupt' corpuscularianism. As far as they were concerned, their doctrine was qualitatively different to that of the ancient atomists, because they were engaged in a different intellectual project. This is despite the fact that an even more important historical identity for seventeenth-century English natural philosophers was their supposed separation from the animism and idolatrous teleology of all the ancient philosophers: this is the theme we turn to now.

---

[351] Esp. since Henry, 'Occult qualities and the experimental philosophy'.

[352] Pyle, *Atomism*, xi (this is already commented on in Lüthy, Murdoch, and Newman, 'Introduction', 8. But see their comments on Lasswitz: 'it is unfortunate that, by way of the second part of his introduction, he did not see fit to treat of the atomism of Democritus, Epicurus, and Lucretius, since this would have enabled him to use these ancient philosophers as a kind of foil against which to measure and point up the differences of the subsequent atomists from the Middle Ages to the seventeenth century that he did investigate' (5)).

[353] Anstey, *Locke*, 31–45, 9.

[354] In Petty's *Discourse made before the Royal Society … concerning the use of duplicate proportion* (London, 1674), very fully discussed in Lewis, *Petty*, 1–9, supplanting Kargon, 'William Petty's mechanical philosophy' (1965).

## 5.4     Ancient philosophy as idolatrous animism

We have already seen hints – not only in more scholarly treatments like Cudworth's, but also in the discussions of the natural philosophers themselves – that the issue of what we would now associate with the concepts of 'animism', 'vitalism', or even 'pantheism' were major concerns of those who engaged with the history of natural philosophy. This will of course come as no surprise to those with even a cursory knowledge of seventeenth-century philosophy: Cartesian dualism, Spinozist monism, Malebranche's occasionalism, and (more importantly than any of these) the general collapse of Aristotelian theories of causation, all raised the problem of the nature of causation and the relationship between the material and immaterial and between God and his creation.[355] This was exacerbated by new speculations on the nature of space, its extension, and its relationship to the attributes of God.[356] But English natural philosophers spoke primarily not of 'animism' or even 'pantheism' but of 'idolatry': this brought them into dialogue with the histories of idolatry and religion epitomised by Vossius's *Theologia gentilis*. The most significant such discussion came in Boyle's hugely important *Free enquiry into the vulgarly receiv'd notion of nature* (1686).[357] Boyle argued that not only well-known animists like Plato and the Stoics but even Aristotle himself had held an idolatrous view of nature that placed an intermediate principle such as an *anima mundi* between God and the world, and in turn conflated the latter with the former; this view was derived from the idolatrous theologies of the near east. He claimed that it also influenced Galenic medicine, with its theories of battling elements and crises as 'Nature's' method of curing illness. This he contrasted with the world-view of the new philosophers like himself, which safely preserved the distance between God and his creation while recognising his operation in the world.[358]

We might interpret Boyle's claims in various ways. Some historians of science have declared that what Boyle was targeting was Aristotelianism in some 'real' sense, as if his genius extended to correctly analysing the 'true' content of ancient philosophies, which unfold with unyielding logic throughout

---

[355] For Malebranche in England, see McCracken, *Malebranche and British philosophy* (1983); Mander, *The philosophy of John Norris* (2008), 10–13. Oldenburg was preparing a translation of the *De la recherche de la vérité* (1674): Malcolm, 'Oldenburg library', 6.

[356] Grant, *Much ado about nothing* (1981) remains key. See also Copenhaver, 'Jewish theologies of space in the scientific revolution' (1980). There are very many studies of Newton on space: see the citations below.

[357] On the development of the work, see Hunter and Davis, 'The making of Robert Boyle's *Free enquiry into the vulgarly receiv'd notion of nature*' (2007), quotation from 219.

[358] For evidence of Boyle agonising on precisely this point, see Anstey, 'Boyle on occasionalism' (1999).

the course of history: 'What Boyle describes here is, indeed, the *Aristotelian* concept of nature enlarged by what natural philosophy in its history has made out of the Aristotelian ideas'.[359] This follows more generally the classic reading of the scientific revolution as witnessing a shift from (largely Aristotelian) immanent teleology to either non-teleological or 'voluntarist' models.[360] A second type of reading has concerned itself with identifying Boyle's contemporary targets, treating his discussion of ancient doctrines as a cipher for figures like Henry More, Sir Matthew Hale, William Harvey, Francis Glisson, and Ralph Cudworth.[361] This may have been the case. But if Boyle's point was to have any force it had to be made in a historiographical climate in which it was believable to say that Aristotle had conflated God and nature. This had been denied by generations of Aristotelian commentaries and textbooks, many of them still in use in England. As far as they were concerned, Aristotle was not at all animistic, but had preserved the distance between God and nature; often they directly contrasted him with Plato or with other more obviously animistic Greek philosophers. Such a conclusion can be found in many of the most prominent natural philosophical textbooks and the notes readers took from them. Burgersdijk's very popular physics textbook announced that the only thing more absurd than the Stoic and Platonic positing of an *anima mundi* was the equation of it with God; Wendelin, in a long and scholarly discussion, distinguished Aristotelianism from its Platonic–Arabic animistic corruption; Petrus Hurtado's *Universa philosophia*, published in a London edition in 1624, asserted that Aristotle placed God above nature and claimed that animating the heavens was only a Platonic error; Adrian Heereboord's *Philosophia naturalis* (Oxford edition: 1665) equated the scholastic term *natura naturans* with God – exactly the same step as taken by Boyle in the *Free enquiry*; and Magirus's *Physiologia*, used by the undergraduate Newton among others, explained that God was separate from nature and stated that this was why Aristotelian natural philosophy could not discuss the nature of God, a hubristic aim that was

---

[359] Mittelstrass, 'Nature and science in the Renaissance' (1988), 32; see also Deason, 'Reformation theology and the mechanistic conception of nature' (1986), 180, which presents Boyle's claims as a quasi-inevitable logical consequence of the clash between Protestant voluntarism and Aristotelian teleology.

[360] This idea is, in various ways, a central feature of Burtt, *The metaphysical foundations of modern science* (1932), 98ff; Osler, 'From immanent natures to nature as artifice: the reinterpretation of final causes in seventeenth-century natural philosophy' (1996); Shapin, *The scientific revolution* (1996), 28–30; Harrison, *Natural science*, 169–84, *passim*.

[361] Hunter and Davis, 'Making', 258–70, *passim*. Hunter and Davis's work far surpasses the previously influential Jacob, 'Boyle's atomism and the Restoration assault on pagan naturalism' (1978), which claims that Boyle's targets were 'papists' and 'paganising deists', and that the *Free enquiry* was published deliberately in response to James II's religious policies. Shapin and Schaffer, *Leviathan and the air-pump* (1985), 202–7 attempt to render Hobbes another target – the attempt is, to my eyes, unsuccessful.

assigned solely to the 'Platonici'.[362] How did the situation change enough for Boyle to be able to make his iconoclastic claims, and to have them widely accepted?

### 5.4.1  Medicine

The critique, made in a haphazard way, was already known to the anti-Aristotelian tradition. Aristotle had famously defined 'nature' as a teleological 'internal principle of motion' (*Physics*, iii, 192[b]8–15): 'God and nature do nothing in vain' (*De caelo*, 271[a]33). However idolatrous this might sound, early Christian apologists were far more concerned with the more overt animism of the Stoics and Plato, who had posited clear intermediaries between God and nature, most obviously the *anima mundi*. The only exception is a passage in Clemens Alexandrinus's *Protrepticus* in which, during a discussion of the errors of those pagan philosophers who 'being ignorant of the great First Cause' sought 'something higher and nobler' either in the elements or in an hypothetical infinite Mind (νοῦς), Aristotle was claimed to have believed that 'He who is called the Highest is the soul of the universe'.[363] If this was a rare example, it resurfaced in humanist anti-Aristotelianism. As early as the mid-fifteenth century, Lorenzo Valla, speaking of Aristotle's claim that 'God and nature do nothing in vain', was asking 'what is this "nature", some kind of goddess?'[364] Patrizi complained that unlike the fully animated (but subordinate to God) nature of the Platonists and the inanimate nature of Leucippus and Epicurus, Aristotle's 'nature' resembled not an animal but a monster.[365] Francis Bacon also claimed, as part of his attack on the search for final causes,

---

[362] See e.g. Giulio Pace, *Aristotelis Stagiritae, Peripateticorum principiis naturalis auscultationis libri VIII* (Frankfurt, 1596), 45; Burgersdijk, *Collegium physicum*, 344–5 ('Formam mundi, Academici Stoiceque voluerunt esse animam quandam, quâ totus mundus dicatur animatus, & vitam vivere distinctam à vita suarum partium ... Absurdum ergo est, mundo animâ tribuere. Sed multò absurdius, Deum mundi animam appellare. Nam si animam intelligant, quae sit mundi forma informans, blasphema sententia est: si animam formámve assistenté esse velint, excusari poterit sententia ab impietate; sed falsa tamen fuerit, atque absurda'); Wendelin, *Contemplationes physicae*, 55a–98b (esp. 85b), 248a–50b, 269a–78; Petrus Hurtado, *Universa philosophia* (London, 1624 [1st edn=Lyon, 1617]), 276a–b, 366b; Adrian Heereboord, *Philosophia naturalis* (Oxford, 1665), 38 (cf. Boyle, *Free enquiry*, 455); Magirus, *Physiologia Peripatetica*, 5–8, esp. 8. This idea also appears in mid-century English natural philosophy tuition: see BL Sloane MS 2514, 'Cursus Physici pars posterior', fol. 2[v] (one of the first things stated in the whole course is that it was only the Platonists who animated the world); it is still present in the early eighteenth century: Folger MS W.a.89, William Dey, 'Tractatus in physicam particularem': this is an overtly Aristotelian set of natural philosophical *disputationes* where under the heading 'An Coeli sint animati, et an fluidi?' (fol. 14[v]) only the Stoics are listed as those who animated the heavens. See also below for Thomas White.

[363] Clemens Alexandrinus, *Protr.*, v.    [364] Valla, *Dialectical disputations*, 94–103.

[365] Patrizi, *Nova de universis philosophia*, fol. 55[r] (in the chapter 'An mundus sit animatus'): 'Itaque a praestantissimis sapientibus, atque vetustissimis, Zoroastre, Hermete, & Graecis Orpheo, Pythagora, Pythagoreis, Platone, vetustissimo dogmate traditum est, mundum esse

that Aristotle was more culpable than even Plato for replacing God with an idolatrous 'nature'.[366] But these attacks were rare and unsystematic: they never formed the heart of an anti-Aristotelian argument.

A change came in the attack on Aristotle by van Helmont, an attack which placed Aristotle's definition of 'nature' at its centre. This definition, van Helmont argued, compromised God as the first cause. He instead offered his own 'Christian' definition: 'Nature is the decree of God, by which a thing is that which it is, and does what it is decreed to do'.[367] Crucially, as part of his proof that Aristotle's conception of nature was 'idolatrous', van Helmont focused on a famously ambiguous passage from *Generation of animals*, II.3 ($736^b30$–$737^a1$):

Now so far as we can see, the faculty of Soul of every kind has to do with some physical substance which is different from the so-called 'elements' and more divine than they are; and as the varieties of Soul differ from one another in the scale of value, so do the various substances concerned with them differ in their nature. In all cases the semen contains within itself that which causes it to be fertile–what is known as 'hot' substance, which is not fire nor any similar substance, but the *pneuma* which is enclosed within the semen or foam-like stuff, and the natural substance which is in the *pneuma*; and this substance is analogous to the element which belongs to the stars.[368]

This passage, with its allusive hint at a divine element central to life, had already been much contested in the commentary tradition and in Renaissance medicine.[369] For van Helmont it was proof that Aristotle held an idolatrous, animistic conception of nature.[370] In opposition, he proposed that it was not a

---

animatum. Quod & Thales, & Heraclitus, & Democritus, & Stoicorum universa secta docuerunt. Inter hos, duo quasi ridiculi Philosophi, Leucippus, & Epicurus, mundum omnino animo carere asseruerunt, eumque veluti cadaver effecerunt. Inter hos media via ingressus Aristoteles, mundum qui ei perfectissimus rerum omnium est visus, monstrum fecit, dimidia parte animatum, dimidia inanimem'.

[366] Francis Bacon, *De augmentis scientiarum* (London, 1623), 168–70 at 170: 'Atque magis in hâc parte accusandus Aristoteles quàm Plato, quandoquidem Fontem *Causarum Finalium, Deum* scilicet, omiserit, & *Naturam* pro *Deo substituerit; caussasque* ipsas *Finales* potiùs ut Logicae amator, quam Theologiae, amplexus sit'. Elsewhere, Bacon more standardly attributed this kind of error to the Pythagoreans and Platonists: *Novum organum*, 74 (=*OFB*, XI, 100–3). See also Basson, *Philosophia naturalis*, 181–259, on which see Lüthy, 'Basson', 15–18.

[367] van Helmont, *Ortus medicinae*, 46b: 'Ego vero credo, *Naturam jussum Dei, quo res est id quod est, & agit, quod agere jussa est*. Haec est definitio Christiana, è Sacris petita'.

[368] I use the translation from Aristotle, *Generation of animals*, ed. A. L. Peck (London, 1943), 171. Syncretic readings may have been encouraged by the fact that Aristotle elsewhere suggests that the 'τῷ τῶν ἄστρων στοιχείῳ' referred to at the end of this passage was known to ancient philosophers (apart from Anaxagoras, who mistook αἰθήρ for fire) (*De caelo*, I.3, $270^b16$–26).

[369] Two very valuable discussions of how various Renaissance Aristotelian commentators and medical theorists manipulated this passage are Deer, 'Academic theories', 397–419 (on Fernel, Argenterio, Riolan, Zabarella, Paparella, and Caimo) and Hirai, *Medical humanism*, 25–33, 68–75, 92–6, 111–12, 181–5.

[370] Van Helmont, *Ortus medicinae*, 47a–48a, quoting and discussing this passage at length. See further Pagel, *Helmont*, 39.

self-sufficient 'nature' but a divinely guided *archeus* that supplied the 'natural' teleology to the world. The actual pay-off of this was medical. Corrupting previous medical practice, Galen, driven by a hubristic desire to establish 'first qualities' and by his sharing Aristotle's principles, invented the doctrines of battling elements and contraries as the causes of disease.[371] This led to the belief that 'crises' are resolved by a personified '*natura medicatrix*'.[372] In reality, nature operated not from innate contrariety but through *semina* 'commanded by God'.[373]

The 'pagan' animation of the elements was therefore for Helmont a key defect of previous philosophies, especially Aristotelian and Galenic: as we shall see, Boyle undoubtedly drew on this critique. But it was not only anti-Aristotelians who found animist tendencies in the Stagirite. Harvey, despite his generally favourable attitude to Aristotle, challenged Aristotle's positing of the heart as the seat of life in the body, assigning principality to the blood.[374] In chapter 52 of *De generatione*, 'Of the blood in so far as it is the principal part', Harvey advanced his contra-Aristotelian theory by pointing out that although Aristotle denied that 'sensation and movement belong to the blood', the truth of that doctrine was 'obvious from many indications'.[375] Aristotle, Harvey claimed, was going against his own logic, for did he not say in the passage from the *Generation of animals* quoted above that bodies contained a vital principle analogous to the element of the stars, as the 'priest of the omnipotent Creator'? Why would one not then 'affirm that the soul is in the blood' and that 'from it the soul is first stirred and inflamed'?[376] Once again, the ambiguous

---

[371] van Helmont, *Ortus medicinae*, 164–8, esp. 167a–b.

[372] Ibid., 174. The reference to *natura medicatrix* is an obvious allusion to the famous saying attributed to Hippocrates, 'νοσων φνσεις ιητροι' (for which, see Neuburger, 'An historical survey of the concept of nature from a medical viewpoint' (1944)).

[373] van Helmont, *Ortus medicinae*, 168b: 'Semina autem ipsa nullatenus operantur ob scopum similitudinis, aut contraietatis (ut alioqui vulgo putatur) sed duntaxat, quia sic sunt jussa operari à rerum Domino, qui solus scientias, fines, seminibus dedit, sibi soli cognitos à priori'.

[374] Pagel, *Biological ideas*, 222–3; French, *Harvey*, 302–4; Webster, 'Harvey's *De Generatione*'; White, 'Harvey and the primacy of the blood' (1986). For Harvey's 'Aristotelian' vitalism, see also Pagel, 'The reaction to Aristotle in seventeenth-century biological thought' (1953).

[375] Harvey, *Exercitationes de generatione animalium*, 155: 'Utrunque autem, *sensum* scilicet, & *motum*, sanguine inesse; plurimis indiciis fit conspicuum: etiamsi *Aristoteles* id negaverit'. Harvey refers to *Hist. an.*, III, 520[b]19.

[376] Harvey, *De generatione*, 155: 'Enimverò, si is veritate coactus fateatur, inesse ovo, etiam subventaneo, animam: & in genitura, ac sanguine, reperiri *divinum quid, respondens elemento stellarum*; esseque omnipotentis Creatoris *vicarium* … quidni pari ratione affirmemus, animam esse in sanguine; cúmque hic primo generetur, nutriatur, & moveatur, ex eodem quoque animam primùm excitari, & *ignescere*?' See also Harvey, *Exercitatio anatomica de circulatione sanguinis* (London, 1649), 112, 114, where Harvey disagrees with Aristotle's comparison of blood and other hot liquids (both are hot only due to the action of an external agent), suggesting that Aristotle's own discussion of the blood leads to the conclusion that its nature is not caused 'by an external agent' but by 'an internal principle, the regulation of nature': 'Et

passage from the *Generation of animals* about the soul corresponding to the element of the stars was being used to render Aristotle a vitalist. Elsewhere, Harvey implied that the names for this 'mind, foresight, and understanding' in nature adopted in various ancient philosophies – God, *natura naturans, anima mundi* – were effectively interchangeable,[377] a claim that 'traditional' Aristotelians would never have accepted, as we have seen.

Harvey's work on the primacy of the blood informed Francis Glisson's later and far more overtly animist interpretations of the nature of life.[378] His arguments were developed primarily in the context of research into the liver, discussed in the *Anatomia hepatis* (1654), and on the stomach and intestines, which appeared in 1677 as *De ventriculo* but on his own account was completed in 1662 and held back until he 'could produce and bring into the light another Treatise, forerunner to this, on the Life of Nature'.[379] This was the *Tractatus de natura substantiae energetica, seu de vita naturae* (1672). The purpose of this work was to show that 'all matter, organic and inorganic alike, was endowed with life ... and that life was defined in terms of an intrinsic motility which could be activated by inherent perceptivity and appetite (or aversion) within the matter itself'.[380] There is no question of any deliberate heterodoxy here: Glisson's lectures reveal a clear belief in immaterial substance (including a human soul),[381] and he was always careful to categorise the perception of matter as 'natural perception', a vital act qualitatively different

Aristotelis, pultis, vel lactis in modum, exemplo assentior, eò úsque, ut illa elevatio, aut depressio sanguinis, non fiat à vaporibus, aut exhalationibus aut spiritibus, in aliquam formam, vapoream, vel aereiam concitatis, neque fit causata, ab externo agente, sed ab interno principio, regulante natura' (114). At 112, Harvey points out that this will be the subject of a work on the 'generation of parts' – i.e. what would become *De generatione*.

[377] Harvey, *De generatione*, 170: 'Nec cuiquam sane haec attributa convenient, nisi omnipotenti rerum principio, quocunque demum nomine id ipsum appellare libuerit: sive, *mentem divinam*, cum *Aristotele*; sive, cum *Platone, animam mundi*; aut, cum aliis, naturam naturante; vel, cum Ethnicis, *Saturnum*, aut *Jovem*, vel potiùs (ut nos decet) *Creatorem*, ac *Patrem* omnium quae in coelis & terris, à quo animalia, eorumque origines dependent, cujusque nutu, sive effato, fiunt & generantur omnia'. See also the very similar passage at 146–7.

[378] For Harvey's influence on Glisson, as charted through his lectures, see Frank, *Harvey*, 22–4. See also French, *Harvey*, 286, 302–4 (290–1 for Glisson's disagreement with Harvey's account of the forceful systole as witnessing a motion being imposed on the blood); Temkin, 'Classical roots'; Pagel, 'Irritability'; Giglioni, 'Anatomist atheist? The "hylozoistic" foundations of Francis Glisson's anatomical research' (1996), 115–16; Hartbecke, *Metaphysik und Naturphilosophie im 17. Jahruhundert* (2006), 52–65.

[379] Henry, 'Medicine and pneumatology' (1987), 20, quoting and translating Francis Glisson, *Tractatus de ventriculo et intestinis* (London, 1677), sig. A3$^r$; see also Giglioni, 'Anatomist Atheist?', 119–20.

[380] Henry, 'Medicine and pneumatology', 21 (22 for this as a development from *Anatomia hepatis*). See also Giglioni, 'Anatomist atheist?', and for the most concise summary by Glisson himself, *Tractatus de natura substantiae energetica, seu, de vita naturae* (Cambridge, 1672), 217–18.

[381] E.g. BL Sloane MS 3306, fol. 163$^r$.

from a cognitive function.[382] So why and how did Glisson adopt this distinctly idiosyncratic view?

Glisson justified this vision by reference to the history of philosophy, specifically by presenting it as a natural outgrowth of Aristotelian philosophy correctly interpreted (i.e. not as it had been by the scholastics). How did Glisson obtain such an unorthodoxly animist Aristotle? At points he seemed to be accepting the Helmontian critique but turning it into a positive, such as when he claimed that his 'plastic power' (*vis plastica*) had an antecedent in the pseudo-Hippocratic dictum '*naturas esse morborum curatrices*' (i.e. νουσων φυσεις ιητροι), which was itself equivalent both to the *archeus* of the chymists and Aristotle's 'nature' as a principle of movement.[383] But Glisson also supplied a fuller answer, taking some very creative scholarly steps to 'Platonise' Aristotle, at the same time claiming that Plato's immaterial world soul was something far more materialist–vitalist. Taking Plato first, Glisson stated that Plato's admiration for the structure of the world made him realise that it could not consist of 'only a mass of stupid and dead matter; and so he attached a spirit, which he called an *anima mundi*'.[384] This was hardly controversial, but Glisson knew that the traditional interpretation of the Platonic *anima mundi* as an immaterial informing principle was hardly congenial to his purpose. And so he assured his readers that this interpretation was wrong: 'What the true opinion of Plato and the Platonists is, can be easily explained ... if only they will allow the author to be understood on the inadequate concept of material entity. For body is broken up into two inadequate concepts: fundamental substance and energetic nature. Plato's "matter" is the fundamental substance, the "*anima*" is the energetic nature'.[385]

Glisson was aware that this was not the standard interpretation; he saved it using a clever historical–contextual argument: 'Nor should this explanation be considered completely frivolous or absurd, for very frequently the custom in antiquity was to speak of inadequate concepts as if they were really distinct

---

[382] Giglioni, 'Francis Glisson's notion of *confoederatio naturae* in the context of hylozoistic corpuscularianism' (2002), esp. 254.

[383] Glisson, *De natura substantiae energetica*, sig. [c4]ʳ; 191, 256 (these themes are well discussed in Hartbecke, *Metaphysik*, 131–40).

[384] Glisson, *De natura substantiae energetica*, 218: 'Plato, non levis judicii Philosophus, mundi admirabilem fabricam, harmoniam, pulchritudinem, dignitatem contemplatus, non potuit animum inducere ut crederet eum constare ex sola stupida & cadaverosa materiae mole. Adjunxit itaque spiritum, quem *mundi animam* vocavit'.

[385] Ibid., 220: 'Quod verò ad Platonis & Platonicorum sententiam attinet, ea facilè exponi potest ... si modò authorem de inadaequato entitatis materialis conceptu intelligi permiserint. Corpus enim in genere in duos inadaequatos conceptus, subsistentiam fundamentalem & naturam energeticam, resolvitur: Platonis materia est subsistentia fundamentalis, anima est natura energetica'.

things and separable from one another'.[386] Plato's famous attribution of life to an *anima mundi* was thus to be understood as a monism expressed in the awkward dualistic language of the Greeks. This was certainly an original interpretation, but its historical assumptions would have made sense to anyone who had read Digby or even Hobbes on the ancients' reification of qualities and accidents (4.2 above).

Glisson's next step was to make Aristotle into the same type of animist he had just identified in Plato. Here again he drew on a long debate within the Aristotelian commentary tradition, pointing out Aristotle's supposed attribution of intelligence to the celestial spheres.[387] Aristotle stated in *Metaphysics* XII.8 that the external movers of the celestial spheres were of the same kind as the first substance, called Mind (νοῦς), which in the preceding chapter is described by him as 'eternal and immovable and separate from sensible things', and in several places he claimed that the celestial bodies are living beings and hence possess a soul.[388] As one might imagine, these sorts of statements generated much contention in both the pagan and the Christian (and indeed Arabic) commentary traditions. Clemens Alexandrinus critiqued Aristotle and his successor Theophrastus specifically for deifying the firmaments.[389] Simplicius influentially ascribed to Aristotle the view that the celestial bodies have a rational soul; Aristotle's first great Christian commentator, John Philoponus, attacked him for the opinion; Avicenna said the heavens were living; Averroës said they were living and intelligent.[390] These issues were all familiar to seventeenth-century Englishmen, with the added pressure that the Italian Aristotelian naturalists such as Pomponazzi were said to have ascribed Christ's miracles to the celestial intelligences.[391] Compilers of Aristotelian textbooks of natural philosophy knew these accusations and spent many pages attempting to exonerate Aristotle.[392] Glisson instead appropriated them.

He also developed a more novel reinterpretation of Aristotle. In *De anima*, Aristotle was clear that there was a difference between organic and inorganic

---

[386] Ibid., 220: 'Neque haec expositio planè frivola aut absurda videri debet; cùm frequentissimus veteribus mos fuisset de inadaequatis conceptibus tanquam de rebus realiter distinctis & ab invicem separabilibus loqui'. See also 239.

[387] Ibid., 218, 355; see also the long quotation from Suárez at 223–4.

[388] Aristotle, *Met.*, 1073$^a$3-5; 1073$^a$14; *De caelo*, 284$^a$27-8; 292$^b$1-2. See Wolfson, 'The problem of the souls of the spheres' (1962), at 65–6; also Dales, 'The de-animation of the heavens in the middle ages' (1980).

[389] Clemens Alexandrinus, *Protr.*, 5 (followed exactly by Athenagoras, *Leg.*, 6).

[390] Wolfson, 'Souls of the spheres', 70–2.

[391] See e.g. Henry More, *An explanation of the grand mystery of godliness* (Cambridge, 1660), 320, 335.

[392] See the remarkable discussion at Wendelin, *Contemplationes physicae*, 430b–38a, especially the long list of patristic opponents of heavenly animation at 433a and the exclusion of Aristotle from those who animated the heavens at 430b–31a (see also 394b–95a for an attack on Simplicius's reading).

beings: the soul is the form of the living body, which has organs (i.e. functional parts) that strive for an end that contributes to the total end of the organised body.[393] Glisson eroded Aristotle's conflation of life with organisation, claiming it to be a later misunderstanding of his doctrine:

> The view that life is restricted solely to animals and plants, I admit, was the common opinion of the Peripatetics, for which they should be forgiven, because the life of nature, without which their view could not be corrected, had not yet been made known to them. We, however, attribute the life of nature to all bodies indiscriminately; and deduce the difference of plants and animals from other bodies not from thence, but, with Aristotle, from organisation.[394]

Aristotle, then, did not limit life to organised entities. How to justify this historically? One option was to lay emphasis on the definition of 'nature' as an internal principle of motion, and Glisson duly cited *Physics* II, $192^b14$–22, drawing in particular on the fact that Aristotle here emphasised the 'naturalness' of the components of 'artificial' objects: 'The scope of the Philosopher [i.e. Aristotle], in these places, it seems, is to distinguish natural from artificial', where the latter is always made up of the former.[395] But this still left the problem of Aristotle's organic/inorganic distinction. This Glisson again ingeniously attributed to the fluidity of the term '*anima*' (and its relationship to 'life') in ancient philosophical discourse:

> The physical form is a partaker in life not only in plants and animals, but also adds a regulating life to all bodies, even the inanimate. I do not say it adds a soul (*anima*). For customary speech did not require that the physical forms of the elements, minerals and similar be called *animae*. For Aristotle defined *anima* to be the form of an organic body; whence the custom grew of calling elements, stones, and all things which lacked organisation, *inanimate*. However, nothing prevents them, in the natural world, from being alive, but without that peculiar, regulating form of life one finds in a soul, and they enjoy only a natural and inorganic life … It seems that Plato used the expression *anima* in a more general sense for the lively and energetic life of the substance, as we saw above.[396]

---

[393] *De anima*, $412^a29$–$412^b1$. Many other relevant passages are adduced in Whiting, 'Living bodies' (1992).

[394] Glisson, *De natura substantiae energetica*, 226: 'Tertiò, Restringit vitam ad sola animalia & plantas. Quae, fateor, communis erat Peripateticorum sententia, & iis olim condonanda, quòd vita naturae, absque qua efficaciter corrigi nequiverat, iis nondum innotuisset. Nos verò vitam naturae omnibus corporibus promiscuè tribuimus; nec indè differentiam plantarum & animalium ab aliis corporibus, sed ab organizatione, cum Aristotele … deducimus'. It should be noted that part of this key passage is already discussed in Giglioni, 'Anatomist atheist?', 117–18.

[395] Glisson, *De natura substantiae energetica*, 232: 'Scopus Philosophi in istis locis, ut videtur, est, distinguere artificialia à naturalibus'.

[396] Ibid., 244: 'Quod ad secundam suppositionem attinet, dico, formam physicam non solùm in plantis & animalibus esse vitae participem, sed & corporibus omnibus etiam inanimatis vitam modificantem addere. Non dico addere *animam*. Usus enim loquendi non obtinuit ut formae physicae elementorum, mineralium, & similium, vocentur *animae*. Aristoteles enim *animam*

By lessening the importance of Aristotle's amalgamation of '*anima*' and 'life', Glisson could present the core Aristotelian message as residing not in the organic/inorganic distinction, but in the (supposed) amalgamation of an active 'nature' and 'life' to be found in the *Physics*. For Glisson, *'Organic* does not discriminate what is alive from what is not. It means a mere degree in the self-developing activity of life [*qua* 'nature'], corresponding to plants and animals'.[397]

Glisson was certainly not aiming at any kind of pantheism or 'hylozoic' atheism.[398] In his lectures he began not only by affirming his own ultimate substance dualism (i.e. between material and immaterial substance) but also by drawing the standard scholastic distinction between *natura naturans* (God) and *natura naturata*, before warning his students that 'nature' should not be used to mean God (or other incorporeal substances like angels and souls), who is the legislator over this nature – this may well have stemmed from a desire to refute van Helmont's anti-Aristotelian critique, or it may have been standard repetition of neo-scholastic commonplaces.[399] It is also quite likely that Glisson's vitalism was in part a reaction to what he saw as the dangerous consequences of Cartesian dualism.[400] Nonetheless, the Stagirite presented in Glisson and to a lesser extent in Harvey was qualitatively different to the Aristotle of most natural philosophy textbooks or scholarship on the history of philosophy available in mid-century England. The abandonment of hylomorphism was leading everyone – whether Aristotelian or anti-Aristotelian – to reconsider the history of causation theory.

### 5.4.2    Philosophy

Glisson's 'animist' Aristotle was certainly considered dangerous: not only Boyle, but also Henry More and Ralph Cudworth were perturbed by his ideas.[401] Walter Charleton, in anatomy lectures read at the College of Physicians, despite his deep admiration for Glisson's vision, claimed that the latter's views on the life of matter were really just a revival of Platonic

---

definit esse formam corporis organici; unde usus inoluit elementa, lapides, & omnia quae carent organizatione, *inanimata* vocare. Nihil tamen prohibet quin, in natura, viva esse possint; sed destituantur modò istâ peculiari vitâ modificante, quae tribuitur animae, & vitâ tantùm naturali atque inorganicâ gaudeant. Verisimile autem est, Platonem generaliore sensu voce *animae* usum esse, pro natura energetica & viva substantiae in genere, ut suprà visum est'.

[397] Giglioni, 'Anatomist atheist?', 117.

[398] Giglioni seems to countenance the possibility at ibid., 125.

[399] BL MS Sloane 3310, fol. 226ʳ (also discussed at French, *Harvey*, 287). For van Helmont's influence on Glisson in other matters, see Hartbecke, *Metaphysik*, 67–82; Boss, 'Helmont, Glisson, and the doctrine of the common reservoir' (1983); Pagel, 'Irritability'.

[400] See the attack on Descartes's opposition to living nature in *De natura substantiae energetica*, 333.

[401] Henry, 'More, Baxter, Glisson'.

animism, which 'hath [already] been sufficiently impugned by *Aristotle, Lucretius, Gassendus*, and all others, who have refuted *Plato's* Doctrine *de Anima mundi*, upon which it is grounded':[402] had he still been alive, Glisson would have been distraught at what he would have perceived as a coarse misreading of both his own views and the true views of Plato and Aristotle. More and Cudworth, meanwhile, developed fully fledged histories of causation theory of their own, partly to defend the possibility of a non-idolatrous animating principle that was at the same time immaterial.

We can remind ourselves of the historical narrative offered by More in his earlier works, especially *Conjectura Cabbalistica* (1653) and its defences (1662), which we met in Chapter 3: the true Cabbala had been received and preserved (although with some corruptions) by Pythagoras and Plato; its physical and metaphysical parts were then separated and gradually corrupted. From the *Immortality of the soul* (1659) onwards, More affirmed that part of the true Pythagorean tradition was the belief in an *anima mundi*, which he liked to call the 'Spirit of Nature'.[403] As More explained to his acquaintances, other commitments prevented him from making further additions to the *Conjectura*, but he certainly felt that he had more to say.[404] There were other good reasons for him to go back into print: the attacks which he had faced in the 1660s (3.5 above), his continuing disenchantment with Cartesian philosophy and subsequent rethinking of his own,[405] and his gradual familiarisation with, and reaction to, Lurianic Cabbala, commencing in 1670 when Franciscus Mercurius van Helmont introduced him by letter to Christian Knorr von Rosenroth.[406] The key texts are More's *Enchiridion metaphysicum* (1671), the *Opera philosophica* (1679) in which his philosophical works were reprinted with extensive *scholia*, and several controversial pieces arising out of these publications. Here More developed at length his ideas on the immaterial spirit of nature, now called the 'hylarchic principle'. The systematic *Enchiridion metaphysicum* may have been intended – at least in part – for a student audience, which probably explains the absence of More's usual extensive

---

[402] Walter Charleton, *Enquiries into human nature in VI. anatomic praelections in the new theatre of the Royal Colledge of Physicians* (London, 1680), 376–7 (but see e.g. 13–14 for deep praise of Glisson's views on spirits).

[403] More, *Immortality*, 203, 299, 396–7, 499 (I cite only *loci* where historical claims about the 'Spirit of nature' are made).

[404] More to Anne Conway, Nov/Dec 1663, in *The Conway letters: the correspondence of Anne, Viscountess Conway, Henry More and their friends, 1642–1684*, ed. M. H. Nicolson, rev. S. Hutton (Oxford, 1992), 217. Jacob, 'The spirit of nature as "Hylarchic" principle of the universe' (1995) is much fuller than either Greene, 'Henry More and Robert Boyle on the spirit of nature' (1962) or Walker, *Il concetto di spirito o anima* (1986), 47–59.

[405] Gabbey, 'Philosophica Cartesiana triumphata'.

[406] Coudert, 'A Cambridge Platonist's Kabbalist nightmare' (1975); Coudert, *The impact of the Kabbalah in the seventeenth century* (1999), 220–40; Copenhaver, 'Jewish theologies of space', esp. 515–28. I do not repeat here the many detailed findings of these studies.

digressions on the history of philosophy. These came in the *scholia* appended to the 1679 edition. They are important to us for two reasons: More's pre-history of his own 'hylarchic principle', and his approach to the history of theories about the nature of space and God's extension.

It is no surprise to find that the very long *scholium* to xiii.4 (an experimental proof for the hylarchic principle to which Boyle specifically replied) again names Plato and Pythagoras as forerunners in adumbrating an *anima mundi* equivalent to More's own spirit of nature or hylarchic principle. This was to be expected: much of it, after all, is concerned with responding to the German physicist Johann Christoph Sturm, who had followed Boyle and John Beale in claming that More had misinterpreted Boyle's air-pump experiments in his attempt to use them as evidence for his positing of an immaterial animating substance.[407] More here also drew on his new knowledge of Lurianic Cabbala to claim that such a principle was part of the esoteric Hebrew tradition. But what is most important for us is that Aristotle is now unexpectedly added to this list of those who believed in an animating principle.[408] Specifically, More claims that Aristotle's 'nature' that 'does nothing in vain' should be understood as equivalent to More's own spirit of nature/hylarchic principle.[409]

Why did More take this unexpected step, and what were his sources? One possibility is that it was a deliberate attempt to outmanoeuvre Sturm, who had repeatedly emphasised the novelty of More's hylarchic principle, by rendering that principle a part of a more mainstream philosophical tradition.[410] There is, however, another possibility. Also in the *scholia* to the *Enchiridion* (as well as to some of his other texts), More attacked what he saw as the materialist vitalism of Glisson, arguing that the Regius Professor of Medicine had 'allowed himself to slip into Behmenism rather than into Platonism' and that

---

[407] J. C. Sturm, *Epistola ad virum celeberrimum Henricum Morum de spiritu ipsius Hylarchio* (Nurenberg, 1676). For Sturm on the passivity of nature, see Baku, 'Der Streit um den Naturbegriff am Ende des 17. Jahrhunderts' (1891), at 168–71; more generally, see the essays in Gaab et al., eds., *Johann Christoph Sturm* (2004). For Boyle and Beale, see Henry, 'More versus Boyle'.

[408] Henry More, *Opera philosophica* (London, 1679), 224 ('*Principium Hylarchicum* ... istiusmodi Principium non solùm *Pythagoras, Plato, Aristoteles* aliique praeclari Philosophi, quanquam sub aliis nominibus, satis manifestò tenuerint' (=Jacob, *More's Manual of Metaphysics*, ii, 78. I have used Jacob's translations throughout, while always comparing with the original).

[409] More, *Opera philosophica*, 231 (=Jacob, ii, 92–3).

[410] Sturm, *Epistola*, 75, directly answered in More, *Opera philosophica*, 231: 'Ad quod rursus respondeo, Principium hoc nec confictum esse nec novum & inauditum, nisi nomen solummodo intelligas, rem enim ipsam agnoverunt antique Philosophi *Pythagoras, Plato*, ipseque Aristoteles sub nomine τῆς φύσεως, ut quando toties inculcat τὴν φύσιν οὐδὲν μάτην ποιεῖν, Naturam nihil facere frustra, quod intelligendum est omnino de hoc *Spiritu Naturae* quem & Principium *Hylarchicum* appello' (=Jacob, ii, 92–3).

such animating power should be reserved for a spiritual entity – which 'has more relation to divinity' than Glisson's vitalist principle – just as Pythagoras and Plato had (contrary to Glisson's reading of Plato) reserved such action for their immaterial λόγοι σπερματικοί (spermatical principles).[411] Like Cudworth, More considered Glisson an inheritor not of orthodox Aristotelianism but of 'hylozoism': the belief that matter could act by itself.[412] He sought to show this by aligning 'orthodox' Aristotelianim with his own position. Nonetheless, More's engagement with the medical literature inspired him to see Aristotle in a more animist light for his own purposes too. This is supported by a new reference (in the *scholia* to *Immortality of the soul*) to Harvey's aforementioned citation of *Generation of animals*, II (seminal heat as analogous to the element of the stars). But unlike Harvey and Glisson, More claimed that this was evidence not of materialistic vitalism but of Aristotle's belief in an immaterial 'spirit of nature'.[413] In effect, he was trying to separate Harvey from Glisson, and pull the former towards himself.

More also used the *scholia* to *Enchiridion metaphysicum* to develop a historical defence of his ideas from the charge of idolatrous anthropomorphism, predictably laid at his feet by Boyle, Sturm, and others. The 'spirit of nature', he contended, was categorically different from the *anima mundi* of the later Platonists, especially that of Plotinus, because the former was not 'endowed with any sense or reason'.[414] The only life that could be attributed to his principle was a 'plastic life, which contains within itself all the laws of natural motion and union'.[415] At least historically, this was obfuscation, but it was tactically necessary, for this defence was developed against the accusations of anthropomorphism made against him by Sturm and by the jurist Matthew Hale. Hale's thoughts on this issue are a good example of the new ambiguities about ancient causation theory and of how a thinker outside both the academy and the main natural philosophical circles could develop his ideas on the

---

[411] More, *Opera philosophia*, 300–2 (=Jacob, II, 230–2). More's criticisms of Glisson are usefully discussed in Henry, 'More, Baxter, Glisson', although it does not consider any texts apart from the second *Epistola ad V.C.* (=*Opera philosophica*, 565–614).

[412] More, *Epistola ad V.C altera*, in *Opera philosophica*, 608. More also termed this position *buisianismus*, adopting the term from Glisson, *De natura substantiae energetica*, 191–3.

[413] More, *Opera philosophica*, II (separate pagination for all works in this volume), 374: 'Quòd autem heic *Harvaeus* Divinum quid subesse autumet in istis vocibus [Natura analoga elemento astrorum] indè fieri censeo, quòd *Aristoteles*, intelligens Principium verésque Divinum in solis Caelis constituerit; atque proinde efficaciam hujusmodi Principii huc etiam pertingere indigitat'. See also the *scholium* added to *Enthusiasmus triumphatus* (1st edn=1656) in *Opera philosophica*, II, 223, where Aristotle is again directly affirmed to believe in a 'spirit of nature' and compared to the Cabbalists.

[414] More, *Opera philosophica*, I, 328–9 (*scholium* to ch. 28) (=Jacob, I, 137).

[415] More, *Opera philosophica*, 328 (=Jacob, I, 137). See also Henry More, *Remarks upon two late ingenious discourses* (London, 1676), 22–3. For Sturm's accusations of anthropomorphism, see e.g. his *Epistola*, 34.

subject.[416] Like More, Hale was not impressed by what he saw as purely mechanical explanations of natural phenomena. In his works on the gravitation of fluids and on interpreting the results of the Torricelli experiment he proposed quasi-Aristotelian interpretations that drew on the work of the Jesuits Honoré Fabri and Franciscus Linus, defending such maxims as 'nature abhors a vacuum'.[417] As well as rejecting mechanical explanations he also condemned as barren speculation intermediate principles like an *anima mundi* or More's hylarchic principle, which he aligned traditionally with Plato and Pythagoras.[418] Not only were such principles speculative, but they also proposed an unnecessary entity between God and nature.[419] Instead, Hale presented himself as following the Aristotelian dictum that 'only Nature is the *principium motus & quietis*'.[420] Yet he never explained what natural processes this actually involved. He could not return to classic scholastic Aristotelianism, as he saw the hylomorphism that underpinned Aristotle's theory as both an 'artificial contrivance' designed to save the phenomena and a consequence of his paganism.[421] To replace hylomorphism he resorted to a semi-fideist agnosticism coupled with a methodological critique: Aristotelian 'nature' was the analogy for the inexplicable causal chain put in operation by God.[422] This answer is so unsatisfying that one can hardly blame More for replying that this agnosticism could be resolved by admitting that Aristotle's 'nature' was simply the Stagirite 'acknowledg[ing] what I contend for, a Spirit of Nature or Hylostatick Principle, which he must of necessity acknowledge, unless he contradict himself' – what else could be the meaning of *natura nihil agit frustra*?[423]

As well as his 'hylarchical principle', More also defended another quasi-animistic idea: that immaterial substance – including God – was extended, and that space was thus an attribute of God. This had been a concern of More's since

---

[416] For Hale's intellectual career, see Cromartie, *Hale* (195–233 for his natural philosophy). Hale's outsider status was reflected in some comments made by natural philosophical contemporaries: see e.g. John Ray to Edward Lhuyd, 15 May 1697, in *Further correspondence of John Ray*, 270 ('Matthew Hale his *Origination of mankind* I have seen, but could never find in my heart to read, not expecting any great matter from a man of his employ in subjects of that nature'). As for Hale's scholarship, he himself admitted that he was a 'better *Grecian* in the 16th, than in the 66th Year of my Life', and so used Latin editions of the primary sources (*Primitive origination*, sig. [a2]ᵛ).

[417] Cromartie, *Hale*, 214.

[418] Hale, *Primitive origination*, 34, 322 (at 45, Hale is adamant that Aristotle did not attribute life to the whole world).

[419] Ibid., 34, 322; Hale, *An essay touching the gravitation, or non-gravitation of fluid bodies, and the reasons thereof* (London, 1673), 42–5 (the key attack on More's hylarchic principle).

[420] [Matthew Hale], *Difficiles nugae: or observations touching the Torricellian experiment* (London, 1674), 238. Hale's notes on More's *Enchiridion metaphysicum* are LP MS 3498, fols. 1ʳ–33ʳ.

[421] Hale, *Primitive origination*, 9–10; LP MS 3502, 'Magnetical observations', p. 85.

[422] [Hale], *Difficiles nugae*, 55–6, 237–9, 255; [Hale], *Primitive origination*, 292–3.

[423] More, *Remarks*, 138–9.

his correspondence with Descartes of 1648–49, where he denied the Cartesian association of matter and extension and suggested that God possessed immaterial extension.[424] This theme was not emphasised in the history presented in the *Conjectura* and its defences; this may have been because the plan of the *Conjectura* limited More to the first three chapters of Genesis.[425] In the *Enchiridion*, however, this idea was forcefully defended. More offered a canon of those philosophers who acknowledged a 'space or internal space distinct from' matter: 'Leucippus, Democritus, Demetrius, Metrodorus, Epicurus, and even all the Stoics'. This was a significant misuse of his unacknowledged source, pseudo-Plutarch's *De placitis philosophorum* (xviii.3–4).[426] But it is clear that More's aim was to align the Italics into one. This involved claiming that Pythagoras, Democritus, and Epicurus 'numbered internal place among real Entities'. For Pythagoras this was based on the only source to suggest his belief in the void, Aristotle's *Physics* ($213^b23$–7); for Democritus and Epicurus it depended on deliberately playing on Epicurus's ambiguous description of the void as 'ἀναφῆ φύσιν', which More translated and interpreted as 'intangible, i.e. incorporeal, nature'.[427]

Whatever the scholarly deficiencies, it is clear that all this was designed to render Laërtius's Italics – whom More had been attempting to present as inheritors of true Mosaic philosophy since the 1640s – even more compatible with More's own philosophy. The rest of the historical discussion claims that the Cabbalistic concept *māqôm* ('place') referred to the divinity of the immobile extension,[428] a theme expanded upon in the *scholia*, which also includes an attribution of a similar concept to Anaxagoras and uses it to explain away the

---

[424] There is quite a large literature; see e.g. Pacchi, *Cartesio*, 33–4; Jacob, 'Introduction'; Grant, *Nothing*, 221–8; Copenhaver, 'Jewish theologies of space'; Koyré, *From the closed world to the infinite universe* (1957), 125–54; Reid, 'The evolution of Henry More's theory of divine absolute space' (2007); Reid, *The metaphysics of Henry More* (2012), 141–236. I have also benefited from the very illuminating paper by Igor Agostini, 'Henry More and the sources of the doctrine of spiritual extension', presented at the symposium on 'The sources of Cambridge Platonism' at Clare College, Cambridge, 6 April 2013.

[425] As already suggested in Copenhaver, 'Jewish theologies of space', 518.

[426] More, *Opera philosophica*, 158–9 (=Jacob, i, 38–9): 'Sed & Philosophi qui Materiae creationem non crediderunt hujusmodi tamen Spatium agnoverunt, ut *Leucippus, Democritus, Demetrius, Metrodorus, Epicurus, & Stoici* quidem omnes'. Both More's marginal note ('Quòd omnium ferè Philosophorum sententia erat, quanquam Materiam increatam crediderunt, Spatium esse ab ea distinctum sive Locum internum' [my emphasis]) and his subsequent comment ('*Platonem* quidam hisce adjunxerunt') are directly contradicted by *Plac. phil.*, i.18 ('All the natural philosophers from Thales to Plato rejected a vacuum' ['οἱ ἀπὸ Θάλεω φυσικοὶ πάντες μέχρι Πλάτωνος τὸ κενὸν ἀπέγνωσαν']).

[427] More, *Opera philosophica*, 166 (=Jacob, i, 54–55): '*Epicuro* rursus disertis verbis κενὸν καὶ χώραν, *Vacuum & Locum*, τὴν ἀναφῆ φύσιν, *naturam intangibilem*, i.e. incorpoream, appellante'. The Epicurean terms are from *Ad. Herod.*, in DL x.39–40. The extremely ambiguous nature of these terms – an ambiguity admitted by Epicurus himself – is usefully discussed in Sedley, 'Physics and metaphysics' (1999), 367–8.

[428] More, *Opera philosophica*, 167, 169 (=Jacob, i, 57–8, 61).

well-known 'materialistic' statements that could be found in some unnamed church fathers (More was surely thinking of Tertullian).[429] Most importantly, More here again made a concerted effort to claim that the logic of Aristotle's philosophy also led to the concept of an immobile immaterial extension; this despite Aristotle's clear repudiation of the idea of place as extension in favour of defining it as 'the boundary of the containing body at which it is in contact with the contained body' (*Physics*, 212$^a$7–8). First, More pointed to the incompatibility of this definition with Aristotle's own statement that it could only apply to place occupied by body.[430] More positively, he also claimed that Aristotle's description of place (at *Physics*, 208$^b$34–209$^a$1) as 'that without which nothing else can exist, while it can exist without the other', was an acknowledgement of the divine power of internal place.[431] Again, these pseudo-scholarly manoeuvrings seem to have stemmed from a new conviction that Aristotle could be amalgamated – however tentatively – with the Mosaic–Italic canon that More had been placing himself in since the 1640s.[432]

Van Helmont, Harvey, Glisson, and More were working in very different contexts, but there is a good reason to unite them under one over-arching umbrella: the attempt to develop new theories of causation, space, and the relationship between nature, life, and matter in a world that had not entirely rejected Aristotle, but *had* rejected hylomorphism. Consequently, they developed readings of Aristotle that moved him far closer to animism – whether materialist or immaterialist – than most of the commentary or textbook tradition would have allowed. We see already that Boyle was not working in a vacuum. But Boyle did not only draw on these medical and philosophical readings. He also drew on the genre by now well familiar to us: histories of pagan religion and its idolatry.

### 5.4.3    Theology

We return at this point to Parker's *Tentamina de Deo*, turning now to chapters 1–3 of Part II, which consist of a long excursion into the history of pagan philosophy, arguing that the pagans worshipped either the sun or an *anima mundi* as their supreme deity and that the Greek philosophers inherited this idolatrous worldview. The overall purpose of these chapters is to demonstrate that philosophical error stemmed from religious error: specifically that the

---

[429] More, *Opera philosophica*, 169–73 (=Jacob, I, 61–5).

[430] More, *Opera philosophica*, 158 (=Jacob, I, 39).

[431] More, *Opera philosophica*, 168 (=Jacob, I, 59). In reality, the text itself is clear that Aristotle was only arguing for place being something distinct from bodies.

[432] Although it should be added that More was also drawing on a belief in immaterial extended substance already found in the Aristotelian tradition – specifically Julius Caesar Scaliger – as convincingly shown by Agostini, 'Sources of spiritual extension'.

pagans amalgamated God and the world by making him an *anima mundi* –
indeed, the title of the relevant chapter is 'The ancient philosophers held the
world soul to be the supreme divinity'.[433] In these first chapters of Book II,
Parker is again operating in the shadow of Vossius's history of idolatry.
Vossius's huge work was based on the principle that idolatry stemmed from a
misunderstanding of the natural world and its relationship to God, heavily
influenced by Maimonides's claim that starworship was the first idolatry.[434]
In one sense, Parker followed this framework; but where the Dutchman
believed that this idolatrous animism was ultimately monotheistic (a case
later made by Cudworth), Parker believed that this animism was *not* compatible
with the Judaeo–Christian vision of God.

Parker began by offering a simple taxonomy of gentile theology: its two
versions were 'Sabianism', or the worship of the celestial bodies; and
'Hellenism', the worship of the dead.[435] It is quite clear, however, that the
first was far more important, for Parker later states that 'Hellenism' was only
born when political rulers started adopting the names of the stars.[436] We have
already met the Maimonidean context of 'Sabianism', and although Parker was
particularly sceptical about rabbinic historiographical traditions,[437] in this
regard he continued to operate in a rabbinic framework. The worship of the
celestial bodies derived from marvelling at the sun. It began not long after the
flood – Parker here had the philological confidence to correct Selden's conjecture that it was antediluvian, accusing Selden of overindulging in
'Talmudicis nugis'. The custom of worshipping and sacrificing in high places –
not least the pyramids of the Egyptians – derived from a desire to be closer to
the sun. The sun was held to be the supreme deity and was given titles
designating total rule; these names corresponded to the names of the supreme
gods of various pagan nations: Baal, Moloch, and so on. These speculations
allowed Parker to engage in charting the sort of genealogies of the pagan gods

---

[433] II.2: 'Veteres Philosophi Animam Mundi Supremum esse Numen censuerunt'.

[434] Vossius, *Theologia gentilis*, e.g. 22–8. See Wickenden, *Vossius and the humanist concept of
history* (1993), 155–61; Jorink, *Book of nature*, 69–70, although it is not quite correct that for
Vossius 'the pagan cultic forms, which had been so amply described in antiquity, were in fact
the consequeces of a regrettable demise of the knowledge that was enshrined in the Old
Testament': Vossius clearly saw corruption as a gradual post-diluvian (not post-Mosaic)
process. The starworship thesis proved extremely influential: among any number of possible
examples, see e.g. Evelyn, *History of religion*, I, 303–5, explicitly drawing on Maimonides, and
structurally very similar to Parker's account (see also Evelyn's notes on this in BL MS Add.
78368, fol. 5ʳ).

[435] Parker, *Tentamina*, 181: 'Gentilium theologiam Duum generum esse volunt eruditi, alterum
*Sabaismum*, qui cultus Coeli est, siderum, aliarumque naturae partium, prout inter Barbaros,
seu gentes *Graecia* alienas obtinuit: *Hellenismum* laterum, qui si strictim capiatur, solummodo
mortalium seu defunctorum venerationem sonat, sin laxè, totam *Graeciae* Idololatriam
complectitur'.

[436] Ibid., 184–5.     [437] 3.6 above; Levitin, 'Spencer'.

that had been made possible by Scaliger's discovery of chronological synchronisms between sacred and profane history. He paid special attention to the
'sacred obscenities' relating to various fertility gods (such as the permanently
erect Priapus and Baal Peor, long associated with indecency in Talmudic
traditions), attributing belief in them to an idolatrous extrapolation from the
generational power of the sun.[438]

This is not just a scholarly excursus into pagan religious culture, for Parker's
aim is to explain how philosophical error derived from religious error. The
pagans sought to explain the providential operation of the sun and of the stars,
which they had made his partners in divinity. They attributed intelligence to the
stars. The sun was said first to be omniscient, then omnipotent, and to pre-
determine everything. From here it was only a short step to asserting the deity's
omnipresence and to equating God with nature. This connection was first
devised by astrologers so that they could claim to read the divine operations
within the world. Philosophers began to argue that human souls were born from
a divine but corporeal aether.[439] This historicisation of Greek philosophy is
Parker's central concern, and it shapes chapter ii.2, where all of Greek physics
is said to have its origins in the belief in a divine but corporeal *anima mundi*.
For all the philosophers God was nature, and even those who adopted monotheism conceived of him as a world soul; indeed, this is how the universal
theism identified by 'the most noble Herbert [of Cherbury's famous *De religione gentilium* (1663)]' had to be interpreted. The pagans understood 'spirit'
not as an immaterial thing but as a 'very thin substance' (*substantiam perte-
nuem*). In turn, when they spoke of 'mind' (νοῦς) they spoke of a faculty rather
than a substance. Creation, providence, and omnipotence were ascribed to it
and souls were said to arise from and return to it – hence Pythagorean
transmigration. But the connection between *anima mundi* philosophy and
paganism could never be forgotten; for example, it explained Egyptian animal-worship.[440]

Parker deviated substantially from the standard accounts by arguing that *all* of
Greek philosophy was characterised by an animist–idolatrous attitude to nature.

---

[438] Parker, *Tentamina*, 192–3 (no antediluvian sun-worship and attack on Selden), 195–7 (sun-
worship appeared shortly after the flood), 197–8 (worshipping in high places), 201–4, 212–14
(names given to the sun), 205–12 (the 'sacred obscenities').

[439] Parker, *Tentamina*, 219–20 (intelligence attributed to the stars), 225–6 (the sun's omniscience
and omnipotence), 227–33 (astrological origins of this), 224–5 (human souls born from the
aether).

[440] Parker, *Tentamina*, 234–6 (all pagans believed in an *anima mundi* to be some kind of aethereal
matter; Egyptian animal-worship), 236–7 (God was equivalent with nature), 241–2 (even
monotheists believed in an *anima mundi*; citation of 'nobilissimus Herbert'), 247–9 (pagan
philosophers' definitions of 'spirit' and 'mind'). Parker's positive citation of Herbert further
substantiates the thesis that his reputation as a 'deist' only developed later: Serjeantson,
'Herbert of Cherbury before deism' (2001).

Most importantly, he claimed that this worldview was held even by Aristotle.[441] This historiographical revisionism was not humanist ornamentation – it was the key to his whole argument. He was offering the historical 'other' to the *nova et reformata philosophia* of his title. That 'other' was the pagan philosophy that had equated God with nature. Parker was sure that remnants of this pagan philosophy had survived in Christendom through its Aristotelian inheritance.[442] The new philosophy was 'new' precisely because it was cleansed of these pagan imperfections and because it recognised the need for distance between the deity and his creation.

Parker can be categorised as a true pioneer. At the age of twenty-five he became the first Englishman to make a systematic and original attempt to place Greek natural philosophy within the context of ancient religious culture. From where, then, did Parker obtain the inspiration for such a view? We have already seen that he was indebted to the histories of idolatry by Selden and Vossius; but he was also going beyond them in denying that pagan animist idolatry contained monotheism: his key chapter on this topic was entitled, 'Pagan notions about God are wrongly applied to the supreme God whom we honour; rather, they should be understood as referring either to the sun or to the world soul, which the pagans supposed to be supreme divinity'.[443] How did Parker arrive at this deviation from the Vossian framework? In part, at least, it was because he drew on another author who bridged the world of humanism and philosophy, and turned the idolatry literature to his own ends. That was Gassendi, although the influential narrative that he developed on this issue has gone entirely unnoticed. We have already encountered the sophisticated technique that Gassendi resorted to when he could not reinterpret Epicurus in a satisfactory way: he would use a deeply contextual approach to drag all the other pagan philosophers down with Epicurus. This was particularly the case in his discussion of the Epicurean doctrine of the soul. The Epicurean material soul could hardly be defended as orthodox, so Gassendi resorted to redefining the other philosophical options. The Platonists and Pythagoreans had obviously considered individual souls to be part of an *anima mundi*. But after deploying some particularly selective quotations from the Arabic commentators, Gassendi also concluded that 'Aristotle can easily be seen to be drawn to the opinion of the *anima mundi*'.[444] He then extrapolated this conclusion so as to defend the Epicurean position that physical or efficient causes were corporeal, offering a history of philosophy that eroded the differences between all contrary opinions,

[441]  Parker, *Tentamina*, 266–8.    [442]  Ibid., 220.

[443]  Parker, *Tentamina*, 181: 'Gentilium de Deo placita perperam ad Supremum, quem colimus, Deum traduci: Sed aut de Sole aut de Animâ Mundi, quae Suprema Omnium Numina esse censuerunt, intelligi oportere' (this is the title of Bk. II, ch. 1).

[444]  Gassendi, *Syntagma philosophicum*, in *Opera*, II, 243: 'Ex quo obiter intelligitur videri posse facile Aristotelem pertrahi ad opinionem de Anima Mundi'.

ascribing them to the same confused and obscurantist multiplication of causes.[445]

By the standards of textual criticism Gassendi had set himself this was not his most impressive scholarly conclusion, for it depended either on readings from the commentators (whom he had previously chastised as presenting a corrupt Aristotle), especially Averroës's famous doctrine of the unity of the intellect, or on rather strained readings of Aristotle's own works. Here again we encounter a citation of the passage from *Generation of animals* on animal heat as analogous to the element of the stars (Gassendi also drew on the tradition of interpreting Aristotle as attributing intelligence to the celestial spheres). The accusation of animism against the Greek philosophers became a motif throughout Gassendi's works.[446] Indeed, it actually served a dual purpose, allowing Gassendi to explain away Epicurus's unforgivable denial of the soul's immortality.[447] Aware that he could hardly reconcile Epicurus's mortalism with Christian doctrine, Gassendi instead resorted to contextualising him to show that none of the ancient philosophers held an acceptable pneumatology: where Epicurus held the admittedly heinous mortalist view, his Greek counterparts were no better in that the vast majority – and crucially Aristotle was included here – believed in the dissipation of the post-mortem soul into an *anima mundi*.[448]

It is clear that Gassendi was Parker's source because the latter also stated that Epicurus was the only Greek not to think the stars animated.[449] Unlike Gassendi, however, Parker's adoption of this narrative was not designed to defend Epicurus, but to suggest that only the 'new' (i.e. non-pagan) philosophy was compatible with Christian apologetics: this he combined with a range of Christian and Jewish sources on the history of paganism to arrive at his own novel position. The fact that the much-read Gassendi was the key source for this historical argument meant that it became available to a range of thinkers. Unsurprisingly, it was repeated by Gassendi's great English follower Charleton, both in his *apologia* for Epicurus and in his work on the immortality of the soul.[450] One noticeable side-effect was the further depreciation of Averroës and Avicenna – already under suspicion because of association with Pomponazzi – who began to be linked more and more with Plato and Pythagoras as philosophers who placed an intermediate principle between

---

[445] See also Brundell, *Gassendi*, 125.

[446] Gassendi, *Syntagma philosophicum*, in *Opera*, II, 241–4. See also *Syntagma philosophicum*, in *Opera*, I, 155, 296, 520–4, 633–4, 833, 835; *Philosophiae Epicuri syntagma*, in *Opera*, III, 127.

[447] For Gassendi on the soul more generally, see Osler, 'Baptizing'; Michael and Michael, 'Gassendi on sensation and reflection' (1988); and in broader context, Serjeantson, 'Soul', 130–1, 135–6.

[448] Gassendi, *Syntagma philosophicum*, in *Opera*, II, 241–4.     [449] Parker, *Tentamina*, 219.

[450] [Charleton], *Epicurus's morals*, sigs. [a3]ʳ–b3ᵛ; Charleton, *The immortality of the human soul, demonstrated by the light of nature* (London, 1657), 181–2.

God and the world. Such accusations can be found in Hale's *Natural motions*,[451] and in Richard Baxter's popular *Of the immortality of mans soul* (1682), which may well have been indebted to both Baxter's close friend Hale and to another friend, the MP Samuel Gott, who had made similar claims in his *Divine history of the genesis of the world* (1670).[452]

With Parker, we encounter a theme repeatedly emphasised in this book: a historiographical conclusion developed in one context (Gassendi's contextual defence of Epicurus) came to be adopted in many others, not from any direct ideological continuity but simply because the first discussion was considered the best. Parker, as we shall see, was a key source for Boyle, but even his discussion was eclipsed by the extremely long section devoted to various forms of ancient animism in Cudworth's *System*. Cudworth's treatment here is even more complex than that he had offered on the history of atomism; consequently it has not received even remotely adequate treatment since Mosheim in the eighteenth century.

To manage this complexity, we can divide the discussion into three parts. (A) The delineation of two types of ancient animist or vitalist atheism: (1) 'hylozoic', which attributed life to each material entity, and was associated in particular with the early Peripatetic philosopher Strato of Lampsacus (treated in Chapter 3); (2) the 'cosmoplastic', which similarly attributed life to a godless corporeal world, but posited only one vegetative principle of life animating the entire cosmos; this is associated with some later Stoics, especially Boethus of Sidon (also treated in Chapter 3).[453] (B) The positing of a very widespread ancient theistic animism, which either made the world animate and rational (the early Stoics) or posited something akin to Cudworth's own 'plastic nature': an incorporeal organising principle subordinate to the deity, as in Pythagoras, Plato, and Aristotle (primarily treated in a long digression at the end of Chapter 3). (C) The claim that much of pagan polytheism can in fact be explained as an animistic monotheism that also allowed the worship of various

[451] [Hale], *Natural motions*, 25–6.

[452] Samuel Gott, *The divine history of the genesis of the world explicated & illustrated* (London, 1670), 114, 450; Richard Baxter, *Of the immortality of mans souls, and the nature of it and other spirits* (London, 1682), 7–8, and 39 (for friendship and intellectual debt to Gott). For Baxter's friendship with Hale, see Cromartie, *Hale*, 185–91; for Baxter on the soul more generally, see Burton, *Hallowing*, 147–200 (and 109–15 for his intellectual debts to Gott). On the other hand, Benjamin Whichcote suggested that Avicenna's animism differed from that of his predecessors, and had stemmed from his belief that Aristotle's view was 'unworthy of God' (Folger MS V.a.326, fol. 39ᵛ rev. (my foliation)). This disparagement of the Arab commentators was part of a more general Europe-wide trend: Nardi, 'La fine dell'averroismo' (1958).

[453] This 'cosmoplastic' atheism is the only element of Cudworth's discussion of ancient animism which has received concerted recent attention, in two perceptive articles: Giglioni, 'The cosmoplastic system of the universe: Ralph Cudworth on Stoic naturalism' (2008); Sellars, 'Cudworth on Stoic theology'.

parts of the world, and which stemmed from the philosophical equation of the world with God (discussed in various parts of the enormous Chapter 4).[454]

Hylozoic atheism 'makes all Body, as such, and therefore every smallest atom of it, to have *Life* essentially belonging to it (Natural Perception, and Appetite), though without any *Animal Sense* or *Reflexive Knowledge*'.[455] According to Cudworth, its 'first and Chief Assertour' was Strato Lampsacus. None of Strato's works survived, and the standard sources were rather sparse: it was known that after Theophrastus's death he became the third scholarch of the Lyceum and that he devoted himself to natural philosophy especially (earning the monicker 'Φυσικός').[456] However, one important passage from Cicero's *De natura deorum* (i.13.35) castigates him for holding that 'all divine force is resident in nature, which contains, he says, the principles of birth, increase, and decay, but which lacks, as we could remind him, all sensation and form'; others imply his atheism.[457] It is on these that Cudworth built his case, although he added further evidence from Plutarch, interpreting a rather ambiguous passage from *Adversus Colotem* to confirm that Strato held a world of vital but not animated (i.e. rationally directed) parts.[458]

Why did Cudworth so focus on this relatively obscure Aristotelian as a founder of this type of hylozoic atheism? It is often assumed that Cudworth developed this elaborate philological–historical discussion of hylozoic atheism with contemporaries in mind, with Strato simply a cipher for Spinoza.[459] This is an overstatement: Cudworth did refer to Spinoza as a 'kind of Hylozoick

---

[454] Except from Cudworth's claims about the trinitarianism inherent in Pythagoreanism and Platonism (see 6.6 below), ch. 4 has gone virtually unstudied since Mosheim, although some comments can be found in Popkin, 'Polytheism'.

[455] Cudworth, *System*, 105 (it is first introduced at 62).

[456] DL v.3.58–64. The fullest collection of sources is now in R. W. Sharples, 'Strato of Lampsacus: the sources. Texts and translations', in *Strato of Lampsacus: text, translation, and discussion*, eds., M.-L Desclos and W. W. Fortenbaugh (New Jersey, 2011), 5–230.

[457] *Acad.*, ii. 121; *De fin.*, v.5.

[458] Cudworth, *System*, 108–9, discussing Plutarch, *Adv. Col.*, 14 1114F–1115B. The ambiguity of the Greek ('καὶ μὴν τῶν ἄλλων Περιπατητικῶν ὁ κορυφαιότατος Στράτων οὔτ᾽ Ἀριστοτέλει κατὰ πολλὰ συμφέρεται καὶ Πλάτωνι τὰς ἐναντίας ἔσχηκε δόξας περὶ κινήσεως, περὶ νοῦ καὶ περὶ ψυχῆς καὶ περὶ γενέσεως, τελευτῶν τὸν κόσμον αὐτὸν οὐ ζῷον εἶναί φησι, τὸ δὲ κατὰ φύσιν ἔπεσθαι τῷ κατὰ τύχην') later led Bayle into a long digression (in the article on Spinoza, in *Dictionnaire historique et critique* (Rotterdam, 1697), 1083–4, n. A). Cudworth offered his own long digression (109–11) where it is argued that the teleological 'nature' of both Hippocrates and Plato was categorically different from the Stratonical, for both associated it with an animal self-awareness (and also presupposed a higher principle anyway, although in Hippocrates's case that higher principle was, à la Heraclitus, a corporeal one – fire).

[459] Colie, *Light and enlightenment* (1957), 96–7, 126; Passmore, *Cudworth*, 5–6; Israel, *Contested*, 446–9; Hutton, 'Reason and revelation in the Cambridge Platonists, and their reception of Spinoza' (1984), 190. This has been accentuated because Cudworth stated that hylozoism had recently begun to revive (*System*, 145).

Atheist' in a later manuscript[460] but this is the only such reference; his two mentions of Spinoza in the *System* (on other issues) reveal an obvious indifference.[461] Much more likely is that his target was Glisson.[462] But even here, there is a problem: Cudworth's only direct reference to Glisson is entirely positive, congratulating him for recognising that 'all Life cannot be meerly *Accidental* ... but there must of Necessity be, some *Substantial Life*'.[463] It remains likely that Glisson, along with a more general belief in the recent growth of pantheistic tendencies, was the key contemporary target, but there is a bigger point. Strato had already been identified as a key exponent of animist idolatry by Vossius, using the same sources as Cudworth would do.[464] Given Cudworth's frequent use of Vossius (see further below), surely this was his first inspiration? In other words, his driving motive was historiographical rather than contemporary–polemical.

Cudworth's discussion of 'cosmoplastic' atheism was similar, but subtly different, from that of the hylozoic.[465] He claimed that the early Stoics were theists – especially the founder of the sect, Zeno of Citium, as well as Heraclitus[466] and Chrysippus – because although they held the whole world to be corporeal they attributed to it a sentient and rational nature, rendering it an animal.[467] However, this Stoic theism was later corrupted into atheism when the vital principle was no longer classified as an animal but as a vegetable, 'without understanding or sense'.[468] Two pieces of evidence were offered for this claim. The first came from Laërtius (VII.143), who, after reporting the animalistic world of the most famous Stoics added that 'Boethus, however, denies that the cosmos is a living thing'. Cudworth judged that Boethus 'consequently must needs make it [the world] to be but *Corpus Naturâ gubernante, ut Arbores, ut Sata, A Body governed by a Plastick or Vegetative Nature, as Trees, Plants and Herbs*'.[469] From this he concluded that 'it is possible that

---

[460] BL MS Add. 4982, fol. 55ʳ.     [461] Cudworth, *System*, 656, 707.

[462] As first recognised in Pacchi, *Cartesio*, 152–3, and then by Henry, 'Medicine and pneumatology'; Henry, 'Matter of souls'; Giglioni, 'Anatomist atheist?'; Giglioni, 'Panpsychism versus hylozoism' (1995), esp. 42–3.

[463] Cudworth, *System*, 839. To avoid this, Henry, 'Medicine and pneumatology', 111 silently conflates the quotations about Glisson and about the recent rise of hylozoism, while Giglioni, 'Anatomist atheist?', 115, n. 2 gives a long list of putative 'references to Glisson's theory' in the *System*, which turn out to be circular, since they are only references to 'hylozoism' and do not refer to Glisson at all.

[464] See the expanded edition of *De theologia gentili ... editio nova* (Amsterdam, 1668), II, 163. This is already recognised in Israel, *Contested*, 445, who strangely refuses to make the causal connection with Cudworth.

[465] It has already received good treatment in Giglioni, 'Cosmoplastic system' and Sellars, 'Cudworth on Stoic theology', so we cover it relatively quickly.

[466] The connection between Heraclitus (c. 535–475 BC) and the Stoics was a natural one, already made in Cicero, *Nat. Deor.*, III.14.

[467] Cudworth, *System*, 113.     [468] Ibid., 131–2.     [469] Ibid., 133–4.

other Stoicks and Heracliticks, might have done the like before Boëthus, so it is very probable that he had after him many Followers'.[470] Both Mosheim and a more recent commentator have condemned Cudworth for taking this step, which is indeed unjustifiable on modern scholarly grounds.[471] However, it rested on two other historical–philological claims that were much more widely accepted by contemporaries. The first was the 'atheism' which early modern commentators attributed to Pliny the Elder (primarily on the basis of the infamous chapter 'Of God' (*Natural history*, II.5)),[472] and which Cudworth cleverly linked to 'Pseudo-Stoical' cosmoplastic atheism.[473] More fundamental was Cudworth's interpretation of a passage from Seneca's *Naturales quaestiones* (III.29.2), part of which informed the description of Boëthus's philosophy quoted above, of which Cudworth wrote:

> Such a form of atheism as this [i.e. cosmoplastic] is hinted to us in that doubtful passage of *Seneca's, Sive Animal est Mundus* (for so it ought to be read, and not *Anima*) *sive Corpus Naturâ Gubernante, ut Arbores, ut Sata; Whether the whole World be an Animal (i. e. endued with one Sentient and Rational Life) or whether it be only a Body Governed, by (a certain Plastick and Methodical, but Sensless) Nature, as Trees, and other Plants or Vegetables.*[474]

Cudworth suggested that Seneca was ambiguous in his choice between the two options (the world as animal and the world as vegetable), and was thus 'not without a doubtful tincture of this [cosmoloplastic] atheism'.[475] Once again, interpreters have accused Cudworth of scholarly disingenuousness for deviating from the manuscript tradition and emending '*anima*' to '*animal*'.[476] However, the emendation was not Cudworth's: it was first suggested by Lipsius in his *Physiologia Stoicorum* (1604) to defend the idea that like an animal the world contained in itself from its beginning all that was destined to happen to it, including its conflagration.[477] Cudworth was not plucking

---

[470] Ibid., 134.　　[471] *System* 1845, 198, n. 3; Sellers, 'Cudworth on Stoic theology', 131.

[472] See e.g., John Rainolds, *Censura librorum apocryphorum Veteris Testamenti, adversum Pontificios* (2 vols, Oppenheim, 1611), II, cols. 1036–40, although he more conventionally makes Pliny an Epicurean, citing ps.-Plutarch, *Plac. phil.*, I.8. In England, Benjamin Whichcote recorded in his notebook that 'Pliny [was] an enemy to immortality of Souls': Folger MS. V.a.326, fol. 43ᵛ rev. (my foliation).

[473] Cudworth, *System*, 134. Cudworth never explained the connection but he was surely thinking of Pliny's association of God with nature at *Hist. nat.*, II.5.27: 'Per quae declaratur haut dubie naturae potentia idque esse quod deum vocemus'.

[474] Cudworth, *System*, 131.　　[475] Ibid., 134.

[476] *System* 1845, 193, n. 6; Sellers, 'Cudworth on Stoic theology', 131.

[477] Justus Lipsius, *Physiologiae Stoicorum libri tres* (Antwerp, 1604), 133: (after quoting III.29.2–3) 'Initio verborum aliquid mutavi, & *Sive animal*, legi, non *Anima*, ut passim edunt: res ita vult, nec quisquam tam stolidus, qui *Mundum* Animam esse dixerit, sed *Mundi*. At illud ambigitur, sitne sentiens Corpus, an Corpus tantùm. Itaque in ipso Mundi conditu inclusum est, quamdiu vigeat vivatque: ut in quoque animali'. I speculate that Lipsius was aiming for consistency with III.29.3 ('Ut in semine omnis futuri hominis ratio comprehensa est et legem

emendations from the clouds to satisfy his own philosophical intentions, but was engaging with a tradition of early modern readings.[478]

There is no textual evidence for the claim that Cudworth's account of Stoic atheism was covertly targeting Spinoza,[479] an interpretation which seems to read later association between Spinoza and the Stoics (e.g. in Bayle) back into Cudworth. As we have seen, if Cudworth cared about Spinoza at all, he did so only in connection with his discussion of hylozoic/Stratonic atheism. Cudworth did mention that 'some Fanaticks of Latter Times, have made *God to be All*, in a Gross Sence' – he may have been thinking of Jacob Böhme, or simply the common association of illuminationism with a crude pantheism – but even here he made it clear that Stoic pantheism worked 'in somewhat a different way'.[480] There is little cause to suppose that Cudworth thought the late Stoics atheists for any other reason than because he thought it was historically true.

Cudworth's own natural philosophy posited a 'plastic nature': an immaterial and unconscious teleological principle through which God governed the operations of the natural world and which had to be posited in superaddition to mechanism to explain motion and life.[481] This was a simplified and some-what confused appropriation of More's 'Spirit of Nature' by a man who, unlike More, was by vocation not a systematic metaphysician but a philologist.[482] Unsurprisingly, its prehistory is written with far more philological verve by the Regius Professor of Hebrew than by the lowly philosopher. As one would expect, Cudworth attributed the notion to those philosophers who had traditionally been treated as animists, like the Platonists and the Stoics (i.e. the non-atheistic ones), alongside a host of others in whom it was possible to find mention of teleological principles: Empedocles, Hippocrates, and

---

barbae canorumque nondum natus infans habet . . . sic origo mundi non minus solem et lunam et vices siderum et animalium ortus quam quibus mutarentur terrena continuit'). It is worth noting that in his edition of the *Naturales quaestiones*, Lipsius preserved the traditional manuscript reading (*L. Annaei Senecae . . . Opera* (Antwerp, 1605), 718). Unlike Cudworth, Lipsius claimed that the Stoics held God to be an immaterial *anima mundi*; see Hirai, 'Lipsius on the world-soul' (2011).

[478] For Meric Casaubon's dissent from Lipsius on this passage, see p. 342 above.

[479] Israel, *Contested*, 463 (although the discussion is rather ambiguous); Brooke, *Philosophic pride*, 136–7 (despite noting that 'direct evidence is hard to come by'); Sellars, 'Mindless vegetable', esp. 132.

[480] Cudworth, *System*, 306; Giglioni, 'Cosmoplastic system', 326–7; Hutton, 'Henry More and Jacob Boehme' (1990).

[481] Cudworth, *System*, 148; for concise definitions, see 165, 172; for discussions: Passmore, *Cudworth*, 23–8; Petit, 'Ralph Cudworth, un platonisme paradoxal: la nature dans la *Digression concerning the plastick life of nature*' (1997); Jacob, *De naturae natura* (1991), 48–52.

[482] See Jacob, *Naturae natura*, 49–51 for an astute philosophical comparison.

Heraclitus.[483] What is of greatest interest to us is that Cudworth made a concerted effort to convert Aristotle into a Plato-style animist.[484] He began simply by emphasising the teleology inherent in Aristotle's 'nature' by citing dictums including 'God and nature do nothing in vain'.[485] This, as Cudworth well knew, was hardly enough, and he embarked on a long explanation, emphasising its necessity by commenting on Aristotle's ambiguity on such key issues as whether 'nature' was immaterial. The 'vulgar Peripatetics' (by which Cudworth meant hylomorphists) had used this ambiguity to align Aristotle's 'nature' with 'form', but this was a mistake.[486] Instead, it should be associated with an animating spirit. Aristotle not only held the equivalent of a plastic soul as a motive force in animals but also in the world as a whole, as could be seen from the passage in *Parts of animals* ($641^b20$–5) where Aristotle suggests that since there is much more 'order and determinate regularity' in the heavens than in animals, teleological nature, rather than chance, must be the internal principle of the former as much as the latter.[487] This was still far too ambiguous for Cudworth's purposes, but he could then resort to the aforementioned tradition of reading Aristotle as animating the heavens, citing the animist interpretations of Simplicius and Alexander of Aphrodisias as those to be adopted 'whatever the doctrine of the modern Peripatetics be'.[488] And so again, we see the same pattern as we found in Hale, in the medical tradition, and throughout both philosophy and theology: as hylomorphism was dismissed as a medieval corruption, Aristotle more and more came to be interpreted animistically, as a quasi-Platonist. Hence Cudworth's conclusion that he had 'now cleared the *Aristotelick Doctrine* concerning the *Plastic Nature* of the universe, with which the *Platonick* also agrees'.[489]

We should not, therefore, ascribe Cudworth's reinterpretation of Aristotle to his putative 'Platonism': he was taking part in a general early modern

---

[483] Cudworth, *System*, 151–5. Even here Cudworth had to deviate from the accepted interpretations: aware that the Platonic *anima mundi* was rather more rational and conscious than his own plastic nature, he claimed that the Platonists 'seemed to affirm' a dual plastic nature, one 'lodged in all particular souls of animals, brutes and men', another, 'distinct from their higher mundane soul, though subordinate to it, and dependent upon it', an interpretation that rested on a somewhat forced reading of, and back projection from, Plotinus's *Enneads*: see *System*, 165.

[484] Already treated in Hutton, 'Aristotle and the Cambridge Platonists: the case of Cudworth' (1999), esp. 344–7, although my interpretation is somewhat different. Cudworth's old Cambridge colleague, Benjamin Whichcote, had already sought to bring Aristotle and Plato closer together by rendering the Aristotelian *intellectus agens* equivalent to Platonic deiformity of the understanding: see his notebook, Folger MS V.a.326, fol. 34ʳ (my foliation). Whichcote admits to drawing on Julius Caesar Scaliger's *Exotericarum exercitationum liber XV* (Paris, 1557) for this idea. The excellent study by K. Sakamoto, 'Creation, the trinity and *prisca theologia* in Julius Caesar Scaliger' (2010), details Scaliger's attempts to 'Platonise' Aristotle on many of the issues considered here.

[485] Cudworth, *System*, 151.    [486] Ibid., 164.    [487] Ibid., 167–8.    [488] Ibid., 168–71.

[489] Ibid., 171.

re-interpretation of Aristotle's philosophy of causation, something revealed when we realise that his key source was again that most un-Platonic of his contemporaries, Gassendi. This emerges most fully in the gargantuan (but incomplete) chapter 4.[490] As we have seen, its purpose was to render impotent the atheist argument for the absurdity of religion from the example of pagan polytheisms by representing them all as corrupt monotheisms which posited subordinate deities: 'no such thing does at all appear ... as that the Pagans or any others did publicly or professedly assert a *Multitude* of *Unmade Self-existent Deities*'.[491]

Cudworth was here echoing the argument of Vossius (and implicitly dissenting from its modification by Parker). After analysing the near-eastern sages and the Greek theogonists, Cudworth turned to the Greek philosophers. His argument was simple but ingenious: because all the philosophers saw the world as animate, they conceived of it as deiform; because 'the ancient Pagans did physiologize in their theology', they 'προσωποποιεῖν, *speak of the things in nature, and the parts of the world, as persons*'.[492] The key argument appeared in IV.29 where Cudworth posited 'that the pagan theologers did thus generally acknowledge one supreme and universal Numen, appears plainly from hence, because they supposed the whole world to be an animal'.[493] Like Parker, he attributed to the ancients a universal animism, grounded in the belief in an *anima mundi*. But where for Parker this had meant that pagan thought was incompatible with the distant God of Judaeo-Christianity, for Cudworth it implied the logic of monotheism. Some of the pagans, such as the Stoics, took the 'soul of the world, and the whole mundane animal' to be God himself; others, 'conceiving the first and highest God to be an abstract and immoveable mind, and not a soul', placed him above this animated world: this was the case with Plato, Aristotle, and Xenocrates.[494]

How has Aristotle again been added to the list of animists? The answer comes in Cudworth's quotation of a passage from pseudo-Plutarch that stated that 'all [philosophers] assert the world to be an animal, and governed by Providence; only Leucippus, Democritus, and Epicurus ... dissenting, who neither acknowledge the world to be animated, not yet to be governed by Providence, but by an irrational nature'.[495] This passage had already been used to claim that all the ancients were animists very recently, for Gassendi had argued that it proved that Epicurus had been closer to Christianity than all the other ancient philosophers, who were quasi-idolatrous animists.[496]

---

[490] That it is incomplete is admitted at *System*, 632.    [491] Cudworth, *System*, 211.
[492] Ibid., 228; see also 244, 462. Giglioni, 'Cosmoplastic system', 324 somewhat misrepresents Cudworth's use of Vossius.
[493] Cudworth, *System*, 462.    [494] Ibid., 463–4.
[495] Ibid., 462, citing ps.-Plutarch, *Plac. phil.*, II.3.4 (=Stobaeus, *Ecl.*, I.21).
[496] Gassendi, *Syntagma philosophicum*, in *Opera omnia*, I, 158b–159a.

Cudworth chastised the Frenchman: far from bringing Epicurus closer to Christianity, 'according to the Language and Notions of those times, to deny the *Worlds Animation*, and to be an Atheist ... was one and the same thing'.[497] But despite their disagreement, Cudworth and Gassendi's overall historical conclusion was the same: all the ancient philosophers – apart from Democritus, Epicurus, and Leucippus, but crucially including Aristotle – had made the world animate and possessed of an *anima mundi*.

It is remarkable to find two such accomplished scholars using the pseudo-Plutarch passage to claim this, for the passage goes on to say that 'Aristotle is excepted [from the canon of animists], who is somewhat different; he is of the opinion, that the whole world is not acted by a soul in every part of it, nor hath it any sensitive, rational, or intellectual faculties, nor is it guided by reason and Providence in every part of it': both Gassendi and Cudworth simply ignored this continuation. This might seem to be enough to bring charges of scholarly disingenuousness.[498] However, the claim that all the ancient philosophers were animists, while obviously used by Gassendi, Parker, and Cudworth to buttress their own philosophical and theological agendas, also stemmed from a set of genuinely scholarly beliefs about the nature of pagan theology and idolatry, beliefs which had been developed in the first half of the seventeenth century by Selden and especially by Vossius.

Cudworth relied heavily on this scholarship. But he also deviated from it. As we have seen, both Parker and Vossius had followed their original source, Maimonides, in claiming that the first idolatry was starworship. This had allowed Vossius to engage in many genealogical conjectures, such as claiming that according to the philosophical idolatry of the pagans, Venus was ultimately the moon.[499] Cudworth read this as a fundamental misunderstanding of the process of deification of natural bodies in pagan philosophical theology, which had not deified specific bodies, but seen them as parts of a universal deity.[500] But despite these differences, Cudworth shared with Vossius and Parker the image of pagan theology as inherently animistic – 'the worshipping (besides one supreme God) of other created beings, as the ministers of his providence' – that they derived from Maimonides.[501] Indeed, Cudworth supplemented him

---

[497] Cudworth, *System*, 462.    [498] See e.g. Mosheim's note in *System* 1845, II, 175, n. 8.

[499] Vossius, *Theologia gentilis*, 465: 'Sed facilè hunc nodum exsolvimus, distinguendo cum Varrone, & Augustino, triplicem gentium Theologiam; poeticam, philosophicam, & civilem. Ex philosophica de Diis doctrina, Venus est vel Luna, ut vidimus, vel Lucifer [i.e. the morning star], sive Hesperus [i.e. the evening star]'. Vossius was referring to the tripartite division of pagan theology in Varro's *Ant. div.*, V, as discussed in Augustine, *Civ. Dei*, IV.27 and VI.5 (Vossius mistakenly cited IV.37 and VI.4). For the centrality of Varro's schematic to Vossius's whole discussion, see *Theologia gentilis*, 307–9.

[500] Cudworth, *System*, 497.

[501] Ibid., 468–9, citing both the *Guide* (I.36; III.18) and *De idololatria* (although he gives the Hebrew, he was using Dionysius Vossius's edition). Later (471), he notes that the celestial

with other rabbinic testimonies, some well known – such as Joseph Albo's *Sefer ha-'Iḳḳarim* (1425) and the Bible commentaries of David Kimchi and Rashi – but also some more obscure, such as the Pentateuch commentary of the Turkish rabbi Moses Albelda, the *Olat Tamid* ('Perpetual Offering', 1600).[502] And so while we can acknowledge that it was partially driven by a specific apologetic aim, we must also recognise that Cudworth's long discussion of animistic philosophy and polytheism was at the same time a contribution to the 'animisation' of ancient philosophy and religion that was occurring throughout seventeenth-century scholarship, philosophy, and theology.

This is also clear from an examination of Cudworth's greatest critic on this subject, Pierre Bayle, who came to know of Cudworth's opinions from Le Clerc's long reviews of the *System* in the *Bibliotheque choisie*.[503] For Bayle, the near universal animism of the pagans could not be characterised as a monotheism: either God was 'totally distinct' from the world, or he was part of it (whether as a world soul or a material principle), in which case he consisted of parts and thus subject to polytheistic worship.[504] The pagans believed the latter: recognising a universal principle was not the same as separating God from the world – indeed, it was little better than proto-Spinozism.[505] If anything, the pagan philosophers had been worse polytheists

---

bodies which the pagans took for inferior gods, the Jews treated as animated, citing Maimonides, 'Jesude Hatterah', which is of course the *Yesodei ha-Torah*, the first book of Maimonides's *Mishneh Torah*, which Cudworth would have used in the edition by Guilielmus Vorstius, *Constitutiones de fundamentis legis Rabbi Mosis F. Maiiemon* (Amsterdam, 1638) (quotation there at 32).

[502] Cudworth, *System*, 468–71, quoting from Moses ben Jacob Albelda, עולת תמיד (Venice, 1600), fol. 147ʳ. On Albelda (1500–c. 1583), see Heller, *The seventeenth century Hebrew book* (2011), 15. Albo's work was often used as a benchmark of Jewish opinion by Restoration Hebraists: see Levitin, 'Spencer', 60.

[503] The key discussion being the paraphrase of much of Cudworth's argument in *Bibliothèque choisie*, 3 (1704), 11–106. Bayle, who did not read English, admitted that this was his source in his *Continuations des pensées sur les cometes* (Rotterdam, 1705), 331.

[504] See the summary of the argument at Bayle, *Continuations*, 335–6: 'Car quel est l'état de la question lors qu'on veut philosopher touchant l'unité de Dieu? C'est de savoir s'il y a une intelligence parfaitement simple, totalement distinguée de la matiere & de la forme du monde, & productrice de toutes choses. Si l'on afirme cela, l'on croit qu'il n'ya a qu'un Dieu, mais si on ne l'afirme pas, on a beau sifler tous les Dieux du Paganisme, & temoigner de l'horreur pour la multitude des Dieux, on en admetra réellement une infinité, soit que l'on dise que le monde ou que l'ame du monde, ou que le soleil est Dieu, & qu'il n'y en a point d'autre; soit que l'on dise que toutes les creatures sont l'ouvrage d'un seul principe par voie d'émanation, ou par une action immanente. La plupart des temoins de Mr. Cudworth tombent par là. Il lui seroit très mal aisé d'en produire qui aient admis l'unité de Dieu sans entendre une substance composée'.

[505] Ibid., 336: 'Voilà des Paiens, me direz vous, qui n'ont reconu qu'un principle de toutes choses. Cela ne sufit pas vous repondrai-je. Les Spinozistes ne parlent pas autrement. Il faut savoir de plus quelle est la nature qu'ils assignment à ce principe. L'exemptent ils de toute compositions, le separent-ils, le distinguent-ils ou de la forme, ou de la matiere du monde?'

than the people.[506] Cudworth, Bayle argued, must have misread his sources: Diodorus Siculus reported on the horrible polytheist animism of the Egyptians; Xenophanes and Parmenides were proto-Spinozists; and even Plato had held a confused vision of a Godhead that was part of the world.[507]

In reality, however, Bayle's argument was far less different from Cudworth's than he claimed. His own key sources were Gassendi on the animism of all the Greek philosophers apart from Epicurus,[508] and, astonishingly, Parker's *Tentamina*, whose argument that the pagans all took the supreme God to be an *anima mundi* or something similar Bayle praised exorbitantly.[509] Parker, Cudworth, and Bayle had all taken the Vossius–Gassendi turn: they all recognised that pagan philosophy and theology was inherently animistic, and none of them – not even Cudworth – can be classified as a 'syncretist' in any meaningful sense. Cudworth hardly valued pagan animistic philosophy, which he was sure was riddled with errors that led to the positing of many inferior deities; he simply attempted to turn the findings of Vossius and Gassendi to apologetic ends in one way (animism implied monotheism), whereas Parker and Bayle found in those findings another apologetic message (the unique triumph of non-animistic Judaeo-Christian theology).

### 5.4.4   Boyle

Given that the key inspiration for the new, animistic reading of Greek philosophy was Gassendi, it is no surprise that natural philosophers engaged with it as much as theologians and scholars. Particularly interesting here is the case of Thomas Willis, whose *De anima brutorum* (1672) was probably the most important treatise on the soul published by any of the English *neoterici*.[510] In the historical overview that constituted the first chapter of that work Willis drew the traditional distinction between Platonic and Pythagorean *anima mundi* doctrines and Aristotle's hylomorphism; however, when he came to the comparison of the corporeal animal soul with the rational soul in chapter seven, he affirmed (against those who would have the rational soul perform all vital functions in humans) that Plato, Pythagoras, and Aristotle had all believed in an immaterial rational soul that was qualitatively separate from the corporeal because it emerged from, and returned to, an *anima mundi*. For this conclusion

---

[506] Ibid., 120: 'Réellement donc les Philosophes qui semblent avoir enseigné l'unité de Dieu ont été plus polytheistes que le peuple'.

[507] Ibid., 332–5, 342–7.

[508] See esp. ibid., 346–8 for the use of exactly the same part of Gassendi's *Syntagma* as Cudworth.

[509] Ibid., 118–20 (Bayle was particularly impressed with Parker's argument that the pagans had used the term 'spirit' in a wide sense – see p. 415 above).

[510] Serjeantson, 'Soul', 132; the fullest discussions are Frank, 'Willis and his circle'; Wright, 'Locke, Willis, and the seventeenth-century Epicurean soul' (1989); Wallace, 'The vibrating nerve impulse in Newton, Willis, and Gassendi' (2003).

he directly cited Gassendi.[511] We shall recall that Willis also rejected Epicurean materialism as overly reductionist. The two ancient extremes as set up by Gassendi – the atomism of Epicurus and the (supposed) animism of everyone else – were becoming the two extremes between which many English naturalists were claiming to forge a *via media*.

It is at this point that we return to Boyle's seminal work on the 'vulgarly received notion of nature', about which we can reach a similar conclusion. According to Boyle, this animistic view of nature had its roots in ancient idolatrous nature-worship, especially the starworship of the Sabians. From there it fed into Greek philosophy, first through the semi-mythical Orpheus but also in the philosophies of Pythagoras, Plato, Zeno, and crucially Aristotle, who all placed an intermediate principle such as an *anima mundi* between God and the world. It also influenced Galenic medicine, with its theories of battling elements and crises as 'Nature's' method of curing illness.

Boyle's conclusions came from a patchwork of sources. For example, one of Boyle's examples of putative Aristotelian and Galenic anthropomorphism was the theory of elements, where 'each of them [has] its natural Place assign'd it in the Universe', and if one is removed, 'it has a strong incessant Appetite to return to it ... and is now in a place, which *Nature* has qualifi'd to preserve it'.[512] Of course, Boyle had good philosophical reasons for attacking Aristotelian element theory, as set out in the *Sceptical chymist*. But a comparison makes it clear that Boyle was drawing on van Helmont, whose attack on the Galenic personification of the elements and the belief that 'crises' are resolved by a personified '*natura medicatrix*' we have met; Boyle even devoted a notebook entry to the dictum.[513] Both condemned the same Aristotelian definition of 'nature' (*Physics* 192$^b$20–2), and countered it with their own voluntaristic definitions.[514]

But Boyle expanded massively on van Helmont, particularly in his efforts to align Aristotle with traditional animists such as the Stoics and Platonists. He found a prime example of the pre-eminence of the vulgar notion of nature when he considered, like Gassendi, Glisson, and Cudworth, 'what has for many Ages been taught by the School Philosophers from *Aristotle*; namely, that the Coelestial Spheres had their peculiar *Intelligences*, that is, Rational, Immortal, Powerful and Active Beings'.[515] He directly cited key texts in the tradition of 'animist' readings of Aristotle on the celestial intelligences from Origen and Maimonides; another passage from the manuscript version of

---

[511] Willis, *De anima brutorum*, 2–4, 116. Willis was in turn directly quoted on the subject in John Webster, *The displaying of supposed witchcraft* (London, 1677), 314–15.

[512] Boyle, *Free enquiry*, 501.    [513] RS BP198, fol. 3$^r$ (*c.* 1680); see also *Free enquiry*, 537.

[514] van Helmont, *Ortus medicinae*, 46 (this similarity was first noted in Clericuzio, 'From van Helmont to Boyle').

[515] Boyle, *Free enquiry*, 448.

*Christian virtuoso* (1690) has very strong echoes of the discussion by Clemens Alexandrinus on the same subject.[516] More fundamentally, this question was central in the Aristotelian textbook tradition and the reader versed in these arguments can recognise Boyle's distinct references to them; for example, when he expressed sympathy for the view that angels may be more appropriate vicegerents of God than a personified 'nature', he adopted the same solution as Aquinas in his commentary on Lombard's *Sentences*.[517] Boyle, then, was not describing the essentially Aristotelian position, but taking a side in a debate that pre-dated even the humanist commentators; manuscript evidence suggests that he was aware of the controversial nature of his interpretation.[518]

None of these discussions was enough to lead Boyle to his master-narrative: that all ancient philosophies spoke of entities such as an *anima mundi* on the basis of their inheritance from Sabian idolatry. We know the rabbinic roots of the final claim; like Stanley, Boyle cited as his source Hottinger's *Historia orientalis*.[519] But Boyle's narrative then jumped from the Sabians straight to Greek philosophy and the 'Stoical Sect, [which] taught, as *Stobaeus* informs us, that the Sun, Moon, and the rest of the Stars were imbu'd with Understanding and Prudence', and to Aristotelian anthropomorphism.[520] For all his references to the primary texts, Boyle had a contemporary source at hand: Parker's *Tentamina* (and perhaps its extended follow-up, the *Disputationes de Deo*). As we saw, Parker connected the Vossian and Gassendist narratives to argue for the animism of all pagan philosophy: there are repeated textual similarities between Parker and Boyle, from the emphasis on Orpheus to the exact same usage of the Stobaeus passage which claimed that Zeno and the Stoics

---

[516] Boyle, *Christian Virtuoso 1, Appendix*, in *Boyle works*, XII, 414. For Clemens, see p. 405 above. As Hunter and Davis report, the passage is found in the earliest extant manuscript (RS BP1 fols. 95$^{r-v}$) and a copy (RS BP1, fol. 10$^r$) but omitted in the final version (RS BP1, fol. 114$^v$). Clemens's work is listed in Boyle's 'A list of books provided & to be provyded for the collection making by Mr Boyle of books tending to the proofs & defence of the truth of the Christian Religion' (*c.* 1689–91), RS BP186 (Notebook, *c.* 1690), fols. 30$^v$–31$^v$ at 30$^v$ (printed in Anstey, 'The Christian virtuoso and the Reformers' (2000), at 32–4).

[517] Boyle, *Free enquiry*, 460–1; on Aquinas, see Wolfson, 'Souls of the spheres', 87–9. This seems also to have been a pedagogical commonplace: see CUL MS Add. 9597/16/1, 'A system of physicks', *c.* 1650–1700, 27–8 (but see also 33 for scepticism about the intelligences). Conversely, Gassendi called the opinion that angels moved the celestial spheres an 'opinio vulgatissima', and also considered it derived from Aristotle (*Syntagma philosophicum*, in *Opera*, I, 634). In manuscript, Boyle suggested that although traditional astrology was nonsensical, the possibility of a corpuscularian explanation for celestial influence on the sublunary sphere was not to be discounted: BP8, fol. 204$^r$ (text on 'judiciary astrology' and celestial influences, 1660s).

[518] See the cautious insertion of 'and as is very likely Aristotle too' in a passage discussing those 'Heathen Philosophers' who held celestial intelligences to be 'Rational Beings' (RS BP10, fol. 165$^r$, part of a dialogue concerning planetary intelligences and divine beings in heaven, 1680s).

[519] Boyle, *Free enquiry*, 471.

[520] Ibid., 472. The Stobaeus source (not given by Boyle), is *Ecl.*, I.213.15.

attributed understanding and prudence to the sun and the moon.[521] Directly anticipating Boyle, Parker had asserted that the heathen philosophers thus ended up sometimes assigning the name 'Nature' to their deity.[522] By the time of the *Disputationes de Deo* he had developed the Gassendist critique of Aristotle even further, claiming that the latter's atheistic replacement of God with a personified 'Nature' stemmed logically from his eternalism.[523] Boyle had good reasons to accept Parker's testimony. As we have seen, Parker's work was very enthusiastically received in the Royal Society in the mid-1660s (when Boyle began the *Free enquiry*) and Parker had been recommended to him in mid-1666 by Henry Oldenburg, reporting on the praise of John Beale; this was swiftly followed by direct praise from Beale himself.[524] The *Disputationes de Deo* is one of the very few theological works that we can be sure that Boyle owned.[525] The Aristotle that van Helmont, Gassendi, Parker, and Boyle attacked (and Cudworth celebrated) was their own creation, a product of several historiographical traditions: certainly no traditional scholastic Aristotelian would have recognised or accepted him.[526]

After Boyle's hugely influential delineation of the non-animism of 'modern' philosophy, it became even more commonplace to assert that all paganism was animistic.[527] The doctrinal critique merged with the methodological, and the accusation of believing in an *anima mundi* became akin to the accusation of believing in hooked atoms or in Cartesian vortices. At the same time, the continuing problems of causality, of God's operation in the world, and non-mechanical explanation continued to keep the issue of active principles, and thus the ancient philosophies which used them, very much alive.

This was the case as much for scholars as it was for practising natural philosophers. John North (1.4, 4.4 above) took the Gassendian train of thought to its logical conclusion, while deploying his expertise in neoplatonic philosophy to buttress the scholarly case (like many others we have met, he considered

---

[521] Parker, *Tentamina*, 221.

[522] Ibid., 236: 'Obiter notandum est illis *Deum* nonnunqua[m] *Naturae* nomine designari'.

[523] Parker, *Disputationes*, 355–80, e.g. 368: 'Quid enim aliud Dei nomine intelligere possumus quàm praestantem quandam aeternamque Naturam, quae Mundum primùm condidit semperque regit?' Parker made much of Aristotle's putative debt to Ocellus Lucanus on this score (see further p. 303 above).

[524] Oldenburg to Boyle, 8 June 1666, *Boyle correspondence*, III, 168; Beale to Boyle, 31 October 1666, ibid., III, 260. Beale continued to praise Parker to Boyle in the 1680s: see the letters of 26 June and 1 July 1682 in ibid., V, 299–300, 306. For Oldenburg's ownership of Parker's *Tentamina*, see n. 114 above.

[525] RS BP190 ('Notebook, 1684-90'), fols. 8^{r-v}.

[526] For the 'myth' of the vast difference between Aristotelian and mechanical attitudes to teleology, see Carlin, 'Boyle's teleological mechanism and the myth of immanent teleology' (2012).

[527] E.g. Evelyn, *History of religion*, I, 7 (pagans found God everywhere), 21–3 (a discussion of 'nature' with strong echoes of Boyle's).

Gassendi 'not onely a recoverer of $y^e$ Epicurean sect, but [that] his works are [also] a treasury of all philosophy, wherein all opinions are brought upon $y^e$ stage proposed and discussed').[528] Democritus developed a philosophy consisting purely of matter in motion. But Aristotle secured fame because his philosophy 'was suited $y^e$ best in $y^e$ world to secure [the pagan] Religion', with his celestial intelligences, and with 'all his Qualitys natural, Endowments of Gravity, levity, &c. referred to God'. But in reality that 'God' was, following Plato, equivalent to 'Nature':

[Aristotle] guided his phisicks wholly upon his Master Platos foundation and tho he rejected the Newness of the world, and doth not bring in a God, yet he hath a φύσις [Nature], $w^{ch}$ he adores as much and abuseth in Referring Most things to her <to> save his owne Ignorance; And perhaps he is in this more to be blamed then Democritus himself; for if you ask him of Gravity or tendency of body to one place, he Condemnes $y^e$ Question, & thinks you had as good ask why trees send forth blossomes, why Creatures generate, & bring forth, $w^{ch}$ he says ... Nature guides ... It is a poor shift.[529]

In another foreshadowing of Bayle, North thus concluded that atheism was preferable in natural philosophy to Platonic–Aristotelian animism: while the 'Democrtatists, & Epicureans by throwing off God, could not but light on the right way of Explaining things by matter & motion only ... Plato by introducing God, neglected more the particular solution ... To say that God hath planted such a Quality in such a thing, without Explaining of what it Consists, is rediculous'. As had Gassendi concluded, 'and so Epicurus may well deride the rest, for making a refuge in any hard Question'.[530] The congruence between Plato and Aristotle was confirmed by the fact that they were so often reconciled, first by Ammonius (when the Academic Platonists got bored of their own scepticism) and by Alexander Aphrodisias, Themistius, and Olympiodorus, who were all Platonists who nonetheless wrote Aristotle commentaries.[531] But correct, non-animistic, natural philosophy need not lead to atheism: after all, Aristotle, the most non-mechanical, animistic philosopher of them all, believed in the eternity of the world.[532] In reality, Democritus and Epicurus had had to resort to a different form of 'mechanistic' animism. To the question of 'how Gravity should be solved [which] hath always puzzled $y^e$ world', they – although they 'took the best way' – could still only answer that it was an inherent 'principle ... in their Atomes'.[533] North, not writing in apologetic mode, simply avoided Cudworth's dilemma in response to Gassendi's historicisation: the ancients had either been atheists but sensible proto-mechanical natural philosophers (Democritus, Epicurus) or animists and bad natural philosophers (Aristotle, Plato). North made no attempt to claim that good philosophy had necessarily been aligned with good natural theology.

---

[528] BL MS Add. 32514, fol. 199$^v$.     [529] Ibid., fol. 208$^r$.     [530] Ibid., fol. 207$^v$.
[531] Ibid., fols. 208$^r$–209$^v$.     [532] Ibid., fol. 207$^r$, 209$^v$–210$^r$.     [533] Ibid., fol. 210$^r$.

Among those more directly engaged with philosophy, meanwhile, we can find Locke aligning the methodological hubris of the ancients – and, crucially, of Aristotle – with their belief in potentially idolatrous active principles as early as his medical manuscripts of the late 1660s. In the 'Anatomia' manuscript, Locke sought to demonstrate his scepticism about the ability of physic to establish the causes of diseases (see 4.4 above) by complaining of the ancients' ignorance of the principles of animal life, after which, 'not knowing what to conceive it, they went above the clouds for a name and cald it φύσιν ἀνάλογον τῷ τῶν ἄστρων στοιχείῳ [Nature, analogous to the primeval element of the stars]', equivalent to some kind of 'hidden δημιουργός [demiurge]'.[534] The reader will of course have noticed that the Greek quotation is the same one from Aristotle's *Generation of animals* that we have met several times, this time adapted to a methodological theme: Aristotle's hubristic claims to offer causal explanation in natural philosophy were grounded in idolatrous views of 'nature' and its cosmological significance. Locke combined this with a critique of the Helmontian *archeus* as a similarly unfounded teleological principle.[535] He was already acquainted with Boyle by this point,[536] but it is just as likely that this reading was inspired by Gassendi.[537]

In his later works and manuscripts Locke even more forcefully articulated his belief that Aristotle had believed in an *anima mundi* and in turn that agnosticism about the nature of matter in action was preferable to such animism. In his long exchange with Stillingfleet in the 1690s,[538] Locke chastised the bishop's attempts to bring Boyle to his (Stillingfleet's) side; in the 'addenda' posthumously attached to the *Second reply* (1699) Locke commented that there was another sense, 'wherein the word φύσις may be found made use of by the *Greeks* . . . As particularly *Aristotle*, if I mistake not, uses it for a Plastick Power, or a kind of *Anima Mundi*, presiding over the material World, and producing the Order and Regularity of Motions, Formations and Generations in it'.[539] Such sentiments would have been far less conceivable

---

[534] PRO 30/24/46/2, fol. 36ᵛ (Locke, 'Anatomia')[=Walmsley, 'Locke', 283].    [535] Ibid.

[536] For Locke's probable first meeting with Boyle in early 1660, perhaps via Richard Lower, see Woolhouse, *Locke*, 34–5; see also Frank, *Harvey*, 186–7.

[537] Walmsley ('Locke', 118) suggests Sennert, *De consensu et dissensu Galenicorum & Peripateticorum cum chymicis* [1619], in *Opera omnia* (2 vols, Lyon, 1656), I, 200 [*LL* 2617, 230] as Locke's source, but although Sennert does quote and dicuss the passage, he is resolutely positive about it: 'loco, quem omnes rerum naturalium scriptores perpetuò ob oculos habere debebant'. It is true that the direct evidence of Locke's engagement with Gassendi is slight: see the very thorough discussion in Milton, 'Locke and Gassendi', which limits Locke's reading of Gassendi primarily to natural philosophical topics in the early 1660s, which fits our chronology (but it should also be noted that Prof. Milton's interpretation depends at a key point (94) on the anachronistic distinction between 'science' and 'philosophy').

[538] The fullest treatment remains Stewart, 'Stillingfleet and the way of ideas'.

[539] John Locke, 'Addenda' to *Mr Locke's reply to the right reverend the Lord Bishop of Worcester's answer to his second letter* (1699) in *The works of John Locke* (3 vols, London, 1714), I, 576.

even half a century earlier. Most important, though, is a manuscript fragment from *c.* 1690 entitled 'Ignorantia'. Here we find Locke's most explicit statement on the connection between *anima mundi* theories and natural philosophical agnosticism:

> Thus because we cannot comprehend how a blinde jumble of Atoms can frame the curious bodys of animals, nor yet thinke it fit to engage the immediate hand of god in the production of every mite and insect an anima mundi without knowledg and consciousnesse is substituted as the conducter of <physical> generations and productions. But yet how this material unthinkeing soule, (for if it be immaterial it will be yet harder to be understood) should be a better guide and artificer than unthinkeing matter or how it differs from it will be always equally hard to be explained and soe in effect amounts to noe ~~thing~~ more but a new name of noething more intelligible than what we would explain by it.[540]

Altough there is no mention of the ancients it is clear from the above evidence that Locke associated them with the sort of thinking critiqued here. The lesson that ancient philosophy had taught him was that speculation about active principles imbued in matter, and thus talk of 'material souls', was better replaced by an agnosticism that allowed the possible attribution of those powers to matter itself, a lesson that was famously and controversially repeated in the *Essay*.[541]

### 5.4.5   Newton

Similar themes to those in Locke can be found in Newton, albeit heavily modified and in a different natural philosophical context. Indeed, so rich and complex is Newton's engagement with this issue that it forms an apt culmination to all the themes we have encountered in Chapters 4 and 5 concerning natural philosophical method, atomism, and the nature of motion and causation.

The published texts which contain relevant material are (A) the famous General Scholium, first published in the second edition of the *Principia* (1713), in which Newton addressed the theological implications of his philosophy, countered the vortex-based philosophy of Descartes and Leibniz, and defended the methodology behind his conclusions, particularly with the famous

---

See further 512–13 and Edward Stillingfleet, *The Bishop of Worcester's answer to Mr. Locke's second letter* (London, 1698), 87–103.

[540]   Bod. MS Locke c. 33, fol. 27ᵛ, 'Ignorantia' (this fragment is undated, but an earlier entry on the same page is dated '[16]90').

[541]   John Locke, *An essay concerning humane understanding* (London, 1690), 270. For the subsequent controversy, see Yolton, *Thinking matter* (1983); Thomson, *Bodies of thought* (2008), 97–248.

phrase 'hypotheses non fingo';[542] and (B) some of the 'Queries' to the *Opticks* (1704, 1706, 1717) (as well as some of their manuscript drafts).[543] The key manuscript material is to be found in (C) the 'Classical scholia', composed *c.* 1693–94 and intended as historical supplements to Propositions IV to IX of Book III of the *Principia* (ultimately not included). In the 'Classical scholia', animism was a central concern of Newton's:

> Up to now I have explained the properties of gravity. I have not made the least judgement of its cause. However, I will report what the ancients thought about it. The heavens are nearly free of bodies, but are everywhere filled with a certain infinite spirit which they called 'God'. However, bodies move freely in this spirit, perpetually impelled towards one another by its force and natural power, more or less strongly according to the harmonic ratio of the distances: gravity corresponds to this action. Some differentiated this spirit from the highest God, calling it the *anima mundi*.[544]

The final manuscript evidence (D) are the thousands of pages of Newton's notes and prose on the history of ancient religion, composed between the mid-1680s and the early 1700s, and primarily surviving in the Yahuda collection in the National Library in Jerusalem.[545]

Let us begin by quoting the key passages from the General Scholium.

> He [God] rules all things, not as the world soul but as the lord of all. And because of his dominion he is called Lord God *Pantokrator*. For 'god' is a relative word and has

---

[542] The historiography on the General Scholium is vast; particular landmarks – not all the conclusions of which I share – are: Cohen, *Introduction to Newton's* Principia (1971), 240–5; Westfall, *Newton*, 510–11, 748–51; Snobelen, 'The theology of Isaac Newton's General Scholium' (2001); Ducheyne, 'The General Scholium' (2010).

[543] Again, a huge historiography exists: for a starting point, see Shapiro, 'Newton's "experimental philosophy"' and Anstey, 'The methodological origins of Newton's queries' (2004) and the literature cited within both.

[544] RS MS Gregory 247, fol. 14$^v$, printed in Schüller, 'Newton's scholia' (2001), 240. I have slightly modified Schüller's translation ('Hactenus proprietates gravitatis explicui. Causas ejus minime expendo. Dicam tamen quid Veteres hac de re senserint . . . nempe caelos esse corporis prope vacuos . . . sed spiritu tamen quodam infinito quem Deum nominabant ubique . . . impleri . . . corpora autem in spirit illo libereme moveri . . . ejus vi et virtute . . . naturali ad invicem . . . perpetuo impelli, idque magis vel minus pro ratione harmonica distantiarum, & in hic im<pul>su gravitatem consistere. Hunc spiritum aliqui a Deo summo distinxerunt & animam mundi vocarunt') (ellipses replace deletions only, rather than any final text).

[545] See 3.7 above for an introduction. The Classical Scholia have traditionally been interpreted independently of the manuscripts on religion, and Newton subsumed into a loose '*prisca sapientia*' or 'Cambridge Platonist' framework. This reading was made famous by McGuire and Rattansi, 'Pipes', which introduced the Classical Scholia to scholarship. They have already received criticism on this score from Paolo Casini, who was the first to print an edition of the Classical Scholia ('Newton: the Classical Scholia' (1984), esp. 9). But Prof. Casini's edition was also unreliable; it has recently been replaced by a much more satisfactory one prepared by Schüller: 'Newton's scholia'. See further Schüller, *Newtons Scholia aus David Gregorys Nachlaß* (2000). The claim in De Smet and Verhelst, 'Newton's Scholium Generale: the Platonic and Stoic Legacy' (2001) that Newton's chief debts are to Philo and Lipsius is based on loose textual parallels that do not convince. See also 4.5 above.

reference to servants, and godhood [*deitas*] is the lordship of God, not over his own body as is supposed by those for whom God is the world soul, but over servants. The supreme God is an eternal, infinite, and absolute being; but a being, however, perfect, without dominion is not the Lord God . . . He is eternal and infinite, omnipotent and omniscient, that is, he endures from eternity to eternity, and he is present from infinity to infinity; he rules all things, and he knows all things that happen or can happen. He is not eternity and infinity, but eternal and infinite; he is not duration and space, but he endures and is present. He endures always and is present everywhere, and by existing always and everywhere he constitutes duration and space. Since each and every particle of space is *always*, and each and every indivisible moment of duration is *everywhere*, certainly the maker and lord of things will not be *never* or *nowhere*.[546]

Soon after, Newton went on:

He is omnipresent not only *virtually* but also *substantially*; for action requires substance. In him all things are contained and move [Newton's note c: 'This opinion was held by the ancients: for example, by Pythagoras as cited in Cicero, *On the Nature of the Gods*, book 1: Thales; Anaxagoras, Virgil, *Georgics*, book 4, v. 221, and *Aenid*, book 6, v. 726; Philo, *Allegorical Interpretation*, book 1, near the beginning; Aratus in the *Phenomena*, near the beginning. Also by the sacred writers: for example, Paul in Acts 17.27, 28; John in his Gospel 14.2; Moses in Deuteronomy 4.39 and 10.14; David, Psalms 139.7, 8, 9; Solomon, 1 Kings 8.27; Job 22.12, 13, 14; Jeremeiah 23.23, 24. Moreover idolaters imagined that the sun, moon, and stars, the souls of men, and other parts of the world were parts of the supreme god and so were to be worshiped, but they were mistaken'], but he does not act on them nor they on him. God experiences nothing from the motion of bodies; the bodies feel no resistance from God's omnipresence.[547]

Soon after appears the most famous passage on not feigning hypotheses to explain the cause of gravity, for hypotheses, 'whether metaphysical or physical, or based on occult qualities, or mechanical, have no place in experimental philosophy'.[548]

We meet in these very famous passages key aspects of Newton's natural philosophy: his anti-hypothetical methodology; his refusal to posit a cause for gravity; his belief in a 'God of dominion', omnipresent 'substantially' but also comprehensible only by his effects; the idea that some aspects of these truths were known to the ancients. These passages are notoriously ambiguous; Newton's precise views on the nature of God's interaction with the world are especially shrouded in mystery. This shroud can be at least partially lifted if the even more ambiguous and allusive references to the ancients are placed first in

---

[546] Newton, *Principia*, 940–1.

[547] Ibid., 941–2. The marginal note is that of the third edition; that in the 2nd reads: 'This opinion was held by the ancients: Aratus in the *Phenomena*, near the beginning; Paul in Acts 7.27, 28; Moses, Deuteronomy, 4.39 and 10.14; David, Psalms 139.7, 8; Solomon, Kings 8.27; Job 22.12; the prophet Jeremiah, 23.23, 24'.

[548] Ibid., 943. For Newton and 'experimental philosophy', see Shapiro, 'Experimental philosophy'; for Newton's varied comments on 'hypotheses', see Cohen, 'Hypotheses in Newton's philosophy' (1966); Janiak, *Newton*, 15–27. See further 4.5 above.

the context of Newton's references to them not just in the Classical Scholia but also in the Yahuda manuscripts in the National Library of Israel, and second in the context of seventeenth-century attitudes to paganism more generally. On first glance it seems fairly clear who Newton's targets in the General Scholium are: Descartes and his followers – of whom Newton considered Leibniz to be the premier – who claimed, through their vortical 'hypothesis', to explain all the causes of gravity, and who thus also removed God from the world.[549] But two (connected) questions remain unanswered: (1) Whom was Newton targeting with his negative references to an *anima mundi* – already present in drafts for the General Scholium?[550] (2) What precisely did he see as the relationship between his explanation and that of the ancients, so briefly alluded to in the General Scholium itself, but on which much of the complex manuscript material focuses?

The answer to these questions, I propose, is as follows. Newton believed that the most ancient religion, practised before the flood and by Noah and his sons (3.7 above), mapped on to his own physical hypothesis both in content *and* in its level of explanatory agnosticism. That is to say, it recognised both heliocentricism, the inverse-square law, and God's omnipresence, but offered no further philosophical or theological explanation for God's operation in the world. This 'philosophical religion' was corrupted by a combination of idolatries – starworship and Euhemerism – that led to what we might label a 'bad animism': one that posited an *anima mundi* and led to the worship of the world *qua* parts of God. It was this idolatry that impregnated various Greek philosophies – that of Thales, the Pythagoreans, and Aristotle; in another way, it led to the innate gravity of Epicurus. It also lay at the origins of the poisonous discipline of metaphysics, and so could even partially explain the methodological hubris of the Cartesians. The evidence is as follows.

As we have seen, Newton believed that God had revealed to Adam a primitive and minimalist ur-religion, which went hand in hand with certain natural philosophical truths; the practical manifestation of this religion was worship in circular temples surrounding a central fire, preserving the truth of heliocentricism. It was inherited by Noah, from whom it spread throughout the

---

[549] Much of the relevant evidence on Newton's opposition to Leibniz in this regard is collected in Janiak, *Newton*, 70–4, *passim*.

[550] *Unpublished scientific papers of Isaac Newton*, eds., A. R. Hall and M. B. Hall (Cambridge, 1962), 355, 359: 'And if the fixed stars be the centres of similar systems, all these are under the same one dominion. This Being rules all things not as the soul of the world (for he has no body)' (the original is CUL, MS Add. 3965, fol. 361$^r$). See also the later emphatic statement in the second English edition of the *Opticks* (1717), 369: 'And yet we are not to consider the World as the Body of God, or the several Parts thereof, as the Parts of God. He is an uniform Being, void of Organs, Members or Parts, and they are his Creatures subordinate to him, and subservient to his Will; and he is no more the Soul of them, than the Soul of a Man is the Soul of the Species of Things carried through the Organs of Sense into the place of its Sensation . . . '.

Mediterranean world and beyond; even Stonehenge 'seems to be an ancient Prytanaeum'.[551] However, this 'philosophical' religion became corrupt through a mixture of Noachic Euhemerism (i.e. the worship of Noah and his sons) and starworship. Newton was not always precise about this corruption; on one occasion he attributed it to the fact that 'y$^e$ frame of y$^e$ heavens consisting of Sun Moon & Stars being represented by <in> the Prytanaea as y$^e$ real temple of the Deity men were led by degrees to pay a veneration to these sensible objects & began at length to worship them as the <visible> seats of divinity'.[552] However, he seemed to more consistently claim that the first idolatry was the worship of Noah and his sons (a view he derived primarily from Samual Bochart);[553] once this Euhemerism became more widespread, it became commonplace to name the stars after these deified ancestors, gradually leading to full starworship. All this first occurred in Egypt, but again quickly spread throughout the world.[554] It was this step that caused what we might appropriately describe as 'animist idolatry': the deification of the world and the subsequent worship of all its parts,[555] for which Newton offered several pages of evidence – once again focusing in particular on Egypt – the ultimate point of which was to contrast this animist idolatry with the original true religion.

[551] NLI MS Yahuda 41 ('Draft chapters of a treatise on the origin of religion and its corruption', early 1690s), fols. 1$^r$–7$^v$, esp. 3$^r$ for Stonehenge (this whole passage was later deleted). Newton's following words ('Tis said there are two or three <some> pieces of antiquity of y$^e$ same form & structure in Denmark') suggest that he was following the tradition of comparing Stonehenge with the rune-inscribed stones in Scandinavia described in Ole Worm's *Danicorum monumentorum libri sex* (Copenhagen, 1643); the work is not listed in *Newton Library*, but on its popularity in England for analysing Stonehenge, see p. 170, n. 295 above.

[552] NLI MS Yahuda 41, fol. 8$^r$. This is followed by 'ffor tis agreed that Idolatry began in ye worship of the heavenly bodies'; as we have seen, this rings immediate Maimonidean bells; while Newton was certainly very familiar with both the *Guide* and the tractate *Avodah Zarah* (in Dionysius Vossius's edn [Trinity College, Cambridge, classmark: NQ.8.46] (although the dog-earring suggests more interest in Vossius snr's *Theologia gentilis*)), other evidence suggests he may have initially considered Eusebius a better source for starworship as the origin of idolatry: Yahuda MS 41, fol. 8$^r$.

[553] See e.g. NLI MS Yahuda 17.2 (Notes and drafts relating to 'Theologiae gentilis origines philosophiae', 1680s and early 1690s), fol. 10$^r$: 'Saturnum esse Noachum Bochartus in Geographia sacra abunde satis probavit'. Newton's copy of Bochart is *Geographia sacra* (Frankfurt, 1681) (Trinity College, Cambridge, NQ.8.27): there is a high level of dog-earing; unfortunately, much of it has been dutifully removed by subsequent readers.

[554] See e.g. NLI MS Yahuda 41, fols. 9$^{r-v}$; Yahuda MS 17.2, 'Et hujusmodi initijs orta videtur Theologia Siderea ... <cum Gentes aliae Aegyptiorum exemplo doctae, suorum etiam Herorum nomina in astra transferrent.>'; NLI MS Yahuda 17.3, fols. 5$^v$–8$^r$: 'Postquam homines <hi omnes mortui sunt> a quibus Planetae nomina <sua> acceperant, eorum animae et animarum qualitates in coelum <a posteris> translatae sunt et Stellis inditae ... Et sic Astrologia et Theologia gentilis ab astutis sacerdotibus ad promovendum ... studium Astrorum honorem scientia studentium & facultat tum maxime facultates sacerdotij et augendum sacerdotium introductae'.

[555] NLI MS Yahuda 17.2, fols. 14$^{r-v}$.

Scraps of the latter were preserved in the former, making it possible for the exegete to reconstruct the original true religion from its animist corruption.[556]

Newton had developed his own interpretation of ancient religion, but it was still anchored in the standard discussions: Vossius's *Theologia gentilis*, Maimonides on idolatry as translated by Dionysius Vossius, and Bochart's *Geographia sacra*, combined with a generous use of Natale Conti's mythography, which permitted him to claim that ancient texts were infused with allegorically concealed philosophical meaning.[557] What is crucial for us is that Newton then extended this narrative to explain the Greek philosophers, forming a bridge between the work on the history of religion and the Classical Scholia to the *Principia*, and thus also the General Scholium. It was Newton's contention that alongside much of their philosophy and their tendency to hide it underneath allegories, the Greek philosophers inherited from the near east the tradition of 'bad animism' (Newton standardly ascribed its transmission to Orpheus).[558] Part of this transmission did contain true doctrine, not least heliocentricism and the inverse-square law, concealed in the allegories of musical harmony in the heavens.[559] But just as importantly, the Greeks inherited the animistic tendencies of the near-eastern theosophies, which manifested themselves in doctrines such as the *anima mundi*.[560] It was for this reason that Thales made God the 'mind of the world',[561] the Pythagoreans believed in transmigration, Zeno imbued the celestial bodies with intelligence and wisdom, the rest of the Stoics made the heavens parts of Jupiter and claimed that all was alive and possessed of reason, and the Platonists made the stars 'the most pure creatures and intellects' (from which opinion Philo Judaeus imported Greek corruption into Judaism).[562] Newton was here relying heavily on Cudworth: an

---

[556] For a concise statement of the contrast, see NLI MS Yahuda 17.3, fols. 8ᵛ–9ʳ, 'Religionems tamen cum ~~tra~~ doctrina de transmigrationem animarum & cultu astrorum et elementorum <~~et~~ ~~statuarum~~> coepisse credendum non est … Fuit enim alia religio ~~qua~~ his omnibus antiquior, qua ignis <~~sacer~~> ~~perpetuus~~ in medio ~~are~~ loci sacri ad sacrificia peragenda ~~ardeb~~ perpetuò ar<d>ebat'.

[557] This is well brought out in Casini, 'Classical scholia', 10–11; Newton owned the 1612 edition of Conti's *Mythologiae* [1567] (*Newton Library*, 125).

[558] NLI MS Yahuda 17.2, fol. 18ʳ: 'Graeci autem ex Aegypto Astro<no>miam primitus ~~derivarunt.~~ <acceperunt>. Ibi Orpheus … theologiam & Mythologiam ~~qua Graecia tam~~ et Pythagoras symbola figurarum et numeroru[m] <ad occultandam philosophiam didicere>'.

[559] NLI MS Yahuda 17.2, fols. 18ʳ⁻ᵛ.

[560] For a clear statement, see NLI MS Yahuda 17.3, fol. 12ʳ: 'Ad corruptionem religionis <illius> antiquae ~~qua~~ accesserunt corruptiones multae in philosophia quam religio illa adumbrabat'.

[561] NLI Yahuda 17.1 ('Notes on ancient religions'), fol. 10ᵛ: 'Thales mentem mundi statuit Deum'.

[562] NLI MS Yahuda 17.1, fol. 10ᵛ; NLI MS Yahuda 17.3, fol. 14ʳ: 'Quinetiam Philosophi antiqui transmigrationem a<ni>marum docentes, non ~~nomina~~ solum ~~sed etiam animas~~ <nomina> majorum suorum ~~Planetis indidere. Stellis <astris> et elementis indidere astris indidere as ste~~ stellis et asterismis indidere, sed etiam animas eorum in cœlos migrasse et in stellis sibi dicatis fulgere docebant tradebant [sic] … Et hinc Zeno apud Stobæum ait Solem et Lunam et singula

English quotation from Plotinus directly follows Cudworth's translation (without acknowledgement).[563] But the point is not that Cudworth is Newton's key 'source': Newton was operating in the context of a whole range of new historiography which had found the pagans to be animists. Newton's and Cudworth's polemical points were different: where the latter wanted to show that the pagans' animation of the world was a sign of their theism, Newton, who agreed with this, also wanted to go further and – like Boyle – present it as an idolatrous corruption of a non-animist philosophical religion. And like Boyle, he also found this corruption in Aristotle, whose granting of intelligences to the celestial spheres he presented as yet another inheritance of the semi-correct, semi-idolatrous animism.[564]

Understanding that for Newton the history of philosophy had to be read in the context of the history of religion is the key that lets us understand both the Classical Scholia and the relevant parts of the General Scholium and the Queries to the *Opticks*. In the Classical Scholia we find the same message about the animism of the ancient philosophers, albeit stripped of the history of religion context. Let us quote in full a passage from the Scholium to proposition IX (i.e. on universal attraction and its causes according to the ancients):

Up to this point I have explained the properties of gravity. I have not made the slightest consideration about its cause. However, I would like to relate what the ancients thought about this. Thales believed all bodies to be animate, inferring it from magnetic and electrical attractions ... And from the same reasoning he had to attribute the attraction of gravity to the soul of that matter. Hence he taught that everything is full of Gods, understanding by 'Gods' animate bodies. In the same way, Pythagoras held the sun and the planets to be Gods, and said of the sun, on account of its vast force of attraction, that it is τὴν τοῦ Διὸς φυλακήν, the prison of Jupiter; that is to say, a body endowed with the greatest divine force, which locked the planets in their orbits. And for these mystical philosophers Pan was the highest deity, who breathed into this world the harmonic ratio, and played it melodically just like a musical instrument; on a par is that statement of Orpheus: Ἁρμονίαν κόσμοιο κρέκων φιλοπαίγμονι μολπῇ. And from there they called God 'harmony', and composed the *anima mundi* from harmonic numbers. Moreover, they

---

astrorum aliorum esse intelligentem ac sapientem igneum ignem. Et Stoici (teste Augustino lib 4 de e<C>iv. Dei c. 11) dicunt omnia sidera partes Iovis esse & omnia vivere atque rationales animas habere & ideo sine controversia Deos esse. Et Philo libro de somnijs ~~docet~~ <~~dicit~~> ~~stellam esse unamquamque esse animal et mentem purissimam~~ ~~quod Opifici mundi placuit omnes ejus partes animalibus imp~~ <ex mente Platonicorum dicit> Stellas ~~et~~<s>se animalia et mentes purissimas, easque <et alibi> in eodem libro <vocat ~~etiam~~ eas> incorruptibiles et immortales animas'.

[563] Compare NLI MS Yahuda 17.3, fol. 14ʳ ('~~Et ex hac sente~~ Et Plotinus: ~~the whole corporeal world is made a God by yᵉ soul thereof & yᵉ Sun is also a God because animated as likewise are all yᵉ starrs thereof Gods. Docuit~~ <~~Tradidit~~> ~~etiam Plotinus~~ <~~tradit quod vult~~> <Per animam suam hic mundus Deus est, sed et Sol Deus est quia animatus et eadem de causa stellæ re sunt Dij>', with Cudworth, *System*, 593.

[564] NLI MS Yahuda 17.3, fol. 14ᵛ: 'Idem docuit Aristoteles per intelligentias coelestibus orbibus affixas'.

said that the planets move in their orbits due to the force of their souls, that is due to the gravitational force originating from the activity of the souls. And so we find from here the birth of the Peripatetic opinion of intelligences moving the solid celestial spheres.[565]

A variant adds further detail, connecting these philosophers specifically to those who believed in an *anima mundi* and thus animated not just the planets but the whole world.[566] These passages are somewhat ambiguous in that it might appear from them that Newton *agreed* with the animist ancients.[567] But we know from the above that Newton thought that while the philosophers *had* inherited parts of the correct cosmology from the near-eastern sages, they had also inherited its later animistic corruptions, corruptions that manifested themselves most clearly in the philosophers' postulation of an *anima mundi*.

Returning finally to the General Scholium we find the same bipartite allusion to the ancient philosophers, now even more ambiguous. They are mentioned *positively* in a marginal note for having recognised that 'in [God] all things are contained and move'. But the *negative* references to *anima mundi* theories which came earlier in the General Scholium are also references to the Greek philosophers, and to their positing of extraneous animistic principles, a practice they inherited from their idolatrous predecessors in the near east.[568]

---

[565] RS MS 247, fol. 13ʳ (=Schüller, 238). Although using it as a guide, I have significantly modified Schüller's translation, which is at a few points deficient ('Hactenus proprietates gravitatis explicui. Causam ejus minime expendo. Dicam tamen quid Veteres hac de re senserint. Thales corpora omnia pro animatis habuit ... id colligens ex attractionibus magneticis et electricis .... Et eodem argumento attractionem gravitatis ad animam materiae referre debuit. Hinc Omnia Deorum plena esse docuit, per Deos intelligens corpora animata. Et eodem sensu Pythagoras ... pro Diis habuit Solem et Planetas ... & Solem propter ingentem ejus vim attractivam dixit esse τὴν τοῦ Διὸς φυλακήν carcer Jovis, id est corpus vi ... Divina quam maxima praeditum, quae Planetae in orbibus suis incarcerantur. Et mysticis Philosophis Pan erat Numen supremum hunc Mundum tamquam instrumentum musicum ratione harmonica inspirans & modulate tractans, juxta illud Orphei, Ἁρμονίαν κόσμοιο κρέκων φιλοπαίγμονι μολπῇ. Indeque Deum et harmoniam nominabant et animam mundi ex numeris harmonicis compositam. Planetas autem vi animarum suarum ... in orbibus suis moveri dicebant id est vi gravitatis ab actione animarum oriundae. Unde nata videtur Peripateticorum de Intellig<en>tiis ... orbes solidos ... moventibus opinio' (ellipses signify deletions only)). Schüller's notes usefully detail the sources, both those cited and implied. McGuire and Rattansi, 'Pipes of Pan', 119–20 misunderstand this passage, not recognising that Newton is criticising theories that posit an *anima mundi*, notwithstanding his praise for their recognising the need for God to act in the world. The passage from fol. 14ᵛ (n. 544 above) is a variant.

[566] RS MS 247, fol. 14ᵛ (=Schüller, 240).

[567] Particularly misleading in this regard are the words of David Gregory, that Newton 'will spread himself in exhibiting the agreement of this philosophy with that of the Ancients and principally with that of Thales' (*Newton correspondence*, iii, 338). Again, the key point Newton wanted to convey is that while Thales and others *were* right to posit an animating principle, they were methodologically *wrong* to offer a full natural philosophical explanation by positing an *anima mundi*.

[568] At this point I thus broadly agree with the interpretation at McGuire and Rattansi, 'Pipes of Pan', 120–1, '[according to Newton's history], nature operating according to these divine ratios, could scarcely be dependent on the guidance of an intermediate world soul'.

It has been claimed that the General Scholium is an esoteric manifestation of Newton's antitrinitarianism and that the passages about God's dominion (without the need for an *anima mundi*) cited above were in particular markers of his heresy.[569] There can be no doubt that Newton's thoughts about God's dominion were intimately connected to his antitrinitarianism. He believed that trinitarianism was a corruption of early Christianity that stemmed in part from the same idolatrous impulses and philosophies that produced *anima mundi* theories (the reference above to Philo's acceptance of Platonic animism is part of that story).[570] But the claims in the General Scholium are about God's operation in the world, not about his relationship to his son; if we are to identify a hidden 'target' for the comments in the General Scholium, it is the ancient philosophers (and, by definition, their modern followers), not trinitarian Christians. That Newton's antitrinitarianism was connected to his natural philosophical statements does not mean that each of those natural philosophical statements contained an esoteric antitrinitarian message.

There are still two further complications. The first is Newton's attitude to the ancient atomists' solution to the problem of motion and action at a distance. In Query 28 to the Opticks (20 in the Latin edition, 1706), consisting primarily of a rejection of the Cartesian idea of fluid material substance comprising the space between particles, Newton seems to speak quite positively of the atomists' attribution of innate motion to their particles, at least as compared to the modern mechanists (i.e. Cartesians):

And for rejecting such a Medium [i.e. a Cartesian fluid aether], we have the Authority of those the oldest and most celebrated Philosophers of *Greece* and *Phoenicia*, who made a *Vacuum*, and Atoms, and their Gravity of Atoms, the first Principles of their Philosophy; tacitly attributing Gravity to some other Cause than dense Matter. Later Philosophers [i.e. Cartesians] banish the Consideration of such a Cause out of natural Philosophy, feigning Hypotheses for explaining all things mechanically . . .[571]

We can better understand these comments in light of the historical manuscripts. Like Cudworth, Newton considered atomism to be far more widespread than the standard sources would allow, attributing it to both the Ionics (who followed Thales) and the Italics (who followed Pythagoras).[572] That Cudworth

---

[569] Esp. in Snobelen, 'Gods of Gods'. Nor am I entirely convinced by Prof. Ducheyne's claim (*Business*, 249–52) that the biblical references dropped from earlier drafts (specifically C-draft) of the General Scholium would have 'revealed his anti-Trinitarian agenda': there is no such thing as an 'antitrinitarian' biblical passage, and we only know that these passages fitted Newton's antitrinitarian agenda because we *already* know that he was an antitrinitarian.

[570] See, Goldish, *Judaism*, 141–62 ('Kabbalah and the corruption of the primitive church'); Mandelbrote, 'Isaac Newton reads the fathers' (2006).

[571] Newton, *Opticks* [1717], 343–4 (=Isaac Newton, *Optice: sive de reflexionibus, refractionibus, inflexionibus & coloribus lucis libri tres* (London, 1706), 314).

[572] E.g. RS MS 247, fol. 10ᵛ [=Schüller, 228–31] ('Ex Atomis autem corpora composuere philosophi tam Jonici ~~Thales~~ quam Italici').

was his source here is certain, for he elsewhere traced atomism back to Moschus the Phoenician, listing a very similar genealogy to his Cambridge predecessor.[573] This was a claim made as part of the Scholium to Proposition VI, where Newton claimed that the ancients were aware of the proportionality of mass and gravity, attributing this gravity even to atoms themselves.[574] Crucially, for Newton this meant that the atomists were in fact engaged with the same problem as all the other philosophers: accounting for motion, gravity, and action at a distance.[575] Where some had resorted to an *anima mundi*, the atomists had resorted to innate gravitation.[576]

It is this that explains Newton's deviation from Cudworth, on whom he took notes and whose classification of Democritus and Epicurus as atheists he disputed.[577] Where Cudworth had seen Epicurus and Democritus's materialism as an effective denial of God, for Newton their attribution of innate motion to particles was a sign of their partaking in the (albeit corrupt) animistic–theistic tradition (in this he agreed with his old Trinity colleague John North). There is clear evidence that Newton thought that in ascribing such extraneous causes (i.e. separate from God's omnipresence and omnipotence) for motion, the atomists – like the animists – were inheriting from the ancient theosophical tradition.[578] However, while the later atomists – Democritus and Epicurus – spoke of innate gravity, the earlier ones, especially the Pythagoreans,

---

[573] In a draft for an addition to Corollary 2 of Proposition VII (imperfectly transcribed at Casini, 'Classical scholia', 36–8), CUL Add. MS 3965.12, fols. 270$^r$–71$^r$. For the relevant notes from Cudworth, see 'Newton's *Out of Cudworth*', in Popkin and Force, *Essays*, 207–13, at 207–8.

[574] Schüller, 225–30. Newton's main 'source' was a reading of Lucretius, *Rer. nat.*, II.184–205, but he also offered an ingenious reading of Aristotle, *De caelo*, 308$^b$.

[575] As Newton makes clear at fol. 10$^v$ (=Schüller, 229): 'Lucretius taught this [innate gravitation] based on the view of Epicurus, Epicurus based on the views of Democritus and older philosophers'.

[576] Newton also found support for this connection between atomism and animism in Macrobius's *In. Somn.*, I.14.9; see RS MS 247, fol. 7$^r$ [=Schüller, 242–3] ('Plato dixit animam essentiam se moventem, Xenocrates numerum se moventem, Pythagoras et Philolaus Harmoniam, – Democritus spiritum insertum atomis hac facilitate motus, ut corpus illi omne sit pervium Macrob . . . l. 1. C. 14') (this is a virtual paraphrase of Macrobius, the dash before 'Democritus' indicating an excluded set of further examples). See also CUL MS Add. 3970 (Draft Versions of the 'Queries'), fol. 620$^v$, discussing 'active principles': 'Gravity was recconed among the laws of motion & by the ancient Philosophers who attributed gravity to their Atoms in vacuo'.

[577] 'Newton's *Out of Cudworth*' (see also Sailor, 'Newton's debt to Cudworth' (1988)). Newton took down specifically the passage derived from Gassendi about all ancient philosophers apart from Democritus, Leucippus, and Epicurus being animists that we encountered at p. 424 above.

[578] CUL MS Add. 3965.12, fols. 270$^r$–271$^r$, esp. 271$^r$: 'Epicurum verò haec [i.e. universal gravitation] a philosophis mysticis didicisse verisimile est cum Heraclides et Pythagoram et Orphei sectatores stellas omnes esse mundos in <infinito> aethere infinito dicerent ut habet Plutarchus lib. 2 de plact. Philos. c. 13' (see McGuire and Rattansi, 'Pipes', 114–15). This is also hinted at in a key passage on atomism from Plutarch, which although used in the Classical Scholia, is first found in Newton's notes on ancient religion to connect the atomists to the animists like Thales and Pythagoras: compare NLI MS Yahuda MS. 17.1, fol. 10$^v$ with RS MS 247, fol. 10$^v$ (=Schüller, 229).

recognised the need for explanatory agnosticism in the face of God's omnipotence, symbolised in their representing atomic interrelation through musical harmonies:

The ancient Philosophers who held Atoms & Vacuum attributed gravity to Atoms without telling us the means unless perhaps in figures: as by calling God Harmony & <representing> him & matter by the God Pan & his Pipe, or by calling the Sun the prison of Jupiter because he keeps the Planets in their orbs. Whence it seems to have been an ancient opinion that matter depends upon a Deity for its <laws of> motion as well as for its existence.[579]

When Newton announced that 'we cannot say that all Nature is not alive',[580] he was announcing the need precisely for this kind of explanatory agnosticism, recognised by the Pythagoreans but not by the Epicureans.[581] Like the animist Greeks, the latter corrupted the original philosophical religion that found God immanent in the world without ever quite explaining that immanence. But even they were preferable to the Cartesians, who removed him from the world altogether. And so just like Boyle and Willis, Newton was presenting his philosophy as a *via media* between those who over-animated the world, ascribing to it an *anima mundi*, and the Epicureans, who ascribed all animation to innate gravitation.

This brings us to a final problem. As we have seen, Newton differentiated between (1) the original true religion, which posited an omnipresent God without explaining how that omnipresence worked; (2) a religious and philosophical corruption of that religion which manifested itself as animism and Democritean–Epicurean atomism (also animist in the sense that it attributed innate motion to atoms); and (3) Cartesian mechanism, which was neither true nor animist, because it removed God from nature altogether. This taxonomy is aptly summarised in a passage from Newton's (anonymously published) 'Account' (1715) of the Royal Society's epistolary report on the calculus priority dispute:

---

[579] CUL MS Add. 3970, fol. 619$^r$. See also later on the same page: 'And since all matter duly formed is attended with signes of life & all ~~things <natural>~~ <things> are framed w$^{th}$ perfect & art & wisdom ... if there be an universal life & all space be the sensorium of a thinking being ... the laws of motion <arising from life or will> may be of universal extent ... To some such laws the ancient Philosophers seem to have eluded when they ~~called God Have said that God was~~ <called God> H[arm]ony, & ~~<attributing musick ot the spheres represented>~~ <signified> his actuating the matter & harmonically ~~proportion~~ by the God Pan's playing upon a Pipe & <attribute musick to the spheres> made the distances & motions of the heavenly bodies to be harmonical & ... represented the Planets by the seven strings of Apollo's Harp'.

[580] CUL MS Add. 3970, fol. 620$^v$.

[581] But it was *not* the same as positing Aristotelian occult causes, which were themselves methodologically hubristic since they posited a cause when none was known: *Opticks* [1717], 376–7 (Query 31).

The one [philosophy—i.e. that of Newton himself] teaches that God (the God in whom we live and move and have our being) is omnipresent, but not as a soul of the world: the other [i.e. the Cartesio-Leibnizian] that he is not the Soul of the World, but INTELLI-GENTIA SUPRAMUNDANA, an Intelligence above the Bounds of the World; whence it seems to follow that he cannot do any thing within the Bounds of the World, unless by an incredible Miracle.[582]

This is as we would expect it to be. And yet in one manuscript, composed around the same period, Newton seemed to state that Cartesianism was an outgrowth of 'bad animism'. Beginning 'Metaphysics is founded in Innate Ideas, Newton's philosophy in phenomena demonstrated through mathematics', and going on to discuss Descartes's *Principles of Philosophy* III.47, Newton wrote:

But Cartesius nowhere proves that the thinking thing [*rem cogitantem*] is a power or faculty of cogitation, nor all things to be extended extension, nor that extension is a mobile thing [*rem mobilem*], nor that the motion of bodies consists only in relative transfer without an inertial force, nor that a thinking thing is present in no space, nor God not to be substantially omnipresent, nor that we have ideas of substances. All these are mere hypotheses. Metaphysics has its origin in the ancient theogony of the pagans, in which all the peoples imagined the Sun, Moon, Stars, <Elements>, Intelligences, human souls, animals and all which is in nature to be either parts of God or His powers. The consequence of which was that nature became God. In this philosophy the Pagans founded their idolatry. And Moses, abrogating the cult of the parts of the world, condemned this philosophy and established the omnipresent God of Dominion apart from the natural world.[583]

---

[582] [Isaac Newton], 'An account of the book entituled *Commercium Epistolicum*', *Philosophical Transactions*, 342 (Jan and Feb 1715), 173–224 at 224 (=*Philosophical writings*, ed. A. Janiak (Cambridge, 2004), 115).

[583] CUL MS Add. 9597.2.14, fol. 4$^r$: 'Metaphysica in ... Idaeis innatis, Philo<so>phia Newtoni in Phaenomenis <per mathematicis Demonstrationibus> fundatur ... Sic nec vim aut facultatem cogitandi rem cogitantem esse aut rem omnem extensam extentionem esse, aut extentionem rem mobilem esse, aut motum corporum in sola translatione relativa sane vi inertiae consistere, aut rem cogitantem nilli spatio praesentem esse, aut Deum non esse omnipraesentem per substantiam suam aut nos Idaeas habere substantiarum Cartesius alicubi probavit. Haec omnia sunt merae hypotheses. Metaphysicae Metaphysica <ubique> ab antiqua Gentium Theogonia originem habuit qua utique Gentes Solem Lunam Stellas <Elementa>, Deos omnes <Intelligentias>, animas humanas <animalia> & omnia mundi [one illegible word] quae in rerum natura sunt vel partes esse Dei summi vel <ejus> potentias <esse> fingebant. adeoque naturam ipsam esse Deum Unde consequens est quod ipsa rerum Natura sit Deus summus. In hac Philosophiam <Gentes> idololatriam suam fundabant. Et Moses [illegible word] <abrogando> cultum partium rerum a Deo conditaram hanc Philosophiam damnavit stellarum partium mundi, damnavit hanc philosophiam ac Dom. Deum omnipraesentem a Natura & rerum natura diversum stabilivit'. My attention was brought to this passage by Ducheyne, 'General Scholium', 260–1, where the whole passage is transcribed, but with several errors. Prof. Ducheyne suggests a date of 1713–15 and that 'it was probably composed in the same period as the drafts to the General Scholium', (n. 181), but another passage in the MS bundle, a draft for an 'Avertissement au Lecteur' (fol. 1$^r$), refers to 'D$^r$ Clarks 4$^{th}$ Reply', i.e. that contained in *A collection of papers, which passed between the late Learned Mr. Leibnitz, and Dr. Clarke, in the years 1715 and 1716* (London, 1717). It is of course

How has Descartes suddenly become an inheritor of 'bad animism'? The answer, it seems to me, is that Newton is saying that Descartes is an inheritor not of animism, but of the metaphysics of innate ideas, which, just like animism, had its origins in pagan theology and philosophy. What Newton is really saying here is that Descartes was an inheritor of pagan idolatrous 'metaphysics' not doctrinally but methodologically. Both claimed to know something about the nature of God or about is relationship with the world that was simply unknowable. This was the essence of the 'metaphysics' that Newton rejected in favour of knowing God only from phenomena. The unspoken assumption here would be that Descartes was a kind of Platonist, an assumption we have already found most potently developed by Parker. Again and again we come back to the same theme: the history of philosophy had become inseparable from the history of religion.

We may now present a full taxonomy of Newton's vision of the history of philosophy:

| Philosophy | Theological status | Method |
|---|---|---|
| 1. Original philosophical-religion | Non-animist; recognised God's presence in the world | – |
| 2. Its first corruption, originating in Egypt | Animist; equated God with the material world | Metaphysical |
| 3. Atomists | Animist; attributed innate motion to matter | (unclear) |
| 4. Cartesian | Non animist; tending to atheism; removed God from the world | Metaphysical |

This has significant implications for the understanding of Newton's natural philosophy more broadly. Newton rejected all claims about God's relationship with the world that were not made on the basis of natural (or 'experimental') philosophy. He was not doing metaphysics and he did not have an elaborate conception of the relationship between God and space; this is precisely why the things he said about these subjects in the General Scholium were negative: God is not eternity and infinity, nor duration and space.[584] Most crucially, this means that Newton, while he did think that it was clear from nature that God was omnipresent and active in the world, did not think that it was known *how* this operation happened – including in the case of gravity. Like Willis, Boyle, and Locke, he presented his philosophy as a *via media* between the non-teleological

possible that Newton had seen it before publication, but this still suggests a composition date of *c.* 1715–17.

[584]  *Principia*, 941. My reading goes against the grain of recent Newton scholarship, much of which has sought to find in the General Scholium and other texts an elaborate metaphysics of God's relationship with space. For full details, see Levitin, 'General scholium'.

mechanism of Epicirus and Descartes and the overly teleological animism of the other Greek philosophers (now including Aristotle), while remaining self-consciously agnostic about how action at a distance and teleology actually occurred.

## 5.5    Conclusion

Post-1660, English natural philosophers – albeit through very different means and for very different reasons – adopted two historiographical obsessions: that the atomism of Epicurus was reductionist and speculative and that all the pagan philosophers had animated the world in a way that was idolatrous and which the 'new' philosophy must avoid. I hope to have shown the centrality of these ideas to the likes of Boyle, Willis, and Newton, among many others. It remains only to reiterate the historiographical implications. First, the old idea that Epicurus or Epicureanism was central to the self-identity of English natural philosophy can finally be abandoned. The vast majority of the advocates of microparticulate matter theories in seventeenth-century England saw themselves as walking a fine tightrope between the reductionism of Epicurus and the qualitative matter theories of others. Those others were often represented as animists, a category that was expanded to include not only the usual suspects – the Platonists and the Stoics foremost among them – but also such unexpected and important figures as Aristotle. This assumption informed some of the most important programmatic statements of the English 'new science', most notably Boyle's *Free enquiry*, and Newton's 'General Scholium'.

# 6    Philosophy in the early church

It will be clear by now that the relationship between pagan philosophy and Judaism and Christianity was a central concern not just of scholars and theologians but also the wider literate elite more generally. We saw in Chapter 3 in particular that a major source of historiographical revisionism against the ideas of Mosaic philosophy and the Israelite origins of pagan wisdom stemmed from a newly critical attitude towards the Hellenistic Jewish and patristic sources which had most forcefully promoted such a vision. That revisionism also affected attitudes to the relationship between philosophy, theology, and revelation in the early church itself.[1] In his seminal account of the intellectual sources of chapters fifteen and sixteen of Gibbon's *Decline and Fall*, J. G. A. Pocock has argued that such a development – which he assigns to a generation of historically minded Protestant theologians starting from *c.* 1680, especially Jean Le Clerc – constituted a crucial component of a 'Protestant Enlightenment' of which the key feature was the replacement of theology with the history of theology, where that history in turn turned out to be the history of philosophical speculation about the divine.[2] I agree with Professor Pocock's identification of this development; I cannot agree with the dating, or with the category of 'enlightenment'.[3] It will be argued that these shifts not only occurred earlier but also stemmed directly from, and were

---

[1]  For early modern patristics, see the studies discussed in Levitin, 'Sacred history', and Quantin, 'Document, histoire, critique dans l'érudition ecclésiastique' (2004).

[2]  Pocock, *Barbarism*, v, 89–214, esp. 89–136 for Le Clerc. Although not cited by Prof. Pocock, the key previous treatment remains Glawe, *Die Hellenisierung*.

[3]  Prof Pocock's reading – while by far the most sophisticated – follows in a long tradition. J. Z. Smith has pointed to elements of the anti-Platonic discourse in the mid-sixteenth-century heretic Michael Servetus, only to conclude that 'the needed sophistication began to enter the theological discussion in 1700' with the publication of Jacques Souverain's *Le Platonisme devoilée: Drudgery divine* (1990), 17. Kristine Haugen, in a valuable article, has argued that Anglican scholars such as John Mill and Richard Bentley turned to biblical criticism to the detriment of historical defences of the doctrine of the trinity because of heterodox historicisations of orthodox dogma; her canon of historical challengers is thus focused exclusively on the late seventeenth- and early eighteenth-century heterodox, Charles Blount, John Toland, and Anthony Collins ('Transformation in the trinity doctrine in English scholarship' (2001), at 151). This follows the tradition of claiming that Toland's *Amyntor* (1699) 'turned the whole fabric of "Primitive Christianity" on its head': Duffy, 'Primitive Christianity revived' (1977), 298. The very full

formed within, the form of late humanist scholarship developed in the late sixteenth and seventeenth centuries. The story, however, is not linear, for as this scholarship was appropriated by divines – both in England and elsewhere – it was turned to new ends and took on new shapes. Neither was it limited to any one theological issue – even if debates about the divinity of Christ were always close to the centre – for it was the product of the larger seventeenth-century historicisations of Second Temple Judaism, early Christianity, and paganism which we have encountered so often already, and of the increasingly sophisticated approach to the history of philosophy, including its late antique mutations.[4]

## 6.1    Sources

Many of the relevant sources we have already met at the outset of Chapter 3, for they were the same church fathers and ecclesiastical historians – mainly but not always Greek – who sought to deflect accusations of anti-intellectualism by positing a Judaic origin for pagan truth. Some of them went further by suggesting that pagan philosophers, especially Plato, had adumbrated aspects of Christian theology. Such narratives were sometimes autobiographical, as in the most famous case, Justin Martyr, who in the prologue to his apologetic *Dialogue with Trypho* described his attempts to grasp God through Stoicism and Aristotelianism, coming closest to the divine through Platonism, before his final conversion to Christianity by an unidentified old sage.[5] Even if he claimed that it was 'eclectic philosophy' that paved the way for the divine, Clemens Alexandrinus nonetheless quoted the Pythagorean Numenius: 'what is Plato but Moses speaking Greek?'[6] Plato's *Parmenides* and *Timaeus* contained terminology that sounded distinctly trinitarian, specifically in their talk of a creator 'Mind' emanating 'Reason' (λόγος) and 'Soul', and it was particularly tempting to adopt such syncretisms (especially as they could be discovered in

---

survey of similar developments in Germany in Lehmann-Brauns, *Weisheit in der Weltgeschichte* similarly focuses only on late seventeenth-century 'anti-apologetic' writers (see e.g. 27–33 on Jacob Thomasius). Israel, *Enlightenment contested*, 421–7 mentions some of the issues in passing, but refuses to countenance the possibility that anyone before 1670 was capable of independent thought. Lim, *The crisis of the trinity in early modern England* (2012), 271–320 ('Platonic captivity or sublime mystery? The trinity and the Gospel of John in early modern England') discusses some of the issues, but misses almost all of the key evidence because of the curious belief that seventeenth-century Anglicans were not interested in 'grammatical-historical exegesis', citing for this – of all people – Cardinal Newman (279–80).

[4] Tigerstedt, *The decline and fall of the neoplatonic interpretation of Plato* (1974) remains very valuable, despite some important gaps.
[5] Justin Martyr, *Tryph.*, 2–3. For all the further allusions to this story in Justin's works, see Hofer, 'The old man as Christ in Justin's "Dialogue with Trypho"' (2003).
[6] Clemens Alexandrinus, *Strom.*, I.22.150. See further Droge, *Homer or Moses*, 124–51.

later neoplatonists like Plotinus) when some of Christianity's key opponents –
especially Porphyry – were themselves Platonists.[7] The epistemology of such
claims could be varied and indeterminate. Sometimes it was ascribed purely to
inheritance from Judaism; Origen implied that Plato had read the Old
Testament; Augustine first accepted and then rejected this judgement.[8] Justin,
who was the first to claim that Plato held trinitarian views, asserted that Plato
had knowledge of Jewish traditions while also holding a more idealistic vision
of the process, ascribing to the philosophers the ability to partake in Christ as
the λόγος, a vision that was particularly useful for anti-Jewish polemic as the
God who appeared to the patriarchs in the Old Testament theophanies could be
re-described as the Messiah.[9] This vision was taken up by those with much
more advanced historiographical tools at their disposal, namely the ecclesiastical historians, most importantly Eusebius. But as well as reiterating the
compatibility of Platonism and Christian theology,[10] Eusebius added new
elements to the syncretic mixture. He discussed at some length the
Hellenistic Jew Philo Judaeus, whose learning and philosophical approach he
praised and from whose *De vita contemplativa* he took an account of an ascetic,
allegorising, and philosophical Egyptian sect, the Therapeutae (Θεραπευταί) –
which even included female members – that Eusebius took to be Christians of
the type who had accompanied the apostles and renounced worldly possessions
(as in Acts 2:45).[11]

Yet by the time Eusebius was writing, new pressures had created ambiguity
about the philosophy–Christianity relationship. Justin's conversion narrative,
after all, already implied the fundamental superiority of faith to any worldly
philosophy. Others, most notably Tertullian, adopted a more dogmatically anti-
intellectualist tone. But even more problematic was the issue of heresy.
Mentioned only briefly in Acts (8:9–24), Simon Magus was in Justin already
the chief heresiarch; he was portrayed as a magician but compared to a
philosopher.[12] From him, according to the key work of Christian heresiology,
Irenaeus's *Adversus haereses* (*c.* 180), stemmed the various 'gnostic' heresies
of Basilides, Valentinus, and Marcion, with their substitution of emanationism
and a Platonic sounding 'Demiurge' for a creator God. Irenaeus claimed that
some gnostics, worshipping in the gentile manner, crowned images of Christ –
whose esoteric doctrine they professed to possess – 'along with the images of
the philosophers of the world'; Tertullian associated Valentinus' 'trinity of
man' with Platonism as part of a chapter on 'pagan philosophy as the parent

---

[7] In lieu of listing the many relevant *loci* here, I permit myself to direct the reader to Hillar, *From logos to trinity* (2012).

[8] Origen, *Cont. Cels.*, vi.7; Augustine, *Doc. Christ.*, ii.28.43; *Civ. Dei*, viii.11.

[9] Droge, *Homer or Moses*, 65–72 collects the evidence.     [10] Ibid., 168–93.

[11] Eusebius, *Hist. eccl.*, ii.17–18.     [12] Justin Martyr, *Apolog. I*, 26.

of heresies'.[13] Eusebius relied heavily on the accounts of Justin and Irenaeus, with the subsequent agonising about philosophy's heresiarchical potential.[14]

Yet if these 'heretics' – and here we have the origins of the concept – could easily be portrayed as outsiders, a greater challenge was explaining the theological controversy over the nature of Christ's divinity that shook the church in the fourth century; it is no coincidence that the continuator of Eusebius's *Historia Ecclesiastica*, Socrates, found the origins of the debate between Alexander, bishop of Alexandria and Arius, who denied the eternity of the Son, in excessive 'philosophical minuteness'.[15] Arianism was declared heterodox by the Nicene Council convened by Constantine in 325 and the Second Ecumenical Council in Constantinople in 381 – the noble Roman soldier–historian Ammianus Marcellinus commented that there had been so many intermediary councils that 'since throngs of bishops hastened hither and thither on the public-horses to the various synods' the postal service was overwhelmed[16] – but its impact as the 'archetypal heresy' was vast, and required explanation. Already in the early fifth century, Cyril of Alexandria suggested that there was a direct similarity between the Platonic trinity of hypostases and the subordinationist scheme of Arius; around the same time Theodoret of Cyr's *Curatio morborum Graecorum* at points developed similarly anti-Platonic sentiments.[17] Just as important was the connected condemnation of Origen, a canonical and very important church father whose works were well known; not only was he formally condemned by the Council of Alexandria (400) and the Fifth Ecumenical Council at Constantinople (553) but his subordinationist trinitarianism and belief in the pre-existence of souls also led to him becoming the prime model of philosophical (and specifically Platonic) hubris, not least in the hands of his former pupil Jerome.[18]

Finally, Eusebius also referred to the spiritualist, mystical, and sometimes theurgic philosophy that we now know as 'neoplatonism'; specifically, he made reference to one Ammonius Saccas (third century) who had supposedly taught both Plotinus and Origen (although we now know that this was another, pagan, Origen): Porphyry in his *Contra Christianos* had claimed that Ammonius had turned away from Christianity upon taking up philosophical studies and Eusebius virulently denied this (we now believe that there were also two men called Ammonius).[19] We may remind ourselves that Stanley was already recognising neoplatonism as a religious as much as a philosophical movement

---

[13] Irenaeus, *Adv. haer.*, 1.25.6; Tertullian, *Praes. haer.*, 7.

[14] Eusebius, *Hist. eccl.*, II.13, although Eusebius is very reticent to posit explanations for Simon's heresies, partially explaining the license of early modern exegetes in offering such explanations.

[15] Socrates, *Hist. eccl.*, 1.5.     [16] Ammianus Marcellinus, *Hist. Rom.*, XXI.16.18.

[17] Now charted and discussed at length in Siniossoglou, *Plato and Theodoret* (2008).

[18] Jerome, *Cont. Ruf.*, 1.14.

[19] Eusebius, *Hist. eccl.*, VI.19.1–12, quoting Porphyry. For the (sparse) evidence and the modern debates usefully collected, see Edwards, 'Ammonius, teacher of Origen' (1993).

(2.3 above) – part of our story is how the consequences of this recognition unfolded.

The above narrative is well known; the same may be said of its early Renaissance reception. Any educated Renaissance figure would have come across Aquinas's statement that the pagans could not have known the mystery of the trinity and that Origen and Arius had been led to their erroneous denial of consubstantiality by their Platonism.[20] The anti-scholastic elements of the humanist movement from the start inspired challenges to this view, challenges that were crucially couched in a historical mode: already Petrarch was stating that it was Plato rather than Aristotle who had dominated the intellectual culture of the Mediterranean in the centuries after Christ.[21] It is therefore of little surprise that Ficino's analysis of the Platonic trinity, unlike the naïve triumphalism of Justin, was cautious and historically minded: like Moses and the Hebrew prophets (from whom Ficino believed Plato had inherited his knowledge) Plato had developed a 'preliminary, anticipatory' vision of the trinity that captured the triune causality but not the consubstantiality of Father, Son, and Holy Spirit. This was understandable, for Christ had not yet been revealed, but it was inexcusable in the later neoplatonists, whose subordinationism was equivalent to Arianism despite their access to the Gospel of John, and who were to be contrasted with the 'true' Christian Platonists Origen and Dionysius the Areopagite.[22] The idea of Jewish pre-adumbration of the trinity was helped by the meshing of Platonic histories with Cabbala – this is only a philosophisation of a type of Christian apologetic applied to the Talmud and Midrashim since Raymundus Martini's *Pugio fidei* (1278) (finally published from manuscript in 1651).[23]

Yet the ambiguities that even Ficino had to acknowledge unsurprisingly led to fierce criticisms. Aldus Manutius might market his edition of Origen as preparatory to a future edition of Plato, but anti-Platonists like Paolo Cortese, Bishop of Urbino, responded with renewed condemnations of Origen's obsession with Greek philosophy, a condemnation he never escaped despite – or perhaps because of – the defences and editions of his works by those sympathetic to Cabbalism like Pico's disciple Egidio da Viterbo (1469–1532) and the

---

[20] Aquinas, *Summa Theologica*, I.32.1.

[21] Hankins, 'Humanism, scholasticism, and Renaissance philosophy' (2007), at 41.

[22] See the seminal discussion in Allen, 'Marsilio Ficino on Plato, the neoplatonists and the Christian doctrine of the trinity' (1984); also Hankins, *Plato*, 357; and for this view more broadly Walker, *Ancient theology*, 40–1, 80–1, 101–3, 114. The *locus classicus* for the inability of neoplatonist works to capture full biblical truth is Augustine, *Conf.*, vii.9; see similarly Basil, *Hom.*, 16.

[23] For Pico's vision, see 3.1 above; for his derivation of the trinity from his 'Cabbala' and from pre-Christian philosophy, see Farmer, *Syncretism*, 219, n. 2.1; Schmidt-Biggemann, *Philosophia perennis* (2004), 93–5; Schmidt-Biggemann, *Kabbala*, 70–130; Wirszubski, *Encounter*.

important Catholic Hebraist Gilbert Génébrard (1535–97).[24] Historicised anti-Platonism reached a peak in a work by a scholar from Gallipoli, Giovanni Battista Crispo (*c.* 1550–98), entitled *De ethnicis philosophis caute legendis* (1594) of which only the section on the dangers of reading Plato was published.[25] Crispo's combative text attacked not only the pagan philosophers and the Cabbala but also the early fathers' mingling of philosophy and theology, which, according to him, led to almost every historical heresy and culminated in Protestantism.[26]

### 6.1.1    A new early Christianity

It may be assumed that the main ingredients for our story are here already in place,[27] but although we shall encounter Crispo's influence on English scholars, anti-Platonism in itself was not enough. If our story is in many ways about the destruction and inversion of the Eusebian narrative, before we can tell it we must outline its deeper roots in some elements of the new approach to early Christianity that developed in European scholarship in the eighty or so years before the outbreak of civil war in England.

For all his strengths, a major historiographical deficiency in Eusebius was his vision of an early church born fully formed *ex nihilo*. The rise of Hebraic scholarship from the early sixteenth century, however, led exegetes like Sebastian Münster (1488–1552) to posit connections between Second Temple Judaism and early Christianity, an approach cemented in the foundational work of Protestant ecclesiastical history, the *Magdeburg centuries*.[28] The history of this discovery remains to be written, but some of its implications for our subject have been explored in a series of works by Joanna Weinberg and Anthony Grafton. The remarkable Italian Jew Azariah de' Rossi (1511/12–77), in his *Me'or Enayim* (1573–75), demonstrated that far from representing orthodox Judaism, Philo (alongside the *Letter of Aristeas*) represented a non-orthodox

---

[24]  Wind, 'The revival of Origen' (1954), at 417; Walker, 'Origène en France' (1969); and now by far the fullest discussion: Mandelbrote, 'Origen against Jerome in early modern Europe' (2010), esp. 115–18.

[25]  Giovanni Battista Crispo, *De ethnicis philosophis caute legendis* (Rome, 1594); a second title-page reads 'De Platoni caute legendo'. See Romano, 'Crispo, Giovan Battista', in *Dizionario biografico degli Italiani* (Rome, 1960–), xxx, 806–8, esp. 807 for the other parts, which supposedly survived in manuscript; Malusa, 'Renaissance antecedents', 46–8; Glawe; *Hellenisierung*, 24–6; Hanegraaff, *Esotericism*, 90–3; Kraye, 'Ficino in the firing line' (2002), 394–7.

[26]  See e.g. the denunciation of Origen as 'indefensible' at Crispo, *De ethnicis philosophis*, 143–4.

[27]  As it is in Glawe, *Hellenisierung*, 38, followed by Hanegraaff, *Esotericism*, 93.

[28]  Grafton and Weinberg, *Casaubon*, 189. More generally, see Lyon, 'Baudouin, Flacius, and the plan for the Magdeburg Centuries' (2003); Backus, *Historical method*, 358–74; Scheible, *Die Entstehung der Magdeburger Zenturien* (1966).

philosophical–allegorical strand of Greek Judaism.[29] Scaliger developed de' Rossi's conclusions in two ways. First, he demonstrated that Philo's 'Therapeutae' were not, as Eusebius had suggested, early Christians, but in fact the ascetic Jewish sect the Essenes. Although the precise details of this finding remained contentious, it became a standard conclusion among some of those who analysed Scaliger's finding, such as the Flemish Hebraist Johannes Drusius and the Jesuit Nicolas Serarius, that the Essenes were some of the first converts to Christianity (Drusius and Serarius disagreed on whether this was a good or bad thing, anticipating some of the debates we shall meet below).[30] It is of some importance that Josephus had already mapped the Jewish sects onto Greek philosophical ones: the Essenes onto Pythagoreans, the Pharisees onto the Stoics, and (by implication only) the Sadducees onto Epicureans:[31] if Josephus had only made the analogy for the ease of his Greek readers, early modern exegetes would forge directly historical connections. Second, Scaliger solved a long-standing exegetical problem by identifying the ἑλληνισταί (Hellenists) mentioned in Acts 6.1 – identified since Erasmus as Jews who lived in the Greek and Roman lands of the Empire – as Greek-speaking Jews who used only the Septuagint, a conclusion quickly accepted by Isaac Casaubon, among others.[32]

Early Christianity now began to look – although we should not overestimate the speed of the process – like a movement situated in a Graeco-Judaic context. Casaubon suggested that Paul and the apostles, in their attempts to convert the gentiles, perhaps unwisely incorporated elements of pagan mystagogic vocabulary into the primitive faith.[33] The same context helped to expose and explain the philosophic forgeries, most notably the *Hermetica*, which could now be assigned to Christians (whether gnostic or 'orthodox') over-eager to convert the pagans addicted to philosophy.[34] As this approach was disseminated, especially in the Dutch Republic, it opened the possibility of new ways of reading both the New Testament and the church fathers. The vitriolic debate between Daniel Heinsius and Claude Saumaise on whether the Greek of the

---

[29] Azariah de' Rossi, *The light of the eyes*, ed. and trans. J. Weinberg (New Haven and London, 2001), 129–30 (on Philo's lack of knowledge of the original versions of the Torah), 135 (on his Platonism), 138–40 (on his allegorical methods). See also the seminal piece by Weinberg: 'The quest for the historical Philo' (1988).

[30] Schmidt, 'The Hasidaeans and the ancient Jewish "sects": a seventeenth-century controversy' (2011); Shuger, *The Renaissance Bible* (1998), 50–1, 215–16, n. 114 to ch. 1

[31] Josephus, *Ant. Jud.*, xv.371 (Essenes=Pythagoreans); *Vita*, 12 (Pharisees=Stoics); *Ant. Jud.*, xv.173, xviii.16, x.277–81 (Sadducees's denial of afterlife and fate). For other *loci* and Josephus's possible intentions, see Mason, *Flavius Josephus on the Pharisees* (1991), 125–8.

[32] Grafton, *Scaliger*, ii, 413–20; Grafton, 'Joseph Scaliger et l'histoire du Judaïsme Hellénistique' (1992); Grafton and Weinberg, *Casaubon*, 153–63.

[33] Glawe, *Hellenisierung*, 21–4; Levitin, 'Spencer'.

[34] Grafton, 'Protestant versus prophet', now supplemented by Grafton and Weinberg, *Casaubon*, 30–42; and *Das Ende*, ed. Mulsow.

New Testament was a dialect was largely philological, but it also touched on historical issues relevant to us, such as Philo's Platonism.[35] A more directly historical message could be extracted from Grotius's New Testament commentaries (1641–50).[36] This approach should not necessarily be aligned with 'secularisation'; indeed, it is more plausible to see Grotius's attempt to connect theological ideas like typology with contextual and philological explanations as a re-assertion of God's providential power and wisdom. Nonetheless, it remains the case that his commentaries became a storehouse of historical information, much of which directly affected our subject. At points this was a matter of historicising theological method: some putative typological concurrences had to be understood as adherence to the ancient Jewish allegorical custom of presenting an allusion as a citation.[37] The idea that the literal sense had to be understood allegorically, and that this had something to do with the philosophical culture in which the Bible was written, would prove important, as we shall see. More straightforwardly, Grotius also placed the intentions of the evangelists in a context that was often philosophical. When Paul spoke of abstinence from meat and drink at Colossians 2:16–17 he must have been referring to the practices not of the Jews but of the Pythagoreans.[38] When he instructed Timothy (1 Tim. 1:4) not to give heed to 'endless genealogies' (γενεαλογίαις) this could be shown to be a reference not just to the emanationist systems of the gnostics but also connected to Persian, Pythagorean, and neoplatonic metaphysics.[39] And in his notes to John 1:2, Grotius affirmed that Origen had been the first to transfer the term 'hypostasis' (ὑπόστασις) from Platonic philosophy into the church to refer to a person of the trinity.[40]

---

[35] Saumaise, for example, argued that Philo's Platonism was not equivalent to a general 'Hellenism': [Claude Saumaise], *Funus linguae Hellenisticae* (Leiden, 1643), 130–1 ('Caeterum si Philo, ob linguae Ebraicae ignorantiam, *Hellenista* censendus est, ut velle hic videtur Hellenisticarius, stylum etiam eius Hellenisticum videri oportet. Si est, Platonis quoque orationem Hellenistico stylo conditam haberi necesse est. Nam ad Platonis ideam maxime adspirat, eamque optime exprimit Philo. Unde veteres Critici de eo iactarunt, ἢ Πλάτων φιλωνίζει, ἢ Φίλων πλατωνίζει'). The final quotation – 'either Plato philonises or Philo platonises' – is from Jerome's *De viris illustribus*, 11.7, where it is already advertised as a Greek proverb. For the important subject of Philo's Christian reputation, I have drawn on Runia, *Philo in early Christian literature* (1993) (313–14 for the proverb, which must have been circulating independently of Jerome). The fullest discussion of the debate remains the seminal article by H. de Jonge, 'The study of the New Testament' (1975), at 95–6; see also de Jonge, 'The study of the New Testament in the Dutch universities, 1575–1700' (1981), 117.

[36] de Jonge, 'Hugo Grotius: exégète du Nouveau Testament' (1984); de Jonge, 'Grotius' view of the Gospels and the Evangelists' (1994).

[37] Drouin, *L'exégèse*, 99–109; Laplanche, *L'écriture*, 330–44; Beaude, 'L'accomplissement des prophéties chez Richard Simon' (1976); Nellen, 'Tension', 816.

[38] Hugo Grotius, *Annotationes in Novum Testamentum* (3 vols, Amsterdam & Paris, 1641–50), ii, 636.

[39] Ibid., ii, 692–3.

[40] Ibid., i, 851 ('Hypostaseon distinctionem Origenes & post eum alii vocavere. Sed notandum est hanc vocem ὑποστάσεων, ut & Τριάδος, ὁμοουσίου & alias quasdam non à primis Christianis

These last concerns about the philosophical vocabulary used to express trinitarianism were developed most fully in the work of the Jesuit Denis Petau (1583–1652). Petau, who had not only known Casaubon during the latter's time in Paris but also encouraged the career of Lucas Holstenius – the early seventeenth century's greatest specialist on neoplatonism[41] – was along with Cardinal Jacques Davy Du Perron (1556–1618) a pioneer of the anti-scholastic, patristic-focused, and text-critical 'positive theology'.[42] Petau argued in the second volume of his *Theologica dogmatica*, 'De trinitate' (1644), that almost all the ante-Nicenes had held a subordinationist trinitarianism, incompatible with post-Nicene orthodoxy and inspired and expressed in the language of Platonic philosophy; the forged pseudo-Hermes was just one testimony to this effect.[43] This was far in advance of any historical–philological arguments that any Socinians had been able to offer; even Michael Servetus had confined most of his criticisms to Aristotelian–scholastic trinitarianism of the type espoused by Peter Lombard.[44] Despite some contemporary accusations there can be no doubt about Petau's orthodoxy;[45] his position was more a developmental one in which Catholic 'tradition' was an unfolding process.[46] His work is better seen as an example of how historical criticism could serve Catholic argument and how a wide range of European confessions were investing in post-Scaliger critical humanism while turning it to theological ends. Nonetheless, it brought the question of the Platonism of the ante-Nicene fathers to the forefront of European scholarship. Where Petau could argue that the testimony of later Latin fathers was sufficient, no such option was available to those *avant garde* members of the English Church for whom only ante-Nicene testimony could function as a witness to the true faith.

usurpatas, cùm contra μίαν ὑπόστασιν dixerit Athanasius, synodi Nicena & Sardicensis & Romanae synodi aliquot, sed desumtas ex Platonicis scriptoribus sensu nonnihil immutato').

[41] Rietbergen, *Power*, 260. On Holstenius and his contacts with England, see further 2.2 above.

[42] Quantin, *Le catholicisme classique et les pères de l'église* (1999), esp. 103–11; Neveu, *Érudition et religion aux XVIIe et XVIIIe siècles* (1994), 333–63; Guelluy, 'L'évolution des méthodes théologiques à Louvain' (1941).

[43] Denis Petau, *Theologica dogmata* (5 vols, Paris, 1644–50), II: *In quo de sanctissima Trinitate agitur* (1644), 8–9. For Petau, see Glawe, *Hellenisierung*, 26–33; Hofmann, *Theologie, Dogma und Dogmenentwicklung im theologischen Werk Denis Petau's* (1976), esp. 194–208; Karrer, *Die Historisch-Positive Methode des Theologen Dionysius Petavius* (1970), esp. 181–4. The first manifestation of Petau's interest in Christian neoplatonism is his important edition of Synesius, Συνεσίου επισκόπου Κυρήνης τα άπαντα ευρισκόμενα. *Synesii episcopi Cyrenensis opera*, ed. D. Petau (Paris, 1612): see e.g. his commentary (separate pagination), 30.

[44] Although he also briefly mentioned possible Platonic influence on Jerome's allegorical–trinitarian interpretation of Matt. 13:33: 'On the errors of the trinity' [1531] in *Two treatises of Servetus on the trinity*, trans. E. M. Wilbur (Cambridge [MA], 1932), 41–2, 67; indeed, he argued that pagans would laugh at trinitarian arguments: 53. For vague and unscholarly statements about the non-existence of the trinity in scripture or the early church by Socinus himself, see e.g. Faustus Socinus, *Opera omnia* (2 vols, Amsterdam, 1656), I, 323. See further Mortimer, *Socinianism*, 15–22.

[45] For the accusations, see Galtier, 'Petau et la Préface de son De Trinitate' (1931).

[46] Fumaroli, 'Des deux Antiquités dans l'érudition jésuite française du XVIIe siècle' (1981).

## 6.2    The early church in philosophical context

As these words suggest, Petau's challenge was of particular importance in England where, from the 1620s, the new type of hyper-ceremonialist and sacerdotalist conformists like Laud and Richard Montagu – drawing on the scholarship and prestige of émigré scholars like Casaubon and Marcantonio de Dominis – invested heavily in a patristic identity for the Church, even if it was 'only after the Restoration [that] the reference to antiquity become essential to the new synthesis which, by that time, can fairly be called Anglicanism'.[47] Englishmen attempted to defeat the Catholics at their own game: Du Perron had 'shifted the debate from doctrine to history, from the Fathers "as Doctors" to the Fathers "as witnesses of the Customes and practise of the Church of their times"', anticipating Petau in his insistence that ante-Nicene testimony was insufficient to establish such witnesses, and that the authority of Roman Catholic tradition was therefore requisite.[48] This move towards a more historical patristic theology proved extremely popular in Catholic France.[49] It was a particularly powerful sparring tool against Protestants: Du Perron argued that it was impossible to save the doctrine of the trinity on the basis of the testimonies of the ante-Nicenes, let alone scripture, without the help of later tradition: an Arian would happily submit to the judgement of the ante-Nicenes.[50] For patristically minded Protestants, Petau's argument was therefore only a development of Du Perron's.

English suspicions had fallen on Petau as early as 1638. Responding to the accusation of the Jesuit Edward Knott that *sola scriptura* was a sure road to Socinianism, William Chillingworth pointed out that the Catholic Petau's notes to his edition of Epiphanius (1622) had already undermined the patristic, tradition-based case for the trinity.[51] This was slightly disingenuous, for Chillingworth and the Great Tew Circle of which he was such an important

---

[47] Quantin, *Antiquity*, 148–9, 397–8.

[48] Ibid., 216, quoting Jacques Davy Du Perron, *The reply of the most illustrious Cardinall of Perron, to the Answeare of the most excellent King of Great Britaine*, trans. Elizabeth Cary, Lady Falkland (Douai, 1630 [French original=1620]), 23–4.

[49] Quantin, *Catholicisme classique*, 79–82.

[50] Jacques Davy Du Perron, *Replique a la Response du serenissime Roy de la Grand Bretagne* (Paris, 1620), 729; Du Perron, *Reply*, 436. On all this, see Quantin, *Antiquity*, 221.

[51] William Chillingworth, *The religion of Protestants* (Oxford, 1638), sigs. §§§ᵛ–§§§2ʳ. Chillingworth is referring to the section in Petau's 'Animadversiones', in *Epiphanii . . . operum omnium*, ed. and trans. D. Petau (2 vols, Paris, 1622), ii, 276–90. For Knott's accusation, see his *Charity maintained by Catholiques* (London, 1634), 105. In a clever (if by then unscholarly) twist, Knott employed the history of philosophy for his own apologetic purposes: 'And as for some truths peculiar to Christians, (for Example, the mystery of the Blessed Trinity &c.) the only setting them downe in *Writing* is not inough to be assured that such a *Writing* is the undoubted word of God: otherwise some sayings of *Plato, Trismegistus, Sybills, Ovid* &c. must be esteemed Canonicall Scripture, because they fall upon some truths proper to Christian Religion' (49).

member had adopted a sceptical approach to patristic authority, drawing on the great Reformed manual of anti-patristic scepticism, Jean Daillé's *Traicté de l'employ des saincts peres*, published in late 1631, which itself had drawn on Du Perron and Petau to argue for the unreliability of the ante-Nicenes.[52] Daillé posited that the obscurity of the fathers had proceeded 'not from their Ignorance, but rather from their great Learning' leading to their 'mixing with the Christian Philosophy' many other traditions.[53] This was itself not unexpected since they wrote not to expound an unchanging orthodoxy but adapted their opinions to suit particular targets, whether Jews, heretics, or pagans.[54] It was no wonder then that they used either pagan tools or even things 'contrary to what [they] themselves believed', as Jerome had already pointed out.[55] The crucial implication of all this was that the fathers' learning made the idea of them as 'witnesses' unsustainable.

Daillé's work became the standard go-to text for Protestant anti-patristics. In their attempts to develop an irenic front against Rome, the Great Tew group and their intellectual successors used his ideas extensively;[56] the role of philosophy in the early church was a particularly tempting example to draw on. An important example can be found in *The liberty of prophesying*, the plea for mutual toleration in *adiaphora* based on the Apostles' Creed published in 1647 by the strict episcopalian and future bishop of Down and Connor Jeremy Taylor (by then deprived of his living and in retirement in Wales).[57] Early Christianity had nothing to do with philosophy; indeed, it was indulgence in philosophy that led to false traditions, such as Clement's belief that the apostles, upon their own deaths, had preached to the gentiles in Hell, which he 'proved ... only by the Testimony of the Book of *Hermes*'; and that the Greek philosophers had been saved, again only on the authority of the apocryphal books of Peter and Paul.[58]

---

[52] Quantin, 'Context et signification du *Traité de l'emploi des saints Pères* de Jean Daillé' (2006). For the impact in England, see Quantin, *Antiquity*, 228–51, *passim*. The above passage from Petau's Epiphanius is already used in the same way in Jean Daillé, *Traicté de l'employ des saincts peres* (Geneva, 1632), 130 [=Jean Daillé, *A treatise concerning the right use of the fathers*, ed. T. Smith (London, 1651), 80–1 (all translations from this version)]. On Smith, see Hammond, 'Thomas Smith: a beleaguered humanist of the Interregnum' (1983), supplemented and corrected by Quantin, *Antiquity*, 247–8.

[53] Daillé, *Traicté*, 134–6 (=*Treatise*, 86–7), instancing Clemens Alexandrinus specifically.

[54] Daillé, *Traicté*, 152–3 (=*Treatise*, 95).

[55] Daillé, *Traicté*, 176–9 (=*Treatise*, 111–13), quoting at length Jerome, *Epist.* 48, 13.

[56] Quantin, *Antiquity*, 209–51.

[57] McAdoo, *Jeremy Taylor* (1997); Spurr, *The Restoration Church of England* (1991), 137, *passim*; Spurr, 'Taylor, Jeremy', *ODNB*; Quantin, *Antiquity*, 242–7 for his patristics, esp. 247 for strong similarities with Chillingworth.

[58] Jeremy Taylor, *Of the liberty of prophesying* [1647] in *Treatises* (London, 1648), 94. Taylor does not give references, but they must be Clemens Alexandrinus, *Strom.*, II.9 (Taylor has made an error here that betrays his anti-philosophical prejudices, for Clement refers not to Hermes but to the Shepherd of Hermas) and *Strom.*, I.4, 20, VI.5 (the reference to the apocryphal *Preaching of Peter* can be found in the last of these).

This of course raised the issue of how the early Christians had dealt with heresy, which Taylor ingeniously solved by claiming that heresies were errors not of the understanding but of the will: the gnostics' error was antinomianism – to believe that 'no matter how men liv'd, so they did but believe aright' – an error that in fact stemmed from distinguishing moral life and theological belief in a manner possible only 'if we speak like Philosophers', but not 'when we speak like Christians'.[59] But philosophy could only be a secondary cause of heresy, and thus not the way to its extirpation: heresies were all 'of the same nature … not of a nicety in dispute, not a question of secret Philosophy … but open defiances of all Faith, of all sobriety, and of all sanctity'.[60] Taylor repeated Socrates' statement that the origins of the Arian controversy were in philosophical disputatiousness, adding to it a long quotation from a famous letter of Constantine to Alexander and Arius in which the emperor chastised them for failing to recognise that even the sectarian philosophers maintain a degree of harmony despite disagreements.[61] Constantine subdued Arius not because of the latter's doctrinal error but because he 'behav'd himself so seditiously and tumultuarily'; after he calmed down he was left to his own devices.[62]

These were not widely held opinions. The use of Daillé and the scepticism about patristic authority developed by anti-episcopalians during the Civil Wars and Interregnum tended not towards this kind of irenicism but towards a scripturalism which 'went hand in hand with Calvinism'.[63] As always, the sticking point was heresy and especially the trinity.[64] Both the importation of Socinian works from the Low Countries and the rise of domestic antitrinitarianism could focus attention back on patristic testimony. Some English antitrinitarians confined themselves strictly to biblical grounds – this was the case in Paul Best's *Mysteries discovered* (1647), although even he had a historical theory of the origins of the corruption, ascribing it to 'Semipagan Christians of the third Century in the Western Church' who also fathered Roman Catholicism.[65] But it was the foremost English antitrinitarian John Biddle

---

[59]  Taylor, *Liberty*, 24.    [60]  Ibid., 31.

[61]  Ibid., 45; Eusebius, *Vit. Const.*, II.71; Socrates, *Hist. eccl.*, I.7.

[62]  Taylor, 'The epistle dedicatory', in *Treatises*, 19–20.    [63]  Quantin, *Antiquity*, 253.

[64]  For the general problem of heresy in this period, see Coffey, 'Defining heresy and orthodoxy in the puritan revolution' (2006); Worden, *God's instruments* (2012), 63–90 ('Toleration and Protectorate'); Mortimer, *Socinianism*, 177–204.

[65]  Paul Best, *Mysteries discovered* (London, 1647), 11. Best, who had studied at St Catharine's College, Cambridge and fought against the Hapsburgs in the Thirty Years War (when he met Socinians), was by this point in prison, where he had been since February 1645, having circulated some of his ideas in manuscript. When brought before parliament on 4 April 1646, Best claimed that 'he acknowledged the Holy and Heavenly Trinity; and doth not speak against it; but hoped to be saved by it: But said further, That he denieth the Tripersonality of *Athanasius*; and that it is *Romish*, and Popish': *Journal of the House of Commons: vol. IV: 1644–1646* (London, 1802), 500. See Mortimer, *Socinianism*, 158–60; McLachlan, *Socinianism in seventeenth-century England* (1951), 149–62; Smith, 'Paul Best, John Biddle, and antitrinitarian heresy in seventeenth-century England' (2006).

(1615/16–1662), who spent (intermittently) a decade in prison for his beliefs, who first developed a 'historical' antitrinitarianism in England.[66] Again, most of Biddle's antitrinitarian works were strongly scripturalist, but in 1647 he supplemented them with a book entitled *The testimonies of Irenaeus, Justin Martyr, Tertullian, Novatianus, Theophilus, Origen … concerning that one God, and the person of the Holy Trinity*. It consisted mostly of quotations (and translations of them) from these fathers, clearly selected for their ante-Nicene pedigree, designed to show that none of them held the Son co-eternal with the Father. Justin Martyr, 'coming out of *Plato's* School to the contemplation of the Gospel' and thus 'imagining *John* the Evangelist to be of the same opinion with *Plato*', did believe in the pre-existence of the Logos-Son, but even he did not believe him eternal.[67] Referring to patristic testimony 'not that I much regard them … but for the sake of the Adversaries, who continually crake *the Fathers, the Fathers*', Biddle declared that all the earliest fathers were not trinitarians in the modern sense, even if 'they went awry in imagining two Natures in Christ; which came to pass … partly because they were great Admirers of *Plato*' (the Nicene Council was even more 'beholding to the Platonists').[68]

It is tempting to assume that Biddle had read Petau: the argument is structurally so similar that it is difficult to know where else he could have got his ideas. However, the only authority he cited was that of Justus Lipsius, according to whom the fathers 'did in outward profession so put-on Christ, as that in heart they did not put-off Plato'.[69] Lipsius had indeed used a formulation very similar to this in an early chapter of his *Manuductio ad Stoicam philosophiam* (1604) in which he defended the use of philosophy by Christians as long as it was accompanied by the required caution.[70] And yet, I rather doubt that this was Biddle's direct source, for

---

[66] On Biddle, McLachlan, *Socinianism*, 163–217 remains key. See also Mortimer, *Socinianism*, 160–3, 224–9; Smith, 'Anti-trinitarian heresy'.

[67] [John Biddle], *The testimonies of Irenæus, Justin Martyr, Tertullian, Novatianus, Theophilus, Origen, (who lived in the two first centuries after Christ was born, or thereabouts;) … concerning that one God, and the person of the Holy Trinity* (London, [1653]), 38–9; Biddle had earlier quoted the famous passage in which Justin claimed that Plato's creation account mapped on to the Mosaic (19–23) (quoting Justin, *Apolog. I*, 59). See also 15 for Irenaeus's putative subordinationism.

[68] [Biddle], *Testimonies*, 83–4, 86.     [69] Ibid., 84.

[70] Justus Lipsius, *Manuductionis ad Stoicam philosophica libri tres* (Antwerp, 1604), 6 ('Nihil ii verae & sobriae philosophiae damnatum aut rejectum eunt: sed aut Sophisticam culpant, aut nimium eius studium et honorem. Nam, ut scias, primis illis Ecclesiae temporibus non dederant, qui Christum ore adsumerent, & Platonem animo non exuerent: qui miscerent etiam dogmata, & sacra illa profanis pravâ subtilitate temperarent. Inde errorum rivi, & haereses: et jure merito Patres in hos tales incurrunt'). Tellingly, the chapter is entitled 'Philosophiam non damnari, nec alienam, imò utilem Christianis esse. Tricas tamen & cavillos vitandos, & cum modo habendam' (5). See also 10–11 for many patristic citations proving that 'many of our [i.e. Christian] leading men also [like Cicero] sided with this faction [i.e. the Platonists]' ('Et plerique etiam nostrorum procerum tabellam in hanc partem dimittunt').

John Owen in his 1643 attack on Arminianism (his first published book) had already pointed out that

It is true indeed, some of the ancient Fathers, before the rising of the *Pelagian* heresie; who had so put on Christ, as *Lipsius* speaks, that they had not fully put off *Plato*, have unadvisedly dropt some speeches, seeming to grant, that divers men before the Incarnation, living μετὰ λόγου, according to the dictates of right reason, might be saved without faith in Christ.[71]

Interestingly, Owen combined this with the testimony of Casaubon's first anti-Baronian exercitation about the philosophical optimism of the fathers. If this was a source for Biddle, as I suspect it was, it is a nice example of how the linguistic shadows of unconnected scholarship could inform vernacular heterodoxy.

Biddle sought to strike at what he thought was a central tension in Reformed trinitarian apologetics: against the papists Protestant controversialists refuted the authority of the fathers, but against him they happily brought them forward.[72] There was certainly a truth to this, but with the reassertion of scripturalism and Reformed scholasticism, Interregnum divines proved quite happy to acknowledge the philosophical dalliances of the ante-Nicenes, and thus abandon them in favour of the supposedly clear trinitarian testimonies in the Bible and of Aristotelian–metaphysical distinctions as found in the tomes of Reformed scholasticism. The greatest puritan heresy-hunter of them all, the Presbyterian Thomas Edwards, claimed that 'a Godly Minister' told him that 'he heard an Independent Minister maintain ... that Organs are a sanctified adjunct in the service of God'; he compared this to '*Origen* and some others versed in *Plato's* Philosophy, br[inging] in opinings into the Church according to *Plato's* doctrine': both were examples of 'wanton men who ... brought ... into doctrines of Faith and Worship such opinions and practises still as have been most suitable to their genius and education'.[73] Familiar with the works and statements of both Best and Biddle, Edwards made no effort to defend the fathers, preferring to rest on 'Orthodox Divines' – that is to say modern Reformed divinity.[74] A similar view is evident in the works published on the eve of the Restoration by Henry Hickman, a 'sternly Calvinist tutor at

---

[71] John Owen, Θεομαχία Αὐτεξουσιαστική, or, a display of Arminianisme (London, 1643), 118. The term 'μετὰ λόγου' had been used by Justin to connect Christ as *logos* with the exercise of reason (e.g. *First Apology*, 46, *Second Apology*, 8, 10). Lim, *Trinity*, 60, 306 notes this passage in Biddle, but fails to spot the connection with Owen (I do not see how Lipsius is a key source for Souverain, as Dr Lim claims at 309).

[72] [Biddle], *Testimonies*, 82–3.

[73] Thomas Edwards, *The third part of Gangraena* (London, 1646), 13–14. See Hughes, *Gangraena and the struggle for the English Revolution* (2004), esp. 55–129; Hughes, 'Thomas Edwards's *Gangraena* and heresiological traditions' (2006).

[74] Edwards, *Gangraena, third part*, 87–8 (reporting on Biddle, whose manuscripts he claimed to have read); Thomas Edwards, *The first and second part of Gangraena* (London, 1646), 114;

Magdalen [Oxford]'.[75] The fathers were 'not fit to be appealed to, in some Controversies now a foot in Christendom', in part because those before Augustine, 'urged by *Paynims* [i.e. pagans], Philosophers in those dayes … extended the power of Free-will unto the uttermost … especially having then no cause to fear any enemie at home … there being yet no Pelagians sprung up in the world'.[76] Writing against a neo-Laudian treatise on the positivity of sin, Hickman claimed that he had the fathers on his side even though they 'did not write in the Scholasticall stile and strain': his list of authorities, however, was strictly post-Nicene (Basil the Great, Gregory of Nyssa, Maximus the Confessor, John Damascene, Gregory of Nazianzus, and pseudo-Dionysius) and he only quoted them on the question of the Aristotelian category of privation, when he could 'strengthen my opinion from the Schoolmen, among whom I have an Army to a man'.[77] He concluded that the Laudian zeal for antiquity and dismissal of 'the niceties of the School' and 'supernatural Philosophy' (i.e. scholastic metaphysics) would lead to Socinianism.[78]

Nowhere is the highly ambiguous nature of orthodox Reformed engagement with ante-Nicene trinitarianism (or lack thereof) more profoundly represented than in the work of Francis Cheynell, a member of the Westminster Assembly, sent by parliament as one of the Visitors to Oxford, made President of St John's, and appointed Lady Margaret Professor of Divinity in 1648.[79] Cheynell had already written against Socinianism in 1643, displaying his solid knowledge of continental Socinian and anti-Socinian works,[80] so in 1650 the university commissioned him 'to set forth a book in vindication of the Trinity'.[81] Very early, Cheynell made his exegetical principles clear. Scripture was the only guide, to be supplemented 'with some discourses in *Aristotle's* Metaphysicks'

---

32–3 (familiarity with Best's manuscripts); see also the praise of 'Geneva' as the 'sharpe[st] enemy' of heretical error at 159–60.

[75] Worden, *God's instruments*, 91–193 ('Politics, piety, and learning: Cromwellian Oxford'), at 170 (also 174–5 for Magdalen as 'the college which came closest to meeting the Puritan ideal', under the mastership of Thomas Goodwin); Quantin, *Antiquity*, 257, 260, 264, 338–9; Wright, 'Hickman, Henry', *ODNB*.

[76] Henry Hickman, *Laudensium apostasia* (London, 1660), 4–5.

[77] Henry Hickman, Πατρο-σχολαστικο-δικαίωςις, *or a justification of the fathers and schoolmen: shewing, that they are not self-condemned for denying the positivity of sin* (Oxford, 1659), 56–9. Hickman was writing against Thomas Pierce, Αυτοκατάκρισις, *or, self-condemnation, exemplified* (London, 1658), 162; see also 100–1 for strong attacks on 'Schoolmen' and for Calvin being directly opposed to the 'Fathers piety'. For Pierce, see the very full account in Parkin, 'Pierce, Thomas', *ODNB*.

[78] Hickman, *Laudensium apostasia*, 49–50.

[79] Worden, *God's instruments*, 97–8, 159–60; Quantin, *Antiquity*, 260–3, Mortimer, *Socinianism*, 109–14, 126–7, 172–4.

[80] Francis Cheynell, *The rise, growth, and danger of Socinianisime* (London, 1643). Much of the work in fact consists of attacks on Laudians.

[81] Worden, *God's instruments*, 159, n. 460, quoting Oxford University Archives, Register of Convocation, T., 97

which help elucidate God's nature.[82] This was an obvious defence of Calvinist explanations of the trinity and all further references to Aristotle came in defences of explicitly Calvinist statements: Cheynell acknowledged that opponents would attack such explanations as 'Philosophical, Scholastical, Metaphysical', but proceeded to defend 'these Metaphysical notions' as 'subservient helps in a subordinate way'.[83] Citing admonitions to scripturalism from Cyril and Clement, he claimed that the fathers were 'as we use to say ... *Puritane[s]*'.[84] This undermined the papist claim that Protestantism inevitably led to Socinianism: Cheynell had earlier cited the same passages from Du Perron and Petau as had been given by Chillingworth.[85] Putting a rather positive spin on a letter of Jerome's which condemned the confusion engendered by the terminology of '*hypostases*', he considered that the post-Nicene fathers had all agreed on the terminology, 'upon some of [the same] considerations' as those of Calvinist orthodoxy.[86] But most remarkable is his attack – in a Latin dedication to Edward Reynolds, Oxford vice-chancellor – on all attempts to defend the trinity on the basis of the philosophical 'pious frauds' of the early Church.[87] This acceptance of Casaubon's vocabulary – so inimical to 'patristic' episcopalians like Montagu – combined with the belief that any vestiges of trinitarianism in Plato were just evidence of plagiarism from the Jews,[88] is a nice example of how far the Calvinist theological leaders of the 1640s were prepared to distance themselves from patristic (or at least ante-Nicene) apologetics. 'To argue for *sola Scriptura* from the deficient christology of the ante-Nicene Fathers had definitely become too dangerous a game',[89] at least for adherents of Reformed theological method. Scripture was to come together with *post*-Nicene orthodoxy,[90] defended through Reformed scholasticism.

Only one Calvinist divine attempted to defend the ante-Nicenes against Biddle: Nicholas Estwick, minister of Warkton in Northamptonshire, in 1656.[91] As

---

[82] Francis Cheynell, *The divine triunity of the Father, Son, and Holy Spirit* (London, 1650), 4.

[83] Ibid., 86, 105, 109, 147. For his defence of Calvin's *autotheos* theory, see below.

[84] Ibid., 13–14, see also 15–17.    [85] Ibid., 15; Cheynell, *Socinianisme*, 50.

[86] Cheynell, *Divine triunity*, 89. Cheynell cites Jerome, *Epist.* 87, but it is in fact *Epist.* 15.

[87] Cheynell, *Divine triunity*, sigs. [A5]ᵛ–[A6]ʳ: 'Suspectae autem fidei sunt, quae de Trinitatis mysterio ex quibusdam laciniis, Sibyllarum carminibus, Hydapsis, M. Trismegisti, Platonis, & aliorum Scriptis Doctores nominis bene magni collegerunt. *In Trismegisto qui Mose antiquior est* (credite posteri) τὸ ὁμοούσιον *occurrit; narrantur in super nonnulla, quae post Christum acciderunt*. Multa denique fraude parum piâ confinxit non nemo, ut Religionis Christianae Gentilibus fidem faceret, quorum apud curiosissimos disciplinarum, nec non Antiquitatum scrutatores nec vola, nec vestigium extat. *Omnia autem adulterina & supposititia tanquam vana rejicimus, damnamus*'.

[88] Ibid., 5; see also there: 'and it is conceived that Christians have inserted such passages into the works of Heathens'.

[89] Quantin, *Antiquity*, 339.

[90] Cheynell, *Divine triunity*, sig. [A6]ʳ (note the entirely *post*-Nicene canon of fathers listed).

[91] There is a summary (but not of the historical arguments) in Lim, *Trinity*, 152–7, which also covers Estwick's Πνευματολογια, *or a treatise of the Holy Ghost* (London, 1648), which does

befitting his confessional identity, Estwick relied primarily on scriptural and Reformed–scholastic arguments; but he did devote one hundred pages to confuting Biddle's patristic case. The story of Justin's conversion demonstrated only that the fathers abandoned Plato before turning to Christ.[92] The fathers had used Platonic vocabulary when evangelising to the gentiles, but this was a purely tactical step; Plato understood λόγος as 'operative reason in God', not as a 'subsistence distinct from God', as did the Christians.[93] If the ante-Nicenes had spoken incautiously it was because Arianism had not appeared to force them into linguistic precision; nonetheless they must be 'favourably expounded'; the later councils can have been 'no innovation, but a continuation of the faith which they received from their Predecessors' more precisely defined.[94] This reasoning was entirely standard, for it had been famously deployed by Jerome.[95] Estwick thought it sufficient to save Origen.[96] Remarkably, Estwick cited Petau in support of this position, claiming that 'The Holy Fathers were sound in the faith of the Trinity: yet when they disputed with the Gentiles touching the Christian faith, the better to perswade them to condescend to the capacity of the hearers for their benefit, spake lesse accurately and conformed their notions of the Christian Religion to *Plato's* form of speaking.'[97] But the whole point of Petau's (and Du Perron's) position was that Jerome's argument was insufficient to save the ante-Nicenes: it was impossible to penetrate beyond the Platonic vocabulary of the ante-Nicenes to save 'orthodox' trinitarianism without the divine light of the councils themselves. Petau had undermined the key hermeneutic that preserved ante-Nicene orthodoxy, and this anti-Jerome conclusion had already been adopted in England by the Great Tew writers.[98] The Reformed scholastics who dominated Interregnum Oxford – while they sometimes in private expressed concern about Du Perron's and Petau's destructive treatment of the ante-Nicenes[99] – were simply not invested enough in

---

not contain patristic arguments, suggesting that Biddle's publications did indeed bring such issues to the fore.

[92] Nicholas Estwick, *Mr Bidle's confession of faith touching the Holy Trinity, wherein his chief designe to overthrow that sacred mystery and the deity of our Blessed Saviour is examined and confuted* (London, 1656), 342, 404.

[93] Ibid., 404–5; see also 362.     [94] Ibid., 318–19, 403.

[95] Jerome, *Adv. Ruf.*, II.17. Augustine had made the same point about those who wrote on free will before Pelagius (*Contra Julianum Pelagianum*, VI.22). Estwick cited both at *Trinity*, 318–19 (mistakenly citing book I of Jerome).

[96] Estwick, *Trinity*, 364–6.     [97] Ibid., 405, citing Petau's *De trinitate*; also at 362.

[98] Lucius Cary, Viscount Falkland, 'The Lord of Faulklands reply', in *Sir Lucius Cary, late Lord Viscount of Falkland, his discourse of infallibility, with an answer to it: and his Lordships reply. Never before published* (London, 1651), 77–8, explicitly deferring to Du Perron (discussed at Quantin, *Antiquity*, 221).

[99] See the Interregnum-era theological notebook of Thomas Brathwaite of Queen's College, Oxford, CUL MS Dd.12.57, fol. 80ʳ: 'The Dʳˢ of yᵉ Romish Church deny [i.e. affirm] very plainely & frequently that the Trinity cannot be proved by Scripture . . . Card. Perron Book 3. C. 2. of his reply to K. James tells yᵉ world yᵗ Eusebius was an Arrian, yᵉ same also of Irenaeus & Tertullian'.

patristic authority to be particularly concerned about developing a scholarly rebuttal.

Yet there was one important and connected issue on which they expended much energy, and on which Cheynell, their chief spokesman on the trinitarian issue, consequently resorted to patristic argument. This was the claim of Calvin and a host of his followers that '*Christ is God of himselfe*', which Cheynell defended from 'Papists, Arminians, Socinians, and some bitter Lutherans', by arguing that their 'Platonical raptures' (i.e. subordinationism) could be confronted with the testimonies of '*Plato's* corrivall' pseudo-Dionysius, as well as a host of post-Nicenes: Athanasius, Basil, Epiphanius, Nazianzen, John Damascene, and even the ante-Nicenes Justin Martyr and Origen, whose well-known errors he rather unexpectedly ascribed to the 'fraud, ignorance, or malice of such as made too bold with his Works'.[100] Calvin, arguing against the early antitrinitarians Servetus and Valentine Gentile (*c.* 1520–66), had claimed both in his *Expositio impietatis Valentini Gentilis* (1561) and in the definitive edition of the *Institutio Christianae religionis* (1559) that Christ was 'God of himself', and that this was compatible with Nicene and even ante-Nicene orthodoxy.[101] This strict reaction against subordinationism was quickly jumped upon by Catholic critics who attacked it as entirely unwarranted by either scripture or tradition. In 1569, Gilbert Génébrard coined the term 'αὐτόθεοσ' (*autotheos*) to describe Calvin's putatively heretical deviation from Nicene orthodoxy; he was followed much more fully by Petau.[102]

Just as crucially, Calvin's idea was dismissed as scholastic triviality by Arminian theologians starting from Arminius himself.[103] He complained that Calvin 'was at variance with . . . the whole of the ancient Church, both Greek and Latin, which had always taught, that *the Son had his Deity from the Father by eternal generation*';[104] his successor Simon Episcopius was much more overt about contrasting the corrupt scholastic trinity of Calvin with the 'true'

---

[100] Cheynell, *Divine triunity*, 234. Cheynell never stated whether he had rejected the authenticity of ps.-Dionysius, but it is difficult to imagine that he had not: whatever the case, he clearly valued his testimony, for he also suggested the paraphrase of the *Corpus Dionysiacum* by the Byzantine George Pachymeres (1242–*c.* 1310), the first Greek edition of which was published in 1561 as *Paraphrasis in omnia Dionysii Areopagitae* (Paris, 1561).

[101] John Calvin, *Expositio impietatis Valentini Gentilis* (Geneva, 1561); Calvin, *Institutionis Christianae religionis* . . . [1559] (London, 1576), I.13.20, 23–9, pp. 53, 55–60. See Muller, *Post-Reformation Reformed dogmatics. Vol.* IV: *the Triunity of God* (2003), 324–32. Ellis, *Calvin, classical trinitarianism, and the aseity of the son* (2012) is of limited use to historians.

[102] Gilbert Génébrard, *De S. Trinitate libri tres contra huius aevi Trinitarios, Antitrinitarios, & Autotheanos* (Paris, 1569), esp. 43. On Génébrard, see also n. 24 above. Petau, *Theologica dogmata*, II, 616–23. The useful discussion in Hampton, *Anti-Arminians* (2008), 166–71 mentions Génébrard's and Petau's criticisms without giving citations.

[103] Muller, 'The Christological problem in the thought of Jacobus Arminius' (1988) places great emphasis on this as the heart of Arminius's theology.

[104] Jacobus Arminius, 'Declaration of the sentiments' [1608], in *The works of James Arminius*, trans. J. Nichols and W. Nichols (3 vols, London, 1825–6), I, 628.

ante-Nicene position which he openly admitted was subordinationist.[105] This was taken even further by Episcopius's successor as professor of theology at the Remonstrant seminary in Amsterdam, Étienne de Courcelles (Stephanus Curcellaeus), who in his preface to Episcopius's *Opera* (1650) questioned even the term ὁμοούσιος – pointing out that it was not even used in the same manner at Nicaea as it was by modern divines – and more generally condemned all scholastic philosophical language of trinitarianism with reference to Lorenzo Valla.[106]

The virulently anti-Arminian Cheynell thus had very good reasons to defend the ante-Nicene heritage of Reformed–scholastic orthodoxy against what he presented as the Platonic subordinationism of modern Catholics and Arminians. Nor was he the only one among the Calvinist heavyweights of the Interregnum to do this. The leading Independent Thomas Goodwin, installed as president of Magdalen College, Oxford in 1650, also offered a Reformed scholastic defence of the trinity which upheld Calvin's *autotheos* – the Westminster Assembly in which Goodwin had been a key participant had already criticised a clause in the Nicene Creed for implicitly contradicting Calvin – at the same time as condemning *all* trinitarian errors as stemming from Platonism.[107] But the 'λόγος' terminology used by John deeply troubled Goodwin: he noted that all the other apostles had used simply 'Son of God', and so suggested that John was probably using it only to combat the emana-tionist heretics mentioned by Irenaeus, being the only apostle to live long enough to see them develop.[108] Paul's warning about 'vain philosophy'

---

[105] Hampton, *Anti-Arminians*, 171–4.

[106] Stephanus Curcellaeus, 'Praefatio', in *M. Simonis Episcopii … Opera theologica* (2 vols, Amsterdam, 1650–65), I, sigs. ***2ᵛ–***3ʳ. Following Bellarmine and Rivet, Courcelles also rejected the authenticity of Justin's *Expositio rectae fidei*, which spoke of the τρόποι ὑπάρξεως (manners of existence) of the divine persons, thus depriving the scholastics of an important ante-Nicene crux. An English edition was published as *M. Simonis Episcopii … Opera theologica … editio secunda, cum autographo accuratissime collata* (2 vols, London, 1665–78). Courcelles is badly understudied, but for this subject see Mortimer, *Socinianism*, 153, which slightly overstates the case ('he also insisted that Christianity was completely viable without the concept of the Trinity and without the philosophical terms alien to the early Christians') and the discussion of his subordinationism as later expressed in his own *Opera theologica* (Amsterdam, 1675) in Hampton, *Anti-Arminians*, 174–5. As far as I can tell, the fullest biographical discussion remains Arnold Poelenburg, 'Oratio funebris in obitum clar-issimi viri D. Stephani Curcellaei', in the *Opera theologica*, but see also Vermeulen, 'Strategies and slander in the Protestant part of the republic of letters' (2002). On Valla, see 6.4 below.

[107] Thomas Goodwin, 'The knowledge of God the Father, and his Son Jesus Christ', in *The works of Thomas Goodwin*, ed. J. Nichol (12 vols, Edinburgh, 1861–66), IV, 404, 416. For his views on *autotheos*, see Jones, *Why heaven kissed earth* (2010), 112–16; for the Westminster Assembly: Quantin, *Antiquity*, 253. For the probable pre-1660 dating of Goodwin's works, which had until recently been seen as the product of post-Restoration nonconformity (follow-ing Hill, *The experience of defeat* (1984), 179), see Lawrence, 'Transmission and transforma-tion: Thomas Goodwin and the puritan project' (2002), chs. 1–2, which also very usefully charts the consistency of his Calvinism. For Goodwin's central role in 1650s Oxford, see Worden, *God's instruments*, 119–20, 122–3, 125–6, 128–9, 141–5.

[108] Goodwin, 'The knowledge of God', 416, 420, 450–1.

concerned precisely this Platonic speculation about the Godhead.[109] John had only used 'λόγος' because it had previously been used by the Jews to refer to the Messiah, as witnessed by the Targums (see below): Plato's and Philo's mistaken use of it also derived from the Jews.[110] This obviously raised big problems about the ante-Nicenes, problems that Goodwin solved by the simple policy of ignoring them in favour of Reformed, Jesuit, and Dominican scholasticism, as he did throughout the rest of his writings.[111]

Already we see quite clearly the tensions between the demands of Reformed orthodoxy and ante-Nicene vocabulary: neither Socinianism nor a particularly developed criticism was necessary for them to come to the fore. These tensions even manifested themselves in some unexpected places. Thomas Barlow, the leading seventeenth-century English Calvinist pedagogue, attacked in his metaphysics textbook (1637) the idea that metaphysics could explain the doctrine of the trinity: to defend this claim he turned to history, asserting that any counter-claim depended on the absurd forgery-filled histories of Steuco, and citing the first chapter of Casaubon's *Exercitationes* to back himself up.[112] But, Barlow continued, Aristotelian metaphysics *could* be combined with scripture to talk about God's nature: this of course was the essence of Reformed scholasticism.[113] This ultimately theological debate between strict Calvinists and their subordinationist critics would play a central role in all historicisations of trinitarian dogma through to Le Clerc and beyond.

That the Calvinists had good reason to fear is revealed by the *Theologia veterum* (1657), a late life work of one of the key Laudians, Peter Heylyn.[114] Throughout his works, Heylyn consistently insisted that 'patristic doctrines had been assailed by the imperialism of Calvinistic ideas'.[115] It is thus no surprise to find him citing Génébrard and Arminius to dismiss Calvin's *autotheos* – 'I professe my self uncapable of these *Schoole-niceties*' – in favour of a view of Christ as having received his being and essence from the Father, albeit not (Heylyn furiously insisted) in the ultra-subordinationist sense implied by Gentile.[116] More striking is his open reference to Platonism in this regard: St John and Plato had both followed the Jewish use of 'λόγος' and John 'made choyce rather of this *notion* then of any other, in the front entrance of his *Gospel*, because it was so known and acceptable both to *Jew* and

---

[109] Ibid., 450–1.     [110] Ibid., 418.

[111] Jones, *Goodwin*, 59–62, although the selectiveness of Godwin's use of the fathers is not recognised here.

[112] Barlow, *Exercitationes aliquot metaphysicae*, 97–9.

[113] Ibid., 101. For Barlow on metaphysics *qua* natural theology, see 4.2 above.

[114] See now Milton, *Laudian and royalist polemic in seventeenth-century England* (2007), esp. 152–61.

[115] Quantin, *Antiquity*, 127; also 154, 161–2, 181, 191, 199, 248–9.

[116] Peter Heylyn, *Theologia veterum, or, the summe of Christian theologie, positive, polemical, and philological, contained in the Apostles creed, or reducible to it* (London, 1654), 37–8.

*Gentile*.[117] Heylyn here referred to the biblical commentary of the Jesuit Juan de Maldonado (*c.* 1533–83), which argued at length for the compatibility of Platonic notions with Christian trinitarianism, defending them by reference to the very frequent use of מימרא דיי (*Memra Yahweh*, 'the Word of God') in the Targums, supposedly equivalent both to Plato's and to John's *Logos*.[118] And so for Heylyn, Paul's words did not render scripture incompatible with philosophy, as long as that did not involve 'medling with the *Protestant* Writers of the forein Churches' [i.e. Calvinists].[119] The story of Justin's conversion was a lesson about philosophy's limited but necessary propaedeutic function.[120] Any Platonic corruption was limited to a later period, specifically to such papist doctrines as mediation by saints and angels and purgatory.[121]

Affirming the Platonism of the fathers thus informed the Laudian attack on the Calvinists. But this investment came at a scholarly cost, for the Casaubonian identification of 'pious forgeries' could not be accepted: 'I dare not so far disparage those good *Catholick* writers as to believe they would support so strong an edifice with so weak a prop, or borrow help from *falshood* to evict the *truth*'. Porphyry and the other anti-Christian philosophers would have surely recognised if the ante-Nicenes were using philosophical forgeries.[122] As Laudian divines invested in the critical scholarship on paganism in the early church, they rejected half of its findings.

## 6.3    A new patristics

The Reformed were happy to abandon the ante-Nicenes altogether, without, for the most part, much in the way of historical scholarship to support their trinitarian position; their episcopalian opponents, much more keen on patristic arguments, veered between optimism at the opportunities that such arguments offered for attacks on the Reformed and caution about its results, not least concerning the fathers' immersion in pagan philosophy. The tension between

---

[117] Heylyn, *Theologia veterum*, 113.

[118] Juan de Maldonado, *Commentarii in quatuor evangelistas ... Hac quarta editione omnia diligentius recognita, ac emendata* (Lyon, 1602 [1st edn=1601), 1256a–b; 1259b–60a; 1263: after mentioning Philo, Hermes Trismegistus, and Plato: 'Quos Philosophos non dubium ab antiquis Haebraeis & hausisse sententiam, & vocabulum accepisse. Voluit ergo Ioannes accommodate ad usum loqui: voluit intelligi'. For a small example of Maldonado's general Hebraic learning, see Grafton and Weinberg, *Casaubon*, 221–2; for his biography, especially during his time at the Collège de Clermont, see Prat, *Maldonat et l'Universite de Paris au XVIe siecle* (1856), esp. 480–510 for his work on the *Commentarii* upon return to Rome in 1580, and for their successful reception. For the general value set upon the Targums by seventeenth-century English scholars and divines, see Feingold, 'The humanities', 471.

[119] Heylyn, *Theologia veterum*, (20–1) ('A preface ... concerning the *antiquity* & *authority* of the ... Apostles Creed', separate bracketed pagination).

[120] Ibid., 29–30. This was also a commonplace in philosophic pedagogy: see e.g. Heereboord, *Meletemata philosophica*, 22–6.

[121] Heylyn, *Theologia veterum*, 432–4, 428.    [122] Ibid., 112–13.

the scholarly acknowledgement of the 'Platonic' subordinationism of the ante-Nicenes and the implications this had for patristic authority would prove long-standing. It developed fully in the context of a renewed episcopalian investment in patristic scholarship. In response to defeat and to Calvinist scripturalism, leading disenfranchised divines proceeded further down the path initially trod by Heylyn, spurred on by such landmark scholarly achievements as Ussher's publication of the uninterpolated Latin version of Ignatius's letters in 1645.[123] As 'beleaguered episcopalians ... felt it less and less advisable to attack the use of the Fathers in religious controversies',[124] as they announced episcopacy as a fundamental of the Church, and as they decisively turned against Daillé, so they had to unpack the implications of continental scholarship on the philosophical culture that their beloved ante-Nicenes inhabited. The roots of this tension are already evident in Montagu, who simultaneously attempted to appropriate the lustre of Casaubon's scholarship while reacting vehemently against the possibility that the orthodox fathers had perpetrated 'pious frauds'; no doubt Heylyn's comments quoted above were inspired by similar considerations.[125] We can trace the development of this tension in some detail in the cases of three of the key players in the survival, re-establishment, and re-definition of the theological and intellectual identity of the episcopalian church: Henry Hammond, Herbert Thorndike, and John Pearson.

Hammond's central role in shaping the surviving church is well known;[126] his career as a religious scholar is rather less well served. Certainly he invested in the authority of the fathers as judges of scripture – and thus as central guides to doctrine and ecclesiology – in a manner that made little concession to the qualifications of previous decades, at the same time accepting Du Perron's vision of the fathers as witnesses.[127] Hammond's hugely popular *Paraphrase and annotations* on the New Testament (1653) passionately defended a philological–historical exegetical method against claims to direct illuminationism or self-interpreting scripture.[128] As part of this contextual approach he explained scores of passages as intended against the gnostic heretics who had already

[123] Quantin, 'La difficile édition princeps de l'épître de Barnabé, de Rome à Amsterdam' (2006), at 138–59; Quantin, *Antiquity*, 267–8; supplanting de Quehen, 'Ignatian controversy'.

[124] Quantin, *Antiquity*, 267.

[125] See Richard Montagu, *Analecta ecclesiasticarum exercitationum* (London, 1622), sigs. b3$^{r-v}$, and the discussion in Quantin, *Antiquity*, 147–8.

[126] Packer, *The transformation of Anglicanism* (1969) remains the fullest treatment; see also Spurr, *Restoration Church*, 10–13 for his importance. For elements of his theology, see McGiffert, 'Henry Hammond and covenant theology' (2005); Lettinga, 'Covenant theology turned upside down' (1993); Mortimer, *Socinianism*, 119–46, *passim*.

[127] Quantin, *Antiquity*, 267–73; Hardy, '*Ars Critica*', 245–51, esp. 245–6 for Hammond's disapproval of the 'pious forgeries' thesis as it had been deployed by David Blondel.

[128] Henry Hammond, *A paraphrase, and annotations upon all the books of the New Testament* (London, 1653), 'A Postscript Concerning New Light, or Divine Illumination' (separate pagination), esp. I, IV–VI.

appeared during the apostolic period. An anecdote – perhaps late – tells of how Ussher and others feared to approach Hammond because he would 'deafen them with constant and annoying talk of the gnostics'.[129] This approach immediately involved Hammond with the history of philosophy, for he could show – more fully than predecessors who had made similar interpretative claims – the contextual meaning of specific anti-gnostic passages. Paul had warned Titus to avoid 'foolish genealogies' (Titus 3:9) and Irenaeus had begun his anti-gnostic work with a reference to them; Hammond could elaborate by explaining that these were derived from a mixture of philosophical, especially Pythagorean, demonology and *askesis* and the genealogies of the Gods in theogonic poetry like Orpheus.[130] Gnosticism – with its programme of abstinence from marriage and meat – was a strange mix of Pythagoreanism and Judaism, designed to appeal to both Hebrews and gentiles during the period of persecutions.[131]

Although he defended his approach as inspired by the fathers' own exegetical methods, there can be little doubt that Hammond was hugely indebted to Grotius's *Annotationes*. Grotius had spent even longer explaining the Greek philosophical background to the 'genealogies' attacked by Paul.[132] And yet, Hammond's approach was far more reductionist than that of the Dutchman. For, example, where Grotius supposed 2 Thess. 2:3–12 to refer partly to Caligula and partly to Simon Magus, Hammond insisted – via a rather stretched reading – that the whole passage referred to Simon.[133] There were several reasons for this move. First, it allowed him to push much further the position taken by Grotius on the identity of antichrist, known by modern theologians as 'preterism': the references were not to the papacy, but to the contemporary enemies of the early Christians. It is no coincidence that it is in Hammond's essay 'de Antichristo' in his *Dissertationes quatuor* (1651) that he most developed the gnostic reading. By this point this had strong anti-puritan implications; it also touched on the history of philosophy, as both Grotius

---

[129] The earliest version that I know of is in Stephen Le Moyne, *In varia sacra notae et observationes* (2 vols, Leiden, 1685), II, 598 ('Non quod Omnia ad Gnosticos trahenda existimarim, quod operoso molimine contendebat olim Hamondus, unde olim Usserio & aliis doctos debebat ludibrium, qui illo accedente se vereri Ludentes significabant, ne illis aures obtunderet frequenti & importuna Gnosticorum memoria'). Le Moyne might have heard the story from William Sancroft, with whom he was in contact (e.g. Bod. MS Tanner 29, fol. 6ʳ). Ironically, it was Ussher who inspired Hammond's historical work of the 1650s by communicating to him the attacks on Ussher's Ignatius by David Blondel: Packer, *Hammond*, 37–8.

[130] Hammond, *Paraphrase*, 690a–91a (on Coloss. 2, cross-referenced to 1 Tim. 1:4), 725a (on 1 Tim. 1:4, cross-referenced to Titus 3:9).

[131] Hammond, *Paraphrase*, 692b; Hammond, 'De Antichristo', in *Dissertationes quatuor quibus episcopatus jura ex S. Scripturis & Primaeva Antiquitate adstruuntur* (London, 1651), 5: 'Licere temporibus persecutionum, aut Judaismum aut Gentilismum simulare, dogma Gnosticum'.

[132] Grotius, *Annotationes in NT*, II, 693.

[133] Ibid., II, 677–83; Hammond, 'De Antichristo', 25–33.

and Hammond saw the second beast of Rev. 13 as representing the Pythagorean magic practised by opponents of Christianity like Apollonius of Tyana.[134] Second, Hammond's focus on the gnostics allowed him to elevate patristic authority. A famous passage from the lost history of Hegesippus (quoted in Eusebius) stating that the Church only remained virginal until the death of the last apostle was often quoted by Reformed writers to condemn arguments from patristic tradition; Hammond could now argue that Hegesippus was referring to the corruptions introduced by the gnostics, against which both the apostles and the fathers were bulwarks.[135] More specifically, it allowed him to defend such contentious patristic texts as the Epistle of Barnabas, recently (1642) published by Ussher: Barnabas's allegorical language was explicable as an attack on gnostic interpretations of biblical passages, 'also mystically and cabbalistically interpreted'.[136]

Hammond did not seem to see that arguing that the 'orthodox' and the 'heretics' had spoken the same philosophical–mystical language was a dangerous game to play; others would be more perceptive.[137] He believed that this method would be particularly useful against the pretences of the Socinians, who were 'contrary to the *doctrine* or *practise* of the *first ages* of the *Universal Church*, upon this one presumption of preferring their *own reason*'.[138] This belief that the Socinians were ahistoricist rationalists would inform a great deal of Anglican scholarship, as we shall see. But Hammond himself never

---

[134] Grotius, *Annotationes in NT*, I, 1051–3; Hammond, *Paraphrase*, 971b–2a; Hammond, 'De Antichristo'. For Hammond as follower of Grotius in this regard, see van den Berg, 'Grotius' views on antichrist and apocalyptic thought in England' (1994), esp. 176–7; *Heaven upon earth* (2006), 152–5; Brady, *The contribution of British writers between 1560 and 1830 to the interpretation of Revelation 13.16–18* (1983), 157–64. For the politico–ecclesiological backstory, see Milton, *Catholic and Reformed*, 93–127.

[135] Eusebius, *Hist. eccl.*, III.32.7–8; Quantin, *Antiquity*, 70–1, 272; Henry Hammond, *A continuation of the defence of Hugo Grotius, in answer to the review of his annotations* (London, 1657), 35–6.

[136] Hammond, 'De antichristo', 22–3: 'Et, ut id obiter dicam, *Apostoli Barnabe*, quae non ita pridem prodiit, *Epistola*, ex hoc uno *Gnosticorum* charactere, commodè explicari poterit, alias (ut complicatum, & prolixum aenigma) certissimam lectoribus *crucem* factura. Isti quippe *Simonis* affectae γνῶσιν, i.e. *Scriptura sacrae mysticè* interpretandae facultatem sibi arrogantes, multa *veteris Testamenti mysteria* ad impuros usus suos accommodabant ... Hinc *Barnabas* hâc ferè universâ *Epistolâ* suâ, *veteris Instrumenti* loca quamplurima *mysticè* etiam, & *cabalisticè* exposita ... *Gnosticorum* doctrinis opponit'. For Barnabas, see Backhouse, *The editio princeps of the Epistle of Barnabas* (1883).

[137] Whether Hammond read Petau's *Theologica Dogmata* is unclear: after being charged with following his ecclesiological doctrines by Sheldon, he only admitted to reading in the late 1630s Petau's controversial works as attacked in Walo Messalinus [i.e. Claude Saumaise], *De Episcopis et Presbyteris contra D. Petavium Loiolitam dissertatio prima* (Leiden, 1641), i.e. Petau's *Dissertationum ecclesiasticarum libri duo* (Paris, 1641): see Hammond's letters to Wren of 14 and 21 October 1651, in N. Pocock, 'Illustrations of the state of the church' (1850), 293–5.

[138] Henry Hammond, *A letter of resolution to six quaeres, of present use in the Church of England* (London, 1652), 31–2 (in the essay 'Of the way of resolving controversies, which are not clearly stated and resolved in the Scriptures', the most overt statement of his principles).

developed such a defence, understandably focusing on issues of ecclesiology and the nature of the church. As far as he was concerned, the biblical λόγος was explicable by the מימרא דיי of the Targums; the term must have been in long use among the Jews, and thus its presence in Gospels other than John's and in Plato: no surprise that the pagan neoplatonist Amelius cried, 'This barbarian is of our Plato's opinion, that the word of God is in the order of principles' upon reading the beginning of John's Gospel.[139] We have already met this conclusion in Maldonado, but it had recently been powerfully restated by Grotius, almost certainly Hammond's source.[140] As we shall see, it was very popular. For Hammond, it also informed his anti-Calvinism, allowing him (at least in private) to question Calvin's *autotheos* theory: the Judaeo–Platonic trinity of the Targums and the ante-Nicenes was far more subordinationist (without being Arian) than the hyper-equal persons sharing the same essence of the Calvinists.[141]

Nonetheless, it can hardly have brought total relief to base one's defence for the key dogma of Christianity on late Jewish texts. The Socinians Martin Ruar and Guilielmus Vorstius had already (1646) devoted a whole learned work to arguing for the incompatibility of *logos* language with Jewish writings, especially the Targums.[142] In England, Anthony Wotton had questioned the trinitarian reading as early as 1611.[143] John Owen – much happier to defend the doctrine of the trinity on the basis of scripture and Reformed scholasticism – argued that Grotius's admission of Platonic vocabulary, use of Philo, and reliance 'only' on the Targums would promote Arianism.[144] This was all very well if one could fall back on Reformed scholasticism – as Owen could – but for patristically minded theologians it was a disastrous conclusion: as Owen no doubt intended it to be. The more critical scholarship delineated the Platonic vocabulary of early Christianity, the more the supposed

---

[139] Hammond, *Paraphrase*, 203a–b, commenting on 'ὑπηρέται τοῦ λόγου' in Luke 1:2 (cross-referenced at John. 1:1, 293). The reference to Amelius's statement is only found in Christian sources: Eusebius, *Praep. Ev.*, XI.19; Theodoret, *Graecarum Affectionum Curatio*, 2; Cyrill, *Cont. Jul.*, 8. Mortimer, *Socinianism*, 128 claims that Hammond 'began to undercut the theological reasoning which underpinned the doctrine of the Trinity as laid out in the Church's Creeds': this seems far too strong: Hammond, after all, believed that John's primary purpose was 'To demonstrate, and declare the *divinity of Christ*' (*Paraphrase*, 4).

[140] Grotius, *Annotationes in NT*, I, 849, mentioning the 'innumerable examples' ('exempla ... innumera') of the term in the Targums. See also Hammond, *Continuation*, 18.

[141] See his letter to Matthew Wren, 10 Jun 1651, in N. Pocock, 'Illustrations of the state of the church' (1849), 292–3.

[142] [Martin Ruar and Guilielmus Vorstius?], *Disceptatio de verbo vel sermone Dei, cujus creberrima fit mentio apud paraphrastas chaldaeos Jonathan, Onkelos & Thargum Hierosolymitanum* ([Amsterdam], 1646). I follow the attribution of authorship in Knijff et al., *Bibliographia Sociniana* (2004), 95.

[143] Lim, *Trinity*, 291–2.

[144] John Owen, *A review of the annotations of Hugo Grotius, in reference unto the doctrine of the deity, and satisfaction of Christ* (Oxford, 1656), 15–17.

*logos*-language of the Targums became essential proof of the divine origins of that vocabulary.

For episcopalians, Hammond's works became a model of a confident histor-ical approach to scripture and questions of controversial theology. Herbert Thorndike – a veteran of the defence of episcopacy and conformist scholarly programmes (he was in charge of the Syriac portion of Walton's polyglot) – defended an even stronger patristically grounded position in works published on the eve, and during the first decade, of the Restoration.[145] On the issues that concern us, there are some clear similarities with Hammond. Directly citing him, Thorndike pointed out in his massive *Epilogue to the tragedy of the Church of England* (1659) the dependence of gnosticism on Pythagorean–Platonic philosophy and magic.[146] Philosopher-magicians were therefore one of the groups to whom the title 'antichrist' could be applied.[147] This answered any possible objections to patristic authority made on the authority of the passage from Hegesippus.[148] Paul's warning to the Colossians thus targeted the Platonism and Pythagoreanism that inspired gnosticism.[149] The encounter with philosophy was central to the identity of both the apostolic and the ante-Nicene church.

Unlike Hammond, however, Thorndike also attempted to explain how 'orthodox' trinitarianism could be shown to have withstood that encounter by meeting head-on the case made both by antitrinitarians[150] and Du Perron and Petau. Stressing the limits of private scriptural interpretation, however ration-alist, Thorndike insisted that against Socinians 'we must have recourse to that

---

[145] For Thorndike's ambiguous status among fellow episcopalians, and thus unjustified valorisa-tion by the Oxford Movement, see Spurr, *Restoration Church*, 395. The fullest study is Miller, 'The doctrine of the Church in the thought of Herbert Thorndike' (1990). Quantin, *Antiquity*, 352–66 is essential for his patristics.

[146] Herbert Thorndike, *An epilogue to the tragedy of the Church of England* (London, 1659), 'Of the covenant of grace' (separate pagination), 91. See also 84–5, 154, 218; 'The lawes of the Church', 291.

[147] Thorndike, *Epilogue*, 'Covenant of grace', 84–5. See also Thorndike, *The right of the Church in a Christian state* (London, 1649), 'A Review' (separate pagination), CLXVI–CLXVII. Thorndike was certainly not as dogmatic as Hammond about the gnostic hypothesis, even if he followed his preterism. See Thorndike, 'The Reformation of the Church of England better than that of the Council of Trent', in *The theological works of Herbert Thorndike* (6 vols, Oxford, 1844–56), v, 502–16, esp. 513 for references to Hammond and Grotius.

[148] Thorndike, *Epilogue*, 'Of the principles of Christian truth', 174–5; 'Covenant of grace', 82.

[149] Thorndike, *Epilogue*, 'Covenant of grace', 85.

[150] Lim, *Trinity*, 134–42, suggests that Biddle was Thorndike's main target, on the basis of the identification in the nineteenth-century Tractarian edition of his works. In reality, Thorndike admitted to deriving most of his knowledge of Socinian doctrines – specifically those of Johann Crell – from Johannes Botsaccus's *Anticrellius* (Danzig, 1642) ('Covenant of grace', 121–2). This work was well enough known in England to be suggested as recommended reading in [Thomas Barlow?], *A library for younger schollers: compiled by an English scholar-priest around 1655*, eds., A. DeJordy and H. F. Fletcher (Urbana, 1961), 47.

which the most ancient Fathers of the Church ... have taught us'.[151] Scholastic method was out of the question (an obvious dig at the Calvinists), and Thorndike even cited Petau to the effect that patristic testimony was incompatible with the 'stiffness' of the schoolmen; elsewhere he carefully admitted his own subordinationism, clearly implying his rejection of Calvinist *autotheos*.[152]

Yet he knew that Petau had also argued that the ante-Nicenes had strayed into Arianism 'out of a desire to reconcile the faith, with the doctrine of *Plato* and his followers'.[153] Thorndike's response was twofold. Like Heylyn and Hammond before him, he turned to Grotius's Targum-based thesis, even going so far as to suggest that Philo and the Essenes may have been Christians after all, Scaliger and the subsequent fifty years of scholarship notwithstanding. He also added references to the *logos*-language of the apocryphal *Book of Wisdom*, arguing that the fathers thus sought to 'reconcile ... with the rule of faith' the *logos* traditions of Judaism, and 'not the doctrine of Plato'.[154] Unsurprisingly, Thorndike had to labour hard to explain why a non-canonical book of the Hebrew Bible was central to Christian dogma, especially when Grotius had already argued that the *Book of Wisdom*, while written by a post-Ezra Jew, had been translated by a Christian who supplemented it with Christological doctrine; even Jerome had long ago mentioned the possible ascription of it to Philo.[155] Thorndike's second anti-Petau argument was even more involved. Even 'if his opinion be admitted', Thorndike countered, 'there will remain evidence enough for the tradition of faith; even in their [i.e. the fathers'] writings, whose skill in the Scriptures goes not the right way to maintain it'.[156] This, claimed Thorndike, was enough to drive a wedge between 'the learned Jesuit' and Du Perron: where the latter claimed that 'we hold

---

[151] Thorndike, *Epilogue*, 'Covenant of Grace', 90.

[152] Ibid., 117, 120: 'it cannot be denied, that the Sonne and the holy Ghost, though honoured with the titles, works, attributes, and worship of God, are neverthelesse expressed and signified by the Scriptures, as depending upon the Father, and as something of his, namely his Sonne and his Spirit, though the same God also neverthelesse ... Nor let any man think, that there is any danger of *Arrius* his heresie in all this'.

[153] Ibid., 125.

[154] Ibid., 125, 115 (directing the reader to 'those things, which *Grotius* upon the beginning of S. *Johns* Gospel, (whereof hitherto I maintaine the true meaning) and upon other Texts which I have imployed to that purpose, hath observed out of the Chaldee Paraphrase, *Philo* the Jew, and others of that nation, besides diverse Heathen Philosophers, whose sayings, otherwise ungrounded, seem to come from the sense of that people'); and 'Principles of Christian truth', 227 (on Philo, directly citing Grotius for the congruence between his *logos* and that of John); 'The lawes of the Church', 369–70 (on Essenes being Christians).

[155] Grotius, *Annotationes ad VT*, III, 35; Jerome, 'Preface to the Books of Solomon', *Vulgate*. See further Runia, *Philo*, 331–2. For Thorndike's answer, see *Epilogue*, 'Principles of Christian truth', 214, claiming that such *apocrypha* were used as catechistical literature for prospective converts from Judaism, on the authority of ps.-Athanasius, *Synopsis Scripturae Sacrae* (Thorndike does not give a specific reference, but he was surely thinking of 2: Ἐκτὸς δὲ τούτων εἰσὶ πάλιν ἕτερα βιβλία τῆς αὐτῆς Παλαιᾶς Διαθήκης, οὐ κανονιζόμενα μὲν, ἀναγινωσκόμενα δὲ μόνον τοῖς κατηχουμένοις ταῦτα· Σοφία Σολομῶνος ... ' [*PG*, 28, 287]).

[156] Thorndike, *Epilogue*, 'Covenant of grace', 125.

the Faith of the holy Trinity originally, from the decree of the council of *Nicaea*, and from that authority of the Church which maintaineth it', Petau's developmental story was compatible with the true 'reason whereupon that decree was grounded and made: That is, from the meaning of the Scriptures expressed and limited by the Tradition of the Church'.[157] Some of the fathers – especially Origen – had expressed themselves incautiously, but this was not to derogate from true tradition; nor was the use of new technical vocabulary at Nicaea a sign that the meaning of that vocabulary was not held by the ante-Nicenes.[158] Origen – whose works Thorndike planned to edit – had not even espoused his opinions publicly.[159] The church could not introduce new doctrines, only clarify old ones.

Structurally, these arguments were not new (although they had not previously been applied to this issue in this way).[160] But it was precisely such claims that Petau's contextualist argument was designed to negate, and to separate his position from Du Perron's was fundamentally to miss the point. Thorndike displayed a deliberate disregard for historical differences in theological language – 'I do not understand why I should make any more of this difference of language … [that] was on foot in the ancient Church about the terms of *hypostasis*, in the blessed Trinity'[161] – but Petau's work had been based precisely on a historical positioning of theological terms in philosophical context. Indeed, Thorndike opened himself up to charges of hypocrisy, for he was quite happy to make subtle and sophisticated linguistic comparisons when he was claiming Platonic origins for the 'heretical' doctrines of the gnostics.[162] By the time Thorndike came to restate his principles in Latin in 1670, he completely reconsidered the grounds on which patristic authority was based, placing it in the position held in the church by any father, rather than on their status as witnesses. 'He thereby got rid of a number of embarrassing objections, but paid for this by having to exclude from his definition of Fathers most ante-Nicene writers.'[163] There can be little doubt that this move – which pushed Thorndike even further from any standard Reformed position – was taken

---

[157] Ibid.

[158] For Origen: Thorndike, 'Principles of Christian truth', 93; 'Covenant of grace', 69, 121; for terminology: 'Covenant of grace', 128–9, 155.

[159] Thorndike, *Epilogue*, 'Principles of Christian truth', 168; 'Covenant of grace', 127, 128. Thorndike's manuscripts towards an edition of Origen, partially acquired through Isaac Vossius and partially collated from exemplars owned by Patrick Young, are Trinity College, Cambridge, MSS B.7.4, B.8.10, B.9.10–11; see Mandelbrote, 'Vossius and the Septuagint', 86 n. 7, 89; Thorndike to Sancroft, 18 Dec 1657, BL MS Harl. 3785, fol. 38$^{r-v}$; Grant, 'Erasmus' *Modus orandi deum*, Origen's *De oratione*, and Cambridge Trinity College MS 194 (B.8.10)' (1998).

[160] Athanasius, *Ad Afros Epistola Synodica*, 6 for the use of non-scriptural terminology (cited in this regard at Thorndike, *Epilogue*, 'Principles of Christian truth', 189); Vincent of Lérins, *Commonitorium*, 28 for the distinction between private opinions and church doctrine; p. 463 above for Jerome on continuity despite linguistic differences.

[161] Thorndike, *Epilogue*, 'Covenant of grace', 161.

[162] Thorndike, *Epilogue*, 'The lawes of the Church', 291.     [163] Quantin, *Antiquity*, 362.

partly with Petau's challenge in mind.[164] Thorndike was the last of the great Anglican patristic scholars to deny entirely Petau's case for philosophical intermingling in early Christian theology.

The level of pressure exerted by Petau's findings is evident in the work of an even better patristic scholar than Thorndike, John Pearson, as we can see from the relevant part of his very popular *Exposition of the Apostles Creed*, first published in 1659. Pearson's 1672 refutation of Daillé on the Ignatian epistles would make him a hero of episcopalian patristics, and we have already encountered his fascination with the pagan philosophers who opposed Christianity while appropriating some of its key doctrines.[165] This fascination also manifested itself in the *Exposition*.[166] On the trinity, though, Pearson was far more hesitant to make such comparisons. As was by now becoming standard among episcopalian divines, he rejected – at some length, and explicitly on the authority of the 'Ancient Fathers' – Calvin's thesis of Christ being of his own essence.[167] Remarkably, he finished a long note on the term ὁμοούσιος with the phrase 'De voce ὁμοούσιος, vide *Dionys. Petau*. De Trinit.'.[168] This invocation of Petau in an anti-Calvinist argument was justified, but it raised the question of the Jesuit's case against the ante-Nicenes. This Pearson only answered briefly in another note on John 1:1. He resorted, as had his predecessors Hammond and Thorndike, to Jewish precedent, pointing to the many instances of מימרא דיי in the Targums and in the *Book of Wisdom*, and even to the translation of one of the Hebrew names of God, 'El Shaddai' (אל שדי), into 'λόγος' in some copies of Ezekiel 1:24 in the Septuagint. The last was a particularly dubious argument, as the additional 'φωνὴ τοῦ λόγου' appears only in the Codex Alexandrinus, and not in other versions, including the Codex Vaticanus, which was the basis for the Cambridge edition (1665) prefaced by Pearson himself.[169] That Philo used λόγος, Pearson continued, was thus not a sign of pagan philosophical influence but of Jewish prefigurement of Christ: 'Nor ought we to look on *Philo Judaeus*

---

[164] See e.g. Herbert Thorndike, *De ratione ac jure finiendi controversias ecclesiae disputatio* (London, 1670), 240.

[165] 2.2 above; Quantin, *Antiquity*, 340–1.

[166] See e.g. John Pearson, *An exposition of the Apostles Creed* (London, 1659), 103 on the 'later Philosophers' who 'though rejecting Christianity, have reproved those of the school of *Plato*, who delivered as the doctrine of their Master, an eternall Companion, so injurious to the Father and Maker of all things', and 108–9 n., on their schooling with Ammonius, whose consistent Christianity Pearson affirms against Porphyry. See also 'Lectiones de Deo et Attributis' [1661], in *Theological works*, I, 104. In Pearson's lifetime, further editions of the *Exposition* were published in 1662, 1669, 1676, and 1683, with many further editions after.

[167] Pearson, *Exposition*, 56–75 (quotation from 56), 269–71.       [168] Ibid., 270–1.

[169] Ibid., 233–4, n. See *Η Παλαια Διαθηκη κατα τους εβδομηκοντα. Vetus Testamentum Graecum ex versione Septuaginta interpretum. Juxta Exemplar Vaticanum Romae editum* (Cambridge, 1665), 352; Pearson's preface is 1–19, separate pagination. Despite this, Pearson continued to use the evidence until the end of his life: see *An exposition of the Creed ... the fifth edition, revised, and now more enlarged* (London, 1683) (this is the last edition to which Pearson contributed), 118.

in this as a *Platonist*, but merely as a *Jew*, who referres his whole doctrine of this λόγος to the first chapter of *Genesis*. And the rest of the *Jewes* before him, who had no such knowledge out of Plato's School, used the same notion'. 'We have no reason to believe', Pearson concluded, that '*S. John* should make use of any other Notion, then what they [i.e. the Jews] before had'; the pedagogical use of the Targums was prevalent in the first centuries, 'which undoubtedly was the cause why *S. John* delivered so great a mystery in so few words, as speaking unto them who at the first apprehension understood him'.[170] Unlike Hammond and Thorndike, Pearson accepted Scaliger's conclusions about the *Hellenistae* as Greek-speaking Jews.[171] However, the Jewish component in the defence against Petau had become so important that acknowledging the full extent of Philo's Hellenism had become too dangerous.

### 6.4     Two early radicals: Hobbes and Beale

Episcopalian divines attempted to adopt the conclusions of Casaubon and Petau while stripping them of their more dangerous features. Anti-episcopalians, as we have seen, tended to undermine patristic authority in favour of Reformed scholasticism. Yet the dangerous possibility existed that both patristic *and* modern theological authority could be rejected as 'philosophical'. This step was of course taken by many civil war and Interregnum critics of university learning, but it found historical exposition in two figures who stood at the margins of recognised intellectual groups: Thomas Hobbes and John Beale.

We have met already Hobbes's historically grounded distaste for Aristotelian essentialism and metaphysics (4.2); before *Leviathan* (1651), these fleetingly manifested themselves in vague complaints against scholastic theology.[172] In the English *Leviathan* these complaints were solidified, the historical target becoming the medieval universities and their modern successors, which 'mingled' Aristotelian metaphysics 'with the Scripture' as part of the deliberate programme of upholding the Roman Catholic kingdom of darkness.[173] But in additions to chapter 46 and the Appendix to the Latin *Leviathan* (1668), as well as repudiating the very peculiar doctrine of the trinity he had developed in the

---

[170] Pearson, *Exposition*, 233–4, n. From the second edition onwards, Pearson added the testimony of Origen, *Cels.*, II.31 reporting that Celsus was told by a Jew that Christians consider the Son of God as the *logos* in an inappropriate fashion, only for Origen to reply that he had never heard any Jew acknowledge the Son of God to be the *logos*. Pearson speculated that Celsus's Jew 'did speake the language of Philo', but that between the time of Celsus and Origen (Pearson estimated 'threescore years') the Jews had 'learnt to deny that notion of λόγος that they might with more colour reject S. John' (*An exposition of the Creed ... the second edition, revised and enlarged* (London, 1662), 130, n.).

[171] Pearson, 'Lectiones in Acta Apostolorum', *Theological works*, I, 344–7.

[172] See the examples in Malcolm, 'General introduction', in Malcolm, I, 47–8.

[173] Hobbes, *Leviathan*, 371; see also 379 (=Malcolm, III, 1076, 1098). See most fully Serjeantson, 'Hobbes'.

English version,[174] Hobbes developed a much fuller account of the philosophical corruption of Christianity, one largely consistent with those offered in the *Historical narration concerning heresie* (1680) and the poetic *Historia ecclesiastica* (published 1688, completed 1671).[175] Of the many thousands converted by the apostles, Hobbes argued, a large proportion were the philosophers who dominated the intellectual world of the Greek-speaking parts of the Roman Empire, the largest part of whom were Aristotelians. These philosophers 'embraced the faith in such a way that, as half-baked Christians, they did not abandon the dogmas of their own masters, retaining those which in some way or other they could reconcile with Christian doctrine'.[176] This was the origin of 'heresies' – the word derived from the Greek term for philosophical sects. Most of these concerned the divinity of Christ: John's Gospel was already written against them. Although Hobbes believed that the philosopher-converts' rhetorical skills gained them high position in the church, he was careful to say that only that which was later defined as heresy had philosophical roots.[177] The Council of Nicaea was called to resolve these debates: 'it briefly summarised the orthodox faith out of the Scriptures themselves, taking no account whatsoever of Greek philosophy ... For at that time most of the Fathers were not philosophers'.[178] Yet the problems began in the next centuries, with attempts at further exposition of the Creed: most specifically, the word ὑπόστασις (*hypostasis*) was introduced, suggesting three substances in the godhead.[179] The word was originally Aristotelian and one of the main culprits for its introduction was Athanasius, although the much later John Damascene is also a favourite target for Hobbes, undoubtedly because of his

---

[174] Hobbes, *Leviathan*, 267–9 (=Malcolm, 776–8). For varying interpretations, see Wright, 'Hobbes and the economic trinity' (1999); Mitchell, 'Luther and Hobbes on the question: who was Moses, who was Christ?' (1991); Warner, 'Hobbes's interpretation of the doctrine of the trinity' (1969).

[175] For the context behind the theological developments of the Latin *Leviathan*, see Malcolm, 'Introduction', 154–8, 179–83 and 195 for a an important characterisation of the nature of the Appendix added there and of Hobbes's theology more generally ('Where Hobbes's unorthodox theology is concerned, it is hard to escape the conclusion that he wrote as he did for one compelling reason above all: he believed that what he wrote was true'), which undercuts the old debate about Hobbes's sincerity (a useful introduction to the recent state-of-play in which can be found in Rose, 'Hobbes among the heretics' (2009)).

[176] Hobbes, *Latin Leviathan*, 316 (=Malcolm, III, 1063–6); Hobbes, *An historical narration concerning heresie and the punishment thereof* (London, 1680), 4; Hobbes, *Historia Ecclesiastica*, eds. and trans., P. Springborg, P. Stablein, and P. Wilson (Paris, 2008), 354–7.

[177] Hobbes, *Historical narration*, 5–6, 4; *Latin Leviathan*, 316, Appendix, 347–8 (=Malcolm, III, 1063–5, 1194).

[178] Hobbes, *Latin Leviathan*, 316–17 (=Malcolm, III, 1065); Appendix, 344 (=Malcolm, III, 1184); the germ of this idea is already in *Leviathan*, 347 (=Malcolm, III, 996). Although see the more negative view of Nicaea at *Historia ecclesiastica*, 368–9.

[179] Hobbes, *Latin Leviathan*, 317 (=Malcolm, III, 1067–9); Appendix, 341–2, 345–6 (Malcolm, III, 1178, 1188); *Historical narration*, 12–13.

overt Aristotelianism.[180] As Aristotelianism – with its abstracted essences – further infiltrated into the church, it gave birth to all the superstitions of Roman Catholicism.[181]

Hobbes's narrative is, in some senses, strikingly conservative. First, he is incredibly polite about the ante-Nicenes and the Nicenes, absolving them of any blame for the philosophical corruptions that destroyed Christianity. Second, he lays all the blame at the feet of the Aristotelians. There is no evidence for the claim that Hobbes held Platonism equally responsible.[182] He considered 'ὑπόστασις' an Aristotelian term even though there is a great deal more evidence for similarity between the Christian usage and that of the neoplatonists. Even more spectacularly, he unequivocally defended both the Johannine λόγος and the Nicene ὁμοούσιος as purely biblical terms, despite their clear Platonic affiliations.[183] The enemy was always Aristotelianism, and Hobbes even suggested that Paul's warnings against philosophy were directed against the Peripatetics.[184] This is supported by Gianni Paganini's finding that Hobbes's key source may have been Lorenzo Valla, who had been the first to condemn as scholastic nonsense the use of the term '*persona*' to represent a

---

[180] For *hypostasis* as an Aristotelian term, see Hobbes, *Latin Leviathan*, Appendix, 330–1 (=Malcolm, III, 1148). Malcolm suggests (1149, n. j) that Hobbes might have been thinking of 'καθ' ὑπόστασιν' in ps.-Aristotle, *De mundo*, 395ᵃ29–30. For Athanasius and John Damascene, see Hobbes, *Latin Leviathan*, Appendix, 360 (=Malcolm, III, 1228–9); *Historical narration*, 8 and esp. 13–14, where it is suggested that Athanasius's banishment by Pope Liberius was the result of his use of '*hypostasis*'. See also *Historia ecclesiastica*, 382–3. Contemporary theological pedagogy certainly used Damascene on these issues: see e.g. CUL MS Add. 4364 ('Tractatus de essentia et attributis Dei', 1652–5), fol. 9ʳ.

[181] Hobbes, *Latin Leviathan*, 320 (=Malcolm, III, 1083–4).

[182] As made in Springborg, 'Introduction' (2008), 184–200. Prof. Springborg does not provide any examples of Hobbes attacking Platonism in this way, instead depending on a strange definition of almost all sixteenth- and seventeenth-century Greek scholarship as 'Platonist' and a subsequent insistence that this hyper-reified 'Platonism' must have been Hobbes's target. But as well as the evidence presented above, see the clear statement in *De corpore*, sig. A3ʳ: 'Nati illis temporibus Ecclesiae (post Apostolis) Doctores primi, dum fidem Christianam contra Gentes ratione naturali defendere conabantur, coeperunt Philosophari etiam ipsi, & placita nonnulla ex Philosophorum Ethnicorum Scriptis Scripturae Sacrae Placitis admiscere. Et primo quidem dogmata admiserunt nonnulla ex *Platone* minùs noxia. Deinde verò etiam ex libris *Physicae Ausculationis*, & *Metaphysicorum* Aristotelis multa inepta & falsa assumentes, Fidei Christianae quasi introductis hostibus arcem prodiderunt'.

[183] Hobbes, *Latin Leviathan*, Appendix, 331–2 (=Malcolm, III, 1150–2), defending ὁμοούσιος as derived from John 1:1, 3 and the Johannine 'Word' as derivable from the Old Testament. The second claim is particularly puzzling, as Hobbes claims that 'often in the Old Testament we read, instead of "what God promised was done", "the word of God which he spoke was done"' – I cannot see what Hobbes might be referring to here. At *Historical narration*, 8, Hobbes claims that in Gen. 1, 'God is said to create every thing by his sole Word' and 'that Christ was that Word, and in the beginning with God, may be gathered out of divers places of *Moses, David*, and other of the Prophets'. These claims are so vague that it is tempting to assume that Hobbes had been influenced by the material gathered by Grotius and others from the Targums without fully understanding it, but I have found no direct evidence for this. See also the mitigated defence of 'ὁμοούσιος' language at ibid., 7–8.

[184] Hobbes, *Latin Leviathan*, 320 (=Malcolm, III, 1081).

divine 'substance'.[185] As well as being attacked by Petau, Valla's account was dismissed by Cheynell, who as we have seen embraced Reformed scholasticism in favour of any supposed ante-Nicene consensus; conversely it was praised by Courcelles.[186] There is thus no reason why Hobbes might not have been familiar with it. However, he completely failed to take the next step that Petau's scholarship forced everyone at least to contemplate: considering the Platonism of the ante-Nicenes. Of course in another sense Hobbes's account was extremely radical, in that it claimed that some of the fathers shared his doubts about immaterial substances, which he also presented as a post-Nicene Aristotelian intrusion.[187] All in all, this was an idiosyncratic account that stood to the side of developments in contemporary scholarship: as far as I can tell, it had no direct influence at all.

No less idiosyncratic – albeit much more private – were the claims of John Beale, known now as a member of the Hartlib Circle and later as an active member of the Royal Society.[188] Beale had studied at Eton, falling under the influence of the irenicist John Hales and of the headmaster Sir Henry Wotton; he later claimed that it was Wotton's influence that pulled him away from the Reformed scholasticism to which he had become addicted. He then proceeded to King's College, Cambridge where he became a Fellow between 1632 and 1640, departing for the sinecure rectorship of Sock Dennis in Somerset – whether his religious or philosophical views had much to do with this departure

---

[185] Paganini, 'Hobbes, Valla and the trinity' (2003).

[186] Cheynell, *Divine triunity*, 68; Courcelles, 'Praefatio', sig. \*\*\*2$^v$; for Petau, see Paganini, 'Trinity', 206. Prof. Paganini insinuates that Hobbes might have been familiar with Petau, as does Richard Tuck ('The civil religion of Thomas Hobbes' (1993), 133–4) but all the evidence points either to the contrary, or at least to the fact that Hobbes fundamentally misunderstood or misused him. Prof. Springborg is so determined to have Hobbes drawing on Petau that she has him reading the 1700 edition of the *Theologica dogmata* – a distinctly unlikely turn of events, given that Hobbes died in 1679 ('A very British Hobbes, or a more European Hobbes?' (2014), 373).

[187] Hobbes, *Latin Leviathan*, 186 (=Malcolm, III, 622), an addition in the Latin on the corporeity of angels, claiming that 'some of the most eminent of the ancient Fathers thought they were corporeal, and some others that they were incorporeal'. Malcolm (623, n. v) suggests a possible source to be John Damascene's claim that angels were immaterial in comparison with man, material in comparison with God (*Exp. fid.*, II.3). Early modern scholars also speculated more widely: Pierre-Daniel Huet suggested in the same year as the Latin *Leviathan* appeared that Origen had held corporeal angels: see his *Origeniana* in Ὠριγενους ... *Origens in Sacras Scripturas commentaria* (3 vols, Rouen, 1668), I, 69. See also *Latin Leviathan*, 316 (=Malcolm, III, 1063–5) (Tertullian's corporealism); Appendix, 360 (=Malcolm, III, 1228–9) (the Nicenes did not use 'incorporeal'; it was introduced by Christians such as the 'Aristotelian philosopher' John Damascene, overtly against Tertullian).

[188] The key studies – albeit with some old-fashioned assumptions – remain those of M. Stubbs ('John Beale, philosophical gardener of Herefordshire, part I' (1982) and 'Part II' (1989)). They are now supplemented by Lewis, 'John Beale's art of memory and its uses' (2005); Goodchild, 'John Evelyn, John Beale and Backbury Hill, Herefordshire' (1991); Leslie, 'The spiritual husbandry of John Beale' (1992); and Poole, 'Two early readers of Milton' (2004), at 77–88 (where much new manuscript evidence is collected). See also Webster, *Great instauration*, 230–1, 478–82.

from Cambridge remains unclear.[189] Similarly ambiguous is his position during the civil wars, to the extent that he was accused of both royalism and
Independency; at some point he developed a complex illuminationist asceticism after going up Buckbury Hill and receiving 'Holy Inspirations' which he
could not write down because when he 'offerd to write pimples would visibly
arise on the backe of my hand, & if I ceasd not pres[en]tly, become a very sore
teter', a condition which lasted for a year spent in meditation and fasting.[190]

In the late 1650s, Beale sought a religious settlement even more minimal
than the Apostles' Creed.[191] In the context of the Interregnum and the irenicism
of the Hartlib Circle this was not particularly striking: more remarkable is
Beale's historical vision of early Christianity, and specifically the role of
philosophy in that history. Beale showed himself much more up-to-date on
matters of early church history than Hobbes, admitting to reading not only
Grotius and the Socinians but also the Hebraist works of Hugh Broughton and
recent texts like William Dell on the history of baptism (1648) and Hammond's
*Annotations*.[192] His views come out most strongly in a letter denying the
efficacy of infant- and water-baptism to Lady Ranelagh. After producing
several patristic authorities demonstrating that infant baptism was an indifferent rite, practised by some and not by others, Beale concluded:

I will not enlarge to shewe in what traduct of time these Elements of water (yea & in
many places of fire also w[th] equall pretence of Authority) of bread & wine, were by all
writers extolld in such high straines, & soe applyed to altars & Sacrifices as if it were the
stratagem thereby to entice all Gentiles by p[a]rcells of their owne rites & Customes to
p[ro]fesse Christianity ... Some will think it more plaine dealinge to acknowledge
that when Emperours, Kings & Princes, all their Armyes & dominions professed
Christianity, as a matter in fashion, then their chiefe Comandrs & Favourites being

---

[189]  Stubbs, 'Beale I', 467–75 gathers a large amount of relevant evidence.
[190]  John Beale to unknown, 28 November 1659, HP 60/1/3A.
[191]  Beale to Hartlib, 26 March 1659, HP 51/102A. Beale claimed that he had been taught 'the
        difference of the Apostles preaching fro[m] ours' by a sermon by the puritan antiquary
        Richard James (1591–1638), which we can identify as that printed as *A sermon ... concerning
        the Apostles preaching and ours* (London, 1630) (Beale to Hartlib, 14 Aug 1658[?], HP 31/1/
        27A). Another important source for Beale was the *De pace et concordia Ecclesiae* (n.p., 1628)
        (I have consulted the 1630 Amsterdam edition) by the Socinian Samuel Przypkovius (see Beale
        to Hartlib, 14 Dec 1658, HP 51/41B, where Beale ascribes it to 'John Graserus', probably
        because of a prefatory quotation from a biblical commentary by Conrad Graserus (see *Pace*,
        sigs. A5[r–v]). For the identity of the author, see *Bibliographia Sociniana*, 89). The book was
        readily available in England: in December 1654, Parliament called in two men found selling the
        book, committed one to the custody of the Serjeant-at-Arms, and referred the book to the same
        committee considering Biddle's works ('The journal of Guibon Goddard, Esq. M.P.' [21 Dec
        1654], in *The diary of Thomas Burton, Esq. Member in the Parliaments of Oliver and Richard
        Cromwell, from 1656 to 1659* (4 vols, London, 1828), I, xcciii–cxxv. It was erroneously
        ascribed to John Hales by Wood (*Ath. Ox.* III.413)).
[192]  Beale to Lady Ranelagh, undated (*c.* 1658), HP 27/16/3B–4A; Beale to Hartlib, 26 Jan 1656,
        BL MS Add. 4365, fols. 365[v]–366[r]. See also Beale to Hartlib, 16 Feb 1657, HP 62/24/1A for
        his attentive reading of Selden.

made Bishops & Presbiters, brought in a souldierlike, & Gentile Theologie consisting either of Platonicall & other Philosophicall raptures or of disputable Creeds carried by faction canvesse Sophistry & vote, rather then fitted for simple faith & true Sanctitie.[193]

The dogmatism enshrined by alliance with secular authority, combined with the conversion of pagan philosophers, led to the destruction of the faith. Yet philosophical intermingling undermined the whole enterprise of deriving any patristic 'orthodoxy':

And for those primitive fathers whose authority is soe much claymed & boasted, this I have many yeares agoe undertaken & demonstrated, that all our authenticall confessions as well of Protestants as of Papists, are spun of such a fine thread of new distinctions as will utterly exclude all these old fathers, soe that if they must be called fathers, the fathers & children are very much unlike each other . . . as in the point of baptisme . . . soe in many others of those logicall points w^{ch} are now in a severe & high straine called fundamentall they totally differ in Judgemt w^{th}out breach of affection or communion. True that when they get y^e secular sword on their side, & about the 4th Century they began to divide excomunicate <curse> & murder one another as we now doe . . . yea for 300 yeares together, w^{ch} are undoubtedly the purest times of the Gospell that have yet appeared, we find them [to] differ very much at least very far from all nationall confessions, in the high points of the holy trinity, of the state of the Soul after death, of Prædestination, Freewill & (to omitt particulers) from the maine body of our positive Theologie. Some were wholy for inspiracions as Tertullian & Origen, some were for Platonicall Ideas & raptures as Sinesius, & other semi-christian Philosophers, some soared aloft in the high straines of eloquence as Chrisostome & Nazianzene, some stood more strictly to close reasonings as Iustine y^e Martyr, & Clemens of Alexandria, yet in their severall wayes & <w^{th}> severall opinions they held firmer to y^e bonds of unity & to the substance of Sanctitie then wee doe.[194]

Beale was thus not only looking for 'the simplified piety which he so admired in the early Fathers'.[195] Rather, he held what was in many ways a much more sophisticated vision of the history of early Christianity than Hobbes, who still believed in (or at least wrote of) a 'pure' scriptural ante-Nicene Christianity battling against 'philosophical' heresies and defeated by a 'philosophical' post-Nicene orthodoxy. Beale, on the other hand, accepted that from an early stage Christians had held a huge variety of conflicting philosophical views, and celebrated that they had been allowed to do so before the civil power usurped Christian liberty. At the same time, this brought in more pagans, so that 'the Government was partly gentile, partly christian', with the political consequence that 'Collonells & Captains were Bishops & Presbyters, And the whole lawe of the Westerne christians was a mixeture betweene Roman called Civile, & chris-tian', ultimately leading – 'for shame' – to the foundation of Canon Law.[196]

---

[193] HP 27/16/9B–10A.    [194] HP 27/16/12A–B.    [195] Stubbs, 'Beale I', 477.
[196] Beale to Hartlib, undated (c. 1659), HP 62/7/1A–3B.

The complexity of Beale's historical vision of the political–intellectual developments in the early church is evident from a letter to Hartlib of September 1658, written upon Beale's reading of what must have been one of the first copies of Henry More's *Immortality of the soul* (1659). Recounting how he had been moved to consider the doctrine after reading Pomponazzi and the Socinians, he set about 'to examine the first Christian writers', finding in them 'a generall swarving from our received opinion', their 'Platonicall phansyes' leading to belief either in 'a kind of Pyrgatory', or 'severall kinds of Elysian groves', or 'psychopannychia', or 'other kinds of bodyes in the Resurrection'. The political lesson was clear: 'from this diversity of judgemts, it would bee hard for a generall Councell to take up a peremptory result, That the Immortality of the Soule, was in those first ages receivd for an Article of fayth'. Yet the truth of the doctrine was not sacrificed, for 'wee of the Westerne World, before wee became christian, did from Druides, & Bards, & other such Priests, Poets, & philosophers more incline to the subsistence of separated Soules, than the Inhabitants of the Easte'; thus 'Wee doe to this day outrun many of the Easterne & Greeke churches in apprehending the holy Texts, & true philosophy to import the Immortality of the Soule, according as wee have rec[eive]d it from our Auncestors in an over-spreading Tradition'.[197]

In other words, the history of philosophy revealed not only the confusions of the early church, but also that on some issues the ancient pagan sages had a better knowledge than the early Christians. Beale had conducted what he perceived to be 'a very diligent inquiry into the Wisedome of the Easte',[198] which he associated in particular with the 'gymnosophisticall philosophers, w[ch] were most mighty in deedes, most p[er]fect in operative philosophy, adorned by all poeticall inspirations carried into these quarters of the world by Druides & Bardes'. The putative content of this philosophy was a full-out pantheism that Beale compared to the ideas of Robert Fludd: 'God is substantially present in all the operations of every creature wth a speciall or essentiall residence in man. And by the same inference, wee may apply the Vnction or reall & presentiall operation of Christs spirite in Christians'.[199] Beale carefully differentiated this from the enthusiasm of sects like the Quakers; amazingly, he considered his views compatible with the naturalistic explanations for 'enthusiasm' recently proposed by Meric Casaubon. Whether illuminationist episodes were all 'naturall' or indeed 'divine revelations' was mere 'logomachy, a verball controversy', for 'the visite of Angells, or the possession of Satain is as natural, as the gusts of the Winde', due to the constant presence of God's 'anoinitng Spirite . . .

---

[197] Beale to Hartlib, 27 Sep 1658, HP 51/21A–22A.
[198] Beale to Hartlib, 28 May 1657, HP 25/5/1A–12B.
[199] Beale to Hartlib, 28 Jan 1659, HP 51/65A. See also the mix of admiration and caution about Fludd in Beale to Hartlib, 21 Dec 1658, HP 51/52B–53A.

in his holy people'.[200] Casaubon would have been horrified to find his work used in this way (and probably even more horrified to learn that Beale considered himself the successor of an irenic lineage that ran: Erasmus, King James I, Isaac Casaubon).[201] Beale believed that the early Christians had been ignorant of this tradition of eastern wisdom, themselves not even knowing Hebrew.[202] Rather, its manifestation was to be found in the great opponent of the primitive church, Apollonius of Tyana, about whom Beale is remarkably positive.[203] Scholarship and esotericism had come together to create the most radical account of Christianity's encounter with philosophy written in seventeenth-century England.

## 6.5    Platonism, monasticism, and enthusiasm in the early church

Had they been published, Beale's ideas would have shocked many, even if they lacked the historical detail to have constituted a serious challenge to patristic 'orthodoxy'. The latter could not be said of two antitrinitarian works published on the continent. The first was the *Irenicum Irenicorum* (1658) by Daniel Zwicker, a German physician and committed antitrinitarian who moved to Amsterdam in 1657.[204] Zwicker followed Petau's analysis of the Platonic-subordinationist proto-Arianism of the ante-Nicenes,[205] but he differed fundamentally from both the Jesuit and from all previous Socinians in attributing the invention of trinitarianism to the Platonically inspired gnosticism of Simon Magus and his followers. It was a pupil of Simon who had forged the neo-Platonic *Orphica*, which fooled Justin Martyr – whose 'knowledge and love of Platonic philosophy' made him so keen to provide a false philosophical lineage

---

[200] Beale to Hartlib, undated, HP 62/7/1B–2A. See also the praise for Casaubon's work (i.e. *A treatise concerning enthusiasme*) in Beale to Hartlib, 14 Aug [1658?], HP 31/1/29A, 34A. For his interest in the interpretation of prophetic dreams, see further Stubbs, 'Beale I'. For his quasi-pantheism, see further Leslie, 'Spiritual husbandry', 158–62. See also Beale to Hartlib, 23 Dec 1656, HP 31/1/7A–8B for his extreme dislike of Quakers.

[201] Beale to Hartlib, 23 Nov 1658, HP 51/37B ('Erasmus, King James, Learned Casaubone, & (when they please,) the most iudicious of Protestants & Romanists can agree in it, That a shorter or at least as short a symbole, as y$^t$ w$^{ch}$ is called Apostolicall, may suffice for the building up into saveing fayth').

[202] Beale to Hartlib, 21 June 1657, HP 25/5/24B. Beale's stated source is Petrus Cunaeus, but this was a commonplace.

[203] Beale to Hartlib, 28 May 1657, HP 25/5/10B; Beale to Hartlib, 21 June 1657, HP 25/5/24B. The threat of Apollonius had been rekindled by the positive treatment in Bodin's *Colloquium Heptaplomeres*: see Oldenburg to Hartlib, 27 Aug 1659, *Oldenburg correspondence*, I, 307. On Bodin's work, see Malcolm, 'Jean Bodin and the authorship of the *Colloquium Heptaplomeres*' (2006).

[204] Bietenholz, *Daniel Zwicker* (1997) is very thorough.

[205] Petau is the first authority cited in the historical section: [Daniel Zwicker], *Irenicum irenicorum, seu reconciliatoris Christianorum hodiernorum norma triplex, sana omnium hominum ratio, Scriptura Sacra, & traditiones* ([Amsterdam], 1658), 14.

for Christian truth – into developing a speculative *logos*-theology.[206] Zwicker discovered a 'true', non-trinitarian and non-philosophical primitive Christianity in the early Judaeo-Christian sects, the Ebionites and Nazarenes, evidence for whom was available only in the heresiological works of Irenaeus and Epiphanius, who had both aligned them with Simon's disciple Cerinthus.[207] The general seventeenth-century recognition of the Jewish component of early Christianity had rekindled interest in these figures, including in England, but it was certainly Zwicker's works that brought them greatest attention.[208] (These works were also no doubt popularised by the zealous response of Comenius, who abandoned all his irenicism and supported persecuting Zwicker.)[209] More shocking must have been Courcelles's claim, made from Arminius's theology chair in Amsterdam a year after *Irenicum* was published, that the book contained 'irrefutable testimonies and arguments'.[210]

An alternative use of Petau was made by the German Arian Christoph Sand in his *Nucleus historiae ecclesiasticae* (1669, augmented edition 1676). Sand had visited Oxford in 1664 to work in the Bodleian and college libraries on patristic research for the book.[211] He happily accepted the Platonism of the ante-Nicenes, presenting the Arians as inheritors of a true Platonic tradition stretching from Moses through Pythagoras, Plato, and Philo. It was the gnostics who introduced the concept of ὁμοούσιος, which was taken up by heretics like

---

[206] [Zwicker], *Irenicum*, 15–17 ('Platonicae Philosophiae cognitio & amor'). The Orpheus idea has its germ in Petau, *Theologica dogmata*, II, 31–2. For Orpheus's key role in previous syncretist narratives, see Walker, 'Orpheus'. Zwicker hedged his bets, also claiming that the ante-Nicenes all held the Father to be superior to the Son: as Bietenholz points out, Zwicker 'fails to harmonize his two conflicting theses' (*Zwicker*, 65, and 55–78 for Zwicker's patristics more generally). Another short summary is Mulsow, 'The trinity as heresy' (2002), at 164–6.

[207] Zwicker, *Irenicum*, 73, 109–16. They had already been briefly evoked in this fashion by Servetus: Friedman, 'The myth of Jewish antiquity' (1994), 41.

[208] Thorndike, *Epilogue*, 'Covenant of grace', 88 had already suggested that St John must have met Ebion in the bathhouse, rather than Cerinthus, as reported in Epiphanius, *Panarion*, I.30.24, because Cerinthus flourished in Galatia (*Panarion*, I.28.6). Cheynell, *Socinianisme*, 1–2 commented on earlier Socinians' refusal to align themselves with the Ebionites, referring specifically to Christoph Ostorodt (*c.* 1560–1611). F. Stanley Jones, hagiographising Toland, wrongly refuses to acknowledge Zwicker's importance: 'The genesis, purpose, and significance of John Toland's *Nazarenus*' (2012), 96, n. 21 – this piece is whiggish and, apart from pointing out errors of transcription, adds little to the key study of Toland on this score: Champion, 'Introduction' (1999).

[209] Johannes Amos Comenius to Johann Ludwig Wolzogen, in *De quaestione utrum Dominus Jesus* (Amsterdam, 1659), 45–71; see further Bietenholz, *Zwicker*, 79–104.

[210] Etienne de Courcelles, *Quaternio dissertationum theologicarum* (Amsterdam, 1659), 118 ('Si quis autem forte dubitet an revera antiqui Doctores ita crediderint, ut dico, de Patris praecelentia in Deitate, consulat libellum nuper editum sub titulo *Irenici Irenicorum*, ubi istud irrefragibilibus testimoniis & argumentis demonstratum inveniet').

[211] Wood, *Fasti*, II.280; Mulsow, 'Intertextuality and cultural exchange in late Socinianism' (2005), 55–7 (speculating on contact between Sand and the vaguely defined 'Cambridge Platonists', but offering no evidence); Quantin, *Antiquity*, 342–3.

Sabellius and Paul of Samosata and then approved at Nicaea in an undignified attempt to defeat Arianism.[212]

The eve of the Restoration meanwhile witnessed the re-emergence of another patristic problem: Origen. Indeed, the years 1658–62 have been described as an 'Origenist moment', which included William Spencer's Cambridge edition of *Contra Celsus* (1658), Henry More's *Immortality of the soul* (1659) and *Explanation of the grand mystery of Godliness* (1660), and the works of More's students: George Rust's *Letter of resolution concerning Origen* (1661) and Joseph Glanvill's *Lux orientalis* (1662).[213] The first of these, it should be noted, does not really deserve to be aligned with the other works on this list. It was produced primarily to correct the mistakes in the previously available translation, that of Sigismund Gelen. There is no sign that the translator, William Spencer (d. 1714), a fellow of Trinity College, had any contact with More's circle. He *was* encouraged by Thomas Smith, a colleague of More's at Christ's and the translator of Daillé.[214] But neither Smith nor Spencer showed any inclination towards More's pseudo-'Cabbala' or other outré philosophical speculations. Indeed, Spencer explicitly commented on Origen's heresies, including Pythagorean metempsychosis and his implicit condemnation at Nicaea for holding a quasi-Arian position.[215] All this stemmed from Origen's failure to realise that God's revelation had rendered the mingling of pagan philosophy with theology unnecessary, a realisation that would have saved more than three hundred years of heresy and disputation.[216]

---

[212] Christoph Sand, *Nucleus historiae Ecclesiasticae* (3 pts, [Amsterdam], 1669), I, 192–3. The Council of Antioch (269) had condemned Paul of Samosata's use of ὁμοούσιος, much to the embarassment of the post-Nicenes (e.g. Athanasius, *De synodis*, III.45).

[213] Hutton, 'Henry More and Anne Conway on preexistence and universal salvation' (1996), 113; Hutton, 'More reads the Bible', 194. For Glanvill, see now, with much extra documentation, Lewis, 'Glanvill', esp. 274–6 for Rust's very probable authorship of the anonymous *Letter*.

[214] Thorndike to William Sancroft, 18 Dec 1657, BL MS Harl. 3783, fol. 175ʳ, reporting on his refusal to supply Spencer with his Origen manuscripts despite the entreaties of Smith (this letter was first noted in Haugen, *Bentley*, 53–4). I do not consider *Origen against Celsus: translated from the original into English by James Bellamy, Gent* (London, n.d.) because although assigned to 1660 by the ESTC (and followed in this by Lewis, 'Glanvill', 274 n. 33), the edition is clearly an early eighteenth-century one (e.g. Johann Ernest Grabe is cited at 9): I strongly suspect the date is 1709, just like ESTC R32215.

[215] William Spencer, 'Ad lectorem', in Ὠριγενης κατα Κελσου … *Origenis contra Celsum libri octo. Ejusdem Philocalia* (Cambridge, 1658), sig. *3ʳ. Spencer is simply following Jerome, *Epist. 84*: 'For the council which condemned Arius would surely have condemned Origen too'.

[216] Spencer, 'Ad lectorem', sig. *4ʳ: 'Nimirum deterrebat multos illud magnum & evidens, quod in Origene praecesserat, humanae temeritatis ac divinae castigationis exemplum. Hic enim cùm de mysteriis à Deo Ecclesiae suae revelatis, nullâ necessitate, solâ differendi cupiditate, per Platonicae & Aristotelicae Philosophiae principia, quibus elimatus erat, in libris illis Περί αρχών latiùs disputare voluisset, omnes penè errores, quibus Ecclesia per trecentos & ampliùs annos afflicta fuit, Arianos, Macedonianos, Photinianos, Pelagianos, Deo audaciam perse-quente, accuratè praeformaverat'. Indeed, Spencer was here only plagiarising Cornelius Jansen, *Augustinus seu doctrina S. Augustini de humanae naturae sanitate,*

Spencer, who became rector of Thurnscoe in Yorkshire in 1663, said that he prepared the edition for no reason other than to fill his *otium* while he held no public office.[217] There was nothing strange about editing a patristic author one partially disagreed with: Thorndike, after all, was planning an important edition of Origen despite having no time whatsoever for More's dabblings in Origenist heterodoxies like the pre-existence of the soul.[218]

More and his followers, meanwhile, stuck doggedly to the claim that Origen was an interpreter of a Mosaic Cabbala, and saw no problems in placing him in a genealogy including Pythagoras and Plato, and in More's case an arbitrary host of others, including Aristotle.[219] More claimed that Origen was 'the greatest Light and Bulwark that antient Christianity had'; Glanvill that pre-existence was universally held by all the Jews of Christ's time (he could bring as examples only Philo and Menasseh ben Israel) and that its popularity was only obscured by the later triumph of Aristotelianism.[220] These statements could stem only from utter ignorance of patristic scholarship. They were confined solely to More's circle, having nothing to do with any wider 'Cambridge Platonism': Culverwell, for example, condemned Origen for following Plato's opinions on the soul, as if he 'had scarce read *Genesis*'.[221] Only Rust attempted an original historical argument, claiming that Pythagoras, Plato, and Origen had actually rejected animal metempsychosis and referred to it only allegorically, an argument based on the dubious authority of the obscure Pythagorean Timaeus of Locri.[222]

This obsession with pre-existence stemmed from an extreme anti-Calvinism and consequent desire to defend God's goodness. More, however, also felt that his work was useful against Socinianism, specifically by showing that 'it is very highly improbable that the *Fathers* borrowed the Mystery of the *Trinity* from the School of *Plato*'.[223] This is a sentiment he had espoused as early as 1653,

---

*aegritudine, medicina adversus Pelagianos & Massilienses* (3 vols, Rouen, 1652 [1st edn=Louvain, 1640]), II, 5 (new pagination).

[217] Spencer, 'Ad lectorem', sig. *4ᵛ; *Alum. Cantab.*, IV, 134.

[218] p. 474 above. Spencer's *anti*-Platonic attitudes were recognised by others: see e.g. Daniel Whitby, *Certainty of Christian faith*, 362, n. 61 to ch. 10.

[219] Henry More, *Immortality*, 245–52; [Joseph Glanvill], *Lux orientalis, or, an enquiry into the opinion of the eastern sages concerning the praeexistence of souls* (London, 1662), sigs. B2ᵛ, 2–3, 33–4, 48–9, 115; Glanvill to [Rust?], in Lewis, 'Glanvill', 293; [George Rust], *A letter of resolution concerning Origen and the chief of his opinions* (London, 1661), 45–6, 104–5. More had held the view as early as his *Philosophical poems* of 1647 (see there, 255–81).

[220] More, *Immortality*, 248; Glanvill, *Lux*, 52–6.

[221] Culverwel, *Light of nature*, 88–9. See also Dockrill, 'The heritage of patristic Platonism in seventeenth-century philosophical theology' (1997), 64.

[222] [Rust], *Origen*, 54–5. No reference is given, but Rust must have been thinking of the passage available in *On the nature of the world and the soul*, ed. and trans. T. H. Tobin (Chico [CA], 1985), 73; for Renaissance editions, see Hankins and Palmer, 50.

[223] More, *Mystery of godliness* (London, 1660), 7. More met Christopher Crell in 1662, and was unimpressed by Socinian reasoning: More to Anne Conway, 5 July 1662, 29 Aug 1662, in *Conway letters*, 203–4, 207–8.

perhaps suggesting a familiarity with the work of Petau.[224] Yet More was prepared to entertain the idea that the fathers had adopted Platonic notions:

> Admit that the ancient Fathers were *Platonists*, and brought the Mystery of the *Trinity* into the Church of the Christians, it does not straight follow That it is therefore a *Pagan* or *Heathenish Mystery: Pythagoras* and *Plato* having not received it from *Pagans* or *Heathens*, but from the learned of the *Jews* ... the *Jews* themselves in long succession having received it as a Divine Tradition.[225]

As we have seen, this last point was a common argument, but rather than relying on the Targums, More turned to his favourite Philo.[226] Given these constant concessions to Platonic sources, it is little surprise that another of his followers, Anne Conway, deviated far closer to the position of Sand.[227] More was once again proving himself an amateur who offered more to the opponents of the Church he belonged to than to its defenders.

But even if he was particularly clumsy at doing it, More was articulating the same dilemma that faced much better patristic scholars: embrace the Platonism of the fathers and the historical, apologetic, and confessional benefits that it might bring, or reject it from fear of the subsequent threat to ante-Nicene authority. A further dimension was added when the issue became a component of the most important rhetorical move made by the Restoration church: the positioning of itself as a *via media* between popery and puritanism. The first scholarly step in this direction was taken by Meric Casaubon in his *Treatise concerning enthusiasme* (1655), a denunciation of pretended claims to divine inspiration as explicable naturally, especially as symptoms of melancholy;[228] we have already encountered Beale's spectacular misappropriation of Casaubon's argument. In the third chapter, 'Of Contemplative and Philosophicall Enthusiasme', Casaubon discussed how the 'sublimity both of [Plato's] matter and language' led not only Plato, but even his readers, to 'infatuation'; this included 'some also that made profession of Christianity': thus the fine line between his use by both orthodox fathers and heretics.[229] A specific problem was the idea of a mystical union with God: Casaubon claimed that Plato himself had not adumbrated such views directly but had his doctrine transformed into this position by the 'enthusiastick *Arabs*' like Averroës and, much more importantly, by exponents of a mystical theology like pseudo-Dionysius the Areopagite.[230] Using the edition of the *Corpus*

---

[224] More, *Conjectura Cabbalistica*, sig. A4ᵛ. In a volume of correspondence between More and Henry Hirn there are some notes on Petau's *Theologica Dogmata*, although they are neither in More's nor Hirn's hand (CUL MS Gg.6.11.F, fol. 43ʳ).

[225] More, *Mystery*, 9.        [226] Ibid., 12.

[227] Anne Conway, *The principles of the most ancient and modern philosophy* [1690] (Cambridge, 1996), 10, 23–7, 30–2; see the comprehensive account in Hutton, 'Platonism and the trinity: Anne Conway, Henry More and Christoph Sand' (2005).

[228] On Casaubon, see 2.2, 5.2 above. Casaubon's naturalist critique of enthusiasm is most fully discussed in Heyd, *Enthusiasm*, 72–92 which for the most part ignores the scholarly dimension.

[229] Casaubon, *Enthusiasme*, 52–3.        [230] Ibid., 110–12.

*Dionysiacum* recently published by the Jansenist Charles Hersent, Casaubon pointed out the Platonic elements of its doctrine of mystical union, concluding that 'We find nothing of it . . . in the Gospel of Christ; nothing in ancient Fathers of greatest antiquity'.[231] However, the idea must have been present among pre-Dionysius Christians, because some passages by the Greek bishop Synesius (*c.* 373–414), himself an enthusiastic Platonist, seemed to oppose it.[232]

This was an original reading; even more important was Casaubon's treatment of Maximus the Confessor (*c.* 580–662), whose monasticism and allegorical approach to scripture Casaubon ascribed to his Platonic enthusiasm.[233] In the first edition Casaubon suggested that this philosophy was of use for Jesuits and Calvinists who wanted to stir up kings into a zealous religious frenzy; he also suggested that it lay behind the visions and mystical experiences of a Parisian Carmelite nun that had recently received the approbation of several highly placed French Catholic ecclesiastics, including Cardinal de Bérulle.[234] In the second edition he made an important polemical addition: this divinity, that 'hath its origine from heathen Philosophers', has infected 'a new generation of men, that are called *Quakers*'.[235] The idea that monasticism had pagan philosophical origins was a long-standing one in Protestant polemic,[236] but Casaubon used the latest scholarship on late antique neoplatonism to refine and develop it, and to add Protestant sectarianism to the list of targets.

Casaubon was too good a scholar to believe that he could remain silent on the possibility that Platonism had infected orthodoxy as well as having fathered monasticism and enthuasiasm – he certainly read Petau's Epiphanius and it is difficult to imagine that he did not at least know of the *De trinitate* too.[237] He must also have known that this was one of the greatest challenges to the

---

[231] Ibid., 112–13, drawing on C. Hersent, ed., *In D. Dionysii areopagitae de mystica theologia librum* (Paris, 1626). Casaubon also mentioned his familiarity with the *Theologia mystica seu contemplatio divina religiosorum a calumniis vindicata* (Mayenne, 1627) by the Jesuit Maximilien Sandeus, another defence of the Dionysian method (see Le Gall, *Le mythe de Saint Denis* (2007), 210). Casaubon himself planned to publish 'a Discourse De cultu Dei spirituali, sive per intellectum' (*Enthusiasme*, 111–12).

[232] Casaubon, *Enthusiasme*, 116–17, quoting Synesius, *Dio*, 7.

[233] Casaubon, *Enthusiasme*, 125–30.

[234] Ibid., 124 ('As for her expressions, of Christs drawing her soul into his, and the like; so agreeable, in effect, to those of the *Platonists*, and *Arab* Philosophers . . . I have no suspicion for all that, that she was acquainted with them'). The text was Madeleine de Saint-Joseph, *La vie de soeur Catherine de Jésus* (Paris, 1628) (Casaubon said that it was this work that spurred him to write *Enthusiasme* in the first place (sigs. [¶6]ʳ–[¶8]ʳ)).

[235] Meric Casaubon, *A treatise concerning enthusiasme . . . the second edition: revised, and enlarged* (London, 1656), 173–4.

[236] See esp. Rudolf Hospinian, *De monachis, hoc est de origine et progressu monachatus, ac ordinum monasticorum* (2nd edn, Zurich, 1609 [1st edn=1588]), sig. 2ᵛ, followed in England by e.g., Lancelot Andrewes, *A learned discourse of ceremonies retained and used in Christian churches* (London, 1653), 19–20.

[237] The earliest reference to Petau's Epiphanius is in Meric Casaubon, *A discourse concerning Christ his incarnation* (London, 1646), 27.

ante-Nicene theology to which the Church of England – and he himself – was now claiming to subscribe.[238] Plato, he wrote in 1670, 'hath been stiled by some, the *Patriarch of Heretiks*' and recently used 'to corrupt and adulterate true Christianity' (no doubt this was yet another swipe by an orthodox divine at More's experiments with pre-existence) yet he had been used extensively by the early fathers.[239] 'For any man ... to say, that neither *Plato*, nor his Interpreters, in their discourses about the three principles, or causes (such as are produced out of them, by the antient Fathers, and Writers)' thought about the trinity thus had to be proved a 'bold and groundless assertion'.[240] But in that case, how to save the fathers from the charge of Platonising, and to explain Plato's possession of the mystery in the first place? One solution – adopted by the fathers themselves – was to claim that he derived it from the Jews, but, aware which way the scholarly tide was turning on this issue (Ch. 3 above), Casaubon affirmed that there was little proof for this: it was hardly easy, for example, to prove the *Book of Wisdom* 'to be of that antiquity'.[241] Only one solution remained: 'either *St John* had read *Plato*; or *Plato St John*: or, because the first is as ridiculous to conceive, as the second is impossible ... both had it (as of the one we are sure) from Divine Revelation'.[242] This seems utterly remarkable: was the son of Isaac Casaubon – the great destroyer of syncretism – asserting separate pagan revelation?

But by 'revelation' Casaubon meant something very specific. God, acting by second causes, had allowed some pagans to speak Christian truths without intending it.[243] When the fathers cited Plato 'they must be favourably understood' to have spoken in the same way that the Athenians spoke of their Unknown God (Acts 17:23).[244] In his wisdom, God had arranged matters in such a way as to offer the apostles and fathers an anti-pagan weapon:

If this were not only lawful, but no small argument of wisdom in *St Paul*; how can we make less of it, then a singular providence of God, for the same progress of the Christian Religion, that so many Learned Heathens, and amongst them some, who professed greatest enmity to the truth of it; should give by their interpretations of *Plato*, whether right or wrong, such advantage to Christianity.[245]

What mattered was that the early Christians 'did verily believe, that those interpretations [of Plato] were right and true'. This sincerity was evidenced by the fact that none of the fathers' pagan–Platonic opponents ever accused them

---

[238] See e.g. his insistence on the importance of theology students reading fathers rather than schoolmen in *Of credulity and incredulity, in things natural, civil and divine, wherein, (among other things) a true and faithful account is given of the Platonick philosophy, as it hath reference to Christianity* (London, 1670), 1; see also Casaubon, *Generall learning*, 102–3.

[239] Casaubon, *Credulity* [70], 121–2.    [240] Ibid., 131–2.    [241] Ibid., 135–6.    [242] Ibid., 128.

[243] Ibid., 132–3: 'to say, that by what he [Plato] wrote, he directly, or his Interpreters, intended the Christian Trinity: there may be somewhat of just offence or scandal in that speech'.

[244] Ibid., 133.    [245] Ibid., 130.

of falsifying Plato, in contrast to the gnostics, whose forgeries were immediately noted by Porphyry and Plotinus.[246] Plato's ambiguous trinitarian comments were made not because he was a trinitarian, but so that they could be of use in the later mission to the gentiles. In fact, Casaubon added, Plato's statement that 'the just man will be crucified' (*Republic*, II.361[e]–362[a]) was genuinely prophetic, although again the philosopher had no realisation of what he was saying.[247]

This providential interpretation had its origin in Augustine's *Contra Faustum*:

If any truth about God or the Son of God is taught or predicted in the Sibyl or Sibyls, or in Orpheus, or in Hermes, if there ever was such a person, or in any other heathen poets, or theologians, or sages, or philosophers, it may be useful for the refutation of Pagan error, but cannot lead us to believe in these writers. For while they spoke, because they could not help it, of the God whom we worship, they either taught their fellow-countrymen to worship idols and demons, or allowed them to do so without daring to protest against it.[248]

It was often used as a cautious counterpart to more enthusiastic Christian claims about Plato's theological knowledge: it was already heavily present in Ficino and used by More; we have met Hyde's use of it for Zoroaster in Chapter 2.[249] But, crucially, it was also used by those much more sceptical about such narratives. Juan Luis Vives had most clearly stated it in his 1522 commentary on Augustine's *City of God*:

Many anxiously torment themselves with the question: did the philosophers have any account of the trinity? . . . In truth, the ancient philosophers, if they ever said something about it, it was so obscure, that it is better to assume that they spoke rather than understood it. For they never managed to uncover those *arcana*. It seems to have been enough for them to know the unity of God, and . . . if they said anything about the trinity it was as testimony of the faith to come, to press their own followers with the statements of the teachers [i.e. so that the pagan philosophers could be condemned by Christians out of the texts of their own intellectual forefathers].[250]

Crucially, the same providential reading of history was even accepted by Isaac Casaubon during his attack on the Sibyls and on Hermes, despite his strong

---

[246] Ibid., 130–1.     [247] Ibid., 134–41; Casaubon, *Incarnation*, 19–23.
[248] Augustine, *Faust.*, XIII.15.
[249] Allen, 'Ficino on the trinity', *passim*; More, *Mystery*, 15; 2.7 above.
[250] Augustine, *De civitate Dei libri XXII*, ed. Juan Luis Vives (Basle, 1555 [1st edn=1522]), 578b: 'Torquent se anxie permulti disputatione illa, Noverint ne philosophi rationem aliquam divinae trinitatis . . . Philosophi vero prisci si quid dixerunt quod ad hanc rem faceret, tam obscurum id fuit, ut locutos potius eos, quam intellexisse existimare par sit. Arcana enim illa nihil eis retegi attinebat, Satis videtur fuisse ad unitatem dei, & cunctipotentiam noscendam pervenisse, si quid de trinitate sunt locuti in testimonium venturae pietatis dixisse ad sectatores suos magistrorum sententia premendos' (Vives's note on x.23).

adherence to Calvin's notion that God would not have revealed the truths of the New Testament to the pagans more clearly than to the Jews:

What moves me above all is that it seems contrary to the word of God to suppose that such profound mysteries were declared more openly to the Gentiles than they were to that people whom the Most High God had a special love for and treated as his own, instructing them in his own voice and the voices of his faithful servants. Except it might be said that the Gentile prophets, like Balaam's ass, said things which they did not understand (which also Daniel, that beloved man, records happening to himself [Dan. 12:9]), not for use in the present, but so that future ages might benefit from them, partly to give witness of the eternal providence, partly to prevail in disproving the opinion of the pagans, as Augustine says in *Contra Faustum*, XIII.15. We know how tiny the sparks of truth were that shone on the Jewish people in ancient times. For the whole Law was leading the Jews to Christ, through shadowy types of future events, in the manner of a teacher, as Paul says to the Galatians [3:24].[251]

It should be made clear that this version of the argument was qualitatively different from its adoption by Vives and others: my point is only that Casaubon left open the door (albeit very slightly) for this kind of 'providential' case, which had for others (but not him) the benefit of allowing the fathers to be unwitting players in a providential game (they were citing statements deliberately scattered for them among similarly unwitting pagans by the hand of providence) without diminishing the 'critical' status of the reading: one need not accept any of the pious forgeries or defend the fathers' competence as historians to make this point.

Accordingly, some of Casaubon père's followers, while accepting his 'hard' destructive argument about syncretism, also adopted this milder providential argument for pagan foreknowledge of Christ. We can see this already in

---

[251] Casaubon, *Exercitationes*, 72: 'Ante omnia movet illud me; quod verbo Dei contrarium videtur, existimare, tam profunda mysteria Gentibus fuisse clarius proposita, quàm illi populo quem Deus Opt. Max. ut peculiariter suum dilexit, & suamet ipsius & fidelium suorum servorum voce erudiit. Nisi quis forte dicat, Gentium vates, instar asinae Balaami, ea dixisse quae non intelligebant, (quod & Daniel, vir ille desideriorum, sibi aliquando accidisse commemorat, XII.9.) non in praesentem usum, sed ut seculis post futuris illa prodessent, & post rerum eventum partim aeternae providentiae testimonium exhiberent; partim at Paganorum auctoritatem revincendam valerent, ut docet B. Augustinus contra Faustum, libro XIII. cap. xv. Nam alioqui scimus quam exiles scintillae veritatis priscis temporibus populo Judaico illuxerint. Tota enim lex per obscuros rerum futurarum typos ad Christum Judaeos deducebat, paedagogi instar, ut Paulus ait ad Galatas, III. 24'. My translation from 'What' to 'servants' and from 'We know' to 'Galatians' is taken from Hardy, '*Ars Critica*', 97, which does not include the central part crucial to us, but demonstrates the similarity with Calvin (although the comparison with the Jews is already present in the Augustine, directly after the passage from *Contra Faustum* quoted above). Casaubon mis-cited Daniel: the requisite passage is from Dan. 12.8 ('And I heard, but I understood not . . . '). Notwithstanding the evidence presented here, the contrast between Vives and Casaubon offered in Grafton and Weinberg, *Casaubon*, 34–6 still stands, although Casaubon's acceptance of the providential argument is not noted there, nor in Grafton, 'Protestant versus prophet'.

Grotius, writing specifically on Plato's proleptic references to the crucifix-ion.[252] Thus Meric was not going against his father's anti-syncretist judge-ment – moreover, he cited Vives and Grotius in support of his position.[253] The scholarly and theological pay-off was immense: it offered the apologetic argument that Plato had pre-empted Christian truth, without having to move into speculation about Cabbalistic transmission, Jewish origins, dubious texts like the *Hermetica*, or direct illumination, speculation that had long been disreputable among serious scholars.[254] For a conformist English scholar like Casaubon, this providential 'middle way' between syncretism and purely destructive arguments was particularly useful because it explained the simila-rities between Platonic and patristic vocabulary, undeniable in the wake of the work of Petau and his successors.

Both lines of Casaubon's interpretation were taken up by subsequent writers. In the *Origines sacrae* (1662), Stillingfleet explained that the similarities between Christian doctrine and the pagan neoplatonists – Hierocles, Porphyry, Simplicius – simply stemmed from their schooling by the Christian Ammonius. The neoplatonists hid the source of their knowledge so as to appear more original in their fight against Christianity – it was against this blend of Christianity and Platonism that Tertullian's comments were directed, and Stillingfleet admitted that 'Ammonius himself, and some others of the School of *Alexandria*' (no doubt Origen) 'might be guilty in this kind'.[255] This separation of the neoplatonists (who had access to the Bible) from Plato was by now a standard point, and Stillingfleet drew on the work of Holstenius.[256]

But Stillingfleet further developed this idea in a truly original direction in 1675, in a polemic against Hugh Cressy (1605–74), a former member of the Great Tew circle who converted to Catholicism in the 1640s, becoming a Benedictine monk and a self-professed exponent of a 'mystical theology' that he traced back to Dionysius the Areopagite, whom he dated to the second or third century.[257] Against him, Stillingfleet argued that not only was Dionysian

---

[252] Grotius, *Annotationes in NT*, I, 210 (on Matt. 10:38): ' … videtur mihi non sine divinae providentiae instinctu olim Plato dixisse de republica II, de vero justitiae cultore πάντα κακὰ παθὼν ἀνασχινδυλευθήσεται'.

[253] Casaubon, *Credulity* [70], 132, 135–6.

[254] Ibid., 125–6 for Plato's value compared to the forged texts of Hermes, Zoroaster, and the Sibyls.

[255] Stillingfleet, *Origines sacrae*, 500–4. The old idea that Porphyry had been a Christian before converting to paganism (the source is Socrates, *Hist. eccl.*, III.23) was more or less dead by the mid-seventeenth century, although it could sometimes crop up: see e.g. the theological discourse by J. R. [John Reading, Calvinist divine?], 'Unio veritatis' [1655], Folger MS V.a.200, fol. 20ᵛ.

[256] Stillingfleet, *Origines*, 501; see also Casaubon, *Incredulity*, 124.

[257] See e.g. Hugh Cressy, *Exomologesis, or, a faithfull narration of the occasion and motives of the conversion unto Catholick unity of Hugh-Paulin de Cressy* (2nd edn, Paris, 1653 [1st edn=1647]), 456–70 (462–3 for Dionysius, 460–1 [mispaginated 434–51] for mystical philo-sophy distinguished from 'abstruse, sublime, and Metaphoricall termes' of the 'Philosophy of

mystical theology enthusiastic, but also that it was an enthusiasm that derived from non-Christian sources, for it was far later and stemmed from the neoplatonic opponents of Christianity: Porphyry, Iamblichus, and later Proclus. Seeing that under Christianity 'the common people were become *Philosophers*', the neoplatonists developed an elitist spiritual exercise to rival the new faith, whose central idea was 'advancing the soul to highest perfection' and thereby enacting a mystical union with God.[258] This movement, based in Alexandria, had three sources. First, having studied with Ammonius, the neoplatonists adopted and adapted some Christian language.[259] Second, they took the pneumatology of Plotinus (who Stillingfleet claimed was also an opponent of Christianity), specifically his belief in a rational and a supra-rational soul, the higher of which could escape the body and achieve deiformity.[260] Third, they adopted the theurgy of the *Chaldean Oracles*, which – whenever they were written – were certainly not Christian, because Pico had an Aramaic copy.[261] The result was a doctrine of '*Deiformity* . . . being attainable by the *life* of *Contemplation*'.[262] This doctrine was undoubtedly pagan. Porphyry may have condemned theurgic rites, but this was only because he focused on the perfection of the higher intellectual soul in the belief that it could return to its divine source.[263] Iamblichus took this idea to such a peak of enthusiasm that he believed theurgy could effect levitation.[264] All this was grounded on the hypothesis of the soul's pre-existence and on opposition to Christianity, specifically the idea of Christ's incarnation, which seemed to bring

---

the Platonists'); S[erenus] C[ressy], *Fanaticism fanatically imputed to the Catholick church by Doctour Stillingfleet and the imputation refuted and retorted* (n.p., 1672), 38–9. Cressy was much influenced by the Benedictine mystic Augustine Baker (1575–1641), whose huge *Sancta Sophia: or directions for the prayer of contemplation* (Douay, 1657) he edited (see e.g. Treatise Three, 'Of prayer', 75 (separate pagination) for reference to Dionysius). On Cressy, see Steuert, 'Dom Serenus Cressy' (1948); Tavard, *The seventeenth-century tradition* (1978), 109–26; Trevor-Roper, *Catholics, Anglicans and puritans* (1987), 183–6, 220–1. Cressy's *Fanaticism* was a response to the attack on mystical theology in Edward Stillingfleet, *A discourse concerning the idolatry practised in the Church of Rome and the danger of salvation in the communion of it* (London, 1671), 325–55, where the connection with pagan philosophy is not yet made. Another of Stillingfleet's targets was O. N. [Abraham Woodhead], *The Roman Church's devotions vindicated* (n.p., 1672), all of which is a defence of mystical union with God (6 for reference to Dionysius). On Woodhead, see Slusser, 'Abraham Woodhead' (1971–81).

[258] Edward Stillingfleet, *An answer to Mr. Cressy's Epistle* (London, 1675), 110.

[259] Ibid., 109–10, 125–6.

[260] Ibid., 116–19. Plotinus never mentioned Christianity, but Stillingfleet claimed – quite reasonably – that his denial of bodily resurrection (*Enneads*, iii.6.6 – true awakening being of the soul *away* from the body) might have been an anti-Christian move.

[261] Stillingfleet, *Answer*, 125–7, 109, 111, 130. For Pico, see 2.1 above.    [262] Ibid., 114.

[263] Ibid., 111. Stillingfleet is obviously drawing on Augustine, *Civ. Dei.*, x.30 here.

[264] Stillingfleet, *Answer*, 120; Iamblichus, *Myst.*, iii.5–6. Eunapius in fact reported that Iamblichus denied rumours of his ability to levitate: Eunapius, *Vit. soph.*, 458–60 (not mentioned by Stillingfleet).

God to flesh when their aim was to escape the flesh.[265] These ideas were 'as remote from Christianity' as anything could be. Nonetheless, pseudo-Dionysius had drawn on them extensively. Here Stillingfleet did not have to work hard, for Hersent and other Catholic scholars had already pointed out the many similarities between Dionysius and the neoplatonists, claiming that the latter had drawn on the former. Like Casaubon – whom he knew and whose library he had by now acquired – Stillingfleet gladly accepted their accounts, while reversing the line of transmission.[266] Dionysius's early dating had been rejected by plenty of Catholic heavyweights – including Bellarmine and Petau – whom Stillingfleet simply listed against their co-religionists still clinging to the earlier dating. He did, however, add one powerful contextual point: the Dionysian corpus probably stemmed from the circle of the late fourth-century heretic Apollinaris, whom Nemesius among the ancients and Petau among the moderns had classified as an over-Platonising Christian for his seeming denial of Christ's bodily incarnation, and whose followers were well-known creators of forgeries.[267] The idea of human deiformity infiltrated Western scholasticism because of its congruence with the Arabic-Aristotelian notion of *intellectus agens*, worming itself into the heart of Roman Catholicism.[268] Yet it is clear that Stillingfleet also had one eye on Protestant 'enthusiasts', noting the similarity of the ideas of Jacob Böhme and the Quakers to this neoplatonism.[269]

On a scholarly level, Stillingfleet's was a powerful argument, clearly indebted to the work not only of Casaubon but also of the greatest seventeenth-century expert on the anti-Christian philosophers, Holstenius, who had done much to place them in the context of what we would now call late antique religiosity.[270] We shall find it being appropriated by far more learned scholars.

---

[265] Stillingfleet, *Answer*, 116 (an idea taken directly from Augustine, *Civ. Dei*, x.29); 127 for preexistence.

[266] Stillingfleet, *Answer*, 123–4, 129–31.

[267] Ibid., 132–3; Petau, *Theologica dogmata*, IV, 27–8. For Nemesius, Stillingfleet was simply plundering Petau, but his *De natura hominis* had also been published in a new edition by John Fell as Περι Φυσεως Ανθρωπου ... *De natura hominis ... manuscriptorum codicum collatione* (Oxford, 1671), with comments on Nemesius in the context of neoplatonic anti-Christian philosophy in Fell's 'Praefatio', sigs. A4ᵛ–[A5]ʳ and 'Annotationes', 3, 13–15, 28–9 (separate pagination). This was one of Fell's 'New Year Books': it was ready by early 1670 (Fell to Vossius, 12 March 1670, Bod. MS d'Orville 470, pp. 168–9; Gale to Bernard, 22 March 1670, Bod. MS Smith 8, fol. 131ʳ); Madan, *Oxford books* (1895–1931), III, 2891 identifies the manuscripts used. For Apollinarian forgeries, the key source is Leontius, *De sectis*, 8.

[268] Stillingfleet, *Answer*, 134. The catchiness of this idea is evident from its uptake by Evelyn: *History of religion*, I, 430.

[269] Stillingfleet, *Answer*, 32.

[270] See e.g. Stillingfleet's acceptance (115) of Holstenius's conjecture about the religious–pneumatological content of Porphyry's poem *The Sacred Marriage* (*Vita Plotini*, 15) ('Dissertatio De vita, & scriptis Porphyrii', in Πορφυριου φιλοσοφου Πυθαγορου βιος ... *liber de vita Pythagorae*, ed. L. Holstenius (Rome, 1630), 76 (separate pagination)).

As we saw in Chapter 3, John Spencer claimed that nonconformist scriptural exegesis and 'enthusiastic' individualism was grounded in Platonic allegoresis.[271] In the same year that Stillingfleet's work was published, the leading Independent divine, Robert Ferguson, was forced into offering a counternarrative. Ferguson was writing against the *avant garde* Arminian conformist William Sherlock, who, in his *Discourse concerning the knowledge of Jesus Christ* (1674) attacked as puritan enthusiasm the standard Reformed position that Christ's righteousness is imputed to the believer personally.[272] Although Sherlock had attributed the claim only to an outgrowth of scholastic error, Ferguson, in his *Interest of reason in religion* (1675) – a defence of nonconformists against claims of anti-intellectualism – responded to the Platonic genealogy for puritanism drawn up by Casaubon, whom he never mentioned by name but had clearly read, and Stillingfleet.[273] The idea that a 'person may by Philosophy and Contemplation attain such a degree of Union with God, as to know and understand things by a *contactus* and conjunction of substance with the Deity' was fundamentally different from mainstream Reformed beliefs about union with Christ: it was most evident in the 'passages which occur in *Plotinus, Porphyrius, Jamblichus*, and *Proclus*', and both Catholic mystics and Quakers had inherited it.[274] Unlike Stillingfleet, Ferguson ascribed its first foundation to Origen, who, taking it from Ammonius (whose reputation Ferguson did not defend), inspired the 'Romish *Monasticks*; I mean such of them as are called *Mystick Theologues*' and then the Familists and the radical German Protestant sect of Weigelians.[275] A follower of Owen and thus of Reformed scholastic theological method, Ferguson had no investment in the ante-Nicenes, and so could make the obvious point that Origen was just as culpable for the rise of philosophical mysticism as the pagan Platonists.[276] Indeed, the accusation could be turned directly against conformists, in an obvious swipe at More that is only further proof of how embarrassing his work was to the English Church:

---

[271] 3.6 above.

[272] William Sherlock, *A discourse concerning the knowledge of Jesus Christ, and our union and communion with him* (London, 1674). See Hampton, *Anti-Arminians*, 63–7.

[273] Sherlock, *Discourse*, 200–1 (nonconformist ideas are scholastic). That Ferguson had read Casaubon's *Enthusiasme* is clear from *The interest of reason in religion; with the import & use of scripture-metaphors; and the nature of the union betwixt Christ & believers* (London, 1675), 524, where one of the origins of deiformist philosophy is found in Theophrastus's *Metaphysics*, exactly as in Casaubon, *Enthusiasme*, 114–16 (the argument is too niche and scholarly for Ferguson to have arrived at it independently). On Ferguson, see the very full entry by Zook, 'Ferguson, Robert', *ODNB*.

[274] Ferguson, *Reason*, 524, 526.     [275] Ibid., 525–6.

[276] For his theological method, see e.g. the discussions of the trinity at *Reason*, 180–2, 475–80, and the explicit defence of 'systematic divines' at 395. Recourse to patristic authority was thus only to late judgements, e.g. the Second Council of Constantinople (504–5).

Were our adversaries impartial in their censures, the excess and exorbitancy in this particular will be found to lye among themselves. For if any be guilty of introducing a *Mystick* Theology out of *Plato* and *Proclus*, and of Allegorising the Scripture according to a pretended *Cabala*, they are the men. Nor do any else that I know of, make such Phantastical applications of Scripture to purposes distant from its own, as those who stile themselves sons of the Church of *England*, do.[277]

Elsewhere, Ferguson drew on the work of Crispo to catalogue at length the philosophical errors that had polluted the early church.[278] From the Anglican perspective, however much the scholarly recognition of philosophical corruption was proving a useful tool in anti-Catholic and anti-nonconformist polemics, preventing it from turning upon the precious ante-Nicenes was proving harder and harder.

Perhaps the clearest sense of that tension came in the invariably original, scholarly, and aggressive work of Samuel Parker. As we have seen, Parker, in his *Free and impartial censure of the Platonick philosophie* (1666), dogmatically rejected the fathers' judgements about the Judaic origins of pagan philosophy.[279] Following through on this, he similarly dismissed narratives of Platonic trinitarianism. The idea had its sources in gnostic forgeries like Hermes, pseudo-Zoroaster, and the Sibyls.[280] Ammonius was the first to fail to recognise their fraudulence and to bring them into the church, even though his pagan student Porphyry quickly spotted the impostures.[281] In fact, the neoplatonist 'trinity' had little to do with the Christian, based as it was on emanated ranks of intellectual beings to which there was even sometimes added a fourth (the human soul).[282] This Platonic Godhead had already been adopted by the gnostics, building 'such a kind of Monster, as the Picture of Mr *Hobb's Leviathan*' – here Parker cited Crispo, who was clearly a key source for him.[283]

Parker's work received enthusiastic praise from Beale.[284] Had Parker known what larger principles this shared concern about Platonism in early Christianity stemmed from, he would have been horrified. But as Beale's praise suggests, Parker's work did raise the question of whether the 'orthodox' fathers had also been infected. Rather than answer this question, Parker went down the route of Hales: the problem with heresies – indeed their very definition – was not wrong doctrine, but the desire to set up new sects and opinions. 'Though most of the Primitive Heresies were false and impious, as well as rash and ungrounded, yet that which gave them their denomination, was their vanity and tendency to create mischeivous and destructive Schismes. The way then to prevent

---

[277] Ferguson, *Reason*, 340. See also 385.
[278] Ibid., 242–6, explicitly citing Crispo's *De ethnicis philosophis caute legendis*.
[279] 3.5 above.      [280] Parker, *Censure*, 108–9.      [281] Ibid., 109–10.      [282] Ibid., 110–14.
[283] Ibid., 87–9. See also 31, 39–40 for Crispo.
[284] Oldenburg to Boyle, 8 Jun 1666, *Boyle correspondence*, III, 168; Beale to Boyle, 31 Oct 1666, *ibid.*, 260. Beale convinced Glanvill not to reply to Parker: Lewis, 'Glanvill', 287.

Controversies, and to avoid Schisms, is not to define, but silence groundless and dividing Opinions'.[285] This might seem to favour the traditional historio-graphical view of Parker as a closet Hobbesian who abandoned *jure divino* arguments in favour of the natural law case for civil authority in ecclesiastical matters.[286] This, however, is misleading.[287] Parker's magistrate had authority only over worship, not church government or essential doctrine. Christian emperors like Theodosius only protected and re-affirmed the judgement of the Nicene Council.[288] In a long and interesting discussion of the events surrounding the Nicene Council published in 1684, Parker took on Sand by attempting to divest him of Petau's scholarship. According to Parker, the Jesuit had not claimed that all the ante-Nicenes were Arians 'only because some of them Platonised too much in some Forms of Expression' – only one who reads 'Books only by skimming over Indexes and Contents of Chapters' could extract such a reading.[289] This was a fair analysis of Petau, but it still failed to address the key point that trinitarian 'orthodoxy' was not extractable from the ante-Nicenes. Parker's rather clever thesis was that the whole Nicene and post-Nicene debate was not really one between 'orthodoxy' and a heterodox Arianism – rather, it was one within orthodoxy, between a more dogmatic group and a liberal one led by Eusebius of Nicomedia, who had foolishly taken Arius into communion after his anathematisation from Alexandria, and had then continued to reject the inclusion of 'consubstantial' in the Nicene Creed partly out of linguistic caution and partly out of pride. Arius himself, it followed, was irrelevant, for he had quickly been condemned by almost universal consent.[290] This had the obvious benefit of removing the possibility of 'heretical' intrusions into tradition: all post-Nicene concessions were to the orthodox but over-liberal Eusebius of Nicomedia (it is possible that Parker saw him as equivalent to those Anglicans campaigning for a broader comprehension). But once again this was only a glancing blow at Petau's key thesis: the

---

[285] Parker, *Censure*, 90. At 91, Parker writes 'I conclude therefore in the words of a late Learned and Judicious Divine. *If the Church had stopt and damn'd up the Originals and Springs of Controversies, rather then by the determining for the one part, to give them as it were a Pipe and Conduit to convey them to Posterity, I perswade my self the Church had not suffered that inundation of Opinions, with which at this day it is over-run*'. This source for this quotation is not given: it comes from Hales's famous sermon, *Concerning the abuses of obscure and difficult places of holy Scripture* (London, 1617), 39.

[286] Parkin, 'Hobbism in the Later 1660s', 96–108; Schochet, 'Between Lambeth and Leviathan' (1993); Marshall, 'The ecclesiology of the latitude-men' (1985), 425–6 (incorrectly claiming that 'Parker ... followed Hobbes in the Restoration in making *rex sacerdos*').

[287] As demonstrated convincingly in Rose, 'Ecclesiastical polity'. But this examines only eccle-siological and not theological issues.

[288] Samuel Parker, *The case of the Church of England, briefly and truly stated in the three first and fundamental principles of a Christian church* (London, 1681), 94–5.

[289] Samuel Parker, *Religion and loyalty, or, a demonstration of the power of the Christian church* (2 pts, London, 1684), I, 364, 366.

[290] The whole story is told in great detail at 349–532: it warrants further study.

Jesuit had shown in some detail that Eusebius's vocabulary betrayed Arian sympathies and Parker had to resort to Jerome's tactic of claiming that these were only 'unwary expressions'.[291]

By the 1680s Parker had adopted an approach to the history of early Christianity that sat rather uneasily beside his remarkably critical (in both senses of the word) attitude to the fathers' own capacities as historians of philosophy and theology. He was now claiming that the fathers' belief in philosophical forgeries like the Sibyls should not undermine their authority, because those forgeries were based on real prophecies.[292] Generally, Scaliger and Casaubon had both gone too far as 'Criticks, who care very little what becomes of the truth or falshood of things, so they can shew their censuring Faculty upon words'.[293] Philo's 'Therapeutae' really were Christians, not Graeco–Jewish philosophers.[294] Parker had by this point swallowed a decade of triumphalist Anglican patristic propaganda, most notably William Beveridge's *Codex Canonum Ecclesiae primitivae vindicatus* (1678), the preface of which consisted of an attack on Daillé.[295] Beveridge was a much-respected divine who would become Bishop of St Asaph in 1704; his early scholarly work on oriental languages and chronology was also held in high esteem throughout Europe.[296] Yet in his patristic work he adopted, much more forcefully, the scepticism about Casaubon's findings on patristic forgeries and errors in Eusebius already evident in Montagu, Hammond, and Thorndike: such concessions, he insisted, would undermine the church.[297] Although he had certainly read at least Petau's edition of Epiphanius,[298] he resolutely refused to mention the Jesuit's key thesis about ante-Nicene Platonic-Arianism.

The same may be said of the work that was closest to being the 'official' Anglican response to Daillé, Matthew Scrivener's *Apologia pro S. Ecclesiae patribus* (1672).[299] Scrivener was not uncritical: for example, he accepted Casaubon's judgement about the use of pagan mystagogic language in the

---

[291] Parker, *Religion and loyalty*, 362–3.

[292] Samuel Parker, *A demonstration of the divine authority of the law of nature and of the Christian religion* (London, 1681), xxix–xxxi.

[293] Parker, *Demonstration*, 213–14, see also 215–16 for Casaubon.    [294] Ibid., xxxiv, 245–50.

[295] Quantin, *Antiquity*, 349–52.    [296] Cowie, 'Beveridge, William', *ODNB*.

[297] William Beveridge, *Codex Canonum Ecclesiae primitivae vindicatus et illustratus* (London, 1678), 131–50 (defending the authenticity of the Sibylline Oracles), 364–83 (defending Eusebius on the 'Therapeutae').

[298] Beveridge, *Codex*, 373, clearly following the argument of Petau, 'Animadversiones', in *Epiphanii ... operum omnium*, II, 53 (as already identified in *The theological works of William Beveridge*, ed. P. Bliss (12 vols, Oxford, 1842–48), XII, 247–8).

[299] Quantin, *Antiquity*, 331–9. Scrivener, a vicar of Halingfield, Cambridgeshire, seems to have been supported from an early stage by Sancroft (see Sancroft to Thomas Holdsworth, 24 Sep 1656, Bod. MS Tanner 52, fol. 192ʳ). Handley, 'Scrivener, Matthew', *ODNB* consists almost only of a list of his works.

early church.[300] But despite his preface making much of the use of patristics to oppose Socinians and those, like Episcopius and Courcelles, who had moved towards them because of their rejection of the fathers,[301] he failed to offer any coherent defence of ante-Nicene trinitarianism, or elucidate on the encounter with philosophy. When the fathers had held unorthodox philosophical doctrines, such as John of Thessalonica (d. *c.* 630) on the corporeity of angels, it was on issues on which there was no 'orthodox' church position; earlier, there had been no fixed language to discuss the issue.[302] Scrivener had read Petau, but only used him when it suited his purposes.[303]

A strange situation emerged in that it was Scrivener's nonconformist opponent who took up the ante-Nicene banner against the papists and Socinians. Henry Hickman, who had been ejected at the Restoration, wrote against Scrivener to defend nonconformist scripturalism, mostly by simply echoing Daillé. But even he now admitted that ante-Nicene testimony was important to the fight against antitrinitarianism, specifically referring to the work of Sand.[304] It was clearly with some irony that he noted that such a task would be 'well worthy Mr. *Scriveners* pains, if he be so well versed in the ancient Fathers as he makes shew'.[305] Hickman's own ideas did not go much further than claiming that Origen's Arian-sounding passages could be excused in one 'who wr[ote] so much, and in great haste', an idea and approach he clearly took from Estwick, whom he cited.[306] As we have seen, this was no longer sufficient; moreover it

---

[300] Matthew Scrivener, *Apologia pro S. Ecclesiae patribus, adversus Joannem Dallaeum* (London, 1672), 110–11.

[301] Ibid., sigs. a3$^r$–[a4]$^v$.

[302] Ibid., 160: 'Nec multum dissimile erit responsum ad simile reprehensionem Veterum, docentium, Angelos esse Corporeos, juxta Joan. Thessalonicensem Episcopum. Primò enîm, Nihil hâc in quaestione definitum invenimus ab Ecclesia. Dein, Est res potius Philosophiae quam Fidei ... Verbis enim & loquendi formulis licentia neganda non est, quam quaevis aetas delegerit. Placuit autem priscis Philosophis, aeque ac Christianis, quodlibet subsistens & in rerum natura permanens, *Corpus* nuncupare'. This is a response to Daillé, *Traicté*, 411–13 (=*Treatise*, II, 109).

[303] Scrivener, *Apologia*, 136 (citing the *Theologia dogmatica* for the idea that to understand a father one needs to see what he said consistently, not just at individual points); and 196–7 for use of Petau's Epiphanius. See also Scrivener, *A course of divinity, or an introduction to the knowledge of the true Catholick religion especially as professed by the Church of England* (London, 1674), 505.

[304] [Henry Hickman], *The nonconformists vindicated from the abuses put upon them by Mr. Durel and Scrivener* (London, 1679), 164–5. Hickman also quoted at length a Latin passage from an unnamed Socinian work which claimed that Reformed trinitarianism depended on the same patristic authority that was denied in anti-papal polemics (163–4): the passage is from Joachim Stegmann, *Brevis disquisitio, an et quomodo vulgo dicti Evangelici Pontificios ... solide atque evidenter refutare queant* ([Amsterdam], 1633), 6–7. On this work, see Keseru, 'Religiones rationales in Transylvania' (2000); it was translated by Biddle as *Brevis disquisitio; or, a brief enquiry touching a better way then is commonly made use of, to refute Papists* (London, 1653); see also McLachlan, *Socinianism*, 89. For Hickman, see Quantin, *Antiquity*, 338–9.

[305] Hickman, *Nonconformists vindicated*, 165.        [306] Ibid., 165–7.

sat uneasily with Hickman's continued Daillé-like insistence on the philosophical errors that plagued the fathers and on their dangerous acceptance of
pious forgeries.[307]

For the most part, nonconformists revelled in pointing out the philosophical
conundrums that the fathers had got themselves into and the theological errors
this had generated. In a 'Digression on the mixing of philosophy and theology'
in his *Theologoumena* (1661), John Owen made it clear that the corruption had
occurred early:

The sacred choir of the apostles and the evangels having been removed, he [Satan] again
attempted the task of corrupting the truth of the Gospel, and not without success. That
which he was never able to do in the course of an attack on the truth, he gradually achieved
in the course of a defence of it. For after the generation of men rendered infallible by the
Holy Spirit was gone from the earth, the advocacy of truth arrived into the hands of those
most trained in all the secular arts. Such were Clement, Origen, Tertullian and many others.
To them ... the Word and Spirit of Christ did not suffice against the enemies of truth, and
they were pleased to advance arguments taken from secular science. And when they saw
those they called 'heretics' (since philosophers had clearly lied in claiming the name of
Christ) twisting Scriptural words in ways not intended, they derived new terms for
explaining the truth, attempting to rescue them from the lair of error and deceit. But
with the passing of time, these philosophical arguments, which these learned men had
made use of for the defence of truth, and even the terms used to express this or that article
of faith, became considered as necessary parts of the Christian religion.[308]

This position did not require elaborate scholarship, but Owen must have known
that it – and the zealous Calvinism that it buttressed – were anathema to the
methods of many of his conformist enemies. His old colleague Theophilus Gale
offered a much longer historical justification for the same point.[309] The intrusion

---

[307] Ibid., 157–8, 160–1.

[308] Owen, *Theologoumena*, 513–14: 'Sublato autem sacro *Apostolorum* & *Evangelistarum* Choro,
corrumpendi veritatem *Evangelicam*, iterum opus aggressus est, non sine successu. Quod scilicet
in oppugnatione nunquam potuit, in defensione veritatis sensim obtinuit. Etenim postquam
hominum ὑπὸ Πνεύματος ἁγίου infallibilitèr φερομένων generatio in terris esse desiisset, in
manu virorum omni seculari sapientiâ instructissimorum pervenit veritatis patrocinium. Horum
erant *Clemens, Origines, Tertullianus,* aliiique innumeri. Istis cùm iis armis quae carnalia non sunt,
Verbo scilicet, & Spiritu Christi adversus veritatis hostes uti non sufficeret, placuit etiam rationibus
aggredi è doctrinâ seculari petitis. Cùmque viderint *Haereticos* quos vocarunt (cùm planè
*Philosophi* fuerint Christianum nomen mentiti,) aliorsùm quam opportuit expressa Sacrae
Scripturae verba trahentes, novis vocabulis in expositione veritatis excogitatis, è dolorum &
fallaciarum latebris eos extrahere tentârunt ... Accidit autem temporis progressu, ut Argumenta
ista Philosophica quae in veritatis defensione viri docti usurpaverant, atque termini & vocabula,
quibus hunc vel illum veritatis divinae articulum enuntiaverant, pro necessariis Religionis Jesu
Christi partibus essent habita'. On this work, see 3.5 above.

[309] Elements of which have been usefully discussed in Hutton, 'The neoplatonic roots of Arianism:
Ralph Cudworth and Theophilus Gale' (1983), although this piece does not discuss the
nonconformist theological agenda or Gale's Latin works, and, to my eyes, over-rates Gale's
supposedly 'immense erudition' (143). See similarly Wallace, *Shapers*, 87–120 ('Theophilus
Gale: Calvinism and the ancient theology').

of pagan philosophy – specifically that prevalent in Alexandria – explained virtually all the corruptions of the early church. Gnosticism was nothing else but a corrupt and mystical mix of Christianity and Pythagoreanism.[310] But the orthodox tradition was also infected, primarily through the influence of Ammonius, who – whether he died a Christian or not – certainly took from scripture, but was guilty of not openly revealing his Christianity, not properly acknowledging the hierarchy of sources of his Bible–Plato syncretism, and hiding the sacred sources from his pagan disciples.[311] The sad effects were a pagan neoplatonism that was even more virulently anti-Christian, and a Christian syncretism that was far too incautious.[312] The Platonism of Justin Martyr and Clemens Alexandrinus, attempting to convert pagans through their syncretism, already led to such errors as moral free will, justification by works, the salvation of virtuous pagans, and the idea that God committed sublunary affairs to angels.[313] Origen, however, was the chief culprit. Not only did he introduce well-known errors like pre-existence and Arianism, but he was also responsible for the two greatest corruptions in the history of Christianity. First, his Platonism led him to emphasise free will in a manner that directly prefigured Pelagianism. Second, it led him to found almost every aspect of papism: mystic theology, allegorical reading of scripture, the monastic life, the ideas of perfection in this life and purgatory.[314] Gale insisted on the philosophical origins of Roman Catholicism over many pages. Mystical theology was derived from Pythagorean asceticism, itself connected to the practices of the Essenes, whose Judaism Gale accepted.[315] Much of canon law was traceable to philosophical origins: 'As the Philosophers had their Deified Demons, which took up a good part of their *Natural Theologie*, so also Antichrist had his Canonised Saints, who fill up a great part of his Canon Law'.[316] Even papal church hierarchy had its origins in pagan philosophy; this peculiar thesis depended on Jerome's statement that 'even in Alexandria from the time of Mark the Evangelist until the episcopates of Heraclas and Dionysius the presbyters always named as bishop of one of their own number chosen by themselves', on the basis of which slender fact Gale concluded that '*Papal Primatie* began very early in this Philosophising Church at *Alexandria* ... and we may presume from their too great symbolising with that *Pythagorean Platonic* Schole in point of Discipline'.[317]

This was a rare bit of original thinking on Gale's part, for in reality he was stockpiling historical information on top of a thesis that he had obtained in other Reformed sources. He cited Owen, but his main ideas came from Cornelius Jansen

---

[310] Gale, *Court*, II: *Of philosophie*, sigs. [a4]ʳ–[a4]ᵇ; Gale, *Court*, III: *the vanity of pagan philosophy demonstrated*, 123–30.
[311] Gale, *Of philosophie*, 262–3.     [312] Ibid., 264.     [313] Gale, *Vanity*, 130–2, 140.
[314] Ibid., 132–7.     [315] Ibid., 149–53.
[316] Ibid., 171 (this theme is developed throughout 163–222).
[317] Ibid., 223–4; Jerome, *Epist. 146*, 1.

and his followers: Jansen himself had placed the origins of Pelagianism in early Christian Platonism, and his sympathiser Antoine Godeau, bishop of Vence, published a *Vie de saint Augustin* (1652) in which he reflected at length on 'the incompetence of the Greek Fathers on issues of grace and free will' – both were cited repeatedly by Gale.[318] At other points he quoted old Reformed classics such as Jean Morély's *Traicté de la discipline & police Chrestienne* (1562), which had found philosophical corruption to have been a gradual process beginning well before Nicaea.[319] Yet at the same time, Gale cited conformists and their heroes – Hammond, Stillingfleet, and Grotius (although he of course rejected their equation of antichrist with the gnostics).[320] Although their work had used the history of Christianity's encounter with philosophy very carefully to defend episcopalian themes, Gale's use of it clearly brought out the scholarly tensions: if Plato and Pythagoras infected gnosticism, surely Justin and Clement likewise; if pseudo-Dionysius was guilty of pagan mysticism, neither could Origen be spared. Gale could take these steps because, like Owen, he had no investment in ante-Nicene authority, as his Latin theological work makes clear. Scripture, which was its own interpreter, was sufficient for the resolution of all controversies.[321] Church tradition was neither a source of authority nor a witness.[322] As for the trinity, for all of Plato's theft from the Jews, his trinity was fundamentally different from the Christian.[323] John borrowed his λόγος from the מימרא דיי found 'in the ancient Chaldaic Thargum', itself proving 'that this Character of Jesus was to be found in the Writings of *Moses* and the *Prophets*, who writ long before the Grecian Philosophers'.[324]

## 6.6    The acceptance of Platonism in the early church

Just as conformist scholars seemed to have won the patristic war on ecclesiological issues,[325] they looked to be at risk of losing it on doctrinal ones. No one

---

[318] Gale, *Of Philosophie*, sig. b'; Gale, *Vanity*, 132–3, 138, 142–3; Quantin, *Catholicisme classique*, 208 ('Godeau … s'y étendait sur l'autorité speciale de la doctrine augustinienne, que l'Église avait faite sienne, et sur l'incompétence des Pères grecs sur les questions de la grâce et du libre arbitre'). For Gale's Jansenism, see p. 151, n. 192 above.

[319] Gale, *Vanity*, 137–8, quoting at length Jean Morély, *Traicté de la discipline & police chrestienne* (Lyon, 1562), 100 (Gale mistakenly claims 101). On Morély, see Denis and Rott, *Jean Morély* (1993).

[320] E.g. Gale, *Of philosophie*, 263–4, 265–6; Gale, *Vanity*, 123–5, 128, 223–4. See further the short summary of philosophical corruption at Theophilus Gale, *Philosophia generalis*, 925–8.

[321] Gale, *Idea theologiae*, 48–54, *passim*.    [322] Ibid., 41–4, 155.

[323] Gale, *Philosophia generalis*, 668; Gale, *Vanity*, 48–50; Gale, *Court*, IV: *Reformed philosophie*, 382–6, which is a full-out attack on Cudworth's just published account of the 'Platonic trinity' (6.6 below), with further comments on patristic misappropriation. Gale never cites Petau.

[324] Gale, *Reformed philosophie*, 385–6.

[325] See Quantin, *Antiquity*, 431: 'The ante-Nicene Fathers now appeared to meet almost every requirement of Church of England apologetics. Ignatius proved the apostolic character of episcopacy, Cyprian the independency of bishops from the See of Rome'.

had offered a satisfactory answer to Du Perron and Petau and their thesis was now repeated in Pierre-Daniel Huet's much-read edition of Origen (1668).[326] English Catholics had long insisted that Protestant refusal to acknowledge church authority would lead to Socinianism.[327] They now cited Petau's findings directly to support this assertion.[328] The claim that councils could introduce new words into the explication of doctrine was much better founded on papal ecclesiological principles.[329] When they did not ignore him, Anglicans' use of Petau verged – even more than Parker's – on the openly disingenuous.[330] Nonconformists, meanwhile, began to cite him with some relish, sometimes even alongside Sand; Richard Baxter in particular revelled in this tactic.[331]

---

[326] E.g. Huet, *Origeniana*, 186–7 ('Multum etiam ad defensionem Origenis confert Patrum aliorum exemplum, quibus errores aliqui exciderunt humanitus, quamvis orthodoxam in aliis tenuerint fidem, & inter orthodoxos positi sint. Nam ut alios brevitatis caussa praetermittam, quot recensere possumus, nulla haereseos suspicione aspersos, & de Trinitate tamen falsa & absurda commentos? Venient in hunc ordinem Justinus Martyr, Athenagoras, Theophilus Antiochenus, Clemens Romanus, Gregorius Thaumaturgus, Methodius, Lucianus, & Origenis praecipue discipulus Dionysius Alexandrinus'). Petau is not cited, but the list is clearly derived from him. For Huet's contact with English scholars, see 3.6 above. The Origen edition was being advertised to Englishmen early: see Justel to Oldenburg, 6 Nov 1667, *Oldenburg correspondence*, III, 580.

[327] Of the most prominent, see e.g. Kenelm Digby, *A discourse concerning infallibility in religion written . . . to the Lord George Digby* (London, 1652), 207–8 (George Digby – Protestant member of Great Tew – agreed that the ante-Nicenes were insufficient for proving trinitarianism: *Letters between George Digby and Kenelm Digby*, 33–4: the conclusion was of course minimalist scripturalism); Hugh Cressy, *Roman-Catholick doctrines no novelties* (n.p., 1663), 269–70.

[328] R. H. [=Abraham Woodhead], *The guide in controversies, or a rational account of the doctrine of Roman-Catholicks* (London, 1667), 338.

[329] Cressy, *Exomologesis*, 127–8; Thomas White, *An apology for Rushworth's dialogues wherein the exceptions for the Lords Falkland and Digby and the arts of their commended Daillé discover'd* (Paris, 1654), 84–99. On White, see 4.4, 5.3 above; for his patristics: Quantin, *Antiquity*, 218–20.

[330] Such as when Stillingfleet cited Petau's collection of multiple patristic views on the manner of the procession of the Holy Spirit from the Father to claim that knowledge of that manner was not essential to salvation, because all the fathers had acknowledged that it had proceeded (Edward Stillingfleet, *A rational account of the grounds of Protestant religion* (London, 1665), 1–43, esp. 12, 17, 19, 20, 30, 37–8, 39). But Stillingfleet took the exact opposite approach in the case of Origen's supposed foundation of papal error on purgatory (653, asserting Origen's Platonism). Others simply used Petau on episcopacy and ignored him on trinitarianism: e.g. Thomas Morton, Ἐπίσκοπος Ἀποστολικός, *or the Episcopacy of the Church of England justified to be Apostolical* (London, 1670), xiv.

[331] E.g. Samuel Mather, *A defence of the Protestant Christian religion against popery* (n.p., 1672), 41–2 (Mather was a Calvinist Independent who had been at Magdalen, Oxford, during the Interregnum, was deprived of his living in 1662, and moved to Ireland – Bremer, 'Mather, Samuel', *ODNB*); Richard Baxter, *Richard Baxter's Catholick theologie* (London, 1675), 112 (citing both Petau and Sand for the prevalence of Arianism before Nicaea); see also [Baxter], *Roman tradition examined . . . in the point of transubstantiation* ([London], 1676), 29; Baxter, *The nonconformists plea for peace* (London, 1679), 27–8; Baxter, *Which is the true church?* (London, 1679), 124, 146; Baxter, *Church-history of the government of bishops and their councils abbreviated* (London, 1680), 48–9; Baxter, *The true and only way of concord* (London, 1680), 184–5, Baxter, *The true history of councils enlarged and defended* (London, 1682), 96–7, 125, 130; Baxter, *A treatise of knowledge and love compared* (London, 1689), 57.

Several conformist apologists fell on the tired and by now inadequate excuse: if the ante-Nicenes had used dubious philosophical terminology, it was because heresies had not yet arisen that required precision. This approach is evident in the interesting works of an otherwise obscure rector of Eckington in Derby, Samuel Gardiner (1619–86), who in the late 1670s and early 1680s wrote two ambitious Latin defences of ante-Nicene trinitarianism that we know he sent to Sheldon and Thomas Barlow (who both approved of them) among others and which were certainly read on the continent: Sand responded to him directly and Bayle was still citing his work at the end of the century.[332] Gardiner realised that the real danger came not from Sand but from the Catholics Petau, Du Perron, and Huet, who, he claimed, were only trying to bolster papal authority by insisting on the insufficiency of both scripture and the ante-Nicenes.[333] Sand's own idiosyncratic claims, such as the similarity he posited between the hierarchies of Gods among the pagan philosophers and the Arian trinity (which he thus claimed were part of the same true tradition), Gardiner found both shocking and ridiculous: no pagan philosophers, including Plato, ever claimed several equal supreme Gods.[334] This argument was easy, but when it came to Sand's appropriation of Petau, Gardiner had to rely on the old claims: as Jerome and Augustine had already pointed out, the fathers often spoke incautiously;[335] Origen's work might 'abound' with errors, including on the trinity, but as Athanasius had argued one could still trace the true catholic

He was also used by the last remains of Great Tew: Edward Hyde, Earl of Clarendon, *Animadversions upon a book intituled, Fanaticism fanatically imputed to the Catholic Church* (London, 1673), 199–200.

[332] Gardiner is, as far as I can tell, unknown to scholarship. His will is Hertfordshire Archives, MS D/EHx/F83; sermons that he preached as prebend of Lichfield are John Rylands Library, University of Manchester, MS BAG/12/2/1. He obtained his D.D. from Corpus Christi College, Cambridge: see the act verses, *Supremus magistratus habet summam potestatem circa sacra* ([Cambridge], 1657) [ESTC R177494] and his *De efficacia gratiæ convertentis, ejúsque agendi modo, determinatio habita Cantabrigiæ in scholis theologicis, A.D. 1658. Pro gradu doctoratûs in S.T* (Cambridge, 1660). For Sheldon, see Gardiner to Sheldon, unknown date, Bod. MS Tanner 33, fol. 10ʳ (mentioning an otherwise unknown work on original sin that he considered publishing) and also the claim that Sheldon approved of his work at Samuel Gardiner, *Responsio valedictoria ad secundam Sandii epistolam* (London, 1681), 62. Barlow owned the work, and noted on the flyleaf that he could reach Gardiner by sending a letter to the posthouse in Chesterfield (Bod. classmark: 8°C.306. Linc.). Sand's responses to Gardiner were *Appendix addendorum, confirmandorum & emendandorum ad Nucleum historiae ecclesiasticae* (Cologne [Amsterdam?], 1678), 95–106, 129–58 (106–28 is a further questioning letter from Gardiner to Sand); and Hermann Cingallo [i.e. Sand], *Scriptura trinitatis revelatrix* (Gouda, 1678).

[333] Samuel Gardiner, Ὑποτύπωσις, *sive Catholicae circa SS. trinitatem fidei delineatio ex scriptis partum ante-Nicaenorm desumpta* (London, 1677), 23, 30, 151, 183–4; *Responsio*, 68,

[334] E.g. *Responsio*, 17–18, 'Deus bone! in quae me tempora reservasti ut haec viderem & legerem? . . . '

[335] Gardiner, *Fides*, sigs. [a5]ʳ⁻ᵛ.

faith by reading them carefully;[336] just because the ante-Nicenes did not use the term *homoousios*, it did not mean that they did not express its meaning.[337] Remarkably, Gardiner never tackled the issue of ante-Nicene Platonism head on, his only comment on the cultural difference between then and now being that some of the early fathers' expressions might sound 'harsh' to 'us, whose ears are more accustomed to scholastic phrases'.[338] That Gardiner was not against such scholastic phrases is suggested by his defence of the Calvinist *autotheos*, perhaps explaining why he was so keen to get his work to Barlow.[339]

Those closer to the Anglican mainstream faced the same problems. William Cave (1637–1713), in what was probably the foremost vernacular popularisation of conformist patristics, admitted – citing Huet – that 'it must be confessed that [Origen] was guilty of great mistakes ... having been a long time accurately trained up in the principles and Books of *Plato*', and that 'I doubt not but whoever would parallel his and the *Platonic* principles would find that ... his master-notions were brought out of the School of *Plato*'. Yet Origen had written 'not positively and dogmatically' but 'by way of exercitation', and had travelled too far in a quasi-Arian direction only in the 'heat of disputation' against Sabellius; most importantly, his worst books were written privately, not intended to be circulated and certainly 'not as doctrines to disturb the Church'.[340] Cave – who had certainly read both Petau and Sand – later made exactly the same claim to excuse Eusebius of Caesarea, who had 'so long convers'd with the several Books and Principles of Philosophers, especially the Writings of the *Platonists*', and thus spoke 'uncautiously' like 'many other

---

[336] Ibid., 60 ('In hujus operibus, licet innumeris, etiam in Sanctissimam Trinitatem, erroribus scateant, ab invidis Adversariis insertis ... haud pauca tamen, eaque insignia, in eisdem extant Catholicae fidei testimonia. Athanasius in libro de Decretis Synodi Nicaenae Origenem laudat contra Arianos, additque eos nullum ex antiquis Patribus pro sua haeresi afferre (quicquid nunc Sandius gloriatur) potuisse'). The reference is to Athanasius, *De decret.*, 6.27.

[337] Gardiner, *Responsio*, 46–7.

[338] Gardiner, *Fides*, sig. [a5]ʳ: 'Memineris etiant, quod ipsa res est, Patres Apostolicae fidei tenacissimos nonnunquam durius, nostris praesertim auribus Scholasticorum Phrasibus magis assuetis, locutos fuisse'. See also the uncritical quotation of Clemens Alexandrinus on the Platonic *logos* being the trinity at 55.

[339] Gardiner, *Responsio*, 62–3. See also the distancing away from the subordinationism of Gentilis and Courcelles at 18.

[340] William Cave, *Apostolici, or the history of the lives, acts, death, and martyrdoms of those who were contemporary with, or immediately succeeded the apostles. As also the most eminent of the primitive fathers for the first three hundred years ... the second edition corrected* (London, 1682 [1st edn=1677]), 235–8. There is no adequate study of Cave, who graduated BA from Cambridge in 1656 and enjoyed the patronage of Sancroft (Minton, 'Cave, William', *ODNB*). He was clearly close to the Oxford Greek scholars' circle, especially to Thomas Smith and Henry Dodwell: see e.g. Cave to Smith, 20 Oct 1676, Bod. MS Smith 48, fol. 71ʳ, and several other letters in that volume. The friendship continued post-1688, despite Cave's conformity (e.g. Cave to Smith, MS Smith 46, fols. 189ʳ–90ʳ, sending regards to Dodwell).

*Ante-Nicene* Fathers'.[341] In a similar vein, when one of Sancroft's chaplains, Henry Maurice, responded to the church history of Richard Baxter, he triumphed on almost every ecclesiological point.[342] Yet when he came to the nonconformist's use of Petau, he had to resort to the old reasoning: 'Some of them spoke loosely, in compliance with a Platonick Notion of the Trinity, not fore-seeing what Consequences might be drawn from their Expressions, or how narrowly they should come afterwards to be examin'd'. The fathers 'that followed the *Nicene* Council took all the Ecclesiastical Writers before their time to be of their opinion'. Nonetheless, he admitted, 'it would be a great Service to the Truth, that seems now to labour under some Prejudice, if some learned hand would take the Pains to shew ... how *Petavius* has betray'd the constant Tradition of this Doctrine'.[343]

That no one had yet attempted this task was even more troubling in light of the fascination of some Englishmen – many of them curious laymen – with the more radical aspects of the anti-trinitarian histories of Sand and Zwicker. Edward Sherburne took notes on 'The Nazarin[e]s and Ebionites' in his commonplace book which, without showing any anti-trinitarian intentionality behind them, were objective, curious, and non-judgemental.[344] One wonders whether Thomas Sprat realised how controversial was his casual statement in the *History of the Royal Society* that the Platonism of the fathers begot most of the controversies in the early church.[345] Much more radically, Henry Stubbe wrote a manuscript 'Account of the rise and progress of Mahometanism' (*c.* 1671), the first chapter of which offered a radical treatment of early Christianity: there was an expectation of a Messiah among Hellenistic Jews due to the popularity of Pythagorean Cabalism; the earliest faith was that of the Nazarenes–Ebionites, using only Matthew's Gospel; the conversion of the gentiles brought the influx of much philosophical doctrine; Petau's work showed that 'Platonick Philosophy, produced ... the doctrine of the Trinity'; the fathers had produced pious forgeries which Casaubon and Daillé had shown were not to be trusted; the Gospel of John was made by Hellenistic Jews; modern Christianity was a mixture of the ascetic Essenes and Therapeutae (Stubbe distinguished the two, although he acknowledged both as Jewish sects)

---

[341] Cave, *Ecclesiastici*, 29–30 (see also 41 for a citation of Sand's *Nucleus*). For Petau, see Cave's *Chartophylax ecclesiasticus* (London, 1685), sig. b3ᵛ. He must have been particularly familiar with the Jesuit's Epiphanius, for he planned a new edition, asking Smith to help collate manuscripts (Cave to Smith, Bod. MS Smith 48, fol. 73ʳ).

[342] Quantin, *Antiquity*, 314–15.

[343] [Henry Maurice], *A vindication of the primitive church, and diocesan episcopacy in answer to Mr. Baxter's Church history of bishops* (London, 1682), 115–16. Maurice offered as evidence the well-known advice of Sisinnius (*d.* 427) to Nectarius of Constantinople that against the Arians, dialectics should be dropped in favour of citations from the ante-Nicenes (the sources are Socrates, *Hist. eccl.*, v.10; Sozomen, *Hist. eccl.*, vii.12).

[344] BL MS Sloane 829 (Sherburne's commonplace book), fol. 26ʳ.

[345] Sprat, *History*, 11 (could this have been suggested to him by Beale?).

and 'Doctrines derived from the Gentile Philosophy'; Islam was 'chiefly founded on the Doctines of the Nazarene Christians and the Arrians'.[346]

The more acute members of the English church must have found particularly galling the realisation that it was the historical–critical approach to theology that they themselves had promoted (1.3, 3.2, 6.3 above) that was now being appealed to by their antitrinitarian enemies, and creating dangerous levels of speculation among laymen like Sherburne and Stubbe. This is best demonstrated by the case of Isaac Newton. Newton turned to historical theology in the mid-1670s, when he considered taking a divinity degree. He disputed under Joseph Beaumont, who certainly had no qualms about the trinity. But the historical method that Beaumont used in his teaching[347] led Newton to read Petau,[348] and eventually to a lifetime of speculation and private writing on the history of the Platonic corruption of early non-trinitarian Christianity,[349] culminating in the key manuscripts produced in the 1690s. For all the zealous work that he put in, Newton's narrative was not particularly original or elaborate: he combined his vision of the corruption of pure Noachic religion through animist idolatry with the history of the Platonic corruption of Christianity, claiming that idolatrous Greek philosophy infiltrated into the church through its absorption into the Jewish Cabbala; these theological errors were combined with the political ambitions of Athanasius and the first monks, directly leading to the formation of trinitarianism and popery.[350] Ultimately, Newton's framework was still the Petavian one: the ante-Nicenes were Arian subordinationists.

---

[346] Henry Stubbe, *An account of the rise and progress of Mahometanism with the life of Mahomet*, ed. Hafix Mahmud Khan Shairani (London, 1911), 1–57 (quotations from 29, 53–4), 146. I am reluctant to say more about this work until a proper collation of the relevant manuscripts (BL MSS Sloane 1709, Sloane 1786, Harl. 1876, Harl. 6189, Bod. MS Eng. misc. c.309, Senate House, University of London, MS 537) has been established: it is clear that the manuscript the printed version is based on is highly defective. Holt, *A seventeenth-century defender of Islam* (1972) is a short introduction based on the printed edition. The fullest extant discussion is now Champion, 'Freethinking uses of Islam from Stubbe to Toland' (2010), esp. 463–6, surpassing the previous treatments in Champion, *Pillars*, 120–4 and the deeply unsatisfactory account in Jacob, *Stubbe*, 64–77. See also Mulsow, 'Socinianism, Islam and the radical uses of Arabic scholarship' (2010), esp. 580–1; and more broadly Klein, 'Muslimischer Antitrinitarismus im lutherischen Rostock' (2008). The edition prepared by Matar (2014) reached me too late to evaluate and incorporate into this account.

[347] See p. 139, n. 132 above.

[348] The key manuscript is King's College, Cambridge, MS Keynes 4 (1670s), which consists entirely of notes from Petau on the Platonic trinity: see the pithy summary in the first sentence: 'Petavius <libro primo> Tomo secundo dogmatum Theologicorum <cap.> primo, Platonicorum Philosophorum Trinitatem exponens, probat eos hæc docuisse'. Newton's studies with Beaumont, the key evidence for which was discovered by Scott Mandelbrote, will be explored in a forthcoming study by him and myself.

[349] By far the fullest account is Mandelbrote, 'Newton reads the fathers'.

[350] A full account can be found in Goldish, *Judaism*, 141–62 ('Kabbalah and the corruption of the primitive church'); see also Levitin, 'Historical assumptions'. The most convenient summary in Newton's own words is the Latin one in NLJ MS Yahuda 11, fols. 1ʳ–7ʳ.

By the 1670s, then, the problem of early Christian Platonism was a well-established one. John North, a serious Greek scholar particularly interested in the history of philosophy (1.4 above), Master of Trinity from 1677, and an acquaintance of Newton,[351] put out in 1673 a selection of Platonic writings under the title *De rebus divinis dialogi selecti*. In the short preface, North deployed the old humanist staple that the church fathers had preferred Plato to other philosophers, especially Aristotle.[352] But he made clear that the Plato and Socrates that he was offering were to be celebrated only for their promotion of basic morality and reverence for God and providence; Plato's more 'barren speculations, which fitted the age in which he lived quite well', were tactfully excluded.[353] This was at least in part a function of the work's probable intended audience: BA students studying moral philosophy, rather than divinity.[354] But it also derived from North's caution about the problem of Platonic speculation among the fathers. North intended to write an anti-antitrinitarian work,[355] and his surviving notes show that he considered the modern Arians far more dangerous than the Socinians: where the latter (like the Calvinists) offered only an arid rationalism, the Arians 'ha[d] some Ground of Antiquity, & general acknowledgm$^t$ at one time'.[356] The fathers, just like the later scholastics, had made grievous philosophical errors – North here cited Sprat, showing that the latter's throw-away comments were not missed by everyone.[357] Tertullian had been right to warn his contemporaries against Plato's animistic theology, especially when 'the Christians were [so] willing ... to use y$^e$ allegory of the heathen Theology'.[358]

In the shadow of such anti-syncretism, and the radical rewritings of early church history that it was producing, the Anglican use of the history of philosophy to find new identities for antichrist, the origins of mystical philosophy or nonconformist enthusiasm now appeared unfairly selective. It is not coincidental then that three scholars now took up the task set by Maurice:

[351] See e.g. Newton to North, 21 April 1677, *Newton correspondence*, II, 205–7.

[352] John North, 'Ad lectorem', in *Platonis de rebus divinis dialogi selecti Graece & Latine* (Cambridge, 1673), sig. A3$^v$.

[353] Ibid., sig. A3$^r$: 'Sed quoniam ea esse natura Philosophi scripta jampridem cognoveram, ut, quanquam quaedam auream plane redolent sapientiam nec ab ullo studioso praetermitti debent; plura tamen jejunas speculationes continerent, aetati forte qua vixit ipse, satis accommodas, nunc autem solum cognitionis omnimodae cupidis congruentes; excerpendos quosdam aurae purioris Dialogos censui'.

[354] Probably explaining the work's reprinting in Cambridge in 1683.

[355] North, *Life of North*, 262.

[356] BL MS Add. 32514, fol. 171$^v$; see also 172$^{r-v}$; 'The Arrians indeed may have some countenance of y$^e$ ancient times, in maintaining a great contest, and in y$^e$ opinion of y$^e$ first fathers who did not so distinctly speak of those things. But Socinus can defend himself by no authority but SS. W$^{ch}$ he miserably shakes off, by a strikt Interpretation' and 170$^r$, 175$^{r-v}$ for his insistence on a contextual approach to scripture and the claim that Calvinists get bogged down in logical niceties.

[357] Ibid., fol. 191$^v$.    [358] Ibid., fol. 181$^v$.

answering Petau, or incorporating his findings into an 'Anglican' history. The three were Ralph Cudworth, Henry Dodwell, and George Bull.

As these comments suggest, Cudworth's long discussion of what he called the 'Platonic trinity' is much better understood within the context of English and continental patristic and theological debates than as a facet of his putative 'Platonism'. He noted trinitarian formulations among many pagans – and we should recall his critical defences of the *Chaldean Oracles*, the *Hermetica*, and the *Orphica*[359] – but argued that 'since it cannot well be conceived, how such a *Trinity of Divine Hypostases*, should be first discovered meerly by humane Wit and Reason', and 'since there are in the ancient Writings of the Old Testament, certain significations of a *Plurality* in the *Deity* ... we may reasonably conclude, that ... it was at first ... a *Theology of Divine Tradition or Revelation*, or a *Divine Cabala*'.[360] This has led interpreters to argue that Cudworth valued the Cabbala,[361] but this is very unlikely, especially given his standing as a leading Hebraist, and that he used the term 'cabbala' for any body of esoteric knowledge, even talking of an 'atheistick Cabala'.[362]

Rather, Cudworth's argument was the providential one we already met in Casaubon. The trinity was not really knowledge held by pagans or even Jews but a tool of God in preparation for Christianity:

we cannot but take notice here of a Wonderful Providence of Almighty God, that this Doctrine of a Trinity of Divine *Hypostases*, should find such Admittance and Entertainment in the Pagan World, and be received by the wisest of all their Philosophers, before the times of Christianity; thereby to prepare a more easie way for the Reception of Christianity amongst the Learned Pagans.[363]

The mystery was 'gradually imparted to the World', and only 'sparingly to the Hebrews themselves'.[364] Cudworth was critical of Philo's wayward use of trinitarian vocabulary, and made no attempt to present him as the inheritor of an advanced esoteric doctrine available to the Hebrews.[365]

As far as Cudworth was concerned, Philo's mistake was to call the Word 'Δεύτερον Θεὸν' ('a second God') 'after the Platonick way'.[366] This stemmed from his drawing on the 'bad' Platonist tradition, differentiated from a true, 'good' one. It was this differentiation that Cudworth used to answer Petau. The 'bad' Platonic tradition was a corruption of the true one. It made the third hypostasis a world soul, thus '*confound*[ing] the *Differences* between *God* and the *Creature*'.[367] This pantheism appealed to the anti-Christian neoplatonists, who 'approached nearest to Christianity and the Truth' and so 'by that means

[359] 2.5, 3.6 above. For the *Orphica*, see Cudworth, *System*, 294–307.
[360] Cudworth, *System*, 547–8.    [361] E.g. Parkin, *Cumberland*, 74; Dixon, *Trinity*, 89–90.
[362] Cudworth, *System*, 121.    [363] Ibid., 625.    [364] Ibid., 548.    [365] Ibid., 550
[366] Ibid. As usual Cudworth gives no reference: he is thinking of the passage from Philo's *Questions and answers on Genesis* quoted in Eusebius, *Praep. Ev.*, VII.17.
[367] Cudworth, *System*, 557.

could with greatest confidence, hold up the Bucklers against Christianity and encounter it' while at the same time using the shared '*Platonick Principles*, as they might be understood ... to defend the Pagan *Polytheism* and *Idolatry*'.[368] The key was not to confuse this 'bad' Platonic trinitarianism with that of Plato himself and with that of the church fathers. Petau's great mistake 'was his not distinguishing betwixt that *Spurious Trinity* of some Platonists, wherein the Third *Hypostasis*, was the *Whole Animated World* ... and that other Doctrine of those, who made it not to be the world it self'.[369] But 'saving' Plato in this way involved a radical reinterpretation of his pneumatology. In the *Timaeus* (30[b], 34[b–c], 36[d], 41[d]) Plato had clearly stated that his third hypostasis, 'Soul', was created. To solve this Cudworth had to suppose, 'with Plotinus and others, that Plato held a double Psyche, or soul': one created (the soul of the world), one uncreated ('*Supramundane*, or *Separate*; and which is not so much the *Form*, as the *Artificer* of the *World*').[370] As Le Clerc would later point out, this argument was very weak: using Plotinus to expound Plato was like using seventh-century monks to explain the doctrines of Christ and the apostles.[371] In Cudworth's case it was doubly weak, since his whole case depended on the *difference* between the 'true' Platonic trinity and that of the neoplatonists like Plotinus. The same accusation could be made against his treatment of the eternity of the second hypostasis.[372]

Nonetheless, Cudworth now felt himself in a position to challenge Petau. '*Arius* was no Platonist at all'.[373] It was, in fact, the ante-Nicenes who were both Platonists and orthodox. Petau's list of proto-Arians – Justin Martyr, Athenagoras, Tatianus, Irenaeus, the author of the pseudo-Clementine *Recognitions*, Tertullian, Clemens Alexandrinus, Origen, Gregory Thaumaturgus, Dionysius of Alexandria, Lactantius, and Athanasius himself – was in fact a list of those who held the true position, in line with the Anglican focus on Nicene and ante-Nicene Christianity: 'From all which it appears, that *Arius* did not so much Platonize, as the *Nicene* Fathers and *Athanasius*; who notwithstanding made not *Plato*, but the Scripture, together with Reason deducing natural Consequences therefrom, their Foundation'.[374]

---

[368] Ibid., 558.

[369] Ibid., 576. This was one of Petau's key differences between Platonic and Christian trinitarianism: *Theologica dogmata*, II, 4: 'Tertius porrò Deus manifestè creatus ab iisdem Platonicis putatur; quem & ποίημα nominant'.

[370] Cudworth, *System*, 576.

[371] Jean Le Clerc, *Epistolae criticae et ecclesiasticae* (Amsterdam, 1700), 247: 'Scio virum doctissimum [i.e. Cudworth], cujus Anglicum Opus antea laudavimus, ex *Plotino* aliam sententiam *Platonis* verbis adscribere, & duas Animas Mundi proferre; quarum altera sit ὑπερκόσμιος, & consubstantialis summo Deo, adeóque aeterna, de qua *Plato* silverit; altera verò ἐγκόσμιος, & creata, de qua Philosophus. Sed *Plotino* tot saeculis post *Platonem* nato, nec alia ejus Scripta proferenti, quàm quae habemus; de *Platonis* genuina sententia, non magis crediderim, quàm Monachis VII. Saeculi, de dogmatibus Christi & Apostolorum'.

[372] Cudworth, *System*, 572–5.    [373] Ibid., 575.    [374] Ibid., 579.

This was not just an anti-Catholic (and by extension anti-Socinian) point: it was also an anti-Calvinist one. Having defended Plato and the ante-Nicenes from the charge of Arianism, Cudworth made no attempt to defend them from the charge of subordinationism, instead embracing it, partly on the basis (again) of Plotinus's readings of Plato and partly on Petau's own work.[375] 'The Platonic Christian would ... urge ... that, according to the principles of *Christianity* itself, there must of necessity be some dependence and subordination of the *Persons of the Trinity* ... And thus does there seem not to be so great a *Difference*, betwixt the more *Genuine Platonists*, and the ancient *Orthodox Fathers*, in their Doctrine concerning the Trinity, as is by many conceived.'[376] Petau had demonstrated that even Athanasius had been a subordinationist,[377] but for Cudworth, far from being a manifestation of Platonic waywardness, this was a sign of his orthodoxy. We should certainly read this as an attack on the Calvinist notion of Christ as *autotheos*, explicitly mentioned by Cudworth as having 'no warrant ... from the Scripture', despite its positing by 'some late Divines' (i.e. Calvinists).[378] In fact, the whole idea of the three hypostases sharing a numerical essence could be traced back to the scholastics at the Fourth Lateran Council (1215) and, previously, to the successors of the Nicenes: Gregory of Nyssa (c. 335–95) and Cyril of Alexandria (c. 376–444). But they abused the word ὁμοούσιος, using it to mean something that it never meant before: 'several things having one and the same Singular Essence'. In reality its use by the 'Platonic' ante-Nicenes only ever meant 'Agreement of things, *Numerically differing* from one another, in some *Common Nature*, or *Universal Essence*; or their having a *Generical Unity* or *Identity*'.[379] This distinction between the 'Platonic-subordinationist' Athanasius and the truly 'consubstantialist' Cyril and Gregory had already been proposed by Petau,[380] but where he had used it as part of his developmental narrative, Cudworth used it to insert a wedge between those up to and including Athanasius and those after: 'And therefore some would think, that the Ancient and Genuine *Platonick Trinity*, taken with all its faults, is to be preferred before this *Trinity* of St. *Cyril* and St. *Gregory Nyssen*, and several other reputed Orthodox Fathers'.[381]

Cudworth was therefore using the history of philosophy not to defend 'Platonism' but to make a theological point – that of Episcopius and Courcelles – against what he saw as a late and unjustified scholasticism which had been taken up by the Calvinists.[382] It seems to me that this has little to do with 'erod[ing] the distinction between natural knowledge and revealed

---

[375] Ibid., 580–601.     [376] Ibid., 598, 600.
[377] Ibid., 599, citing Petau, *Theologica dogmata*, ii, 363.     [378] Cudworth, *System*, 574–5.
[379] Ibid., 605.     [380] E.g., Petau, *Theologica dogmata*, ii, 385–6.
[381] Cudworth, *System*, 604.
[382] The only account to recognise this is Hampton, *Anti-Arminians*, 175–6.

knowledge';[383] rather, it is a standard example of seventeenth-century historical theology. In his correspondence with Philipp van Limborch, who sent him the works of both Episcopius and Courcelles, Cudworth regularly spoke of Calvinist divinity in the harshest terms.[384] This sympathy for Arminianism is usually taken as a mark of Cudworth's 'liberalism'.[385] It is certainly true that Cudworth had a very optimistic view of the inclusivity of the Church of England (a position probably easier to hold when one neglects one's parish in favour of university life, as Cudworth did).[386] But Arminianism is not a political or ecclesiological position: it is a set of theological principles. Whatever Cudworth's ecclesiology (and the evidence is very sparse) he held a dogmatic, anti-Calvinist account of the trinity and he believed – like many of his much more intolerant Anglican colleagues – that the ante-Nicenes had to be saved from Petau's challenge.

But attempting to turn Petau against himself led to both scholarly and theological problems. No Anglican apologist had ever drawn such a sharp distinction between the subordinationist Nicenes and their immediate followers: that Cudworth's account was soon accused of Arianism is unsurprising.[387] And yet, some mainstream figures believed that Cudworth had offered

[383]  Harrison, *Religion*, 33; see also Sutcliffe, *Judaism*, 68.

[384]  Cudworth to Limborch, 20 Feb 1668, Universiteitsbibliotheek Amsterdam MS M.21.a (acknowledging receipt of Episcopius's works, describing his and the university's move away from Calvinism).

[385]  The classic statement is Colie, *Light*, esp. 36–48 ('Liberal theology and liberal politics').

[386]  E.g. Cudworth to Limborch, 26 March 1674, Universiteitsbibliotheek Amsterdam MS. M.21.c: 'Utique in hâc nostrâ Ecclesiâ Anglicanâ, tanquam in Arca Noachi omne genus Animalium, (si ita loqui liceat,) Protestantium; Calviniani; Remonstrantes, et credo etiam Sociniani, unà cohabitant; conspirantes sine ulla aperta Discordia, in unam et eandem Externam Communionem. Utinam ea mens, is animus esset, caeteris ubique Terrarum Protestantibus et Reformatis, ut quamvis dissentientes in Dogmatis, Pacem nihilominus non turbarent, nec Communionem scinderent, aut in Schismata abirent, et propterea Conditiones Communionis suae Laxiores proponerent.' The first half of this passage in noted in Colie, *Light*, 40, which does not mention the virulently anti-Catholic follow-up ('Sed quod ad Romanenses et Pontificios attinet, alia, (ut mihi videtur) res est; cum in eorum communionem admitti vix possint, nisi eiusdem cum illis, Idololatria affines'). For Cudworth's neglect of his parish, see the complaints in Thomas White (not the Catholic) to Sancroft, 27 May, year unknown, Bod. MS Tanner 30, fol. 45[r]; see also the similar complaints about his neglect of Clare Hall when Master in Humphrey Henchman to Richard Love, 17 Oct, year unknown, Bod. MS Tanner 49, fol. 32[r].

[387]  John Turner, *A Discourse concerning the Messias ... To which is prefixed a large preface, asserting and explaining the doctrine of the Blessed Trinity against the late writer of the Intellectual system* (London, 1685), xvi–clxiii, esp. lvii, lxiii–lxiv for the recognition that Cudworth was simply adapting Petau. For Turner's long personal vendetta against Cudworth, see Levitin, 'Spencer', 89–90. Surely connected is his long attack on the notion of a connection between the Hebrew and the Pythagorean Tetragrammatons in *Two exercitations* (London, 1684), 199–312. The other well-known early reaction is the 'Letter to Mr. R. Cudworth, D.D.' at the end of the second edition of the Catholic John Warner's anonymous *Anti-Haman ... where in is shewed the conformity of the doctrine, worship, & practice of the Roman Catholick church with those of the purest times* (n.p., 1679), attacking Cudworth's claim that most pagans believed in God's unity.

an answer to Petau. Cave, for example, accepted his distinction between 'good' and 'bad' Platonic trinitarianism, suggesting, *contra* the Jesuit, that Arius had only appropriated the latter, 'stretching the Differences, and gradual Subordination, which the Elder *Platonists* had made amongst the *Hypostases*, into too wide a distance'.[388] On the other hand, Tenison, whose dislike of Cudworth's history of ancient philosophy we have already met, was as critical of the trinitarian side of the story. Contrary to Cudworth's antipathy to Cyril, Tenison directly cited him on the Greek philosophical (i.e. Platonic) origins of Arianism.[389] Plato's subordinationism was linked to his idolatrous belief in the 'government of the World [by] the Genii next to God'. As for Plato's trinity among the early Christians, had it genuinely been orthodox, 'as some would have it, who can find in him the mysteries of the *Athanasian* Articles', it would not have produced 'the earliest Hereticks', who 'believed in another kind of *Logos*'. The allusion is obviously to Cudworth, against whom Tenison could now turn Petau's finding that Arius 'was a very genuine *Platonist*'.[390] Striking at the weakest part of Cudworth's argument, Tenison noted that the idea that Plato had not affirmed the generation of the *logos* could depend only on reading Plato through Plotinus, 'who lived where Christianity was planted'.[391] So idolatrous was Plato's own subordinationism that it closely resembled the worship of the Confucians, who 'own one God ... yet they have Temples for Tutelar Spirits'.[392] Apart from Arius, the only Christian inheritors of Platonic subordinationism were the gnostics who surrounded their images of Christ with those of the Greek philosophers.[393] This of course left Tenison with the problem of answering Petau, a problem exacerbated by the rise in Catholic propaganda after the accession of James II. Tenison pointed out that it was the Socinians who were benefiting from the Jesuit's scholarship; just because the scriptures were sometimes obscure, one need not resort to an infallible authority.[394]

Yet how *were* Protestants to decide? At one point in his response to Petau, Tenison seemed to abandon the fathers as witnesses: 'For the Fathers of the earliest Ages, they were more busied in writing against Heresies, then in explaining of Scriptures'.[395] But in the face of the Restoration Church's

---

[388] Cave, *Ecclesiastici*, 44–5.   [389] Tenison, *Idolatry*, 55–6.   [390] Ibid.   [391] Ibid., 396–8.
[392] Ibid., 81–2.   [393] Ibid., 152–4.
[394] Thomas Tenison, *A discourse concerning a guide in matters of faith with respect especially to the Romish pretence of the necessity of such a one as is infallible* (London, 1683), 39–40; Thomas Tenison, *The difference betwixt the Protestant and Socinian methods in answer to a book written by a Romanist* (London, 1687), 39. The latter is an answer to R. H. [Abraham Woodhead], *The Protestants plea for a Socinian* (London, 1686), 14 for the standard Catholic use of Petau. For similarly evasive answers, see Edward Stillingfleet, *A relation of a conference held about religion at London ... with some gentlemen of the Church of Rome* (London, 1687), 36–7.
[395] Tenison, *Discourse*, 40–1.

triumphant construction of a patristic identity, this move was no longer acceptable. Cudworth's defence – hidden away in the midst of a sprawling treatise on atheism – was never going to be sufficient, and in 1685 George Bull published at Fell's Oxford press his *Defensio fidei Nicaenae* (he had worked on it for many years, completing it in 1680).[396] Bull, secretly ordained in the mid-1650s, was of the generation that felt increasingly little need to make any concessions to the Calvinism that had shaped the theological orthodoxy of the first half of the century: his *Harmonia apostolica* (1670) adopted a clearly anti-Calvinist stance on justification by faith, eliciting a fierce reaction from the remnants of the old guard like Thomas Barlow; this was a move that also involved strong insistence on the authority of the ante-Nicenes, even to the explicit detriment of Augustine.[397] This unashamedly Arminian theology was carried into the *Defensio*, written by the time Bull had been promoted to prebend of Gloucester Cathedral on the recommendation of Tillotson; like Cudworth's *System* the work directly espoused subordinationism, explicitly rejecting scholasticism, the Fourth Lateran Council, and Calvin's self-begotten Christ.[398] While he was familiar with the works of both Sand and Zwicker, Bull knew that it was Petau's scholarship that lay behind them. He was perceptive enough to realise that the usual response to ante-Nicene uncertainty was useless against the Jesuit: 'Bull did not make the point that the Fathers had spoken obscurely or incautiously before heresies arose—this would have been too damaging an admission'.[399] But how then to explain the Platonic vocabulary of the ante-Nicenes? Bull's key claim was that the term ὁμοούσιος – or at least its meaning – was in use well before Nicaea. Old Testament passages referred to Christ's pre-existence. That which the fathers 'related of the apparitions of the Word ... in the Old Testament ... were not empty inventions of their own,

---

[396] George Bull, *Defensio fidei Nicaenae, ex scriptis, quae extant, Catholicorum doctorum, qui intra tria prima Ecclesiae Christianae saecula floruerunt* (Oxford, 1685), sigs. a3ʳ–[a4]ʳ. In his 'Apologia pro Harmonia' Bull had already announced that he had 'some years ago' ('ante aliquot annos') written a historical defence of the ante-Nicenes against Petau: in *Examen censurae, sive, responsio ad quasdam animadversiones antehac ineditas in librum cui titulus Harmonia apostolica* (London, 1676), 13 (new pagination). It is unclear what is the connection between this account and that given in the *Defensio*. Robert Nelson, *The life of Dr. George Bull, late Lord Bishop of St. David's* (London, 1714), 280–4 offers no new information on this score, but the whole work remains the best source for Bull's biography.

[397] Spurr, *Restoration Church*, 311–16; Hampton, *Anti-Arminians*, 49–60; Tyacke, 'Religious controversy', 606–9; Quantin, *Antiquity*, 341–2.

[398] There is a useful summary in Hampton, *Anti-Arminians*, 176–8. Mulsow, 'A German Spinozistic reader of Cudworth, Bull, and Spencer' (2006), states (at 360–1) that 'Bull is honest enough as a philologist to accept that subordinationism played a central role in the early Church', but the position was a philological–*theological* one.

[399] Quantin, *Antiquity*, 345 (344–9 for the patristic principles behind the work); Nelson, *Life*, 281–2 saw this as a particular strength of the work. Although see the usual special pleading for Origen as writing 'privately' at Bull, *Defensio*, 168–9.

but derived from the Apostolic doctrine itself'.[400] The external proof of this was that they 'drew this from the ancient Jewish Cabbala or tradition, or, at any rate, that those things that the apostles had learnt about this through the Holy Spirit fitted perfectly with that tradition'.[401] This was demonstrated by the use of proto-Christian *logos*-vocabulary by Philo, 'but if anyone might suspect Philo of Platonizing in this' (as Petau had) the evidence of the *Book of Wisdom* and of the Targums with their דיי מימרא could be brought forward.[402]

Bull's use of these materials show his limitations as a scholar. He made no attempt to combat Grotius's questioning of the *Book of Wisdom* nor to answer questions on the usefulness of the Targums in this regard. All his Hebraica was taken from the works of Andreas Masius (1514–73) and Paul Fagius: great scholars in their time, but hardly the most up-to-date references (the parish priest Bull admitted that he had written the *Defensio* without access to the latest scholarly literature).[403] The casual reference to Cabbala was by now an embarrasment. These weaknesses in Hebraica were soon leapt upon by antitrinitarians.[404] Bull's best evidence for the early and non-gnostic use of 'ὁμοούσιος', meanwhile, was the *Poemander*, which he acknowledged as a forgery but attempted to save by pointing out that the forger was 'very early, living shortly after the apostles'.[405] All the ante-Nicenes who spoke of Christ's temporal 'birth' as a God spoke metaphorically.[406]

Although Bull accumulated much evidence, these key arguments were by now obsolete. When antitrinitarians attacked his work, he had to amend many of his claims. But like many in the Church invested in a patristic identity there were steps into criticism that he was not prepared to take, such as accepting that the fathers could have been deceived by pious forgeries: Bull even cited Montagu for this judgement.[407] It was left to one defender of the English Church to take on the

---

[400] Bull, *Defensio*, 23: 'Ex his autem manifestum est, quae de apparitionibus τοῦ λόγου, sive Filii Dei, Patriarchis, & viris sanctis sub veteri Testamento factis, tradiderunt Patres primaevi, non illorum vana fuisse commenta; sed ab ipsa Apostolica doctrina derivata'.

[401] Ibid., 23: ' . . . ex antiqua Judaeorum Cabala, sive traditione hausisse: vel certe, quae Apostoli ea de re per Spiritum S. edocti fuerunt, cum traditione illa optime convenire'.

[402] Ibid., 26: 'Ne quis autem Philonem in his πλατωνίζει suspicetur . . . Auctor Judaeus libri, sapientiae Solomonis inscripti, (quem Philone longe antiquiorem, non ipsum fuise Philonem, ut quidam somniarunt, evidentissimis argumentis constat,) eadem de τοῦ λόγου philosophatur'; 26–7 for the Targums.

[403] Ibid., sigs. a4ᵛ–b1ʳ.    [404] See below.

[405] Bull *Defensio*, 51: 'Certe planum fuisse Scriptorem, hoc est, non ipsum Trismegistum, sed Christianum aliquem ejus nomen ementientem, solide probavit Petavius: sed & idem Petavius fatetur, circulatorem illum perantiquum esse, & Paulo post Apostolorum tempora extitisse'.

[406] Quantin, *Antiquity*, 343 lists examples.

[407] George Bull, *Primitiva & Apostolica traditio dogmatis in Ecclesia Catholica recepti, de Jesu Christi Servatoris nostri divinitate . . . contra Danielem Zuickerum ejusque nuperos in Anglica sectatores*, in *Opera omnia*, ed. J. E. Grabe (London, 1703), 29 (new pagination): 'Obiter illud dicam, me in ea esse sententia, ut existimem, ab eodem fonte Sibyllina etiam oracula, à Justino, ac post eum ab aliis, de Christo contra Gentes producta, promanare potuisse. Adduci enim non possum, ut credam, à primitivae Ecclesiae Patribus conficta illa vaticinia, vel ipsis per pias fraudes obtrusa, quemadmodum Viri quidam docti fidenter asserunt; intolerandum convitum

full implications of the work of Casaubon and Petau: Henry Dodwell. In a series of texts published between 1672 and 1710, Dodwell developed 'the most elaborate theory of the authority of antiquity on historical lines', a theory that was consistently sponsored by the Anglican scholarly elite at Oxford but came to be accepted by almost no one, 'whether of the establishment or of the little Nonjuring body to which he adhered from 1691 to 1710'.[408] His scheme described how the providentially assisted fathers of the first centuries preserved, as witnesses, the historical truth of the apostolic period; such providential assistance included the continued ability to perform miracles and the elongation of their lives to maintain unbroken tradition. This was still a Protestant case – 'the point was not to compare the Fathers of the second and third centuries with the Apostles, but to contrast the Fathers and modern interpreters of the apostolic writings'[409] – but it certainly pushed to an extreme the ideas of the difficulty of independent scriptural interpretation and of the fathers as witnsses. The radicalness of Dodwell's position was that – like Daillé – he accepted the discontinuity of ante- and post-Nicene positions; unlike the Huguenot, he believed that historical method could extract the precise meaning of the earliest fathers.[410]

That historical method can be fairly labelled 'contextualist', the key context being pagan philosophy. Yet that contextualism was theologically grounded, as made clear in Dodwell's first publication, the 'Prolegomena' to the posthumous *De obstinatione* (1672) of his old tutor at Trinity College, Dublin, John Stearne (1624–69). Stearne's work was explicitly a work of Christian Stoicism, and Dodwell, who published the manuscript, believed that it required justification in what is a book-length treatment of the relationship between Christianity and philosophy.[411] His case was based on a universalisation of the principle of divine accommodation and economic providence. On topics known naturally – especially those of moral philosophy – no extra revelation was required, and the opinions of the early Christians could be gathered from their reference to the doctrines of

---

(ut cum Montacutio nostro loquar) in sanctos illos Proceres temerè atque inverecundè jactitantes'.

[408] Quantin, *Antiquity*, 366. What I offer in the following is only a meagre supplement to the essential study by Quantin: 'Anglican scholarship gone mad?' (2006). For Dodwell's biography summarised, see Harmsen, 'Dodwell, Henry', *ODNB*. I am not convinced by the interpretations in Leighton 'The religion of the non-jurors and the early British enlightenment' (2002); Leighton, 'Ancienneté among the non-jurors' (2005).

[409] Quantin, *Antiquity*, 376.    [410] Ibid., 382–3.

[411] Henry Dodwell, 'Prolegomena apologetica, de usu dogmatum Philosophicorum, praecipue Stoicorum, in Theologia', in John Stearne, *De obstinatione. Opus posthumum, pietatem Christiano-Stoicam, scholastico more, suadens* (Dublin, 1672). This work is probably the fullest engagement with the idea of Christian Stoicism published in the second half of the seventeenth century, yet it goes unmentioned in any of the numerous works on the early modern Stoicism. On Stearne, professor of medicine at Trinity and founder of the Dublin College of Physicians, see Belcher, 'Memoir of John Stearne' (1865). That Dodwell already held some of these ideas in the preceding years is evident from his letters: see e.g. Dodwell to Bernard, 2 June 1670, Bod. MS Smith 45, pp. 1–6.

contemporary philosophers. On topics known only by revelation, pagan philosophy was useless – Dodwell instanced the Platonists on the trinity – but the Holy
Spirit *had* accommodated itself to the philosophical vocabulary current among
the receivers of the gospel, especially the Hellenistic Jews.[412] In scriptural
exegesis, philosophy, including Reformed scholasticism, was again useless:
'Systematical Divines' work 'from Reasoning alone' upon the words of the
Bible, whereas the 'design of interpreting Scriptures ought to be indeed <not>
to find the sense of Scripture which may be known to be reasonable independently of its being the sense of those passages from whence it is gathered; but
rather to know the sense of the Writers which is therefore to be presumed
reasonable because it was the sense of such writers who were so assisted by the
H. Ghost'.[413] Modern scholasticism was thus useful in *natural* theology;[414]
concomitantly, some of the fathers had made terrible mistakes because they
were poor philosophers: witness the case of Origen.[415] But these were private
opinions. To understand scripture and the early Christians what was required was
not to explain Platonic language through Aristotelian philosophy as it had been
filtered through Arabic ideas, but a contextual understanding of the language
itself.[416] This was evident from a simple equation: 'First, it was the intention of
the Holy Spirit that scripture be accommodated to the capacities of those to whom
it was delivered; second, the character of the age to which scripture was delivered
was philosophical: that of the famous philosophers of the time'.[417] The similarities with Spencer's universal application of the accommodation principle (3.6
above) are striking, and it is no coincidence that Dodwell cited Maimonides's
treatment of the Sabian context of the Levitical Laws as a parallel case.[418]

   This approach served to defend Stearne's Christian Stoicism by demonstrating that in moral philosophy, the late Stoicism of Seneca, Epictetus, and Marcus
Aurelius was compatible with the thoughts of the early Christians.[419] But it also
had a far wider significance, for Dodwell based on it his whole defence of early
Christianity, against nonconformists, papists, and Socinians. Du Perron's (and

---

[412] For a summary, see Dodwell, 'Prolegomena', 20–24; for another, with the specific example of
the Platonists on the trinity included, see Dodwell, *Two letters*, 219–25. This work was popular
enough to be reprinted in London in 1680 and 1691, with some updating.

[413] Dodwell to William Lloyd, 3 Dec 1695, Bod. MS Cherry 22, fol. 42$^r$.

[414] Dodwell, *Two Letters*, 179–80, 205–6, 207–8.      [415] Dodwell, 'Prolegomena', 12–14.

[416] Dodwell, *Two Letters*, sigs. b8$^v$–c$^v$.

[417] Dodwell, 'Prolegomena', 84–5: '*Quòd accommodata fuerit Sacra Scriptura captui
Philosophico illius aevi quo tradita est, idque ex intentione Spiritus Sancti*, per partes facile
probabitur: Primo enim ex intentione Spiritûs Sancti accommodata est Sacra Scriptura captui
illius aevi quo tradita est: Secundò captus aevi, quo tradita est Sacra Scriptura, fuit
Philosophicus ad normam Philosophorum eo saeculo celebrium'.

[418] Dodwell, *Two letters*, 196–7. For further similarities between Dodwell and Spencer, see
Levitin, 'Spencer', 72–3, 76–7.

[419] Dodwell used the work of Gataker, on which see 5.2 above: e.g. 'Prolegomena', 129. See also
the summary at *Two letters*, 225–30.

thus Petau's) dismissal of the ante-Nicenes was negated,[420] and the Socinians' insistence on reason as the only interpreter of scripture was shown to be futile: like the scholastics they failed to see that it was not abstract reason but historical context that explained scripture.[421]

The approach required a whole new research programme.[422] Dodwell undertook that programme primarily to defend episcopacy, in English polemical works published at the height of the Restoration Crisis of 1677–83 and in Latin scholarly dissertations on Cyprian (1682) and Irenaeus (1689). He defended the case that 'by being *disunited* from the *Church*' the Christian believer 'loses his *Union* with *Christ* and all the *Mystical benefits* consequent to that *Union*'.[423] This remarkable contextual–ecclesiological argument was re-articulated at length in Dodwell's Latin works.[424] This mystical union could only be understood in the context of the eclectic but primarily Platonic philosophy which was dominant at the time of its revelation: 'the great design of Christ plainly appears to have been that *Mystical* ἔνωσις [union] so much spoken of in the *Mystical Philosophy* of that Age, and spoken of as the peculiar office of the λόγος'.[425] The main doctrine of the philosophy of the Hellenistic Platonists who expected a Messiah – the key linguistic evidence was to be found in Philo[426] – was the mystical congruence between earthly ectypes and universal archetypes of which the *logos* was the most important:

in this *Mystical* way of arguing from *Archetypal* to *Ectypal* Beings so frequently used in the Scripture in allusion to the *Platonick* Notions then received among the *Hellenists*, the *Archetypes* are supposed to be not only like *Copies* in *imitation* whereof the resemblances in the *Ectypa* were made, but as *Seals* do *produce* their own similitudes, as *Seals* do by application to the wax.[427]

External ceremonies were, according to this framework, mystical ectypes of the union with Christ as *logos*:

---

[420] Dodwell, 'Prolegomena', 108: ' ... ut omnino frustra sit illa, Magni *Perronii* inter alios, querela de deperditis veterum monumentis, ad excludendum *veteris Ecclesiae* de controversiis hodiernis judicium'. See also the allusion to Du Perron identified in Quantin, *Antiquity*, 382. Dodwell had certainly read Petau early in his career: 'Prolegomena', 5.

[421] Dodwell, 'Prolegomena', 87–8; Dodwell, *Dissertationes in Irenaeus*, 85–7. See Quantin, *Antiquity*, 374–5.

[422] Longingly described at *Two letters*, sigs. c3$^{r-v}$.

[423] Henry Dodwell, *Separation of churches from episcopal government, as practiced by the present non-conformists, proved schismatical* (London, 1679), xii.

[424] See e.g. Henry Dodwell, *Dissertationes Cyprianicae* [Oxford, 1684], 20b (also citing Hammond on Philippians 3.20). I am extremely grateful to Jean-Louis Quantin for informing me of his finding that this stand-alone folio edition was published in 1684, and not immediately with the *Sancti Caecilii Cypriani Opera recognita & illustrata*, ed. J. Fell (Oxford, 1682).

[425] Dodwell, *Separation*, 365.

[426] Dodwell had also written a 'Dissertation ... about the Mystical Interpretation of the Old Testament used ... by S. Paul himself': Francis Brokesby to John Woodward, 11 June 1711, CUL MS Add. 7647, no. 137.

[427] Dodwell, *Separation*, 348–9. See Quantin, 'Dodwell', 350.

Hence it came to be the design of the *Primitive Christians* in the great use they made of *Mystical Judaism* for their purpose, to shew that all the externals of the *Law* were only *Ectypal* resemblances of those original *Archetypal Ideas* which were reserved in *Christ* as being that λόγος in whom the *Platonists* and the *Mysticizing Jews* themselves placed their *Ideas*, and that they were reserved with him in *Heaven* before his descent on *earth*.[428]

As Casaubon had long ago suggested, Christian sacraments were designed to emulate pagan mysteries.[429] Porphyry, the most important of the neoplatonists, had explained that sacrifices were 'a natural means of procuring that *Mystical Union* which was designed between the *Gods* and their *Sacrifices*', and this view was 'generally followed by the *Primitive Christians*'.[430] Baptism was clearly such a philosophical–mystical rite: baptism 'into one body' (1 Cor. 12:13) and into union with Christ was reminiscent of the purgatory rites described in the *Chaldean Oracles*,[431] which Dodwell believed to have influenced both Plato and the neoplatonists.[432] It thus 'does not only *represent*, but *apply* the *merits* and *efficacy* of his *Resurrection* to us, so that it must produce in us a like *signature* (ἐκμαγεῖον is the *Platonical* term,) first of a *Mystical Resurrection* from *sin* and a *worldly Life*, and then of our *corporeal Resurrection* from the grave'.[433] More simply, it was a purification more worldly than that of the neoplatonists 'with whom the *Apostles* had to deal', who, believing God to be absent from the corporeal world, attempted to starve themselves out of their bodies and performed 'the most abominable *pollutions* of the *flesh*', the particulars of which 'cannot be mentioned without immodesty'.[434] The Eucharist too had to be contextualised in the world of Hellenistic philosophy: when Christ spoke of the 'true bread from heaven' (John 6:32) he no doubt spoke in accordance with the Hellenistic Jews like Philo, who, 'as well as the *Platonists*, placed [ideas] in *Heaven*, and particularly in the λόγος'.[435] Philo had equated the 'mystical manna' with the *Logos*, and he was clearly of one mind with the 'Adversaries with whom [Christ] had then to deal': it was thus a sign of great 'prudence and cogency' to speak allegorically of heavenly bread, since Christ then 'had nothing more to convince them of in order to the proving that he was the *true Bread*, but only that he was the λόγος'.[436]

[428] Dodwell, *Separation*, 394. See also *Dissertationes Cyprianicae*, 21b, 39a–40a.

[429] Dodwell, *Separation*, 358, 375.

[430] Henry Dodwell, *A discourse concerning the one altar and the one priesthood insisted on by the ancients in their disputes against schism* (London, 1683), 166; Porphyry, *Abst.*, II.42.

[431] Dodwell, *Separation*, 273–4.     [432] Dodwell, *Two letters*, 275–6.

[433] Dodwell, *Separation*, 349. Dodwell does not give a source, but for equivalent use of ἐκμαγεῖον in Plato, see *Theaetetus*, 191ᶜ, 194ᵈ⁻ᵉ, 196ᵃ.

[434] Dodwell, *Separation*, 368–9. Dodwell cites Porphyry's self-starvation upon hearing Plotinus's lectures (Eunapius, *Vit. soph.*, B 456), and Plotinus's detestation of his own body to the extent that he forbade sculptures of himself to be made (Porphyry, *Vit. Plot.*, 1).

[435] Dodwell, *Separation*, 393–4.

[436] Ibid., 395, citing Philo, *Leg. all.*, III.162, 169. There are many more possible references: see Vermès, *Post-Biblical Jewish Studies* (1975), 143–4.

Understood contextually, the sacraments enacted a mystical union with Christ. This was an anti-individualist argument. Neoplatonism led to the belief in individual perfectibility and thus to schismatic heresies like gnosticism, but this was a misunderstanding both of mystical Hellenism and of orthodox Platonism.[437] 'The pretence of abstaining from the external Ordinances under the pretence of Perfection' was already evident in the first ages, derived from the philosophers whose pantheistic cosmologies and belief in the deiformity of the soul led to an anti-conformist enthusiasm: such enthusiasts believed that 'there was no need of going to certain *places* to worship him [God], because he was *every-where*; nay *within* them'.[438] Christianity was always susceptible to this deviant view due to its roots in Hellenistic Judaism, with its allegorical mysticism – Dodwell referenced Aristobulus, the *Letter of Aristeas*, and Philo, showing himself to be a direct successor to de' Rossi – especially the sect of the Essenes, 'who were thus so extremely drawn over to the spiritual sense as even to be inclinable to neglect the *external* observances of the Law'. The Christians 'took this very same method to recommend their own Doctrine to the *Jews*, as the *Jews* had done to recommend theirs to the *Philosophers*' – it was no coincidence that there was no record of Essenes opposing Christianity, unlike the Pharisees and Saducees.[439] This enthusiastic anti-ceremonialism was understandable, given that the early Christians made much of their rejection of Jewish ceremonialism, again using the terms of Greek philosophical asceticism.[440] But it was a fundamental error that led to both monasticism and modern enthusiasm:

It is indeed somewhat surprizing to observe, but he, who shall be pleased to observe, will find it true, that the Enthusiastick style of *Jacob Behmen, Henry Nicholas*, and the *Quakers*, and such other Enemies of *Learning*, such strangers to *Antiquity*, and to the tongues they wrote in, should so agree with the *Platonism* of the *elective Philosophy* I am speaking of.[441]

Dodwell later recommended Stillingfleet's attack on Cressy as useful reading on this matter, a nice example of how vernacular polemical divinity could still inspire much more scholarly works.[442] And he applied the theory to practice, in

---

[437] Dodwell, *Separation*, 210, 217–20. For Platonism, Dodwell paraphrases Cicero, *Somn.*, 21; see also *Dissertationes in Irenaeum*, 312.

[438] Dodwell, *Separation*, 248. Dodwell cites Seneca's famous letter 'On the God within us' (*Epist.* 41) and Porphyry, *Abst.*, II.52.

[439] Dodwell, *Separation*, 249–50.     [440] Ibid., 251–2.

[441] Ibid., 254–5. See also the preface to *Dissertationes Cyprianicae*, sig. a2ᵛ.

[442] Dodwell to Francis Lee, 15 Jan 1698, Bod. MS Cherry 22, fols. 54ᵛ–55ʳ: 'I wish you would also be pleased to see what Bᴾ Stillingfleet has written against Mʳ. Cressy's Sancta Sophix. You will there find that the Mystical Divinity which is the foundation of Quietism was rather derived from the Philosophical Religion invented by the later Platonists, and among them admired by the great enemy of the Christian Religion, Porphyry, than from any Tradition derived from the Apostles. The pretended Areopagite has given it great Authority with those who did not know that he was an Impostor. And it seems to <be> the language of those Platonists that was

a rather moving epistolary exchange with the physician, millenarian, and nonjuror Francis Lee (1661–1719).[443] Lee had become involved with a group of pietists and followers of Böhme during a tour of the continent; perhaps having read Dodwell's works he sought the Irishman's opinion on his stepmother, Jane Lead (1624–1704), a mystic who lived in the Behmenist commune of John Pordage and published several books whose central feature was an androgynous God.[444] Lee was clearly eager to extricate her from the charge of enthusiasm, but Dodwell's curt reply was that her writings on magic were in the tradition of the *Chaldean Oracles* as they were used by Simon Magus, and that her vision of an androgynous God was pre-empted by the gnostics who had drawn on Egyptian philosophy and theology.[445]

In his published works, Dodwell's philological–polemical trump card was the argument that the enthusiasts had failed to recognise that even the philosophers who believed in perfectibility had never claimed that this excused them from initiation into communal mysteries: witness the complex rites of the Pythagoreans themselves, which were another model for the Eucharist.[446] Far from being cautious of the similarities between the Platonic heretics and 'orthodoxy', as Hammond, Stillingfleet, and many others had been, Dodwell refused to believe that either could be understood outside of the same philosophical context.[447] A fully historical interpretation showed that Hellenistic philosophy determined not only participation in the sacraments but also episcopal ecclesiastical structure. In the mystical theology of the pagans, the '*Chief Priests* represented . . . a greater and more sacred *Person* than their own', again the *logos*.[448] The Christian bishop was equivalent to the High Priest of Hellenistic Judaism, as he was ectypal of the archetypal High Priest (Philo was again the key source).[449] Christianity being 'nothing but a *Mystical*

---

initiated by that Impostor. They seem to understand the Mystical Unity of a coalescence with God and Christ, which certaintly is against yᵉ Doctrine of Christ'.

[443] On Lee, see Gibbons, 'Lee, Francis', *ODNB*.

[444] See Smith, 'Jane Lead's wisdom' (1984).

[445] Dodwell to Lee, 23 Aug 1698, Bod. MS Cherry 22, fols. 60ᵛ–61ʳ.

[446] Dodwell, *Separation*, 260–2. See also *Dissertationes Cyprianicae*, 5b.

[447] Dodwell, 'Prolegomena', 79.

[448] Dodwell, *One altar*, 191–2. So thorough was Dodwell's treatment of the neoplatonists that he became an authority on the subject outside of the theological context to which he was deploying it: see e.g. the use of his work in the very learned biblical commentary (perhaps by Daniel Whitby) at Folger, MS X.d.29(5), fol. 14ᵛ.

[449] Dodwell, *One altar*, 204–6, with a long quotation from Philo, *Vit. Mos.*, III.14 about the garments of the High Priest representing the world. See also Henry Dodwell, *Occasional communion fundamentally destructive to the discipline of the primitive catholick church* (London, 1705), 156–62; Dodwell, *Dissertationes Cyprianicae*, 40b; Dodwell to Lloyd, 3 Dec 1695, Bod. MS Cherry 22, fol. 42ᵛ: 'it is very clear from Philo also as well as the Writers of the N.T. that the Archetypal Priesthood was ascribed to the λόγος, and that it was by them believed that the efficacy even of the Jewish Priesthood was derived from its Union with that Archetypal Priesthood as an Authorized Representative of it by the Divine appointment so as

*Judaism*', it was clear that 'the *Primitive Christians* understood their *Bishop* to answer the Office of the *High Priest*'.[450]

Dodwell himself recognised that this contextualist approach was not for the masses.[451] This was another step in the Anglican sociology of knowledge in which scholar-priests became essential to establishing ecclesiological and liturgical practice. Even at this stage it was a step too far: Dodwell may in theory have preserved the autonomy of scripture, but in practise it was hard to see what independent reading of scripture could contribute. Even more problematically, Dodwell's scholarship led him to become what Richard Baxter would label a 'strange kind of Nonconformist'. As Jean-Louis Quantin has shown, Dodwell's historicising impulse led to severe and permanent doubts about the Athanasian Creed, doubts that rendered him incapable of joining the priesthood. Professor Quantin summarises that 'it is not clear whether he may even have disagreed with some positive teachings of the Athanasian Creed', or simply considered its formulations late and its damnatory clauses thus invalid.[452] Although he rarely referred to him, Dodwell had read Petau early in life.[453] He certainly did not accept the Jesuit's claim that the ante-Nicenes were proto-Arians, as is made clear in a long letter to his friend William Lloyd, where Dodwell argues that Christ's membership of the Melchizedekian rather than Aaronical priesthood (Heb. 7:1–27), when understood through the Platonic filter, certainly rendered him eternal.[454] But that same Platonic filter, Dodwell thought, also rendered the Calvinist notion of *autotheos* nonsensical.[455] Might he, like Cudworth, have seen the flowering of over-dogmatic insistence on consubstantiality in the immediately post-Nicene period as the root of error? It would be good to know what Socinian books he read that led 'some notions come into my mind which my cooler thoughts would not so probably have suggested', as he told Thomas Smith.[456] Despite Smith's advice to the contrary, he attended the only Socinian meeting that he could find in London in 1675.[457] One can only speculate on the amazed reactions of this tiny

---

not onely to signify but also to oblige the λόγος to ratify in heaven what was transacted by his Authorized Representative on Earth'.

[450] Dodwell, *One altar*, 231, 239.

[451] Henry Dodwell, 'An answer to six queries proposed to a *Gentlewoman* of the Church of England, by an emissary of the Church of ROME, fitted to a gentlewomans capacity', in *Two short discourses against the Romanists* (London, 1676), sigs. A2ᵛ–3ʳ (separate pagination).

[452] Quantin, 'Dodwell', 337–41. The key evidence is Dodwell's letter to Barlow, Queen's College, Oxford, MS 279, fols. 177ʳ⁻ᵛ.

[453] n. 420 above.    [454] Bod. MS Cherry 22, fol. 43ʳ.

[455] Dodwell, *Separation*, 240. Might this be why Dodwell applied to the Calvinist Barlow for clarification? Barlow himself happily believed that an orthodox consensus lasted for some time after Nicaea: see his inaugural lecture as Lady Margaret Professor of Divinity: Queen's College, Oxford, MS 235, p. 14: 'De quibus [i.e. the explication of the trinity] synodus Nicenae, Athanasius, patrisque pro aliquot secula subsequentes, modeste et orthodoxe … '.

[456] Dodwell to Smith, 22 June 1675, Bod. MS Smith 49, fol. 119ʳ.

[457] Dodwell to Smith, 3 July 1675, Bod. MS Smith 49, fol. 121ʳ.

urban congregation upon having the leading patristic scholar in the country arrive and quote Greek at them.

As Professor Quantin has already suggested, Dodwell, for all his brilliance and idiosyncrasy, cannot be read in a vacuum: his case demonstrates the preparedness of Restoration Oxford to welcome into its fold genuine originality.[458] The same may be said of Dodwell's treatment of the encounter between Christianity and philosophy. For all his originality, he was happy to acknowledge his debt to figures like Stillingfleet. Fifty years of scholarship had established the importance of the philosophical context to understanding the fathers. Dodwell's role was to universalise that scholarship, and to refuse to compartmentalise it to specific polemical tasks.

## 6.7     The trinitarian controversy

Dodwell finished his letter to Smith with remarkable prescience:

Whatever they [the Socinians] are at present, yet they are the most likely to prevail on the Genius of this Age, and therefore I cannot but conceive it very usefull to inform my self particularly of the Principles and humour of that Part of them which is in this City in order to the more effectual opposing them as I may have hereafter.[459]

What he probably meant was that the taste for an ahistorical rationalism would ferment the heresy of 'these witty men, who pretend to expound these antient monuments without dealing in coaeval monuments'.[460] In reality, the great trinitarian crisis of the 1690s[461] did not emerge from rationalism. First, it stemmed from a degree of *de facto* liberalisation of printing after James II's Declaration for the liberty of conscience of April 1687 (and more generally post-1688) that was taken advantage of by the philanthropist Thomas Firmin, who personally sponsored the majority of anti-trinitarian publications.[462] Second, it stemmed from the continuation of the theological split within orthodoxy, as William Sherlock pushed to the extreme the anti-Calvinist subordinationist trinity of the Arminians and many of his Anglican colleagues.[463]

---

[458] Quantin, 'Dodwell', 355, questioning, to my mind quite rightly, the interpretation offered in Trevor-Roper, *Archbishop Laud* (1940), 117.

[459] Bod. MS Smith 49, fol. 121ʳ.     [460] Bod. MS Cherry 22, fol. 43ᵛ.

[461] See Trowell, 'Unitarian and/or Anglican' (1996); Greig, 'Gilbert Burnet and the trinitarian controversy of the 1690s' (1993); Dixon, *Disputes*, esp. 98–129; Lim, *Trinity*, 305–9. All these studies ignore the continental theological–scholarly dimension. A very thorough bibliographical introduction can be found in Bianchi, 'Some sources for a history of English Socinianism' (1985).

[462] On the remarkably well-connected Firmin, see *The life of Mr. Thomas Firmin, late citizen of London* (London, 1698); *An account of Mr. Firmin's religion* (London, 1698); and *A vindication of the memory of the late excellent and charitable Mr. Firmin* (London, 1699), all anonymous; and Stephenson, 'Thomas Firmin' (1949).

[463] See now Hampton, *Anti-Arminians*, 129–91, which is certainly the most theologically informed discussion of the whole trinitarian controversy; see also Thiel, 'The Trinity and

Most ironically, historical narratives of the type Dodwell had pioneered were central to both antitrinitarian and trinitarian arguments.[464] The very first salvo on the antitrinitarian side, Stephen Nye's *Brief history of the Unitarians* (1687), cited Petau alongside Sand and claimed that early Christianity saw a gradual degeneration from the primitive pure monotheism of the Nazarenes and other Jewish Christians (whose writings were later destroyed by the Arians and trinitarians) first to the proto-Arian *logos*-theology of Justin and Origen, then to Arianism, then to the idea of the eternity of Christ proclaimed at Nicaea, and finally to that of consubstantiality proclaimed by the post-Nicenes.[465] Soon after, Nye explicitly inserted Platonism into the story. The ante-Nicenes were, as Cudworth had suggested, Platonist trinitarians, but their strange kind of subordinationism or 'semi Arianism', now revived by Cudworth and Sherlock, was so obviously tritheistic that it had been replaced by the scholastic 'nominal' trinitarianism of three persons in one essence, lately defended by the Calvinist Robert South against Sherlock, but itself philosophically nonsensical, as Cudworth had shown.[466] South had already accused Sherlock of following Cudworth's Plato over 'General Councils, and the Universal constant use of the Church', by which South – not particularly invested in patristics – clearly meant the Athanasian Creed and Reformed orthodoxy.[467] This accusation was not unfounded, since Sherlock had argued that Petau and Cudworth had shown definitively that when the Nicenes spoke of the persons of the trinity as being ὁμοούσιος, they 'did not understand this word of a Numerical but Specifick Sameness of Nature: or the agreement of things, numerically differing from one another in the same common Nature', although he did attempt to vindicate 'from the Mis-representations and hard Censures of *Petavius* and Dr. *Cudworth*' those post-Nicenes – especially Gregory of Nyssa and Cyril of

---

human personal identity' (2000), at 219–43; Reedy, *Robert South* (1992), 137–42; Antognazza, *Leibniz on the trinity and the incarnation* (2008 [1999]), 91–2, 94–7, 100–2.

[464]  See Dockrill, 'The authority of the fathers in the great trinitarian debates of the 1690s' (1990), which does not recognise the central importance of Petau's work.

[465]  [Stephen Nye], *A brief history of the Unitarians, called also Socinians* ([London], 1687), 26–8, 32–3; see also the classification of Episcopius as an Arian at 34–5. On Nye, who despite his anti-trinitarianism never left his position as rector of Little Hormead, Hertfordshire, see McLachlan, *Socinianism*, 320–3; McLachlan, *The story of a nonconformist library* (1923), 53–86.

[466]  [Stephen Nye], *A letter of resolution concerning the doctrines of the Trinity and the Incarnation* ([London], 1691), 11, 15–17; [Nye], *Some thoughts upon Dr. Sherlock's Vindication of the Doctrin* [sic] *of the Holy Trinity* ([London], 1691]), 1; [Nye], *Considerations on the explications of the doctrine of the Trinity by Dr. Wallis, Dr. Sherlock, Dr. S—th, Dr. Cudworth, and Mr. Hooker* (London, 1692), 10–11, 13–14, 15–17, 18–19 (for Cudworth as 'moderate Arian'); [Nye], *Considerations on the explications of the doctrine of the Trinity occasioned by four sermons preached by His Grace the Lord Arch-Bishop of Canterbury* ([London], 1694), 16. For South's scholastic attack on Sherlock, see Hampton, *Anti-Arminians*, 143–50.

[467]  Robert South, *Tritheism charged upon upon Dr. Sherlock's new notion of the trinity* (London, 1695), 232.

Alexandria – who had gone further and 'placed the Essential Unity of the Divine Nature in the sameness of Essence'.[468]

Nye was thus doing little more than pointing out the differences between the two supposedly 'orthodox' camps: one which had to acknowledge the Platonism and the subordinationism of the Nicene and ante-Nicene fathers, the other which had to resort to scholasticism to preserve the orthodoxy of strict consubstantiality. Nye agreed with Cudworth that the ante-Nicenes were Platonists and that the Cambridge man had shown that the commonly accepted 'Scholastic Trinity is a pure jargonry; y$^e$ Philosophy of Gotham' which was 'invented by P. Lombard', and 'was never Authorised by any public authority, except of y$^e$ Lateran Council'.[469] And yet Cudworth's own trinity not only 'revisited the error' of Calvin's old Arian enemy Gentile, but it also showcased the Platonic corruptions that destroyed the primitive Nazarene faith.[470] Petau and Sand had long shown the Platonism behind trinitarian language: without the Jesuitical recourse to church authority this left nothing but pagan polytheism.[471] The usual defence of the fathers – that they spoke incautiously before the rise of non-trinitarian heresy – was nonsensical, for the first Jewish converts like the Nazarenes certainly did not hold Christ's divinity.[472] To rely on the Cabbala as Bull had done was almost as bad as relying on pagan and Christian forgeries like the Sibyls and Hermes.[473]

The antitrinitarian attack, then, involved little new scholarship, but depended mostly on pointing out the divisions that had been established within 'orthodoxy' over the previous fifty years. Only in their identification with the early

---

[468] William Sherlock, *A vindication of the doctrine of the holy and ever blessed trinity and the incarnation of the Son of God . . . the second edition* (London, 1691 [1st edn=1690]), 106–9 and 109–49 for the defence of the post-Nicenes, with many references to Petau. See also [William Sherlock], *A defence of Dr. Sherlock's notion of a trinity in unity* (London, 1694), 24–5 (Petau used against the standard definition of consubstantiality), 83 (for the authority of Plato on replacing the use of 'person' with 'mind'). South attempted to respond by collapsing the difference between Sherlock's ante- and post-Nicene positions: *Animadversions upon Dr. Sherlock's book* (London, 1693), 174–90 (he does not address the accusation of Platonism). Thomas Holdsworth, *Impar conatui* (London, 1695), vehemently attacks Sherlock, Cudworth, and Petau, claiming them all to be disproved by Bull. But conversely, see the defence of Petau and Cudworth as both supposedly supporting the orthodox position in J. B., *The doctrine of the fathers and schools consider'd concerning the articles of a trinity of divine persons* (London, 1695), 102–18: a nice example of the fluidity of 'orthodoxy' that had been introduced by the Jesuit's work.

[469] Nye to unknown, 17 Nov 1703, BL MS Add. 4367, fol. 99$^r$. See also [Nye], *Considerations* [1693], 10, 15–16.

[470] BL MS Add. 4367, fol. 103$^r$.

[471] [Stephen Nye?], *A defence of the Brief history of the Unitarians* ([London], 1691), 5; [Nye], *Letter of resolution*, 3; [Nye], *An accurate examination of the principal texts usually alledged for the divinity of our Saviour* ([London], 1692), 44–5; [Nye], *The trinitarian scheme of religion . . . considered* (London, 1692), 4–5; [Nye], *Considerations* [1694], 20; [Nye], *The agreement of the Unitarians with the Catholick Church* ([London], 1697), 54.

[472] [Nye], *Letter of resolution*, 11.   [473] [Nye], *Letter of resolution*, 15–17.

Jewish Christians did the antitrinitarians make a new positive case, although this was cribbed from the references gathered by Sand and especially Zwicker; all the evidence was derived from the heresiographers and nothing new was available. In fact, the argument probably weakened the antitrinitarian position. The longest antitrinitarian historical statement, a work entitled *The judgment of the fathers concerning the doctrine of the Trinity* (1695) written directly against Bull and probably also by Nye,[474] presented the Nazarenes, Ebionites, and their descendants as the only true Christians in the first century and a half. This involved denying the authenticity of 'orthodox' texts adduced by Bull such as the Epistle of Barnabas, the Pastor of Hermas, and the Ignatian Epistles, and questioning G. J. Vossius's late dating for the Apostles' Creed.[475] These texts, and Vossius's redating, had been almost universally accepted among scholars, and the author offered no new evidence against them.[476] The polemical point, however, was obvious: by negating these testimonies Bull's earliest authority became Justin Martyr, whose ideas could be dismissed as Platonic fancy.[477] Far more powerful were the arguments against Bull's deployment of putative Judaic precedents for Platonic language. 'I cannot but wonder' stated the author, 'that a Protestant Divine should believe the Jewish *Cabbala*'.[478] The *Book of Wisdom* was a Christian forgery, as Grotius had argued.[479] The Targums meanwhile spoke of the *logos* not 'in the Platonick sense; namely, as a Person, or as a God: but only in the Jewish and Socinian Sense; namely, as the Energy and Power of God'.[480] This powerful argument only fell apart over

---

[474] *The judgment of the fathers concerning the doctrine of the trinity; opposed to Dr. G. Bull's Defence of the Nicene faith. Part I.* ([London], 1695). The widely accepted attribution to an otherwise invisible 'Thomas Smalbroke' stems from R. Wallace in 'Historical sketch of the trinitarian controversy' (1845), 289–90, based on manuscript notes signed '"T" or "F" Smalbroke' in a copy of Nye's *History of the Unitarians* (1687) (I have been unable to trace this copy). The content of the notes was, according to Wallace, incorporated into a second edition of the *History* (1691), where they appear without attribution. Wallace claims that 'it is highly improbable that a person transcribing into his own copy of the first edition of a work the alterations made by the author in a second edition, would take the liberty of changing the phraseology'. Nye would later defend himself from accusations by Pierre Allix that he authored the work: *The doctrine of the holy trinity, and the manner of our Saviour's divinity* (London, 1701), 164. On the basis of these flimsy factoids, Wallace's attribution to 'Smalbroke' was taken up in McLachlan, *Nonconformist library*, 72–4, from where it eventually entered the ESTC and has been uncritically accepted by e.g. Myllykoski, 'Christian Jews'; Goldish, 'The battle for "true" Jewish Christianity' (1999), 148–9. In reality, the textual similarities with Nye's works are striking (compare e.g. the treatment of the Cabbala at 58 with [Nye], *Letter of resolution*, 15–16). The author also admits (47) to writing *Considerations* [1694], all the essays in which were definitely by Nye (McLachlan, *Nonconformist library*, 70–1). Therefore, the author will herewith be cited as '[Nye?]'.

[475] [Nye?], *Judgment of the fathers*, 7–29.

[476] Quantin, *Antiquity*, 242, 267, 284, 294, 340–1, 346 n. 125; G. J. Vossius, *Disseratationes tres de tribus symbolis, Apostolico, Athanasiano, et Constantinopolitano* (Amsterdam, 1642), 1–36. They had just been conveniently translated by William Wake as *The genuine epistles of the apostolical fathers* (London, 1693).

[477] [Nye?], *Judgment of the fathers*, 49.     [478] Ibid., 58.     [479] Ibid., 60.     [480] Ibid., 61.

the case of Philo, who, the antitrinitarian author had to claim, was a Platonic Christian: a claim not only completely outdated but also very stupid given his earlier case for the uniquely non-Platonic Jewish Christianity that supposedly existed before *c.* 150.[481] Nonetheless, the incontrovertible point about the fundamental difference between the Platonic and scholastic trinities and how they cancelled each other out could again be made. It was remarkable that Bull had espoused his subordinationist trinity when a contrary orthodoxy 'ha[d] been followed by all the Divinity-Chairs in *Christendom*, from about the Year 1200', even if Bull's was 'the Doctrine of the Fathers'.[482]

The fullest use of Sand and Zwicker was in fact made by a little-known former Cambridge mathematician, Gilbert Clerke (1626–*c.* 1697),[483] who, writing in Latin, repeated their accusation against the trinitarians of 'bringing their opinions about the Son of God not from Scripture but from the Platonic school and from their own brains'.[484] This involved the usual condemnation of Justin Martyr as the fountainhead of Platonic corruption.[485] Clerke's only original thesis seems to have been that the Athanasian trinitarianism which followed the Platonic derived from Tertullian's adoption of the Montanist heresy.[486] A similarly low level of originality was to be found in the third tract in the same volume, which was by Samuel Crell (1660–1747), who regularly travelled to London in the 1690s.[487] Arguing that 'all the works of those followers of the Apostles who did not rush headlong into Platonism were lost',[488] he identified precisely the deflowering of the primitive church

---

[481] Ibid., citing Eusebius, who in fact never directly claims Philo as a Christian (all the references are *Hist. eccl.*, II.4.2, II.5.6, II.16–17, II.17.1, II.18.8).

[482] [Nye?], *Judgment of the fathers*, 74.

[483] For Clerke, who resigned his fellowship at Sidney Sussex College, Cambridge, in 1655, see Mandelbrote, 'Clerke, Gilbert', *ODNB*. As well as accusing him of plagiarism from Zwicker and Sand, Nelson claimed that he was 'flung' towards Socinianism by his revulsion at mid-century antinomianism ('Life of Bull', 501, 512): if true, this is interesting evidence of seventeenth-century conversion experiences.

[484] Gilbert Clerke, 'Ante-Nicenismus', in *Tractatus tres; quorum qui prior Ante-Nicenismus dicitur ... in secundo brevis responsio ordinatur ad D. G. Bulli Defensionem Synodi Nicenae* ([London], 1695), sig. A3ᵛ, ' ... Ante-Nicenos, qui non ex Scripturis, sed sui-ipsorum cerebro, & Scholâ Platonis, sententiam suam de filio Dei exprompserint'.

[485] Clerke, 'Ante-Nicenismus', 3–11.

[486] Ibid., 23–4. Clerke was following a hint in Jonas Szlichtyng's *De SS. Trinitate, de moralibus N. & V. Testamenti praeceptis, itemque de sacris, eucharistiae, & baptimi ritibus* ([n.p.], 1637), 9–11. Curiously, this opinion has recently been revived: McGowan, 'Tertullian and the "heretical" origins of the "orthodox" trinity'(2006).

[487] On Crell, see Mulsow, *Moderne aus dem Untergrund* (2002), 85–113, and on his travels to London and English contacts: Mulsow, 'New Socinians', 61–3 (although some claims are unsubstantiated, e.g. 'men such as John [sic – Matthew] Tindal and Anthony Collins were among those who had helped finance the publication of his books').

[488] [Samuel Crell], 'Vera & Antiqua Fides de Divinitate Christi asserta', in *Tractatus Tres*, 178: 'Atque hic rogandus est Lector, ut animum advertat periisse libros omnes Apostolicorum discipulorum quicunque in Platonismum non irruerent praecipites; inter alios vel casu perditos, vel industria deletos, etiam Christianorum qui erant ex circumcisione libros lugemus, quos

mentioned by Hegesippus to the expulsion from Judea of the Jewish Christians, alongside the Jews themselves, in the reign of Hadrian, facilitating the triumph of 'the Platonic faith'.[489]

These arguments often played into the hands of trinitarian apologists. Bull, in a work written in response to the publication of the *Judgment of the fathers* and Clerke's *Tractatus tres*, could gleefully point out that Crell's argument was based on a twisted quotation from Sulpicius Severus's *Chronica*: the true one in fact stated that it was the Jewish Christians who benefited from Hadrian's expulsion of the Jews and that of them 'amost all believed in Christ as God while continuing in the observance of the law'.[490] By 1694 Bull had developed an elaborate counter-narrative that separated the Jewish Christians into two groups: the Nazarenes who combined observance of the Levitical law with 'catholic' trinitarianism and the heretical Ebionites.[491] Yet on the issues of the Platonic vocabulary of the ante-Nicenes and its differences from the stark consubstantialism of the post-Nicenes, the antitrinitarians – drawing freely on Petau, Sand, and now Cudworth – seemed to have the upper hand. Some trinitarians resorted to claiming naïvely that Plato must have taken his *logos* language from the Jews, as did the veterans John Wallis (who even cited Theophilus Gale)[492] and Thomas

inter Hegesippus fama notissimus, primorum temporum historiam Ecclesiasticam contexuerat; eique, à Platonizantibus Christianis qui imputantur errores, in causa sunt, quòd historia desideratissimâ privemur'.

[489] Ibid., 179–80: 'Jam haec magni momenti res est, & notatu dignissima; per illam utíque Hegesippus fatalem Epochen disignat, quando Episcopi Christiani, qui non ita pridem Ethnici Philosophi, Nazarenis Episcopis successerint, & consequenter, quando Platonismus purae & simplicis veritatis quam Jacobi succesores praedicaverant, in locum subiverit. Atque hoc accidit sub ipso Adriani imperio, i.e. quum Judaei universi unà cum Christiani circumcises abacti essent ex Judaea. Sulpitius Severus, lib. 2. cap. 45. Non sine causa dixit *fidem Christianam*, i.e. [juxta opinionem suam] fidem Platonicam, *lucrum fecisse non exiguum ex illa dispersione:* quippe quòd tunc temporis, quum Platonismo viam obstruere non poterat fides primitiva, quam Nazareni integram & illibatam servassent; fatale malum longè latéque se diffuderit, & rapidi fluminis instar turbidis imbribus aucti, & conciti, per omnem diffluxit Ecclesiam, imò nec ipsi Hierosolymitanae pepercit'. In modern editions, the passage quoted rather loosely by Crell occurs at Sulpicius Severus, *Chronica*, II.31.

[490] George Bull, *Primitiva & Apostolica Traditio*, 17 (it is unclear when exactly this posthumous work was written, but from the obvious polemical investement in the trinitarian controversy, one supposes c. 1695–99); Sulpicius Severus, *Chronica*, II.31: 'Quod quidem Christianae Fidei proficiebat, quia tum paene omnes Christum Deum sub legis observatione credebant'. A similar argument is made in William Basset, *An answer to the Brief history of the Unitarians* (London, 1693), 125–7.

[491] George Bull, *Judicium Ecclesiae Catholicae trium primorum seculorum de necessitate credendi quod Dominus noster Jesus Christus sit verus Deus* (Oxford, 1694), 50–4. This rather ambitious argument, based on a reinterpretation of Justin, *Tryph.*, 45–7, was attacked in [Nye?], *Judgment of the fathers*, 32–45.

[492] John Wallis, *Three sermons concerning the sacred trinity* (London, 1691), 99–100. Because of this, McGuire and Rattansi try to straitjacket Wallis into a 'Platonist' canon ('Pipes', 133–4). Wallis later used Petau to argue for subordinationism: *A seventh letter, concerning the sacred Trinity* (London, 1691), 12.

Long.[493] Even Archbishop Tillotson made this point, although he also added the much more impressive one that St. John's Platonic vocabulary could be explained by his writing against the Platonic gnostics: like Dodwell he concluded that the Socinians were incapable of understanding texts in context.[494] His episcopal colleague Gilbert Burnet admitted that 'many of the Fathers' were over-excited by the convenient Platonic vocabulary, saying 'many things which intimate that they believed an inequality between the Persons, and a Subordination of the Second and Third to the First'; they were then opposed by those asserting that 'the Deity was one Numerical Being'.[495] This obvious extrapolation from Cudworth was treated as an admission of defeat by Nye.[496]

The abandonment of the fathers by Burnet – a highly idiosyncratic member of the Church of England whose Scottish education was unlikely to instil much patristic fervour[497] – was not representative. Unfortunately for the Church, few serious scholars stepped up to the plate. Dodwell's only reply to the idea that the trinity was a Platonic fable, a reply again based on the idea that 'even the Apostles themselves' spoke of Christ as the archetypal *logos*, was hidden away in a brief passage in an appendix to a work on the Roman historian Velleius.[498] On 19 October 1695 Evelyn dined with Thomas Gale at St Paul's school, Gale showing him 'many curious passages out of some ancient Platonists' MSS. concerning the H. Trinity, which this great and learned person would publish ... if he was encouraged, and eased of the burden of Teaching'.[499]

---

[493] Thomas Long, *An answer to a Socinian treatise, call'd The naked Gospel* (London, 1691), 36–7, wheeling out the old references to patristic authorities, Augustine (*Civ. Dei*, x.29), and those that referred to Amelius (n. 139 above). On Long, see Chamberlain, 'Long, Thomas', *ODNB*. The long section on the ante-Nicenes in Luke Milbourne, *Mysteries in religion vindicated* (London, 1692), 411–81, simply ignores the accusation of Platonism, despite familiarity with Petau and Zwicker (462).

[494] John Tillotson, *Sermons concerning the divinity and incarnation of our blessed Saviour* (2nd edn, London, 1695 [1st edn=1693]), 7–8 (including reference to the Targums), 20, 269–71, 9–14, 14–15: 'And this was the great and fatal mistake of *Socinus*, to go to interpret Scripture merely by Criticising upon words ... without regard to the true Occasion upon which they were made, and without any manner of knowledge and insight into the History of the Age in which they were written'.

[495] Gilbert Burnet, *Four discourses delivered to the clergy of the Diocess of Sarum* (London, 1694), 'II. The divinity and death of Christ', 97–8; see also 100–1. Burnet was almost certainly influenced by Le Clerc: see below and 2.6 above.

[496] Nye, *Considerations* [1694], 16. Burnet was also attacked by Samuel Hill in *A vindication of the primitive fathers against the imputations of Gilbert Lord Bishop of Sarum* (London, 1695), esp. 54–9, deploying the providentialist argument for any trinitarian language in Plato. For the high-church Hill, a prominent controversialist in the two decades after the revolution of 1688, see Greig, 'Hill, Samuel', *ODNB*.

[497] See in general Greig, 'Burnet and nonconformity'.

[498] Henry Dodwell, *Annales Velleiani, Quintilianei, Statiani* (Oxford, 1698), 'Dissertatio miscellanea II. De editi a Cl. Rigaltio Commodiani aetate', sigs. Uu2$^{r-v}$ (first identified in Quantin, *Antiquity*, 388).

[499] Evelyn, *Diary*, v, 221.

Given Gale's expertise on neoplatonism this would have been a major publication, but nothing seems to have come of it.[500]

It was left to a Huguenot refugee to offer the fullest scholarly defence. Pierre Allix (1641–1717) had succeeded Daillé as pastor of the Huguenot church at Charenton and became the highest profile Huguenot minister in England after emigrating upon the Revocation of the Edict of Nantes, building up many religious as well as scholarly contacts (one of whom was Dodwell, whose works he read carefully).[501] Allix was a respected Hebraist[502] and he took it upon himself to defend Bull's weak Judaic arguments against the cavils of the author of the *Judgment of the fathers*: the result was published in 1699 as *The judgement of the ancient Jewish church, against the Unitarians*.[503]

Allix's argument was that trinitarianism had existed among the Israelies but that most evidence of it had later been eroded by the post-Christ Jews.[504] The work was learned and critical. He rubbished Nye's idea that the works of Philo were second-century Christian forgeries while admitting that Eusebius's belief that the Therapeutae were Christians was nonsense.[505] He acknowledged that the Targums, especially Jonathan, contained later additions but argued that these additions would only have been made to strengthen the Jewish aspects, not the Christian ones; in any case, Onkelos was not corrupt.[506] And he was generally sceptical about the Cabbala,[507] preferring to base his arguments on Philo, the Targums, a few Midrashim, and the apocryphal scriptures, especially the *Book of Wisdom*, which he saved from Grotius's destructive arguments by pointing out that Nachmanides cited the Aramaic version and that Azariah de' Rossi had believed it ancient.[508] It was absurd to insinuate, as had the author of

---

[500]  On Gale, see 3.6 above.

[501]  See Larminie, 'Allix, Peter [Pierre]', *ODNB*; Gwynn, 'Conformity, non-conformity and Huguenot settlement in England' (2006), 37; Gwynn, 'The Huguenots and non-conformity' (2011), 146–7; Allix to Dodwell, Feb 1688, Bod. MS Eng. lett. c.28, fols. 19$^r$–20$^r$. He was also in contact with Thomas Smith (e.g. Bod. MS Smith 46, fols. 5$^r$–8$^r$) and Beveridge (see Allix to John Batteley, 24 May [unknown year], Bod. MS Tanner 29, fol. 30$^r$). Further study is very desirable.

[502]  Grudgingly praised even by the otherwise unimpressible Bernard: see Bernard to Thomas Smith, 20 Aug 1687, Bod. MS Smith 47, fol. 50$^r$, commenting on Allix's *Réflexions sur les livres de l'écriture sainte, pour établir la verité de la religion chrétienne* (London, 1687).

[503]  Pierre Allix, *The judgement of the ancient Jewish church, against the Unitarians* (London, 1699), xvi–xvii. Two years earlier, Allix had entered the lists on the subject anonymously: [P. Allix], *The fathers vindicated, by a Presbyter of the Church of England* (London, 1697). The ESTC attributes the work to John Deacon, but textual similarities to the *Judgement of the ancient Jewish church* suggest that it is almost certainly by Allix. A copy in CUL (classmark 3.36.32) has been marked 'Pierre Allix D.D.' on the title page in a contemporary hand.

[504]  A useful discussion is Goldish, 'Allix's polemics', although it does not recognise Allix's authorship of *Fathers vindicated*.

[505]  Allix, *Judgement*, 76, 80–1; [Allix], *Fathers vindicated*, 127–9.

[506]  Allix, *Judgement*, 88–90, 95–7.

[507]  See the definition adopted at [Allix], *Fathers vindicated*, 122–3.

[508]  Allix, *Judgement*, 68–9, 343. For Nachmanides, Allix probably just took the claim directly from de' Rossi: *Azariah de' Rossi's observations on the Syriac New Testament: a critique of the*

the *Judgment of the fathers*, that the Targums had been corrupted by 'Platonic' Christians: why would the Jews then accept them?[509] The *logos*-theology of scripture was therefore derived from the Jews, who had consistently spoken of and expected a divine Messiah.[510] Philo was thus a key witness for scriptural vocabulary.[511] Of the contested fathers, Justin's conversion story showed that he rejected Platonism in favour of 'the Doctrine of *Moses* and the Prophets'.[512] Later, the Jews had a political reason for rejecting their proto-trinitarian theology: having been crushed by the Romans they framed 'more carnal notions concerning the Kingdom of the Messias: Fancying that he should come as a victorious Prince, to conquer, and to avenge them to their Enemies'.[513] The non-trinitarian Nazarenes were mistaken in their belief that they followed traditional Jewish doctrine; instead, they followed the innovatory anti-Christian political Judaism.[514]

Yet when it came to the accusation of Platonism, Allix had to resort to the uncritical acceptance of patristic testimonies that he had elsewhere rejected. This he covered under a veneer of Casaubonian criticism: Plato's trinity was extremely obscure, and Eusebius was wrong to adduce it in defence of Christianity.[515] And Philo, like the widely discredited Aristobulus, had indeed been a syncretist who sometimes followed Platonic expressions because he wanted to demonstrate the dependence of paganism on Judaism.[516] But ultimately both Josephus and the 'Antient Fathers' were right: 'if *Plato* had any distinct Notions in Religion, he most certainly had them from the *Jews* while he sojourned in *Egypt*', probably through Pythagoras.[517] Paul's complaints against 'false genealogies' were directed at the Platonists and at the Platonic–Pythagorean Cabbala that had by then already sprung up among the Jews.[518] At the same time (and somewhat in contradiction): was it likely that fishermen had parroted the works of Plato?[519]

## 6.8      Enlightenment?

Allix's discussion was certainly of a high scholarly calibre, especially in its treatment of Hebraica. It became the go-to citation for many trinitarians, including Bull himself.[520] The accusation of Platonic corruption had led to a state where the defence of *the* key Christian doctrine had come to rest on an

---

*Vulgate by a sixteenth-century Jew*, ed. J. Weinberg (London, 2005), 86–7. See also the slightly different reasons in [Allix], *Fathers vindicated*, 121–2.

[509] Allix, *Judgement*, 357–8.      [510] Ibid., 253–65.      [511] Ibid., 313–18.

[512] Ibid., 318–22 at 319, 360–1; [Allix], *Fathers vindicated*, 93–109.

[513] Allix, *Judgement*, 39.      [514] Ibid., xvii; [Allix], *Fathers vindicated*, 64–76.

[515] Allix, *Judgement*, 355.      [516] Ibid., 355–7; for Aristobulus see Ch. 3 above.

[517] Ibid., 357, 362, 354 (for Pythagoras).      [518] Ibid., 263.

[519] Ibid., 359–60; [Allix], *Fathers vindicated*, 118.

[520] Bull, *Primitiva & Apostolica Traditio*, 20.

apocryphal book of the Old Testament, the Targums, and a Hellenistic Jew who everyone agreed was unreliable. It is in this context that we must approach Jean Le Clerc, to whose works, which a contemporary claimed were in 'every body's hands' in England, Allix was recommended as an antidote.[521] Professor Pocock has claimed that Le Clerc's repeated insistence on the Platonic component of ante-Nicene debate, especially on the trinity, and the heavily contextualist methodology used to defend it, were manifestations of the application of a 'Lockean theory of knowledge' to a 'critical approach to Christian history', all of which coalesced into an 'early Enlightenment—meaning the period during which Christian scholarship came to be dominated by critical method' deployed for the end of toleration, and whose beginnings can be dated and connected to the political events of the 1680s.[522] I would like to offer a slightly different picture, one in which the connection between scholarship and the politics of toleration that has defined almost all work on Le Clerc is moved to the background in favour of a focus on scholarly continuity.

Professor Pocock's subtle account depends on the idea that Le Clerc's contextual method was grounded in the application of Locke's theory of knowledge; indeed, that Locke's *Essay* prompted 'a new start' in ecclesiastical history and that Le Clerc's '*critique* [of the fathers] can be traced back to Locke and 1688'.[523] The evidence for this is a letter from Le Clerc to Locke of July 1688 in which the former stated that the *Essay* – of which he had published a well-known 'Abrégé' – had 'much confirmed in me [Le Clerc] some thoughts which I have had touching the manner of explaining the writings of the ancients'.[524] There can be no doubt that from the late 1680s Le Clerc started to use more frequently – although still not particularly frequently – the fashionable language of 'ideas' and their linguistic correlates (or lack thereof) in his historical work. Yet as his own words suggest, Locke's work only confirmed in him ideas that he held already. These were derived from long-available sources, some of which we have encountered in this book. Take, for example, this passage from 1685:

To write the history of a book is not simply to say when and by whom it was written, which copyists transcribed it, and what faults they committed in doing so. It is not

---

[521] William Wotton, *Some thoughts concerning a proper method of studying divinity*, ed. H. Cotton (Oxford, 1818 [1st edn=London, 1734], 40 (from internal evidence, this work was composed in the 1710s).

[522] Pocock, *Barbarism*, v, 89–92, 99. For Le Clerc, see further 2.6, 3.7, 5.3 above. For readings of him as an 'enlightened' pioneer who replaced theology with reason and so 'liberated' ecclesiastical history, see Pitassi, *Entre croire et savoir*, 83–91; Marshall, *Toleration*, esp. 477–501.

[523] Pocock, *Barbarism*, v, 95.

[524] Le Clerc to Locke, 13/23 July 1688, *Locke correspondence*, III, 487–8 ('Vôtre troisiéme Libre m'a beaucoup confirmé en diverses pensées que j'avois euës touchant la maniere d'expliquer les écrits des Anciens'). Prof. Pocock silently amalgamates this letter with that of 4/14 Oct 1688 (*Locke correspondence*, III, 506–7). For the 'Abrégé', published in the spring 1688 edition of the *BUH*, see Hill and Milton, 'The Epitome (Abrégé) of Locke's *Essay*' (2003).

enough to tell us who translated it and to recount the faults of the version, nor to teach us about who commented on it, and the defects of these commentaries. We must also be told, if possible, with what purpose the author wrote it, what circumstances urged him to take up the pen, and to what opinion or events he makes allusion to in the work, especially when discussing a book which does not contain general reflections or eternal truths, which are the same in all ages and among all the world's peoples.[525]

As examples of such an approach, Le Clerc offered the treatments of the Mosaic Law by Marsham and Spencer, Grotius and Hammond's commentaries on John's apocalypse, and the edition of Horace recently published by André Dacier.[526] Within a year he was applying these principles to the question of Nicene trinitarianism, citing Petau and Courcelles to the effect that for many of the ante-Nicenes 'ὁμοούσιος' meant only a shared general nature, not a shared numerical essence, against Bull's recently published *Defensio* (although he in turn cited Bull's defence of subordinationism against Catholic and Reformed orthodoxy, a nice example of even his involvement in confessional disputes).[527]

If all this by now sounds familiar, it is because it is – the product of a century of theological conflict. Le Clerc had in fact defended Courcelles's position as early as 1681 in a work that directly influenced Sherlock.[528] In the late 1680s he elaborated these ideas in a series of publications, the vitriolic English reaction to which deeply surprised him, and not entirely unjustly: first because he was mostly repeating ideas that had already been adumbrated in England and second because the nature of his reception fell very much outside of his control. In 1688 he published in his periodical, the *Bibliothèque universelle et historique*, reviews of several patristic editions that were in reality less reviews and

---

[525] [Le Clerc], *Sentimens*, 'Sentimens ... sur l'Histoire Critique en général' 6: 'Faire l'Histoire d'un Livre n'est pas simplement dire quand & par qui il a été fait, quels Copistes l'ont transcrit, & quelles fautes ils ont commises en le transcrivant. Il ne suffit pas de nous dire qui l'a traduit, & de nous faire remarquer les defauts de sa Version; ni meme de nous apprendre qui l'a commenté, & ce qu'il y a de défectueux dans ces Commentaires. Il faut encore nous découvrir, si cela se peut, dans quel dessein l'Auteur l'a composé, quelle occasion lui a fait prendre la plume, & à quelles opinions, ou à quels évenemens, il peut faire allusion dans cet Ouvrage, sur tout lors qu'il ne s'agit pas d'un livre qui contiene des réflexions générales, ou des veritez éternelles, qui sont les memes dans tous les Siécles, & parmi tous les peuples du monde'. That Simon has *not* followed this method is stated at 8, throwing doubt on the standard attribution of strong influence of Simon on Le Clerc (e.g. Pitassi, *Le Clerc*, 12–16, *passim*; Pocock, *Barbarism*, v, 92–3). See also Ch. 3, n. 450 above.

[526] [Le Clerc], *Sentimens*, 14–15, 16–17, 19. For Le Clerc and Spencer, see 3.7 above. I know of no serious treatment of Dacier. Le Clerc's 1688 comments to Locke were made after a discussion of Hebrew poetry: for his approach, and its deep debt to discussions stretching back to the sixteenth century, see now Haugen, 'Hebrew poetry', 21–2.

[527] [Jean Le Clerc], *Défense des sentimens de quelques Théologiens de Hollande* (Amsterdam, 1686), 75–82.

[528] Liberius a Sancto Amore [Jean Le Clerc], *Epistolae theologicae: in quibus varii scholasticorum errores castigantur* ([Amsterdam], 1679 [1681]). South recognised the influence of this work on Sherlock: *Tritheism charged*, 84–7. See also the useful discussion at Hampton, *Anti-Arminians*, 141–2.

more historical attacks on the faults of the fathers. To understand an author one had to understand his intellectual world, and the intellectual world of the post-apostolic fathers was Greek philosophy: Clemens Alexandrinus, for example, was so obsessed with philosophy that he believed it played the same role for the Greeks as prophecy did for the Jews.[529] Unfortunately, this engendered a dangerous syncretism, especially with Platonic philosophy – whose terms sometimes appeared similar to those of the Bible – and especially on the doctrine of the trinity.[530] This was a lesson in contextualism: most who begin to study the fathers did not realise that a grounding in Platonic philosophy is essential to understand their meaning.[531] Yet there was also a theological message: the fathers speculated freely and were not to be reduced to a 'system' of orthodoxy: a message for which Le Clerc cited not any of his supposedly 'enlightened' counterparts but the old stalwart of Protestant anti-patristics, Daillé.[532] All this was much expanded in another long essay on Eusebius, with further references to Petau and Huet; Bull was again condemned for not noting the differences between the Platonic discourses of specific numerical and general unity.[533] Eusebius meanwhile, was classified as an Arian – a conclusion that should not have been particularly controversial since it had been reached by Athanasius, Jerome and the Second Council of Nicaea (787) as well as Petau.[534] Another essay on Gregory Nazianzen similarly pointed to his Platonic vocabulary, and his failure to assert numerical unity.[535]

It was at this point that Le Clerc's problems in England began. The essay on Eusebius was translated and published as the *Defence* (1691) of the *Naked Gospel* (1690), the well-known statement of doctrinal minimalism by Arthur Bury, the rector of Exeter College, Oxford, which would launch a protracted controversy in the university, finally leading to the confirmation of Bury's deprivation in 1695.[536] Contrary to speculation,[537] the translation was not by

---

[529]  *BUH*, 10 (1688), 'Clementis Alexandrini Opera Graece & Latini . . . Coloniae 1688', 199.
[530]  Ibid., 207–8.    [531]  Ibid., 211.    [532]  Ibid., 222–3.
[533]  *BUH*, 10 (1688): 'Eusebii Pamphilicae . . . Praeparatio Evangelica . . . Demonstratione Evanglica . . . Colon. 1688', 415, 419.
[534]  Petau, *Theologica dogmata*, II, 56–72. See also the references to Petau, Huet, and Courcelles in the review of Isaac Barrow's posthumous *Opuscula* (London, 1687), *BUH*, 10 (1688), 31
[535]  *BUH*, 18 (1690), 'S. P. N. Gregorii Nazianzeni Theologi Opera . . . Coloniae 1690', 25–9.
[536]  [Arthur Bury], *The naked Gospel* ([London], 1690). See 88–9 for a discussion of the meaning of 'mystery' in the early church clearly drawn (without attribution) from Casaubon. The ESTC lists two London editions and an Oxford edition in 1690 alone. For the subsequent controversy, see most fully Tyacke, 'Religious controversy' (1997), 616–18; also Champion, *Pillars*, 107–8.
[537]  That Le Clerc wrote the work to defend Bury is wrongly asserted in Nuovo, 'Introduction' (2012), xxiii. A different rumour was that Le Clerc appreciated the work so much that he later appropriated it for his own: Wallace, 'Historical sketch', 135, Wallace, *Antitrinitarian biography* (1850), I, 207, through which it has entered the ESTC. The original source must be Nelson, *Life*, 374. Pocock, *Barbarism*, V, 106–7 remains agnostic. Le Clerc received the work from Benjamin Furly (Le Clerc to Locke, 22 Oct/1 Nov 1690, *Locke correspondence*, IV, 150–1), discussing it in a review in *BUH*, 19 (1690), 364–442.

Le Clerc, for the polemical preface went much further in its views than he ever did, pontificating on how 'the simple Primitive Chastity of the Gospel was defil'd with the Ceremonies, and the vain *Philosophy* of the *Pagans:* How *Platonic Enthusiasm* was impos'd upon the World for *Faith, Mystery* and *Revelation*, by cloyster'd Ecclesiasticks'.[538] The essays on Clemens Alexandrinus and Gregory Nazianzen were translated, also without Le Clerc's permission,[539] and published in 1696 and 1701[540] with prefaces advertising their usefulness to the trinitarian controversy.[541] This was the last type of notoriety that Le Clerc, desperate for a clerical appointment in England,[542] wanted. Certainly his association with Socinianism was by now cemented, and both public[543] and private[544] English condemnations followed.

Responding in part to the warnings of his friend Gilbert Burnet, Le Clerc attempted to demonstrate that his elucidation of a Platonic context was compatible with non-Arian trinitarianism. In 1695 he published a commentary on the beginning of John's Gospel, in which he defended his orthodoxy by attacking the 'Alogian' hypothesis that that Gospel was a forgery by Cerinthus.[545] Since no modern antitrinitarian had actually espoused this opinion the argument was of little importance: far more important was Le Clerc's claim that John had written his Gospel not just against the gnostics, as Irenaeus, Jerome, and most other exegetes had suggested, but against the Platonism of Philo Judaeus. But John himself 'seems to have had a respect'[546] for Platonism, and his λόγος

---

[538] *An historical vindication of The naked Gospel recommended to the University of Oxford* ([n.p.], 1690), sig. A2ʳ.

[539] As he himself stated: Jean Le Clerc, *A supplement to Dr. Hammond's Paraphrase and annotations on the New Testament* (London, 1699) (a translation of some of the notes in *Novum Testamentum Domini nostri Jesu Christi, ex versione vulgata, cum paraphrasi et adnotationibus Henrici Hammondi* (Amsterdam, 1698)), iii–iv (a new preface added to this English edition); Le Clerc, *Epistolae criticae*, 71, suggesting it may have been a French Socinian. Perhaps this was Charles Le Cène, who had a history of publishing Socinian works? On Le Cène, who had by the 1690s moved to Holland, and his English connections, see Marshall, 'Huguenot thought after the revocation of the Edict of Nantes' (2001), 389–90.

[540] Jean Le Clerc, *The lives of Clemens Alexandrinus, Eusebius Bishop of Cæsarea, Gregory Nazianzen, and Prudentius the Christian poet* (London, 1696); Le Clerc, *The lives of the primitive fathers . . . with their several opinions about the deity of Christ. Which may give some light to the late dipsutes concerning the Trinity* (London, 1701). For other unauthorised translations of Le Clerc, see 3.7 above.

[541] Le Clerc, *Lives* [1696], sig. [A3]ʳ.    [542] Brogi, 'Le Clerc et l'Église anglicane'.

[543] South, *Tritheism charged*, 85–6; F. B., *A free but modest censure on the late controversial writings and debates . . . with brief remarks on Monsieur Le Clerc's Ars critica* (London, 1698), 26–31.

[544] See e.g. the copy of Le Clerc's *Ars critica* (2nd edn, London, 1698) in Trinity College, Cambridge (classmark: II.10.103) acquired by Edward Rudd in 1699, with Latin comments on Le Clerc's putative Socinianism written on the flyleaf.

[545] The source is Epiphanius, *Pan.*, LI. For Le Clerc's attack, see Jean Le Clerc, *XVIII. Prima commata capitis primi Evangelii S. Joannis paraphrasi et animadversionibus* (Amsterdam, 1695), 11–15.

[546] These words appear in the new preface added in Le Clerc, *Supplement*, 155.

should be translated not as 'Word' but as 'Reason', in accordance with Platonic opinion.[547] The second claim was not particularly original: Petau had already pointed out that many of the Greek fathers had used the term in this way.[548] The first was more original, although of course it rested on more than a century of analysis of Philo *qua* Platonist, beginning with de' Rossi.

Le Clerc made the claim in the context of a project of translating into Latin and supplementing Hammond's *Paraphrase*, where the target of John's words was ascribed to philosophical gnosticism. Professor Pocock suggests that Le Clerc's deviation from Hammond derived from political differences: where Hammond posited a debate between 'orthodox' and 'heretic', 'Le Clerc remains in a position to use Lockean philosophy, and the theology arising from it, as arguments for toleration. Apostles and philosophers, orthodox and heterodox, are struggling with the same language difficulties and should treat each other with respect'.[549] Indeed, he questions why Le Clerc chose to translate Hammond in the first place.[550] The reality seems far more simple: Le Clerc translated Hammond because he thought him an excellent example of historical criticism of the New Testament and he rejected his gnostic hypothesis not for political but for scholarly reasons: he thought it dangerous to apply the evidence for later gnostic beliefs gathered by Irenaeus to John's contemporaries.[551] As we have seen, he was not the first to find Hammond overly obsessed with gnosticism: it hardly took enlightened tolerationism.[552] The idea that John opposed Philo stemmed from this scepticism about early gnosticism: in the absence of better evidence it was preferable to assume that John had opposed those whose Platonic notions were

---

[547] The germ of both these opinions is already in *BUH*, 10, 400–2.

[548] Petau, *Theologica dogmata*, II, 539–46; Le Clerc acknowledges the influence at *Supplement*, 156.

[549] Pocock, *Barbarism*, V, 122.

[550] Ibid., 119 ('Le Clerc's decision to expend labour in translating and improving his work is hard to explain without supposing a complex relationship with English churchmanship, persisiting after he had lost all hope of an English position; he cites a great many English authorities in his writings').

[551] See e.g. le Clerc, *Prima commata*, 38–9: 'In voce *Unigenitus* [i.e. from Joh. 1:14] latet forte ἀντίθετις aliqua ad Philonis doctrinam, qui Λόγον, non μονογενῆ *unigenitum*, sed tantùm πρωτότοκον *primogenitum*, & πρεσβύτατον *antiquissimum Angelorum* vocitare solet. Vult *Grotius* Gnosticos hîc damnari, qui alium Λόγον, alium Μονογενῆ faciebant; sed nescio an jam inventae essent futiles illae *Pleromatis Syzygiae*, cùm Joannes scripsit', and the attack on Irenaeus for reading back the doctrines of the later Valentinians into the earlier gnostics, 39–40. ('Respici vult *Irenaeus* πλήρωμα, quod tribuit non modò *Valentinianis*, sed etiam *Cerintho* ... Non audemus tamen ei prorsus assentiri, ob sequentes rationes ... ').

[552] Le Clerc repeats the accusation throughout the commentary: see the English translation, *Supplement*, e.g. VI, 254–5, 466 (on 'vain philosophy' in Coloss. 2:8), 542. Among Englishmen, even Le Clerc's critics agreed with him that Hammond had over-stretched the gnostic thesis: see e.g. Daniel Whitby, *A paraphrase and commentary upon all the epistles of the New Testament* (London, 1700), sig. [A4]ʳ, pointing out that he wants to supply an 'Antidote' to le Clerc's animadversions on Hammond, but that he nonetheless agrees with the Huguenot's dismissal of Hammond's 'darling Opinion' about the gnostics.

well known, that is to say the Hellenistic Jews like Philo, than to assume gnostic opponents for whom there was no evidence.[553] Grotius had already demonstrated that Philo's works were known to the author of the Epistle to the Hebrews,[554] and the Alexandrian Jew had also understood λόγος as 'Reason'.[555] But there were important differences between John and Philo. First and most important, Philo's *logos* was God's instrument in the creation of the world, whereas John said it of God himself.[556] Second, when John affirmed that 'all things' were made by the *logos*, he was opposing the Epicurean belief that things had come about by chance, strains of which had even appeared in Philo (who, despite his Platonism, had claimed that venomous reptiles were not created providentially but by the heating of internal moisture).[557]

Although building on previous scholarship, this was a clever interpretation that allowed Le Clerc to demonstrate the non-Arianism of John while continuing to berate the church fathers for subsequent Platonic confusions that they had introduced, a task he continued in his famous *Ars critica* (1696).[558] On the Platonism of the ante-Nicene trinity, which did not share one numerical essence, Le Clerc openly relied on Petau, Courcelles, Huet, and Cudworth.[559] Needless to say, this was not enough for an English church that had invested so heavily in the authority of the ante-Nicenes.[560] At the same time, Le Clerc's insistence on Eusebius's Arianism came back to haunt him: William Cave, whom he had accused of

---

[553] Le Clerc, *Prima commata*, 16: 'Quamvis tacuissent memorati Scriptores [Irenaeus and others who wrote on apostolic intentions], non difficulter ex ipsa re conjecturam ducere potuissemus; cùm enim Scriptores celebres & Sectae Haereticorum in Religionem Judaïcam & Christianam intulissent varias voces Platonicas, antequàm Joannes scriberet; videamúsque eum easdem voces, singulari sensu, primum Christianorum Scriptorum usurpare, & quidem ab ipso Evangelii sui initio; facile fuit conjicere Apostolorum ad eorum hominum sermonem alludere, & quo sensu usurpari eae voces possint Christianos docere'. For Philo's contemporary notoriety, see 17.

[554] Le Clerc mentions this at *Prima commata*, 17 without giving a reference, but see e.g. Grotius, *Annotationes in NT*, II, 811–12.

[555] Le Clerc, *Prima commata*, 24–5, quoting from Philo, *De creat.*, 20.

[556] Le Clerc, *Prima Commata*, 29: 'Hoc tamen inter *Joannem* & *Philonem* interest, quod cùm *Joannes* docuerit Λόγον Θεὸν εἶναι *esse Deum*, nimirum, summum, Philosophus Judaeus velit dici Mundum *per eum* creatum, quòd sit ea in re Dei instrumentum'.

[557] Ibid., 30–1, quoting a fragment of Philo's lost *De providentia* preserved in Eusebius, *Praep. Ev.*, VIII.14.

[558] Jean Le Clerc, *Ars critica* (2nd edn, London, 1698 [1st edn=London, 1696]), 3, 75, 144–7, 180, 224. For this work in the context of its genre, see Grafton, *What was history*, 2–20, 48–9.

[559] Le Clerc, *Ars critica*, 224; for a summary of the argument, see 145: 'cùm vox ὁμοούσιος, ex Platonicorum usu, significaret *ejusdem speciei* . . . nulla est ratio existimandi hac voce significatum fuisse *unicam numero* Essentiam Patris, & Filii. Nihil sanè occurrit in Disputationibus *Homousianorum*, quod suadere possit alia in re controversiam Arianam sitam fuisse, nisi quòd Ariani *Essentiam* filii parem non esse *Essentiae* Patris contenderent: *Homoousiani* verò paritatem propugnarent; quod Viri doctissimi copiose ostenderunt' – the marginal note reveals that the 'learned men who have clearly shown this' were Courcelles and Cudworth.

[560] *The Reverend and learned Dr. Hammond, and his paraphrase and annotations on the New Testament, vindicated from the rude and unjust reflections made upon him and them by Monsieur Le Clerc* (London, 1699), esp. 40–2, 83. This work is anonymous, but in the copy

writing panegyric rather than history for denying the fact, entered the lists against him, unsurprisingly also accusing him of Socinianism.[561] Le Clerc's dependence on Petau is aptly demonstrated by the fact that Cave spent more time confuting the Jesuit than the Arminian.[562] Like Bull, Cave's argument was that all ante-Nicene passages which placed the Son below the Father implied only subordinationism, not a rejection of a shared essence.[563] By now this was obviously to skirt the main issue and in an answer dedicated to Tenison, Le Clerc threw back at Cave all the evidence for the Platonic context of early Christianity, constantly citing Petau, Courcelles, and Cudworth – Cave resolutely refused to discuss Platonism, even in a further reply.[564]

It is difficult to see why any of this constitutes a distinctive 'enlightenment'. Le Clerc was certainly virulently anti-patristic, but as Cave pointed out and as Le Clerc himself affirmed, his position was in principle no more radical than that advanced by Daillé sixty years previously (even if it was based on much more sophisticated scholarship).[565] His whole argument was anchored in a theological debate as old as Du Perron, and, more widely, in a recognition of the syncretisms in early Christian culture as old as Casaubon. Le Clerc himself celebrated the superiority to the fathers of critics not since the 1680s, but since the sixteenth century.[566] He used Hammond because of Hammond's investment in critical scholarship, not despite a lack of it.[567]

This was the English clerical scholars' great problem. They had invested in critical scholarship and it had paid rich dividends in the justification of episcopacy in works and commentaries that Le Clerc admired enough to republish.[568] But in the case of the encounter with philosophy they could not find

---

in Trinity College, Cambridge (classmark: I.1.21), the dedication is signed, in a contemporary hand, 'John Edwards' (sig. A3ᵛ). The polemical style certainly fits Edwards, as does the Calvinist insistence on the direct inspiration of scripture (18); the intimation of personal acquaintance with Hammond (8) does not rule him out, although I have not found any corroborative evidence of such an acquaintance.

[561] William Cave, *Scriptorum Ecclesiasticorum historia literaria facili & perspicua methodo digesta. Pars altera* (London, 1698), 'Dissertatio tertia: de Eusebii Caesariensis Arianismo adversus Joannem Clericum', 61–88.

[562] Ibid., 63, 81–3.      [563] Summarised at ibid., 64.

[564] Le Clerc, *Epistolae criticae*, 37–8, 42–5, 67–8, 96–7, 99, 109. Cave's further reply is *Epistola apologetica adversus iniquas Joannis Clerici criminationes* (London, 1700).

[565] Cave, 'De Eusebii Arianismo', 61; Cave, *Epistola apologetica*, 18–21 (Cave even still cited the Vincentian rule against Le Clerc, as if this was now of any relevance); Le Clerc, *Epistolae criticae*, 114–56 is a long defence of Daillé, including a dismissal of Scrivener at 117. See also *Lives* [1696], 42; *Ars critica*, 7. For the comparable importance of Daillé's work to Pierre Bayle, see the important study by Ruth Whelan, 'The wage of sin is orthodoxy' (1988).

[566] Le Clerc, *Epistolae criticae*, 151–2.

[567] See the celebration of Hammond and Grotius as superior to Justin and Irenaeus at *Epistolae criticae*, 154.

[568] S. *Patrum qui temporibus Apostolicis floruerunt, Barnabae, Clementis, Hermae, Ignatii, Polycarpi opera edita et inedita* ... ed. Le Clerc (2 vols, Antwerp, 1698), with lavish praise for Beveridge at I, sig. [*4]ʳ and Pearson and Ussher at II, sig. *2ʳ.

satisfactory answers to Petau, with the exception of Cudworth and Dodwell, both of whose works Le Clerc admired greatly, even if he certainly did not share the latter's ecclesiology.[569] Le Clerc's greatest novelty lay in his amalgamation of these old findings into a fully developed narrative of the history of the relationship between Jews, Christians, and Greek philosophers. As we have already seen (2.6, 3.7) he was very sceptical about narratives of Hebrew primacy, preferring to see all similarities between Jewish and pagan philosophy as flowing from the latter to the former, after the Babylonian captivity and the Alexandrian conquests. The fathers had been extremely stupid to accept the fables about ancient Hebrew wisdom and Judaic primacy offered by the Hellenistic Jews.[570] These Jews, especially in Alexandria, swayed in part by Plato's assertion of the Unity of the Supreme Being, adopted Platonic terminology in the three centuries before Christ's birth.[571] In reality, the Greeks had had no contact with the Jews: Le Clerc cited the same Lactantius passage as had Samuel Parker and a host of others (see Ch. 3).[572] Cudworth – whom he otherwise admired – had been wrong to imply that Plato had followed a Jewish tradition.[573] The various Jewish sects had been mapped onto Greek philosophical sects by Josephus because they had actually derived from them.[574] The *Book of Wisdom* and the Targums, with their Platonic *logos*-vocabulary, were, like Philo, also the product of this syncretist culture. For this final finding, Le Clerc cited the old Socinian work by Ruar and Vorstius, which he may have had a hand in republishing in 1700.[575] Le Clerc thus connects the histories we have told in Chapters 2, 3, and 6.

## 6.9     Conclusion

We need not chart the culmination of the Platonic corruption debate in the *Platonisme devoilé* (1700) by the Huguenot Socinian Jacques Sourverain, who,

---

[569] For Le Clerc's admiration for Dodwell, see e.g. *S. Patrum qui temporibus Apostolicis floruerunt*, I, 140; *BUH*, 10, 381–2 (=*Lives* [1696], 64); Le Clerc to Locke, 1/11 April 1692, *Locke correspondence*, IV, 434, Quantin, 'Dodwell', 347, and specifically for the philosophical context of early Christianity, see the huge quotation from Dodwell's *Two letters* in *Supplement*, 6–9.

[570] Le Clerc, *Lives* [1696], 22–3; *Epistolae criticae*, 229–35, 304.

[571] Le Clerc, *Lives* [1696], 79–80.

[572] Le Clerc, *Epistolae criticae*, 228, and more broadly, 220–54.        [573] Ibid., 238–9.

[574] Ibid., 306–8.

[575] Ibid., 277–80; 305; Le Clerc, *Supplement*, 120–1. It was republished as *Bilibra veritatis et rationis de מימרא די seu verbo Dei, librae Joh. Stephani Rittangelii ... opposita* ([n.p.], 1700), with a short 'Praefatio' which is attributed, without explanation, to Le Clerc in *Bibliographia Sociniana*, 95. The earliest example of such an attribution that I have been able to find is David Clement, *Bibliothèque curieuse historique et critique* (4 vols, Hannover, 1753), IV, 246, again not providing any evidence.

as recent scholarship has shown, had numerous English connections.[576] That work is now celebrated as a cornerstone of a putative 'early enlightenment', a concept which I hope might now seem, at least in this context, rather more questionable. Professor Pocock has spoken of Le Clerc as the 'Quentin Skinner of the early enlightenment', who 'replaced theology with the history of theology'.[577] Yet if anyone deserves this epithet it is Dodwell, who formalised the rule that the only account of trinitarian vocabulary could be a historical–contextual one.[578] The hyper-sacerdotalist Dodwell of course does not fit any category of 'enlightenment', suggesting that, as Le Clerc would say, we are imposing the inappropriate vocabulary upon the past.[579] Similarly, the connection between Le Clerc's scholarship and his political views has to be softened. There can be no doubt that he was in favour of Lockean tolerationism, but the extent to which this had much impact on the specifics of his historical arguments is doubtful. Is it really so surprising that a scholar trained in Calvinist Geneva did not have a high opinion of the post-apostolic fathers?

Le Clerc did not want to change the world. He wanted to change theological education: a great many of his works in the 1680s and 1690s have this explicit stated aim.[580] Nonetheless, the wide dissemination of his reviews certainly had an impact. But even that impact was unpredictable and has to be understood in the context of a long humanism. John Evelyn, who took many notes on the history of religion and theology, and was never reluctant to make adverse comments when he suspected heterodoxy, was remarkably neutral about Le Clerc's ideas on Platonic terminology among the ante-Nicenes and about the meaning of the Johannine *logos*.[581] Even more interesting is the case of

---

[576] [Jacques Souverain], *Le Platonisme devoilé, ou essai touchant le Verbe Platonicien* ([Amsterdam], 1700); [Souverain], *Platonism unveil'd: or an essay concerning the notions and opinions of Plato, and some antient and modern divines his followers, in relation to the Logos* ([London], 1700). See Glawe, *Hellenisierung*, 115–32; Mulsow, 'Jacques Souverain, Samuel Crell et les cryptosociniens de Londres' (2000). For Souverain's troubles with the English Huguenot church, and for more on his contacts with Locke, see the important account in Marshall, 'Thought', 383–4, 390–2, drawing on much of the key manuscript evidence.

[577] Pocock, *Barbarism*, v, 99; Pocock, 'Historiography and enlightenment' (2008), 87.

[578] Le Clerc, meanwhile, still discussed abstracted theological terms in his pedagogical philosophical works: *Ontologia, sive de ente in genere* [1692] in *Opera philosophica* (4 vols, Amsterdam, 1700), i, 323–427. Le Clerc conceived of 'ontology' as a replacement for Aristotelian 'metaphysics' (324): what precisely he meant by this, and how he arrived at it, is worth further investigation.

[579] See further Levitin, 'Sacred history'.

[580] As well as the *Logica, Ontologia*, and the *Pneumatologia*, see the express comments to this effect in *Ars critica*, xiii. See also the earlier [Charles Le Cène and Jean Le Clerc], *Entretiens sur diverses matieres de theologie: où l'on examine particulierement les questions de la grace immédiate, du franc-arbitre, du peché originel, de l'incertitude de la metaphysique, & de la prédestination* (Amsterdam, 1685).

[581] BL MS Evelyn, Add 78332, 'Adversaria', fols. 48ᵛ, 49ᵛ (respectively, praise for the *Ars critica* and notes on Platonic terminology in early trinitarianism from that work), fol. 54ʳ (notes on Le

Abraham Hill.[582] Reading Le Clerc's journals in the early eighteenth century, Hill took acerbic notes such as 'as Philosophy was in the time of the fathers full of nonsense so their Theology was much infected with it'.[583] But he did not stop there, going back through the whole array of seventeenth- and late sixteenth-century scholarship to investigate these conclusions: Vossius's edition of Barnabas's Epistles for the allegorical methods of the fathers,[584] Spencer and Marsham on whether the Jews had taken from the Egyptians,[585] Petau on the ante-Nicenes,[586] Hammond and Dodwell on the early relationship between 'orthodox' and 'heretic',[587] and Isaac Casaubon for the idea that there were 'Among the heathen many Mysterys to which none were admitted without passing through many degrees, wherein they were much imitated by the Christians in the celebration of the Lords supper'.[588] Le Clerc's work, then, was important in spreading the critical humanism from which it emerged. But this only underlines the continuities within the long humanist tradition.

Clerc's annotations to Hammond regarding the meaning of John's 'λόγος'). See also fol. 6$^v$ for condemnation of the fathers for believing the pseudo-pagan forgeries.

[582] See 3.7 above.

[583] BL MS Sloane 2891, Abraham Hill, commonplace book, fol. 195$^r$; the reference is to the *Bibliothèque choisie*, 25 (1712), 320.

[584] BL MS Sloane 2891, fol. 196$^r$.     [585] Ibid., fol. 129$^r$.     [586] Ibid., fol. 44$^r$.

[587] Ibid., fol. 35$^r$.

[588] Ibid., fol. 32$^r$. Also cited are Stillingfleet's *Irenicum* and the *Bibliotheque choisie*, 19 (1709), 230–2.

# 7   Conclusion

The series of 'pre-critical' surveys of the history of thought written in Europe between the 1650s and 1680s vividly illustrate both the humanists' pious traditionalism, and placid syncretism, in intellectual matters and the total bankruptcy of humanist intellectual attitudes and tastes in the face of late seventeenth-century *critique*.[1]

The above view, notwithstanding the idiosyncratically bombastic expression, is based on long scholarly traditions, and is prevalent throughout the historiography. It has now been shown to be unsubstantiated. I hope to have offered a vision of seventeenth-century intellectual life – at least in England – that not only demonstrates the vitality and variety of humanist engagement with the history of philosophy, but also its centrality to almost all intellectual culture. Far from deploying a tired and uncritical 'pious syncretism', by the middle of the seventeenth-century scholars and clerics, and following them natural philosophers and men and women of letters more generally, had all invested in the critical scholarship of Scaliger, Casaubon, Vossius, Selden, and Holstenius. As a result, by the 1640s figures like Stanley, Pearson, and Meric Casaubon were developing anti-syncretist accounts of ancient philosophy that – while having apologetic pay-offs – could hardly be described as 'traditional' or reduced to the theology they subscribed to. This process was only assisted by the vast investment in historical apologetics that continued after the Restoration. Works like Stillingfleet's *Origines sacrae*, Parker's *Tentamina de Deo*, and Cudworth's *True intellectual system* – and the myriad of other texts that we have encountered – were the products of this investment. Each of them engaged, in their own way, with various continental traditions of historiography of philosophy and religion, engagements that can only be explained by examining what, as scholars, they were actually *doing* (and certainly not by reductionist labels like 'latitudinarianism' and 'Cambridge Platonism'). Even more

---

[1]   Israel, *Enlightenment contested*, 472.

importantly, radically new and controversial works like Spencer's *De legibus Hebraeorum* and Hyde's *Historia religionis veterum Persarum* – works which undoubtedly had vast readership and influence throughout eighteenth-century Europe and thus continue to be assigned places in a dubious and ill-defined pantheon of 'enlightenment' – were the products of this investment.

This investment *worked*. Even important figures outside the formal academic structure, like Marsham and Stanley, co-existed in the same world as the scholar divines Pearson, Thorndike, Meric Casaubon, and Edward Bernard, and as the European men of letters – most notably Isaac Vossius – who valued them both as scholars and as friends.[2] Marsham, it is true, could not have written his work of technical chronology within the academy, but the fact remains that he was an 'outsider' working happily with the 'insiders', rather than against them. True 'outsiders', by contrast, bring the success of the investment in scholarship into relief. Theophilus Gale was one such outsider. His insistence on Mosaic roots for all philosophy was simply out of date by the 1670s, an anachronism that is explicable by his being excluded from the academic mainstream, by choice and by force. However much we extol the successes of nonconformist intellectual culture – and Anglophone historiography has for a long time extolled the disenfranchised – in the world of scholarship, they were left behind. Gale had previously been classified as having a familial relationship to 'Cambridge Platonism'. As we have seen, this claim is based on a misunderstanding of the evidence, and the belief that any engagement with ancient philosophy is a tell-tale sign of such an affiliation. If readers are to take away any one point from this study, it is that such classifications are redundant. There was no such thing as a Cambridge Platonist view of the history of philosophy. Henry More, often taken as representative of the group, was another outsider. This was partly because, unlike almost all others within English academic life, he never 'grew out' of philosophy. While this meant that he developed by far the most advanced metaphysics of any seventeenth-century Englishman, it placed him out-of-kilter with mainstream intellectual culture, particularly as he entirely failed to substantiate the pre-history he offered for his philosophy with up-to-date scholarship. For the most part, More was an embarrassment to his nominal allies within the Church and the universities, and a godsend to their opponents. The same certainly cannot be said for his friend Cudworth. As I hope to have shown, there are very good reasons for aligning Cudworth (not personally but professionally) with figures such as More's *opponents* Joseph Beaumont or Herbert Thorndike. Cudworth was a scholarly prodigy who earned his high institutional status precisely because of

---

[2] Throughout, I have only touched incidentally on Vossius's role as the glue between English scholars, but this is a topic that requires more study. For now, see the huge amount of relevant evidence gathered in Mandelbrote, 'Vossius and the Septuagint'.

his high scholarly status. The attempt to read him as a 'philosopher' or to reify his views into 'Platonism' have done more to obscure than reveal his actual intellectual identity. Far from being the remnant of a 'Renaissance' 'Platonic' tradition, Cudworth was part of an advanced scholarly elite that approached the ancient world (including the philosophy of Plato and the neoplatonists) through the tools offered by the European scholars of the first half of the seventeenth century. Even his rehabilitation of *spuria* such as the *Hermetica* needs to be understood in this context: challenging Isaac Casaubon did not place him outside of the Casaubonian framework.

As these words suggest, I hope to have offered a vision of English intellectual culture that is rather more European than that one still tends to find in the literature. The English case is only one – albeit a particularly interesting and intense one (for the reasons above) – in the general process of change that from the late sixteenth century came gradually to create the conditions for the existence of the humanities as we understand them today. As scholars studied the ancient world more and more intensively, they came to abandon the aim of extracting ideals from that world, and instead began to contextualise it, and to write histories that emphasised historical distance. It should be noted that there is an important distinction to be made here, one that we have already encountered on several occasions. That seventeenth-century histories of ancient philosophy did not attempt to extract ideals does not mean that they did not have apologetic or didactic purposes – like almost all history, they very frequently did (although there is a big difference between the explicit apologetic aims of a work like Cudworth's and the latent assumptions behind Stanley's *History* or Hyde's *Historia*). What it does mean is that they accepted that the ancient past was different, and that apologetics could only be built on that recognition. 'Syncretisim' this certainly was not.

It was precisely this institutional, mainstream investment in critical and contextualist humanist scholarship that caused the tensions that have previously been assigned to 'heterodoxy', 'latitudinarianism', or 'early enlightenment'. The cases of Cudworth, Parker, Dodwell, and Spencer all demonstrate how arguments that were designed, at one level or another, to defend 'orthodoxy', all faced tensions when it actually came to doing the scholarship. While Dodwell's is probably the most spectacular case, Parker's is perhaps the most instructive. In the 1660s, he invested heavily in the new 'critical' approach, chastising the church fathers for believing the Judaic fables about the Mosaic origins of pagan philosophy that had recently been re-espoused by More and Glanvill. And yet by the 1680s he was rejecting some of the key findings of the same critical approach, in order to save the church fathers. It was precisely the investment in criticism – *not* its rejection – that caused problems for 'orthodoxy'. The weapons that had secured victory in the scholarly battle over episcopacy were proving incapable of defeating Petau. And yet the 'orthodox' reaction was still not re-entrenchment, but the spectacular if self-destructive syntheses of Cudworth and Dodwell. Again, this had nothing to do with 'latitudinarianism' or a simplistic connection between 'liberal' churchmanship and 'critical' scholarship. On the contrary, the more one was invested in a discrete confessional identity, the more one invested in critical humanism to defend it. Dodwell, Cudworth, Spencer, Hyde, Parker and the scores of other figures that we have met were the products of a specific sociology of knowledge actively encouraged by the post-Laudian church. It was their scholarship that Le Clerc engaged with, and the tensions within it that he explored. He did so using the resources that they – and their European predecessors – had developed. To attempt to limit this story to a post-1680 Hazardian 'crise' is to erode the reality of confessionalised scholarship in favour of simplistic and chronologically convenient model building.

Throughout, we have seen that humanist culture was not replaced or defeated by 'science' or any other shibboleth of a nebulous 'modernity'. Figures as diverse as Sherburne and the many natural philosophers who took part in the debates about Genesis and Mosaic philosophy in the 1680s and 1690s had feet in both camps. 'Ancients versus moderns' had nothing to do with any of this: it was an irrelevant side issue that flared up for a short time in the 1690s. Even more importantly, debates about the history of philosophy played a key role in actual natural philosophical discourse, both about method and about doctrine. The full extent of this role has not previously been recognised partly because historians of science tend to avoid these issues, but also because intellectual history remains far too detached from institutional history. In many ways, the history of the success of the 'new philosophy' is the history of the *novatores* rendering their methods acceptable to the institutionalised mainstream. Since mainstream methodological discourse was still in large part historical, historical claims were hugely important to this process. In particular, learned medicine was so central to the triumph of experimentalism precisely because it was in medical pedagogy and among the fellows of the Royal College of Physicians that a successful historically grounded methodological rhetoric was developed, in contrast to the failure of the Royal Society apologists like Sprat and Glanvill to achieve the same aim. Texts like Petty's and Glissons's medical lectures should be foregrounded much more prominently in histories of the rise of 'experimental philosophy': they were at least as, if not more, important for the development and justification of experimentalism as Glanvill's oft-cited *apologiae*, because they could amalgamate that experimentalism with the traditional rhetoric of university natural philosophy and medicine, and their histories.

At the same time, the neoterics were not afraid of radically rewriting the history of natural philosophy when it came to questions of doctrine. I hope that I have shown once and for all that the historiographical obsession with English

'Epicureanism' in natural philosophy is unjustified. Apart from Charleton, no one subscribed to Gassendi's vision of Epicurean philosophy as the basis either of natural philosophical method, or for a methodologically justifiable matter theory. Epicurus was incompatible with the methodological backstories the experimentalists had adopted for themselves. Ironically, Gassendi's influence was greatest not on the topic of Epicurus, but on the other Greek philosophers, for he was crucial in convincing Englishmen that the Greek philosophical past stemmed from – and indeed was defined by – an idolatrous animation of the world. Here we have perhaps the closest amalgamation between natural philosophical and clerical–humanist discourse: the Boyle of the *Free enquiry* and the Newton of the General Scholium were speaking the same language as the Parker of the *Tentamina* and the Cudworth of chapter 4 of the *System*, and, in turn, the continental scholars who inspired them. These humanist salvoes were not ornamental or lazy concessions to literary culture: it is simply impossible to understand what Newton is saying in the General Scholium if we do not appreciate the scholarly world from which he is coming and in which he is operating. This is not easy. It involves abandoning comforting old certainties like 'Cambridge Platonism', and reading many texts that on first sight have very little to do with the new philosophy. But this is precisely why the history of scholarship is indispensible to wider histories of early modern intellectual change. Gassendi's vision of Epicurus may have proved a failure, but it was his historically grounded approach, not the a-historical 'dreams' of Descartes, that chimed most with English intellectual culture.

Can all this be tied up into what Anglophone historiography so loves: an overarching 'argument'? I hope I have offered two already: first, the continuing vitality in England of a European-wide humanist scholarly culture among not just scholars but the whole intellectual community; second, the uselessness of reified 'isms' like 'Platonism' and 'Epicureanism' in an age when *all* men and women of letters engaged reflexively with the ancient philosophical past.[3] But if, as I am suggesting, the emphasis should be on singularity of experience and scholarly endeavour, and not on convenient philosophical abstraction, can the history I have told be subsumed to any wider narrative of intellectual change?

I will suggest one such narrative, already hinted at throughout this book. The greatest transformation of seventeenth-century English intellectual culture was not the replacement of one philosophy with another, but rather the death of the ideal of the philosopher-theologian, an intellectual *persona* encapsulated in the figure of the metaphysician. In the first half of the seventeenth century, that figure existed – as it did far longer in Germany[4] – in the guise of the Reformed

---

[3] For a different but not unconnected statement of the dangers of reification, see Condren, *Argument*; Condren, *Language*.

[4] Hunter, *Rival enlightenments* (2001).

scholastic. Now, as we have seen, broadly 'Aristotelian' philosophy textbooks continued to be in use throughout the century. But at the level of intellectual elites, 'philosophy' (excepting its 'experimental' variant) became ever more unfashionable. The standard story of 'enlightenment' tends to favour the victory of 'philosophy' over both theology and humanism.[5] What this book seems to confirm is the tough lot of philosophy in our period. The more everyone – including philosophers themselves – accepted the conclusions of the late humanists, and especially the conclusion that almost all the philosophical ideas inherited from antiquity (and which were not?) were the products of a specific and contingent historical context, one in which pagan theology provided both the conceptual and linguistic framework for the development of thought, the more 'philosophy' as it was widely recognised came to be seen as a dangerous and even anachronistic throwback to paganism itself. To make a rather obvious point, I know of no one who wrote a history of the triumph of philosophy over 'irrational' theology. Hobbes, surely the most likely person to do that, wrote exactly the opposite: a narrative of philosophy's corrosive effects on the basic truths of natural religion. When the Dutch physician Lodewijk Meyer published a *Philosophia S. Scripturae interpres* (1666), no one in England took his claims seriously.[6] As the distinction between natural and dogmatic theology grew sharper, philosophy came to be aligned sometimes, but relatively rarely, with the successes of the former, but much more frequently with the failures of the latter. Concomitantly, the ideal of the philosopher-theologian *qua* metaphysician dwindled in importance until its espousal late in the century – in opposition to Locke – in either Anglican or Roman Catholic hands could be subject to either incomprehension or direct ridicule.[7]

This state of affairs did not go uncommented upon. Stubbe, for example, believed that while Glanvill's historical dismissal of metaphysics was completely wrongheaded in terms of the debate over the history of natural philosophical method, it would have very dangerous consequences for the study of *divinity*, where metaphysics was of crucial importance.[8] But it was permitted to

---

[5] Although this story is now under attack, most prominently in Edelstein, *The Enlightenment: a genealogy* (2010).

[6] See the late response: John Wilson, *The Scriptures genuine interpretation asserted or, a discourse concerning the right interpretation of Scripture wherein a late excertation, intitled, Philosophia S. Scripturae Interpres, is examin'd, and the Protestant doctrine in that point vindicated* (London, 1678). Wilson develops many of the points we have met: the best early interpreters of scripture were *non*-philosophical (97–8); a grudging acceptance of the Platonic element in some ante-Nicene fathers (115).

[7] For Stillingfleet's attempts to rescue the doctrine of the trinity against Locke by returning to scholastic–metaphysical language, see Stewart, 'Stillingfleet and the way of ideas'; for a structurally related attempt by the Catholic polemicist John Sergeant and for wider pedagogical contexts, see Levitin, 'Reconsidering John Sergeant, critic of Locke' (2010).

[8] Stubbe, *Non Plus*, 1. Glanvill failed to answer the charge: *Answer*, 64–5.

go on precisely because the English church had happily chosen the humanist path. It is no coincidence that so many of our chapters have finished with Le Clerc. As we have seen, Professor Pocock has claimed that 'Le Clerc [took] a long step towards replacing theology with the history of theology in a language world'.[9] In reality, this is a step that the English church had been taking for almost a century.[10] Experimental philosophy, meanwhile, could flourish because its exponents made sure again and again to point out that it was neither speculative nor metaphysical, without – crucially – ever quite denying that it was philosophy. To a significant extent they did this by writing natural philosophy's history. Philosophy had been replaced by the history of philosophy on the one hand, and experimentalism masquerading as traditional natural philosophy on the other.

---

[9] Pocock, 'Historiography and enlightenment'.

[10] See 1.3. above. More broadly, I hope to present this as the subject of my next monograph, provisionally entitled *An age of erudition*.

# Bibliography

## Manuscripts

This listing is confined to manuscripts cited in the main text. The descriptions are summary, and in the case of composite collections, describe the whole collection (although sometimes with reference to specific items mentioned in the main text).

### Amsterdam

#### Universiteitsbibliotheek Amsterdam
M.21.a–d    [Correspondence of Ralph Cudworth and Philipp van Limborch]

### Cambridge

#### Emmanuel College
3.2.6    [MS of the *Yasna*, belonging to Thomas Hyde]

#### King's College
Keynes 4    [Isaac Newton, notes from Petau's *Theologica dogmata*, 1670s]

#### St John's College
MS 91    [Ulugh Beg, *Zīj-i Sultānī*, annotated by John Greaves]
K.17    [John Milner's trans. of the Targum on Chron. 1–2 (1662)]

#### Trinity College
B.7.4    [Herbert Thorndike's MS of Origen's *Epistola ad Africanum*]
B.8.10    [Herbert Thorndike's MSS of Origen's *Super Matthaeum* and *De oratione*]
B.9.10–11    [Herbert Thorndike's MS of Origen's *In Ioannem*]
O.4.23    [Thomas Gale's MS of Damascius's *On first principles*]
O.IIa.1    [Robert Hooke papers]
R.9.5–7    [John Pearson's notes on Hesychius]
R.9.18–19    [Greek MS, including a DL owned by Thomas Gale]
R.13.32    [Thomas Gale papers]
R.16.38    [Papers, including part of Newton's 'Out of Cudworth']

*University Library*

| | |
|---|---|
| Add. 84 | [Papers of John and Simon Patrick] |
| Add. 102 | [Cambridge philosophy commonplace book belonging to Edmundus Laeus] |
| Add. 697–9 | [Divinity exercises by students of Joseph Beaumont] |
| Add. 2610 | [Notes by John Spencer] |
| Add. 3313–18 | [Book lists of William Herbert] |
| Add. 3965 | [Isaac Newton papers] |
| Add. 3970 | [Isaac Newton papers] |
| Add. 3996 | [Isaac Newton, Trinity notebook] |
| Add. 4364 | ['Tractatus de essentia et attributis Dei', 1652–55] |
| Add. 7514 | [Early poems and translations by Thomas Stanley] |
| Add. 7570 | [John Woodward papers] |
| Add. 7647 | [John Woodward papers] |
| Add. 8861[2] | [Thomas Millington, Inaugural lecture as Sedleian Professor of Natural Philosophy, 12 Apr 1675] |
| Add. 8861[3] | [Notes on ancient Judaism, *c.* 1660] |
| Add. 9597.2 | [Isaac Newton papers] |
| Add. 9597.16.1 | ['A system of physicks', *c.* 1650–1700] |
| Dd.4.52 | ['Loci communes theologiae', mid-seventeenth century] |
| Dd.9.44 | [John Smith commonplace book] |
| Dd.12.57 | [Thomas Brathwaite, theological notebooks] |
| Gg.3.7–15 | [Thomas Stanley's notes] |
| Gg.3.7.16 | [Thomas Stanley, Ἀκροθίνια. Exercitatio philologica de primitiis ac decimis praedae ad versum IV capitis VII Epistolae ad Hebraeos'] |
| Gg.6.11.F | [Correspondence between Henry More and Henry Hirn] |
| Kk.3.1 | [Joseph Beaumont's lectures on Romans] |
| Kk.5.38 | [William Lloyd's correspondence with Antoine Pagi] |
| Kk.6.7 | ['Philosophia universalis, vulgo metaphysica' (1664) belonging to Hugh Smith] |
| Ll.v.1 | [Notes by Abednego Seller] |
| Oo.6.91 | [Notes by Abednego Seller, including from Thomas Stanley's MSS] |

*Gloucester*

*Gloucestershire Record Office*

| | |
|---|---|
| D3549/2/4/24 | [Chronological notes by William Lloyd] |

*Hertford*

*Hertfordshire Archives*

| | |
|---|---|
| D/EHx/F83 | [Samuel Gardiner, will] |

*Jerusalem*

*National Library of Israel [accessed via www.newtonproject.sussex.ac.uk/]*

| | |
|---|---|
| Yahuda 9.1 | [Newton's 'Treatise on revelation'] |
| Yahuda 11 | [Newton, 'Prooemium' and first chapter on church history] |
| Yahuda 17.1 | [Newton's notes on ancient religions] |
| Yahuda 17.2 | [Newton's notes and drafts relating to the 'Theologiae gentilis origines Philosophiae', 1680s and early 1690s] |
| Yahuda 17.3 | [Newton's further notes on ancient religion] |
| Yahuda 41 | [Newton's 'The original of religions'] |

*Lincoln*

*Lincolnshire Archives*

| | |
|---|---|
| Tur.14.1.7 | [Will of Samuel Pickering] |

*London*

*British Library*

| | |
|---|---|
| APAC Eur. E.192a | [Correspondence of Thomas Hyde and Thomas Bowrey] |
| Arundel gr. 531 | [Greek fragments, incl. of DL, later collated by Thomas Gale] |
| Add. 4292 | [Correspondence of Walter Needham and others] |
| Add. 4293 | [Correspondence of Walter Needham and others] |
| Add. 4367 | [Correspondence of Stephen Nye and others] |
| Add. 4978–82 | [Ralph Cudworth papers] |
| Add. 4986–7 | [Ralph Cudworth, commentaries on Daniel] |
| Add. 28927 | [Correspondence of Thomas Hyde and others] |
| Add. 32506 | [Roger North papers] |
| Add. 32514 | [Roger North's notes from John North's papers, neat copy] |
| Add. 32517 | [Roger North's notes from John North's papers, rough copy] |
| Add. 32544 | [Roger North, 'PHYSICA, an essay on natural philosophy'] |
| Add. 32545 | [Roger North, 'Autobiographical notes, and draughts, more or less imperfect, of essays on natural philosophy'] |
| Add. 32546 | [Roger North, treatise and notes on natural philosophy] |
| Add. 32548 | ['Loci phisiologici, ordine fortuito'] |
| Add. 72891 | [William Petty papers, including medical lectures] |
| Add. 78314 | [John Evelyn papers] |
| Add. 78328 | [John Evelyn papers] |
| Add. 78332 | [John Evelyn papers] |
| Add. 78351 | [John Evelyn papers] |
| Add. 78367 | [John Evelyn papers] |
| Add. 78368 | [John Evelyn papers, incl. notes for the *History of religion*] |
| Burney 369 | [Correspondence of Meric Casaubon and others] |
| Egmont 47131 | [Various correspondence, including John Woodward's] |
| Harl. 1876 | [Henry Stubbe on the rise of Islam] |
| Harl. 3783 | [Various correspondence, including William Sancroft's] |
| Harl. 3785 | [Various correspondence, including William Sancroft's] |

| | |
|---|---|
| Harl. 4153 | [Kenelm Digby papers] |
| Harl. 5676 | [Bentley's notes from Stanley's Callimachus] |
| Harl. 6189 | [Henry Stubbe on the rise of Islam] |
| Roy. 16B | [Thomas Hyde's Persian MSS] |
| Royal Appendix 72 | [Correspondence of Isaac Vossius and others] |
| Sloane 35 | [Henry Stubbe library catalogue] |
| Sloane 528 | [Nathaniel Highmore, 'Observationes de signis morborum' and other tracts] |
| Sloane 543 | [Nathaniel Highmore, commonplace book] |
| Sloane 546 | [Nathaniel Highmore, 'Anatomia restaurata'] |
| Sloane 547 | [Nathaniel Highmore, 'Anatomia restaurata', corrected draft] |
| Sloane 656 | [Walter Needham, 'Institutiones medicae' (1670s)] |
| Sloane 824 | [Edward Sherburne papers] |
| Sloane 829 | [Edward Sherburne papers] |
| Sloane 832 | [Edward Sherburne papers] |
| Sloane 836 | [Edward Sherburne papers] |
| Sloane 837 | [Edward Sherburne papers] |
| Sloane 857 | [Edward Sherburne's library catalogue] |
| Sloane 1324 | [Anomymous mid-seventeenth-century treatise on natural philosophy] |
| Sloane 1326 | [Henry Power papers and correspondence] |
| Sloane 1346 | [Henry Power's library catalogue] |
| Sloane 1709 | [Henry Stubbe on the history of Islam] |
| Sloane 1775 | [Sloane papers, including unattributed translation of Book VII of Burnet's *Archaelogiae*] |
| Sloane 1786 | [Sloane papers, including notes by Everard Maynwaringe and Stubbe on the rise of Islam] |
| Sloane 1950 | [Nehemiah Grew's papers, including on the history of astronomy, and his 'Short account of Thales, Solon, Socrates, and other antient philosophers, and their different systems of philosophy'] |
| Sloane 2514 | ['Cursus physici pars posterior sive specialis de variis corporum speciebus'] |
| Sloane 2891 | [Abraham Hill, commonplace book] |
| Sloane 3306–15 | [Medical lectures and theses taught by Francis Glisson] |
| Sloane 3323 | [Hans Sloane papers, including catalogue of Thomas Hyde's oriental books and papers] |
| Sloane 3413 | [Walter Charleton, commonplace book] |
| Sloane 3433 | ['Disciplinae physicae', 1685] |
| Sloane 3828 | [Hans Sloane papers, including Hooke's readings at the RS] |
| Sloane 4038 | [Correspondence of Hans Sloane and others, including Thomas Hyde] |
| Sloane 4039 | [Sloane papers, including biography of John Beaumount] |
| Sloane 4066 | [Correspondence of Thomas Hyde and others] |

*Dr Williams's Library*

| | |
|---|---|
| 201/38 | [Edward Stillingfleet papers and correspondence] |

*Lambeth Palace Library*

| | |
|---|---|
| 674 | [Correspondence, including that of John Spencer] |
| 870 | ['Jo. Spenceri Literae et Declamationes in Acad. Cantabrig.'] |
| 943 | [Correspondence, including that of John Spencer] |
| 953 | [Correspondence of Thomas Tenison and others] |
| 3498 | [Matthew Hale papers] |
| 3502 | [Matthew Hale papers] |

*National Archives*

PRO Prob/11/392, fol. 230$^v$ [Ralph Cudworth, will]
PRO 30/24/47/2, fols. 47$^4$–56$^r$ [John Locke, 'De arte med[ica]']

*Royal Society*

| | |
|---|---|
| BP1 | [Boyle papers] |
| BP7 | [Boyle papers] |
| BP8 | [Boyle papers] |
| BP9 | [Boyle papers] |
| BP10 | [Boyle papers] |
| BP18 | [Boyle papers] |
| BP28 | [Boyle papers] |
| BP32 | [Boyle papers] |
| BP186 | [Boyle papers] |
| BP190 | [Boyle papers] |
| BP198 | [Boyle papers] |
| EL/H3/79 | [Various papers and correspondence, including Edmond Halley's] |
| Gregory 247 | [Newton, 'Classical scholia'] |
| Hooke Folio | [Notes from Royal Society meetings by Robert Hooke] |
| RBC 7.391 | ['Concerning the motion of light by Mr Halley, 19 October 1692'] |
| RBC 7.364 | [Halley, 'Some observations on the motion of the sun, 18 October 1693'] |

*Society of Antiquaries*

| | |
|---|---|
| 447.2 | [Correspondence of Michael Lort] |

*Senate House*

| | |
|---|---|
| 537 | [Henry Stubbe on the rise of Islam] |

*Los Angeles*

*William Andrews Clarke Memorial Library*

| | |
|---|---|
| fn563Z | [Part of Newton's 'Out of Cudworth'] |

*Maidstone*

*Centre for Kentish Studies*

| | |
|---|---|
| U1121 E5 | [John Marsham papers] |
| U1121 E7 | ['Catalogus librorum Bibliothecae Marshamianae'] |

| U1121 Z25 | [John Marsham papers] |
| U1300 C1 | [Correspondence of John Marsham] |
| U1300 Z10 | ['Robert Marsham's Biography of Sir John [Marsham]'] |

### Manchester

*John Rylands Library, University of Manchester*
| BAG/12/2/1 | [Samuel Gardiner, sermons] |

### Nottingham

*Nottingham University Library*
| Mi LM 15/1 | [Francis Willughby commonplace book]. |

### Oxford

*Bodleian Library*
| Ashmole 1817b | [Correspondence of Edward Lhuyd and others] |
| Auct. S.6.16 | [Aeschylus with notes by Thomas Stanley and others] |
| Ballard 5 | [Various correspondence] |
| Ballard 24 | [Correspondence of William Lloyd and others] |
| Ballard 39 | [Various correspondence] |
| Cherry 22 | [Correspondence of Henry Dodwell and others] |
| Cherry 23 | [Correspondence of Henry Dodwell and others] |
| D'Orville 468 | [Correspondence of Isaac Vossius and others] |
| D'Orville 470 | [Correspondence of Isaac Vossius and others] |
| D'Orville 478 | [Correspondence of various scholars] |
| Eng. lett.c.16 | [Correspondence of Thomas Stanley and others] |
| Eng. lett.c.28 | [Correspondence of Henry Dodwell and others] |
| Eng. misc.c.309 | [Henry Stubbe on the rise of Islam] |
| Hyde 36 | [Hyde's Tamerlane] |
| Linc. D.5.13 | [Collation of Manilius by Edward Bernard] |
| Lister 36 | [Papers and correspondence of Martin Lister] |
| Locke c. 28 | [Locke papers, including 'Division of the sciences'] |
| Locke c. 42A | [John Locke medical and scientific commonplace book, 1679–94] |
| Locke c. 42B | [John Locke commonplace book] |
| Locke d. 11 | [John Locke, 'Lemma physica'] |
| Locke f. 14 | [John Locke notebook, *c.* 1659–67] |
| Locke f. 15 | [John Locke memorandum book, 1677–78] |
| Locke f. 32 | [John Locke, notes on the Old Testament] |
| Marshall 134 | [Correspondence of Thomas Marshall] |
| Rawl. A7171 | [Various papers, including Pepys's 'Notes of discourses touching religion'] |
| Rawl. G.193 | [Aeschylus with notes by Thomas Stanley and others] |
| Rawl. Q.b.3 | [Edward Sherburne's later library catalogue] |

| | |
|---|---|
| Rawl. letters 52 | [Correspondence of Theophilus Gale] |
| Rawl. letters 53 | [Correspondence of Theophilus Gale] |
| Rawl. letters 54 | [Correspondence of Theophilus Gale] |
| Rawl. letters 59 | [Correspondence of Theophilus Gale] |
| Rawl. letters 104 | [Correspondence of Theophilus Gale] |
| Rawl. letters 83 | [Correspondence of G. J. Vossius and others] |
| Rawl. letters 84 c | [Correspondence of G. J. Vossius and others] |
| Rawl. letters 84 f | [Correspondence of G. J. Vossius and others] |
| Selden supra 106 | [Third edn of Selden's *De Diis Syris*] |
| Selden supra 108 | [Selden correspondence] |
| Selden supra 109 | [Selden correspondence] |
| Smith 5 | [Correspondence of Thomas Smith and others] |
| Smith 6 | [Correspondence of Thomas Smith and others] |
| Smith 8 | [Correspondence of Thomas Smith and others] |
| Smith 13 | [Papers of Walter Charleton] |
| Smith 45 | [Correspondence of Thomas Smith and others] |
| Smith 46 | [Correspondence of Thomas Smith and others] |
| Smith 47 | [Correspondence of Thomas Smith and others] |
| Smith 48 | [Correspondence of Thomas Smith and others] |
| Smith 49 | [Correspondence of Thomas Smith and others] |
| Smith 50 | [Correspondence of Thomas Smith and others] |
| Smith 53 | [Correspondence of Thomas Smith and others] |
| Smith 63 | [Correspondence of Thomas Smith and others] |
| Smith 65 | [Correspondence of Thomas Smith and others] |
| Smith 72 | [Correspondence of Thomas Smith and others] |
| Smith 88 | [Correspondence of Thomas Smith and others] |
| Tanner 21 | [Correspondence of Thomas Tanner and others] |
| Tanner 24 | [Correspondence of Thomas Tanner and others] |
| Tanner 29 | [Correspondence of Thomas Tanner and others] |
| Tanner 30 | [Correspondence of Thomas Tanner and others] |
| Tanner 33 | [Correspondence of Thomas Tanner and others] |
| Tanner 49 | [Correspondence of Thomas Tanner and others] |
| Tanner 52 | [Correspondence of Thomas Tanner and others] |
| Wood F.39 | [Correspondence of Anthony Wood] |
| Wood F.44 | [Correspondence of Anthony Wood] |

*Corpus Christi College*
| | |
|---|---|
| 158 | [Damascius, *Of first principles*] |

*Queens College*
| | |
|---|---|
| 235 | [Thomas Barlow, inaugural lecture as Lady Margaret Professor of Divinity] |
| 279 | [Thomas Barlow papers] |

*Sheffield*
Hartlib Papers

*Washington, DC*

*Folger Shakespeare Library*

| | |
|---|---|
| V.a.200 | [J. R. [John Reading?], 'Unio veritatis' (1655)] |
| V.a.284–99 | [John Ward diaries] |
| V.a.326 | [Benjamin Whichcote commonplace book] |
| V.a.472 | [John Rastrick notebook, early eighteenth century] |
| V.b.15 | [Mid seventeenth-century English commonplace book] |
| V.b.108 | [Henry Fairfax's divinity commonplace book] |
| V.b.110 | [Henry Oxenden commonplace book, *c.* 1640s–60s] |
| V.b.154 | [Thomas Hatton's commonplace book, *c.* 1680] |
| V.b.254 | [Anonymous English commonplace book, *c.* 1700] |
| W.a.89 | [William Dey, 'Tractatus in physical particularem'] |
| X.d.29 | [Biblical commentary, perhaps by Daniel Whitby?] |

## Libri Annotati and Unique Copies

*Cambridge*

*Parker Library, Corpus Christi College*

| | |
|---|---|
| B.1.21 | John Spencer's copy of Louis Cappel, *Commentarii et notae criticae in Vetus Testamentum* (Amsterdam, 1689). |
| M.8.33 | John Spencer's copy of Maimonides, Moses, *Doctor perplexorum: ad dubia & obscuriora Scripturae loca rectiùs intelligenda*, ed. Johann Buxtorf (Basel, 1629). |

*Pembroke College*

| | |
|---|---|
| L.C.ii.159 | Thomas Stanley's copy of Aeschylus, *Tragoediae septem*, ed. P. Vettori (Venice, 1552). |

*Trinity College*

| | |
|---|---|
| II.10.103 | Edward Rudd's copy of Jean Le Clerc, *Ars critica* (2nd edn, London, 1698). |
| NQ 8.27 | Newton's copy of Samuel Bochart's *Geographica sacra* (Frankfurt, 1681). |
| NQ 8.46 | Newton's copy of G. J. Vossius's *De theologia gentili* (Amsterdam, 1641) and D. Vossius's translation of Maimonides, *De idolalatria liber* (Amsterdam, 1641). |
| NQ 8.56 | Newton's copy of Thomas Burnet's *Archaeologiae philosophicae* (London, 1692). |
| NQ 16.150 | Newton's copy of Thomas Burnet, *Telluris theoria sacra* (London, 1681–89). |
| NQ 17.18 | Newton's copy of John Spencer, *De legibus Hebraeorum ritualibus* (Cambridge, 1683–85). |

## University Library

| | |
|---|---|
| 3.36.32 | A marked copy of [Allix, Pierre], *The fathers vindicated, by a Presbyter of the Church of England* (London, 1697). |
| Adv.a.27.7 | William Brouncker's presentation copy of Walter Charleton, *Physiologia Epicuro-Gassendo-Charltoniana* (London, 1654). |
| Adv.a.44.11 | John Spencer's copy of his own *De legibus Hebraeorum* (Cambridge, 1683–85). |
| Adv.a.44.15 | Thomas Stanley's copy of Diogenes Laërtius, *De vitis dogmatis et apophthegmatis eorum qui in philosophia clarerunt libri X*, ed. T. Aldobrandini (Rome, 1594). |
| Adv.b.44.1–8 | Thomas Stanley's copy of Aeschlys, *Tragoediae septem*, ed. T. Stanley (London, 1663). |
| Adv.c.27.4 | Thomas Burnet's self-annotated copy of his own *Telluris theoria sacra ... libri duo posteriores* (London, 1689). |
| Adv.d.44.5 | Edward Sherburne's copy of Manilius, *Astronomicon*, ed. J. Scaliger (2nd edn, Leiden, 1600). |
| Adv.e.44.2 | Thomas Stanley's copy of Aeschylus, *Tragoediae septem*, ed. A. F. Robortello (Venice, 1552). |
| N.3.41 | Copy of Adrian Heereboord, *Meletemata philosophica* (Amsterdam & London, 1680 [1st edn=Amsterdam, 1665]) belonging to a student at Corpus Christi College. |
| Pet. 2.2. | John Patrick's copy of Marcus Friedrich Wendelin's *Contemplationes Physicae* (Cambridge, 1648). |

## Kansas City

### Linda Hall Library for Science, Engineering and Technology

| | |
|---|---|
| D59.M36 1676 | [Newton's copy of John Marsham, *Canon chronicus ... nunc longè emendatior in Germaniâ recusus* (Leipzig, 1676)]. |

## London

### British Library

| | |
|---|---|
| 676.g.17 | John Sheffield, Duke of Buckingham's copy of Ralph Cudworth, *The true intellectual system of the universe* (London, 1678). |
| 3105 f.1. | Thomas Tenison's copy of John Spencer, *De legibus Hebraeorum* (Cambridge, 1683–85). |
| Eve.A.123 | John Evelyn's copy of Theophilus Gale, *Court of the Gentiles* (1669–78). |

## Oxford

### Bodleian Library

| | |
|---|---|
| 8°A.72. Linc | Thomas Barlow's copy of Ιεροκλεους φιλοσοφου Υπομνημα εις τα τῦν Πυθαγορειων ἔπη τὰ χρυσα. *Hierocli* |

|                    | *Philosophi commentarius in aurea Pythagoreorum carmina* (London, 1654). |
|--------------------|---|
| 8°C 306 Linc.      | Thomas Barlow's copy of Samuel Gardiner's, *Responsio valedictoria ad secundam Sandii epistolam in Vindicias Nuclei sui Historiae ecclesiasticae conscriptam* (London, 1681). |
| MSS Top. Oxon.b.8–9 | Anthony Wood, *Athenae Oxoniensis. An exact history of all the writers and bishops who have had their education in the ... University of Oxford ... The second edition*, ed. T. Tanner (London, 1721), with additions and inserts by Wood. |
| G. Pamph. 1688(6)  | University of Cambridge Act verses, 1604: *Corpora humana non fiunt indes imbecilliora; Mundus secundum Aristotelem non est aeternus* ([Cambridge], [1604?]). |
| 4°Rawl.49          | Walter Charleton, *Epicurus's morals, collected partly out of his owne Greek text, in Diogenes Laertius, and partly out of the rhapsodies of Marcus Antoninus, Plutarch, Cicero, & Seneca* (London, 1656), presentation copy to Thomas Belassis, Viscount Faconberg. |

## Printed Primary Sources

The bibliographies of printed primary and secondary sources are confined to works cited in the main text. The alphabetical order is of the first element of the name that bears a capital letter.

de Acosta, José, *The natural and morall histories of the East and West Indies* (London, 1604).

*Acta eruditorum* (1686).

*Acta eruditorum quae Lipsiae publicantur supplementa*, 2 (1696).

Ainsworth, Henry, *Annotations upon the first books of Moses* (Amsterdam, 1621 [1st edn=1616]).

  *Annotations upon the five books of Moses* (London, 1627).

Alexander Aphrodisiensis, *Alexander Aphrodisias: enarratio de anima ex Aristotelis institutione. Neudruck der 1. Ausgabe Brescia 1495*, ed. E. Kessler (Stuttgart, 2008).

Allatius, Leo, ed., *Socratis, Antisthenis, et aliorum Socraticorum epistolae* (Paris, 1637).

  *Apes urbanae, sive de viris illustribus* (Rome, 1633).

Allix, Pierre, *Réflexions sur les livres de l'écriture sainte, pour établir la verité de la religion chrétienne* (London, 1687).

  *The fathers vindicated, by a Presbyter of the Church of England* (London, 1697).

  *The judgement of the ancient Jewish church, against the Unitarians* (London, 1699).

Andreae, Samuel, *Examen generale Cabbale philosophicae D. Henrici Mori* (Herborn, 1670).

Andrewes, Lancelot, *A learned discourse of ceremonies retained and used in Christian churches* (London, 1653).

Anquetil-Duperron, Abraham Hyacinthe, *Zend-Avesta, ouvrage de Zoroastre, contenant les idées théologiques, physiques & morales de ce législateur, les cérémonies du culte religieux qu'il a établi, & plusieurs traits importans relatifs à l'ancienne histoire des Parses* (3 vols, Paris, 1771).

Annius, Joannes, *Antiquitatum libri quinque* (Wittenberg, 1612 [1st edn=Rome, 1498]).

[Anon.] *Histrio-Mastix. A whip for Webster* in Thomas Hall, *Vindiciae Literarum* (London, 1654).

*Anthropologie abstracted: or the idea of humane nature reflected in briefe philosophicall, and anatomicall collections* (London, 1655).

*A letter to Mr. Henry Stubs, concerning his censure* (London, 1670).

*A catalogue of books printed for Thomas Basset, and are to be sold at his shop at the George near Cliffords Inne in Fleet-Street* (London, 1672).

*The life of Mr. Thomas Firmin, late citizen of London* (London, 1698).

*An account of Mr. Firmin's religion; and of the present state of the Unitarian controversy* (London, 1698).

*A vindication of the memory of the late excellent and charitable Mr. Firmin* (London, 1699).

[John Edwards?] *The Reverend and learned Dr. Hammond, and his paraphrase and annotations on the New Testament, vindicated from the rude and unjust reflections made upon him and them by Monsieur Le Clerc* (London, 1699).

*The lives of the ancient philosophers … extracted from Diogenes Laertius, Casaubon, Menagius, Stanley, Gassendus, Charleton …* (London, 1702).

*The life of the Reverend Humphrey Prideaux* (London, 1748).

Arbuthnot, John, *An examination of Dr. Woodward's account of the deluge* (London, 1697).

ps.-Archytas, *Über die Kategorien. Texte zur griechischen Aristoteles-Exegese*, ed. T. A. Szlezák (Berlin, 1972).

Arminius, Jacobus, 'Declaration of the sentiments' [1608], in *The works of James Arminius*, trans., J. Nichols and W. Nichols (3 vols, London, 1825–6).

Augustine, *De civitate Dei libri XXII*, ed. J. L. Vives (Basle, 1555 [1st edn=1522]).

Bacon, Francis, *Of the proficience and advancement of learning, divine and humane* (London, 1605) [=*OFB*, IV, ed. M. Kiernan (Oxford, 2000)].

*Novum Organum* (London, 1620) [=*OFB*, XI, eds., G. Rees and M. Wakely (Oxford, 2004)].

*De augmentis scientiarum* (London, 1623).

Bainbridge, John, *Canicularia* (Oxford, 1648).

Baker, Augustine, *Sancta Sophia: or directions for the prayer of contemplation* (Douay, 1657).

[Baker, Thomas], *Reflections upon learning* (London, 1699).

Baldi, Bernardino, *Cronica de Matematici, overo Epitome dell'istoria delle vite loro* (Urbino, 1707).

Bampfield, Francis, *A grammatical opening of some Hebrew words and phrases in the beginning of the Bible* (London, 1684).

Barlow, Thomas, *Exercitationes aliquot metaphysicae, de Deo: quod sit objectum metaphysicae* (Oxford, 1658 [1st edn=1637]).

[?], *A library for younger schollers: compiled by an English scholar-priest around 1655* eds., A. DeJordy and H. F. Fletcher (Urbana, 1961).

Baron, Robert, *Metaphysica generalis* (London, 1658).

Barrow, Isaac, *'Epistola lectori', Archimedis opera; Apollonii Pergaei conicorum libri IIII; Theodosii Sphaerica* (London, 1675).

*Lectiones mathematicae XXIII, in quibus principia matheseôs generalia exponuntur* (London, 1685).

*The usefulness of mathematical learning explained and demonstrated*, trans. J. Kirkby (London, 1734).

*The theological works of Isaac Barrow, D.D.*, ed. A. Napier (9 vols, Cambridge, 1859).

Basset, William, *An answer to the Brief history of the Unitarians* (London, 1693).

Basson, Sébastien, *Philosophiae naturalis adversus Aristotelem libri XII* (Geneva, 1621).

Bathurst, Ralph, *The life and literary remains of Ralph Bathurst, M.D.*, ed. T. Warton (2 vols, London, 1761).

Baxter, Richard, *The reasons of the Christian religion the first part . . . also an appendix defending the soul's immortality against the Somatists or Epicureans and other pseudo-philosophers* (London, 1667).

*Richard Baxter's Catholick theologie plain pure, peaceable, for pacification of the dogmatical word warriours* (London, 1675).

*Roman tradition examined . . . in the point of transubstantiation* ([London], 1676).

*The nonconformists plea for peace* (London, 1679).

*Which is the true church?* (London, 1679).

*Church-history of the government of bishops and their councils abbreviated* (London, 1680).

*The true and only way of concord of all the Christian churches* (London, 1680).

*The true history of councils enlarged and defended* (London, 1682).

*Of the immortality of mans souls, and the nature of it and other spirits* (London, 1682).

*A treatise of knowledge and love compared in two parts* (London, 1689).

Bayle, Pierre, *Lettre à M. L. A. D. C. Docteur de Sorbonne, où il est prouvé par plusieurs raisons . . . que les cometes ne sont point le presage d'aucun malheur* ([Rotterdam], 1682).

*Dictionnaire historique et critique* (Rotterdam, 1697).

*Dictionnaire historique et critique* (2nd edn, 3 vols, Amsterdam, 1702).

*Continuations des pensées sur les cometes* (Rotterdam, 1705).

*The general dictionary, historical and critical* (10 vols, London, 1734–41).

*Pensées diverses sur la comète: edition critique*, ed. A. Prat (2 vols, Paris, 1939).

Beaumont, John, *Considerations on a book, entituled The theory of the earth* (London, 1693).

Beaumont, Joseph, *Some observations upon the apology of Dr. Henry More* (Cambridge, 1665).

Becher, Johann, *Oedipus chymicus* (Amsterdam, 1664).

Bentley, Richard, *'Cl. Viro Oanni Millio'*, in Ἰωάννου Ἀντιοχεως του επικλην Μαλάλα χρονικη ιστορια *Joannis Antiocheni cognomento Malalae historia chronica* (Oxford, 1691).

*A dissertation upon the epistles of Phalaris, Themistocles, Socrates, Euripides, and others* (London, 1697).

*A dissertation upon the epistles of Phalaris, with an answer to the objections of the honourable Charles Boyle* (London, 1699).

Berkelius, Abrahamus, *Genuina Stephani Byzantini De urbibus et populis fragmenta ... accredit Hannonis Carthaginensium Regis Periplus* (Leiden, 1674).

Bernard, Edward, *De mensuris et ponderibus antiquis* (Oxford, 1688).

*Orbis eruditi literaturam à charactere Samaritico hunc in modum favente Deo deduxit Eduardus Bernardus* (Oxford, 1689).

ed., *Catalogi librorum manuscriptorum Angliae et Hiberniae* (Oxford, 1697).

*Bibliotheca Bernardina*, ed. E. Millington (London, 1697).

Best, Paul, *Mysteries discovered* (London, 1647).

Beveridge, William, *Codex Canonum Ecclesiae primitivae vindicatus et illustratus* (London, 1678).

*The theological works of William Beveridge*, ed. P. Bliss (12 vols, Oxford, 1842–48).

Beza, Theodore, ed. and trans., *Iesu Christi D.N. Novum testamentum, sive Novum foedus*, ed. and trans. T. Beza (2nd edn, Geneva, 1582 [1st edn=1565]).

*Bibliothèque choisie*, 1 (1703).

*Bibliothèque choisie*, 3 (1704).

*Bibliothèque choisie*, 7 (1705).

*Bibliothèque choisie*, 19 (1709).

*Bibliothèque choisie*, 25 (1712).

*Bibliothèque universelle et historique*, 7 (1687).

*Bibliothèque universelle et historique*, 10 (1688).

*Bibliothèque universelle et historique*, 18 (1690).

*Bibliothèque universelle et historique*, 19 (1690).

[Biddle, John,] *The testimonies of Irenæus, Justin Martyr, Tertullian, Novatianus, Theophilus, Origen, (who lived in the two first centuries after Christ was born, or thereabouts;) as also, of Arnobius, Lactantius, Eusebius, Hilary, and Brightman; concerning that one God, and the person of the Holy Trinity* (London, [1653]).

Biggs, Noah, *Mataeotechnia medicinae praxeos, the vanity of the craft of physick ... with an humble motion for the reformation of the universities* (London, 1651).

Birch, Thomas, 'An historical and critical account of the life and writings of Mr. John Greaves', in *The miscellaneous works of Mr. John Greaves* (2 vols, London, 1737).

*The history of the Royal Society of London* (4 vols, London, 1756–57).

'Account of the life and writings of Ralph Cudworth', in R. Cudworth, *The true intellectual system of the universe*, ed. T. Birch (4 vols, London, 1820).

Blomberg, W. N., *An account of the life and writings of Edmund Dickinson* (London, 1739).

Blondel, David, *Des Sibylles célébrées tant par l'antiquité payenne que par les saincts perés* (Paris, 1649).

Blount, Charles, *Anima mundi, or, an historical narration of the opinions of the ancients concerning man's soul after this life* (London, 1679).

*Janua scientiarum, or, a compendious introduction to geography, chronology, government, history, philosophy, and all genteel sorts of literature* (London, 1684).

*The oracles of reason*, ed. C. Gildon (London, 1693).

Blount, Thomas Pope, *Censura celebriorum authorum, sive, Tractatus in quo varia virorum doctorum de clarissimis cujusque seculi scriptoribus judicia traduntur* (London, 1690).

Boate, G., and Boate, A., *Philosophia naturalis reformata. Id est, philosophiae Aristotelicae accurata examinatio, ac solida confutatio. Et novae ac verioris introductio* (Dublin, 1641).

Bochart, Samuel, *Geographia sacra* (Caen, 1646).

*Geographia sacra* (3rd edn, London, 1692 [1st edn=1646]).

Bohun, Ralph, *Discourse concerning the origine and properties of wind* (Oxford, 1671).

Bolnest, Edward, *Medicina instaurata, or, a brief account of the true grounds and principles of the art of physick* (London, 1665).

Bonfrerio, Jacobo, *Pentateuchus Moysis commentario illustratus* (Antwerp, 1625).

Borrichius, Olaus, *De ortu, et progressu chemiae dissertatio* (Copenhagen, 1668).

*Hermetis Aegyptiorum et chemicorum sapientia ab Hermanni Conringi animadversionibus vindicata* (Copenhagen, 1674).

B[ostocke], R[ichard], *The difference between the auncient phisicke, first taught by the godly forefathers . . . and the latter phisicke proceeding from idolaters, ethnickes, and heathen* (London, 1585).

Botsaccus, Johannes, *Anticrellius* (Danzig, 1642).

Boulduc, Jacques, *De ecclesia ante legem* (Paris, 1630 [1st edn=Lyon, 1626]).

Boyle, Charles, *Dr. Bentley's Dissertations on the epistles of Phalaris . . . examin'd* (London, 1698).

Boyle, Robert, *The early essays and ethics of Robert Boyle*, ed. J. Harwood (Carbondale and Edwardsville, 1991).

*The works of Robert Boyle*, eds., M. Hunter and E. B. Davis (14 vols, London, 1999–2000).

*The correspondence of Robert Boyle*, eds., M. Hunter, A. Clericuzio, and L. M. Principe (6 vols, London, 2001).

*Boyle on Atheism*, ed. J. J. MacIntosh (Toronto, 2005).

Bray, Thomas, *Bibliotheca parochialis: or, a scheme of such theological heads both general and particular, as are more peculiarly requisite to be well studied by every pastor of a parish* (London, 1697).

Brent, William, *A discourse upon the nature of eternitie* (London, 1655).

Brokesby, Francis, *Of education with respect to grammar schools, and the universities; concluding with direction to young students at the universities* (London, 1701).

[Brown, Thomas] 'Preface', in *Twelve dissertations out of Monsieur Le Clerk's Genesis* (London, 1696).

Browne, Thomas, *Pseudodoxia epidemica* (London, 1646).

*The works of Sir Thomas Browne*, ed. G. Keynes (4 vols, London, 1928–31).

Brucker, Johann Jakob, *The history of philosophy, from the earliest times to the beginning of the present century*, trans. W. Enfield (2 vols, London, 1791 [1st edn=Leipzig, 1742–44]).

Budgell, Gilbert, *A discourse of prayer* (London, 1690).

Bull, George, *Examen censurae, sive, responsio ad quasdam animadversiones antehac ineditas in librum cui titulus Harmonia apostolica* (London, 1676).

*Defensio fidei Nicaenae, ex scriptis, quae extant, Catholicorum doctorum, qui intra tria prima Ecclesiae Christianae saecula floruerunt* (Oxford, 1685).

*Judicium Ecclesiae Catholicae trium primorum seculorum de necessitate credendi quod Dominus noster Jesus Christus sit verus Deus* (Oxford, 1694).

*Opera omnia*, ed. J. E. Grabe (London, 1703).

Bulstrode, Whitelocke, *An essay of transmigration, in defence of Pythagoras* (London, 1692).

Bulteel, J., ed., *The Apophthegmes of the ancients taken out of Plutarch, Diogenes Laertius, Elian, Atheneus, Stobeus, Macrobius, and others. Collected into one volume for the benefit and pleasure of the ingenious* (London, 1683).

Burgersdijk, Franco, *Collegium phyiscum, disputationibus XXXII* (Cambridge, 1650 [1st edn=Leiden, 1637]).

Burnet, Gilbert, *Four discourses delivered to the clergy of the Diocess of Sarum* (London, 1694).

Burnet, Thomas, *Telluris theoria sacra: orbis nostri origenem & mutationes generales* (2 vols, London, 1681, 1689).

*The theory of the earth: containing an account of the original of the earth* (2 vols, London, 1684, 1690).

*An answer to the late exceptions made by Mr. Erasmus Warren* (London, 1690).

*A short consideration of Mr. Erasmus Warren's defence* (London, 1691).

*Archaeologiae philosophicae: sive doctrina antiqua de rerum originibus* (London, 1692).

*Archaelogiae philosophicae: or the ancient doctrine concerning the originals of things* (London, 1736).

*Doctrina antiqua de rerum originibus: or, an inquiry into the doctrine of the philosophers of all nations* (London, 1736).

[Bury, Arthur], *The naked Gospel. Discovering I. What was the Gospel which our Lord and his apostles preached? II. What additions and alterations later ages have made in it? III. What advantages and damages have thereupon ensued?* ([London], 1690).

Buxtorf, Johann, *Tractatus de punctorum vocalium … in libris Veteris Testamenti* (Basle, 1648).

Bysshe, Edward, *Παλλαδίου, περι τῶν τῆς Ἰνδίας ἐθνῶν καὶ τῶν Βραγμανων. Palladius de Gentibus Indiae et Bragmantibus. S. Ambrosius De Moribus Brachmanorum. Anonymus de Bragmanibus. Quorum Priorem & Postremum nunc primum in lucem protulit ex Bibliotheca Regia Edoardus Bissaeus* (London, 1665).

Calvin, John, *Expositio impeitatis Valentini Gentilis* (Geneva, 1561).

*Institutionis Christianae religionis* (London, 1576 [1st edn=Geneva, 1559]).

Cappel, Louis, *Arcanum punctationis revelatum* (Leiden, 1624).

Cartwright, Christopher, *Electa thargumico-rabbinica; sive, annotationes in Genesim* (London, 1648).

Cary, Viscount Falkland, Lucius, 'The Lord of Faulklands reply', in *Sir Lucius Cary, late Lord Viscount of Falkland, his discourse of infallibility, with an answer to it: and his Lordships reply. Never before published* (London, 1651).

Cary, Robert, *Palæologia chronica. A chronological account of ancient time* (London, 1677).

Casaubon, Isaac, *Animadversionum in Athenaei Dipnosophistas* (London, 1600).

*De rebus sacris & ecclesiasticis exercitationes XVI* (Frankfurt, 1615 [1st edn=London, 1614]).

'Notae ad Diogenes Laertii Libros', *in Λαερτιου Διογενους Περι Βίων Δογματων και Αποφθεγματων των εν φιλοσοφία ευδοκομησάντων ... Laertii Diogenes de vitis dogmatis et apophthegmatis eorum qui in philosophia claruerunt, libri X,* ed. G. Ménage (London, 1664).

Casaubon, Meric, 'Notes', in *Marcus Aurelius Antoninus the Roman emperor, his meditations concerning himselfe* (London, 1634).

'In Marci Antonini De seipso & ad seipsum libros, notae', in *Marci Antonini Imperatoris De seipso et ad seipsum libri XII* (London, 1643).

*The originall cause of temporall evils* (London, 1645).

*A discourse concerning Christ his incarnation, and exinanition* (London, 1646).

'In Hierocles Commentarium Notae, & Emendationes', in *Hierocles de providentia & fato* (London, 1655).

*A treatise concerning enthusiasme* (London, 1655).

*A treatise concerning enthusiasme ... the second edition: revised, and enlarged* (London, 1656).

*De nupera Homeri* (London, 1659).

'Notae, & emendationes', in *Λαερτιου Διογενους Περι Βίων Δογματων και Αποφθεγματων των εν φιλοσοφία ευδοκομησάντων ... Laertii Diogenes de vitis dogmatis et apophthegmatis eorum qui in philosophia claruerunt, libri X,* ed. G. Ménage (London, 1664).

*Of credulity and incredulity, in things natural, civil and divine* (London, 1668).

*A letter ... to Peter du Moulin* (Cambridge, 1669).

*Of credulity and incredulity, in things natural, civil and divine, wherein, (among other things) a true and faithful account is given of the Platonick philosophy, as it hath reference to Christianity* (London, 1670).

*Generall Learning: A seventeenth-century treatise on the formation of the General Scholar by Meric Casaubon,* ed. R. Serjeantson (Cambridge, 1999).

Castle, George, *The chymical Galenist: a treatise wherein the practise of the ancients is reconcil'd to the new discoveries in the theory of physick; shewing, that many of their rules, methods, and medicins, are useful for the curing of diseases in this age* (London, 1667).

Cave, William, *Apostolici, or the history of the lives, acts, death, and martyrdoms of those who were contemporary with, or immediately succeeded the apostles. As also the most eminent of the primitive fathers for the first three hundred years ... the second edition corrected* (London, 1682 [1st edn=1677]).

*Ecclesiastici, or, the history of the lives, acts, death & writings, of the most eminent fathers of the church, that flourist in the fourth century* (London, 1683).

*Chartophylax ecclesiasticus* (London, 1685).

*Scriptorum Ecclesiasticorum historia literaria facili & perspicua methodo digesta. Pars altera* (London, 1698).

*Epistola apologetica adversus iniquas Joannis Clerici criminationes* (London, 1700).

Chaeremon, *Chaeremon: Egyptian priest and Stoic philosopher: the fragments,* ed. and trans. P. W. van der Horst (Leiden, 1984).

Chalcidius, *Chalcidii V.C. Timaeus de Platonis translatus,* ed. J. Meursius (Leiden, 1617).

Chardin, Jean, *Voyages de monsieur le chevalier Chardin en Perse et autres lieux de l'orient* (3 vols, Amsterdam, 1711).

Charleton, Walter, *The darkness of atheism dispelled by the light of nature* (London, 1652).

*Physiologia Epicuro-Gassendo-Charltoniana* (London, 1654).

*Epicurus's morals, collected partly out of his owne Greek text, in Diogenes Laertius, and partly out of the rhapsodies of Marcus Antoninus, Plutarch, Cicero, & Seneca* (London, 1656).

*The immortality of the human soul, demonstrated by the light of nature* (London, 1657).

*Chorea gigantum, or, the most famous antiquity of Great-Britan [sic], vulgarly called Stone-Heng, standing on Salisbury Plain, restored to the Danes* (London, 1663).

*Enquiries into human nature in VI. anatomic praelections in the new theatre of the Royal Colledge of Physicians* (London, 1680).

*The harmony of natural and positive divine laws* (London, 1682).

Cheynell, Francis, *The rise, growth, and danger of Socinianisime* (London, 1643).

*The divine triunity of the Father, Son, and Holy Spirit, or, the blessed doctrine of the three coessentiall subsistents in the eternall Godhead without any confusion or division of the distinct subsistences or multiplication of the most single and entire Godhead* (London, 1650).

Chillingworth, William, *The religion of Protestants* (Oxford, 1638).

Clarke, Samuel, *A collection of papers, which passed between the late Learned Mr. Leibnitz, and Dr. Clarke, in the years 1715 and 1716* (London, 1717).

Clement, David, *Bibliothèque curieuse historique et critique Catalogue raisonné de livres dificiles a trouver* (4 vols, Hannover, 1753).

Clerke, Gilbert, *Tractatus tres; quorum qui prior Ante-Nicenismus dicitur ... in secundo brevis responsio ordinatur ad D. G. Bulli Defensionem Synodi Necenae* ([London], 1695).

Colomiès, Paul, *Opuscula* (Utrecht, 1669).

Comenius, Johannes Amos, *A reformation of schooles designed in two excellent treatises* (London, 1642).

*De quaestione utrum Dominus Jesus* (Amsterdam, 1659).

Confucius, *Confucius Sinarum philosophus sive scientia Sinensis* (Paris, 1687).

Conring, Hermann, *De Hermetica Aegyptiorum vetere et Paracelsicorum nova medicina liber unus* (Helmstadt, 1648).

*De hermetica medicina libri duo* (Helmstadt, 1669).

Conway, Anne, *The Conway letters: the correspondence of Anne, Viscountess Conway, Henry More and their friends, 1642–1684*, ed. M. H. Nicolson, rev. S. Hutton (Oxford, 1992).

*The principles of the most ancient and modern philosophy* [1690] (Cambridge, 1996).

Cooper, William, *Catalogus librorum ... Guliemi Outrami* (London, 1681).

*Corpus inscriptorum Latinarum* (17 vols, Berlin, 1853—).

Cortesius, Joan Baptista, *Miscellaneorum medicinalium decades denae* (Messina, 1625).

Coste, Pierre 'Discours sur la philosophie ancienne et moderne où l'on fait en abregé l'histoire de cette science', in Pierre Sylvain Régis, *Cours entire de philosophie ou système général selon les principes de M. Descartes* (Amsterdam, 1691).

Cotta, John, *A short discoverie of the unobserved dangers of severall sorts of ignorant and unconsiderate practisers of physicke in England* (London, 1612).

Coumbus, Realdus, *De re anatomica* (Paris, 1562).

Couplet, Phillipe, '*Philosophorum Sinensium Principis Confucii Vita*', in *Confucius Sinarum philosophus sive scientia Sinensis* (Paris, 1687).

Cowley, Abraham, *A proposition for the advancement of experimental philosophy* (London, 1661).

    'To Mr. Hobs', *The works of Mr Abraham Cowley* (5th edn, London, 1679 [1st edn=1668]).

[Coxe, Daniel], *A discourse wherein the interest of the patient in reference to physick and physicians is soberly debated* (London, 1669).

Creech, Thomas, 'Notes upon the first book', in *Lucretius his six books of epicurean philosophy and Manilius his five books containing a system of the ancient astronomy and astrology together with the philosophy of the Stoicks* (London, 1700).

[Crell, Samuel], 'Vera & Antiqua Fides de Divinitate Christi asserta', *Tractatus tres; quorum qui prior Ante-Nicenismus dicitur ... in secundo brevis responsio ordinatur ad D. G. Bulli Defensionem Synodi Necenae* ([London], 1695).

Cressy, Hugh, *Exomologesis, or, a faithfull narration of the occasion and motives of the conversion unto Catholick unity of Hugh-Paulin de Cressy* (2nd edn, Paris, 1653 [1st edn=1647]).

    *Roman-Catholick doctrines no novelties, or, An answer to Dr. Pierce's court-sermon, miscall'd the primitive rule of Reformation* (n.p., 1663).

    *Fanaticism fanatically imputed to the Catholick church by Doctour Stillingfleet and the imputation refuted and retorted* (n.p., 1672).

Crispo, Giovanni Battista, *De ethnicis philosophis caute legendis* (Rome, 1594).

Croft, Herbert, *Some animadversions upon a book intituled, The theory of the earth* (London, 1685).

Cudworth, Ralph, *A discourse concerning the true notion of the Lords Supper* (London, 1641).

    *The true intellectual system of the universe: the first part; wherein all the reason and philosophy of atheism is confuted; and its impossibility demonstrated* (London, 1678).

    *Bibliotheca Cudworthiana sive catalogus variorum librorum plurimus facultatibus* (London, 1692).

    *A treatise concerning eternal and immutable morality* (London, 1731).

    *A treatise of freewill*, ed. J. Allen (London, 1838).

    *A treatise concerning eternal and immutable morality, with a Treatise of freewill*, ed. S. Hutton (Cambridge, 1996).

Culverwell, Nathanial, *An elegant and learned discourse of the light of nature* (London, 1652).

    *An elegant and learned discourse of the light of nature*, eds., R. A. Greene and H. MacCallum (Toronto, 1971).

Cumberland, Richard, *Origines gentium antiquissimae; or, attempts for discovering the times of the first planting of nations in several tracts* [*c.* 1680] (London, 1724).

Curcellaeus, Stephanus, 'Praefatio', in *M. Simonis Episcopii ... Opera theologica* (2 vols, Amsterdam, 1650–65).

    *Opera* (Amsterdam, 1675).

Cyprian, *Sancti Caecilii Cypriani Opera recognita & illustrata*, ed. J. Fell (Oxford, 1682).

Dacier, André, *La vie de Pythagore, ses Symbols, ses Vers Dorez, & la vie d'Hierocles* (Paris, 1706).

*The Life of Pythagoras, with his Symbols and Golden Verses. Together with the Life of Hierocles* (London, 1707).

Daillé, Jean, *Traicté de l'employ des saincts peres* (Geneva, 1632).

*A treatise concerning the right use of the fathers*, trans T. Smith (London, 1651).

Deichgräber, K., ed., *Die griechische Empirikerschule: Sammlung der Fragmente und Darstellung der Lehre* (Berlin, 1965).

Dell, William, *The tryal of spirits both in teachers & hearers* (London, 1653).

Descartes, René, *Oeuvres de Descartes*, eds., C. Adam and P. Tannery (12 vols, Paris, 1897–1910).

Dhabhar, B. N., ed., *Saddar Nasár and Saddar Bundehesh* (Bombay, 1909).

Dickinson, Edmund, *Delphi phoenicizantes sive, tractatus, in quo Græcos, quicquid apud Delphos celebre erat ... è josuæ historiâ, scriptisque sacris effinxisse rationibus haud inconcinnis ostenditur* (Oxford, 1655)

*Physica vetus et vera* (London, 1702).

Digby, Kenelm, *Two treatises, in the one of which, the nature of bodies; in the other, the nature of mans soule; is looked into: in way of discovery, of the immortality of reasonable soules* (Paris, 1644).

*Letters between the Lord George Digby, and Sir Kenelm Digby knight concerning religion* (London, 1651).

*A discourse concerning infallibility in religion written ... to the Lord George Digby* (London, 1652).

Diodati, Giovanni, *Pious annotations, upon the Holy Bible* (London, 1643).

Diogenes Laërtius, *Διογένους Λαερτίου περὶ Βίων, δογμάτων καὶ ἀποφθεγμάτων τῶν ἐν φιλοσοφία εὐδοκιμησάντων Βιβλία, ι. Diogenis Laertii de vitis, dogmatis & apophthegmatis eorum qui in philosophia claruerunt, libri X ... cum annotationibus Henr. Stephani* (Geneva, 1570).

*Διογένους Λαερτίου περὶ Βίων, δογμάτων καὶ ἀποφθεγμάτων τῶν ἐν φιλοσοφία εὐδοκιμησάντων Βιβλία, ι. Diogenis Laertii de vitis, dogmatis & apophthegmatis eorum qui in philosophia claruerunt, libri X ... Is. Casauboni Notae ad lib. Diogenis, multo auctiores & emendatiores* (Geneva, 1593).

*Διογένους Λαερτίου περὶ Βίων, δογμάτων καὶ ἀποφθεγμάτων τῶν ἐν φιλοσοφία εὐδοκιμησάντων Βιβλία, ι. Diogenis Laertii de vitis, dogmatis & apophthegmatis eorum qui in philosophia claruerunt, libri X*, ed. and trans. T. Aldobrandini (Rome, 1594).

*Λαερτιου Διογενους Περι Βίων Δογματων και Αποφθεγματων των εν φιλοσοφία ευδοκομησάντων ... Laertii Diogenes de vitis dogmatis et apophthegmatis eorum qui in philosophia claruerunt, libri X*, ed. G. Ménage (London, 1664).

*The lives, opinions, and remarkably sayings of the most famous ancient philosophers*, trans., T. Fetherstone, S. White, E. Smith, J. Philips, R. Kippax, W. Baxter, R. M., and S. White (2 vols, London, 1688).

*Diogenis Laertii de vitis, dogmatibus et apophthegmatibus clarorum philosophorum libri X*, ed. M. Meibom (2 vols, Amsterdam, 1692).

ps.-Dionysius, *Paraphrasis in omnia Dionysii Areopagitae* (Paris, 1561).

Dodwell, Henry, *Two letters of advice I. For the susception of Holy Orders, II. For studies theological, especially such as are rational* (Dublin, 1672).

'Prolegomena apologetica, de usu dogmatum Philosophicorum, praecipue Stoicorum, in Theologia', in John Stearne, *De obstinatione. Opus posthumum, pietatem Christiano-Stoicam, scholastico more, suadens* (Dublin, 1672).

*Two short discourses against the Romanists* (London, 1676).

*Separation of churches from episcopal government, as practiced by the present non-conformists, proved schismatical* (London, 1679).

*A discourse concerning the one altar and the one priesthood insisted on by the ancients in their disputes against schism* (London, 1683).

*Dissertationes Cyprianicae* (Oxford, 1684).

*Dissertationes in Irenaeum* (Oxford, 1689).

*Praelections academicae in schola historices Camdeniana* (Oxford, 1692).

'Dissertatio prima. De vero Peripli, qui Hannonis nomine circumfertur, tempore', in *Geographiae veteris scriptores graeci minores*, ed. J. Hudson (Oxford, 1698).

*Annales Velleiani, Quintilianei, Statiani. Seu vitae P. Velleii paterculi, M. Fabii quintiliani, P. Papinii statii, (obiterque Juvenalis,) pro temporum ordine, dispositae* (Oxford, 1698).

*De veteribus Graecorum Romanorumque cyclis* (2 vols, Oxford, 1701–02).

*Occasional communion fundamentally destructive to the discipline of the primitive catholick church* (London, 1705).

[Duncon, Eleazar], *The copy of a letter written by E.D. Doctour of physicke to a gentleman ... The latter is a discourse of emperiks or unlearned physitians, wherein is plainly proved that the practise of all those which have not beene brought up in the grammar and university, is always confused, commonly dangerous, and often deadly* (London, 1606).

Du Perron, Jacques Davy, *Replique a la Response du serenissime Roy de la Grand Bretagne* (Paris, 1620).

*The reply of the most illustrious Cardinall of Perron, to the Answeare of the most excellent King of Great Britaine*, trans. Elizabeth Cary, Lady Falkland (Douai, 1630).

Duport, James, 'Apologiae pro Aristotele, contra novos philosophos. Seu pro veteribus contra nuperos Novatores', in *Musae subsecivae, se, poetica stromata* (Cambridge, 1676).

Duppa, Brian, *The correspondence of Bishop Brian Duppa and Sir Justinian Isham, 1650–1660*, ed. G. Isham (Northampton, 1951).

Dury, John, *The reformed librarie-keeper, with a supplement to the reformed-school* (London, 1650).

Edwards, John, *A compleat history: or, survey of all the dispensations and methods of religion* (London, 1699).

Edwards, Thomas, *The first and second part of Gangraena, or, a catalogue and discovery of many of the errors, heresies, blasphemies and pernicious practices of the sectaries of this time, vented and acted in England in these four last years* (London, 1646).

*The third part of Gangraena. Or, a new and higher discovery of the errors, heresies, blasphemies, and insolent proceedings of the sectaries of these times* (London, 1646).

Empedocles, *L'Empédocle de Strasbourg*, eds., A. Martin and O. Primavesi (Strasbourg, 1999).

Ent, George, *Apologia pro circulatione sanguinis* (London, 1641).

Episcopius, Simon, *Opera theologica* (2 vols, Amsterdam, 1650–65).

> *Opera theologica . . . editio secunda, cum autographo accuratissime collata* (2 vols, London, 1665–78).

d'Espagnet, Jean, *Enchiridion physicae restitutae* (Paris, 1608).

> *La philosophie naturelle restablie en sa purete* (Paris, 1651).

Estienne, Henri, ed., *Poesis philosophica, vel saltem reliquiae poesis philosophicae Empedoclis, Parmenidis, Xenophanis, Cleanthis, Timonis, Epicharmi; adiuncta sunt Orphei illius carmina qui a suis appellatus fuit ὁ Θεολόγος; item, Heracliti et Democriti loci quidam et eorum epistolae* (Geneva, 1573).

Estwick, Nicholas, *Πνευματολογια, or a treatise of the Holy Ghost* (London, 1648).

> *Mr Bidle's confession of faith touching the Holy Trinity, wherein his chief designe to overthrow that sacred mystery and the deity of our Blessed Saviour is examined and confuted* (London, 1656).

Eugenius Philalethes [i.e., Thomas Vaughan], *Anima magica abscondita: or a discourse of the universall spirit of nature* (London, 1650).

Eutychius, *Contextio Gemmaru, sive Eutychii Patriarchae Alexandrini Annales*, eds., J. Selden and E. Pococke (2 vols, Oxford, 1658).

Evelyn, John, *An essay on the first book of T. Lucretius Carus De rerum natura* (London, 1656).

> *The history of religion: a rational account of the true religion*, ed. R. M. Evanson (2 vols, London, 1850).

> *The diary and correspondence of John Evelyn, F.R.S.*, ed. W. Bray (4 vols, London, 1854–57).

> *The diary of John Evelyn*, ed. E.S. de Beer (6 vols, Oxford, 1951).

F. B., *A free but modest censure on the late controversial writings and debates of the Lord Bishop of Worcester and Mr. Locke, Mr. Edwards and Mr. Locke, the Honorable Charles Boyle, Esq., and Dr. Bently together with brief remarks on Monsieur Le Clerc's Ars critica* (London, 1698).

al-Farghānī, Abū al-ʿAbbās Aḥmad ibn Muḥammad ibn Kathīr, *Muhammedis Fil. Ketiri Ferganensis, qui vulgo Alfraganus dicitur, elementa astronomica, Arabicè & Latinè*, ed. and trans. J. Golius (Amsterdam, 1669).

Fagius, Paul, *Exegesis sive expositio dictionum Hebraicarum literalis & simplex, in quatuor capita Geneseos, pro studiosis linguae hebraicae* (Isny im Allgäu, 1542).

Farissol, Abraham ben Mordechai, *Igeret orḥot shalem, id est, Itinera mundi, sic dicta nempe cosmographia*, ed. and trans. T. Hyde (Oxford, 1691).

Fell, John, 'Praefatio', and 'Annotationes', in Nemesius, *Περι Φυσεως Ανθρωπου . . . De natura hominis . . . manuscriptorum codicum collatione*, ed. J. Fell (Oxford, 1671).

Fell, Samuel, *Primitiae, sive oratio habita Oxonia in schola theologica* (Oxford, 1627).

Ferguson, Robert, *The interest of reason in religion; with the import & use of scripture-metaphors; and the nature of the union betwixt Christ & believers* (London, 1675).

Fernel, Jean, *On the hidden causes of things*, ed. and trans., J. M. Forrester and J. Henry (Leiden, 2005 [1st edn=1548]).

Flavel, John, *Tractatus de demonstratione methodicus & polemicus . . . in usum Juventutis in Collegio Wadhami apud Oxonienses privatis praelectionibus traditus*, ed. A. Huish (Oxford, 1619, repr. 1624, 1651).

Flood, Robert, *Philosophia Moysaica* (Gouda, 1638).

*Mosiacall philosophy grounded upon the essential truth, or eternal sapience* (London, 1659).

Flower, Samuel, 'A Letter from Mr. F. A. Esq; R. S. S. to the publisher, with a paper of Mr. S. Flowers containing the exact draughts of several unknown characters, taken from the ruines at Persepolis', *Philosophical Transactions*, 17 (1693), 775–7.

Foster, Samuel, *Elliptical, or azimuthal horologiography* (London, 1654).

*Miscellanies, or Mathematical lucubrations of Mr. Samuel Foster published and many of them translated into English by . . . John Twysden* (London, 1659).

Frommenius, Andreas, *Synopsis metaphysica*, ed. P. Claussen (Oxford, 1669, repr. 1691).

Fulman, William and Gale, Thomas, eds., *Rerum Anglicarum scriptorum veterum* (Oxford, 1684).

Gaffarel, Jacques, *Curiositez inouyes sur la sculpture talismanique des Persans* (Paris, 1629).

*Unheard-of curiosities: concerning the talismanical sculpture of the Persians* (London, 1650).

Gage, Thomas, *A new survey of the West-Indies: or, The English American his travel by sea and land* (London, 1677).

Gale, Theophilus, *The court of the gentiles: or a discourse touching the original of human literature . . . from the Scriptures, and Jewish church* (5 vols, 1669–77).

*The true idea of Jansenisme, both historick and dogmatick* (London, 1669).

*Idea theologiae, tam contemplativae quam activae, ad formam s. Scripturae delineata* (London, 1673).

*Philosophia generalis, in duas partes disterminata* (London, 1676).

'A Summary of the Two Covenants', in William Strong, *A discourse of the two covenants*, ed. Theophilus Gale (London, 1678).

Gale, Thomas, *Opuscula mythologica, ethica et physica* (Cambridge, 1671).

*Opuscula mythologica, ethica et physica* (Amsterdam, 1688).

Gardiner, Samuel, *Supremus magistratus habet summam potestatem circa sacra* ([Cambridge], 1657).

*De efficacia gratiæ convertentis, ejúsque agendi modo, determinatio habita Cantabrigiæ in scholis theologicis, A.D. 1658. Pro gradu doctoratûs in S.T* (Cambridge, 1660).

Ὑποτύπωσις, *sive Catholicae circa SS. trinitatem fidei delineatio ex scriptis partum ante-Nicaenorm desumpta* (London, 1677).

*Responsio valedictoria ad secundam Sandii epistolam in Vindicias Nuclei sui Historiae ecclesiasticae conscriptam* (London, 1681).

Gassendi, Pierre, *Exercitationes paradoxicae adversus Aristoteleos* (Amsterdam, 1649 [1st edn=Grenoble, 1624]).

*Animadversiones in decimum librum Diogenis Laertii* (3 vols, Lyon, 1649).

*Opera omnia* (6 vols, Lyon, 1658).

*Three discourses of happiness, virtue, and liberty collected from the works of the learn'd Gassendi, by Monsieur Bernier* (London, 1699).

Gataker, Thomas, 'Praeloquium', in Marcus Aurelius, *De rebus suis, sive de eis quae ad se pertinere censebat*, ed. and trans. T. Gataker (Cambridge, 1652).

Gaule, John, *Pus-mantia the mag-astro-mancer, or, the magicall-astrologicall-diviner posed, and puzzled* (London, 1652).

Gaulmin, Gilbert, ed., *De vita et morte Mosis, libri tres, cum observationibus* (Paris, 1629).

Gaza, Theodorus, 'In libros de animalibus praefatio', *Aristotelis Stagiritae operum, tomus secundus* (Leiden, 1549 [1st edn, 1476]).

Génébrard, Gilbert, *De S. Trinitate libri tres contra huius aevi Trinitarios, Antitrinitarios, & Autotheanos* (Paris, 1569).

Geraldus, Lilius, *De Deis gentium varia et multiplex historia* (Basle, 1548).

Gigon, P., ed., *Vita Aristotelis Marciana* (Berlin, 1962).

[Timothy Goodwin [?]], 'The life and character of ... Edward Stillingfleet', in Edward Stillingfleet, *Works* (6 vols, London, 1709–10), I, 1–53.

[Glanvill, Joseph], *Lux orientalis, or, an enquiry into the opinion of the eastern sages concerning the praeexistence of souls* (London, 1662).

*Scepsis scientifica* (London, 1665).

*Plus ultra, or, the progress and advancement of knowledge since the days of Aristotle* (London, 1668).

*Praefatory answer to Mr. Henry Stubbe* (London, 1671).

*A further discovery of M. Stubbe* (London, 1671).

*Essays on several important subjects in philosophy and religion* (London, 1676).

Glisson, Francis, *De rachitide, sive, morbo puerili* (London, 1650).

*Tractatus de natura substatiae energetica, seu, De vita naturae* (Cambridge, 1672).

*Tractatus de ventriculo et intestinis* (London, 1677).

Goddard, Guibon, 'The journal of Guibon Goddard, Esq. M.P.' [21 Dec 1654], in *The diary of Thomas Burton, Esq. Member in the Parliaments of Oliver and Richard Cromwell, from 1656 to 1659* (4 vols, London, 1828).

Goddard, Jonathan, *A discourse setting forth the unhappy condition of the practice of physick in London* (London, 1670).

Goodwin, Thomas, *The works of Thomas Goodwin*, ed. J. Nichol (12 vols, Edinburgh, 1861–66).

Gott, Samuel, *An essay of the true happiness of man in two books* (London, 1650).

*The divine history of the genesis of the world explicated & illustrated* (London, 1670).

Greaves, John, *Astronomica quaedam ex traditione Shal Cholgii Persae una cum Hypothesibus Planetarum* (London, 1650).

ed., *Epochae celebriores, astronomis, historicis, chronologis Chataiorum ... ex traditione Ulugh Beigi* (London, 1650).

*The Miscellaneous works of Mr. John Greaves* (2 vols, London, 1737).

Grotius, Hugo, *De veritate religionis Christianae. Editio nova, additis annotationibus, in quibus testimonia* (Leiden, 1640).

*Annotationes in Novum Testamentum* (3 vols, Amterdam & paris, 1641–50).

*Annotationes ad Vetus Testamentum* (Paris, 1644).

*Philosophorum sententiae de fato* (Amsterdam, 1648).

Gruter, Jan, *Inscriptionum Romanarum corpus absolutissimum* (Paris, 1616).

Hakewill, George, *An apologie of the power and providence of God in the government of the world* (Oxford, 1627).

Hale, Matthew, *An essay touching the gravitation, or non-gravitation of fluid bodies, and the reasons thereof* (London, 1673).

*Difficiles nugae: or observations touching the Torricellian experiment* (London, 1674).

*The primitive origination of mankind, considered and examined according to the light of nature* (London, 1677).

*Observations touching the principles of natural motions* (London, 1677).

Hales, John, *Concerning the abuses of obscure and difficult places of holy Scripture, and remedies against them* (London, 1617).

Hall, John, *Poems* (Cambridge, 1646).

Hall, Thomas, *Vindiciae literarum, the schools guarded, or the excellency and usefulnesse of humane learning in subordination to divinity* (London, 1654).

Halley, Edmund, 'A discourse of the rule of the decrease of the height of the mercury in the barometer', *Philosophical Transactions*, 16 (1686), 104–16.

'A short account of the cause of the saltness of the ocean … to discover the age of the world', *Philosophical Transactions*, 29 (1714–16), 296–300.

'Some considerations about the cause of the universal deluge', *Philosophical Transactions*, 33 (1724–25), 118–23.

'Farther thoughts upon the same subject', *Philosophical Transactions*, 33 (1724–25), 123–5.

*The correspondence and papers of Edmond Halley*, ed. E. F. MacPike (Oxford, 1932).

Hallywell, Henry, *Deus justificatus; or, the divine goodness vindicated and cleared* (London, 1668).

Hammond, Henry, *Of superstition* (Oxford, 1645).

*Dissertationes quatuor quibus episcopatus jura ex S. Scripturis & Primaeva Antiquitate adstruuntur* (London, 1651).

*A letter of resolution to six quaeres, of present use in the Church of England* (London, 1652).

*A paraphrase, and annotations upon all the books of the New Testament* (London, 1653).

*A continuation of the defence of Hugo Grotius, in answer to the review of his annotations* (London, 1657).

Harmer, Thomas, *Observations on divers passages of Scripture … the second edition … enlarged with many new observations* (2 vols, London, 1776 [1st edn=1764]).

Harris, John, *Remarks on some late papers relating to the universal deluge* (London, 1697).

*The atheistical objections against the being of God and his attributes fairly considered and fully refuted* (London, 1698).

Harris, Walter, *Pharmacologia anti-empirica, or, a rational discourse of remedies both chymical and Galenical* (London, 1683).

[Harvey, Gideon], *The accomplisht physician* (London, 1670).

Harvey, William, *Exercitatio anatomica de motu cordis et sanguinis in animalibus* (Frankfurt, 1628).

*Exercitationes de generatione animalium* (London, 1651).

*Disputations touching the generation of animals*, ed. and trans. G. Whitteridge (Oxford, 1981).

Hearne, Thomas, *Remarks and collections of Thomas Hearne* (11 vols, Oxford, 1885–1921).

Heereboord, Adrian, *Philosophia naturalis* (Oxford, 1665).

*Meletemata philosophica* (Amsterdam & London, 1680 [1st edn=Amsterdam, 1665]).

van Helmont, Johannes Baptista, *Ortus medicinae* (Amsterdam, 1648).

*Oriatrike or, physick refined* (London, 1662).

Herbert, Edward, *De religione gentilium, errorumque apud eos causis* (Amsterdam, 1663).

Herbert, William, *Catalogue of books in various languages . . . among others . . . [the] library of the late Mr. William Herbert* (London, 1795).

*Catalogue of the library of William Herbert* (London, 1796).

*Catalogue of the entire and curious library of a late well-known collector* (London, 1798).

*Catalogue of a choice and valuable library, the property of a gentleman* (London, 1798).

Hersent, Charles, ed., *In D. Dionysii areopagitae de mystica theologia librum, apparatus, interpretatio, notae, commentarii, paraphrasis, in quibus de supremo divinae contemplationis gradu, unione scilicet et ignoratione luculentissime agitur, praemissa est theologiae mysticae apologia adversus ejus obtrectatores* (Paris, 1626).

Heurnius, Johannes, 'Commentaria', in Hippocrates, *Prolegomena, et prognosticorum libri tres* (Leiden, 1597).

Heylyn, Peter, *Cosmographie in four bookes: containing the chorographie and historie of the whole world* (London, 1652).

*Theologia veterum, or, the summe of Christian theologie, positive, polemical, and philological, contained in the Apostles creed, or reducible to it according to the tendries of the antients both Greeks and Latines* (London, 1654).

Hickman, Henry, Πατρο-σχολαστικο-δικαίωαις, *or a justification of the fathers and schoolmen: shewing, that they are not self-condemned for denying the positivity of sin* (Oxford, 1659).

*Laudensium apostasia: or A dialogue in which is shewen, that some divines risen up in our church since the greatness of the late archbishop, are in sundry points of great moment, quite fallen off from the doctrine received in the Church of England* (London, 1660).

*The nonconformists vindicated from the abuses put upon them by Mr. Durel and Scrivener* (London, 1679).

Hierocles, Ιεροκλεους φιλοσοφου Υπομνημα εις τα τῶν Πυθαγορειων ἔπη τὰ χρυσα. *Hierocli Philosophi commentarius in aurea Pythagoreorum carmina* (London, 1654).

*De providentia & fato* (London, 1655).

*Hieroclis Philosophi Alexandrini commentarius in Aurea Carmina, De Providentia & Fato*, ed. P. Needham (Cambridge, 1709).

Highmore, Nathaniel, *Corpris humani disquisitio anatomica* (The Hague, 1651).

*The history of generation* (London, 1651).

Hill, Samuel, *A vindication of the primitive fathers against the imputations of Gilbert Lord Bishop of Sarum* (London, 1695).

Hippocrates, *Prolegomena, et prognosticorum libri tres* (Leiden, 1597).

ps.-Hippocrates, *The laughing philosopher. Being a letter from Hippocrates the physician to his friend Damagetus, concerning the madness of Democritus* (London, 1736).

*Histoire des ouvrages des sçavans*, 1 (December 1687).

Hobbes, Thomas, *Leviathan* (London, 1651).

*Elementorum philosophiae sectio prima de corpore* (London, 1655).

*Six lessons to the professors of the mathematiques* (London, 1656).

*An historical narration concerning heresie and the punishment thereof* (London, 1680).

*Critique du De mundo de Thomas White*, eds., J. Jacquot and H. W. Jones (Paris, 1973).

*Historia Ecclesiastica*, ed. and trans., P. Springborg, P. Stablein, and P. Wilson (Paris, 2008).

*Leviathan*, ed. N. Malcolm (3 vols, Oxford, 2012).

Hodges, Nathaniel, *Vindiciae medicinae et medicorum* (London, 1665).

Holdsworth, Thomas, *Impar conatui* (London, 1695).

Holstenius, Lucas, 'Dissertatio De vita, & scriptis Porphyrii', in Πορφυριου φιλοσοφου Πυθαγορου βιος … *liber de vita Pythagorae*, ed. L. Holstenius (Rome, 1630).

*Notae et castigationes postumae in Stephani Byzantii Ethnika, quae vulgo Peri poleōn inscribuntur* (Leiden, 1684).

*Lucae Holstenii epistolae ad diversos*, ed. J. F. Boissonade (Paris, 1817).

Hooke, Robert, *Micrographia, or, some physiological descriptions of minute bodies made by magnifying glasses* (London, 1665).

'An account of a book', *Philosophical Transactions*, 17 (1693), 796–812.

*The posthumous works of Robert Hooke*, ed. R. Waller (London, 1705).

*The diary of Robert Hooke*, eds., H. Robinson and W. Adams (London, 1935).

'Lectures of things requisite to a ntral history', in D. R. Oldroyd, 'Some writings of Robert Hooke on procedures for the prosecution of scientific inquiry, including his "Lectures of things requisite to a ntral history"', *NRRS*, 41 (1987), 145–67, at 151–9.

Horn, Georg, *De statu ecclesiae Britannicae hodierno, liber commentarius; una cum appendice eorum, quae in Synodo Glasguensi contra episcopus decreta sunt* (Danzig, 1647).

*Rerum Britannicarum libri septem* (Leiden, 1648).

*Historiae philosophicae libri VII* (Leiden, 1655).

Hospinian, Rudolf, *De monachis, hoc est de origine et progressu monachatus, ac ordinum monasticorum* (2nd edn, Zurich, 1609 [1st edn=1588]).

Hottinger, Johann Heinrich, *Historia orientalis: ex variis orientalium monumentis collecta* (Zürich, 1651).

Hudson, John, ed., *Geographiae veteris scriptores graeci minores* (Oxford, 1698).

Huet, Pierre-Daniel, *Origeniana in* Ωριγενους … *Origens in Sacras Scripturas commentaria* (3 vols, Rouen, 1668).

*Demonstratio evangelica ad serenissimum delphinium* (Paris, 1679).

*Demonstratio evangelica* (3rd edn, Paris, 1690).

Hughes, George, *An analytical exposition of the whole first book of Moses, called Genesis … delivered in a mornings exercise on the Lords Day* (London, 1672).

Huntington, Robert, 'A Letter from Dublin … concerning the porphyry pillars of Egypt', *Philosophical Transactions*, 14 (1684), 624–9.

*D. Roberti Huntingtoni, Episcopi Rapotensis, epistolae*, ed. T. Smith (London, 1704).

Hurtado, Petrus, *Universa philosophia* (London, 1624 [1st edn=Lyon, 1617]).

Hutchinson, Lucy, *On the principles of Christian religion, addressed to her daughter; and on theology*, ed. J. Hutchinson (London, 1817).

Hyde, Thomas, 'In Ulugh Beighi Tabulas Stellarum fixarum Commentarii', in Ulugh Beg, *Tabulae longitudinis et latitudinis stellarum fixarum*, ed. and trans. T. Hyde (Oxford, 1665).

*Historia Tîmûri Arabicè ac Latiné* (Oxford, 1675) [Wing H3879A].

'De mensuris & ponderibus Sinensium epistola', in Edward Bernard, *De mensuris et ponderibus antiquis libri tres* (Oxford, 1688).

*De ludis orientalibus* (Oxford, 1694).

*Historia religionis veterum Persarum, eorumque magorum prospectus* ([Oxford], 1699) [Wing H3872A].

*Historia religionis veterum Persarum, eorumque Magorum* (Oxford, 1700).

*Syntagma dissertationum*, ed. G. Sharp (Oxford, 1767).

Hyde, Earl of Clarendon, Edward, *Animadversions upon a book intituled, Fanaticism fanatically imputed to the Catholic Church* (London, 1673).

Iamblichus, *De vita Pythagorae, & protrepticae orationes ad philosophiam*, ed. J. Arcerius (2 vols, [Heidelberg], 1598).

*In Nichomachi arithmeticam introductionem*, ed. S. Tennulius (Arnhem, 1668).

*De mysteriis liber*, ed. T. Gale (Oxford, 1678).

*Exhortation to philosophy … including the letters of Iamblichus and Proclus' commentary on the Chaldean oracles*, ed. and trans., T. M. Johnson and S. Neuville (Grand Rapids, 1988 [1st edn=1907]).

*De mysteriis*, ed. and trans., E. C. Clarke, J. M. Dillon, and J. P. Hershbell (Leiden, 2004).

Ingelo, Nathaniel, *Bentivolio and Urania in four bookes* (London, 1660).

Jackson, Arthur, *A help for the understanding of the Holy Scripture … the first part. Containing certain short notes of exposition upon the five books of Moses* (Cambridge, 1643).

James, Richard, *A sermon delivered in Oxford. Concerning the Apostles preaching and ours* (London, 1630).

Jansen, Cornelius, *Augustinus seu doctrina S. Augustini de humanae naturae sanitate, aegritudine, medicina adversus Pelagianos & Massilienses* (3 vols, Rouen, 1652 [1st edn=Louvain, 1640]).

Jenkin, Robert, *The reasonableness and certainty of the Christian religion* (London, 1700).

Johnson, William, *Agyrto-Mastix, or, some brief animadversions upon two late treatises; … Galeno-Pale; … the Poor man's physitian* (London, 1665).

Jonsius, Johannes, *De scriptoribus historiae philosophiae libri IV* (Frankfurt, 1659).

Josephus, Flavius, *Antiquitatum Judaicarum libri quatuor priores, et pars magna quinti*, ed. E. Bernard (Oxford, 1700).

*Journal des Sçavans*, 3 (1675).

*Journal of the House of Commons: vol. IV: 1644–1646* (London, 1802).

Judah ha-Levi, הכוזרי, ed. and trans. Judah b. Tibbon (Venice, 1594).

*Liber Cosri*, ed. and trans. J. Buxtorf jnr (Basel, 1660).

Kidder, Richard, *A commentary on the five books of Moses: with a dissertation concerning the author or writer of the said books* (London, 1694).

Kircher, Athanasius, *Obeliscus Pamphilius, hoc est interpretatio nova et hucusque intentata Obelisci Hieroglyphici* (Rome, 1650).

L. P., *Two essays sent in a letter from Oxford* (London, 1695).

Lascaris, Constantine, *Institutiones* (Ferrara, 1510).

[Le Clerc, Jean], *Epistolae theologicae: in quibus varii scholasticorum errores castigantur* ([Amsterdam], 1679 [1681]).

> *Sentimens de quelques theologiens de Holland sur l'histoire critique du Vieux Testament* (Amsterdam, 1685).

> *Défense des sentimens de quelques Théologiens de Hollande* (Amsterdam, 1686).

> *Five letters concerning the inspiration of the Holy Scriptures* (London, 1690).

> 'Praefatio', and 'Notae interpretis in Oracula Chaldaica', in Thomas Stanley, *Historia philosophiae orientalis. Recensuit, ex Anglica lingua in Latinam transtulit, notis in oracula Chaldaica & indice philologico auxit Joannes Clericus* (Amsterdam, 1690).

> *An historical vindication of The naked Gospel recommended to the University of Oxford*, unknown trans. ([n.p.], 1690).

> *Ontologia et pneumatologia* (Amsterdam, 1692).

> *Logica: sive ars ratiocinandi* (London, 1692).

> *Genesis sive Mosis prophetae liber primus* (Amsterdam, 1693).

> *XVIII. Prima commata capitis primi Evangelii S. Joannis paraphrasi et animadversionibus* (Amsterdam, 1695).

> *Pentateuchus, sive Mosis prophetae libri quinque* (Amsterdam, 1696).

> *Twelve dissertations out of Monsieur Le Clerk's Genesis* (London, 1696).

> *The lives of Clemens Alexandrinus, Eusebius Bishop of Cæsarea, Gregory Nazianzen, and Prudentius the Christian poet: containing an impartial account of their lives and writings, together with several curious observations upon both. Also a short history of Pelagianism* (London, 1696).

> *Physica, sive, de rebus corporeis* (London, 1696).

> *Ars critica* (2 vols, Amsterdam, 1697).

> *Ars critica* (2nd edn, London, 1698).

> *Opera philosophica* (Amsterdam, 1698) (further edns, 1704, 1710, 1722).

> *Compendium historiae universalis* (Amsterdam, 1698).

> *S. Patrum qui temporibus Apostolicis floruerunt, Barnabae, Clementis, Hermae, Ignatii, Polycarpi opera edita et inedita ... recensuit & notulas aliquot adspersit Joannes Clericus* (2 vols, Antwerp, 1698).

> *Novum Testamentum Domini nostri Jesu Christi, ex versione vulgata, cum paraphrasi et adnotationibus Henrici Hammondi* (Amsterdam, 1698).

> *A supplement to Dr. Hammond's Paraphrase and annotations on the New Testament* (London, 1699).

> *Epistolae criticae et ecclesiasticae* (Amsterdam, 1700).

> 'Praefatio', in *Bilibra veritatis et rationis de מימרא ד"י seu verbo Dei, librae Joh. Stephani Rittangelii ... opposita. Praemissa est disceptatio de verbo Dei cujus creberrima fit mentio apoud Chaldaeos Paraphrastas* ([n.p.], 1700).

> *Opera philosophica* (4 vols, Amsterdam, 1700).

> *The lives of the primitive fathers ... with their several opinions about the deity of Christ. Which may give some light to the late disputes concerning the Trinity* (London, 1701).

*Veteris testamenti prophetae . . . cum ejusdem commentario philologico et paraphrasi* (Amsterdam, 1731).

*Epistolario*, eds., M. Grazia and M. Sina (4 vols, Florence, 1987–97).

and [Le Cène, Charles], *Entretiens sur diverses matieres de theologie: où l'on examine particulierement les questions de la grace immédiate, du franc-arbitre, di peché originel, de l'incertitude de la metaphysique, & de la prédestination* (Amsterdam, 1685).

Leigh, Edward, *A treatise of divinity* (London, 1646).

Leland, John, *The divine authority of the Old and New Testament asserted* (2 vols, London, 1739–40).

Le Moyne, Stephen, *In varia sacra notae et observationes* (2 vols, Leiden, 1685).

Lightfoot, John, *A few, and new observations, upon the booke of Genesis* (London, 1642).

Lister, Martin, 'The manner of making steel . . . with a guess at the way the ancients used to steel their picks, for the cutting or hewing of porphyry', *Philosophical Transactions*, 17 (1693), 865–70.

Lipsius, Justus, *Opera omnia* (Antwerp, 1600).

*Physiologiae Stoicorum libri tres* (Antwerp, 1604).

*Manuductionis ad Stoicam philosophica libri tres* (Antwerp, 1604).

Lloyd, David, *Dying and dead mens living words published* (London, 1668).

Lloyd, William, *A chronological account of the life of Pythagoras . . . with an epistle to the Rd Dr. Bentley, about Porphyry's and Jamblichus's lives of Pythagoras* (London, 1699).

Locke, John, *An essay concerning humane understanding* (London, 1690).

*Some thoughts concerning education* (London, 1693).

*The works of John Locke* (3 vols, London, 1714).

*An early draft of Locke's essay, together with excerpts from his journals*, eds., R. I. Aaron and J. Gibb (Oxford, 1936).

Lodwick, Francis, *On language, theology, and utopia*, eds., F. Henderson and W. Poole (Oxford, 2011).

Long, Thomas, *An answer to a Socinian treatise, call'd The naked Gospel* (London, 1691).

Lord, Henry, *A display of two forraigne sects in the East Indies vizt: the sect of the Banians the ancient natives of India and the sect of the Persees the ancient inhabitants of Persia* (London, 1630).

Lovell, Archibald, *A summary of material heads which may be enlarged and improved into a compleat answer to Dr. Burnet's Theory of the earth* (London, 1696).

Lowth, William, *A vindication of the divine authority and inspiration of the writings of the Old and New Testament* (Oxford, 1692).

Lucretius, *De rerum natura*, ed. G. Nardi (Florence, 1647).

*Six books De natura rerum done into English verse, with notes*, ed. and trans. T. Creech (Oxford, 1682).

Lusitanus, Zacutus, *Opera omnia* (2 vols, Lyon, 1657 [1st edn=1649]).

M. S. [Matthew Smith?], *A philosophical discourse of the nature of rational and irrational souls* (London, 1695).

Madeleine de Saint-Joseph, *La vie de soeur Catherine de Jesus* (Paris, 1628).

Maimonides, Moses, *Doctor perplexorum: ad dubia & obscuriora Scripturae loca rectiùs intelligenda*, ed. Johann Buxtorf (Basel, 1629).

*De idololatria liber*, ed. D. Vossius (Amsterdam, 1641).

Magirus, Johann, *Physiologiae Peripateticae libri sex cum commentariis* (Cambridge, 1642 [1st edn=Frankfurt, 1597]).

Majercik, R., ed., *The Chaldean oracles: text, translation, and commentary* (Leiden, 1989).

al-Makīn Ğirğis al-'Amīd, *Historia Saracenica*, ed. and trans. T. Erpenius (Leiden, 1625).

Maldonado, Juan de, *Commentarii in quatuor evangelistas … Hac quarta editione omnia diligentius recognita, ac emendata* (Lyon, 1602 [1st edn=1601]).

Manley, Roger, *The history of the late warres in Denmark* (London, 1670).

Marcus Aurelius, *Meditations concerning himselfe*, ed. and trans. M. Casaubon (London, 1634).

    *Marci Antonini Imperatoris De seipso et ad seipsum libri XII*, ed. M. Casaubon (London, 1643).

    *De rebus suis, sive de eis quae ad se pertinere censebat*, ed. and trans. T. Gataker (Cambridge, 1652).

Marsham, John, *Diatriba chronologica* (London, 1649).

    *Chronicus canon Aegyptiacus, Ebraicus, Graecus et disquisitiones* (London, 1672).

    *Canon chronicus … nunc longè emendatior in Germaniâ recusus* (Leipzig, 1676).

Marvell, Andrew, *The rehearsal transpros'd. The second part* (London, 1673).

Masters, Robert, *The history of the college of Corpus Christ* (Cambridge, 1753).

Mather, Samuel, *A defence of the Protestant Christian religion against popery* (n.p., 1672).

[Maurice, Henry], *A vindication of the primitive church, and diocesan episcopacy in answer to Mr. Baxter's Church history of bishops, and their councils abridged: as also to some part of his Treatise of episcopacy* (London, 1682).

Maynwaringe, Edward, *Medicus absolutus adespotos* (London, 1668).

    *The pharmacopoeian physician's repository* (London, 1670).

    *Praxis medicorum antiqua et nova* (London, 1671).

Mayow, John, *Tractatus quinque medico-physici* (Oxford, 1674).

Meldrum, George (*praeses*), *Theses philosophicae quas posuerunt adolescentes, laureæ Magisterialis candidati, in inclyta universitatis Abredonensis* (Aberdeen, 1659).

Ménage, Gilles, 'In Diogenes Laertius observationes et emendationes', in *Λαερτιου Διογενους Περι Βίων Δογματων και Αποφθεγματων των εν φιλοσοφία ευδοκομησάντων … Laertii Diogenes de vitis dogmatis et apophthegmatis eorum qui in philosophia claruerunt, libri X*, ed. G. Ménage (London, 1664).

    *Historia mulierum philosopharum* (Lyon, 1690).

Menasseh ben Israel, *De creatione problemata XXX* (Amsterdam, 1635).

Meursius, Johannes, 'Notae', in *Chalcidii V.C. Timaeus de Platonis translatus*, ed. J. Meursius (Leiden, 1617).

    *Denarius Pythagoricus. Sive, de numerorum, usque ad denarium, qualitate, ac nominibus, secundum Pythagoricos* (Leiden, 1631).

Milbourne, Luke, *Mysteries in religion vindicated, or, the filiation, deity and satisfaction of our Saviour asserted against Socinians and others* (London, 1692).

Milner, John, *Conjectanea in Isaiam ix, I, II. Item in parallela quaedam veteris ac novi testamenti, in quibus versionis 70. Interpretum … cum textu Hebraeo conciliationem* (London, 1673).

Milton, John, *The reason of church-government urg'd against prelaty* (London, 1641).

Montagu, Richard, *Analecta ecclesiasticarum exercitationum* (London, 1622).

Moses ben Jacob Albelda, תמיד עולת (Venice, 1600).

More, Henry, *Philosophical Poems* (Cambridge, 1647).

*Observations upon Anthroposophia Theomagica* (London, 1650).

*The second lash* . . . (London, 1651).

*Conjectura Cabbalistica or, a conjectural essay of interpreting the minde of Moses* (London, 1653).

*An antidote against atheisme* (London, 1653).

*The immortality of the soul* (London, 1659).

*An explanation of the grand mystery of godliness* (Cambridge, 1660).

*A collection of several philosophical writings* (London, 1662).

*A modest enquiry into the mystery of iniquity* (London, 1664).

*Enchiridion metaphysicum, sive, de rebus incorporeis succincta & luculenta dissertatio* (London, 1671).

*Remarks upon two late ingenious discourses the one, an essay touching the gravitation and non-gravitation of fluid bodies, the other, observations touching the Torricellian experiment, so far forth as they may concern any passages in his Enchiridium Metaphysicum* (London, 1676).

*Opera omnia* (London, 1679).

*Opera philosophica* (London, 1679).

'Annotations', in George Rust, *Two choice and useful Treatises* (London, 1682).

*Collection of several philosophical writings* (London, 1712).

*Manual of metaphysics*, ed. and trans. A. Jacob, (Hildesheim, 1995).

Morély, Jean, *Traicté de la discipline & police chrestienne* (Lyon, 1562).

[Morgan, Thomas], *The moral philosopher* (London, 1737).

Mornay, Phillipe Du-Plessis, *A worke concerning the trewness of the Christian religion*, trans. P. Sidney (London, 1587).

al-Nadīm, Muḥammad ibn Isḥāq Ibn, *The Fihrist of al-Nadīm: a tenth-century survey of Muslim culture*, ed. & trans. B. Dodge (2 vols, New York, 1970).

Nardi, Giovanni, 'De funeribus Aegyptiorum', in Lucretius, *De rerum natura*, ed. G. Nardi (Florence, 1647).

Needham, Peter, 'Praefatio', *Hieroclis Philosophi Alexandrini commentarius in Aurea Carmina, De Providentia & Fato*, ed. P. Needham (Cambridge, 1709).

Needler, Benjamin, *Expository notes, with practical observations: towards the opening of the five first chapters of the first book of Moses called Genesis* (London, 1655 [i.e. 1654]).

N[edham], M[archamont], *Medela medicinae. A plea for the free profession, and a renovation of the art of physick* (London, 1665).

Nelson, Robert, *The life of Dr. George Bull, late Lord Bishop of St. David's* (London, 1714).

Nemesius, Περι Φυσεως Ανθρωπου . . . *De natura hominis* . . . *manuscriptorum codicum collatione*, ed. J. Fell (Oxford, 1671).

Newton, Isaac, *Optice: sive de reflexionibus, refractionibus, inflexionibus & coloribus lucis libri tres* (London, 1706).

'An account of the book entituled Commercium Epistolicum', *Philosophical Transactions*, 342 (Jan and Feb 1715), 173–224.

*Opticks* . . . *the second edition, with additions* (London, 1717).

*The opticks* (Dover, 1952).

*Unpublished scientific papers of Isaac Newton*, eds., A. R. Hall and M. B. Hall (Cambridge, 1962).

*The mathematical papers of Isaac Newton*, ed. D. T. Whiteside (8 vols, Cambridge, 1967–81).

*Certain philosophical questions: Newton's Trinity notebook*, eds., J. E. McGuire and M. Tamny (Cambridge, 1983).

*The Principia. Mathematical principles of natural philosophy* [1687], eds., and trans., I. B. Cohen and A. Whitman (Berkeley, 1999).

*Philosophical writings*, ed. A. Janiak (Cambridge, 2004),

Nicholls, William, *A conference with a theist. Wherein I. Are shewn the absurdities in the pretended eternity of the world. II. The difficulties in the Mosaick creation are cleared. III. The lapse of mankind is defended, against the objections of Archæologiæ philosophicæ, The oracles of reason, &c.* (London, 1696).

Nicomachus, *Introduction to arithmetic*, trans. M. L. D'Ooge (London, 1926).

Nicolson, William, *Letters on various subjects*, ed. J. Nichols (2 vols, London, 1809).

*The London diaries of William Nicolson, Bishop of Carlisle, 1702–1718*, ed. C. Jones (Oxford, 1985).

Nizolio, Mario, *De veris principiis et vera ratione philosophandi contra pseudophilosophos libri IV* [1553], ed. Q. Breen (2 vols, Rome, 1956).

North, John, 'Ad lectorem', in *Platonis de rebus divinis dialogi selecti Graece & Latine* (Cambridge, 1673).

North, Roger, *The life of the honourable Sir Dudley North . . . and . . . Dr. John North* (London, 1744).

*The life of the lord keeper North by Roger North*, ed. M. Chan (Lewiston [NY], 1995).

*Nouvelles de la république des lettres*, 48 (November 1709).

[Nye, Stephen], *A brief history of the Unitarians, called also Socinians in four letters, written to a friend* ([London], 1687).

*A letter of resolution concerning the doctrines of the Trinity and the Incarnation* ([London], 1691).

*Some thoughts upon Dr. Sherlock's Vindication of the Doctrin [sic] of the Holy Trinity* ([London], 1691).

*A defence of the Brief history of the Unitarians* ([London], 1691).

*An accurate examination of the principal texts usually alledged for the divinity of our Saviour* ([London], 1692).

*The trinitarian scheme of religion, concerning almighty God and mankind considered both before and after the (pretended) fall* (London, 1692).

*Considerations on the explications of the doctrine of the Trinity by Dr. Wallis, Dr. Sherlock, Dr. S—th, Dr. Cudworth, and Mr. Hooker as also on the account given by those that say the Trinity is an unconceivable and inexplicable mystery* (London, 1692).

*Considerations on the explications of the doctrine of the Trinity occasioned by four sermons preached by His Grace the Lord Arch-Bishop of Canterbury* ([London], 1694).

*The judgment of the fathers concerning the doctrine of the trinity; opposed to Dr. G. Bull's Defence of the Nicene faith. Part I. The doctrine of the Catholick Church, during the first 150 years of Christianity; and the explication of the unity of God (in a trinity of divine persons) by some of the following fathers, considered* ([London], 1695).

*The agreement of the Unitarians with the Catholick Church being also a full answer to the infamations of Mr. Edwards and the needless exceptions of my Lords the Bishops of Chichester, Worcester and Sarum, and of Monsieur De Luzancy* ([London], 1697).

*The doctrine of the holy trinity, and the manner of our Saviour's divinity: as they are held in the Catholic church, and the Church of England* (London, 1701).

Ocellus Lucanus, *De universi natura*, ed. L. Nogarola (Venice, 1559).

*De universi natura*, ed. and trans. C. E. Vizzanius (Bologna, 1646).

[Oldenburg, Henry], 'An account of some books', *Philosophical Transactions*, 3 (1668), 779–88.

'An account of some books', *Philosophical Transactions*, 19 (1675), 296–301.

Origen, *Against Celsus: translated from the original into English by James Bellamy, Gent* (London, n.d. [1709]).

Outram, William, *De sacrificiis libri duo* (London, 1677).

Owen, John, Θεομαχία Ἀυτεξουσιαστικῇ, *or, a display of Arminianisme* (London, 1643).

*A review of the annotations of Hugo Grotius, in reference unto the doctrine of the deity, and satisfaction of Christ. With a defence of the charge formerly laid against them* (Oxford, 1656).

*Theologoumena pantodapa, sive, de natura, ortu progressu, et studio verae theologiae, libri sex* (Oxford, 1661).

Pace, Giulio, *Aristotelis Stagiritae, Peripateticorum principiis naturalis auscultationis libri VIII* (Frankfurt, 1596).

Panvinio, Onoforio, *De ludis circensibus* (Venice, 1600).

Pappus, *Pappi Alexandrini collectionis quae supersunt e libris manuscriptis edidit*, ed. and trans. F. Hultsch (3 vols, Berlin, 1876–78).

Parker, Samuel, *Tentamina physico-theologica de Deo: sive, theologica scholastica ad normam novae & reformatae philosophiae concinnata & duobus libris comprehensa* (London, 1665).

*A free and impartial censure of the Platonick philosophie* (Oxford, 1666).

*An account and nature of the divine dominion and goodnesse* in *A free and impartial censure of the Platonick philosophie* (2nd edn, Oxford, 1667).

*Disputationes de Deo* (London, 1678).

*The case of the Church of England, briefly and truly stated in the three first and fundamental principles of a Christian church* (London, 1681).

*A demonstration of the divine authority of the law of nature and of the Christian religion in two parts* (London, 1681).

*Religion and loyalty, or, a demonstration of the power of the Christian church within it self* (2 pts, London, 1684).

Partliz, Simeon, *Medici systematis harmonici* (Frankfurt, 1625).

*A new method of physick: or, a short view of Paracelsus and Galen's practice*, trans. N. Culpeper (London, 1654).

Patrick, Simon, *A commentary upon the first book of Moses, called Genesis* (London, 1695).

Patrizi, Francesco, *Discussionum Peripateticarum tomi IV* (4 vols, Basle, 1581 [1st edn=1571]).

*Nova de universis philosophia* (Venice, 1593 [1st edn=Ferrara, 1591]).

Pearson, John, 'Prolegomena de Editione, Autore, & Opere', in *Hierocles de Providentia & Fato* (London, 1655).

*An exposition of the Apostles Creed* (London, 1659).

ed., *Critici sacri: sive doctissimorum virorum in SS. Biblia annotationes, & tractatus*, ed. J. Pearson (9 vols, London 1660).

*An exposition of the Creed . . . the second edition, revised and enlarged* (London, 1662).

'Reverendissimo doctissimóque viro Aegidio Menagio', in *Λαερτιου Διογενους Περι Βίων Δογματων και Αποφθεγματων των εν φιλοσοφία ευδοκομησάντων . . . Laertii Diogenes de vitis dogmatis et apophthegmatis eorum qui in philosophia claruerunt, libri X*, ed. G. Ménage (London, 1664).

ed., *Η Παλαιά Διαθήκη κατά τους Εβδομήκοντα Vetus Testamentum Graecum ex versione Septuaginta interpretum* (Cambridge, 1665).

*An exposition of the Creed . . . the fifth edition, revised, and now more enlarged* (London, 1683).

*The minor theological works of John Pearson*, ed. E. Churton (2 vols, Oxford, 1844).

Pemble, William, *De formarum origine* (London, 1629).

Petau, Denis, 'Notae', in *Συνεσίου επισκόπου Κυρήνης τα απαντα ευρισκόμενα. Synesii episcopi Cyrenensis opera*, ed. D. Petau (Paris, 1612).

'Animadversiones', in *Epiphanii Constantiae sive Salaminis in Cypro, episcopi, operum omnium . . .* ed. and trans. D. Petau (2 vols, Paris, 1622).

*De doctrina temporum* (2 vols, Paris, 1627).

*Dissertationum ecclesiasticarum libri duo* (Paris, 1641).

*Theologica dogmata* (5 vols, Paris, 1644–50).

Petty, William, *Discourse made before the Royal Society . . . concerning the use of duplicate proportion* (London, 1674).

*The Petty papers.*, ed. Marquis of Landsdowne (2 vols, London, 1927).

*William Petty on the order of nature: an unpublished manuscript treatise*, ed. R. Lewis (Tempe [AR], 2012).

Pfaff, C. M., 'Dissertatio Praeliminaris', in John Spencer, *De legibus Hebraeorum*, (Tübingen, 1732).

Philo Judaeus, *Philonis Iudaei . . . lucubrationes omnes*, ed. S. Gelen (Basle, 1561).

Pico della Mirandola, Giovanni, 'Preface', quoted and trans. in S. A. Farmer, *Syncretism in the West: Pico's 900 theses (1486). The evolution of traditional religious and philosophical systems* (Tempe, 1998).

Pierce, Thomas, *Αυτοκατάκρισις, or, self-condemnation, exemplified in Mr. Whitfield, Mr. Barlee, and Mr. Hickman . . . Mr Calvin, Mr Beza, Mr Zuinglius, Mr Piscator, Mr Rivet, and Mr Rollock: but more especially on Doctor Twisse, and Master Hobbs* (London, 1658).

des Places, E., ed., *Oracles chaldaïques, avec un choix de commentaires anciens* (3rd edn, rev. A. Segonds, Paris, 1996).

Plato, *Platonis de rebus divinis dialogi selecti Graece & Latine*, ed. J. North (Cambridge, 1673, repr. 1683).

Plutarch, *Plutarchi Chaeronensis omnium quae extant operum* (2 vols, Paris, 1624).

*Lives* (5 vols, London, 1684).

Pococke, Edward, *Specimen historiae Arabum, sive Gregorii Abul Farajii Malatiensis, de origine & moribus Arabum* (Oxford, 1650).

*Historia compendiosa dynastiarum, authore Gregorio Abul-Pharajio* (Oxford, 1663).

Poelenburg, Arnold, 'Oratio funeribus in obitum clarissimi viri D. Stephani Curcellaei', in *Opera theologica* (Amsterdam, 1675).

Pomponazzi, Pietro, *Tractatus de immortalitate animae* (Bologna, 1516).

Porphyry, *Lettera ad Anebo*, ed. and trans. A. R. Sodano (Naples, 1958).

Power, Henry, *Experimental philosophy, in three books containing new experiments microscopical, mercurial, magnetical* (London, 1664).

Prat, J. M., *Maldonat et l'Universite de Paris au XVIe siecle* (Paris, 1856).

Prideaux, John, *Hypomnemata logica, rhetorica, physica, metaphysica, pneumatica, ethica, politica, oeconomica* (Oxford, 1650).

Prideaux, Humphrey, *The Old and New Testament connected in the history of the Jews and neighbouring nations* (4th edn, 2 vols, London, 1718 [1st edn=1716–18]).

*Letters of Humphrey Prideaux to John Ellis 1674–1722*, ed. E. M. Thompson (London, 1875).

[Przypkovius, Samuel] *De pace et concordiae Ecclesiae* ([Amsterdam], 1630 [1st edn=1628]).

Quercetanus, Joseph, *Liber de priscorum philosophorum verae medicinae materia* (Geneva, 1603).

*Ad veritatem Hermeticae medicinae ex Hippocratis veterumque decretis ac therapeusi* (Paris, 1604).

*The practise of chymicall, and hermeticall physicke*, trans. T. Timme (London, 1605).

Raleigh, Walter, *The history of the world* (London, 1617 [1st edn=1614]).

Randolph, Thomas, *Aristippus, or, the joviall philosopher presented in a private shew* (London, 1630).

Ray, John, *Miscellaneous discourses* (London, 1692).

*Three physico-theological discourses* (London, 1693).

*The correspondence of John Ray*, ed. E. Lankester (London, 1848).

*The further correspondence of John Ray*, ed. R. W. T. Gunther (London, 1928).

Reyner, E., *A treatise of the necessity of humane learning for a Gospel-preacher* (London, 1663).

Richardson, John, *Choice observations and explanations upon the Old Testament . . . to which are added some further and larger observations of his upon the whole book of Genesis* (London, 1655).

Rigaud, S. J., *The correspondence of scientific men of the seventeenth century* (2 vols, Oxford, 1846).

Rivet, André, *Theologicae et scholasticae exercitationes CXC in Genesin* (Leiden, 1633).

Robinson, Tancred, *A Letter sent to Mr. William Wotton . . . concerning some Late Remarks* (n.p., n.d. [1697]).

*New observations on the natural history of this world of matter* (London, 1696).

Robinson, Thomas, *The anatomy of the earth* (London, 1694).

Ross, Alexander, *The first booke of questions and answers upon Genesis* (London, 1620).

*Rerum Judaicarum memorabiliorum* (4 vols, London, 1617–32).

*Commentum de terrae motu circulari* (London, 1634).

*The philosophical touch-stone: or observations upon Sir Kenelm Digbie's discourses* (London, 1645).

*The new planet no planet* (London, 1646).

*The marrow of historie* (London, 1650).

*The history of the world the second part . . . being a continuation of the famous history of Sir Walter Raleigh* (London, 1652).

de' Rossi, Azariah ben Moses, *The light of the eyes*, ed. and trans. J. Weinberg (New Haven and London, 2001).

*Azariah de' Rossi's observations on the Syriac New Testament: a critique of the Vulgate by a sixteenth-century Jew*, ed. J. Weinberg (London, 2005).

Rualdus, Joannes, 'Vita Plutarchi Chaeronensis', in *Plutarchi Chaeronensis omnium quae extant operum* (2 vols, Paris, 1624).

[Ruar, Martin and Vorstius, Guilielmus?], *Disceptatio de verbo vel sermone Dei, cujus creberrima fit mentio apud paraphrastas chaldaeos Jonathan, Onkelos & Thargum Hierosolymitanum* ([Amsterdam], 1646).

*Bilibra veritatis et rationis de* מימרא ד"יי *seu verbo Dei, librae Joh. Stephani Rittangelii . . . opposita. Praemissa est disceptatio de verbo Dei cujus creberrima fit mentio apoud Chaldaeos Paraphrastas* ([n.p.], 1700).

Rust, George, *A letter of resolution concerning Origen and the chief of his opinions* (London, 1661).

*Two choice and useful treatises* (London, 1682).

S. W., *A vindication of the doctrine contained in Pope Benedict XII* (Paris, 1659).

Saumaise, Claude, *Plinianae exercitationes in Caii Iulii Solini polyhistora* (Paris, 1629).

'Notae et animadversiones in Epictetum et Simplicium', in *Simplicii commentarius in enchiridion Epicteti ex libris veteribus emendatus* (Leiden, 1640).

*De Episcopis et Presbyteris contra D. Petavium Loiolitam dissertatio prima* (Leiden, 1641).

*Funus linguae Hellenisticae, sive confutatio Exercitationis de Hellenistis et lingua Hellenistica* (Leiden, 1643).

Sand, Christoph, *Nucleus historiae Ecclesiasticae* (3 pts, [Amsterdam], 1669).

*Appendix addendorum, confirmandorum & emendandorum ad Nucelum historiae ecclesiasticae . . . quarum prima est autoris ejusdem ad D. Samuelem Gardinerum scriptam defensionem* (Cologne [Amsterdam?], 1678).

*Scriptura trinitatis revelatrix* (Gouda, 1678).

Sanderson, Robert, *Logicae artis compendium* (Oxford, 1615).

*Physicae scientiae compendium* (Oxford, 1671).

Sandeus, Maximilien, *Theologia mystica seu contemplatio divina religiosorum a calumniis vindicata* (Mayenne, 1627).

*Physicae scientiae compendium* (Oxford, 1671).

Scaliger, Joseph, *Thesaurus temporum Eusebii Pamphili* (Leiden, 1606).

*Elenchus Trihaeresii Nicolai Serarii . . . eiusdem delirium fanaticum & impudentissimum mendacium, quo Essenos Monachos Christianos fuisse contendit, validisssimis argumentis elusum* (Franeker, 1605).

Scaliger, Julius Caesar, *Exotericarum exercitationum liber XV* (Paris, 1557).

*Juliii Ceasaris Scaligeri in libros duos, qui inscribuntur de Plantis, Aristotele Authore, libri duo* (Marburg, 1598).

Scheffer, Johann, *De natura et constitutione philosophiae Italicae, seu Pythagoricae* (Uppsala, 1664).

Schickhard, Wilhelm, בחינת הפירושים *Bechinath Happeruschim, hoc est examinis commentationum Rabbinicarum in Mosen prodromus* (Tübingen, 1624).

Scrivener, Matthew, *Apologia pro S. Ecclesiae patribus, adversus Joannem Dallaeum* (London, 1672).

*A course of divinity, or an introduction to the knowledge of the true Catholick religion especially as professed by the Church of England* (London, 1674).

Securis, John, *A detection and querimonie of the daily enormities and abuses comitted [sic] in physic concernyng the three parts therof: that is, the physitions part, the part of the surgeons, and the arte of poticaries* ([London], 1566).

Selden, John, *De Diis Syris* (London, 1617).

*The historie of tithes* (London, 1618).

*De jure naturali & gentium, iuxta disciplinam Ebraeorum libri septem* (London, 1640).

*Joannis Seldeni jurisconsulti opera omnia*, ed. D. Wilkins (London, 1726).

Seneca, *L. Annaei Senecae ... Opera*, ed. J. Lipsius (Antwerp, 1605).

*Medea*, ed. and trans. E. Sherburne (London, 1648).

Sennert, Daniel, *De Chymicorum cum Aristotelicis et Galenicis consensu ac dissensu* (Paris, 1633).

*Hypomnemata physica* (Frankfurt, 1636).

*Institutionum medicinae libri quinque* (Wittenberg, 1644).

*Opera omnia* (4 vols, Lyon, 1656).

Servetus, Michael, *Two treatises of Servetus on the trinity*, trans. E. M. Wilbur (Cambridge [MA], 1932).

Severinus, Petrus, *Idea medicinae philosophicae* (Basle, 1571).

al-Shahrastānī, Muḥammad, *Livre des religions et des sects*, eds., and trans., D. Gimaret, G. Monnot, and J. Jolivet (2 vols, Paris, 1986).

Sharp, George, 'Προλεγομενα de vita et scriptis doctissimi viri Thomae Hyde, S.T.P', in Thomas Hyde, *Syntagma dissertationum*, ed. G. Sharp (Oxford, 1767), i–xxiv.

Sharp, Thomas, *The life of John Sharp ... Archbishop of York*, ed. T. Newcome (London, 2 vols, 1825).

Sheffield, Duke of Buckingham, John, *The works of John Sheffield, Earl of Mulgrave, Marquis of Normandy, and Duke of Buckingham* (London, 1723).

Sherburne, Edward, *Seneca's answer, to Lucilius his quaere; why good men suffer misfortunes seeing there is a divine providence?* (London, 1648).

ed. and trans., *The sphere of Marcus Manilius* (London, 1675).

*The tragedies of L. Annaeus Seneca the philosophers; viz. Medea, Phaedra and Hippolytus, Troades, or the Royal Captives, and the rape of Helen ... to which is prefixed the life and death of Seneca the philosopher* (London, 1702).

Sherley, Thomas, *A philosophical essay declaring the probable causes whence stones are produced in the greater world* (London, 1672).

Sherlock, William, *A discourse concerning the knowledge of Jesus Christ, and our union and communion with him* (London, 1674).

*A vindication of the doctrine of the holy and ever blessed trinity and the incarnation of the Son of God ... the second edition* (London, 1691 [1st edn=1690]).

*A defence of Dr. Sherlock's notion of a trinity in unity* (London, 1694).

Simon, Richard, *Histoire critique du vieux testament* (Paris, 1680 [1st edn=1678]).

*A critical history of the Old Testament*, trans. [H. Dickinson] (London, 1682).

*Bibliothèque critique* (4 vols, Paris, 1708–10).

Simpson, William, *Hydrologia chymica* (London, 1669).

    *Zymologia physica, or, a brief philosophical discourse of fermentation, from a new hypothesis of acidum and sulphur* (London, 1675).

    *Philosophical dialogues concerning the principles of natural bodies* (London, 1677).

Smith, John, *Select discourses* (London, 1660).

Smith, Thomas, *Vita clarissimi et doctissimi viri, Edwardi Bernardi* (London, 1704).

    'Huntingtoni vita', in *D. Roberti Huntingtoni, Episcopi Rapotensis, epistolae*, ed. T. Smith (London, 1704).

Socinus, Fautus, *Opera omnia* (2 vols, Amsterdam, 1656).

South, Robert, *Animadversions upon Dr. Sherlock's book, entituled A vindication of the holy and ever-blessed trinity* (London, 1693).

    *Tritheism charged upon upon Dr. Sherlock's new notion of the Trinity and the charge made good* (London, 1695).

[Souverain, Jacques], *Le Platonisme devoilé, ou essai touchant le Verbe Platonicien* ([Amsterdam], 1700).

    *Platonism unveil'd: or an essay concerning the notions and opinions of Plato, and some antient and modern divines his followers, in relation to the Logos* ([London], 1700).

Spencer, John, *A discourse concerning prodigies* (Cambridge, 1663).

    *A discourse concerning vulgar prophecies in A discourse concerning prodigies* (2nd edn, Cambridge, 1665).

    *Dissertatio de Urim & Thummim* (Cambridge, 1669, reiss. 1670).

    *De legibus Hebraeorum ritualibus et earum rationibus, libri tres* (The Hague, 1686 [1st edn=Cambridge, 1683–5]).

    *De legibus Hebraeorum ritualibus et earum rationibus* (Tübingen, 1732).

Spencer, William, 'Ad lectorem', in *Ωριγενης κατα Κελσου ... Origenis contra Celsum libri octo. Ejusdem Philocalia* (Cambridge, 1658).

Sprackling, Robert, *Medela ignorantiae: or a just and plain vindication of Hippocrates and Galen from the groundless imputations of M. N.* (London, 1665).

Sprat, Thomas, *The plague of Athens* (London, 1659).

    *The history of the Royal Society* (London, 1667).

St. Clair, Robert, 'To the Reader', in *The Abyssinian philosophy confuted: or, Telluris theoria neither sacred, nor agreeable to Reason* (London, 1697).

Stanhope, George, ed., *Epictetus his morals, with Simplicius his comment* (London, 1694).

Stanley, Thomas, *The history of philosophy ... containing those on whom the attribute of wise was conferred* (4 vols, London, 1655–62).

    ed. and trans., *Aeschyli tragoediae septem: cum Scholiis Graecis omnibus* (London, 1663).

    *The history of philosophy: containing the lives, opinions, actions and discourses of the philosophers of every sect ... the second edition* (London, 1687).

    *Historia philosophiae orientalis. Recensuit, ex Anglica lingua in Latinam transtulit, notis in oracula Chaldaica & indice philologico auxit Joannes Clericus* (Amsterdam, 1690).

    *The history of philosophy: containing the lives, opinions, actions and discourses of the philosophers of every sect ... the third edition* (London, 1701).

*Historia philosophiae: vitas, opiniones, resque gestas, et dicta philosophorum sectae cujusvis complexa, ex anglico sermone in latinum translata, emendata, variis dissertationibus atque observationibus passim aucta*, ed. and trans. G. Olearius (2 vols, Lepizig, 1711).

*The history of philosophy . . . in which the innumerable mistakes, both in the text and notes of all former editions are corrected . . .* (London, 1743).

*Aeschyli tragoediae quae supersunt*, ed. S. Butler (4 vols, Cambridge, 1809–16).

*The poems and translations of Thomas Stanley*, ed. G. M. Crump (Oxford, 1962).

*The history of philosophy . . . with a new introduction by Knud Haakonssen* (Bristol, 2000).

Starkey, George, *Natures explication and Helmont's vindication* (London, 1657).

Stearne, John, *De obstinatione. Opus posthumum, pietatem Christiano-Stoicam, scholastico more, suadens* (Dublin, 1672).

Stegmann, Joachim, *Brevis disquisitio, an et quomodo vulgo dicti Evangelici Pontificos . . . solide atque evidenter refutare queant* ([Amsterdam], 1633).

*Brevis disquisitio; or, a brief enquiry touching a better way then is commonly made use of, to refute Papists, and reduce Protestants to certainty and unity in religion*, trans. J. Biddle (London, 1653).

Stillingfleet, Edward, *Homo naturâ est zōon politikon* ([Cambridge], 1657) [ESTC S5595].

*Origines sacrae, or, a rational account of the grounds of Christian faith, as to the truth and divine authority of the Scriptures and the matters therein contained* (London, 1662).

*A rational account of the grounds of Protestant religion being a vindication of the Lord Archbishop of Canterbury's relation of a conference* (London, 1665).

*A discourse concerning the idolatry practised in the Church of Rome and the danger of salvation in the communion of it* (London, 1671).

*An answer to Mr. Cressy's Epistle* (London, 1675).

*Origines Britannicae, or, the antiquities of the British churches* (London, 1685).

*A relation of a conference held about religion at London . . . with some gentlemen of the Church of Rome* (London, 1687).

*The Bishop of Worcester's answer to Mr. Locke's second letter* (London, 1698).

*Discourse of the true antiquity of London* (London, 1704).

Strabo, *Res geographia*, ed. I. Casaubon (Geneva, 1587).

Stubbe, H., *The Plus Ultra reduced to a Non Plus* (London, 1670).

*Legends no histories* (London, 1670).

*A reply unto the letter written to Mr Henry Stubbe in defense of the history of the Royal Society* (Oxford, 1671).

*An account of the rise and progress of Mahometanism with the life of Mahomet*, ed. H. M. Khan Shairani (London, 1911).

Sturm, Johann Christoph, *Epistola ad virum celeberrimum Henricum Morum de spiritu ipsius Hylarchio* (Nurenberg, 1676).

Suárez, Francisco, *Metaphysicae disputationes, in quibus universa naturalis theologia ordinate traditur* (Venice, 1605 [original=1597]).

Sydenham, Thomas, *Methodus curandi febres* (London, 1666).

*Observationes medicae circa morborum acutorum historiam et curationem* (London, 1676).

*Epistolae responsoriae duae* (London, 1680).

*Tractatus de podagra et hydrope* (London, 1683).

*The works of Thomas Sydenham*, ed. and trans. R. G. Latham (2 vols, London, 1848–50).

Syncellus, *The chronography of George Synkellos: a Byzantine chronicle of universal history from the creation*, eds., and trans., W. Adler and P. Tuffin (Oxford, 2002).

Synesius, Συνεσίου επισκόπου Κυρήνης τα απαντα ευρισκόμενα. *Synesii episcopi Cyrenensis opera*, ed. D. Pétau (Paris, 1612).

Szlichtyng, Jonasz, *De SS. Trinitate, de moralibus N. & V. Testamenti praceptis, itemque de sacris, eucharistiae, & baptimi ritibus* ([n.p.], 1637).

T. M., *A Letter concerning the present state of physick* (London, 1665).

Tachenius, Otto, *Hippocrates chymicus* (Lyon, 1671 [1st edn=Venice, 1666]).

*Otto Tachenius his Hippocrates chymicus*, trans. J[ohn] W[arr] (London, 1677).

Taylor, Jeremy, *Treatises* (London, 1648).

Temple, William, 'Upon ancient and modern learning', in *Miscellanea . . . the second part* (London, 1690).

Tenison, Thomas, *Of idolatry: a discourse, in which is endeavoured a declaration of, its distinction from superstition; its notion, cause, commencement, and progress* (London, 1678).

*A discourse concerning a guide in matters of faith with respect especially to the Romish pretence of the necessity of such a one as is infallible* (London, 1683).

*The difference betwixt the Protestant and Socinian methods in answer to a book written by a Romanist* (London, 1687).

Thévenot, Melchisédech, *Relations de divers voyages curieux* (4 vols, Paris, 1663–72).

T[hompson], J[ames], *Helmont disguised: or, the vulgar errours of impericall and unskilfull practisers of physick confuted* (London, 1657).

Thomson, George, *Galeno-pare: or, a chymical trial of the Galenist, that their dross in physick may be discovered* (London, 1665).

Thoresby, Ralph, *Vicaria Leodiensis* (London, 1724).

Thorndike, Herbert, *The right of the Church in a Christian state* (London, 1649).

*An epilogue to the tragedy of the Church of England* (London, 1659).

*De ratione ac jure finiendi controversias ecclesiae disputatio* (London, 1670).

*The theological works of Herbert Thorndike*, ed. J. H. Parker (6 vols, Oxford, 1844–56).

Tillotson, John, *Sermons concerning the divinity and incarnation of our blessed Saviour preached in the Church of St. Lawrence Jewry* (2nd edn, London, 1695 [1st edn=1693]).

Timaeus Locrus, *On the nature of the world and the soul*, ed. and trans. T. H. Tobin (Chico [CA], 1985).

Toland, John, *Dissertationes duae, Aedeisidaemon et origines Judaicae* (The Hague, 1709).

Turner, John, *Two exercitations. The first attempting to demonstrate that the Jews till after the return from . . . Babylon, were not allowed the publick and promiscuous use of the canonical books of the Old Testament. The second concerning the . . . Tetragrammaton* (London, 1684).

*Boaz and Ruth . . . With a discovery of several things, as well in the Eastern, as the Roman antiquities, never yet explained or understood by any* (London, 1685).

*A Discourse concerning the Messias ... To which is prefixed a large preface, asserting and explaining the doctrine of the Blessed Trinity against the late writer of the Intellectual system* (London, 1685).

Twells, Leonard, 'The life of ... Pocock', in *The theological works of ... Pococke*, ed. L. Twells (2 vols, London, 1740).

Twysden, John, *Problematum quorundam mathematicorum ... analytica solutio, et constructio* (London, 1659).

*Disquisition touching the sibyls and the sibylline writings in which their number, antiquity, and by what spirit they were inspired, are succinctly discussed, the objections made by Opsopaeus, Isaac Casaubon, David Blondel, and others, are examined, as also the authority of those writings asserted* (London, 1662).

*Medicina veterum vindicata, or, an anwer to a book, entitled Medela medicinae* (London, 1666).

*The use of the general planishpere, called the analemma* (London, 1685).

Ulugh Beg, *Tabulae longitudinis et latitudinis stellarum fixarum*, ed. and trans. T. Hyde (Oxford, 1665).

Ursinus, Johannes Henricus, *De Zoroastre Bactriano, Hermete Trismegisto, Sanchoniathone Phoenicio eorumque scriptis et aliis contra Mosaicae scripturae antiquitatem exercitationes familiares* (Nürnberg, 1661).

Ussher, James, *The whole works of the most Rev. James Ussher, D.D.*, ed. C. R. Elrington (17 vols, Dublin, 1847–64).

Valla, Lorenzo, *Dialectical disputations* [1439], eds., and trans., B. P. Copenhaver and L. Nauta (2 vols, Cambridge [MA], 2012).

[Vaughan, Henry], *The man mouse taken in a trap* (London, 1650).

*The moor scour'd again* (London, 1651).

de Veil, Charles-Marie, *A letter to the Honourable Robert Boyle ... defending the divine authority of the Holy Scripture* (London, 1683).

Vesalius, Andreas, *De humani corporis fabrica* (Basle, 1555).

Vives, Juan Luis, 'De Aristotelis operibus censura', in Aristotle, *Opera* (12 vols, Venice, 1560).

*On education: a translation of the De trandendis disciplinis of Juan Luis Vives*, ed. and trans. F. Watson (Cambridge, 1913).

Vizzanius, Emmanuel, 'Praefatio', in *Ocellus Lucanus philosophus De universi natura*, ed. and trans. C. E. Vizzanius (Bologna, 1646).

Vorstius, Guilelmus, *Constitutiones de fundamentis legis Rabbi Mosis F. Maiiemon* (Amsterdam, 1638).

Vossius, Gerardus Joannes, *De historicis Graecis libri quatuor* (London, 1624).

*De theologia gentili, et physiologia Christiana; sive de origine ac progressu idololatriae* (Amsterdam, 1641).

*Disseratationes tres de tribus symbolis, Apostolico, Athanasiano, et Constantinopolitano* (Amsterdam, 1642).

*De artis poeticae natura, ac constitutione liber* (Amsterdam, 1647).

*De philosophia et philosophorum sectis libri II* (The Hague, 1658).

*De theologia gentili ... editio nova* (Amsterdam 1668).

*Doctissimi clarissimique Gerardi Johan. Vossii et Clarorum virorum ad eum epistolae*, ed. P. Colomiès (London, 1690).

Wake, William, *The genuine epistles of the apostolical fathers, S. Barnabas, S. Ignatius, S. Clement, S. Polycarp, the Shepherd of Hermas, and the martyrdoms of St. Ignatius and St. Polycarp* (London, 1693).

Walker, George, *The history of the creation, as it is written by Moses in the first and second chapters of Genesis, plainly opened and expounded* (London, 1641).

Walker, Henry, בראשית *The creation of the world being an exposition on the Hebrew in the first chapter of Genesis* (London, 1649).

Wallis, John, *A treatise of algebra, both historical and practical. Shewing, the original, progress, and advancement thereof, from time to time; and by what steps it hath attained to the height at which now it is* (London, 1685).

*Three sermons concerning the sacred trinity* (London, 1691).

*A seventh letter, concerning the sacred Trinity* (London, 1691).

*Opera mathematica* (3 vols, London, 1693–99).

*The correspondence of John Wallis*, eds., P. Beeley and C. J. Scriba (3 vols, Oxford, 2003–12).

Walton, Brian, ed., *S. S. Biblia sacra polyglotta* (6 vols, London, 1655–57).

Ward, John, *The lives of the professors of Gresham College* (London, 1740).

[Ward, Seth and Wilkins, John], *Vindiciae academiarum containing some briefe animadversions upon Mr Websters book stiled, The examination of academies* (Oxford, 1654).

[Warner, John], *Anti-Haman ... where in is shewed the conformity of the doctrine, worship, & practice of the Roman Catholick church with those of the purest times* (n.p., 1679).

*The considerator considered: or, a brief view of certain considerations upon the Biblia polyglotta* (London, 1659).

Warren, Erasmus, *Geologia: or a discourse concerning the earth before the deluge* (London, 1690).

*A defence of the Discourse concerning the earth before the flood* (London, 1691).

*Some reflections upon the Short consideration* (London, 1691).

Warton, Thomas, 'The life of Ralph Bathurst', in *The life and literary remains of Ralph Bathurst, M.D.* (2 vols, London, 1761).

Webb, John, *The antiquity of China, or an historical essay, endeavouring a probability that the language of the empire of China is the primitive language spoken through the whole world before the confusion of Babel* (London, 1669, reiss. 1678).

Webster John, *Metallographia: or, an history of metals* (London, 1671).

*The displaying of supposed witchcraft* (London, 1677).

Wendelin, Marcus Friedrich, *Contemplationum physicarum sectio I. Quae physiologiae generalis, de principiis & affectionibus corporis naturalis* (Cambridge, 1648).

West, E. W., trans., 'Sad-Dar', in *Pahlavi Texts III* (Oxford, 1885), 253–361.

Whiston, William, *A new theory of the earth* (London, 1696).

*Memoirs of the life and writing of Mr William Whiston ... the second edition, corrected* (London, 1753 [1st edn=1749–50]).

Whitby, Daniel, *An endeavour to evince the certainty of Christian faith in general* (London, 1671).

*A paraphrase and commentary upon all the epistles of the New Testament* (London, 1700).

White, John, *A commentary upon the three first chapters of the first book of Moses called Genesis* (London, 1656).

White, Thomas, *De mundo dialogi tres* (Paris, 1642).

*Institutionum peripateticarum ad mentem summi viri clarissimíque philosophi Kenelmi Equitis Digbaei, pars theorica: item appendix theologica de origine mundi* (London, 1647).

*An apology for Rushworth's dialogues wherein the exceptions for the Lords Falkland and Digby and the arts of their commended Daillé discover'd* (Paris, 1654).

*Peripateticall Institutions* (London, 1656).

*Sciri, sive, Sceptices & scepticorum jure disputationis exclusio* (London, 1663).

*An exclusion of scepticks from all title to dispute: being an answer to The vanity of dogmatizing* (London, 1665).

[Wilkins, John], *The discovery of a world in the moone* (London, 1638).

*A discourse concerning a new planet* (London, 1640).

*Mathematicall magick, or the wonders that may be performed by mechanicall geometry* (London, 1648).

*Ecclesiastes, or, a discourse concerning the gift of preaching* (3rd edn, London, 1651 [1st edn=1646]).

*Le monde dans la lune, divisé en deux livres. Le premier, prouvant que la lune peut ester un monde, le second, que la terre peut-estre une Planette. De la Traduction du Sr de la Montagne* (Rouen, 1656).

*Ecclesiastes: or, a discourse concerning the gift of preaching ... the seventh edition*, ed. J. Williams (London, 1690).

Willis, Francis, *Synopsis physicae tam Aristotelicae, quam novae ad usum scholae accommodata* (London, 1690).

Willis, Thomas, *Diatribae duae medico-philosophicae* (London, 1659).

*Diatribae duae medico philosophicae ... editio secunda, ab authore recognita, atque ab eodem multiplici auctario lucupleta* (London, 1660).

*De anima brutorum quae hominis vitalis ac sensitiva est, exercitationes duae* (London, 1672).

*Pharmaceutice rationalis, sive, Diatriba de medicamentorum operationibus in humano corpore* (Oxford, 1674).

*Pharmaceutice rationalis ... pars secunda* (Oxford, 1675).

*Dr. Willis's practice of physick* (London, 1684).

*Thomas Willis's Oxford lectures*, ed. K. Dewhurst (Oxford, 1980).

Windet, James, *De vita functorum statu, ex Hebraoerum atque Graecorum comparatis sententiis concinnatus* (London, 1663).

ed. and trans., Olympiodorus, *Vita Platonis, in Diogenis Laertii de vitis, dogmatibus et apophthegmatibus clarorum philosophorum libri X*, ed. M. Meibom (2 vols, Amsterdam, 1692).

Witsius, Hermann, *Aegyptiacam et ΔΕΚΑΦΥΛΟΝ. Sive de Aegyptiacorum sacrorum cum Hebraicis collatione libri tres* (Amsterdam, 1696).

Wolff, Johann Christoph, *Manichaeismus ante Manichaeos, et in Christianismo redivivus* (Hamburg, 1707).

Wood, Anthony à, *The life and times of Anthony Wood, antiquary, of Oxford, 1632–1695* (5 vols, Oxford, 1891–1900).

[Woodhead, Abraham], *The guide in controversies, or a rational account of the doctrine of Roman-Catholicks concerning the ecclesiastical guide in controversies of religion* (London, 1667).

*The Roman Church's devotions vindicated* (n.p., 1672).

*The Protestants plea for a Socinian* (London, 1686).

Woodward, John, *An essay toward a natural history of the earth* (London, 1695).

*An account of some Roman urns, and other antiquities . . . with brief reflections upon the antient and present state of London* (London, 1713).

*Naturalis historia telluris* (London, 1714).

*The natural history of the Earth, illustrated, inlarged, and defended*, ed. and trans. B. Holloway (London, 1726).

*Of the wisdom of the antient Egyptians . . . a discourse concerning their arts, their sciences, and their learning* (London, 1777).

Worm, Ole, *Danicorum Monumentorum libri sex* (Copenhagen, 1643).

Worthington, John, *The diary and correspondence of Dr John Worthington*, eds., J. Crossley and R. C. Christie (2 vols, London, 1847–86).

Wotton, William, *Reflections upon ancient and modern learning* (London, 1694).

*Some thoughts concerning a proper method of studying divinity*, ed. H. Cotton (Oxford, 1818 [1st edn=London, 1734]).

Wren, Christopher, 'Oratio inauguralis, habita Londini in collegio Greshamensi per Christophorum Wren, A.M. astronomiae professorem electum, ann. 1657, aetatis suae 25', in John Ward, *The lives of the Professors of Gresham College* (London, 1740).

'Inaugural oration as Gresham Professor of astronomy' (1657), in Stephen Wren, *Parentalia* (London, 1750).

*Memoirs of the life and works of Sir Christopher Wren*, ed. J. Elmes (London, 1823).

Younge, Richard, *The drunkard's character* (London, 1638).

Zabarella, Jacopo, *De naturalis scientiae constitutione* (Venice, 1586).

*Opera logica* (4th edn, Venice, 1600 [1st edn=1578]).

[Zwicker, Daniel] *Irenicum irenicorum, seu reconciliatoris Christianorum hodiernorum norma triplex, sana omnium hominum ratio, Scriptura Sacra, & traditiones* ([Amsterdam], 1658).

## Printed secondary sources

Åkerman, S., *Queen Christina of Sweden and her circle: the transformation of a seventeenth century philosophical libertine* (Leiden, 1991).

Albrecht, M., *Eklektik: Eine Begriffsgeschichte mit Hinweisen auf die Philosophie- und Wissenschaftsgeschichte* (Stuttgart, 1994).

Allan, D., 'Ross, Alexander', *ODNB*.

'"An Ancient Sage Philosopher": Alexander Ross and the defence of philosophy', *The Seventeenth Century*, 16 (2001), 68–94.

Allen, D. C., 'The rehabilitation of Epicurus and his theory of pleasure in the early Renaissance', *Studies in Philology* 41 (1941), 1–15.

'The predecessors of Champollion', *Proceedings of the American Philosophical Society*, 104 (1960), 527–47.

*The legend of Noah: Renaissance rationalism in art, science, and letters* (Illinois, 1963).

*Mysteriously meant: the rediscovery of pagan symbolism and allegorical interpretation in the Renaissance* (Baltimore, 1970).

Allen, M. J. B., 'Marsilio Ficino on Plato, the neoplatonists and the Christian doctrine of the trinity', *Renaissance Quarterly*, 37 (1984), 555–84.

'Marsilio Ficino, Hermes Trismegistus and the Corpus Hermeticum', in *New perspectives on Renaissance thought*, eds., J. Henry and S. Hutton (London, 1990), 38–47.

*Synoptic Art: Marsilio Ficino on the history of Platonic interpretation* (Florence, 1998).

Anselment, R. A., 'Thomas Sprat's *The plague of Athens*; Thucydides, Lucretius, and the "Pindaric Way"', *Bulletin of the John Rylands University Library of Manchester*, 78 (1996), 3–20.

Anstey, P., 'Boyle on occasionalism: an unexamined source', *JHI*, 60 (1999), 57–81.

*The philosophy of Robert Boyle* (London, 2000).

'The Christian virtuoso and the Reformers: are there Reformation roots to Boyle's natural philosophy?', *Lucas*, 27/8 (2000), 5–40.

'Robert Boyle and the heuristic value of mechanism', *SHPS*, 33 (2002), 161–74.

'Boyle on seminal principles', *SHPS*, 33 (2002), 597–630.

'Locke, Bacon and natural history', *ESM*, 7 (2002), 65–92.

'The methodological origins of Newton's queries', *Studies in the History and Philosophy of Science*, 35 (2004), 247–69.

'Experimental versus speculative natural philosophy', in *The science of nature in the seventeenth century*, eds., P. R. Anstey and J. A. Schuster (Leiden, 2005), 215–42.

*John Locke and natural philosophy* (Oxford, 2011).

'John Locke and Helmontian medicine', in *The body as object and instrument of knowledge: embodied empiricism in early modern science*, eds., C. T. Wolfe and O. Gal (Dordrecht, 2010), 93–117.

'The matter of medicine: new medical matter theories in mid-seventeenth-century England', in *Vanishing matter and the laws of motion: Descartes and beyond*, eds., D. Jalobeanu and P. R. Anstey (London, 2011), 61–79.

'Francis Bacon and the classification of natural history', *ESM*, 17 (2012), 11–31.

ed., *The Oxford handbook of British philosophy in the seventeenth century* (Oxford, 2013).

and Hunter, M., 'Robert Boyle's "Designe about natural history"', *ESM*, 13 (2008), 83–126.

and Burrows, J., 'John Locke, Thomas Sydenham, and the authorship of two medical essays', *Electronic British Library Journal* (2009), article 3.

and Campbell, K., Jacovides, M., 'Locke's experimental philosophy', *Metascience*, 22 (2013), 1–22.

and Vanzo, A., 'The origins of early modern experimental philosophy', *IHR*, 22 (2012), 499–518.

Antognazza, M. R., *Leibniz on the trinity and the incarnation: reason and revelation in the seventeenth century* (Yale, 2008 [Italian original=1999]).

Ariew, R., *Descartes and the last scholastics* (Ithaca, 1999).

Arnold, M., 'Thomas Stanley's *Aeschylus*: Renaissance practical criticism of Greek Tragedy', *Illinois Classical Studies*, 9 (1984), 229–49.

van Asselt, W. J., 'Covenant theology as relational theology: the contributions of Johannes Cocceius (1603–1669) and John Owen (1618–1683) to a living Reformed theology', in *The Ashgate research companion to John Owen's theology*, eds., K. M. Kapic and M. Jones (Aldershot, 2012), 65–84.

Aslanian, S. D., *From the Indian Ocean to the Mediterranean: the global trade networks of Armenian merchants from New Julfa* (Berkeley, 2011).

Assmann, J., *Moses the Egyptian: the memory of Egypt in Western monotheism* (Cambridge [MA], 1997).

Asso, C., 'Erasmus redivivus. Alcune osservazioni sulla filologia Neotestamentaria de Jean Le Clerc', in *Vico Nella Storia della Filologia*, eds., S. Caianiello and A. Viana (Naples, 2004), 79–115.

Auvray, P., *Richard Simon (1638–1712)* (Paris, 1974).

Backhouse, J. H., *The editio princeps of the Epistle of Barnabas by Archbishop Ussher . . . with a dissertation on the literary history of that edition* (Oxford, 1883).

ed., *The reception of the church fathers in the West* (2 vols, Leiden, 1997).

Baku, G., 'Der Streit um den Naturbegriff am Ende des 17. Jahrhunderts', *Zeitschrift für Philosophie und philosophische Kritik*, 98 (1891), 162–90.

Barbour R., *English Epicures and Stoics: ancient legacies in early Stuart culture* (Amherst, 1998).

'Anonymous Lucretius', *Bodleian Library Record*, 23 (2010), 105–11.

and Norbrook, D., 'Introduction', in Lucy Hutchinson, *The translation of Lucretius*, eds., R. Barbour, D. Norbrook, and M. C. Zerbino (Oxford, 2012), xv–clxvi.

Barducci, M., 'Clement Barksdale, translator of Grotius: Erastianism and episocpacy in the English church, 1651–1658', *The Seventeenth Century*, 25 (2010), 265–80.

'Political and ecclesiological contexts for the early English translations of Grotius's De Veritate (1632–1686)', *Grotiana*, 33 (2012), 70–87.

Barnes, A., *Jean Le Clerc (1657–1736) et la République des Lettres* (Paris, 1938).

Beaude, P.-M., 'L'accomplissement des prophéties chez Richard Simon', *Revue des Sciences Philosophiques et Théologiques*, 60 (1976), 3–35.

Beck, R., 'Thus spake not Zarathustra: Zoroastrian pseudepigrapha of the Greco-Roman world', in M. Boyce and F. Grenet, *A history of Zoroastrianism, vol. III: Zoroastrianism under Macedonian and Roman rule* (Leiden, 1991), 491–565.

Beddard, R. A., 'Restoration Oxford and the remaking of the Protestant establishment', in *The history of the University of Oxford, vol. IV: seventeenth-century Oxford*, ed. N. Tyacke (Oxford, 1997), 803–62.

'Tory Oxford', in *The history of the University of Oxford, vol. IV: seventeenth-century Oxford*, ed. N. Tyacke (Oxford, 1997), 863–906.

van Beeck, F. J., 'Introduction', in *The poems and translations of Sir Edward Sherburne*, ed., F. J. van Beeck (Assen, 1961), xvii–xlv.

Beiser, F. C., *The sovereignty of reason: the defense of rationality in the early English Enlightenment* (Princeton [NJ], 1996).

Belcher, T. W., 'Memoir of John Stearne', *Dublin Journal of Medical Science*, 39 (1865), 436–66.

Ben-Chaim, M., 'Empowering lay belief: Robert Boyle and the moral economy of experiment', *Science in Context*, 15 (2002).

Ben-Zaken, A., *Cross-cultural scientific exchanges in the eastern Mediterranean, 1560–1660* (Baltimore [MD], 2010).

Benin, S. D., 'The "cunning of God" and divine accommodation', *JHI*, 45 (1984), 179–91.

*The footprints of God: divine accommodation in Jewish and Christian thought* (New York, 1993).

Bennett, J. A., 'A study of *Parentalia*, with two unpublished letters of Sir Christopher Wren', *Annals of Science*, 30 (1973), 129–47.

Bercovitch, S., 'Empedocles in the English Renaissance', *Studies in Philology*, 65 (1968), 67–80.

van den Berg, J., 'Menasseh ben Israel, Henry More and Johannes Hoornbeeck on the pre-existence of the soul', in *Menasseh ben Israel and his world*, eds., Y. Kaplan, H. Méchoulan, and R. H. Popkin (Leiden, 1989), 98–116.

'Grotius' views on antichrist and apocalyptic thought in England', in *Hugo Grotius, theologian*, eds., H. J. M. Nellen and E. Rabbie (Leiden, 1994), 169–84.

Bergemann, L., *Ralph Cudworth—System Aus Transformation: Zur Naturphilosophie Der Cambridge Platonists Und Ihrer Methode (Transformationen Der Antike)* (Berlin, 2012).

Bernier, J., *La critique du Pentateuque de Hobbes à Calmet* (Paris, 2010).

Bianchi, D., 'Some sources for a history of English Socinianism: a bibliography of 17th-century English Socinian writings', *Topoi*, 4 (1985), 91–120.

Bidez, J., and Cumont, F., *Les Mages hellénisés* (2 vols, Paris, 1938).

Bietenholz, P. G., 'Sigismundus Gelenius of Prague, c. 1498–early 1554', in *Contemporaries of Erasmus: a biographical register of the Renaissance and Reformation, Vols* I-III, eds., P. G. Bietenholz and T. B. Deutscher (Toronto, 1985).

*Daniel Zwicker, 1612–1678: peace, tolerance and God the One and only* (Florence, 1997).

Birrell, T. A., 'The reconstruction of the library of Isaac Casaubon', in *Hellinga: Festschrift*, ed. A. R. A. Croiset van Uchelen (Amsterdam, 1980), 59–68.

'The library of Sir Edward Sherburne', in *The book trade and its customers, 1450–1900: historical essays for Robin Myers*, eds., A. Hunt, G. Mandelbrote, and A. Shell (Winchester, 1997), 189–204.

Black, S. B., 'Marsham, John', *ODNB*.

Blackwell, C., 'Epicurus and Boyle, Leclerc and Locke: "Ideas" and their redefinition in Jacob Brucker's *Historia Philosophica Doctrinae de Ideis'*, in *Il vocabulario della Republique des lettres, terminologia filosofica e storia della filosofia*, ed. M. Fattori (Florence, 1997), 70–90.

'Thales philosophus: the beginning of philosophy as a discipline', in *History and the disciplines: the reclassification of knowledge in early-modern Europe*, ed. D. R. Kelley (Rochester, 1997), 61–8.

'Sturm, Morhof and Brucker vs. Aristotle: three eclectic natural philosophers view the Aristotelian method', *Method and order in Renaissance philosophy of nature*, eds., D. A. Di Liscia, E. Kessler, and C. Methuen (Aldershot, 1998), 49–77.

and Kusukawa, S., eds., *Philosophy in the sixteenth and seventeenth centuries: conversations with Aristotle* (Aldershot, 1999).

Blair, A., 'Mosaic physics and the search for a pious natural philosophy in the late Renaissance', *Isis* 91 (2000), 32–58.

Blau, A., 'Uncertainty and the history of ideas', *History and Theory*, 50 (2011), 358–72.

Blau, J. L., *The Christian interpretation of the Cabala in the Renaissance* (New York, 1944).

Blok, F. F., *Isaac Vossius and his circle: his life until his farewell to Queen Christina of Sweden*, trans. C. van Heertum (Groningen, 2000 [Dutch orig.=1999]).

Blom, F. J. M., 'Lucas Holstenius (1596–1661) and England', in *Studies in seventeenth-century English literature, history and bibliography*, eds., G. A. M. Janssens and F. G. A. M. Aarts (Amsterdam, 1984).

Blom, H., and Winkel, L., 'Introduction', in *Grotius and the Stoa*, eds., H. W. Blom and L. C. Winkel (Assen, 2004), 3–21.

Blum, P. R., '"Cognitio falsitatis vera est." Benedictus Pererius critico della magia e della cabala', in *La magia nell'Europa moderna: tra antica sapienza e filosofia naturale*, eds., F. Meroi and E. Scapparone (Florence, 2007), 345–62.

Blundell, B., *Pierre Gassendi: from Aristotelianism to a new natural philosophy* (Dordrecht, 1987).

Booth, E., *'A Subtle and Mysterious Machine': the medical world of Walter Charleton (1619–1707)* (Dordrecht, 2005).

Boss, J. M. N., '"Doctrina de circulatione sanguinis haud immutat antiquam medendi methodum": an unpublished manuscript (1662) by Francis Glisson (1597–1677) on implications of Harvey's physiology', *Physis. Rivista Internazionale di Storia della Scienza*, 20 (1978), 309–36.

'Helmont, Glisson, and the doctrine of the common reservoir in the seventeenth-century revolution in physiology', *BJHS*, 16 (1983), 261–72.

Bossier, F., 'Traductions latines et influences du Commentaire In de Caelo des Simplikios', in *Simplicius, sa vie, son oeuvre, sa survie*, ed. I. Hadot (Berlin and New York, 1987), 298–325.

Boter, J. G., 'Epictetus', *CTC*, ix, 1–54.

Bots, H., Hillenaar, H., Janssen, J., Van der Korst, J., and Van Lieshout, L., eds., *De 'Bibliothèque Universelle et Historique' (1686–1693): een periodiek als trefpunt van geletterd Europa* (Amsterdam, 1981).

Boyce, M., *A history of Zoroastrianism* (3 vols, Leiden, 1975–91).

*Zoroastrians: their religious beliefs and practices* (London, 1979).

Brach, J.-P., 'Mathematical esotericism: some perspectives on Renaissance arithmology', in *Hermes in the academy*, eds., W. J. Hanegraaff and J. Pijnenburg (Amsterdam, 2009), 75–90.

Brady, D., *The contribution of British writers between 1560 and 1830 to the interpretation of Revelation 13.16–18 (the number of the beast)* (Tübingen, 1983).

Braun, L., *Histoire de l'histoire de la philosophie* (Paris, 1973).

Bravo, B., 'Critice in the sixteenth and seventeenth centuries and the rise of the notion of historical criticism', in *History of scholarship*, eds., C. Ligota and J.-L. Quantin (Oxford, 2006), 135–96.

Breen, Q., 'Introduction', in M. Nizolio, *De veris principiis et vera ratione philosophandi*, ed. Q. Breen (2 vols, Rome, 1955), i, i–lxxiv.

Bremer, F. J., 'Mather, Samuel', *ODNB*.

Brink, C. O., *English classical scholarship* (New York, 1986).

Brockliss, L., and Jones, C., *The medical world of early modern France* (Oxford, 1997).

Brogi, S., 'Jean Le Clerc et l'Église anglicane', in *Les relations franco-anglaises aux XVIIe et XVIIIe siècles: périodiques et manuscrits clandestins*, ed. G. Artigas-Menant (Paris, 2007), 117–44.

Brooke, C., 'How the Stoics became Atheists', *HJ*, 49 (2006), 387–402.

*Philosophic pride: Stoicism and political thought from Lipsius to Rousseau* (Princeton, 2012).

Browne, A., 'J. B. van Helmont's attack on Aristotle', *Annals of Science*, 36 (1979), 575–91.

Brown, C. C., 'The mere numbers of Henry More's Cabbala', *Studies in English Literature, 1500–1900*, 10 (1970), 143–53.

Buchwald, J., and Feingold, M., *Newton and the origins of civilization* (Princeton, 2013).

Burnett, S. G., 'Later Christian Hebraists', in *Hebrew Bible/Old Testament: the history of its interpretation, vol.* ii: *from the Renaissance to the Enlightenment*, ed. M. Saebø (Göttingen, 2008) ii, 785–801.

Burnham, F. B., 'The More-Vaughan controversy: the revolt against philosophical enthusiasm', *JHI*, 35 (1974), 33–49.

Burns, W. E., '"Our lot is fallen into an age of wonders": John Spencer and the controversy over prodigies in the early Restoration', *Albion*, 27 (1995), 237–52.

   *An age of wonders: prodigies, politics, and providence in England, 1657–1727* (Manchester, 2002).

   'Glanvill, Joseph', *ODNB*.

Burstein, S. M., 'Images of Egypt in Greek historiography', in *Ancient Egyptian literature: history and forms*, ed. A. Loperino (Leiden, 1996), 591–604.

Burton, S. J. G., *The hallowing of logic: the trinitarian method of Richard Baxter's Methodus Theologiae* (Leiden, 2012).

Burtt, E. A., *The metaphysical foundations of modern science* (London, 1932).

Bylebyl, J. J., 'Teaching *Methodus medendi* in the Renaissance', in *Galen's method of healing*, eds., F. Kudlien and R. J. Durling (Leiden, 1991), 157–89.

Campagnolo, M., 'Entre Théodore de Bèze et Erasme de Rotterdam: Isaac Casaubon', in *Théodore de Bèze (1519–1605): Actes du colloque de Genève*, ed. I. Backus (Geneva, 2007), 195–217.

Campanini, S., 'Le fonti ebraiche del *De harmonia mundi* di Francesco Zorzi', *Annali di Ca'Foscari*, 38 (1999), 29–74.

   'Eine späte Apologie der Kabbala. Die Abdita divinae Cabalae Mysteria des Jacques Gaffarel', in *Topik und Tradition. Prozesse der Neuordnung von Wissensüberlieferungen des 13. bis 17. Jahrhunderts*, eds., T. Frank, U. Kocher, and U. Tarnow (Göttingen, 2007), 325–51.

Cantlie, H. A., 'Gideon Harvey', *Annals of Medical History*, 3 (1921), 204–37.

Carabelli, G., *Tolandiana: materiali bibliografici per lo studio dell'opera e della fortuna di John Toland (1670–1722)* (Florence, 1975).

Carlin, L., 'Boyle's teleological mechanism and the myth of immanent teleology', *SHPS*, 43 (2012), 54–63.

Carpenter, E., *Thomas Tenison, archbishop of Canterbury* (Michigan, 1948).

Carroll, R. T., *The common sense philosophy of religion of Bishop Edward Stillingfleet* (The Hague, 1975).

Carter, H., *A history of the Oxford University Press: to the year 1780* (Oxford, 1975).

Casini, P., 'Newton: the Classical Scholia', *History of Science*, 22 (1984), 1–58.

   'The Pythagorean myth: Copernicus to Newton', in *Copernico e la questione copernica in Italia*, ed. L. Pepe (Florence, 1996), 183–99.

Catana, L., *The historiographical concept 'system of philosophy': its origin, nature, influence and legitimacy* (Leiden, 2008).

   'The history of the history of philosophy, and the lost biographical tradition', *BJHP*, 20 (2012), 619–25.

Cecon, K., 'Robert Boyle's experimental programme: some interesting examples of the use of subordinate cuases in chemistry and pneumatics', *Intellectual History Review*, 25 (2015), 81–96.

Celenza, C. S., 'Pythagoras in the Renaissance: the case of Marsilio Ficino', *Renaissance Quarterly*, 52 (1999), 667–711.

Chalmers, A., 'The lack of excellency of Boyle's mechanical philosophy', *SHPS*, 24 (1993), 541–64.

'Experiment versus mechanical philosophy in the work of Robert Boyle: a reply to Anstey and Pyle', *SHPS*, 33 (2002), 191–7.

'Boyle and the origins of modern chemistry: Newman tried in the fire', *SHPS*, 41 (2010), 1–10.

'Understanding science through its history: a response to Newman', *SHPS*, 42 (2011), 150–3.

'Intermediate causes and explanations: the key to understanding the scientific revolution', *SHPS*, 43 (2012), 551–62.

Chamberlain, J. S., 'Long, Thomas', *ODNB*.

Champion, J. A. I., *The pillars of priestcraft shaken: the Church of England and its enemies 1660–1730* (Cambridge, 1992).

'Legislators, impostors, and the politic origins of religion: English theories of "imposture" from Stubbe to Toland', in *Heterodoxy, Spinozism, and free thought in early-eighteenth-century Europe: studies on the Traité des trois imposteurs*, eds., S. Berti, F. Charles-Daubert, and R. H. Popkin (Dordrecht, 1996), 333–56.

'Richard Simon and biblical criticism in Restoration England', in *Everything connects: in conference with Richard Popkin*, eds., J. Force and D. Katz (Leiden, 1999), 37–61.

'Introduction', in John Toland, *Nazarenus*, ed. J. A. I. Champion (Oxford, 1999).

'"I remember a Mahometan story of Ahmed ben Edris": freethinking uses of Islam from Stubbe to Toland', *Al-Qantara*, 31 (2010), 443–80.

Chan, M., and Kassler, J. C., *Roger North: materials for a chronology of his writings* (Kensington [NSW], 1989).

Chapman, A., 'Edmond Halley's use of historical evidence in the advancement of science', *NRRS*, 48 (1994), 167–91.

Chen, B., 'Politics and letters: Gisbert Cuper as servant of two republics', in *Double agents: cultural and political brokerage in early modern Europe*, eds., M. Keblusek and B. V. Noldus (Leiden, 2011), 71–95.

Chevalier, P., ed., *Dionysiaca: Recueil donnant l'ensemble des traductions latines des ouvrages attribués au Denys de l'Aréopage* (2 vols, Paris, 1937–50).

Christianson, P., *Discourse on history, law, and governance in the public career of John Selden, 1610–1635* (Toronto, 1996).

Churton, E., 'Memoir of the life and writings of John Pearson', in *The minor theological works of John Pearson*, ed. E. Churton (2 vols, Oxford, 1844), i, xiii–cxxxvi.

Chwolsohn, D., *Die Ssabier und der Ssabismus* (2 vols, St Petersburg, 1856).

Cifoletti, G., 'The creation of the history of algebra in the sixteenth century', in *L'Europe mathématique: histoires, mythes, identités*, eds., C. Goldstein, J. Gray, and J. Ritter (Paris, 1996), 123–44.

Clark, S., 'Gaule, John', *ODNB*.

Clarke, D. M., and C. Wilson, eds., *The Oxford handbook of philosophy in early modern Europe* (Oxford, 2011).

Claydon, T., 'Latitudinarianism and apocalyptism in the worldview of Gilbert Burnet', *HJ*, 51 (2008), 577–97.

Cleary, J. J., *Aristotle and mathematics: aporetic method in cosmology and metaphysics* (Leiden, 1995).

Clericuzio, A., 'A redefinition of Boyle's chemistry and corpuscular philosophy', *Annals of Science*, 47 (1990), 561–89.

'From van Helmont to Boyle: a study of the transmission of Helmontian chemical and medical theories in seventeenth-century England', *BJHS*, 26 (1993), 303–34.

'Carneades and the chemists: a study of *The sceptical chymist* and its impact on seventeenth-century chemisty', in *Robert Boyle recosidered*, ed. M. Hunter (Cambridge, 1994), 79–90.

'L'atomisme de Gassendi et la philosophie corpusculaire de Boyle', in *Gassendi et l'Europe (1592–1792)*, ed. S. Murr (Paris, 1997), 227–35.

*Elements, principles and corpuscles. A study of atomism and chemistry in the seventeenth century* (Dordrecht, 2000).

'Gassendi, Charleton and Boyle on matter and motion', in *Late medieval and early modern corpuscular matter theories*, eds., C. Lüthy, J. E. Murdoch, and W. Newman (Leiden, 2001), 467–83.

'Maynwaring, Everard', *ODNB*.

'Sherley, Thomas', *ODNB*.

Clucas, S., 'The atomism of the Cavendish circle: a reappraisal', *The Seventeenth Century*, 9 (1994), 247–73.

Coffey, J., 'A ticklish business: defining heresy and orthodoxy in the puritan revolution', in *Heresy, literature and politics in early modern English culture*, eds., D. Loewenstein and J. Marshall (Cambridge, 2006), 108–36.

Cohen, E. H., and Ross, J. S., 'The commonplace book of Edmond Halley', *NRRS*, 40 (1985), 1–40.

Cohen, I. B., 'Hypotheses in Newton's philosophy', *Physis. Rivista Internazionale di Storia della Scienza*, 8 (1966), 163–84.

*Introduction to Newton's Principia* (Cambridge, 1971).

Cole, F. J., 'Henry Power on the circulation of blood', *Journal of the History of Medicine*, 12 (1657), 291–324.

Coleman-Norton, P. R., 'The authorship of the *Epistola de Indicis Gentibus et de Bragmanibus*', *Classical Philology*, 21 (1926), 154–60.

Colie, R., *Light and enlightenment* (Cambridge, 1957).

Collier, K. B., *Cosmogonies of our fathers: some theories of the seventeenth and the eighteenth centuries* (New York, 1934).

Cope, J. I., 'The cupri-cosmits: Glanvill on latitutdinarian anti-enthusiasm', *Huntington Library Quarterly*, 17 (1954), 269–86.

*Joseph Glanvill: Anglical apologist* (St. Louis, 1956).

Corneanu, S., *Regimens of the mind: Boyle, Locke, and the cultura animi tradition* (Chicago, 2012).

Cornelius, P., *Languages in seventeenth- and early eighteenth-century imaginary voyages* (Geneva, 1965).

Cornwall, R. D., 'Nicholls, William', *ODNB*.

Condren, C., *The language of politics in seventeenth-century England* (London, 1994).

*Argument and authority in early modern England* (Cambridge, 2006).

Cook, H. J., *The decline of the old medical regime in Stuart London* (Ithaca, 1986).

'The Society of Chemical Physicians, the new philosophy, and the Restoration court', *Bulletin of the History of Medicine*, 61 (1987), 61–77.

'Physicians and the new philosophy: Henry Stubbe and the virtuosi-physicians', in *The medical revolution in the seventeenth century*, eds., R. French and A. Wear (Cambridge, 1989), 246–71.

'The new philosophy and medicine in seventeenth-century England', in *Reappraisals of the scientific revolution*, eds., D. C. Lindberg and R. S. Westman (Cambridge, 1990), 397–436.

Copenhaver, B. P., 'Jewish theologies of space in the scientific revolution: Henry More, Joseph Raphson, Isaac Newton and their predecessors', *Annals of Science*, 37 (1980), 489–548.

'Introduction', in *Hermetica: the Greek Corpus Hermeticum and the Latin Asclepius*, ed. and trans. B. P. Copenhaver (Cambridge, 1992).

'Did science have a Renaissance?', *Isis*, 83 (1993), 387–407.

Costello, W. T., *The scholastic curriculum at early seventeenth century Cambridge* (Cambridge [MA], 1958).

Coudert, A. P., 'A Cambridge Platonist's Kabbalist nightmare', *JHI*, 36 (1975), 633–52.

'Henry More, the Kabbalah, and the Quakers', in *Philosophy, science, and religion in England, 1640–1700*, eds., R. Kroll, R. Ashcraft, and P. Zagorin (Cambridge, 1992), 31–67.

*The impact of the Kabbalah in the seventeenth century: the life and thought of Francis Mercury van Helmont (1614–1698)* (Leiden, 1999).

Coughlan, P., 'Natural history and historical nature: the project for a natural history of Ireland', in *Samuel Hartlib and universal Reformation: studies in intellectual communication*, eds., M. Greengrass, M. Leslie, and T. Raylor (Cambridge, 1994), 298–318.

Cowie, B. W., 'Beveridge, William', *ODNB*.

Cragg, G. R., *From Puritanism to the age of reason: a study of changes in religious thought within the Church of England* (Cambridge, 1950).

Cranz, F. E., 'Alexander Aphrodisiensis', *CTC*, I, 77–135, II, 411–22, VII, 296–8 (addenda by C. Vecce).

Crocker, R., 'Mysticism and enthusiasm in Henry More', in *Henry More: tercentenary studies*, ed. S. Hutton (Dordrecht, 1990), 137–55.

*Henry More, 1614–1687: a biography of the Cambridge Platonist* (Dordrecht, 2003).

Cromartie, A., *Sir Matthew Hale, 1609–1676: law, religion and natural philosophy* (Cambridge, 1995).

Crowther, K. M., 'Sacred philosophy, secular theology: the Mosaic physics of Levinus Lemnius (1505-1568) and Francisco Valles (1524–1592)', in *Nature and scripture in the Abrahamic religions*, eds., J. M. van der Meer and S. Mandelbrote (2 vols, Leiden, 2008), I, 397–428.

Crump, G. M., 'Thomas Stanley's manuscript of his poems and translations', *Transactions of the Cambridge Bibliographical Society* II.5 (1958), 359–65.

'Introduction', in *The poems and translations of Thomas Stanley*, ed. G. M. Crump (Oxford, 1962), xxi–lxiv.

Cumont, F., *Astrology and religion among the Greeks and Romans* (New York, 1912).

Cunningham, A., 'Thomas Sydenham: epidemics, experiment and the "Good Old Cause"', in *The medical revolution in the seventeenth century*, eds., R. French and A. Wear (Cambridge, 1989), 164–90.

    *The anatomical Renaissance: the resurrection of the anatomical projects of the ancients* (Aldershot, 1997), 167–90.

    'The transformation of Hippocrates in seventeenth-century Britain', in *Reinventing Hippocrates*, ed. D. Cantor (Aldershot, 2002), 91–116.

Curran, B., 'The Renaissance afterlife of ancient Egypt (1400–1650)', in *The wisdom of Egypt: changing visions through the ages*, eds., P. Ucko and T. Champion (London, 2003), 101–32.

    *The Egyptian Renaissance: the afterlife of ancient Egypt in early modern Italy* (Chicago, 2007).

    and A. Grafton, 'A fifteenth-century site report on the Vatican obelisk', *JWCI*, 58 (1995), 234–48.

Dal Pra, M., 'Giovanni Jonsio', *Rivista di storia della filosofia*, 3 (1948), 159–69.

Dales, R. C., 'The de-animation of the heavens in the middle ages', *JHI*, 41 (1980), 531–50.

Dan, J., 'Menasseh ben Israel: attitude towards the Zohar and Lurianic Kabbalah', in *Menasseh ben Israel and his world*, eds., Y. Kaplan, H. Méchoulan, and R. H. Popkin (Leiden, 1989), 199–206.

Dannenfeldt, K. H., 'Hermetica philosophica', *CTC*, I, 137–50, II, p. 423, III, 425 (addenda by M.-T. D'Alverny).

    'Oracula Chaldaica', *CTC*, 157–64, VII, 326–29 (addenda by I. Klutstein).

    'The pseudo-Zoroastrian oracles in the Renaissance', *Studies in the Renaissance*, 4 (1957), 7–30.

    'Egypt and the Egyptian antiquities in the Renaissance', *Studies in the Renaissance*, 6 (1959), 7–27.

Darley, G., *John Evelyn: living for ingenuity* (New Haven, 2006).

Davies, C. S. L., 'The youth and education of Christopher Wren', *English Historical Review*, 123 (2008), 1–28.

De Smet R., and Verhelst, K., 'Newton's Scholium Generale: the Platonic and Stoic Legacy—Philo, Justus Lipsius and the Cambridge Platonists', *History of Science*, 39 (2001), 1–30.

Dear, P., *Discipline and experience: the mathematical way in the scientific revolution* (Chicago, 1995).

    'Method and the study of nature', in *The Cambridge history of seventeenth-century philosophy*, eds., D. Garber and M. Ayers (2 vols, 1998), I, 147–77.

    'Circular argument: Descartes' vortices and their crafting as explanations of gravity', in *The science of nature in the seventeenth century*, eds., P. R. Anstey and J. A. Schuster (Leiden, 2005), 81–98.

    'What is the history of science the history *of?* Early modern roots of the ideology of modern science', *Isis*, 96 (2005), 390–406.

Deason, G. B., 'Reformation theology and the mechanistic conception of nature', in *God and nature: historical essays on the encounter between Christianity and science*, eds., D. C. Lindberg and R. L. Numbers (Berkley and Los Angeles, 1986), 167–92.

Debus, A. G., 'An Elizabethan history of medical chemistry', *Annals of Science*, 18 (1964), 1–29.

    *The English Paracelsians* (London, 1965).

'Mathematics and nature in the chemical texts of the Renaissance', *Ambix*, 15 (1968), 1–28.

'Introduction', in *Science and education in the seventeenth century: the Webster-Ward debate* (New York, 1970).

'Parcelsian medicine: Noah Biggs and the problem of medical reform', in *Medicine in seventeenth century England*, ed. A. G. Debus (Berkeley, 1974), 33–48.

*The chemical philosophy: Paracelsian science and medicine in the sixteenth and seventeenth centuries* (2 vols, New York, 1977).

'Thomas Sherley's *Philosophical essay* (1672): Helmontian mechanism as the basis of a new philosophy', *Ambix*, 27 (1980), 124–35.

*The French Paracelsians* (Cambridge, 1991).

Deitz, L., '"Falsissima est ergo haec de triplici substantia Aristotelis doctrina". A sixteenth-century critic of Aristotle—Francesco Patrizi da Cherso on privation, form, and matter', *ESM*, 2 (1997), 227–50.

'Francesco Patrizi da Cherso's criticism of Aristotle's logic', *Vivarium*, 45 (2007), 113–24.

Del Torre, M.A., *Le origini moderne della storiografia filosofica* (Florence, 1976).

Denis P., and Rott, J., *Jean Morély (ca 1524–1594) et l'Utopie d'une démocratie dans l'eglise* (Geneva, 1993).

Dennehy M., and Ramond, C., eds., *La philosophie naturelle de Robert Boyle* (Paris, 2009).

Des Chene, D., *Physiologia: natural philosophy in late Aristotelian and Cartesian thought* (Ithaca, 1996).

Deuse, W., 'Celsus im Prooemium von "De medicina": Römische Aneignung griechischer Wissenschaft', *Aufstieg und Niedergang der römischen Welt*, 37 (1993), 819–41.

Dewhurst, K., *Dr Thomas Sydenham (1624–1689): his life and original writings* (Berkeley, 1966).

'Introduction', in *Richard Lower's 'Vindicatio'. A defence of the experimental method* (Oxford, 1983).

Di Liscia, D. A., Kessler, E., and Methuen, C., eds., *Method and order in Renaissance philosophy of nature* (Aldershot, 1998).

Diestel, L., *Geschichte des Alten Testamentes in der christlichen kirche* (Jena, 1869).

Dijkstra, J. H. F., 'Mysteries of the Nile? Joseph Scaliger and ancient Egypt', *Aries. Journal for the Study of Western Esotericism*, 9 (2009), 59–82.

*Dizionario biografico degli Italiani* (Rome, 1960—).

Dobbs, B. J. T., 'Studies in the natural philosophy of Sir Kenelm Digby, I', *Ambix*, 18 (1971), 1–25.

'Studies in the natural philosophy of Sir Kenelm Digby, II', *Ambix*, 20 (1973), 143–63.

'Newton's *Commentary* on *The Emerald Tablet* of Hermes Trismegistus: its scientific and theological significance', in *Hermeticism and the Renaissance*, eds., I. Merkel and A. G. Debus (Washington, 1988), 182–91.

Dockrill, D., 'The authority of the fathers in the great trinitarian debates of the 1690s', *Studia Patristica*, 18 (1990), 335–47.

'The heritage of patristic Platonism in seventeenth-century philosophical theology', in *The Cambridge Platonists in philosophical context*, eds., G. A. J. Rogers, J. M. Vienne, and Y. C. Zarka (Dordrecht, 1997), 55–77.

and Lee, J. M., 'Reflections on an episode in Cambridge latitudinarianism: Henry More's Epistle Dedicatory to Gilbert Sheldon of his *Enchiridion Metaphysicum*', in *Tradition and traditions: prudentia*, eds., D. Dockrill and R. G. Tanner (London, 1994), 207–23.

Dod, B. G., 'Aristoteles Latinus', in *The Cambridge history of later medieval philosophy: from the rediscovery of Aristotle to the disintegration of scholasticism, 1100–1600*, eds., N. Kretzmann, A. Kenny and J. Pinborg (Cambridge, 1982), 45–79.

Domski, M., 'The constructible and the intelligible in Newton's philosophy of geometry', *Philosophy of Science*, 70 (2003), 1114–24.

'Newton as historically-minded philosopher', in *Discourse on a new method: reinvigorating the marriage of history and philosophy of science*, eds., M. Dickson and M. Domski (LaSalle, 2010), 65–90.

Donini, P., 'The history of the concept of eclecticism', in *The question of 'eclecticism'*, eds., A. A. Long and J. M. Dillon (Berkeley, 1988), 15–33.

Dorandi, T., *Laertiana. Capitoli sulla tradizione manoscritta e sulla storia del testo delle Vite dei filosofi di Diogene Laerzio* (Berlin, 2009).

Douglas, D. C., *English scholars* (London, 1939).

Droge, A. J., *Homer or Moses? Early Christian interpetations of the history of culture* (Tübingen, 1989).

Droixhe, D., 'La crise de l'hébreu langue-mère au XVIIe siècle', in *La république des lettres et l'histoire du judaïsme antique: XVIe-XVIIIe siècles*, eds. C. Grell and F. Laplanche (Paris, 1992), 65–99.

Drouin, S., *Théologie ou libertinage? L'exégèse allégorique à l'âge des Lumières* (Paris, 2010).

Ducheyne, S., 'The General Scholium: some notes on Newton's published and unpublished endeavours', *Lias*, 33 (2010), 223–74.

*The main business of natural philosophy: Isaac Newton's natural-philosophical methodology* (Dordrecht, 2012).

Duffy, E., 'Primitive Christianity revived: religious renewal in Augustan England', in *Renaissance and renewal in Christian history*, ed., D. Baker (Oxford, 1977), 287–300.

Dunlop, K., 'What geometry postulates: Newton and Barrow on the relationship of mathematics to nature', in *Interpreting newton: critical essays*, eds., A. Janiak and E. Schliesser (Cambridge, 2012), 69–102.

Dupront, A., *Pierre-Daniel Huet et l'exégèse comparatiste au xviie siècle* (Paris, 1930).

Durling, R. J., 'A chronological census of Renaissance editions and translations of Galen', *JWCI*, 24 (1961), 230–305.

Dweck, Y., *The scandal of Kabbalah: Leon Modena, Jewish mysticism, early modern Venice* (Princeton, 2011).

Edelstein, D., *The Enlightenment: a genealogy* (Chicago, 2010).

Edwards, M., 'Aristotelianism, Descartes, and Hobbes', *HJ*, 50 (2005), 449–64.

Edwards, M., 'Ammonius, teacher of Origen', *Journal of Ecclesiastical History*, 44 (1993), 169–81.

van der Eijk, P. J., *Diocles of Carystus: a collection of the fragments with translation and commentary* (2 vols, Leiden, 2001).

El Daly, O., 'Mummies as medicine', *Discussion in Egyptology*, 48 (2000), 49–65.

Ellenzweig, S., *The fringes of belief: English literature, ancient heresy, and the politics of freethinking, 1660–1760* (Stanford, 2008).

Elmer, P., *The library of Dr. John Webster: the making of a seventeenth-century radical* (London, 1986).

Elukin, J., 'Maimonides and the rise and fall of the Sabians: explaining Mosaic laws and the limits of Scholarship', *JHI*, 63 (2001), 619–37.

Enenkel, K. A. E., 'The making of 16th-century mythography: Giraldi's *Syntagma de Musis* (1507, 1511, and 1539), *De deis gentium historia* (ca. 1500–1548) and Julien de Havrech's *De cognominibus deorum gentilium* (1541)', *Humanistica Lovaniensia*, 51 (2002), 9–53.

Farmer, S. A., *Syncretism in the West: Pico's 900 theses (1486). The evolution of traditional religious and philosophical systems* (Tempe, 1998).

Fattori, M., '*Signum* in Francis Bacon: dal mondo del sacro al mondo degli uomini', in *Signum: IX colloquio internazionale del Lessico Intellecttuale Europeo*, ed. M. Bianchi (Florence, 1999), 235–61.

Feingold, M., *The mathematicians' apprenticeship: science, universities and society in England, 1560–1640* (Cambridge, 1984).

'Isaac Barrow: divine, scholar, mathematician', *Before Newton: the life and times of Isaac Barrow* (Cambridge, 1990), 1–104.

'Patrons and professors: the origins and motives for the endowment of University Chairs—in particular the Laudian Professorship of Arabic', in *The 'Arabick', interest of the natural philosophers in the seventeenth-century England*, ed. G. A. Russell (Leiden, 1994), 109–27.

'The humanities', in *The history of the University of Oxford, vol. IV: seventeenth-century Oxford*, ed. N. Tyacke (Oxford, 1997), 211–357.

'The mathematical sciences and the new philosophies', in *The history of the University of Oxford, vol. IV: seventeenth-century Oxford*, ed. N. Tyacke (Oxford, 1997), 359–448.

'Oriental studies', in *The history of the University of Oxford, vol. IV: seventeenth-century Oxford*, ed. N. Tyacke (Oxford, 1997), 449–504.

'Aristotle and the English universities in the seventeenth century: a re-evaluation', in *European universities in the age of Reformation and Counter-Reformation*, ed. H. Robinson-Hammerstein (Dublin, 1998), 149–68.

'Mathematicians and naturalists: Sir Isaac Newton and the Royal Society', in *Isaac Newton's natural philosophy*, eds. J. Z. Buchwald and I. B. Cohen (Cambridge [MA], 2001), 77–102.

'The origins of the Royal Society revisited', *The practice of reform in health, medicine, and science, 1500–2000: essays for Charles Webster*, eds. M. Pelling and S. Mandelbrote (Aldershot, 2005), 167–83.

'"Experimental philosophy": the history and meaning of a concept' (forthcoming).

and Gouk, P. M., 'An early critic of Bacon's *Sylva sylvarum*: Edmund Chilmead's treatise on sound', *Annals of Science*, 40 (1983), 139–57.

Feisenberger, H. A., ed., *Sale catalogues of libraries of eminent persons: vol. XI: scientists* (London, 1975).

Feldhay, R., 'The use and abuse of mathematical entities: Galileo and the Jesuits revisited', in *The Cambridge companion to Galileo*, ed. P. Machamer (Cambridge, 1998), 80–145.

Ferrier, R. W., *A journey to Persia: Jean Chardin's portrait of a seventeenth-century empire* (London, 1996).

Festugière, A.-J., *La révélation d'Hermès Trismégiste* (4 vols, Paris, 1950).

Findlen, P., *Possessing nature: museums, collecting and scientific culture in early modern Italy* (Berkeley, 1994).

Finocchiaro, M. A., 'The biblical argument against Copernicanism and the limitation of biblical authority: Ingoli, Foscarini, Galileo, Campanella', in *Nature and scripture in the Abrahamic religions*, eds., J. M. van der Meer and S. Mandelbrote (2 vols, Leiden, 2008), I, 627–64.

Firby, N. K., *European travellers and their perceptions of Zoroastrians in the seventeenth and eighteenth centuries* (Berlin, 1988).

Fisch, H., 'The scientist as priest: a note on Robert Boyle's natural theology', *Isis*, 44 (1953), 252–65.

Fisher, S., 'Gassendi's atomist account of generation and heredity in plants and animals', *Perspectives on Science*, 11 (2003), 484–512.

Fleischmann, W. B., 'Lucretius', *CTC*, II, 349–66.

Fleitmann, S., *Walter Charleton (1620–1707), 'Virtuoso': Leben und Werk* (1986).

Floridi, L., *Sextus Empiricus: the transmission and recovery of Pyrrhonism* (Oxford, 2002).

Flower, M., 'Thomas Stanley (1525–1678): a bibliography of his writings in prose and verse, 1647–1743', *Transactions of the Cambridge Bibliographical Society*, 1 (1950), 138–72.

Force, J., *William Whiston: honest Newtonian* (Cambridge, 1985).

'Newton, the Lord God of Israel and knowledge of nature', in *Jewish Christians and Christian Jews* (Dordrecht, 1993), 131–58.

Forrester, J. M., and Henry, J., 'Introduction', in Jean Fernel, *On the hidden causes of things*, eds. and trans. J. M. Forrester and J. Henry (Leiden, 2005 [1st edn=1548]).

Foster, M., 'Sir Kenelm Digby as man of religion and thinker', *Downside Review*, 106 (1988), 35–58, 101–25.

Fouke, D. C., *The enthusiastical concerns of Dr. Henry More: religious meaning and the psychology of delusion* (Leiden, 1997).

Fowden, G., *The Egyptian Hermes: a historical approach to the late pagan mind* (Cambridge, 1986).

Fowler, C. F., *Descartes on the human soul: philosophy and the demands of Christian doctrine* (Dordrecht, 1999).

Fraenkel, E., 'Prolegomena', in Aeschylus, *Agamemnon*, ed. E. Fraenkel (3 vols, Oxford, 1959).

Frank, G., Leinkauf, T., and Wriedt, M., eds., *Die Patristik in der frühen Neuzeit: Die Relektüre der Kirchenväter in den Wissenschaften des 15. bis 18. Jahrhundert* (Stuttgart, 2006).

Frank, R. G., 'The John Ward diaries: mirror of seventeenth century science and medicine', *Journal of the History of Medicine*, 29 (1974), 147–79.

*Harvey and the Oxford physiologists: a study of scientific ideas* (Berkeley, 1980).

'Thomas Willis and his circle: brain and mind in seventeenth-century medicine', in *The languages of psyche: mind and body in enlightenment thought*, ed. G. S. Rousseau (Oxford, 1990), 107–40.

'Medicine', in *The history of the University of Oxford, vol. IV: seventeenth-century Oxford*, ed. N. Tyacke (Oxford, 1997), 507–58.

French, R., *William Harvey's natural philosophy* (Cambridge, 1994).

*Medicine before science: the business of medicine from the middle ages to the enlightenment* (Cambridge, 2003).

Fried, M. N., *Edmond Halley's reconstruction of the lost book of Apollonius's Conics* (Dordrecht, 2011).

Friedenwald, H., *The Jews and medicine* (2 vols, Baltimore, 1944).

Friedman, J., 'The myth of Jewish antiquity: new Christians and Christian-Hebraica in early modern Europe', in *Jewish Christians and Christian Jews: from the Renaissance to the enlightenment*, eds., R. H. Popkin and G. M. Weiner (Dordrecht, 1994), 35–56.

Fück, J., *Die arabischen Studien in Europa bis den Anfang des 20. Jahrhunderts* (Leipzig, 1955).

Fumaroli, M., 'Temps de croissance et temps de corruptions: des deux Antiquités dans l'érudition jésuite française du XVIIᵉ siècle', *XVIIᵉ siècle*, 131 (1981), 149–68.

'Les Abeilles et les araignées', in *La querelle des ancients et des modernes*, ed. A.-M. Lecoq (Paris, 2001), 7–218.

Gaab, H., Leich, P., and Löffladt, G., eds., *Johann Christoph Sturm (1635–1703)* (Frankfurt, 2004).

Gabbey, A., 'Philosophia Cartesiana triumphata: Henry More (1646–1671)', in *Problems of Cartesianism*, eds., T. M. Lennon, J. M. Nicholas, and J. W. Davis (Kingston, 1982), 171–250.

'The *Principia*: a treatise on "mechanics"?', in *The investigation of difficult things*, eds., P. M. Harman and A. E. Shapiro (Cambridge, 1992), 305–22.

'Between *ars* and *philosphia naturalis*: reflections on the historiography of early modern mechanics', in *Renaissance and revolution: humanists, scholars, craftsmen and natural philosophers in early modern Europe* (Cambridge, 1993), 133–45.

Gabriel, F., 'L'ordo alexandrine: Sa'id ibn Batriq, Selden, et la hiérarchie ecclésiale. De l'Orient chrétien à l'ecclésiologie primitive', *Annuaire de l'Institut Michel Villey*, 3 (2011), 419–50.

Gabrieli, V., *Sir Kenelm Digby, un ingelse italianato nell'età della controriforma* (Rome, 1957).

Galtier, P., 'Petau et la Préface de son De Trinitate', *Recherches de Science Religieuse*, 21 (1931), 462–76.

Ganzenmüller, W., 'Wandlungen in der geschichtlichen Betrachtung der Alchemie', *Chymia*, 3 (1950), 143–54.

Garber, D. and Ayers, M., eds., *The Cambridge history of seventeenth-century philosophy* (2 vols, Cambridge, 1998).

Garin, E., *La filosofia come sapere storico* (Bari, 1959).

Garrison, J. W., 'Newton and the relation of mathematics to natural philosophy', *JHI*, 48 (1987), 609–27.

Gascoigne, J., *Cambridge in the age of the enlightenment: science, religion and politics from the Restoration to the French Revolution* (Cambridge, 1988).

'The wisdom of the Egyptians and the secularisation of history in the age of Newton', in *The uses of antiquity: the scientific revolution and the classical tradition*, ed. S. Gaukroger (Dordrecht, 1991), 171–212.

Gatti, H., 'Frances Yates's Hermetic Renaissance in the documents held in the Warburg Institute archive', *Aries*, 2 (2002), 193–210.

Gaukroger, S., *Francis Bacon and the transformation of early modern philosophy* (Cambridge, 2001).

*The emergence of a scientific culture: science and the shaping of modernity, 1210–1685* (Oxford, 2006).

Gause, A., 'Hammond, William', *ODNB*.

Gentile, S., *Marsilio Ficino e il ritorno di Ermete Trismegisto* (Florence, 1999).

Gibbons, B. J., 'Lee, Francis', *ODNB*.

Gigante, M., 'Ambrogio Traversai interprete di Diogene Laerzio', in *Ambrogio Traversari nel VI centenario della nascita* (Florence, 1988), 367–459.

Giglioni, G., 'Anatomist atheist? The "hylozoistic" foundations of Francis Glisson's anatomical research', in *Religio medici: medicine and religion in seventeenth century England*, eds., O.P. Grell and A. Cunningham (Aldershot, 1996), 115–35.

'Francis Glisson's notion of *confoederatio naturae* in the context of hylozoistic corpuscularianism', *Revue d'histoire des sciences*, 55 (2002), 239–62.

'Glisson, Francis', *ODNB*.

'The cosmoplastic system of the universe: Ralph Cudworth on Stoic naturalism', *Revue d'histoire des sciences*, 61/2 (2008), 313–31.

Gillespie, S., 'Lucretius in the English Renaissance', in *The Cambridge companion to Lucretius*, eds., S. Gillespie and P. Hardie (Cambridge, 2007), 242–53.

Gingerich, O., *An annotated census of Copenicus' 'De revolutionibus' (Nuremberg, 1543 and Basel, 1566)* (Leiden, 2002).

Glawe, W., *Die Hellenisierung des Christentums in der Geschichte der Theologie von Luther bis auf die Gegenwart* (Berlin, 1912).

Golden, S. A., 'Dryden's praise of Dr Charleton', *Hermathena*, 103 (1966), 59–65.

*Jean Le Clerc* (New York, 1972).

Goldgar, A., *Impolite Learning: conduct and community in the republic of letters, 1680–1750* (New Haven and London, 1995).

Goldie, M., 'The Cambridge Platonists', *ODNB*.

Goldish, M., *Judaism in the theology of Sir Isaac Newton* (Dordrecht, 1998).

Goodchild, P., '"No phantasticall Utopia, but a reall place": John Evelyn, John Beale and Backbury Hill, Herefordshire', *Garden History*, 19 (1991), 105–27.

Goulding, R., *Defending Hypatia: Ramus, Savile, and the Renaissance rediscovery of mathematical history* (Dordrecht, 2010).

Grafton, A., 'Joseph Scaliger and historical chronology: the rise and fall of a discipline', *History and Theory*, 14 (1975), 156–185.

'Rhetoric, philology and Egyptomania in the 1570s: J. J. Scaliger's invective against M. Guilandinus' papyrus', *JWCI*, 52 (1979), 167–94.

'Protestant versus prophet: Isaac Casaubon on Hermes Trismegistus', *JWCI*, 46 (1983), 78–93.

*Joseph Scaliger* (2 vols, Oxford, 1983–93).

'The availability of ancient works', in *The Cambridge history of Renaissance philosophy*, eds., C. B. Schmitt and Q. Skinner (Cambridge, 1988), 767–91.

'Barrow as Scholar', in *Before Newton: the life and times of Isaac Barrow*, ed. M. Feingold (Cambridge, 1990), 291–302.

*Defenders of the text: the traditions of scholarship in an age of science, 1450–1800* (Cambridge [MA], 1991).

'Joseph Scaliger et l'histoire du Judaïsme Hellénistique', in *La république des letters et l'histoire du Judaïsme antique, XVIe-XVIIe siècles*, eds., C. Grell and F. Laplanche (Paris, 1992), 51–63.

'The new science and the traditions of humanism', in *The Cambridge companion to Renaissance humanism*, ed. J. Kraye (Cambridge, 1996), 203–23.

'From apotheosis to analysis: some late Renaissance histories of classical astronomy', in *History and the disciplines: the reclassification of knowledge*, ed. D. R. Kelley (Rochester, 1997), 261–76.

*The footnote: a curious history* (London, 1997).

'Kircher's chronology', in *Athanasius Kircher: the last man who knew everything*, ed. P. Findlen (New York and London, 2004), 171–87.

*What was history? The art of history in early modern Europe* (Cambridge, 2007).

'Isaac Vossius, chronologer', in *Isaac Vossius (1618–1689): between science and scholarship*, eds., E. Jorink and D. van Miert (Leiden, 2012), 43–84.

and J. Weinberg, *I have always loved the Holy Tongue: Isaac Casaubon, the Jews, and a forgotten chapter in Renaissance scholarship* (Cambridge [MA], 2011).

Grant, E., *Much ado about nothing: theories of space and vacuum from the middle ages to the scientific revolution* (Cambridge, 1981).

Grant, J. N., 'Erasmus' *Modus orandi deum*, Origen's *De oratione*, and Cambridge Trinity College MS 194 (B.8.10)', *Humanistica Lovaniensia*, 48 (1998), 42–59.

Greaves, R. L., 'Pemble, William', *ODNB*.

Greenblatt, S., *The swerve: how the Renaissance began* (New York, 2011).

Greene, R. A., 'Henry More and Robert Boyle on the spirit of nature', *JHI*, 32 (1962), 451–74.

'Whichcote, the candle of the Lord and synderesis', *JHI*, 51 (1991), 617–44.

and MacCallum, H., 'Introduction', in *An elegant and learned discourse of the light of nature*, eds., R. A. Greene and H. MacCallum (Toronto, 1971).

Greengrass, M., Leslie, M., Raylor, T., *Samuel Hartlib and universal Reformation: studies in intellectual communication* (Cambridge, 1994).

Gregory, T., 'Studi sull'atomismo del Seicento', in *Giornale critico della filosofia italiana*, 43 (1964), 38–65; 45 (1966), 44–63; 46 (1967), 528–41.

Greig, M., 'The reasonableness of Christianity? Gilbert Burnet and the trinitarian controversy of the 1690s', *Journal of Ecclesiastical History*, 44 (1993), 631–51.

'Gilbert Burnet and the problem of non-conformity in Restoration Scotland and England', *Canadian Journal of History*, 32 (1997), 1–24.

'Hill, Samuel', *ODNB*.

Grell, O. P., ed., *Paracelsus: the man and his reputation, his ideas and their transformation* (Leiden, 1998).

Gribbe, C., 'John Owen, Renaissance man? The evidence of Edward Millington's Bibliotheca Oweniana (1684)', in *The Ashgate research companion to John Owen's theology*, eds., K. M. Kapic and M. Jones (Aldershot, 2012), 97–112.

Griffin, M. I. J., jnr., *Latitudinarianism in the seventeenth-century Church of England*, ed. L. Freedman (Leiden, 1992).

Grunert F., and Vollhard, F., eds., *Historia literaria. Neuordnungen des Wissens im 17. und 18. Jahrhundert* (Berlin, 2007).

Gruys, J. A., *The early printed editions (1518–1664) of Aeschylus: a chapter in the history of classical scholarship* (The Hague, 1981).

Guelluy, R., 'L'évolution des methods théologiques à Louvain d'Erasme à Jansénius', *Revue d'Histoire Ecclésiastique*, 37 (1941), 31–144.

Gueroult, M., *Dianoématique: histoire de l'histoire de la philosophie* (3 vols, Paris, 1979–88).

Guicciardini, N., *Reading the Principia: the debate on Newton's mathematical methods for natural philosophy from 1687 to 1736* (Cambridge, 1999).

*Isaac Newton on mathematical certainty and method* (Cambridge [MA], 2009).

Guinsburg, A. M., 'Henry More, Thomas Vaughan and the late Renaissance magical tradition', *Ambix*, 27 (1980), 36–58.

Gurlt, E., *Geschichte der Chirurgie und ihrer Ausübung: Volkschirurgie—Alterthum—Mittelalter—Renaissance* (3 vols, Berlin, 1898).

Gundlach, F., *Catalogus professorum Academiae Marburgensis* (Marburg, 1927).

Güthenke, C., 'Shop Talk. Reception studies and recent work in the history of scholarship', *Classical Receptions*, 1 (2009), 104–15.

Gwynn, R., 'Conformity, non-conformity and Huguenot settlement in England in the later seventeenth century', in *The religious culture of the Huguenots, 1660–1750*, ed. A. Dunan-Page (Aldershot, 2006), 23–42.

'Strains of worship: the Huguenots and non-conformity', in *The Huguenots: history and memory in transnational context* (Leiden, 2011), 121–52.

Hadot, P., 'La survie du Commentaire de Simplicius sur le *Manuel d'Epictète* du XVe au XVIIe siècles: Perotti, Politien, Steuchus, John Smith, Cudworth', in *Simplicius, sa vie, son oeuvre, sa survie*, ed. I. Hadot (Berlin and New York, 1987), 326–67.

Häfner, R., 'Das Erkenntnisproblem in der Philologie um 1700: Zum Verhältnis von Polymathie und Aporetik bei J. F. Reimmann, Chr. Thomasius und J. A. Fabricius', in *Philologie und Erkenntni: Beiträge zu Begriff und Problem frühneuzeitlicher 'Philologie'*, ed. R. Häfner (Tübingen, 2001), 95–128.

*Die Götter im Exil: Frühneuzeitliches Dichtungsverständnis im Spannungsfeld christlicher Apologetik und philogischer Kritik (ca.1590–1736)* (Tübingen, 2003).

'Shaping early modern comparative studies: the significance of Christoph Arnold (1627–1685)', in *Patristic tradition and intellectual paradigms in the 17th century*, eds., S.-P. Bergjan and K. Pollmann (Tübingen, 2010), 3–18.

Hall, A. R., *The revolution in science, 1500–1750* (London, 1983).

*Henry More: magic, religion and experiment* (Oxford, 1990).

Hall, M. B., 'Hero's *Pneumatica*: a study of its transmission and influence', *Isis*, 40 (1949), 38–48.

'The establishment of the mechanical philosophy', *Osiris*, 10 (1952), 412–41.

'Acid and alkali in seventeenth-century chemistry', *Archives Internationales d'Histoire des Sciences*, 9 (1956), 13–28.

*Robert Boyle and seventeenth century chemistry* (Cambridge, 1958).

Halleux, R., 'La controverse sur les origines de la chimie, de Paracelse à Borrichius', in *Acta Conventus neo-Latini Turonensis*, ed. J. C. Margolin (2 vols, Paris, 1980), II, 807–19.

Hämeen-Anttila, J., *The last pagans of Iraq: Ibn Waḥshiyya and his Nabatean Agriculture* (Leiden, 2006).

Hamilton, A., *The apocryphal apocalypse: the reception of the second book of Esdras (4 Ezra) from the Renaissance to the Enlightenment* (Oxford, 1999).

*The Copts and the West, 1439–1822: the European discovery of the Egyptian church* (Oxford, 2006).

'Huntington, Robert', *ODNB*.

Hammond, P., 'Thomas Smith: a beleaguered humanist of the Interregnum', *Bulletin of the Institute of Historical Research*, 56 (1983), 180–94.

Handley, S., 'Scrivener, Matthew', *ODNB*.

'Seller, Abednego', *ODNB*.

Hanegraaff, W. J., 'Beyond the Yates paradigm: the study of Western esotericism between counterculture and new complexity', *Aries*, 1 (2001), 5–37.

*Esotericism and the academy: rejected knowledge in Western culture* (Cambridge, 2012).

Hankins, J., *Plato in the Italian Renaissance* (2 vols, Leiden, 1990).

'Socrates in the Italian Renaissance', in *Socrates, from antiquity to the Enlightenment*, ed. M. B. Trapp (Aldershot, 2007), 179–208.

'Humanism, scholasticism, and Renaissance philosophy', in *The Cambridge companion to Renaissance philosophy*, ed. J. Hankins (Cambridge, 2007), 30–48.

and Palmer, A., *The recovery of ancient philosophy in the Renaissance* (Florence, 2008).

Hankinson, R. J., *Cause and explanation in ancient Greek thought* (Oxford, 2001).

Harrison, C. W., 'The ancient atomists and English literature of the seventeenth century', *Harvard Studies in Classical Philology*, 45 (1934), 1–74.

Harrison, P., *'Religion' and the religions in the English enlightenment* (Cambridge, 1990).

*The Bible, Protestantism, and the rise of natural science* (Cambridge, 1998).

'The influence of Cartesian cosmology in England', in *Descartes' natural philosophy*, eds. S. Gaukroger, J. Schuster, and J. Sutton (London, 2000), 168–92.

Hartbecke, K., *Metaphysik und Naturphilosophie im 17. Jahruhundert. Francis Glissons Substanztheorie in ihrem ideengeschichtlichen Kontext* (Tübingen, 2006).

Hartnup, K., *'On the beliefs of the Greeks': Leo Allatios and popular orthodoxy* (Leiden, 2004).

Harwood, J., 'Introduction', in *The early essays and ethics of Robert Boyle*, ed. J. Harwood (Carbondale and Edwardsville, 1991), xv–lxix.

Haskell, F., *History and its images: art and the interpretation of the past* (New Haven, 1993).

Hasper, P. J., 'Aristotle's diagnosis of atomism', *Apeiron*, 39 (2006), 121–56.

Hatfield, G., 'Metaphysics and the new science', in *Reappraisals of the scientific revolution*, eds., D. C. Lindberg and R. S. Westman (Cambridge, 1990), 93–166.

Hatzimichali, M., *Potamo of Alexandria and the emergence of eclecticism in late Hellenistic philosophy* (Cambridge, 2011).

Haugen, K. L., 'Transformation in the trinity doctrine in English scholarship: from the history of beliefs to the history of texts', *Archiv für Religionsgeschichte* 3 (2001), 149–161.

*Richard Bentley: poetry and enlightenment* (Cambridge [MA], 2011).

'Hebrew poetry transformed, or, scholarship invincible between Renaissance and Enlightenment', *JWCI*, 75 (2012), 1–29.

Hazard, P. *La Crise de la conscience européenne* (Paris, 1935) [=*The European mind (1680–1715)*, trans. J. Lewis May (London, 1953)].

Hedley, D., *Coleridge, philosophy and religion: aids to reflection and the mirror of spirit* (Cambridge, 2000).

Heller, H. J., *The seventeenth century Hebrew book: an abridged thesaurus* (Leiden, 2011).

Henderson, F., 'Unpublished material from the memodrandum book of Robert Hooke, Guildhall Library MS 1758', *NRRS*, 61 (2007), 129–75.

Heninger, S. K., *Touches of sweet harmony: Pythagorean cosmology and Renaissance poetics* (Huntington, 1974).

'Some Renaissance versions of the Pythagorean tetrad', *Studies in the Renaissance*, 8 (1961), 7–35.

Henry, J., 'Atomism and eschatology: Catholicism and natural philosophy in the Interregnum', *BJHS*, 15 (1982), 211–39.

'Occult qualities and the experimental philosophy: active principles in pre-Newtonian matter theory', *History of Science*, 24 (1986), 335–81.

'Medicine and pneumatology: Henry More, Richard Baxter, and Francis Glisson's *Treatise on the energetic nature of substance*', *Medical History*, 31 (1987).

'Henry More versus Robert Boyle: the spirit of nature and the nature of providence', in *Henry More: tercentenary studies*, ed. S. Hutton (Dordrecht, 1990), 55–76.

'Sir Kenelm Digby, recusant philosopher', in *Insiders and outsiders in seventeenth-century philosophy*, eds. G. A. J. Rogers, T. Sorell, and J. Kraye (London, 2010), 43–75.

Herklotz, I., *Die Academia Basiliana: griechische Philologie, Kirchengeschichte und Unionsbemühungen im Rom der Barberini* (Rome, 2008).

Hessayon, A., *'Gold tried in the fire': the prophet TheaurauJohn Tany and the English revolution* (Aldershot, 2007).

Hesse, M. B., 'Hooke's philosophical algebra', *Isis*, 57 (1966), 67–83.

Heyd, M., *'Be Sober and Reasonable': the critique of enthusiasm in the seventeenth and early eighteenth centuries* (Leiden, 1995).

Hill, C., *The experience of defeat: Milton and some contemporaries* (New York, 1984).

Hill, J., and Milton, J. R., 'The Epitome (*Abrégé*) of Locke's Essay', in *The philosophy of John Locke: new perspectives*, ed. P. R. Anstey (London, 2003), 3–25.

Hillar, M., *From logos to trinity: the evolution of religious beliefs from Pythagoras to Tertullian* (Cambridge, 2012).

Hirai, H., 'Le concept de semence de Pierre Gassendi entre les théories de la matière et les sciences de la vie au XVIIᵉ siècle', *Medicina nei Secoli*, 15 (2003), 205–26.

*Le concept de semence dans les théories de la matière à la Renaissance: De Marsile Ficin à Pierre Gassendi* (Turnhout, 2005).

'Atomes vivants, origine de l'âme et génération spontanée chez Daniel Sennert,' *Bruniana & Campanelliana*, 13 (2007), 477–95.

'The invisible hand of God in seeds: Jacob Schegk's theory of plastic faculty', *ESM*, 12 (2007), 377–404.

'Lecture néoplatonicienne d'Hippocrate chez Fernel, Cardan et Gemma', in *Pratique et pensée médicales à la Renaissance*, ed. J. Vons (Paris, 2009), 241–56.

*Medical humanism and natural philosophy: Renaissance debates on matter, life and the soul* (Leiden, 2011).

'Lipsius on the world-soul between Roman cosmic theology and Renaissance "prisca theologia"', in *Justus Lipsius and Natural Philosophy*, eds. H. Hirai and J. Papy (Brussels, 2011), 63–79.

Hochstrasser, T. J., *Natural law theories in the early enlightenment* (Cambridge, 2000).

Hofer, A., 'The old man as Christ in Justin's "Dialogue with Trypho"', *Vigiliae Christianae*, 57 (2003), 1–21.

Hofmann, M., *Theologie, Dogma und Dogmenentwicklung im theologischen Werk Denis Petau's* (Frankfurt am Main, 1976).

Holt, P. M., 'The treatment of Arab history by Prideaux, Ockley and Sale', in *Historians of the middle east*, eds. B. Lewis and P. M. Holt (London, 1962), 290–302.

  *A seventeenth-century defender of Islam: Henry Stubbe (1632–76) and his book* (London, 1972).

Holzhey, H., 'Der Philosoph im 17. Jahruhundert', in *Grundriss der Greschichte der Philosophie begründet von Friedrich Ueberweg. Die Philosophie des 17. Jahrhunderts. Band 1: Allgemeine Themen. Iberische Halbinsel/Italien*, ed. J.-P. Schobinger (Basel, 1998), 3–30.

Hopfner, T., *Orient und griechische Philosophie* (Leipzig, 1925).

Horbury, W., 'Spencer, John', *ODNB*.

  'John Spencer (1630–93) and Hebrew study', *Letter of the Corpus Association*, 78 (1999), 12–23.

Housman, A. E., 'Introduction', in Manilius, *Astronomicon*, ed. A. E. Housman (5 vols, Cambridge, 1937).

Howell, K. H., 'Natural knowledge and textual meaning in Augustine's interpretation of Genesis: the three functions of natural philosophy', in *Nature and scripture in the Abrahamic religions*, eds. J. M. van der Meer and S. Mandelbrote (2 vols, Leiden, 2008), I, 117–145.

Hughes, A., 'Popular presbyterianism in the 1640s and 1650s: the cases of Thomas Edwards and Thomas Hall', in *England's long Reformation, 1500–1800*, ed. N. Tyacke (London, 1998), 235–59.

  'Thomas Edwards's *Gangraena* and heresiological traditions', in *Heresy, literature and politics in early modern English culture*, eds. D. Loewenstein and J. Marshall (Cambridge, 2006), 137–59.

  *Gangraena and the struggle for the English Revolution* (Oxford, 2004).

Hughes, J. T., *Thomas Willis, 1621–1675: his life and work* (London, 1991).

Hull, F., 'John Marsham, a forgotten antiquary', *Archaelogia Cantiana*, 83 (1968), 49–54.

Hunt, R. W., 'Introduction', in H. O. Coxe, *Bodleian Library Quarto Catalogues II: Laudian Manuscripts … reprinted from the edition of 1858–1885 …* (Oxford, 1973).

Hunter, I., *Rival enlightenments: civil and metaphysical philosophy in early modern Germany* (Cambridge, 2001).

  'The university philosopher in early modern Germany', in *The philosopher in early modern Europe*, eds., C. Condren, S. Gaukroger, and I. Hunter (Cambridge, 2006), 35–65.

Hunter, M., *Science and society in Restoration England* (Cambridge, 1981).

  'Ancients, moderns, philologists, and scientists', *Annals of Science*, 39 (1982), 187–92.

  *Establishing the new science: the experience of the early Royal Society* (Woodbridge, 1989).

  'Latitudinarianism and the "ideology" of the early Royal Society: Thomas Sprat's *History of the Royal Society* (1667) reconsidered', in *Philosophy, science, and religion in England, 1640–1700*, eds. R. Kroll, R. Ashcraft, and P. Zagorin (Cambridge, 1992), 199–229.

*The Royal Society and its fellows, 1660–1700: the morphology of an early scientific institution* (2nd edn, Stanford in the Vale, 1994).

*Science and the shape of orthodoxy: intellectual change in late seventeenth-century Britain* (Woodbridge, 1995).

*Robert Boyle (1627–91): scrupulosity and science* (Woodbridge, 2000).

*The Boyle papers: understanding the manuscripts of Robert Boyle* (Aldershot, 2007).

'Robert Boyle and the early Royal Society: a reciprocal exchange in the making of Baconian science', *BJHS*, 40 (2007), 1–23.

*Boyle: between God and science* (New Haven, 2009).

'Robert Boyle's early intellectual evolution: A reappraisal', *Intellectual History Review*, 25 (2015), 5–19.

ed., *Robert Boyle by himself and his friends* (London, 1994).

ed., *Robert Boyle reconsidered*, ed. M. Hunter (Cambridge, 1994).

and Davis, E. B., 'The making of Robert Boyle's *Free enquiry into the vulgarly receiv'd notion of nature*', in *The Boyle papers: understanding the manuscripts of Robert Boyle* (Aldershot, 2007), 219–76.

Hutton, S., 'The neoplatonic roots of Arianism: Ralph Cudworth and Theophilus Gale', in *Socinianism and its role in the culture of the XVIth to XVIIIth Centuries*, ed. L. Szczucki (Warsaw, 1983), 139–45.

'Reason and revelation in the Cambridge Platonists, and their reception of Spinoza', in *Spinoza in der Frühzeit seiner Religiösen Wirkung*, eds. K. Gründer and W. Schmidt-Biggemann (Heidelberg, 1984), 181–200.

'Henry More and Jacob Boehme', in *Henry More: tercentenary studies*, ed. S. Hutton (Dordrecht, 1990), 158–71.

'Edward Stillingfleet, Henry More, and the decline of *Moses Atticus*: a note on seventeenth-century Anglican apologetics', in *Philosophy, science, and religion in England, 1640–1700*, eds., R. Kroll, R. Ashcraft, and P. Zagorin (Cambridge, 1992), 68–84.

'Science, philosophy, and atheism: Edward Stillingfleet's defence of religion', in *Scepticism and irreligion in the seventeenth and eighteenth centuries*, eds., R. H. Popkin and A. Vanderjagt (Leiden, 1993), 102–21.

'Henry More and Anne Conway on preexistence and universal salvation', in *'Mind senior to the world': Stoicismo e origenismo nella filosofia platonica del Seicento inglese*, ed. M. Baldi (Milan, 1996), 113–26.

'Platonism and the trinity: Anne Conway, Henry More and Christoph Sand', in *Socinianism and Arminianism: antitrinitarians, Calvinists and cultural exchange in seventeenth-century Europe*, eds., M. Mulsow and J. Rohls (Leiden, 2005), 209–24.

'Henry More, Anne Conway and the Kabbalah: a cure for the Kabbalistic nightmare', in *Judaeo-Christian intellectual culture in the seventeenth century*, ed. A. P. Coudert (Leiden, 1999), 27–42.

'Aristotle and the Cambridge Platonists: the case of Cudworth', in *Philosophy in the sixteenth and seventeenth centuries: conversations with Aristotle*, eds., C. Blackwell and S. Kusukawa (Aldershot, 1999), 337–49.

'The Cambridge Platonists', in *A companion to early modern philosophy*, ed. S. Nadler (London, 2002), 308–19.

'Smith, John', *ODNB*.

'Iconisms, enthusiasm, and Origen: Henry More reads the Bible', in *Scripture and scholarship in early modern England*, eds., A. Hessayon and N. Keene (Aldershot, 2006), 192–207.

Idel, M., 'The magical and neoplatonic interpretations of the Kabbalah in the Renaissance', in *Jewish thought in the sixteenth century*, ed. B. D. Cooperman (Cambridge [MA], 1983), 186–242.

'Jewish Kabbalah and Platonism in the Middle Ages and Renaissance', in *Neoplatonism and Jewish thought*, ed. L. E. Goodman (Albany, 1992), 319–51.

'Prisca theologia in Marsilio Ficino and some Jewish treatments', in *Marsilio Ficino: his theology, his philosophy, his legacy*, eds., M. J. B. Allen and V. Rees (Leiden, 2002), 137–58.

'Jewish thinkers versus Christian Kabbalah', in *Christliche Kabbala*, ed. W. Schmidt-Biggemann (Ostfildern, 2003), 49–65.

'Kabbalah, Platonism and prisca theologia: the case of R. Menasseh Ben Israel', in *Menasseh ben Israel and his world* (Leiden, 1989), 207–19.

Iliffe, R., 'Isaac Newton: Lucatello Professor of mathematics', in *Science incarnate: historical embodiments of natural knowledge*, eds., C. Lawrence and S. Shapin (Chicago, 1998), 121–55.

Isler, H., *Thomas Willis, 1621–1675: doctor and scientist* (New York, 1968 [German original=1965]).

Israel, J. I., 'Philosophy, history of philosophy, and *l'histoire de l'esprit humain*: a historiographical question and problem for philosophers', in *Teaching new histories of philosophy*, ed. J. B. Schneewind (Princeton, 2004), 329–344.

*Enlightenment contested: philosophy, modernity, and the emancipation of man, 1670–1752* (Oxford, 2006).

Ito, Y., 'Hooke's cyclic theory of the earth in the context of seventeenth century England', *BJHS*, 21 (1988), 295–314.

Iversen, E., *The myth of Egypt and its hieroglyphs in European tradition* (Princeton [NJ], 1993 [1st edn=Copenhagen, 1961]).

'Egypt in classical antiquity. A résumé', in *Hommages à Jean Leclant*, eds., C. Berger, G. Clerc, and N. Grimal (Cairo, 1994), 295–305.

Jacob, A., 'Henry More's *Psychodia Platonica* and its Relationship to Marsilio Ficino's *Theologia Platonica*', *JHI*, 44 (1985), 503–22.

*De naturae natura: a study of idealistic conceptions of nature and the unconscious* (Stuttgart, 1991).

'Introduction', in Henry More, *Manual of metaphysics*, ed. and trans. A. Jacob, (Hildesheim, 1995), i–lxxvi.

'The spirit of nature as "Hylarchic" principle of the universe', in Henry More, *Manual of metaphysics*, ed. and trans. A. Jacob, (Hildesheim, 1995), ii, i–xlix.

Jacob, J. R., *Robert Boyle and the English revolution* (London, 1977).

'Boyle's atomism and the Restoration assault on pagan naturalism', *Social Studies of Science*, 8 (1978), 211–33

*Hebry Stubbe, radical Protestantism and the early enlightenment* (Cambridge, 1983).

Jacob, M. C. and Lockwood, W. A., 'Political millenarianism and Burnet's *Sacred theory*', *Science Studies*, 2 (1972), 265–79.

Jacquart, D., 'Minima in twelfth-century medical texts from Salerno', in *Late medieval and early modern corpuscular matter theories*, eds., C. Lüthy, J. E. Murdoch, and W. Newman (Leiden, 2001), 39–56.

Jacquot J., and Jones, H. W., 'Introduction', in Hobbes, *Critique du De mundo de Thomas White*, eds., J. Jacquot and H. W. Jones (Paris, 1973), 9–102.

Jahn, M., 'A bibliographical history of John Woodward's *An essay toward a natural history of the earth*', *Journal of the Society of the Bibliography of Natural History*, 6 (1974), 181–213.

Janiak, A., *Newton as philosopher* (Cambridge, 2008).

Jardine, L., 'Dr Wilkins's boy wonders', *NRRS*, 58 (2004), 107–29.

Jardine, N., 'Galileo's road to truth and the demonstrative regress', *SHPS*, 7 (1976), 277–31.

    'Keeping order in the school of Padua', in *Method and order in Renaissance philosophy of nature: the Aristotle commentary tradition*, eds., D. A. Di Liscia, E. Kessler, and C. Methuen (Aldershot, 1997), 183–209.

Jaumann, H., ed., *Die europäische Gelehrtenrepublik im Zeitalter des Konfessionalismus* (Wiesbaden, 2001).

Jehasse, J., *Renaissance de la critique: l'essor de l'humanisme érudit de 1560 à 1614* (Saint Etienne, 1976).

Johns, A., 'Prudence and pedantry in early modern cosmology: the trade of Al Ross', *History of Science*, 35 (1997), 23–59.

Johnson, M. R., 'Was Gassendi an Epicurean?', *History of Philosophy Quarterly*, 20 (2003), 339–60.

Johnston, S. I., *Hekate soteira: a study of Hekate's role in the Chaldean oracles and related literature* (Atlanta, 1990).

Joly, B., 'Les references à la philosophie antique dans les débats sur l'alchimie au début du XVIIe siècle', in *Alchimie: Art, histoire et myths*, eds., D. Kahn and S. Matton (Paris/Milan, 1995), 671–90.

Jones, H., *The Epicurean tradition* (London, 1989).

Jones, M., *Why heaven kissed earth: the Christology of the puritan Reformed orthodox theologian, Thomas Goodwin (1600–1680)* (Göttingen, 2010).

Jones, R. F., *Ancients and moderns: a study of the rise of the scientific movement in seventeenth-century England* (2nd edn, Berkeley, 1961).

Jones, W. R., 'Brown, Thomas', *ODNB*.

de Jong, A., *Traditions of the Magi: Zoroastrianism in Greek and Latin literature* (Leiden, 1997).

de Jonge, H. J, 'The study of the New Testament', in *Leiden University in the seventeenth century*, eds., T. H. Lunsingh Scheurleer and G. H. M. Posthumus Meyjes (Leiden, 1975), 64–109.

    'The study of the New Testament in the Dutch universities, 1575–1700', in *History of Universities*, 1 (1981), 113–29.

    'Hugo Grotius: exegete du Nouveau Testament', in *The world of Hugo Grotius (1583–1645)* (Amsterdam, 1984), 176–93.

    'Grotius' View of the Gospels and the Evangelists', in *Hugo Grotius, theologian*, eds., H. J. M. Nellen and E. Rabbie (Leiden, 1994), 65–74.

Joost-Gaugier, C. L., *Pythagoras and Renaissance Europe: finding heaven* (Cambridge, 2009).

Jorink, E., *Reading the book of nature in the Dutch golden age, 1575–1715* (Leiden, 2010 [Dutch original=2006]).

Joy, L. S., *Gassendi the atomist: advocate of history in an age of science* (Cambridge, 1987).

'Epicureanism in Renaisance moral and natural philosophy', *JHI*, 53 (1992), 573–83.

Jue, J. K., *Heaven upon earth: Joseph Mede (1586–1638) and the legacy of millenarianism* (Dordrecht, 2006).

Jungkuntz, R., 'Fathers, heretics and Epicureans', *The Journal of Ecclesiastical History*, 17 (1966), 3–10.

Kaehler, S. A., 'Der Kampf zwischen Theologie und Philosophie, 1680–1702', in *Die Philipps-Universität zu Marburg, 1527–1927*, eds. H. Hermlink and S. A. Kaehler (Marburg, 1927), 299–331.

Kákosy, L., 'Plato and Egypt. The Egyptian tradition', in *Gedenkschrift István Hahn*, ed. G. Németh (Budapest, 1993), 25–8.

'Egypt in ancient Greek and Roman thought', in *Civilizations of the ancient near east*, eds., J. M. Sasson, J. Baines, G. Beckman, and K. S. Rubinson (New York, 1995), 3–14.

Kangro, H., 'Erklärungswert und Schwierigkeiten der Atomhypothese und ihrer Anwendung auf chemische Probleme in der ersten Hälfte des 17. Jahrhunderts', *Technikgeschichte*, 35 (1968), 14–36.

Kaplan, B., *'Divulging of Useful Truths in Physick': the medical agenda of Robert Boyle* (Baltimore, 1993).

Kaplan, Y., Méchoulan, H., and Popkin, R. H., eds., *Menasseh ben Israel and his world* (Leiden, 1989).

Kargon, R. H., 'Walter Charleton, Robert Boyle and the acceptance of Epicurean atomism in England', *Isis*, 55 (1964), 184–92.

'William Petty's mechanical philosophy', *Isis*, 56 (1965), 63–6.

'Newton, Barrow and the hypothetical physics', *Centaurus*, 11 (1966), 46–56.

*Atomism in England from Hariot to Newton* (Oxford, 1966).

Karrer, L., *Die Historisch-Positive Methode des Theologen Dionysius Petavius* (Munich, 1970).

Kassler, J. C., *The honourable Roger North (1651–1734): on life, morality, law and tradition* (Ashgate, 2009).

Katchen, A. L., *Christian Hebraists and Dutch rabbis: seventeenth century apologetics and the study of Maimonides' Mishneh Torah* (Cambridge [MA], 1984).

Katz, D. S., 'The Abendana brothers and the Christian Hebraists of seventeenth-century England', *Journal of Ecclesiastical History*, 40 (1989), 28–52.

Keblusek, M., 'The exile experience. Royalist and Anglican book culture in the Low Countries (1640–1660)', in *The bookshop of the world. The role of the Low Countries in the book-trade, 1473–1941*, eds., L. Hellinga, A. Duke, and J. Harskamp (Houten, 2001), 151–8.

'A tortoise in the shell: Royalist and Anglican experience of exile in the 1650s', in *Literatures of exile in the English Revolution and its aftermath, 1640–1690*, ed. P. Major (Aldershot, 2010), 79–91.

Keene, N., 'John Fell: education, erudition and the English Church in late seventeenth-century Oxford', *History of Universities*, 18 (2003), 62–101.

Kelley, D., *The descent of ideas: the history of intellectual history* (Aldershot, 2002).

Kenney, E. J., *The classical text: aspects of editing in the age of the printed book* (Berkeley, 1974).

Keseru, G., 'Religiones rationales in Transylvania', in *György Enyedi and central European Unitarianism*, eds., M. Balázs and G. Keserű (Budapest, 2000), 125–36.

Kessler, E., 'The intellective soul', in *The Cambridge history of Renaissance philosophy*, eds., C. B. Schmitt and Q. Skinner (Cambridge, 1988), 484–534.

'The transformation of Aristotelianism during the Renaissance', in *New perspectives on Renaissance thought*, eds., J. Henry and S. Hutton (London, 1990), 137–47.

and Lohr, C. H., and Sparn, W., eds., *Aristotelismus und Renaissance* (Wiesbaden, 1988).

Kibre, P., *Hippocrates Latinus: repertorium of Hippocratic writings in the Latin Middle Ages* (New York, 1985).

Kidd, C., *Before nationalism: ethnicity and nationhood in the Atlantic world, 1600–1800* (Cambridge, 1999).

Killeen, K., *Biblical scholarship, science and politics in early modern England: Thomas Browne and the thorny place of knowledge* (Farnham, 2009).

King, H., 'Hodges, Nathaniel', *ODNB*.

King, L. S., *The road to medical Enlightenment, 1650–1695* (New York, 1970).

Kirsop, W., 'Prolégomènes à une étude de la publication et de la diffusion des *Opera omnia* de Gassendi', in *Materia actuosa: antiquité, âge classique, lumières* (Paris, 2000), 207–15.

Klein, D., 'Muslimischer Antitrinitarismus im lutherischen Rostock. Zacharias Grapius der Jüngere und die Epistola theologica des Ahmed ibn Abdallāh', in *Wahrnehmung des Islam zwischen Reformation und Aufklärung*, eds., D. Klein and B. Platow (Munich, 2008), 41–60.

Klempt, A., *Die Säkularisierung der universalhistorischen Auffassung im 16. Und 17. Jahrhundert* (Berlin, 1960).

Klutstein, I., 'Marsile Ficin et les "Oracles Chaldaïques"', in *Marsilio Ficino e il ritorno di Platone*, ed. G. C. Garfagnini (Florence, 1976), 331–8.

*Marsilio Ficino et la théologie ancienne: Oralces Chaldaïques, Hymnes Orphiques, Hymnes de Proclus* (Florence, 1987).

Knijff, P., Visser, S. J., and Visser, P., *Bibliographia Sociniana: a bibliographical reference tool for the study of Dutch Socinianism and antitrinitarianism* (Amsterdam, 2004).

Knoepfler, D., *La Vie de Ménédème d'Érétrie de Diogène Laërce: contribution à l'histoire et à la critique du texte des Vies des Philosophes* (Basel, 1991).

Knoespel, K. J., 'Interpretative strategies in Newton's *Theologiae gentilis origines philosophicae*', in *Newton and religion: context, nature and influence*, eds., J. Force and R. H. Popkin (Dordrecht, 1999), 179–202.

Kollerstrom, N., 'The hollow world of Edmond Halley', *Journal for the History of Astronomy*, 23 (1992), 185–92.

Korsten, F., *Roger North (1651–1734) virtuoso and essayist* (Amsterdam and Maarssen, 1981).

'Thomas Baker's *Reflections upon learning*', in *Studies in seventeenth century English literature, history and bibliography*, eds., G. A. M. Janssens and F. G. A. M. Aarts (Amsterdam, 1984), 133–48.

*A catalogue of the library of Thomas Baker* (Cambridge, 1990).

Koyré, A., *From the closed world to the infinite universe* (Baltimore, 1957).

Kraye, J., 'The pseudo-Aristotelian *Theology* in sixteenth- and seventeenth-century Europe', in *Pseudo- Aristotle in the middle ages*, eds., J. Kraye, W. F. Ryan, and C. B. Schmitt (London, 1986), 265–86.

'Daniel Heinsius and the author of *De mundo*', in *The uses of Greek and Latin: historical essays*, eds., A.C. Dionissoti, A. Grafton, and J. Kraye (London, 1988), 171–97.

'Aristotle's God and the authenticity of "De mundo": an early modern controversy', *JHP*, 28 (1990), 339–58.

'"Ethnicorum omnium sanctissimus": Marcus Aurelius and his *Meditations* from Xylander to Diderot', in *Humanism and early modern philosophy*, eds., J. Kraye and M. Stone (London, 2000), 107–34.

'Ficino in the firing line: a renaissance neoplatonist and his critics', in *Marsilio Ficino: his theology, his philosophy, his legacy*, eds., M. J. B. Allen and V. Rees (Leiden, 2002), 377–97.

'The legacy of ancient philosophy', in *The Cambridge companion to Greek and Roman philosophy*, ed. D. Sedley (Cambridge, 2003), 323–52.

'Philology, moral philosophy and religion in Thomas Gataker's edition of Marcus Aurelius's *Meditations* (1652)', in *Ethik—Wissenschaft oder Lebenskunst? Modelle der Normenbegründung von der Antike bis zur Frühen Neuzeit*, eds., S. Ebbersmeyer and E. Kessler (Münster, 2007), 293–307.

'Pagan philosophy and patristics in Erasmus and his contemporaries', *Erasmus of Rotterdam Society Yearbook*, 31 (2011), 33–60.

Ryan, W. F., and Schmitt, C. B., eds., *Pseudo-Aristotle in the Middle Ages* (London, 1986).

Kristeller, P. O., *The philosophy of Marsilio Ficino* (New York, 1943).

*Aristotelismo e sincretismo nel pensiero di Pietro Pomponazzi* (Padua, 1983).

Kroll, R., 'The question of Locke's relation to Gassendi', *JHI*, 45 (1984), 339–59.

*The material word: literate culture in the Restoration and early eighteenth century* (Baltimore, 1991).

Kusukawa, S., 'Bacon's classification of knowledge', in *The Cambridge companion to Bacon,* ed. M. Peltonen (Cambridge, 1996), 47–74.

Labib-Rahman, L., 'Sir Jean Chardin, the great traveller (1642–1712/13)', *Proceedings of the Huguenot Society*, 23 (1977–82), 309–18.

Lagrée, J., 'Lumière naturelle et notions communes: Herbert de Cherbury et Culverwell', in *'Mind senior to the world': stoicismo e origenismo nella filosofia platonica del Seicento inglese*, ed. M. Baldi (Milan, 1996), 35–54.

Lake, P., 'The Laudians and the argument from authority', in *Court, country and culture: essays on early modern British history in honor of Perez Zagorin*, eds., B. Y. Kunze and D. D. Brautigam (New York, 1992), 149–75.

Laplanche, F., *L'écriture, le sacré et l'histoire: érudits et politiques Protestants devant la Bible en France au XVIIe siècle* (Amsterdam, 1986).

'Grotius et les religions du paganisme dans les *Annotationes in Vetus Testamentum*', in *Hugo Grotius, Theologian*, eds., H. J. M. Nellen and E. Rabbie (Leiden, 1994), 53–64.

Larminie, V., 'Allix, Peter [Pierre]', *ODNB*.

Lasswitz, K., *Geschichte der Atomistik vom Mittelalter bis Newton* (2 vols, Hamburg and Leipzig, 1890).

Laursen, J. C., 'Temporizing after Bayle: Isaac de Beausobre and the Manicheans', in *The Berlin refuge 1680–1780: learning and science in European context*, eds., S. Pot, M. Mulsow, and L. Danneberg (Leiden, 2003), 89–113.

Laven, H., *The 'Acta Eruditorum' under the editorship of Otto Mencke: the history of an international learned journal between 1682 and 1707*, trans. L. Richards, (Amsterdam, 1990 [Dutch orig.=1986]).

Le Gall, J.-M., *Le mythe de Saint Denis: entre Renaissance et Révolution* (Seyssel, 2007).

Lehmann-Brauns, S., *Wisheit in der Weltgeschichte: Philosophiegeschichte zwischen Barock und Aufklärung* (Tübingen, 2004).

Lehnus, L., 'Callimaco redivivo tra Th. Stanley e R. Bentley', *Eikasmos*, 2 (1991), 285–309.

Leighton, C. D. A., 'The religion of the non-jurors and the early British enlightenment: a study of Henry Dodwell', in *History of European Ideas*, 28 (2002), 247–62.

'Ancienneté among the non-jurors: a study of Henry Dodwell', *History of European Ideas*, 31 (2005), 1–16.

Leijenhorst, C., 'Franceso Patrizi's Hermetic philosophy', in *Gnosis and Hermeticism from antiquity to modern times*, eds., R. van den Broek and W. J. Hanegraaff (Albany, 1998), 125–46.

*The mechanization of Aristotelianism: the late Aristotelian setting of Thomas Hobbes' natural philosophy* (Leiden, 2002).

Leng, T., *Benjamin Worlsey (1618–1677): trade, interest and the spirit in revolutionary England* (New York, 2008).

Lennox, J. G., 'The comparative study of animal development: William Harvey's Aristotelianism', in *The problem of animal generation in early modern philosophy*, ed. J. E. H. Smith (Cambridge, 2006), 21–46.

Leospo, E., *La Mensa Isiaca di Torino* (Leiden, 1978).

Leslie, M., 'The spiritual husbandry of John Beale', in *Culture and cultivation in early modern England*, eds., M. Leslie and T. Raylor (Leicester, 1992), 151–72.

Lettinga, N., 'Covenant theology turned upside down: Henry Hammond and Caroline Anglican moralism', *Sixteenth-Century Journal*, 24 (1993), 653–69.

Levine, J., *Dr Woodward's shield: history, science, and satire in Augustan England* (Berkeley, 1977).

*The Battle of the Books: history and literature in the Augustan Age* (Ithaca [NY], 1991).

*Between the ancients and the moderns: Baroque culture in Restoration England* (London, 1999).

'Latitudinarians, neoplatonists, and the ancient wisdom', in *Philosophy, science, and religion in England, 1640–1700*, eds., R. Kroll, R. Ashcraft, and P. Zagorin (Cambridge, 1992), 85–108.

'Deists and Anglicans: the ancient wisdom and the idea of progress', in *The margins of orthodoxy: heterodox writing and cultural response, 1660–1750*, ed. R. D. Lund (Cambridge, 1995), 219–40.

*Between the ancients and the moderns: Baroque culture in Restoration England* (New Haven, 1999).

Levitin, D., 'Reconsidering John Sergeant's attacks on Locke's *Essay*', *Intellectual History Review*, 20 (2010), 457–77.

'Matthew Tindal's *Rights of the Christian Church* (1706) and the church-state relationship', *HJ*, 45 (2011), 717–40.

'From sacred history to the history of religion: paganism, Judaism, and Christianity in European historiography from Reformation to "enlightenment"', *HJ*, 55 (2012), 1117–60.

'John Spencer's *De legibus Hebraeorum* and "enlightened" sacred history: a new interpretation', *JWCI*, 76 (2013), 49–92.

'Edmund Halley and the eternity of the world revisited', *NRRS*, 67 (2013), 315–29.

'Rethinking English physico-theology: Samuel Parker's *Tentamina de Deo* (1665)', *ESM*, 19 (2014), 28–75.

'"Made up from many experimentall notions". The Society of Apothecaries, medical humanism, and the rhetoric of experience in 1630s London', *Journal of the History of Medicine and Allied Sciences* (2015).

'Egyptology, the limits of antiquarianism, and the origins of conjectural history, *c.* 1680–1740: new sources and perspectives', *History of European Ideas* (2015).

'The historical assumptions behind the General Scholium: a non-metaphysical Newton', in *Newton's General Scholium after 300 years*, eds., S. Ducheyne, S. Mandelbrote and S. Snobelen (forthcoming).

'Newton and scholastic philosophy', *British Journal for the History of Science* (forthcoming, 2015).

Lewis, E., 'Walter Charleton and early modern eclecticism', *JHI*, 62 (2001), 651–64.

Lewis, R., '"The Best Mnemonicall Expedient". John Beale's art of memory and its uses', *The Seventeenth Century*, 20 (2005), 113–44.

'Of "Origenian Platonisme": Joseph Glanvill on the pre-existence of souls', *Huntington Library Quarterly*, 69 (2006), 267–300.

*Language, mind and nature: artificial languages in England from Bacon to Locke* (Cambridge, 2007).

*William Petty on the order of nature: an unpublished manuscript treatise* (Temple [AR], 2012).

Ligota, C., 'Der apologetische Rahmen der Mythendeutung im Frankreich des 17. Jahrhunderts (P. D. Huet)', *Mythographie der frühen Neuzeit: ihre Anwendung in den Künsten*, ed. W. Killy (Wiesbaden, 1984), 148–61.

'Annius of Viterbo and historical method', *JWCI*, 50 (1987), 44–56.

and Quantin, J.-L., 'Introduction', in *History of scholarship*, eds. C. Ligota and J.-L. Quantin (Oxford, 2006), 1–38.

Lim, P., *Mystery unveiled: the crisis of the trinity in early modern England* (Oxford, 2012).

Lloyd Jones, G., *The discovery of Hebrew in Tudor England: a third language* (Manchester, 1983).

Lohr, C. H., *Latin Aristotle commentaries, II: Renaissance authors* (Florence, 1988).

'Metaphysics', in *The Cambridge history of Renaissance philosophy*, eds., C. B. Schmitt and Q. Skinner (Cambridge, 1988), 537–638.

'The sixteenth-century transformation of the Aristotelian natural philosophy', in *Aristotelismus und Renaissance*, eds., E. Kesller, C. H. Lohr, and W. Sparn (Wiesbaden, 1988), 89–100.

'Renaissance Latin translations of the Greek commentaries on Aristotle', in *Humanism and early modern philosophy*, eds., J. Kraye and M. W. F. Stone (London, 2000), 24–40.

Lolordo, A., *Pierre Gassendi and the birth of early modern philosophy* (Cambridge, 2007).

Long, P., 'Humanism and science', in *Renaissance humanism: foundations, forms and legacy*, ed. A. Rabil (3 vols, Philadelphia, 1988), iii, 468–512.

Longo, M., 'A "critical" history of philosophy and the early enlightenment: Johann Jacob Brucker', in Santinello ii, 477–578.

Longrigg, J., *Greek Rational medicine: philosophy and medicine from Alcmaeon to the Alexandrians* (London, 1993).

Lonie, I. M., 'The "Paris Hippocratics": teaching and research in Paris in the second half of the sixteenth century', in *The medical Renaissance of the sixteenth century*, eds., A. Wear, R. K. French, and I. M. Lonie (Cambridge, 1985), 155–72.

Loop, J., 'Johann Heinrich Hottinger (1620–1667) and the "Historia Orientalis"', *Church History and Religious Culture*, 88 (2008), 169–203.

Lorimer, W.L., *The text tradition of Pseudo-Aristotle 'De mundo'* (Oxford, 1924).

Loveman, K., 'Samuel Pepys and "Discourses touching religion" under James II', *English Historical Review*, 127 (2012), 46–82.

de Lubac, H., *Exégèse médiévale, les quatre sens de l'écriture* (2 vols, Paris, 1959–61).

Lüthy, C., 'Atomism, Lynceus, and the fate of 17th-century microscopy', *ESM*, 1 (1996), 1–27.

'Thoughts and circumstances of Sébastien Basson. Analysis, micro-history, questions', *ESM*, 2 (1997), 1–73.

'What to do with seventeenth-century natural philosophy? A taxonomic problem', *Perspectives on Science*, 8 (2000), 164–95.

'The fourfold Democritus on the stage of early modern science', *Isis*, 91 (2000), 443–79.

'An Aristotelian watchdog as avant-garde physicist: Julius Caesar Scaliger', *The Monist*, 84 (2001), 542–61.

'Atoms and corpuscles. Kurd Lasswitz and the historiography of atomism', *Intellectual News*, 11/12 (2003), 7–16.

*David Gorlaeus (1591–1612): an enigmatic figure in the history of philosophy and science* (Amsterdam, 2013).

and Newman, W. R., '"Matter" and "form": by way of a preface', *ESM*, 2 (1997), 215–26.

and Murdoch, J. E., and Newman, W. R., eds., *Late medieval and early modern corpuscular matter theories* (Leiden, 2001).

and Murdoch, J. E., and Newman, W. R., 'Introduction: corpuscles, atoms, particles and minima', in *Late medieval and early modern corpuscular matter theories*, eds., C. Lüthy, J. E. Murdoch, and W. Newman (Leiden, 2001), 1–38.

Luxon, T. H., *Literal figures: Puritan allegory and the Reformation crisis in representation* (Chicago, 1995).

Lyon, G. B., 'Baudouin, Flacius, and the plan for the Magdeburg Centuries', *JHI*, 64 (2003), 253–72.

Maber, R. G., *Publishing in the republic of letters: the Ménage-Graevius-Wetestein correspondence, 1679–1692* (Amsterdam, 2005).

Maclean, I., *Interpretation and meaning in the Renaissance: the case of law* (Cambridge, 1992).

'Foucault's Renaissance episteme: an Aristotelian counterblast', *JHI*, 59 (1998), 149–66.
*Logic, signs and nature in the Renaissance: the case of learned medicine* (Cambridge, 2002).
Madan, F., *Oxford books* (3 vols, Oxford, 1895–1931).
Mahoney, E. P., 'Neoplatonism, the Greek commentators, and Renaissance Aristotelianism', in *Neoplatonism and Christian thought*, ed. D. J. O'Meara (Albany, 1982), 169–77, 264–82.
Mahoney, M. S., 'Barrow's mathematics: between ancients and moderns', in *Before Newton: the life and times of Isaac Barrow*, ed. M. Feingold (Cambridge, 1990), 179–249.
Mayo, T., *Epicurus in England (1650–1725)* (Dallas, 1934).
Majercik, R., 'Introduction', in *The Chaldean Oracles: text, translation, and commentary by Ruth Majercik* (Leiden, 1989), 1–45.
Malcolm, N., 'Biographical register', in *Hobbes Correspondence*, II.
*Aspects of Hobbes* (Oxford, 2002).
'Private and public knowledge: Kircher, esotericism, and the republic of letters', in *Athanasius Kircher: the last man who knew everything*, ed. P. Findlen (New York and London, 2004), 297–309.
'The library of Henry Oldenburg', *Electronic British Library Journal* (2005), article 7.
'Jean Bodin and the authorship of the *Colloquium Heptaplomeres*', *JWCI*, 69 (2006), 95–150.
'The name and nature of *Leviathan*: political symbolism and biblical exegesis', *IHR*, 17 (2007), 21–39.
'The 1649 English Translation of the Koran: its Origins and Significance', *JWCI*, 75, (2012), 261–95.
'General introduction', in Thomas Hobbes, *Leviathan*, ed. N. Malcolm (3 vols, Oxford, 2012), I, 1–195.
Malet, A., 'Isaac Barrow on the mathematization of nature: theological voluntarism and the rise of geometrical optics', *JHI*, 58 (1997), 265–87.
Malusa, L., 'Renaissance antecedents to the historiography of philosophy', in Santinello I, 3–65.
'The first general histories of philosophy in England and the Low Countries', in Santinello I, 163–71.
Mancosu, P., *Philosophy of mathematics and mathematical practice in the seventeenth century* (Oxford, 1996).
Mandelbrote, S., '"A duty of the greatest moment": Isaac Newton and the writing of biblical criticism', *BJHS*, 26 (1993), 281–302.
'Isaac Newton and Thomas Burnet: biblical criticism and the crisis of late seventeenth-century England', in *The books of nature and scripture*, eds. J. E. Force and R. H. Popkin (Dordrecht, 1994), 149–78.
*Footprints of the lion: Isaac Newton at work* (Cambridge, 2001).
'The authority of the Word: manuscript, print and the text of the Bible in seventeenth-century England', in *The uses of script and print, 1300–1700*, eds. J. Crick and A. Walsham (Cambridge, 2004), 135–56.
'William Petty and Anne Green: medical and political reform in Commonwealth Oxford', in *The practice of reform in health, medicine and science, 1500–2000* (Aldershot, 2005), 125–49.

'Beaumont, John', *ODNB*.

'Burnet, Thomas', *ODNB*.

'Clerke, Gilbert', *ODNB*.

'Ray, John', *ODNB*.

'"Then this nothing can be plainer": Isaac Newton reads the fathers', in *Die Patristik in der frühen Neuzeit*, eds., G. Frank, T. Leinkauf, and M. Wried (Stuttgart, 2006), 277–97.

'Biblical hermeneutics and the sciences, 1700–1900: an overview', in *Nature and scripture in the Abrahamic religions*, eds., J. van der Meer and S. Mandelbrote (2 vols, Leiden, 2008), II, 3–40.

'Origen against Jerome in early modern Europe', in *Patristic tradition and intellectual paradigms in the 17th century*, eds., S.-P. Bergjan and K. Pollmann (Tübingen, 2010), 106–35.

'Isaac Vossius and the Septuagint', in *Isaac Vossius (1618–1689): between science and scholarship*, eds., E. Jorink and D. van Miert (Leiden, 2012), 85–118.

Mander, W. J., *The philosophy of John Norris* (Oxford, 2008).

Manning, G., 'Three biased reminders about hylomorphism in early modern science and philosophy', in *Matter and form in early modern science and philosophy*, ed. G. Manning (Leiden, 2012), 1–32.

Manuel, F. E., *Isaac Newton, historian* (Cambridge, 1963).

Manzo, S. A., 'Francis Bacon and atomism: a reappraisal', in *Late medieval and early modern corpuscular matter theories*, eds., C. Lüthy, J. E. Murdoch, and W. Newman (Leiden, 2001), 209–44.

Marshall, J., 'The ecclesiology of the latitude-men, 1660–1689: Stillingfleet, Tillotson and "Hobbism"', *Journal of Ecclesiastical History*, 26 (1985), 407–27.

*John Locke: resistance, religion and responsibility* (Cambridge, 1994).

'Huguenot thought after the revocation of the Edict of Nantes: toleration, "Socinianism", integration and Locke', in *From strangers to citizens: the integration of immigrant communities in Britain, Ireland and Colonial America, 1550–1750* (Portland [OR], 2001), 383–96.

*John Locke, toleration, and early enlightenment culture* (Cambridge, 2006).

Marshall, P. J., 'Thomas Hyde: stupor mundi', *The Hakluyt Society* (London, 1982), 1–11.

'Hyde, Thomas', *ODNB*.

Marshall, W., 'Tenison, Thomas', *ODNB*.

Martin, C., *Subverting Aristotle: religion, history and philosophy in early modern science* (Baltimore, 2014).

Mason, S., *Flavius Josephus on the Pharisees: a composition-critical study* (Leiden, 1991).

Mayor, J. E. B., and Scott, R. F., *Admissions to the college of St John the Evangelist* (Cambridge, 1882–93).

Mazzi, C., *Leone Allacci e la Palatina di Heidelberg* (Bologna, 1893).

McAdoo, H. R., *The spirit of Anglicanism: a survey of Anglican theological method in the seventeenth century* (London, 1965).

*Jeremy Taylor: Anglican theologian* (Keady, 1997).

McColley, G., 'The Ross-Wilkins controversy', *Annals of Science*, 3 (1938), 153–89.

McCracken, C. J., *Malebranche and British philosophy* (Oxford, 1983).

McDowell, N., *Poetry and allegiance in the English civil wars: Marvell and the cause of wit* (Oxford, 2008).

McGiffert, M., 'Henry Hammond and covenant theology', *Church History*, 74 (2005), 255–85.

McGowan, A., 'Tertullian and the "heretical" origins of the "orthodox" trinity', *Journal of Early Christian Studies*, 14 (2006), 437–57.

McGuire, J. E., 'Newton's "Principles of philosophy": an intended Preface for the 1704 *Optics* and a related draft fragment', *BJHS*, 5 (1970), 178–86.

and Rattansi, P. M., 'Newton and the "Pipes of Pan"', *NRRS*, 21 (1966), 108–43.

McKenzie, D. F., *The Cambridge University Press, 1696–1712: a bibliographical study* (2 vols, Cambridge, 1966).

McKitterick, D., *A history of Cambridge University Press* (3 vols, 1992–2004).

McLachlan, H. J., *The story of a nonconformist library* (Manchester, 1923).

*Socinianism in seventeenth-century England* (Oxford, 1951).

Meinel, C., 'Early seventeenth-century atomism. Theory, epistemology, and the insufficiency of experiment', *Isis*, 79 (1988), 68–103.

van Melsen, A. G. M., *From atomos to atom. The history of the concept of atom*, trans. H. J. Koren (New York, 1960 [1st Engl. edn=Pittsburgh, 1952; 1st Dutch edn=Amsterdam, 1949]).

Melton, F. T., *Sir Robert Clayton and the origins of English deposit banking, 1658–1685* (Cambridge, 1986).

de Menasce, J. P., 'Zoroastrian Pahlavi Writings', in *The Cambridge history of Iran. vol. III: the Seleucid, Parthian and Sasanian periods,* ed. E. Yarshater (2 vols, Cambridge, 1983, 2000), II, 1166–1195.

Mercier, R., 'English orientalists and mathematical astronomy', in *The 'Arabick' interest of the natural philosophers in the seventeenth-century England*, ed. G. A. Russell (Leiden, 1994), 158–214.

Merkel I., and Debus, A. G., eds., *Hermeticism and the Renaissance: intellectual history and the occult in early modern Europe* (Washington, 1988).

Messeri, M., *Causa e spiegazione: la fisica di Pierre Gassendi* (Milan, 1985).

Meynell, G. G., *Materials for a biography of Dr Thomas Sydenham* (Folkestone, 1988).

'Sydenham, Locke and Sydenham's *De peste sive febre pestilentiali*', *Medical History*, 36 (1993), 330–2.

'A database for John Locke's medical notebooks and medical reading', *Medical History*, 42 (1997), 473–86.

'Locke as pupil of Peter Stahl', *Locke Studies*, 1 (2001), 221–7.

'John Locke and the Preface to Thomas Sydenham's *Observationes medicae*', *Medical History*, 50 (2006), 93–110.

Michael, E., 'Daniel Sennert on matter and form. At the juncture of the old and the new', *ESM*, 2 (1997), 272–99.

'Sennert's sea change: atoms and causes', in *Late medieval and early modern corpuscular matter theories*, eds., C. Lüthy, J. E. Murdoch, and W. Newman (Leiden, 2001), 331–62.

and Michael, F. S., 'Gassendi on sensation and reflection: a non-Cartesian dualism', *History of European Ideas*, 9 (1988), 583–95.

Micheli, G., 'The history of philosophy in Germany in the second half of the seventeenth century', in Santinello I, 371–476.

van Miert, D., 'The limits of transconfessional contact in the Republic of Letters around 1600: Scaliger, Casaubon, and their Catholic correspondents', in *Between Scylla and Charybdis: learned letter writers navigating the reefs of religious and political controversy in early modern Europe*, eds., J. De Landtsheer and H. Nellen (Leiden, 2011), 367–408.

Mikkeli, H., *An Aristotelian response to Renaissance humanism: Jacopo Zabarella on the nature of the arts and sciencies* (Helsinki, 1992).

'The foundation of an autonomous natural philosophy: Zabarella on the classification of arts and sciences', in *Method and order in Renaissance philosophy of nature*, eds., D. A. Di Liscia, E. Kessler, and C. Methuen (Aldershot, 1998), 211–28.

*Hygiene in the early modern medical tradition* (Helsinki, 1999).

Miller, J., 'Innate ideas in Stoicism and Grotius', in *Grotius and the Stoa*, eds., H. W. Blom and L. C. Winkel (Assen, 2004), 157–76.

'Grotius and Stobaeus', *Grotiana*, 26–28 (2005–07), 104–26.

Miller, P., 'The "antiquarianisation" of Biblical scholarship and the London polyglot Bible (1653–57)', *JHI*, 62 (2001), 463–82.

'Taking paganism seriously: anthropology and antiquarianism in early seventeenth-century histories of religion', *Archiv für Religionsgeschichte*, 3 (2001), 183–209.

Milton, A., *Catholic and Reformed: The Roman and Protestant churches in English Protestant thought, 1600–1640* (Cambridge, 1995).

'The creation of Laudianism: a new approach', in *Politics, religion and popularity in early Stuart Britain*, eds. T. Cogswell, R. Cust, and P. Lake (Cambridge, 2002), 162–84.

*Laudian and royalist polemic in seventeenth-century England: the career and writings of Peter Heylyn* (Manchester, 2007).

Milton, J. R., 'Locke and Gassendi: a reappraisal', *in English philosophy in the age of Locke*, ed. M.A. Stewart (Oxford, 2000), 87–110.

Minton, G. E., 'Cave, William', *ODNB*.

Mitchell, J., 'Luther and Hobbes on the question: who was Moses, who was Christ?', *The Journal of Politics*, 53 (1991), 676–700.

Mittelstrass, J., 'Nature and science in the Renaissance', *in Metaphysics and the philosophy of science in the seventeenth and eighteenth centuries*, ed. R. S. Woolhouse (Dordrecht, 1988), 17–44.

Momigliano, A., *Alien wisdom: the limits of Hellenization* (Cambridge, 1971).

*On pagans, Jews and Christians* (Middletown [CT], 1987).

Moody, M. E., 'A man of a thousand: the reputation and character of Henry Ainsworth, 1569/70–1662', *Huntington Library Quarterly*, 45 (1982), 200–14.

Moore, N. and Wallis, P., 'Twysden, John', *ODNB*.

Moraux, P., *Der Aristotelismus bei den Griechen von Andronikos bis Alexander von Aphrodisias* (2 vols, Berlin, 1975–84).

Morgan, J., *Godly learning: Puritan attitudes towards reason, learning, and education, 1560–1640* (Cambridge, 1986).

'Sprat, Thomas', *ODNB*.

'Science, England's "Interest" and universal monarchy: the making of Thomas Sprat's *History of the Royal Society*', *History of Science*, 47 (2009), 27–54.

Morison, S., *John Fell, the University Press and the 'Fell' types* (Oxford, 1967).

Mortimer, S., *Reason and religion in the English revolution: the challenge of Socinianism* (Cambridge, 2010).

Muccillo, M., 'La storia della filosofia presocratica nelle "Discussiones peripateticae" di Francesco Patrizi da Cherso', *La cultura*, 13 (1975), 48–105.

'La biblioteca greca di Francesco Patrizi', in *Bibliothecae selectae: da Cusano a Leopardi*, ed. E. Canone (Florence, 1993), 73–118.

*Platonismo, Ermetismo e 'Prisca Theologia': ricerche di storiografia filosofica rinascimentale* (Florence, 1996).

Muller, R. A., 'The debate over the vowel points and the crisis in orthodox hermeneutics', *Journal of Medieval and Renaissance Studies*, 10 (1980), 53–72.

'The Christological problem in the thought of Jacobus Arminius', *Nederlands Archief voor Kerkgeschiendenis*, 68 (1988), 145–63.

*After Calvin: studies in the development of a theological tradition* (Oxford, 2003).

*Post-Reformation Reformed dogmatics: the rise and development of Reformed orthodoxy, ca. 1520 to ca. 1725* (4 vols, 2nd edn, Grand Rapids, 2003).

Mulligan, L., '"Reason", "right reason", and "revelation" in mid-seventeenth-century England', in *Occult and scientific mentalities in the Renaissance,* ed. B. Vickers (Cambridge, 1984), 375–402.

Mulsow, M., 'Orientalistik im Kontext der sozinianischen und deistischen Debatten um 1700. Spencer, Crell, Locke und Newton', *Scientia Poetica*, 2 (1998), 27–57.

'Jacques Souverain, Samuel Crell et les cryptosociniens de Londres', in *J. Souverain, Lettre à Mr\*\*\* touchant l'apostasie*, eds., S. Matton and E. Labrousse (Paris, 2000), 49–63.

'John Seldens *De Diis Syris*: Idolatriekritik und vergleichende Religionsgeschichte im 17 Jahrhundert', *Archiv für Religionsgeschichte*, 3 (2001), 1–24.

'Antiquarianism and idolatry: the "historia" of religions in the seventeenth century', in *Historia: empiricism and erudition in early modern Europe*, eds., G. Pomata and N. G. Siraisi (Cambridge [MA], 2005), 181–210.

*Moderne aus dem Untergrund: radikale Frühaufklärung in Deutschland 1680–1720* (Hamburg, 2002).

'The trinity as heresy: Socinian counter-histories of Simon Magus, Orpheus, and Cerinthus', in *Histories of heresy in early modern Europe*, ed. J. C. Laursen (New York, 2002), 161–70.

'A German Spinozistic reader of Cudworth, Bull, and Spencer: Johann Georg Wachter and his *Theologia Martyrum* (1712)', in *History of scholarship*, eds., C. Ligota and J.-L. Quantin (Oxford, 2006), 357–85.

'Socinianism, Islam and the radical uses of Arabic scholarship', *Al-Qantara*, 31 (2010), 549–86.

ed., *Das Ende des Hermetismus: historische Kritik und neue Naturphilosophie in der Spätrenaissance: Dokumentation und Analyse der Debatten um die Datierung der hermetischen Schriften von Genebrard bis Casaubon (1567–1614)* (Tübingen, 2002).

and Zedelmaier, H., eds., *Die Praktiken der Gelehrsamkeit in der frühen Neuzeit* (Tübingen, 2001).

and Assmann, J., eds., *Sintflut und Gedächtnis: Erinnern und Vergessen des Ursprungs* (Munich, 2006).

Mund-Dopchie, M., 'Hanno', *CTC*, xiii, 49–55.

Mungello, D. E., *Curious land: Jesuit accommodation and the origins of Sinology* (Stuttgart, 1985).

Munk, W., *The Roll of the Royal College of Physicians of London*, *vol.* I (London, 1861).

Murdoch, J. E., 'Aristotle on Democritus's argument against infinite divisibility in *De generatione et corruptione*, book I, Chapter 2', in *The commentary tradition on Aristotle's 'De generatione et corruptione'*, eds., J. M. M. H. Thijssen and H. A. G. Braakhuis (Turnhout, 1999), 87–102.

'The medieval and Renaissance tradition of *minima naturalia*', in *Late medieval and early modern corpuscular matter theories*, eds., C. Lüthy, J. E. Murdoch, and W. Newman (Leiden, 2001), 91–123.

Nadler, S., *A companion to early modern philosophy* (London, 2002).

Nardi, B., 'La fine dell'averroismo', in *Saggi sull'aristotelismo padovano dal secolo XIV al XVI* (Florence, 1958), 443–55.

Nauta, L., *In defense of common sense: Lorenzo Valla's humanist critique of scholastic philosophy* (Cambridge [MA], 2009).

Neal, K., *From discrete to continuous: the broadening of number concepts in early modern England* (Dordrecht, 2002).

Nellen, H. J. M., 'De vitae termino. An epistolary survey by Johan van Beverwijck (1632–1639)', in *Acta Conventus Neo-Latini Hafniensis*, eds., A. Moss, P. Dust, P. G. Schmidt, J. Chomarat, and F. Tateo (Binghamton [NY], 1994), 731–40.

'Growing tension between church doctrines and critical exegesis', in *Hebrew Bible/ Old Testament: the history of its interpretation, vol.* II*: from the Renaissance to the Enlightenment*, ed. M. Saebø (Göttingen, 2008), 802–26.

Nelson, E., *The Hebrew republic: Jewish sources and the transformation of European political thought* (Cambridge [MA], 2010).

Neuburger, M., 'An historical survey of the concept of nature from a medical viewpoint' *Isis*, 35 (1944), 16–28.

Neumann, H.-P., 'Atome, Sonnenstäubchen, Monaden. Zum Pythagoreismus im 17. und 18. Jahrhundert', in *Auflklärund und Esoterik. Rezeption–Integration–Konfrontation*, eds., M. Neugebauer-Wölk and A. Rudolph (Tübingen, 2008), 205–82.

Neveu, B., *Érudition et religion aux XVIIe et XVIIIe siècles* (Paris, 1994).

Newman, W. R., 'Thomas Vaughan as an interpreter of Agrippa von Nettesheim', *Ambix*, 29 (1982), 125–40.

*Gehennical fire: the lives of George Starkey: an American alchemist in the scientific revolution* (Chicago, 1994).

'The alchemical sources of Robert Boyle's corpuscular philosophy', *Annals of Science*, 53 (1996), 567–85.

'Experimental corpuscular theory in Aristotelian alchemy: from Geber to Sennert', in *Late medieval and early modern corpuscular matter theories*, eds., C. Lüthy, J. E. Murdoch, and W. Newman (Leiden, 2001), 291–330.

*Atoms and alchemy: chymistry and the experimental origins of the scientific revolution* (Chicago, 2006).

'How not to integrate the history and philosophy of science: a reply to Chalmers', *SHPS*, 41 (2010), 203–13.

and Principe, L. M., 'Alchemy vs. chemistry: the etymological origins of a historiographic mistake', *ESM*, 3 (1998), 32–65.

and Principe, L. M., *Alchemy tried in the fire: Starkey, Boyle, and the fate of Helmontian chymistry* (Chicago, 2002).

Nicolson, M. H., 'Christ's College and the latitude men', *Modern Philosophy*, 27 (1929), 36–53.

Nielsen, O. L., 'A seventeenth-century physician on God and atoms. Sebastian Basso', in *Meaning and inference in medieval philosophy*, ed. N. Kretzmann (Dordrecht, 1988), 297–369.

Noreña, C. G., *Juan Luis Vives* (The Hague, 1970).

Norman, L. F., *The shock of the ancient: literature and history in early modern France* (Chicago, 2011).

Nuovo, V., 'Introduction', in John Locke, *Vindications of the Reasonableness of Christianity*, ed. V. Nuovo (Oxford, 2012).

Nutton, V., '"Prisci dissectionum professores": Greek texts and Renaissance anatomists', in *The uses of Greek and Latin: historical essays*, eds., A. C. Dionisotti, A. Grafton, and J. Kraye (London, 1988), 111–26.

'Hippocrates in the Renaissance', *Dujhoffs Archiv*, 27 (1989), 420–39.

'Wittenberg anatomy', in *Medicine and the Reformation*, eds., O. P. Grell and A. Cunningham (London, 1993), 11–32.

O'Malley, C. F., *Adreas Vesalius of Brussels, 1514–1564* (Berkeley, 1964).

O'Meara, D.J., 'Plotinus', *CTC*, VII, 55–74.

Oldroyd, D. R., 'Some writings of Robert Hooke on procedures for the prosection of scientific inquiry, including his "Lectures of things requisite to a ntral history"', *NRRS*, 41 (1987), 145–67.

'Geological controversy in the seventeenth century: Hooke vs Wallis and its aftermath', in *Robert Hooke: new studies*, eds., M. Hunter and S. Schaffer (Woodbridge, 1989), 207–33.

Osborn, J. M., 'Thomas Stanley's lost "Register of Friends"', *Yale University Library Gazette* (1958), 1–26.

Osborne, C., 'Ralph Cudworth's *The true intellectual system of the universe* and the presocratic philosophers', in *The presocratics from the Latin middle ages to Hermann Diels*, eds., O. Primavesi and K. Luchner (Stuttgart, 2011), 215–235.

Osler, M. J., 'Baptizing Epicurean atomism: Pierre Gassendi on the immortality of the soul', in *Religion, science, and worldview*, eds., M. J. Osler and P. L. Farber (Cambridge, 1985), 163–83.

'Introduction', in *Atoms, pneuma, and tranquitlity: Epicurean and Stoic themes in European thought*, ed. M. J. Osler (Cambridge, 1991).

'Ancients, moderns and the history of philosophy: Gassendi's Epicurean project', in *The rise of modern Philosophy*, ed. T. Sorell (Oxford, 1993).

*Divine will and the mechanical philosophy: Gassendi and Descartes on contingency and necessity in the created world* (Cambridge, 1994).

'From immanent natures to nature as artifice: the reinterpretation of final causes in seventeenth-century natural philosophy', *The Monist*, 79 (1996), 388–407.

'When did Gassendi become a libertine?', in *Heterdoxy in early modern science and religion*, eds., J. H Brooke and I. Maclean (Oxford, 2005), 169–92.

Osmond, P. H., *Isaac Barrow: his life and times* (London, 1944).

Oster, M., 'Highmore, Nathaniel', *ODNB*.

Pacchi, A., *Cartesio in Inghilterra: da More a Boyle* (Bari, 1973), 3–48.

Packer, J., *The transformation of Anglicanism, 1643–1660: with special reference to Henry Hammond* (Manchester, 1969).

Paganini, G., 'Hobbes, Valla and the trinity', *BJHP*, 11 (2003), 183–218.

Pagel, W., 'The reaction to Aristotle in seventeenth-century biological thought: Campanella, Van Helmont, Glanvill, Charleton, Harvey, Glisson, Descartes', in *Science, medicine and history*, ed. E. A. Underwood (2 vols, Oxford, 1953), I, 489–509.

'Harvey and Glisson on irritability: with a note on van Helmont', *Bulletin of the History of Medicine*, 41 (1967), 497–514.

*William Harvey's biological ideas* (Basel, 1967).

*New light on William Harvey* (Basel, 1976).

*Paracelsus: an introduction to philosophical medicine in the era of the Renaissance* (2nd rev. edn, Basel, 1982).

*Joan Baptista van Helmont: reformer of science and medicine* (Cambridge, 1982).

Palmerino, C. R., 'Pierre Gassendi's *De Philosophia Epicuri Universi* rediscovered', *Nuntius*, 14 (1998), 131–62.

Parente, F., 'Spencer, Maimonides, and the history of religion', in *History of scholarship*, eds., C. Ligota and J.-L. Quantin (Oxford, 2006), 277–304.

Parenty, H., *Isaac Casaubon, Helléniste: Des studia humanitatis à la philologie* (Geneva, 2009).

Parkin, J., *Science, religion and politics in Restoration England: Richard Cumberland's De Legibus Naturae* (Woodbridge, 1999).

'Hobbism in the later 1660s: Daniel Scargill and Samuel Parker', *HJ*, 42 (1999), 85–108.

'Pierce, Thomas', *ODNB*.

Parry, G., *The trophies of time: English antiquarians of the seventeenth century* (Oxford, 1995).

'Thomas Browne and the uses of antiquity', in *Sir Thomas Browne: the world proposed* (Oxford, 2008), 63–79.

Partington, J. R., 'The life and work of John Mayow', *Isis*, 47 (1956), 217–30, 405–17.

Pasnau, R., 'Form, substance, and mechanism', *The Philosophical Review*, 113 (2004), 31–88.

Passmore, J. A., *Ralph Cudworth: an interpretation* (Cambridge, 1951).

Patrides, C. A., 'Introduction', in John Smith, *Select Discourses* (New York, 1979).

Pattison, M., 'Tendencies of religious thought in England from 1688 to 1750', *Essays and reviews* (London, 1860).

Payne, L. M., 'Sir Charles Scarburgh's Harveian Oration, 1662', *Journal of the History of Medicine and Allied Sciences*, 12 (1957), 158–64.

Pedersen, S., 'Festschriftiness', *London Review of Books*, 33.19 (October 2011), 31–2.

Péllisier, L. G., 'Les amis d'Holstenius', *Revue des Langues Romanes*, 35 (1891), 321–78, 503–47.

Pelseneer, J., 'Une opinion inédite de Newton sur l'analyse des anciens' à propos de l'Analysis Geometrica de Hugo de Omerique', *Isis*, 14 (1930), 155–65.

Perani, M., *Gugliemo Raimondo Moncada alias Flavio Mitridate. Un ebreo converso siciliano* (Palermo, 2008).

Perilli, L., *Menodoto di Nicomedia: contributo a una storia Galeniana della medicina empirica* (Leipzig, 2004).

Petersson, R. T., *Sir Kenelm Digby, the ornament of England, 1603–1665* (London, 1956).

Petit, A., 'Ralph Cudworth, un platonisme paradoxal: la nature dans la *Digression concerning the plastick life of nature*', in *The Cambridge Platonists in philosophical context*, eds. G. A. J. Rogers, J.-M. Vienne, and Y.-C. Zarka (Dordrecht, 1997), 101–10.

Pfeiffer, R., *History of classical scholarship: from the beginnings to the end of the Hellenistic Age* (Oxford, 1968).

*History of classical scholarship from 1300 to 1850* (Oxford, 1976).

Philip, I. G., 'Letter from Thomas Hyde, Bodley's librarian, 1665–1701', *The Bodleian Library Record*, 3 (1950–51), 40–5.

Piaia, G., 'Foreword to the English edition', in Santinello II, v–vi.

'The histories of philosophy in France in the age of Descartes', in Santinello II, 3–92.

'Philosophical historiography in France from Bayle to Deslandes', in Santinello II, 93–176.

'Cartesianism and history: from the rejection of the past to a "critical" history of philosophy', in *Translatio Studiorum: ancient, medieval and modern bearers of intellectual history*, ed. M. Sgarbi (Leiden, 2012), 141–54.

Pigney, S., 'Theophilus Gale (1628–79), nonconformist scholar and intellectual: an introduction to his life and writings', *Journal of the United Reformed Church History Society*, 7 (2007), 407–20.

'Theophilus Gale and historiography of philosophy', in *Insiders and outsiders in seventeenth-century philosophy*, eds. G. A. J. Rogers, T. Sorell, and J. Kraye (New York and Oxford, 2010), 76–99.

Pitassi, M. C., *Entre croire et savoir. Le problème de la méthode critique chez Jean Le Clerc* (Leiden, 1987).

Pluta, O., 'The transformations of Alexander of Aphrodisias' interpretation of Aristotle's theory of the soul', in *Renaissance readings of the Corpus Aristotelicum*, ed. M. Pade (Copenhagen, 2001), 147–66.

Pocock, J. G. A., *The ancient constitution and the feudal law: a study of English historical thought in the seventeenth century* (Cambridge, 1957; reissued with a retrospect, 1987).

'Post-puritan England and the problem of the enlightenment', in *Culture and politics from puritanism to the enlightenment*, ed. P. Zagorin (Berkeley, 1980), 91–111.

'Clergy and commerce: the conservative enlightenment in England', in *L'età dei lumi*, eds., R. Ajello, E. Cortese, and V. P. Mortari (2 vols, Naples, 1985), I, 523–68.

'Within the margins: the definitions of orthodoxy', in *The margins of orthodoxy: heterodox writing and cultural response, 1660–1750*, ed. R. D. Lund (Cambridge, 1995), 33–53.

'Historiography and enlightenment: a view of their history', *Modern Intellectual History*, 5 (2008), 83–96.

*Barbarism and religion, vol.* V. *Religion: the first triumph* (Cambridge, 2011).

'Review of S. Pincus, *1688: The first modern revolution*', *Common Knowledge*, 17 (2011), 186–9.

Pocock, N., 'Illustrations of the state and church during the Great Rebellion', *The Theologian and Ecclesiastic*, 9 (1850).

Pomata, G., and Siraisi, N. G., eds., *Historia: empiricism and erudition in early modern Europe*, (Cambridge [MA], 2005).

Poole, H. H., 'Milner, John', *ODNB*.

Poole, W., 'Two early readers of Milton: John Beale and Abraham Hill', *Milton Quarterly*, 38 (2004), 76–99.

'Francis Lodwick's creation: theology and natural philosophy in the early Royal Society', *JHI*, 66 (2005), 245–63.

'The Genesis narrative in the circle of Robert Hooke and Francis Lodwick', in *Scripture and scholarship in early modern England*, eds. A. Hessayon and N. Keene (Aldershot, 2006), 41–58.

'Sir Robert Southwell's dialogue on Thomas Burnet's theory of the earth: "C & S discourse of Mr Burnetts Theory of the Earth" (1684): contexts and an edition', *The Seventeenth Century*, 23 (2008), 72–104.

'Introduction', in *The Man in the Moone*, ed. W. Poole (Ontario, 2009).

*The world makers: scientists of the Restoration and the search for the origins of the earth* (Oxford, 2010).

'The evolution of George Hakewill's *Apologie or declaration of the power and providence of God*, 1627–1637: academic contexts, and some new angles from manuscripts', *Electronic British Library Journal* (2010), Article 7.

'Heterodoxy and Sinology: Isaac Vossius, Robert Hooke and the early Royal Society's use of Sinology', in *The intellectual consequences of religious heterodoxy 1600–1750*, eds., S. Mortimer and J. Robertson (Leiden, 2012), 134–54.

'Loans from the library of Sir Edward Sherburne and the 1685 English translation of Xenophon', *The Library*, 14 (2013), 80–7.

'John Fell's New Year Books again' (forthcoming).

Popkin, R. H., 'The philosophy of Bishop Stillingfleet', *JHP*, 9 (1971), 303–19.

'Newton and Maimonides', in *A straight path: studies in medieval philosophy and culture* (Washington, 1988), 216–29.

'Some further comments on Newton and Maimonides', in *Essays on the context, nature, and influence of Isaac Newton's theology*, eds., J. E. Force and R. H. Popkin (Dordrecht, 1990), 1–8.

'The crisis of polytheism and the answers of Vossius, Cudworth and Newton', in *Essays on the context, nature, and influence of Isaac Newton's theology*, eds., J. E. Force and R. H. Popkin (Dordrecht, 1990), 9–26.

'Polytheism, deism and Newton', in *Essays on the context, nature, and influence of Isaac Newton's theology*, eds., J. E. Force and R. H. Popkin (Dordrecht, 1990), 27–42.

Popper, N., '"Abraham, Planter of Mathematics": histories of mathematics and astrology in early modern Europe', *JHI*, 67 (2006), 87–106.

*Walter Ralegh's* History of the world *and the historical culture of the late Renaissance* (Chicago, 2012).

Porter, R., *The making of geology: earth science in Britain 1660–1815* (Cambridge, 1977).

Porter, S., 'University and society', in *The history of the University of Oxford, vol. IV: seventeenth-century Oxford*, ed. N. Tyacke (Oxford, 1997), 25–104.

Potter, A. C., *The library of Harvard University: descriptive and historical notes* (3rd edn, Cambridge [MA], 1915 [1st edn=1903]).

Praz, M., 'Stanley, Sherburne and Ayres as translators and imitators of Italian, Spanish and French poets', *Modern Language Review*, 20 (1925), 280–94.

Primavesi, O., 'Henri II Estienne über philosophische Dichtung: Eine Fragmentsammlung als Beitrag zu einer poetologischen Kontroverse', in *The presocractics from the Latin Middle Ages to Hermann Diels*, eds. O. Primavesi and K. Luchner (Stuttgart, 2011), 157–96.

Principe, L. M., 'Virtuous romance and romantic virtuoso: the shaping of Robert Boyle's literary style', *JHI*, 56 (1995), 377–97.

*The aspiring adept: Robert Boyle and his alchemical quest* (New Jersey, 1998).

'Castle, George', *ODNB*.

'Dickinson, Edmund', *ODNB*.

Prosperi, V., *Di soavi licor gli orli del vaso: La fortuna di Lucrezio dal l'Umanismo alla Controriforma* (Turin, 2004).

Puliafito, A. L., 'Searching for a new physics: metaphysics of light and ancient knowledge in Francesco Patrizi da Cherso', in *Magia, alchimia, scienza dal '400 al '700: L'influsso di Ermete Trismegisto*, eds., C. Gilly and C. van Heertum (2 vols, Florence, 2002), 237–51.

Pumfrey, S., 'The spagyric art: or, the impossible work of separating pure from impure Paracelsianism: a historiographical analysis', in *Paracelsus: the man and his reputation, his ideas and their transformation*, ed. O. P. Grell (Leiden, 1998), 21–52.

Purvery, M., *The Royal Society: concept and creation* (Cambridge [MA], 1967).

Pyle, A., *Atomism and its critics: from Democritus to Newton* (Bristol, 1995).

Quantin, J.-L., *Le catholicisme classique et les pères de l'église: un retour aux sources (1669–1713)* (Paris, 1999).

'Document, histoire, critique dans l'érudition ecclésiastique des temps modernes', *Recherches de Science Religieuse* 92 (2004), 597–635.

'Un manuel anti-patristique: context et signification du *Traité de l'emploi des saints Pères* de Jean Daillé (1632)', in *Die Patristik in der frühen Neuzeit*, eds., G. Frank, T. Leinkauf, and M. Wried (Stuttgart, 2006), 299–325.

'L'Orthodoxie, la censure et la gloire: la difficile édition princeps de l'épître de Barnabé, de Rome à Amsterdam (1549–1646)', in *'Editiones principes' delle opera dei padri greci e latini* (Florence, 2006), 103–62.

'Anglican scholarship gone mad? Henry Dodwell (1641–1711) and Christian antiquity', in *History of scholarship*, eds., C. Ligota and J.-L. Quantin (Oxford, 2006), 305–56.

'Du Chrysostome latin au Chrysostome grec: une histoire européene (1518–1613)', in *Chrysostomosbilder in 1600 Jahren: Facetten der Wirkungsgeschichte eines Kirchenvaters* (Berlin, 2008), 267–346.

*The Church of England and Christian antiquity: the construction of a confessional identity in the 17th century* (Oxford, 2009).

'John Selden et l'étude de l'Antiquité chrétienne: Érudition, critique et anticléricalisme', *Annuaire de l'institute Michel Villey*, 3 (2011), 339–90.

'Reason and reasonableness in French ecclesiastical scholarship', *Huntington Library Quarterly*, 74 (2011), 401–36.

de Quehen, H., 'Politics and scholarship in the Ignatian controversy', *Seventeenth Century*, 13 (1998), 69–84.

'Bentley, Richard', *ODNB*.

'Prideaux, Humphrey', *ODNB*.

'Sherburne, Edward', *ODNB*.

Rademaker, C. S. M., *Life and work of Gerardus Joannes Vossius (1577–1649)* (Assen, 1981).

and van der Lem, G. A. K., *Inventory of the correspondence of Gerardus Joannes Vossius (1577–1649)* (Assen, 1993).

Ramsey, R., 'China and the ideal of order in John Webb's *An Historical Essay*', *JHI*, 62 (2001), 483–503.

Randall, J., *The school of Padua and the emergence of modern science* (Padua, 1961).

Rapp, C., 'Friedrich Nietzsche and pre-Platonic philosophy', in *The presocratics from the Latin middle ages to Hermann Diels*, eds., O. Primavesi and K. Luchner (Stuttgart, 2011), 335–58.

Rappaport, R., 'Hooke on earthquakes: lectures, strategy and audience', *BJHS*, 19 (1986), 129–46.

*When geologists were historians, 1665–1750* (New York, 1997).

'Questions of evidence: an anonymous tract attributed to John Toland', *JHI*, 58 (1997), 339–48.

Rattansi, P. M., 'The Helmontian-Galenist controversy in Restoration England', *Ambix*, 12 (1964), 1–23.

Raven, C. E., *John Ray, naturalist: his life and works* (2nd edn, Cambridge, 1950).

Raylor, T., 'Hobbes, Payne, and a Short tract on first principles', *HJ*, 44 (2001), 29–58.

Real, H. J., *Untersuchungen zur Lukrez-Übersetzung von Thomas Creech* (Berlin, 1970).

Reedy, G., *The Bible and reason: Anglicans and scripture in late seventeenth-century England* (Philadelphia, 1985).

*Robert South (1634–1716): an introduction to his life and sermons* (Cambridge, 1992).

Rees, G. 'Atomism and "subtlety" in Francis Bacon's philosophy', *Annals of science*, 37 (1980), 549–71.

and Wakely, M., 'Introduction', in *The Instauratio magna Part II: Novum organum and associated texts*, eds. M. D Reeve. and M. Wakely (=*OFB*, xi) (Oxford, 2004).

'Acidalius on Manilius', *The Classical Quarterly*, 41 (1991), 226–39.

Rehnman, S., 'John Owen: a Reformed scholastic at Oxford', in *Reformation and scholasticism: an ecumenical enterprise*, eds., W. J. van Asselt and E. Dekker (Grand Rapids, 2001), 181–204.

*Divine discourse: the theological methodology of John Owen* (Grand Rapids, 2002).

Reid, J., 'The evolution of Henry More's theory of divine absolute space', *JHP*, 45 (2007), 79–102.

*The metaphysics of Henry More* (Dordrecht, 2012).

Reif, S. C., *Hebrew manuscripts at Cambridge University Library: a description and introduction* (Cambridge, 1997).

Reiner, H., 'Die Entstehung der Lehre vom bibliothekarischen Ursprung des Namens Metaphysik. Geschichie einer Wissenschaftslegende', *Zeitschrift für philosophische Forschung*, 9 (1955), 77–99.

Repetzki, M. M., 'Preface', in *John Evelyn's translation of Titus Lucretius Carus de rerum natura: an old-spelling critical edition* (Frankfurt, 2000).

Revard, S., 'Translation and imitation of Joannes Secundus' *Basia* during the era of the civil war and protectorate in England', *Acta Conventus Neo-Latini Abulensis* (Tempe [AR], 2000), 553–61.

'Thomas Stanley and "A Register of Friends"', in *Literary circles and cultural communities in Renaissance England*, eds., C. J. Summers and T.-L. Pebworth (New York and London, 2000), 148–172.

Reventlow, H. G., 'English deism and anti-deist apologetic', in *Hebrew Bible/Old Testament: the history of its interpretation, vol. II: from the Renaissance to the Enlightenment*, ed. M. Saebø (Göttingen, 2008), 851–74.

Reverdin, O., 'Isaac Casaubon et Genève de 1596 à 1614', in *Mélanges offerts à M. Paul-E. Martin par ses amis, ses collègues et ses élèves* (Geneva, 1961), 503–21.

'En guise d'épilogue: Brève évocation de la Ποίησις φιλόσοφος (Poesis Philosophica), recueil composé et imprimé à Genève, en 1573, par Henri Estienne', in *Hermann Diels (1848–1922) et la Science de L'antiquité*, eds., W. M. Calder III and J. Mansfeld (Geneva, 1999), 295–8.

Reynolds L. D., and Wilson, N., *Scribes and scholars: a guide to the transmission of Greek and Latin literature* (Oxford, 1991).

Rietbergen, P., *Power and religion in Baroque Rome: Barberini cultural policies* (Leiden, 2006).

Rivers, I., *Reason, grace, and sentiment: a study of the language of religion and ethics in England, 1660–1780* (2 vols, Cambridge, 1991).

Roberts, R. S., 'Jonathan Goddard. *Discourse concerning physick and the many abuses thereof by apothecaries*, 1668: A lost work or a ghost?' *Medical History*, 8 (1964), 190–1.

Robinson, H. W., 'An unpublished letter of Dr Seth Ward relating to the early meetings of the Oxford Philosophical Society', *NRRS*, 7 (1950), 68–71.

Roger, J., 'The Cartesian model and its role in eighteenth-century "Theories of the earth"', in *Problems of Cartesianism*, eds., T. Lennon, J. Nicholas, and J. Davis (Kingston, 1982), 95–113.

Roitman, A. D., '"This people are descendants of Chaldeans" (Judith 5:6): its literary form and historical setting', *Journal of Biblical Literature*, 113 (1994), 245–63.

Rolet, S., 'Invention et exégèse symbolique à la Renaissance: Le "tombeau d'Aureolus" dans les *Antiquitates Mediolanenses* d'Alciat et les *Hieroglyphica* de Valeriano', *Albertiana*, 5 (2002), 109–40.

Romano, A., 'Crispo, Giovan Battista', in *Dizionario biografico degli Italiani* (Rome, 1960–), xxx, 806–8.

van Rooden, P. T., *Theology, biblical scholarship, and rabbinical studies in the seventeenth century: Constantijn L'Empereur (1591–1648), professor of Hebrew and theology at Leiden* (Leiden, 1989).

Roos, A. M., *The salt of the earth: natural philosophy, medicine, and chymistry in England, 1650–1750* (Leiden, 2007).

*Web of nature: Martin Lister (1639–1712), the first arachnologist* (Leiden, 2011).

Rose, J., 'Hobbes among the heretics', *HJ*, 52 (2009), 493–511.

'The ecclesiastical polity of Samuel Parker', *The Seventeenth Century*, 25 (2010), 350–76.

Rose, P. L., and Drake, S., 'The pseudo-Aristotelian Questions of Mechanics in Renaissance culture', *Studies in the Renaissance*, 18 (1971), 65–104.

Rosenblatt, J. P., *Renaissance England's chief rabbi: John Selden* (Oxford, 2006).

Rossi, P., *Francis Bacon: from magic to science*, trans. S. Rabinovitch (London, 1968 [Italian original= 1957]).

'Sulle origini dell'idea di progresso', in *Immagini della scienza* (Roma, 1977), 15–69.

'Francesco Bacone e la tradizione filosofica', *Atti dell'Istituto Lombardo di scienze e lettere*, 88 (1955), 33–93.

*The dark abyss of time: the history of the earth and the history of nations from Hooke to Vico*, trans., L. Cochrane (Chicago, 1984 [Italian orig.=1979]).

Ruelle, C. A., 'Praefatio', in *Damascii Successoris . . . De primis principiis, in Platonis Parmenidem*, ed. C. A. Ruelle (Paris, 1889), i–xxi.

Runia, D. T., *Philo in early Christian literature* (Assen, 1993).

'What is doxography?', in *Ancient histories of medicine: essays in medical doxography and historiography in classical antiquity*, ed. P. J. van der Eijk (Leiden, 1999), 33–55.

and Mansfield, J., *Aëtiana: the method and intellectual context of a doxographer. Vol. I: the sources* (Leiden, 1997), 1–41.

Sachau, E., 'Contributions to the knowledge of Parsee literature', *Journal of the Royal Asiatic Society*, 4 (1869), 229–83.

Sailor, D. B., 'Moses and atomism', *JHI*, 25 (1964), 3–16.

'Newton's debt to Cudworth', *JHI*, 49 (1988).

Sakamoto, K., 'Creation, the trinity and *prisca theologia* in Julius Caesar Scaliger', *JWCI*, 73 (2010), 195–207.

Salaman, C., 'Echoes of Egypt in Hermes and Ficino', in *Marsilio Ficino: his theology, his philosophy, his legacy*, eds., M. J. B. Allen and V. Rees (Leiden, 2001), 115–36.

Sandys, J. E., *A history of classical scholarship* (3 vols, Cambridge, 1903–8).

Sankey, M. D., 'Sheffield, John', *ODNB*.

Santinello, G., ed., *Storia delle storie generali della filosofia: Delle origini rinascimentali alla 'historia philosophica'* (Brescia, 1981), trans. as Santinello I.

ed., *Storia delle storie generali della filosofia: Dall'eta cartesiana a Brucker*, trans. as Santinello II.

ed., *Storia delle storie generali della filosofia: Il secondo illuminismo e l'età kantiana* (Padua, 1988).

ed., *Storia delle storie generali della filosofia: L'età hegeliana* (1995, 2004).

ed., *Storia delle storie generali della filosofia: Il secondo Ottocento* (Rome, 2004).

Sargent, R.-M., *The diffident naturalist: Robert Boyle and the philosophy of experiment* (Chicago, 1995).

Saveson, J. E., 'Descartes' influence on John Smith, Cambridge Platonist', *JHI*, 20 (1959), 258–63.

'Differing reactions to Descartes among the Cambridge Platonists', *JHI*, 21 (1960), 560–7.

Schaffer, S., 'Halley's atheism and the end of the world', *NRRS*, 32 (1977), 17–40.

Scheible, H., *Die Entstehung der Magdeburger Zenturien. Ein Beitrag zur Geschichte der historiographischen Methode* (Gütersloh, 1966).

Schepelern, H. D., 'Introduction', in *Olai Borrichii itinerarium 1660–1665: the journal of the Danish polyhistor Ole Borch*, ed. H. D. Schepelern (Copenhagen, 1983), vii–xliii.

Schibli, H. S., *Hierocles of Alexandria* (Oxford, 2002).

Schironi, F., *From Alexandria to Babylon: near eastern languages and Hellenistic erudition in the Oxyrhynchus glossary* (Berlin, 2009).

Schmidt, F., 'The Hasidaeans and the ancient Jewish "sects": a seventeenth-century controversy', in *Sects and sectarianism in Jewish history*, ed. S. Stern (Leiden, 2011), 187–204.

Schmidt-Biggemann W., *Philosophia perennis: historical outlines of Western spirituality in ancient, medieval and early modern thought* (Dordrecht, 2004).

'History and prehistory of the Cabala of JHSUS', in *Hebrew to Latin, Latin to Hebrew: the mirroring of two cultures in the age of humanism*, ed. G. Busi (Berlin, 2006), 223–41.

*Geschichte der christlichen Kabbala. 15. und 16. Jahrhundert* (Stuttgart, 2012).

and Stammen T., eds., *Jacob Brucker (1696–1770): Philosoph und Historiker der europäischen Aufklärung* (Berlin, 1998).

Schmitt, C. B., 'Aristotle as a cuttlefish: the origin and development of an image', *Studies in the Renaissance*, 12 (1965), 60–72.

*Gianfrancesco Pico della Mirandola (1469–1533) and his critique of Aristotle* (The Hague, 1967).

*Cicero Scepticus: a study of the influence of the Academica in the Renaissance* (The Hague, 1972).

*Aristotle and the Renaissance* (Cambridge [MA], 1983).

'The rediscovery of ancient skepticism in modern times', in *The skeptical tradition*, ed. M. F. Burnyeat (Berkeley, 1983), 225–51.

*The Aristotelian tradition and the Renaissance universities* (London, 1984).

'William Harvey and Renaissance Aristotelianism: a consideration of the *Praefatio to "De generatione animalium"* (1651)', in *Humanismus und Medizin*, eds., G. Keil and R. Schmitz (Winheim, 1984), 117–38.

'Olympiodorus', *CTC*, ii, 199–204.

'Theophrastus', *CTC*, ii, 239–322.

'Aristotle among the physicians', in *The medical Renaissance of the sixteenth century*, eds., A. Wear, R. K. French, and I. M. Lonie (Cambridge, 1985), 1–15.

'The rise of the philosophical textbook', in *The Cambridge history of Renaissance philosophy*, eds., C. B. Schmitt and Q. Skinner (Cambridge, 1988), 792–804.

and Cranz, F. E., *A Bibliography of Aristotle Editions, 1501–1600* (2nd edn, Baden-Baden, 1984).

Schneider, U. J., 'Eclecticism and the history of philosophy', *History and the disciplines: the reclassification of knowledge in early modern Europe*, ed. D. R. Kelley (Rochester, 1997), 83–102.

'Eclecticism rediscovered', *JHI*, 59 (1998), 173–82.

Schochet, G., 'Between Lambeth and Leviathan: Samuel Parker on the church of England and political order', in *Political discourse in early-modern Britain*, eds., N. Phillipson and Q. Skinner (Cambridge, 1993), 189–208.

Scholem, G., 'The beginnings of the Christian Kabbalah', in *The Christian Kabbalah: Jewish mystical books and their Christian interpreters*, ed. J. Dan (Cambridge [MA], 1997), 17–51.

Schuler, R. M., 'Some spiritual alchemies of seventeenth-century England', *JHI*, 41 (1980), 293–318.

Schüller, V., *Newtons Scholia aus David Gregorys Nachlaß zu den Propositionen IV–IX Buch III seiner Principia* (Berlin, 2000).

'Newton's scholia from David Gregory's estate on the propositions IV through IX book III of his Principia', in *Between Leibniz, Newton, and Kant: philosophy and science in the eighteenth century*, ed. W. Lefèvre (Dordrecht, 2001), 213–65.

Schuster, J. A., '"Waterworld": Descartes' vortical celestial mechanics—a gambit in the natural philosophical contest of the early seventeenth century', in *The science of nature in the seventeenth century: patterns of change in early modern natural philosophy*, eds. P. Anstey and J. Schuster (Dordrecht, 2005), 35–80.

Schütt, H.-P., *Die Adoption des 'Vaters der modernen Philosophie'* (Frankfurt, 1998).

Secret, F., *Les Kabbalistes Chrétiens de la Renaissance* (Neuilly-sur-Seine, 1964).

'Gilbert Gaulmin et l'histoire comparée des religions', *Revue de l'histoire des religions*, 177 (1970), 35–63.

Sedley, D., 'Physics and metaphysics', in *The Cambridge history of Hellenistic philosophy*, eds., K. Algra, J. Barnes, J. Mansfeld, and M. Schofield (Cambridge, 1999), 355–411.

Sellars, J., 'Is God a mindless vegetable? Cudworth on Stoic theology', *IHR*, 21 (2011), 121–33.

'Stoics against Stoics in Cudworth's *A treatise of freewill*', *BJHP*, 20 (2012), 935–52.

Sellin, P., *Daniel Heinsius and Stuart England* (Leiden, 1968).

Serjeantson, R. W., 'Introduction', in *Generall learning: A seventeenth-century treatise on the formation of the General Scholar by Meric Casaubon*, ed. R. Serjeantson (Cambridge, 1999), 1–65.

'Herbert of Cherbury before deism: the early reception of *De Veritate*', *The Seventeenth Century*, 16 (2001), 217–38.

'Thomas Farnaby', in *British rhetoricians and logicians, 1500–1660*, ed. E. A. Malone (Detroit, 2001), 108–16.

'Hobbes, the universities, and the history of philosophy', in *The philosopher in early modern Europe*, eds., C. Condren, S. Gaukroger, and I. Hunter (Cambridge, 2006), 113–39.

'"Human understanding" and the genre of Locke's *Essay*', *IHR*, 18 (2008), 157–71.

'David Hume's *Natural history of religion* (1757) and the end of modern Eusebianism', *The intellectual consequences of religious heterodoxy*, eds., J. Robertson and S. Mortimer (Leiden, 2011), 267–96.

'The soul', in *The Oxford handbook of philosophy in early modern Europe*, eds., D. M. Clarke and C. Wilson (Oxford, 2011), 119–41.

'Becoming a philosopher in seventeenth-century Britain', in *The Oxford handbook of British philosophy in the seventeenth century*, ed. P. Anstey (Oxford, 2013), 9–38.

'The philosophy of Francis Bacon in early Jacobean Oxford, with an edition of an uknown manuscript of the *Valerius Terminus*', *HJ*, 56 (2013), 1087–106.

'The education of Francis Willughby' (forthcoming).

Sgarbi, M., *The Aristotelian tradition and the rise of British empiricism: logic and epistemology in the British Isles (1570–1689)* (Dordrecht, 2013).

Shackelford, J., *A philosophical path for Paracelsian medicine: the ideas, intellectual context, and influence of Petrus Severinus (1540/2–1602)* (Copenhagen, 2004).

Shalev, Z., 'Measurer of all things: John Greaves (1602–1652), the Great Pyramid, and early modern metrology', *JHI*, 63 (2002), 555–75.

*Sacred words and worlds: geography, religion, and scholarship, 1550–1700* (Leiden, 2012).

Shapin, S., 'Robert Boyle and mathematics: reality, representation, and experimental practice', *Science in Context*, 2 (1988), 23–58.

*A social history of truth: civility and science in seventeenth-century England* (Chicago, 1994).

*The scientific revolution* (Chicago, 1996).

and Schaffer, S., *Leviathan and the air-pump: Hobbes, Boyle, and the experimental life* (Princeton, 1985).

Shapiro, A. E., *Fits, passions, and paroxysms* (Cambridge, 1993).

'Newton's "experimental philosophy"', *ESM*, 9 (2004), 185–217.

Shapiro, B. J., *John Wilkins, 1614–1672: an intellectual biography* (Berkeley, 1969).

*Probability and certainty in seventeenth-century England* (Princeton, 1983).

Sharp, L., 'Walter Charleton's early life, 1620–1659, and relationship to natural philosophy in mid-seventeenth century England', *Annals of Science*, 30 (1973), 311–40.

Sharples, R. W., 'Strato of Lampsacus: the sources. Texts and translations', in *Strato of Lampsacus: text, translation, and discussion*, eds., M.-L Desclos and W. W. Fortenbaugh (New Jersey, 2011), 5–230.

Sheehan, J., 'Sacred and profane: idolatry, antiquarianism and the polemics of distinction in the seventeenth century', *Past and Present*, 192 (2006), 35–66.

Shelford, A. G., *Transforming the republic of letters: Pierre-Daniel Huet and European intellectual life, 1650–1720* (Rochester, 2007).

'Thinking geometrically in Pierre-Daniel Huet's *Demonstratio evangelica* (1679)', *JHI*, 63 (2002), 599–617.

Sherlock, P., 'Bysshe, Sir Edward', *ODNB*.

Shuger, D. K., *The Renaissance Bible: scholarship, sacrifice and subjectivity* (Berkeley, 1998).

Sicherl, M., *Die Handschriften, Ausgaben und Übersetzungen von Iamblichos 'De Mysteriis'* (Berlin, 1957).

Sider, S., 'Horapollo', *CTC*, VI, 15–30 and VIII, 325.

Silk, M., 'Numa Pompilius and the idea of civil religion in the West', *Journal of the American Academy of Religion*, 72 (2004), 863–96.

Siniossoglou, N., *Plato and Theodoret: the Christian appropriation of Platonic philosophy and the Hellenic intellectual resistance* (Cambridge, 2008).

Siraisi, N., *Avicenna in Renaissance Italy* (Princeton, 1987).

'Giovanni Argenterio and sixteenth-century medical innovation: between princely patronage and academic controversy', *Osiris*, 2.6 (1990), 161–80.

*The clock and the mirror: Girolamo Cardano and Renaissance medicine* (Princeton, 1997).

'In search of the origins of medicine: Egyptian medicine and some Renaissance physicians', in *Inventing genealogies*, eds., V. Finucci and K. Brownlee (Durham [NC], 2001), 235–61.

*History, medicine, and the traditions of Renaissance learning* (Ann Arbor, 2007).

'Medicine, 1450–1620, and the history of science', *Isis*, 103 (2012), 491–514.

Slusser, M., 'Abraham Woodhead (1608–78): some research notes, chiefly about his writings', *Recusant History*, 15 (1971–81), 406–22.

Small, A., and Small, C., 'John Evelyn and the garden of Epicurus', *JWCI*, 60 (1997), 194–214.

Smith, C. F., 'Jane Lead's wisdom: women and prophecy in seventeenth-century England', *Poetic prophecy in Western literature*, eds., J. Wojcik and R. J. Frontain (Michigan, 1984), 55–63.

Smith, J. E. H., ed., *The problem of animal generation in early modern philosophy* (Cambridge, 2006).

'Introduction', in *The problem of animal generation in early modern philosophy*, ed. J. E. H. Smith (Cambridge, 2006), 1–20.

*Divine machines, Leibniz and the sciences of life* (Princeton, 2011).

Smith, J. Z., *Drudgery divine. On the comparison of early Christianities and the religions of late antiquity* (Chicago, 1990).

Smith, N., '"And if God was one of us": Paul Best, John Biddle, and anti-trinitarian heresy in seventeenth-century England', in *Heresy, literature and politics in early modern English culture*, eds., D. Loewenstein and J. Marshall (Cambridge, 2006), 160–84.

Smith, P. H., 'Science on the move: recent trends in the history of early modern science', *Renaissance Quarterly*, 62 (2009), 345–75.

Smith, W. D., *The Hippocratic tradition* (Ithaca, 1979).

Snobelen, S. D., '"God of Gods, and Lord of Lords": the theology of Isaac Newton's General Scholium to the *Principia*', *Osiris*, 16 (2001), 169–208.

Solaro, G., *Lucrezio: Biografie umanistiche* (Bari, 2000).

Snobelen, S. D., '"Not in the language of astronomers": Isaac Newton, the scriptures, and the hermeneutics of accommodation', in *Nature and scripture in the Abrahamic religions*, eds., J. M. van der Meer and S. Mandelbrote (2 vols, Leiden, 2008), I, 491–530.

Soll, J., *Publishing the Prince: history, reading, and the birth of political criticism* (Ann Arbor, 2005).

Sorell, T., 'Hobbes and Aristotle', in *Philosophy in the sixteenth and seventeenth centuries: conversations with Aristotle*, eds., C. Blackwell and S. Kusukawa (Aldershot, 1999), 364–79.

Southgate, B. C., 'Cauterising the tumour of Pyrrhonism: Blackloism vs skepticism', *JHI*, 53 (1992), 631–45.

*'Covetous of truth': the life and work of Thomas White, 1593–1676* (Dordrecht, 1993).

Spellman, W. M., *The latitudinarians and the Church of England, 1660–1700* (Athens [GA], 1993).

Spiller, M. R. G., *'Concerning Natural Experimental Philosophie': Meric Casaubon and the Royal Society* (The Hague, 1980).

Spinks, B. D., 'Outram, William', *ODNB*.

Springborg, P., 'Introduction', in Thomas Hobbes, *Historia Ecclesiastica*, eds. and trans. P. Springborg, P. Stablein, and P. Wilson (Paris, 2008).

'A very British Hobbes, or a more European Hobbes?', *BJHP*, 22 (2014), 368–86.

Spurr, J., '"Latitudinarianism" and the Restoration Church', *HJ*, 31 (1988), 61–82.

'"Rational religion" in Restoration England', *JHI*, 49 (1988), 563–85.

*The Restoration Church of England, 1646–1689* (New Haven, 1991).

'Taylor, Jeremy', *ODNB*.

von Staden, H., 'Haeresis and heresy: the case of the *haireseis iatrikai*', in *Jewish and Christian self-definition, vol. III: self-definition in the Greek and Roman world*, eds., B. F. Meyer and E. P. Sanders (London, 1982), 76–100, 199–206.

'Rupture and continuity: Hellenistic reflections on the history of medicine', in *Ancient histories of medicine: essays in medical doxography and historiography in classical antiquity*, ed. P. J. van der Eijk (Leiden, 1999), 143–88.

'Celsus as historian', in *Ancient histories of medicine: essays in medical doxography and historiography in classical antiquity*, ed. P. J. van der Eijk (Leiden, 1999), 251–94.

Stanley Jones, F., 'The genesis, purpose, and significance of John Toland's *Nazarenus*', in *The rediscovery of Jewish Christianity: from Toland to Baur*, ed. F. Stanley Jones (Atlanta, 2012), 91–104.

Stanwood, P. G., 'Stobaeus and classical borrowing in the Renaissance, with special reference to Richard Hooker and Jeremy Taylor', *Neophilologus*, 59 (1985), 141–6.

Stausberg, M., *Faszination Zarathushtra: Zoroaster und die Europäische Religionsgeschichte der Frühen Neuzeit* (2 vols, Berlin, 1998).

'Von den Chaldäischen Orakeln zu den Hundert Pforten und darüber hinaus: Das 17. Jahrhundert als rezeptionsgeschichtliche Epochenschwelle', in *Archiv für Religionsgeschichte*, 3 (2001), 257–72.

*Die Religion Zarathushtras: Geschichte, Gegenwart, Rituale* (3 vols, Stuttgart, 2002–4).

Steinmetz, D. C., and Kolb, R., eds., *Die Patristik in der Bibelexegese des 16. Jahrhunderts* (Wiesbaden, 1999).

Stephen, L., *History of English thought in the eighteenth century* (2 vols, London, 1881).

Steuert, D. H., 'A study in Recusant prose: Dom Serenus Cressy, 1605–74', *The Downside Review*, 66 (1948).

Stevenson, L. G., '"New diseases" in the seventeenth century', *Bulletin of the History of Medicine*, 39 (1965), 1–21.

Stewart, I., 'Mathematics as philosophy: Barrow and Proclus', *Dionysius*, 18 (2000), 151–81.

Stewart, L., *The rise of public science: rhetoric, technology, and natural philosophy in Newtonian Britain, 1660–1750* (Cambridge, 1992).

'Harris, John', ODNB.

Stewart, M. A., 'Stillingfleet and the way of ideas', *English philosophy in the age of Locke*, ed. M. A. Stewart (Oxford, 2000), 245–80.

Stinger, C. L., *Humanism and the church fathers: Ambrogio Traversari (1386–1439) and Christian antiquity in the Italian Renaissance* (New York, 1977).

Stolzenberg, D., 'The Egyptian crucible of truth and superstition: Athanasius Kircher and the hieroglyphic doctrine', in *Antike Weisheit und kulturelle Praxis: Hermetismus in der Frühen Neuzeit*, eds., A.-C. Trepp and H. Lehmann (Göttingen, 2001), 145–64.

*Egyptian Oedipus: Athanasius Kircher and the secrets of antiquity* (Chicago, 2013).

Stroumsa, G. G., 'Isaac de Beausobre revisited: the birth of Manichaean studies', in *Studia Manichaica. IV. Internationaler Kongreß zum Manichäismus, Berlin, 14.-18. Juli 1997*, eds. R. E. Emmerick, W. Sundermann, and P. Zieme (Berlin, 2000), 601–12.

'John Spencer and the roots of idolatry', *History of Religions*, 40 (2001), 1–23.

'Thomas Hyde and the birth of Zoroastrian studies', in *Jerusalem Studies in Arabic and Islam*, 26 (2002), 216–30.

*A new science: the discovery of religion in the age of reason* (Cambridge [MA], 2010).

Stubbs, M., 'John Beale, philosophical gardener of Herefordshire, part I. Prelude to the Royal Society (1608–1663)', *Annals of Science*, 39 (1982), 463–89.

'Part II: the improvement of agriculture and trade in the Royal Society (1663–1683)', *Annals of Science*, 46 (1989), 323–63.

Sutcliffe, A., *Judaism and enlightenment* (Cambridge, 2003).

Sundermann, W., 'How Zoroastrian is Mani's dualism?', in *Manicheismo e oriente Christiano antico*, eds., L. Cirillo and A. van Tongerloo (Louvain, 1997), 343–60.

Sykes, N., *From Sheldon to Secker: aspects of English church history 1660–1768* (Cambridge, 1959).

Tambrun-Krasker, B., ed. and trans., *Μαγικὰ λόγια τῶν ἀπὸ Ζωροάστρου μάγων ... Ἐξήγησις εἰς τὰ αὐτὰ λόγια: Oracles chaldaïques. Recension de Georges Gémiste Pléthon* (Brussels, 1995).

'Marsile Ficin et le "Commentaire" de Pléthon sur les "Oracles Chaldaïques"', *Academia*, 1 (1999), 9–48.

*Pléthon: Le retour de Platon* (Paris, 2006).

Tavard, G. H., *The seventeenth-century tradition: a study in Recusant thought* (Leiden, 1978).

Taylor, E. G. R., 'The English worldmakers of the seventeenth century and their influence on the earth sciences', *Geographical Review*, 38 (1948), 104–12.

Taylor, J. E., *Jewish women philosophers of first-century Alexandria: Philo's 'Therapeutae' reconsidered* (Oxford, 2003).

Temkin, O., 'Celsus' "On medicine" and the ancient medical sects', *Bulletin of the Institute of the History of Medicine*, 3 (1935), 249–64.

'The classical roots of Glisson's doctrine of irritation', *Bulletin of the History of Medicine*, 38 (1964), 297–328.

*Galenism: rise and decline of a medical philosophy* (Ithaca, 1973).

*The double face of Janus* (Baltimore, 1977).

Terrall, M., 'Natural philosophy for fashionable readers', in *Books and the sciences in history*, eds., M. Frasca-Spada and N. Jardine (Cambridge, 2000), 239–44.

Thiel, U., 'The trinity and human personal identity', in *English philosophy in the age of Locke*, ed. M. A. Stewart (Oxford, 2000).

Thompson, M. P., 'Reception theory and the interpretation of historical meaning', *History and Theory*, 32 (1993), 248–72.

Thouard, D., 'Hamann and the history of philosophy', in *History of scholarship*, eds., C. Ligota and J.-L. Quantin (Oxford, 2006), 413–36.

Tigerstedt, E. N., *The decline and fall of the neoplatonic interpretation of Plato* (Helsinki, 1974).

Timpanaro, S., *The genesis of Lachmann's method*, trans. G. Most (Chicago, 2005 [Italian orig.=1963]).

Tite, C. G. C., *The manuscript library of Sir Robert Cotton* (London, 1994).

Todd, R. B., 'Themistius', *CTC*, VIII, 57–102.

Tolomio, I., 'The "historica philosophica" in the sixteenth and seventeenth centuries', in Santinello I, 66–160.

Toomer, G.J., *Easterne wisedome and learning: the study of Arabic in seventeenth-century England* (Oxford, 1996).

'Selden's *Historie of Tithes*: genesis, publication, aftermath', *Huntington Library Quarterly*, 65 (2002), 345–78.

*John Selden: A life in scholarship* (2 vols, Oxford, 2009).

Trevor-Roper, H., *Archbishop Laud 1573–1645* (London, 1940).

*Catholics, Anglicans and puritans: seventeenth-century essays* (London, 1987).

*History and the enlightenment* (New Haven, 2010).

Trowell, S., 'Unitarian and/or Anglican: the relationship of Unitarianism to the Church from 1687 to 1698', *Bulletin of the John Rylands University Library of Manchester*, 78 (1996), 77–101.

Tuck, R., 'The civil religion of Thomas Hobbes', in *Political discourse in early modern Britain*, eds., N. Phillipson and Q. Skinner (Cambridge, 1993), 120–38.

'The institutional setting', in *The Cambridge history of seventeenth-century philosophy*, eds., D. Garber and M. Ayers (Cambridge, 1998), I, 9–32.

Tulloch, J., *Rational theology and Christian philosophy in England in the seventeenth century* (2 vols, London, 1874).

Turnbull, G. H., 'John Hall's letters to Samuel Hartlib', *Review of English Studies*, 4 (1953), 221–33.

Turner, A. J., 'Hooke's theory of the Earth's axial displacement: some contemporary opinion', *BJHS*, 7 (1974), 166–70.

Tutino, S., *Thomas White and the Blackloists: between politics and theology during the English Civil War* (Aldershot, 2008).

Tuveson, E., 'Swift and the world makers', *JHI*, 11 (1950), 54–74.

Tyacke, N., 'Religious controversy', in *The history of the University of Oxford, vol.* IV*: seventeenth-century Oxford*, ed. N. Tyacke (Oxford, 1997), 569–619.

*Aspects of English Protestantism, c. 1530–1700* (Manchester, 2001).

*Universal Magazine, The*, 94 (1794).

Vasoli, C., *Francesco Patrizi da Cherso* (Rome, 1989).

*Quasi sit Deus: studi su Marsilio Ficino* (Lecce, 1999).

Vermès, G., *Post-Biblical Jewish Studies* (Leiden, 1975).

Vermeulen, C. L., 'Strategies and slander in the Protestant part of the republic of letters: image, friendship and patronage in Etienne de Courcelles' correspondence', in *Self-presentation and social identification: the rhetorics and pragmatics of letter writing in early modern times*, eds., T. Van Houdt, J. Papy, G. Tournoy, and C. Matheeussen (Leuven, 2002), 247–80.

Walker, D. P., 'Orpheus the theologian and Renaissance Platonists', *JWCI*, 16 (1953), 100–20.

'Origène en France', in *Courants religieux et humanisme à la fin du XVe et au début du XVIe siècle* (Paris, 1969), 101–19.

*The ancient theology* (Ithaca, 1972).

*Il concetto di spirit o anima in Henry More e Ralph Cudworth* (Naples, 1986).

Wallace, D. D., jr., *Shapers of English Calvinism, 1660–1714: variety, persistence, and transformation* (Oxford, 2011).

Wallace, R., 'Historical sketch of the trinitarian controversy from the accession of William III to the passing of the Blasphemy Act', *The Christian Reformer* (1845), 133–40, 278–90.

*Antitrinitarian biography* (3 vols, London, 1850).

Wallace, W., 'The vibrating nerve impule in Newton, Willis, and Gassendi: first steps in a mechanical theory of communication', *Brain and Cognition*, 51 (2003), 66–94.

Wallace, W. W., 'Newton's early writings: beginning of a new direction', in *Newton and the new direction in science*, eds., G. V. Coyne, M. Heller, and J. Życiński (Vatican City, 1988), 23–44.

Wallis, P., 'Harvey, Gideon', *ODNB*.

'Mapletoft, John', *ODNB*.

Walmsley, J. C., '"Morbus"—Locke's early essay on disease', *ESM*, 5 (2000), 366–93.

'Sydenham and the development of Locke's natural philosophy', *BJHP*, 16 (2008), 65–83.

Ward, C. E., '*Religio Laici* and father Simon's *History*', *Modern Language Notes*, 61 (1946).

Warner, D. H. J., 'Hobbes's interpretation of the doctrine of the trinity', *Journal of Religious History*, 5 (1969), 299–313.

Wear, A., 'William Harvey and the "way of the anatomists"', *History of Science*, 21 (1983), 223–49.

Webster, C., 'Water as the ultimate principle of nature: the background to Boyle's Sceptical Chymist', *Ambix*, 13 (1965), 96–107.

'Harvey's *De generatione*: its origins and relevance to the theory of circulation', *BJHS*, 3 (1967), 263–74.

'Henry Power's experimental philosophy', *Ambix*, 14 (1967), 150–78.

'English medical reformers of the Puritan Revolution: a background to the "Society of Chymical Physitians"', *Ambix*, 14 (1967), 16–41.

'Henry More and Descartes: some new sources', *BJHS*, 4 (1969), 359–77.

'The Helmontian George Thomson and William Harvey: the revival and applications of splenectomy to physiological research', *Medical History*, 15 (1971), 154–67.

*From Paracelsus to Newton: magic and the making of modern science* (New York, 1982).

*The great instauration: science, medicine and reform, 1626–1660* (2nd edn, Oxford, 2002 [1st edn=1975]).

Weinberg, J., 'The quest for the historical Philo in sixteenth-century Jewish historiography', in *Jewish history: essays in honour of Chumen Abramsky*, eds., A. Rapoport-Albert and S. Zipperstein (London, 1988), 163–87.

Weinstein, D., *Savonarola and Florence: prophecy and patriotism in the Renaissance* (Princeton, 1970).

Westfall, R. S., *The construction of modern science* (Cambridge, 1971).

*Science and religion in seventeenth-century England* (Michigan, 1973).

'The role of alchemy in Newton's career', in *Reason, experiment and mysticism in the Scientific Revolution*, eds., M. L. Righini Bonelli and W. R. Shea (Michigan, 1975), 189–232.

*Never at rest: a biography of Isaac Newton* (Cambridge, 1980).

Westman, R., *Plutarch gegen Kolotes. Seine Schrift 'Adversus Kolotem' als philosophiegeschichtliche Quelle* (Helsinki, 1955).

Whelan, R., 'The wage of sin is orthodoxy: the *Confessions* of Saint Augustine in Bayle's *Dictionnaire*', *JHP*, 26 (1988) 195–206.

Whitaker, V. K., 'Francesco Patrizi and Francis Bacon', in *Francis Bacon's legacy of texts,* ed. W. A. Sessions (New York, 1990), 89–104.

White, J. S., 'William Harvey and the primacy of the blood', *Annals of Science*, 43 (1986), 239–55.

Whitehouse, H., *Ancient Egypt and Nubia in the Ashmolean museum* (Oxford, 2009).

Whiting, J., 'Living bodies', in *Essays on Aristotle's De anima*, eds., M. C. Nussbaum and A. O. Rorty (Oxford, 1992).

Whitteridge, G., 'Introduction', in W. Harvey, *Disputations touching the generation of animals*, trans. G Whitteridge (Oxford, 1981).

Wickenden, N., *G. J. Vossius and the humanist concept of history* (Assen, 1993).

Wijngaards, A. N. M., *De 'Bibliothèque Choisie' van Jean Le Clerc: een Amsterdams geleerdentijdschrift uit de jaren 1703 tot 1713* (Amsterdam, 1986).

von Wilamowitz-Moellendorff, U. *History of classical scholarship*, trans. A. Harris (London, 1982 [German 1st edn=1921]).

Williams, A., *The common expositor: an account of the commentaries on Genesis, 1527–1633* (Chapel Hill, 1948).

Williams, A. V., 'Hyde, Thomas', *Encyclopaedia Iranica* (London, 1982–), XII, fasc. 6, 590–2.

Willmoth, F., *Sir Jonas Moore: practical mathematics and Restoration science* (Woodbridge, 1993).

Wilson, C., *Epicureanism at the origins of modernity* (Oxford, 2008).

Wilson, E., and Vinson, E., 'Thomas Stanley's translations and borrowings from Spanish and Italian poems', *Revue de Littérature Comparée*, 32 (1958), 548–56.

Wind, E., 'The revival of Origen', in *Studies in art and literature for Belle da Costa Greene*, ed. D. Miner (London, 1954), 412–24.

Wirszubski, C., *Pico della Mirandola's encounter with Jewish mysticism* (Cambridge [MA], 1989).

Wojcik, J., *Robert Boyle and the limits of reason* (Cambridge, 1997).

Wolff, E., 'L'Utilisation du texte du Lucrèce par Gassandi dans le *Philosophiae Epicuri Syntagma* (1649)', in *Présence de Lucrèce*, ed. R. Poignault (Tours, 1999), 327–43.

Wolffe, M., 'Hughes, George', *ODNB*.

Wolfson, H. A., *Philo* (2 vols, Cambridge [MA], 1947).

'The problem of the souls of the spheres: from the Byzantine commentaries on Aristotle through the Arabs and St. Thomas to Kepler', *Dumbarton Oaks Papers*, 16 (1962), 65–93.

Wood, P. B., 'Methodology and apologetics: Thomas Sprat's "History of the Royal Society"', *BJHS*, 13 (1980), 1–26.

Woodhouse, C. M., *George Gemistos Plethon: the last of the Hellenes* (Oxford, 1986).

Woolf, D. R., *The idea of history in early Stuart England: erudition, ideology, and the 'light of truth' from the accession of James I to the Civil War* (Toronto, 1990).

Woolhouse, R., *Locke: a biography* (Cambridge, 2007).

Worden, B., *God's instruments: political conduct in the England of Oliver Cromwell* (Oxford, 2012).

Wright, G., 'Hobbes and the economic trinity', *BJHP*, 7 (1999), 397–428.

Wright, J. P., 'Locke, Willis, and the seventeenth-century Epicurean soul', in *Atoms, pneuma, and tranquility: Epicurean and Stoic themes in European thought*, ed. M. J. Osler (Cambridge, 1989), 239–58.

Wright, S., 'Hickman, Henry', *ODNB*.

Yates, F. A., *Giordano Bruno and the Hermetic Tradition* (London, 1964).

Yolton, J. W., *Thinking matter: materialism in eighteenth-century Britain* (Minnesota, 1983).

Young, B., *Religion and enlightenment in eighteenth-century England: theological debate from Locke to Burke* (Oxford, 1998).

van der Zande, J. 'August Ludwig Schlözer and the English *Universal History*', in *Historikerdialoge: Geschichte, Mythos und Gedächtnis Im Deutsch-britischen kulturellen Austausch 1750–2000*, eds., S. Berger, P. Lambert, and P. Schumann (Göttingen, 2003), 135–56.

Zook, M., 'Ferguson, Robert', *ODNB*.

## Unpublished Secondary Works

Agostini, I., 'Henry More and the sources of the doctrine of spiritual extension', paper presented at the symposium on *'The sources of Cambridge Platonism'*, Clare College, Cambridge, 6 April 2013.

Bulman, W., 'Constantine's Enlightenment: culture and religious politics in the early British Empire, c. 1648-1710' (unpublished PhD thesis, Princeton University, 2009).

Cerbu, T. J.-M., 'Leone Allacci (1587–1669): the fortunes of an early Byzantinist' (unpublished PhD thesis, Harvard University, 1986).

Day, S., 'Nathaniel Culverwell's *Elegant and learned discourse on the light of nature* (1652) in institutional and philosophical context' (unpublished BA dissertation, University of Cambridge, 2009).

Deer, L. A., 'Academic theories of generation in the Renaissance: the contemporaries and successors of Jean Fernel' (unpublished PhD thesis, University of London, Warburg Institute, 1980).

Fishman, J. H., 'Edward Stillingfleet, Bishop of Worcester (1635–99): Anglican bishop and controversialist' (unpublished PhD thesis, University of Wisconsin, 1977).

Hardy, N. J. S., 'The *ars critica* in early modern England' (unpublished DPhil thesis, University of Oxford, 2012).

Keene, N., 'Critici Sacri: biblical criticism in England c. 1650–1710' (unpublished PhD thesis, University of London, 2004).

Lawrence, M. T., 'Transmission and transformation: Thomas Goodwin and the puritan project' (unpublished PhD thesis, University of Cambridge, 2002).

Lewis, M. A., 'The educational influence of Cambridge Platonism: tutorial relationships and student networks at Christ's College, Cambridge, 1641–1688' (unpublished PhD thesis, University of London, 2010).

Malet, A., 'Studies on James Gregorie (1638–1675)' (unpublished PhD thesis, Princeton University, 1989).

Miller, E. C., 'The doctrine of the Church in the thought of Herbert Thorndike (1598–1672)' (unpublished DPhil thesis, University of Oxford, 1990).

Stephenson, H., 'Thomas Firmin' (unpublished DPhil thesis, University of Oxford, 1949).

Walmsley, J. C., 'John Locke's natural philosophy (1632–1671)' (unpublished PhD thesis, King's College, University of London, 1998).

Wilmott, M. J., 'Francesco Patrizi da Cherso's humanist critique of Aristotle' (unpublished PhD thesis, University of London, The Warburg Institute, 1984).

# Index

*Note*: all names are ordered by the first element of the name that bears a capital letter. For subjects that are discussed throughout the book, such as 'philosophy', references are given only to specific issues raised about the concept or individual debates about it. Titles of primary sources appear only when they are discussed in the body of the text, not the notes. Names of modern historians appear only when they are mentioned in the body of the text. Greek and Hebrew terms with no direct English equivalent are listed at the end.

# IDEAS IN CONTEXT

*Edited by*

## DAVID ARMITAGE, RICHARD BOURKE, JENNIFER PITTS, AND JOHN ROBERTSON